Lecture Notes in Computer Science 2404

Edited by G. Goos, J. Hartmanis, and J. van Leeuwen

Springer
Berlin
Heidelberg
New York
Barcelona
Hong Kong
London
Milan
Paris
Tokyo

Ed Brinksma   Kim Guldstrand Larsen (Eds.)

Computer Aided Verification

14th International Conference, CAV 2002
Copenhagen, Denmark, July 27-31, 2002
Proceedings

Springer

Series Editors

Gerhard Goos, Karlsruhe University, Germany
Juris Hartmanis, Cornell University, NY, USA
Jan van Leeuwen, Utrecht University, The Netherlands

Volume Editors

Ed Brinksma
University of Twente, Department of Computer Science
P. O. Box 217, 7500 AE Enschede, The Netherlands
E-mail: brinksma@cs.utwente.nl

Kim Guldstrand Larsen
Aalborg University, Department of Computer Science
Fredrik Bajers Vej 7, 9220, Aalborg Ø, Denmark
E-mail: kgl@cs.auc.dk

Cataloging-in-Publication Data applied for

Die Deutsche Bibliothek - CIP-Einheitsaufnahme

Computer aided verification : 14th international conference ; proceedings /
CAV 2002, Copenhagen, Denmark, July 27 - 31, 2002. Ed Brinksma ;
Kim Guldstrand Larsen (ed.). - Berlin ; Heidelberg ; New York ; Barcelona ;
Hong Kong ; London ; Milan ; Paris ; Tokyo : Springer, 2002
　　(Lecture notes in computer science ; Vol. 2404)
　　ISBN 3-540-43997-8

CR Subject Classification (1998): F.3, D.2.4, D.2.2, F.4.1, I.2.3, B.7.2, C.3

ISSN 0302-9743
ISBN 3-540-43997-8 Springer-Verlag Berlin Heidelberg New York

Springer-Verlag Berlin Heidelberg New York
a member of BertelsmannSpringer Science+Business Media GmbH

http://www.springer.de

© Springer-Verlag Berlin Heidelberg 2002
Printed in Germany

Typesetting: Camera-ready by author, data conversion by DA-TeX Gerd Blumenstein
Printed on acid-free paper　　SPIN 10873641　　06/3142　　5 4 3 2 1 0

Preface

This volume contains the proceedings of the conference on *Computer Aided Verification* (CAV 2002), held in Copenhagen, Denmark on July 27-31, 2002. CAV 2002 was the 14th in a series of conferences dedicated to the advancement of the theory and practice of computer-assisted formal analysis methods for software and hardware systems. The conference covers the spectrum from theoretical results to concrete applications, with an emphasis on practical verification tools, including algorithms and techniques needed for their implementation. The conference has traditionally drawn contributions from researchers as well as practitioners in both academia and industry.

This year we received 94 regular paper submissions out of which 35 were selected. Each submission received an average of 4 referee reviews. In addition, the CAV program contained 11 tool presentations selected from 16 submissions. For each tool presentation, a demo was given at the conference. The large number of tool submissions and presentations testifies to the liveliness of the field and its applied flavor.

The CAV 2002 program included a tutorial day with three invited tutorials by Wolfgang Thomas (Aachen) on *Infinite Games and Verification*, Patrick Cousot (ENS Paris) on *Abstraction in Software Verification* and Thomas A. Henzinger (Berkeley) on *The Symbolic Approach to Hybrid Systems*. The conference also included two invited talks by Sharad Malik (Princeton) on *The Quest for Efficient Boolean Satisfiability Solvers* and Gerard J. Holzmann (Bell Labs) on *Software Analysis and Model Checking*. In addition, there were three workshops associated with CAV 2002:

- PAPM-PROBMIV: Process Algebras and Performance Modeling/Probabilistic Methods in Verification.
- RT-TOOLS: Workshop on Real-Time Tools.
- RV: Run-Time Verification.

The publication of these workshop proceedings was managed by their respective chairs, independently of the present proceedings.

We would like to thank all the Program Committee members and the sub-referees who assisted in their work. Our thanks also go to the Steering Committee members and last year's organizers for their helpful advice. The Local Organization Chair, Jens Christian Godskesen, deserves our gratitude for his contributions throughout the preparations. We would also like to thank the invited speakers and invited tutorial speakers, the authors of submitted papers, and all the participants of the conference. Special thanks go to Brian Nielsen for installing and managing the START Conference system and to Ole Høgh Jensen for the production of the final proceedings.

This year, CAV was part of the Federated Logic Conference (FLoC 2002), and was organized jointly with CADE (Conference on Automated Deduction),

FME (Formal Methods Europe), ICL (International Conference on Logic Programming), LICS (Logic in Computer Science), RTA (Rewriting Techniques and Applications), and TABLEAUX (Automated Reasoning with Analytic Tableaux and Related Methods). In particular, the invited talk given by Sharad Malik was joint with CADE 2002, and the paper also appears, in identical form, in the proceedings of CADE 2002. In addition, FLoC included 31 workshops associated with the different conferences. We would like to acknowledge the help of the FLoC 2002 steering committee Moshe Y. Vardi (General Chair), Neil D. Jones (Conference Chair), Ulrich Firbach (CADE), Edmund M. Clarke (CAV), Dines Bjørner (CAV), Catuscia Palamidessi (ICLP), Samson Abramsky (LICS), Nachum Dershowitz (RTA), Reiner Hähnle (TABLEAUX), Harald Ganzinger (Associate General Chair), and Dana Scott (IFCOLOG).

Finally, we gratefully acknowledge support from IBM, Esterel Technologies, IT-U of Copenhagen, the Department of Computer Science at Aalborg University, Twente University, and BRICS.

May 2002   Ed Brinksma and Kim Guldstrand Larsen

Matthew Dwyer
Niklas Een
Cindy Eisner
Kousha Etessami
Monica Farkash
Jean-Claude Fernandez
D. Fink
Dana Fisman
Emmanuel Fleury
Martin Fränzle
Carl Chr. Frederiksen
L. Fribourg
Dimitra Giannakopoulou
Patrice Godefroid
Jean Goubault-Larrecq
Susanne Graf
Claudia Gsottberger
Elsa Gunter
Alan Hartman
Frederic Herbreteau
Holger Hermanns
Gerard Holzmann
Hardi Hungar
Radu Iosif
S. Iyer
Damir Jamsek
Somesh Jha
Ranjit Jhala
HoonSang Jin
Damien Joly
Bengt Jonsson
Bernhard Josko
Marcin Jurszinski
Vineet Kahlon
M. Kaltenbach
Joost-Pieter Katoen
Felix Klaedtke
Nils Klarlund
Jens Knoop
Olga Kouchnarenko
Hillel Kugler

Robert P. Kurshan
Yassine Lakhnech
Rom Langerak
Jim Larus
Jerome Leroux
Xavier Leroy
Bing Li
Angelika Mader
Monika Maidl
Rupak Majumdar
Oded Maler
Freddy Mang
Panagiotis Manolios
Nicolas Markey
Ken McMillan
Jon Millen
Mark Minas
Sebastian Moedersheim
Oliver Möller
In-Ho Moon
Remi Morin
Laurent Mounier
Leonardo de Moura
Markus Müller-Olm
Uwe Nestmann
Juergen Niehaus
Oliver Niese
Thomas Noll
Abelardo Pardo
Corina Pasareanu
Charles Pecheur
Wojciech Penczek
Paul Pettersson
Claudine Picaronny
Nir Piterman
Shaz Qadeer
Sriram K. Rajamani
Kavita Ravi
S. Ray
E. Reeber
Iris Reuveni

Grigore Rosu
Sitvanit Ruah
Harald Ruess
John Rushby
Oliver Rüthing
Theo Ruys
Hassen Saidi
Jun Sawada
Viktor Schuppan
Helmut Seidl
Ohad Shaham
Elad Shahar
Gil Shurek
Maria Sorea
Robert Staerk
Christian Stehno
M. Sustik
Gregoire Sutre
Ashish Tiwari
Richard J. Trefler
Jan Tretmans
Stavros Tripakis
Tomas Uribe
Moshe Vardi
Miroslav Velev
Luca Vigano
S. Vinod
Willem Visser
T. Wahl
Chao Wang
Farn Wang
Ingo Wegener
Jon Whittle
Thomas Wilke
Harro Wimmel
Burkhart Wolff
Heisung Yoo
Emmanuel Zarpas
Wenhui Zhang
C. Zhou
Lenore Zuck

Table of Contents

Invited Talks

Invited Tutorials

Symbolic Model Checking

Abstraction/Refinement and Model Checking

Compositional/Structural Verification

Timing Analysis

SAT Based Methods

Symbolic Model Checking

Extended Model Checking

Tool Presentations

Code Verification

Regular Model Checking and Acceleration

Model Reduction

Software Analysis and Model Checking

Gerard J. Holzmann

Bell Laboratories, Lucent Technologies,
Murray Hill, New Jersey 07974, USA.
gerard@research.bell-labs.com

Abstract. Most software developers today rely on only a small number of techniques to check their code for defects: peer review, code walkthroughs, and testing. Despite a rich literature on these subjects, the results often leave much to be desired. The current software testing process consumes a significant fraction of the overall resources in industrial software development, yet it cannot promise zero-defect code. There is reason to hope that the process can be improved. A range of tools and techniques has become available in the last few years that can asses the quality of code with considerably more rigor than before, and often also with more ease. Many of the new tools can be understood as applications of automata theory, and can readily be combined with logic model checking techniques.

1 Introduction

Humans occasionally make mistakes, even programmers do. Even though mistakes are generally unpredictable, within fixed domain we can often predict fairly accurately just how many mistakes will be made. For programmers in industrial software development, the residual software defect ratio (the number of latent faults that remain in the code at the end of the development process) is normally somewhere between 0.5 and 5 defects per one thousand lines of non-comment source code [H01]. Curiously, this ratio is not unique to programming.

The New York Times appears seven times a week, with an average of 138,000 words per weekday issue, and 317,000 per Sunday issue [AM02]. Despite great care in fact checking, proof reading and spell checking, inevitably seven times a week a list appears of the most important mistakes that made it into print on the previous day. On average, the list of corrections contains 10 entries per day. At an average of ten words per sentence, this gives a fairly predictable residual defect density of one defect per one thousand sentences written.

So without knowing anything about the particulars of a given industrially produced software product, one thing is generally safe to assume: it has bugs. The same is of course true for all industrial products, but what makes the problem unique in software is that the effects of even very minor programming mistakes can cause major system failures. It is very hard to contain the potential effects of a software defect, especially in distributed systems software.

We will not argue in this paper that traditional software testing, peer reviews and code walkthroughs can or should be replaced wholesale. Most studies agree that this combination of techniques effectively catches the majority of design and coding errors. Yet, undeniably at the end of this process the residual software defect density ratio is not zero. Even at a low residual defect density of 0.1 defect per one thousand lines of

D. Brinksma and K. G. Larsen (Eds.): CAV 2002, LNCS 2404, pp. 1-16, 2002.

```
do {
          lock( &devExt->writeListLock );
          nPacketsOld = nPackets;
          request = devExt->WriteListHeadVa;
          if (request && request->status)
          {       devExt->WriteListHeadVa = request->nxt;
                  unlock(&devExt->writeListLock);
                  /* ... */
                  nPackets++;
          }
} while (nPackets != nPacketsOld);
unlock(&devExt->writeListLock);
```

Fig. 1. Sample Device Driver Code from [BR01]

code, a ten million line source package will have an expected 10^3 latent defects. To reduce this number, we need to devise complementary analysis and testing techniques. It should also be noted that no-one really knows how many latent defects there *really* are in any given software product. All we can tell is how many of these defects eventually lead to customer complaints, in the years following product delivery. The industry average of 0.5 to 5 defects per one thousands lines of code is based on a count of the typical numbers of those customer complaints. We can suspect that the *true* number of latent defects is at least an order of magnitude higher, more likely in the range of 0.5 to 5 defects per one hundred lines of source code. Looking for latent software defects, then, is not quite like looking for needles in a haystack. Almost any new technique that differs sufficiently from traditional testing should be expected to intercept enough extra defects to justify its application. How could we devise such alternate techniques?

In this paper we will look at three such techniques that have proven to be effective in the software development process, and we will try to show that these techniques have interesting new applications that can be understood in terms of automata theory. The three techniques we will discuss are:

- □ Static Analysis,
- □ Runtime monitoring, and
- □ Logic Model Checking.

2   Static Analysis

Static analysis is the art of making predictions about a program's runtime behavior based on a direct analysis of its source code. Much of the work in this area is based on the foundational work in abstract interpretation by Cousot and Cousot, e.g. [CC76].

As a motivating example we will take a look at a snippet of C device driver code, reproduced in Figure 1. The code is slightly abbreviated from the original that appeared in [BR01]. We have highlighted three procedure calls: one call on **lock** and two on **unlock**. As in [BR01] we want to check if this piece of code respects the normal locking discipline that says that it would be an error if a single thread could:

- □ Attempt to lock the resource when it already holds that lock,
- □ Attempt to unlock the resource when it does not currently hold the lock,
- □ Terminate execution with the lock still in effect.

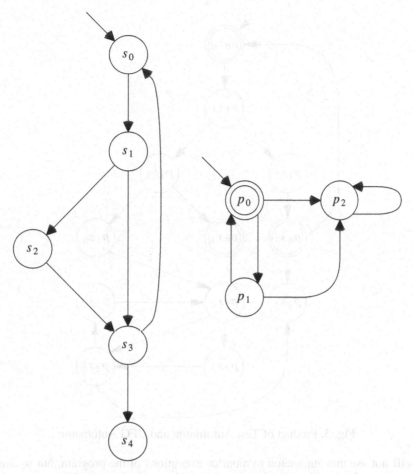

Fig. 2. Control Flow Graph for Figure 1 (left)
and Test Automaton for Locking Property (right)

These types of problems can be found frequently in device driver code, as demonstrated convincingly in [E00].

The first step in the formalization of this code is to generate the control flow graph, as shown in abstract form on the left in Figure 2. The control flow graph can be defined as a labeled transition system: an annotated automaton. Since we are only interested in the occurrences of the calls to lock and unlock, we have marked all other actions as **other**. These actions can be considered *skip* statements for the purpose of the initial analysis we will do.

The property we want to check for, the faithful observance of a locking discipline, can also be formalized as an automaton, as illustrated on the right in Figure 2. This property automaton has three states, p_0, p_1, and p_2. The initial state, p_0, is also marked as an accepting state, by which we express that all finite runs that start in p_0 should terminate in p_0. State p_2 is really an error state. Any transition into that state may immediately be flagged as an error.

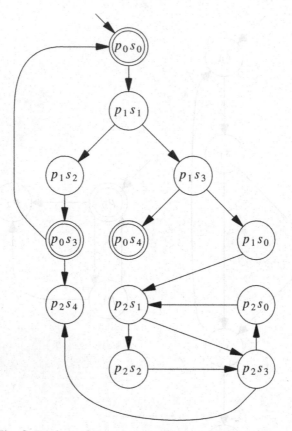

Fig. 3. Product of Test Automaton and CFG Automaton

We will not use this automaton to monitor executions of the program, but to analyze the source code directly. To do so, we in effect try to match the test automaton against the abstracted control flow graph. The formal mechanism for this is to compute the synchronous product of two automata: the automaton that corresponds to an abstracted version of the control flow graph and the automaton for the property.

The product automaton, illustrated in Figure 3, can be defined in a standard way as a synchronization on labels, where **other** is treated as a silent τ move that requires no synchronization. It can be computed without ever attempting to really execute the program from Figure 1.

There are two end-states in this product automaton: $p_2 s_4$ and $p_0 s_4$, but only $p_0 s_4$ is accepting. There are also two strongly connected components: C1 = { $p_0 s_0$, $p_1 s_1$, $p_1 s_2$, $p_0 s_3$ }, and C2 = { $p_2 s_1$, $p_2 s_2$, $p_2 s_3$, $p_2 s_0$ }, only one of which contains accepting states (C1). Any feasible finite path that starts in $p_0 s_0$ and that ends in $p_2 s_4$ would correspond to a violation of the locking property. Similarly, any feasible infinite path that reaches $p_2 s_1$ corresponds to a violation.

By computing the product automaton we can narrow down the search for potential violations of the locking discipline to the analysis of just two types of paths:

$$[p_0s_0 \rightarrow p_1s_1 \rightarrow p_1s_2 \rightarrow p_0s_3]^+ \rightarrow p_2s_4, \text{ and}$$
$$p_0s_0 \rightarrow p_1s_1 \rightarrow p_1s_3 \rightarrow p_1s_0 \rightarrow p_2s_1 \rightarrow \cdots$$

where the superfix + indicates a repetition of one or more times of the immediately preceding execution fragment enclosed in square brackets. Mapped onto executions through just the control flow graph from Figure 2, this reduces to:

$$[s_0 \rightarrow s_1 \rightarrow s_2 \rightarrow s_3]^+ \rightarrow s_4, \text{ and}$$
$$s_0 \rightarrow s_1 \rightarrow s_3 \rightarrow s_0 \rightarrow s_1 \rightarrow \cdots$$

The shortest example of the first path corresponds in source form to:

```
s0:  lock ( &devExt->writeListLock );
     nPacketsOld = nPackets;
     request = devExt->WriteListHeadVa;
s1:  if (request && request->status)      /* true */
     devExt->WriteListHeadVa = request->nxt;
s2:  unlock(&devExt->writeListLock);
     /* ... */
     nPackets++;
s3:  if (nPackets != nPacketsOld);         /* false */
     unlock(&devExt->writeListLock);
s4:  end
```

Similarly, the second path reads in source form:

```
s0:  lock ( &devExt->writeListLock );
     nPacketsOld = nPackets;
     request = devExt->WriteListHeadVa;
s1:  if (request && request->status)       /* false */
s3:  if (nPackets != nPacketsOld);         /* true */
s0:  lock ( &devExt->writeListLock );
     . . .
```

The analysis problem now reduces to determining whether or not these two path fragments are feasible, i.e., whether or not they could occur in a real execution. The feasibility of the two paths is determined by the conditionals that are evaluated along the path. For the first path this means that we should check if the conditionals at s1 and s3 can evaluate to *true* and *false* respectively, given the history of steps that precede them.

In general, this problem is undecidable, so we have no hope of building a general algorithm that can reliably come up with the correct answer in each case. In many practical cases though even partial knowledge of the semantics of C suffices to resolve the question. There is insufficient information to determine if the conditional at s1 could be *true* or *false*, since we do not know the value of the variable request, which is derived from devExt->WriteListHeadVa. We can, however, tell that the condition at s3 could not possibly evaluate to false in this path, given the only two preceding manipulations of the variables involved. If we reduce the path to just the access to the two variables that appear in the condition this becomes clear:

```
           nPacketsOld = nPackets;
           nPackets++;
    s3:    if (nPackets != nPacketsOld);        /* false */
```

Clearly, the condition must evaluate to *true*, not *false*, in this context.

For the second path we can come to a similar conclusion. Reducing it to the manipulations of the variables from the second condition we get:

```
           nPacketsOld = nPackets;
    s3:    if (nPackets != nPacketsOld);        /* true */
```

which again is infeasible in any context. The resolution to these two cases can be done quickly with a theorem prover, or with decision procedures for Pressburger arithmetic, such as the Omega tool from [K96] or the Newton tool described in [BR01]. In the Bell Labs tool UNO, a simple builtin decision procedure is used for the most commonly occurring cases [H02]. Since quick responses from the analyzer are as important as the generation of definitive results for all cases that are in principle decidable, UNO errs on the side of caution and restricts itself to the analysis of only the cases that can be decided most efficiently.

2.1 User-Definable Properties

The UNO tool, defined more fully in [H02], is an attempt to construct a static analyzer that can accept a range of user-defined properties, within the bounds of what is expressible in its property specification language. The basic propositions that can be expressed in this language can refer to data-flow tags that are computed by the tool and attached to the nodes in the control flow graphs of each function. Automata specifications are constructed from these propositions with the normal control-flow syntax of ANSI-C. The locking discipline, for instance as defined by the automaton from Figure 2, is easily expressible by this language, but much richer sets of properties can also be defined. The algorithms used in UNO are relatively straightforward. The tool computes product automata (cf. Figure 3) and performs basic path analysis. It has three basic properties built-in that allow the tool to hunt down what are often said to be the most commonly occurring types of defects in C programs: use of *u*ninitialized variables, *n*il-pointer dereferencing errors, and *o*out-of-bound array indexing errors.

The notion that one can allow the user to freely define program specific properties as automata, and perhaps even derive such automata from logic formulae, to perform *static* analysis is in itself not new. As far as we can tell the first to propose the use of finite state machines to specify properties for static analysis was W.E. Howden [H87]. A version of this idea was used more recently in Engler's work [E00]. In [BR01] the idea of user-defined properties is also used in a clever way that makes it possible to connect static analysis to an approach that is based on logic model checking.

All approaches we discuss here have strengths and weaknesses. If we have to pick a weakness for the approaches based on static analysis it would have to be the decidability problem: determining whether or not paths are feasible. Significant progress has been made on tackling this problem, as noted starting with the work of Cousot and Cousot. The work in this area is already exploited in some very effective commercial tools, such as Polyspace in France, and KLOCwork accelerator in the US.

3 Runtime Monitoring

There are two ways in which we can attempt to side-step the decidability issue that has to be confronted in approaches based on static analysis. One way is to execute the code directly for specific input values, and then monitor the execution for compliance with the requirements. The second way is to execute the code not directly, but symbolically, in abstract form. Admittedly, these approaches too have their weaknesses. For the first approach it is the inability to secure proper coverage, and for the second approach it is computational complexity. We will come back to these issues below. In this section we will discuss direct execution methods based on runtime monitoring, and in the next section we will discuss abstraction methods. Our aim again is to see if these methods can be linked to a standard automata theoretic framework.

The basic idea in runtime monitoring is again simple. We define a test automaton for a property of interest and run it along with an executing system. To be able to check for compliance of the system execution with the test automaton we now instrument the source code to emit signals of all events of interest (i.e., all events that appear in the property to be tested). The monitor can run as a separate process, perhaps even remotely, and tracks the system execution with the help of the signals emitted by the running program. It updates the state of the property automaton, and flags errors as soon as they can be detected.

To do so for the locking property we will have to instrument the code in such a way that not only the basic calls to lock and unlock are recorded, but also the parameters that are passed to those procedures.

Our automata now become extended automata, and can store some data (i.e., references to the locked objects). A clever use of this feature was made in the Eraser algorithm, described in [S97]. The purpose of the algorithm is again to detect locking violations by runtime monitoring, but this time the analysis is focused on the detection of potential data races that are not prevented by the use of locking primitives. The source code is now instrumented not to directly flag calls to lock and unlock, but to flag read and write accesses to shared objects. Each signal to the runtime monitor indicates the object that is referenced, whether the event is a read (r) or a write (w), and the set of locks that is held by the executing process at the moment of access. The automaton used in the algorithm is shown in Figure 4.

The automaton records the transitions that the monitor will make for a single specific shared object. (Each object is monitored by a separate automaton.) We have marked each action in Figure 4 with one or more numbers, with the following meaning.

☐ A zero mark (0) indicates a read (r) or write (w) access by the *first* thread to access the shared data object. A write access in initial state s_0 corresponds to an initialization event. It is an error for a shared object to be read before it is initialized. To reflect this, we added a transition to an error state .

☐ Transitions marked with a one (1) indicate the first access to the shared object by a new thread (i.e., different from the thread that initialized the object).

☐ On all transitions marked with a two (2) the set of locks held by the current thread is recorded in set L.

☐ On all transitions marked with (3) L is assigned a new value that is equal to the intersection of the set of locks held by the current thread and the old value of L.

☐ The transition marked with (4) is taken when lockset L becomes empty, causing an error to be reported by the runtime monitor.

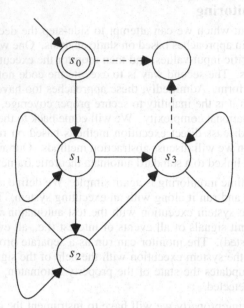

Fig. 4. Eraser Automaton from [S97] (error state added.)

Locking violations are only reported in state s_3, which can only be reached if at least two different threads have attempted to write to the shared object. The reason is clear: it is not an error if the shared object is only updated by a single thread, while all competing threads restrict themselves to read access.

The Eraser algorithm has the attractive and curious property that a lock violation need not actually occur for the monitor to be able to detect that it *could* occur in some future execution of the code.

Algorithms based on runtime monitoring have been included in successful commercial tools. The Eraser algorithm, for instance, is included in Compaq's Visual Threads tool [H00]. None of the widely used runtime monitoring tools appear to allow for user-defined properties though, an extension that should readily be possible. We will explore such extensions in a little more detail in the next subsection.

3.1 Liveness

The methods sketched so far use standard finite automata defined over finite strings, or executions. They can capture safety, but not liveness properties. It is possible to extend the capability of a runtime monitor to liveness properties, capturing also more general properties expressed in linear temporal logic.

Consider a system requirement expressed as an LTL formula. The negation of , capturing the possible violations of , can be converted into a Büchi automaton with a standard procedure, e.g. [GP95]. As before, runtime monitor will track an execution of the system under test, call it , with the help of automaton . This time, though, the transitions in the automaton are labeled not with events from the executions in , but with boolean expressions on an abstract representation of the system

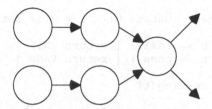

Fig. 5. Runtime Monitoring Context for Checking Liveness Properties
: LTL requirement; : test automaton; : runtime tester;
: system under test; : abstraction function

state of itself. This context is illustrated in Figure 5.

The abstract system state of is computed by an abstraction function . The abstraction function must preserve all information that is relevant to the checking of requirement , but no more. In many cases, this abstract representation of the system state of can be considerably smaller than the full representation of the system state.

The source code from system is now instrumented to invoke function at specific points in its execution. Each time function is invoked, it passes its results to the runtime monitor , which uses it to update the state of automaton . After each such transition can declare either a *pass* or a *fail* result, where the *pass* results will typically be silent, and the *fail* results could lead to an abort.

A *pass* result means that has not yet been able to detect a potential violation of requirement ; a *fail* result means that a potential violation was found. Once a *fail* result has been issued, this result persists throughout the remainder of the execution, until system is reinitialized (reset or restarted). It is also possible that loses track of the execution, being unable to construe a counter-example to the requirement. In that case will move to a state where only *pass* results are issued for the remainder of the execution, again until system is reinitialized.

The cause of a *fail* result can be the existence of a true implementation error in , but it can also be an error in the definition of the requirement, an error in the definition of the abstraction function , or an error in the determination of the invocation points for . Since a *fail* always produces an execution trace, the source of a false negative can be analyzed with the help of that trace and repaired. As in all tests, an absence of failure does not imply that requirement cannot be violated by executions of system . It means that did not exhibit any violations of that were detectable under abstraction .

We can be brief about the definition of here. It is a critical step, but no different from the problem of defining abstraction functions in more standard applications of logic model checking. The abstraction function will in general be property sensitive, to assure that everything that is directly or indirectly visible to the property is preserved. can be derived with the help of static analysis techniques, but it can also be determined experimentally by a human tester.

A more critical point in the definition of the runtime monitor is to determine how it could reasonably conclude Büchi acceptance based on only finite executions of . To do so must be able to detect the occurrence of execution cycles through Büchi acceptance states in automaton . We will distinguish two cases. The simple case

```
Verdict
function d_check (Ustate u)        # B is deterministic
{
        if ( t == fail ) { return FAIL }
        if ( t == pass ) { return PASS }

        if Accepting(t)
        {
              if state u is in set States(t)
              {
                      t = fail
                      return FAIL
              } else
              {
                      States(t) += u
        }       }

        if empty Succ(u,t)
        {
              t = pass                  # B is incomplete
        } else
        {
              t = Succ(u,t)
        }

        return PASS
}
```

Fig. 6. Checking Liveness with a Deterministic Test Automaton

where   is assumed to be deterministic, and the harder case where   can be non-deterministic. In neither case do we require   to be completely defined.

For deterministic   , a simple algorithm for   is shown in Figure 6. The notation used is as follows:

```
t:             the current state of automaton
u:             last observed abstract state of system
Succ(u,t):     function returning the successor state
               in  , if any, given current state t and
               abstract system state u
States(t):     a set of abstract system states associated
               with t
Accepting(t):  boolean function that returns true if t is
               a Büchi acceptance state
x += y:        add element (or set) y to set x
```

Assume that   invokes the function *d_check* with parameter *u* encoding the abstract representation of the current system state of U. Function *d_check* returns a *pass/fail* verdict for each such call. The tester   maintains the automaton state for   in a global variable *t* whose value persists across calls. Variable *t* can have two special values. The special value *fail* means that a failure has been detected and the automaton will now issue only *fail* results until   is reinitialized. The special value *pass* means that the automaton was incomplete, causing   to lose track of the execution. Only *pass*

```
Verdict
function nd_check (Ustate u)      # B non-deterministic
{
        if ( t == fail )              { return FAIL }
        if ( t == pass )              { return PASS }

        xt = empty                    # next state set in B
        for each ot in t              # current states in B
        {
                if {u,ot} in Pairs(ot)
                {
                        t = fail
                        return FAIL
                }

                if Accepting(ot)
                {
                        Pairs(ot) += {u,ot}
                }

                for each nt in Succ(u,ot)
                {
                        Pairs(nt) += Pairs(ot)
                        xt += nt
                }
        }

        if empty xt
        {
                t = pass              # B is incomplete
        } else
        {
                t = xt
        }

        return PASS
}
```

Fig. 7. Checking Liveness with a Non-Deterministic Test Automaton

results will be issued now, again until   is reinitialized.

The essence of the algorithm is that for every visit to a Büchi acceptance state in   the tester remembers the encoding of abstract system state u. A repeat visit to the state with the same encoding u points at a potential cyclic execution of   that violates the requirement (by satisfying its negation in).

The same type of algorithm could be used for a non-deterministic automaton   , but it may lead to more false negatives than necessary. The algorithm in Figure 7, due to Mihalis Yannakakis, is more precise. The following notation differs from the one used in Figure 6:

```
t:              the set of current states of automaton
Pairs(t):       a set of pairs {u,b} associated with automaton
                state t of previously seen combinations of
                abstract system state u and accepting automaton
                state b
```

Pairs of abstract system states and accepting automaton states that have been encountered in the current execution are now propagated forward in the execution, until a repeat is seen. The algorithms in Figures 6 and 7 are claimed to have the following properties.

☐   If system   cannot violate requirement   , then in any execution of   the tester will report *pass* at every step.

☐   If any monitored execution of system   violates requirement   , then the tester will report *fail* at the earliest point in the execution where the violation can be conclusively detected under abstraction   .

☐   If system   can violate requirement   , but the monitored executions of   do not demonstrate this, then tester   may or may not report a *fail*.

4   Logic Model Checking

The best known example of an automata based approach to software verification is logic model checking. In applications of model checking to software verification, there are some flies in the ointment again that often prevent us from claiming more than best effort results. For fundamental reasons, model checking techniques cannot be applied blindly to arbitrary program code written in the currently popular programming languages (cf. [S65]). To apply a model checking algorithm we need to create an abstract, finitary, representation of the source code: a verification model. The verification model is traditionally constructed by hand, and is therefore subject to human error. Human error can introduce both defects that the real system does not have and it can hide defects that the real system does have. Errors of the first type are mostly harmless, since they will trigger false negatives that can be repaired after an analysis of an error trace. Errors of the second type, however, can lead to false positives, which are much harder to diagnose.

Another, often forgotten, potential source of error is in the definition of the properties. Defining properties is unavoidably a human effort, and it is therefore quite predictable that they will in some cases be incorrect. Again, it is easily repaired if a bad property leads to a false negative, but we should also consider the possibility of false positives.

To reduce one source of potential error we can try to extract automata models mechanically from source code. There have been several promising attempts to do so. For Java, this includes the Bandera toolset [CD00] from Kansas State University, and the Pathfinder tools from NASA Ames Research Center [HP00,VP00,VH00]. For C this includes the Bebop toolset from Microsoft [BR01], and our own   tool, e.g. [HS00], [HS02]. The judicious application of abstraction techniques is key to the success of these techniques. One can use property based slicing [T95,HD00], predicate abstraction techniques [VP00], static analysis, and theorem proving techniques to justify the abstractions.

In the application of   , abstraction functions are recorded in a lookup table that acts as a filter for the source code. Abstraction is only applied to basic statements and conditionals; the control-flow structure of the source code is preserved. To apply the

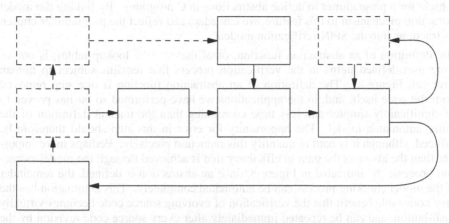

Fig. 8.   Model Extraction Framework
(Dashed arrows are user-defined steps; solid arrows are automated steps)

abstraction and generate the system model, the source code is first parsed, with a standard compiler front-end.   uses a simple ANSI-C parser to perform this step. The parse tree for each function in the source code is converted into a control-flow graph, which becomes the basis for model extraction, as illustrated in Figure 8.   The edges in the control-flow graph correspond to the basic statements in the source language (e.g., assignments and function calls).   Most nodes will have a single outgoing edge, encoding normal sequential control flow.   Nodes without any outgoing edges correspond to function termination points.   Nodes with more than one outgoing edge correspond to decision points, and are labeled with the criterion that is to be used for the selection of an outgoing edge. For a standard if-then-else construct, the condition is an expression, and there are two outgoing edges: one labeled *true* and the other labeled *false*. For C-style switch statements, there can be more outgoing edges, each labeled with a different numeric value for the switch expression.

The abstraction function in   is applied only to the labels on the edges in the control-flow graph. The abstraction can result in certain operations to be hidden completely (as if they are sliced away from the program text), others to be modified in accordance with the coarsening of selected data types, and still others may be preserved as is.   Conditions can similarly be removed completely, and replaced with non-deterministic selections, they may be modified in accordance with data type mappings, or they can be preserved as is.

4.1 Functions to Automata

The   model extraction process targets C functions as the primary focus of abstractions.   As part of a   test harness setup (not shown in Figure 8), the user must define the specific C functions that are to be converted into SPIN automata models, and provide a context for those models.   Typically there is one main control function per thread of execution, and that control function will be targeted for model extraction. The functions converted into SPIN models will often call subsidiary functions to perform smaller computational chores.   Those subsidiary functions are best left in the code, and invoked as-is as embedded C-code, or abstracted with the help of a stub-function.   The notion used here is that the definition of functions is the main vehicle for a programmer to define abstractions in C programs. By linking the model extraction mechanism to this feature, we can adapt and reflect the programmer chosen abstractions into the SPIN verification models.

The definition of an abstraction function, or of the   lookup tables, is one of three user-defined items in the verification process that remains subject to human error (cf. Figure 8). The definition of an abstraction function is one step removed from the code itself, and, in the applications we have performed so far has proven to be significantly simpler and less time consuming than the manual definition of the entire automaton model. The opportunity for error in this step should therefore be reduced, although it is hard to quantify this reduction precisely. Perhaps more important than the above is the gain in efficiency that is achieved through the model extraction process. As indicated in Figure 8, once an abstraction is defined, the remainder of the model checking process can be automated completely. This automation has the very noticeable benefit that the verification of evolving source code becomes virtually push-button, and can be repeated immediately after every source code revision by the programmers.

4.2 Vacuity Checking

When the model checker returns a *pass* verdict, it means that it was unable to construct a counter-example to a correctness claim. Since the claim is derived from a user-defined property this still leaves the possibility that the claim is ill-defined and vacuously true. In the   application to the verification of the PathStar® call processing code [HS00], we supported a simple vacuity check by generating a graphical version of the ω test automaton, coloring each state in the automaton remained unreached in all model checking attempts for the property from which it was generated. We normally expect that all but a few final states in the automaton are reached. If only the initial state is reached, or a minority of all the remaining states, this most likely indicates a vacuous result. A more thorough method of vacuity checking can be found in [KV99].

4.3 Main Benefits

The   tool grew out of an attempt to come up with a thorough method to check the call processing software for a commercial switching product, called the PathStar® Access Server. We pursued this approach over a period of eighteen months, working with the developers of the target software from the initial design for the code in 1998 to after commercial sales for the product began in 2000. The project was successful in demonstrating that the approach based on model checking could intercept a significantly larger fraction of the design and coding errors in the software than traditional testing techniques: we measured a difference of approximately one order of magnitude in effectiveness, as measured by the number of defects found with each method [HS00]. We also succeeded in realizing our original goal of automating almost the entire verification trajectory by driving all our software from a web-browser that gave access to a database of verification results, and allowed users to enter new properties, start verification runs, and retrieve the results of such runs. We have also applied   in several smaller projects with similar results, e.g. [GH02].

Although the   approach side-steps the need for the time-consuming construction of verification models, we have found that some of the remaining tasks can still be challenging. Once a   test harness has been defined, the remainder of a verification exercise is relatively simple and requires no substantial investments of time or skill, even if the source code continues to evolve. But the initial construction of a test harness requires thought, and experimentation [HS02]. The test harness defines which functions are converted into SPIN process threads, how these threads are connected (i.e., how internal communication from the C code is lifted into a communication mechanism that is visible to SPIN). Most important in the definition of the test harness, though, is the definition of abstraction functions that populate the lookup tables, and that determine which state information from the C code should be tracked in the SPIN models. If we could succeed in simplifying, or even automating, these tasks, the value of this approach would be increased significantly.

5 Conclusion

The aim of this paper is to show that many of the new approaches to software testing are based on, or can be understood as applications of, automata theory. User-defined temporal properties may be checked with approaches based on run-time monitoring, static analysis, and of course in standard applications of logic model checking. In logic model checking considerable gains can be made by finding ways to extract automata models directly from program source code. Not all problems are solved in this domain, but perhaps we are beginning to see the types of checking capabilities that might be ahead.

Acknowledgements

The author is grateful to Mihalis Yannakakis and Klaus Havelund for many inspiring discussions on the topics covered in this paper. The work on   was done jointly with Margaret Smith and greatly benefited from the collaboration with Ken Thompson and Phil Winterbottom in the first application to PathStar®.

References

[BR01]   T. Ball, S.K. Rajamani, Automatically Validating Temporal Safety Properties of Interfaces, *Proc. SPIN 2001 Workshop on Model Checking of Software*, Springer LNCS 2057, May 2001, Toronto, pp. 103-122.

[CD00]   J. Corbett, M. Dwyer, et. al. Bandera: Extracting Finite-state Models from Java Source Code. *Proc. ICSE 2000*, Limerick, Ireland.

[CC76]   P. Cousot, R. Cousot, Static Determination of Dynamic Properties of Programs, In B. Robinet, (Ed.), *Proc. 2nd Int. Symp. on Programming*, Paris, France, April 1976, pp. 106-130.

[H00]   J.J. Harrow, Runtime checking of multithreaded applications with Visual Threads. *Proc. SPIN 2000 Workshop on Spin Model Checking and Software Verification*, Springer LNCS 1885, August/Sept. 2001, Stanford University, pp. 331-343.

[HD00]   J. Hatcliff, M.B. Dwyer, and H. Zheng, Slicing software for model construction, *Journal of Higher-Order and Symbolic Computation*.

[E00]   D. Engler, B. Chelf, A. Chou, and S. Hallem, Checking system rules using system-specific, programmer-written compiler extensions. *Proc. 4th Symp. on Operating Systems Design and Implementation (OSDI)*, Usenix Organization, San Diego, CA., Oct. 22-25, 2000.

[GP95]   R. Gerth, D. Peled, M. Vardi, P. Wolper, Simple On-the-fly Automatic Ver-
          ification of Linear Temporal Logic, *Proc. Symp. on Protocol Specification
          Testing and Verification*, Warsaw, Poland, 1995, pp. 3-18.

[GH02]   P.R. Gluck, G.J. Holzmann Using Spin Model Checking for Flight Software
          Verification, *Proc. 2002 Aerospace Conference*, IEEE, March 2002, Big
          Sky, MT, USA.

[HP00]   K. Havelund, T. Pressburger Model Checking Java Programs Using Java
          PathFinder *Int. Journal on Software Tools for Technology Transfer*.

[H97]   G.J. Holzmann, The model checker . *IEEE Trans. on Software Engineer-
          ing*, Vol 23, No. 5, pp. 279-295, May 1997.

[H01]   G.J. Holzmann, Economics of Software Verification, *Proc. Workshop on
          Program Analysis for Software Tools and Engineering*, ACM, Snowbird,
          Utah, USA, June 2001.

[HS00]   G.J. Holzmann, and M.H. Smith, Automating software feature verification,
          Bell Labs Technical Journal, April-June 2000, pp. 72-87.

[HS02]   G.J. Holzmann, and M.H. Smith,   1.0 User Guide, Technical
          Report, Bell Labs, February 28, 2002, 64 pgs.

[H02]   G.J. Holzmann, Static source code checking for user-defined properties,
          Proc. IDPT 2002, 6th World Conference on Integrated Design & Process
          Technology, Pasadena, CA, USA, June 2002.

[H87]   W.E. Howden, *Functional Program Testing and Analysis*, McGraw Hill,
          1987.

[K96]   W. Kelly, V. Maslov, W. Pugh, E. Rosser, T. Shpeisman, and D. Wonna-
          cott, *The Omega calculator and library*, Version 1.1.0. Technical Report
          November 18, 1996, University of Maryland.

[KR88]   B.W. Kernighan, and D.M. Ritchie, *The C Programming Language, 2nd
          Edition*, Prentice Hall, Englewood Cliffs, N.J., 1988.

[KV99]   O. Kupferman, M.Y. Vardi, Vacuity detection in temporal model checking,
          Conf. on Correct Hardware Design and Verification Methods, Springer-
          Verlag, LNCS 1703, 1999, pp. 82-96.

[AM02]   L. Amster, D.L. McClain (Eds.), *Kill Duck Before Serving, Red Faces at
          The New York Times*, Publ. St. Martin's Griffin, New York, 2002, 172 pgs.

[S97]   S. Savage, M. Burrows, G. Nelson, P. Sobalvarro, and T.E. Anderson.
          Eraser: A dynamic data race detector for multithreaded programming. *ACM
          Transactions on Computer Systems*, Vol. 15, No. 4, pp. 391-411, 1997.

[S65]   C. Strachey, An impossible program, Computer Journal, Vol. 7, No. 4, Jan-
          uary 1965, p. 313.

[T95]   F. Tip, A survey of program slicing techniques. *Journal of Programming
          Languages*, Vol. 3, No. 3, Sept. 1995, pp. 121-189.

[VP00]   W. Visser, S. Park, and J. Penix, Applying predicate abstraction to model
          checking object-oriented programs. *Proc. 3rd ACM SOGSOFT Workshop
          on Formal Methods in Software Practice*, August 2000.

[VH00]   W. Visser, K. Havelund, G. Brat, and S. Park, Model checking programs.
          Proc. Int. Conf. on Automated Software Engineering, Sept. 2000.

The Quest for Efficient Boolean Satisfiability Solvers

Lintao Zhang and Sharad Malik

Department of Electrical Engineering, Princeton University
Princeton, NJ 08544
{lintaoz,sharad}@ee.Princeton.edu

Abstract. The classical NP-complete problem of Boolean Satisfiability (SAT) has seen much interest in not just the theoretical computer science community, but also in areas where practical solutions to this problem enable significant practical applications. Since the first development of the basic search based algorithm proposed by Davis, Putnam, Logemann and Loveland (DPLL) about forty years ago, this area has seen active research effort with many interesting contributions that have culminated in state-of-the-art SAT solvers today being able to handle problem instances with thousands, and in same cases even millions, of variables. In this paper we examine some of the main ideas along this passage that have led to our current capabilities. Given the depth of the literature in this field, it is impossible to do this in any comprehensive way; rather we focus on techniques with consistent demonstrated efficiency in available solvers. For the most part, we focus on techniques within the basic DPLL search framework, but also briefly describe other approaches and look at some possible future research directions.

1. Introduction

Given a propositional formula, determining whether there exists a variable assignment such that the formula evaluates to true is called the Boolean Satisfiability Problem, commonly abbreviated as SAT. SAT has seen much theoretical interest as the canonical NP-complete problem [1]. Given its NP-Completeness, it is very unlikely that there exists any polynomial algorithm for SAT. However, NP-Completeness does not exclude the possibility of finding algorithms that are efficient enough for solving many interesting SAT instances. These instances arise from many diverse areas - many practical problems in AI planning [2], circuit testing [3], software verification [4] can be formulated as SAT instances. This has motivated the research in practically efficient SAT solvers.

This research has resulted in the development of several SAT algorithms that have seen practical success. These algorithms are based on various principles such as resolution [5], search [6], local search and random walk [7], Binary Decision Diagrams [8], Stälmarck's algorithm [9], and others. Gu *et al.* [10] provide an excellent review of many of the algorithms developed thus far. Some of these algorithms are **complete**, while others are **stochastic** methods. For a given SAT instance, complete SAT solvers can either find a solution (i.e. a satisfying variable assignment) or prove that no solution exists. Stochastic methods, on the other hand, cannot prove the instance to be unsatisfiable even though they may be able to find a

D. Brinksma and K. G. Larsen (Eds.): CAV 2002, LNCS 2404, pp. 17-36, 2002.

solution for certain kinds of satisfiable instances quickly. Stochastic methods have applications in domains such as AI planning [2] and FPGA routing [11], where instances are likely to be satisfiable and proving unsatisfiability is not required. However, for many other domains (especially verification problems e.g. [4, 12]), the primary task is to prove unsatisfiability of the instances. For these, complete SAT solvers are a requirement.

In recent years search-based algorithms based on the well-known Davis-Logemann-Loveland algorithm [6] (sometimes called the DPLL algorithm for historical reasons) are emerging as some of the most efficient methods for complete SAT solvers. Researchers have been working on DPLL-based SAT solvers for about forty years. In the last ten years we have seen significant growth and success in SAT solver research based on the DPLL framework. Earlier SAT solvers based on DPLL include Tableau (NTAB) [13], POSIT [14], 2cl [15] and CSAT [16] among others. They are still appearing occasionally in the literature for performance comparison reasons. In the mid 1990's, Silva and Sakallah [17], and Bayardo and Schrag [18] proposed to augment the original DPLL algorithm with non-chronological backtracking and conflict-driven learning. These techniques greatly improved the efficiency of the DPLL algorithm for structured (in contrast to randomly generated) SAT instances. Many practical applications emerged (e.g. [4, 11, 12]), which pushed these solvers to their limits and provided strong motivation for finding even more efficient algorithms. This led to a new generation of solvers such as SATO [19], Chaff [20], and BerkMin [21] which pay a lot of attention to optimizing various aspects of the DPLL algorithm. The results are some very efficient SAT solvers that can often solve SAT instances generated from industrial applications with tens of thousands or even millions of variables. On another front, solvers such as satz [22] and cnfs [23] keep pushing the ability to tackle hard random 3-SAT instances. These solvers, though very efficient on random instances, are typically not competitive on structured instances generated from real applications.

A DPLL-based SAT solver is a relatively small piece of software. Many of the solvers mentioned above have only a few thousand lines of code (these solvers are mostly written in C or C++, for efficiency reasons). However, the algorithms involved are quite complex and a lot of attention is focused on various aspects of the solver such as coding, data structures, choosing algorithms and heuristics, and parameter tuning. Even though the overall framework is well understood and people have been working on it for years, it may appear that we have reached a plateau in terms of what can be achieved in practice – however we feel that many open questions still exist and present many research opportunities.

In this paper we chart the journey from the original basic DPLL framework through the introduction of efficient techniques within this framework culminating at current state-of-the-art solvers. Given the depth of literature in this field, it is impossible to do this in any comprehensive way; rather, we focus on techniques with consistent demonstrated efficiency in available solvers. While for the most part, we focus on techniques within the basic DPLL search framework, we will also briefly describe other approaches and look at some possible future research directions.

2. The Basic DPLL Framework

Even though there were many developments pre-dating them, the original algorithm for solving SAT is often attributed to Davis and Putnam for proposing a resolution-based algorithm for Boolean SAT in 1960 [5]. The original algorithm proposed suffers from the problem of memory explosion. Therefore, Davis, Logemann and Loveland [6] proposed a modified version that used search instead of resolution to limit the memory required for the solver. This algorithm is often referred to as the DPLL algorithm. It can be argued that intrinsically these two algorithms are tightly related because search (i.e. branching on variables) can be regarded as a special type of resolution. However, in the future discussion we will regard search-based algorithms as their own class and distinguish them from explicit resolution algorithms.

For the efficiency of the solver, the propositional formula instance is usually presented in a Product of Sum form, usually called a **Conjunctive Normal Form** (**CNF**). It is not a limitation to require the instance to be presented in CNF. There exist polynomial algorithms (e.g. [24]) to transform any propositional formula into a CNF formula that has the same satisfiability as the original one. In the discussions that follow, we will assume that the problem is presented in CNF. A SAT instance in CNF is a logical **and** of one or more **clauses**, where each clause is a logical **or** of one or more **literals**. A literal is either the positive or the negative occurrence of a **variable**.

A propositional formula in CNF has some nice properties that can help prune the search space and speed up the search process. To satisfy a CNF formula, each clause must be satisfied individually. If there exists a clause in the formula that has all its literals assigned value 0, then the current variable assignment or any variable assignment that contains this will not be able to satisfy the formula. A clause that has all its literals assigned to value 0 is called a **conflicting clause**.

```
DPLL(formula, assignment) {
  necessary = deduction(formula, assignment);
  new_asgnmnt = union(necessary, assignment);
  if (is_satisfied(formula, new_asgnmnt))
    return SATISFIABLE;
  else if (is_conflicting(formula, new_asgnmnt))
    return CONFLICT;
  var = choose_free_variable(formula, new_asgnmnt);
  asgn1 = union(new_asgnmnt, assign(var, 1));
  if (DPLL(formula, asgn1)==SATISFIABLE)
    return SATISFIABLE;
  else {
    asgn2 = union (new_asgnmnt, assign(var, 0));
    return DPLL(formula, asgn2);
  }
}
```

Fig. 1. The recursive description of DPLL algorithm

Traditionally the DPLL algorithm is written in a recursive manner as shown in Fig. 1. Function `DPLL()` is called with a formula and a set of variable assignments. Function `deduction()` will return with a set of the necessary variable assignments that can be deduced from the existing variable assignments. The recursion will end if the formula is either satisfied (i.e. evaluates to 1 or **true**) or unsatisfied (i.e. evaluates to 0 or **false**) under the current variable assignment. Otherwise, the algorithm will choose an unassigned variable from the formula and branch on it for both phases. The solution process begins with calling the function `DPLL()` with an empty set of variable assignments.

In [25], the authors generalized many of the actual implementations of various solvers based on DPLL and rewrote it in an iterative manner as shown in Fig. 2. The algorithm described in Fig. 2 is an improvement of algorithm in Fig. 1 as it allows the solver to backtrack non-chronologically, as we will see in the following sections. Different solvers based on DPLL differ mainly in the detailed implementation of each of the functions shown in Fig. 2. We will use the framework of Fig. 2 as the foundation for our discussions that follow.

The algorithm described in Fig. 2 is a branch and search algorithm. Initially, none of the variables is assigned a value. We call unassigned variables **free** variables. First the solver will do some preprocessing on the instance to be solved, done by function `preprocess()` in Fig. 2. If preprocessing cannot determine the outcome, the main loop begins with a branch on a free variable by assigning it a value. We call this operation a **decision** on a variable, and the variable will have a **decision level** associated with it, starting from 1 and incremented with subsequent decisions. This is done by function `decide_next_branch()` in Fig. 2. After the branch, the problem is simplified as a result of this decision and its consequences. The function `deduce()` performs some reasoning to determine variable assignments that are needed for the problem to be satisfiable given the current set of decisions. Variables that are assigned as a consequence of this deduction after a branch will assume the same decision level as the decision variable. After the deduction, if all the clauses are satisfied, then the instance is satisfiable; if there exists a conflicting clause, then the

```
status = preprocess();
if (status!=UNKNOWN) return status;
while(1) {
  decide_next_branch();
  while (true) {
    status = deduce();
    if (status == CONFLICT) {
      blevel = analyze_conflict();
      if (blevel == 0)
        return UNSATISFIABLE;
      else backtrack(blevel);
    }
    else if (status == SATISFIABLE)
        return SATISFIABLE;
    else break;
  }
}
```

Fig. 2. The iterative description of DPLL algorithm

current branch chosen cannot lead to a satisfying assignment, so the solver will backtrack (i.e. undo certain branches). Which decision level to backtrack to is determined by the function `analyze_conflict()`. Backtrack to level 0 indicates that even without any branching, the instance is still unsatisfiable. In that case, the solver will declare that the instance is unsatisfiable. Within the function `analyze_conflict()`, the solver may do some analysis and record some information from the current conflict in order to prune the search space for the future. This process is called **conflict-driven learning**. If the instance is neither satisfied nor conflicting under the current variable assignments, the solver will choose another variable to branch and repeat the process.

3. The Components of a DPLL SAT Solver

In this section of the paper, we discuss each of the components of a DPLL SAT solver. Each of these components has been the subject of much scrutiny over the years. This section focuses on the main lessons learnt in this process.

3.1 The Branching Heuristics

Branching occurs in the function `decide_next_branch()` in Fig. 2. When no more deduction is possible, the function will choose one variable from all the free variables and assign it to a value. The importance of choosing good branching variables is well known - different branching heuristics may produce drastically different sized search trees for the same basic algorithm, thus significantly affect the efficiency of the solver. Over the years many different branching heuristics have been proposed by different researchers. Not surprisingly, comparative experimental evaluations have also been done (e.g. [26, 27]).

Early branching heuristics such as Bohm's Heuristic (reported in [28]), Maximum Occurrences on Minimum sized clauses (MOM) (e.g. [14]), and Jeroslow-Wang [29] can be regarded as greedy algorithms that try to make the next branch generate the largest number of implications or satisfy most clauses. All these heuristics use some functions to estimate the effect of branching on each free variable, and choose the variable that has the maximum function value. These heuristics work well for certain classes of instances. However, all of the functions are based on the statistics of the clause database such as clause length etc. These statistics, though useful for random SAT instances, usually do not capture relevant information about structured problems.

In [26], the author proposed the use of literal count heuristics. Literal count heuristics count the number of unresolved (i.e. unsatisfied) clauses in which a given variable appears in either phase. In particular, the author found that the heuristic that chooses the variable with dynamic largest combined sum (DLIS) of literal counts in both phases gives quite good results for the benchmarks tested. Notice that the counts are state-dependent in the sense that different variable assignments will give different counts. The reason is because whether a clause is unresolved (unsatisfied) depends on the current variable assignment. Because the count is state-dependent, each time the function decide_next_branch() is called, the counts for all the free variables need to be recalculated.

As the solvers become more and more efficient, calculating counts for branching dominates the run time. Therefore, more efficient and effective branching heuristics are needed. In [20], the authors proposed the heuristic called Variable State Independent Decaying Sum (VSIDS). VSIDS keeps a score for each phase of a variable. Initially, the scores are the number of occurrences of a literal in the initial problem. Because modern SAT solvers have a learning mechanism, clauses are added to the clause database as the search progresses. VSIDS increases the score of a variable by a constant whenever an added clause contains the variable. Moreover, as the search progresses, periodically all the scores are divided by a constant number. In effect, the VSIDS score is a literal occurrence count with higher weight on the more recently added clauses. VSIDS will choose the free variable with the highest combined score to branch. Experiments show that VSIDS is quite competitive compared with other branching heuristics on the number of branches needed to solve a problem. Because VSIDS is state independent (i.e. scores are not dependent on the variable assignments), it is cheap to maintain. Experiments show that the decision procedure using VSIDS takes a very small percentage of the total run time even for problems with millions of variables.

More recently, [21] proposed another decision scheme that pushes the idea of VSIDS further. Like VSIDS, the decision strategy is trying to decide on the variables that are "active recently". In VSIDS, the activity of a variable is captured by the score that is related to the literal's occurrence. In [21], the authors propose to capture the activity by conflicts. More precisely, when a conflict occurs, all the literals in the clauses that are responsible for the conflict will have their score increased. A clause is responsible for a conflict if it is involved in the resolution process of generating the learned clauses (described in the following sections). In VSIDS, the focus on "recent" is captured by decaying the score periodically. In [21], the scores are also decayed periodically. Moreover, the decision heuristic will limit the decision variable to be among the literals that occur in the last added clause that is unresolved. The experiments seem to indicate that the new decision scheme is more robust compared with VSIDS on the benchmarks tested.

In other efforts, satz [22] proposed the use of look-ahead heuristics for branching; and cnfs [23] proposed the use of backbone-directed heuristics for branching. They share the common feature that they both seem to be quite effective on difficult random problems. However, they are also quite expensive compared with VSIDS. Random SAT problems are usually much harder than structured problems of the same size. Current solvers can only attack hard random 3-SAT problems with several hundred variables. Therefore, the instances regarded as hard for random SAT is generally much smaller in size than the instances considered hard for structured problems. Thus, while it may be practical to apply these expensive heuristics to the smaller random problems, their overhead tends to be unacceptable for the larger well-structured problems.

3.2 The Deduction Algorithm

Function deduce() serves the purpose of pruning the search space by "look ahead". When a branch variable is assigned a value, the entire clause database is simplified. Function deduce() needs to determine the consequences of the last decision to make the instance satisfiable, and may return three status values. If the instance is satisfied under the current variable assignment, it will return SATISFIABLE; if the instance contains a conflicting clause, it will return CONFLICT; otherwise, it will return UNKNOWN and the solver will continue to branch. There are various mechanisms with different deduction power and run time costs for the deduce function. The correctness of the algorithm will not be affected as long as the deduction rules incorporated are valid (e.g. it will not return SATISFIABLE when the instance contains a conflicting clause under the assignment). However, different deduction rules, or even different implementations of the same rule, can significantly affect the efficiency of the solver.

Over the years several different deduction mechanisms have been proposed. However, it seems that the **unit clause rule** [6] is the most efficient one because it requires relatively little computational power but can prune large search spaces. The unit clause rule states that for a certain clause, if all but one of its literals has been assigned the value 0, then the remaining (unassigned) literal must be assigned the value 1 for this clause to be satisfied, which is essential for the formula to be satisfied. Such clauses are called **unit clauses**, and the unassigned literal in a unit clause is called a **unit literal**. The process of assigning the value 1 to all unit literals is called **unit propagation**, or sometimes called **Boolean Constraint Propagation (BCP)**. Almost all modern SAT solvers incorporate this rule in the deduction process. In a SAT solver, BCP usually takes the most significant part of the run time. Therefore, its efficiency is directly related to the implementation of the BCP engine.

3.2.1 BCP Mechanisms

In a SAT solver, the BCP engine's function is to detect unit clauses and conflicting clauses after a variable assignment. The BCP engine is the most important part of a SAT solver and usually dictates the data structure and organization of the solver.

A simple and intuitive implementation for BCP is to keep counters for each clause. This scheme is attributed to Crawford and Auton [13] by [30]. Similar schemes are subsequently employed in many solvers such as GRASP [25], rel_sat [18], satz [22] etc. For example, in GRASP [25], each clause keeps two counters, one for the number of value 1 literals in the clause and the other for the number of value 0 literals in the clause. Each variable has two lists that contain all the clauses where that variable appears as a positive and negative literal, respectively. When a variable is assigned a value, all the clauses that contain this literal will have their counters updated. If a clause's value 0 count becomes equal to the total number of literals in the clause, then it is a conflicting clause. If a clause's value 0 count is one less than the total number of literals in the clause and the value 1 count is 0, then the clause is a unit clause. A counter-based BCP engine is easy to understand and implement, but this scheme is not the most efficient one. If the instance has m clauses and n variables, and on average each clause has l literals, then whenever a variable gets assigned, on the average $l\,m\,/\,n$ counters need to be updated. On backtracking from a conflict, we need to undo the counter assignments for the variables unassigned during the backtracking. Each undo for a variable assignment will also update $l\,m\,/\,n$ counters on average. Modern solvers usually incorporate learning mechanisms in the search process (described in the next sections), and learned clauses often have many literals. Therefore, the average clause length l is quite large, thus making a counter-based BCP engine relatively slow.

In [30], the authors of the solver SATO proposed the use of another mechanism for BCP using head/tail lists. In this mechanism, each clause has two pointers associated with it, called the head and tail pointer respectively. A clause stores all its literals in an array. Initially, the head pointer points to the first literal of the clause (i.e. beginning of the array), and the tail pointer points to the last literal of the clause (i.e. end of the array). Each variable keeps four linked lists that contain pointer to clauses. The linked lists for the variable v are `clause_of_pos_head(v)`, `clause_of_neg_head(v)`, `clause_of_pos_tail(v)` and `clause_of_neg_tail(v)`. Each of these lists contains the pointers to the clauses that have their head/tail literal in positive/negative phases of variable v. If v is assigned with the value 1, `clause_of_pos_head(v)` and `clause_of_pos_tail(v)` will be ignored. For each clause C in `clause_of_neg_head(v)`, the solver will search for a literal that does not evaluate to 1 from the position of the head literal of C to the position of the tail literal of C. Notice the head literal of C must be a literal corresponding to v in negative phase. During the search process, four cases may occur:

1)   If during the search we first encounter a literal that evaluates to 1, then the clause is satisfied, we need to do nothing.

2)   If during the search we first encounter a literal l that is free and l is not the tail literal, then we remove C from `clause_of_neg_head(v)` and add C to head list of the variable corresponding to l. We refer to this operation as moving the head literal, because in essence the head pointer is moved from its original position to the position of l.

3)   If all literals in between these two pointers are assigned value 0, but the tail literal is unassigned, then the clause is a unit clause, and the tail literal is the unit literal for this clause.

4)   If all literals in between these two pointers and the tail literal are assigned value 0, then the clause is a conflicting clause.

Similar actions are performed for `clause_of_neg_tail(v)`, only the search is in the reverse direction (i.e. from tail to head).

Head/tail list method is faster than the counter-based scheme because when the variable is assigned value 1, the clauses that contain the positive literals of this clause will not be visited at all and vice-versa. As each clause has only two pointers, whenever a variable is assigned a value, the status of only m/n clauses needs to be updated on the average, if we assume head/tail literals are distributed evenly in either phase. Even though the work needed to be done for each update is different from the counter-based mechanism, in general head/tail mechanism is still much faster.

For both the counter-based algorithm and the head/tail list-based algorithm, undoing a variable's assignment during backtrack has about the same computational complexity as assigning the variable. In [20], the authors of the solver Chaff proposed another BCP algorithm called 2-literal watching. Similar to the head/tail list algorithm, 2-literal watching also has two special literals for each clause called *watched literals*. Each variable has two lists containing pointers to all the watched literals corresponding to it in either phase. We denote the lists for variable v as pos_watched(v) and neg_watched(v). In contrast to the head/tail list scheme in SATO, there is no imposed order on the two pointers within a clause, and each of the pointers can move in either direction. Initially the watched literals are free. When a variable v is assigned value 1, for each literal p pointed to by a pointer in the list of neg_watched(v) (notice p must be a literal of v with negative phase), the solver will search for a literal l in the clause containing p that is not set to 0. There are four cases that may occur during the search:

1) If there exists such a literal l and it is not the other watched literal, then we remove pointer to p from neg_watched(v), and add pointer to l to the watched list of the variable corresponding to l. We refer to this operation as moving the watched literal, because in essence one of the watched pointers is moved from its original position to the position of l.

2) If the only such l is the other watched literal and it is free, then the clause is a unit clause, with the other watched literal being the unit literal.

3) If the only such l is the other watched literal and it evaluates to 1, then we need to do nothing.

4) If all literals in the clause is assigned value 0 and no such l exists, then the clause is a conflicting clause.

2-literal watching has the same advantage as the head/tail list mechanism compared with the literal counting scheme. Moreover, unlike the other two mechanisms, undoing a variable assignment during backtrack in the 2-literal watching scheme takes constant time. This is because the two watched literals are the last to be assigned to 0, so as a result, any backtracking will make sure that the literals being watched are either unassigned, or assigned to one. Thus, no action is required to update the pointers for the literals being watched. Therefore, it is significantly faster than both counter-based and head/tail mechanisms for BCP. In Fig. 3, we show a comparison of 2-literal watching and head/tail list mechanism.

In [31], the authors examined the mechanisms mentioned above and introduced some new deduction data structures and mechanisms. In particular, the experiments suggest that the mechanism called Head/Tail list with Literal Sifting actually outperforms the 2-literal watching mechanism for BCP. However, the experiments are carried out in a framework implemented in Java. The authors admit that it may not represent the actual performance if implemented in C/C++.

3.2.2 Other Deduction Mechanisms

Besides the unit clause rule, there are other rules that can be incorporated into a deduction engine. In this section, we briefly discuss some of them. We want to point out that though many of the deduction mechanisms have been shown to work on certain classes of SAT instances, unlike the unit clause rule, none of them seems to work without deteriorating the overall performance of the SAT solver for general SAT instances.

One of the most widely known rules for deduction is the **pure literal rule** [6]. The pure literal rule states that if a variable only occurs in a single phase in all the unresolved clauses, then it can be assigned with a value such that the literal of the variable in that phase evaluates to 1. Whether a variable satisfies the pure literal rule

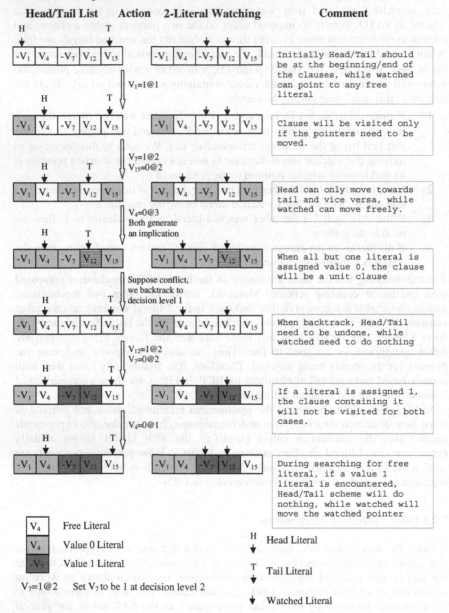

Fig. 3. Comparison of Head/Tail List and 2-Literal Watching

is expensive to detect during the actual solving process, and the consensus seems to be that incorporating the pure literal rule will generally slow down the solving process for most of the benchmarks encountered.

Another explored deduction mechanism is equivalence reasoning. In particular, eqsatz [32] incorporated equivalence reasoning into the satz [22] solver and found that it is effective on some particular classes of benchmarks. In that work, the equivalence reasoning is accomplished by a pattern-matching scheme for equivalence clauses. A related deduction mechanism was proposed in [33]. There, the authors propose to include more patterns in the matching process for simplification purpose in deduction.

The unit literal rule basically guarantees that all the unit clauses are consistent with each other. We can also require that all the 2 literal clauses be consistent with each other and so on. Researchers have been exploring this idea in the deduction process in works such as [34, 35]. In particular, these approaches maintain a transitive closure of all the 2 literal clauses. However, the overhead of maintaining this information seems to far outweigh any benefit gained from them on the average.

Recursive Learning [36] is another reasoning technique originally proposed in the context of learning with a logic circuit representation of a formula. Subsequent research [37] has proposed to incorporate this technique in SAT solvers and found that it works quite well for some benchmarks generated from combinational circuit equivalence checking problems.

3.3 Conflict Analysis and Learning

When a conflicting clause is encountered, the solver needs to backtrack and undo the decisions. Conflict analysis is the procedure that finds the reason for a conflict and tries to resolve it. It tells the SAT solver that there exists no solution for the problem in a certain search space, and indicates a new search space to continue the search.

The original DPLL algorithm proposed the simplest conflict analysis method. For each decision variable, the solver keeps a flag indicating whether it has been tried in both phases (i.e. flipped) or not. When a conflict occurs, the conflict analysis procedure looks for the decision variable with the highest decision level that has not been flipped, marks it flipped, undoes all the assignments between that decision level and current decision level, and then tries the other phase for the decision variable. This method is called **chronological backtracking** because it always tries to undo the last decision that is not flipped. Chronological backtracking works well for random generate SAT instances and is employed in some SAT solvers (e.g satz [22]).

For structured problems (which is usually the case for problems generated from real world applications), chronological backtracking is generally not efficient in pruning the search space. More advanced conflict analysis engines will analyze the conflicting clauses encountered and figure out the direct reason for the conflict. This method will usually backtrack to an earlier decision level than the last unflipped decision. Therefore, it is called **non-chronological backtracking**. During the conflict analysis process, information about the current conflict may be recorded as clauses and added to the original database. The added clauses, though redundant in the sense that they will not change the satisfiability of the original problem, can often help to prune search space in the future. This mechanism is called **conflict-directed learning**. Such learned clauses are called **conflict clauses** as opposed to **conflicting clauses**, which refer to clauses that generate conflicts.

Non-chronological backtracking, sometimes referred to as **conflict-directed backjumping**, was proposed first in the Constraint Satisfaction Problem (CSP) domain (e.g. [38]). This, together with conflict-directed learning, were first incorporated into a SAT solver by Silva and Sakallah in GRASP [25], and by Bayardo and Schrag in rel_sat [18]. These techniques are essential for efficient solving of structured problems. Many solvers such as SATO [19] and Chaff [20] have incorporated similar technique in the solving process.

Previously, learning and non-chronological backtracking have been discussed by analyzing implication graphs (e.g. [17, 39]). Here we will formulate learning as an alternate but equivalent resolution process and discuss different schemes in this framework.

Researchers have adapted the conflict analysis engine to some deduction rules other than the unit clause rule in previous work (e.g. [33, 37]). However, because the unit clause rule is usually the only rule that is incorporated in most SAT solvers, we will describe the learning algorithm that works with such a deduction engine. In such a solver, when a variable is implied by a unit clause, the clause is called the **antecedent** of the variable. Because the unit clause rule is the only rule in the deduction engine, every implied variable will have an antecedent. Decision variables, on the other case, have no antecedents.

In conflict driven learning, the learned clauses are generated by resolution. Resolution is a process to generate a clause from two clauses analogous to the process of **consensus** in the logic optimization domain (e.g. [40]). Resolution is given by

$$(x + y)\,(y' + z) \equiv (x + y)\,(y' + z)(x + z)$$

The term $(x + z)$ is called the **resolvent** of clause $(x + y)$ and $(y' + z)$. Because of this, we have

$$(x + y)\,(y' + z) \rightarrow (x+z)$$

Similar to the well-known consensus law (e.g. [40]), the resulting clause of resolution between two clauses is redundant with respect to the original clauses. Therefore, we can always generate clauses from original clause database by resolution and add the generated clause back to the clause database without changing the satisfiability of the original formula. However, randomly choosing two clauses and adding the resolvent to the clause database will not generally help the solving process. Conflict-driven learning is a way to generate learned clauses with some direction in the resolution process.

The pseudo-code for conflict analysis is shown in Fig. 4. Whenever a conflicting clause is encountered, `analyze_conflict()` will be called. Function `choose_literal()` will choose a literal from the clause. Function `resolve(cl1, cl2, var)` will return a clause that contains all the literals in cl1 and cl2 except for the literals that corresponds to variable var. Note that one of the input clauses to `resolve()` is a conflicting clause (i.e. all literals evaluate to 0), and the other is the antecedent of the variable *var* (i.e. all but one literal evaluate to 0). Therefore, the resulting clause will have all literals evaluating to 0, i.e. it will still be a conflicting clause.

```
analyze_conflict(){
    cl = find_conflicting_clause();
    while (!stop_criterion_met(cl)) {
        lit = choose_literal(cl);
        var = variable_of_literal( lit );
        ante = antecedent( var );
        cl = resolve(cl, ante, var);
    }
    add_clause_to_database(cl);
    back_dl = clause_asserting_level(cl);
    return back_dl;
}
```

Fig. 4. Generating Learned Clause by Resolution

The clause generation process will stop when some predefined stop criterion is met. In modern SAT solvers, the stop criterion is that the resulting clause be an **asserting clause**. A clause is asserting if the clause contains all value 0 literals; and among them only one is assigned at current decision level. After backtracking, this clause will become a unit clause and force the literal to assume another value (i.e. evaluate to 1), thus bringing the search to a new space. We will call the decision level of the literal with the second highest decision level in an asserting clause the **asserting level** of that clause. The asserting clause is a unit clause at its asserting decision level.

In addition to the above asserting clause requirement, different learning schemes may have some additional requirements. Different learning schemes differ in their stop criterion and the way to choose literals. Notice the stop criterion can always be met if function choose_literal() always chooses the literal that is assigned last in the clause. If that is the case, the resolution process will always resolve the conflicting clause with the antecedent of the variable that is assigned last in the clause. After a certain number of calls to resolve(), there will always be a time when the variable that is assigned last in the clause is the decision variable of the current decision level. At this time, the resulting clause is guaranteed to be an asserting clause. The SAT solver rel_sat [18] actually uses this stop criterion, i.e. it requires that the variable that has the highest decision level in the resulting clause be a decision variable. The literal corresponding to this variable will be a unit literal after backtracking, resulting in essentially flipping the decision variable.

In [39], the authors discussed a scheme called the FirstUIP scheme. The FirstUIP scheme is quite similar to the rel_sat scheme but the stop criterion is that it will stop when the *first* asserting clause is encountered. In [17], the authors of GRASP use a similar scheme as the FirstUIP, but add extra clauses other than the asserting clause into the database. If function choose_literal() does not choose literals in reversed chronological order, then extra mechanisms are needed to guarantee that the stop criterion can be met. Some of the schemes discussed in [39] may need function choose_literal() to choose literals that are not in the current decision level.

Different learning schemes affect the SAT solver's efficiency greatly. Experiments in [39] show that among all the discussed schemes, FirstUIP seems to be the best on the benchmarks tested. Therefore, recent SAT solvers (e.g. Chaff [20]) often employ this scheme as the default conflict-driven learning scheme.

Conflict-driven learning will add clauses to the clause database during the search process. Because added clauses are redundant, deleting some or all of them will not affect the correctness of the algorithm. In fact, the added clauses will slow down the deduction engine, and keeping all added clauses may need more memory for storage than the available memory. Therefore, it is often required for the solver to delete some of the less useful learned clauses and learned clauses that have too many literals. There are many heuristics to measure the usefulness of a learned clause. For example, rel_sat [18] proposes to use relevance to measure a clause's usefulness, while BerkMin [21] use the number of conflicts that involve this clause in the history to measure a clause's usefulness. These measures seem to work reasonably well.

3.4 Data Structure for Storing Clause Database

Current state-of-the-art SAT solvers often need to solve instances that are quite large in size. Some instances generated from circuit verification problems may contain millions of variables and several million clauses. Moreover, during the SAT solving process, learned clauses are generated for each conflict encountered and may further increase the dataset size. Therefore, efficient data structures for storing the clauses are needed.

Most commonly, clauses are stored in a linear way (sometimes called **sparse matrix representation**), i.e. each clause occupies its own space and no overlap exists between clauses. Therefore, the dataset size is linear in the number of literals in the clause database. Early SAT solvers (e.g. GRASP [25], rel_sat [18]) use pointer heavy data structures such as linked lists and array of pointers pointing to structures to store the clause database. Pointer heavy data structures, though convenient for manipulating the clause database (i.e. adding/deleting clauses), are not memory efficient and usually cause a lot of cache misses during the solving process because of lack of access locality. Chaff [20] uses a data structure that stores clause data in a large array. Because arrays are not as flexible as linked lists, some additional garbage collection code is needed when clauses are deleted. The advantage of the array data structure is that it is very efficient in memory utilization. Moreover, because an array occupies contiguous memory space, access locality is increased. Experiments shows that the array data structure has a big advantage compared with linked lists in terms of cache misses that translates to substantial speed-up in the solving process.

Researchers have proposed schemes other than sparse matrix representation for storing clauses. In [41], the authors of the solver SATO proposed the use of a data structure called **trie** to store clauses. A trie is a ternary tree. Each internal node in the trie structure is a variable index, and its three children edges are labeled Pos, Neg, and DC, for positive, negative, and don't care, respectively. A leaf node in a trie is either True or False. Each path from root of the trie to a True leaf represents a clause. A trie is said to be ordered if for every internal node V, Parent(V) has a smaller variable index than the index of variable V. The ordered trie structure has the nice property of being able to detect duplicate and tail subsumed clauses of a database quickly. A clause is said to be tail subsumed by another clause if its first portion of the literals (a prefix) is also a clause in the clause database. For example, (a + b + c) is tail subsumed by (a + b). Fig. 5 shows a simple clause database represented in a trie structure.

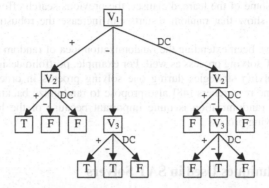

Fig. 5. A trie data structure representing clauses (V_1+V_2) $(V_1'+V_3)$ $(V_1'+V_3')(V_2'+V_3')$

An ordered trie has obvious similarities with Binary Decision Diagrams. This has naturally led to the exploration of decision diagram style set representations. In [42] and [43], the authors have experimented with using Zero-suppressed Binary Decision Diagrams (ZBDDs) [44] to represent the clause database. A ZBDD representation of the clause database can detect not only tail subsumption but also head subsumption. Both authors report significant compression of the clause database for certain classes of problems.

Based on current experimental data it does not seem that the data compression advantages of the trie and ZBDD data structures are sufficient to justify the additional maintenance overhead of these data structures compared to the sparse matrix representation.

3.5 Preprocess, Restart and Other Techniques

Preprocess aims at simplifying the instances before the regular solving begins in order to speed up the solving process. Usually the preprocessor of a SAT solver is just an extra deduction mechanism applied at the beginning of the search. Because the preprocessor will only be applied once in the solving process, it is usually possible to incorporate some deduction rules that are too expensive to be applied at every node of the search tree. The preprocessor can be applied on-line (within the solver) or off-line (it produces an equivalent instance to be fed to a solver). In [45], the authors give an overview of some of the existing preprocessing techniques and find that the result of applying simplification techniques before the regular search is actually mixed.

The time required for solving similar SAT instances often varies greatly for complete algorithms. Two problems that are exactly the same except for the variable order may require totally different times to solve by a certain SAT solver (e.g. one can be solved in seconds while the other takes days). In [46], the authors proposed to use **random restart** to cope with this phenomenon. Random restart randomly throws away the already searched space and starts from scratch. This technique is applied in modern SAT solvers such as Chaff [20] and BerkMin [21]. In these cases, when restart is invoked, even though the current search tree is abandoned, because the solver still keeps some of the learned clauses, the previous search effort is not totally lost. Experiments show that random restarts can increase the robustness of certain SAT solvers.

Researchers have been extending the randomization idea of random restart to other aspects of the SAT solving process as well. For example, portfolio design [47] aims at using different solving strategies during one solving process in order to make the solver robust. Some researchers [48] also propose to randomize backtracking. All in all, it seems that randomization is quite important because of the heavy tail [49] nature of SAT solving process.

4. Other Techniques Used in SAT Solvers

In this section, we briefly discuss some of the other techniques used to solve SAT problems besides the basic DPLL search.

The original Davis Putnam algorithm [5] was based on resolution. A well-known problem of the resolution-based algorithm is that the solver tends to blow up in memory. Because of this, resolution based algorithm is seldom employed in modern SAT solvers. In [42], the authors propose the use of ZBDDs to represent clauses in a resolution-based solver and utilize the compression power of decision diagrams to control the memory blowup. Their experiment shows that for certain classes of SAT problems, the resolution-based approach shows very good results.

Stalmärck's algorithm [9] is a patented proprietary algorithm for solving SAT. Stalmärck's algorithm use breath-first search in contrast to the depth-first search employed by DPLL. There are commercial implementations of SAT solvers based on this algorithm [50]. HeerHugo [51] is a publicly available solver that claims to be using an algorithm similar to the Stalmärk's algorithm.

Another approach is to use stochastic algorithms. Stochastic algorithms cannot prove a SAT instance to be unsatisfiable. However, for some hard satisfiable instances, stochastic methods may find solutions very quickly. Currently, two of the more successful approaches to the stochastic method are random walk based algorithms such as walksat [7] and Discrete Lagrangian-Based global search methods such as DLM [52].

For more about other SAT solving techniques, we refer the readers to a survey[10].

5. Conclusions and Future Works

In this paper, we briefly discussed some of the techniques employed in modern Boolean Satisfiability solvers. In particular, we concentrated on the procedure based on the DPLL search algorithm. In recent years, SAT solvers based on DPLL search have made phenomenal progress. Efficient SAT solvers such as Chaff [20] are deployed in industrial strength applications for hardware verification and debugging. In these environments, the SAT solver routinely encounters instances with thousands or even millions of variables. Therefore, it is of great importance to increase the capacity and efficiency of the SAT solver.

Even though researchers have been working on SAT engines for quite a long time, there is still a lot of work that remains to be done. First of all, the overall understanding of SAT instances is still quite limited. For example, though there exist some rough ideas about the difficulty of SAT problems (e.g. [53, 54]), it is still not clear how can we estimate the hardness of a given problem without actually solving it. Experimental evaluation of different SAT solving algorithms is more like an art than a science because it is easy to tune a solver to a given set of benchmarks, but the parameters may not work for the same benchmarks with some simple permutation (e.g.[55]). On the application side, currently most of the applications use SAT solvers as blackboxes and no interaction is possible between the applications and the SAT solvers. Application specific knowledge can help a lot in the solving process as demonstrated in [56]. For a particular application, custom implementation of a SAT solver may also be helpful (e.g. [57]). All in all, we believe there are still many research topics to be explored. As more and more applications utilize SAT solvers as deduction and reasoning engine, we believe many new algorithms will emerge and push the envelope for efficient implementations even further.

Acknowledgments

The authors would like to thank Dr. Aarti Gupta for suggestions and help in improving the paper.

6. References

[1] S. A. Cook, "The complexity of theorem-proving procedures," presented at Third Annual ACM Symposium on Theory of Computing, 1971.

[2] H. Kautz and B. Selman, "Planning as Satisfiability," presented at European Conference on Artificial Intelligence(ECAI-92), 1992.

[3] P. Stephan, R. Brayton, and A. Sangiovanni-Vencentelli, "Combinational Test Generation Using Satisfiability," IEEE Transactions on Computer-Aided Design of Integrated Circuits and Systems, vol. 15, pp. 1167-1176, 1996.

[4] D. Jackson and M. Vaziri, "Finding Bugs with a Constraint Solver," presented at International Symposium on Software Testing and Analysis, Portland, OR, 2000.

[5] M. Davis and H. Putnam, "A computing procedure for quantification theory," Journal of ACM, vol. 7, pp. 201-215, 1960.

[6] M. Davis, G. Logemann, and D. Loveland, "A machine program for theorem proving," Communications of the ACM, vol. 5, pp. 394-397, 1962.

[7] B. Selman, H. Kautz, and B. Cohen, "Local Search Strategies for Satisfiability Testing," in Cliques, Coloring, and Satisfiability: Second DIMACS Implementation Challenge, DIMACS Series in Discrete Mathematics and Theoretical Computer Science, vol. 26, D. S. Johnson and M. A. Trick, Eds.: American Methematical Society, 1996.

[8] R. E. Bryant, "Graph-Based Algorithms for Boolean Function Manipulation," IEEE Transactions on Computers, vol. C-35, pp. 677-691, 1986.

[9] G. Stålmarck, "A system for determining prepositional logic theorems by applying values and rules to triplets that are generated from a formula." US Patent N 5 27689, 1995.

[10] J. Gu, P. W. Purdom, J. Franco, and B. W. Wah, "Algorithms for the Satisfiability (SAT) Problem: A Survey," in *DIMACS Series in Discrete Mathematics and Theoretical Computer Science*: American Mathematical Society, 1997.

[11] G.-J. Nam, K. A. Sakallah, and R. A. Rutenbar, "Satisfiability-Based Layout Revisited: Detailed Routing of Complex FPGAs Via Search-Based Boolean SAT," presented at ACM/SIGDA International Symposium on Field-Programmable Gate Arrays (FPGA'99), Monterey, California, 1999.

[12] A. Biere, A. Cimatti, E. M. Clarke, and Y. Zhu, "Symbolic Model Checking without BDDs," presented at Tools and Algorithms for the Analysis and Construction of Systems (TACAS'99), 1999.

[13] J. Crawford and L. Auton, "Experimental results on the cross-over point in satisfiability problems," presented at National Conference on Artificial Intelligence (AAAI), 1993.

[14] J. W. Freeman, "Improvements to Propositional Satisfiability Search Algorithms," in *Ph.D. Thesis, Department of Computer and Information Science*: University of Pennsylvania, 1995.

[15] A. V. Gelder and Y. K. Tsuji, "Satisfiability Testing with more Reasoning and Less guessing," in *Cliques, Coloring and Satisfiability: Second DIMACS Implementation Challenge, DIMACS Series in Discrete Mathematics and Theoretical Computer Science*, M. Trick, Ed.: American Mathematical Society, 1995.

[16] O. Dubois, P. Andre, Y. Boufkhad, and J. Carlier, "SAT v.s. UNSAT," in *Cliques, Coloring and Satisfiability: Second DIMACS Implementation Challenge, DIMACS Series in Discrete Mathematics and Theoretical Computer Science*, D. S. Johnson and M. Trick, Eds., 1993.

[17] J. P. Marques-Silva and K. A. Sakallah, "Conflict Analysis in Search Algorithms for Propositional Satisfiability," presented at IEEE International Conference on Tools with Artificial Intelligence, 1996.

[18] R. Bayardo and R. Schrag, "Using CSP look-back techniques to solve real-world SAT instances," presented at National Conference on Artificial Intelligence (AAAI), 1997.

[19] H. Zhang, "SATO: An efficient propositional prover," presented at International Conference on Automated Deduction (CADE), 1997.

[20] M. Moskewicz, C. Madigan, Y. Zhao, L. Zhang, and S. Malik, "Chaff: Engineering an Efficient SAT Solver," presented at 39th Design Automation Conference, 2001.

[21] E. Goldberg and Y. Novikov, "BerkMin: a Fast and Robust SAT-Solver," presented at Design Automation & Test in Europe (DATE 2002), 2002.

[22] C. M. Li and Anbulagan, "Heuristics based on unit propagation for satisfiability problems," presented at the fifteenth International Joint Conference on Artificial Intelligence (IJCAI'97), Nagayo, Japan, 1997.

[23] O. Dubois and G. Dequen, "A backbone-search heuristic for efficient solving of hard 3-SAT formulae," presented at International Joint Conference on Artificial Intelligence (IJCAI), 2001.

[24] D. A. Plaisted and S. Greenbaum, "A Stucture-preserving Clause Form Translation," *Journal of Symbolic Computation*, vol. 2, pp. 293-304, 1986.

[25] J. P. Marques-Silva and K. A. Sakallah, "GRASP -- A New Search Algorithm for Satisfiability," presented at IEEE International Conference on Tools with Artificial Intelligence, 1996.

[26] J. P. Marques-Silva, "The Impact of Branching Heuristics in Propositional Satisfiability Algorithms," presented at the 9th Portuguese Conference on Artificial Intelligence (EPIA), 1999.

[27] J. N. Hooker and V. Vinay, "Branching rules for satisfiability," *Journal of Automated Reasoning*, vol. 15, pp. 359-383, 1995.

[28] M. Buro and H. Kleine-Buning, "Report on a SAT competition," Technical Report, University of Paderborn 1992.

[29] R. G. Jeroslow and J. Wang, "Solving propositional satisfiability problems," *Annals of Mathematics and Artificial Intelligence*, vol. 1, pp. 167-187, 1990.

[30] H. Zhang and M. Stickel, "An efficient algorithm for unit-propagation," presented at International Symposium on Artificial Intelligence and Mathematics, Ft. Lauderdale, Florida, 1996.

[31] I. Lynce and J. P. Marques-Silva, "Efficient data structures for backtrack search SAT solvers," presented at Fifth International Symposium on the Theory and Applications of Satisfiability Testing, 2002.

[32] C. M. Li, "Integrating equivalency reasoning into Davis-Putnam Procedure," presented at National Conference on Artificial Intelligence (AAAI), 2000.

[33] I. Lynce and J. P. Marques-Silva, "Integrating Simplification Techniques in SAT Algorithms," presented at Logic in Computer Science Short Paper Session (LICS-SP), 2001.

[34] A. V. Gelder and Y. K. Tsuji, "Satisfiability Testing with more Reasoning and Less guessing," in *Cliques, Coloring and Satisfiability: Second DIMACS Implementation Challenge, DIMACS Series in Discrete Mathematics and Theoretical Computer Science*, D. S. Johnson and M. Trick, Eds.: American Mathematical Society, 1993.

[35] S. T. Chakradhar and V. D. Agrawal, "A Transitive Closure Based Algorithm for Test Generation," presented at Design Automation Conference (DAC), 1991.

[36] W. Kunz and D. K. Pradhan, "Recursive Learning: A New Implication Technique for Efficient Solutions to CAD-problems: Test, Verification and Optimization," *IEEE Transactions on Computer-Aided Design of Integrated Circuits and Systems*, vol. 13, pp. 1143-1158, 1994.

[37] J. P. Marques-Silva, "Improving Satisfiability Algorithms by Using Recursive Learning," presented at International Workshop on Boolean Problems (IWBP), 1998.

[38] P. Prosser, "Hybrid algorithms for the constraint satisfaction problem," *Computational Intelligence*, vol. 9, pp. 268-299, 1993.

[39] L. Zhang, C. Madigan, M. Moskewicz, and S. Malik, "Efficient Conflict Driven Learning in a Boolean Satisfiability Solver," presented at International Conference on Computer Aided Design (ICCAD), San Jose, CA, 2001.

[40] G. Hachtel and F. Somenzi, *Logic Sysntheiss and Verification Algorithms*: Kluwer Academic Publishers, 1996.

[41] H. Zhang and M. Stickel, "Implementing Davis-Putnam's method," Technical Report, University of Iowa 1994.

[42] P. Chatalic and L. Simon, "Multi-Resolution on Compressed Sets of Clauses," presented at International Conference on Tools with Artificial Intelligence, 2000.

[43] F. Aloul, M. Mneimneh, and K. Sakallah, "Backtrack Search Using ZBDDs," presented at International Workshop on Logic Synthesis (IWLS), 2001.

[44] S. I. Minato, "Zero-Suppressed BDDs for Set Manipulation in Combinatorial Problems," presented at 30th Design Automation Conference (DAC), 1993.

[45] I. Lynce and J. P. Marques-Silva, "The Puzzling Role of Simplification in Propositional Satisfiability," presented at EPIA'01 Workshop on Constraint Satisfaction and Operational Research Techniques for Problem Solving (EPIA-CSOR), 2001.

[46] C. P. Gomes, B. Selman, and H. Kautz, "Boosting Combinatorial Search Through Randomization," presented at National Conference on Artificial Intelligence (AAAI), Madison, WI, 1998.

[47] B. A. Huberman, R. M. Lukose, and T. Hogg, "An Economics approach to hard computational problems," *Science*, vol. 275, pp. 51-54, 1997.

[48] I. Lynce and J. P. Marques-Silva, "Complete unrestricted backtracking algorithms for Satisfiability," presented at Fifth International Symposium on the Theory and Applications of Satisfiability Testing, 2002.

[49] C. P. Gomes, B. Selman, N. Crator, and H. Kautz, "Heavy-tailed phenomena in satisfiability and constraint satisfaction problems," *Journal of Automated Reasoning*, vol. 24(1/2), pp. 67-100, 1999.

[50] "Prover Proof Engine," Prover Technology.

[51] J. F. Groote and J. P. Warners, "The propositional formula checker HeerHugo," *Journal of Automated Reasoning*, vol. 24, 2000.

[52] Y. Shang and B. W. Wah, "A Discrete Lagrangian-Based Global-Search Method for Solving Satisfiability Problems," *Journal of Global Optimization*, vol. 12, pp. 61-99, 1998.

[53] I. Gent and T. Walsh, "The SAT Phase Transition," presented at European Conference on Artificial Intelligence (ECAI-94), 1994.

[54] M. Prasad, P. Chong, and K. Keutzer, "Why is ATPG easy?," presented at Design Automation Conference (DAC99), 1999.

[55] F. Brglez, X. Li, and M. Stallmann, "The role of a skeptic agent in testing and benchmarking of SAT algorithms," presented at Fifth International Symposium on theTheory and Applications of Satisfiability Testing, 2002.

[56] O. Strichman, "Pruning techniques for the SAT-based Bounded Model Checking Problem," presented at 11th Advanced Research Working Conference on Correct Hardware Design and Verification Methods (CHARM'01), 2001.

[57] M. Ganai, L. Zhang, P. Ashar, A. Gupta, and S. Malik, "Combining Strengths of Circuit-based and CNF-based Algorithms for a High-Performance SAT Solver," presented at Design Automation Conference (DAC'02), 2002.

On Abstraction in Software Verification*

Patrick Cousot[1] and Radhia Cousot[2]

[1] École normale supérieure, Département d'informatique,
45 rue d'Ulm, 75230 Paris cedex 05, France
Patrick.Cousot@ens.fr www.di.ens.fr/~cousot/
[2] CNRS & École polytechnique, Laboratoire d'informatique,
91128 Palaiseau cedex, France
Radhia.Cousot@polytechnique.fr lix.polytechnique.fr/~rcousot

Abstract. We show that the precision of static abstract software checking algorithms can be enhanced by taking explicitly into account the abstractions that are involved in the design of the program model/abstract semantics. This is illustrated on reachability analysis and abstract testing.

1 Introduction

Most formal methods for reasoning about programs (such as deductive methods, software model checking, dataflow analysis) do not reason directly on the trace-based operational program semantics but on an approximate model of this semantics. The abstraction involved in building the model of the program semantics is usually left implicit and not discussed. The importance of this abstraction appears when it is made explicit for example in order to discuss the soundness and (in)completeness of temporal-logic based verification methods [1,2].

The purpose of this paper is to discuss the practical importance of this abstraction when designing static software checking algorithms. This is illustrated on reachability analysis and abstract testing.

2 Transition Systems

We follow [3,4] in formalizing a hardware or software computer system by a transition system $\langle S, t, I, F, E \rangle$ with set of states S, transition relation $t \subseteq (S \times S)$, initial states $I \subseteq S$, erroneous states $E \subseteq S$, and final states $F \subseteq S$.

An example is that of automatic program manipulation techniques based on the operational semantics of a programming language $\mathcal{L}$. Then there is a computable function mapping any program $p \in \mathcal{L}$ to a (symbolic computer representation of the) transition relation $t[\![p]\!]$ (as well as $I[\![p]\!]$, $F[\![p]\!]$ $E[\![p]\!]$).

---

* This work was supported in part by the RTD project IST-1999-20527 DAEDALUS of the european IST FP5 programme.

A program execution trace $\sigma \in S^\infty$ is a maximal non-empty finite ($\sigma \in S^+$) or infinite ($\sigma \in S^\omega$) sequence $\sigma_0 \ldots \sigma_i \ldots$ of states $\sigma_i \in S$. Execution starts with an initial state $\sigma_0 \in I$. Any state σ_i is related to its successor state σ_{i+1} as specified by the transition relation t so that $\langle \sigma_i, \sigma_{i+1} \rangle \in t$. The sequence $\sigma = \sigma_0 \ldots \sigma_i \ldots \sigma_n$ is finite (of length $|\sigma| = n + 1$) if and only if the last state is erroneous $\sigma_n \in E$ (because of an anomaly during execution) or final $\sigma_n \in F$ (because of normal termination). All other states have a successor (formally $\forall s \in S \setminus (E \cup F) : \exists s' \in S : \langle s, s' \rangle \in t$) in which case execution goes on normally, may be for ever (for infinite traces σ of length $|\sigma| = \omega$).

3   Reachability

Let $t^\star$ be the reflexive transitive closure of the binary relation t. Let $\mathrm{post}[t]\, X$ be the post-image of X by t, that is the set of states which are reachable from a state of X by a transition t: $\mathrm{post}[t]\, X \stackrel{\text{def}}{=} \{s' \in S \mid \exists s \in X : \langle s, s' \rangle \in t\}$ [5,6]. Let $\mathrm{lfp}^{\subseteq} \varphi$ be the least fixpoint of a monotone map φ on a poset $\langle L, \sqsubseteq \rangle$ when it exists (e.g. $\langle L, \sqsubseteq \rangle$ is a cpo or a complete lattice). We have $\mathrm{post}[t^\star]\, I = \mathrm{lfp}^{\subseteq} \mathcal{F}[t]I$ where $\mathcal{F}[t]I(X) \stackrel{\text{def}}{=} I \cup \mathrm{post}[t]\, X$ [3,5]. Given a specification $Q \subseteq S$, the *reachability problem* considered in [5] consists in proving that $\mathrm{post}[t^\star]\, I \subseteq Q$.

Inverse problems consist in considering the inverse t^{-1} of the relation t [3]. We let $\mathrm{pre}[t]\, X \stackrel{\text{def}}{=} \mathrm{post}[t^{-1}]\, X$ be the pre-image of X by t that is the set of states from which there exists a possible transition t to a state of X: $\mathrm{pre}[t]\, X = \{s \in S \mid \exists s' \in X : \langle s, s' \rangle \in t\}$. From $(t^\star)^{-1} = (t^{-1})^\star$ we have $\mathrm{pre}[t^\star]\, F = \mathrm{post}[(t^\star)^{-1}]\, F = \mathrm{lfp}^{\subseteq} \mathcal{F}[t^{-1}]F = \mathrm{lfp}^{\subseteq} \mathcal{B}[t]F$ where $\mathcal{B}[t]F(X) \stackrel{\text{def}}{=} F \cup \mathrm{pre}[t]\, X$ [3,4].

Dual problems [3] consist in considering the dual $\neg \circ \varphi \circ \neg$ of monotone functions φ on complete boolean lattices where $\neg X \stackrel{\text{def}}{=} S \setminus X$ and $f \circ g(x) = f(g(x))$. The dual notions are $\widetilde{\mathrm{post}}[r]\, X \stackrel{\text{def}}{=} \neg \mathrm{post}[r](\neg X)$ so that $\widetilde{\mathrm{post}}[r]\, X = \{s' \mid \forall s : \langle s, s' \rangle \in r \implies s \in X\}$ and $\widetilde{\mathrm{pre}}[r]\, X \stackrel{\text{def}}{=} \neg \mathrm{pre}[r](\neg X) = \{s \mid \forall s' : \langle s, s' \rangle \in r \implies s' \in X\}$. Dual fixpoint characterizations follow from Park's dual fixpoint theorem for monotone functions on complete boolean lattices $\mathrm{gfp}\, \varphi = \neg \mathrm{lfp}\, \neg \circ \varphi \circ \neg$ [6].

4   Program Testing

Program testing was extended beyond reachability analysis to liveness properties such as termination [3,6]. The specifications considered in [3] are of the form:

$$\mathrm{post}[t^\star]\, I \implies (\neg E) \wedge \mathrm{pre}[t^\star]\, F .$$

Informally such a specification states that the descendants of the initial states are never erroneous and can potentially lead to final states.

By choosing different user specified invariant assertions Iv for $(\neg E)$ and intermittent assertions It for F, these forms of specification were slightly extended by [7] under the name "abstract debugging" to:

$$\mathrm{post}[t^\star]\, I \implies \mathrm{Iv} \wedge \mathrm{pre}[t^\star]\, \mathrm{It} .$$

If the states $\langle p, m \rangle \in S$ consist of a program point $p \in P$ and a memory state $m \in M$ then, when P is finite, the user can specify local invariant assertions Iv_p attached to program points $p \in \text{Pv} \subseteq P$ and local intermittent assertions It_p attached to program points $p \in \text{Pt}$ so that

$$\text{Iv} = \{\langle p, m \rangle \mid p \in \text{Pv} \implies \text{Iv}_p(m)\}$$
$$\text{and} \qquad \text{It} = \{\langle p, m \rangle \mid p \in \text{Pt} \wedge \text{It}_p(m)\} \, .$$

Otherwise stated, the descendants of the initial states always satisfy all local invariant assertions (which always holds) and can potentially lead to states satisfying some local intermittent assertion (which will sometime hold).

Consider for example, the factorial program below (the random assignment ? is equivalent to the reading of an input value or the passing of an unknown but initialized parameter value and <> is $\neq$). A specification that this factorial program should always terminate normally states that any execution should always reach program point 6. The termination requirement can be very simply specified as comments in the program text which specify the following local invariant and intermittent assertions:

```
0: n := ?; 1: f := 1;      Iv_p(n, f) = n, f ∈ [−∞, +∞], p = 1, ..., 6;
2: while (n <> 0) do       It_p(n, f) = false,          p = 1, ..., 5;
   3: f := (f * n);        It_6(n, f) = true .
   4: n := (n - 1)
5: od;
6: sometime true;;
```

5 Exact Formal Methods

Deductive methods were certainly the first considered to solve the reachability problem $\text{post}[t^*] \, I \subseteq Q$ that is $\text{lfp}^{\subseteq} \, \mathcal{F}[t] I \subseteq Q$ exactly. By *exact*, we mean that one directly reason on the small-step operational semantics $\langle S[\![p]\!], t[\![p]\!], I[\![p]\!], F[\![p]\!], E[\![p]\!] \rangle$ of the considered program $p \in \mathcal{L}$.

5.1 Exact Deductive Methods

By Park fixpoint induction, we have $\text{lfp}^{\subseteq} \, \mathcal{F}[t] I \subseteq Q$ if and only if $\exists J : \mathcal{F}[t] I(J) \subseteq J \wedge J \subseteq Q$ that is $\exists J : I \subseteq J \wedge \text{post}[t] \, J \subseteq J \wedge J \subseteq Q$. This is Floyd's inductive proof method, subgoal induction for the inverse problem and contrapositive methods for dual problems [8].

Human interaction is necessary both to help discover the inductive argument J and to assist the prover to check the verification conditions $I \subseteq J$, $\text{post}[t] \, J \subseteq J$ and $J \subseteq Q$ because the implication $\subseteq$ is not decidable. In general the transition relation $t[\![p]\!]$ is specified by a formal semantics of a programming language so that the formula $\text{post}[t[\![p]\!]]$ can be computer-generated by structural induction on the syntax of program $p \in \mathcal{L}$, although human interaction is again needed since these formulae must be simplified. Moreover, the invariant J is program specific so the proof is not reusable and may have to be completely redone when the program is modified.

5.2   Exact Model Checking

When the set S of states is finite, model checking [9,10,11] consists in computing exactly $\mathrm{lfp}^{\sqsubseteq} \mathcal{F}[t]I$ and checking that the fixpoint iterates are all included in Q. Efficient data structures and algorithms have been developped for boolean encodings such as BDDs [12]. To prove $\mathrm{lfp}^{\sqsubseteq} \mathcal{F}[t]I \nsubseteq Q$, one can prove that there exist an iterate of $\mathcal{F}[t]I$ which is not included in Q using SAT [13]. Unfortunately this can only be used for debugging and does not presently scale up beyond a few thousands boolean variables.

In practice the transition system $\langle S, t, I, F, E \rangle$ is in general not that of the semantics $\langle S[\![p]\!], t[\![p]\!], I[\![p]\!], F[\![p]\!], E[\![p]\!] \rangle$ of the considered computer system $p \in \mathcal{L}$ but an abstraction of this semantics. This abstraction is often done by hand and its correctness is not discussed. The abstract interpretation framework [4,5] is a formal basis for making the abstraction explicit and for proving its soundness and (in)completeness.

6   Abstract Interpretation

Abstract Interpretation [3] is a theory of abstraction of structures. Let us recall a few basic elements of this theory [4].

An abstraction is defined by a Galois connection $\langle L, \sqsubseteq \rangle \xrightarrow[\alpha]{\gamma} \langle L^\natural, \sqsubseteq^\natural \rangle$ that is by definition $\forall x \in L : \forall y \in L^\natural : \alpha(x) \sqsubseteq^\natural y \iff x \sqsubseteq \gamma(y)$. The intuition is that, in the concrete world L, any element $x \in L$ can be approximated by any x' such that $x \sqsubseteq x'$ (for example x is a property which implies a weaker one x'). In the abstract world $L^\natural$, x can be approximated by any y such that $x \sqsubseteq \gamma(y)$. The best or more precise such abstract approximation is $y = \alpha(x)$. It is an upper approximation since $x \sqsubseteq \gamma \circ \alpha(x)$. It is the more precise since for any other abstract approximation y, $x \sqsubseteq \gamma(y) \implies \gamma \circ \alpha(x) \sqsubseteq \gamma(y)$.

In order to abstract fixpoints, let us recall the following classical results in abstract interpretation [3,4,5]:

Theorem 1 (Fixpoint Abstraction). *If* $\langle L, \sqsubseteq, \bot, \top, \sqcup, \sqcap \rangle$ *and* $\langle L^\natural, \sqsubseteq^\natural, \bot^\natural, \top^\natural, \sqcup^\natural, \sqcap^\natural \rangle$ *are complete lattices,* $\langle L, \sqsubseteq \rangle \xrightarrow[\alpha]{\gamma} \langle L^\natural, \sqsubseteq^\natural \rangle$ *is a Galois connection, and* $F \in L \xmapsto{mon} L$, *then* $\alpha(\mathrm{lfp}^{\sqsubseteq} F) \sqsubseteq \mathrm{lfp}^{\sqsubseteq^\natural} \alpha \circ F \circ \gamma$.

Proof. In a Galois connection, α and γ are monotonic, so by Tarski's fixpoint theorem, the least fixpoints exist. So let $Q^\natural \overset{\text{def}}{=} \mathrm{lfp}^{\sqsubseteq^\natural} \alpha \circ F \circ \gamma$. We have $\alpha \circ F \circ \gamma(Q^\natural) = Q^\natural$ whence $F \circ \gamma(Q^\natural) \sqsubseteq \gamma(Q^\natural)$ by definition of Galois connections. It follows that $\gamma(Q^\natural)$ is a postfixpoint of F whence $\mathrm{lfp}^{\sqsubseteq} F \sqsubseteq \gamma(Q^\natural)$ by Tarski's fixpoint theorem or equivalently $\alpha(\mathrm{lfp}^{\sqsubseteq} F) \sqsubseteq^\natural Q^\natural = \mathrm{lfp}^{\sqsubseteq^\natural} \alpha \circ F \circ \gamma$. □

Theorem 2 (Fixpoint Approximation). *If* $\langle L^\natural, \sqsubseteq^\natural, \bot^\natural, \top^\natural, \sqcup^\natural, \sqcap^\natural \rangle$ *is a complete lattice,* $F^\natural, \bar{F}^\natural \in L^\natural \xmapsto{mon} L^\natural$, *and* $F^\natural \sqsubseteq^\natural \bar{F}^\natural$ *pointwise, then* $\mathrm{lfp}^{\sqsubseteq^\natural} F^\natural \sqsubseteq^\natural \mathrm{lfp}^{\sqsubseteq^\natural} \bar{F}^\natural$.

Proof. We have $F^\sharp(\mathrm{lfp}^{\sqsubseteq^\sharp} \bar{F}^\sharp) \sqsubseteq^\sharp \bar{F}^\sharp(\mathrm{lfp}^{\sqsubseteq^\sharp} \bar{F}^\sharp) = \mathrm{lfp}^{\sqsubseteq^\sharp} \bar{F}^\sharp$ whence $\mathrm{lfp}^{\sqsubseteq^\sharp} F^\sharp \sqsubseteq^\sharp$ $\mathrm{lfp}^{\sqsubseteq^\sharp} \bar{F}^\sharp$ since $\mathrm{lfp}^{\sqsubseteq^\sharp} F^\sharp = \bigsqcap^\sharp \{X \mid F^\sharp(X) \sqsubseteq^\sharp X\}$ by Tarski's fixpoint theorem. $\square$

7   Abstract Interpretation Based Formal Methods

In order to reduce the need for human-interaction as in deductive methods some form of abstraction is needed. This consists in replacing program properties by abstract ones. For example a set of traces $X \subseteq S^\infty$ can be abstracted by sets of reachable states $\alpha(X)$ where $\alpha \in \wp(S^\infty) \mapsto \wp(S)$ is $\alpha(X) \stackrel{\mathrm{def}}{=} \{\sigma_i \mid \sigma \in X \wedge 0 \leqslant i < |\sigma|\}$ and $\gamma \in \wp(S) \mapsto \wp(S^\infty)$ is $\gamma(Y) \stackrel{\mathrm{def}}{=} \{\sigma \in S^\infty \mid \forall i < |\sigma| : \sigma_i \in Y\}$ so that $\langle \wp(S^\infty), \subseteq \rangle \xleftarrow[\alpha]{\gamma} \langle \wp(S), \subseteq \rangle$. For reachability, a further abstraction $\langle \wp(S), \subseteq \rangle \xleftarrow[\alpha]{\gamma} \langle L^\sharp, \sqsubseteq^\sharp \rangle$ leads, by Th. 1 & 2 to $\mathrm{post}[t^\star] I \subseteq \gamma(\mathrm{lfp}^{\sqsubseteq^\sharp} \mathcal{F}^\sharp)$ where $\alpha \circ \mathcal{F}[t]I \circ \gamma \sqsubseteq^\sharp \mathcal{F}^\sharp$ pointwise, so that $\mathrm{lfp}^{\sqsubseteq^\sharp} \mathcal{F}^\sharp \sqsubseteq^\sharp Q^\sharp$ implies $\mathrm{post}[t^\star] I \subseteq \gamma(Q^\sharp)$. Depending on the scope of the abstraction, there are essentially two approaches:

- In static program analysis, an abstraction $\alpha[\![p]\!]$ has to be conceived by the designer for all programs $p \in \mathcal{L}$ of a programming language $\mathcal{L}$;
- In abstract software model checking, a specific abstraction α is designed by the end-user for each particular program.

We now examine the consequences of these two possible choices.

7.1   Static Program Analysis

In static program analysis, the abstract interpreter is given any program $p \in \mathcal{L}$ of a programming language $\mathcal{L}$, establishes equations $X = \mathcal{F}^\sharp[\![p]\!](X)$ or constraints $\mathcal{F}^\sharp[\![p]\!](X) \sqsubseteq^\sharp X$ where $\alpha[\![p]\!] \circ \mathcal{F}[t[\![p]\!]]I[\![p]\!] \circ \gamma[\![p]\!] \sqsubseteq^\sharp \mathcal{F}^\sharp[\![p]\!]$ and computes or effectively upper approximates $\mathrm{lfp}^{\sqsubseteq^\sharp} \mathcal{F}^\sharp[\![p]\!]$.

There is no need for the user to manually design the abstract interpreter, which is done by specialists. Hence there is no easy fine tuning of the abstract interpreter for a particular specification and a particular program. A consequence of this generality is that there will always be some program on which the analyzer will produce false alarms.

To minimize false alarms, infinite abstract domains are definitely needed in program analysis for precision (and sometimes efficiency or ease of programming of the program analyzer). The argument given in [14] uses reachability analysis with the attribute-independent interval domain [5] for the family of programs of the form:

```
x := 0; while (x < n) do x := (x + 1) od;;
```

where **n** is a given integer constant. It is easy to prove that for any $n > 0$, an interval analyzer [5] will discover ranges of possible values for numerical variables as follows (each program point has been numbered and a corresponding local invariant (given between parentheses) provides the possible values of the variables when reaching that program point. The uninitialized value Ω is denoted _0_.):

```
0: { x:_0_ }
   x := 0;
1: { x:[0,n] }
   while (x < n) do
      2: { x:[0,n - 1] }
         x := (x + 1)
      3: { x:[1,n] }
   od
4: { x:[n,n] }
```

The argument is then as follows:

1. for any given n it is possible to find an abstract domain (here $\{\Omega,\ [0,n],$ $[0, n-1],\ [1,n],\ [n,n]\}$) and to redesign a corresponding program analyzer (and its correctness proof) so that the above result can be computed by this specific analyzer for the specific abstract domain corresponding to this particular n [15].

2. Any single program analyzer being able to analyze the entire infinite family of programs must use an abstract domain containing the $\subseteq$-strictly increasing chain $[1,n]$, $n > 0$, hence an infinite abstract domain, as well as a widening, to cope with non termination ($+\infty$ (respectively $-\infty$) typed +oo (resp. -oo) denotes the greatest (resp. smallest) machine representable integer):

```
0: { x:_0_ }
   x := 0;
1: { x:[0,+oo] }
   while (0 < 1) do
      2: { x:[0,+oo] }
         x := (x + 1)
      3: { x:[1,+oo] }
   od
4: { x:_|_ }
```

Program point 4 is not reachable which is denoted by the bottom value $\perp$ (typed _|_).

7.2   Abstract Model Checking

Most abstractions considered in abstract model checking [16,17] are state to state abstractions $\wp(S) \mapsto \wp(S^\sharp)$ of the form $\alpha(X) = \{\alpha(s) \mid s \in X\}$ for a given state abstraction $\alpha \in S \mapsto S^\sharp$, see [1, sec. 14, p. 23]. Then we have $\langle\wp(S),$ $\subseteq\rangle \xleftarrow[\alpha]{\gamma} \langle\wp(S^\sharp), \subseteq\rangle$ where $\gamma(Y) \overset{\text{def}}{=} \{x \in S \mid \alpha(x) \in Y\}$. This is of the form $\langle\wp(S),$ $\subseteq\rangle \xleftarrow[\text{post}[\alpha]]{\widetilde{\text{pre}}[\alpha]} \langle\wp(S^\sharp), \subseteq\rangle$ which is a slight generalization when the state-to-state abstraction is relational ($\alpha \subseteq S \times S^\sharp$) and not simply functional ($\alpha \in S \mapsto S^\sharp$).

The need for restricting to state-to-state abstractions follows from the requirement in abstract model-checking to model-check the abstract semantics which, in order to be able to reuse existing model-checkers, must have the form of a transition system on (abstract) states. Indeed $\alpha \circ \text{post}[t] \circ \gamma$ is $\text{post}[t^\sharp]$ by defining $t^\sharp \overset{\text{def}}{=} \{\langle s^\sharp, s'^\sharp \rangle \mid \exists s, s' \in S : \langle s, s^\sharp \rangle \in \alpha \wedge \langle s, s' \rangle \in t \wedge \langle s', s'^\sharp \rangle \in \alpha\}$, $I^\sharp \overset{\text{def}}{=} \{s^\sharp \mid \exists s \in I : \langle s, s^\sharp \rangle \in \alpha\}$, etc.

Contrary to a common believe not all abstractions are state-to state. So some abstract semantics (using e.g. the interval abstraction [5] or the polyhedral abstraction [18]) are beyond the scope of abstract model checking. Some model checking publications use these abstractions or similar ones which are not state based, e.g. [19]. But then they use abstract interpretation based techniques such as fixpoint approximation, widening/narrowing, etc. to check safety (mainly reachability) properties as considered in Sec. 7.1.

In (abstract) model-checking, all efforts are concentrated on the design of the (abstract) model $\langle S^\sharp, t^\sharp, I^\sharp, F^\sharp, E^\sharp \rangle$. By [15], the abstract model can always be chosen to be boolean, finite and even small enough so that a model-checker will always succeed. Not surprisingly, [15] shows that for reachability problems, the discovery of the adequate abstract model is logically equivalent to the discovery of an inductive invariant J while the soundness proof is logically equivalent to the inductive proof $\text{post}[t] J \subseteq J$ (as considered in Sec. 5.1). So the human effort which was placed in the assistance of a prover for deductive methods is now placed in the design of an (abstract) model, which is a significant saving only when the abstract model is not proved correct. However these abstractions developed for a specific program and an explicit specification of that program are not reusable hence extremely expensive to design.

7.3 Automatic Abstraction and Abstraction Refinement

Predicate abstraction [20] is the per example automatization of the design of specific program analyzers by computing $\alpha[p] \circ \mathcal{F}[t[p]] I[p] \circ \gamma[p]$ for a given program p with a theorem prover/proof assitant/algebraic simplifier. It is based on the use of abstract domains using finite sets of predicates in disjunctive normal form. The abstract domain is refined on a spurious counter example basis [21]. This is an instance of domain refinement in abstract interpretation [22] but for the fact that infinite-disjunctions are handled heuristically to cope with uncomputability.

Beyond the limitations on the automatic use of theorem provers, the huge cost of the refinement process, the precision of the method as analyzed by [21] may be insufficient. This is because widening by dropping conjuncts in disjuncts [21] is not equivalent to the extrapolations to limits involved in abstract domains. An example is:

```
x := 100; y := -200;
while x <> 0 do x := (x - 1); y := (y + 2) od;;
always { y = 0 }
```

which is easily and automatically handled by the linear equalities abstract domain [23] (which satisfies the ascending chain condition) since the loop invariant $2x - y = 0$ and $x = 0$ implies $y = 0$.

7.4   Abstract Software Model Checking

At first sight, abstract testing is model-checking [9,10,11] of the temporal formula[3]:

$$\Box(\bigwedge_{p \in Pv} at_p \implies Iv_p) \wedge \Diamond(\bigvee_{p \in Pt} at_p \wedge It_p) \tag{1}$$

for a small-step operational semantics $\langle S, t, I \rangle$ of the program (or more precisely, abstract model-checking since abstract interpretation is involved).

Note that with state to state abstraction, the correctness of the formula in the abstract does not imply its correctness in the concrete (see [1,2]). A simple counter-example would be the termination of:

```
n := ?; f := 1; b := true;
while ((n <> 0) | b) do f := (f * n); n := (n - 1) od;;
```

where memory states $\langle n, f, b \rangle$ are abstracted by $\langle n, f \rangle$. So the verification of (1) cannot be done with upper approximations only and would also require a lower approximation or the use of a variant function [1,2].

7.5   Abstract Testing

Since lower approximations are hard to design and the handling of both lower and upper approximations is computationally complex, abstract testing uses upper approximations only. This consists in automatically computing local upper approximations A_p, $p \in P$, such that for $A \overset{\text{def}}{=} \{\langle p, m \rangle \mid A_p(m)\}$ we have:

$$(\text{post}[t^\star] I \wedge Iv \wedge \text{pre}[t^\star] It) \implies A .$$

The information provided by A is $(\neg A \wedge \text{post}[t^\star] I) \implies (\neg Iv \vee \widetilde{\text{pre}}[t^\star] \neg It)$, that is reachable states not satisfying A either do not satisfy the invariant assertion Iv or must inevitably lead to a violation of the intermittent assertion It. So A should be checked at checking-time or run-time to forestall errors. This consists in considering the transition system $\langle S, t', I', F, E \rangle$ where $t' \overset{\text{def}}{=} t \cap (S \times A)$ and $I' \overset{\text{def}}{=} I \cap A$. If $S = P \times M$ then defining $t_{pp'} \overset{\text{def}}{=} \{\langle\langle p, m \rangle, \langle p', m' \rangle\rangle \in t\}$ and $\text{succ}(p) \overset{\text{def}}{=} \{p' \in P \mid t_{pp'} \neq \varnothing\}$, we have $t = \bigcup_{p' \in \text{succ}(p)} t_{pp'}$. An economical way to check A is to use local checks (denoted : ! : in the examples below). This consists in considering $t' = \bigcup_{p' \in \text{succ}(p)} t'_{pp'}$ where $t'_{pp'} \overset{\text{def}}{=} t_{pp'}$ if $\text{post}[t_{pp'}] A_p \implies A_{p'}$ and $t'_{pp'} \overset{\text{def}}{=} t_{pp'} \cap (S \times A_{p'})$ otherwise. If A is taken in computer-language representable abstract domains, the transformed transition system $\langle S, t', I', F, E \rangle$ corresponds to a transformed program, which is a simple form of program monitoring [24].

The automatic analysis of the above factorial program leads to the following result [25,26]:

---

[3] The temporal operator $\Box Q$ denotes the set of sequences of states such that all states satisfy Q, $\Diamond Q$ denotes the set of sequences containing at least one state satisfying Q and the predicate $at\, p$ holds in all states which control point is p.

```
0: { n:_0_; f:_0_ }
   n := ?;
1:!: { n:[0,+oo]; f:_0_ }
   f := 1;
2: { n:[0,+oo]; f:[1,+oo] }
   while (n <> 0) do
      3: { n:[1,+oo]; f:[1,+oo] }
         f := (f * n);
      4: { n:[1,+oo]; f:[1,+oo] }
         n := (n - 1)
      5: { n:[0,+oo-1]; f:[1,+oo] }
   od
6: { n:[0,0]; f:[1,+oo] }
```

The analysis automatically discovers the condition $n \geq 0$ which should be checked at program point 1 (as indicated by :!:), since otherwise a runtime error or nontermination is inevitable. Then the computed invariants will always hold. For example the final value of n is 0 whereas f $\geq$ 1.

8   Precise Fixpoint Checking in the Presence of Approximations

All approximate formal methods considered in Sec. 7 involve fixpoint approximations. These approximations, such as widenings [5], can be simply ignored in model-checking of finite-state transition systems. However, *in the presence of approximations*, fixpoint approximation check can be made more precise than the fixpoint computations involved in traditional abstract model-checking [16,17].

8.1   Fixpoint Approximation Check

A first illustration is for the fixpoint approximation check $\text{lfp}^{\sqsubseteq} \mathcal{F} \sqsubseteq Q$ where $\langle L, \sqsubseteq, \bot, \top, \sqcup, \sqsupseteq \rangle$ is a complete lattice, $\mathcal{F} \in L \xmapsto{\text{mon}} L$ is monotonic and $\text{lfp}^{\sqsubseteq} \mathcal{F}$ is the $\sqsubseteq$-least fixpoint of $\mathcal{F}$. An example is reachability analysis of Sec. 3.

In (abstract) model-checking, one computes iteratively $\text{lfp}^{\sqsubseteq} \mathcal{F}$ and then checks that $\text{lfp}^{\sqsubseteq} \mathcal{F} \sqsubseteq Q$ (or uses a strictly equivalent check, see [27, p. 73] and Sec. 10 below).

In abstract testing, one computes iteratively an upper-approximation J of $\text{lfp}^{\sqsubseteq} \lambda X \cdot Q \sqcap \mathcal{F}(X)$ with acceleration of the convergence of the iterates by widening/narrowing [5,6]. The convergence criterion is:

$$(Q \sqcap \mathcal{F}(J)) \sqsubseteq J . \tag{2}$$

Then the invariance check has the form:

$$\mathcal{F}(J) \sqsubseteq Q . \tag{3}$$

This is sound, by the following theorem:

Theorem 3. *If* $\langle L, \sqsubseteq, \bot, \top, \sqsubseteq, \sqsupseteq \rangle$ *is a complete lattice,* $\mathcal{F} \in L \xmapsto{\ mon\ } L$ *is monotonic and* $Q, J \in L$, *then:*

$$(Q \sqcap \mathcal{F}(J)) \sqsubseteq J \wedge \mathcal{F}(J) \sqsubseteq Q \implies \mathrm{lfp}^{\sqsubseteq} \mathcal{F} \sqsubseteq Q$$

Proof. We have $\mathcal{F}(J) = \mathcal{F}(J) \sqcap \mathcal{F}(J) \sqsubseteq Q \sqcap \mathcal{F}(J)$ [by (3)] $\sqsubseteq J$ [by (2)] proving $\mathcal{F}(J) \sqsubseteq J$ by transitivity whence $\mathrm{lfp}^{\sqsubseteq} \mathcal{F} \sqsubseteq J$ by Tarski's fixpoint theorem. By definition of fixpoints and monotony, it follows that $\mathrm{lfp}^{\sqsubseteq} \mathcal{F} = \mathcal{F}(\mathrm{lfp}^{\sqsubseteq} \mathcal{F}) \sqsubseteq \mathcal{F}(J)$ $\sqsubseteq Q$ [by (3)]. By transitivity, we conclude $\mathrm{lfp}^{\sqsubseteq} \mathcal{F} \sqsubseteq Q$ as required. $\qquad\square$

The reason why abstract testing uses more involved computations is that in the context of infinite state systems, and for a given abstraction, the approximation of the more complex expression is in general more precise than the abstraction of the trivial expression. Consider for example interval analysis [5] of the simple loop accessing sequentially an array $A[1], \ldots, A[100]$. The result of the analysis [26] is too approximate to statically check that the index i is within the array bounds 1 and 100 :

```
Reachability from initial states;    0: { i:_0_ }
i := 0;                              i := 0;
while (i <> 100) do                  1: { i:[0,+oo] }
    i := (i + 1);                    while (i <> 100) do
    skip % array access %               2: { i:[0,+oo] }
od;;                                    i := (i + 1);
                                        3: { i:[1,+oo] }
                                        skip
                                     4: { i:[1,+oo] }
                                     od
                                     5: { i:[100,100] }
```

However by explicit conjunction with the array access invariant $0 < i \leqslant 100$ (the evaluation of the runtime check always B has the effect of blocking the program execution when the assertion B does not hold), the static analysis now proves that the array out of bound error is impossible:

```
Reachability from initial states;    0: { i:_0_ }
i:=0;                                i := 0;
while i <> 100 do                    1: { i:[0,100] }
    i := i + 1;                      while (i <> 100) do
    always ((0 < i) & (i <= 100))        2: { i:[0,99] }
od;;                                    i := (i + 1);
                                        3: { i:[1,100] }
                                        always ((0 < i) & (i <= 100))
                                     4: { i:[1,100] }
                                     od
                                     5: { i:[100,100] }
```

Experimentally, acceleration of the convergence may even lead to a faster convergence of the more precise analysis.

8.2   Fixpoint Meet Approximation

A second illustration of the possible refinement of fixpoint computation algorithms in the presence of abstraction is the upper-approximation of the descendants of the initial states which are ancestors of the final states. An (abstract) model-checking algorithm (such as [28]) computes a conjunction of forward and backward fixpoints. The forward and backward analyses of the factorial program, respectively yield:

```
Reachability from initial states;        Ancestors of final states;
0: { n:_0_; f:_0_ }                       0: { n:[-oo,+oo]?; f:[-oo,+oo]? }
   n := ?;                                   n := ?;
1: { n:[-oo,+oo]; f:_0_ }                 1: { n:[0,+oo]; f:[-oo,+oo]? }
   f := 1;                                   f := 1;
2: { n:[-oo,+oo]; f:[-oo,+oo] }           2: { n:[0,+oo]; f:[-oo,+oo]? }
   while (n <> 0) do                         while (n <> 0) do
      3: { n:[-oo,+oo]; f:[-oo,+oo] }          3: { n:[1,+oo]; f:[-oo,+oo] }
      f := (f * n);                            f := (f * n);
      4: { n:[-oo,+oo]; f:[-oo,+oo] }          4: { n:[1,+oo]; f:[-oo,+oo]? }
      n := (n - 1)                             n := (n - 1)
      5: { n:[-oo,+oo-1]; f:[-oo,+oo] }        5: { n:[0,+oo]; f:[-oo,+oo]? }
od                                        od
6: { n:[0,0]; f:[-oo,+oo] }               6: { n:[-oo,+oo]?; f:[-oo,+oo]? }
```

The intersection is therefore:

```
   0: { n:_0_; f:_0_ }
      n := ?;
   1: { n:[-oo,+oo]; f:_0_ }
      f := 1;
   2: { n:[0,+oo]; f:[-oo,+oo]? }
      while (n <> 0) do
         3: { n:[1,+oo]; f:[-oo,+oo] }
         f := (f * n);
         4: { n:[1,+oo]; f:[-oo,+oo] }
         n := (n - 1)
         5: { n:[0,+oo-1]; f:[-oo,+oo] }
      od
   6: { n:[0,0]; f:[-oo,+oo] }
```

Abstract testing iterates an alternation between forward and backward fixpoints [3,29]. For the factorial program, the analysis is more precise (since it can now derive that f is positive):

```
Reachability/ancestry analysis for initial/final states;
   0: { n:_0_; f:_0_ }
      n := ?;
   1:!: { n:[0,+oo]; f:_0_ }
      f := 1;
   2: { n:[0,+oo]; f:[1,+oo] }
      while (n <> 0) do
```

```
3: { n:[1,+oo]; f:[1,+oo] }
   f := (f * n);
4: { n:[1,+oo]; f:[1,+oo] }
   n := (n - 1)
5: { n:[0,+oo-1]; f:[1,+oo] }
od
6: { n:[0,0]; f:[1,+oo] }
```

Now $\mathcal{F}$ and $\mathcal{B}$ can be approximated by their abstract interpretations $\mathcal{F}^\sharp \sqsupseteq \alpha \circ \mathcal{F} \circ \gamma$ of $\mathcal{F}$ and $\mathcal{B}^\sharp \sqsupseteq \alpha \circ \mathcal{B} \circ \gamma$ of $\mathcal{B}$. A better approximation than $\mathrm{lfp}^{\sqsubseteq^\sharp} \mathcal{F}^\sharp \sqcap^\sharp \mathrm{lfp}^{\sqsubseteq^\sharp} \mathcal{B}^\sharp$ was suggested in [3]. It is calculated as the limit of the *alternating fixpoint computation*:

$$\dot{X}^0 = \mathrm{lfp}^{\sqsubseteq^\sharp} \mathcal{F}^\sharp \text{ or } \mathrm{lfp}^{\sqsubseteq^\sharp} \mathcal{B}^\sharp \tag{4}$$

$$\dot{X}^{2n+1} = \mathrm{lfp}^{\sqsubseteq^\sharp} \lambda X \cdot (\dot{X}^{2n} \sqcap^\sharp \mathcal{B}^\sharp(X)), \qquad n \in \mathbb{N} \tag{5}$$

$$\dot{X}^{2n+2} = \mathrm{lfp}^{\sqsubseteq^\sharp} \lambda X \cdot (\dot{X}^{2n+1} \sqcap^\sharp \mathcal{F}^\sharp(X)), \quad n \in \mathbb{N} \tag{6}$$

For soundness, we assume:

$$\mathrm{lfp}^{\sqsubseteq} \mathcal{F} \sqcap \mathrm{lfp}^{\sqsubseteq} \mathcal{B} = \mathrm{lfp}^{\sqsubseteq} \lambda X \cdot (\mathrm{lfp}^{\sqsubseteq} \mathcal{F} \sqcap \mathcal{B}(X)) \tag{7}$$

$$= \mathrm{lfp}^{\sqsubseteq} \lambda X \cdot (\mathrm{lfp}^{\sqsubseteq} \mathcal{B} \sqcap \mathcal{F}(X)) \tag{8}$$

$$= \mathrm{lfp}^{\sqsubseteq} \lambda X \cdot (\mathrm{lfp}^{\sqsubseteq} \mathcal{F} \sqcap \mathrm{lfp}^{\sqsubseteq} \mathcal{B} \sqcap \mathcal{B}(X)) \tag{9}$$

$$= \mathrm{lfp}^{\sqsubseteq} \lambda X \cdot (\mathrm{lfp}^{\sqsubseteq} \mathcal{F} \sqcap \mathrm{lfp}^{\sqsubseteq} \mathcal{B} \sqcap \mathcal{F}(X)) \tag{10}$$

so that there is no improvement when applying the alternating fixpoint computation to $\mathcal{F}$ and $\mathcal{B}$ (such as the exact forward $\mathrm{post}[t^\star]\,I$ and backward $\mathrm{pre}[t^\star]\,F$ collecting semantics). However, when considering approximations $\mathcal{F}^\sharp$ of $\mathcal{F}$ and $\mathcal{B}^\sharp$ of $\mathcal{B}$, not all information can be collected in one pass. So the idea is to propagate the initial assertion forward so as to get a final assertion. This final assertion is then propagated backward to get stronger necessary conditions to be satisfied by the initial states for possible termination. This restricts the possible reachable states as indicated by the next forward pass. Going on this way, the available information on the descendant states of the initial states which are ascendant states of the final states can be improved on each successive pass, until convergence. A specific instance of this computation scheme was used independently by [30] to infer types in flowchart programs.

The correctness of the alternating fixpoint computation follows from the following [3]:

Theorem 4 (Alternating Fixpoint Approximation). *If* $\langle L, \sqsubseteq, \bot, \top, \sqcup, \sqcap \rangle$ *and* $\langle L^\sharp, \sqsubseteq^\sharp, \bot^\sharp, \top^\sharp, \sqcup^\sharp, \sqcap^\sharp \rangle$ *are complete lattices,* $\langle L, \sqsubseteq \rangle \xrightarrow[\alpha]{\gamma} \langle L^\sharp, \sqsubseteq^\sharp \rangle$ *is a Galois connection,* $\mathcal{F} \in L \xrightarrow{mon} L$ *and* $\mathcal{B} \in L \xrightarrow{mon} L$ *satisfy the hypotheses (9) and (10),* $\mathcal{F}^\sharp \in L^\sharp \xrightarrow{mon} L^\sharp$, $\mathcal{B}^\sharp \in L^\sharp \xrightarrow{mon} L^\sharp$, $\alpha \circ \mathcal{F} \circ \gamma \sqsubseteq^\sharp \mathcal{F}^\sharp$, $\alpha \circ \mathcal{B} \circ \gamma \sqsubseteq^\sharp \mathcal{B}^\sharp$ *and the sequence* $\langle \dot{X}^n, n \in \mathbb{N} \rangle$ *is defined by (4), (5) and (6) then* $\forall k \in \mathbb{N} : \alpha(\mathrm{lfp}^{\sqsubseteq} \mathcal{F} \sqcap \mathrm{lfp}^{\sqsubseteq} \mathcal{B}) \sqsubseteq^\sharp \dot{X}^{k+1} \sqsubseteq^\sharp \dot{X}^k$.

Proof. Observe that by the fixpoint property, $\dot{X}^{2n+1} = \dot{X}^{2n} \sqcap^\sharp \mathcal{B}^\sharp(\dot{X}^{2n+1})$ and $\dot{X}^{2n+2} = \dot{X}^{2n+1} \sqcap^\sharp \mathcal{F}^\sharp(\dot{X}^{2n+2})$, hence $\dot{X}^{2n} \sqsubseteq^\sharp \dot{X}^{2n+1} \sqsubseteq^\sharp \dot{X}^{2n+2}$ since $\sqcap^\sharp$ is the greatest lower bound for $\sqsubseteq^\sharp$ so that $\dot{X}^k$, $k \in \mathbb{N}$ is a decreasing chain.

We have $\alpha(\text{lfp}^{\sqsubseteq} \mathcal{F} \sqcap \text{lfp}^{\sqsubseteq} \mathcal{B}) \sqsubseteq^\sharp \alpha(\text{lfp}^{\sqsubseteq} \mathcal{F})$ since α is monotone and $\alpha(\text{lfp}^{\sqsubseteq} \mathcal{F}) \sqsubseteq^\sharp \text{lfp}^{\sqsubseteq^\sharp} \mathcal{F}^\sharp$ by Th. 2, thus proving the proposition for $k = 0$.

Let us observe that $\alpha \circ \mathcal{F} \circ \gamma \sqsubseteq^\sharp \mathcal{F}^\sharp$ implies $\mathcal{F} \circ \gamma \sqsubseteq \gamma \circ \mathcal{F}^\sharp$ by definition of Galois connections so that in particular for an argument of the form $\alpha(X)$, $\mathcal{F} \circ \gamma \circ \alpha \sqsubseteq \gamma \circ \mathcal{F}^\sharp \circ \alpha$. In a Galois connection, $\gamma \circ \alpha$ is extensive so that by monotony and transitivity $\mathcal{F} \sqsubseteq \gamma \circ \mathcal{F}^\sharp \circ \alpha$.

Assume now by induction hypothesis that $\alpha(\text{lfp}^{\sqsubseteq} \mathcal{F} \sqcap \text{lfp}^{\sqsubseteq} \mathcal{B}) \sqsubseteq^\sharp \dot{X}^{2n}$, or equivalently, by definition of Galois connections, that $\text{lfp}^{\sqsubseteq} \mathcal{F} \sqcap \text{lfp}^{\sqsubseteq} \mathcal{B} \sqsubseteq \gamma(\dot{X}^{2n})$. Since $\mathcal{F} \sqsubseteq \gamma \circ \mathcal{F}^\sharp \circ \alpha$, it follows that $\lambda X \cdot \text{lfp}^{\sqsubseteq} \mathcal{F} \sqcap \text{lfp}^{\sqsubseteq} \mathcal{B} \sqcap \mathcal{F}(X) \sqsubseteq \lambda X \cdot \gamma(\dot{X}^{2n}) \sqcap \gamma \circ \mathcal{F}^\sharp \circ \alpha(X) = \lambda X \cdot \gamma(\dot{X}^{2n} \sqcap \mathcal{F}^\sharp \circ \alpha(X))$ since, in a Galois connection, γ is a complete meet morphism. Now by hypothesis (9), we have $\text{lfp}^{\sqsubseteq} \mathcal{F} \sqcap \text{lfp}^{\sqsubseteq} \mathcal{B} = \text{lfp} \lambda X \cdot (\text{lfp}^{\sqsubseteq} \mathcal{F} \sqcap \text{lfp}^{\sqsubseteq} \mathcal{B} \sqcap \mathcal{F}(X)) \sqsubseteq^\sharp \text{lfp} \lambda X \cdot \gamma(\dot{X}^{2n} \sqcap \mathcal{F}^\sharp \circ \alpha(X))$ by Th. 2. Let G be $\lambda X \cdot \dot{X}^{2n} \sqcap \mathcal{F}^\sharp(X)$. In a Galois connection, $\alpha \circ \gamma$ is reductive so that by monotony $G \circ \alpha \circ \gamma \sqsubseteq^\sharp G$ and $\alpha \circ \gamma \circ G \circ \alpha \circ \gamma \sqsubseteq^\sharp G \circ \alpha \circ \gamma$, whence, by transitivity, $\alpha \circ \gamma \circ G \circ \alpha \circ \gamma \sqsubseteq^\sharp G$. By Th. 1, we have $\alpha(\text{lfp} \gamma \circ G \circ \alpha) \sqsubseteq^\sharp \text{lfp} \alpha \circ \gamma \circ G \circ \alpha \circ \gamma \sqsubseteq^\sharp \text{lfp} G$ by Th. 2. Hence, $\text{lfp} \lambda X \cdot \gamma(\dot{X}^{2n} \sqcap \mathcal{F}^\sharp \circ \alpha(X)) \sqsubseteq \gamma(\text{lfp} \lambda X \cdot \dot{X}^{2n} \sqcap \mathcal{F}^\sharp(X))$ so that by transitivity we conclude that $\alpha(\text{lfp}^{\sqsubseteq} \mathcal{F} \sqcap \text{lfp}^{\sqsubseteq} \mathcal{B}) \sqsubseteq^\sharp \dot{X}^{2n+1}$.

The proof that $\alpha(\text{lfp}^{\sqsubseteq} \mathcal{F} \sqcap \text{lfp}^{\sqsubseteq} \mathcal{B}) \sqsubseteq^\sharp \dot{X}^{2n+2}$ is similar, using hypothesis (9) and by exchanging the rôles of $\mathcal{F}$ and $\mathcal{B}$.   □

It is interesting to note that the computed sequence (4), (5) and (6) is optimal (see [3]). A similar result holds when replacing one least fixpoint by a greatest fixpoint [31].

If the abstract lattice does not satisfy the descending chain condition then [3] also suggests to use a narrowing operator $\triangle$ [5] to enforce convergence of the downward iteration $\dot{X}^k$, $k \in \mathbb{N}$. The same way a widening/narrowing approach can be used to enforce convergence of the iterates for $\lambda X \cdot \dot{X}^{2n} \sqcap \mathcal{F}^\sharp(X)$ and $\lambda X \cdot \dot{X}^{2n+1} \sqcap \mathcal{B}^\sharp(X)$.

8.3   Local Iterations

A third illustration that the precision of static abstract software checking algorithms can be enhanced by taking explicitly into account the abstractions is the local iterations [32] to handle tests, backward assignments, etc. Below is an example of program static analysis, without local iterations:

```
Reachability from initial states;
0: { x:_0_; y:_0_; z:_0_ }
   x := 0;
1: { x:[0,0]; y:_0_; z:_0_ }
   y := ?;
```

```
2: { x:[0,0]; y:[-oo,+oo]; z:_0_ }
   z := ?;
3: { x:[0,0]; y:[-oo,+oo]; z:[-oo,+oo] }
   if (((x = y) & (y = z)) & ((z + 1) = x)) then
      4: { x:[0,0]; y:[0,0]; z:[-1,-1] }
         skip
      5: { x:[0,0]; y:[0,0]; z:[-1,-1] }
   else
      6: { x:[0,0]; y:[-oo,+oo]; z:[-oo,+oo] }
         skip
      7: { x:[0,0]; y:[-oo,+oo]; z:[-oo,+oo] }
   fi
8: { x:[0,0]; y:[-oo,+oo]; z:[-oo,+oo] }
```

The precision of the same program with the same abstract domain is greatly enhanced with local iterations:

```
Forward reductive analysis from initial states;
0: { x:_0_; y:_0_; z:_0_ }
   x := 0;
1: { x:[0,0]; y:_0_; z:_0_ }
   y := ?;
2: { x:[0,0]; y:[-oo,+oo]; z:_0_ }
   z := ?;
3: { x:[0,0]; y:[-oo,+oo]; z:[-oo,+oo] }
   if (((x = y) & (y = z)) & ((z + 1) = x)) then
      4: { x:_|_; y:_|_; z:_|_ }
         skip
      5: { x:_|_; y:_|_; z:_|_ }
   else
      6: { x:[0,0]; y:[-oo,+oo]; z:[-oo,+oo] }
         skip
      7: { x:[0,0]; y:[-oo,+oo]; z:[-oo,+oo] }
   fi
8: { x:[0,0]; y:[-oo,+oo]; z:[-oo,+oo] }
```

When applied to tests without side-effects, the idea of the local iterations is to iterate the abstract evaluation of the test. From { x:[0,0]; y:[-oo,+oo]; z:[-oo,+oo] }, the abstract interpretation of the test (x = y) yields y:[0,0], the test (y = z) provides no information on y and z while ((z + 1) = x) yields z:[-1,-1]. Iterating once more, the tests (x = y) and ((z + 1) = x) provide no new information while (y = z) is false and so is the conjunction (((x = y) & (y = z)) & ((z + 1) = x)). It follows that program point 4 is not reachable.

9   Counter-Examples to Erroneous Designs

Another important element of comparison between model-checking and abstract testing concerns the conclusions that can be drawn in case of failure of the automatic verification process. The model checking algorithms usually provide a counter-example [12]. This is not directly possible in the abstract since the necessary over-approximation leads to the consideration of inexisting program executions which should not be proposed as counter-examples. Nevertheless, in abstract model checking, counterexamples can be found in the concrete [33,34], provided concrete program transformers can be effectively computed (e.g. when the concrete transition system is finite). Because of the uncomputability of the programming language semantics, this is not always possible with abstract testing (e.g. for non-termination).

However, abstract testing can provide necessary conditions for the specification to be (un-)satisfied. These automatically calculated conditions can serve to abstract program slicing as a guideline to discover the errors. They can also be checked at run-time to start the debugging mode before the error actually happens. For example the analysis of the following factorial program with a termination requirement leads to the necessary pre-condition $n \geqslant 0$:

```
Ancestors of final states;        0: { n:[-oo,+oo]?; f:[-oo,+oo]? }
n := ?;                           n := ?;
f := 1;                           1: { n:[0,+oo]; f:[-oo,+oo]? }
while (n <> 0) do                 f := 1;
    f := (f * n);                 2: { n:[0,+oo]; f:[-oo,+oo]? }
    n := (n - 1)                  while (n <> 0) do
od;;                              3: { n:[1,+oo]; f:[-oo,+oo]? }
                                  f := (f * n);
                                  4: { n:[1,+oo]; f:[-oo,+oo]? }
                                  n := (n - 1)
                                  5: { n:[0,+oo]; f:[-oo,+oo]? }
                                  od
                                  6: { n:[-oo,+oo]?; f:[-oo,+oo]? }
```

Indeed when this condition is not satisfied, i.e. when initially $n < 0$, the program execution may not terminate or may terminate with a run-time error (arithmetic overflow in the above example). The following static analysis with this erroneous initial condition $n < 0$ shows that the program execution never terminates properly so that the only remaining possible case is an incorrect termination with a run-time error ($\perp$, typed _|_, is the false invariant hence denotes unreachability in forward analysis and impossibility to reach the goal in backward analysis):

```
Reachability from initial states;  0: { n:_|_; f:_|_ }
initial n < 0;                     initial (n < 0);
f := 1;                            1: { n:[-oo,-1]; f:_0_ }
while (n <> 0) do                  f := 1;
    f := (f * n);                  2: { n:[-oo,-1]; f:[-oo,1] }
    n := (n - 1)                   while (n <> 0) do
od;;                               3: { n:[-oo,-1]; f:[-oo,1] }
                                   f := (f * n);
                                   4: { n:[-oo,-1]; f:[-oo,0] }
                                   n := (n - 1)
                                   5: { n:[-oo,-2]; f:[-oo,0] }
                                   od
```

$$6: \{ \; n:\_|\_; \; f:\_|\_ \; \}$$

Otherwise stated, infinitely many counter-examples are simultaneously provided by this counter-analysis. Except in the case of bounded cyclicity, concrete nontermination counterexamples would be hard to exhibit for infinite state transition systems.

10 Contrapositive Reasoning

For the last element of comparison between concrete and abstract software verification, observe that in model-checking, using a set of states or its complement is equivalent as far as the precision of the result is concerned (but may be not its efficiency). For example, as observed in [27, p. 73], the Galois connection $\langle \wp(S), \subseteq \rangle \xrightleftharpoons[\text{post}[r]]{\widetilde{\text{pre}}[r]} \langle \wp(S), \subseteq \rangle$ (where $r \subseteq S \times S$ and $\widetilde{\text{pre}}[r] \, X \overset{\text{def}}{=} \{ s \mid \forall s' : \langle s, s' \rangle \in r \implies s' \in X \}$) implies that the invariance specification check $\text{post}[t^\star] \, E \subseteq Q$ is equivalent to $\widetilde{\text{pre}}[t^\star] \, \neg Q \subseteq \neg E$ (or $\text{pre}[t^\star] \, \neg Q \subseteq \neg E$ for total deterministic transition systems [6]). Otherwise stated a forward positive proof is equivalent to a backward contrapositive proof, as observed in [8]. So the difference between the abstract testing algorithm of [4,5,6] and the model-checking algorithm of [9,10,11] is that abstract testing checks $\text{post}[t^\star] \, I \subseteq Q$ while model-checking verifies $\widetilde{\text{pre}}[t^\star] \, \neg Q \subseteq \neg I$, which is equivalent for finite transition systems as considered in [9,10,11].

However, when considering infinite state systems the negation may be approximate in the abstract domain. For example the complement of an interval as considered in [5] is not an interval in general. So the backward contrapositive checking may not yield the same conclusion as the forward positive checking. For example when looking for a pre-condition of an out of bounds error for the following program:

```
Ancestors of final states;
i:=0;
while i <> 100 do
  i := i + 1;
  if (0 < i) & (i <= 100) then
    skip % array access %
  else
    final (i <= 0) | (100 < i) % out of bounds error %
  fi
od;;
```

the predicate (i <= 0) | (100 < i) cannot be precisely approximated with intervals, so the analysis is inconclusive:

```
0: { i:[-oo,+oo]? }
  i := 0;
1: { i:[-oo,+oo-1] }
  while (i <> 100) do
```

```
      2: { i:[-oo,+oo-1] }
         i := (i + 1);
      3: { i:[-oo,+oo] }
         if ((0 < i) & (i <= 100)) then
         4: { i:[-oo,+oo-1] }
            skip
         5: { i:[-oo,+oo-1] }
         else {((i <= 0) | (100 < i))}
         6: { i:[-oo,+oo] }
            final ((i <= 0) | (100 < i))
         7: { i:[-oo,+oo-1] }
         fi
      8: { i:[-oo,+oo-1] }
   od
9: { i:_|_ }
```

However both the forward positive and backward contrapositive checking may be conclusive. This is the case if we check for the lower bound only:

```
Ancestors of final states;
i:=0;
while i <> 100 do
   i := i + 1;
   if (0 < i) then
      skip % array access %
   else
      final (i <= 0) % out of lower bound error %
   fi
od;;
```

This is shown below since the initial invariant is false so the out of lower bound error is unreachable and similarly for the upper bound:

```
0: { i:_|_ }                      0: { i:_|_ }
   i := 0;                           i := 0;
1: { i:[-oo,-1] }                 1: { i:[101,+oo-1] }
   while (i <> 100) do               while (i <> 100) do
   2: { i:[-oo,-1] }                 2: { i:[100,+oo-1] }
      i := (i + 1);                     i := (i + 1);
   3: { i:[-oo,0] }                  3: { i:[101,+oo] }
      if (0 < i) then                   if (i <= 100) then
      4: { i:[-oo,-1] }                 4: { i:[101,+oo-1] }
         skip                              skip
      5: { i:[-oo,-1] }                 5: { i:[101,+oo-1] }
      else {(i <= 0)}                   else {(100 < i)}
      6: { i:[-oo,0] }                  6: { i:[101,+oo] }
         final (i <= 0)                    final (100 < i)
      7: { i:[-oo,-1] }                 7: { i:[101,+oo-1] }
      fi                                fi
   8: { i:[-oo,-1] }                 8: { i:[101,+oo-1] }
   od                                od
```

```
9: { i:_|_ }                         9: { i:_|_ }
```

Both analyzes could be done simultaneously by considering both intervals and their dual, or more generally finite disjunctions of intervals. More generally, completeness may always be achieved by enriching the abstract domain [22]. To start with, the abstract domain might be enriched with complements, but this might not be sufficient and indeed the abstract domain might have to be enriched for each primitive operation, thus leading to an abstract algebra which might be quite difficult to implement if not totally inefficient. Moreover limit abstract values in the abstract domains require infinite iterations so that the exact abstract domain refinement may not be computable (see Sec. 7.3).

11   Conclusion

As an alternative to program debugging, formal methods have been developed to prove that a semantics or a model of the program satisfies a given specification. Abstraction was first considered in contexts in which false alarms are quite acceptable (e.g. static program analysis in compilation [5], overestimation of worst-case execution time [35], etc) to applications in which false alarms are unsatisfactory (e.g. software verification). For example in compile-time boundedness checking, a selectivity of 90% will lead to significant performance improvements in execution times whereas such a selectivity rate is not acceptable to prove that no unexpected interrupts can be raised in large embedded critical real-time software. By concentrating on models of programs rather than on their semantics, these formal methods have had more successes for finding bugs than for actual correctness proofs of full programs. Beyond the design and maintenance cost of models of complex programs and their unreliability, the basic idea of complete program verification underlying the deductive and model checking methods has been abandoned in favor of debugging. Because of theoretical and practical limitations, these approaches will be hard to scale up for complex programs as considered in the DAEDALUS project (over 250 000 lines of C) e.g. for boundedness checking or liveness analysis.

Abstract interpretation based methods offer techniques which, in the presence of approximation, can be viable and powerful alternatives to both the exhaustive search of model-checking and the partial exploration methods of classical debugging. There are essentially two approaches:

- *General-purpose static analyzers* automatically provide a program model by an approximation of its semantics chosen to offer a good average cost/precision compromize. Such analyzers are reusable and so their development cost can be shared among many users;
- *Specializable static analyzers* provide the user with the capability to tune the abstractions to achieve high-precision by chosing among a predefined set of wide-spectrum parameterized approximations. The refinement is on the local choice of abstract domains which automatically induces a more precise abstract semantics. This should ensure the soundness of the abstraction,

and at least for specific classes of programs lead to very precise and efficient analyzes going much beyond examples modelled by hand.

References

1. Cousot, P., Cousot, R.: Temporal abstract interpretation. In: 27th POPL, Boston, USA, ACM Press (2000) 12–25
2. Schmidt, D.: From trace sets to modal-transition systems by stepwise abstract interpretation. Submitted for publication (2001)
3. Cousot, P.: Méthodes itératives de construction et d'approximation de points fixes d'opérateurs monotones sur un treillis, analyse sémantique de programmes. Thèse d'État ès sciences mathématiques, Université scientifique et médicale de Grenoble, Grenoble, France (1978)
4. Cousot, P., Cousot, R.: Systematic design of program analysis frameworks. In: 6th POPL, San Antonio, USA, ACM Press (1979) 269–282
5. Cousot, P., Cousot, R.: Abstract interpretation: a unified lattice model for static analysis of programs by construction or approximation of fixpoints. In: 4th POPL, Los Angeles, USA, ACM Press (1977) 238–252
6. Cousot, P.: Semantic foundations of program analysis. In Muchnick, S., Jones, N., eds.: Program Flow Analysis: Theory and Applications. Prentice-Hall (1981) 303–342
7. Bourdoncle, F.: Abstract debugging of higher-order imperative languages. In: Proc. ACM SIGPLAN '93 Conf. PLDI. ACM SIGPLAN Not. 28(6), Albuquerque, USA, ACM Press (1993) 46–55
8. Cousot, P., Cousot, R.: Induction principles for proving invariance properties of programs. In Néel, D., ed.: Tools & Notions for Program Construction. Cambridge U. Press (1982) 43–119
9. Clarke, E., Emerson, E.: Synthesis of synchronization skeletons for branching time temporal logic. In: IBM Workshop on Logics of Programs. Yorktown Heights, USA, LNCS 131, Springer-Verlag (1981)
10. Clarke, E., Emerson, E., Sistla, A.: Automatic verification of finite-state concurrent systems using temporal logic specifications. TOPLAS 8 (1986) 244–263
11. Queille, J.P., Sifakis, J.: Verification of concurrent systems in Cesar. In: Proc. Int. Symp. on Programming. LNCS 137. Springer-Verlag (1982) 337–351
12. Burch, J., Clarke, E., McMillan, K., Dill, D., Hwang, L.: Symbolic model checking: 10^{20} states and beyond. Inform. and Comput. 98 (1992) 142–170
13. Biere, A., Cimatti, A., Clarke, E., Fujita, M., Zhu, Y.: Symbolic model checking using SAT procedures instead of BDDs. In: Proc. 36th Conf. DAC '99. New Orleans, USA. ACM Press (21–25 June 1999) 317–320
14. Cousot, P., Cousot, R.: Comparing the Galois connection and widening/narrowing approaches to abstract interpretation, invited paper. In Bruynooghe, M., Wirsing, M., eds.: Proc. 4th Int. Symp. PLILP '92. Leuven, Belgium, 26–28 Aug. 1992, LNCS 631, Springer-Verlag (1992) 269–295
15. Cousot, P.: Partial completeness of abstract fixpoint checking, invited paper. In Choueiry, B., Walsh, T., eds.: Proc. 4th Int. Symp. SARA '2000. Horseshoe Bay, USA, LNAI 1864. Springer-Verlag (2000) 1–25
16. Clarke, E., Grumberg, O., Long, D.: Model checking and abstraction. TOPLAS 16 (1994) 1512–1542

17. Cleaveland, R., Iyer, P., Yankelevitch, D.: Optimality in abstractions of model checking. In Mycroft, A., ed.: Proc. 2nd Int. Symp. SAS '95. Glasgow, UK, 25–27 Sep. 1995, LNCS 983. Springer-Verlag (1995) 51–63

18. Cousot, P., Halbwachs, N.: Automatic discovery of linear restraints among variables of a program. In: 5th POPL, Tucson, USA, ACM Press (1978) 84–97

19. Halbwachs, N.: About synchronous programming and abstract interpretation. Sci. Comput. Programming **31** (1998) 75–89

20. Graf, S., Loiseaux, C.: A tool for symbolic program verification and abstraction. In Courcoubetis, C., ed.: Proc. 5th Int. Conf. CAV '93. Elounda, Grece, LNCS 697, Springer-Verlag (1993) 71–84

21. Katoen, J.P., Stevens, P., eds.: Relative Completeness of Abstraction Refinement for Software Model Checking. In Katoen, J.P., Stevens, P., eds.: Proc. 8th Int. Conf. TACAS '2002. Grenoble, France, LNCS 2280, Springer-Verlag (2002)

22. Giacobazzi, R., Ranzato, F., Scozzari, F.: Making abstract interpretations complete. J. ACM **47** (2000) 361–416

23. Karr, M.: Affine relationships among variables of a program. Acta Informat. **6** (1976) 133–151

24. Cousot, P., Cousot, R.: Systematic design of program transformation frameworks. In: 29th POPL, Portland, USA, ACM Press (2002) 178–190

25. Cousot, P.: The Marktoberdorf'98 generic abstract interpreter. http://www.di.ens.fr/~cousot/Marktoberdorf98.shtml (1998)

26. Cousot, P.: Calculational design of semantics and static analyzers by abstract interpretation. NATO Int. Summer School 1998 on Calculational System Design. Marktoberdorf, DE. Organized by F.L. Bauer, M. Broy, E.W. Dijkstra, D. Gries and C.A.R. Hoare. (1998)

27. Cousot, P., Cousot, R.: Refining model checking by abstract interpretation. Aut . Soft . Eng. **6** (1999) 69–95

28. Berezin, S., Clarke, E., Jha, S., Marrero, W.: Model checking algorithms for the μ-calculus. Tech. rep. tr-cmu-cs-96-180, Carnegie Mellon University, USA, (1996)

29. Cousot, P., Cousot, R.: Abstract interpretation and application to logic programs. J. Logic Programming **13** (1992) 103–179 (The editor of J. Logic Programming has mistakenly published the unreadable galley proof. For a correct version of this paper, see http://www.di.ens.fr/~cousot.).

30. Kaplan, M., Ullman, J.: A general scheme for the automatic inference of variable types. J. ACM **27** (1980) 128–145

31. Massé, D.: Combining forward and backward analyzes of temporal properties. In Danvy, ., Filinski, A., eds.: Proc. 2nd Symp. PADO '2001. Århus, Danmark, 21–23 May 2001, LNCS 2053, Springer-Verlag (2001) 155–172

32. Granger, P.: Improving the results of static analyses of programs by local decreasing iterations. In Shyamasundar, R., ed.: Proc. 12th FST & TCS. New Delhi, India, 18–20 Dec. 1992, LNCS 652, Springer-Verlag (1992) 68–79

33. Clarke, E., Grumberg, O., Jha, S., Lu, Y., Veith, H.: Counterexample-guided abstraction refinement. In Emerson, E., Sistla, A., eds.: Proc. 12th Int. Conf. CAV '00. Chicago, USA, LNCS 1855, SPRINGER (2000) 154–169

34. Giacobazzi, R., Quintarelli, E.: Incompleteness, counterexamples and refinements in abstract model-checking. In Cousot, P., ed.: Proc. 8th Int. Symp. SAS '01. Paris, France, LNCS 2126, Springer-Verlag (2001) 356–373

35. Ferdinand, C., Heckmann, R., Langenbach, M., Martin, F., Schmidt, M., Theiling, H., Thesing, S., Wilhelm, R.: Reliable and precise WCET determination for a real-life processor. In Henzinger, T., Kirsch, C., eds.: Proc. 1st Int. Workshop ESOP '2001. Volume 2211 of LNCS. Springer-Verlag (2001) 469Ñ–485

The Symbolic Approach to Hybrid Systems

Thomas A. Henzinger

University of California, Berkeley

A hybrid system is a dynamical system whose state has both a discrete component, which is updated in a sequence of steps, and a continuous component, which evolves over time. Hybrid systems are a useful modeling tool in a variety of situations, including the embedded (digital) control of physical (analog) plants, robotics, circuits, biology, and finance. We survey a computational approach to the verification and control of hybrid systems which is based on the symbolic discretization of continuous state changes. On the theoretical side, we classify infinite, hybrid state spaces as to which finite, discrete abstractions they admit. This classification enables us to apply concepts and results from concurrency theory, model checking, and game theory to hybrid systems. On the practical side, we discuss several options for implementing the symbolic approach to hybrid systems, and point to existing tool support.

D. Brinksma and K. G. Larsen (Eds.): CAV 2002, LNCS 2404, p. 57, 2002.

Infinite Games and Verification
(Extended Abstract of a Tutorial)

Wolfgang Thomas

Lehrstuhl für Informatik VII, RWTH Aachen
52056 Aachen, Germany
thomas@informatik.rwth-aachen.de

Abstract. The purpose of this tutorial is to survey the essentials of
the algorithmic theory of infinite games, its role in automatic program
synthesis and verification, and some challenges of current research.

1   Background and Motivation

The research on infinite games in theoretical computer science is based on a
mixture of several motivations:

1. The beautiful classical theory of infinite games, as developed in descriptive
   set theory, lacks an algorithmic content. Such an algorithmic orientation is
   provided by the automata theoretic approach to infinite games, originating
   in work of Church, Büchi, McNaughton, and Rabin about fourty years ago.
2. Determinacy results for infinite games are closely related to complementation
   results for logics and automata; thus, infinite games help to analyze logical
   theories (the most prominent being the monadic theory S2S of two successor
   functions, see e.g. [Th97]).
3. Games are a natural model of reactive computation, and infinite games are
   thus a faithful representation of nonterminating reactive systems (for which
   control problems can be solved in terms of providing winning strategies).
4. The model-checking problem for logics like the μ-calculus can be formulated
   as the question to determine the winner of an infinite game.

The purpose of this tutorial is to explain the core of the algorithmic (and
automata theoretic) theory of infinite games. In the present extended abstract,
only some key notions are explained, without technical details and proofs. In the
tutorial, more will be said about topics of current research as listed in Section 6
of this abstract.

2   The Terminological Framework

We consider infinite two-person games with perfect information; the two players
are called 0 and 1. A game is specified by a directed *game graph* (also called arena
of the game) and a *winning condition*, which singles out those infinite plays which

D. Brinksma and K. G. Larsen (Eds.): CAV 2002, LNCS 2404, pp. 58–65, 2002.

are won by player 0 (the others are won by player 1). The game graph $G = (V, E)$ is equipped with a partition of its vertex set V into sets V_0, V_1. A *play* over G from vertex v_0 is a sequence $\pi = v_0 v_1 \ldots$ of vertices built up for $i = 0, 1, \ldots$ as follows: If $v_i \in V_0$ then player 0 chooses v_{i+1} as next vertex (otherwise player 1 chooses v_{i+1}), in both cases respecting the condition that that $(v_i, v_{i+1}) \in E$. The winning condition for player 0 can be given by a logical formula which expresses a certain property of a play π, or by an acceptance condition from the theory of ω-automata applied to π. If the vertex set V is infinite, one usually assumes a finite coloring of the vertices and expresses the winning condition by referring to the induced sequence of vertex colors rather than to the vertices themselves. In the sequel, up to the last section, we assume that the game graph is finite.

A *strategy* for player p is a function which maps each play prefix $v_0 \ldots v$ ending in a vertex $v \in V_p$ to a suitable "next vertex", i.e. some v' with $(v, v') \in E$. In the automata theoretic framework, two special kinds of strategies are essential: A strategy is *positional* (or: *memoryless*) if its value for a play prefix $v_0 \ldots v$ only depends on the last (or "current") vertex v, and it is called *finite-state* if it can be computed by a finite automaton with output (upon reading $v_0 \ldots v$ as input). A *winning strategy* for player 0 leads to a play won by player 0 whatever choice of vertices is done by player 1. One says that player 0 *wins* a given game *from* v_0 if he has a winning strategy for plays starting in v_0. The set of these initial vertices v_0 forms the *winning region* W_0 of player 0. A game is determined if the winning region of player 1 is the complement set $W_1 = V \setminus W_0$. All games to be considered here are determined.

In the classical theory of Gale-Stewart games, a game involves the infinite binary tree as game arena, and the winning condition is just given by an abstract set of plays. The presentation of games by game graphs and logical formulas or by ω-automata (as winning conditions) raises algorithmic problems which are not relevant in the classical framework:

1. To decide for a given vertex v_0 whether it belongs to the winning region of player 0, and
2. if possible to construct a program which executes a winning strategy for player 0, [1] and
3. to minimize the complexity for determining a winning strategy, as well as to reduce the complexity of the strategy itself. For finite-state strategies the latter can mean to minimize the number of states of the respective strategy automata.

By "solving a game" we mean a solution to questions (1) and (2).

Sometimes, a reactive system can be modelled in this framework of infinite games, by identifying player 0 with a control component and player 1 with the environment. The winning condition corresponds to the specification which the

---

[1] It should be noted that in general one cannot infer a computable winning strategy for player 0 from the fact that the winning region of player 0 is decidable; see e.g. [Th95].

control component has to meet under all possible behaviours of the environment. A solution to question (1) amounts to the test whether the specification allows a solution, item (2) is concerned with the synthesis of a correct controller, and item (3) with optimizations of this synthesis. In the present tutorial, we stay with "linear-time specifications" and the case of complete information; [KV99] is a reference where branching-time specifications and incomplete information are treated.

3   Topological Classification of Winning Conditions

If the winning condition of a game is expressible in propositional temporal logic or in the monadic logic S1S, one can apply the well-known transformation of such formulas into deterministic ω-automata, say with a Muller acceptance condition. Using such a transformation of a formula φ into a deterministic automaton $\mathcal{A}_\varphi$, one can proceed from the given game graph G to the product $G \times \mathcal{A}_\varphi$, in which a play π over G becomes the pair (π, ρ), where ρ is the run of $\mathcal{A}_\varphi$ on input π. For this induced play, the winning condition φ is captured by the Muller acceptance condition applied to ρ. The *Muller games*, i.e. games with a Muller winning condition, are thus a framework general enough for most applications in synthesis and verification.

The set of all plays over a game graph can naturally be viewed as a topological space (called Cantor space for finitely branching graphs and Baire space for countably branching ones). Properties of plays are classified in the so-called Borel hierarchy, its first level consisting of the closed and open sets. For the question of solving games, it is useful to locate the set of winning plays in this hierarchy. Six basic cases have to be distinguished (for more background see e.g. [MP92]):

1. "reachability games" (or "guarantee games"), where a play is a win for player 0 iff it reaches at some time a vertex of a given "target set",
2. "safety games", where a play is a win for player 0 iff it remains within a given set of vertices,
3. games with boolean combinations of conditions 1 and 2 as winning conditions, the so-called "obligation games" or "weak Muller games", where the set of vertices visited in a play determines whether it is a win for player 0,
4. "recurrence games" (or "Büchi games"), where a play is a win for player 0 iff it meets a given set of "target vertices" infinitely often,
5. "persistence games", in which a play is a win for player 0 if from some point onwards, only vertices of a predefined vertex set occur,
6. games with boolean combinations of conditions 4 and 5 as winning conditions, where the set of vertices visited infinitely often in a play determines whether it is a win for player 0.

The games of item 3 are captured by an automata theoretic winning condition due to Staiger and Wagner, the games of item 6 are the Muller games.

The basis of most strategy constructions is the solution of reachability games: Starting from the set T of target vertices, one computes by an inductive process the sets A_i (for $i = 1, 2, \ldots$) of those vertices from which player 0 can ensure to reach T within i moves. If the game graph is finitely branching, the union of the A_i, called the "0-attractor of T", is the winning region of player 0. On this region, there is a positional winning strategy for player 0 (which just has to ensure that the distance to T decreases in each step).

Variants and extensions of this construction also allow to solve the safety games, the recurrence games, and the persistence games, in each case only by means of positional strategies. Another pleasant feature of these games is that their solution is possible in polynomial time (in fact, linear time in the case of reachability and safety games).

4 Game Simulations and Parity Conditions

The weak Muller games and the Muller games involve some complications, mainly due to the fact that positional winning strategies do no more suffice. In fact, there is a sequence of game graphs G_n with $O(n)$ vertices such that any winning strategy solving a certain associated weak Muller game requires a strategy automaton with at least 2^n states. Similarly, for the Muller games a lower bound of $n!$ can be established ([DJW97]). In ω-automata theory, one can consider the Rabin or the Streett condition instead of the Muller condition; in these cases, player 0 (resp. player 1) can win with a positional strategy, but the other player again needs in general some memory in order to win.

At this point, the so-called parity winning conditions are very convenient: They allow to reach the expressive power of the weak Muller and the Muller condition, but at the same time admit solutions by positional winning strategies. A parity winning condition refers to a coloring of the vertices of a game graph by finitely many integers (formally presented by a function $c : V \to C$ with finite $C \subseteq \mathbb{Z}$). With respect to the parity condition, a play $\pi = v_0 v_1 \ldots$ is a win for player 0 if the maximal color occurring infinitely often in the sequence $c(v_0) c(v_1) \ldots$ is even. The weak parity condition just requires that the maximal color occurring at all (rather than infinitely often) has to be even.

A nested computation of attractor sets suffices to solve a weak parity game, including the (polynomial time) construction of positional winning strategies for the two players on their respective winning regions. The solution of parity games is harder; there are exponential time algorithms for computing the winning regions of the two players and corresponding positional winning strategies, and it is presently open whether a polynomial time solution exists. Below we give a more detailed discussion.

To verify that the weak parity condition and the parity condition are indeed enough to capture the weak Muller and the Muller condition, respectively, we use a notion of game simulation (see [Th95]): It involves a transformation of a game over a graph $G = (V, E)$ with winning condition φ into a "simulating game" over a (usually larger) game graph $G' = (V', E')$ with a (usually simpler) winning condition φ'. In the cases considered here, the vertex set V' will be a product $V \times S$ for a finite set S (in which a certain element s_0 is designated). A play π from v through G will determine a well-defined play π' through G' from (v, s_0). The simulation relation $(G, \varphi) \leq (G', \varphi')$ holds if for a play π over G we have that π satisfies φ iff π' satisfies φ'. It turns out that a weak Muller game over $G = (V, E)$ is simulated by a weak parity game over a graph $G' = (V \times 2^V, E')$, and that a Muller game over $G = (V, E)$ can be simulated by a parity game over a graph $G' = (V \times S, E')$ where S is the set of permutations of the V-elements. The first simulation is a variant of the subset construction (namely, in the second component of a V'-vertex the V-vertices visited so far in a play are collected). The second simulation involves sequences of vertices rather than sets, namely the "latest appearance record", i.e. the visited states in the order of their most recent visit.

One can combine the simulation of weak Muller games and Muller games by weak parity games and by parity games, respectively, with the construction of positional winning strategies for the latter. Altogether one obtains finite-state strategies for the weak Muller games and the Muller games. The idea is to use the auxiliary set S introduced in the game simulation as the set of states of a strategy automaton. Also other games where winning strategies involve memory (e.g., Streett games) can be solved by such a reduction to parity games.

5   Parity Games and μ-Calculus Model-Checking

To find an efficient solution for parity games is one of the central open problems in the the verification of state-based systems. As Emerson, Jutla, and Sistla [EJS93] have shown, the model-checking problem for the μ-calculus is polynomial-time reducible to the problem of solving parity games. To show this, one transforms (in polynomial time) a given finite Kripke structure $\mathcal{K}$ with designated state s_0 and a μ-calculus formula φ into a game graph $G_{(\mathcal{K}, s_0, \varphi)}$ equipped with a parity condition. The vertices of the game graph are pairs (s, ψ) or (s, X) where s is a state s from $\mathcal{K}$, ψ is a subformula of φ, and X is a fixed point variable occurring in φ. The number of colors reflects the alternation depth of φ. The construction ensures that $(\mathcal{K}, s_0) \models \varphi$ iff over $G_{(\mathcal{K}, s_0, \varphi)}$ player 0 has a winning strategy from vertex (s_0, φ). (For details the reader may consult the recent monograph [Sti01].)

Also fragments and variants of the μ-calculus can be handled in this game theoretical setting. For example, the Computation Tree Logic CTL leads to a weak parity game.

For the solution of parity games, the available upper bounds do so far not allow to infer a polynomial time algorithm. To be specific, one considers the decision problem whether a vertex of a finite game graph of a parity game belongs to the winning region of player 0. It is known that this problem is in NP ∩ co-NP, and even in the slightly more restricted complexity class UP ∩ co-UP (see [Jur98]). There are several algorithms whose exponential time behavior is due to an exponent $d/2$ where d is the number of colors. Another algorithm (presented in [VJ00]) uses an elegant scheme of "strategy improvement", in which a sequence of positional strategies of player 0 is constructed ending with a uniform winning strategy over the winning region of player 0: Each initial choice of a positional strategy by player 0 is answered by a "best response strategy" of player 1 (again positional), from which player 0 can continue by a local improvement of his strategy, then again obtaining a "best response" of player 1, and so on until player 0 reaches a strategy where no local improvement is possible. (We have to skip the definitions of "best response" and "local improvement" here.) While it is easy to see that each round in this improvement scheme costs only polynomial time, the number of improvement steps can (so far) only be bounded by the number of all possible positional strategies of player 0 (which is exponential in the number of vertices). On the other hand, no family of example graphs seems to be known where the outlined algorithm has to carry out an exponential number of improvement steps.

6   Selected Topics of Current and Future Research

We close by listing a number of fields and problems which are subject of present research or seem to be promising future steps in developing the theory of infinite games. A look into the literature will show that this list is far from complete.

1. *Games over pushdown transition graphs.* The core results of the theory over finite game graphs have been lifted to pushdown graphs (see [Wa00]). However, computational results and efficiency considerations now have to incorporate a new parameter, the "size of a state" (which is the length of the word representing the state).

2. *Games over other infinite graphs.* It is well-known that over slightly more general graphs than the pushdown graphs, an algorithmic solution even of the simplest games (reachability games) fails. This is not only true for recursive graphs in general, but also for quite restricted classes like the "ground tree rewriting graphs" (where vertices are finite trees and the edge relation is defined in terms of ground rewriting rules).

3. *Games with winning conditions of Borel level greater than 2.* For infinite graphs, even for pushdown graphs, it is reasonable to consider winning conditions which transcend the level of Muller condition, i.e. which are located on higher levels of the Borel hierarchy, but which still admit algorithmic solutions.

4. *Games over structured transition systems.* The flat representation of a system by a game graph does not, in general, provide an appropriate system model. In distributed systems, different winning strategies have to be devised for different components ([PR90], [MT01]). Another research direction is to provide methods for solving games over hierarchical systems.

5. *Timed systems, optimality of strategies.* The subject of strategy synthesis over timed systems has attracted much attention; see e.g. [AMPS98] and [AM99]. Rather than to optimize strategy automata w.r.t. their number of states, other criteria for optimization become now relevant. For example, one tries to ensure that waiting times between different events are minimized.

6. *Nondeterministic strategies.* In hierarchical design, a way of strategy construction is desirable where the idea of refinement can be applied. Nondeterministic strategies are a possible approach; refinement steps would narrow down the nondeterminism.

7. *Compositional strategy construction.* In contrast to model-checking (where a logical specification can be handled by decomposing a formula according to its construction), we do not know of such a compositional approach for solving infinite games; indeed, their solution rests on the presentation of winning conditions by ω-automata. A practical theory would have to offer a more structured method in which logical operators enter.

References

[AMPS98] E. Asarin, O. Maler, A.Pnueli, J. Sifakis, Controller Synthesis for Timed Automata, Proc. IFAC Symposium on System Structure and Control, 469-474, Elsevier, Amsterdam 1998. 63

[AM99] E. Asarin, O. Maler, As Soon as Possible: Time Optimal Control for Timed Automata, Hybrid Systems (F. Vaandrager et al. Eds.): Computation and Control, Lecture Notes in Computer Science 1569 (1999), 19-30. 63

[EJS93] E. A. Emerson, C. S. Jutla, A. P. Sistla, On model checking for fragments of μ-calculus, in: CAV'93 (C. Coucoubetis, Ed), Lecture Notes in Computer Science **697** (1993), 385-396. 62

[DJW97] S. Dziembowski, M. Jurdzinski, I. Walukiewicz, How much memory is needed to win infinite games?, Proc. 12th IEEE Symp. on Logic in Computer Science, 1997, 99-110. 61

[Ju98] M. Jurdzinski, Deciding the winner in parity games is in UP∩co-UP, *Inform. Processing Letters* **68** (1998), 119-124. 62

[KV99] O. Kupferman, M. Y. Vardi, Church's problem revisited, *Bull. Symb. Logic* **5** (1999), 245-263. 60

[MP92] Z. Manna, A. Pnueli, *The Temporal Logic of Reactive and Concurrent Programs*, Springer-Verlag, Berlin-Heidelberg-New York 1992. 60

[MT01] P. Madhusudan, P. S. Thiagarajan: Distributed Controller Synthesis for Local Specifications. Proc. ICALP 2001, Lecture Notes in Computer Science 2076 (2001), 396-407. 63

[PR90] A. Pnueli, R. Rosner, Distributed reactive systems are hard to synthesize, Proc. 31st IEEE Symp. on Foundation of Computer Science, 1990, 746-757. 63

[Sti01] C. Stirling, *Modal and Temporal Properties of Processes*, Springer-Verlag, New York 2001. 62

[Th95] W. Thomas, On the synthesis of strategies in infinite games, in: STACS'95 (E. W. Mayr, C. Puech, Eds.), Lecture Notes in Computer Science **900** (1995), 1-13. 59, 61

[Th97] W. Thomas, Languages, automata, and logic, in: *Handbook of Formal Languages* (G. Rozenberg, A. Salomaa, Eds.), Vol. 3, Springer-Verlag, Berlin Heidelberg 1997. 58

[VJ00] J. Vöge, M. Jurdzinski, A strategy improvement algorithm for solving parity games, CAV 2000, Lect. Notes in Computer Science **1855** (2000), 202-215. 62

[Wal00]   I. Walukiewicz, Pushdown processes: games and model-checking, *Information and Computation* **157** (2000), 234-263. 63

Symbolic Localization Reduction with Reconstruction Layering and Backtracking

Sharon Barner, Daniel Geist and Anna Gringauze

IBM Haifa Research Lab, Haifa Israel

Abstract. Localization reduction is an abstraction-refinement scheme for model checking which was introduced by Kurshan [12] as a means for tackling state explosion. It is completely automatic, but despite the work that has been done related to this scheme, it still suffers from computational complexity. In this paper we present algorithmic improvements to localization reduction that enabled us to overcome some of these problems. Namely, we present a new symbolic algorithm for path reconstruction including incremental refinement and backtracking. We have implemented these improvements and compared them to previous work on a large number of our industrial examples. In some cases the improvement was dramatic. Using these improvements we were able to verify circuits that we were not previously able to address.

1 Introduction

The directions in which contemporary research is tackling the state explosion problem are quite diversified. Structural model reductions are performed, various optimizations are published, and bounded model checking [4] is gaining momentum. Formal verification activity has also somewhat shifted from verification to falsification or as it is popularly called "bug hunting". This paper concentrates on a method which is called localization reduction or iterative abstraction refinement. The strength of this method is in verification and therefore it is complimentary to the methods such as bounded model checking and partial search whose main strength is in falsification.

Localization reduction with counterexample guided refinement was introduced by Kurshan [12]. Localization reduction is an iterative technique that starts with an abstraction of the model under verification and tries to verify the specification on this abstraction. When a counterexample is found a *reconstruction* process is executed to determine if it is a valid one. If the counterexample is found to be bogus (or spurious), then the abstract model is refined to eliminate the possibility of this counterexample in the next verification iteration. The details are described in Section 2.

Note that the localization technique either leaves a variable unchanged or replaces it by a non-deterministic abstraction. A similar approach is described by Balarin and Sangiovanni-Vincentelli [2]. Another refinement technique has been proposed by Lind-Nelson and Andersen [14]. They use under and over-approximation in order to handle all CTL. Their approximation techniques enable them to avoid rechecking the entire model after each refinement step while guaranteeing completeness.

There are abstraction-refinement techniques that do not use counterexamples to refine the abstraction [13, 16]. A technique proposed by Govindaraju and Dill [10] uses under approximation techniques and counterexamples to verify the specification. The refinement technique used there is different - it randomly chooses a concrete state corresponding to the first spurious state in the abstract counter example and tries to construct a real counterexample starting with the image of this state under the transition relation. Furthermore, the paper is limited to handling of safety properties and non-cyclic counterexamples.

D. Brinksma and K. G. Larsen (Eds.): CAV 2002, LNCS 2404, pp. 65-77, 2002.
© Springer-Verlag Berlin Heidelberg 2002

A general abstraction method using a counterexample guided refinement was recently proposed by Clarke et al. in [7]. Wang et al. have reported the use of an ATPG solver for reconstruction [19]. Clarke et al. [9] have reported similar work where they used the GRASP [18] SAT solver to perform reconstruction. Gupta and Clarke have used spectral analysis to perform refinement[11]. The algorithms reported in this paper are implemented using BDDs but some of them can be implemented otherwise and can be used in conjunction with SAT or ATPG based implementations.

The steps of the abstraction refinement process described in this paper are no different than those described by Clarke et al. [7]. However an implementation of the methods described in Clarke et al. resulted for the most part with state explosion when they were attempted on our current industrial examples. We therefore improved the algorithms described by Clarke et al. and as result achieved dramatic improvements in some cases of real industrial examples.

Our improvements are described in Section 4. Most of the improvements were on path reconstruction and we also changed the way refinement is done. Since localization reduction is most effective when a property passes (as can be seen in the results in Section 5), it may seem that concentration on the refinement process would be more appropriate. However, since the refinement is guided by the counterexample, the reconstruction phase also calculates information that is crucial for the refinement phase. Therefore, improving reconstruction also improves refinement.

We have implemented the changes to localization reduction and used them on some of our designs. The new algorithms enabled us to verify circuits which we could not handle previously and in some cases the improvement was dramatic.

The rest of the paper is organized as follows. The next section describes localization reduction in detail. Section 3 defines the notation we use. Section 4 describes our algorithms. Section 5 details experimental results. We conclude in Section 6 with some suggestions for future work.

2 Overview of Localization Reduction Process

The process of localization reduction is depicted in Figure 1. Given a model M and an ACTL [8] formula φ where the model checking problem $M \models \varphi$, is too large for a model checker to handle, the localization reduction method works as follows: first a heuristic process is executed in order to obtain an abstract model M' of M such that $M \prec M'$ where $\prec$ is the simulation relation. Next, the model checking problem $M' \models \varphi$, is submitted to a model checker. Note that although M' may contain more behavior than M, it's structure and description are much simpler so the model checker is able to resolve the problem without reaching state explosion. The resolution may result in a "pass" or a "fail". In the case of a "pass" (i.e. $M' \models \varphi$ is true), the process can terminate because $M \prec M'$ and this implies that $M \models \varphi$. However, in the case of a "fail", the counter-example path, π' generated is valid for M' but may not have a corresponding execution path π in M. In this case it is necessary to validate that there is a corresponding path in M. This process is called "reconstruction". If a path π is successfully reconstructed then the process terminates. However, if reconstruction is not possible then π' is considered to be "spurious and the next iteration is started by heuristically

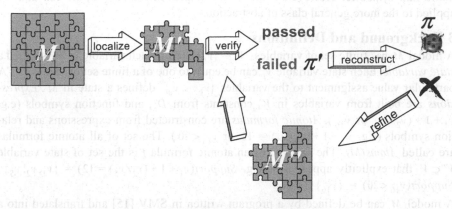

Fig. 1. The localization reduction process

refining and replacing M' with M'' such that $M \prec M'' \prec M'$. This process of iterative refinement continues until a "pass" is returned, or reconstruction of a "fail" is successful, or eventually state explosion is reached during model checking.

2.1 Improvements
Aside from state explosion in model checking, the abstraction refinement has two additional difficulties:

1. The reconstruction operation can in itself explode.

2. When reconstruction fails, the refinement operation is usually guided by trying to determine from the path π', what are the inconsistencies of this path and the model M. This is usually defined as a NP hard problem [7].

The methods of Clarke et al. explore all concrete paths which correspond to a certain abstract path starting from the initial states. In case there is no such concrete path they refine the model. Since these algorithms still suffer from state explosion we improved them in the following ways:

1. The path reconstruction was significantly changed:

   a. Incremental reconstruction: Instead of trying to reconstruct π' directly on model M, our algorithm performs successive reconstructions on model $M_i, i = 1 \ldots k$ where $M = M_k \prec \ldots M_1 \prec M$.

   b. Partial search and backtracking: Instead of trying to find all paths that correspond to π' the algorithm selects a subset of such paths and continues reconstruction. It is therefore possible to backtrack when a dead end is reached. The details are described in Section 4.2.

2. The refinement criterion is essentially the same as in Clarke et al. [7] however the method of computation takes advantage of the fact that we are handling a restricted class of abstractions (as described next).

We chose to restrict the class of abstractions we support to a subset of those supported in Clarke et al. While Clarke et al. support very general abstraction we confined ourselves to variable projection because with the general abstraction you need more refinement iterations and the benefit is small. Overall, our new method is entirely automatic and symbolic. However, some of the improvements we report can also be applied to the more general class of abstractions.

3 Background and Definitions

A model M has finite set of variables $V = \{v_1, ..., v_n\}$. Each variable in V is called a *state variable*. Each state variable v_i can be equal to one of a finite set of values D_i. A particular value assignment to the variables $\{v_1, ..., v_n\}$ defines a state in M. *Expressions* are built from variables in V, constants from D_i, and function symbols (e.g. $v_1 + 1 + (v_2/v_5)$ or v_{16}). *Atomic formulas* are constructed from expressions and relation symbols (e.g. $v_1 + 1 + (v_2/v_5) = 12$ or $v_{16} < 20$). The set of all atomic formulas are called *Atoms(M)*. The *Support* of an atomic formula f is the set of state variable $V' \subseteq V$ that explicitly appear in f (e.g. $Support(v_1 + 1 + (v_2/v_5) = 12) = \{v_1, v_2, v_5\}$, $Support(v_{16} < 20) = \{v_{16}\}$).

A model M can be defined by a program written in SMV [15] and translated into a *Kripke structure* $K = (S, I, R, L)$ Where $S = D_1 \times ... \times D_n$, is a set of states, $I \subseteq S$, is a set of Initial states $R \subseteq S \times S$, is a transition relation and $L : S \rightarrow 2^{Atoms(M)}$ is a labeling of the states in S given by $L(s) = \{f \in Atoms(M) \mid s \models f\}$. Based on the Kripke structure K of M, formulas of the ACTL temporal logic can be constructed and evaluated (i.e. model checked). For a detailed definition of ACTL see [8].

Localization reduction involves abstraction of the model M (and its associated structure K). There is more than one way to obtain an abstract model of M. We now describe the type of abstraction used in this paper.

Definition 1 *(State projection) Given a state $s = (v_1, ..., v_n)$ and a subset of the state variables $V' \subseteq V$ where*

1. $m = |V'|$.

2. Let $i_1, ..., i_m$ be the indices in increasing order of the state variables that belong to V', then $v'_1 = v_{i_1}, v'_2 = v_{i_2}, ..., v_m = v'_{i_m}$.

The state projection of s on V' is the m-tuple $s' = (v_1', ..., v_m')$ which satisfies $s' = \exists(V/V')s(V)$ and denoted by $proj(s, V')$.

Intuitively, the state s is projected onto the coordinates of the variables contained in V'.

Definition 2 *(Set projection) Given a set of states S and a set of state variables V', The set projection S' of the set S on V' is defined as $S' = \{proj(s, V') \mid s \in S\}$.*

Definition 3 *(Model projection) Given a Kripke structure K which represents a model M and a subset of the state variables $V' \subseteq V$ we define a model projection K' of K with respect to V' which represents a model M' as follows:*

1. V' is the set of state variables of M'.

2. $K' = (S', I', R', L')$ where:

$S' = proj(S, V')$.

$I' = proj(I, V')$.

$R' = \{(s'_1, s'_2) \mid s'_1 = proj(s_1, V'), s'_2 = proj(s_2), (s_1, s_2) \in R\}\}$.

$L'(s') = \{f \in Atoms(M') \mid s' \models f\}$.

where $Atoms(M')$ is the subset of $Atoms(M)$ where only variables that belong to V' appear.

Note that its easy to see that $M \prec M'$ by definition of model projection, and that model projection defines a family of model abstractions for M that has a partial order with respect to $\prec$.

From here on and throughout the paper, the term *abstraction* will mean projection type of abstraction. The choice of projection as an abstraction is intuitive when working with Binary Decision Diagrams (BDDs). Projection of a set can be calculated by existential quantification which is a standard operation of BDD packages [6].

Definition 4 (Path projection) The projection of path $\pi = \{s_0, s_1, ..., s_k\}$ *on a set of variables* V' *is a set of paths* $\Pi' = \{S_0', S_1', ..., S_k'\}$ *, where for all i,* $S_i' = proj(s_i, V')$ *. We denote* $\Pi_i' \equiv S_i'$ *.*

Note that a projection of a path has a set of states as path elements, so it corresponds to a set of paths in the original model. We make this distinction by denoting a set of paths (and its elements) with capital letter.

Since the Kripke structures we handle are derived from hardware implementations the transition relations obtained can be partitioned according to the state variables as follows: $R = \bigcap R_i$ where $R_i \subseteq S_i \times V_i'$, S_i is a projection of S onto some $Supp_i \subseteq V$ and V_i' is a projection of S' onto $\{v_i'\}$. We call $Supp_i$ the *support* of variable v_i. Intuitively the next value of each state variable in the model is independent of the next values of other variables of the model and the support is the state variables which appear in the atomic formula that describes the next state behavior (in practice some variables may be optimized out if the formula is equivalent to one that does not contain them). The support induces a graph on the state variables, where each variable is a node and there is an edge between v_i and v_j if $v_j \in Supp_i$.

The Support of a set of state variables is defined to be the union of the supports of the variables belonging to the set.

We are now ready to describe the abstraction refinement algorithms we improved.

4 The Abstraction Refinement Process

As mentioned in Section 1 our abstraction-refinement process follows the same steps as described in Clarke et al. We now describe the differences that make it more practical.

4.1 Initial Abstraction

Given a Model M and a model checking problem $M \models \varphi$, our initial abstraction M' is obtained by projection of M onto the set of state variables that are in the Support of the atomic formulas of φ. Then we utilize a model checker to resolve $M' \models \varphi$. In the case where a false answer is returned, we continue the process with reconstruction.

4.2 Trace Reconstruction

4.2.1 Reconstructing a Finite Path

Given a path Π' in the abstract model M', the purpose of trace reconstruction is to find a path π of M such that Π' is a projection of π.

Let M be the original model and $V = \{v_0, v_1, ..., v_n\}$ denote the original set of variables. Assume that we have model M' which is projection of the original model on the

```
reconstruct (Π', M', M ) {
    Π⁰ = Π';
    i = 1;
    U:=variables_of(M');
    while ( (U ≠ ∅) ∧ (Πⁱ ≠ ∅) ) {
        U := choose_n_variables(support(U)/U) ∪ U;
        M'' := project_model(M, U);
        Πⁱ⁺¹ := reconstruct_one_layer(Πⁱ, M', M'');
        if(Πⁱ⁺¹ = ∅) return ∅; /*refinement needed */
        i = i + 1;
    }
    return choose_one_counter_example(Πⁱ);
}
```

Fig. 2. Layered reconstruction

set of variables $V' = \{v'_0, v'_1, ..., v'_m\}$, where $m \le n$. Let also $\Pi = \{S_0, S_1, ..., S_k\}$ be the counter example for the original formula in the projected model.

Generally, the counter example (path) reconstruction algorithm analyzes the reachable state space for the variables in V/V', where all search steps are performed inside $\bigcup_{0 \le i \le k} S_i$. In [7], the algorithm iteratively performs consequent image computations using the model M, intersecting each i-th step with S_i before the next image computation, till no further step is possible or the end is reached. In the former case we have a spurious counter example, and in the latter case the counter example is proved real. However, this algorithm often leads to state space explosion, because in many practical cases $|V/V'|$ is significantly greater than $|V'|$.

In this section we present some techniques to overcome the state space explosion problem. First, we introduce the notion of *layer*

4.2.2 The Layering Reconstruction Algorithm
Definition 5 *layer*.

1. $U_0 = V'$ is a layer.

2. Any set $U_i \subseteq support\left(\bigcup_{0 \le k \le i-1} U_k\right) / \left(\bigcup_{0 \le k \le i-1} U_k\right)$ is a layer.

With the notion of layer we can divide the variable dependency graph into disjoint sets of variables (or layers), such that each variable in the layer is in the direct dependency of some variable(s) in one of the previous layers.

We divide the set V/V' into layers, and perform the layer reconstruction algorithm below iteratively, each time by computing an additional layer of variables and adding it to the abstract model. On the i-th iteration, the partially reconstructed counter example $\Pi^i = \{S_0^i, S_1^i, ..., S_k^i\}$ is produced.

Let Π be a path in the abstract model. Our algorithm for the path reconstruction is shown on Figure 2. The function **reconstruct** accepts an abstract path Π', an abstract model M' and a concrete model M. The algorithm performs layer by layer reconstruction iteratively, each time reconstructing one more layer, till all the variables are reconstructed ($U = \emptyset$)or no further reconstruction is possible and the refinement is done ($\Pi^i = \emptyset$). For layer computation (**choose_n_variables**), the next layer can be chosen

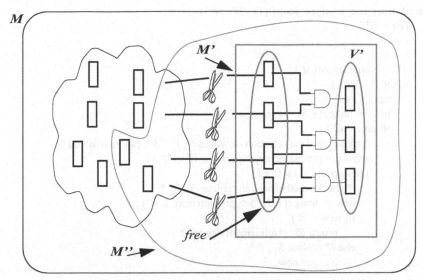

Fig. 3. The Abstract Model Structure

to be the entire support of the previous layer. However, on the first iteration of the loop we give priority to the support of the variables that were added to the model in the last refinement stage since they are the most suspect as ones that will force another refinement. In further iterations we take the support of the entire set of variables in the current model.

The advantage of layered reconstruction is twofold: first, we only reconstruct a few variables at a time while the rest are restricted to a very small subset. This maintains the state space we work on very small and avoid state explosion. Secondly, we can detect that a refinement is required early, many iterations before we actually obtain the entire concrete model.

4.2.3 Reconstructing one Layer

Reconstruction of one layer is different depending if Π' contains a loop or not. In the case of a simple path (no loop) we have implemented two algorithms. As explained above, the straightforward algorithm described in [7] suffers from state explosion. Both our algorithms try to alleviate that problem. The first one is faster and in usually good enough but when it fails due to the fact that too many variables are added back to the model, we apply our second algorithm which employs backtracking.

4.2.3.1 Reconstructing without a Loop (Algorithm 1)

The function **reconstruct_one_layer_no_loop1** accepts an abstract path Π' an abstract model M' and an intermediate model M''. We first try to reconstruct the path for model M''. Note that we do not care what the values of those new variables will be at each point of the reconstructed path except that the path has to be valid in M'' and its projection on the abstract model should be Π'. We therefore iteratively perform forward steps starting from I'', the initial set of M'' and conjunct each step with the corresponding step in Π'. This is no different so far than what is done in [7]. However, if we reach a dead end (i.e. the conjunction becomes empty) instead of proceeding to refine the model we try to modify Π' to be consistent with M''.

```
reconstruct_one_layer_no_loop1 (Π', M', M'' ) {
    last = |Π'| − 1 ;
    s := S_0 ;
    i := 0;
    V' := variables_of(M') ;
    while (i < last) {
        next_s := S_{i+1} ;
        new := image(s, M'') ∩ next_s ;
        if( new = ∅ ) {
            /* try to see if the selection of values in V''/V' can be changed */
            suspect := preimage(project(next_s, V' ), M' ) ;
            if ((suspect ∩ s) ≠ ∅ ) {
                /* check whether we can replace S_{i+1} */
                new := image(s, M'') ∩ project(next_s, V') ;
                if( new = ∅ )
                    return ∅ ; /*refinement needed */
                else /* replace S_{i+1} */
                    S_{i+1} := new;
            }
            else
                return ∅ ; /*refinement needed */
        }
        i := i+1;
    }
    return Π ;
}
```

Fig. 4. The first reconstruction algorithm (without a loop)

The choice of the specific Π' is arbitrary and is done mainly to avoid state explosion. Thus, we can modify it during reconstruction. Note that in addition to values of variables in V', Π' also contains values for the Support of V'. These variables are "cut" from their behavior logic and have completely free (nondetermimistic) behavior as shown in Figure 3. One can change the values of these free variables in Π' as long as this change is consistent with M'' (and therefore, also M'). The resulting path will still be a valid counter-example of the formula φ. Figure 4 details the algorithm: whenever Π' is found to be inconsistent with M'', we project the offending state onto V' and perform a preimage computation. That is, we preserve the values of V' and discard the other values. We try to find other values for V''/V' in order to make the state consistent with the model. Notice that we avoid preimage computations of M'' which tends to explode.

In most cases the algorithm presented in this section gives good results. However, in some of the hard cases we add backtracking to reconstruction.

4.2.3.2 Reconstructing without a Loop (Algorithm 2)

Layering is not sufficient to avoid explosion because at each iteration, the Π^i counter example is getting larger (because all the possible counter examples which comply with Π^{i-1} are searched). However, only one such counter example would suffice, and may be found in less effort than all of them. In order to exploit this, we combine under-approximation of a partially reconstructed counter example with backtracking. The

```
reconstruct_one_layer_no_loop2( Π', M', M'' ) {
    last = |Π'| – 1 ;
    for(i := 0 to last -1) S_i^all = ∅ ;
    V' := variables_of(M') ;
    S_0 := I'' ∩ project(S_0, V') ;
    i = 0 ;
    while ( i ≥ 0 and i < last ){
        prev := project(S_i, V' );
        new := project(S_{i+1}, V' );
        step := preimage(new, M'') ;
        if ( step ∩ S_i ≠ ∅ ) /* step forward */ {
            S_{i+1} = image(step, M'') ∩ S_{i+1} ;
            S_{i+1} = subset(S_{i+1}) ;
            i = i + 1 ;
        }
        else if ((step ∧ prev) ≠ ∅ ) /* backtracking */ {
            S_i = (preimage(S_{i+1}, M'') ∩ prev) / S_i^all ;
            if (S_i = ∅ ) return ∅ ;
            S_i = subset(S_i) ;
            S_i^all = S_i^all ∪ S_i ;
            i = i – 1 ;
        }
        else return ∅ ; / *refinement is needed */
    }
    return Π ;
}
```

Fig. 5. Reconstruction with backtracking

basic idea is, when reconstructing one layer of variables, to use subsets of real forward steps (image computations), as long as possible, and try backtracking when a dead end is reached.

Figure 5 shows the function **reconstruct_one_layer_no_loop2** for reconstruction with backtracking. The algorithm performs forward and backward steps (image and preimage computations) as long as possible. The forward step is done if the next step of the path is consistent with the forward computation using the model M'', till the trace is reconstructed and the bad states reached, or no forward step intersects the next state. In the latter case, backtracking is done - the algorithm performs backward steps and chooses different behavior for V''/V' till the forward step is again possible or a backward step cannot be performed anymore. This can happen if we checked all the possible values of V''/V' for the current state, or there is no backward step from the current state that intersects with the previous state. Note that we also employ underapproximation by doing subsetting [17] to avoid state explosion. In our experiments, we used subsetting to reduce the BDD size down to 5000 BDD nodes.

4.2.3.3 Reconstruction of a path with a Loop

To reconstruct an abstract path containing a loop (due to a liveness formula) we have to additionally ensure that the concrete path contains one as well. The concrete model sometimes contains some variable which acts like a "counter". That is, it changes cyclically independent of the abstract model and it is the root cause of our failure to

```
reconstruct_a_loop( Π', M', M'' ) {
    old := TRUE;
    new := S_0 ;
    last = |Π'| – 1 ;
    while(((new ∩ old) ≠ ∅) ∧ (new ≠ old)) {
        i := 1;
        new :=new ∩ old ;
        old := new;
        step := new;
        while(i <= last) {
            step := image(step, M') ∩ S_i ;
            if( step = ∅ )
                refine;
            else {
                S_i := step;
                i := i + 1 ;
            }
            new := step;
        }
    }
    if((new ∩ old) ≠ ∅ ) {
        S_0 := new;
        return extract_loop_trace( Π', M' );
    }
    else
        refine;
}
```

Fig. 6. Reconstruction with loop

find a loop using the naive approach. However, if we look for a concrete path that includes traversal of the abstract loop a few times, then we may succeed in finding one which contains a concrete loop. It is possible to try a naive approach using one of the algorithms in Section 4.2.3.1 or 4.2.3.2 and then test if the reconstructed path contains a loop and if not proceed to refinement. However, in some cases we have found that this leads to refinement right away although it is possible to find a loop using the abstract path. In [7], the approach taken was to unwind the loop a sufficient number of times and then reconstruct it. Our approach was to implement a fixed point algorithm.

The algorithm depicted in Figure 6 describes how this is done. The input path Π' is assumed to be the abstract loop without the tail leading to it from the initial state. The algorithm performs a forward fixed point algorithm to find a loop with length that is a product of $|\Pi'| - 1$. On termination of the fixed point, if $(\text{new} \cap \text{old}) \neq \emptyset$, a concrete loop exists. However, its possible that not all states in S_0 are on a loop and therefore **extract_loop_trace** chooses an arbitrary state from S_0 and iteratively performs backward steps from it until some state in S_0 is encountered more than once. This is similar to the algorithm described in [5] by Biere et al. that proves a tableau construction by showing how a concrete path can be constructed from path with a loop that satisfies the tableau.

```
refine( S_i, S_{i+1}, M', M'' ) {
    V' := variables_of(M') ;
    prev := project(S_i, V') ;
    D := differ(image(prev, M''), S_{i+1}) ;
    if( D ⊆ V ) {
        new := project(S_{i+1}, V') ;
        D := differ(preimage(new, M''), S_i) ;
    }
    return add_to_model(M' ,D );
}
```

Fig. 7. Refinement

4.3 Refinement

When reconstruction fails, it's necessary to refine the model. In the family of abstractions we use, this means adding back state variables from the original model that were eliminated in the previous abstraction. The decision which subset of variables to add back can be formulated as an NP-complete problem [7]. We need to find a small set of state variables that don't belong to the set V, for which values cannot be found such that a path π can be reconstructed from Π'. We use the first element of Π' that cannot be reconstructed (S_{i+1}) and its preceding element (S_i) and try to find for which variables in the set V''/V we could not find valid values consistent with M''. We use a heuristic function $differ(A, B)$ where $(A \cap B = \varnothing)$ The function tries to find the minimal set of variables P s.t. $proj(A, P) \cap proj(B, P) = \varnothing$. The actual implementation of differ is heuristic. At first, $P = V''$. We randomly choose variables from V''/V to eliminate until we no longer have $proj(A, P) \cap proj(B, P) = \varnothing$. Since the result of this algorithm depends on the order that we choose variables, we attempt this algorithm with different variable sequences according to a predefined number of attempts.

5 Results

The experimentation with the new algorithms was conducted using hard cases that we accumulated from industrial design groups that use our model checker for the purpose of their verification work. The cases were diverse: they were from different designs from different design groups, and had a significantly different number of state variables. Comparing to easy cases did not seem meaningful as obviously localization will not perform better on them because of the extra overhead. For example, we ran the texas 97 benchmarks [1] but most of them completed in less than a second without localization reduction. The tests were all done on a 375Mhz IBM pSereis 640 with a PowerPC3-2 processor and a 4MB L2 cache and 1G of memory.

The results are divided into two tables of safety and liveness. The first column describes the type of design the example was taken from. The second column gives the number of state variables in the examples. The third column details wether the property passed or failed. The rest of the columns detail the results of the different algorithms run on the example - giving run time (sec) and memory requirement. A "Memory" entry means that the run reached the limit of 1G. Some of these examples were ones that we could not verify even with 2G of memory which is the current limit of a 32 bit application on the IBM pSereis 640. We run all algorithms using dynamic BDD reordering.

In Table 1 we compared 4 algorithms. All of the algorithms performed On-The-Fly model checking [3]: without localization, with Clarke et al.'s algorithm, with Layering and the algorithm in Section 4.2.3.1, and with layering and the algorithm in Section 4.2.3.2.

Table 1: Results for safety formulas

Name	No. Vars	Verif. Result	Without Local.	Clarke et al.	Layer+ Alg1	Layer+ Alg2
Infiniband 1	396	passed	Memory	Memory	54s/43M	134s/47M
Infiniband 2	377	passed	Memory	0.95s/33M	4.32s/33M	4.19s/33M
Ethernet 1	86	passed	1601s/87M	657s/189M	243s/88M	287s/88M
CPU 1	123	passed	599s/92M	Memory	85s/99M	335s/93M
Queue CRM	79	passed	148s/45M	75s/42M	34s/41M	28s/41M
Ethernet 2	156	passed	Memory	14211s/185M	Memory	9.4s/31M
CPU 2	105	failed	595s/62M	N/A	405s/50M	229s/50M
CPU 3	167	failed	1943s/96M	Memory	28963s/ 192M	1096s/ 103M

In Table 2 we compared 3 algorithms: without localization. With localization and no fixed point, and with localization and the algorithm in Section 4.2.3.3.

The results in Table 1 indicate that when a safety property passes the improvement in time and memory requirements can be 2 orders of magnitude. This is due to the fact that the examples are verified using a much smaller model. When the property fails, it usually requires much more iterations of refinement and the results are either comparable to the result without localization or worse than it. There was only one case (Infiniband 2) where the algorithm of Clarke et al. did better - in this case there were no refinement iterations required, thus our improvements were unnecessary but even with the overhead they added the example ran much faster than without localization.

Table 2: Results for liveness formulas

Name	No. Vars	Verif. Result	Without Local.	Layer+ Naive	Layer+ Fixed Point
Infiniband 3	366	passed	Memory	7.87/33M	7.7s/33M
Ethernet 3	41	failed	1.57s/27M	10.9s/27M	8.9s/27M
CPU 4	66	passed	28s/132M	22s/99M	23s/98M
CPU 5	66	failed	35s/132M	534s/131M	349s/128M

For liveness (Table 2), we also observed an order of magnitude improvement in some cases (Infiniband 3 is an example) but the results were not as consistent as for safety. There were cases where the result was significantly better than without localization. Note also that the fixed point algorithm was not better than the naive approach (except for example CPU 5). This indicates that perhaps doing more refinement can be easier than trying to locate a concrete loop which traverses the abstract loop more than once.

6 Conclusions

We presented improvements to symbolic localization reduction that gave us dramatic improvements in the verification of some hard industrial examples. The improvements were mainly in the reconstruction process. The algorithms we presented were found to be most effective in the cases where the property is a safety property and passes. However, we have also shown that it can give orders of magnitude improvement on liveness formulas that pass. Thus this method is complimentary to the bounded model checking methods which generally work better when the property fails.

For future work we intend to investigate ways to improve counterexample reconstruction of liveness properties since our results in these cases are not as consistent as with safety. We also intend to combine some of our algorithms such as layering with the satisfiability based reconstruction techniques reported in [9,19] which we believe can further speed-up the results described here.

References

[1] The texas97 verification benchmarks. http://vlsi.colorado.edu/ vis/texas-97/.

[2] F. Balarin and A. Sangiovanni-Vincentelli. An iterative approach to language containment. In Computer Aided Verification, pages 29–40, 1993.

[3] I. Beer, S. Ben-David, and A. Landver. On-the-fly model checking of rctl formulas. In Computer Aided Verification, pages 184–194, 1998.

[4] A. Biere, A. Cimatti, E. M. Clarke, and Y. Zhu. Symbolic model checking without BDDs. In Proc. of TACAS, 1999.

[5] A. Biere, E. M. Clarke, and Y. Zhu. Multiple state and single state tableaux for combining local and global model checking. In Correct System Design, pages 163–179, 1999.

[6] K. S. Brace, R. L. Rudell, and R. E. Bryant. Efficient Implentation of a BDD Package. In 27th ACM/IEEE Design Automation Conference, pages 40–45. ACM/IEEE, 1990.

[7] E. M. Clarke, O. Grumberg, S. Jha, Y. Lu., H. Veith. Counterexample-guided abstraction refinement. In Computer Aided VerificationI, pages 154–169, 2000.

[8] E. M. Clarke, O. Grumberg, and D. Peled. MIT Press, 2000.

[9] E. M. Clarke, Y. Lu, P. Chauhan, and A. Gupta. Automatic abstraction by counterexample-guided refinement. Private Communication.

[10] S. G. Govindaraju and D. L. Dill. Verification by approximate forward and backward reachability. In Inter. Conf.on Computer Aided Design, 1998.

[11] A. Gupta and E. M. Clarke. Using fourier analysis for abstraction-refinement in model checking. Private Communication.

[12] R. P. Kurshan. Computer-Aided-Verification of Coordinating Processes. Princeton University Press, 1994.

[13] W. Lee, A. Pardo, J. Jang, G. Hachtel, and F. Somenzi. Tearing based automatic abstraction for ctl model checking. In Inter. Conf.on Computer Aided Design, pages 76–81, 1999.

[14] J. Lind-Nielsen and H. Andersen. Stepwise ctl model checking of state/event systems. In Computer Aided Verification, pages 316–327, 1999.

[15] K. L. McMillan. The SMV System DRAFT. Carnegie Mellon University, Pittsburgh, PA, 1992.

[16] A. Pardo and G. Hachtel. Incremental ctl model checking using bdd subsetting. In IEEE DAC,, 1998.

[17] K. Ravi and F. Somenzi. High-density reachability analysis. In ICCAD, 1995.

[18] G. P. M. Silva and K. A. Sakallah. GRASP – a search algorithm for propositional satisfiability. IEEE Trans. on Computers, 44:506–516, 1999.

[19] D. Wang, P. Ho, J. Long, J. Kukula, Y. Zhu, T. Ma, and R. Damiano. Formal property verification by abstraction refinement with formal, simulation and hybrid engines. In 38th IEEE DAC, pages 35–40, 2001.

Modeling and Verifying Systems
Using a Logic of Counter Arithmetic
with Lambda Expressions
and Uninterpreted Functions

Randal E. Bryant[1,2], Shuvendu K. Lahiri[2], and Sanjit A. Seshia[1]

[1] School of Computer Science, Carnegie Mellon University
Pittsburgh, PA
{Randy.Bryant,Sanjit.Seshia}@cs.cmu.edu
[2] Electrical and Computer Engineering Department, Carnegie Mellon University
Pittsburgh, PA
shuvendu@ece.cmu.edu

Abstract. In this paper, we present the logic of Counter Arithmetic
with Lambda Expressions and Uninterpreted Functions (CLU). CLU
generalizes the logic of equality with uninterpreted functions (EUF) with
constrained lambda expressions, ordering, and successor and predecessor
functions. In addition to modeling pipelined processors that EUF has
proved useful for, CLU can be used to model many infinite-state systems including those with infinite memories, finite and infinite queues
including lossy channels, and networks of identical processes. Even with
this richer expressive power, the validity of a CLU formula can be efficiently decided by translating it to a propositional formula, and then
using Boolean methods to check validity. We give theoretical and empirical evidence for the efficiency of our decision procedure. We also describe
verification techniques that we have used on a variety of systems, including an out-of-order execution unit and the load-store unit of an industrial
microprocessor.

1   Introduction

Systems with parameters of finite but arbitrary or large size are often modeled
as infinite-state systems. Such systems include superscalar processors, communication protocols with unbounded channels, and networks of an arbitrary number
of identical processes. Modeling and verification methods for these systems must
trade off between the expressiveness of the modeling formalism and the efficiency
and automation of the tool. Tools based on very general logics can express a variety of systems but require greater human assistance.

To verify pipelined processors, Burch and Dill presented a logic of equality
with uninterpreted functions (EUF) [10], and then added interpreted operations
read and *write* to model unbounded, random-access memories. EUF thus allows
for abstract modeling of both data and data operations, as well as unbounded

D. Brinksma and K. G. Larsen (Eds.): CAV 2002, LNCS 2404, pp. 78–92, 2002.
© Springer-Verlag Berlin Heidelberg 2002

memories. In previous work, we presented PEUF, a logic of positive equality with uninterpreted functions [7]. PEUF has the same expressive power as EUF, but allows for a more efficient decision procedure based on Boolean methods. The main source of efficiency is a technique for transforming a PEUF formula into a propositional formula whose validity can be checked using either BDDs or a satisfiability solver. The advantages of using PEUF have been demonstrated in reasoning about pipelined processors [22].

In this paper, we continue our research into logics that have an efficient transformation into propositional logic. We generalize EUF to yield a logic of Counter Arithmetic with Lambda Expressions and Uninterpreted Functions (CLU). The generalizations are of two kinds. The first is to include a restricted class of lambda expressions as a means of defining state variables that are functions or predicates. As we will discuss, this generalization subsumes the need for special *read* and *write* operations. The second is to introduce ordering and a highly restricted fragment of Peano arithmetic we call *counter arithmetic*. We do this by use of the interpreted predicate symbol "$<$" and interpreted function symbols **succ** (the successor function) and **pred** (the predecessor function). As with EUF, we consider only a quantifier-free subset of first-order logic. However, our generalizations give us richer expressiveness in modeling both data and control.

We make two main contributions in this paper. First, we demonstrate the expressiveness of CLU by modeling constructs found in several infinite-state systems, including processors, communication protocols, and unbounded process arrays. Second, we describe our decision procedure for CLU that retains the efficiencies of the decision procedure for PEUF. We give theoretical and empirical evidence for our procedure's efficiency, comparing it with the Stanford Validity Checker (SVC) [3]. We have built UCLID[1], a tool in which systems modeled using CLU can be specified and checked for safety properties and have applied it to a variety of systems including an out-of-order processor core, pipelined processors, a complex load-store unit from an industrial microprocessor, a cache coherence protocol, and the Alternating Bit Protocol. Our analysis of examples is more general than that possible by many traditional model-checking approaches in that we can handle arbitrary-size data structures and infinite data types without abstracting them away.

Related Work A range of specification and verification methods currently exist for infinite-state systems. However, most of these methods are specialized for classes of problems. For example, for communication protocols, existing queue representations include QDDs [5] and regular expressions [1]. Regular expressions have also been used to model networks of identical processes and systems operating on unbounded data structures such as stacks [15,6]. While regular expressions are good for modeling control based on the form of process arrays or data structures, they cannot be used to model data and operations on data. In contrast, CLU can be used to model both data and control. The applicability of

---

[1]   UCLID stands for "Uninterpreted functions, Counter arithmetic and Lambda expressions for Infinite Domains"

QDDs is restricted to modeling queues. Bultan et al. [9] have used Presburger arithmetic to model process networks. Presburger arithmetic is a very powerful as it allows quantification and integer addition. However it suffers two drawbacks: First, the worst-case complexity of checking validity of formulas in this logic is prohibitively high [11], and second, adding uninterpreted functions to the logic makes it undecidable. The theory of *separation predicates* [19] differs from CLU in that it has neither uninterpreted functions nor lambda expressions, but can have real valued variables. Our work complements techniques for deciding this logic (e.g., [4,20]) by adding the benefits of positive equality. Theorem proving systems (e.g., PVS [17] or HOL [13]) that use higher order logic can clearly express all the systems that CLU can, but at the cost of reduced automation and efficiency. Compositional model checking [14] can verify both safety and liveness properties and is effective when the system can be easily decomposed into components based on modularity, temporal separation, or if a "unit of work" uses a small finite amount of resources, but it still suffers from state explosion. The role played by lambda expressions in our logic is very similar to that played by state variables of infinite-length array-type in Cadence SMV.

The rest of the paper is organized as follows. In the next two sections, we present the syntax and semantics of CLU, and show how it can be used to model various systems. We next discuss our decision procedure for CLU, and describe UCLID, the verification tool we have built. Finally, we present results demonstrating the efficiency of our decision procedure, and conclusions.

2   Counter Arithmetic with Lambda Expressions and Uninterpreted Functions

Expressions in CLU describe a means of computing four different types of values. *Boolean* expressions yield **true** or **false**. We also refer to Boolean expressions as *formulas*. *Integer* expressions, also referred to as *terms*, yield integer values. *Predicate* expressions denote functions from integers to Boolean values. *Function* expressions, on the other hand, denote functions from integers to integers. Figure 1 summarizes the expression syntax.

The simplest truth expressions are the values **true** and **false**. Boolean expressions can also be formed by comparing two term expressions for equality (referred to as an *equation*) or for ordering (referred to as an *inequality*), by applying a predicate expression to a list of term expressions, and by combining Boolean expressions using Boolean connectives. Integer expressions can be integer variables, used only as the formal arguments of lambda expressions. They can also be formed by applying a function expression (including interpreted functions **succ** and **pred**) to a set of integer expressions, or by applying the *ITE* (for "if-then-else") operator. The *ITE* operator chooses between two values based on a Boolean control value, i.e., $ITE(\textbf{true}, x_1, x_2)$ yields x_1 while $ITE(\textbf{false}, x_1, x_2)$ yields x_2. Function expressions can be either function symbols, representing uninterpreted functions, or lambda expressions, defining the value of the function as an integer expression containing references to a set of argument variables. Func-

$$bool\text{-}expr ::= \textbf{true} \mid \textbf{false} \mid \neg bool\text{-}expr \mid (bool\text{-}expr \wedge bool\text{-}expr)$$
$$\mid (bool\text{-}expr \vee bool\text{-}expr) \mid (int\text{-}expr {=} int\text{-}expr) \mid (int\text{-}expr {<} int\text{-}expr)$$
$$\mid predicate\text{-}expr(int\text{-}expr, \ldots, int\text{-}expr)$$
$$int\text{-}expr ::= int\text{-}var \mid ITE(bool\text{-}expr, int\text{-}expr, int\text{-}expr)$$
$$\mid \textbf{succ}(int\text{-}expr) \mid \textbf{pred}(int\text{-}expr)$$
$$\mid function\text{-}expr(int\text{-}expr, \ldots, int\text{-}expr)$$
$$predicate\text{-}expr ::= predicate\text{-}symbol \mid \lambda\, int\text{-}var, \ldots, int\text{-}var\,.\, bool\text{-}expr$$
$$function\text{-}expr ::= function\text{-}symbol \mid \lambda\, int\text{-}var, \ldots, int\text{-}var\,.\, int\text{-}expr$$

Fig. 1. Expression Syntax. Expressions can denote computations of Boolean values, integers, or functions yielding Boolean values or integers

tion symbols of arity 0 are also called *symbolic constants*. They denote arbitrary integer values. Since these symbols are instantiated without any arguments, we will omit the parentheses, writing a instead of $a()$. Similarly, predicate expressions can be either predicate symbols, representing uninterpreted predicates, or lambda expressions, defining the value of the predicate as a Boolean expression containing references to a set of argument variables. Predicate symbols of arity 0 are also called *symbolic Boolean constants*. They denote arbitrary Boolean values. We will also omit the parentheses following the instantiation of such a predicate.

Notice that we restrict the parameters to a lambda expression to be integers, and not function or predicate expressions. There is no way in our logic to express any form of iteration or recursion. The lambda expressions in CLU are very useful for modeling, as we show in Section 3, but, in the theoretical sense, they do not add expressive power to the logic.

An integer variable x is said to be *bound* in expression E when it occurs inside a lambda expression for which x is one of the argument variables. We say that an expression is *well-formed* when it contains no unbound variables. The value denoted by a well-formed expression in CLU is defined relative to an interpretation I of the function and predicate symbols. Let $\mathcal{Z}$ denote the set of integers. Interpretation I assigns to each function symbol of arity k a function from $\mathcal{Z}^k$ to $\mathcal{Z}$, and to each predicate symbol of arity k a function from $\mathcal{Z}^k$ to $\{\textbf{true}, \textbf{false}\}$. Given an interpretation I of the function and predicate symbols and a well-formed expression E, we can define the *valuation* of E under I, denoted $[E]_I$, according to its syntactic structure. The valuation of E is either a Boolean value, an integer, a function from integers to Boolean values, or a function from integers to integers, according to whether E is a Boolean expression, an integer expression, a predicate expression, or a function expression, respectively. We omit the details. A well-formed formula F is *true under interpretation I* if $[F]_I$ is **true**. It is *valid* when it is true under all possible interpretations.

In earlier work [7], it was shown that formulas in PEUF can be efficiently decided by only considering *maximally diverse interpretations*. We will show in Section 4 how the benefits of PEUF are retained to yield an efficient decision procedure for CLU.

3   System Modeling

In this section, we give representative examples of structures modeled using CLU. We use a record notation to represent data structures that are characterized by multiple CLU expressions.

3.1   Memories

Lambda notation allows us to model the effect of a sequence of read and write operations on a memory. At any point of system operation, a memory is represented by a function expression M denoting a mapping from addresses to values. The initial state of the memory is given by an uninterpreted function symbol m_0 indicating an arbitrary memory state. The effect of a write operation with integer expressions A and D denoting the address and data values yields a function expression M':

$$M' = \lambda\,addr\,.\,ITE(addr = A,\,D,\,M(addr))$$

Other forms of memory can be modeled as well. For example, we can model a Content Addressable Memory (CAM) that stores associations between keys and data. We represent a CAM C at any point in the system operation by two expressions: a predicate expression $C.present$ such that $C.present(k)$ is true for any key k that is stored in the CAM, and a function expression $C.data$, such that $C.data(k)$ yields the data associated with key k, assuming the key is present. As an initial state in invariant checking we can represent a CAM C having an arbitrary state by letting $C.present = p_0$ and $C.contents = c_0$, where p_0 (respectively, c_0) is an uninterpreted predicate (resp., function).

Insertion into a CAM is expressed by the operation $Insert(C, K, D)$. This operation yields a new CAM C' where:

$$C'.present = \lambda\,key\,.\,key = K \vee C.present(key)$$
$$C'.data = \lambda\,key\,.\,ITE(key = K,\,D,\,C.data(key))$$

On the other hand, the effect of deleting the entry associated with key K is expressed by the operation $Delete(C, K)$. This operation yields a new CAM C' where

$$C'.present = \lambda\,key\,.\,\neg(key = K) \wedge C.present(key)$$
$$C'.data = C.data$$

3.2 Queues

A queue of arbitrary length can be modeled as a record Q having components $Q.contents$, $Q.head$, and $Q.tail$. Conceptually, the contents of the queue are represented as some subsequence of an infinite sequence, where $Q.contents$ is a function expression mapping an integer index i to the value of sequence element i. $Q.head$ is an integer expression indicating the index of the head of the queue, i.e., the position of the oldest element in the queue. $Q.tail$ is an integer expression indicating the index at which to insert the next element. In general, we require $Q.head \leq Q.tail$ as an invariant property. Q is modeled as having an arbitrary state by letting $Q.contents = c_0$, $Q.head = h_0$, and $Q.tail = t_0$, where c_0 is an uninterpreted function and h_0 and t_0 are symbolic constants satisfying the constraint $h_0 \leq t_0$. This constraint is enforced by including it in the antecedent of the formula whose validity we wish to check.

The operation testing if the queue is empty can be expressed quite simply as:

$$isEmpty(Q) = (Q.head = Q.tail)$$

Using this operation we can define the following three operations on the queue:

1. $Pop(Q)$: The pop operation on an non-empty queue returns a new queue Q' with the first element removed; this is modeled by incrementing the head.

$$Q'.head = ITE(isEmpty(Q),\ Q.head,\ \mathbf{succ}(Q.head))$$

2. $First(Q)$: This operation returns the element at the head of the queue, provided the queue is non-empty. It is defined as $Q.contents(Q.head)$.

3. $Push(Q, X)$: Pushing data item X into Q returns a new queue Q' where

$$Q'.tail = \mathbf{succ}(Q.tail)$$
$$Q'.contents = \lambda i\ .\ ITE(i = Q.tail,\ X,\ Q.contents(i))$$

Assuming we start in a state where $h_0 \leq t_0$, $Q.head$ will never be greater than $Q.tail$ because of the conditions under which we increment the head.

Bounded length queues can be similarly expressed, with an additional constraint in the case of the push operation disallowing a push when the queue is full. In particular, to bound a queue to a maximum length of k (where k is an integer, not a symbolic constant), we add the condition for pushing that $Q.tail$ is incremented only when $Q.tail < \mathbf{succ}^k(Q.head)$, where $\mathbf{succ}^k$ indicates k compositions of the successor operation. We can use similar guard conditions to to model lossy behavior and duplication as well.

3.3 Process Arrays

Lambda expressions can be used to represent systems containing an arbitrary number of identical processes, such as an array of processors in a cache coherence protocol. For each integer state variable of the process state, we define a function expression S, where $S(i)$ denotes the value of this state variable for process i. Similarly, we represent a Boolean state variable as a predicate expression.

We implement an interleaving model of concurrency in CLU by defining a process identifier state variable pid that is updated on each step of operation to designate a single active process. Given uninterpreted function symbols A and N of arity 1, pid is defined as having a value equal to $A(ctr)$, where ctr is an integer state variable with initial value c_0 and next state value ctr' defined as $ctr' = N(ctr)$. Since our verifier checks the validity of the formula for all possible interpretations of A and N, it will include the case where each successive value of ctr is unique. The different possible interpretations of A will then cover all possible sequences of process identifiers. Other concurrency models (e.g., parallel updates to elements of the process array that satisfy a predicate) can also be implemented quite readily.

As an example, consider an array $Add1$ of processes each having a single state variable indicating the value of a counter. On each step of operation, one process is selected to increment its counter. The process state table for this array is thus a table of counts represented by a lambda expression $cntTbl$. The initial value of $cntTbl$ is given by an uninterpreted function symbol c_0 of arity 1 and the next state expression is given by

$$cntTbl' = \lambda i \,.\, ITE(i = pid, \mathbf{succ}(cntTbl(i)), cntTbl(i))$$

3.4 Observations

Uninterpreted functions provide a natural means for abstracting data and data operations. Lambda expressions provide a powerful notation for describing state transformations. Counter arithmetic provides us the ability to express counters and some forms of pointers. The combination of these three modeling constructs enables CLU to express a wide variety of data structures and system types.

4 Decision Procedure

Assume we start with a well-formed formula F_{ver} in CLU expressing some desired system property. The decision procedure must determine whether it is *valid*, i.e., true under all possible interpretations of the function and predicate symbols. Through a sequence of transformations, described below, we convert a formula over the logic to a propositional formula and then use a Boolean satisfiability checker to determine validity.

Expand Lambda Applications Since CLU syntax does not permit recursion or iteration, each lambda application can be expanded by *beta-substitution*, i.e., by replacing each argument variable with the corresponding argument term. Let us call the resulting formula F_{exp}.

Identify P-Function Symbols As with PEUF, we can exploit the restricted uses of equations and inequalities to greatly reduce the number of interpretations that must be encoded when we reduce the formula to propositional logic. As described in [ ], we can automatically analyze an arbitrary formula to determine those function symbols that satisfy the restrictions of p-functions. The general idea is to determine the polarity of each equation, i.e., whether it appears under an even (positive) or odd (negative) number of negations. Terms can then be classified as either p-terms, i.e., used only under positive equalities, or g-terms, i.e., general terms. Function symbols for which all applications are p-terms can then be classified as p-function symbols. Applications of p-function symbols can be encoded in propositional logic with fewer symbolic variables than can those of general "g-function" symbols. The extensions required for CLU are to deal with inequalities and the successor and predecessor operations.

The first stage in the analysis labels the subformulas occurring in F_{exp} as being *negative* and/or *positive*. First, we start by labeling F_{exp} as being positive. In addition, for each term of the form $ITE(F, T_1, T_2)$, we label F as being both negative and positive. Then we recursively label the subformulas as follows: If formula $F \doteq F_1 \wedge F_2$ is labeled as being positive (respectively, negative), then so are F_1 and F_2. Similarly for $F \doteq F_1 \vee F_2$. If formula $F \doteq \neg F_1$ is labeled as being positive (respectively, negative), then F_1 is labeled as being negative (respectively, positive).

Once the subformulas have been labeled, we identify which subterms in F_{exp} must be considered g-terms. We start by considering every formula $F \doteq T_1 = T_2$ that was labeled as being negative, as well as every inequality $T_1 < T_2$. For these, we must mark T_1 and T_2 as g-terms. Then we recursively label the subterms as follows: If $T \doteq ITE(F, T_1, T_2)$ was labeled as a g-term, then so must be T_1 and T_2. If $T \doteq \mathbf{succ}(T_1)$ was labeled as a g-term, then so must be T_1. Similarly for $T \doteq \mathbf{pred}(T_1)$.

Finally, we classify each function symbol as either a p-function or a g-function symbol. For function symbol f, if any term of the form $f(T_1, \ldots, T_k)$ was labeled as a g-term, then f must be classified as a g-function symbol. Otherwise, it is a p-function symbol.

Remove Function and Predicate Applications As described in [ ], we can replace all applications of uninterpreted functions or predicates of nonzero arity by terms containing only symbolic constants. Our method differs from the more common method introduced by Ackermann [2] in that it replaces each term by a nested series of ITE operations rather than a single symbolic constant. Our method makes it possible to exploit positive equality in encoding possible instantiations of the constants.

As an example, if function symbol f has three occurrences: $f(a_1)$, $f(a_2)$, and $f(a_3)$, then we would generate 3 new symbolic constants vf_1, vf_2, and vf_3. We would then replace all instances of $f(a_1)$ by vf_1, all instances of $f(a_2)$ by $ITE(a_2 = a_1, vf_1, vf_2)$, and all instances of $f(a_3)$ by $ITE(a_3 = a_1, vf_1, ITE(a_3 = a_2, vf_2, vf_3))$.

Predicate applications can be removed by a similar process. In eliminating applications of some predicate p, we introduce symbolic Boolean constants $vp_1, vp_2, \ldots$.

This leaves us with a formula F_{const} containing only symbolic constants, ITEs, successors, predecessors, equations, inequalities, and logical connectives.

Partition into Subdomains We first split the set of symbolic constants V into two sets V_p and V_g. V_p consists of those symbolic constants occurring in F_{exp} that were classified as p-function applications, as well as those constants vf_i that were introduced when eliminating an application of some p-function symbol f. The remaining symbolic constants are in V_g.

We then partition the set of symbolic constants into classes $V_1, \ldots, V_n$. Each constant in V_p is assigned to its own class. Constants in V_g are grouped according to whether their values may be compared by equations or inequalities. We start by assigning each constant in V_g to its own class. We then compute the *dependency* set for each term in F_{const}, denoting some subset of variables in V_g to which this term could evaluate. While doing this, we merge some of the classes so that each dependency set is a subset of some class. For term $T \doteq v$, its dependency set is $\emptyset$ if $v \in V_p$ and is $\{v\}$ if $v \in V_g$. For term $T \doteq \mathbf{succ}(T_1)$, its dependency set is the same as that of T_1. Similarly for $T \doteq \mathbf{pred}(T_1)$. For $T \doteq ITE(F, T_1, T_2)$, its dependency set is the union of those of T_1 and T_2. If the dependency sets of T_1 and T_2 are subsets of two distinct classes, then we merge those classes. For each equation $T_1 = T_2$ and each inequality $T_1 < T_2$, we perform a similar merging if the dependency sets of T_1 and T_2 are subsets of distinct classes.

Compute Ranges For each symbolic constant v in F_{const} we must determine the maximum amount it can be incremented or decremented by successor and predecessor operations. We do this by labeling each distinct term T in F_{const} by an its lower bound $l(T)$ and its upper bound $u(T)$. These bounds indicate the range over which the term may be decremented or incremented.

The labeling can be implemented as a fixed-point computation, starting with $l(T) = u(T) = 0$ for each term T. Labels are then updated according to the following rules: Eventually, this process will reach a point where the bounds do not change. We then use the values of $l(v)$ and $u(v)$ to determine the range of offsets for symbolic constant v.

Term T	Lower Bound	Upper Bound
$ITE(F, T_1, T_2)$	$l(T_1) \leftarrow \min(l(T_1), l(T))$ $l(T_2) \leftarrow \min(l(T_2), l(T))$	$u(T_1) \leftarrow \max(u(T_1), u(T))$ $u(T_2) \leftarrow \max(u(T_2), u(T))$
$\mathbf{succ}(T_1)$	$l(T_1) \leftarrow \min(l(T_1), l(T) + 1)$	$u(T_1) \leftarrow \max(u(T_1), u(T) + 1)$
$\mathbf{pred}(T_1)$	$l(T_1) \leftarrow \min(l(T_1), l(T) - 1)$	$u(T_1) \leftarrow \max(u(T_1), u(T) - 1)$

Instantiate Subdomains For each class V_i we compute its range as:

$$range(V_i) = \sum_{v \in V_i} (u(v) - l(v) + 1).$$

This determines the size of the finite instantiation we must consider for each symbolic constant in V_i.

Suppose there are K different classes and let M be the maximum value of $range(V_i)$ for any class V_i. Let $k = \lceil \log_2 K \rceil$ and $m = \lceil \log_2 M \rceil$. Then we encode each symbolic constant as a vector of $k + m$ Boolean formulas v. For variable v in class V_i, the high order k elements of v correspond to the binary encoding of i. If class V_i contains just a single constant v, then the low order m elements of v are simply the binary representation of $-l(v)$. Since $l(v)$ must be less than or equal to zero, the effect of this is to bias the value used to encode variable v such that this value will never be decremented below zero by any of the **pred** operations. Otherwise, for each variable v we must introduce m' Boolean variables $\boldsymbol{x}_v \doteq x_v^{m'-1}, \ldots, x_v^0$, where $m' = \lceil \log_2 |V_i| \rceil$. The low order m elements of v are then the Boolean formulas expressing the bit-level representation of $\boldsymbol{x}_v - l(v)$.

We then recursively translate F_{const} into a symbolic Boolean formula, where each term is represented as a vector of $k + m$ formulas and each subformula as a single Boolean formula. Each symbolic constant v is represented by the vector $\boldsymbol{v}$, while each symbolic Boolean constant is represented by a Boolean variable. ITE operators are translated to perform a bit-wise multiplexing of the arguments. Successor and predecessor operations are translated as bit-level incrementers and decrementers. Equations and inequalities are translated as comparators. Boolean connectives are translated as Boolean operators.

This translation process takes advantage of the positive equality structure of the formula in a manner similar to that described in [ ]. Each symbolic constant in V_p is assigned a fixed bit pattern, greatly reducing the number of Boolean variables required. Beyond the optimizations described here, we could exploit the equation structure between g-terms using some of the techniques described in [18]. However, many of these optimizations cannot be used when terms are compared by inequalities.

Let F_{bool} denote the resulting Boolean formula. We can then use Boolean satisfiability to see if $\neg F_{bool}$ is satisfiable. If it is, then our decision procedure generates a counterexample to the macro-expanded formula F_{exp} by constructing a partial interpretation of the function and predicate symbols over bit vectors of length $k + m$. If $\neg F_{bool}$ is not satisfiable, then we have determined that the original formula F_{ver} is valid.

Analysis The decision procedure is efficient because the translation to propositional logic only gives rise to a low-degree polynomial blowup in the formula size. Suppose we represent a formula in CLU as a directed acyclic graph (DAG). The size of the formula is the number of nodes in its DAG representation. Consider the CLU formula F_{exp} of size N in which all lambda applications have been expanded. Assuming that the arities of function and predicate symbols are bounded, we can prove that the size of the final propositional formula F_{bool} is $O((N + M^2 + P^2)lg(N))$, where M and P are the number of function and predicate application terms in F_{exp} respectively (including applications of **succ** and **pred**). The M^2 and P^2 terms come from introducing nested *ITE* expressions while eliminating function and predicate applications, and the $lg(N)$ comes from the binary encoding of integer symbolic constants.

In practice, the number of function and predicate applications is far smaller than the total number of DAG nodes, and so the size of F_{bool} grows as $O(Nlg(N))$. In the worst case, expanding lambda applications can result in an exponential blowup in formula size. In our experience, however, the expressions tend to have a linear structure, with each lambda instantiated only once. With this structure, there is no blowup from lambda expansion.

Modifications The decision procedure described above uses small-domain instantiation to encode integer symbolic constants. We have also experimented with using Boolean variables to encode equations, as in previous work on PEUF [8]. The latter method performs better in some cases because it directly encodes equations that control system operation. For brevity, we omit a detailed comparison from this paper.

5   UCLID

We have built UCLID, a tool to specify and verify systems modeled in CLU. The UCLID specification language can be used to specify a state machine, where the state variables either have primitive types — Boolean, enumerated, or (unbounded) integer — or are functions of integer arguments that evaluate to these primitive types. Details about the specification language may be found in the user's guide [21]. We mention one notable feature about the internal encoding of enumerated types in UCLID. A enumerated type E of k values is encoded as an integer sequence $\{z_E, \mathbf{succ}(z_E), \ldots, \mathbf{succ}^{k-1}(z_E)\}$, where a different symbolic constant z_E is used for each type E. Since variables of an enumerated type can only be compared for equality against other variables of the same enumerated type[2], the decision procedure assigns the function symbol z_E to its own singleton subdomain, and encodes values of the enumerated type with exactly $\lceil lg(k) \rceil$ bits.

The UCLID verification engine comprises of a symbolic simulator that can be "configured" for different kinds of verification tasks, and a decision procedure for CLU. The following verification methods are supported:

1. *Bounded property checking*: The system is symbolically simulated for a fixed number of steps starting from a reset state. At each step, the decision procedure is invoked to check the validity of a safety property. If the property fails, we generate a counterexample trace from the reset state.

---

[2] Enforced by the type-checker in the UCLID front-end

2. *Inductive invariant checking*: The system is initialized in a most general state satisfying the invariant to be proved, symbolically simulated for one step, and the invariant is checked on the resulting state.
3. *Proving simulation diagrams*, showing that a specification machine simulates an implementation machine. This includes the method of *correspondence checking* for superscalar processors, such as in the style of Burch and Dill [10]. UCLID allows the user to set the values of control variables at different steps of the symbolic simulation. For example, in verifying pipelined processors, this allows the user to specify the steps at which the pipeline must be flushed.

UCLID's decision procedure checks the satisfiability of $\neg F_{bool}$ using either a BDD package or a SAT solver. A very useful feature of UCLID is its ability to generate counterexample traces, like a model checker. A counterexample to a CLU formula F_{ver} is a partial interpretation I to the function and predicate symbols in the formula, which is generated from a satisfying assignment to $\neg F_{bool}$. If the system has been symbolically simulated for k steps, then the interpretation I generated above can be applied to the expressions at each step, thereby resulting in a complete counterexample trace for k steps.

We have used UCLID to model and check safety properties of a variety of systems, including an out-of-order execution unit, a complex load-store unit of an industrial microprocessor, a cache coherence protocol [12], a 5-stage DLX pipeline, and the Alternating Bit Protocol. In particular, using bounded property checking we can handle models with large state spaces such as the load-store unit (which has about 150 state variables with over half of integer type, after abstraction from RTL). The specifications of most of these models are available on the UCLID website [21].

6 Decision Procedure Benchmarking

We have run experiments to compare UCLID's decision procedure with decision procedures for logics of comparable expressiveness, such as the Stanford Validity Checker (SVC) [3]. SVC can decide a superset of CLU, including, in addition, linear arithmetic and bit-vector arithmetic. Most of the example formulas were generated by performing bounded property checking for some number of steps. By varying the number of steps we can generate benchmark formulas of different lengths. All experiments were run on an Intel Pentium III 550 MHz processor with 256 MB of main memory running Linux. For satisfiability checking, we used the mChaff version of the Chaff SAT solver [16].

Figure 2 shows empirical results comparing UCLID against SVC 1.1 over a set of valid formulas. We can draw four conclusions. First, the conversion from F_{exp} to F_{bool} agrees with the theoretical $O(Nlg(N))$ bound. Second, exploiting positive equality has substantial benefits as deciding satisfiability of $\neg F_{bool}$ is much faster. Third, for the CLU logic, UCLID's decision procedure scales better than SVC, outperforming it for large formulas. The times for UCLID, even on the largest formulas, are less than 2 minutes. Finally, the time taken in converting

F_{exp} to F_{bool} dominates the time taken by Chaff for small formulas, but the conversion overhead reduces for larger formulas.

7 Conclusions and Future Work

Extending EUF by constrained lambda expressions, ordering and counter arithmetic substantially increases the range of systems that can be modeled without losing the benefits of the efficient decision procedure based on PEUF. Moreover, recent advances in building efficient Boolean satisfiability solvers lend support to our approach of deciding formulas in richer logics via efficient translations to propositional logic.

In terms of future work, we have extended the method of encoding equations with Boolean variables to integer equations and inequalities with constant offsets. We have built some support for quantifiers in CLU using automatic quantifier instantiation heuristics. Finally, we are also working on extending the verification capabilities of UCLID to handle some form of reachability analysis.

Model	steps	#(int vars) in F_{exp}	#(p-vars) in F_{exp}	#(prop vars) in F_{bool}	F_{exp} size	F_{bool} size	UCLID time (sec.)				SVC time (sec.)
							Conversion	SAT	Total	No + (total)	
Load-Store	6	33	14	76	218	942	1.15	0.06	1.21	1.66	10.86
Unit	8	70	23	180	1085	4481	7.81	0.61	8.42	11.61	1851.60
	10	104	39	317	2467	16453	27.46	3.16	30.62	62.87	> 1 day
	12	149	65	466	4553	54288	78.00	33.09	111.09	295.35	> 1 day
Out-of-order	7	39	19	79	735	3658	4.58	0.20	4.78	9.79	2.96
Execution	9	53	24	158	1970	13775	16.29	2.00	18.29	37.71	102.35
Unit	11	67	30	255	3929	37179	44.90	17.00	61.90	149.46	4257.38
Cache	10	26	10	75	1829	6254	5.97	0.32	6.29	26.50	11.49
Coherence	12	30	12	102	2782	12144	11.72	4.41	16.13	165.91	231.12
Protocol	14	34	14	133	3939	21468	20.16	40.92	61.08	> 1 hr.	6640.00
DLX Pipeline	–	105	73	205	639	9476	11.13	2.09	13.22	1897	20.58

Fig. 2. Experimental results for decision procedure. "steps" indicates the number of steps of symbolic simulation, except when the formula was generated in correspondence checking. F_{exp} denotes the original CLU formula and F_{bool} the final propositional formula UCLID generates. "int-vars" is the number of integer symbolic constants in F_{exp} after eliminating function applications, and "p-vars" is number of those symbolic constants that correspond to p-function applications. "UCLID time – Total" is the time taken by our decision procedure. This time has two components: the time for converting F_{exp} into F_{bool}, labeled "Conversion", and the time taken by the SAT solver, labeled "SAT". "UCLID time – No +" indicates the time taken without exploiting positive equality in the conversion. "SVC time" is the time taken by SVC 1.1 to decide F_{exp}

Acknowledgments

This research was supported in part by the Semiconductor Research Corporation, Contract RID 684, and by the Gigascale Research Center, Contract 98DT-660. The third author was supported in part by a National Defense Science and Engineering Graduate Fellowship.

References

1. P. Abdulla, A. Bouajjani, and B. Jonsson. On-the-fly analysis of systems with unbounded, lossy FIFO channels. In *CAV'98*, LNCS 1427, pages 305–318. 79
2. W. Ackermann. *Solvable Cases of the Decision Problem*. 1954. 85
3. C. Barrett, D. Dill, and J. Levitt. Validity checking for combinations of theories with equality. In *FMCAD'96*, LNCS 1166, pages 187–201. 79, 89
4. A. J. C. Bik and H. A. G. Wijshoff. Implementation of Fourier-Motzkin elimination. Technical Report 94-42, Dept. of Computer Science, Leiden University, 1994. 80
5. B. Boigelot, P. Godefroid, B. Willems, and P. Wolper. The power of QDDs. In *SAS '97*, pages 172–186. 79
6. A. Bouajjani, B. Jonsson, M. Nilsson, and T. Touili. Regular model checking. In *CAV 2000*, LNCS 1855, pages 403–418. 79
7. R. E. Bryant, S. German, and M. N. Velev. Exploiting positive equality in a logic of equality with uninterpreted functions. *ACM Transactions on Computational Logic*, 2(1):93–134, January 2001. 79, 82, 85, 87
8. R. E. Bryant and M. N. Velev. Boolean satisfiability with transitivity constraints. In *CAV 2000*, LNCS 1855, pages 85–98. 88
9. T. Bultan, R. Gerber, and W. Pugh. Symbolic model checking of infinite state systems using Presburger arithmetic. In *CAV '97*, LNCS 1254, pages 400–411. 80
10. J. R. Burch and D. L. Dill. Automated verification of pipelined microprocessor control. In *CAV '94*, LNCS 818, pages 68–80. 78, 89
11. M. J. Fischer and M. O. Rabin. Super-exponential complexity of Presburger arithmetic. *Proc. SIAM-AMS*, 7:27–41, 1974. 80
12. Steven German. Personal communication. 89
13. M. J. C. Gordon and T. F. Melham. *Introduction to HOL: A Theorem Proving Environment for Higher-Order Logic*. 1993. 80
14. R. Jhala and K. McMillan. Microarchitecture verification by compositional model checking. In *CAV 2001*, LNCS 2102, pages 396–410. 80
15. Y. Kesten, O. Maler, M. Marcus, A. Pnueli, and E. Shahar. Symbolic model checking with rich assertional languages. In *CAV '97*, LNCS 1254, pages 424–435. 79
16. M. Moskewicz, C. Madigan, Y. Zhao, L. Zhang, and S. Malik. Chaff: Engineering an efficient SAT solver. In *Design Automation Conference (DAC'01)*, pages 530–535, June 2001. 89
17. S. Owre, J. M. Rushby, and N. Shankar. PVS: A prototype verification system. In *CADE '92*, LNAI 607, pages 748–752. 80
18. A. Pnueli, Y. Rodeh, O. Shtrichman, and M. Siegel. Deciding equality formulas by small-domain instantiations. In *CAV '99*, LNCS 1633, pages 455–469. 87
19. V. Pratt. Two easy theories whose combination is hard. Technical report, Massachusetts Institute of Technology, 1977. Cambridge, Mass. 80

20. O. Strichman, S. A. Seshia, and R. E. Bryant. Deciding separation formulas with SAT. In *Proc. Computer-Aided Verification (CAV'02)*, July 2002. This volume. 80
21. UCLID. Available at http://www.cs.cmu.edu/~uclid. 88, 89
22. M. N. Velev and R. E. Bryant. Effective use of Boolean satisfiability procedures in the formal verification of superscalar and VLIW microprocessors. In *Design Automation Conference (DAC '01)*, pages 226–231, June 2001. 79

Combining Symmetry Reduction
and Under-Approximation
for Symbolic Model Checking

Sharon Barner[1,2] and Orna Grumberg[1]

[1] Computer Science Department, Technion
Haifa 32000, Israel
{skeidar,orna}@cs.technion.ac.il
[2] IBM Haifa Research Lab
Haifa, Israel

Abstract. This work presents a collection of methods, integrating *symmetry reduction*, *under-approximation*, and *symbolic model checking* in order to reduce space and time for model checking. The main goal of this work is *falsification*. However, under certain conditions our methods provide *verification* as well.

We first present algorithms that perform on-the-fly model checking for temporal safety properties, using symmetry reduction. We then extend these algorithms for checking liveness properties as well.

Our methods are fully automatic. The user should supply some basic information about the symmetry in the verified system. However, the methods are *robust* and work correctly even if the information supplied by the user is incorrect. Moreover, the methods return correct results even in case the computation of the symmetry reduction has not been completed due to memory or time explosion.

We implemented our methods within IBM's model checker RuleBase, and compared the performance of our methods with that of RuleBase. In most cases, our algorithms outperformed RuleBase with respect to both time and space.

1   Introduction

This work presents a collection of methods, integrating *symmetry reduction*, *under-approximation*, and *symbolic model checking* in order to reduce space and time for model checking. The main goal of this work is *falsification*, that is, proving that a given system does not satisfy its specification. However, under certain conditions our methods provide also *verification*, i.e., they prove that the system satisfies its specification.

Our methods are fully automatic. The user should supply some basic information about the symmetry in the verified system. However, the methods are *robust* and work correctly even if the information supplied by the user is incorrect. Moreover, the methods return correct results even in case the computation of the symmetry reduction has not been completed due to memory or time explosion.

D. Brinksma and K. G. Larsen (Eds.): CAV 2002, LNCS 2404, pp. 93–106, 2002.
© Springer-Verlag Berlin Heidelberg 2002

Temporal logic model checking [6] is a technique that accepts a finite state model of a system and a temporal logic specification and determines whether the system satisfies the specification. The main problem of model checking is its high memory requirements. *Symbolic model checking* [15], based on BDDs [4], can handle larger systems, but is still limited in its capacity. Thus, additional work is needed in order to make model checking feasible for larger systems.

This work exploits symmetry reduction in order to reduce memory and time used in symbolic model checking. Symmetry reduction is based on the observation that many systems consist of several similar components. Exchanging the role of such components in the system does not change the system's behavior. Thus, system states can be partitioned into equivalence classes called *orbits*, and the system can be verified by examining only representatives from each orbit.

Two main problems arise, however, when combining symbolic model checking with symmetry reduction. One is building the orbit relation and the other is choosing a representative for each orbit. [13] proves that the BDD for the orbit relation is exponential in the number of the BDD variables, and suggests choosing more than one representative for each orbit in order to obtain a smaller BDD for the orbit relation. Yet, this method does not solve the problem of choosing the representatives. The choice of representatives is significant since it strongly influences the size of the BDDs representing the symmetry-reduced model. [11] suggests to choose generic representatives. This approach involves compiling the symmetric program to a reduced model over the generic states. Such a compilation can only be applied to programs written with a special syntax in which symmetry is defined inside the program. [12] introduces an algorithm for explicit model checking which chooses as a representative for an orbit the first state from this orbit, discovered by the DFS. This method avoids choosing the representatives in advance. Unfortunately, it is not applicable to symbolic model checking since performing DFS is very inefficient with BDDs.

We suggest a new approach that avoids building the orbit relation and chooses representatives on-the-fly while computing the reachable states. Unlike [12] the choice of the representatives is guided by BDD criteria. Reachability is performed using an *under-approximation* that, at each step, explores only a subset of the reachable states. Some of the unexplored states are symmetric to the explored ones. By exploiting symmetry information, those states will never be explored. Thus, easier symbolic forward steps are obtained.

We first apply this approach for verifying properties of the form $AG(p)^1$, where p is a boolean formula. If we find a "bad" state that does not satisfy p we conclude that the checked system does not satisfy $AG(p)$. On the other hand, if no "bad" state is found we cannot conclude that the system satisfies $AG(p)$ since reachability with under-approximation does not necessarily explore every reachable state. We next present a special version of the previous algorithm in which the under-approximation is guided by *hints* [3]. Under certain conditions this algorithm can also verify the system.

---

[1] $AG(p)$ means that p holds along every path, in every state on the path.

The algorithms described above are based on reachability, and are often referred to as *on-the-fly* model checking. It is well known how to extend on-the-fly model checking for $AG(p)$ to verifying general *safety temporal properties*. This is done by building an automaton describing the property and running it together with the system. We specify conditions on the automaton that guarantee the correctness of the on-the-fly algorithm also when the automaton runs together with the symmetry-reduced model. The suggested conditions hold for the tableau construction used for symbolic LTL model checking [ ], when restricted to LTL safety properties. They also hold for the satellite used in symbolic model checking of RCTL formulas [ ]. By running the automaton together with the reduced model we save both space and time while verifying these types of formulas.

On-the-fly symbolic model checking cannot handle liveness properties. In order to handle such properties we developed two extensions combining symmetry reduction with classical (not on-the-fly) symbolic model checking. One is easy to perform and is mainly suitable for falsification. The other is more expensive but can handle verification as well.

Previous works expect the user to provide a symmetry group that is also an invariance group [ ]. In many cases two formulas checked on the same model require different invariance groups since each formula breaks differently the symmetry of the model. Thus, the user needs to supply different invariance groups for different formulas. In other works [,] the program is written in a special syntax, which enables finding the invariance group according to this syntax. In these cases only formulas which do not break the symmetry of the model are allowed. In contrast, we build the invariance group automatically, once the symmetry group is given. Supplying the symmetry group usually requires only a high level understanding of the system and therefore is easier than supplying the invariance group.

We implemented our methods within the enhanced model checking tool Rule-Base [ ], developed by the IBM Haifa Research Laboratories, and compared the performance of our methods with that of RuleBase. Our experiments show that our methods performed significantly better, with respect to both time and space, in checking liveness properties. For temporal safety properties they achieved better time requirements. However, their space requirements were worse for small examples and identical for larger ones.

The rest of the paper is organized as follows. Section 2 gives some basic definitions. Section 3 shows how to build the invariance group. Section 4 presents an algorithm for on-the-fly symbolic model checking with symmetry reduction and then introduces hints into this algorithm. Section 5 and 6 handle temporal safety properties and liveness properties, respectively and Section 7 presents our experimental results.

2   Preliminaries

Let AP be a set of atomic propositions. We model a system by a Kripke structure M over AP, $M = (S, S_0, R, L)$ where S is a finite set of states, S_0 is a set of initial states, $R \subseteq S \times S$ is a total transition relation, and $L : S \to 2^{AP}$ is a labeling function which labels each state with the set of atomic propositions true in that state.

As the specification language we use the branching time temporal logic CTL, defined over AP. The semantics of CTL is defined with respect to a Kripke structure. We write $M \models \varphi$ to denote that the formula φ is true in M. For a formal definition of CTL and its semantics see [7]. ACTL is the sub-logic of CTL in negation normal form in which all formulas contain only universal path quantifiers.

The *bisimulation equivalence* and *simulation preorder* are relations over Kripke structures (see [7] for definitions) that have useful logical characterizations. We write $M \equiv_{bis} M'$ to denote that M and M' are bisimulation equivalent and $M \leq_{sim} M'$ to denote that M is smaller than M' by the simulation preorder. The following lemmas relate bisimulation and simulation with logics.

Lemma 1. *[7] For every two Kripke structures M, M′ over AP,*

- *if $M \equiv_{bis} M'$ then $\forall \varphi \in CTL$ over AP, $M' \models \varphi \Leftrightarrow M \models \varphi$.*
- *if $M \leq_{sim} M'$ then $\forall \varphi \in ACTL$ over AP, $M' \models \varphi \Rightarrow M \models \varphi$.*

BDDs: A Binary Decision Diagram (BDD) [4] is a data structure for representing boolean functions. BDDs are defined over boolean variables, they are often (but not always) concise in their memory requirement, and most boolean operations can be performed efficiently on BDD representations. In [15] it has been shown that BDDs can be very useful for representing Kripke structures and performing model checking symbolically. One of the most useful operations in model checking, and in particular on-the-fly model checking, is the *image computation*. Given a set of states S and a binary relation T, represented by the BDDs $S(\bar{v})$ and $T(\bar{v}, \bar{v}')$ respectively, the image computation finds the set of all states related by T to some state in S. More precisely, $Im_T(S(\bar{v})) = \exists \bar{v}(S(\bar{v}) \wedge T(\bar{v}, \bar{v}'))$.

Partial Search: While symbolic model checking can be very efficient, it might still suffer from explosion in the BDD size. One of the solutions is to perform partial search of the reachable state space while avoiding large BDDs [16]. Other methods perform partial search which is guided by the user [3] or by the checked specification [18]. In all these methods the set of reachable states discovered in each step is an under approximation of the set of reachable states which would have been discovered by a BFS. This property enables combining partial search with on-the-fly model checking.

Symmetry: A permutation on a set A, $\sigma : A \to A$ is a one-to-one and onto function. For a set $A' \subseteq A$, $\sigma(A') = \{a | \exists a' \in A' \, \sigma(a') = a\}$. In this paper we use permutations over the set of states of a Kripke structure. Given a CTL formula β and a structure M, $\sigma(\beta)$ refers to applying σ to the set of states in M that satisfy β.

A *permutation group* G is a set of permutations together with the composition operation such that the identity permutation e is in G and G is closed under the inverse and the composition operations. If there exists $\sigma \in G$ such that $\sigma(s) = s'$ we say that the two states s, s' are symmetric.

Definition 1. $\sigma_1, \sigma_2, \ldots, \sigma_k$ *are generators of a permutation group G (denoted $G = \langle \sigma_1, \sigma_2, \ldots, \sigma_k \rangle$) if G is the closure of the set $\{\sigma_1, \sigma_2, \ldots, \sigma_k\}$ under composition operation.*

Definition 2. *A permutation group G is a* symmetry group *of a Kripke structure M if every permutation $\sigma \in G$ preserves the transition relation. That is, $\forall s, s' \in S \; [(s, s') \in R \Leftrightarrow (\sigma(s), \sigma(s')) \in R]$.*

Definition 3. *A symmetry group G of a Kripke structure M is an* invariance group *for formula φ if for every atomic proposition β of φ, every $\sigma \in G$ and $s \in S \; [M, s \models \beta \Leftrightarrow M, \sigma(s) \models \beta]$.*

Given an invariance group G and a Kripke structure M we can partition S into equivalence classes. The equivalence class of s is $[s] = \{s' | \exists \sigma \in G, \; \sigma(s) = s'\}$. Each $[s]$ is called an *orbit* and the relation OR $= \{(s, s') | s, s' \in S \text{ and } [s] = [s']\}$ is called the *orbit relation*

For a Kripke structure $M = (S, S_0, R, L)$ and an invariance group G for φ the *quotient structure* is $M_G = (S_G, S_G^0, R_G, L_G)$ where $S_G = \{ [s] \mid s \in S \}$, $S_G^0 = \{ [s] \mid s \in S_0 \}$, $R_G = \{ ([s], [s']) \mid (s, s') \in R \}$ and $L_G([s]) = L(s)$. In [10,13] it has been proved that $M_G \equiv_{bis} M$. By Lemma 1 we therefore have that for every CTL formula ψ over the same AP as φ, $M_G \models \psi \Leftrightarrow M \models \psi$.

In order to build the quotient structure a representative should be chosen from each orbit In many cases, however, it is easier to choose more than one representative for each orbit. We then define a *representative relation* $\xi \subseteq Rep \times S$ which satisfies $(s, s') \in \xi \Leftrightarrow s \in Rep \wedge [s] = [s']$. In this case we define the structure $M_m = (S_m, S_m^0, R_m, L_m)$ (m for multiple representatives) where $S_m = Rep$, $S_m^0 = \{ s \mid \exists s' \in S_0 \; (s, s') \in \xi \}$, $R_m = \xi^{-1} R \xi$ and $L_m = L$. [13] shows that $M_m \equiv_{bis} M_G \equiv_{bis} M$.

3   Building the Invariance Group

In this section we show how to automatically compute the generators of an invariance group given the generators of a symmetry group.

Our method works as follows. Given a set of generators for a symmetry group G, an invariance group G_{inv} is defined by restricting the generators of G to those σ_i that satisfy $\sigma_i(\beta) = \beta$ for every $\beta \in AP$. The following lemma states the correctness of our approach.

Lemma 2. *Let $\sigma_1, \sigma_2, \ldots, \sigma_k$ be generators of a symmetry group G of a Kripke structure M and let φ be a formula over AP. Then $IG = \{\sigma_i | \forall \beta \in AP, \; \sigma_i(\beta) = \beta\}$ generates an invariance group G_{inv} of M for φ.*

4   Symmetry with On-the-Fly Representatives

The symbolic algorithm **Symmetry_MC** presented in this section is aimed at avoiding the two main problems of symmetry reduction, namely building the orbit relation and choosing a representative for each orbit.

Let $M = (S, S_0, R, L)$ be a Kripke structure and $\sigma_1, \dots, \sigma_k$ be a set of generators of a symmetry group G of M. Also let $\varphi = AG(p)$ where p is a boolean formula. The algorithm **Symmetry_MC**, presented in Figure 1, applies on-the-fly model checking for M and φ, using under-approximation and symmetry reduction.

The algorithm works in iterations. Starting with the set of initial states, at each iteration a subset **under** of the current set of states is chosen. The successors of **under** are computed. However, every state which is symmetric to (i.e., in the same orbit with) a previously reached state is removed. The states that are first found for each orbit are taken to be the orbit representatives. Note that an orbit may have more than one representative if several of its states are reached when the orbit is encountered for the first time. At any step, the set of representatives are checked to see if they include a state that violates p. If such a state is found (line 9) then the computation stops and a counterexample is produced. We then conclude that $M \not\models AG(p)$. A useful optimization can be performed by deleting from memory the BDD for the set `full_reach` immediately after it is used (after line 7). This may avoid memory explosion when computing forward steps.

The set of symmetric states that should be removed are computed using the procedure σ_**Step** (Figure 2) instead of using the orbit relation. For a set of states A and a set of generators $IG = \{ \sigma_1, \dots, \sigma_k \}$, σ_**Step** returns the set of all states belonging to the orbits of states in A according to $G = \langle IG \rangle$. By using σ_**Step** we exploit symmetry information without building the orbit

---

Symmetry_MC(M, φ, $\sigma_1, \dots \sigma_k$)

1   Calculate the generators of the invariance group of M
         $IG = \{\sigma_i|$ for each atomic sub-formula β of φ: $\sigma_i(\beta) = \beta\}$
2   **reach_rep** $= S_0$, i=0
3   while $S_i \neq \emptyset$
4   choose **under** $\subseteq S_i$ (**under** is an under-approximation of S_i)
5             $S_{i+1} = Im_R(\textbf{under})$
6   **full_reach** $= \sigma$_**Step**(**reach_rep**, $\sigma_1, \dots \sigma_k$)
7             $S_{i+1} = S_{i+1}$ / **full_reach**
8   **reach_rep** = **reach_rep** $\cup S_{i+1}$
9   if $S_{i+1} \wedge \neg p \neq \emptyset$
10   generate a counter example and break.
11   i = i+1.

Fig. 1. The algorithm **Symmetry_MC** performs on-the-fly model checking of φ on M, using symmetry reduction

```
        σ_Step(A, σ₁, σ₂, ..., σₖ)
1           sym_states = A;
2           old_sym_states = ∅
3           while old_sym_states ≠ sym_states
4                 old_sym_states = sym_states
5               for i = 1 ... k
6                   new_sym_states = Im_{σ_i}(sym_states)
7                   sym_states = sym_states ∪ new_sym_states
8           return sym_states
```

Fig. 2. σ_**Step** calculates the states belonging to the orbits of states in A. In order to calculate $Im_{\sigma_i}($sym_states$)$, σ_i can be viewed as the binary relation $\bar{v} = \sigma(\bar{v}')$

relation. σ_**Step** is expected to be smaller since it represents a set of states and not a relation. Furthermore it is applied only to reachable states which are usually represented by smaller BDDs. Indeed, our experiments successfully applied σ_**Step** to designs for which building the orbit relation was infeasible.

Computationally, σ_**Step** is quite heavy. To avoid this problem, in most of our experiments we stopped the computation of σ_**Step** before it got to a fixed point. In general there is a tradeoff between the amount of computation in σ_**Step** and the symmetry reduction obtained by **Symmetry_MC**.

4.1   Robustness of Symmetry_MC

We now discuss the robustness of the algorithm **Symmetry_MC** for falsification in the presence of an incomplete σ_**Step** and an incorrect set of generators. Consider first the case in which the computation of procedure σ_**Step** is stopped before a fixed point is reached. σ_**Step** then returns only a subset of the states in the orbits of states in A. In this case, less states are removed from S_{i+1} and as a result **reach_rep** contains more states. Thus, we might have more representatives for each orbit.

Consider now the case in which the algorithm is given an incorrect set of generators. If a "bad" generator (a permutation which associates states that are not symmetric) is given, then σ_**Step** returns states which are not symmetric to any state in **reach_rep**. These states are removed from S_{i+1} and we might not add any representatives of their orbits to **reach_rep**. Thus, **reach_rep** represents an under-approximation of the reachable orbits. Consequently, if there is a state $s \in$ **reach_rep** which does not satisfy p, this state is reachable in the original model and the counterexample generated by **Symmetry_MC** actually exists in the original model. If a "good" generator is missing, then σ_**Step** returns less states and as a result there is more than one representative for each orbit. However, like in the previous case, **reach_rep** contains only reachable states and therefore **Symmetry_MC** generates only real counterexamples. To summarize,

Lemma 3. *Given any set of generators, the algorithm* **Symmetry_MC** *is sound for falsification.*

At termination of **Symmetry_MC**, if reach_rep contains at least one state from each reachable orbit then M_m, defined according to reach_rep (S_m = reach_rep) is bisimilar to M (see Section 2). Thus, if $M_m \models AG(p)$ then $M \models AG(p)$ as well. Note that $M_m \models AG(p)$ can be checked on-the-fly by **Symmetry_MC**.

4.2 Symmetry Reduction Combined with Hints

In this section we present a special case of the algorithm **Symmetry_MC** in which the under-approximation is guided by a sequence of hints given by the user [3]. The algorithm **Hints_Sym**, presented in Figure 3, gets as parameters also a sequence $h_1, \ldots, h_l$ of hints such that $h_l = \text{TRUE}$.

If $\sigma_1, \ldots, \sigma_k$ contain no "bad" generator[2] then our hints guarantee that when $S_i = \emptyset$, reach_rep contains at least one state from each reachable orbit. In this case, the algorithm **Hints_Sym** is suitable for verification as well as falsification.

    Hints_Sym(M, φ, $\sigma_1, \ldots, \sigma_k$, $h_1, \ldots, h_l$)
1   Calculate IG = $\{\sigma_i|$ for each atomic sub-formula β of φ: $\sigma_i(\beta) = \beta\}$
2   reach_rep = S_0, i = 0, hint = h_1, j = 2
3   while $S_i \neq \emptyset$
4   under = $S_i \cap$ hint
5            $S_{i+1} = Im_R(\text{under})$
6   full_reach = σ_Step(reach_rep, $\sigma_1, \ldots \sigma_k$)
7            $S_{i+1} = S_{i+1}/$full_reach
8   reach_rep = reach_rep $\cup S_{i+1}$
9   if $S_{i+1} \wedge \neg p \neq \emptyset$
10   generate counter example and break
11   if $S_{i+1} = \emptyset \wedge j \leq l$
12   hint = $hint_j$
13   j = j+1
14               $S_{i+1} = $ reach_rep
15   i = i+1
16   φ is TRUE

Fig. 3. The algorithm **Hints_Sym** applies on-the-fly model checking of φ on M, using hints and symmetry reduction

---

[2] In many cases, the nonexistence of bad generators can be easily determined by the program syntax [17,8]. In other cases it is expensive but possible to check whether all generators are good.

5   Extension for Temporal Safety Properties

There are several known algorithms which use a construction A_φ for the evaluated formula φ and the product model $M \times A_\varphi$ in order to apply model checking more efficiently. We now show that it is possible to combine symmetry reduction with these algorithms. We first specify the requirements on the construction A_φ so that it can be used with symmetry reduction.

Definition 4. *Given a logic $\mathcal{L}$ and a construction that associates with each $\varphi \in \mathcal{L}$ a structure A_φ, the construction A_φ is safe for symmetry reduction w.r.t. $\mathcal{L}$ if it satisfies the following conditions:*

1. $\exists \psi \forall \varphi \in \mathcal{L}\ (M \models \varphi \Leftrightarrow M \times A_\varphi \models \psi)$.
2. *For every invariance group G_{inv} of M for φ, every $\sigma \in G_{inv}$ and every $(s,t) \in S_{M \times A_\varphi}$, $\sigma((s,t)) = (\sigma(s),t)$* [3].
3. *For every atomic proposition β of ψ and every*
   $(s,t), (s',t) \in S_{M \times A_\varphi}$, $(s,t) \models \beta \Leftrightarrow (s',t) \models \beta$.

The second condition requires that σ is defined only on s and leaves t unchanged. The third condition requires that the truth of all β in ψ depend only on t.

Lemma 4. *For every construction A_φ which is safe for symmetry reduction w.r.t. $\mathcal{L}$, if G is an invariance group of structure M for formula $\varphi \in \mathcal{L}$ then G is an invariance group of structure $M \times A_\varphi$ for formula ψ.*

Corollary 1. *For every construction A_φ which is safe for symmetry reduction w.r.t. $\mathcal{L}$ and for every $\varphi \in \mathcal{L}$ and $\psi \in CTL$, the quotient structure $(M \times A_\varphi)_G$, built for $M \times A_\varphi$ and an invariance group G of M, satisfies $(M \times A_\varphi)_G \models \psi \Leftrightarrow M \models \varphi$.*

Note that using safe construction enables us to find the generators of the invariance group of M according to φ and then to evaluate formula ψ on $M \times A_\varphi$ with symmetry reduction that use the same generators. There are several A_φ constructions which are safe for symmetry reduction w.r.t. logic $\mathcal{L}$. One example is the tableau construction in [ ] when restricted to LTL safety properties. In this case the tableau includes no fairness constraints and it fulfills the requirements of Definition 4. Another safe construction is the satellite for RCTL formulas defined in [ ]. By combining safe construction with symmetry reduction we make symmetry reduction applicable together with a new set of algorithms, like symbolic on-the fly model checking for RCTL and symbolic LTL model checking, for which it was not applicable until now. We implemented our algorithms using the construction introduced in [ ], which enabled us to check RCTL formulas on-the-fly while using a symmetry reduction.

---

[3] since s and $\sigma(s)$ agree on AP, $[(s,t) \in S_{M \times A_\varphi} \Leftrightarrow (\sigma(s),t) \in S_{M \times A_\varphi}]$.

6   Extensions for Liveness Formulas

We now describe two possible extensions that combine classical (not on-the-fly) symbolic model checking with symmetry reduction. These extensions are useful for checking liveness properties, and other properties which cannot be checked on-the-fly.

6.1   Liveness Restricted to Representatives

The purpose of this extension is to falsify ACTL formulas with respect to a structure M, while avoiding the construction of its quotient model M_G. The idea is to get a set of representatives Rep and to construct the restricted model $M|_{Rep}$. The restricted model $M|_A = (S|_A, S_0|_A, R|_A, L|_A)$ is a Kripke structure where $S|_A = A$, $S_0|_A = S_0 \cap A$, $\forall s, s' \in S|_A$ $[(s, s') \in R|_A \Leftrightarrow (s, s') \in R]$ and $\forall s \in S|_A$ $[L|_A(s) = L(s)]$. Since $M|_{Rep} \leq_{sim} M$, we have that for every ACTL formula φ, if $M|_{Rep} \not\models \varphi$ then $M \not\models \varphi$. Thus, φ can be checked on the smaller model $M|_{Rep}$.

Note that in principle this idea works correctly with any set of representatives, even such that does not include a representative for each orbit. There are however advantages to choosing as Rep the set reach_rep which results from the algorithm **Symmetry_MC**. First, reach_rep includes only reachable states. Second, by construction, the states in reach_rep are connected by transitions while an arbitrary set of representatives Rep might not be connected, thus, $M|_{reach\_rep}$ often includes more behaviors than $M|_{Rep}$. Third, the states in reach_rep represent many other states in the system, thus if the system includes a bad behavior, it is more likely that reach_rep will reflect it.

Following the discussion above we suggest the Algorithm **Live_Rep** that works as follows: it first runs **Symmetry_MC** to obtain reach_rep and then performs classical symbolic model checking on $M|_{reach\_rep}$.

6.2   Liveness with the Representative Relation

We now present another possibility for handling liveness properties. It is applicable only if no bad generators exist. This method is more expensive computationally, but is suitable for verification of liveness properties. Similarly to the previous section we first compute reach_rep using the algorithm **Symmetry_MC**. However, now we apply the procedure **Create_ξ**, presented below, in order to compute the representative relation $\xi \subseteq$ reach_rep $\times S$ (see definition in Section 2). Next we construct a new structure $M' = (S', S_0', R', L')$ where $S' =$ reach_rep, $S_0' = \{ s \mid \exists s' \in S_0 \ (s, s') \in \xi \}$, $R' = \xi^{-1} R \xi$ and $L' = L$. Finally, we run classical symbolic model checking on φ and M'.

Lemma 5. *If S' contains at least one representative for each reachable orbit then $M \equiv_{bis} M'$. Otherwise, $M' \leq_{sim} M$.*

Create_$\xi(\sigma_1, \sigma_2 \ldots \sigma_k,$ Rep$)$

1      $\xi(\bar{v}, \bar{v}') = \text{Rep}(\bar{v}) \wedge (\bar{v} = \bar{v}')$

2   old_$\xi(\bar{v}, \bar{v}') = \phi$

3   while old_$\xi(\bar{v}, \bar{v}') \neq \xi(\bar{v}, \bar{v}')$

4   old_$\xi(\bar{v}, \bar{v}') = \xi(\bar{v}, \bar{v}')$

5   for i = 1 ... k

6   new$(\bar{v}, \bar{v}'') = \exists \bar{v}'(\xi(\bar{v}, \bar{v}') \wedge \sigma_i(\bar{v}'', \bar{v}'))$

7          $\xi(\bar{v}, \bar{v}') = \xi(\bar{v}, \bar{v}') \cup$ new$(\bar{v}, \bar{v}')$

8   return $\xi(\bar{v}, \bar{v}')$

Fig. 4. The algorithm **Create_ξ** for computing $\xi \subseteq Rep \times S$. Line 6 is implemented with the operator `compose_odd` [14] which computes $\exists \bar{v}'(\xi(\bar{v}, \bar{v}') \wedge \sigma_i(\bar{v}'', \bar{v}'))$ using only two sets of BDD variables instead of three

If `reach_rep` is the result of the algorithm **Hints_Sym**, then `reach_rep` indeed contains at least one representative for each orbit, and M' is bisimilar to M. Thus, M' can be used for verifying full CTL.

Figure 4 presents the BDD-based procedure **Create_ξ** for building the representative relation ξ for a given set of representatives Rep and a set of generators $\sigma_1, \ldots, \sigma_k$ of an invariance group G of M for φ.

7 Experimental Results

We implemented the algorithms **Hints_Sym**, **Live_Rep**, and **Create_ξ** in the IBM's model checker RuleBase [1]. We ran it on a number of examples which contain symmetry. For each example we tuned our algorithms according to the evaluated formula, the difficulty level of computing the reachable states and the difficulty level of building the transition relation. In most cases, our algorithms outperformed RuleBase with respect to both time and space. In the tables below time is measured by seconds, memory (mem) in bytes, and the transition relation size (TR size) in number of BDD nodes.

The Futurebus Example: We ran the algorithm **Live_Rep** in order to check liveness properties on the Futurebus cache-coherence protocol with a single bus and a single cache line for each processor. The table in Figure 5 presents the results of evaluating the property for a different number of processors. For comparison we ran also the RuleBase classical symbolic model checking algorithm. Both algorithms applied dynamic BDD reordering. The BDD order is very important since the best BDD order for the classical algorithm is different from the best BDD order of our algorithm. In order to obtain a fair comparison between these algorithms we ran each algorithm twice. In the first run each algorithm reordered a BDD without time limit in order to find a BDD order which is good

# of processors	# vars	classic algorithm			Live_Rep		
		time	mem	TR size	time	mem	TR size
5	45	132	43M	144069	101	41M	122769
6	54	607	118M	260625	265	56M	219572
7	63	2852	277M	418701	704	76M	379428
8	72	8470	589M	839055	3313	101M	457781
9	81	81,171	709M	1935394	4571	106M	819871
10	90	-	> 1G	-	4909	120M	642083

Fig. 5. Live_Rep on Future bus example

for this algorithm. The initial order of the second run was the BDD order which was found by the first run.

The most difficult step in the Futurebus example is building the transition relation. By restricting the transition relation to the representatives which were chosen on-the-fly, the transition relation became smaller and as a result the evaluation became easier. Figure 5 shows that both time and space were reduced dramatically using **Live_Rep**. We can also observe that as the number of processes increases, the results improved. This is to be expected, as the increase in the number of the reachable representatives is smaller than the increase in the number of reachable states.

The Arbiter Example: We ran algorithm **Hints_Sym** on an arbiter example with n processes. We checked the arbiter w.r.t. RCTL formulas which were translated to safe A_φ and ψ. For comparison we ran RuleBase on-the-fly model checking and on-the-fly model checking with hints (without symmetry). All algorithms used dynamic BDD reordering and partitioned transition relation [9]. In this case we calculated σ_**Step** only when we changed hints and stopped σ_**Step** before the fixed point has been reached. The table in Figure 6 presents the results of the three algorithms on arbiter with 6,8 and 10 processes. For each case we checked one property that passed and one that failed. We notice that **Hints_Sym** reduced time but not necessarily space. This can be explained by the fact that σ_**Step** produced large intermediate BDDs but resulted in a significant reduction in S_i, thus reduced the computation time of the image steps.

# of processors	status	# vars	on-the-fly		on-the-fly + hints		Hints_Sym	
			time	mem	time	mem	time	mem
6	passed	65	53	40M	39	40M	42	40M
6	failed	65	213	52M	64	41M	51	87M
8	passed	84	581	64M	255	49M	179	87M
8	failed	84	745	71M	524	71M	292	83M
10	passed	105	1470	94M	598	67M	358	92M
10	failed	105	1106	93M	740	73M	520	91M

Fig. 6. Hints_Sym compared to other on-the-fly algorithms

num of generators	num of vars	orbit_to_ξ		Create_ξ	
		time	mem	time	mem
3	16	0.26	26M	0.23	26M
4	20	30.4	33M	1.2	28M
5	24	1017	114M	18	42M
6	28	-	>1.5G	735	132M
6	32	-	>1.5G	29083	1.2G

Fig. 7. Create_ξ compared to Orbit_To_ξ

Comparing Create_ξ and Orbit_To_ξ: [13] presents an algorithm for computing ξ by building the orbit relation and then choosing the representatives. We refer to this algorithm by **Orbit_To_ξ**. We compare this algorithm with **Create_ξ**. Both algorithms find the representative relation $\xi \subseteq Rep \times S$ for the set of representatives Rep chosen according to the lexicographic order. The results in Figure 7 show that **Create_ξ** gave better results in both time and space, We believe that this is due to the fact that it saves less information while building ξ.

Acknowledgment

We thank Cindy Eisner for many helpful discussions. Somesh Jha is thanked for his help with the examples.

References

1. I. Beer, S. Ben-David, C. Eisner, and A. Landver. RuleBase: An industry-oriented formal verification tool. In *Design Automation Conference*, pages 655–660, June 1996. 95, 103
2. I. Beer, S. Ben-David, and A. Landver. On-the-fly model checking of RCTL formulas. In Alan J. Hu and Moshe Y. Vardi, editors, *Proceedings of the 10th International conference on Computer-Aided Verification*, volume 1427 of *LNCS*, pages 184–194. Springer-Verlag, June 1998. 95, 101
3. R. Bloem, K. Ravi, and F. Somenzi. Symbolic guided search for CTL model checking. In *Design Automation Conference*, pages 29–34, June 2000. 94, 96, 100
4. R. E. Bryant. Graph-based algorithms for boolean function manipulation. *IEEE transactions on Computers*, C-35(8):677–691, 1986. 94, 96
5. E. Clarke, O. Grumberg, and H. Hamaguchi. Another look at LTL model checking. *Formal Methods in System Design*, 10(1), 1997. 95, 101
6. E. M. Clarke, E. A. Emerson, and A. P. Sistla. Automatic verification of finite-state concurrent systems using temporal logic specifications. *ACM Transactions on Programming Languages and Systems*, 8(2):244–263, 1986. 94
7. E. M. Clarke, O. Grumberg, and D. A. Peled. *Model Checking*. MIT press, December 1999. 96
8. C. N. Ip and D. L. Dill. Better verification through symmetry. In D. Agnew, L. Claesen, and R. Camposano, editors, *Computer Hardware Description Languages and their Applications*, pages 87–100, Ottawa, Canada, 1993. Elsevier Science Publishers B. V., Amsterdam, Netherland. 95, 100

9. D. Geist and I. Beer. Efficient model checking by automated ordering of transition relation. In David L. Dill, editor, *Proceedings of the sixth International Conference on Computer-Aided Verification CAV*, volume 818, pages 299–310. Springer-Verlag, June 1994. 104

10. E. A. Emerson and A. P. Sistla. Symmetry and model checking. In C. Courcoubetis, editor, *Proceedings of the 5th International conference on Computer-Aided Verification*, volume 697 of *LNCS*. Springer-Verlag, June 1993. 97

11. E. Allen Emerson and Richard J. Trefler. From asymmetry to full symmetry: New techniques for symmetry reduction in model checking. In *Conference on Correct Hardware Design and Verification Methods*, pages 142–156, 1999. 94

12. V. Gyuris and A. P. Sistla. On-the-fly model checking under fairness that exploits symmetry. *Formal Methods in System Design: An International Journal*, 15(3):217–238, November 1999. 94

13. S. Jha. *Symmetry and Induction in Model Checking*. PhD thesis, CMU, 1996. 94, 95, 97, 105

14. S. Katz. Coverage of model checking. Master's thesis, Technion, haifa, Israel, 2001. 103

15. K. L. McMillan. *Symbolic Model Checking: An Approach to the State Explosion Problem*. Kluwer Academic Publishers, 1993. 94, 96

16. K. Ravi and F. Somenzi. High-density reachability analysis. In *Proc. Intl. Conf. on Computer-Aided Design*, pages 154–158, November 1995. 96

17. A. P. Sistla, V. Gyuris, and E. A. Emerson. SMC: a symmetry-based model checker for verification of safety and liveness properties. *Software Engineering and Methodology*, 9(2):133–166, 2000. 95, 100

18. C. Han Yang and David L. Dill. Validation with guided search of the state space. In *Design Automation Conference*, pages 599–604, June 1998. 96

Liveness with $(0, 1, \infty)$-Counter Abstraction*

Amir Pnueli[1], Jessie Xu[2], and Lenore Zuck[2]

[1] Weizmann Institute of Science, Rehovot, Israel
amir@wisdom.weizmann.ac.il
[2] New York University, New York
{jessie,zuck}@cs.nyu.edu

Abstract. We introduce the $(0, 1, \infty)$-*counter abstraction* method by which a parameterized system of unbounded size is abstracted into a finite-state system. Assuming that each process in the parameterized system is finite-state, the abstract variables are limited counters which count, for each local state s of a process, the number of processes which currently are in local state s. The counters are saturated at 2, which means that $\kappa(s) = 2$ whenever 2 *or more* processes are at state s. The emphasis of the paper is on the derivation of an adequate and sound set of fairness requirements (both weak and strong) that enable proofs of liveness properties of the abstract system, from which we can safely conclude a corresponding liveness property of the original parameterized system. We illustrate the method on few parameterized systems, including Szymanski's Algorithm for mutual exclusion. The method is also extended to deal with parameterized systems whose processes may have infinitely many local states, such as the Bakery Algorithm, by choosing few "interesting" state assertions and $(0, 1, \infty)$-counting the number of processes satisfying them.

1 Introduction

Uniform verification of parameterized systems is one of the most challenging problems in verification today. Given a parameterized system $S(N)$: $P[1]\| \cdots \| P[N]$ and a property p, uniform verification attempts to verify $S(N) \models p$ for every $N > 1$. One of the promising approaches to the verification of infinite-state systems (and, due to the unbounded value of the parameter N, parameterized systems are essentially infinite-state) is the method of *finitary abstraction* by which we abstract an infinite-state system into a finite-state one, that can then be model checked. A general theory of finitary abstraction which abstracts a system *together* with the property to be proven is presented in [14], and can be applied to the verification of arbitrary LTL properties, including liveness properties.

---

* This research was supported in part by the Minerva Center for Verification of Reactive Systems, a gift from Intel, the European Community IST project "Advance", and ONR grant N00014-99-1-0131.

D. Brinksma and K. G. Larsen (Eds.): CAV 2002, LNCS 2404, pp. 107–122, 2002.
© Springer-Verlag Berlin Heidelberg 2002

In this paper we present *counter abstraction*, a special finitary abstraction method for parameterized systems. Assume that the processes $P[i]$ in the parameterized system have similar programs, where the program has locations $0, \ldots, L$. Assume first that processes do not have local variables (except for the program counter). In this case, the abstract state space is defined by having abstract variables $\kappa_0, \ldots, \kappa_L$. Abstract variable κ_ℓ is intended to count the number of concrete processes that are at location ℓ. To guarantee that the abstract system is finite-state, we bound the range of κ_ℓ to $[0..2]$. For $k < 2$, $\kappa_\ell = k$ states that precisely k processes are at location ℓ, while $\kappa_\ell = 2$ states that 2 *or more* processes are at location ℓ. Certainly, such an abstraction is adequate for specifying properties of mutual exclusion which requires that the number of processes at critical locations never exceeds 1. The case that processes do possess additional (finite-state) local variables can also be treated by counter abstraction, only in this case we allocate a counter κ_s to each *local state* s of a process. The counter κ_s counts (up to 2) the number of processes whose local state is s.

The idea of this simple abstraction is certainly not new [17] and usually serves as one of the first examples of abstraction and abstract interpretation [ ]. The main contribution of this paper is to present a systematic method for enriching the counter abstraction with an adequate and automatically derivable set of fairness conditions, and illustrate its application to verify effectively and efficiently various liveness properties of parameterized systems.

The method can be applied with no extensions to parameterized systems in which every process has only finitely many local states and the global variables range over finite domains. It can also be extended to deal with systems in which individual processes may have infinitely many local states. The necessary extension is that we identify some state assertions and then allocate (bounded) counters that count the number of processes whose local states satisfy these assertions. This extension is illustrated in Section 5 where we verify the correctness of Szymanski's algorithm and the Bakery Algorithm.

Related Work. The work which obtains results closest to ours is [ ] and previous articles describing the PAX system. They also address the problem of verification of parameterized systems, with emphasis on liveness properties and manage to verify individual accessibility of Szymanski's protocol. One of the differences between the two approaches is that [ ] is based on the method of *predicate abstraction* [ ] by which the abstract space is determined by the assertions appearing in the transition system and in the temporal property to be verified. As a result, the structure of the abstraction varies from case to case and the computation of the added fairness requirements depends on a marking algorithm which has to be re-applied for each case separately, searching for appropriate well-founded ranking. In comparison, we propose a uniform abstraction approach based on the notion of counter abstraction, which allows us to provides a standard recipe for the additional compassion (strong fairness) requirements, as well as additional justice (weak fairness) requirements, which [ ] claims cannot be automatically lifted from the concrete to the abstract systems (unless it is for a distinguished process which is not abstracted). Thus, due to our focus on a single uniform abstraction, we are able to derive a richer set of abstract fairness conditions, including weak as well as strong fairness. Like [9], we also use an implementation of WS1S in order to compute the abstracted system. Another relative advantage of our method is its extended ability to deal with parameterized systems whose individual processes are not necessarily finite-state.

The theory of linear abstraction, as presented in [14], is aimed at verifying liveness (and general LTL) properties. However, the general recipe of abstraction is often too weak to provide a working finitary abstraction. In order to obtain a complete method, it is suggested to augment the system under consideration by an auxiliary monitoring module and abstract the composed system. While this may be theoretically satisfactory, no effective method is provided for designing the augmenting monitor.

The problem of uniform verification of parameterized systems is, in general, undecidable [1]. One approach to remedy this situation, pursued, e.g., in [7], is to look for restricted families of parameterized systems for which the problem becomes decidable. Many of these approaches fail when applied to asynchronous systems where processes communicate by shared variables.

Another approach is to look for sound but incomplete methods. Representative works of this approach include methods based on: explicit induction ([8]), network invariants that can be viewed as implicit induction ([15]), abstraction and approximation of network invariants ([6]), and other methods based on abstraction ([9]). Other methods include those relying on "regular model-checking" (e.g., [12]) that require special *acceleration* procedures and thus involve user ingenuity and intervention, methods based on symmetry reduction (e.g., [10]), or compositional methods (e.g., ([20]) that combine automatic abstraction with finite-instantiation due to symmetry. These works, from which we have mentioned only few representatives, require the user to provide auxiliary constructs and thus do not provide for fully automatic verification of parameterized systems.

2   Parameterized Systems

The systems we consider here consist of a parallel composition of N processes, all executing the same program, that may refer to the id (identity) of the executing process. In addition, the process programs may access a set of global shared variables and each other's local variables. Accesses to the local variables of other processes can be done under existential or universal quantification. A simple example of such a system is MUX-SEM in Fig. 1. There, each of the processes is executing exactly the same code (that does not refer to the id of the executing process), and there are only references to the single shared variable y.

The semaphore instructions "**request** y" and "**release** y" appearing in the program stand, respectively, for $\langle \textbf{when } y = 1 \textbf{ do } y := 0 \rangle$ and $y := 1$. As seen in Fig. 1, we use the simple programming language SPL [19, 18] for presenting programs.

2.1   The Computational Model

For a computational model we use *fair discrete systems*, which is a slight varia-
tion on the *fair transition systems* (FTS) model of [19]. An FDS $\mathcal{D} : \langle V, \Theta, \rho, \mathcal{J}, \mathcal{C} \rangle$
consists of the following components.

- $V = \{u_1, ..., u_n\}$: A finite set of typed *system variables*, containing data and
  control variables. The set of *states* (interpretation) over V is denoted by Σ.
- Θ : The *initial condition* – an *assertion* (first-order state formula) characterizing the initial states.
- ρ : A *transition relation* – an assertion $\rho(V, V')$, relating the values V of the
  variables in state $s \in \Sigma$ to the values V' in a $\mathcal{D}$-successor state $s' \in \Sigma$.
- $\mathcal{J} : \{J_1, ..., J_k\}$: A (possibly parameterized) set of *justice* (*weak fairness*)
  requirements. The justice requirement $J \in \mathcal{J}$ is an assertion, intended to
  guarantee that every computation contains infinitely many J-state (states
  satisfying J).
- $\mathcal{C} : \{\langle p_1, q_1 \rangle, ... \langle p_n, q_n \rangle\}$: A (possibly parameterized) set of *compassion*
  (*strong fairness*) *requirements*. The compassion requirement $\langle p, q \rangle \in \mathcal{C}$ is a
  pair of assertions, intended to guarantee that every computation containing
  infinitely many p-states also contains infinitely many q-states.

We require that every state $s \in \Sigma$ has at least one $\mathcal{D}$-successor. This is often
ensured by including in ρ the *idling* disjunct $V = V'$ (also called the *stuttering*
step). In such cases, every state s is its own $\mathcal{D}$-successor.

The FDS corresponding to program MUX-SEM is presented in Fig. 2.

A *computation* of an FDS $\mathcal{D} : \langle V, \Theta, \rho, \mathcal{J}, \mathcal{C} \rangle$ is an infinite sequence of states
$\sigma : s_0, s_1, s_2, ...$, satisfying the following requirements:

Initiality: s_0 is initial, i.e., $s_0 \models \Theta$.
Consecution: For each $j = 0, 1, ...$, the state s_{j+1} is a $\mathcal{D}$-successor of the
state s_j.
Justice: For each $J \in \mathcal{J}$, σ contains infinitely many J-positions.
Compassion: For each $\langle p, q \rangle \in \mathcal{C}$, if σ contains infinitely many p-positions, then
it also contain infinitely many q-positions.

For an FDS $\mathcal{D}$, we denote by $\mathcal{C}omp(\mathcal{D})$ the set of all computations of $\mathcal{D}$.

$$
\begin{array}{l}
\textbf{in} \quad N : \textbf{natural where } N > 1 \\
\textbf{local } y \;: \textbf{boolean where } y = 1 \\
\displaystyle\overset{N}{\underset{i=1}{\|}} P[i] :: \left[
\begin{array}{l}
\textbf{loop forever do} \\
\left[
\begin{array}{l}
0 : \textbf{Non-Critical} \\
1 : \textbf{request } y \\
2 : \textbf{Critical; release } y
\end{array}
\right]
\end{array}
\right]
\end{array}
$$

Fig. 1. Program MUX-SEM

$$V : \begin{cases} N : \textbf{natural} \\ y : \textbf{boolean} \\ \pi : \textbf{array } [1..N] \textbf{ of } \{0, 1, 2\} \end{cases} \qquad \Theta : y \ \wedge \ N > 1 \ \wedge \ \forall i : [1..N] : \pi[i] = 0$$

$$\rho : \exists i : [1..N] \begin{pmatrix} \pi'[i] = \pi[i] \ \wedge \ y' = y \\ \vee \ \pi[i] = 0 \ \wedge \ \pi'[i] = 1 \ \wedge \ y' = y \\ \vee \ \pi[i] = 1 \ \wedge \ y = 1 \ \wedge \ \pi'[i] = 2 \ \wedge \ y' = 0 \\ \vee \ \pi[i] = 2 \ \wedge \ \pi'[i] = 0 \ \wedge \ y' = 1 \end{pmatrix} \ \wedge$$
$$\forall j \neq i : \pi'[j] = \pi[j] \ \wedge \ N = N'$$

$$\mathcal{J} : \Big\{ \pi[i] \neq 2 \mid i \in [1..N] \Big\} \qquad\qquad \mathcal{C} : \Big\{ \langle \pi[i] = 1 \ \wedge \ y \, , \ \pi[i] = 2 \rangle \mid i \in [1..N] \Big\}$$

Fig. 2. MUX-SEM–The FDS corresponding to program MUX-SEM

2.2 Verification of Parameterized Systems

When verifying properties of a parameterized system Sys, one wants to show that the property of interest is valid for all values of N. We focus on properties that are expressible by a formula φ of the type $\forall i_1, \ldots, i_k : f(i_1, \ldots, i_k)$ where k is a constant independent of N, $i_1, \ldots, i_k$ are indices of processes and f is a temporal formula over the free variables $i_1, \ldots, i_k$. Thus, to show that φ is valid over a parameterized system Sys, it is necessary to show that every computation $\sigma \in Comp(Sys)$, $\sigma \models N \geq k \rightarrow \forall i_1, \ldots, i_k : [1..N] : f(i_1, \ldots, i_k)$.

For example, the safety property of MUX-SEM, requiring that no two processes are ever in the critical section at the same time, is given by $\forall i \neq j : \Box \neg(\pi[i] = 2 \wedge \pi[j] = 2)$. Thus, to prove safety one has to show that for every $N \geq 2$, the property $\forall i \neq j : \Box \neg(\pi[i] = 2 \wedge \pi[j] = 2)$ holds for every computation of $Comp($MUX-SEM$)$.

As stated in the introduction, automatic verification of parameterized systems is notoriously difficult. Many methods, including [2], have been proposed for proving safety properties for a large class of such systems. Our goal here is to automatically prove liveness properties of such systems. It should be noted that the methodology reported here allows for automatic verification of safety properties, at times more efficiently than by other methods.

Our approach is based on the method of *finitary abstraction* introduced in [14]. The idea behind finitary abstraction (as well as other abstraction methods, all inspired by [6]) is to reduce the problem of verifying that a given *concrete* system $\mathcal{D}$ satisfies its (concrete) specifications ψ, into a problem of verifying that some (carefully crafted, finite-state) *abstract* system $\mathcal{D}^\alpha$ satisfies its (finite-state) abstract specifications ψ^α.

We sketch here the basic elements of the method, and refer the reader to [14] for additional details. Consider an FDS $\mathcal{D} = \langle V, \Theta, \rho, \mathcal{J}, \mathcal{C} \rangle$. Assume a set of *abstract variables* V_A and a set of expressions $\mathcal{E}^\alpha$, such that $V_A = \mathcal{E}^\alpha(V)$ expresses the values of the abstract variables in terms of concrete variables. For an assertion p, $\alpha^+(p)$ is the set of abstract states that have *some* p-states abstracted into them, and $\alpha^-(p)$ is the set of abstract states such that *all* states abstracted into them are p-states. Both α^- and α^+ can be generalized to temporal formulae ([14]). The temporal formula ψ^α is obtained by taking $\alpha^-(\psi)$. The abstract system $\mathcal{D}^\alpha$ that corresponds to $\mathcal{D}$ under α is the FDS $(V^\alpha, \Theta^\alpha, \rho^\alpha, J^\alpha, \mathcal{C}^\alpha)$ where $V^\alpha = V_A$, $\Theta^\alpha = \alpha^+(\Theta)$, $\rho^\alpha = \alpha^{++}(\rho)$, $J^\alpha = \bigcup_{J \in \mathcal{J}} \alpha^+(J)$, and $\mathcal{C}^\alpha = \bigcup_{\langle p,q \rangle \in \mathcal{C}} \langle \alpha^-(p), \alpha^+(q) \rangle$ where $\alpha^{++}(\rho) = \exists V, V' : V_A = \mathcal{E}^\alpha(V) \wedge V'_A = \mathcal{E}^\alpha(V') \wedge \rho(V, V')$.

It is proven in [14] that this abstraction method is sound. That is, if $\mathcal{D}^\alpha \models \psi^\alpha$ then $\mathcal{D} \models \psi$. Since formula ψ is an arbitrary temporal formula, this provides a sound abstraction method for verifying liveness as well as safety properties. In the next section we show the procedure above is not sufficient for deriving abstract fairness requirements.

3   Counter Abstraction

We present *counter abstraction*, a simple data abstraction method which is a special case of the finitary abstraction approach. Counter abstraction was studied in several other works (e.g., in [22,17]), but not in the context of fully automatic verification of liveness properties. The standard methodology for abstracting fairness requirements is inadequate when applied to counter abstraction. We show how to derive stronger fairness requirements for abstracted systems in general and counter abstracted systems in particular. These stronger fairness requirements support fully automatic verification of liveness properties.

3.1   Counter Abstracting States and Transitions

Consider a parameterized system Sys described by an SPL program as described in Section 2. Assume that the control variable of processes $(\pi[i])$ ranges over $0, \ldots, L$, and that the shared variables are $y_1, \ldots, y_b$. For simplicity, we assume first that the processes do not have any local variables. Thus, the concrete state variables are N, $\pi[1..N]$, and $y_1, \ldots, y_b$. We define a *counter abstraction* α, where the abstract variables are $\kappa_0, \ldots, \kappa_L : \{0, 1, 2\}$; $Y_1, \ldots, Y_b$ and the abstraction mapping $\mathcal{E}^a$ is given by

$$\kappa_\ell = \left\{ \begin{array}{l} 0 \text{ if } \forall i : [1..N] : \pi[i] \neq \ell \\ 1 \text{ if } \exists i_1 : [1..N] : \pi[i_1] = \ell \wedge \forall i_2 \neq i_1 : \pi[i_2] \neq \ell \\ 2 \text{ otherwise} \end{array} \right\} \text{ for } \ell \in [0..L]$$
$$Y_j = y_j \hspace{6cm} \text{for } j = 1, \ldots, b$$

That is, κ_ℓ is 0 when there are no processes at location ℓ, it is 1 if there is exactly one process at location ℓ, and it is 2 if there are two or more processes at location ℓ.[1]

Since the systems we are dealing with are symmetric, all the processes have initially the same control value. Without loss of generality, assume it is location 0.

---

[1] The upper bound of 2 can be substituted with other positive integer. In particular 1 can be used for most locations.

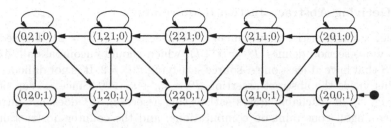

Fig. 3. Counter abstraction of MUX-SEM $(N \geq 5)$

Thus we have that Θ^α is $\kappa_0 = 2 \land \kappa_1 = \cdots = \kappa_L = 0 \land Y_1 = y_1^0 \land \cdots \land Y_b = y_b^0$, where $y_1^0, \ldots y_b^0$ denote the initial values of the concrete shared variables $y_1, \ldots, y_b$.

Next, we obtain ρ^α according to the "recipe" of the previous section. This can be computed automatically using a system supporting the logic WS1S, such as TLV[P] [13] or MONA [11]. Alternately, we can follow the more efficient procedure sketched below. The details are easy to flesh out and omitted here for brevity. For every location ℓ in the SPL program that describes a process, assume the instruction at location ℓ is of the form:

$\ell:$ **if** c **then** [$y := f_1(y)$; **goto** ℓ_1] **else** [$y := f_2(y)$; **goto** ℓ_2]

Suppose c^α is defined and that $\ell \neq \ell_1, \ell_2$. For $i = 1, 2$, let τ_i be the formula

$\kappa_\ell > 0 \land \kappa'_\ell = \kappa_\ell \ominus 1 \land \kappa'_{\ell_i} = \kappa_{\ell_i} \oplus 1 \land \forall j \neq \ell, \ell_i : \kappa_j = \kappa'_j \land y' = f_i(y)$

where $x' = x \oplus 1$ is an abbreviation for: $x' = \min\{x + 1, 2\}$ and $x' = x \ominus 1$ is an abbreviation for: $x' = \max\{0, x - 1\}$. Then, we include in ρ^α the disjunction $c^\alpha \land \tau_1 \lor \neg c^\alpha \land \tau_2$.

Example 1 Fig. 3 presents graphically the FDS obtained by counter abstracting MUX-SEM, where each state displays the values assigned to the abstract variables $\kappa_0, \kappa_1, \kappa_2; Y$. To make the figure more compact, we removed states and transitions that occur only for small values of N (namely, for $N < 5$.) For example, all states where every κ_i is less than two (implying $N < 4$) is removed; so is the transition that leads from $\langle 2, 1, 1; 0 \rangle$ into $\langle 1, 2, 1; 0 \rangle$ (since it implies that $N = 4$.) The initial state is identified by an entry edge. Suppose c^α is defined and that $\ell \neq \ell_1, \ell_2$. For $i = 1, 2$, let τ_i be the formula

$\kappa_\ell > 0 \land \kappa'_\ell = \kappa_\ell \ominus 1 \land \kappa'_{\ell_i} = \kappa_{\ell_i} \oplus 1 \land \forall j \neq \ell, \ell_i : \kappa_j = \kappa'_j \land y' = f_i(y)$

where $x' = x \oplus 1$ is an abbreviation for: $x' = \min\{x + 1, 2\}$ and $x' = x \ominus 1$ is an abbreviation for: $x' = \max\{0, x - 1\}$. Then, we include in ρ^α the disjunction $c^\alpha \land \tau_1 \lor \neg c^\alpha \land \tau_2$.

We note that there are self loops on each of the states, which is to be expected considering we assume there is always an idle transition, and when there are self loops in the concrete systems, they also appear in the abstract system.

Establishing the safety property is now trivial, since the counter abstraction of the safety property $\varphi : \forall i \neq j : \Box \neg(\pi[i] = 2 \land \pi[j] = 2)$ is $\varphi^\alpha = \Box(\kappa_2 \leq 1)$, which trivially holds for MUX-SEM$^\alpha$.

3.2   Deriving Abstract Justice Requirements

Consider a single justice requirement of MUX-SEM J : $(\pi[i] \neq 2)$. The recipe in the previous section defines $J^\alpha = \alpha^+(J)$, which should encompass all abstract states S that have at least one α-source satisfying $\pi[i] \neq 2$. It is not difficult to see that this yields the abstract assertion $J^\alpha = \kappa_0 + \kappa_1 > 0$. Since, as can be seen from Fig. 3, all reachable states satisfy this assertion, J^α does not introduce any meaningful constraint on computations, and the counter abstraction of a system with the requirement J will be equivalent to the system without this requirement. It follows that any liveness property (such as accessibility) that is not valid for system MUX-SEM without the justice requirement J cannot be proven by an abstraction which only abstracts J into $\alpha^+(J)$.

We now develop a method by which stronger abstract justice requirements can be derived. Let φ be an abstract assertion, i.e., an assertion over the abstract state variables V_A. We say that φ *suppresses the concrete justice requirement* J if, for every two concrete states s_1 and s_2 such that s_2 is a ρ-successor of s_1, and both $\alpha(s_1)$ and $\alpha(s_2)$ satisfy φ, $s_1 \models \neg J$ implies $s_2 \models \neg J$.

For example, the abstract assertion $\varphi : \kappa_2 = 1$ suppresses the concrete justice requirement $J : \pi[i] \neq 2$. Indeed, assume two states s_1 and s_2 such that s_2 is a successor of s_1 and both are counter-abstracted into abstract states satisfying $\kappa_2 = 1$. This implies that both s_1 and s_2 have precisely one process executing at location 2. If s_1 satisfies $\neg J = (\pi[i] = 2)$ then the single process executing at location 2 within s_1 must be $P[i]$. Since s_2 is a successor of s_1 and also has a single process executing at location 2, it must also be the same process $P[i]$, because it is impossible for $P[i]$ to exit location 2 and another process to enter the same location all within a single transition.

The abstract assertion φ is defined to be *justice suppressing* if, for every concrete state s such that $\alpha(s) \models \varphi$, there exists a concrete justice requirement J such that $s \models \neg J$ and φ suppresses J.

For example, the assertion $\kappa_2 = 1$ is justice suppressing, because every concrete state s whose counter-abstraction satisfies $\kappa_2 = 1$ must have a single process, say $P[i]$, executing at location 2. In that case, s violates the justice requirement $J : \pi[i] \neq 2$ which is suppressed by φ.

Theorem 1. *Let $\mathcal{D}$ be a concrete system and α be an abstraction applied to $\mathcal{D}$. Assume that $\varphi_1, \ldots, \varphi_k$ is a list of justice suppressing abstract assertions. Let $\mathcal{D}^\alpha$ be the abstract system obtained by following the abstraction recipe described in Section 2 and then adding $\{\neg\varphi_1, \ldots, \neg\varphi_k\}$ to the set of abstract justice requirements. If $\mathcal{D}^\alpha \models \psi^\alpha$ then $\mathcal{D} \models \psi$.*

Thus, we can safely add $\{\neg\varphi_1, \ldots, \neg\varphi_k\}$ to the set of justice requirement, while preserving the soundness of the method.

The proof of the theorem is based on the observation that every abstraction of a concrete computation must contain infinitely many $\neg\varphi$-states for every justice suppressing assertion φ. Therefore, the abstract computations removed from the abstract system by the additional justice requirements can never correspond to abstractions of concrete computations, and it is safe to remove them.

Theorem 1 is very general (not even restricted to counter abstraction) but does not provide us with guidelines for the choice of the justice suppressing assertions. For the case of counter-abstraction, we can provide some practical guidelines, as follows:

G1. If the concrete system contains the justice requirements $\neg(\pi[i] = \ell)$, then the assertion $\kappa_\ell = 1$ is justice suppressing.
G2. If the concrete system contains the justice requirements $\neg(\pi[i] = \ell \wedge c)$, where c is a condition on the shared variables (that are kept intact by the counter-abstraction), then the assertion $\kappa_\ell = 1 \wedge c$ is justice suppressing.
G3. If the concrete system contains the justice requirements $\neg(\pi[i] = \ell)$ and the only possible move from location ℓ is to location $\ell + 1$, then the two assertions $\kappa_\ell > 0 \wedge \kappa_{\ell+1} = 0$ and $\kappa_\ell > 0 \wedge \kappa_{\ell+1} = 1$ are justice suppressing.
G4. If the concrete system contains the justice requirements $\neg(\pi[i] = \ell \wedge c)$, where c is a condition on the shared variables, and the only possible move from location ℓ is to location $\ell+1$, then the assertions $\kappa_\ell > 0 \wedge \kappa_{\ell+1} = 0 \wedge c$ and $\kappa_\ell > 0 \wedge \kappa_{\ell+1} = 1 \wedge c$ are justice suppressing.

Example 2 We state justice properties of MUX-SEM$^\alpha$ according to the above guidelines. Since for MUX-SEM we have the justice $\neg(\pi[i] = 2)$, and since every move from location 2 leads to location 0, then the assertions $\kappa_2 = 1$, $\kappa_2 > 0 \wedge \kappa_0 = 0$, and $\kappa_2 > 0 \wedge \kappa_0 = 1$ are all justice suppressing and their negation can be added to $\mathcal{J}^\alpha$. Similarly, the concrete compassion requirement $\langle \pi[i] = 1 \wedge y, \pi[i] = 2 \rangle$ implies that the concrete assertion $\neg(\pi[i] = 1 \wedge y)$ is a justice requirement for system MUX-SEM. We can therefore add $\neg(\kappa_1 = 1 \wedge y)$ to the abstract justice requirement. Since every move from location 1 leads to location 2, we can also add $\neg(\kappa_1 > 0 \wedge \kappa_2 = 0 \wedge y)$ to the abstract justice requirements.

Note: All justice requirements of MUX-SEM$^\alpha$ have been generated automatically by a general procedure implementing all the rules specified by the guidelines above.

3.3   Proving Liveness

The liveness property one usually associates with parameterized systems is *individual accessibility* of the form $\forall i : \Box(\pi[i] = \ell_1 \rightarrow \Diamond(\pi[i] = \ell_2))$. Unfortunately, counter-abstraction does not allow us to observe the behavior of an individual process. Therefore, the property of individual accessibility cannot be expressed (and, consequently, verified) in a counter-abstracted system. In Section 3.4 we show how to extend counter-abstraction to handle individual accessibility properties.

There are, however, liveness properties that *are* expressible and verifiable by counter abstraction. Such are *livelock freedom* (sometime called *communal accessibility*) properties of the form $\psi : \Box(\exists i : \pi[i] = \ell_1 \rightarrow \Diamond(\exists i : \pi[i] = \ell_2))$, stating that if *some* process is at location ℓ_1, then eventually *some* process (not

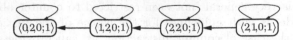

Fig. 4. Reachability graph for χ

necessarily the same) will enter ℓ_2. The counter-abstraction of such a property is $\psi^\alpha : \; \Box(\kappa_{\ell_1} > 0 \rightarrow \Diamond(\kappa_{\ell_2} > 0))$. Model checking that ψ^α holds over Sys^α can be accomplished by standard model checking techniques of response properties. E.g., the procedure in [16] suggests extracting from the state-transition graph of the subgraph of *pending states* and showing that it contains no infinite fair path. A pending state for a property $p \rightarrow \Diamond q$ is any state which is reachable from a p-state by a q-free path.

Example 3 Consider the system MUX-SEM$^\alpha$ of Fig. 3 and the abstract live-lock freedom property $\chi : \Box(\kappa_1 > 0 \rightarrow \Diamond(\kappa_2 > 0))$. In Fig. 4, we present the subgraph of pending states for the property χ over the system MUX-SEM$^\alpha$.

The way we show that this graph contains no infinite fair path is to decompose the graph into maximal strongly connected components and show that each of them is *unjust*. A strongly connected subgraph (SCC) S is unjust if there exists a justice requirement which is violated by all states within the subgraph. In the case of the graph in Fig. 4 there are four maximal SCC's. Each of these subgraphs is unjust towards the abstract justice requirement $\neg(\kappa_1 > 0 \;\wedge\; \kappa_2 = 0 \;\wedge\; y)$ derived in Example 2.

We conclude that the abstract property $\Box(\kappa_1 > 0 \rightarrow \Diamond(\kappa_2 > 0))$ is valid over system MUX-SEM$^\alpha$ and, therefore, the property $\Box(\exists i : \pi[i] = 1 \rightarrow \Diamond(\exists i : \pi[i] = 2))$ is valid over MUX-SEM.

3.4   Proving Individual Accessibility

As indicated before, individual accessibility cannot be directly verified by standard counter abstraction which cannot observe individual processes. To prove individual accessibility for the generic process $P[t]$, we abstract the system by counter abstracting all the processes except for $P[t]$, whom we leave intact. We then prove that the abstracted system satisfies the liveness property (the abstraction of which leaves it unchanged, since it refers to $\pi[t]$ that is kept intact by the abstraction), from which we derive that the concrete system satisfies it as well.

The new abstraction, called "counter abstraction save one", is denoted by γ. As before, we assume for simplicity that the processes possess no local variables except for their program counter. The abstract variables for γ are given by $\kappa_0, \ldots, \kappa_L : [0..2], \Pi : [0..L]; Y_1, \ldots, Y_b$ and for the abstraction mapping $\mathcal{E}^\gamma$ we have $\Pi = \pi[t], Y_k = y_k$ for $k = 1, \ldots, b$, and

$$\kappa_\ell = \left\{ \begin{array}{l} 0 \text{ if } \forall r \neq t : \pi[r] \neq \ell \\ 1 \text{ if } \exists r \neq t : \pi[r] = \ell \;\wedge\; \forall j \notin \{r,t\} : \pi[t] \neq \ell \\ 2 \text{ otherwise} \end{array} \right\} \text{ for } \ell \in [0..L]$$

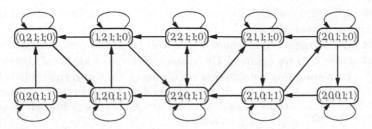

Fig. 5. The states of MUX-SEM$^\gamma$ which are pending with respect to φ

We obtain ρ^γ in the obvious way. For $\mathcal{J}^\gamma$, we include all the justice requirements obtained by the recipe of [14] and the guidelines of Subsection 3.2, with all requirements in $\mathcal{J}$ that relate to $P[t]$. For $\mathcal{C}^\gamma$ we take all the requirements in $\mathcal{C}$ that relate only to $P[t]$. To prove $\varphi : \Box(\Pi = 1 \rightarrow \Diamond(\Pi = 2))$, consider the subgraph of S^γ that consists of all the abstract states that are reachable from a $(\Pi = 1)$-state by a $(\Pi = 2)$-free paths, and show, as before, that this subgraph contains no infinite fair path.

Example 4 Consider the system MUX-SEM$^\gamma$ and the liveness property φ^γ given by $\Box((\Pi = 1) \rightarrow \Diamond(\Pi = 2))$. The subgraph of pending states is presented in Fig. 5. Each state in this graph is labeled by a tuple which specifies the values assigned by the state variables $\langle \kappa_0, \kappa_1, \kappa_2; \Pi; Y \rangle$.

Unlike the previous case, this system has the compassion requirement $\langle \Pi = 1 \land Y, \Pi - 2 \rangle$ associated with $P[t]$. After removing from the graph all states satisfying $\Pi = 1 \land Y$, it is easy to see that no infinite fair paths are left. We can thus conclude that the abstract property $\Box((\Pi = 1) \rightarrow \Diamond(\Pi = 2))$ is valid over MUX-SEM$^\gamma$ and, therefore, $\Box((\pi[t] = 1) \rightarrow \Diamond(\pi[t] = 2))$ is valid over MUX-SEM.

4   Compassion

In Section 3.2 we showed how to derive additional justice requirements for a counter-abstracted system. We now turn to abstract compassion requirements, which do not always correspond to concrete compassion requirements. Here we derive abstract compassion requirements which reflect well-founded properties of some of the concrete data domains. Consider program TERMINATE presented in Fig. 6(a).

The liveness property we would like to establish for this program is given by the formula $\varphi : \Diamond(\forall i : \pi[i] = 1)$, stating that eventually, all processes reach location 1. The counter abstraction for TERMINATE, (assuming $N > 2$), is TERMINATE$^\alpha$, presented in Fig. 6(b), where each state s is labeled by the values state s assigns to the abstract variables κ_0 and κ_1. The abstracted property φ^α is given by $\Diamond(\kappa_0 = 0)$. However, this property is not valid over TERMINATE$^\alpha$, even when we take into account all the justice requirements derived according to Subsection 3.2. These justice requirements force the computation to eventually exit states $\langle 2, 0 \rangle$, $\langle 2, 1 \rangle$, and $\langle 1, 2 \rangle$, but they do not prevent the computation from staying forever in state $\langle 2, 2 \rangle$.

To obtain a fairness requirement which will force the computation to eventually exit state $\langle 2, 2 \rangle$ we augment the system with two additional abstract variables and a corresponding compassion requirement that governs their behavior.

Let $Sys : \langle V, \Theta, \rho, \mathcal{J}, \mathcal{C} \rangle$ be an FDS representing a concrete parameterized system, where the locations of each process are $[0..L]$. We define an *augmented system* $\mathcal{D}^* : \langle V^*, \Theta^*, \rho^*, \mathcal{J}^*, \mathcal{C}^* \rangle$ as follows:

$$V^* : V \cup \{from, to : [-1..L]\}$$
$$\Theta^* : \Theta \wedge (from = -1) \wedge (to = -1)$$
$$\rho^* : \rho \wedge \left(\begin{array}{c} \exists i : [1..N], \ell_1 \neq \ell_2 : [0..L] : \pi[i] = \ell_1 \wedge \pi'[i] = \ell_2 \wedge \\ (from' = \ell_1) \wedge (to' = \ell_2) \\ \vee \forall i : [1..N] : \pi'[i] = \pi[i] \wedge (from' = -1) \wedge (to' = -1) \end{array} \right)$$
$$\mathcal{J}^* : \mathcal{J}$$
$$\mathcal{C}^* : \mathcal{C} \cup \{\langle from = \ell, to = \ell \rangle \mid \ell \in [0..L]\}$$

Thus, system Sys is augmented with two auxiliary variables, *from* and *to*. Whenever a transition causes some process to move from location ℓ_1 to location $\ell_2 \neq \ell_1$, the same transition sets *from* to ℓ_1 and *to* to ℓ_2. Transitions that cause no process to change its location set both *from* and *to* to -1. For every $\ell \in [0..L]$, we add to Sys^* the compassion requirement $\langle from = \ell, to = \ell \rangle$. This compassion requirement represents the obvious fact that, since the overall number of processes is bounded (by N), processes cannot leave location ℓ infinitely many times without processes entering location ℓ infinitely many times.

Comparing the observable behavior of Sys and Sys^*, we can prove the following:

Claim. Let σ be an infinite sequence of V-states. Then σ is a computation of Sys iff it is a V-projection of a computation of system Sys^*.

Thus, the augmentation of Sys does not change its observable behavior.

Consequently, instead of counter-abstracting the system Sys, we can counter-abstract Sys^*. We denote by $Sys^\dagger = (Sys^*)^\alpha$ the counter abstraction of the augmented system Sys^*. In the presence of the auxiliary variable *from*, we can derive

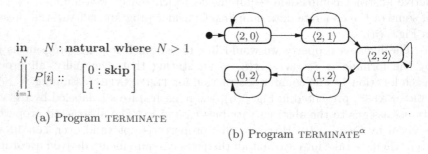

(a) Program TERMINATE

(b) Program TERMINATE$^\alpha$

Fig. 6. Program TERMINATE and its counter abstraction

an even sharper justice requirements and replace the guidelines of Subsection 3.2 by the following single rule:

G5. If the concrete system contains the justice requirements $\neg(\pi[i] = \ell \wedge c)$, where c is a condition on the shared variables and process indices other than i, then we may add to $Sys^\dagger$ the justice requirement $from = \ell \vee \neg(\kappa_\ell > 0 \wedge c^\alpha)$, where c^α is the counter abstraction of c.

Reconsider program TERMINATE. Applying the augmented abstraction, we obtain the following abstraction TERMINATE†, where each state s is labeled by the values s assigns to the variables $\langle \kappa_0, \kappa_1, from, to \rangle$ ($-$ stands for -1):

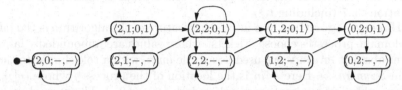

This system is augmented by the additional justice requirement $(from = 0) \vee (\kappa_0 = 0)$ (generated according to G5) and the compassion requirement $\langle from = 0, to = 0 \rangle$.

Taking into account the new justice requirement $(from = 0) \vee (\kappa_0 = 0)$, and the new compassion requirement $\langle from = 0, to = 0 \rangle$, it is easy to see that the program admits no infinite fair paths. It follows that TERMINATE† satisfies $\Diamond(\kappa_0 = 0)$ and, therefore, that the concrete system TERMINATE satisfies $\forall i : \Diamond(\pi[i] \neq 0)$.

5   Examples

We briefly describe two of our test cases: Szymanski's mutual exclusion algorithm [23], described in Fig. 7(a), and the Bakery algorithm, described in Fig. 7(b). The complete FDSs and codes for the test cases are omitted from here for space reasons and can be found in *http://cs.nyu.edu/~zuck/counter*.

Szymanski's Algorithm. Strictly speaking, the algorithm is not symmetric since the instruction in ℓ_6 depends on the id of the executing process. To prove mutual exclusion with a counter abstraction, it was necessary to add an additional abstract variable *lmin* to the abstraction. This variable maintains the location of the process with the minimal index among those in 3..7; *lmin* is 0 when there are no processes in locations 3..7. Once the abstraction mapping of this variable is defined, the abstract transition relation can be automatically computed. Using this abstraction we were able to verify the property of mutual exclusion of the system.

To facilitate the proof of the livelock freedom property $\chi : (\exists i : \pi[i] = 1) \rightarrow \Diamond(\exists i : \pi[i] = 7)$, the abstract system szyman† contains the abstract justice requirements $from = \ell \vee \neg En(\tau)$ for each abstract transition τ departing from location $\ell \neq 0$, where $En(\tau)$ is the enabling condition for τ. Consider, for example, the transition corresponding to a process moving from location 6 to location 7. The enabling condition for the corresponding abstract transition is $\kappa_6 > 0 \,\wedge\, lmin = 6$. Consequently, we include in the abstract FDS the justice requirement $from = 6 \,\vee\, \neg(\kappa_6 > 0 \,\wedge\, lmin = 6)$. In addition, we include in the abstract system the compassion requirements $\langle from = \ell, to = \ell \rangle$, for each $\ell = 0, \ldots, 7$. We were able to verify χ. Note that the auxiliary variable $lmin$ is not required for establishing livelock freedom.

To prove individual accessibility, we applied γ abstraction to szyman*. Some bookkeeping was needed to maintain the value of $lmin$, that was used, as before, to store the location of the non-t process whose index is minimal among those in locations 3..7 (including t.)

The Bakery Algorithm. An interesting feature of the algorithm is the infinite data domain–processes choose "tickets" whose values are unboundedly large. To counter abstract BAKERY, we used a variable $lmin$, with a role similar to the one used in *Szymanski*. Here $lmin$ is the location of the process j whose $(y[j], j)$ is (lexicographically) minimal among those in locations 2..4. The mutual exclusion property of the protocol, $\Box(\kappa_4 < 2)$, as well as the livelock freedom property, $\Box(\kappa_1 > 0 \to \Diamond(\kappa_4 > 0))$ were easily established in TLV (the Weizmann Institute programmable model checker [21]). To establish the individual accessibility property, $\pi[t] = 1 \to \Diamond(\pi[t] = 4)$, we applied γ abstraction to BAKERY*. As in the case of *Szymanski*, some bookkeeping was needed to maintain the value of $lmin$, that was used, as before, to store the location of the non-t process whose index is minimal among those in locations 2..4 (including t.)

Run Time Results In Fig. 8 we give the user run-time (in seconds) results of our various experiments. All verifications were carried in TLV.

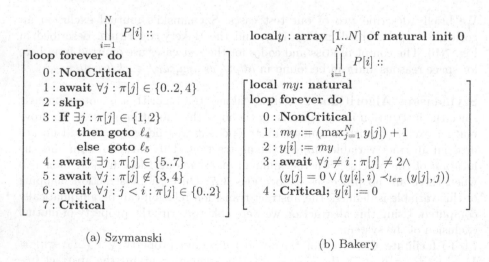

(a) Szymanski

(b) Bakery

Fig. 7. Szymanski's and the Bakery Mutual Exclusion Algorithms

	MUX-SEM (sec)	szyman (sec)	BAKERY (sec)
Mutual Exclusion and Livelock Freedom	0.02	0.69	0.12
Mutual Exclusion and Individual Accessibility (γ abstraction)	0.03	95.87	1.06

Fig. 8. Run time results

6 Conclusions

We have presented the abstraction method of *counter abstraction*. The main novelty and contribution is the derivation of additional fairness conditions (both weak and strong) which enable us to perform automatic verification of interesting liveness properties of non-trivial parameterized systems.

References

1. K. R. Apt and D. Kozen. Limits for automatic program verification of finite-state concurrent systems. *IPL*, 22(6), 1986. 109
2. T. Arons, A. Pnueli, S. Ruah, J. Xu, and L. Zuck. Parameterized verification with automatically computed inductive assertions. In *CAV'01*, pages 221–234, 2001. 111
3. K. Baukus, Y. Lakhnesche, and K. Stahl. Verification of parameterized protocols. *Journal of Universal Computer Science*, 7(2):141–158, 2001. 108, 109
4. N. Bjørner, I. Browne, and Z. Manna. Automatic generation of invariants and intermediate assertions. In 1st *Intl. Conf. on Principles and Practice of Constraint Programming*, volume 976 of *LNCS*, pages 589–623. Springer-Verlag, 1995. 108
5. E. Clarke, O. Grumberg, and S. Jha. Verifying parametrized networks using abstraction and regular languages. In *CONCUR'95*, pages 395–407, 1995. 109
6. P. Cousot and R. Cousot. Abstract interpretation: A unified lattice model for static analysis of programs by construction or approximation of fixpoints. In *POPL'77*. ACM Press, 1977. 108, 111
7. E. Emerson and V. Kahlon. Reducing model checking of the many to the few. In *17th International Conference on Automated Deduction (CADE-17)*, pages 236–255, 2000. 109
8. E. A. Emerson and K. S. Namjoshi. Reasoning about rings. In *POPL'95*, 1995. 109
9. E. Gribomont and G. Zenner. Automated verification of szymanski's algorithm. In B. Steffen, editor, *TACAS'98*, pages 424–438, 1998. 109
10. V. Gyuris and A. P. Sistla. On-the-fly model checking under fairness that exploits symmetry. In *CAV'97*, 1997. 109
11. J. Henriksen, J. Jensen, M. Jørgensen, N. Klarlund, B. Paige, T. Rauhe, and A. Sandholm. Mona: Monadic second-order logic in practice. In *TACAS'95*, 1995. 113
12. B. Jonsson and M. Nilsson. Transitive closures of regular relations for verifying infinite-state systems. In *TACAS'00*, 2000. 109
13. Y. Kesten, O. Maler, M. Marcus, A. Pnueli, and E. Shahar. Symbolic model checking with rich assertional languages. In *CAV'97*, pages 424–435, 1997. 113

14. Y. Kesten and A. Pnueli. Control and data abstractions: The cornerstones of practical formal verification. *Software Tools for Technology Transfer*, 4(2):328–342, 2000. 107, 109, 111, 112, 117

15. D. Lesens, N. Halbwachs, and P. Raymond. Automatic verification of parameterized linear networks of processes. In *POPL'97*, Paris, 1997. 109

16. O. Lichtenstein and A. Pnueli. Checking that finite-state concurrent programs satisfy their linear specification. In *POPL'85*, pages 97–107, 1985. 116

17. B. D. Lubachevsky. An approach to automating the verification of compact parallel coordination programs. *Acta Infromatica*, 21, 1984. 108, 112

18. Z. Manna, A. Anuchitanukul, N. Bjørner, A. Browne, E. Chang, M. Colón, L. D. Alfaro, H. Devarajan, H. Sipma, and T. Uribe. STeP: The Stanford Temporal Prover. Technical Report STAN-CS-TR-94-1518, Dept. of Comp. Sci., Stanford University, Stanford, California, 1994. 109

19. Z. Manna and A. Pnueli. *Temporal Verification of Reactive Systems: Safety.* Springer-Verlag, New York, 1995. 109, 110

20. K. McMillan. Verification of an implementation of Tomasulo's algorithm by compositional model checking. In *CAV'98*, pages 110–121, 1998. 109

21. A. Pnueli and E. Shahar. A platform for combining deductive with algorithmic verification. In *CAV'96*, pages 184–195, 1996. 120

22. F. Pong and M. Dubois. A new approach for the verification of cache coherence protocols. *IEEE Transactions on Parallel and Distributed Systems*, 6(8):773–787, Aug. 1995. 112

23. B. K. Szymanski. A simple solution to Lamport's concurrent programming problem with linear wait. In *Proc. 1988 International Conference on Supercomputing Systems*, pages 621–626, St. Malo, France, 1988. 119

Shared Memory Consistency Protocol Verification Against Weak Memory Models: Refinement via Model-Checking*

Prosenjit Chatterjee, Hemanthkumar Sivaraj, and Ganesh Gopalakrishnan

School of Computing, University of Utah
{prosen,hemanth,ganesh}@cs.utah.edu
http://www.cs.utah.edu/formal_verification/cav02.html

Abstract. *Weak shared memory consistency models*, especially those used by modern microprocessor families, are quite complex. The bus and/or directory-based protocols that help realize shared memory multiprocessors using these microprocessors are also exceedingly complex. Thus, the *correctness problem* – that all the executions generated by the multiprocessor for any given concurrent program are also allowed by the memory model – is a major challenge. In this paper, we present a formal approach to verify protocol implementation models against weak shared memory models through automatable *refinement checking* supported by a *model checker*. We define a taxonomy of weak shared memory models that includes most published commercial memory models, and detail how our approach applies over all these models. In our approach, the designer follows a prescribed procedure to build a highly simplified intermediate abstraction for the given implementation. The intermediate abstraction and the implementation are concurrently run using a model-checker, checking for refinement. The intermediate abstraction can be proved correct against the memory model specification using theorem proving. We have verified four different Alpha as well as Itanium memory model implementations[1] against their respective specifications. The results are encouraging in terms of the uniformity of the procedure, the high degree of automation, acceptable run-times, and empirically observed bug-hunting efficacy. The use of parallel model-checking, based on a version of the parallel Murφ model checker we have recently developed for the MPI library, has been essential to finish the search in a matter of a few hours.

1 Introduction

Modern weak shared memory consistency models [1,2,3,4] allow subtle reorderings among *load*s and *store*s falling into multiple storage classes to permit aggressive compiler optimizations, hide load latencies, and maintain I/O semantics

---

* This work was supported by NSF Grants CCR-9987516 and CCR-0081406

[1] We designed both these protocols - one with a split-transaction bus and one with Scheurich's optimization - as there are no public domain Itanium protocols as far as we know.

D. Brinksma and K. G. Larsen (Eds.): CAV 2002, LNCS 2404, pp. 123–136, 2002.
© Springer-Verlag Berlin Heidelberg 2002

as well as legacy compatibility. Since these specifications are the basis for many generations of microprocessors, manufacturers are committed to formal methods for specifying them. Unfortunately, simple and intuitive formal specification methods that apply across a wide range of weak memory models are yet to be developed. In this paper, we address this problem and propose a parameterizable operational model that can cover a wide range of modern weak memory models. The bus and/or directory-based protocols that help realize shared memory multiprocessors using modern microprocessors are also exceedingly complex. Thus, in addition to the specification problem, formal verification of shared memory consistency protocols against weak shared memory models remains largely unsolved [2,]. Most reported successes have been either for far simpler memory models such as cache coherence or sequential consistency (e.g., [, , ,]), or approaches that took advantage of existing architectural test program suites and created finite-state abstractions for them [10].

In this paper, we present a methodology that systematically applies to a wide spectrum of weak architectural memory consistency models. Basically, we instantiate our parameterizable operational model to obtain a finite-state approximation to the weak memory model of interest. We then take the finite-state model of the protocol under verification, and subject these models to 'lockstep' execution, to check for a simulation (refinement) relation: whether an event that can be fired on the interface of the implementation can be accepted by the specification. The execution happens within the explicit-state enumeration model-checker Murφ that we have recently ported to run on our in-house Network Testbed[2] using the MPI library. We demonstrate our results on four different Alpha as well as Itanium memory model implementations against their respective specifications. The results are encouraging in terms of reduced effort, potential for reuse of models, the degree of automation, run-times, and bug-hunting efficacy (it found many subtle coding errors). To the best of our knowledge, no other group has hitherto verified this variety of protocols against modern weak memory models.

Approach to Verification: Instead of using a model-checker to verify a temporal logic formula, we use it to check for the existence of a refinement mapping between an implementation model and an abstract model. While operational models are well suited for this purpose, if they are non-deterministic, an inefficient backtracking search would be needed. To illustrate this difficulty, consider one source of internal non-determinism - namely *local bypassing* (otherwise known as *read forwarding*). Local bypassing allows a *load* to pick its value straight out of the store buffer, as opposed to allowing the store to post globally, and then reading the global store. Consider the operational-style specification of a memory model, such as the one illustrated in Figure 1(b) (the details of this figure are not important for our illustration). Consider one such model M_1, and make an *identical copy* calling it M_2. Let the external events of M_1 and M_2 (its alphabet) be *load* and *store*. Certainly we expect M_2 to refine M_1. However, both M_2

---

[2] http://www.emulab.net

and M_1 can have different executions starting off with a common prefix, signifying non-determinism. For instance, if P1 runs program $store(a, 1)$; $load(a)$, and P2 runs program $load(a)$, one execution of M_1 obtained by annotating *loads* with the returned values is

Exec1 $= P1 : store(a, 1)$; $P1 : load(a, 1)$; $P2 : load(a, 1)$

while an execution of the M_2 is

Exec2 $= P1 : store(a, 1)$; $P1 : load(a, 1)$; $P2 : load(a, \top)$,

where $\top$ is the initial value of a memory location. Note that Exec2 exercises the bypass option while Exec1 didn't do so. However such bypass events are invisible in high-level operational models that employ only the external *loads* and *stores*. Therefore, in the above example, even though the *load* values disagreed, we cannot throw an error, but must backtrack and search another internal execution path. However, by enriching the alphabet of our example to $\Sigma' = \{store_{p1}(a, 1), store_g(a, 1), load(a, 1), load(a, \top)\}$, where $store_{p1}$ refers to the store being visible to P1 and $store_g$ refers to the store being visible globally (these being internal events), Exec1 and Exec2 can be elaborated into Exec1' and Exec2', and these executions do not disagree on *load* after a common prefix:

Exec1' $= P1 : store_{p1}(a, 1)$; $P1 : load(a, 1)$; $store_g(a, 1)$; $P2 : load(a, 1)$,

Exec2' $= P1 : store_{p1}(a, 1)$; $P1 : load(a, 1)$; $P2 : load(a, \top)$; $store_g(a, 1)$.

In general, there are many sources to non-determinism than just local bypassing, and all of them must be determinized, essentially resulting in a situation where each *load* is associated with a *unique* past store event. In Section 6, we sketch how this approach can be applied to a wide range of weak memory models. In Section 2, we illustrate the visibility order approach on the Alpha memory model. The use of internal events in writing specifications is, fortunately, already accepted in practice (e.g., [2,3,11]). Most approaches in this area specify the so called *visibility order* of executions in terms of the enriched alphabet.

Creating *Imp*, *Imp_{abs}*, and the *Spec* Models: In our approach, verification is divided into two distinct phases. First, an intermediate abstraction Imp_{abs} which highly simplifies the implementation Imp is created, and Imp is verified against it through model-checking. Next, Imp_{abs} is verified against $Spec$, the visibility-order based specification of the memory model. We believe (as we will demonstrate) that Phase 1 can in itself be used as a very effective bug-hunting tool. Phase 2 can be conducted using theorem-proving, similar to [12], as detailed on our webpage. This paper is mostly about Phase 1. For a large class of implementations, Phase 2 does not vary, as the same Imp_{abs} results from all these implementations, thus permitting verification reuse. In fact, most Imp_{abs} models we end up creating are the same as *operational style* models, such as the UltraSparc operational model of [13] or the Itanium operational model [4]. We also expect the designer who creates Imp to be annotating it with internal events. However, since such annotations are designer assertions as to when (they think) the internal events are happening, it should be something a designer who has studied the visibility order $Spec$ must be able to do.

The creation of Imp_{abs} is based on the following observation. Most proto-col implementations possess two distinct partitions: a small *internal* partition containing the *load* and *store* buffers, and a *much larger external* partition. containing the *cache, main memory*, and the (multiple) buses and directories (see Section 3 for an illustration). For a wide spectrum of memory models, Imp_{abs} is obtained by retaining the internal partition and replacing the external partition by a highly simplified operational structure which, in most cases, is a single-port memory (see Section 4 for an illustration). This approach also enables consis-tent annotation of the internal and external partitions of Imp and Imp_{abs} with events from the enriched alphabet. Another significant advantage is that we can *share* the internal partition during model-checking, explained as follows.

Why Sharing the Internal Partition is Possible: A specification state is a pair $\langle spec\_int\_part, spec\_ext\_part \rangle$ and an implementation state is a pair $\langle imp\_int\_part, imp\_ext\_part \rangle$. Typically, all the 'int_part's and 'ext_part's are bit-vectors of hundreds of bits. Let $\langle i_i, i_e \rangle$ be an implementation state and let $\langle s_i, s_e \rangle$ be the corresponding specification state (starting with the respective initial states). The state vector maintained during reachability is $\langle i_i, i_e, s_i, s_e \rangle$. We then select an eligible external event e from the enriched external alpha-bet and perform it on the implementation, advancing the verification state to $\langle i_i', i_e', s_i, s_e \rangle$. This state is *not* stored. If the same event e cannot be performed on the specification, an error-trace is generated; else, it is performed and the state is advanced to $\langle i_i', i_e', s_i', s_e' \rangle$. Since we can retain the same internal partition, i_i' and s_i' are always the same - and so we can share their bits, reducing the state vector to $\langle i_i', i_e', s_e' \rangle$. To sum up, since we do not multiply out states, the number of states generated during reachability is the *same* as the number of reachable states in the implementation model, and the state-vector size grows only by s_e.

Handling Protocols where the Temporal and Logical Orders Differ: In many aggressive protocols, the *logical* order of events (the "explanation") is dif-ferent from the *temporal* order in which the protocol performs these events. Con-sider an optimization described by Scheurich in the context of an invalidation-based directory protocol. In the unoptimized version, a store request sent to the directory causes invalidations to be sent to each read-shared copy. The store can proceed only after the invalidations have been performed. Under the optimiza-tion, read-sharers merely queue the invalidations, sending "fake" acknowledge-ments back to the directory, and perform the invalidations only later. Thus, even after a processor P_1 writes new data to the line, a *ld* from some other proces-sor P_2 to the same cache line can read stale data. Thus, in the logical order, the new stores must be situated after the loads, even though in temporal order, the store is done before the loads on the stale lines. Such issues are not addressed in most prior work. The creation of the intermediate abstraction Imp_{abs} helps us partition our concerns [14]. Details appear on our webpage.

Handling Protocols with Large State-Spaces: Shared memory consistency protocols can easily have several billions of states, with global dependencies caused by pointers and directory entries that defy compact representation using BDDs. We find the use of a parallel model-checker almost essential to make things practical. In some cases, we aborted runs that took more than 55 hours (due to thrashing) on sequential model-checkers on machines with 1GB memory, when they finished in less than a few hours on our parallel model-checker.

Summary of Results: We applied our method to an implementation of the Alpha processor [15] that was modeled after a multiprocessor using the Compaq (DEC) Alpha 21264 microprocessor. The cache coherence protocol is a Gigaplane-like split transaction bus [16] protocol. We also verify an Alpha implementation with an underlying cache coherence protocol using multiple interleaved buses, modeled after the Sun $Ultra^{TM}$ $Enterprise^{TM}$ 10000 [17]. Both these implementations were verified with and without Scheurich's optimization. These four Alpha processor protocols finished in anywhere between 54 to 240 minutes on 16 processors, visiting up to 250 million states. The diameter of the reachability graph (indicating the highest degree of attainable parallelism if one cuts the graph along its diameter and distributes it) was in excess of 5,000. The highest numbers reported in [18] using their *original* Parallel $Mur\varphi$ on the Stanford FLASH as well as the SCI protocols were around 1 million states and a diameter of 50. While designer insight is required in selecting the external partition, the effort is not *case* specific, but instead *class* specific. As shown in Section 6, we can taxonomize memory models into four categories, and once and for all develop external partitions for each branch of the taxonomy. Designer insight is required in attaching events to the abstract model. The "final property" verified in our approach is quite simple: to reiterate, it is that the loads completing in the implementation and specification models return the same data. We therefore think that our method has the right ingredients for being scaled up towards considerably more aggressive protocols - including directory protocols.

Related Work: See [1] for a survey and [5] for a recent workshop. We showed how to port Collier's architectural testing work [19] to model-checking [10] and extend Collier's work to weak memory models [20]. In [21], event sequences generated by protocol implementations are verified by a much simpler trustworthy protocol processor. In [22,23], shared memory consistency models are described in an operational style. In [6], sequential consistency verification, including parameterized model-checking is addressed. To our knowledge, we are the first to verify eight different protocols against two different weak memory models using a uniform approach. While we model "only" two processors, memory locations, as well as data values, we end-up getting trillions of transitions. We believe that before we can attempt parameterized verification, we must conquer the complexity of these "small" instance verifications. Weak memory models for Java are also under active study [24,25].

2 Alpha Memory Model Specification

A concurrent shared memory Alpha program is viewed as a set of sequences of instructions, one sequence per processor. Each sequence captures *program order* at that processor. An *execution* obtained by running the shared memory program is similar to the program itself, except that each *load(a)* now becomes *load(a,return_value)*. Every instruction in an execution can be decomposed into one or two[3] *events* (*local* and *global* in the latter case; in the former case, we shall use the words 'instruction' and 'event' synonymously). Each event t is defined as a tuple (p, l, o, a, d) where $p(t)$ is the processor in whose program t originates from, $l(t)$ is the label of instruction t in p's program, $o(t)$ is the event type (load/store/etc.), $a(t)$ is the memory address, and $d(t)$ the data. All instructions except st are decomposed into exactly one event. Each st is decomposed into a st_{local} and a st_{global}. An *execution* obeys Alpha memory model if all the memory events of the *execution* form at least one total order which obeys the *Per Processor Order* stipulated by the memory model, and the *Read Value* Rule stipulated by the memory model. In addition, the st_{global} events must form a total order. (Note that this total order may not respect program order of st instructions.) The *Read Value Rule* specifies the data value to be returned by the load events in an execution. The *Per Processor Order* respects both program order as well as data dependence. The fact that st_{global} operations form a single total order is modeled by generating only 'one copy' of a st_{global} event corresponding to each st instruction, and situating the st_{global} events in the total order '$\rightarrow$'. Since Alpha allows local bypassing, we split any store instruction t into two events t^{local} and t^{global} (and also create the corresponding tuples) where $o(t^{local})=st_{local}$ and $o(t^{global})=st_{global}$. More specifically, an execution satisfies the Alpha memory model if there exists a logical total order '$\rightarrow$' of all the ld, st_{local} and st_{global} events and memory fence events present in the execution, such that '$\rightarrow$' satisfies the following clauses:

1. *Per Processor Order*: Let t_1 and t_2 be two events s.t $p(t_1) = p(t_2)$, $l(t_1) < l(t_2)$ (t_1 appears earlier in program order than t_2).
   (a) If $a(t_1) = a(t_2)$ and,
       i. $o(t_1) = st_{local}$, $o(t_2) = ld$, or
       ii. $o(t_1) = ld$, $o(t_2) = st_{local}$, or
       iii. $o(t_1) = st_{local}$, $o(t_2) = st_{local}$,
       iv. $o(t_1) = ld$, $o(t_2) = ld$, or
       v. $o(t_1) = st_{global}$, $o(t_2) = st_{global}$
       then $t_1 \rightarrow t_2$.
   (b) If there exists a fence(MB) instruction t_f s.t. $l(t_1) < l(t_f) < l(t_2)$ then $t_1 \rightarrow t_2$.
2. *Read Value*: This definition follows the style in which *Read Value* is defined in [1] for TSO. Formally, let t_1 be a load (ld) event. Then the data value of t_1 is the data value of the most recent local event, if present; if not, it

---

[3] In general, as discussed later, there could be more events.

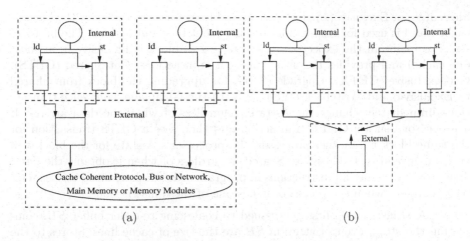

(a)   (b)

Fig. 1. (a) The alpha implementation model, and (b) The alpha intermediate abstraction

is the most recent global store event (in the total order relation $\rightarrow$) to the same memory location as t_1. *i.e.*,

(a) if
  i. $p(t_1) = p(t_2), a(t_1) = a(t_2), t_2^{local} \rightarrow t_1 \rightarrow t_2^{global}$ and
  ii. there does not exist a st instruction t_3 s.t $p(t_1) = p(t_3), a(t_1) = a(t_3)$ and $t_2^{local} \rightarrow t_3^{local} \rightarrow t_1$.
  then $d(t_1) = d(t_2^{local})$;

(b) else if
  i. $a(t_1) = a(t_2)$, $t_2^{global} \rightarrow t_1$ and
  ii. there does not exist a st instruction t_3 s.t $a(t_1) = a(t_3)$ and $t_2^{global} \rightarrow t_3^{global} \rightarrow t_1$.
  then $d(t_1) = d(t_2^{global})$;

(c) else, $d(t_1)$ is the "initial memory value" (taken to be $\top$ in our paper).

3   Alpha Implementation Model

In the Alpha implementation of each processor is separated from its cache (situated in the external partition) with a coalescing re-order store buffer SB and a re-order read buffer RB (situated in the internal partition). Caches are kept coherent with a write-invalidate coherence protocol [11]. The data structure of caches is a two dimensional array C where, for event t, $C[p(t)][a(t)].a$ refers to data value of address $a(t)$ at processor $p(t)$, and $C[p(t)][a(t)].st$ refers to its address state (A-state)[4]. We begin with a brief explanation of our memory consistency protocol. This protocol is the same as the one used in [16] to describe a Gigaplane-like split-transaction bus. Memory blocks may be cached Invalid(I),

---

[4] We overload the selectors ".a" and ".st" for notational brevity.

Shared(S), or Exclusive(E). The A-state (address state) records how the block is cached and is used for responding to subsequent bus transactions. The protocol seeks to maintain the expected invariants (e.g, a block is Exclusive in at most one cache) and provides the usual coherent transactions: Get-Shared (GETS), Get-Exclusive (GETX), Upgrade (UPG, for upgrading the block from Shared to Exclusive) and Writeback (WB). As with the Gigaplane, coherence transactions immediately change the A-state, regardless of when the data arrives. If a processor issues a GETX transaction and then sees a GETS transaction for the same block by another processor, the processor's A-state for the block will go from Invalid to Exclusive to Shared, regardless of when it obtains the data. The processor issues all instructions in program order. Below, we specify exactly what happens when the processor issues one of these instructions.

1. st: A st instruction first gets issued to coalescing re-order buffer SB, completing the st_{local} event. Entries in SB are the size of cache lines. Stores to the same cache line are coalesced in the same entry and if two stores write to the same word, the corresponding entry will hold the value written by the store that was issued later. Entries are eventually deleted (flushed) from SB to the cache, although not necessarily in the order in which they were issued to the write buffer. Before deleting, the processor first makes sure there is no earlier issued ld instruction to the same address pending in RB (if any, those RB instructions must be completed before deleting that entry from SB). It then checks if the corresponding block's A-state is Exclusive(E). If not, the coherence protocol is invoked to change the A-state to E. Once in E state, the entry is deleted from SB and written into the cache atomically, thus completing the st_{global} event.

2. ld: To issue a ld instruction, the processor first checks in its SB for a st instruction to the same word. If there is one, the ld gets its value from it. If there is no such word, the processor buffers the ld in RB. In future, when an address is in E or S state, all ld entries to that same address in RB gets its data from cache and are then deleted from the buffer. ld entries to different words in RB can be deleted in any relative order. There is no overlap between the issuing of lds and the flushing of sts to the same address once E state is obtained.

3. MB: Upon issuing a MB instruction, all entries in SB are flushed to the cache and all entries in RB are deleted after returning their values from cache, hence completing the corresponding MB event[5]. While flushing an entry from SB, the processor checks that there is no earlier issued ld instruction to the same address residing in RB. We call this entire process as $flush_{imp}$.

4   The Intermediate Abstraction

The Alpha abstract model retains the internal data partition of the implementation *without any changes*. However, the cache, the cache coherent protocol, bus and main memory in the implementation which belong to the external partition are all replaced by a single port main memory M in the abstract model.

---

[5] Appropriate cache entries need to be in E state before flushing

Table 1. Completion steps of all events of implementation and abstract model

Event	Implementation	Operational Model
$ld(t)$ $(SB_{p(t)}hit)$	read from $SB_{p(t)}$	read from $SB_{p(t)}$
$ld(t)$ $(SB_{p(t)}miss)$	Issue to $RB_{p(t)}$; $C[p(t)][a(t)].st=$S or E and $d(t) \leftarrow C[p(t)][a(t)].a$	Issue to $RB_{p(t)}$; $d(t) \leftarrow M[a(t)]$
$st_{local}(t)$	Issue($SB_{p(t)}, t$)	Issue($SB_{p(t)}, t$)
$st_{global}(t)$	$C[p(t)][a(t)].st=$E and $C[p(t)][a(t)].a \leftarrow d(t)$	$M[a(t)] \leftarrow d(t)$
$MB(t)$	$flush_{imp}$	$flush_{abstract}$

This replacement follows the rules of the thumb we have presented in Section 6 for dealing with memory models obeying write atomicity (as is the case with the Alpha model). We now take a look at how each of the instructions get implemented. As with the implementation, the processor issues all instructions in program order.

1. st: A st instruction first gets issued to SB just as in the implementation, completing the st_{local} event. At any time, an entry anywhere in SB can be deleted from the buffer and written to the single port memory M atomically, provided there is no earlier issued ld instruction to that address pending in RB. This completes the st_{global} event.

2. ld: Similarly, as in implementation, a ld instruction tries to hit SB and on a miss, it gets buffered in RB. However, any entry in RB can be deleted once it receives its data from M, both the steps being performed in one atomic step. Entries to same address get their data values from M at the same time.

3. MB: Upon issuing a MB instruction, all entries in SB are flushed to M and all entries in RB are deleted after returning their values from M. While flushing from SB the processor checks that there is no earlier issued load event to the same address residing in RB. We call this entire process as $flush_{abstract}$.

5 Model-Checking Based Refinement

The events $st_{local}, st_{global}, ld$ and MB have been defined for both the implementation and the abstract model. Every event of the implementation is composed of multiple steps. However, in the abstract model each event except ld is composed of a single atomic step. For example, for a st_{global} event to complete, if the

---

[5] Here $d(t) \leftarrow C[p(t)].[a(t)].a$ refers to the load instruction t receiving its data from the updated cache entry

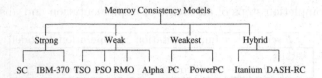

Memory Model	Splitting of store instructions	External Partition
Strong	store unsplit	single port memory
Weak	store split to local and global	single port memory
Weakest	store split to local and $(p+1)^6$ globals	memory and re-order buffer per processor
Hybrid	store split to local and $(p+1)$ globals	memory and re-order buffer per processor

Fig. 2. (a) Memory model classes, and (b) Splitting of store and external partition for each class

concerned address's A-state is Invalid, the processor will need to send a request on the bus to get an Exclusive copy. During this process many intermediate steps take place which include other processors and main memory reacting to the request. However, if a miss occurs while handling the st_{global} event in the abstract model, the entry in SB can be deleted and atomically written to single port memory.

Synchronization Scheme: The discovery of the synchronization sequences between the implementation and the specification is the crux of our verification method. Table 5 provides an overview of the overall synchronization scheme. This table compares the completion steps of both the implementation and the abstract

Table 2. Experimental results

Cache Coherent Protocol	Alpha Implementation			Itanium Implementation		
	States ($\times 10^6$)	Transitions ($\times 10^6$)	Time (hrs)	States ($\times 10^6$)	Transitions ($\times 10^6$)	Time (hrs)
Split Trans. Bus	64.16	470.52	0.95	111.59	985.43	1.75
Split Trans. Bus with Scheurich's Opt.	251.92	1794.96	3.42	325.66	2769.77	4.80
Multiple Interleaved Buses	255.93	1820.38	3.65	773.27	2686.89	10.97
Multiple Interleaved Buses with Scheurich's Opt.	278.02	1946.67	3.90	927.31	3402.41	12.07

model, and highlights all synchronization points. Let us briefly elaborate the actions taken for ld entry in RB to complete. In the implementation, coherence actions are first invoked to promote the cache line into an Exclusive or Shared state. Thereafter, the implementation receives data from the bus and at this point completes the ld event. At this point, the model-checker will immediately make the same event complete in the abstract model by simply returning the data from $M[a(t)]$ through the multiplexor switch. Synchronization happens if the same datum is returned. In general, the last step that completes any event in the implementation and the single step that completes the same event in the abstract model are performed atomically.

The synchronization scheme for instructions that may get buffered and get completed later are slightly more elaborate. Basically, synchronization must be performed both when the instruction is entered into the buffer and later when they complete. For example, since a ld instruction may miss the SB and hence may not complete immediately, we will have to synchronize both the models when ld gets buffered, and finally synchronize again when the ld event completes. The synchronization of MB is accomplished indirectly, by the already existing synchronizations between the models at ld or st_{global}. This is because an MB completes when the above instructions occurring before it complete. Our experimental results are summarized in Table 5.

6   Creation of Intermediate Abstractions, Imp_{abs}

In our verification methodology, the abstract model always retains, without change, the internal partition of the implementation. However, the *external* partition is considerably simplified. Designer insight is required in the selection of a simplified external partition, as this depends on the memory model under examination. In this section we categorize memory models into four classes and show how a common external partition can be derived for memory models belonging to a particular memory model class, thus providing a systematic approach to deriving the abstract model. The four classes of memory models are as follows:

$\boxed{Strong:}$ requires *Write atomicity* and does not allow local bypassing. (e.g. Sequential Consistency,IBM-370).

$\boxed{Weak:}$ requires *Write atomicity* and allows local bypassing (e.g. Ultra Sparc TSO,PSO and RMO,Alpha)

$\boxed{Weakest:}$: does not require *Write atomicity* and allows local bypassing (e.g. PowerPC,PC).

$\boxed{Hybrid:}$: supports weak load and store instructions that come under memory model *Weakest* and also support strong load and store instructions that come under *Strong* or *Weak* memory model classes (e.g. Itanium, DASH-RC).

Depending upon the category a memory model falls under, we split a store instruction into one or more events. Load instructions for any memory model can

---

[6] p is number of processors

always be treated as a single event. Here are a few examples of splitting events. In case of Sequential Consistency, we do not split even the stores as sequential consistency demands a single global total order of the loads and stores. For a weak memory model such as the Ultra Sparc TSO, we split the store instruction into two events, a local store event (which means that the store is only visible to the processor who issued it) and a global event (which means that the store event is visible to all processors). Since the *Weakest*[7] category of memory models lack write atomicity, we need to split stores into $p+1$ events, where p is number of processors, thus ending up with a local store event and p global events (global event i would mean that the store event is visible to processor i). Figure 2(b) summarizes these splitting decisions for various memory models. It also shows the nature of the external partition chosen for various memory models.

In case of *Strong* and *Weak* memory models, the external partition is just a single port memory M. The intuition behind having M is that both these classes of memory models require *Write Atomicity* and hence a store instruction should be visible to all processors instantaneously. *Weakest* and *Hybrid* memory models require more involved data structures where each processor i has its own memory M_i and also a re-ordering buffer that takes in incoming store instructions posted by different processors including itself from their SB. Store instructions residing in this buffer eventually get flushed to memory. The combination of M_i and a re-ordering buffer simulates a processor seeing store instructions at different times and different relative order as that of another processor. An algorithm that generates the correct external partition given a memory model has been designed. A remotely executable web-based tool is also available for experimenting with the operational models thus generated.

7   Conclusions

In this paper, we presented a uniform verification methodology that applies across a spectrum of architectural memory consistency models and handles a variety of consistency protocols. We report experiments involving eight different protocols and two different weak memory models. Our approach fits today's design flow where aggressive, performance oriented protocols are first designed by expert designers, and handed over to verification engineers. The verification engineer can follow a systematic method for deriving an abstract reference model. Our approach does not require special training to use, and can benefit from the use of multiple high-performance PCs to conduct parallel/distributed model checking, thereby covering large state spaces. In ongoing work, we are verifying directory based implementations for the Alpha and Itanium memory models. We are also working on several optimizations to speed-up model checking as well as exploring alternatives to model-checking.

---

[7] Note that the abstract models for *weakest* memory models can also be used as abstract models for strong models. For example, the Lazy Caching protocol of Gerth [9] can be used as an abstract model for sequential consistency.

References

1. Sarita V. Adve and Kourosh Gharachorloo. Shared memory consistency models: A tutorial. Computer, 29(12):66-76, December 1996. 123, 127
2. http://research.microsoft.com/users/lamport/tla/wildfire-challenge.html. 123, 124, 125
3. Gil Neiger, 2001. http://www.cs.utah.edu/mpv/papers/neiger/fmcad2001.pdf. 123, 125
4. Prosenjit Chatterjee and Ganesh Gopalakrishnan. Towards a formal model of shared memory consistency for intel itanium. In ICCD, pages 515-518, 2001. 123, 125
5. Mpv: Workshop on specification and verification of shared memory systems, 2001. http://www.cs.utah.edu/mpv/. 124, 127
6. Thomas Henzinger, Shaz Qadeer, and Sriram Rajamani. Verifying sequential consistency on shared-memory multiprocessor systems. In CAV, LNCS 1633, pages 301-315,1999. 124, 127
7. Shaz Qadeer. Verifying sequential consistency on shared-memory multiprocessors by model checking. Technical report, SRC, December 2001. Research Report 176. 124
8. Anne Condon and Alan J. Hu. Automatable verification of sequential consistency. In Symposium on Parallel Algorithms and Architectures (SPAA), July 2001. 124
9. Michael Merritt. Guest editorial: Special issue on shared memory systems. Distributed Computing, 12(12):55-56, 1999. 124, 134
10. Ratan Nalumasu, Rajnish Ghughal, Abdel Mokkedem, and Ganesh Gopalakrishnan. The 'test model-checking' approach to the verification of formal memory models of multiprocessors. In CAV, LNCS 1427, pages 464-476, 1998. 124, 127
11. D. Sorin et.al. Specifying and verifying a broadcast and a multicast snooping cache coherence protocol. Technical Report #1412, CS Department, U. Wisconsin, Madison, March 2000. 125, 129
12. Seungjoon Park. Computer Assisted Analysis of Multiprocessor Memory Systems. PhD thesis, Stanford University, jun 1996. Department of Computer Science. 125
13. David L. Weaver and Tom Germond. The SPARC Architecture Manual - Version 9. P T R, Prentice-Hall, Englewood Cliffs, NJ 07632, USA, 1994. 125
14. Prosenjit Chatterjee. Formal specification and verification of memory consistency models of shared memory multiprocessors. Master's thesis, Univ Utah, School of Computing, 2002. 126
15. Anne Condon, Mark Hill, Manoj Plakal, and David Sorin. Using lamport clocks to reason about relaxed memory models. In Proceedings of HPCA-5, January 1999. 127, 128
16. A.Singhal et.al. Gigaplane: A high performance bus for large smps. In Proc. 4th Annual Symp on High Performance Interconnects, Stanford University, pages 41-52, 1996. 127, 129
17. The Ultra Enterprise 10000 Server, http://www.sun.com/servers/highend/10000/ 127
18. Ulrich Stern and David Dill. Parallelizing the Muro verifier. Formal Methods in System Design, 18(2):117-129, 2001. (Journal version of their CAV 1997 paper). 127
19. W. W. Collier. Reasoning About Parallel Architectures. Prentice-Hall, Englewood Cliffs, NJ, 1992. 127

20. Rajnish Ghughal and Ganesh Gopalakrishnann. Verification methods for weaker shared memory consistency models. In Jose Rolim et al. (Eds.), editor, *Proc. FMPPTA*, pages 985-992, May 2000. LNCS 1800. 127

21. Jason F. Cantin, Mikko H. Lipasti, and James E. Smith. Dynamic verification of cache coherence protocol. In ?, June 2001. Workshop on Memory Performance Issues, in conjunction with ISCA. 127

22. David L. Dill, Seungjoon Park, and Andreas Nowatzyk. Formal specification of abstract memory models. In Gaetano Borriello and Carl Ebeling, editors, *Research on Integrated Systems*, pages 38-52. MIT Press, 1993. 127

23. P. Ladkin, L. Lamport, B. Olivier, and D. Roegel. Lazy caching in TLA. *Distributed Computing*, 1997. 127

24. Jeremy Manson and William Pugh. Core semantics of multithreaded Java. In *ACM Java Grande Conference*, June 2001. 127

25. Yue Yang, Ganesh Gopalakrishnan, and Gary Lindstrom. Formalizing the java memory model for multithreaded program correctness and optimization. Technical Report UUCS-02-011, University of Utah, School of Computing, 2002. Also at http://www.cs.utah.edu/-yyang/research. 127

Automatic Abstraction
Using Generalized Model Checking

Patrice Godefroid[1] and Radha Jagadeesan[*2]

[1] Bell Laboratories, Lucent Technologies
god@bell-labs.com
[2] Department of Computer Science, Loyola University of Chicago
radha@cs.luc.edu

Abstract. Generalized model checking is a framework for reasoning about partial state spaces of concurrent reactive systems. The state space of a system is only "partial" (partially known) when a full state-space exploration is not computationally tractable, or when abstraction techniques are used to simplify the system's representation. In the context of automatic abstraction, generalized model checking means checking whether there exists a concretization of an abstraction that satisfies a temporal logic formula. In this paper, we show how generalized model checking can extend existing automatic abstraction techniques (such as predicate abstraction) for model checking concurrent/reactive programs and yield the three following improvements: (1) any temporal logic formula can be checked (not just universal properties as with traditional conservative abstractions), (2) correctness proofs and counter-examples are both guaranteed to be sound, and (3) verification results can be more precise. We study the cost needed to improve precision by presenting new upper and lower bounds for the complexity of generalized model checking in the size of the abstraction.

1 Introduction

How to broaden the scope of model checking to reactive software is currently one of the most challenging open problems related to computer-aided verification. Essentially two approaches have been proposed and are still actively being investigated. The first approach consists of adapting model checking into a form of systematic testing that simulates the effect of model checking while being applicable to (Unix-like) processes executing arbitrary code [10]; although counter-examples reported with this approach are sound, it is inherently incomplete for large systems. The second approach consists of automatically extracting a model out of a software application by statically analyzing its code, and then of analyzing this model using traditional model-checking algorithms (e.g., [2,6,25,21,14]); although automatic abstraction may be able to prove correctness, counter-examples are generally unsound since abstraction usually introduces unrealistic behaviors that may yield to spurious errors being reported when analyzing the model.

---

* Supported in part by NSF.

D. Brinksma and K. G. Larsen (Eds.): CAV 2002, LNCS 2404, pp. 137–151, 2002.
© Springer-Verlag Berlin Heidelberg 2002

Recently [11], we showed how automatic abstraction can be performed to verify arbitrary formulas of the propositional μ-calculus [17] in such a way that both correctness proofs and counter-examples are guaranteed to be sound. The key to make this possible is to represent abstract systems using richer models that distinguish properties that are true, false and unknown of the concrete system. Examples of such richer modeling formalisms are partial Kripke structures [3] and Modal Transition Systems [19,11]. Reasoning about such systems requires 3-valued temporal logics [3], i.e., temporal logics whose formulas may evaluate to *true*, *false* or $\perp$ ("unknown") on a given model. Then, by using an automatic abstraction process that generates by construction an abstract model which is less complete than the concrete system with respect to a completeness preorder logically characterized by 3-valued temporal logic, every temporal property that evaluates to *true* (resp. *false*) on the abstract model automatically holds (resp. does not hold) of the concrete system, hence guaranteeing soundness of both proofs and counter-examples; in case a property evaluates to $\perp$ on the model, a more complete (i.e., less abstract) model is then necessary to provide a definite answer concerning this property of the concrete system. This approach is applicable to check arbitrary formulas of the propositional μ-calculus (thus including negation and arbitrarily nested path quantifiers), not just universal properties as with a traditional "conservative" abstraction that merely simulates the concrete system. It is shown in [11] that building a 3-valued abstraction can be done using existing abstraction techniques at the same computational cost as building a conservative abstraction.

In this paper, we build upon this previous work and study the use of *generalized model checking* in the context of automatic abstraction. Generalized model checking was introduced in [4] as a way to improve precision when reasoning about partially defined systems. Specifically, given a model M and a temporal-logic formula ϕ, the generalized model-checking problem is to decide whether there exists a complete system M' that is more complete than M and that satisfies the formula ϕ. The model M can thus be viewed as a partial solution to the satisfiability problem for ϕ which reduces the solution space to complete systems that are more complete than M with respect to a completeness preorder. Generalized model checking is thus a generalization of both satisfiability and model checking. Algorithms and complexity bounds for the generalized model-checking problem for various temporal logics were presented in [4].

We present here several new results. First, we study the complexity of generalized model checking in the size of the abstraction $|M|$, and provide new upper and lower bounds for various temporal logics. We show that the worst-case runtime complexity of generalized model checking for the temporal logics LTL and CTL can be quadratic in $|M|$, but that generalized model checking can be solved in time linear in $|M|$ in the case of *persistence* properties, i.e., properties recognizable by *co-Büchi automata*. Complexity in the size of the abstraction is important in practice since the abstraction can be large and hence is often the main limiting factor that prevents obtaining verification results.

Second, we show how generalized model checking can help improve precision of verification via automatic abstraction. We present a new process for iterative abstraction refinement that takes advantage of the techniques introduced here. Iterative abstraction refinement [, ,] in the context of predicate abstraction [ ] is a process for automatically refining an abstraction that is guided by spurious counter-examples found at higher levels of abstraction. In contrast with abstractions used in traditional program analysis, iterative abstraction refinement using predicate abstraction has thus the advantage of making it possible to adapt the level of abstraction dynamically on a demand-driven basis guided by the verification needs. Unfortunately, refining an abstraction can be an expensive operation since successive abstraction refinements can generate exponentially larger abstractions. Better precision when analyzing an abstraction is therefore critical to avoid unnecessary refinements of this abstraction. We believe generalized model checking is a useful addition to existing techniques for automatic abstraction since it can help an iterative "abstract-check-refine" verification process terminate sooner and more often by providing better analysis precision for a cost polynomial (quadratic or linear) in the size of the abstraction.

2   Background: Generalized Model Checking

In this section, we recall the main ideas and key notions behind the framework of [, , ,] for reasoning about partially defined systems. Examples of modeling formalisms for representing such systems are *partial Kripke structures* (PKS) [ ], *Modal Transition Systems* (MTS) [,] or *Kripke Modal Transition Systems* (KMTS) [ ].

Definition 1. *A* KMTS *M is a tuple* $(S, P, \overset{must}{\longrightarrow}, \overset{may}{\longrightarrow}, L)$, *where S is a nonempty finite set of states, P is a finite set of atomic propositions,* $\overset{may}{\longrightarrow} \subseteq S \times S$ *and* $\overset{must}{\longrightarrow} \subseteq S \times S$ *are transition relations such that* $\overset{must}{\longrightarrow} \subseteq \overset{may}{\longrightarrow}$, *and* $L : S \times P \to \{true, \bot, false\}$ *is an* interpretation *that associates a truth value in* $\{true, \bot, false\}$ *with each atomic proposition in P for each state in S. An MTS is a KMTS where* $P = \emptyset$. *A PKS is a KMTS where* $\overset{must}{\longrightarrow} = \overset{may}{\longrightarrow}$.

The third value $\bot$ (read "unknown") and *may*-transitions that are not *must*-transitions are used to model explicitly a loss of information due to abstraction concerning, respectively, state or transition properties of the concrete system being modeled. A standard, *complete* Kripke structure is a special case of KMTS where $\overset{must}{\longrightarrow} = \overset{may}{\longrightarrow}$ and $L : S \times P \to \{true, false\}$, i.e., no proposition takes value $\bot$ in any state. It can be shown that PKSs, MTSs, KMTSs and variants of KMTSs where transitions are labeled and/or two interpretation functions L^{may} and L^{must} are used [ ], are all equally expressive (i.e., one can translate any formalism into any other). In this paper, we will use KMTSs since they conveniently generalize models with *may*-transitions only, which are used with traditional conservative abstractions. Obviously, our results also hold for other equivalent formalisms (exactly as traditional model-checking algorithms and complexity bounds apply equally to systems modeled as Kripke structures or Labeled Transition Systems, for instance).

In interpreting propositional operators on KMTSs, we use Kleene's strong 3-valued propositional logic [16]. Conjunction $\wedge$ in this logic is defined as the function that returns *true* if both of its arguments are *true*, *false* if either argument is *false*, and $\perp$ otherwise. We define negation $\neg$ using the function 'comp' that maps *true* to *false*, *false* to *true*, and $\perp$ to $\perp$. Disjunction $\vee$ is defined as usual using De Morgan's laws: $p \vee q = \neg(\neg p \wedge \neg q)$. Note that these functions give the usual meaning of the propositional operators when applied to values *true* and *false*.

Propositional modal logic (PML) is propositional logic extended with the modal operator AX (which is read "for all immediate successors"). Formulas of PML have the following abstract syntax: $\phi ::= p \mid \neg\phi \mid \phi_1 \wedge \phi_2 \mid AX\phi$, where p ranges over P. The following 3-valued semantics generalizes the traditional 2-valued semantics for PML.

Definition 2. *The value of a formula ϕ of 3-valued PML in a state s of a KMTS* $M = (S, P, \overset{must}{\longrightarrow}, \overset{may}{\longrightarrow}, L)$, *written $[(M, s) \models \phi]$, is defined inductively as follows:*

$$[(M, s) \models p] = L(s, p)$$
$$[(M, s) \models \neg\phi] = comp([(M, s) \models \phi])$$
$$[(M, s) \models \phi_1 \wedge \phi_2] = [(M, s) \models \phi_1] \wedge [(M, s) \models \phi_2]$$
$$[(M, s) \models AX\phi] = \begin{cases} true \ if \ \forall s' : s \overset{may}{\longrightarrow} s' \Rightarrow [(M, s') \models \phi] = true \\ false \ if \ \exists s' : s \overset{must}{\longrightarrow} s' \wedge [(M, s') \models \phi] = false \\ \perp \quad otherwise \end{cases}$$

This 3-valued logic can be used to define a preorder on KMTSs that reflects their degree of completeness. Let $\leq$ be the *information ordering* on truth values, in which $\perp \leq true$, $\perp \leq false$, $x \leq x$ (for all $x \in \{true, \perp, false\}$), and $x \not\leq y$ otherwise.

Definition 3. *Let* $M_A = (S_A, P, \overset{must}{\longrightarrow}_A, \overset{may}{\longrightarrow}_A, L_A)$ *and* $M_C = (S_C, P, \overset{must}{\longrightarrow}_C,$ $\overset{may}{\longrightarrow}_C, L_C)$ *be KMTSs. The* completeness preorder $\preceq$ *is the greatest relation* $\mathcal{B} \subseteq$ $S_A \times S_C$ *such that* $(s_a, s_c) \in \mathcal{B}$ *implies the following:*

- $\forall p \in P : L_A(s_a, p) \leq L_C(s_c, p)$,
- *if* $s_a \overset{must}{\longrightarrow}_A s'_a$, *there is some* $s'_c \in S_C$ *such that* $s_c \overset{must}{\longrightarrow}_C s'_c$ *and* $(s'_a, s'_c) \in \mathcal{B}$,
- *if* $s_c \overset{may}{\longrightarrow}_C s'_c$, *there is some* $s'_a \in S_A$ *such that* $s_a \overset{may}{\longrightarrow}_A s'_a$ *and* $(s'_a, s'_c) \in \mathcal{B}$.

This definition allows to abstract M_C by M_A by letting truth values of propositions become $\perp$ and by letting *must*-transitions become *may*-transitions, but all *may*-transitions of M_C must be preserved in M_A. We then say that M_A is *more abstract*, or *less complete*, than M_C. The inverse of the completeness preorder is also called *refinement preorder* in [19,15,11]. Note that relation $\mathcal{B}$ reduces to a simulation relation when applied to MTSs with *may*-transitions only.

It can be shown that 3-valued PML logically characterizes the completeness preorder [3,15,11].

Theorem 1. *Let* $M_A = (S_A, P, \overset{must}{\longrightarrow}_A, \overset{may}{\longrightarrow}_A, L_A)$ *and* $M_C = (S_C, P, \overset{must}{\longrightarrow}_C,$ $\overset{may}{\longrightarrow}_C, L_C)$ *be KMTSs such that* $s_a \in S_A$ *and* $s_c \in S_C$, *and let* Φ *be the set of all formulas of 3-valued PML. Then,*

$$s_a \preceq s_c \text{ iff } (\forall \phi \in \Phi : [(M_A, s_a) \models \phi] \leq [(M_C, s_c) \models \phi]).$$

In other words, KMTSs that are "more complete" with respect to $\preceq$ have more definite properties with respect to $\leq$, i.e., have more properties that are either *true* or *false*. Moreover, any formula ϕ of 3-valued PML that evaluates to *true* or *false* on a KMTS has the same truth value when evaluated on any more complete structure. This result also holds for PML extended with fixpoint operators, i.e., the propositional μ-calculus [3].

In [11], we showed how to adapt the abstraction mappings of [8] to construct abstractions that are less complete than a given concrete program with respect to the completeness preorder.

Definition 4. *Let* $M_C = (S_C, P, \overset{must}{\longrightarrow}_C, \overset{may}{\longrightarrow}_C, L_C)$ *be a (concrete) KMTS. Given a set* S_A *of abstract states and a total[1] abstraction relation on states* $\rho \subseteq S_C \times S_A$, *we define the (abstract) KMTS* $M_A = (S_A, P, \overset{must}{\longrightarrow}_A, \overset{may}{\longrightarrow}_A, L_A)$ *as follows:*

- $a \overset{must}{\longrightarrow}_A a'$ *if* $\forall c \in S_C : c\rho a \Rightarrow (\exists c' \in S_C : c'\rho a' \wedge c \overset{must}{\longrightarrow}_C c')$;
- $a \overset{may}{\longrightarrow}_A a'$ *if* $\exists c, c' \in S_C : c\rho a \wedge c'\rho a' \wedge c \overset{may}{\longrightarrow}_C c'$;
- $L_A(a, p) = \begin{cases} true & \text{if } \forall c : c\rho a \Rightarrow L_C(c, p) = true \\ false & \text{if } \forall c : c\rho a \Rightarrow L_C(c, p) = false \\ \bot & \text{otherwise} \end{cases}$

The previous definition can be used to build abstract KMTSs.

Theorem 2. *Given a KMTS* M_C, *any KMTS* M_A *obtained by applying Definition 4 is such that* $M_A \preceq M_C$.

Given a KMTS M_C, any abstraction M_A less complete than M_C with respect to the completeness preorder $\preceq$ can be constructed using Definition 4 by choosing the inverse of ρ as $\mathcal{B}$ [11]. When applied to MTSs with *may*-transitions only, the above definition coincides with traditional "conservative" abstraction. Building a 3-valued abstraction can be done using existing abstraction techniques at the same computational cost as building a conservative abstraction [11].

Since by construction $M_A \preceq M_C$, any temporal-logic formula ϕ that evaluates to *true* (resp. *false*) on M_A automatically holds (resp. does not hold) on M_C. It is shown in [4] that computing $[(M_A, s) \models \phi]$ can be reduced to two traditional (2-valued) model-checking problems on regular fully-defined systems (such as Kripke structures or Labeled Transition Systems), and hence that 3-valued model-checking for any temporal logic L has the same time and space complexity as 2-valued model checking for the logic L.

---

[1] That is, $(\forall c \in S_C : \exists a \in S_A : c\rho a)$ and $(\forall a \in S_A : \exists c \in S_C : c\rho a)$.

However, as argued in [ ], the semantics of $[(M, s) \models \phi]$ returns $\perp$ more often than it should. Consider a KMTS M consisting of a single state s such that the value of proposition p at s is $\perp$ and the value of q at s is $true$. The formulas $p \vee \neg p$ and $q \wedge (p \vee \neg p)$ are $\perp$ at s, although in all complete Kripke structures more complete than (M, s) both formulas evaluate to $true$. This problem is not confined to formulas containing subformulas that are tautological or unsatisfiable. Consider a KMTS M' with two states s_0 and s_1 such that $p = q = true$ in s_0 and $p = q = false$ in s_1, and with a may-transition from s_0 to s_1. The formula $AXp \wedge \neg AXq$ (which is neither a tautology nor unsatisfiable) is $\perp$ at s_0, yet in all complete structures more complete than (M', s_0) the formula is $false$. This observation is used in [ ] to define an alternative 3-valued semantics for modal logics called the $thorough$ semantics since it does more than the other semantics to discover whether enough information is present in a KMTS to give a definite answer. Let the $completions$ $\mathcal{C}(M, s)$ of a state s of a KMTS M be the set of all states s' of complete Kripke structures M' such that $s \preceq s'$.

Definition 5. *Let ϕ be a formula of any two-valued logic for which a satisfaction relation $\models$ is defined on complete Kripke structures. The truth value of ϕ in a state s of a KMTS M under the* thorough *interpretation, written $[(M, s) \models \phi]_t$, is defined as follows:*

$$[(M, s) \models \phi]_t = \begin{cases} true & if\ (M', s') \models \phi\ for\ all\ (M', s')\ in\ \mathcal{C}(M, s) \\ false & if\ (M', s') \not\models \phi\ for\ all\ (M', s')\ in\ \mathcal{C}(M, s) \\ \perp & otherwise \end{cases}$$

It is easy to see that, by definition, we always have $[(M, s) \models \phi] \leq [(M, s) \models \phi]_t$. In general, interpreting a formula according to the thorough three-valued semantics is equivalent to solving two instances of the generalized model-checking problem [ ].

Definition 6 (Generalized Model-Checking Problem). *Given a state s of a KMTS M and a formula ϕ of a (two-valued) temporal logic L, does there exist a state s' of a complete Kripke structure M' such that $s \preceq s'$ and $(M', s') \models \phi$?*

This problem is called *generalized model-checking* since it generalizes both model checking and satisfiability checking. At one extreme, where $M = (\{s_0\}, P, \xrightarrow{must} = \xrightarrow{may} = \{(s_0, s_0)\}, L)$ with $L(s_0, p) = \perp$ for all $p \in P$, all complete Kripke structures are more complete than M and the problem reduces to the satisfiability problem. At the other extreme, where M is complete, only a single structure needs to be checked and the problem reduces to model checking.

Algorithms and complexity bounds for the generalized model-checking problem for various temporal logics were presented in [ ]. In the case of branching-time temporal logics, generalized model checking has the same complexity in the size of the formula as satisfiability. In the case of linear-time temporal logic, generalized model checking is EXPTIME-complete in the size of the formula, i.e., harder than both satisfiability and model checking, which are both PSPACE-complete in the size of the formula for LTL. Figure 1 summarizes the complexity

Logic	MC	SAT	GMC
Propositional Logic	Linear	NP-complete	NP-complete
PML	Linear	PSPACE-complete	PSPACE-complete
CTL	Linear	EXPTIME-complete	EXPTIME-complete
μ-calculus	NP∩co-NP	EXPTIME-complete	EXPTIME-complete
LTL	PSPACE-complete	PSPACE-complete	EXPTIME-complete

Fig. 1. Known results on the complexity in the size of the formula for (2-valued and 3-valued) model checking (MC), satisfiability (SAT) and generalized model checking (GMC)

results of [4]. These results show that the complexity in the size of the formula of computing $[(M, s) \models \phi]_t$ (GMC) is always higher than that of computing $[(M, s) \models \phi]$ (MC).

Regarding the complexity in the size of the model $|M|$, it is only shown in [4] that generalized model checking can be solved in time quadratic in $|M|$. In the next two sections, we refine this result by presenting new upper and lower bounds for the complexity of generalized model checking in the size of the model for various classes of temporal properties. Our algorithms and constructions make use of automata-theoretic techniques (e.g., see [18]). For basic notions of automata theory (including definitions of nondeterministic/alternating/weak Büchi automata on words and trees), please refer to [18]. Let us simply recall that a co-Büchi acceptance condition is the dual of a Büchi acceptance condition: an infinite execution w satisfies a co-Büchi acceptance condition F if it does not intersect the set F of (rejecting) states infinitely often (i.e., $Inf(w) \cap F = \emptyset$), while an infinite execution w satisfies a Büchi acceptance condition F if it intersects the set F of (accepting) states infinitely often (i.e., $Inf(w) \cap F \neq \emptyset$).

3 Generalized Model Checking for LTL

We first consider the case of properties expressed as linear-time temporal-logic (LTL) formulas [20]. To begin, we recall the following property of LTL: if ϕ is an LTL formula and (M, s) is a complete Kripke structure, $(M, s) \not\models \phi$ is *not* logically equivalent to $(M, s) \models \neg\phi$. Indeed, if $\mathcal{L}(M, s)$ denotes the language of ω-words represented by (M, s), the former statement is equivalent to $\exists w \in \mathcal{L}(M, s) : w \not\models \phi$ while the latter is equivalent to $\forall w \in \mathcal{L}(M, s) : w \models \neg\phi$, which in turn is equivalent to $\forall w \in \mathcal{L}(M, s) : w \not\models \phi$.

Therefore, computing $[(M, s) \models \phi]_t$ in the LTL case reduces to only one generalized model-checking problem, namely "does there exists a completion (M', s') of (M, s) such that $(M', s') \models \phi$?", plus a second problem of the form "does there exists a completion (M', s') of (M, s) such that $(M', s') \not\models \phi$?". This second problem is easier to solve than generalized model checking.

Theorem 3. *Given a state s of a KMTS M and a LTL formula ϕ, checking whether there exists a state s' of a complete Kripke structure M' such that $s \preceq s'$*

and $(M', s') \not\models \phi$ *can be done in time linear in* $|M|$ *and is PSPACE-complete in* $|\phi|$.

Proof. (Sketch)[2] For any two infinite sequences $w = a_1 a_2 \ldots$ and $w' = a'_1 a'_2 \ldots$, let $w \leq w'$ denote that $\forall i > 0 : \forall p \in P : L(a_i, p) \leq L(a'_i, p)$. It is easy to show that $\exists (M', s') : s \preceq s' \wedge (M', s') \not\models \phi$ iff $\exists w \in \mathcal{L}(M, s) : \exists w' : w \leq w' \wedge w' \not\models \phi$. The latter condition can be reduced to checking nonemptiness of a nondeterministic Büchi word automaton A defined by a product construction of the KMTS (M, s) and of a nondeterministic Büchi automaton $A_{\neg \phi}$ accepting the set of ω-words violating the property ϕ. This product construction does not distinguish *may* and *must* transitions of M and attempts to match all of these to transitions of $A_{\neg \phi}$; occurrences of value $\bot$ in M are matched to both values *true* and *false* in $A_{\neg \phi}$; the size of A is therefore linear in $|M|$. Checking nonemptiness of the resulting Büchi automaton A can be done in time linear in $|A|$ (hence linear in $|M|$). By analogy with traditional model checking, it is easy to show that the problem is also PSPACE-complete in $|\phi|$.

Computing $[(M, s) \models \phi]_t$ for an LTL formula ϕ can thus be done using the following procedure:

1. Check whether $(M, s) \times A_{\neg \phi} = \emptyset$. By the previous theorem, this can be done in time linear in $|M|$ and is PSPACE-complete in $|\phi|$. If the outcome of this check is positive (i.e., the product is empty), then all completions of (M, s) satisfy ϕ, and $[(M, s) \models \phi]_t = true$; otherwise, continue.
2. Check whether $\exists (M', s') : s \preceq s' \wedge (M', s') \models \phi$ (generalized model checking). As recalled in the previous section, this can be done in time quadratic in $|M|$ and is EXPTIME-complete in $|\phi|$. (Intuitively, this check is more expensive since it requires checking that $\forall w \in \mathcal{L}(M, s) : \exists w' : w \leq w' \wedge w' \models \phi$, which includes an alternation of $\forall$ and $\exists$.) If the outcome of this check is positive, we have $[(M, s) \models \phi]_t = \bot$; otherwise, all completions of (M, s) violate ϕ, and $[(M, s) \models \phi]_t = false$.

Because Step 2 of the above procedure requires solving an instance of the generalized model-checking problem, the time needed to compute $[(M, s) \models \phi]_t$ using the generalized model-checking algorithm of [ ] can be quadratic in $|M|$. Unfortunately, the lower bound provided by the following theorem shows that it is unlikely this quadratic complexity can be reduced in the general case.

Theorem 4. *The problem of checking emptiness of nondeterministic Büchi tree automata is reducible in linear time and logarithmic space to the generalized model-checking problem for LTL properties represented by nondeterministic Büchi word automata.*

Since the worst-case run-time complexity of the best known algorithm for checking emptiness of nondeterministic Büchi tree automata is quadratic in the size of the automaton [ ], it is therefore unlikely that the generalized model-checking problem for LTL can be solved using better than quadratic time in $|M|$ in the worst case.

---

[2] Complete proofs are omitted in this extended abstract due to space limitations.

However, we now identify an important class of LTL formulas for which the generalized model-checking problem can be solved in time linear in $|M|$. This class is the class of *persistence properties* [20]. Persistence properties can be represented by LTL formulas of the form $\Diamond \Box p$ (where $\Diamond$ is read "eventually" and $\Box$ is read "always" [20]). Persistence properties also correspond to languages of ω-words recognizable by *co-Büchi automata*.

Theorem 5. *The generalized model-checking problem for LTL persistence properties can be solved in time linear in the size of the model.*

Proof. (Sketch) Every persistence property can be represented by a co-Büchi automaton A_ϕ. A_ϕ can then easily be transformed into a *weak* (Büchi or co-Büchi) nondeterministic automaton A'_ϕ accepting the same language and of size linear in $|A_\phi|$. Generalized model checking can then be reduced to checking emptiness of an alternating Büchi word automaton $A_{(M,s_0),\phi}$ over a 1-letter alphabet defined using a product construction of the KMTS (M, s_0) and the weak Büchi automaton A'_ϕ. If A'_ϕ is weak, $A_{(M,s_0),\phi}$ is also weak. Moreover, the size of $A_{(M,s_0),\phi}$ is linear in $|M|$. Since checking emptiness of a weak alternating Büchi word automaton over a 1-letter alphabet can be done in linear time [18], we obtain a decision procedure for the generalized model-checking problem of LTL persistence properties that is linear in $|M|$.

Of practical interest, persistence properties include all safety properties (LTL formulas of the form $\Box p$), as well as guarantee properties (LTL formulas of the form $\Diamond p$) and obligation properties (boolean combinations of safety and guarantee properties) [20]. Examples of LTL properties that are not persistence properties are response properties (LTL formulas of the form $\Box \Diamond p$).

4   Generalized Model Checking for BTL

We now consider the case of branching-time temporal logics (BTL) such as propositional modal logic (e.g., see [23]), CTL [5] or the propositional μ-calculus [17]. In the case of a BTL formula ϕ, computing $[(M, s) \models \phi]_t$ reduces to two generalized model-checking problems, namely "does there exist two completions (M', s') and (M'', s'') of (M, s) such that $(M', s') \models \phi$ and $(M'', s'') \not\models \phi$?", the latter statement being equivalent to $(M'', s'') \models \neg\phi$.

Given a CTL formula ϕ, the worst-case run-time complexity of computing $[(M, s) \models \phi]_t$ for a CTL formula ϕ using the generalized model-checking algorithm of [4] is quadratic in $|M|$. The next theorem provides a lower bound similar to the one given in Theorem 4 in the LTL case.

Theorem 6. *The problem of checking emptiness of nondeterministic Büchi tree automata is reducible in linear time and logarithmic space to the generalized model-checking problem for CTL properties represented by nondeterministic Büchi tree automata.*

As in the LTL case, we can identify classes of properties for which generalized model checking can be done in time linear in $|M|$.

Theorem 7. *The generalized model-checking problem for BTL properties recognizable by nondeterministic co-Büchi tree automata can be solved in time linear in the size of the model.*

Proof. (Sketch) BTL properties recognizable by nondeterministic co-Büchi tree automata are also recognizable by weak tree automata. One can then use a product construction of such a weak tree automaton with a KMTS M to define a weak alternating Büchi word automaton A over a 1-letter alphabet and of size linear in $|M|$ such that generalized model checking can be reduced to checking emptiness of this alternating automaton. A key observation to prove the linear bound on $|M|$ is that generalized model checking on a KMTS M can be reduced to generalized model checking on a PKS M' of size linear in M, hence showing that not all (exponentially many) subsets of *may*-transitions of M need be considered when checking branching properties of the set of all possible completions of M. Since checking emptiness of a weak alternating Büchi word automaton over a 1-letter alphabet can be done in linear time [18], we obtain a decision procedure for generalized model-checking that is linear in $|M|$.

The previous theorem generalizes Theorem 5 since tree automata are generalizations of word automata. Examples of CTL properties that are recognizable by nondeterministic co-Büchi tree automata are AGp and EFp. In contrast, CTL formulas such as $AGAFp$ and $AGEFp$ are not recognizable by co-Büchi tree automata. As a corollary to the previous theorem, it is easy to show that the generalized model checking for any PML formula can be solved in linear time in $|M|$. Finally note that in order to compute $[(M, s) \models \phi]_t$ in time linear in $|M|$, both ϕ and $\neg\phi$ need be recognizable by co-Büchi tree automata.

5   Application to Automatic Abstraction

The usual procedure for performing verification via predicate abstraction and iterative abstraction refinement is the following (e.g., see [1,9]).

1. Abstract: compute an abstraction M_A that simulates the concrete prgm M_C.
2. Check: given a universal property ϕ, decide whether $M_A \models \phi$.
   - if $M_A \models \phi$: stop (the property is proved: $M_C \models \phi$).
   - if $M_A \not\models \phi$: go to Step 3.
3. Refine: refine M_A (possibly using a counter-example found in Step 2). Then go to Step 1.

Since M_A simulates M_C, one can only prove the correctness of universal properties (i.e., properties over all paths) of M_C by analyzing M_A in Step 2. Note that the three steps above can also be interleaved and performed in a strict demand-driven fashion as described in [13].

The purpose of this paper is thus to advocate a new procedure for automatic abstraction.

1. Abstract: compute an abstraction M_A using Def. 4 such that $M_A \preceq M_C$.
2. Check: given *any* property ϕ,

(a) (3-valued model checking) compute $[M_A \models \phi]$.
   - if $[M_A \models \phi] = true$ or $false$: stop (the property is proved (resp. disproved) on M_C).
   - if $[M_A \models \phi] = \perp$, continue.
(b) (generalized model checking) compute $[M_A \models \phi]_t$.
   - if $[M_A \models \phi]_t = true$ or $false$: stop (the property is proved (resp. disproved) on M_C).
   - if $[M_A \models \phi] = \perp$, go to Step 3.
3. Refine: refine M_A (possibly using a counter-example found in Step 2). Then go to Step 1.

This new procedure strictly generalizes the traditional one in several ways. First, any temporal logic formula can be checked (not just universal properties). Second, all correctness proofs and counter-examples obtained by analyzing any abstraction M_A such that $M_A \preceq M_C$ are guaranteed to be sound (i.e., hold on M_C) for any property (by Theorem 1 of Section 2). Third, verification results can be more precise than with the traditional procedure: the new procedure will not only return *true* whenever the traditional one returns *true* (trivially, since the former includes the latter), but it can also return *true* more often thanks to a more thorough check using generalized model-checking, and it can also return *false*. The new procedure can thus terminate sooner and more often than the traditional procedure — the new procedure will never loop through its 3 steps more often than the traditional one. Remarkably, each of the 3 steps of the new procedure can be performed at roughly the same cost as the corresponding step of the traditional procedure: as shown in [ ], building a 3-valued abstraction using Definition 4 (Step 1 of new procedure) can be done at the same computational cost as building a conservative abstraction (Step 1 of traditional procedure); computing $[M_A \models \phi]$ in Step 2.a can be done at the same cost at traditional (2-valued) model checking [ ]; following the results of Sections 3 and 4, computing $[M_A \models \phi]_t$ in Step 2.b can be more expensive than Step 2.a, but is still polynomial (linear or quadratic) in the size of M_A; Step 3 of the new procedure is similar to Step 3 of the traditional one (in the case of LTL properties for instance, refinement can be guided by error traces found in Step 2 as in the traditional procedure). Finally note that the new procedure could also be adapted so that the different steps are performed in a demand-driven basis following the work of [ ].

6 Examples

We now give examples of programs, models and properties where computing $[(M, s) \models \phi]_t$ returns a more precise answer than $[(M, s) \models \phi]$.

Consider the three programs shown in Figure 2, where x and y denote variables, and f denotes some unknown function. The notation "x,y = 1,0" means variables x and y are simultaneously assigned to values 1 and 0, respectively. Consider the two predicates p: "is x odd?" and q: "is y odd?". Figure 2 shows an example of KMTS model for each of the three programs. These models can

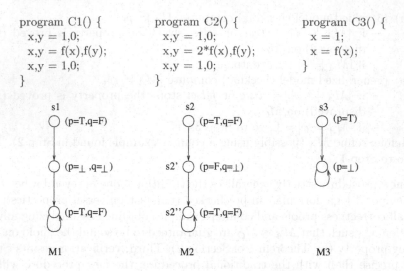

Fig. 2. Examples of programs and models

be computed automatically using Definition 4, predicate abstraction techniques and predicates p and q, so that by construction they satisfy Theorem 2. Each model is a KMTS with *must*-transitions only and with atomic propositions p and q whose truth value is defined in each state as indicated in the figure.

Consider the LTL formula $\phi_1 = \Diamond q \Rightarrow \Box(p \vee q)$. While $[(M_1, s_1) \models \phi_1] = \bot$, $[(M_1, s_1) \models \phi_1]_t = true$. In other words, using the thorough interpretation yields a more definite answer in this case. Note that the gain in precision obtained in this case is somewhat similar to the gain in precision that can be obtained using an optimization called *focusing* [1] aimed at recovering some of the imprecision introduced when using *cartesian abstraction* (see [1,11]).

Consider now the formula $\phi_2 = \Diamond q \wedge \Box(p \vee \neg q)$ evaluated on (M_2, s_2). In this case, we have $[(M_2, s_2) \models \phi_2] = \bot$, while $[(M_2, s_2) \models \phi_2]_t = false$. Again, using the thorough interpretation yields a more definite answer, although solving a generalized model-checking problem is necessary to return a negative answer. Indeed, one needs to prove in this case that there exists a computation of (M_2, s_2) (namely $s_2 s_2' s_2''^\omega$ – there is only one computation in this simple example) that does not have any completion satisfying ϕ_2, which itself requires using alternating automata and can thus be more expensive as discussed in Section 3. Another example of formula is $\phi_2' = \bigcirc q \wedge \Box(p \vee \neg q)$ (where $\bigcirc$ is read "next" [20]). Again we have that $[(M_2, s_2) \models \phi_2'] = \bot$, while $[(M_2, s_2) \models \phi_2']_t = false$. Note that, although ϕ_2' is an LTL safety formula and hence is within the scope of analysis of existing tools ([2], [6], etc.), none of these tools can prove that ϕ_2' does not hold: this result can only be obtained using generalized model checking.

Last, consider (M_3, s_3) and formula $\phi_3 = \Box p$. In this case, we have both $[(M_3, s_3) \models \phi_3] = [(M_3, s_3) \models \phi_3]_t = \bot$, and the thorough interpretation cannot produce a more definite answer than the standard 3-valued interpretation.

7   Conclusions

We have introduced generalized model checking as a way to improve precision of automatic abstraction for the verification of temporal properties of programs. In this context, generalized model checking means checking whether there exists a concretization of an abstraction M that satisfies a temporal logic formula ϕ.

We believe generalized model checking is quite practical despite its seemingly higher complexity than that of model checking. Indeed, a higher worst-case complexity in the size of the formula (for instance, EXPTIME-complete instead of PSPACE-complete for LTL formulas) may not be too troublesome since formulas are usually quite short and checking algorithms typically behave better than the worst case in practice. Perhaps more importantly, we showed in this paper that generalized model checking may require in general quadratic time in the size of the abstraction, which may be a more severe limitation, but that it can be solved in linear time for important classes of properties including safety properties. In any case, generalized model checking can help an iterative "abstract-check-refine" verification process terminate sooner and more often by providing better analysis precision for a cost only polynomial in the size of the abstraction, which in turn may prevent the unnecessary generation and analysis of possibly exponentially larger refinements of that abstraction.

References

1. T. Ball, A. Podelski, and S. K. Rajamani. Boolean and Cartesian Abstraction for Model Checking C Programs. In *Proceedings of TACAS'2001 (Tools and Algorithms for the Construction and Analysis of Systems)*, volume 2031 of *Lecture Notes in Computer Science*. Springer-Verlag, April 2001. 139, 146, 148
2. T. Ball and S. Rajamani. The SLAM Toolkit. In *Proceedings of CAV'2001 (13th Conference on Computer Aided Verification)*, Paris, July 2001. 137, 148
3. G. Bruns and P. Godefroid. Model Checking Partial State Spaces with 3-Valued Temporal Logics. In *Proceedings of the 11th Conference on Computer Aided Verification*, volume 1633 of *Lecture Notes in Computer Science*, pages 274–287, Trento, July 1999. Springer-Verlag. 138, 139, 140, 141
4. G. Bruns and P. Godefroid. Generalized Model Checking: Reasoning about Partial State Spaces. In *Proceedings of CONCUR'2000 (11th International Conference on Concurrency Theory)*, volume 1877 of *Lecture Notes in Computer Science*, pages 168–182, University Park, August 2000. Springer-Verlag. 138, 139, 141, 142, 143, 144, 145, 147
5. E. M. Clarke and E. A. Emerson. Design and Synthesis of Synchronization Skeletons using Branching-Time Temporal Logic. In D. Kozen, editor, *Proceedings of the Workshop on Logic of Programs,* Yorktown Heights, volume 131 of *Lecture Notes in Computer Science*, pages 52–71. Springer-Verlag, 1981. 145
6. J. C. Corbett, M. B. Dwyer, J. Hatcliff, S. Laubach, C. S. Pasareanu, Robby, and H. Zheng. Bandera: Extracting Finite-State Models from Java Source Code. In *Proceedings of the 22nd International Conference on Software Engineering*, 2000. 137, 148

7. P. Cousot and R. Cousot. Temporal Abstract Interpretation. In *Proceedings of the 27th ACM Symposium on Principles of Programming Languages*, pages 12–25, Boston, January 2000.

8. D. Dams. *Abstract interpretation and partition refinement for model checking*. PhD thesis, Technische Universiteit Eindhoven, The Netherlands, 1996.   141

9. S. Das and D. L. Dill. Successive Approximation of Abstract Transition Relations. In *Proceedings of LICS'2001 (16th IEEE Symposium on Logic in Computer Science)*, pages 51–58, Boston, June 2001.   139, 146

10. P. Godefroid. Model Checking for Programming Languages using VeriSoft. In *Proceedings of the 24th ACM Symposium on Principles of Programming Languages*, pages 174–186, Paris, January 1997.   137

11. P. Godefroid, M. Huth, and R. Jagadeesan. Abstraction-based Model Checking using Modal Transition Systems. In *Proceedings of CONCUR'2001 (12th International Conference on Concurrency Theory)*, volume 2154 of *Lecture Notes in Computer Science*, pages 426–440, Aalborg, August 2001. Springer-Verlag.   138, 139, 140, 141, 147, 148

12. S. Graf and H. Saidi. Construction of Abstract State Graphs with PVS. In *Proceedings of the 9th International Conference on Computer Aided Verification*, volume 1254 of *Lecture Notes in Computer Science*, pages 72–83, Haifa, June 1997. Springer-Verlag.   139

13. T. Henzinger, R. Jhala, R. Majumdar, and G. Sutre. Lazy Abstraction. In *Proceedings of the 29th ACM Symposium on Principles of Programming Languages*, Portland, January 2002.   139, 146, 147

14. G. J. Holzmann and M. H. Smith. A Practical Method for Verifying Event-Driven Software. In *Proceedings of the 21st International Conference on Software Engineering*, pages 597–607, 1999.   137

15. M. Huth, R. Jagadeesan, and D. Schmidt. Modal Transition Systems: a Foundation for Three-Valued Program Analysis. In *Proceedings of the European Symposium on Programming (ESOP'2001)*, volume 2028 of *Lecture Notes in Computer Science*. Springer-Verlag, April 2001.   139, 140

16. S. C. Kleene. *Introduction to Metamathematics*. North Holland, 1987.   140

17. D. Kozen. Results on the Propositional Mu-Calculus. *Theoretical Computer Science*, 27:333–354, 1983.   138, 145

18. O. Kupferman, M. Y. Vardi, and P. Wolper. An Automata-Theoretic Approach to Branching-Time Model Checking. *Journal of the ACM*, 47(2):312–360, March 2000.   143, 145, 146

19. K. G. Larsen and B. Thomsen. A Modal Process Logic. In *Proceedings of Third Annual Symposium on Logic in Computer Science*, pages 203–210. IEEE Computer Society Press, 1988.   138, 139, 140

20. Z. Manna and A. Pnueli. *The Temporal Logic of Reactive and Concurrent Systems: Specification*. Springer-Verlag, 1992.   143, 145, 148

21. K. S. Namjoshi and R. K. Kurshan. Syntactic Program Transformations for Automatic Abstraction. In *Proceedings of the 12th Conference on Computer Aided Verification*, volume 1855 of *Lecture Notes in Computer Science*, pages 435–449, Chicago, July 2000. Springer-Verlag.   137

22. F. Nielson, H. R. Nielson, and C. Hankin. *Principles of Program Analysis*. Springer-Verlag, 1999.

23. M. Y. Vardi. Why is Modal Logic So Robustly Decidable? In *Proceedings of DIMACS Workshop on Descriptive Complexity and Finite Models*. AMS, 1997.   145

24. M. Y. Vardi and P. Wolper. Automata-Theoretic Techniques for Modal Logics of Programs. *Journal of Computer and System Science*, 32(2):183–221, April 1986. 144

25. W. Visser, K. Havelund, G. Brat, and S. Park. Model Checking Programs. In *Proceedings of ASE'2000 (15th International Conference on Automated Software Engineering)*, Grenoble, September 2000. 137

Property Checking via Structural Analysis

Jason Baumgartner[1], Andreas Kuehlmann[2], and Jacob Abraham[3]

[1] IBM Enterprise Systems Group, Austin, TX 78758
[2] Cadence Berkeley Labs, Berkeley, CA 94704
[3] The University of Texas, Austin, TX 78712

Abstract. This paper describes a structurally-guided framework for the
decomposition of a verification task into subtasks, each solved by a specialized algorithm for overall efficiency. Our contributions include the
following: (1) a structural algorithm for computing a bound of a state-
transition diagram's diameter which, for several classes of netlists, is sufficiently small to guarantee completeness of a bounded property check;
(2) a robust backward unfolding technique for structural target enlargement: from the target states, we perform a series of *compose-based* pre-
image computations, truncating the search if resource limitations are
exceeded; (3) similar to frontier simplification in symbolic reachability
analysis, we use induction via *don't cares* for enhancing the presented target enlargement. In many practical cases, the verification problem can be
discharged by the enlargement process; otherwise, it is passed in simplified form to an arbitrary subsequent solution approach. The presented
techniques are embedded in a flexible verification framework, allowing
arbitrary combinations with other techniques. Extensive experimental
results demonstrate the effectiveness of the described methods at solving
and simplifying practical verification problems.

1 Introduction

Due to the complexity of modern hardware designs, formal verification methods are finding increasing utilization to augment the coverage shortcomings of
test-based validation approaches. There are two primary methodologies for the
verification of safety properties. Inductive methods use a provided or computed
invariant to prove that no initial state can reach a state that violates a property (a *target state*). State traversal techniques employ exact or approximate
search to find a trajectory from an initial state to a target state; unreachability
is proven if a search exhausts without finding such a trajectory. Because of their
exponential complexity, exact state traversal techniques – whether symbolic or
explicit – are applicable only to small or modestly-sized designs.

Numerous approximate techniques have been proposed to address the capacity limitations of exact state traversal. Overapproximating the set of reachable
states is useful to prove a target unreachable if all target states remain outside
the overapproximation, though cannot readily demonstrate reachability otherwise. For example, design partitioning [4] can be applied to overapproximate
the set of reachable states by exploring components whose sizes are tractable for

D. Brinksma and K. G. Larsen (Eds.): CAV 2002, LNCS 2404, pp. 151–165, 2002.
© Springer-Verlag Berlin Heidelberg 2002

exact traversal. Similarly, the concept of a *free fence* [11] is suggested for proving the correctness of a property by *localization*.

Conversely, underapproximate techniques are useful to demonstrate reachability of targets, but are generally incapable of proving their unreachability. For example, bounded model checking (BMC) [1] is based upon a satisfiability check of a finite k-step unfolding of the target. If it can be proven that the diameter of the design is smaller or equal to k, BMC becomes complete and can thereby also prove unreachability. A similar underapproximate method is based upon a bounded backward unfolding of the design starting from the target. The unfolded structure comprises an enlarged target which can be used to either directly discharge the verification problem or to produce a new, simplified problem to be solved by a subsequent verification flow.

An inductive proof requires an invariant that implies the property. The base step of a k-step inductive proof checks that the invariant holds during the first k time-steps. The inductive step must then show that asserting the invariant during time-steps $i, \ldots, (i + k - 1)$ implies that it continues to hold at time-step $(i + k)$. The typical drawback of inductive schemes is the intrinsic difficulty in determining a powerful enough invariant that is inductive and also implies correctness of the property. However, for many practical problems, backward unfolding results in an inductive invariant after several steps.

In this paper we show how the above-mentioned techniques can be synergistically combined to exploit their individual strengths. We first calculate an overapproximation of the diameter of the design using a novel structural algorithm. This bound has shown significant practical utility in precluding "redundantly large" unfoldings, and obviating more costly unbounded proof techniques. We next alternate between SAT-based forward unfolding and inductive backward BDD-based unfolding to attempt to solve the property. The forward analysis is useful for quickly hitting shallow targets, and also efficiently discharges our induction hypothesis for the backward analysis. The backward analysis is useful for proving unreachability, and renders a simpler problem – the enlarged target – otherwise. This iteration terminates if the unfolding depth surpasses the estimated diameter or if some resource limitations are exceeded. In the first case unreachability is proven; in the latter the enlarged target is passed to a subsequent solution approach. As demonstrated by our experiments, our technique efficiently solves many practical targets, and otherwise offers a significant reduction capability, hence the enlarged target is often much easier to discharge than the original.

2   Netlists: Syntax and Semantics

Definition 1. A *netlist* is a tuple $N = \langle \langle V, E \rangle, G, T, Z \rangle$ comprising a directed graph with vertices V and edges $E \subseteq V \times V$, a semantic mapping from vertices to gate types $G : V \mapsto types$, and a set of *targets* $T \subseteq V$ correlating to a set of properties $AG(\neg t), \forall t \in T$. The function $Z : V \mapsto V$ is the initial value mapping.

Our gate *types* define a set of constants, primary inputs (nondeterministic bits), registers, and combinational gates with various functions, whose semantics are provided in Definition 2. The type *register* is our only sequential gate type; all others are combinational. The type of a gate may place constraints upon its incoming edge count – e.g., registers and inverters have an indegree of one. We assume that every directed cycle comprises one or more registers – i.e., there are no combinational cycles.

Definition 2. The *semantics of a netlist* N are defined in terms of semantic traces: $0, 1$ valuations to gates over time. We denote the set of all legal traces associated with a netlist by $P \subseteq [V \times \mathbb{N} \mapsto \{0, 1\}]$, defining P as the subset of all possible functions from $V \times \mathbb{N}$ to $\{0, 1\}$ which are consistent with the following rule. The value of gate v at time i in trace p is denoted by $p(v, i)$.

$$p(v, i) = \begin{cases} c & : v \text{ is a constant vertex with value } c \in \{0, 1\} \\ s^i_{v_p} & : v \text{ is a primary input with sampled value } s^i_{v_p} \\ G_v\big(p(u_1, i), ..., p(u_n, i)\big) & : v \text{ is a combinational gate and } G_v = G(v) \\ p(u_1, i - 1) & : v \text{ is a register and } i > 0 \\ p\big(Z(v), 0\big) & : v \text{ is a register and } i = 0 \end{cases}$$

Term u_j denotes the source vertex of the j-th incoming edge to v, implying $(u_j, v) \in E$.

The initial values of a netlist represent the values that registers can take at time 0; note that this function is ignored for non-register types. For a set of vertices $U \subseteq V$, let $regs(U) = \{v \subseteq U : G(v) = register\}$, and let $coi(U)$ be the set of vertices in the cone of influence of U. We assume that $coi\big(Z(regs(V))\big)$ contains no registers. Furthermore, we do not allow combinational cycles, which makes Definition 2 well-formed. We say that target t is *hit* in trace p at time i if $p(t, i) = 1$. A *state* is a mapping from registers to $0, 1$ values. We refer to the set of states for which there exists a primary input mapping that hits $t \in T$ as the set of *target states*.

Definition 3. The *diameter*[1] of $U \subseteq V$, denoted by $d(U)$, is the minimum $d \in \mathbb{N}$ such that for any trace p and $\forall i, j \geq 0$, there exists a trace p' such that $p\big(regs(coi(U)), i\big) = p'\big(regs(coi(U)), i\big)$ and $p(U, i+j+d) = p'(U, i+k)$ for some $0 \leq k < d$.

In other words, if any state s' is reachable from state s, then s' is reachable in less than d steps from s. By this definition, the diameter of a purely combinational cone is 1; the diameter of mod c-counter is c. Clearly $AG(\neg t)$ iff $\forall p \in P. \bigwedge_{i=0}^{d(t)-1} \big(p(t, i) = 0\big)$.

---

[1] Our definition of diameter is generally one greater than the standard definition for graphs.

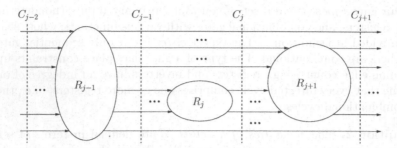

Fig. 1. Slice of TSAP structure

3 Diameter Approximation

In this section, we discuss a structural algorithm for computing an upper bound $\hat{d}(t) \geq d(t)$ on the diameter of target t. The goal is to find a practically tight overapproximation such that bounded search can be applied in a complete manner. A simple bound is $2^{|regs(coi(t))|}$, though this bound is often too weak to be of any practical value. Semantic approaches at obtaining a bound [1, 13] are of formidable complexity – often greater than a BMC of the target itself.

There are two characteristics of practical netlists which may be exploited to structurally compute a tighter diameter bound. First, netlists seldom represent monolithic strongly connected graphs. Instead, they often comprise multiple maximal strongly connected components (SCCs); an approximation of diameter can thus be derived from an estimation of the individual SCC diameters. Second, although the overapproximate diameter of a component is generally exponential in its register count, several commonly occurring structures have much tighter bounds. For example, as proven in Theorem 1, the diameter of a single memory *row* comprising n registers is 2 instead of 2^n; acyclic registers only cause a linear, rather than multiplicative increase in diameter.

Definition 4. A *topologically sorted acyclic partitioning (TSAP)* of V into n components is a labeling $comp : V \mapsto \{1, 2, \ldots, n\}$ such that $\forall u, v \in V.((u, v) \in E \Rightarrow comp(u) \leq comp(v))$.

Let $R_i = \{v : comp(v) = i\}$ denote the i-th component of a TSAP. Let $C_i = R_i \cup \{u : \exists v.((u, v) \in E \wedge u \in \bigcup_{j=1}^{i-1} R_j \wedge v \in \bigcup_{j=i+1}^{n} R_j)\}$. Set C_i adds to R_i the elements of lower-numbered components which fan out to higher-numbered components. For example, in Figure 1, some elements of component R_{j-1} are included in C_j and C_{j+1}, though no elements of R_j are included in C_{j+1} since no outgoing edges from R_j have sinks beyond R_{j+1}. We distinguish between the following specific types of components of a TSAP. Let x_i be a register vertex and y_i be the source of the incoming edge to x_i, denoting the present-state and next-state function of the corresponding register, respectively.

– A *combinational component* (*CC*) contains only non-register vertices.

- A *constant register component* (*NC*) contains only register vertices whose incoming edges are sourced by their outputs; i.e. $y_i = x_i$.
- An *acyclic register component* (*AC*) contains only register vertices whose incoming edges are inputs to the component.
- A *memory register component* (*MC*) is composed solely of a set of $r \times c$ registers and combinational gates, for $r \geq 1$ and $c \geq 1$. The next-state functions of the registers have the form: $y_{i,j} = (x_{i,j} \wedge \bigwedge_{k=1}^{w} \neg load_{i,k}) \vee \bigvee_{k=1}^{w} (data_{i,j,k} \wedge load_{i,k})$, for $1 \leq i \leq r$ and $1 \leq j \leq c$, where $data_{i,j,k}$ and $load_{i,k}$ are inputs to the component. Let $rows(R_i) = r$ for *MC* R_i.
- A *queue register component* (*QC*) is composed solely of a set of $r \times c$ registers and combinational gates, for $r > 1$ and $c \geq 1$. The next-state functions of the registers have the form: $y_{1,j} = (x_{1,j} \wedge \bigwedge_{k=1}^{w} \neg load_k) \vee \bigvee_{k=1}^{w} (data_{j,k} \wedge load_k)$; $y_{i,j} = (x_{i,j} \wedge \bigwedge_{k=1}^{w} \neg load_k) \vee (x_{i-1,j} \wedge \bigvee_{k=1}^{w} load_k)$, for $1 < i \leq r$ and $1 \leq j \leq c$, where $data_{j,k}$ and $load_k$ are inputs to the component. Let $rows(R_i) = r$ for *QC* R_i.
- All remaining components are *general components* (*GC*). Let $|regs(R_i)|$ denote the number of registers in *GC* R_i, which must be greater than 0. If there exists a combinational path from an input of R_i to any combinational gate $u \in R_i$, and $\exists v.((u,v) \in E \wedge v \notin R_i)$, we say that the *GC* is *Mealy*.

Note that *MC*s and *QC*s are generalized for w write ports. Further generalizations are possible, though we have found these adequate for commonly-occurring structures. *NC*s may have constant initial values (in which case they should be simplified by constant propagations) or symbolic initial values (e.g., implementing *forall* variables).

Our approximation of the diameter of a target t is based upon a TSAP of its *coi*. We prefer TSAPs with maximally-sized *AC*s, *NC*s, *MC*s, and *QC*s to ensure tighter approximation, which are obtained by first partitioning $coi(t)$ into maximal SCCs, then selectively clustering components so as not to introduce cycles.

Let $\epsilon(i) = 0$ if $i = 0$, or if $(C_{i-1} \cap C_i \neq \emptyset)$, or if R_i is a *Mealy GC*; otherwise $\epsilon(i) = 1$. Further, let $\delta(i) = 1 - \epsilon(i)$. Term $\epsilon(i)$ denotes whether R_i constitutes a cut between components $R_1 \ldots R_{i-1}$ and components $R_{i+1} \ldots R_n$, and $\delta(i) = \neg\epsilon(i)$. In Figure 1, only R_{j-1} constitutes a cut (provided that it is not a *Mealy GC*), hence $\epsilon(j-1) = 1$, whereas $\epsilon(j) = \epsilon(j+1) = 0$. The following formulas for computing $D(i)$ and $S(i)$ provide the key to our diameter estimation for R_i. Let $Q : R_i \mapsto \{CC, NC, AC, MC, QC, GC\}$ denote the type of component R_i.

$$
D(i) = \begin{cases}
1 & : i = 0 \\
D(i-1) & : i > 0 \wedge Q(R_i) \in \{CC, NC, AC\} \\
D(i-1) \cdot (rows(R_i) + \delta(i)) & : i > 0 \wedge Q(R_i) \in \{MC, QC\} \\
D(i-1) \cdot (D_i - \epsilon(i)) + \epsilon(i) & : i > 0 \wedge Q(R_i) = GC
\end{cases}
$$

$$
S(i) = \begin{cases}
0 & : i = 0 \\
S(i-1) & : i > 0 \wedge Q(R_i) \in \{CC, NC, GC\} \\
S(i-1) + \epsilon(i) & : i > 0 \wedge Q(R_i) \in \{MC, QC\} \\
S(i-1) + 1 & : i > 0 \wedge Q(R_i) = AC
\end{cases}
$$

Term D_i represents an upper-bound on the diameter $GC\,R_i$; clearly $2^{|regs(R_i)|}$ is conservative. We may use other estimation techniques, such as approximate reachability analysis [ ], to find tighter bounds on the diameter of a GC. Note that the recurrence diameter [ ] must be used with such an approach due to possible input constraints to the GC in the composed netlist.

Theorem 1. The value $D(i) + S(i)$ is an upper-bound on the diameter of component R_i. Further, term $\hat{d}(t) = D(i) + S(i)$ is an upper-bound on the diameter of target t for $comp(t) = i$.

Proof. Our proof is based upon the hypothesis that for cut C_i, any arbitrarily-ordered succession of c reachable valuations is producible within $c \cdot D(i) + S(i)$ time-steps. The theorem follows from assigning $c = 1$. We will prove this hypothesis by induction on i. The intuition behind this hypothesis is that component R_{i+1} may transition from each state only upon a distinct valuation of C_i. Therefore, in order to ensure that we attain an upper bound on the diameter of R_{i+1}, we generally must wait for a succession of $c = D(i+1)$ valuations to C_i.

Our base case has $i = 1$. If $Q(R_1) \in \{NC, CC\}$, we obtain $D(1) = 1$ and $S(1) = 0$. This result is correct, since any valuation producible by C_1 is producible every time-step due to its lack of sequential behavior. $Q(R_1)$ cannot be MC, QC, or AC since those types require other components to drive their inputs. Finally, if $Q(R_1) = GC$, then $D(1) = D_1$ which is an upper bound on the diameter of C_1 by definition, hence our proof obligation is satisfied.

We next proceed to the inductive step. If $Q(R_{i+1}) = NC$, then our result is correct by the base case analysis since such components have no inputs sourced by other components. If $Q(R_{i+1}) = CC$, then our result is correct by hypothesis, noting that R_{i+1} is a purely combinational function of C_i and primary inputs. If $Q(R_{i+1}) = AC$, then $D(i+1) = D(i)$ and $S(i+1) = S(i) + 1$. This result is correct since the initial values of an AC have semantic importance only at time 0, and since an AC merely delays some values of C_i by one time-step. If $Q(R_{i+1}) \in \{MC, QC\}$, then we obtain $D(i+1) = D(i) \cdot \big(rows(R_{i+1}) + \delta(i+1)\big)$ and $S(i+1) = S(i) + \epsilon(i+1)$. This result is correct by noting that it can take at most $c \cdot D(i) + S(i)$ time-steps to reach any possible succession of c valuations to C_i by hypothesis. If $\delta(i+1) = 1$, then C_i fans out to C_{i+2}, meaning that we generally must wait for $c = \big(rows(R_{i+1}) + 1\big)$ valuations to C_i to be sure that we have an upper bound on the diameter of C_{i+1}. If $\delta(i+1) = 0$, then we need only wait for $c = rows(R_{i+1})$ valuations to C_i, plus one extra time-step for the *load* to take effect upon C_{i+1}. Lastly, if $Q(R_{i+1}) = GC$, then $D(i+1) = D(i) \cdot \big(D_{i+1} - \epsilon(i+1)\big) + \epsilon(i+1)$ and $S(i+1) = S(i)$, where D_{i+1} is defined as an upper-bound on the diameter of R_{i+1}. For $\epsilon(i+1) = 0$ this result is obvious. Otherwise, note that any trace segment begins in one state of R_{i+1}, and $c = (D_{i+1} - 1)$ transitions, which must initiate within $c \cdot D(i) + S(i)$ time-steps, plus one for the final transition to complete, is sufficient to put R_{i+1} into any of its subsequently-reachable states. Hence $D(i+1) = D(i) \cdot (D_{i+1} - 1) + 1$ time-steps satisfies our obligation. $\square$

We lastly observe that localization [11] has shown significant practical utility in quickly proving unreachability, and possibly enhancing reachability analysis. Localization consists of using a cut frontier (the *free fence*) to isolate an over-approximate localized *coi* for target t, yielding localized target t'. Term $\hat{d}(t')$ may be useful to enable bounded analysis, rather than often-more-expensive unbounded analysis, to solve t' since localized cones may often have structurally-calculatable shallow diameters. This technique may be useful not only to analyze certain localized cones more efficiently, but also to select better localized cones. For example, one may incrementally add gates to a localized cone to make it as large as possible – hence the overapproximation becomes tighter, as long as the incremental additions preserve a shallow diameter.

4   Target Enlargement

A k-step enlargement of target t incrementally computes the set of states that can reach t in k transitions. If an initial state becomes part of the enlarged target during this process, the target is proven reachable. Otherwise, if during the current enlargement step no new states are enumerated that have not been encountered in "shallower" steps, the target is proven unreachable. If $k \geq d(t)$ steps are performed without reaching an initial state, unreachability can be inferred. If at any step the computing resources exceed a given limit, the enlargement process is truncated and the verification problem is reformulated based upon the states enumerated during shallower steps (refer to Figures 2 and 3).

Target enlargement is based upon pre-image computation, for which there are three primary techniques: (1) transition-relation based methods [2,16,15,9], (2) transition-function based methods using the *constrain* operator [4], and (3) transition-function based methods using the *compose* operator [6]. We utilize the latter, since the set of registers in the support of each iteration of a target enlargement is often a small subset of those in the entire *coi* of the target. This precludes entailing unnecessary computational complexity, and well-suits our goal of rendering a simpler problem with as few registers as possible – the enlarged target – if the target is not solved during enlargement.

Figure 2 shows the pseudocode for our target enlargement algorithm. In step 1, $BSAT(N, t, i)$ denotes a SAT-based bounded check of target t using unfolding depth i. We use $BSAT$ to attempt to hit the target as well as to discharge our induction hypothesis for the the subsequent backward analysis. We use SAT rather than BDD-based analysis since the former is often more efficient for bounded analysis. If the overapproximate diameter is surpassed in the bounded search, we discharge the target in step 1b.

If $BSAT$ is inconclusive, we perform *compose-based* pre-image computations[2]. We apply early quantification of primary input variables to keep the intermediate BDD size small; as soon as the last composition which has a given primary

---

[2] We may alternatively iterate between $BSAT$ and pre-image computation with resource bounds.

Algorithm Enlarge($N, t, k, \hat{d}(t)$)

1. for ($i = 0$; $i < k$; i++)
   (a) Apply $BSAT(N, t, i)$. If t is reachable, then **return** REACHABLE with $BSAT$ trace.
   (b) If $i = \hat{d}(t)$, then **return** UNREACHABLE.
2. Build BDD_0 for t over the primary inputs and registers in its transitive fanin.
3. Existentially quantify primary inputs from BDD_0.
4. for ($i = 1$; $i \leq k$; i++)
   (a) Compute MLP [12] schedule $S = (v_1, \ldots, v_s)$ for registers supporting BDD_{i-1}.
   (b) Rename all variables v in BDD_{i-1} to v', forming BDD_i.
   (c) for ($j = 1$; $j \leq |S|$; j++)
       i. $BDD_i = $ bdd_compose(BDD_i, v'_j, f_{v_j}), which substitutes f_{v_j} in place of variable v'_j in BDD_i, where f_{v_j} is the BDD for the next-state function of v_j.
       ii. Perform early quantification of primary inputs from BDD_i.
       iii. Minimize BDD_i with bdd_compact [8] using $BDD_0 \ldots BDD_{i-1}$ as *don't cares*.
       iv. If BDD_i is too large, assign $k = i - 1$ and **return** BDD_{i-1}.
   (d) If BDD_i is 0, then **return** UNREACHABLE.
5. **return** BDD_k.

Fig. 2. Algorithm **Enlarge** for target enlargement

input i in its support is performed, we may quantify i. We utilize a modified MLP algorithm [12] for our quantification and composition scheduling. At each MLP scheduling step, we either schedule a composition, or "activate" an input to simplify future scheduling decisions – initially, all primary inputs are "inactive." Our goal is to minimize the lifetime of input variables, from activation until quantification, and to delay the introduction of registers. Each composition step eliminates one next-state register variable v', and introduces zero or more present-state register variables v and primary inputs. The following modifications of the MLP algorithm have proven to be the most useful:

- At each scheduling step, we schedule compositions of all registers with no inactive primary inputs in their support which introduce at most one register not already in the BDD support. Each such composition eliminates the corresponding v' variable from the BDD support, and adds at most one v variable to the support, which is typically beneficial for minimizing peak BDD size. We next schedule compositions of all registers with zero inactive, and nonzero active, inputs in their support, regardless of their register support, to force input quantification.
- If no register satisfies the above criteria, we instead activate an input. When choosing which input i to activate, we select one which is in the support of an unscheduled register with the fewest, though non-zero, inactive inputs in its support. Ties are broken to minimize the total number of registers not already in the BDD support which would need to be introduced before i could be quantified.

After each quantification, the intermediate BDD_i is simplified by the bdd_compact operator [ ], using the BDDs of previous iterations as *don't cares*[3]. Effectively, this simplification attempts to prove inductiveness of the target; the corresponding hypothesis was previously discharged by $BSAT$. The resulting simplified BDD'_i satisfies the relation $BDD_i \setminus \bigcup_{j=0}^{i-1} BDD_j \subseteq BDD'_i \subseteq \bigcup_{j=0}^{i} BDD_j$ and $size(BDD'_i) \leq size(BDD_i)$, where $size(BDD_i)$ represents the node count of BDD_i. The bdd_compact operation cannot introduce new variables into the support of a BDD, but may eliminate some. Hence it is well-suited for our goal of minimizing the support of each pre-image step and thereby of the enlarged target. It is also this goal that prompts us to keep each BDD_i distinct. Using don't cares instead of constraints weakens our unreachability analysis, thus a fixed-point may never be reached. However, as demonstrated by our experimental results, many targets can be solved or significantly simplified which affirms the chosen trade-off of precision versus computational efficiency.

If the BDD size at any step exceeds a given limit, the enlargement process is truncated and the BDD of the previous iteration is returned. This prevents exceedingly large enlarged targets which could harm the subsequent verification flow. We have found that this approach – from structure to BDDs back to structure – is more effective in a flexible toolset than enlargement by purely structural transformation [ ]. The latter does tend to yield large, redundant structures which may seriously hinder subsequent BDD- or simulation-based analysis methods. In contrast, our enlargement approach often reduces the size of the target cone and thus enhances any subsequent verification approach.

Using SAT rather than BDDs for an inductive proof may occasionally be more efficient. However, if unsuccessful, our BDD-based result can be reused to directly represent the *simplified* function of the k-step enlarged target. A similar reuse is not possible for a SAT-based method. In [ ] it is proposed to apply cubes obtained during an inductive SAT call as "lighthouses" to enhance the ability to subsequently hit targets; such an incomplete approach, however, precludes the structural reductions of our technique.

5   Top-Level Algorithm

In this section we discuss the overall flow of our decomposition algorithm **Verify** which is illustrated in Figure 3. We first determine a limit on the number of enlargement steps and then call the algorithm **Enlarge** on target t. If **Enlarge** returns a *reachable* or *unreachable* solution, this result is returned. Otherwise a structure representing the enlarged target is added to N. This is performed by creating a new netlist N' which encodes the function of the BDD of the enlarged target. The output gate of N', denoted as t', is a combinational function over the

---

[3] A similar reachability-based approach would exploit states that can hit t within k time-steps as don't cares when assessing reachability of a state that can hit t in exactly k steps. With this observation, we may use these don't cares also to simplify the next-state functions of registers, which may further reduce the complexity for a subsequent verification flow.

registers in N. The composition of N and N', denoted as $N \parallel N'$, is then passed to a subsequent verification flow to attempt to solve t'. For example, we may next apply retiming and combinational optimizations [9] which have the potential to further reduce the netlist size before another application of **Verify** is attempted. This effectively applies the presented approach as a reentrant engine in a general *transformation-based verification* [9] flow. If a subsequent engine demonstrates unreachability of t', then t is also unreachable. If the subsequent verification flow hits t', we use simulation and another $BSAT$ in step 6 to undo the effects of the enlargement on the trace. Because of its speed, a simulation preprocessing for eliminating easy-to-hit targets as step 0 may be useful in a robust toolset.

Algorithm Verify (N, t)

1. Determine a limit on number of enlargement steps
   $k = \min \left(user\_specified\_limit, \hat{d}(t) \right)$.
2. Invoke algorithm **Enlarge**$(N, t, k, \hat{d}(t))$ to enlarge the target. If the problem is solved (*result* $\in$ {REACHABLE, UNREACHABLE}) **return** *result* with any applicable trace.
3. Synthesize the BDD for the enlarged target from step 2 into netlist N', compose N' onto N, and declare new target $t' \in V(N')$. This results in a new problem ($N \parallel N', t'$).
4. Utilize an arbitrary verification flow to attempt to solve ($N \parallel N', t'$).
5. If step 4 yields UNREACHABLE **return** UNREACHABLE.
6. If step 4 yields REACHABLE with a trace p, undo the effects of the enlargement by the following steps:
   (a) Complete p over N with simulation up to the first hit of t' to obtain p'. This is needed because the cone-of-influence of t and t' may differ and p may be only partial.
   (b) Cast $BSAT(N, t, k)$ from the last state of p', which must be satisfiable, to obtain p''.
   (c) Concatenate p'' onto p', overwriting the last time-step of p' with the first time-step of p'', to obtain p'''.
   (d) **return** REACHABLE with p'''.

Fig. 3. Top-level algorithm **Verify**

Theorem 2. Algorithm **Verify** (N, t) is sound and complete.

The proof of Theorem 2 is straight-forward, and omitted due to space limitations.

6   Experimental Results

In this section we provide experimental results. All experiments were run on an IBM ThinkPad model T21 running RedHat Linux 6.2, with an 800 MHz Pentium III and 256 MB main memory. We set the peak BDD size to 2^{17} nodes, and capped $BSAT$ (using a structural SAT solver [10]) to 10 seconds per target with an upper-bound of fifty steps.

Our first set of experiments were performed on the ISCAS89 benchmark netlists. The results are provided in Table 6. Since these benchmarks have no specified properties, we labeled each primary output of these netlists as a target. Column 1 gives the name of the benchmark and Column 2 provides the number of registers that are included in the various component types: constants (NCs), acyclic (ACs), table cells (MCs or QCs), and complex (GCs). Column 3 lists the average diameter $\hat{d}$ of all targets t with $\hat{d}(t) \leq 20$ and their count. These are candidates to be discharged with BMC. The bound of 20 was chosen arbitrarily as being typically efficient for bounded search. The next columns provide results for two distinct runs: first a standard run using the techniques as described in the previous sections, and second a "reduction-only" run which does not apply $BSAT$ to solve the problem. Instead, if $BSAT$ would solve the target in i steps, our enlargement is performed to depth $j = i - 1$; if $j < 1$, we only build BDD_0 in **Enlarge**. For the standard run in Column 4 we report the number of targets in the netlist, the number of targets which are hit, and the number of targets that are proven unreachable. The number of unreachable results proven with BDDs is provided in parenthesis. In Column 5 we report the accumulated size of the coi's of unsolved targets in terms of the number of registers and primary inputs, and the number eliminated in the corresponding enlarged cones. Column 6 reports the average number of seconds spent per target, and the peak memory usage. For the reduction-only run we report coi sizes and reduction results (similar to Column 5) in Column 7.

There are several noteworthy points in Table 6. Our techniques solve most targets whether reachable or unreachable, regardless of netlist size – 1575 of 1615 targets are solved. Though the "difficulty" of these targets is unknown, this is an indication of the robustness of our approach. Many registers are non-complex: 26% are acyclic registers, and 6% are table cells. For netlists with unsolved targets, we achieve an average reduction per netlists of 5.3% in register count and 5.0% in primary input count, and a cumulative reduction of 12.2% for registers and 10.3% for primary inputs. A total of 381 targets have a diameter of less than 20. Our reduction-only run yields an average reduction per netlist of 13.9% in registers and 13.0% in primary inputs.

In Table 6 we provide a similar analysis for randomly-selected targets from the IBM Gigahertz Processor (GP). Most targets, 254 out of 284, are solved. A large fraction of the registers is non-complex: 1% are constants, 57% are acyclic, and 10% are table cells. A total of 91 targets have a diameter of less than 20. We achieve an average reduction per netlist of 12.1% in registers and 11.1% in primary inputs. The reduction-only run yields an average reduction per netlist of 54.9% in registers and 54.8% in primary inputs, and a cumulative reduction of 70.6% of registers and 69.5% of primary inputs.

We now discuss several netlists in more detail. Netlist LIBBQn is a large table-based netlist. Forward reachability analysis of the optimized [10] cone of a single unreachable target with a diameter of three (comprising 442 registers and 134 primary inputs) requires 172.3 seconds and 25 MB with a MLP [12] algorithm, with sift variable ordering enabled and a random initial ordering. Our

Table 1. Experimental results for the ISCAS89 benchmarks

Model	regs in: NC;AC; MC+QC; GC	Avg. d < 20; Count	Standard Run |T|;Rch; Unrch (BDDs)	regs (inputs) Eliminated ; Sum	Time/|T| (s); Mem (MB)	Reduction-Only Run regs (inputs) Eliminated ; Sum
PRO-LOG	0 ; 107 ; 1 ; 28	1.5 ; 6	73 ; 69 ; 4 (0)	0 (0); 0 (0)	0.07 ; 15	146 (126) ; 2044 (1438)
S1196	0 ; 18 ; 0 ; 0	3.3 ; 14	14 ; 14 ; 0 (0)	0 (0); 0 (0)	0.08 ; 12	24 (56); 88 (196)
S1238	0 ; 18 ; 0 ; 0	3.3 ; 14	14 ; 14 ; 0 (0)	0 (0); 0 (0)	0.08 ; 12	24 (56); 88 (196)
S1269	0 ; 9 ; 17 ; 11	4.0 ; 2	10 ; 10 ; 0 (0)	0 (0); 0 (0)	0.10 ; 15	289 (145); 296 (152)
S13207_1	0 ; 314 ; 128 ; 196	1.7 ; 51	152 ; 131 ; 12 (9)	26 (0); 527 (18)	1.02 ; 107	3155 (302); 24244 (2172)
S1423	0 ; 3 ; 16 ; 55	1.0 ; 1	5 ; 5 ; 0 (0)	0 (0); 0 (0)	0.13 ; 15	2 (0); 278 (69)
S1488	0 ; 0 ; 0 ; 6	0.0 ; 0	19 ; 18 ; 0 (0)	0 (0); 6 (8)	0.74 ; 23	0 (0); 114 (152)
S1494	0 ; 0 ; 0 ; 6	0.0 ; 0	19 ; 18 ; 0 (0)	0 (0); 6 (8)	0.89 ; 23	0 (0); 114 (152)
S1512	0 ; 0 ; 1 ; 56	0.0 ; 0	21 ; 10 ; 0 (0)	8 (8); 437 (283)	8.22 ; 24	135 (93); 837 (543)
S15850_1	0 ; 99 ; 124 ; 311	2.3 ; 112	150 ; 135 ; 8 (1)	451 (54); 1450 (174)	0.68 ; 63	2425 (321); 9683 (1301)
S208_1	0 ; 0 ; 0 ; 8	0.0 ; 0	1 ; 1 ; 0 (0)	0 (0); 0 (0)	0.27 ; 15	0 (0); 8 (10)
S27	0 ; 1 ; 2 ; 0	2.0 ; 1	1 ; 1 ; 0 (0)	0 (0); 0 (0)	0.23 ; 12	0 (0); 3 (4)
S298	0 ; 0 ; 1 ; 13	0.0 ; 0	6 ; 6 ; 0 (0)	0 (0); 0 (0)	0.12 ; 15	22 (6); 54 (18)
S3271	0 ; 6 ; 0 ; 110	7.0 ; 1	14 ; 14 ; 0 (0)	0 (0); 0 (0)	0.11 ; 15	0 (0); 1248 (339)
S3330	0 ; 103 ; 1 ; 28	1.0 ; 6	73 ; 73 ; 0 (0)	0 (0); 0 (0)	0.08 ; 15	146 (125); 2044 (1442)
S3384	0 ; 111 ; 0 ; 72	7.8 ; 4	26 ; 26 ; 0 (0)	0 (0); 0 (0)	0.09 ; 15	26 (25); 2587 (425)
S344	0 ; 0 ; 4 ; 11	3.3 ; 3	11 ; 10 ; 1 (0)	0 (0); 0 (0)	0.09 ; 15	6 (2); 129 (75)
S349	0 ; 0 ; 4 ; 11	3.0 ; 3	11 ; 10 ; 1 (0)	0 (0); 0 (0)	0.09 ; 15	3 (1); 126 (74)
S35932	0 ; 0 ; 0 ; 1728	0.0 ; 0	320 ; 320 ; 0 (0)	0 (0); 0 (0)	2.01 ; 105	0 (0); 331776 (11200)
S382	0 ; 6 ; 0 ; 15	0.0 ; 0	6 ; 6 ; 0 (0)	0 (0); 0 (0)	1.71 ; 15	34 (6); 96 (18)
S38584_1	0 ; 47 ; 4 ; 1375	1.0 ; 38	304 ; 301 ; 1 (0)	0 (0); 1377 (24)	1.54 ; 88	17925 (458); 105273 (2564)
S386	0 ; 0 ; 0 ; 6	0.0 ; 0	7 ; 7 ; 0 (0)	0 (0); 0 (0)	0.07 ; 14	0 (1); 42 (43)
S400	0 ; 6 ; 0 ; 15	0.0 ; 0	6 ; 6 ; 0 (0)	0 (0); 0 (0)	1.72 ; 15	34 (6); 96 (18)
S420_1	0 ; 0 ; 0 ; 16	0.0 ; 0	1 ; 1 ; 0 (0)	0 (0); 0 (0)	0.25 ; 15	0 (0); 16 (18)
S444	0 ; 6 ; 0 ; 15	0.0 ; 0	6 ; 6 ; 0 (0)	0 (0); 0 (0)	1.80 ; 15	34 (6); 96 (18)
S4863	0 ; 62 ; 0 ; 42	0.0 ; 0	16 ; 16 ; 0 (0)	0 (0); 0 (0)	0.09 ; 15	0 (0); 1664 (784)
S499	0 ; 0 ; 0 ; 22	0.0 ; 0	22 ; 22 ; 0 (0)	0 (0); 0 (0)	0.09 ; 16	0 (0); 484 (22)
S510	0 ; 0 ; 0 ; 6	0.0 ; 0	7 ; 4 ; 0 (0)	0 (0); 18 (57)	6.64 ; 25	0 (0); 42 (133)
S526N	0 ; 0 ; 1 ; 20	0.0 ; 0	6 ; 2 ; 0 (0)	8 (2); 64 (12)	10.44 ; 27	10 (2); 96 (18)
S5378	0 ; 115 ; 0 ; 64	2.0 ; 2	49 ; 47 ; 1 (1)	4 (0); 164 (33)	0.59 ; 26	165 (37); 7087 (1456)
S635	0 ; 0 ; 0 ; 32	0.0 ; 0	1 ; 0 ; 0 (0)	0 (0); 32 (2)	18.23 ; 15	0 (0); 32 (2)
S641	0 ; 7 ; 0 ; 12	1.0 ; 3	24 ; 23 ; 1 (1)	0 (0); 0 (0)	0.09 ; 15	64 (64); 319 (338)
S6669	0 ; 181 ; 0 ; 58	3.0 ; 37	55 ; 55 ; 0 (0)	0 (0); 0 (0)	0.08 ; 15	16 (0); 3061 (1466)
S713	0 ; 7 ; 0 ; 12	1.0 ; 3	23 ; 22 ; 1 (1)	0 (0); 0 (0)	0.10 ; 15	64 (64); 304 (323)
S820	0 ; 0 ; 0 ; 5	5.3 ; 18	19 ; 19 ; 0 (0)	0 (0); 0 (0)	0.23 ; 13	0 (0); 90 (324)
S832	0 ; 0 ; 0 ; 5	5.3 ; 18	19 ; 19 ; 0 (0)	0 (0); 0 (0)	0.25 ; 13	0 (0); 90 (324)
S838_1	0 ; 0 ; 0 ; 32	0.0 ; 0	1 ; 1 ; 0 (0)	0 (0); 0 (0)	0.29 ; 15	0 (0); 32 (34)
S9234_1	0 ; 45 ; 9 ; 157	1.2 ; 21	39 ; 37 ; 2 (0)	0 (0); 0 (0)	0.06 ; 16	146 (24); 1786 (317)
S938	0 ; 0 ; 0 ; 32	0.0 ; 0	1 ; 1 ; 0 (0)	0 (0); 0 (0)	0.33 ; 15	0 (0); 32 (34)
S953	0 ; 23 ; 0 ; 6	2.0 ; 3	23 ; 23 ; 0 (0)	0 (0); 0 (0)	0.13 ; 15	23 (8); 143 (288)
S967	0 ; 23 ; 0 ; 6	2.0 ; 3	23 ; 23 ; 0 (0)	0 (0); 0 (0)	0.14 ; 15	23 (8); 143 (288)
S991	0 ; 0 ; 0 ; 19	3.9 ; 17	17 ; 17 ; 0 (0)	0 (0); 0 (0)	0.08 ; 13	64 (564); 67 (629)

compose-based search requires 34.7 seconds and 16 MB for the same BDD conditions. However, because of its small diameter, the presented approach can solve the target using SAT in 0.46 seconds and 16 MB. After one step of enlargement, the cone drops to 380 registers and 132 primary inputs; the second step solves the target.

L_FLUSHn is a largely feed-forward netlist. For one target with 38 registers and 47 primary inputs, reachability analysis of the optimized target with MLP requires 1.20 seconds and 11 MB. Optimization [ ] plus retiming [ ] with MLP solves the target in 0.60 seconds with 13 MB. *Compose-based* search requires 0.50 seconds and 9 MB. Due to a shallow diameter of three, our techniques solve the target using SAT in 0.19 seconds with 9 MB. The first two steps of enlargement of this target reduce it to 4 then 2 registers, and 3 then 2 primary inputs, respectively. The third step hits the target.

Table 2. Experimental results for GP netlists

Model	regs: NC;AC; MC+QC; GC	Avg. d < 20; Count	Standard Run			Reduction-Only Run
			|T|;Rch; Unrch (BDDs)	regs (inputs) Eliminated ; Sum	Time/|T| (s); Mem (MB)	regs (inputs) Eliminated ; Sum
CP_RAS	0 ; 279 ; 66 ; 315	0.0 ; 0	2 ; 2 ; 0 (0)	0 (0); 0 (0)	0.61 ; 19	1 (0); 554 (131)
CLB_CNTL	0 ; 29 ; 2 ; 19	0.0 ; 0	2 ; 2 ; 0 (0)	0 (0); 0 (0)	0.24 ; 15	0 (0); 84 (12)
CR_RAS	0 ; 96 ; 6 ; 329	0.0 ; 0	1 ; 0 ; 0 (0)	0 (0); 401 (99)	3.55 ; 24	0 (0); 401 (99)
D_DASA	0 ; 16 ; 81 ; 18	0.0 ; 0	2 ; 2 ; 0 (0)	0 (0); 0 (0)	0.24 ; 15	11 (17); 20 (25)
D_DCLA	0 ; 382 ; 1 ; 754	0.0 ; 0	2 ; 1 ; 1 (1)	0 (0); 0 (0)	7.65 ; 44	273 (67); 469 (133)
D_DUDD	0 ; 30 ; 28 ; 71	4.4 ; 5	22 ; 14 ; 8 (6)	0 (0); 0 (0)	1.15 ; 25	491 (353); 1009 (725)
I_IBBQn	0 ; 623 ; 1488 ; 0	2.9 ; 15	15 ; 8 ; 7 (0)	0 (0); 0 (0)	0.28 ; 60	190 (30); 2169 (437)
I_IFAR	0 ; 303 ; 11 ; 99	0.0 ; 0	2 ; 2 ; 0 (0)	0 (0); 0 (0)	0.31 ; 16	8 (0); 101 (35)
I_IFPF	11 ; 893 ; 44 ; 598	0.0 ; 0	1 ; 1 ; 0 (0)	0 (0); 0 (0)	2.72 ; 40	745 (152); 746 (154)
L3_SNP1	25 ; 529 ; 39 ; 82	0.0 ; 0	5 ; 4 ; 1 (0)	0 (0); 0 (0)	1.21 ; 22	7 (0); 595 (164)
L_EMQn	5 ; 146 ; 6 ; 66	0.0 ; 0	1 ; 0 ; 1 (1)	0 (0); 0 (0)	11.57 ; 18	127 (89); 127 (89)
L_EXEC	12 ; 421 ; 0 ; 102	0.0 ; 0	2 ; 2 ; 0 (0)	0 (0); 0 (0)	0.47 ; 18	433 (200); 433 (200)
L_FLUSHn	6 ; 198 ; 0 ; 4	3.7 ; 7	7 ; 6 ; 1 (0)	0 (0); 0 (0)	0.11 ; 12	128 (170); 165 (222)
L_INTRo	14 ; 143 ; 12 ; 5	2.9 ; 29	30 ; 24 ; 6 (0)	0 (0); 0 (0)	0.06 ; 12	750 (626); 830 (672)
L_LMQo	28 ; 690	0.0 ; 0	16 ; 0 ;	0 (0);	14.01 ; 39	2568 (1512)
	4 ; 133	0.0 ; 0	8 (8)	2592 (1512)	14.01 ; 39	5160 (3024)
L_LRU	0 ; 142 ; 20 ; 75	0.0 ; 0	12 ; 5 ; 7 (7)	0 (0); 0 (0)	6.27 ; 19	721 (192); 721 (192)
L_PFQo	13 ; 1936 ;	1.0 ; 1	67 ; 0 ;	0 (0); 0 (0)	10.99 ; 77	10318 (3036);
	18 ; 84	1.0 ; 1	67 (66)	0 (0); 0 (0)	10.99 ; 77	10318 (3036)
L_PNTRn	3 ; 228 ; 10 ; 11	2.0 ; 23	31 ; 0 ; 31 (8)	0 (0); 0 (0)	2.92 ; 19	1057 (1023); 1057 (1023)
L_PRQn	34 ; 366 ; 106 ; 265	2.0 ; 8	10 ; 0 ; 8 (2)	24 (8); 36 (12)	0.30 ; 19	42 (16); 54 (20)
L_SLB	3 ; 135 ; 6 ; 27	1.0 ; 1	3 ; 1 ; 2 (0)	0 (0); 0 (0)	0.16 ; 15	1 (1); 61 (29)
L_TBWKn	0 ; 202 ; 117 ; 14	0.0 ; 0	21 ; 1 ; 3 (3)	2 (0); 291 (238)	17.07 ; 26	36 (28); 342 (280)
M_CIU	0 ; 343 ; 10 ; 424	0.0 ; 0	6 ; 1 ; 5 (0)	0 (0); 0 (0)	0.24 ; 18	775 (60); 775 (60)
SIDECAR	3 ; 109 ; 32 ; 455	0.0 ; 0	1 ; 0 ; 0 (0)	1 (0); 137 (13)	18.64 ; 27	1 (0); 137 (13)
S_SCU1	1 ; 232 ; 4 ; 136	0.0 ; 0	3 ; 2 ; 1 (1)	0 (0); 0 (0)	0.66 ; 24	386 (142); 579 (213)
V_CACH	5 ; 94 ; 15 ; 59	0.0 ; 0	1 ; 0 ; 1 (1)	0 (0); 0 (0)	0.61 ; 16	86 (21); 86 (21)
V_DIR	6 ; 91 ; 13 ; 68	0.0 ; 0	2 ; 2 ; 0 (0)	0 (0); 0 (0)	0.20 ; 15	33 (16); 33 (16)
V_SNPM	65 ; 846 ; 134 ; 376	2.0 ; 1	2 ; 1 ; 1 (0)	0 (0); 0 (0)	1.27 ; 32	905 (266); 905 (266)
W_GAR	0 ; 159 ; 0 ; 83	1.0 ; 1	7 ; 6 ; 0 (0)	4 (0); 86 (37)	2.43 ; 20	4 (0); 500 (224)
W_SFA	0 ; 22 ; 0 ; 42	0.0 ; 0	8 ; 8 ; 0 (0)	0 (0); 0 (0)	0.08 ; 15	42 (21); 112 (56)

One target of netlist S15850_1 comprises 476 registers, primarily complex, and 55 primary inputs. MLP-based analysis is infeasible on this cone, even after optimization [10] plus retiming [9] which yields 397 registers. However, the first five steps of structural enlargement of this target reduce it to 475, 38, 36, 35, and finally 24 registers, and to 55, 55, 14, 13, and 13 primary inputs, respectively. MLP-based forward reachability hits the 5-step-enlarged target in 10 iterations with a combined effort of 2.5 seconds and 23MB. The only other approach that is able to hit this target is a 15-step *BSAT* which requires 7.3 seconds and 14MB. For an unreachable target BMC would not have been applicable. Traditional approaches of target enlargement would be ineffective on this netlist since they do not offer any reduction capability, without which the enlarged target remains infeasibly complex.

7   Conclusion

We have presented an efficient framework for decomposing a verification task into multiple subtasks. Our techniques are capable of solving or simplifying most problems, and comprise a useful component of a more general *transformation-based verification* toolset. We first calculate the number of time-steps k to use for bounded search via a novel structural algorithm for diameter overapproximation. For many practical netlists, this analysis yields a sufficiently small bound on the diameter to allow bounded model checking to discharge the proof. Otherwise, we iteratively perform SAT-based forward search and inductive *compose-based* backward search for *structural target enlargement*. If the property is not solved by the above, we construct a simpler enlarged target and pass it to a subsequent verification approach. While inherently performing a *temporal* decomposition of the verification task, our approach is capable of *spatially* reducing the target size and complexity, thus the enlarged target is often significantly simpler to discharge than the original. We use simulation and BMC to *complete* any traces obtained on the target-enlarged netlist for undoing the effects of the transformation. Extensive experimental results demonstrate the effectiveness of the proposed techniques in solving and simplifying problems.

References

1. Armin Biere, Alessandro Cimatti, Edmund M. Clarke, and Yunshan Zhu. Symbolic model checking without BDDs. In *5th International Conference on Tools and Algorithms for Construction and Analysis of Systems*, March 1999. 152, 154, 156
2. J. R. Burch, E. M. Clarke, D. E. Long, K. L. McMillan, and D. L. Dill. Symbolic model checking for sequential circuit verification. *IEEE Transactions on Computer-Aided Design*, 13(4), April 1994. 157
3. H. Cho, G. Hachtel, E. Macii, B. Pleisser, and F. Somenzi. Algorithms for approximate FSM traversal based on state space decomposition. *IEEE Transactions on Computer-Aided Design*, 15(12), Dec. 1996. 151, 156
4. O. Coudert, C. Berthet, and J. C. Madre. Verification of sequential machines using Boolean functional vectors. In *IMEC-IFIP International Workshop on Applied Formal Methods for Correct VLSI Design*, Nov. 1989. 157
5. Luca de Alfaro, Thomas A. Henzinger, and Freddy Y. C. Mang. Detecting errors before reaching them. In *Computer-Aided Verification*, July 2000. 157
6. Thomas Filkorn. Functional extensions of symbolic model checking. In *Computer-Aided Verification*, June 1991. 157
7. Malay K. Ganai. *Algorithms for Efficient State Space Search*. PhD thesis, University of Texas at Austin, May 2001. 159
8. Youpyo Hong, Peter A. Beerel, Jerry R. Burch, and Kenneth L. McMillan. Safe BDD minimization using don't cares. In *Proc. 34th ACM/IEEE Design Automation Conference*, June 1997. 158, 159
9. Andreas Kuehlmann and Jason Baumgartner. Transformation-based verification using generalized retiming. In *Computer-Aided Verification*, July 2001. 160, 162, 163
10. Andreas Kuehlmann, Malay K. Ganai, and Viresh Paruthi. Circuit-based Boolean reasoning. In *Proc. 38th ACM/IEEE Design Automation Conference*, June 2001. 160, 161, 162, 163
11. Robert P. Kurshan. *Computer-Aided Verification of Coordinating Processes*. Princeton University Press, 1994. 152, 157
12. In-Ho Moon, Gary D. Hachtel, and Fabio Somenzi. Border-block triangular form and conjunction schedule in image computation. In *Formal Methods in Computer-Aided Design*, Nov. 2000. 158, 161
13. Mary Sheeran, Satnam Singh, and Gunnar Stalmarck. Checking safety properties using induction and a SAT-solver. In *Formal Methods in Computer-Aided Design*, Nov. 2000. 154

14. Poul F. Williams, Armin Biere, Edmund M. Clarke, and Anubhav Gupta. Combining decision diagrams and SAT procedures for efficient symbolic model checking. In *Computer-Aided Verification*, July 2000. 159

15. C. Han Yang and David L. Dill. Validation with guided search of the state space. In *Proc. 35th ACM/IEEE Design Automation Conference*, June 1998. 157

16. Jun Yuan, Jian Shen, Jacob Abraham, and Adnan Aziz. On combining formal and informal verification. In *Computer-Aided Verification*, June 1997. 157

Conformance Checking for Models
of Asynchronous Message Passing Software

Sriram K. Rajamani and Jakob Rehof

Microsoft Research
{sriram,rehof}@microsoft.com

Abstract. We propose a notion of *conformance* between a specification S and an implementation model I extracted from a message-passing program. In our framework, S and I are CCS processes, which soundly abstract the externally visible communication behavior of a message-passing program. We use the extracted models to check that programs do not get *stuck*, waiting to receive or trying to send messages in vain. We show that our definition of stuckness and conformance capture important correctness conditions of message-passing software. Our definition of conformance was motivated by the need for *modular* reasoning over models, leading to the requirement that conformance preserve substitutability with respect to stuck-freeness: If I conforms to S, and P is any environment such that $P \mid S$ is stuck-free, then it follows that $P \mid I$ is stuck-free. We present a simple algorithm for checking if I conforms to S, when I and S obey certain restrictions.

1 Introduction

Checking behavioral properties of concurrent software using model checking is an active area of current research [7,9,19]. We are interested in extracting message-passing skeletons from concurrent message-passing software, and using model checking to check properties on the skeletons. For this approach to be scalable, we require users to annotate each module with a *behavioral signature*. In our framework [12,3], if F is a module which can communicate with its environment by sending and receiving messages on channels $x_1, \ldots, x_n$, then a signature of F is a CCS process $S(x_1, \ldots, x_n)$ describing the messaging behavior of F on those channels. Each module is then analyzed in isolation to check if its implementation *conforms* with its signature. This requires that a model of the implementation of F is extracted and compared to the signature. Like signatures, implementation models are CCS processes. If I is an implementation model and S is its signature (specification), we use the notation $I \leq S$ to denote that I conforms to S. For our modular reasoning to be sound with respect to a property φ, the conformance relation $\leq$ needs to obey the following *substitutability* property: If $I \leq S$ and P is any environment such that $P \mid S$ satisfies φ then $P \mid I$ satisfies φ ($P \mid S$ denotes the parallel composition of P and S). Substitutability enables a module's behavioral signature to be used instead of a module in invocation contexts, and hence enables model checking to scale.

D. Brinksma and K. G. Larsen (Eds.): CAV 2002, LNCS 2404, pp. 166–179, 2002.
© Springer-Verlag Berlin Heidelberg 2002

We are interested in checking if message-passing software is *stuck-free*. i.e, that a message sent by a sender will not get stuck without some receiver ever receiving it, and a receiver waiting for a message will not get stuck without some sender ever sending it. Stuck-freeness is a safety property, and in general any safety property [10,17] can be encoded as stuck-freeness. Thus, we desire our conformance relation $\leq$ to satisfy substitutability with respect to stuck-freeness: If $I \leq S$ and P is any environment such that $P \mid S$ is stuck-free, then $P \mid I$ is stuck-free.

A widely used conformance relation is *simulation* [13]. Module I is simulated by module S, written $I \leq^s S$ if every externally visible action α performed by I can also be performed by S such that, if I' and S' are the states of I and S respectively after performing action α, then $I' \leq^s S'$. Simulation does not satisfy substitutability with respect to stuck-freeness due to two reasons: First, while simulation prevents the implementation from doing actions not allowed by the specification, it does not require the implementation to do any particular action. Second, simulation does not distinguish between external nondeterminism that arises due to the ability of the environment to give different inputs, and internal nondeterminism that arises from underspecification or abstraction.

This paper makes the following contributions:

- We present a novel definition of conformance that satisfies substitutability with respect to stuck-freeness. The definition distinguishes between external and internal nondeterminism, requires implementations to do certain actions, and allows implementations that are nonterminating (Section 4).
- We present an algorithm that dualizes specifications using a so-called "mirror construction" to transform a conformance checking problem to a standard invariant checking problem on a product model. Based on this algorithm, a restricted form of conformance checking can be done using an off-the-shelf model checker for invariant checking as a back-end (Section 5).
- We present extensions to the definition of conformance and the checking algorithm to handle cases where the programmer expects certain operations to possibly get stuck, using "weak" send and receive operations (Section 6).

We have implemented a conformance checker as part of a subtype relation checker in a behavioral type system for asynchronous message-passing software. In this paper, we focus entirely on the notion of conformance between CCS models and our algorithm for checking it, assuming that CCS models are extracted from programs. We refer to [12,3] for the problem of model extraction.

2   Background and Related Work

Two traditional notions of conformance between models are language containment [18] and simulation [13]. The former adopts a linear-time view and latter a branching-time view. Our conformance relation is used to define model abstraction in the framework of a behavioral type system [3] where CCS processes [13,14] are used as specifications and models of π-calculus programs [14]. Sound model abstractions in that system are limited to simulation relations (see [ ] for details), and consequently we consider simulation (denoted by $\leq^s$) as a starting point for our investigation.

In this paper, we focus on *stuck-freeness* of communication. Informally, stuck-freeness means that a message sent by a sender will not get stuck without some receiver ever receiving it, and a receiver waiting for a message will not get stuck without some sender ever sending it. This is often an important property in asynchronous software systems. For example, an asynchronous exception may be implemented as a message send operation, and in this case, stuck-freeness of the send operation means that the exception gets caught. Also, asynchronous functions typically get invoked by sending messages to them, and they return results be sending messages back to the caller. In this case, stuck-freeness of the receive operation on the side of the caller means that the caller eventually gets a result.

As mentioned earlier, substitutability is necessary for modular reasoning. Simulation does not preserve substitutability for being stuck-free. For example, let $I_1 = \mathbf{0}$ and $S_1 = x!\#y!$, where $\mathbf{0}$ is the inactive null process, $x!$ denotes a send operation on channel x, and $y!$ denotes a send operation on channel y. The connective $\#$ denotes internal choice. Then $I_1 \leq^s S_1$ holds, but if we consider the environment $P = \texttt{select } x? + y?$ (where $\texttt{select } x? + y?$ denotes an external choice of a receive operation on channel x and a receive operation on channel y), then $P \mid S_1$ is stuck-free, whereas $P \mid I_1$ is stuck, waiting to receive on either channel x or channel y. The difficulty here is that the implementation does not implement *any* of the internal choices that the specification allows.

As another example, if $I_2 = x?$ (receive on x) and $S_2 = \texttt{select } x? + y?$ (external choice of either receive on x or receive on y), we have that $I_2 \leq^s S_2$. Further, for an environment $P = y!$, we have that $P \mid S_2$ is stuck-free, whereas $P \mid I_2$ gets stuck. The difficulty here is that the implementation does not implement *all* of the external choices that the specification prescribes.

The distinction between external and internal choice, and the implications for conformance has been noticed before [,]. The notion of alternating simulation proposed in [ ] requires the implementation to provide a *subset* of internal choices allowed by the specification and a *superset* of external choices prescribed by the specification. We denote alternating simulation by the symbol $\leq^a$. However, alternating simulation still does not preserve substitutability for being stuck-free. To illustrate this, consider an example with $I_3 = \texttt{select } (x? \texttt{ -> } y?) + y?$, and $S_3 = x? \texttt{->} y?$. By the definition of $\leq^a$, we have that $I_3 \leq^a S_3$. If $P = (x! \mid y!)$, we have that $P \mid S_3$ is stuck-free but $P \mid I_3$ can get stuck if the interaction on channel y happens first. The difficulty here is that the implementation allows a superset of the external choices prescribed by the specification.

Our definition of conformance was motivated by the above examples. Unlike simulation, we distinguish between internal and external choice [ ]. If the specification is an internal choice, then we require the implementation to implement at least one of the choices. If the specification is an external choice, then we require the implementation to implement exactly all of the choices. Further, we allow arbitrary number of silent internal actions (to allow loops to be abstracted) in the implementation. The formal definition of conformance, and a precise description of how it differs from simulation and alternating simulation can be found in Section 4.

Our notion of conformance and the algorithm for conformance checking are inspired by Dill's work on asynchronous circuit verification [ ]. In asynchronous circuits, there is no buffering and an output from one component must be instantaneously received by another component. In asynchronous software, messages are typically queued. Both the conformance relation and the checking algorithm change in subtle ways to reflect this queueing. For example, the process $x! \mid y! \mid x? \text{->} y?$ is an erroneous process in Dill's framework since a receiver for the send $y!$ is not immediately available. However, our framework allows $y!$ to block until the interaction on x succeeds and then proceed to have an interaction on y.

An alternative approach to obtain modularity is to reason with context-sensitive abstractions as in [ ]. In the context of CSP [ ], notions of failures and divergence have been used in model checkers such as FDR [ ]. Traces and failures can be used to express various notions of refinement between interfaces as in [ ]. Tools have been built to check simulations and bisimulations between CCS processes [ ].

3   Models

Our model language is a variant of CCS as presented in [ ], where we distinguish between internal and external choice [ ]. Our *processes* (ranged over by I, M, M', P, Q, R, S etc.) are defined as follows.

$$M ::= \mathbf{0} \mid X \mid \texttt{select } I_1 + \ldots + I_n \mid O_1 \# \ldots \# O_n \quad \text{(Processes)}$$
$$\mid (M_0 \mid M_1) \mid (\nu x)M \mid \mu X.M$$

$$I \ ::= x? \text{->} M \qquad\qquad\qquad\qquad\qquad \text{(Guarded expressions)}$$
$$O ::= x!.M$$

Here, $x!.M$ is a process that sends on channel x and continues as M. Process $x? \text{->} M$ receives on channel x and continues as M. We use the symbol $\#$ for internal choice and $+$ for external choice. The process $\texttt{select } x? \text{->} M + y? \text{->} M'$ either receives on x and continues as M, or it receives on y and continues as M'. The process $x!.M \# y!.M'$ continues as either $x!.M$ or as $y!.M'$. We write $x!$ as shorthand for $x!.\mathbf{0}$ and $x?$ as shorthand for $x? \text{->} \mathbf{0}$. We also sometimes write $x? \text{->} M + y? \text{->} M'$ as shorthand for $\texttt{select } x? \text{->} M + y? \text{->} M'$ (*i.e.*, we sometimes leave out the keyword $\texttt{select}$). Label X is used to encode looping in $\mu X.M$. We write $*M$ as an abbreviation for $\mu X.(M \mid X)$.

Given a set of channels $\overline{x}$, the set of *actions* over $\overline{x}$ is defined to be $\{x, x?, x! \mid x \in \overline{x}\} \cup \tau, \epsilon$. The action x is called a *reaction* on channel x. The actions $x?$ and $x!$ are called *commitments* on channel x. Intuitively, two commitments $x?$

Structural Congruence

Structural congruence $\equiv$ is the least congruence relation (equivalence relation closed under term contexts) closed under the following rules, together with renaming and reordering of bound variables and reordering of terms in a summation (either internal or external choice). The set of free names of P is denoted $\mathsf{fn}(P)$.

$$P \mid \mathbf{0} \equiv P \qquad P \mid Q \equiv Q \mid P \qquad P \mid (Q \mid R) \equiv (P \mid Q) \mid R$$

$$(\nu x)\mathbf{0} \equiv \mathbf{0} \qquad \mu X.P \equiv P[\mu X.P/X] \qquad (\nu x)(\nu y)P \equiv (\nu y)(\nu x)P$$

$$\frac{x \notin \mathsf{fn}(P)}{P \mid (\nu x)Q \equiv (\nu x)(P \mid Q)} \qquad \frac{P \equiv P' \quad Q \equiv Q'}{P \mid Q \equiv P' \mid Q'}$$

Labeled Reduction

$$x!.P \mid \mathsf{select}\ (\ldots + x? \mathbin{->} Q + \ldots) \xrightarrow{x} P \mid Q \qquad [\text{REACT}]$$

$$x!.P \xrightarrow{x!} P \quad [\text{O-COMM}] \qquad \mathsf{select}\ (\ldots + x? \mathbin{->} P + \ldots) \xrightarrow{x?} P \qquad [\text{I-COMM}]$$

$$(\ldots \#x!.P\# \ldots) \xrightarrow{\epsilon} x!.P \qquad [\text{I-CHOICE}]$$

$$\frac{P \xrightarrow{x} P'}{(\nu x)P \xrightarrow{\tau} (\nu x)P'} \quad [\text{TAU}] \qquad \frac{P \xrightarrow{\ell} P' \quad \ell \notin \{x, x?, x!\}}{(\nu x)P \xrightarrow{\ell} (\nu x)P'} \quad [\text{RES}]$$

$$\frac{P \equiv P' \quad P' \xrightarrow{\ell} Q' \quad Q' \equiv Q}{P \xrightarrow{\ell} Q} \quad [\text{S-CONG}] \qquad \frac{P \xrightarrow{\ell} P'}{P \mid Q \xrightarrow{\ell} P' \mid Q} \quad [\text{PAR}]$$

$$\frac{P \xrightarrow{\epsilon} P' \quad P' \xrightarrow{\ell} P''}{P \xrightarrow{\ell} P''} \quad [\epsilon\text{-LEFT}] \qquad \frac{P \xrightarrow{\ell} P', P' \xrightarrow{\epsilon} P''}{P \xrightarrow{\ell} P''} \quad [\epsilon\text{-RIGHT}]$$

Eta rules

$$\frac{P \xrightarrow{x} P'}{(\eta x)P \xrightarrow{x} (\eta x)P'} \quad [\text{ETA1}] \qquad \frac{P \xrightarrow{\ell} P' \quad \ell \notin \{x, x?, x!\}}{(\eta x)P \xrightarrow{\ell} (\eta x)P'} \quad [\text{ETA2}]$$

Fig. 1. Structural congruence and labeled reduction on CCS processes

and $x!$ on the channel x between two parallel processes can be combined into a reaction x. The action τ is called *silent reaction*, and ϵ is called *null action*.

Figure 1 defines the labeled reduction relation on processes adapted from the commitment and reaction semantics given in [14]. Note that the reduction relation distinguishes between internal and external choice. Internal choice is handled by the rule I-CHOICE where the process chooses the send operation, and external choice is handled by the rule REACT where the environment chooses the receive operation. As indicated by rule S-CONG in Figure 1, reduction is modulo structural congruence. Note that in addition to the usual rules for the restriction operator ν we have rules ETA1 and ETA2 for the restriction operator η. This operator is the same as ν, only with different observability properties: The expression $(\eta\overline{x})P$ is simply meta-notation for a ν-abstraction whose interactions can be observed. This notation is needed to state our substitutability property.

We extend labeled reduction to sequences of actions as well, with ϵ satisfying left and right cancellation under concatenation (rules ϵ-LEFT and ϵ-RIGHT). We write $M_1 \xrightarrow{*} M_2$ if M_1 can transition to M_2 using some sequence of actions. We write M^* to denote the set $\{M' \mid M \xrightarrow{*} M'\}$.

We say that channel x is *bound* in $(\nu x)M$. If x is not bound in M' we say that x is *free* in M'. We say that M is an *end-state* if there are no α and M' such that $M \xrightarrow{\alpha} M'$. If $M \equiv (\eta\overline{x})(P \mid Q)$ is an end-state, and either (1) $P \equiv x!.M_1$, where $x \in \overline{x}$, or (2) $P \equiv \texttt{select } (x_{i_1}? \rightarrow M_1 + x_{i_2}? \rightarrow M_2 + \ldots + x_{i_k}? \rightarrow M_k)$ where $\{x_{i_1}, x_{i_2}, \ldots, x_{i_k}\} \in \overline{x}$, then we say that *M is stuck because of P*. M is *stuck* if there exists some P such that *M is stuck because of P*. M is *stuck-free* if no element of M^* is stuck.

Implementation models are defined to be subset of processes satisfying the following property:

A1. For every free channel x, we have x is either used exclusively for sending or exclusively for receiving, and

Assumption A1 is for technical convenience. It is not a fundamental restriction since a bidirectional communication can be achieved using two unidirectional channels, one in either direction. Finally, *Specification models* are defined to be the subset of implementation models that do not contain name restriction, ν.

4   Conformance

Conformance is a binary relation (written $\leq$) between implementation models and specification models. We define conformance in two steps: (1) first we give a definition for specification models that do not have parallel composition, (2) next we extend it to specification models with parallel composition.

Let I be an implementation model and let S be a specification model such that S does not have parallel composition. Informally, I conforms to S if every commitment of I on a free channel can be performed by S, and if S is an internal choice of send operations, then I can perform at least one of the specified send operations, and if S is an external choice of receive operations then I can perform exactly all of the specified receive operations, and such conformance holds recursively after performing corresponding actions in I and S. The formal definition follows.

Definition 1. *I conforms to S, written $I \leq S$ if I and S have the same set of free channels and there exists a binary relation $H \subseteq I^* \times S^*$ such that the following conditions hold:*

D1. $\langle I, S \rangle \in H$.

D2. *For every $\langle P, Q \rangle \in H$ and every commitment α on a free channel we have that if $P \xrightarrow{\tau^*.\alpha} P'$ then there exists $Q' \in Q^*$ such that $Q \xrightarrow{\alpha} Q'$ and $\langle P', Q' \rangle \in H$.*

D3. *For every $\langle P, Q \rangle \in H$, if $Q = (x_1!.Q_1)\# (x_2!.Q_2)\# \cdots \#(x_n!.Q_n)$, then for all P' such that $P \xrightarrow{\tau^*} P'$, either there exists P'' such that $P' \xrightarrow{\tau} P''$, or there exists $1 \leq i \leq n$ and $P_i \in I^*$ such that $P' \xrightarrow{x_i!} P_i$, and $\langle P_i, Q_i \rangle \in H$.*

D4. *For every $\langle P, Q \rangle \in H$, if $Q = (x_1?\text{->}Q_1)+(x_2?\text{->}Q_2)+\cdots+(x_n?\text{->}Q_n)$, then for all P' such that $P \xrightarrow{\tau^*} P'$, either there exists P'' such that $P' \xrightarrow{\tau} P''$, or for all $1 \leq i \leq n$ there exists $P_i \in I^*$ such that $P' \xrightarrow{x_i?} P_i$, and $\langle P_i, Q_i \rangle \in H$.*

We extend conformance to specification models with parallelism by requiring structural similarity in the implementation and specification: we say that $I_1 \mid I_2 \leq S_1 \mid S_2$ if $I_1 \leq S_1$ and $I_2 \leq S_2$.

Properties Conformance is stronger than both simulation ($\leq^s$) and alternating simulation ($\leq^a$). Simulation is obtained by removing conditions D3 and D4 from the definition. Alternating simulation is obtained by removing condition D3, and weakening condition D2 to consider only send commitments on free channels. We recall some examples from Section 2 to illustrate the differences between simulation, alternating simulation and conformance. If $I_1 = \mathbf{0}$ and $S_1 = x!\#y!$, we have that $I_1 \leq^s S_1$, but $I_1 \not\leq S_1$ since condition D3 is violated. If $I_2 = x?$ and $S_2 = x? + y?$, we again have that $I_2 \leq^s S_2$, but $I_2 \not\leq S_2$ since condition D4 is violated. Finally, if $I_3 = \mathtt{select}\ (x? \text{ -> } y?) + y?$, and $S_3 = x? \text{ -> } y?$, we have that $I_3 \leq^a S_3$, but $I_3 \not\leq S_3$ since condition D2 is violated for commitment $y?$ from I_3.

We also note that simulation and alternating simulation are incomparable. For example, $I_2 \leq^s S_2$, but $I_2 \not\leq^a S_2$, and $I_3 \leq^a S_3$, but $I_3 \not\leq^s S_3$.

We have intentionally stated the definition for conformance to allow the implementation to perform an arbitrary number of internal τ actions. This is in accordance with usual practice in typed programming languages, which allows nonterminating implementations. For example, most type systems will allow the function $\mathtt{foo(x)} = \mathtt{while(true)}\ \{\mathtt{skip}\};\ \mathtt{return(x+1)}$ with a nonterminating while loop to be typed with the type signature $int \rightarrow int$.

Conformance is not the largest relation satisfying substitutability for being stuck-free. For example, with $I = x? \mid y?$ and $S = \mathtt{select}\ x? \text{ -> } y?$, we have that any environment P such that $P \mid I$ gets stuck would also make $P \mid S$ stuck.

The example shows that it is sometimes possible to sequentialize an implementation in the specification with respect to stuck-freeness. Alternating simulation would accept $I \leq^a S$, but as shown above, $\leq^a$ does not always respect substitutability for stuck-freeness. The following theorem states that conformance obeys substitutability for being stuck-free. A proof of the theorem can be found in [15].

Theorem 1. *Let I be any implementation model and S be any specification model, with the same set of free channels $\bar{x}$. If $I \leq S$, then for any process P if $(\eta\bar{x})(P \mid S)$ is stuck-free, then $(\eta\bar{x})(P \mid I)$ is stuck-free.*

Example Suppose a service F can be called with channel parameters x , y and e for sending back responses to the caller. Suppose further that F asynchronously calls two other services G and H (using response channels z and w, respectively) to produce its responses on x and y, respectively. Finally, assume that H may either respond normally or raise an exception by sending a message on a channel Err, in which case F will throw an exception by sending on e. An implementation of F could be as shown below, declared with behavioral signature $x!.(y!\#e!)$. We wish to decide whether F conforms to its signature, given only the signatures (and no implementations) for G and H.

```
G(z) : z!
H(w) : w! # Err!


F(x,y) : x!.(y! # e!)
{
  try{
    async(z,w){G(z), H(w)}{
      select z? -> { send x; select w? -> send y;}}
  } catch Err {throw e}
}
```

A model for the body of F is constructed by substituting the signatures for G and H at the call sites, yielding the CCS model M_F shown below. Notice that the asynchronous calls to G and H are run concurrently, and the exception handler is modeled by waiting to receive on Err in the select statements. Because the channels z and w are used internally by F to receive responses from G and H, these channels are restricted using the ν operator.

$$M_F = (\nu z)(\nu w)(z! \mid (w!\#Err!) \mid$$
$$(\texttt{select } (z? \rightarrow x!.(\texttt{select } (w? \rightarrow y!) + (Err? \rightarrow e!)) + (Err? \rightarrow e!)))$$

Checking conformance of F to its signature, we decide whether $M_F \leq x!.(y!\#e!)$. We find that the conformance test fails: if H throws an exception before F has sent its response on x, then no response will be sent on x at all. An environment expecting, according to the signature of F, a response on x followed by a message on either y or e, will be stuck. The problem can be fixed either by changing the signature of F or by changing the implementation of F. A signature that would work is $(x!.(y!\#e!))\#e!$. This signature does not promise much to the environment, and it suggests that one would rather want to change the implementation of F to conform to its original signature. This could be done by sequentializing the calls to G and H, by first waiting for G to respond and only then calling H afterwards. Or, perhaps better, one could throw the exception e only after sending on x. Notice that, by restricting z and w used for internal communication with G and H in F, conformance allows us to avoid exposing that communication in the signature of F. This is essential for a scalable module system.

5   Mirrors

Given an implementation model I and a specification model S, we would like to check if $I \leq S$ using a state space exploration on I. If S and I obey certain restrictions, then there is a simple and elegant way to do this by constructing a so called *mirror* of S and a so called *serialization* of I. Using this construction we can perform conformance checking using any off-the-shelf model checker.

In order to describe the necessary restrictions for our mirror construction, we impose two restrictions on processes:

A2. Specifications and implementations do not have mixed selects. Formally, every external choice of the form $(x_1? \text{->} M_1 + x_2? \text{->} M_2 + \cdots + x_k? \text{->} M_k)$, either all the x_i are free channels or all the x_i are bound channels.

A3. Specifications do not contain hidden internal nondeterminism. Formally, the condition means that for all T_1 such that $T \xrightarrow{*} T_1$, we have that for every commitment α, whenever $T_1 \xrightarrow{\alpha} T_2$ and $T_1 \xrightarrow{\alpha} T_3$, it is the case that $T_2 \equiv T_3$.

Finally, we strengthen the conformance relation $\leq$ to a stronger relation $\preceq$ by strengthening condition D4. in Definition 1 as follows:

D4'. For every $\langle P, Q \rangle \in H$, if $Q = (x_1? \text{->} Q_1) + (x_2? \text{->} Q_2) + \cdots + (x_n? \text{->} Q_n)$, then for all P' such that $P \xrightarrow{\tau^*} P'$, either there exists P'' such that $P' \xrightarrow{\tau} P''$, or $P' = (x_1? \text{->} P_1) + (x_2? \text{->} P_2) + \cdots + (x_n? \text{->} P_n)$ such that $\langle P_i, Q_i \rangle \in H$ for $1 \leq i \leq n$.

Since D4' is stronger than D4, the strengthened relation $\preceq$ satisifies Thorem 1. We give an algorithm for checking $\preceq$ below.

For a specification S without parallel composition, we can construct a *mirror* process $\mathcal{M}(S)$ that represents all possible environments that S can potentially be composed with. Let $\overline{x} = \{x_1, x_2, \ldots, x_n\}$ be the set of free channels in the specification. The definition of $\mathcal{M}(.)$ is given in Figure 2, by structural induction on the specification. The definition uses an error process Err which is used to denote one kind of failure in the conformance check.

$$\mathcal{M}(0) = 0$$

$$\mathcal{M}\left((x_{i_1}?\text{->}P_1) + \ldots + (x_{i_k}?\text{->}P_k)\right) = (x_{i_1}!.\mathcal{M}(P_1))\# \ldots \#(x_{i_k}!.\mathcal{M}(P_k))$$
$$\#(x_{j_1}!.Err\#x_{j_2}!.Err\#x_{j_m}!.Err)$$
$$\text{where } \{x_{j_1}, \ldots, x_{j_m}\} = \overline{x} \setminus \{x_{i_1}, \ldots, x_{i_k}\}$$

$$\mathcal{M}\left((x_{i_1}!.P_1)\# \ldots \#(x_{i_m}!.P_m)\right) = (x_{i_1}?\text{->}\mathcal{M}(P_1)) + \ldots + (x_{i_m}?\text{->}\mathcal{M}(P_m))$$

$$\mathcal{M}(X) = X$$

$$\mathcal{M}(\mu X.M) = \mu X.\mathcal{M}(M)$$

Fig. 2. Mirror construction

For an implementation model I, with free channels $\overline{x}$, we construct a *serialized* process $\mathcal{R}(S)$ that serializes all communications on free channels using a lock implemented by two global channels acq and rel. The definition of the serialization function $\mathcal{R}(.)$ is given in Figure 3, by structural induction on the implementation.

Note that our assumption A2. that external choices are either over free channels, or over bound channels, but not a mixture of both free and bound channels is used in the definition of $\mathcal{R}(.)$. Let $L = \mu X.acq!.rel?\text{->}X$ be a process that implements a lock. Given an implementation I and specification S, in order to check if $I \preceq S$, we check if $\mathcal{M}(I) \mid \mathcal{R}(S) \mid L$ neither gets stuck in certain ways (mentioned below) nor reaches the error process Err.

Before making this statement precise, we need a weaker notion of stuckness. We say that M is a τ-*end-state* if for all $M \xrightarrow{\omega} M'$, we have that $\omega \in \tau^*$. If $M \equiv (\eta\overline{x})(P \mid Q)$ is a τ-end-state, and either (1) $P \equiv x!.M_1$, where $x \in \overline{x}$, or (2) $P \equiv \texttt{select}(x_{i_1}?\text{->}M_1 + x_{i_2}?\text{->}M_2 + \ldots + x_{i_k}?\text{->}M_k)$ where $\{x_{i_1}, x_{i_2}, \ldots, x_{i_k}\} \in \overline{x}$, then we say that M is τ-*stuck because of* P. M is τ-*stuck* if there exists some P such that M is τ-*stuck because of* P.

The following theorem contains our algorithm for checking conformance $I \preceq S$ via the process $\mathcal{M}(I) \mid \mathcal{R}(S) \mid L$. A proof of the theorem can be found in [15].

Theorem 2. *Let I be any implementation model and S be any specification model, with the same set of free channels $\overline{x}$. Let $L() = \mu X.acq!.rel?\text{->}X$ be a process that implements a lock using two channels acq and rel that are not present in I or S. We have that $I \preceq S$ iff the following three conditions hold for all processes $\hat{M} \equiv (\eta(\overline{x}, acq, rel))(\mathcal{M}(\hat{S}) \mid \mathcal{R}(\hat{I}) \mid \hat{L})$, such that $(\eta(\overline{x}, acq, rel))(\mathcal{M}(S) \mid \mathcal{R}(I) \mid L) \xrightarrow{*} (\eta(\overline{x}, acq, rel))(\mathcal{M}(\hat{S}) \mid \mathcal{R}(\hat{I}) \mid \hat{L})$:*

C1. $\hat{S} \not\equiv Err$
C2. $\hat{M}$ is not τ-stuck because of $\mathcal{R}(\hat{I})$
C3. $\hat{M}$ is not stuck because of $\mathcal{M}(\hat{S})$

$$\mathcal{R}(0) = 0$$

$$\mathcal{R}\big((x_{i_1}?\text{->}P_1) + \ldots + (x_{i_k}?\text{->}P_k)\big) = acq?\text{->}\left(\begin{array}{l}(x_{i_1}?\text{->}rel!.\mathcal{R}(P_1)) + \ldots + \\ (x_{i_k}?\text{->}rel!.\mathcal{R}(P_k))\end{array}\right)$$
$$\text{if } \{x_{j_1}, \ldots, x_{j_m}\} \subseteq \overline{x}$$

$$\mathcal{R}\big((y_{i_1}?\text{->}P_1) + \ldots + (y_{i_k}?\text{->}P_k)\big) = \big((y_{i_1}?\text{->}\mathcal{R}(P_1)) + \ldots + (y_{i_k}?\text{->}\mathcal{R}(P_k))\big)$$
$$\text{if } \{y_{j_1}, \ldots, y_{j_m}\} \cap \overline{x} = \phi$$

$$\mathcal{R}\big((z_{i_1}!.P_1)\# \ldots \#(z_{i_m}!.P_m)\big) = \big((\mathcal{T}(z_{i_1}).\mathcal{R}(P_1)\# \ldots \#(\mathcal{T}(z_{i_m}).\mathcal{R}(P_m))\big),$$
$$\text{where } \mathcal{T}(z_{i_k}) = \begin{array}{l} z_{i_k}! \text{ if } z_{i_k} \notin \overline{x}, \text{ and} \\ acq?\text{->}z_{i_k}!.rel! \text{ if } z_{i_k} \notin \overline{x} \end{array}$$

$$\mathcal{R}(X) = X$$

$$\mathcal{R}(\mu X.M) = \mu X.\mathcal{R}(M)$$

$$\mathcal{R}(M_0 \mid M_1) = \mathcal{R}(M_0) \mid \mathcal{R}(M_1)$$

$$\mathcal{R}((\nu x)M) = (\nu x)\mathcal{R}(M)$$

Fig. 3. Serialization

6   Weak Send and Receive

Our definition of stuckness so far assumes that send and receive operations must always succeed. This is not always feasible. A parallel search program spawns off a number of child processes, and after the first process to discover the item reports success, the remaining processes are disregarded by the parent. We do not wish to regard the program as stuck, even though all child processes but one could be sending messages in vain. We distinguish between operations that are intended to succeed and operations that are allowed not to succeed by referring to the latter as *weak send* and *weak receive* operations, respectively, and we introduce special syntax for the weak operations. This allows us to treat them differently in checking conformance. We introduce the extended syntax for send and receive operations:

$$M ::= \ldots \mid \underline{\text{select}}\ I_1 + \ldots + I_n$$
$$O ::= \ldots \mid \underline{x}!.M$$

Here, a *weak receive* is of the form $\underline{\text{select}}\ I_1 + \ldots + I_n$, and allows all of the receives specified in I_1 through I_n to not succeed. Similarly, a *weak send* $\underline{x}!.M$ is allowed not to succeed. Notice that we allow internal choices of mixed mode. For example, the expression $x!.M_1 \# \underline{y}!.M_2$ is allowed, and if the left branch is chosen, then it leads to the operation $x!.M_1$ where the send is required to succeed, whereas choosing the right branch leads to $\underline{y}!.M_2$, which may or may not succeed.

We need to extend our notions of conformance ($\leq$) and conformance checking for the weak constructs. Consider first a weak send, $\underline{x}!$. We require that $\underline{x}! \leq x!$ holds, but on the other hand, $x! \not\leq \underline{x}!$. Intuitively, the operation $x!$ requires more of any operating environment than the operation $\underline{x}!$: the former operation gets *stuck* in an environment that does not offer the corresponding receive on x. Hence, substitutability is preserved for this extension of $\leq$. Similarly, we require that $\underline{\text{select}}\,I \leq \text{select}\,I$ holds, but on the other hand $\text{select}\,I \not\leq \underline{\text{select}}\,I$.

We extend our conformance check to handle the weak operations by extending the notion of mirrors, as follows:

$$\mathcal{M}\left(\underline{\text{select}}\,(I_1 + \ldots + I_n)\right) = \mathcal{M}\left(\text{select}\,(I_1 + \ldots + I_n)\right)\#0$$

$$\mathcal{M}\left((\xi_1!.P_1)\#\ldots\#(\xi_n!.P_n)\right) = \text{select}\,(\tilde{\xi}_1?\text{->}\mathcal{M}(P_1)) + \ldots + (\tilde{\xi}_n?\text{->}\mathcal{M}(P_n))$$

where ξ ranges over channels of the usual form x or of the weak form $\underline{x}$, and where we define $\tilde{\xi} = \tilde{x}$, if $\xi = \underline{x}$, and $\tilde{\xi} = x$, if $\xi = x$. In this defintion, the special receive form $\text{select}\,(\tilde{x}?\text{->}\mathcal{M}(P))$ (with action $\tilde{x}?$) is used to mirror the weak send. This form is used internally by the conformance checker and defines an extended notion of *stuckness*, capturing the conformance relation with weak send. Thus, the process $\text{select}(\tilde{x}?\text{->}0) \mid x!.0$ is classified as stuck, corresponding to the fact that the conformance relation $x! \leq \underline{x}!$ does *not* hold. On the other hand, the process $\text{select}\,(\tilde{x}?\text{->}0) \mid \underline{x}!.0$ is not classified as stuck (and it reacts normally on x), so the conformance relation $\underline{x}! \leq x!$ holds. We also change the notion of stuckness to allow for weak receives with no corresponding send. For example, we do not classify $\underline{\text{select}}\,(x?\text{->}0) \mid 0$ as stuck. The mirror of the weak receive, as defined above, adds the choice of the null process 0 to the previous definition of $\mathcal{M}$. Hence, weak receive specification $\underline{\text{select}}\,I$ requires implementation to be prepared to handle the situation where no input arrives. By our previous notion of stuckness, we have that $\text{select}\,(x?\text{->}0) \mid 0$ is stuck. It follows (by our definitions above) that

$$\text{select}\,(x?\text{->}0) \mid \mathcal{M}(\underline{\text{select}}\,(x?\text{->}0)) = \text{select}\,(x?\text{->}0) \mid x!.0\#0$$

can evolve to an end-state, so the conformance relation $\text{select}\,(x?\text{->}0) \leq \underline{\text{select}}\,(x?\text{->}0)$ does *not* hold.

7 Conclusion

Scalable model checking of models extracted from message-passing software requires that components be abstracted by simpler specifications. Existing definitions of conformance between a component and its abstraction —simulation and alternating simulation— do not satisfy substitutability for stuck-freeness. We presented a new definition of conformance that has this property. Our definition of conformance is stronger than both simulation and alternating simulation. We gave a simple algorithm to check if an implementation I conforms to a specification S, assuming certain restictions on I and S, by serializing I, dualizing S

and doing a state space exploration on the product. We have implemented the algorithm using the SPIN model checker, as a back-end for a behavioral type checker for message-passing software.

Acknowledgments

We thank Cedric Fournet, Tony Hoare, Gerard Holzmann, Jim Larus and Bill Roscoe for very helpful discussions.

References

1. R. Alur, T. A. Henzinger, O. Kupferman, and M. Y. Vardi. Alternating refinement relations. In *CONCUR 98: Concurrency Theory*, LNCS 1466, pages 163–178. Springer-Verlag, 1998. 168
2. E. Brinksma, B. Jonsson, and F. Orava. Refinining interfaces of communicating systems. In *TAPSOFT 91: Theory and Practice of Software Development*, LNCS 494, pages 297–312. Springer-Verlag, 1991. 169
3. S. Chaki, S. K. Rajamani, and J. Rehof. Types as models: Model checking message-passing programs. In *POPL 02: ACM Principles of Programming Languages*, pages 45–57. ACM, 2002. 166, 167, 168
4. R. J. Cleaveland, J. Parrow, and B. Steffen. The Concurrency Workbench: a semantics-based tool for the verification of finite-state systems. *ACM Transactions on Programming Languages and Systems*, 15(1):36–72, 1993. 169
5. L. de Alfaro and T. A. Henzinger. Interface theories for component-based design. In *EMSOFT 01: Embedded Software*, LNCS, pages 148–165. Springer-Verlag, 2001. 168
6. D. L. Dill. *Trace Theory for Automatic Verification of Speed-Independent Circuits.* MIT Press, 1988. 169
7. M. Dwyer, J. Hatcliff, R. Joehanes, S. Laubach, C. Pasareanu, Robby, W. Visser, and H. Zheng. Tool-supported program abstraction for finite-state verification. In *ICSE 01: International Conference on Software Engineering*, pages 177–187. ACM, 2001. 166
8. C. A. R. Hoare. *Communicating Sequential Processes.* Prentice Hall, 1985. 168, 169
9. G. J. Holzmann. Logic verification of ANSI-C code with Spin. In *SPIN 00: SPIN Workshop*, LNCS 1885, pages 131–147. Springer-Verlag, 2000. 166
10. L. Lamport. Proving the correctness of multiprocess programs. *IEEE Transactions on Software Engineering*, SE-3(2):125–143, 1977. 167
11. Kim G. Larsen and Robin Milner. A compositional protocol verification using relativized bisimulation. *Information and Computation*, 99:80–108, 1992. 169
12. J. R. Larus, S. K. Rajamani, and J. Rehof. Behavioral types for structured asynchronous programming. Technical report, Microsoft Research, 2001. 166, 167
13. R. Milner. *Communication and Concurrency.* Prentice Hall, 1989. 167
14. R. Milner. *Communicating and Mobile Systems: the π-Calculus.* Cambridge University Press, 1999. 167, 169, 171
15. S. K. Rajamani and J. Rehof. Conformance checking for models of asynchronous message passing software. Technical report, Microsoft Research, 2002. 173, 175
16. A. W. Roscoe. *The Theory and Practice of Concurrency.* Prentice Hall, 1998. 169

17. F. B. Schneider. Enforceable security policies. *ACM Transactions on Information and System Security*, 3(1):30–50, February 2000. 167
18. M. Y. Vardi and P. Wolper. An automata-theoretic approach to automatic program verification. In *LICS 86: Logic in Computer Science*, pages 322–331. IEEE Computer Society Press, 1986. 167
19. W. Visser, K. Havelund, G. Brat, and S. Park. Model checking programs. In *ICASE 00: Automated Software Engineering*, pages 3–12, 2000. 166

A Modular Checker for Multithreaded Programs

Cormac Flanagan[1], Shaz Qadeer[1], and Sanjit A. Seshia[2]*

[1] Compaq Systems Research Center
Palo Alto, CA
[2] School of Computer Science, Carnegie Mellon University
Pittsburgh, PA

Abstract. Designing multithreaded software systems is prone to errors due to the difficulty of reasoning about multiple interleaved threads of control operating on shared data. Static checking, with the potential to analyze the program's behavior over all execution paths and for all thread interleavings, is a powerful debugging tool. We have built a scalable and expressive static checker called Calvin for multithreaded programs. To handle realistic programs, Calvin performs modular checking of each procedure called by a thread using specifications of other procedures and other threads. The checker leverages off existing sequential program verification techniques based on automatic theorem proving. To evaluate the checker, we have applied it to several real-world programs. Our experience indicates that Calvin has a moderate annotation overhead and can catch defects in multithreaded programs, including synchronization errors and violation of data invariants.

1 Introduction

Mission-critical software systems, such as operating systems and databases, are often multithreaded. Ensuring the reliability of these systems is an important but difficult problem. Design of multithreaded software is particularly prone to errors because of subtle interactions between multiple interleaved threads of control operating on shared data. Static checking can analyze the program's behavior over all execution paths and for all thread interleavings. However, current static checking techniques do not scale to large programs.

A common way to achieve scalability is to use modularity, i.e., to analyze each component of the system separately using a specification of other components. A standard notion of modularity for sequential programs is *procedure-modular* reasoning [17], where a call site of a procedure is analyzed using a precondition/postcondition specification of that procedure. But this style of procedure-modular reasoning does not generalize to multithreaded programs [5,15]. An orthogonal notion of modularity for multithreaded programs is *thread-modular* reasoning [14], which avoids the need to explicitly consider all possible interleavings of threads. This technique analyzes each thread separately using a specification, called an *environment assumption*, that constrains the updates

---

* Supported in part by a NDSEG Fellowship.

D. Brinksma and K. G. Larsen (Eds.): CAV 2002, LNCS 2404, pp. 180–194, 2002.

to shared variables performed by interleaved actions of other threads. But this style of thread-modular reasoning handles a procedure call by the inherently non-scalable method of inlining the procedure body. Consequently, approaches based purely on any one of procedure-modular or thread-modular reasoning are inadequate for large programs with many procedures and many threads.

In this paper, we describe a combination of thread-modular and procedure-modular reasoning for verifying safety properties of multithreaded programs. In our methodology, the specification of each procedure consists of an environment assumption and an abstraction. The environment assumption, as in pure thread-modular reasoning, is a two-store predicate that constrains updates to shared variables performed by interleaved actions of other threads. The abstraction is a program that simulates the procedure implementation in an environment that behaves according to the environment assumption. Since each procedure may be executed by any thread, the implementation, environment assumption and abstraction of each procedure are parameterized by the thread identifier tid.

For each procedure p and for each thread tid, there are two proof obligations. First, the abstraction of p must simulate the implementation of p. Second, each step of the implementation must satisfy the environment assumption of p for every thread other than tid. It is sound to prove these obligations by inlining the abstractions rather than the implementations of the called procedures. Moreover, these obligations need to hold only in an environment that behaves according to the environment assumption of p. We reduce the two checks to verifying the correctness of a sequential program and present an algorithm to produce this sequential program. We leverage existing techniques for verifying sequential programs based on verification conditions and automatic theorem proving. Our approach is scalable since each procedure is verified separately using an environment assumption to model other threads and abstractions to model called procedures.

We have implemented our methodology for multithreaded Java [ ] programs in a checking tool called Calvin. We have applied Calvin to several multithreaded programs, the largest of which is a 1500 line portion of the web crawler Mercator [ ]. Our experience indicates that Calvin has the following useful features:

1. It naturally scales to programs with many procedures and threads since each procedure implementation is analyzed separately using the specifications for the other threads and procedures.
2. The checker is sufficiently expressive to handle the variety of synchronization idioms commonly found in systems code, e.g., readers-writer locks, producer-consumer synchronization, and time-varying mutex synchronization [ ]. Yet, it uses the conceptually simple framework of reducing the verification of multithreaded programs to the well-studied problem of verifying sequential programs.
3. Although a procedure abstraction can describe complex behaviors (and in an extreme case could detail every step of the implementation), in general the appropriate abstraction for a procedure is concise. In addition, the necessary environment assumption annotations are simple and intuitive for

programs using common synchronization idioms, such as mutexes or reader-writer locks.

Related Work. In an earlier paper [9], we presented an implementation of thread-modular reasoning for Java programs. However, a procedure call could be handled only by inlining the procedure body.

Static checkers have been built for detecting data races in multithreaded programs [2,6,8,20]; however, these tools are limited to checking a small subset of the synchronization mechanisms found in systems code. Moreover, these tools cannot verify invariants or check refinement of abstractions.

Recently, a few tools for checking invariants on multithreaded programs have appeared. These tools are based on a combination of abstract interpretation and model checking. The Bandera toolkit [7] uses programmer-supplied data abstractions to translate multithreaded Java programs into the input languages of various model checkers. Yahav [21] describes a method to model check multi-threaded Java programs using a 3-valued logic [19] to abstract the store. Since these tools explicitly consider all interleavings of the multiple threads, they have difficulty scaling to large programs. Ball et al. [4] present a technique for model checking a software library with an unspecified number of threads, but this method applies only when all the threads are identical and finite-state.

The compositional principle underlying our technique is assume-guarantee reasoning, of which there are several variants. We refer the reader to our earlier paper [9] for a detailed discussion; here we only discuss the closely related work of Jones [14] and Abadi and Lamport [1]. Abadi and Lamport consider a composition of components, where each component modifies a separate part of the store. Their system is general enough to model a multithreaded program since a component can model a collection of threads operating on shared state and signaling among components can model procedure calls. However, their proof rule does not allow each thread in a component to be verified separately. The proof rule of Jones does allow each thread in a multithreaded program to be verified separately; however the program for each thread does not have any procedure calls. Our work can be viewed as a synthesis of the two approaches, which is necessary to tackle the verification of programs that have a large number of procedures and threads.

2   The Parallel Language Plato

Verifying properties of multithreaded programs in a large and realistic language such as Java is quite complex. To help structure and modularize this process, our checker first translates the given Java program into a simpler intermediate language. This translation eliminates many of the complexities of the Java programming language and is outlined elsewhere [16]. In this paper, we focus on the subsequent verification of the resulting intermediate program, which we assume is expressed in the idealized language *Plato* (parallel language of atomic operations).

Plato syntax

$S \in Stmt ::=$	**skip**	no op	$\mathcal{B} \in$	$Defn$	$= Proc \rightarrow Stmt$
	$\mid \{p\}X$	atomic op	$P \in$	$Program ::=$	$S_1 \parallel \cdots \parallel S_n$
	$\mid S \square S$	choice	$\sigma \in$	$Store$	$= Var \rightarrow Value$
	$\mid S; S$	composition	$X, Y \in$	$Action$	$\subseteq Store \times Store$
	$\mid S^*$	iteration			
	$\mid p()$	procedure call			

A Plato program P is a parallel composition $S_1 \parallel \cdots \parallel S_n$ of several statements, or *threads*. The program executes by interleaving atomic steps of its various threads. The threads interact through a shared store σ, which maps program variables to values. The sets of variables and values are left intentionally unspecified, as they are mostly orthogonal to our technical presentation. Statements in the Plato language include the empty statement **skip**, atomic operation $\{p\}X$ (described below), sequential composition $S_1; S_2$, the nondeterministic choice construct $S_1 \square S_2$, which executes either S_1 or S_2, the iteration statement S^*, which executes S some arbitrary number of times, and procedure calls. The set *Proc* contains the procedure names and the mapping $\mathcal{B}$ provides the implementation corresponding to a procedure name. To simplify our presentation, the language does not include procedure arguments or return values.

Perhaps the most notable aspect of Plato is that it does not contain constructs for conventional primitive operations such as assignment and assertions. Instead, such primitive operations are combined into a general mechanism called an *atomic operation* $\{p\}X$, where p is a state predicate that should hold in the pre-state of the operation, and X is an *action*, or two-state predicate that describes the transition from the pre-state to the post-state.

To execute the atomic operation $\{p\}X$ from a pre-state σ, if $p(\sigma)$ does not hold, then the execution terminates in a special state **wrong** indicating that an error occurred. Otherwise an arbitrary post-store σ' is chosen that satisfies the constraint $X(\sigma, \sigma')$, and the execution of the program continues with the new store σ'. If no post-store σ' satisfies the constraint $X(\sigma, \sigma')$, then the thread blocks; execution proceeds only on the other threads.

Although an action X is a two-state predicate, it is typically written as a formula in which primed variables refer to their value in the post-store σ', and unprimed variables refer to their value in the pre-store σ. In addition, for any action X and set of variables $V \subseteq Var$, we use the notation $\langle X \rangle_V$ to mean the action that satisfies X and only allows changes to variables in V between the pre-store and the post-store, and we use $\langle X \rangle$ to abbreviate $\langle X \rangle_\emptyset$. Finally, we abbreviate the atomic operation $\{\mathbf{true}\}X$ to simply the action X. We also allow state predicates and actions to refer to thread identifier **tid**, a non-zero integer parameter that uniquely identifies the currently executing thread.

Expressing conventional constructs in Plato

$$\text{x = } e \stackrel{\text{def}}{=} \langle x' = e \rangle_x \qquad\qquad \text{if } (e) \{ S \} \stackrel{\text{def}}{=} (\text{assume } e; S) \square (\text{assume } \neg e)$$

$$\text{assert } e \stackrel{\text{def}}{=} \{e\}\langle \text{true} \rangle \qquad \text{while } (e) \{ S \} \stackrel{\text{def}}{=} (\text{assume } e; S)^*; (\text{assume } \neg e)$$

$$\text{assume } e \stackrel{\text{def}}{=} \langle e \rangle \qquad\qquad \text{CAS(l,e,n)} \stackrel{\text{def}}{=} \left\langle \begin{array}{l} \wedge\, 1 \neq e \Rightarrow (1' = 1 \wedge n' = n) \\ \wedge\, 1 = e \Rightarrow (1' = n \wedge n' = 1) \end{array} \right\rangle_{1,n}$$

Using atomic operations, Plato can express many conventional constructs, including assignment, assert, assume, if, and while statements. In addition, atomic operations can also express less common constructs, such as the atomic compare-and-swap instruction CAS(l,e,n), which tests if variable l has value e and swaps the values of n and l if the test passes; otherwise their values are unchanged.

2.1   Semantics

The execution of a Plato program is defined as an interleaving of the executions of its individual, sequential threads, and is formalized as a transition system. A *sequential state* Φ is either a pair of a store and a statement, or the special state **wrong** (indicating that the execution went wrong by failing an assertion).

$$\Phi \in SeqState ::= (\sigma, S) \mid \textbf{wrong}$$

In the sequential state (σ, S), the statement S identifies the code remaining to be executed, thus avoiding the need for a program counter. Given the environment $\mathcal{B}$ associating procedure names with their implementations, the semantics of an individual thread i is defined via the transition relation $\rightarrow_i$ on sequential states. We write $\mathcal{B} \vdash (\sigma, S) \rightarrow_i \Phi$ to indicate the execution of the "first instruction" in S from store σ, interpreting any occurrence of tid in S as i. This instruction may go wrong, yielding $\Phi = \textbf{wrong}$, or it may terminate normally, yielding a sequential state $\Phi = (\sigma', S')$ consisting of a (possibly modified) store σ' and a statement S' that remains to be executed.

A *parallel state* Θ is either a pair of a store and a program (representing the threads being executed), or the special state **wrong**.

$$\Theta \in ParState ::= (\sigma, P) \mid \textbf{wrong}$$

We write $\mathcal{B} \vdash (\sigma, P) \rightarrow_p \Theta$ to indicate the execution of a single sequential step of an arbitrarily chosen thread in P from store σ. If that sequential step terminates normally, then execution continues with the resulting post-state. If the sequential step goes wrong, then so does the entire execution. The details of the transition relations $\rightarrow_i$ and $\rightarrow_p$ are given in our technical note [11].

SimpleLock program

```
// module Top                          // module Mutex
int x = 0;                             int m = 0;

void t1() {        void t2() {         void acquire() {      void release()
   acquire();         acquire();          var t = tid;       {
   x++;               x = 0;              while (t == tid)      m = 0;
   assert x > 0;      release();            CAS(m,0,t);       }
   release();      }                    }
}                                       }
```

3 Overview of Modular Verification

We start by considering an example that provides an overview and motivation of our modular verification method. The multithreaded program SimpleLock consists of two modules, Top and Mutex. The module Top contains two threads that manipulate a shared integer variable x (initially zero) protected by a mutex m. The module Mutex provides acquire and release operations on that mutex. The mutex variable m is either the (non-zero) identifier of the thread holding the lock, or else 0, if the lock is not held by any thread. The implementation of acquire is non-atomic, and uses busy-waiting based on the atomic compare-and-swap instruction (CAS) described earlier. The local variable t cannot be modified by other threads. We assume the program starts execution by concurrently calling procedures t1 in thread 1 and t2 in thread 2.

We would like the checker to verify that the assertion in t1 never fails. This assertion should hold because x is protected by m and because we believe the mutex implementation is correct.

To avoid considering all possible interleavings of the various threads, our checker performs thread-modular reasoning, and relies on the programmer to specify an *environment assumption* constraining the interactions among threads. In particular, the environment assumption $E_{\mathtt{tid}}$ for thread tid summarizes the possible effects of interleaved atomic steps of other threads. For SimpleLock, an appropriate environment assumption is:

$$E_{\mathtt{tid}} \stackrel{\mathrm{def}}{=} \begin{aligned}&\wedge\ \mathtt{m} = \mathtt{tid} \Rightarrow \mathtt{m} = \mathtt{m}'\\ &\wedge\ \mathtt{m} = \mathtt{tid} \Rightarrow \mathtt{x} = \mathtt{x}'\\ &\wedge\ I \Rightarrow I'\end{aligned}$$

The first two conjuncts states that if thread tid holds the lock m, then other threads cannot modify either m or the protected variable x. The final conjunct states that every action preserves the invariant that whenever the lock is not held, x is at least zero:

$$I \stackrel{\mathrm{def}}{=} \mathtt{m} = 0 \Rightarrow \mathtt{x} \geq 0$$

This invariant is necessary to ensure, after t1 acquires the lock and increments x, that x is strictly positive.

3.1   Thread-Modular Verification

For small programs, it is not strictly necessary to perform procedure modular
verification. Instead, our checker could inline the implementations of acquire
and release at their call sites. Suppose that *InlineBody*(S) inlines the implementation of called procedures in a statement S. Then *InlineBody*($\mathcal{B}$(t1)) enjoys
the following technical property:

"*InlineBody*($\mathcal{B}$(t1))" is simulated by E_2^* from the set of states satisfying
m $= 0 \wedge$ x $= 0$ with respect to the environment assumption E_1.

The notion of simulation is formalized later in the paper. For now, the stated
property intuitively means that, when executed from an initial state where both x
and m are zero, each action of procedure t1 does not go wrong and satisfies E_2,
provided that each interleaved action of the other thread satisfies E_1.

The procedure t2 enjoys a corresponding property with the roles of E_1 and E_2
swapped. Using assume-guarantee reasoning, our checker infers from these two
facts that the SimpleLock program does not go wrong, no matter how the scheduler chooses to interleave the execution of the two threads.

3.2   Adding Procedure-Modular Verification

Analyzing a large system is impossible using the simple approach sketched above
of inlining procedure implementations at call sites. Instead, our checker performs
a procedure-modular analysis that uses procedure specifications to model called
procedures. We next tackle the question: what is the appropriate specification
for the procedure acquire in a multithreaded program?

A traditional precondition/postcondition specification for acquire is:

requires I;   modifies m;   ensures m $=$ tid $\wedge$ x ≥ 0

This specification records that m can be modified by the body of acquire and
asserts that, when acquire terminates, m is equal to the current thread identifier and that x is at least 0. This last postcondition is crucial for verifying the
assertion in t1.

However, although this specification suffices to verify the assertion in t1,
it suffers from a serious problem: it mentions the variable x, even though x
should properly be considered a private variable of the separate module Top.
This problem arises because the postcondition, which describes the final state
of the procedure's execution, needs to record store updates performed during
execution of the procedure, both by the thread executing this procedure, and
also by other concurrent threads (which may modify x).

In order to overcome the aforementioned problem and still support modular
specification and verification, we propose a generalized specification language
that can describe intermediate atomic steps of a procedure's execution, and
need not summarize effects of interleaved actions of other threads.

In the case of acquire, the appropriate specification is that acquire first
performs an arbitrary number of *stuttering* steps that do not modify m; it then

performs a single atomic action that acquires the lock; after which it may perform additional stuttering steps before returning. This code fragment $\mathcal{A}(\texttt{acquire})$ concisely specifies this behavior:

$$\mathcal{A}(\texttt{acquire}) \overset{\text{def}}{=} \langle \texttt{true} \rangle^*; \langle \texttt{m} = 0 \wedge \texttt{m}' = \texttt{tid} \rangle_\texttt{m}; \langle \texttt{true} \rangle^*$$

This abstraction specifies only the behavior of thread $\texttt{tid}$ and therefore does not mention x. Our checker validates the specification of acquire by checking that the statement $\mathcal{A}(\texttt{acquire})$ is a correct abstraction of the behavior of acquire, i.e.: the statement $\mathcal{B}(\texttt{acquire})$ is simulated by $\mathcal{A}(\texttt{acquire})$ from the set of states satisfying $\texttt{m} = 0$ with respect to the environment assumption $\texttt{true}$.

After validating a similar specification for release, our checker replaces calls to acquire and release from the module Top with the corresponding abstractions $\mathcal{A}(\texttt{acquire})$ and $\mathcal{A}(\texttt{release})$. If $InlineAbs$ denotes this operation of inlining abstractions, then $InlineAbs(\mathcal{B}(\texttt{t}i))$ is free of procedure calls, and so we can apply thread-modular verification, as outlined in Section 3.1, to the module Top. In particular, by verifying that "$InlineAbs(\mathcal{B}(\texttt{t1}))$" is simulated by E_2^* from the set of states satisfying $\texttt{m} = 0 \wedge \texttt{x} = 0$ with respect to E_1, and verifying a similar property for t2, our checker infers by assume-guarantee reasoning that the complete SimpleLock program does not go wrong.

4   Modular Verification

In this section, we formalize our modular verification method sketched in the previous section. Consider the execution of a procedure p by the current thread $\texttt{tid}$. We assume p is accompanied by a specification consisting of three parts: (1) an invariant $\mathcal{I}(p) \subseteq Store$ that must be maintained by all threads while executing p, (2) an environment assumption $\mathcal{E}(p) \in Action$, parameterized by $\texttt{tid}$, that models the behavior of threads executing concurrently with $\texttt{tid}$'s execution of p, and (3) an abstraction $\mathcal{A}(p) \in Stmt$, also parameterized by $\texttt{tid}$, that summarizes the behavior of thread $\texttt{tid}$ executing p. The abstraction $\mathcal{A}(p)$ may not contain any procedure calls.

In order for the abstraction $\mathcal{A}(p)$ to be correct, we require that the implementation $\mathcal{B}(p)$ be simulated by $\mathcal{A}(p)$ with respect to the environment assumption $\mathcal{E}(p)$. Informally, this simulation requirement holds if, assuming other threads perform actions consistent with $\mathcal{E}(p)$, each action of the implementation corresponds to some action of the abstraction. The abstraction may allow more behaviors than the implementation, and may go wrong more often. If the abstraction does not go wrong, then the implementation also should not go wrong and each implementation transition must be matched by a corresponding abstraction transition. When the implementation terminates the abstraction should be able to terminate as well.

We formalize the notion of simulation between (multithreaded) programs. A relation $R \subseteq Store \times Program \times Program$ is a simulation relation if, whenever we have $R(\sigma, S_1 \parallel \ldots \parallel S_n, T_1 \parallel \ldots \parallel T_n)$ then the following conditions hold:

1. if $S_i = \textbf{skip}$ then $\mathcal{B} \vdash (\sigma, T_i) \rightarrow_i^* (\sigma, \textbf{skip})$.

2. if $\mathcal{B} \vdash (\sigma, S_i) \rightarrow_i$ **wrong** then $\mathcal{B} \vdash (\sigma, T_i) \rightarrow_i^*$ **wrong**
3. if $\mathcal{B} \vdash (\sigma, S_i) \rightarrow_i (\sigma', S_i')$ holds then there exists a statement T_i' such that
   $\mathcal{B} \vdash (\sigma, T_i) \rightarrow_i^* (\sigma', T_i')$ holds and
   $R(\sigma',\ S_1 \parallel \ \cdots\ \parallel S_i' \parallel \ \cdots\ \parallel S_n,\ T_1 \parallel \ \cdots\ \parallel T_i' \parallel \ \cdots\ \parallel T_n)$.

A program P is *simulated* by a program Q from a set of states Σ if there exists a simulation relation R such that $R(\sigma, P, Q)$ holds for each state $\sigma \in \Sigma$. A statement B is *simulated* by a statement A with respect to an environment assumption E from a set of states Σ, if for all non-zero integers j, we have that the program $(B \parallel E^*)[\mathtt{tid} := j]$ is simulated by $(A \parallel E^*)[\mathtt{tid} := j]$ from Σ.

The implementation $\mathcal{B}(p)$ must also satisfy two other properties. While a thread $\mathtt{tid}$ executes p, every atomic operation must preserve the invariant $\mathcal{I}(p)$ and satisfy the environment assumption $\mathcal{E}(p)[\mathtt{tid} := j]$ of every thread j other than $\mathtt{tid}$. We can check that $\mathcal{B}(p)$ is simulated by $\mathcal{A}(p)$ and also satisfies the aforementioned properties by checking that $\mathcal{B}(p)$ is simulated by a derived abstraction $\hat{\mathcal{A}}(p)$ obtained from $\mathcal{A}(p)$ as follows: for every atomic operation $\{p\}X$ in $\mathcal{A}(p)$, replace X by the action

$$X \wedge (\mathcal{I}(p) \Rightarrow \mathcal{I}'(p)) \wedge \forall j : (j \neq 0 \wedge j \neq \mathtt{tid} \Rightarrow \mathcal{E}(p)[\mathtt{tid} := j]).$$

Moreover, this simulation must hold only in an environment that preserves the invariant $\mathcal{I}(p)$. Therefore, we also define a derived environment assumption

$$\hat{\mathcal{E}}(p) \stackrel{\text{def}}{=} \mathcal{E}(p) \wedge (\mathcal{I}(p) \Rightarrow \mathcal{I}'(p)).$$

In order to check simulation for a procedure p, we first inline the derived abstractions for procedures called from $\mathcal{B}(p)$. We use $InlineAbs : Stmt \rightarrow Stmt$ to denote this abstraction inlining operation. We also require that for any procedure q called from p, the environment assumption of p must ensure the environment assumption of q $(\mathcal{E}(p) \Rightarrow \mathcal{E}(q))$, and the invariant of p must ensure the invariant of q $(\mathcal{I}(p) \Rightarrow \mathcal{I}(q))$. Finally, if the program starts by executing a set of concurrent procedure calls $t_1() \parallel \cdots \parallel t_n()$, then we require that the initial store satisfy the invariant $\mathcal{I}(t_i)$ of every t_i and that $InlineAbs(\mathcal{B}(t_i))$ ensures the environment assumption of the other threads. As formalized in the following theorem, if all these conditions hold, then the multithreaded program will not go wrong. Thus, this theorem formalizes our method for combining procedure-modular and thread-modular verification.

Theorem 1. *Let $P = t_1() \parallel \cdots \parallel t_n()$ be a parallel program. Let Init be the set of initial stores of the program. Suppose the following conditions hold.*

1. *For all procedures $p \in Proc$, the statement $InlineAbs(\mathcal{B}(p))$ is simulated by $\hat{\mathcal{A}}(p)$ from $\mathcal{I}(p)$ with respect to the environment assumption $\hat{\mathcal{E}}(p)$.*
2. *For all procedures $p, q \in Proc$, if p calls q then $\mathcal{E}(p) \Rightarrow \mathcal{E}(q)$ and $\mathcal{I}(p) \Rightarrow \mathcal{I}(q)$.*
3. *Init satisfies the invariant $\mathcal{I}(t_i)$ for all $i \in 1..n$.*
4. *Let G be the action $\forall j \in 1..n : (j \neq \mathtt{tid} \Rightarrow \hat{\mathcal{E}}(t_j)[\mathtt{tid} := j])$. For all $i \in 1..n$, the statement $InlineAbs(\mathcal{B}(t_i))[\mathtt{tid} := i]$ is simulated by $G^*[\mathtt{tid} := i]$ from Init with respect to the environment assumption $\hat{\mathcal{E}}(t_i)[\mathtt{tid} := i]$.*

Then

1. *the program P is simulated by $\mathcal{A}(t_1) \parallel \ldots \parallel \mathcal{A}(t_n)$ from Init.*
2. *for any store $\sigma \in Init$, we have $\mathcal{B} \vdash (\sigma, P) \not\to_p^* \textbf{wrong}$ and if $\mathcal{B} \vdash (\sigma, P) \to_p^*$ (σ', P') then σ' satisfies $\mathcal{I}(t_i)$ for all $i \in 1..n$.*

Discharging the proof obligations in this theorem requires a method for checking simulation, which is the topic of the following section.

5   Checking Simulation

In this section, we present a method for checking simulation between two statements without procedure calls. We first look at the simpler problem of checking that the atomic operation $\{p\}X$ is simulated by $\{q\}Y$. This simulation holds if (1) whenever $\{p\}X$ goes wrong, then $\{q\}Y$ also goes wrong, i.e., $\neg p \Rightarrow \neg q$, and (2) whenever $\{p\}X$ performs a transition, $\{q\}Y$ can perform a corresponding transition or may go wrong, i.e., $p \wedge X \Rightarrow \neg q \vee Y$. The conjunction of these two conditions can be simplified to $(q \Rightarrow p) \wedge (q \wedge X \Rightarrow Y)$.

The following atomic operation $sim(\{p\}X, \{q\}Y)$ checks simulation between the atomic operations $\{p\}X$ and $\{q\}Y$; it goes wrong from states for which $\{p\}X$ is not simulated by $\{q\}Y$, and otherwise behaves like $\{p\}X$. The definition uses the notation $\forall Var'$ to quantify over all primed (post-state) variables.

$$sim(\{p\}X, \{q\}Y) \stackrel{\text{def}}{=} \{(q \Rightarrow p) \wedge (\forall Var'. \; q \wedge X \Rightarrow Y))\}(q \wedge X)$$

We extend our method to check simulation between an implementation B and an abstraction A from a set of states Σ with respect to an environment assumption E. We assume that the abstraction A consists of n atomic operations ($\{\textbf{true}\}Y_i$ for $i \in 1..n$) interleaved with stuttering steps $\{\textbf{true}\}K$, preceded by an asserted precondition $\{pre\}\langle\textbf{true}\rangle$, and ending with the assumed postcondition $\{\textbf{true}\}\langle post\rangle$:

$$A \stackrel{\text{def}}{=} \quad \{pre\}\langle\textbf{true}\rangle;$$
$$(\{\textbf{true}\}K^*; \{\textbf{true}\}Y_1); \; \ldots; \; (\{\textbf{true}\}K^*; \{\textbf{true}\}Y_n);$$
$$\{\textbf{true}\}K^*; \{\textbf{true}\}\langle post\rangle$$

This restriction on A enables efficient simulation checking and has been sufficient for all our case studies. Our method can be generalized to arbitrary abstractions A at the cost of more complexity.

Our method translates B, A, and E into a sequential program such that if that program does not go wrong, then B is simulated by A with respect to E. We need to check that whenever B performs an atomic operation, the statement A performs a corresponding operation. In order to perform this check, the programmer needs to add a *witness* variable pc ranging over $\{1, 2, \ldots, n+1\}$ to B, to indicate the operation in A that will simulate the next operation performed in B. An atomic operation in B can either leave pc unchanged or increment it by 1. If the operation leaves pc unchanged, then the corresponding operation in A is K. If the operation changes pc from i to $i + 1$, then the corresponding operation in A is Y_i. Thus, each atomic operation in B needs to be simulated by the following atomic operation:

$$W \stackrel{\text{def}}{=} \{\texttt{true}\}(\bigvee_{i=1}^{n}(pc = i \wedge pc' = i + 1 \wedge Y_i) \vee (pc = pc' \wedge K))$$

Using the above method, we generate the sequential program $[\![B]\!]_A^E$ which performs the simulation check at each atomic action, and also precedes each atomic action with the iterated environment assumption that models the interleaved execution of other threads. Thus, the program $[\![B]\!]_A^E$ is obtained by replacing every atomic operation $\{p\}X$ in the program B with $E^*; sim(\{p\}X, W)$. The following program extends $[\![B]\!]_A^E$ with constraints on the initial and final values of pc.

$$\texttt{assume } pre \wedge \Sigma \wedge pc = 1; [\![B]\!]_A^E; E^*; \texttt{assert } post \wedge pc = n + 1$$

This program starts execution from the set of states satisfying the precondition pre and the initial predicate Σ and asserts the postcondition $post$ at the end. Note that this sequential program is parameterized by the thread identifier $\texttt{tid}$. If this program cannot go wrong for any nonzero interpretation of $\texttt{tid}$, then we conclude that B is simulated by A from Σ with respect to E. We leverage existing sequential analysis techniques (based on verification conditions and automatic theorem proving) for this purpose.

6   Implementation

We have implemented our modular verification method for multithreaded Java programs in an automatic checking tool called Calvin. For the sake of simplicity, our checker assumes a sequentially consistent memory model and that reads and writes of primitive Java types are atomic (although neither of these assumptions is strictly consistent with Java's current memory model).

In Java, threads are objects of type $\texttt{Thread}$. Therefore, in our implementation the current thread identifier $\texttt{tid}$ refers to the object corresponding to the currently executing thread. The implicit lock associated with each Java object is modeled by including in each object an additional abstract field $\texttt{holder}$ of type $\texttt{Thread}$, which is either null or refers to the thread currently holding the lock.

6.1   Checker Architecture

The input to Calvin is an annotated Java program. In addition to the usual field and method declarations, a Java class can contain invariants, environment assumptions, procedure abstractions, and assertions to be checked. An invariant and an environment assumption are declared once for each class. The environment assumption $\mathcal{E}(p)$ (invariant $\mathcal{I}(p)$) for a procedure p is the conjunction of the environment assumptions (invariants) in (1) the class containing p, and (2) all those classes whose methods are transitively called by p.

Calvin parses, type checks, and translates the annotated input Java program into an intermediate representation language similar to Plato. Calvin then uses the techniques of this paper, as summarized by Theorem 1, to verify the intermediate representation of the program. To verify that each procedure p satisfies its specification, Calvin first inlines the abstraction of any procedure call from p. If the abstraction is not provided, then the implementation is inlined instead. Next, Calvin uses the simulation checking technique of the previous section to generate a sequential "simulation checking" program S. To check the correctness of S, Calvin translates it into a verification condition [12] and invokes the automatic theorem prover Simplify [18] to check the validity of this verification condition.

If the verification condition is valid, then the procedure implements its specification and the stated invariants and assertions are true. Alternatively, if the verification condition is invalid, then the theorem prover generates a counterexample, which is then post-processed into an appropriate error message in terms of the original Java program. The error message may identify an atomic step that violates one of the stated invariants, environment assumptions, or abstraction steps. The error message may also identify an assertion that could go wrong. This assertion may be explicit, as in the SimpleLock program, or implicit, for example, that a dereferenced pointer is never null.

The implementation of Calvin leverages extensively off the Extended Static Checker for Java [10], a powerful checking tool for sequential Java programs.

6.2   Optimizations

Calvin reduces simulation checking to the correctness of the sequential "simulation checking" program. The simulation checking program is often significantly larger than the original procedure implementation, due in part to the iterated environment assumption inserted before each atomic operation. To reduce verification time, Calvin simplifies the program before attempting to verify it. In addition to traditional sequential optimization techniques, we have found the following two additional optimizations particularly useful for simplifying the simulation checking program.

In all our case studies, the environment assumptions were reflexive and transitive. Therefore, our checker optimizes the iterated environment assumption E^* to the single action E after using the automatic theorem prover to verify that E is indeed reflexive and transitive.

The environment assumption of a procedure can typically be decomposed into a conjunction of actions mentioning disjoint sets of variables, and any two such actions commute. Moreover, assuming the original assumption is reflexive and transitive, each of these actions is also reflexive and transitive. Consider an atomic operation that accesses a single shared variable v. An environment assertion is inserted before this atomic operation, but all actions in the environment assumption that do not mention v can be commuted to the right of this operation, where they merge with the environment assumption associated with the next atomic operation. Thus, we only need to precede each atomic operation with the actions that mention the shared variable being accessed.

7   Applications

7.1   The Mercator Web Crawler

Mercator [ ] is a web crawler which is part of Altavista's Search Engine 3 product. It is multithreaded and written entirely in Java. Mercator spawns a number of *worker* threads to perform the web crawl and write the results to shared data structures in memory and on disk. To help recover from failures, Mercator also spawns a *background* thread that writes a snapshot of its state to disk at regular intervals. Synchronization between these threads is achieved using two kinds of locks: Java monitors and *readers-writer* locks.

We focused our analysis efforts on the part of Mercator's code (~1500 LOC) that uses readers-writer locks. We first provided a specification of the readers-writer lock implementation in terms of two abstract variables—`writer`, a reference to a `Thread` object and `readers`, a set of references to `Thread` objects. If a thread owns the lock in write mode then `writer` contains a reference to that thread and `readers` is empty, otherwise `writer` is `null` and `readers` is the set of references to all threads that own the lock in read mode. The procedure `beginWrite` acquires the lock in write mode by manipulating a concrete boolean variable `hasWriter`. The annotations specifying the abstraction of `beginWrite` and the corresponding Plato code are shown below.

```
/*@
requires holder == tid
modifies hasWriter
action:
also_modifies writer
ensures writer == null
      && writer' == tid
*/
public void beginWrite()
```

$$\{\text{holder} = \text{tid}\}\langle\text{true}\rangle;$$
$$\{\text{true}\}\langle\text{true}\rangle_{\text{hasWriter}}{}^{*};$$
$$\{\text{true}\}\left\langle\begin{array}{l}\wedge\text{writer} = \text{null}\\\wedge\text{writer}' = \text{tid}\end{array}\right\rangle_{\{\text{hasWriter},\text{writer}\}};$$
$$\{\text{true}\}\langle\text{true}\rangle_{\text{hasWriter}}{}^{*}$$

The next step was to annotate and check the clients of `ReadersWriterLock` to ensure that they follow the synchronization discipline for accessing shared data. The part of Mercator that we analyzed uses two readers-writer locks—L1 and L2. We use the following `writable_if` annotation to state that before modifying the variable `tbl`, the background thread should always acquire lock L1 in write mode, but a worker thread need only acquire the mutex on lock object L2.

```
/*@ writable_if  (tid == backgroundThread && L1.writer == tid)
             || (tid instanceof Worker && L2.holder == tid) */
private long[][]tbl; // the in-memory table
```

We did not find any bugs in the part of Mercator that we analyzed; however, we injected bugs of our own, and Calvin located those. In spite of inlining all non-public methods, the analysis took less than 10 minutes for all except one public method. The exception was a method of 293 lines (after inlining non-public method calls), on which the theorem prover ran overnight to report no errors.

7.2   The java.util.Vector Library

We ran Calvin on `java.util.Vector` class (~400 LOC) from JDKv1.2. There are two shared fields: an integer `elementCount`, which keeps track of the number of valid elements in the vector, and an array `elementData`, which stores the elements. These variables are protected by the mutex on the `Vector` object.

```
/*@ writable_if this.holder == tid */
protected int elementCount;
/*@ writable_if this.holder == tid */
protected Object elementData[];
```

Based on the specifications, Calvin detected a race condition illustrated in the following excerpt.

```
public int lastIndexOf(Object elem) {
    return lastIndexOf(elem, elementCount-1); // RACE!
}
public synchronized int lastIndexOf(Object elem, int index) {
    ....
        for (int i = index; i >= 0; i--)
            if (elem.equals(elementData[i]))
    ....
}
```

Suppose there are two threads manipulating a `Vector` object v. The first thread calls `v.lastIndexOf(Object)`, which reads `v.elementCount` without acquiring the lock on v. Before the first thread calls `lastIndexOf(Object,int)`, the other thread removes all elements from `v.elementData` and resets it to an array of length 0, and sets `v.elementCount` to 0. Now the first thread tries to access `v.elementData` based on the old value of `v.elementCount` and triggers an array out-of-bounds exception. An erroneous fix for this race condition is as follows:

```
public int lastIndexOf(Object elem) {
    int count;
    synchronized(this) { count = elementCount-1; }
    return lastIndexOf(elem, count);
}
```

Even though the lock is held when `elementCount` is accessed, the original defect still remains. RCC/Java [ ], a static race detection tool, caught the original defect in the `Vector` class, but will not catch the defect in the modified code. Calvin, on the other hand, still reports this error as what it is: a potential array out-of-bounds error.

References

1. M. Abadi and L. Lamport. Conjoining specifications. *ACM TOPLAS*, 17(3):507–534, 1995. 182
2. A. Aiken and D. Gay. Barrier inference. In *Proc. 25th POPL*, pages 243–354, 1998. 182
3. K. Arnold and J. Gosling. *The Java Programming Language*. Addison-Wesley, 1996. 181

4. T. Ball, S. Chaki, and S. Rajamani. Parameterized verification of multithreaded software libraries. In *TACAS*, pages 158–173, 2001. 182

5. A. Birrell, J. Guttag, J. Horning, and R. Levin. Synchronization primitives for a multiprocessor: A formal specification. In *Proc. 11th SOSP*, pages 94–102, 1987. 180

6. C. Boyapati and M. Rinard. A parameterized type system for race-free Java programs. In *Proc. OOPSLA*, pages 56–69, 2001. 182

7. M. Dwyer, J. Hatcliff, R. Joehanes, S. Laubach, C. Pasareanu, Robby, W. Visser, and H. Zheng. Tool-supported program abstraction for finite-state verification. In *Proc. 23rd ICSE*, pages 177–187, 2001. 182

8. C. Flanagan and S. N. Freund. Type-based race detection for Java. In *Proc. PLDI*, pages 219–232, 2000. 182, 193

9. C. Flanagan, S. N. Freund, and S. Qadeer. Thread-modular verification for shared-memory programs. In *Proc. 11th ESOP*, pages 262–277, 2002. 181, 182

10. C. Flanagan, K. R. M. Leino, M. Lillibridge, C. Nelson, J. Saxe, and R. Stata. Extended static checking for Java. In *Proc. PLDI*, 2002. 191

11. C. Flanagan, S. Qadeer, and S. A. Seshia. A modular checker for multithreaded programs. Technical Note 2002-001, Compaq Systems Research Center, 2002. 184

12. C. Flanagan and J. B. Saxe. Avoiding exponential explosion: Generating compact verification conditions. In *Proc. 28th POPL*, pages 193–205, 2001. 191

13. A. Heydon and M. Najork. Mercator: A scalable, extensible web crawler. In *Proc. 8th WWW Conf.*, pages 219–229, December 1999. 181, 192

14. C. B. Jones. Tentative steps toward a development method for interfering programs. *ACM TOPLAS*, 5(4):596–619, 1983. 180, 182

15. L. Lamport. Specifying concurrent program modules. *ACM TOPLAS*, 5(2):190–222, 1983. 180

16. K. R. M. Leino, J. B. Saxe, and R. Stata. Checking Java programs via guarded commands. Technical Note 1999-002, Compaq Systems Research Center, 1999. 182

17. B. Liskov and J. Guttag. *Abstraction and Specification in Program Development*. MIT Press, 1986. 180

18. C. G. Nelson. Techniques for program verification. Technical Report CSL-81-10, Xerox Palo Alto Research Center, 1981. 191

19. M. Sagiv, T. Reps, and R. Wilhelm. Parametric shape analysis via 3-valued logic. In *Proc. 26th POPL*, pages 105–118, 1999. 182

20. N. Sterling. WARLOCK — a static data race analysis tool. In *USENIX Tech. Conf. Proc.*, pages 97–106, Winter 1993. 182

21. E. Yahav. Verifying safety properties of concurrent Java programs using 3-valued logic. In *Proc. 28th POPL*, pages 27–40, 2001. 182

Automatic Derivation of Timing Constraints by Failure Analysis

Tomohiro Yoneda[*][1], Tomoya Kitai[2], and Chris Myers[**][3]

[1] National Institute of Informatics
Tokyo 101-8430, Japan
yoneda@nii.ac.jp
[2] Tokyo Institute of Technology
Tokyo 152-8552, Japan
kitai@yt.cs.titech.ac.jp
[3] University of Utah
Salt Lake City UT 84112, USA
myers@ece.utah.edu

Abstract. This work proposes a technique to automatically obtain timing constraints for a given timed circuit to operate correctly. A designated set of delay parameters of a circuit are first set to sufficiently large bounds, and verification runs followed by failure analysis are repeated. Each verification run performs timed state space enumeration under the given delay bounds, and produces a failure trace if it exists. The failure trace is analyzed, and sufficient timing constraints to prevent the failure is obtained. Then, the delay bounds are tightened according to the timing constraints by using an ILP (Integer Linear Programming) solver. This process terminates when either some delay bounds under which no failure is detected are found or no new delay bounds to prevent the failures can be obtained. The experimental results using a naive implementation show that the proposed method can efficiently handle asynchronous benchmark circuits and nontrivial GasP circuits.

Keywords: Trace theoretic verification, Failure analysis, Timed circuits, Timing constraints.

1 Introduction

In order to obtain high performance systems, it is necessary to design circuits with aggressive and complex sets of timing constraints. GasP circuits [ ] are a prime example of such highly *timed circuits*, i.e., circuits that don't work as expected, unless strict timing constraints on delay parameters are satisfied. In particular, the correctness of GasP circuits depends on the fact that (1) no hazards occur, (2) hold time constraints are satisfied for some signal transitions, and (3) short circuits caused by turning on all transistors in the path between the power supply and ground either never occur or occur only for a very short time. It is, however, not easy to check if the circuit satisfies all these constraints

[*] This research is supported by JSPS Joint Research Projects.
[**] This research is supported by NSF CAREER award MIP-9625014, NSF Japan Program award INT-0087281, and SRC grant 99-TJ-694.

D. Brinksma and K. G. Larsen (Eds.): CAV 2002, LNCS 2404, pp. 195–208, 2002.
© Springer-Verlag Berlin Heidelberg 2002

by simulation or static timing analysis due to the complexity of the timing constraints. Therefore, formal verification is essential.

This work uses a formal verification tool VINAS-P [2]. VINAS-P is based on a timed version of trace theoretic verification [3], and time Petri nets are used for modeling both specifications and circuits. VINAS-P checks safety properties. Bad behavior such as a hazard, hold time violation, and a short circuit can be detected as safety failures. VINAS-P uses partial order reduction which explores only a reduced state space that is sufficient to detect failures, which enables us to verify much larger circuits than a traditional total order method.

Although a formal verifier is very effective to prove a given circuit is correct with respect to the specification, for an incorrect circuit, it simply generates a failure trace. In the case of VINAS-P, it shows for a failure trace a waveform of selected signals. This is useful to understand what is going on in a circuit, but, it is not easy to see why the failure occurs, or how the failure can be eliminated. When we tried to verify the GasP circuits, failure traces were actually produced again and again. Although almost all these failures are caused by incorrect delay settings, obtaining the appropriate delays or conditions for them is a difficult problem. This motivates this work, which proposes a way to obtain sufficient timing conditions on delays for correct behavior of timed circuits by analyzing failure traces produced by the verifier.

In the proposed method, several delay parameters are selected to be examined, and initially, some large integer bounds are set to them. Then, the model is verified. If a failure trace is provided by the verifier, then our algorithm analyzes it, and suggests a set of candidates for additional timing constraints. Those timing constraints are sorted using heuristics, and the most appropriate one is chosen by the algorithm. The rest of the constraints are used when backtracking occurs. The selected timing constraint is added to the initial timing constraints, meaning the delay bounds are tightened. Then, an ILP (Integer Linear Programming) solver is invoked to update the delay bounds. This new set of delay bounds are used for the next verification run. This process of verification, analysis of failure traces to obtain timing constraints, and updating the delay bounds are fully automatic, and it is repeated until verification succeeds or no consistent timing constraints are found. Integer delay bounds and ILP are used in order to guarantee the termination of this process.

The rest of this paper is organized as follows. Section 2 refers to related works. Section 3 briefly introduces the verification method. Section 4 shows an example to explain the proposed method intuitively. In Section 5, the algorithms to analyze a failure trace and obtain timing constraints to eliminate the failure are proposed. The heuristics used for performance improvement are also shown there. Section 6 shows experimental results using a naive implementation. Finally, Section 7 summarizes the discussion.

2   Related Works

The same problem discussed in this paper is solved by two different but similar approaches. In [4], Negulescu proposes a method where a timed circuit is represented by an untimed model, called a process, and untimed state space enumeration is done. When a failure is detected, they analyze it by hand and construct a new model that avoids the failure. This process of untimed verification and reconstruction of the model is repeated until no failure is detected or model reconstruction fails due to inconsistency. Another approach is proposed in [5,6]. This approach also uses untimed models and untimed verification. In this approach, all possible failures of a circuit are generated by one state enumeration, and then timing constraints are obtained automatically by analyzing the state graph. The constraints obtained by this approach are not those on delays but those on ordering of signal transitions. Thus, their goal is slightly different from ours.

Another work that we need to mention is a verification of timed systems using relative timing method, which is proposed in [7]. Its goal is to verify timed circuits, not to obtain timing constraints. But, in their method, a detected failure is checked if it is legal with respect to the given delay bounds, and if so, a new model that excludes the failure is reconstructed. Verification and reconstruction are repeated similarly to Negulescu's method, but automatically. While it may be possible to combine this work and Negulescu's work to achieve the same result as ours, it is not clear how effective this would be since it has not been attempted.

The biggest difference between these works and our work is that only our method uses timed state space enumeration. The authors of the above works claim that the advantage of their works is that the verification of timed systems can be reduced to that of untimed systems. It is apparent that the complexity of untimed verification is much smaller than that of timed verification. Our claim is, however, that a huge number of failures may be detected if a timed circuit is analyzed as an untimed circuit, i.e., many but unrealistic failure traces can be produced by the untimed analysis. This makes the cost to obtain timing constraints fairly large. If the initial delay bounds can be suitably reduced to realistic ones, our method may work more efficiently. Probably, the only way to compare both approaches is to implement our idea and to compare the results for many examples. This is one of the goals of this paper.

Another difference is in adding timing constraints. Our method uses updated delay bounds. Thus, the cost of each verification run is almost the same. On the other hand, in the method proposed in [4] and [7], an additional timing constraint is represented by a process or a transition system, and the composition of the original model and the model for the additional timing constraint is verified in the next run. It is possible that this more complicated model may require more BDD nodes and increase the verification cost. The method in [5] does not suffer from this problem, because no model reconstruction is done. However, their method does not obtain constraints on delays but ordering of signal transitions, and hence, it seems difficult to verify, for example, hold time violation. In order to obtain constraints on delays, model reconstruction or a re-verification step (in our case) is necessary in each iteration, because there are potentially many constraints that eliminate a particular failure, and searching appropriate combinations of constraints to eliminate all possible failures step by step with backtracking is much easier than obtaining all possible combinations on the first try. For this reason, our problem cannot be modeled by a uniform ILP problem.

It's also necessary to mention that there are many works[8,9,10, and others] to verify timed systems using timed automata. Although this work uses time Petri nets to model timed circuits, because a tool based on them is available for us, we believe that the technique proposed in this paper can be easily applied to timed automaton based tools. Furthermore, although our tool uses the DBM analysis to handle real-time constraints, the proposed technique can also be applied to discrete-time analysis methods.

3   Verification Method

The underlying verification method used in this work is the timed extension of trace theoretic verification [ ]. In our method, each circuit element, called a module, is modeled by a time Petri net.

A time Petri net consists of *transitions* (thick bars), *places* (circles), and *arcs* between transitions and places. A *token* (large dot) can occupy a place, and when every source place of a transition is occupied, the transition becomes *enabled*. Each transition has two times, the *earliest firing time* and the *latest firing time*. In this work, it is assumed that these times are integers. An enabled transition becomes ready to fire (i.e., *firable*) when it has been continuously enabled for its earliest firing time, and cannot be continuously enabled for more than the latest firing time, i.e., it must fire unless it is disabled. The firing of a transition occurs instantly. It consumes tokens in its source places and produces tokens into its destination places.

A module is defined as (I, O, N), where I and O are sets of input and output wires, respectively, and N is a time Petri net. A firing of a transition changes the value of a wire that is related to the transition, and the direction of change $(0 \rightarrow 1$ or $1 \rightarrow 0)$ is represented by $+$ or $-$ in its name. A transition that is related to an output wire of the module is called an *output transition*. An *input transition* is defined similarly.

A timed circuit is modeled by a set of modules. In a set of modules, an input transition fires only in synchronization with the corresponding output transition in some different module. Thus, the earliest and latest firing times of an input transition is considered to be $[0, \infty]$. If an output transition is firable and every corresponding input transition is disabled in a module, the state is called a *failure state*, and the verifier reports a *failure trace*, which is a sequence of all transitions fired between the initial state and the failure state.

A specification is also modeled as a module. If a circuit behaves differently from its specification, an output from a circuit module cannot be accepted by the specification, and it is detected as a failure. In addition, bad behavior such as a hazard, hold time violation, and a short circuit can be detected as failures inside circuit modules.

4   A Small Example

Let's consider a circuit shown in Figure 1(a), where the delay bounds of the inverter and OR gate are $[d_{inv}, D_{inv}]$ and $[d_{or}, D_{or}]$. The initial state of this circuit is $(a, b, c, d) = (1, 0, 0, 0)$, and its behavior is expected as follows (See Figure 1(b)): When c is raised, d goes up. Then, a and c are lowered in this order. During these input changes, the circuit keeps d high. Finally, when a is raised again, d goes down, and the circuit goes back to the initial state. Hence,

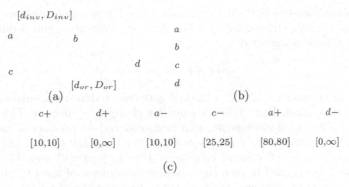

Fig. 1. A circuit and its environment

Fig. 2. Two possible cases to prevent the failure

the environment of this circuit can be expressed by $(\{d\}, \{a, c\}, N_s)$, where N_s is a time Petri net shown in Figure 1(c) [1]. The delay bounds for $c+$ and $u-$ are $[10,10]$, while those for $c-$ and $a+$ are $[25,25]$ and $[80,80]$, respectively. Note that d is an input of this environment and it fires in synchronization with the circuit output.

Assume that the following initial constraints for the circuit delay bounds are given.

$$5 \leq d_{inv} \leq 50, \quad 5 \leq D_{inv} \leq 50, \quad 5 \leq d_{or} \leq 50, \quad 5 \leq D_{or} \leq 50,$$
$$d_{inv} + 2 \leq D_{inv} \leq d_{inv} + 30, \qquad d_{or} + 2 \leq D_{or} \leq d_{or} + 30 \tag{1}$$

The constraints of the form $d_{inv} + 2 \leq D_{inv}$ are used to avoid tight delay bounds, and those of the form $D_{inv} \leq d_{inv} + 30$ are for reducing the state space. These and the lower bounds are also important to avoid imbalanced delay assignment such as assigning total delay to one gate and zero to the others. Actually, these initial delay bounds should be determined depending on the device technology used to implement the circuits. Now, the problem to be solved is to find some delay bounds, satisfying the above constraints, under which the circuit behaves correctly with its environment. Although it is desired that maximal possible delay bounds are found, it is beyond the scope of this paper.

The first step of our algorithm is to obtain initial delay bounds from (1) using a ILP solver. In this case, they are

$$d_{inv} = 5, \ D_{inv} = 35, \ d_{or} = 5, \ D_{or} = 35.$$

---

[1] More precisely, this is defined as a *mirror* of a specification, where their input set (output set) is equal to the output set (input set) of the circuit.

The details about the ILP solver and the objective function used are mentioned in Section 6. Using these delay bounds, the first verification run is done, and the following failure is detected: [2]

$$c+;\ d+;\ a-;\ c-;\ b+$$

This failure means that after $c-$, the OR gate tries to lower its output d because b is low at that time. But, before its output change, $b+$ occurs. This violates a property called semi-modularity, and is considered to produce a hazard. This failure can be prevented, if (a) $b+$ occurs later than the output change $d-$, or (b) $b+$ occurs before the input change $c-$ (See Figure 2(a) and (b)). Note that the failure is prevented in case (b), because the output of the OR gate is stable during these input changes. Suppose that our algorithm first tries case (a). In order to obtain the constraint for (a), the algorithm examines the casuals of $b+$ and $d-$. $b+$ is caused by $a-$, while $d-$ is caused by $c-$ and $c-$ is caused by $a-$ in the environment. Hence, to make $b+$ occur later than $d-$, the following constraint is necessary.

$$25 + D_{or} < d_{inv} \tag{2}$$

Note that the largest delay is used for the OR gate, while the smallest delay is used for the inverter. This ensures the above ordering $(d-;\ b+)$ even in the worst case.

For constraints (1) and (2), the ILP solver gives the delay bounds

$$d_{inv} = 33,\ D_{inv} = 50,\ d_{or} = 5,\ D_{or} = 7,$$

and the second verification run with these delay bounds produces the following failure.

$$c+;\ d+;\ a-;\ c-;\ d-$$

This failure occurs, because the circuit produces $d-$ although it is not expected in the environment (i.e., $d-$ is not enabled after $c-$). In other words, to prevent this failure, $d-$ should be prevented. This is possible if $b+$ occurs before $c-$. Again, the algorithm checks their casuals, and finds that both $b+$ and $c-$ are caused by $a-$. Hence, the following constraint is obtained.

$$D_{inv} < 25 \tag{3}$$

For constraints (1), (2), and (3), however, the ILP solver gives no solution due to inconsistency.

Now, the algorithm backtracks to the most recent selection point, and chooses case (b) instead. This constraint is actually the same as the above one, and constraint (3) is obtained. For constraints (1) and (3), the ILP solver gives

$$d_{inv} = 5,\ D_{inv} = 24,\ d_{or} = 5,\ D_{or} = 35,$$

and the third verification run reports no failure. Hence, the above delay bounds are the solution of our problem.

---

[2] Every gate is modeled by a time Petri net [ ], and it contains internal transitions other than input or output transitions. A failure trace includes internal transitions, but here, they are omitted for simplicity.

The main technical issue of our algorithm is to automatically obtain a constraint to prevent the given failure by analyzing the failure trace and the structure of the Petri nets. Another issue is that the correctness of the algorithm depends on the backtracking. In the above example, one backtrack occurs. Many backtrackings, of course, decreases the performance of the algorithm. Our algorithm uses a heuristic to choose appropriate constraints, which is simple, but very effective. These issues are discussed in the following section.

5   Failure Analysis

This section presents the algorithm that is used to perform analysis to derive sufficient timing constraints to avoid failures.

5.1   Finding A and B Events

When a failure trace is given, our algorithm first finds two events, called event A and event B, such that the failure is caused because event A occurs before event B, and that the failure may be prevented by firing event B before event A. For a failure trace, there can exist several event A's and B's. In the above example, for case (a), A is $b+$ and B is $d-$, and for case (b), A is $c-$ and B is $b+$. In order to handle cases where event B may not be even enabled, event A and B are extended so that they have an offset. That is, an AB-candidate with respect to a failure trace $\mathcal{F}$ is a three tuple $\langle t_A, t_B, \mathit{off} \rangle_{\mathcal{F}}$, where t_A is a transition that fires in $\mathcal{F}$, t_B is a transition that is enabled in the state where t_A fires, such that firing t_B certainly off time units earlier than t_A may be able to prevent $\mathcal{F}$. $\mathcal{F}$ is omitted from this notation if there is no confusion.

Let's consider modules M_1, M_2 shown in Figure 3 and their failure trace $\mathcal{F} = a+;\ t_4;\ t_2;\ t_1;\ b+(out)$. This failure trace starts when an output transition $a+(out)$ of M_2 fires in its initial marking $\mu_0 = \{p_0, p_5\}$ as well as the corresponding input transition $a+(in)$ of M_1. The failure occurs in a marking $\mu_3 = \{p_3, p_4, p_7\}$ because $b+(out)$ of M_1 fires before its input transition $b+(in)$ of M_2 becomes enabled. Thus, one way to prevent this failure is to fire t_6 before $b+(out)$. Note that an input transition is assumed to have $[0, \infty]$ bound, and so it becomes ready to fire immediately when it is enabled. In this example, however, t_6 is not yet enabled when $b+(out)$ of M_1 fires. Thus, the net is traversed upward, and an enabled transition t_5 is found. Since t_6 takes D_6 time units to fire in a worst case, it is necessary to fire t_5 D_6 time units earlier than $b+(out)$. Hence, $\langle b+(out), t_5, D_6 \rangle$ is obtained. This AB-candidate is computed by force_fire($b+(in), b+(out), 0, \mu_3, \emptyset$), where force_fire($t, t_A, \mathit{off}, \mu, T_D$) obtains a set of AB-candidates in a marking μ to force t to fire certainly off time units earlier than t_A without firing transitions in T_D, and it is defined as follows.

1. If $t \in T_D$, then force_fire($t, t_A, \mathit{off}, \mu, T_D$) $= \emptyset$. T_D is used to terminate looping.
2. Otherwise, if t is enabled in μ, then

$$\text{force\_fire}(t, t_A, \mathit{off}, \mu, T_D) = \{\langle t_A, t, \mathit{off} \rangle\}.$$

$M_2(\{b\}, \{a\}, N_2)$ t_7

    p_5 p_6

          p_7 p_8 p_9

$a+ (out)$ $b+ (in)$

      t_4 t_5 t_6

       p_2 $b+ (out)$

$a+ (in)$ Bounds for t_i

   p_1 t_1 p_4 are $[d_i, D_i]$,

                          bounds for $a + (out)$

p_0 are $[d_{a+}, D_{a+}]$,

$M_1(\{a\}, \{b\}, N_1)$ t_2 p_3 t_3 and so on.

Fig. 3. An example of a module set

3. Otherwise, for some empty place $p \in \bullet t - \mu$,

$$\text{force\_fire}(t, t_A, \textit{off}, \mu, T_D) =$$
$$\bigcup_{t' \in \bullet p} \text{force\_fire}(\text{out\_trans}(t'), t_A, \textit{off} + \text{Lft}(t), \mu, T_D \cup \{t\}),$$

where out_trans(t') is the output transition that corresponds to t' (if t' is an output transition, then out_trans$(t') = t'$), and Lft(t) is the latest firing time of t. Note that it is sufficient to check some empty source place p of t because at least p needs a token in order to enable t. On the other hand, all source transitions of p should be checked, because it is unknown which source transition produces a token to p.

There are, however, other ways to prevent the above failure. For example, if t_3 fires before t_1, this failure is prevented, because the output transition $b +$ (out) is no longer enabled. Furthermore, if t_7 fires before t_4 and $b + (out)$, this failure is prevented. The method used in our work to cover all these cases is to try every transition t_c that lost the chance to fire in the failure trace, i.e., our method obtains every AB-candidate for firing transition t_c such that $t_c \in$ conflict(t) where t is a transition that fired in the failure trace and conflict(t) is a set of transitions that are in conflict with t. Since this method may produce unnecessary AB-candidates, removing them is probably necessary in order to improve the performance, but this is left as future work. Hence, the following obtain_AB$(\mathcal{F})$ obtains a set of all AB-candidates for a failure trace $\mathcal{F}$, where in_trans(t, M) is a set of input transitions of module M that correspond to output transition t, M_{in} is the module whose input transition causes a failure, $l = |\mathcal{F}|$, t_i is the i-th transition in $\mathcal{F}$ (i.e., t_{l-1} is the failure transition), and μ_i is the marking where t_i fires (i.e., μ_0 is the initial marking).

$$\text{obtain\_AB}(\mathcal{F}) = \bigcup_{t' \in \text{in\_trans}(t_{l-1}, M_{in})} \text{force\_fire}(t', t_{l-1}, 0, \mu_{l-1}, \emptyset) \cup$$
$$\bigcup_{i=0}^{l-2} \left(\bigcup_{t' \in \text{conflict}(t_i)} \text{force\_fire}(\text{out\_trans}(t'), t_i, 0, \mu_i, \emptyset) \right)$$

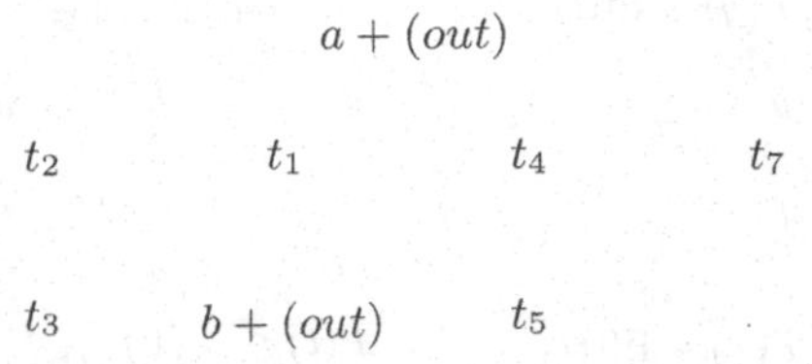

$$a + (out)$$

$$t_2 \qquad\qquad t_1 \qquad\qquad t_4 \qquad\qquad t_7$$

$$t_3 \qquad b + (out) \qquad t_5$$

Fig. 4. Timing relations implied by the failure trace $\mathcal{F}$

5.2   Obtaining Constraints

Once AB-candidates are found, the next step is to construct timing constraints for each AB-candidate. This is done based on the timing relations implied by the given failure trace. A failure trace gives two kinds of timing relations, called *causal relation* and *preceding relation*.

If transition u is the unique parent of transition t, i.e., the firing of u causes t to become enabled, the firing time of t, denoted by $T(t)$, must satisfy the following relation.

$$\mathsf{Eft}(t) \leq T(t) - T(u) \leq \mathsf{Lft}(t)$$

This is a causal relation. If t has two or more parents $u_1, u_2, \cdots$, the verification algorithm chooses one parent, say u_p, that decides the firing time of t. Such a parent is called a *true parent*. Since a true parent must fire later than the other parents in order to actually cause its child transition, the following relation is also necessary besides the above causal relation.

$$T(u_1) \leq T(u_p), \ \ T(u_2) \leq T(u_p), \ \ \cdots$$

These are called preceding relations. Furthermore, if two or more transitions $t_1, t_2, \cdots$ are in conflict, and t_k wins the conflict, then the following relation is necessary to express that t_k fires earlier than any other conflicting transitions.

$$T(t_k) \leq T(t_1), \ \ T(t_k) \leq T(t_2), \ \ \cdots$$

These are also preceding relations. Precisely, this relation is necessary for all transitions in a ready set [3], which is a set of transitions that should be interleaved in the state.

Consider again the modules shown in Figure 3 and the failure trace $\mathcal{F} = a+;\ t_4;\ t_2;\ t_1;\ b + (out)$. The timing relations implied by this failure trace can be illustrated as shown in Figure 4. In this figure, which is called a *failure graph*, a node represents a transition that fires or gets enabled in the failure trace. A normal arrow from u to t indicates the causal relation (i.e., $\mathsf{Eft}(t) \leq T(t) - T(u) \leq \mathsf{Lft}(t)$), while a dotted arrow indicates the preceding relation (i.e., $T(u) \leq T(t)$).

Now, consider an AB-candidate $\langle b + (out), t_5, D_6 \rangle$ to construct its timing constraints for firing t_6 certainly earlier than $b + (out)$. The first step to obtain the constraints is to find the common ancestor of t_5 and $b + (out)$ in the failure graph. In this example, it's $a + (out)$. This means that $a + (out)$ determines the firing times of both t_5 and $b + (out)$, and so the constraints should be related to minimal delay $T(y) + \mathsf{Eft}(u)$ maximal delay $T(y) + \mathsf{Lft}(u)$

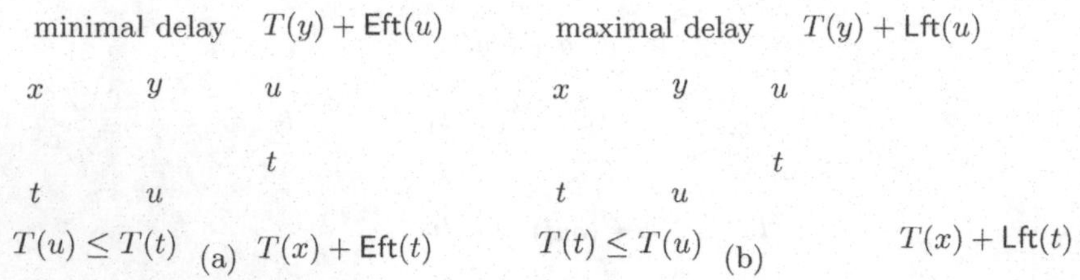

$x \qquad y \qquad u$ $x \qquad y \qquad u$

t t

$t \qquad u$ $t \qquad u$

$T(u) \leq T(t)$ (a) $T(x) + \mathsf{Eft}(t)$ $T(t) \leq T(u)$ (b) $T(x) + \mathsf{Lft}(t)$

Fig. 5. Paths by preceding relation

the delays between $a + (out)$ and those two events. Next, in order to guarantee the above relation between t_6 and $b + (out)$, the maximal delay from $a + (out)$ to t_5 plus D_6 must be smaller than the minimal delay from $a + (out)$ to $b + (out)$. From the causal relation of $\mathcal{F}$, this is expressed as follows.

$$D_4 + D_5 + D_6 < d_1 + d_{b+}$$

Note that bounds for t_i are denoted by $[d_i, D_i]$, bounds for $a + (out)$ are $[d_{a+}, D_{a+}]$, and so on. In addition to the above constraint, the effect of the preceding relation should be considered. When computing minimal delay up to t, suppose that there is a preceding relation $T(u) \leq T(t)$ as shown in Figure 5(a). Due to this constraint, if u fires late enough, the earliest firing time of t is not decided by $T(x) + \mathsf{Eft}(t)$, but decided by $T(y) + \mathsf{Eft}(u)$. This means that the path shown by the dotted arrow in the figure should also be considered for the minimal delay path. Since it is difficult to check if u certainly fires late enough, both paths (i.e., $x \to t$ and $y \to u \to t$) need to be considered. Similarly, for the maximal delay computation, the dotted arrow in Figure 5(b) should be considered. Hence, another constraint like

$$D_7 + D_5 + D_6 < d_1 + d_{b+}$$

is also necessary.

5.3   Heuristics to Select Constraints

Since the algorithms shown in the previous sections obtain constraints for considering all possibilities to prevent the given failure, many constraints are often generated, Thus, it is very important to select an appropriate one from them. This subsection shows simple heuristics for this purpose.

Let $v(d)$ be a value assigned to a delay d by the ILP solver for the most recent verification run, and for an expression $E = d_1 + d_2 + \cdots$, let $v(E)$ be $v(d_1) + v(d_2) + \cdots$. A *weight* of a constraint $L < R$ is $v(L) - v(R)$, where L and R are expressions. The idea is that the weight of a constraint implies how much effort is necessary to satisfy the constraint based on the current delay assignment. For example, for the current delay assignment such as $v(d_1) = 10$, $v(d_2) = 50$, and $v(D_3) = 60$, it may be easier to satisfy a constraint $D_3 < d_2$ rather than to satisfy $D_3 < d_1$, because d_2 should be increased by more than 10 for the former, while d_3 should be increased by more than 50 for the latter. This is represented by the weights 10 and 50, respectively. Note that a constraint with negative weight is illegal, because such a constraint is supposed to be already satisfied under the current delay assignment, and it cannot prevent the given failure.

If a constraint that is too strong is selected, an inconsistency may be detected after several verification runs, and backtracking occurs. On the other hand, even if a constraint that is too weak is selected, a stronger constraint can be added later to obtain a suitable constraint set. Hence, our heuristics select a constraint with the smallest nonnegative weight. For the example shown in Section 4, the weight of constraint (2) is 55, and that of (3) is 10. Hence, if this heuristic is used, case (b) is selected first, and no backtracking occurs.

5.4   Overall Procedure

The whole procedure that repeats the verification runs and adds new constraints is shown in Figure 6. This procedure takes two inputs, M and con_set. M is a set of time Petri nets representing the circuit and its specification. When the procedure is called for the first time, the initial constraints for the circuit delay bounds like (1) in Section 4 is set to con_set. This procedure first calls an ILP solver (line 3). Currently, we use a public domain ILP solver called lp_solve (ver 3.1a, ftp://ftp.ics.ele.tue.nl/pub/lp_solve/). An ILP solver computes an optimal integer assignment to variables for maximizing or minimizing an objective function under a given set of constraints. For delays $d_1, D_1, d_2, D_2, \cdots$ where d_i is a lower bound of the delay and D_i is an upper bound, our algorithm uses the following objective function f and tries to maximize it.

$$f = (D_1 - 2d_1) + (D_2 - 2d_2) + \cdots$$

From our experience, the most suitable solutions such that the difference between lower bounds and upper bounds are large and that lower bounds are fairly small are obtained by this objective function. $stat$ in line 3 indicates "infeasible", if the constraint set is inconsistent. In this case, the procedure returns with "impossible" for backtracking (line 4). Otherwise, $bounds$ contains an optimal assignment to the delay bounds. In line 5, the bounds of M are modified according to this delay assignment, and M' is obtained. This M' is used for the verification in line 6. If the verifier returns "success", this means that a set of timing constraints under which the circuit works as expected are obtained, and so, the procedure terminates (line 7). Otherwise, the verifier produces a failure trace $failure$. In line 8, this $failure$ is analyzed as mentioned in the previous subsections, and a set of new timing constraints are obtained. Those timing constraints are sorted based on their weights (line 9), and each constraint con with a nonnegative weight is added to con_set in this order for the recursive call of "obtain_timing_constraints"(line 11). If it returns, it means that no solution is obtained under $con\_set \cup \{con\}$, and so, the next constraint in the new_con' is tried by the foreach loop (line 10 and line 11). If every constraint causes inconsistency, the procedure returns with "impossible" for backtracking (line 12).

By selecting a constraint with a nonnegative weight, it is guaranteed that the constraint certainly reduces the space of the delay bounds. Therefore, since the earliest and latest firing times are integer, this procedure always terminates.

```
 1:   obtain_timing_constraints(M, con_set)
 2:   begin
 3:      (stat, bounds) = ILP(con_set);
 4:      if (stat == infeasible) then return(impossible);
 5:      M' = modify_bounds(M, bounds);
 6:      (stat, failure) = verify(M');
 7:      if (stat == success) then exit(success);
 8:      new_con = analyze_failure(failure);
 9:      new_con' = sort(new_con);
10:      foreach con ∈ new_con'
11:         if weight(con) ≥ 0 then obtain_timing_constraints(M, con_set ∪ {con});
12:      return(impossible);
13:   end
```

Fig. 6. Overall procedure

On the other hand, when the procedure terminates with "impossible", is it really impossible to eliminate the failure? If so, the procedure is called *complete*. In order to prove its completeness, it is necessary to show that the algorithm to find an AB-candidate covers all cases to eliminate failures, and that the constraints obtained are not unnecessarily strict. This is not yet proven formally. The selection of objective function as well as errors in the ILP solutions certainly affect the performance (i.e., the number of backtrackings) and the quality of the results (i.e., the width of the delay bounds), but we do not believe that the completeness is affected by them.

6   Experimental Results

In order to demonstrate the proposed method, the VINAS-P verifier has been modified so that it produces a set of timing constraints for a detected failure trace. This program corresponds to lines 6 ⋯ 8 in Figure 6. Then, a Perl script has been developed to naively implement the rest of the procedure.

In this section, two sets of experimental results are shown. The first set of experiments have been done using some asynchronous benchmark circuits from [6]. The second and third columns of Table 1 show the number of signals and the number of gates in each circuit. "#timed states" shows the number of timed states in the circuits with the final bounds (i.e., the circuits that pass verification). The next two columns show the number of verification runs and the number of backtracks needed to obtain the final constraint sets. The CPU times for the overall procedure are shown in the column "CPU" (all CPU times are shown in seconds). The column "CPU-[6]" is quoted from [6], where the experiments were done on a 450MHz 1GB Ultra SPARC60 machine. According to the authors of that paper, the data comes from a proof-of-concept prototype that is not yet optimized for run-time and thus does not incorporate many of the known speed-up techniques and optimizations for untimed analysis. In addition, the majority of the the run-time is taken up in the process for optimizing constraint sets that can be made much more efficient. Our experiments have been performed on a Pentium II 333MHz, 128MB Linux machine, and as mentioned,

Table 1. Experimental results (1)

name	#signals	#gates	#timed states	#verify	#backtracks	CPU	CPU-[ ]
alloc-outbound	15	11	85	4	0	1.36	13.08
mp-forward-pkt	13	10	57	3	0	0.93	0.89
dff	8	6	67	6	0	1.48	27.17
sbuf-send-pkt2	17	13	113	7	0	2.69	69.97
converta	14	12	98	7	0	2.36	113.12
ram-read-sbuf	22	16	161	7	0	3.08	127.98

Table 2. Experimental results (2)

name	#signals	#gates	#timed states	#verify	#backtracks	CPU	CPU (last)
gasp4	27	32	817	9	0	2.07	0.11
gasp8	51	64	65147	10	0	752.17	717.77
square9	82	81	3017	11	2	21.26	2.04

our current implementation is also very naive. Thus, we consider that these data demonstrate that the performance of our method based on time analysis is at least comparable to those of their method based on untimed analysis.

If the sorting by the constraints' weights (line 9 of Figure 6) is turned off, 10 verification runs and 5 backtrackings are needed for the "alloc-outbound" circuit. This shows the effectiveness of the heuristics shown in Section 5.3.

The second set of experiments [3] use several GasP circuits shown in [ ] and [ ]. These circuits have fairly large state spaces, but our method can handle them as shown in Table 2. Almost all CPU times are spent for the final verification of the correct circuits as shown in the last column (CPU (last)), and the process to obtain the timing constraint sets is performed within a rather short time. These experiments have been performed on a Pentium III 1GHz, 2MB Linux machine. In these experiments, the CPU times for ILP is negligible compared with those for state space enumeration. Thus, from a performance point of view, using ILP instead of LP is not too costly.

7   Conclusion

This paper describes a new method for the derivation of timing constraints that guarantee the correctness of timed circuit implementations. This approach uses an automatic technique in which a failure trace is analyzed to find pairs of events and obtain associated new timing constraints that can eliminate the failure trace. This method has been automated around the VINAS-P tool, and our initial verification results are very promising.

In the future, we plan to develop better heuristics to avoid generating useless AB-candidates. We also plan to perform a formal analysis to show that our method is complete in that when no constraints can be found, no solution can exist.

---

[3] The source files and results of these experiments can be downloaded from
http://yoneda-www.cs.titech.ac.jp/~yoneda/tcs-data/data.tar.gz.

Acknowledgement

The authors would like to thank Peter Beerel and Hoshik Kim for helping us to understand their method and giving their latest experimental results, and to thank Bill Coates and Ian Jones for helpful comments to model GasP circuits.

References

1. Ivan Sutherland and Scott Fairbanks. GasP: A minimal FIFO control. In *Proc. International Symposium on Advanced Research in Asynchronous Circuits and Systems*, pages 46–53. IEEE Computer Society Press, March 2001. 195, 207
2. http://yoneda-www.cs.titech.ac.jp/~yoneda/pub.html. 196
3. Tomohiro Yoneda and Hiroshi Ryu. Timed trace theoretic verification using partial order reduction. In *Proc. of Fifth International Symposium on Advanced Research in Asynchronous Circuits and Systems*, pages 108–121, 1999. 196, 198, 200, 203
4. Radu Negulescu and Ad Peeters. Verification of speed-dependences in single-rail handshake circuits. In *Proc. International Symposium on Advanced Research in Asynchronous Circuits and Systems*, pages 159–170, 1998. 196, 197
5. Hoshik Kim. Relative timing based verification of timed circuits and systems. In *Proc. International Workshop on Logic Synthesis*, June 1999. 197
6. Hoshik Kim, Peter A. Beerel, and Ken Stevens. Relative timing based verification of timed circuits and systems. In *Proc. International Symposium on Advanced Research in Asynchronous Circuits and Systems*, pages 115–124, 2002. 197, 206, 207
7. Marco A. Peña, Jordi Cortadella, Alex Kondratyev, and Enric Pastor. Formal verification of safety properties in timed circuits. In *Proc. International Symposium on Advanced Research in Asynchronous Circuits and Systems*, pages 2–11. IEEE Computer Society Press, April 2000. 197
8. Rajeev Alur and David Dill. Automata for modeling real-time systems. *LNCS 600 Real-time: Theory in Practice*, pages 45–73, 1992. 197
9. Marius Bozga, Oded Maler, and Stavros Tripakis. Efficient Verification of Timed Automata Using Dense and Discrete Time Semantics. In *Proc. of 10th IFIP WG10.5 Advanced Research Working Conference on Correct Hardware Design and Verification Methods*, LNCS 1703, pages 125–141, 1999. 197
10. Marius Minea. *Partial order reduction for verification of timed systems*. PhD thesis, Carnegie Mellon University, 1999. 197
11. Jo Ebergen. Squaring the FIFO in GasP. In *Proc. International Symposium on Advanced Research in Asynchronous Circuits and Systems*, pages 194–205. IEEE Computer Society Press, March 2001. 207

Deciding Separation Formulas with SAT[*]

Ofer Strichman, Sanjit A. Seshia, and Randal E. Bryant

Computer Science, Carnegie Mellon University, Pittsburgh, PA
{ofers,sanjit,bryant}@cs.cmu.edu

Abstract. We show a reduction to propositional logic from a Boolean combination of inequalities of the form $v_i \geq v_j + c$ and $v_i > v_j + c$, where c is a constant and v_i, v_j are variables of type **real** or **integer**. Equalities and uninterpreted functions can be expressed in this logic as well. We discuss the advantages of using this reduction as compared to competing methods, and present experimental results that support our claims.

1 Introduction

Recent advances in SAT solving make it worthwhile to try and reduce hard decision problems, that were so far solved by designated algorithms, to the problem of deciding a propositional formula. Modern SAT solvers can frequently decide formulas with hundreds of thousands of variables in a short amount of time. They are used for solving a variety of problems such as AI planning, Automatic Test Pattern Generation (ATPG), Bounded Model Checking, and more. In this paper we show such a reduction to SAT from a theory of *separation predicates*[1], i.e., formulas that contain the standard Boolean connectives, as well as predicates of the form $v_i \triangleright v_j + c$ where $\triangleright \in \{>, \geq\}$, c is a constant, and v_i, v_j are variables of type **real** or **integer**. The other inequality signs as well as equalities can be expressed in this logic. Uninterpreted functions can be handled as well since they can be reduced to Boolean combinations of equalities[ ].

Separation predicates are used in verification of timed systems, scheduling problems, and more. Hardware models with ordered data structures have inequalities as well. For example, if the model contains a queue of unbounded length, the test for $head \leq tail$ introduces inequalities. In fact, most inequalities in verification conditions, Pratt observed [ ], are of this form. Furthermore, since theorem provers can decide mixed theories (by invoking an appropriate

---

[*] This research was supported in part by the Office of Naval Research (ONR) and the Naval Research Laboratory (NRL) under contract no. N00014-01-1-0796, and the Gigascale Research Center under contract 98-DT-660. The second author is supported in part by a National Defense Science and Engineering Graduate Fellowship.

[1] The term *separation predicates* is adopted from Pratt[ ], who considered 'separation theory', a more restricted case in which all the constraints are of the form $v_i \leq v_j + c$, and conjunction is the only Boolean operator allowed. This logic is also known as 'difference logic'.

decision procedure for each logic fragment[11]), restricting our attention to separation predicates does not mean that it is helpful only for pure combinations of these predicates. Rather it means that the new decision procedure can shorten the verification time of any formula that contains a significant number of these predicates.

The reduction to SAT we suggest is based on two steps. First, we encode the separation predicates as new Boolean variables. Second, we add constraints on these variables, based on an analysis of the transitivity of the original predicates. A similar framework was used by Bryant et al. to reduce equality predicates [4]. The current work can therefore be seen as a natural extension of their work to the more general segment of logic, namely a logic of separation predicates.

2   SAT vs. Other Decision Procedures

There are many methods for deciding a formula consisting of a conjunction of separation predicates. For example, a known graph-based decision procedure for this type of formulas (frequently attributed to Bellman, 1957) works as follows: given a conjunction of separation predicates φ, it constructs a *constraints graph*, which is a directed graph $G(V, E)$ in which the set of nodes is equal to the set of variables in φ, and node v_i has a directed edge with 'weight' c to node v_j iff the constraint $v_i \leq v_j + c$ is in φ. It is not hard to see that φ is satisfiable iff there is no cycle in G with a negative accumulated weight. Thus, deciding φ is reduced to searching the graph for such cycles. Variations of this procedure were described, for example in [9], and are implemented in theorem provers such as Coq[2]. The Bellman-Ford algorithm [6] can find whether there is a negative cycle in such a graph in polynomial time, and is considered as the standard in solving these problems. It is used, for example, when computing Difference Decision Diagrams (DDD) [7]. DDD's are similar to BDDs, but instead of Boolean variables, their nodes are labeled with separation predicates. In order to compute whether each path in the DDD leads to '0' or '1', the Bellman-Ford procedure is invoked separately for each path.

Most theorem provers can decide the more general problem of linear arithmetic. Linear arithmetic permits predicates of the form $\sum_{i=1}^{n} a_i v_i \rhd a_{n+1}$ (the coefficients $a_1 \ldots a_{n+1}$ are constants). They usually apply variable elimination methods, most notably the Fourier-Motzkin technique [8], which is used in PVS, ICS , IMPS and others. Other approaches include the graph-theoretic analysis due to Shostak [10], the Simplex method, the Sup-Inf method, and more. All of these methods, however, need to be combined with case-splitting in order to handle disjunctions. Normally this is the bottleneck of the decision process, since the number of sub-problems that need to be solved is worst case exponential. One may think of case-splitting as a two steps algorithm: first, the formula is converted to Disjunctive Normal Form (DNF); second, each clause is solved separately. Thus, the complexity of this problem is dominated by the size of the generated DNF. For this reason modern theorem provers try to refrain from explicit case-splitting. They apply 'lazy' case-splitting (splitting only when encountering a disjunction) that only in the worst case generates all possible sub-formulas as described above. One exception to the need for case splitting in the presence of disjunctions is DDDs. DDDs do not require explicit case-splitting, in the sense that the DDD data structure allows term sharing. Yet the number of sub-problems that are solved can still be exponential.

Reducing the problem to deciding a propositional formula (SAT) obviously does not avoid the potential exponential blow-up. The various branching algorithms used in SAT solvers can also be seen as case-splitting. But there is a difference between applying case-splitting to formulas and splitting the domain. While the former requires an invocation of a (theory-specific) procedure for deciding each case considered, the second is an instantiation of the formula with a finite number of assignments. Thus, the latter amounts to checking whether all clauses are satisfied under one of these assignments.

This difference, we now argue, is the reason for the major performance gap between CNF - SAT solvers and alternative decision procedures that have the same theoretical complexity. We will demonstrate the implications of this difference by considering three important mechanisms in decision procedures: *pruning*, *learning* and *guidance*. In the discussion that follows, we refer to the techniques applied in the Chaff [8] SAT solver. Most modern SAT solvers work according to similar principles.

- *Pruning*. Instantiation in SAT solvers is done by following a binary decision tree, where each decision corresponds to choosing a variable and assigning it a Boolean value. This method makes it very easy to apply pruning: once it discovers a contradictory partial assignment a, it backtracks, and consequently all assignments that contain a are pruned. It is not clear whether an equivalent or other pruning techniques can be applied in case-splitting over formulas, other than stopping when a clause is evaluated to true (or false, if we check validity).
- *Learning*. Every time a conflict (an unsatisfied clause) is encountered by Chaff, the partial assignment that led to this conflict is recorded, with the aim of preventing the same partial assignment from being repeated. In other words, all assignments that contain a 'bad' sub-assignment that was encountered in the past are pruned. Learning is applied in different ways in other decision procedures as well. For example, PVS records sub-goals it has proven and adds them as an antecedent to yet unproven sub-goals, with the hope it will simplify their proofs. In regard to separation theory, we are not aware of a specific learning mechanism, but it's not hard to think of one. Our argument in this case is therefore not that learning is harder or impossible in other decision procedures - rather that by reducing problems to SAT, one benefits from the existing learning techniques that were already developed and implemented over the years.
- *Guidance*. By 'guidance' we mean prioritizing the internal steps of the decision procedure. For example, consider the formula $\varphi_1 \lor \varphi_2$, where φ_1 is unsatisfiable and hard to solve, and φ_2 is satisfiable but easy to solve. If the clauses are solved from left to right, solving the above formula will take

longer than solving $\varphi_2 \vee \varphi_1$. We experimented with several such formulas in both ICS and PVS, and found that changing the order of expressions can have a significant impact on performance, which means that guidance is indeed problematic in the general case.

The success of guidance depends on the ability to efficiently estimate how hard it is to process each sub formula and/or to what extent it will simplify the rest of the proof. Both of these measures are easy to estimate in CNF-SAT solving, and hard to estimate when processing more general sub formulas. Guidance in SAT is done when choosing the next variable and Boolean value in each level in the decision tree. There are many heuristics for making this choice. For example: choose the variable and assignment that satisfies the largest number of clauses. Thus, the hardness of what will remain to prove after each decision is estimated by the number of unsatisfied clauses.

Not only that these mechanisms are harder to integrate in the alternative procedures, they become almost impossible to implement in the presence of mixed theories (what can be learned from solving a sub-goal with e.g. bit-vectors that will speed up another sub-goal with linear arithmetic, even if both refer to the same variables?). This is why reducing mixed theories to a common theory like propositional logic makes it easier to enjoy the potential speedup gained by these techniques. Many decidable theories that are frequently encountered in verification have known efficient reductions to propositional formulas. Therefore a similar reduction from separation predicates broadens the logic that can be decided by solving a single SAT instance.

3   A Graph Theoretic Approach

Let φ be a formula consisting of the standard propositional connectives and predicates of the form $v_i \rhd v_j + c$ and $v_i \rhd c$, where c is a constant, and v_i, v_j are variables of type `real` (we treat integer variables in Section 5). We decide φ in three steps, as described below. A summary of the procedure and an example will be given in Section 3.4.

3.1   Normalizing φ

As a first step, we normalize φ.

1. Rewrite $v_i \rhd c$ as $v_i \rhd v_0 + c$.[2]
2. Rewrite equalities as conjunction of inequalities.
3. Transform φ to Negation Normal Form (NNF), i.e., negations are allowed only over atomic predicates, and eliminate negations by reversing inequality signs[3].

---

[2] $v_0 \notin \varphi$ can be thought of as a special variable that always has a coefficient '0' (an idea adopted from [10]).

[3] This step is only required for the integer case, described in Section 5.

4. Rewrite '$<$' and '$\leq$' predicates as '$>$' and '$\geq$', e.g., rewrite $v_i < v_j + c$ as $v_j > v_i - c$.

The normalized formula has no negations, and all predicates are of the form $v_i > v_j + c$ or $v_i \geq v_j + c$

3.2 Boolean Encoding and Basic Graph Construction

After normalizing φ, our decision procedure abstracts all predicates by replacing them with new Boolean variables. By doing so, the implicit transitivity constraints of these predicates are lost. We use a graph theoretic approach to represent this 'lost transitivity' and, in the next step, to derive a set of constraints that compensate for this loss.

Let $G_\varphi(V, E)$ be a weighted directed multigraph, where every edge $e \in E$ is a 4-tuple (v_i, v_j, c, x) defined as follows: v_i is the source node, v_j is the target node, c is the weight, and $x \in \{>, \geq\}$ is the type of the edge. We will denote by $s(e), t(e), w(e)$ and $x(e)$ the source, target, weight, and type of an edge e, respectively. We will also define the dual edge of e, denoted $\hat{e}$, as follows:

1. if $e = (i, j, c, >)$, then $\hat{e} = (j, i, -c, \geq)$.
2. if $e = (i, j, c, \geq)$, then $\hat{e} = (j, i, -c, >)$.

Informally, $\hat{e}$ represents the complement constraint of e. Thus, $\hat{\hat{e}} = e$.

We encode φ and construct G_φ as follows:

1. *Boolean encoding and basic graph construction*
   (a) Add a node for each variable in φ.
   (b) Replace each predicate of the form $v_i \triangleright v_j + c$ with a Boolean variable $e_{i,j}^{c,\triangleright}$, and add $(v_i, v_j, c, \triangleright)$ to E.
2. *Add dual edges.*
   For each edge $e \in E$, $E := E \cup \hat{e}$.

The dual edges are needed only if φ was not transformed to NNF in step 3 of Section 3.1. In the rest of this section we assume that this is the case.

We denote the encoded Boolean formula by φ'. Since every edge in G_φ is associated with a Boolean variable in φ' (while its dual is associated with the negation of this variable), we will refer to edges and their associated variables interchangeably when the meaning is clear from the context.

3.3 Identifying the Transitivity Constraints

The transitivity constraints imposed by separation predicates can be inferred from previous work on this logic [,]. Before we state these constraints formally, we demonstrate them on a simple cycle of size 2. Let $p1 : v_1 \triangleright_1 v_2 + c_1$ and $p2 : v_2 \triangleright_2 v_1 + c_2$ be two predicates in φ. It is easy to see that if $c_1 + c_2 > 0$ then $p1 \wedge p2$ is unsatisfiable. Additionally, if $c1 + c2 = 0$ and at least one of $\triangleright_1, \triangleright_2$ is equal to '$>$', then $p1 \wedge p2$ is unsatisfiable as well. The constraints on the other

	$x(\mathcal{C})$	Rules
$l_1:$	'$\geq$'	**R1, R2**
$l_2:$	'$>$'	**R3, R4**
$l_3:$	else	**R2, R3**

	$x(T)$	$x(B)$	Rules
$l'_1:$	'$\geq$'	'$>$'	**R1', R2'**
$l'_2:$	'$>$'	'$\geq$'	**R3', R4'**
$l'_3:$		else	**R2', R3'**

R1 : if $w(\mathcal{C}) > 0$, $\bigwedge_{e_i \in \mathcal{C}} e_i = 0$

R2 : if $w(\mathcal{C}) \leq 0$, $\bigvee_{e_i \in \mathcal{C}} e_i = 1$

R3 : if $w(\mathcal{C}) \geq 0$, $\bigwedge_{e_i \in \mathcal{C}} e_i = 0$

R4 : if $w(\mathcal{C}) < 0$, $\bigvee_{e_i \in \mathcal{C}} e_i = 1$

R1' : if $w(T) > w(B)$, $\bigwedge_{e_i \in T} e_i \rightarrow \bigvee_{e_j \in B} e_j$

R2' : if $w(T) \leq w(B)$, $\bigwedge_{e_i \in B} e_i \rightarrow \bigvee_{e_j \in T} e_j$

R3' : if $w(T) \geq w(B)$, $\bigwedge_{e_j \in T} e_j \rightarrow \bigvee_{e_i \in B} e_i$

R4' : if $w(T) < w(B)$, $\bigwedge_{e_i \in B} e_i \rightarrow \bigvee_{e_j \in T} e_j$

(a) *Cycles*   (b) *Transitive sub-graphs*

Fig. 1. Transitivity requirements of cycles (a) and transitive sub-graphs (b)

direction can be inferred by applying the above constraints to the duals of $p1$ and $p2$: if $c1 + c2 < 0$, or if $c1 + c2 = 0$ and at least one of $\rhd_1, \rhd_2$ is equal to '$<$', then $\neg p1 \wedge \neg p2$ is unsatisfiable.

We continue by formalizing and generalizing these constraints.

Definition 1. *A* directed path *of length m from v_i to v_j is a list of edges $e_1...e_m$ s.t. $s(e_1) = v_i$, $t(e_m) = v_j$ and $\forall_{i=1}^{m-1} t(e_i) = s(e_{i+1})$. A directed path is called* simple *if no node is repeated in the path.*

We will use capital letters to denote directed paths, and extend the notations $s(e)$, $t(e)$ and $w(e)$ to paths, as follows. Let $T = e_1...e_m$ be a directed path. Then $s(T) = s(e_1)$, $t(T) = t(e_m)$ and $w(T) = \sum_{i=1}^{m} w(e_i)$. $x(T)$ is defined as follows:

$$x(T) = \begin{cases} \geq & \text{if } \forall_{i=1}^{m} x(e_i) = \text{'}\geq\text{'} \\ > & \text{if } \forall_{i=1}^{m} x(e_i) = \text{'}>\text{'} \\ \sim & \text{otherwise} \end{cases}$$

We also extend the notation for dual edges to paths: if T is a directed path, then $\hat{T}$ is the directed path made of the dual edges of T.

Definition 2. *A* Transitive Sub-Graph (TSG) $\mathcal{A} = T \cup B$ *is a sub-graph comprised of two directed paths T and B, $T \neq B$, starting and ending in the same nodes, i.e., $s(T) = s(B)$ and $t(T) = t(B)$. $\mathcal{A}$ is called* simple *if both B and T are simple and the only nodes shared by T and B are $s(T)(= s(B))$ and $t(T)(= t(B))$.*

The transitivity requirements of a directed cycle[4] $\mathcal{C}$ and a TSG $\mathcal{A}$ are presented in Fig. 1. These requirements can be inferred from previous work on this logic, and will not be formally proved here.

Both sets of rules have redundancy due to the dual edges. For example, each cycle $\mathcal{C}$ has a dual cycle $\hat{\mathcal{C}}$ with an opposite direction and $w(\mathcal{C}) = -w(\hat{\mathcal{C}})$. Applying the

---

[4] By a 'directed cycle' we mean a closed directed path in which each sub-cycle is iterated once. It is obvious that iterations over cycles do not add transitivity constraints.

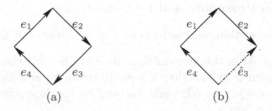

Fig. 2. A cycle (a) and a possible dual transitive sub-graph (b). Solid edges represent strict inequality ($>$) while dashed edges represent weak inequalities ('$\geq$')

four rules to both cycles will yield exactly the same constraints. We can therefore consider cycles in one direction only. Alternatively, we can ignore **R3** and **R4**, since the first two rules yield the same result when applied to the dual cycle. Nevertheless we continue with the set of four rules for ease of presentation.

Definition 3. *A cycle* C *(alternatively, a* TSG $\mathcal{A}$*) is satisfied by assignment* α*, denoted* $\alpha \models C$*, if* α *satisfies its corresponding constraints as defined in Fig. 1.*

We will denote by $\alpha(e)$ the Boolean value assigned to e by an assignment α. We will use the notation $\alpha \not\models_i C$, $1 < i < 4$, to express the fact that rule **R**i is applied to C and is not satisfied by α.

Proposition 1. *Let* $\mathcal{A} = T \cup B$ *and* $C = T \cup \hat{B}$ *be a* TSG *and a directed cycle in* G_φ*, respectively. Then* $\alpha \models \mathcal{A}$ *iff* $\alpha \models C$.

(Proofs for all propositions in this article can be found in the full version of this article [13]).

Example 1. We demonstrate the duality between TSG's and cycles with a cycle C where $x(C) =$'$>$' and $w(C) > 0$ (Fig. 2(a)). Assume α assigns 1 to all of C edges, i.e., $\alpha(C) = 1$. Consequently, $\alpha \not\models_3 C$.

We construct $\mathcal{A}$ from C by substituting e.g., e_3 with its dual (Fig. 2(b)). $\mathcal{A}$ is a TSG made of the two directed paths $T = e_4, e_1, e_2$ and $B = \hat{e}_3$, that satisfy $x(T) =$'$>$', $x(B) =$ '$\geq$' and $w(T) > w(B)$ (because $w(B) = -w(e_3)$). According to Fig. 1(b), we apply **R3'** and **R4'**. But since $\alpha(\hat{e}_3) = \neg\alpha(e_3) = 0$, **R3'** is not satisfied. Thus, $\alpha \not\models_{3'} \mathcal{A}$.   □

Proposition 1 implies that it is sufficient to concentrate on either TSG's or cycles. In the rest of this paper we will concentrate on cycles, since their symmetry makes them easier to handle.

The following proposition will allow us to concentrate only on *simple* cycles.

Proposition 2. *Let* C *be a non simple cycle in* G_φ*, and let* α *be an assignment to* C *edges. If* $\alpha \not\models C$ *then there exists a sub-graph of* C *that forms a simple cycle* C' *s.t.* $\alpha \not\models C'$.

Thus, our decision procedure adds constraints to φ' for every simple cycle in G_φ according to Fig. 1(a).

3.4   A Decision Procedure and Its Complexity

To summarize this section, our decision procedure consists of three stages:

1. Normalizing φ. After this step the formula contains only the '>'and '$\geq$'signs.
2. Deriving φ' from φ by encoding φ's predicates with new Boolean variables. Each predicate adds an edge and its dual to the inequality graph G_φ, as explained in Section 3.2
3. Adding transitivity constraints for every simple cycle in $G\varphi$ according to Fig. 1(a).

Example 2. Consider the formula $\varphi : x > y - 1 \vee \neg(z > y - 2 \wedge x \geq z)$. After step 2 we have $\varphi' : e_{x,y}^{-1,>} \vee \neg(e_{z,y}^{-2,>} \wedge \neg e_{z,x}^{0,>})$ (for simplicity we only refer to strict inequality predicates in φ', while the weak inequality predicates are referred to by a negation of their duals). Together with the dual edges, G_φ contains one cycle with weight 1 consisting of the vertices x, y, z, and the dual of this cycle. Considering the former, according to **R3** we add to φ' the constraint $\neg e_{x,y}^{-1,>} \vee \neg(\neg e_{z,y}^{-2,>}) \vee \neg e_{z,x}^{0,>}$. The constraint on the dual cycle is equivalent and is therefore not computed. $\square$

This example demonstrates that the suggested procedure may generate redundant constraints (yet none of them makes the procedure incomplete). There is no reason to consider cycles that their edges are not conjoined in the DNF of φ. In [12] we prove this observation and explain how the above procedure can be combined with *conjunctions matrices* in order to avoid redundant constraints. The conjunction matrix of φ is a $|E| \times |E|$ matrix, computable in polynomial time, that state for each pair of predicates in φ whether they would appear in the same clause if the formula was transformed to DNF. This information is sufficient for concluding whether a given cycle ever appears in a DNF clause. Only if the answer is yes, we add the associated constraint. We refer the reader to the above reference for more details on this improvement (note that the experiments in Section 6 did not include this optimization).

Complexity. The complexity of enumerating the constraints for all simple cycles is linear in the number of cycles. There may be an exponential number of such cycles. Thus, while the number of variables is fixed, the number of constraints can be exponential (yet bounded by $2^{|E|}$). SAT is exponential in the number of variables and linear in the number of constraints. Therefore the complexity of the SAT checking stage in our procedure is tightly bounded by $O((2^{|E|})^2) = O(2^{2|E|})$, which is similar to the complexity of the Bellman-Ford procedure combined with case-splitting. The only argument in favor of our method is that in practice SAT solvers are less sensitive to the number of variables, and are more affected by the connectivity between them. The experiments detailed in Section 6 proves that this observation applies at least to the set of examples we tried. The SAT phase was never the bottleneck in our experiments; rather it was the generation of the formula.

Thus, the more interesting question is whether the cycle enumeration phase is easier than case splitting, as both are exponential in $|E|$. The answer is that normally there are significantly more clauses to derive and check than there are cycles to enumerate. There are two reasons for this: first, the same cycles can be repeated in many clauses; second, in satisfiable formulas many clauses do not contain a cycle at all.

4   Compact Representation of Transitivity Constraints

Explicit enumeration of cycles will result in 2^n constraints in the case of Fig. 3(a), regardless of the weights on the edges. In many cases this worst case can be avoided by adding more edges to the graph. The general idea is to project the information that is contained in a directed path (i.e., the accumulated weight and type of edges in the path) to a single edge. If there are two or more paths that bear the same information, the representation will be more compact. In Section 4.2 we will elaborate on the implication of this change on the complexity of the procedure.

4.1   From Cycles to Triangles

The main tool that we will use for deriving the compact representation is *chordal graphs*. Chordal graphs (a.k.a. triangulated graphs) are normally defined in the context of undirected, unweighted graphs. A chordal graph in that context is a graph in which all cycles of size 4 or more contain an internal chord (an edge between non adjacent vertices). Chordal graphs were used in [4] to represent transitivity constraints (of equality, in their case) in a concise way. We will use them for the same purpose. Yet, there are several aspects in which G_φ is different from the graph considered in the standard definition: G_φ is a directed multigraph with two types of edges, the edges are weighted and each one of them has a dual.

Definition 4. *Let C be a simple cycle in G_φ. Let v_i and v_j be two non adjacent nodes in C. We denote the path from v_i to v_j by $T_{i,j}$. A chord e from v_i to v_j is called $T_{i,j}$-accumulating if it satisfies these two requirements:*

1. $w(e) = w(T_{i,j})$
2. $x(e) =$ '$\geq$' *if* $x(T_{i,j}) =$ '$\geq$' *or if* $x(T_{i,j}) =$ '$\sim$' *and* $x(T_{j,i}) =$ '$>$'. *Otherwise* $x(e) =$ '$>$'.

This definition refers to the case of one path between i and j, and can be easily extended if there is more than one such path. Note that the definition of $x(e)$ relies on $x(T_{j,i})$, which is based on the edges of the 'other side' of the cycle. Since there can be more than one path $T_{j,i}$, and each one can have different types of edges, making the graph chordal may require the addition of two edges between i and j, corresponding to the two types of inequality signs. As will be shown in Section 4.2, our decision procedure refrains from explicitly checking all the paths $T_{j,i}$. Rather it adds these two edges automatically when $x(T_{i,j}) =$ '$\sim$'.

Definition 4 gives rise to the following observation:

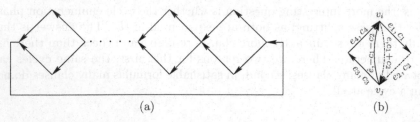

Fig. 3. (a) In a closed n-diamonds shape there are 2^n simple cycles. (b) The edge e accumulates the path $T_{i,j} = (e_1, e_2)$

Proposition 3. *Let e be a $T_{i,j}$-accumulating chord in a simple cycle C, and let $C' = (C \cup e) \setminus T_{i,j}$. The following equivalences hold: $x(C) = x(C')$ and $w(C) = w(C')$.*

Example 3. In Fig. 3(b), each edge is marked with its identifier e_i and weight c_i. By Definition 4, e is a $T_{i,j}$-accumulating chord. Let $C' = (C \cup e) \setminus T_{i,j} = (e, e_3, e_4)$. Then as observed in Proposition 3, $x(C') = x(C) = '\sim'$ and $w(C') = w(C) = \Sigma_{i=1}^{4} c_i$.   □

Definition 5. *G_φ is called* chordal *if all simple cycles in G_φ of size greater or equal to 4 contain an accumulating chord.*

We leave the question of how to make G_φ chordal to the next section. We first prove the following proposition:

Proposition 4. *Let C be a simple cycle in a chordal graph G_φ, and let α be an assignment to the edges of C. If $\alpha \not\models C$ then there exists a simple cycle C' of size 3 in G_φ s.t. $\alpha \not\models C'$.*

4.2   The Enhanced Decision Procedure and Its Complexity

Based on the above results, we change the basic decision procedure of Section 3. We add a stage for making the graph chordal, and restrict the constraints addition phase to cycles of size 3 or less:

1. In the graph construction stage of Section 3.2, we add a third step for making the graph chordal:

    3. *Make the graph chordal.*
        While $V \neq \emptyset$
        (a) Choose an unmarked vertex $i \in V$ and mark it.
        (b) For each pair of edges $(j, i, c_1, x_1), (i, k, c_2, x_2) \in E$, where j and k are unmarked vertices and $j \neq k$:
            *   Add $(j, k, c_1 + c_2, x_1)$ and its dual to E.
            *   If $x1 \neq x2$, add $(j, k, c_1 + c_2, x_2)$ and its dual to E.

2. Rather than enumerating constraints for all simple cycles, as explained in Section 3.3, we only concentrate on cycles of size 2 and 3.

Various heuristics can be used for deciding the order in which vertices are chosen in step 3(a). Our implementation follows a greedy criterion: it removes the vertex that results in the minimum number of added edges.

Proposition 5. *The graph G_φ, as constructed in step 3, is chordal.*

Although Definition 5 requires accumulating chords in cycles larger than 3, the above procedure adds accumulating chords in triangles as well (i.e., one of the edges of the triangle accumulates the other two). It can be shown that it is sufficient to constrain these cycles (rather than all cycles of size 3) and cycles of size 2. With this improvement, the number of constraints becomes linear in the number of added edges. We skip the formalization and proof of this improvement due to space restrictions.

We now have all the necessary components for proving the soundness and the completeness of this procedure:

Proposition 6. *φ is satisfiable if and only if φ' is satisfiable.*

Complexity. In the worst case the process of making the graph chordal can add an exponential number of edges. Together with the complexity of SAT, it makes the procedure double exponential. However, in many cases it can reduce the complexity: consider, for example, a graph similar to the one in Fig. 3(a), where all the diamonds are 'balanced', i.e., the accumulated weight of the top and bottom paths of each diamond are equal (for example, in the frequently encountered case where all weights are equal to '0'). In this case the number of added edges is linear in n. Thus, in this case the size of the formula and the complexity of generating it is smaller than in the explicit enumeration method of Section 3.

5   Integer Domains

In our discussion so far we assumed that all variables in the formula are of type `real`. We now extend our analysis to *integer separation predicates*, i.e., predicates of the form $v_i \rhd v_j + c$, where v_i and v_j are declared as integers (predicates involving both types of variables are assumed to be forbidden). We add a preprocessing stage right after φ is normalized:

1. Replace all integer separation predicates of the form $v_i \rhd v_j + c$ where c is not an integer with $v_i \geq v_j + \lceil c \rceil$.
2. For each integer predicate of the form $v_i > v_j + c$, add to φ the constraint $v_i > v_j + c \rightarrow v_i \geq v_j + c + 1$

The procedure now continues as before, assuming all variables are of type `real`.

Example 4. Consider the unsatisfiable formula $\varphi : x > y + 1.2 \wedge y > x - 2$ where x and y are integers. After the preprocessing step $\varphi : x \geq y + 2 \wedge y > x - 2 \wedge (y > x - 2 \rightarrow y \geq x - 1)$. □

The following proposition justifies the preprocessing stage:

Proposition 7. *Let φ^I be a normalized combination of integer separation predicates, and let φ^R be the result of applying the preprocessing stage to φ^I. Then φ^I is satisfiable iff φ^R is satisfiable.*

6   Experimental Results

To test whether checking the encoded propositional formula φ' is indeed easier than checking the original formula φ, we generated a number of sample formulas and checked them before and after the encoding. We checked the original formulas with the ICS theorem prover, and checked the encoded formula φ' with the SAT solver Chaff [8].

First, we generated formulas that have the 'diamond' structure of Fig. 3(a), with D conjoined diamonds. Although artificial examples like this one are not necessarily realistic, they are useful for checking the decision procedure under controlled conditions. Each diamond had the following properties: the top and bottom paths have S conjoined edges each; the top and bottom paths are disjointed; the edges in the top path represent strict inequalities, while the edges in the bottom path represent weak inequalities. Thus, there are 2^D simple conjoined cycles, each of size $(D \cdot S + 1)$.

Example 5. The formula below represents the diamond structure that we used in our benchmark for $S = 2$. For better readability, we use the notation of edges rather than the one for their associated Boolean variables. We denote by $t_i^j(b_i^j)$ the jth node in the top (bottom) path of the ith diamond. Also, for simplicity we chose a uniform weight c, which in practice varied as we explain below.
$\bigwedge_{i=1}^{D}((v_i, t_i^1, c, >) \wedge (t_i^1, v_{i+1}, c, >) \vee (v_i, b_i^1, c, \geq) \wedge (b_i^1, v_{i+1}, c, \geq)) \wedge (v_{i+1}, v_1, c, >)$
□

By adjusting the weights of each edge, we were able to control the difficulty of the problem: first, we guaranteed that there is only one satisfying assignment to the formula, which makes it more difficult to solve (e.g., in Example 5, if we assign $c = -1$ for all top edges, and $c = (D - 1)$ for all bottom edges, and $c = S \cdot D - 1$ for the last, closing edge, only the path through the top edges is satisfiable); second, the weights on the bottom and top paths are uniform (yet the diamonds are not balanced), which, it can be shown, causes a quadratic growth in the number of added edges and constraints. This, in fact, turned out to be the bottleneck of our procedure. As illustrated in the table, Chaff solved all SAT instances in negligible time, while the procedure for generating the CNF formula (titled 'CNF') became less and less efficient. However, in all cases except the last one, the combined run time of our procedure was faster than the three theorem provers we experimented with. The table in Fig. 4 includes results for 7 cases. The results clearly demonstrate the easiness of solving the propositional encoding in comparison with the original formula. As a more realistic test, we experimented with formulas that are generated in hardware

Topology		Separation			
D	S	ICS	CNF	Chaff	Total
3	2	< 1	< 1	< 1	< 1
4	2	5.9	< 1	< 1	< 1
5	2	95.1	< 1	< 1	< 1
7	4	*	< 1	< 1	< 1
100	5	*	32	< 1	33
250	5	*	754	1.6	756
500	5	*	*		

Fig. 4. Results in seconds, when applied to a diamond-shaped graphs with D diamonds, each of size S. '*' denotes run time exceeding 10^4 sec

verification problems. To generate these formulas we used the UCLID verification tool [5]. These hardware models include a load-store unit from an industrial microprocessor, an out-of-order execution unit, and a cache coherence protocol. The formulas were generated by symbolically simulating the models for several steps starting from an initial state, and checking a safety property at the end of each step. Fig. 5(a) summarizes these results. Finally, we also solved formulas generated during symbolic model checking of timed systems. These examples are derived from a railroad crossing gate controller that is commonly used in the timed systems literature. Fig. 5(b) shows the results for these formulas.

Model	Steps	ICS	Separation		
			CNF	Chaff	Total
Load-	1	< 1	< 1	< 1	< 1
Store	2	87.1	< 1	< 1	< 1
unit	3	*	90	1	91
Out-of-	2	< 1	< 1	< 1	< 1
order unit	3	*	2.9	< 1	3
Cache	1	< 1	< 1	< 1	< 1
protocol	2	1.8	< 1	< 1	< 1

Model	ICS	Separation		
		CNF	Chaff	Total
RailRoad-2	52	< 1	< 1	< 1
RailRoad-12	15.2	< 1	< 1	< 1
RailRoad-13	189	< 1	< 1	< 1
RailRoad-14	49.6	< 1	< 1	< 1

(a)   (b)

Fig. 5. Results in seconds, when applied to formulas generated by symbolically simulating several hardware designs (a) and symbolic model checking of timed systems(b)

Acknowledgments

We thank S. German for giving us the cache-protocol example, and S. Lahiri for helping with the experimens. The first author also wishes to thank D. Kroening for his guidance through the maze of algorithms that various theorem provers use.

References

1. W. Ackermann. *Solvable cases of the Decision Problem.* Studies in Logic and the Foundations of Mathematics. North-Holland, Amsterdam, 1954. 209
2. B. Barras, S. Boutin, C. Cornes, J. Courant, J. C. Filliatre, E. Giménez, H. Herbe-lin, G. Huet, C. Mu noz, C. Murthy, C. Parent, C. Paulin, A. Saïbi, and B. Werner. The Coq Proof Assistant Reference Manual – Version V6.1. Technical Report RT-0203, INRIA, August 1997. revised version distributed with Coq. 210
3. A. J. C. Bik and H. A. G. Wijshoff. Implementation of Fourier-Motzkin elimination. Technical Report 94-42, Dept. of Computer Science, Leiden University, 1994. 210
4. R. Bryant, S. German, and M. Velev. Processor verification using efficient reductions of the logic of uninterpreted functions to propositional logic. *ACM Transactions on Computational Logic*, 2(1):1–41, 2001. 210, 217
5. R. E. Bryant, S. K. Lahiri, and S. A. Seshia. Modeling and verifying systems using a logic of counter arithmetic with lambda expressions and uninterpreted functions. In *Proc. Computer-Aided Verification (CAV'02)*, July 2002. This volume. 221
6. T. Cormen, C. Leiserson, and L. Rivest. *Introduction to Algorithms.* MIT press. 210
7. J. Møller, J. Lichtenberg, H. R. Andersen, and H. Hulgaard. Difference decision diagrams. In *Proceedings 13th International Conference on Computer Science Logic*, volume 1683 of *LNCS*, pages 111–125, 1999. 210
8. M. Moskewicz, C. Madigan, Y. Zhao, L. Zhang, and S. Malik. Chaff: Engineering an efficient SAT solver. In *Proc. Design Automation Conference (DAC'01)*, 2001. 211, 220
9. V. Pratt. Two easy theories whose combination is hard. Technical report, Massachusetts Institute os Technology, 1977. Cambridge, Mass. 209, 210, 213
10. R. Shostak. Deciding linear inequalities by computing loop residues. *J. ACM*, 28(4):769–779, October 1981. 210, 212, 213
11. R. Shostak. Deciding combinations of theories. *J. ACM*, 31(1):1–12, 1984. 210
12. O. Strichman. Optimizations in decision procedures for propositional linear inequalities. Technical Report CMU-CS-02-133, Carnegie Mellon University, 2002. 216
13. O. Strichman, S. A.Seshia, and R. E.Bryant. Reducing separation formulas to propositional logic. Technical Report CMU-CS-02-132, Carnegie Mellon University, 2002. 215

Probabilistic Verification
of Discrete Event Systems
Using Acceptance Sampling

Håkan L. S. Younes and Reid G. Simmons

School of Computer Science, Carnegie Mellon University
Pittsburgh, PA 15213, U.S.A.

Abstract. We propose a model independent procedure for verifying properties of discrete event systems. The dynamics of such systems can be very complex, making them hard to analyze, so we resort to methods based on Monte Carlo simulation and statistical hypothesis testing. The verification is probabilistic in two senses. First, the properties, expressed as CSL formulas, can be probabilistic. Second, the result of the verification is probabilistic, and the probability of error is bounded by two parameters passed to the verification procedure. The verification of properties can be carried out in an anytime manner by starting off with loose error bounds, and gradually tightening these bounds.

1 Introduction

In this paper we consider the problem of verifying properties of discrete event systems. We present a procedure for verifying probabilistic real-time properties of such systems based on Monte Carlo simulation and statistical hypothesis testing. The verification procedure is not tied to any specific model of discrete event systems—we only require that *sample execution paths* for the systems can be generated—but it is mainly intended for verification of systems with complex dynamics such as generalized semi-Markov processes (GSMPs) [14, 8] for which no symbolic methods exist, or semi-Markov processes (SMPs) [11] for which current symbolic and numeric methods do not yield a practical solution.

Since we are using sampling, we cannot guarantee that our verification procedure always produces the correct answer. A key result, however, is that we can bound the probability of error with two parameters α and β, where α is the largest acceptable probability of incorrectly verifying a true property, and β is the largest acceptable probability of incorrectly verifying a false property.

The number of sample execution paths required to verify certain properties can be large, but our procedure can be used in an anytime manner by first verifying a property with loose error bounds, and then successively tighten the error bounds to obtain more accurate results.

We adopt the continuous stochastic logic (CSL) as our formalism for expressing probabilistic real-time properties of discrete event systems. CSL has previously been proposed as a formalism for expressing temporal and probabilistic properties of continuous-time Markov chains (CTMCs) [3, 4, 5] and SMPs [12].

D. Brinksma and K. G. Larsen (Eds.): CAV 2002, LNCS 2404, pp. 223–235, 2002.

The problem of verifying properties of GSMPs has been considered before, but in a qualitative setting where it is checked whether a property holds with probability one or greater than zero [ ]. With our approach, we are able to verify whether a property holds with at least (or at most) probability θ, for an arbitrary probability threshold θ. Kwiatkowska et al. [ ] present an algorithm for verifying probabilistic timed automata against properties expressed in probabilistic timed CTL, but the complexity of their algorithm makes it seem practically infeasible. Infante López et al. [ ] propose a method for verifying CSL properties of SMPs. They conclude, however, that verifying time-bounded CSL formulas using their algorithm can become numerically very complex, and the negative complexity results carry over to GSMPs.

2 Discrete Event Systems

The verification procedure we present in this paper is model independent, and only requires that we can generate sample execution paths for a discrete event system we want to verify. Because of the model independence, we choose not to introduce any specific model for discrete event systems, but instead focus only on relevant properties of such systems. We will typically use discrete event simulation [ ] to generate sample execution paths, but our verification procedure could conceivably be used to verify probabilistic real-time properties of hybrid dynamic systems as well given that we have an appropriate simulator.

At any point in time, a discrete event system occupies some state $s \in S$, where S is a set of states.[1] Let AP be a fixed, finite set of atomic propositions. We then define a labeling function $L : S \to 2^{AP}$ assigning to each state $s \in S$ the set $L(s)$ of atomic propositions that hold in s. The system remains in a state s until the occurrence of an event, at which point the system instantaneously transitions to a state s' (possibly the same state as s). Events can occur at any point along a continuous time-axis.

Execution Paths. An execution path σ of a discrete event system is a sequence

$$\sigma = s_0 \xrightarrow{t_0} s_1 \xrightarrow{t_1} s_2 \xrightarrow{t_2} \dots \ ,$$

with $s_i \in S$ and $t_i > 0$ being the time spent in state s_i before an event triggered a transition to state s_{i+1}. If the lth state of path σ is absorbing, then we set $s_i = s_l$ for all $i > l$, and $t_i = \infty$ for all $i \geq l$.

Let $\sigma[i] = s_i$, for $i \geq 0$, be the ith state along the path σ, let $\delta(\sigma, i) = t_i$ be the time spent in state s_i, let $\tau(\sigma, i) = \sum_{j=0}^{i-1} \delta(\sigma, j)$ be the time elapsed before entering the ith state, and let $\sigma(t) = \sigma[i]$ with i being the smallest index such that $t \leq \tau(\sigma, i+1)$. We denote the set of all paths starting in state s by $Path(s)$. For any given model, we need to define a σ-algebra on the set $Path(s)$ and a

---

[1] We do not require S to be finite. In fact, for GSMPs it is convenient to think of a state s as some discrete state features s' coupled with a set of real-valued clock settings c for currently enabled events (see [,]).

probability measure on the corresponding measurable space, or else we will not be able to talk about the probability of a set of paths satisfying a property. This is not a serious restriction, however, because it can be done for the models we typically use for discrete event systems. It is done in [5] for CTMCs and in [12] for SMPs, and can be done in a similar way for GSMPs (cf. [13]).

3 Continuous Stochastic Logic

Aziz et al. [3] propose the continuous stochastic logic (CSL) as a formalism for expressing properties of CTMCs. CSL—inspired by CTL [7] and its extensions to continuous-time systems [1, 2]—adopts temporal operators and probabilistic path quantification from PCTL [10].

We adopt the version of CSL used by Baier et al. [5], excluding their steady-state probability operator and unrestricted temporal operators[2], and present a semantics for CSL formulas interpreted over discrete event systems. The semantics is model dependent only through the definition of execution paths.

CSL Syntax. A CSL formula is either a state formula or a path formula. The formulas of CSL are inductively defined as follows:

1. tt is a state formula.
2. $a \in AP$ is a state formula.
3. If ϕ is a state formula, then so is $\neg\phi$.
4. If ϕ_1 and ϕ_2 are state formulas, then $\phi_1 \wedge \phi_2$ is a state formula.
5. If ρ is a path formula and $\theta \in [0,1]$, then $\Pr_{\geq\theta}(\rho)$ is a state formula.[3]
6. If ϕ is a state formula, then $X\phi$ (next state) is a path formula.
7. If ϕ_1 and ϕ_2 are state formulas and $0 \leq t < \infty$, then $\phi_1 \, \mathcal{U}^{\leq t} \, \phi_2$ (until) is a path formula.

Other Boolean connectives and path operators are derived in the usual way. For example, $\Pr_{\geq\theta}(\Diamond^{\leq t}\phi)$ can be written as $\Pr_{\geq\theta}(\text{tt}\,\mathcal{U}^{\leq t}\,\phi)$.

CSL Semantics. The truth value of a state formula is determined in a specific state. The formula $\Pr_{\geq\theta}(\rho)$ holds in a state s iff the probability of the set of paths starting in s and satisfying ρ is at least θ.

The truth value of a path formula is determined over a specific execution path. The semantics of the next and until operators is standard. The formula $X\phi$ is true over a path σ iff ϕ holds in the state after the first transition. If the initial state along σ is absorbing, there is no next state so the formula is false. The formula $\phi_1 \, \mathcal{U}^{\leq t} \, \phi_2$ is true over a path σ iff ϕ_2 holds in some state along σ at time $x \in [0,t]$, and ϕ_1 holds in all prior states along σ. We inductively define the satisfaction relation $\models$ as follows:

---

[2] We need the time-bound on the temporal operators to set a limit on the simulation time for the generation of sample execution paths.

[3] With the sampling based verification procedure we propose, it is not meaningful to distinguish between $\Pr_{\geq\theta}(\rho)$ and $\Pr_{>\theta}(\rho)$. We can therefore write $\Pr_{\leq\theta}(\rho)$ as $\neg\Pr_{\geq\theta}(\rho)$, which means we only need to consider one comparison operator.

1. $s \models \mathrm{tt}$ for all $s \in S$.
2. $s \models a$ iff $a \in L(s)$.
3. $s \models \neg\phi$ iff $s \not\models \phi$.
4. $s \models \phi_1 \wedge \phi_2$ iff $s \models \phi_1$ and $s \models \phi_2$.
5. $s \models \mathrm{Pr}_{\geq\theta}(\rho)$ iff $\mathrm{Pr}\{\sigma \in Path(s) \mid \sigma \models \rho\} \geq \theta$.
6. $\sigma \models X\phi$ iff $\delta(\sigma, 0) < \infty$ and $\sigma[1] \models \phi$.
7. $\sigma \models \phi_1 \, \mathcal{U}^{\leq t} \, \phi_2$ iff $\sigma(x) \models \phi_2$ for some $x \in [0, t]$ and $\sigma(y) \models \phi_1$ for all $y \in [0, x)$.

The probability measure $\mathrm{Pr}\{\ldots\}$ must be well defined, as described in the previous section.

4   Probabilistic Verification

Given a discrete event system M and a state s of M, we want to verify that a property—expressed as a state formula ϕ in CSL—holds in s. In other words, we desire to test if $s \models \phi$.

The complexity of general discrete event systems makes them hard to analyze, and we resort to methods based on Monte Carlo simulation and statistical hypothesis testing. This means that in general we will not be able to answer with certainty whether a given property holds, but we will at least be able to bound the likelihood of error.

More specifically, given s and ϕ, let H_0 be the hypothesis that ϕ holds in s, and let H_1 be the alternative hypothesis (i.e. that ϕ does not hold in s). The probability of accepting H_1 given that H_0 holds is required to be at most α, and the probability of accepting H_0 if H_1 holds should be no more than β. The error bounds α and β are supplied as parameters to the verification procedure, which is devised so that less effort (on average) is required to verify a property with more relaxed error bounds.

4.1   Verifying Probabilistic Properties

The possibility of error in our verification procedure arises from the way we verify probabilistic properties $\phi = \mathrm{Pr}_{\geq\theta}(\rho)$ given a state s. Let p be the (unknown) probability that ρ holds over paths starting in s. If $p \geq \theta$, then ϕ holds in s.

We use simulation (typically discrete event simulation) to generate sample paths starting in s. Let Y be a binary random variable with parameter p such that $\mathrm{Pr}[Y = 1] = p$. Sample paths over which ρ holds represent samples $y_i = 1$ of Y, and remaining sample paths represent samples $y_i = 0$ of Y. Using these samples, we would like to test the hypothesis $p \geq \theta$ against the alternative hypothesis $p < \theta$, but we are forced to relax the hypotheses in order to freely be able to choose error bounds α and β.

For this purpose we introduce an indifference region of width $2 \cdot \delta$. Let $p \geq \theta + \delta$ be H_0 and let $p \leq \theta - \delta$ be H_1. We use acceptance sampling to test H_0 against H_1. The outcome of the acceptance sampling test is that we accept either H_0 or H_1, so the two events "accept H_0" and "accept H_1" are mutually exclusive and exhaustive. Note, however, that for a non-zero δ the two hypotheses H_0 and H_1 are not exhaustive although they are mutually exclusive. Let H_2 be the hypothesis that neither H_0 nor H_1 holds. H_2 represents indifference, and holds if the probability of ρ being true over paths starting in s is within δ of θ.

We are given the following guarantees by an acceptance sampling test:

$$\Pr[H_0 \text{ holds} \mid \text{accept } H_1] \leq \alpha$$
$$\Pr[H_1 \text{ holds} \vee H_2 \text{ holds} \mid \text{accept } H_1] \geq 1 - \alpha$$
$$\Pr[H_1 \text{ holds} \mid \text{accept } H_0] \leq \beta$$
$$\Pr[H_0 \text{ holds} \vee H_2 \text{ holds} \mid \text{accept } H_0] \geq 1 - \beta$$

The formula ϕ is definitely true if H_0 holds, and definitely false if H_1 holds, but if H_2 holds we have no information about the truth value of ϕ. Recall, however, that H_2 represents indifference—i.e. the true probability of ρ holding over paths starting in s is sufficiently close to θ that we are indifferent to whether it actually is below or above θ. In case H_2 holds we interpret this to mean that ϕ is true if we accepted H_0, and false if we accepted H_1. With this interpretation, we obtain the desired error bounds $\Pr[\phi \mid \text{accept } H_1] \leq \alpha$ and $\Pr[\neg\phi \mid \text{accept } H_0] \leq \beta$.

Nested Probabilistic Operators. The above results for formulas $\phi = \Pr_{\geq\theta}(\rho)$ hold if we can determine the truth value of ρ over sample paths without error. In case ρ contains probabilistic operators, there is some probability at most α' of ρ being true over a sample path σ if it is verified to be false, and some probability at most β' of ρ being false over σ if it is verified to be true. We need to take the possibility of error into account in the acceptance sampling test, and we here present a modification of Wald's sequential probability ratio test [16] that deals with this situation. We choose the sequential probability ratio test because of its strong average performance measured in the number of samples required to reach a decision.

We can model the situation of imprecise samples in general terms as follows. Let Y be a binary random variable with unknown parameter p such that $\Pr[Y = 1] = p$. Our goal is to test the hypothesis H_0 that $p \geq p_0$ (for $p_0 = \theta + \delta$) against the hypothesis H_1 that $p \leq p_1$ (for $p_1 = \theta - \delta$). We want the probability of accepting H_1 given that H_0 holds to be at most α, and the probability of accepting H_0 given that H_1 holds to be at most β. If we could generate samples of Y, then we could accomplish our goal using the unmodified sequential probability ratio test, but instead we can only generate samples from a binary random variable Z related to Y in the following way:

$$\Pr[Z = 1 \mid Y = 1] \geq 1 - \alpha'$$
$$\Pr[Z = 0 \mid Y = 1] \leq \alpha'$$
$$\Pr[Z = 1 \mid Y = 0] \leq \beta'$$
$$\Pr[Z = 0 \mid Y = 0] \geq 1 - \beta'$$

Given these constraints and the total probability formula, we can obtain bounds on the unconditional probability $\Pr[Z = 1]$:

$$p(1 - \alpha') \leq \Pr[Z = 1] \leq 1 - (1 - p)(1 - \beta') \qquad (1)$$

We now want to use the sequential probability ratio test to test hypothesis H_0 against H_1 given samples of Z.

The sequential probability ratio test is carried out as follows. At each stage of the test, calculate the quantity

$$\frac{p_{1m}}{p_{0m}} = \frac{\prod_{i=1}^{m} \Pr[Z = z_i \mid p = p_1]}{\prod_{i=1}^{m} \Pr[Z = z_i \mid p = p_0]} ,$$

where z_i is the sample of Z generated at stage i. Accept H_0 if

$$\frac{p_{1m}}{p_{0m}} \geq \frac{1 - \beta}{\alpha} . \qquad (2)$$

Accept H_1 if

$$\frac{p_{1m}}{p_{0m}} \leq \frac{\beta}{1 - \alpha} . \qquad (3)$$

Otherwise, generate an additional sample and repeat the termination test. This test procedure respects the error bounds α and β.[4]

We cannot compute the fraction p_{1m}/p_{0m} because $\Pr[Z = 1]$ is unknown to us, but we can obtain upper and lower bounds for the fraction, which can then be used to devise a modified test respecting the error bounds α and β.

Let d_m denote the number of samples, of the first m samples, equal to 1. We can then write the fraction p_{1m}/p_{0m} as

$$\frac{p_{1m}}{p_{0m}} = \frac{(\Pr[Z = 1 \mid p = p_1])^{d_m} (1 - \Pr[Z = 1 \mid p = p_1])^{m - d_m}}{(\Pr[Z = 1 \mid p = p_0])^{d_m} (1 - \Pr[Z = 1 \mid p = p_0])^{m - d_m}} .$$

Let I_i be the interval $[p_i(1 - \alpha'), 1 - (1 - p_i)(1 - \beta')]$. We know from (1) that $\Pr[Z = 1 \mid p = p_i] \in I_i$. A lower bound for p_{1m}/p_{0m} can be obtained by finding a $\check{p}_1 \in I_1$ that minimizes p_{1m} and a $\hat{p}_0 \in I_0$ that maximizes p_{0m}. Conversely, an upper bound for the fraction can be obtained by finding a $\hat{p}_1 \in I_1$ that maximizes p_{1m} and a $\check{p}_0 \in I_0$ that minimizes p_{0m}. We then have the bounds

$$\frac{(\check{p}_1)^{d_m} (1 - \check{p}_1)^{m - d_m}}{(\hat{p}_0)^{d_m} (1 - \hat{p}_0)^{m - d_m}} \leq \frac{p_{1m}}{p_{0m}} \leq \frac{(\hat{p}_1)^{d_m} (1 - \hat{p}_1)^{m - d_m}}{(\check{p}_0)^{d_m} (1 - \check{p}_0)^{m - d_m}}$$

for the fraction p_{1m}/p_{0m}. Given these bounds, it is safe to accept H_0 if

$$\frac{(\check{p}_1)^{d_m} (1 - \check{p}_1)^{m - d_m}}{(\hat{p}_0)^{d_m} (1 - \hat{p}_0)^{m - d_m}} \geq \frac{1 - \beta}{\alpha} \qquad (4)$$

---

[4] There is a slight approximation involved in the stopping criteria of the test. See [16] for details.

since then surely condition (2) holds. Likewise, it is safe to accept H_1 if

$$\frac{(\hat{p}_1)^{d_m}(1-\hat{p}_1)^{m-d_m}}{(\check{p}_0)^{d_m}(1-\check{p}_0)^{m-d_m}} \leq \frac{\beta}{1-\alpha} \tag{5}$$

since then surely condition (3) holds. By replacing the original stopping criteria (2) and (3) with the new stopping criteria (4) and (5) we obtain a sequential acceptance sampling test that can handle imprecise samples. We now need to find the appropriate values for $\check{p}_i$ and $\hat{p}_i$.

Proposition 1. *Let* $f(x) = x^{d_m}(1-x)^{m-d_m}$. *For* $d_m \in I_i$, $\hat{p}_i = d_m/m$ *and*

$$\check{p}_i = \begin{cases} p_i(1-\alpha') & \text{if } f(p_i(1-\alpha')) < f(1-(1-p_i)(1-\beta')) \\ 1-(1-p_i)(1-\beta') & \text{otherwise} \end{cases}.$$

If $d_m/m < p_i(1-\alpha')$, *then* $\hat{p}_i = p_i(1-\alpha')$ *and* $\check{p}_i = 1-(1-p_i)(1-\beta')$. *Otherwise if* $d_m/m > 1-(1-p_i)(1-\beta')$, *then* $\hat{p}_i = 1-(1-p_i)(1-\beta')$ *and* $\check{p}_i = p_i(1-\alpha')$.

Proof. For $d_m = 0$, $f(x) = (1-x)^m$ is monotonously decreasing in the interval $[0,1]$. For $d_m = m$, $f(x) = x^m$ is monotonously increasing in the interval $[0,1]$. Otherwise for $0 < d_m < m$, $f(0) = f(1) = 0$. The first derivative of $f(x)$ is $f'(x) = d_m x^{d_m-1}(1-x)^{m-d_m} - (m-d_m)x_m^d(1-x)^{m-d_m-1}$. We can find a local maximum of $f(x)$ in the open interval $(0,1)$ by setting $f'(x) = 0$:

$$d_m x^{d_m-1}(1-x)^{m-d_m} = (m-d_m)x_m^d(1-x)^{m-d_m-1} \implies$$

$$d_m(1-x) = (m-d_m)x \implies x = \frac{d_m}{m}$$

Thus, $f(x)$ has a local maximum at d_m/m. $\qquad\square$

The stopping criteria (4) and (5) reduce to the regular stopping criteria for the test if $\alpha' = \beta' = 0$, as expected. With imprecise samples, the average number of samples required before a decision can be reached will increase, but it is worth noting that the choice of α' and β' can be made independent of the values for α and β.

4.2 Verifying Compound State Formulas

When verifying a compound state formula ϕ such as $\neg\phi_1$ or $\phi_1 \wedge \phi_2$ in a state s, we first test parts that do not involve any probabilistic operators. The truth value of those parts can be determined with certainty, and results in a reduced formula ϕ'. If ϕ reduces to either true or false we are done. Otherwise all parts of ϕ' contain probabilistic operators, and we need to propagate appropriate error bounds to the test of the parts in order to obtain the desired error bounds for the compound formula.

Negation. For a negation $\neg\phi_1$, assume inductively that we can obtain the error bounds α_1 and β_1 for ϕ_1. By setting $\beta_1 = \alpha$ and $\alpha_1 = \beta$, we obtain the required error bounds for $\neg\phi_1$.

Conjunction. For a conjunction $\phi_1 \wedge \cdots \wedge \phi_n$, the situation is slightly more complicated. We want to accept the conjunction as true if all conjuncts are true, and reject the conjunct as false if some conjunct is false.

First assume that we can verify each conjunct ϕ_i as true with error bounds α_i and β_i. This means that the probability of ϕ_i being false is at most β_i, which implies that the probability of the whole conjunction being false is at most $\sum_{i=1}^{n} \beta_i$. We can thus achieve a verification error of at most β in this case if we choose the β_i's so that $\sum_{i=1}^{n} \beta_i = \beta$. Without any further information about the complexity of each ϕ_i, the natural choice is $\beta_i = \beta/n$.

Now assume that we can verify some conjuncts ϕ_i as false with error bounds α_i and β_i. This means that the probability of ϕ_i being true is at most α_i, which implies that the probability of the whole conjunction being true is at most $\max_{i=1}^{n} \alpha_i$. By setting $\alpha_i = \alpha$, we achieve the desired error bound α on the verification of the whole conjunction.

We combine these two results into a complete verification procedure for conjunctions. In order to minimize the expected verification effort, we use a two-step procedure. The first step is a "fast reject" step, in which we verify each conjunct ϕ_i with error bounds α and β', where β' can be chosen arbitrarily. If we can verify any ϕ_i as false using these bounds, we can conclude with sufficient confidence that the whole conjunction is false. We will want to choose β' high so that the number of samples required to verify each ϕ_i in the first step is low, but not too high because it would lower the chance of verifying any ϕ_i as false.

If we verify each conjunct as true in the first step, we perform a second step corresponding to a "rigorous accept". Again we verify each conjunct ϕ_i with $\alpha_i = \alpha$, but this time with $\beta_i = \beta/n$. If we verify any conjunct ϕ_i as false using these bounds, we can conclude with sufficient confidence that the whole conjunction is false, but we can also conclude with sufficient confidence that the conjunction is true if we verify each conjunct as true.

4.3   Verifying Path Formulas

When verifying $\Pr_{\geq \theta}(\rho)$ in a state s, we need to determine the truth value of the path formula ρ over sample execution paths starting in the given state. A sample path σ is generated by simulation. We only generate as much of a path that is needed to determine the truth value of ρ with sufficient confidence.

The Next Operator. To verify a path formula $\rho = X\phi$ with error bounds α and β over a path starting in the state s, we sample a next state s'. We then verify ϕ in s' with α and β as error bounds. If s is a terminal state, we can conclude without error that ρ is false.

The Until Operator. A path formula $\rho = \phi_1 \, \mathcal{U}^{\leq t} \, \phi_2$ holds over a path σ if ϕ_2 holds in $\sigma[0]$, or if ϕ_2 holds in $\sigma[i]$ and ϕ_1 holds in all states $\sigma[j]$ for $j < i$. Let $\phi_i^{(j)}$ represent the proposition that ϕ_i holds in the state $\sigma[j]$, and let n be the smallest index such that $\tau(\sigma, n) > t$. Then the path formula ρ holds over σ iff

$$\bigvee_{i=0}^{n-1} \left(\phi_2^{(i)} \wedge \bigwedge_{j=0}^{i-1} \phi_1^{(j)} \right) , \qquad (6)$$

which can be verified in the same way as a compound state formula.

Equation (6) is a disjunction of size n, with the ith disjunct being a conjunction of size $i + 1$. In the worst case, we will have to verify each disjunct with error bounds α/n and β in order to verify the whole formula with error bounds α and β. In that case we may have to verify each component of the ith disjunct with error bounds α/n and $\beta/(i+1)$, which can require quite a few samples if n is large. This will happen if both ϕ_1 and ϕ_2 contain probabilistic operators and we verify the path formula ρ as true.

The problem of verifying an until formula simplifies significantly if either ϕ_1 or ϕ_2, or both, can be verified without error. In the simples case, without any nested probabilistic operators, we only need to expand the path σ until either ϕ_2 becomes true, or ϕ_1 becomes false or the time limit is exceeded. In the former case the until formula holds with certainty, while in the latter case we can conclude with certainty that the until formula is false.

5   Performance Evaluation

The performance of our procedure for verifying a formula on the form $\phi = \Pr_{\geq\theta}(\rho)$ in a state s depends primarily on the number of samples n needed by the acceptance sampling test used. If we are using a sequential test, such as Wald's sequential probability ratio test [16], then n is a random variable. Let $E_p[n]$ denote the expected number of samples required by the test given that p is the true probability of ρ holding over paths starting in s. We can expect to need more samples the closer p is to the probability threshold θ.

The expected number of samples depends not only on p and θ, but also on the parameters δ, α, and β. In addition, if there are nested probabilistic operators so that we need to use the modified test as described earlier in this paper, then the average number of samples also depends on the parameters α' and β' corresponding to the maximum error in the verification of a nested formula.

Figure 1 shows the average number of samples as a function of p for three different values of θ, and with the remaining parameters fixed. The data is based on 5,000 tests for each of 201 equidistant values of p. Similar data is shown in Fig. 2 but with θ fixed and δ varying, and in Fig. 3 the error bounds α and β are varying. Finally, Fig. 4 shows how the average number of samples increases with an increase in α' and β'. The dotted curve is the same in all four figures.

As can be seen, the number of samples is typically very low, suggesting that the proposed verification procedure can be quite efficient. Note however that if we are verifying a formula with nested probabilistic operators, then for each sample generated for the outer probabilistic operator, we need to generate several samples to verify the inner probabilistic operator. Given one level of nesting, if

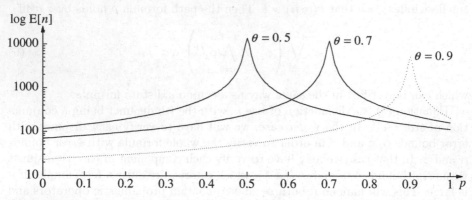

Fig. 1. Expected number of samples for different values of θ, with $\delta = 0.01$, $\alpha = \beta = 0.01$, and $\alpha' = \beta' = 0$

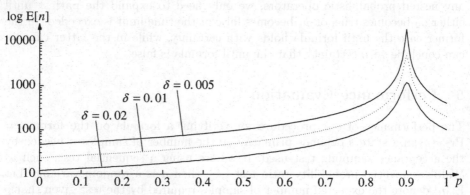

Fig. 2. Expected number of samples for different values of δ, with $\theta = 0.9$, $\alpha = \beta = 0.01$, and $\alpha' = \beta' = 0$

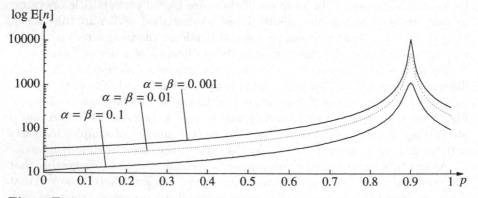

Fig. 3. Expected number of samples for different values of α and β, with $\theta = 0.9$, $\delta = 0.01$, and $\alpha' = \beta' = 0$

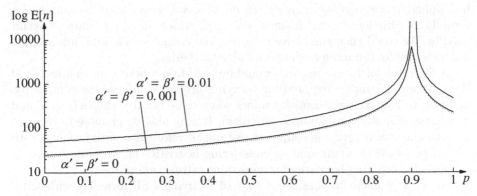

Fig. 4. Expected number of samples for different values of α' and β', with $\theta = 0.9$, $\delta = 0.01$, and $\alpha = \beta = 0.01$

the expected number of samples for the outer probabilistic operator is n_o, and we need n_i samples on average for the inner operator, then $n_o \cdot n_i$ is the expected number of samples needed to verify the whole formula. The total number of required samples grows rapidly with the level of nesting, but this does not seem to be a problem in practice since CSL formulas typically have at most one level of nesting—if any at all.

There is no definite upper bound on the number of samples required by the sequential probability ratio test. If this is a problem, as it can be when verifying nested probabilistic formulas, then a truncated test can be used. Wald [16] suggests a method for choosing an upper bound on the number of samples so that the given error bounds, for all practical purposes, are still respected.

6   Discussion

We have presented a model independent procedure for verifying properties of discrete event systems. The properties are expressed as CSL formulas, and we have shown how to interpret these formulas given a definition of sample execution paths of a discrete event system. The definition of sample execution paths, as well as the probability measure on sets of paths, is the only model dependent component of the framework we have discussed.

Because of the complex nature of many discrete event systems, we depend on Monte Carlo simulation and statistical hypothesis testing in order to verify CSL formulas. Our verification procedure takes two parameters, α and β, where α is the highest acceptable probability of incorrectly verifying a true formula, and β is the highest acceptable probability of incorrectly verifying a false formula.

Using sequential acceptance sampling the number of samples required for verifying a CSL formula is typically low, but can be high for verifying certain formulas—in particular formulas of the form $\Pr_{\geq \theta}(\phi_1 \, \mathcal{U}^{\leq t} \, \phi_2)$, where both ϕ_1 and ϕ_2 contain probabilistic operators. Our verification procedure can, however, be applied in an anytime manner. To do this, we would start by verifying a formula ϕ with loose error bounds α and β, which should produce a result quickly. We could then successively tighten the error bounds, and obtain more accurate results the more resources we give the verifier.

A direction for future research would be to obtain a better understanding of the number of samples required for verifying properties of varying complexity, and how to best choose parameter values when there is a free choice (e.g. α' and β' in case of nested probabilistic formulas). It may also be possible to increase performance when verifying conjunctions (and therefore also until formulas with nested probabilistic operators) by considering heuristics for ordering conjuncts (cf. variable ordering heuristics for constraint satisfaction problems [6]).

Another problem to consider is that of verifying CSL formulas with unrestricted temporal operators and the steady-state operator, which requires developing techniques for evaluating the long-run behavior of a discrete event system. Work on output analysis for simulation of transient and steady-state quantities in operations research (see, e.g., [9]) may be applicable. Also, the algorithm proposed by Infante Lopéz et al. [12] is reported to scale well to SMPs in the case of unrestricted temporal operators and the steady-state operator, and a similar approach may be fruitful even for more general models of discrete event systems.

References

[1] Rajeev Alur, Costas Courcoubetis, and David Dill. Model-checking for real-time systems. In *Proceedings of the Fifth Annual IEEE Symposium on Logic in Computer Science*, pages 414–425, Philadelphia, PA, June 1990. IEEE Computer Society Press. 225

[2] Rajeev Alur, Costas Courcoubetis, and David Dill. Model-checking for probabilistic real-time systems. In J. Leach Albert, B. Monien, and M. Rodríguez Artalejo, editors, *Proceedings of the 18th International Colloquium on Automata, Languages and Programming*, volume 510 of *Lecture Notes in Computer Science*, pages 115–126, Madrid, Spain, July 1991. Springer. 224, 225

[3] Adnan Aziz, Kumud Sanwal, Vigyan Singhal, and Robert Brayton. Verifying continuous time Markov chains. In Rajeev Alur and Thomas A. Henzinger, editors, *Proceedings of the 8th International Conference on Computer Aided Verification*, volume 1102 of *Lecture Notes in Computer Science*, pages 269–276, New Brunswick, NJ, July/August 1996. Springer. 223, 225

[4] Adnan Aziz, Kumud Sanwal, Vigyan Singhal, and Robert Brayton. Model-checking continuous-time Markov chains. *ACM Transactions on Computational Logic*, 1(1):162–170, July 2000. 223

[5] Christel Baier, Joost-Pieter Katoen, and Holger Hermanns. Approximate symbolic model checking of continuous-time Markov chains. In Jos C. M. Baeten and Sjouke Mauw, editors, *Proceedings of the 10th International Conference on Concurrency Theory*, volume 1664 of *Lecture Notes in Computer Science*, pages 146–161, Eindhoven, the Netherlands, August 1999. Springer. 223, 225

[6] James R. Bitner and Edward M. Reingold. Backtrack programming techniques. *Communications of the ACM*, 18(11):651–656, November 1975. 234

[7] E. M. Clarke, E. Allen Emerson, and A. Prasad Sistla. Automatic verification of finite-state concurrent systems using temporal logic specifications. *ACM Transactions on Programming Languages and Systems*, 8(2):244–263, April 1986. 225

[8] Peter W. Glynn. A GSMP formalism for discrete event systems. *Proceedings of the IEEE*, 77(1):14–23, January 1989. 223, 224

[9] Peter W. Glynn and Donald L. Iglehart. Simulation methods for queues: An overview. *Queueing Systems*, 3:221–255, 1988. 234

[10] Hans Hansson and Bengt Jonsson. A logic for reasoning about time and reliability. *Formal Aspects of Computing*, 6(5):512–535, 1994. 225

[11] Ronald A. Howard. *Dynamic Probabilistic Systems*, volume II. John Wiley & Sons, New York, NY, 1971. 223

[12] Gabriel G. Infante López, Holger Hermanns, and Joost-Pieter Katoen. Beyond memoryless distributions: Model checking semi-Markov chains. In Luca de Alfaro and Stephen Gilmore, editors, *Proceedings of the 1st Joint International PAPM-PROBMIV Workshop*, volume 2165 of *Lecture Notes in Computer Science*, pages 57–70, Aachen, Germany, September 2001. Springer. 223, 224, 225, 234

[13] Marta Kwiatkowska, Gethin Norman, Roberto Segala, and Jeremy Sproston. Verifying quantitative properties of continuous probabilistic timed automata. In Catuscia Palamidessi, editor, *Proceedings of the 11th International Conference on Concurrency Theory*, volume 1877 of *Lecture Notes in Computer Science*, pages 123–137, State College, PA, August 2000. Springer. 224, 225

[14] Klaus Matthes. Zur Theorie der Bedienungsprozesse. In Jaroslav Kožešník, editor, *Transactions of the Third Prague Conference on Information Theory, Statistical Decision Functions, Random Processes*, pages 513–528, Liblice, Czechoslovakia, June 1962. Publishing House of the Czechoslovak Academy of Sciences. 223

[15] Gerald S. Shedler. *Regenerative Stochastic Simulation*. Academic Press, Boston, MA, 1993. 224

[16] Abraham Wald. Sequential tests of statistical hypotheses. *Annals of Mathematical Statistics*, 16(2):117–186, June 1945. 227, 228, 231, 233

Checking Satisfiability of First-Order Formulas by Incremental Translation to SAT

Clark W. Barrett, David L. Dill, and Aaron Stump

{barrett,dill,stump}@cs.stanford.edu

Abstract. In the past few years, general-purpose propositional satisfiability (SAT) solvers have improved dramatically in performance and have been used to tackle many new problems. It has also been shown that certain simple fragments of first-order logic can be decided efficiently by first translating the problem into an equivalent SAT problem and then using a fast SAT solver. In this paper, we describe an alternative but similar approach to using SAT in conjunction with a more expressive fragment of first-order logic. However, rather than translating the entire formula up front, the formula is incrementally translated during a search for the solution. As a result, only that portion of the translation that is actually relevant to the solution is obtained. We describe a number of obstacles that had to be overcome before developing an approach which was ultimately very effective, and give results on verification benchmarks using CVC (Cooperating Validity Checker), which includes the Chaff SAT solver. The results show a performance gain of several orders of magnitude over CVC without Chaff and indicate that the method is more robust than the heuristics found in CVC's predecessor, SVC.

Keywords: Satisfiability, Decision Procedures, Propositional Satisfiability, First-Order Logic.

1 Introduction

Automated tools to check the satisfiability (or dually, the validity) of formulas are of great interest because of their versatility. Many practical problems can be reduced to the question of whether some formula is valid in a given logical theory.

Different approaches have been taken to developing general-purpose decision procedures. At one extreme, propositional satisfiability (SAT) solvers are blazingly fast, but only operate on propositional formulas, a very limited input language. At another extreme, general purpose first- or higher-order theorem provers are capable of proving some sophisticated results, but since their logics are undecidable, a result cannot be guaranteed.

A middle road is to develop fast decision procedures for specific decidable first-order theories. One interesting way to do this which has recently seen a lot of research activity is to translate the problem to SAT and then use a fast SAT solver to obtain a solution. By using appropriate tricks to reduce the time

D. Brinksma and K. G. Larsen (Eds.): CAV 2002, LNCS 2404, pp. 236–249, 2002.
© Springer-Verlag Berlin Heidelberg 2002

and space required for the translation, this approach seems to work well for simple theories such as the theory of equality with uninterpreted functions [3, 12]. However, it is not clear how or whether such an approach would work for other decidable theories.

We propose a method designed to be more generally applicable: given a satisfiability procedure Sat_{FO} for a conjunction of literals in some first-order theory, a fast SAT-based satisfiability procedure for *arbitrary* quantifier-free formulas of the theory can be constructed by abstracting the formula to a propositional approximation and then incrementally refining the approximation until a sufficiently precise approximation is obtained to solve the problem. The refinement is accomplished by using Sat_{FO} to diagnose conflicts and then adding the appropriate *conflict clauses* to the propositional approximation.

In Section 2, we briefly review propositional satisfiability. We then describe the problem in Section 3. Section 4 describes our approach to solving the problem using SAT, and Section 5 describes a number of difficulties that had to be overcome in order to make the approach practical. Section 6 describes some related work, and in Section 7, we give results obtained using CVC [15], a new decision procedure for a combination of theories in a quantifier-free fragment of first-order logic which includes the SAT solver Chaff [10]. We compare with results using CVC without Chaff and with our best previous results using SVC [1], the predecessor to CVC. The new method is generally faster, requires significantly fewer decisions, and is able to solve examples that were previously too difficult.

2   Propositional Satisfiability

The SAT problem is the original classic NP-complete problem of computer science. A propositional formula is built as shown in Fig. 1 from propositional variables (i.e. variables that can either be assigned *true* or *false*) and Boolean operators ($\land$, $\lor$, $\neg$). Given such a formula, the goal of SAT is to find an assignment of *true* or *false* to each variable which results in the entire formula being *true*.

Instances of the SAT problem are typically given in conjunctive normal form (CNF). As shown in Fig. 1, CNF requires that the formula be a conjunction of *clauses*, each of which is a disjunction of propositional literals. In Section 4.1, we describe a well-known technique for transforming any propositional formula into an equisatisfiable propositional formula in conjunctive normal form.

Although the SAT problem is NP-complete, a wide variety of techniques have been developed that enable many examples to be solved very quickly. A large number of publicly distributed algorithms and benchmarks are available [14]. Chaff [10] is a SAT solver developed at Princeton University. As with most other SAT solvers, it requires that its input be in CNF. It is widely regarded as one of the best performing SAT solvers currently available.

```
propositional formula ::= true | false |
propositional variable
        | propositional formula ∧ propositional
formula
        | propositional formula ∨ propositional formula
        | ¬propositional formula

CNF formula ::= (clause ∧ ... ∧
clause)

clause ::= (propositional literal ∨ ... ∨
propositional literal)

propositional literal ::= propositional variable
        | ¬propositional variable
```

Fig. 1. Propositional logic and CNF

```
formula ::= true | false | literal
        | term = term
        | predicate symbol(term, ..., term)
        | formula ∧ formula
        | formula ∨ formula
        | ¬formula

literal ::= atomic formula | ¬atomic formula

atomic formula ::= atomic term = atomic term
        | predicate symbol(atomic term, ...,
atomic term)

term ::= atomic term
        | function symbol(term, ..., term)
        | ite(formula, term, term)

atomic term ::= variable | constant symbol
        | function symbol(atomic term,
..., atomic term)
```

Fig. 2. A quantifier-free fragment of first-order logic

3   The Problem

We will show how to use SAT to aid in determining the satisfiability of a formula ϕ in a language which is much more expressive than propositional logic: the basic variant of quantifier-free first-order logic shown in Fig. 2. Note that in the remainder of the paper, the term "literal" by itself will be used to refer to an atomic formula or its negation, as defined in Fig. 2. This differs from the term "propositional literal" which we will use as in the previous section to mean a propositional variable or its negation. A small difference between this logic and conventional first-order logic is the inclusion of the **ite** (*if-then-else*) operator which makes it possible to compactly represent a term which may have one of two values depending on a Boolean condition, a situation which is common in applications. An **ite** expression contains a formula and two terms. The semantics are that if the formula is true, then the value of the expression is the first term, otherwise the value of the expression is the second term. Note that while both formulas and terms may contain proper Boolean sub-expressions, *atomic* formulas and *atomic* terms do not.

Formulas in the logic of Fig. 2 are intended to be interpreted with respect to some first-order theory which gives meaning to the function, predicate, and constant symbols in the formula. The theory of integer linear arithmetic, for example, defines function symbols like "+" and "-", predicate symbols like "<", and ">", and arbitrary integer constant symbols. For a given theory and formula, the formula is *satisfiable* if it is possible to assign values to the variables in the formula from elements of the domain associated with the theory in a way that makes the formula true.

Significant research has gone into fast algorithms for determining the satisfiability of conjunctions of literals with respect to some logical theory (or combination of theories) [2,11,13]. CVC, for example, is such a decision procedure which includes theories for arithmetic, arrays, abstract data types, and uninterpreted functions. We do not address the issue of constructing such decision procedures here, but rather assume that we are given a decision procedure Sat_{FO} for determining the satisfiability, with respect to a theory of interest, of a conjunction of literals in the logic of Fig. 2.

The problem we will address is how to use such a decision procedure to construct an efficient SAT-based decision procedure for the satisfiability of arbitrary formulas (i.e. not just conjunctions of literals).

4   Checking Satisfiability
of Arbitrary Formulas Using SAT

Suppose we have, as stated, a core decision procedure Sat_{FO} for determining the satisfiability of conjunctions of literals, and we wish to determine whether an arbitrary formula ϕ is satisfiable.

An obvious approach would be to use propositional transformations (such as distributivity and DeMorgan's laws) to transform ϕ into a logically equivalent

```
CheckSat(decisions,φ)
   φ := Simplify(decisions,φ);
   IF φ ≡ false THEN RETURN ∅;
   IF ¬Sat_FO(decisions) THEN RETURN ∅;
   IF φ ≡ true THEN RETURN decisions;
   Choose the first atomic formula α appearing in φ.
   result := CheckSat(decisions ∪ {α},φ);
   IF result = ∅ THEN
      result := CheckSat(decisions ∪ {¬α},φ);
   RETURN result;
```

Fig. 3. Simple recursive algorithm for checking satisfiability

disjunction of conjunctions of literals and then test each conjunct for satisfiability using Sat_{FO}. Unfortunately, this transformation can increase the size of the formula exponentially, and is thus too costly in practice.

The approach taken by CVC's predecessors is equivalent to the recursive algorithm shown in Fig. 3. The algorithm takes two parameters: the decisions made so far, and the formula whose satisfiability is in question. The formula is first simplified relative to the decisions. Then, a number of base cases are checked: if the formula is *false* or the decisions are inconsistent, the algorithm returns ∅ (indicating that no satisfying assignment was found); if the formula is *true*, then the set *decisions* describes a consistent state in which the formula is satisfied. If none of the base cases hold, then a case-split is done on the first atomic formula α in ϕ. The algorithm is then called recursively: first considering the case when α is *true* and then considering the case when α is *false*. Although this approach is straightforward and works well in some cases, it is not very robust: small changes or differences in formulas can cause a dramatic change in the number of decisions made and the amount of time taken.

Our new approach is designed to be fast and robust. The key idea is to incrementally form a propositional abstraction of a first-order formula. Consider an abstraction function *Abs* which maps first-order formulas to propositional formulas. It is desirable that the abstraction have the following two properties:

1. For any formula ϕ, if $Abs(\phi)$ is unsatisfiable, then ϕ is unsatisfiable.
2. If $Abs(\phi)$ is satisfiable, then the abstract solution can either be translated back into a solution for ϕ or be used to refine the abstraction.

We first describe a process for determining an appropriate initial propositional abstraction *Abs*. We then describe how to refine the abstraction if the proof attempt is inconclusive.

4.1 Computing a Propositional Abstraction of a First-Order Formula

The basic idea of the process is to replace non-propositional formulas with propositional variables. Each syntactically distinct atomic formula α is replaced with a new propositional variable, p_α. Syntactically identical atomic formulas are replaced with the same propositional variable.

The result would be a purely propositional formula if not for the **ite** operator. Handling this operator requires a bit more work. We use a transformation which preserves satisfiability and eliminates the **ite** expressions. First, each **ite** term t is replaced with a new term variable v_t. Again, syntactically identical terms are replaced with the same variable. Then for each syntactically distinct term $t \equiv \mathbf{ite}(a, b, c)$ that is replaced, the following formula is conjoined to the original formula: $(a \rightarrow v_t = b) \wedge (\neg a \rightarrow v_t = c)$. By repeating this process, all **ite** operators can be eliminated (in linear time), and in the resulting formula, all terms are atomic. Atomic formulas can then be replaced by propositional variables, as described above, and the resulting formula is purely propositional.

To convert the resulting propositional formula to CNF in linear time, we employ a standard technique [ ]: a new propositional variable is introduced for each syntactically distinct non-variable sub-formula. Then, a set of CNF clauses is produced for each sub-formula which describes the relationship of the formula to its children. The translations for each of the standard Boolean operators are as follows.

$$a := \neg b \longrightarrow (a \vee b) \wedge (\neg a \vee \neg b) .$$
$$a := b \wedge c \longrightarrow (a \vee \neg b \vee \neg c) \wedge (\neg a \vee b) \wedge (\neg a \vee c)$$
$$a := b \vee c \longrightarrow (\neg a \vee b \vee c) \wedge (a \vee \neg b) \wedge (a \vee \neg c)$$

Now, suppose that $Abs(\phi)$ is satisfiable and that the solution is given as a conjunction ψ of propositional literals. This solution can be converted into an equivalent first-order solution by inverting the abstraction mapping on the solution (replacing each propositional variable p_α in ψ with α). Call the result $Abs^{-1}(\psi)$. Since $Abs^{-1}(\psi)$ is a conjunction of literals, its satisfiability can be determined using Sat_{FO}. If $Abs^{-1}(\psi)$ is satisfiable, then in the interpretation which satisfies it, the original formula ϕ must reduce to *true*, and thus ϕ is satisfiable. Otherwise, the result of the experiment is inconclusive, meaning that the abstraction must be refined. We describe how to do this next.

4.2   Refining the Abstraction

An obvious approach to refining the abstraction is to add a clause to the propositional formula that rules out the solution determined to be invalid by Sat_{FO}. Since ψ is a conjunction of propositional literals, applying de Morgan's law to $\neg\psi$ yields a standard propositional clause. Thus, $Abs(\phi) \wedge \neg\psi$ is a refinement of the original abstraction which rules out the invalid solution ψ. Furthermore, the refinement is still in CNF as required. We call the clause $\neg\psi$ a a *conflict clause* because it captures a set of propositional literals which conflict, causing an inconsistency. This is in accordance with standard SAT terminology. However, in standard SAT algorithms, conflict clauses are obtained by analyzing a clause which has become false to see which decisions made by the SAT solver are responsible. In our approach, the conflict clause is obtained by an agent outside of the SAT solver. After refining the abstraction by adding a conflict clause, the SAT algorithm can be restarted. By repeating this process, the abstraction will hopefully be refined enough so that it can either be proved unsatisfiable by the SAT solver or the solution ψ provided by SAT can be shown to map to a satisfying assignment for the original formula.

5   The Difficult Path to Success

There are a surprising number of roadblocks on the way from the previous idea to a practical algorithm. In this section we describe some of these and our solutions.

5.1   Redundant Clauses

The most severe problem with the naive approach outlined above is that it tends to produce an enormous number of redundant clauses. To see why, suppose that SAT computes a solution consisting of $n + 2$ propositional literals, but that only the last two propositional literals contribute to the inconsistency of the equivalent first-order set of literals. Then, for each assignment of values to the other n propositional variables which leads to a satisfying solution, the refinement loop will have to add another clause. In the worst case, the refinement loop will have to add 2^n clauses. This is particularly troubling because a single clause, one containing just the two contributing propositional literals would suffice.

In order to avoid the problem just described, the refinement must be more precise. In particular, when Sat_{FO} is given a set of literals to check for consistency, an effort must be made to find the *smallest* possible subset of the given set which is still inconsistent. Then, a clause derived from *only these* literals can be added to the propositional formula.

One possible way to implement this is to minimize the solution by trial and error: starting with n literals, pick one of the literals and remove it from the set. If the set is still inconsistent, leave that literal out; otherwise, return it to the set. Continue with each of the other literals. At the end, the set will contain a minimal set of literals. Unfortunately, this approach requires having Sat_{FO} process $O(n)$ literals n times for each iteration of the refinement loop (where n is the number of variables in the abstract formula). A few experiments with this approach quickly reveal that it is far too costly to give a practical algorithm.

A more practical solution, though one which is not trivial to implement, is to have the decision procedure Sat_{FO} maintain enough information to be able to report directly which subset of a set of inconsistent literals is responsible for the inconsistency.

Fortunately, through a discussion with Cormac Flanagan [ ], we realized that this is not difficult to do in CVC. This is because CVC is a proof-producing decision procedure, meaning that it is possible to have CVC generate an actual proof of any fact that it can prove. Using the infrastructure for proof production in CVC, we implemented a mechanism for generating *abstract proofs*. In abstract proof mode, CVC just tracks the external assumptions that are required for each proof. The result is that when a set of literals is reported by CVC to be inconsistent, the abstract proof of inconsistency contains exactly the *subset* of those literals that would be used to generate a proof of the inconsistency. The abstract proof thus provides a subset which is known to be inconsistent. This subset is not guaranteed to be minimal, but we found that in most cases it is very close to minimal. Since the overhead required to keep track of abstract proofs is small (typically around 20%), abstract proofs provide an efficient and practical solution for eliminating the problem of redundant clauses.

5.2   Lazy vs. Eager Notification

The approach described in the previous section is *lazy* (see the note in Section 6 below) in the sense that the SAT solver is used as a black box and the first-order procedure Sat_{FO} is not invoked until a solution is obtained from the SAT solver. Unfortunately, as shown in Table 3, the lazy approach becomes impractical for problems which require many refinements. In contrast, an *eager* approach is to notify the first-order procedure Sat_{FO} of every decision that is made (or unmade) by the SAT solver. Then, if an inconsistency is detected by Sat_{FO}, it is immediately diagnosed, providing a new conflict clause for SAT. The SAT algorithm then continues, never having to be restarted.

The performance advantages of the eager approach are significant. The disadvantages are that it requires more functionality of both the SAT solver and the decision procedure Sat_{FO}. The SAT solver is required to give notification every time it makes (or revokes) a decision. Furthermore, it must be able to accept new clauses in the middle of solving a problem (CVC includes a modified version of Chaff which has this functionality). The eager approach also requires Sat_{FO} to be *online*: able quickly to determine the consistency of incrementally more or fewer literals. Fortunately, CVC has this property.

5.3   Decision Heuristics

The decision heuristics used by Chaff and other SAT solvers consider every variable a possible target when choosing a new variable to do a case split on. However, in the abstracted first-order formula, not all variables are created equally. For example, consider an **ite** expression: $\mathbf{ite}(\alpha, t_1, t_2)$, and suppose that t_1 and t_2 are both large non-atomic terms. If the propositional variable associated with α is set to *true*, then all of the clauses generated by the translation of t_2 can be ignored since they can no longer affect the value of the original formula. Unfortunately, the SAT solver doesn't have this information, and as a result it can waste a lot of time choosing irrelevant variables. This problem has been addressed by others [5], and our solution is similar. We annotate the propositional variables with information about the structure of the original formula (i.e. parent/child relationships). Then, rather than invoking the built-in heuristic for variable selection, a depth-first search (DFS) is performed on the portion of the original formula which is relevant. The first variable corresponding to an atomic formula which is not already assigned a value is chosen. Although this can result in sub-optimal variable orders in some cases, it avoids the problem of splitting on irrelevant variables. Table 4 compares results obtained using the built-in Chaff decision heuristic with those obtained using the DFS heuristic. These are discussed in Section 7.

5.4   SAT Heuristics and Completeness

A somewhat surprising observation is that some heuristics used by SAT solvers must be disabled or the method will be incomplete. An example of this is the "pure literal" rule. This rule looks for propositional variables which have the property that only one of their two possible propositional literals appears in the formula being checked for satisfiability. When this happens, all instances of the propositional literal in question can immediately be replaced with *true*, since if a solution exists, a solution will exist in which that propositional literal is *true*.

However, if the formula is an abstraction of a first-order formula, it may be the case that a solution exists when the propositional literal is *false* even if a solution does not exist when the propositional literal is *true*. This is because the propositional literal is actually a place-holder for a first-order literal whose truth may affect the truth of other literals. Propositional literals are guaranteed to be independent of each other, while first-order literals are not. Because of this, there is no obvious way to take advantage of pure literals and the rule must be disabled. Fortunately, this was the only such rule that had to be disabled in Chaff.

5.5   Theory-Specific Challenges

Finally, a particularly perplexing difficulty is dealing with first-order theories that need to do case splits in order to determine whether a set of literals is satisfiable. For example, consider a theory of arrays with two function symbols, *read* and *write*. In this theory, $read(a, i)$ is a term which denotes the value of array a at index i. Similarly, the term $write(a, i, v)$ refers to an array which is identical to a everywhere except possibly at index i, where its value is v. Now, consider the following set of literals in this theory: $\{read(write(a, i, v), j) = x, x \neq v, x \neq a[i]\}$. In order for the array decision procedure to determine that such a set of literals is inconsistent, it must first do a case split on $i = j$. However, such additional case splits by the theories can cost a lot of time. Furthermore, they may not even be necessary to solve the problem. We found it difficult to find a strategy for integrating such case splits without adversely affecting performance. Our solution was to preprocess the formulas to try to eliminate such case splits. In particular, for the array theory, every instance of $read(write(a, i, v), j)$ is rewritten to $\mathbf{ite}(i = j, v, read(a, i))$. Furthermore, in order to increase the likelihood of being able to apply this rewrite, every instance of $read(\mathbf{ite}(a, b, c), v)$ is rewritten to $\mathbf{ite}(a, read(b, v), read(c, v))$. These rewrites were sufficient to obtain reasonable performance for our examples. However, we suspect that for more complicated examples, something more sophisticated may be required.

6   Related Work

Flanagan, Joshi, and Saxe at Compaq SRC have independently developed a very similar approach to combining first-order decision procedures with SAT [ ]. Their translation process is identical to ours. Furthermore, their approach to generating conflict clauses is somewhat more sophisticated than ours. However, their prototype implementation is lazy (the nomenclature of "lazy" versus "eager" is theirs). Also it only includes a very limited language and its performance is largely unknown. Unfortunately, we have not been able to compare directly with their implementation.

De Moura, Ruess, and Sorea at SRI have also developed a similar approach using their ICS decision procedure [ ]. However, ICS is unable to produce minimal conflict clauses, so they use an optimized variation of the trial and error method described in Section 5.1 to minimize conflict clauses. Also, as with the Compaq approach, their implementation is lazy and its performance unknown. Though they do not report execution times, they do provide their benchmarks, and our implementation using CVC with Chaff was able to solve all of them easily.

It would also be interesting to compare with the approach for solving problems in the logic of equality with uninterpreted functions by translating them (up front) to SAT problems. We made an attempt to perform direct comparisons with [ ], but their benchmarks are not provided in the language of equality with uninterpreted functions, and unfortunately, it is not clear how to translate them. As a result, we were unable to run their benchmarks. We suspect that our approach would be competitive with theirs. However, since the logic is so simple, it is not clear that a more general approach like ours would be better.

7   Results

We implemented the approach described above in the CVC decision procedure using the Chaff SAT solver, and tested it using a suite of processor verification benchmarks. The first three benchmarks are purely propositional formulas from Miroslav Velev's superscalar suite (http://www.ece.cmu.edu/~mvelev). The next three are also from Velev's DLX verification efforts, but they include array and uninterpreted function operations. The rest are from our own efforts in processor verification and also include array and uninterpreted function operations.

These were run using gcc under linux on an 800MHz Pentium III with 2GB of memory. The best overall results were obtained by using an eager notification strategy and the DFS decision heuristic. Table 1 compares these results to results obtained by using CVC without Chaff (using the recursive algorithm of Fig. 3). As can be seen, the results are better, often by several orders of magnitude, in every case but one (the easiest example which is solved by both methods very quickly). These results show that CVC with Chaff is a significant improvement over CVC alone.

Table 1. Results comparing CVC without Chaff to CVC combined with Chaff

Example	CVC without Chaff		CVC+Chaff	
	Decisions	Time (s)	Decisions	Time (s)
bool-dlx1-c	?	> 10000	2522	1.14
bool-dlx2-aa	?	> 10000	792	0.81
bool-dlx2-cc-bug01	?	> 10000	573387	833
v-dlx-pc	8642456	5082	6137	6.10
v-dlx-dmem	2888268	2820	2184	3.48
v-dlx-regfile	29435	37.6	3833	6.64
dlx-pc	515	0.68	529	1.04
dlx-dmem	6031	4.50	1276	1.90
dlx-regfile	6386	5.27	2739	4.12
pp-bloaddata-a	93714	79.1	1193	1.80
pp-bloaddata	345569	338	4451	4.51
pp-dmem2	367877	338	2070	1.52

Our goal in integrating Chaff into CVC was not only to test the feasibility of the approach, but also to produce a tool that could compete with and improve upon the best results obtained by our previous tool, SVC. SVC uses a set of clever but somewhat ad hoc heuristics to improve on the performance obtained by the algorithm of Fig. 3 by learning which atomic formulas are best to split on [ ]. Table 2 compares the results obtained by SVC with the results obtained by CVC with Chaff.

SVC performs particularly well on the last 6 examples, a fact which is not too surprising since these are old benchmarks that were used to tune SVC's heuristics. However, SVC's performance on the first six examples shows that it's heuristics are simply not flexible enough to handle a large variety of formulas. CVC, on the other hand produces good results fairly consistently. Even in the four cases where CVC is slower than SVC, the number of decisions is comparable, and in all other cases the number of decisions required by CVC is much less. This is encouraging because it means that CVC is finding shorter proofs, and additional performance gains can probably be obtained by tuning the code. Thus, overall, CVC seems to perform better and to be more robust than SVC, which is the goal we set out to accomplish.

7.1   Comparing Different Strategies

Finally, we show experimental results for some of the different strategies discussed in the previous section. First, just to drive the point home, we show a simple comparison of the naive (lazy without minimal conflict clauses), lazy (with minimal conflict clauses), and eager (with minimal conflict clauses) implementations on some simple examples. As can be seen, the naive and lazy approaches quickly become impractical.

Next, we compare two versions of the eager approach with minimal conflict clauses: one using the standard Chaff decision heuristics, and one using the DFS

Table 2. Results comparing SVC to CVC

Example	SVC		CVC+Chaff	
	Decisions	Time (s)	Decisions	Time (s)
bool-dlx1-c	11228452	776	2522	1.14
bool-dlx2-aa	?	> 10000	792	0.81
bool-dlx2-cc-bug01	?	> 10000	573387	833
v-dlx-pc	4620149	503	6137	6.10
v-dlx-dmem	199540	31.7	2184	3.48
v-dlx-regfile	74600	18.2	3833	6.64
dlx-pc	384	0.15	529	1.04
dlx-dmem	655	0.21	1276	1.90
dlx-regfile	936	0.27	2739	4.12
pp-bloaddata-a	902	0.66	1193	1.80
pp-bloaddata	35491	5.35	4451	4.51
pp-dmem2	47989	7.54	2070	1.52

Table 3. Results comparing naive, lazy, and eager implementations

Example	Naive		Lazy		Eager
	Iterations	Time (s)	Iterations	Time (s)	Time (s)
read0	77	0.14	17	0.09	0.07
pp-pc-s2i	?	> 10000	82	1.36	0.10
pp-invariant	?	> 10000	239	5.81	0.22
v-dlx-pc	?	> 10000	6158	792	3.22
v-dlx-dmem	?	> 10000	?	> 10000	4.12

Table 4. Variable selection by Chaff vs. by depth-first search

Example	Chaff		DFS	
	Decisions	Time (s)	Decisions	Time (s)
bool-dlx1-c	1309	0.69	2522	1.14
bool-dlx2-aa	4974	2.36	792	0.81
bool-dlx2-cc-bug01	10903	11.4	573387	833
v-dlx-pc	4387	3.22	6137	6.10
v-dlx-dmem	5221	4.12	2184	3.48
v-dlx-regfile	6802	5.85	3833	6.64
dlx-pc	39833	19.0	529	1.04
dlx-dmem	34320	18.8	1276	1.90
dlx-regfile	47822	35.5	2739	4.12
pp-bloaddata-a	8695	5.47	1193	1.80
pp-bloaddata	9016	5.56	4451	4.51
pp-dmem2	3167	2.24	2070	1.52

heuristic discussed in Section 5.3. The results are shown in Table 4. As can be seen, DFS outperforms the standard technique on all but four examples. Two of these are purely Boolean test cases, and so the DFS method wouldn't be expected to provide any advantage. For purely propositional formulas, then, (or first-order formulas that are *mostly* propositional), the standard Chaff technique is probably better. It is particularly interesting to note how badly DFS does on the example "bool-dlx2-cc-bug01". One area for future work is trying to find a way to automatically choose between or combine these two methods.

More information about these and other benchmarks (as well as the benchmarks themselves) is available from http://verify.stanford.edu/barrett/CAV02. CVC is available from http://verify.stanford.edu/CVC.

Acknowledgments

We'd like to thank the anonymous reviewers for many helpful suggestions. This work was partially supported by the National Science Foundation Grant CCR-9806889, and ARPA/AirForce contract number F33615-00-C-1693.

References

1. C. Barrett, D. Dill, and J. Levitt. Validity Checking for Combinations of Theories with Equality. In Mandayam Srivas and Albert Camilleri, editors, *Formal Methods In Computer-Aided Design*, pages 187–201, 1996. 237
2. Clark W. Barrett. *Checking Validity of Quantifier-Free Formulas in Combinations of First-Order Theories*. PhD thesis, Stanford University, 2002. 239
3. R. Bryant, S. German, and M. Velev. Exploiting Positive Equality in a Logic of Equality with Uninterpreted Functions. In *11th International Conference on Computer-Aided Verification*, pages 470–482, 1999. 237
4. Leonardo de Moura, Harald Ruess, and Maria Sorea. Lazy Theorem Proving for Bounded Model Checking over Infinite Domains. In *18th International Conference on Automated Deduction*, 2002. 245
5. L. e Silva, L. Silveira, and J. Marques-Silva. Algorithms for Solving Boolean Satisfiability in Combinational Circuits. In *Proceedings of the IEEE/ACM Design, Automation and Test in Europe Conference (DATE)*, March 1999. 243
6. C. Flanagan. Private Communication, 2000. 242
7. Cormac Flanagan, Rajeev Joshi, and James B. Saxe. The Design of An Efficient Theorem Prover using Explicated Clauses. 2002. In Preparation. 245
8. Tracy Larrabee. Test pattern generation using Boolean satisfiability. *IEEE Transactions on Computer-Aided Design*, 11(1):4–15, January 1992. 241
9. Jeremy R. Levitt. *Formal Verification Techniques for Digital Systems*. PhD thesis, Stanford University, 1999. 246
10. M. Moskewicz, C. Madigan, Y. Zhao, L. Zhang, and S. Malik. Chaff: Engineering an Efficient SAT Solver. In *Proceedings of the 39th Design Automation Conference*, 2001. 237
11. G. Nelson and D. Oppen. Simplification by cooperating decision procedures. *ACM Transactions on Programming Languages and Systems*, 1(2):245–57, 1979. 239

12. A. Pnueli, Y. Rodeh, O. Shtrichman, and M. Siegel. Deciding Equality Formulas by Small-Domain Instantiations. In *11th International Conference on Computer-Aided Verification*, pages 455–469, 1999. 237, 245

13. H. Ruess and N. Shankar. Deconstructing Shostak. In *16th Annual IEEE Symposium on Logic in Computer Science*, pages 19–28, June 2001. 239

14. Laurent Simon. The Sat-Ex Site. http://www.lri.fr/~simon/satex/satex.php3. 237

15. A. Stump, C. Barrett, and D. Dill. CVC: a Cooperating Validity Checker. In *14th International Conference on Computer-Aided Verification*, 2002. 237

Applying SAT Methods
in Unbounded Symbolic Model Checking

Ken L. McMillan

Cadence Berkeley Labs

Abstract. A method of symbolic model checking is introduced that
uses conjunctive normal form (CNF) rather than binary decision diagrams (BDD's) and uses a SAT-based approach to quantifier elimination.
This method is compared to a traditional BDD-based model checking approach using a set of benchmark problems derived from the compositional
verification of a commercial microprocessor design.

1   Introduction

Symbolic model checking [6,7] is a method of verifying temporal logic properties
of transition systems that relies on a symbolic representation of sets (*i.e.*, as
formulas rather than as an explicit lists). In the finite state case, this method
has become identified with Binary Decision Diagrams [4] (BDD's), a canonical
form for Boolean formulas that has proved to be quite efficient for this purpose in
practice. Because of the success of BDD's, and related structures, other forms of
expressing Boolean functions in symbolic model checking have remained largely
unexplored. In this work, we will consider the use of conjunctive normal form
(CNF) as a representation in symbolic model checking. The use of this form
makes it possible to adapt efficient algorithms used in solving the satisfiability
problem (SAT) to the most important operation in symbolic model checking,
quantifier elimination.

In particular, we will show that, with a slight modification, modern SAT algorithms based on the Davis-Logemann-Loveland (DLL) approach can be used
to eliminate universal quantifiers from an arbitrary Boolean formula, producing
a result in CNF. This makes it possible, using standard methods, to compute
a CNF formula equivalent to the CTL formula AXp, where p is an arbitrary
Boolean formula. This in turn makes it possible to evaluate any CTL formula
using fixed point characterizations of the CTL operators (and, in fact, the formulas of the more general μ-calculus).

We will observe that this procedure, using CNF and SAT-based quanti-
fier elimination, can be exponentially more efficient than model checking using
BDD's, in cases where the resulting fixed points have compact representations in
CNF, but not as BDD's. We will also compare the SAT-based approach with the
BDD-based approach on a set of benchmark model checking problems derived
from microprocessor verification.

D. Brinksma and K. G. Larsen (Eds.): CAV 2002, LNCS 2404, pp. 250–264, 2002.
© Springer-Verlag Berlin Heidelberg 2002

Related Work In the past, SAT methods have been applied in model checking in a variety of ways. In *bounded model checking* [2], the transition relation of a system is unfolded k times, allowing any counterexamples of up to k states to be found using a SAT solver. Unless a bound on the length of counterexamples is known, however, this method cannot actually verify the given property, it can only produce counterexamples. The method presented here is not bounded, and produces a guarantee of correctness when the property is true.

SAT solvers have also been used in a hybrid method to detect when a fixed point has been reached, while quantifier elimination is performed by other means (generally by the expansion of the quantifier as $\exists v.f = f\langle 0/v\rangle \vee f\langle 1/v\rangle$, followed by some simplification method). Examples of this approach include [3,1,17]. Because of the expense of quantifier elimination in this method, it is usually limited to sequential machines with a very small number of inputs (typically zero or one). By contrast, the approach presented here uses SAT methods in the actual quantifier elimination step, and is not limited in terms of the number of inputs (examples with hundreds of inputs have been verified). SAT algorithms have also been used to, in effect, generate a disjunctive decomposition for BDD-based image computations [9]. Here, BDD's are not used – the image computation is entirely based on SAT methods and produces a result in CNF.

Finally, another approach to using SAT in model checking is based on unfolding the transition relation to the length of the longest "shortest path" between two states [15]. The fact that this length has been reached can be verified using a SAT solver. Thus, unlike bounded model checking, the method can provide a guarantee of correctness for any property. Unfortunately, the longest "shortest path" can be exponentially longer than the diameter of the state space (for example, the longest shortest path for an n-bit register is 2^n, while the diameter is 1). The method presented here does not involve unfolding the transition relation, and requires a number of iterations bounded by the diameter, as does traditional symbolic model checking.

Outline of this Paper In section 2 we outline the standard DLL approach to SAT using conflict-based learning. We first consider the satisfiability problem for CNF formulas, then use this result verify the validity of arbitrary Boolean formulas. In section 3, this basic algorithm is extended to convert an arbitrary Boolean formula into CNF, rather than simply checking its validity. In section 4 we extend this algorithm to eliminate universal quantifiers in the result. We also consider the problem of quantifier elimination under a restriction (*i.e*, a "don't care" condition). In section 5, we then apply this quantifier elimination procedure in a symbolic CTL model checking algorithm, and show how to detect convergence of the fixed point series. Finally, in section 6, we compare this approach to a standard method using BDD's.

2   The Basic SAT Algorithm

The satisfiability problem (SAT) is to determine whether a Boolean formula in conjunctive normal form (CNF) has a satisfying assignment. We sketch here a generalized SAT algorithm using conflict-based learning, introducing only sufficient detail to allow understanding of the algorithms that follow. Details of the implementation are crucial for performance, but are not covered here. The reader may refer, for example, to [16,13] for a detailed treatment.

Preliminaries Let $\mathcal{V}$ be a finite set of *variables* and let $\mathcal{B}$ stand for the set $\{0,1\}$. A *literal* is a variable $v \in \mathcal{V}$, or its negation $\neg v$. A *clause* is a disjunction of a set of zero or more literals $l_1 \vee \cdots \vee l_n$ (where the disjunction of zero literals is taken to mean the constant 0). A CNF formula is a conjunction of a set of zero or more clauses $c_1 \wedge \cdots \wedge c_n$ (where a conjunction of zero clauses taken to mean the constant 1). In the sequel, we will speak of a clause as a *set* of literals, and a CNF formula as a *set* of clauses, the disjunction or conjunction, respectively, of these sets being implicit. A clause will be said to be *trivial* if it contains both a variable v and its negation $\neg v$. A trivial clause is equivalent to the constant 1. In the sequel, will will take "clause" to mean "non-trivial clause".

An *assignment* is a partial function from $\mathcal{V}$ to $\mathcal{B}$. An assignment is said to be *total* when its domain is $\mathcal{V}$. A total assignment A is said to be *satisfying* for formula f when $f(A)$, the value of f given A under the usual interpretation of the Boolean connectives, is 1. We will equate an assignment A with a conjunction of a set of literals, specifically the set containing $\neg v$ for all $v \in \text{dom}(A)$ such that $A(v) = 0$ and v for all $v \in \text{dom}(A)$ such that $A(v) = 1$. Thus, for example, we will take $a \wedge \neg b$ to stand for the assignment $\{(a,1),(b,0)\}$.

Boolean Constraint Propagation The basic SAT algorithm builds up an assignment by making a sequence of arbitrary decisions. During this process, additional implied assignments are generated by a process called *Boolean constraint propagation* (BCP). That is, given an assignment A and a clause c in the CNF formula, if all the literals in the clause but one are false in A, then the remaining literal must be true in any satisfying assignment extending A. Thus, this *implied* literal can be added to A without loss of generality. BCP builds an *implication graph*, a DAG in which the vertices are literals, and each vertex is implied by its predecessors.

More formally, for a given CNF formula f and assignment A, let the *implication graph* $\text{IG}(A,f)$ be a directed acyclic graph (V,E), where V is a set of literals. For any vertex $l \in V$, let $\text{preds}(v)$ denote $\{l' \in V \mid (l',l) \in V\}$. The implication graph has the following properties:

- Every literal in A is a root.
- For every vertex l not in A, the CNF formula f contains the clause $l \vee \bigvee_{m \in \text{preds}(l)} \neg m$. We will denote this clause $\text{cl}(l,A,f)$.
- For all $v \in \mathcal{V}$, V does not contain both v and $\neg v$.

We also assume that the graph is maximal, in the sense that no extension of the graph satisfies the above conditions. Note, however, that the above conditions do not uniquely define the implication graph. We will refer to literals in A as the "roots" of the graph, although technically one-literal clauses in f (unit clauses) can also induce vertices with no predecessors.

As an example, suppose that $f = (\neg a \vee b) \wedge (\neg b \wedge c \wedge d)$ and $A = a \wedge \neg c$. A possible implication graph $\mathrm{IG}(A, f)$ is shown below:

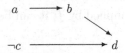

We will denote by A_f the assignment induced by the implication graph $\mathrm{IG}(A, f)$. That is, $A_f = \bigwedge V$, where $(V, E) = \mathrm{IG}(A, f)$. In our example, $A_f = a \wedge \neg c \wedge b \wedge d$. It is straightforward to show by induction on the edge relation E that $f \wedge A$ implies A_f.

Conflict-Based Learning Given an assignment A, a clause is said to be in *conflict* when all of its literals are false in A_f. If any clause in the CNF formula f is in conflict, then our assignment A cannot be extended to a satisfying assignment. In this case, a technique called *conflict-based learning* is used to deduce a new clause that will, in effect, prevent us from becoming blocked in the same way in the future. This new clause, called the *conflict clause*, is deduced by resolving existing clauses in f using the implication graph as a guide.

First, we must define *resolution*. Given two clauses of the form $c_1 = v \vee A$ and $c_2 = \neg v \vee B$, we say that the *resolvent* of c_1 and c_2 is $A \vee B$, provided $A \vee B$ is non-trivial (*i.e*, contains no contradictory literals). For example, the resolvent of $a \vee b$ and $\neg a \vee \neg c$ is $b \vee \neg c$, while $a \vee b$ and $\neg a \vee \neg b$ have no resolvent, since $b \vee \neg b$ is trivial. It is easy to see that any two clauses have at most one resolvent. The resolvent of c_1 and c_2 (if it exists) is a clause that is implied by $c_1 \wedge c_2$ (in fact, it is exactly $(\exists a)(c_1 \wedge c_2)$).

Now, suppose that $c = l_1 \wedge \cdots \wedge l_n$ is a clause in f that is in conflict. We know that the implication graph contains the literals $\neg l_1 \ldots \neg l_n$. Further suppose that some literal $l_i \in c$ is not in A (*i.e.*, is not a root of the implication graph). Then by definition f contains the clause $\mathrm{cl}(\neg l_i, A, f) = \neg l_i \vee \neg m_1 \vee \cdots \vee \neg m_k$ where $m_1 \ldots m_k$ are the predecessors of $\neg l_i$ in the implication graph. The resolvent of c and $\mathrm{cl}(\neg l_i, A, f)$ is a clause that is itself in conflict.

As an example, suppose that that we add the clause $(\neg b \vee \neg d)$ to the example above. This clause is in conflict, since the implication graph contains both b and d. Taking the resolvent of $\mathrm{cl}(d, A, f) = (\neg b \wedge c \wedge d)$ with the conflicting clause $(\neg b \vee \neg d)$, we obtain an implied clause $(\neg b \vee c)$, which is also in conflict. Resolving this clause with $\mathrm{cl}(b, A, f) = (\neg a \vee b)$, we obtain another implied clause $(\neg a \vee c)$, also in conflict.

The following is a generic conflict-based learning procedure that takes a clause in conflict and produces an implied clause (also in conflict) by repeatedly applying resolution steps until some termination condition T is satisfied, or no further steps are possible:

```
0        procedure deduce(c, A, f)
1        while ¬T and exists l ∈ c such that ¬l ∉ A
2                let c = resolvent of cl(¬l, A, f) and c
3        return c
```

Since the resulting clause is implied by f, it can be added to f without changing its satisfiability.

Basic SAT Procedure We now put together the methods of Boolean constraint propagation and conflict-based learning to obtain a generic procedure for determining the satisfiability of a CNF formula f:

```
0        procedure SAT(f)
1        let A = ∅
2        repeat
3                if f contains 0 return "unsatisfiable"
4                else if some clause c in conflict
5                        add clause deduce(c, A, f) to f
6                        remove some literals from A
7                else if A_f is total, return "satisfiable"
8                else
9                        choose a literal l such that l ∉ A and ¬l ∉ A
10                       add l to A
```

The procedure heuristically guesses new literals (*i.e.*, decisions) to add to the assignment A. If at any point a conflict occurs in the implication graph IG(A, f), we call the procedure deduce to generate an implied clause, which is added to f, and then we "backtrack", removing some literals from A. Otherwise, the procedure terminates when either the implied assignment A_f is total (in which case we have a satisfying assignment) or the empty clause **0** is deduced (in which case the f is unsatisfiable). We assume throughout that the implication graph IG(A, f) is updated incrementally to reflect any changes in A or f.

Note that there are many heuristic choices to be made in this procedure. Notable among these are the choice of which literals to add to A (the decision heuristic), the choice of literals to eliminate by resolution in the conflict-based learning procedure, and the order of building the implication graph. These heuristic choices vary between solvers and strongly effect the efficiency of the procedure, but are essentially orthogonal to the methods introduced here.

Proving Validity of Arbitrary Boolean Formulas Given an arbitrary Boolean formula (not in CNF), there is a standard procedure for constructing a CNF formula that is unsatisfiable exactly when p is valid. We assume a set of *input variables* $V_I \subset V$, and a Boolean formula p over V_I. For simplicity, we also assume p uses only disjunction and negation, and contains no double negation (*i.e.* subformulas of the form $\neg\neg q$). For every subformula q of the form $r \vee s$, we introduce a distinct variable v_q. To each subformula of p we can now associate a literal l_q, which is q if q is an input, v_q if q is a disjunction, and $\neg v_r$ if q is of the form $\neg r$. Now, we construct a CNF formula CNF(p), which contains, for each subformula q of the form $r \vee s$, the clauses

$$\{(v_q \vee \neg l_r), (v_q \vee \neg l_s), (\neg v_q \vee l_r \vee l_s)\}$$

It is not difficult to show that for any assignment A to V_I, there is a unique satisfying assignment A' of CNF(p) consistent with A, and such that $A'(l_p) = p(A)$. A a result, the CNF formula CNF(p) $\wedge \neg l_p$ is unsatisfiable exactly when p is valid.

3   Characterizing Boolean Functions in CNF

Now, given an arbitrary formula p, rather than checking the validity of p, we wish to construct an equivalent formula to p in conjunctive normal form. This can be done by a slight modification of the basic SAT algorithm. Briefly, we construct a SAT problem for the validity of p, and run the SAT algorithm as described above. However, if a satisfying assignment is found, instead of terminating, we construct a new clause that is in conflict (*i.e.*, rules out the satisfying assignment) and continue the procedure. This new clause, which we will call a *blocking clause*, must have the following properties:

- It must contain only variables in V_I,
- It must be false in the current assignment A_f, and
- It must be implied by $l_p \wedge$ CNF(p).

The following procedure uses blocking clauses to compute a CNF formula χ equivalent to p:

```
0        procedure toCNF(p)
1        let f = CNF(p) ∧ ¬l_p, χ = 1, and A = ∅
2        repeat
3                if f contains 0, return χ
4                else if some clause c in conflict
5                        add clause deduce(c, A, f) to f
6                        remove some literals from A
7                else if A_f is total
8                        choose a blocking clause c'
9                        add c' to f and χ
10               else
11                       choose a literal l such that l ∉ A and ¬l ∉ A
12                       add l to A
```

Each time a satisfying assignment is obtained, the procedure generates a new clause whose complement characterizes a set of satisfying assignments (*i.e.*, it rules out a set of cases where p is false). When the CNF formula becomes unsatisfiable, these clauses precisely characterize p. We can argue partial correctness of this procedure as follows. The procedure maintains the invariant that p implies χ (since only clauses implied by p are added to χ). Further, at all times f is equivalent to $\text{CNF}(p) \wedge \neg l_p \wedge \chi$. Thus, on termination, when $f = 0$, there is no assignment that makes p false and χ true, in other words, χ implies p. If the procedure terminates, therefore, χ is a CNF formula equivalent to p.

Of course, the important question is how to choose a blocking clause when a satisfying assignment is reached. Such a clause can be generated using the conflict-based learning procedure. However, to ensure that the conflict clause we generate involves only input variables, we must use an alternate implication graph to generate it, in which all the roots are assignments to input variables.

Such a graph can be generated in the following way. Suppose we have a satisfying assignment A_f for f. Let $A' = A_f \downarrow V_I$ (the projection of A_f onto the input variables) and let $f' = \text{CNF}(p) \wedge \chi$. We can show that $A'_{f'} = A_f$, that is, the implication graph $\text{IG}(A', f')$ induces the same assignment as $\text{IG}(A, f)$. This can be argued as follows: first, we know that A_f is a satisfying assignment for f', since f' contains a subset of the clauses in f. Further, since $\text{CNF}(p)$ determines the non-input variables as a function of the input variables, it follows that A_f is the *unique* satisfying assignment consistent with A'. Finally, since the truth value of any subformula of p can be inferred from the truth values of its own immediate subformulas, it follows that the assignment $A'_{f'}$ is total. Since A' implies $A'_{f'}$ and A_f is the *only* satisfying assignment consistent with A', it follows that $A'_{f'} = A_f$.

Now, in particular, since f contains the clause $(\neg l_p)$, it follows that the clause (l_p) is in conflict in $\text{IG}(A', f')$. As a result, by computing $c' = \texttt{deduce}(l_p, A', f')$, we obtain a clause that is implied by $\text{CNF}(p) \wedge l_p$ (since this implies f'), and is in conflict (*i.e.*, false in the current assignment). Further, we can ensure that c' involves only input variables by modifying the termination condition T in $\texttt{deduce}$ so that resolution may terminate only when c' contains only input literals. This must eventually occur since all the roots of the implication graph $\text{IG}(A', f')$ are input literals. Thus c' is a blocking clause.

Clearly, it would be wise from a performance point of view to maintain the alternate implication graph $\text{IG}(A', f')$ incrementally, updating it as changes occur in A_f. In this way we avoid reconstructing the entire graph each time a satisfying assignment is found. Further, there is no need to add a literal to A' if that literal is already implied by the existing assignment. Thus, A' will typically be smaller than $A_f \downarrow V_I$, which will generally result in shorter blocking clauses.

As an example, suppose that $p = (a \wedge b) \vee c$, and suppose that we have guessed the assignment $A = a$. A possible implication graph is shown in (a) below. Note that the literal $\neg l_p$ always occurs in the implication graph because f includes the unit clause $(\neg l_p)$. At this point, we have a satisfying assignment. Projecting onto the input variables, we have $A' = a \wedge \neg b \wedge \neg c$. The resulting alternate implication graph $IG(A', f')$ is shown in (b) below. Note that the implied assignment is the same as in the original graph, and further, clause (l_p) is in conflict. Thus, we begin the conflict-based learning process with clause (l_p). We first eliminate l_p, to obtain $(l_{a \wedge b} \vee c)$. Since this contains a non-input variable $v_{a \wedge b}$, we must continue. Thus, we eliminate $l_{a \wedge b}$, obtaining the blocking clause $(b \vee c)$. Adding this clause, we undo the assignment to a and continue. Suppose we once again guess $A = a$. This time, instead of reaching a satisfying assignment, we find the new clause $(b \vee c)$ in conflict. Thus, we perform the normal conflict analysis, obtaining the conflict clause $(\neg a)$. Propagating implications, this yields a new satisfying assignment where $A' = \neg a \wedge b \wedge \neg c$. This in turn yields the blocking clause $(a \vee c)$. This clause is in conflict in the empty assignment, thus, the standard conflict analysis infers the empty clause, and the procedure terminates, returning the CNF formula $(b \vee c) \wedge (a \vee c)$.

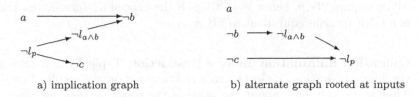

a) implication graph   b) alternate graph rooted at inputs

4   Quantification and Image Computations

As noted in the introduction, in order to compute AXp, we need to be able to eliminate universal quantifiers. That is, given a Boolean formula p, and a set of variables $W = w_1, \ldots, w_n$, we would like to construct a Boolean formula equivalent to $\forall W.p$. This is quite easily done if p is a CNF formula, as we simply delete all the literals of the form w_i or $\neg w_i$. That is, the universal quantifier distributes over the conjunction, and also over the disjunction within a clause, since the literals in the clause have independent support. It follows that to compute a CNF formula for $\forall W.p$, we have only to convert p to CNF form using procedure toCNF and then delete the literals w_i and $\neg w_i$ from the result. This procedure may be highly inefficient however. In the extreme case, we may generate an exponentially large CNF formula for p, which then becomes equivalent to the single clause $\mathbf{0}$ when quantification is applied.

To alleviate his problem, we can introduce the quantification step into the SAT algorithm itself. This yields the following procedure:

```
0        procedure forall(W, p)
1        let f = CNF(p) ∧ ¬l_p, χ = 1, and A = ∅
2        repeat
3                if f contains 0, return χ
4                else if some clause c in conflict
5                        add clause deduce(c, A, f) to f
6                        remove some literals from A
7                else if A_f is total
```

8		choose a blocking clause c'
8a		remove literals of form w_i or $\neg w_i$ from c'
9		add c' to f and χ
10	else	
11		choose a literal l such that $l \notin A$ and $\neg l \notin A$
12		add l to A

This differs from the previous algorithm only in the addition of line 8a, which universally quantifies the variables $w_1, \ldots, w_n$ in the blocking clause c'. This procedure maintains the invariant that $\forall W.p$ implies χ (since c' is always implied by p, it follows that $\forall W.c'$ is always implied by $\forall W.p$). Further, at all times f is equivalent to $\mathrm{CNF}(p) \wedge \neg l_p \wedge \chi$. Thus, on termination, when $f = \mathbf{0}$, there is no assignment that makes p false and χ true, in other words, χ implies p, hence $\forall W.\chi$ implies $\forall W.p$, hence $\chi \Rightarrow \forall W.p$. If the procedure terminates, therefore, χ is a CNF formula equivalent to $\forall W.p$.

Quantifier Elimination under a Restriction Typically in a symbolic model checking application, we are given a restriction r on the result of an operation. That is, we only care about the value of the resulting formula when r is true. In this case, we would like to evaluate $(\forall W.p) \downarrow r$, which is defined to mean some formula g such that $r \wedge g = r \wedge \forall W.p$. This can be accomplished using the quantifier elimination procedure **forall** by simply replacing $\mathrm{CNF}(p)$ with $\mathrm{CNF}(p) \wedge \mathrm{CNF}(r) \wedge l_r$. This in effect restricts the satisfying assignments to those that satisfy r. When the algorithm terminates, χ is a CNF formula for $(\forall W.p) \downarrow r$. Further, in the case when $r \Rightarrow \forall W.p$, there is no satisfying assignment, hence the algorithm returns $\chi = \mathbf{1}$. This is a useful property, as we will shortly observe.

5   Symbolic Model Checking Using SAT Methods

We now consider the use of the above quantifier elimination algorithm in symbolic CTL model checking. We assume the reader is familiar with the temporal logic CTL, as defined by Clarke and Emerson [ ], and with symbolic model checking methods [ ]. To give a symbolic CTL model checking algorithm using a given representation for Boolean functions, it suffices to give an algorithm for reducing the formula AXp, where p is a Boolean formula, into the given form. The remaining operators of the logic can then be derived using standard equivalences and fixed point characterizations.

Briefly, we assume a set of state variables $\mathcal{S} = s_1, \ldots, s_n$ and a set of combinational variables $W = w_1, \ldots, w_k$. The transition relation of the model is given by a set of equations of the form $s_i' = \delta_i(\mathcal{S}, W)$. For a given propositional formula p, we can characterize AXp as:

$$AXp = \forall W.\, p \langle \delta_i / s_i \rangle$$

That is, we can compute a CNF formula equivalent to AXp by syntactically substituting each s_i by δ_i, and then applying our universal quantifier elimination algorithm to the combinational variables $w_i, \ldots, w_k$. Now, for example, we can compute AGp, using the "frontier set simplification" method, as the conjunction of the following sequence:

$$Z_1 = p$$

$$Z_{i+1} = (AX\ Z_i) \downarrow \bigwedge_{j=1}^{i} Z_j$$

To evaluate the "frontier set" Z_{i+1}, we can use our algorithm for quantifier elimination under a restriction. This sequence converges when $\bigwedge_{j=1}^{i} Z_j \Rightarrow (AX\ Z_i)$, in which case Z_{i+1} is the constant $\mathbf{1}$. This gives us a way to detect convergence without solving an additional SAT problem, and yields the following procedure for computing a Boolean formula equivalent to AGp:

```
0      procedure AG(p)
1         let Z = Q = p
2         while Z ≠ 1
3              let Z = (∀W. p⟨δᵢ/sᵢ⟩) ↓ Q
4              let Q = Q ∧ Z
5         return Q
```

It is straightforward to derive algorithms for the other CTL modalities using their fixed point characterizations. Note that the existential modalities can be obtained using the duality $EXp = \neg AX\neg p$.

6   Comparison with BDD-Based Symbolic Model Checking

We now compare this approach to symbolic model checking using SAT techniques to a standard approach using binary decision diagrams (BDD's). In our experiments, both techniques use the same fixed point iteration for AGp (though we will also compare to a BDD method using a forward traversal method). The BDD-based technique is implemented in the Cadence SMV system.[1] It uses a "conjunctive partitioning" approach [5] to the reverse image computation. It also uses "dynamic variable ordering" [14] to optimize the BDD variable order during the computation. The quantifier elimination algorithm forall was implemented by modifying the ZCHAFF SAT solver [13] from Princeton University. The decision variable heuristics and implication graph mechanism in that solver are unchanged. The implementation is quite inefficient, in that it reconstructs the entire implication graph $IG(A', f')$ when a satisfying assignment is found, rather than maintaining this structure incrementally. Thus, there is considerable room for improvement in performance results presented. All computations are

---

[1] http:/www-cad.eecs.berkeley.edu/~kenmcmil

performed on workstation using a 900MHz Pentium III processor, and the Linux operating system.

A Simple Example To begin with, it is generally held that BDD's provide a more compact representation for Boolean functions than, for example CNF. However, there are some interesting cases where the CNF form can be exponentially more compact than the BDD form. Consider, for example, the following simple sequential machine that we will call swap. The state of swap consists of n k-bit binary numbers, $x_0, \ldots, x_{n-1}$. We assume that $n \leq 2^k$. The input to the machine is a number i, in the range $0, \ldots, n-1$. At each step, the machine swaps the values of x_i and $x_{i-1 \bmod n}$. In the initial state of the machine, we have, for all j, $x_j = j$. We would like to check the property $AG(x_0 \neq x_1)$, that is, the first two numbers are always different. What is interesting about this problem is that $AG(x_0 \neq x_1)$ is precisely the set of states such that all the x_i's are distinct. This is similar to a situation that occurs in real systems that rely on the fact that no resource is allocated to two different users.

We note that the BDD representing the fact that "all the x_i's are distinct" is exponential for any variable order. On the other hand, there is a cubic CNF representation for this proposition, of the form:

$$\bigwedge_i \bigwedge_{j>i} \bigwedge_v (x_i \neq v \vee x_j \neq v)$$

Of course, since our SAT-based algorithm does not compute a *minimal* CNF formula for AGp, we are not guaranteed to obtain a result of this size. However, it is plausible that the CNF-based technique could perform exponentially better than a BDD-based technique on this example.

In fact, this turns out to be the case. Figure 1 plots the run time performance of a BDD-based model checker and our SAT-based model checker in computing $AG(x_0 \neq x_1)$, as we increase n, letting $k = \lceil \log_2 n \rceil$. The BDD-based model checker was stopped at $n = 10$, having exhausted 250MB of memory. We note that in fact the BDD run time is increasing exponentially, while the time for the SAT-based model checker increases approximately as $n^{4.5}$. Similar results are also obtained using BDD's with a forward traversal approach. It appears therefore, that the CNF approach can be more efficient than binary decision diagrams in some cases.

Microprocessor Verification Benchmarks We now compare these two techniques on a more substantial set of benchmarks. These are publicly available model checking problems derived from the compositional verification of one unit of a commercial microprocessor design, using techniques describe in [10].[2] All of

---

[2]   The design is the PicoJava II (TM) design from Sun Microsystems, Inc. The RTL-level source code for this design is available from Sun Microsystems. The benchmark suit is described at http://www-cad.eecs.berkeley.edu/~kenmcmil, and can be generated from the source code using the Cadence SMV tool.

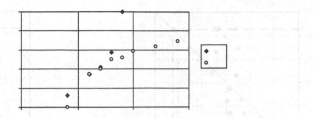

Fig. 1. Run time for SAT- and BDD-based model checkers on swap

the formulas to be checked in this benchmark suite are of the form AGp, where p is Boolean, and all are true in the initial states (*i.e.*, no counterexamples are generated).

These benchmark problems, as generated by the Cadence SMV system, contain a large number of functionally equivalent nodes. This is due partly to the fact that the logic in the RTL design description is unoptimized, and also to the fact that the abstraction steps performed by Cadence SMV can generate many redundant expressions. The benchmarks were preprocessed using a technique called "BDD sweeping" [11] to combine functionally equivalent nets, since this technique was found by Kuehlmann and Baumgartner to substantially improve the performance of SAT-based bounded model checking at little expense.[3]

In the algorithm for AGp, we also perform a lightweight optimization of the CNF formula that results from the quantifier elimination procedure. This procedure is based on a ZBDD representation of the clause set, and results in the elimination of some subsumed clauses, and resolution of some clause pairs (*i.e.*, it can resolve $a \vee b$ and $a \vee \neg b$ to a). This is done because the quantifier elimination procedure is observed to produce many redundant clauses. The time required for this optimization is generally small compared to the total run time, but it is not included in run time figures presented below, which are therefore slightly optimistic.

The left graph in figure 2 plots the performance of the SAT-based method against the performance of the BDD-based method. Points above the diagonal line indicate a faster run time for the BDD-based technique, while points below the line indicate a faster time for the SAT-based approach. A time of 1800 seconds indicates that a computation was stopped at 1800 seconds without completing. This time is indicated by the heavy dashed lines in the figure. In no case was a computation stopped because of memory exhaustion.

For reference, right graph compares the run times of the "backward" SAT-based approach against a forward traversal method using BDD's. This comparison is less direct, but it shows at least that the previous comparison is not a "straw man".

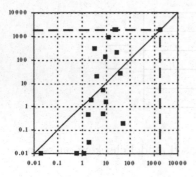
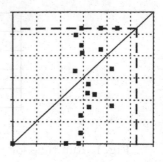

Fig. 2. Microprocessor verification benchmark

What we observe in this experiment is that, while the total run time is much smaller for the BDD-based technique, for most individual problems, the SAT-based method is faster (in some cases by two orders of magnitude). In the direct comparison, the SAT-based method performed better in 11 cases, while the BDD-based method performed better in 7 cases. However, the graph clearly shows that the variance in run times is greater for the SAT-based method than for the BDD-based method. Overall, this is a promising result, since there is likely to be much room for improvement in the SAT-based methods, especially given the highly inefficient implementation of the procedure that was used in the comparison. It suggests at the very least that it would be a good policy to devote a short time to model checking using the SAT-based method before trying the BDD-based approach.

7   Conclusion

We have observed that a traditional DLL-style SAT solver can be modified to perform quantifier elimination on Boolean formulas, producing a result in CNF. This in turn provides a basis for symbolic model checking that is not based on BDD's. This may provide an advantage over BDD-based model checking in the case when the CNF form is more compact than the BDD form (which may happen, for example, when resource allocation is involved), or if the SAT-based image computation step proves to be faster than the BDD-based approach. In a preliminary benchmark comparison against a standard BDD-based approach, the new approach appears promising, especially given the relative maturity of BDD-based model checkers.

In particular, there are several ways in which the current implementation might be improved. In the first place, as mentioned above, our implementation is highly inefficient, since it does not maintain the implication graph incrementally (no self-respecting SAT solver would do this!). Secondly, the BDD-based approach is using the "conjunctive partitioning" method, based on early quantification to simplify the representation of the transition relation. Without this technique, it is unlikely that any of the benchmarks could be completed. On the other hand, the SAT-based method is computing the reverse image in a single step. It is possible that computing the image incrementally, using the early quantification technique, would also improve the performance of the SAT-based method correspondingly. Finally, the method suffers from the fact that "blocking clauses" may only contain input variables. It is straightforward to construct examples that produce an exponentially large number of blocking clauses simply because quantified clauses cannot be learned that involve larger subformulas. In fact, an ordinary SAT solver that could only learn clauses over input variables would be quite inefficient. If a solution can be found for this problem, a dramatic improvement in performance might result.

References

1. P. A. Abdulla, P. Bjesse, and N. Een. Symbolic reachability analysis based on SAT-solvers. In TACAS 2000, volume 1785 of *LNCS*. Springer-Verlag, 2000. 251
2. A. Biere, A. Cimatti, E. M. Clarke, and Y. Zhu. Symbolic model checking without BDDs. In TACAS 1999, pages 193-207, 1999. 251
3. P. Bjesse. Symbolic model checking with sets of states represented as formulas. Technical Report CS-1999-100, Department of Computer Science, Chalmers technical university, March 1999. 251
4. R. E. Bryant. Graph-based algorithms for boolean function manipulation. *IEEE Transactions on Computers*, C-35(8), 1986. 250
5. J. R. Burch, E. M. Clarke, and D. E. Long. Symbolic model checking with partitioned transition relations. In A. Halaas and P. B. Denyer, editors, VLSI '91, Edinburgh, Scotland, August 1991. 259
6. J. R. Burch, E. M. Clarke, K. L. McMillan, D. L. Dill, and J. Hwang. Symbolic model checking: 10^{2^0} states and beyond. In *Proceedings of the Fifth Annual Symposium on Logic in Computer Science*, June 1990. 250
7. O. C., C. Berthet, and J.-C. Madre. Verification of synchronous sequential machines based on symbolic execution. In Joseph Sifakis, editor, *Automatic Verification Methods for Finite State Systems, International Workshop, Grenoble, France*, volume 407 of *Lecture Notes in Computer Science*. Springer-Verlag, June 1989. 250
8. E. M. Clarke and E. A. Emerson. Synthesis of synchronization skeletons for branching time temporal logic. In Dexter Kozen, editor, *Logic of Programs: Workshop*, volume 131 of *Lecture Notes in Computer Science*, Yorktown Heights, New York, May 1981. Springer-Verlag. 258
9. A. Gupta, Z. Yang, P. Ashar, and A. Gupta. SAT-based image computation with application in reachability analysis. In *FMCAD* 2000, pages 354-371, 2000. 251
10. R. Jhala and K. L. McMillan. Microarchitecture verification by compositional model checking. 2001. 260
11. A. Kuehlmann and F. Krohm. Equivalence checking using cuts and heaps. In *Design Automation Conf.*, pages 263-268, 1997. 261
12. K. L. McMillan. Symbolic *Model Checking*. Kluwer, 1993. 258

13. M. W. Moskewicz, C. F. Madigan, Y. Z., L. Z., and S. Malik. Chaff: Engineering an efficient SAT solver. In *Design Automation Conference,* pages 530-535, 2001. 252, 259
14. R. Rudell. Dynamic variable ordering for binary decision diagrams. In *Proc. Intl. Conf. on Computer-Aided Design,* pages 42-47, 1993. 259
15. M. Sheeran, S. Singh, and G. Stalmarck. Checking safety properties using induction and a sat-solver. In *Formal Methods in Computer Aided Design,* 2000. 251
16. J. P. M. Silva and K. A. Sakallah. Grasp-a new search algorithm for satisfiability. In *Proceedings of the International Conference on Computer-Aided Design,* November 1996, 1996. 252
17. P. F. Williams, A. Biere, E. M. Clarke, and A. Gupta. Combining decision diagrams and SAT procedures for efficient symbolic model checking. In *Computer Aided Verification,* pages 124-138, 2000. 251

SAT Based Abstraction-Refinement Using ILP and Machine Learning Techniques[*]

Edmund Clarke[1], Anubhav Gupta[1], James Kukula[2], and Ofer Strichman[1]

[1] Computer Science, Carnegie Mellon University, Pittsburgh, PA
{emc,anubhav,ofers}@cs.cmu.edu
[2] Synopsys, Beaverton, OR
kukula@synopsys.com

Abstract. We describe new techniques for model checking in the counterexample guided abstraction/refinement framework. The abstraction phase 'hides' the logic of various variables, hence considering them as inputs. This type of abstraction may lead to 'spurious' counterexamples, i.e. traces that can not be simulated on the original (concrete) machine. We check whether a counterexample is real or spurious with a SAT checker. We then use a combination of Integer Linear Programming (ILP) and machine learning techniques for refining the abstraction based on the counterexample. The process is repeated until either a real counterexample is found or the property is verified. We have implemented these techniques on top of the model checker NuSMV and the SAT solver Chaff. Experimental results prove the viability of these new techniques.

1 Introduction

While state of the art model checkers can verify circuits with several hundred latches, many industrial circuits are at least an order of magnitude larger. Various conservative abstraction techniques can be used to bridge this gap. Such abstraction techniques must preserve all the behaviors of the concrete system, but may introduce behaviors that are not present originally. Thus, if a universal property (i.e. an ACTL* property) is true in the abstract system, it will also be true in the concrete system. On the other hand, if a universal property is false in the abstract system, it may still be true in the concrete system. In this case, none of the behaviors that violate the property in the abstract system can be reproduced in the concrete system. Counterexamples corresponding to these behaviors are said to be *spurious*. When such a counterexample is found, the abstraction can be refined in order to eliminate the spurious behavior. This

[*] This research was sponsored by the Semiconductor Research Corporation (SRC) under contract no. 99-TJ-684, the National Science Foundation (NSF) under grant no. CCR-9803774, the Office of Naval Research (ONR), and the Naval Research Laboratory (NRL) under contract no. N00014-01-1-0796. The views and conclusions contained in this document are those of the author and should not be interpreted as representing the official policies, either expressed or implied, of SRC, NSF, ONR, NRL, the U.S. government or any other entity.

D. Brinksma and K. G. Larsen (Eds.): CAV 2002, LNCS 2404, pp. 265–279, 2002.
© Springer-Verlag Berlin Heidelberg 2002

process is repeated until either a real counterexample is found, or the abstract system satisfies the property. In the latter case, we know that the concrete system satisfies the property as well, since the abstraction is conservative.

There are many known techniques, some automatic and some manual, for generating the initial abstraction and for abstraction/refinement. The automatic techniques are more relevant to this paper, not only because our method is fully automatic, but also because of the clear practical advantage of automation. Our methodology is based on an iterative abstraction/refinement process. Abstraction is performed by selecting a set of latches or variables and making them *invisible*, i.e., they are treated as inputs. In each iteration, we check whether the abstract system satisfies the specification with a standard OBDD-based symbolic model checker. If a counterexample is reported by the model checker, we try to simulate it on the concrete system with a fast SAT solver. In other words, we generate and solve a SAT instance that is satisfiable if and only if the counterexample is real. If the instance is not satisfiable, we look for the *failure state*, which is the last state in the longest prefix of the counterexample that is still satisfiable. Note that this process can not be easily performed with a standard circuit simulator, because the abstract counter example does not include values for all inputs.

We use the failure state in order to refine the abstraction. The abstract system has transitions from the failure state that do not exist in the concrete system. We eliminate these transitions by refining the abstraction, i.e., by making some variables visible that were previously invisible. The problem of selecting a small set of variables to make visible is one of the main issues that we address in this paper. It is important to find a small set in order to keep the size of the abstract state space manageable. This problem can be reduced to a problem of separating two sets of states (abstraction unites concrete states, and therefore refining an abstraction is the opposite operation, i.e., separation of states). For realistic systems, generating these sets is not feasible, both explicitly and symbolically. Moreover, the minimum separation problem is known to be NP-hard [ ]. We combine *sampling* with Integer Linear Programming (ILP) and machine learning to handle this problem. Machine learning algorithms are successfully used in a wide range of problem domains like data mining and other problems where it is necessary to extract implicit information from a large database of samples[ ]. These algorithms exploit ideas from a diverse set of disciplines, including information theory, statistics and complexity theory.

The closest work to the current one that we are aware of was described in [ ]. Like the current work, they also use an automatic, iterative abstraction/refinement procedure that is guided by the counterexample, and they also try to eliminate the counterexample by solving the state-separation problem. But there are three main differences between the two methods. First, their abstraction is based on replacing predicates of the program with new input variables, while our abstraction is performed by making some of the variables invisible (thus, we hide the entire logic that defines these variables). The advantage of our approach is that computing a minimal abstraction function becomes easy.

Secondly, checking whether the counterexample is real or spurious was performed in their work symbolically, using OBDDs. We do this stage with a SAT solver, which for this particular task is extremely efficient (due to the large number of solutions to the SAT instance). Thirdly, they derive the refinement symbolically. Since finding the coarsest refinement is NP-hard, they present a polynomial procedure that in general computes a sub-optimal solution. For some well defined cases the same procedure computes the optimal refinement. We, on the other hand, avoid the complexity by considering only samples of the states sets, which we compute explicitly. By doing so we also pay the price of optimality: this procedure yields a refinement step which is not necessarily optimal (i.e., we do not necessarily find the smallest number of invisible variables that should become visible in order to eliminate the counterexample). Yet we suggest a method for efficient sampling, which in most cases allows us to efficiently compute an optimal refinement.

The work of [7] should also be mentioned in this context, since it is very similar to [5], the main difference being the refinement algorithm: rather than computing the refinement by analyzing the abstract failure state, they combine a theorem prover with a greedy algorithm that finds a small set of previously abstracted predicates that eliminate the counterexample. They add this set of predicates as a new constraint to the abstract model.

Previous work on abstraction by making variables invisible (this technique was used under different names in the past) include the localization reduction of Kurshan [8] and many others (see, for example [1,9]). The localization reduction follows the typical abstraction/refinement iterative process. It starts by making all but the property variables invisible. When a spurious counterexample is identified, it refines the system by making more variables visible. The variables made visible are selected according to the variable dependency graph and information that is derived from the counterexample. The candidates in the next refinement step are those invisible variables that are adjacent on the variable dependency graph to currently visible variables. Choosing among these variables is done by extracting information from the counterexample. Another relevant work is described in [14]. They use 3-valued simulation to simulate the counterexample on the concrete model and identify the invisible variables whose values in the concrete model conflict with the counterexample. Variables are chosen from this set of invisible variables by various ranking heuristics. For example, like localization, they prefer variables that are close on the variable dependency graph to the currently visible variables.

The rest of the paper is organized as follows. In the next section we briefly give the technical background of abstraction and refinement in model checking. In section 3 we describe our counterexample guided abstraction/refinement framework. We elaborate in this section on how the counterexample is being checked and how we refine the abstraction. We also describe refinement as a learning problem. In sections 4 and 5 we elaborate on our separation techniques. These techniques are combined with the efficient sampling technique, which is described in section 6. We give experimental results in section 7, which proves the viability of our methods comparing to a state of the art model checker (Cadence SMV). We discuss conclusions and future work in section 8.

2   Abstraction in Model Checking

We start with a brief description of the use of abstraction in model checking (for more details refer to [ ]). Consider a program with a set of variables $V = \{x_1, \ldots, x_n\}$, where each variable x_i ranges over a non-empty domain D_{x_i}. Each state s of the program assigns values to the variables in V. The set of all possible states for the program is $S = D_{x_1} \times \cdots \times D_{x_n}$. The program is modeled by a transition system $M = (S, I, R)$ where

1. S is the set of states.
2. $I \subseteq S$ is the set of initial states.
3. $R \subseteq S \times S$ is the set of transitions.

We use the notation $I(s)$ to denote the fact that a state s is in I, and we write $R(s_1, s_2)$ if the transition between the states s_1 and s_2 is in R.

An abstraction function h for the system is given by a surjection $h : S \to \hat{S}$, which maps a concrete state in S to an abstract state in $\hat{S}$. Given a concrete state $s_i \in S$, we denote by $h(s_i)$ the abstract state to which it is mapped by h. Accordingly, we denote by $h^{-1}(\hat{s})$ the set of states s such that $h(s) = \hat{s}$.

Definition 1. *The* minimal abstract transition system $\hat{M} = (\hat{S}, \hat{I}, \hat{R})$ *corresponding to a transition system* $M = (S, I, R)$ *and an abstraction function h is defined as follows:*

1. $\hat{S} = \{\hat{s} \mid \exists s. \ s \in S \wedge h(s) = \hat{s}\}$.
2. $\hat{I} = \{\hat{s} \mid \exists s. \ I(s) \wedge h(s) = \hat{s}\}$
3. $\hat{R} = \{(\hat{s}_1, \hat{s}_2) \mid \exists s_1. \ \exists s_2. \ R(s_1, s_2) \wedge h(s_1) = \hat{s}_1 \wedge h(s_2) = \hat{s}_2\}$

Intuitively, minimality means that $\hat{M}$ can start in state $h(s)$ if and only if M can start in state s , and $\hat{M}$ can transition from $h(s)$ to $h(s')$ if and only if M can transition from s to s'.

For simplicity, we restrict our discussion to model checking of **AG**p formulas, where p is a non-temporal propositional formula. The theory can be extended to handle any safety property, because such formulas have counterexamples that are finite paths.

Definition 2. *A propositional formula p respects an abstraction function h if for all $s \in S$, $h(s) \models p \Rightarrow s \models p$.*

The essence of conservative abstraction is the following preservation theorem[ ], which is stated without proof.

Theorem 1. *Let $\hat{M}$ be an abstraction of M corresponding to the abstraction function h, and p be a propositional formula that respects h. Then $\hat{M} \models$ **AG**$p \Rightarrow M \models$ **AG**p*

The converse of the above theorem is not true, however. Even if the abstract model invalidates the specification, the concrete model may still satisfy the specification. In this case, the abstract counterexample generated by the model checker is *spurious*, i.e. it does not correspond to a concrete path. The abstraction function is too coarse to validate the specification, and we need to refine it.

Definition 3. *Given a transition system $M = (S, I, R)$ and an abstraction function h, h' is a* refinement *of h if*

1. *For all $s_1, s_2 \in S$, $h'(s_1) = h'(s_2)$ implies $h(s_1) = h(s_2)$.*
2. *There exists $s_1, s_2 \in S$ such that $h(s_1) = h(s_2)$ and $h'(s_1) \neq h'(s_2)$.*

3   Abstraction-Refinement

Based on the above definitions, we now describe our *counterexample guided abstraction refinement* procedure. Given a transition system M and a safety property φ:

1. Generate an initial abstraction function h.
2. Model check $\hat{M}$. If $\hat{M} \models \varphi$, then $M \models \varphi$. Return TRUE.
3. If $\hat{M} \not\models \varphi$, check the counterexample on the concrete model. If the counterexample is real, $M \not\models \varphi$. Return FALSE.
4. Refine h, and go to step 2.

The above procedure is complete for finite state systems. Since each refinement step partitions at least one abstract state, the number of loop iterations is bounded by the number of concrete states. In the next subsections, we explain in more detail how we perform each step.

3.1   Defining an Abstraction Function

We partition the set of variables V into two sets: the set of *visible* variables which we denote by $\mathcal{V}$ and the set of *invisible* variables which we denote by $\mathcal{I}$. Intuitively, $\mathcal{V}$ corresponds to the part of the system that is currently believed to be important for verifying the property. The abstraction function h abstracts out the irrelevant details, namely the invisible variables. The initial abstraction in step 1 and the refinement in step 4 correspond to different partitions of the set of variables. As an initial abstraction, $\mathcal{V}$ includes the variables in the property φ. In each refinement step, we move variables from $\mathcal{I}$ to $\mathcal{V}$, as we will explain in sub-section 3.3.

More formally, let $s(x)$, $x \in V$ denote the value of variable x in a state s. Given a set of variables $U = \{u_1, \ldots, u_p\}$, $U \subseteq V$, s^U denotes the portion of s that corresponds to the variables in U, i.e. $s^U = (s(u_1)\ldots s(u_p))$. Let $\mathcal{V} = \{v_1, \ldots, v_k\}$. The partitioning defines our abstraction function $h : S \to \hat{S}$. The set of abstract states is $\hat{S} = D_{v_1} \times \cdots \times D_{v_k}$ and the abstraction function is simply $h(s) = s^{\mathcal{V}}$.

Given h, we need to compute the minimal abstraction. For an arbitrary system M and abstraction function h, it is often too expensive or impossible to construct the minimal abstraction $\hat{M}[ ]$. However, our abstraction function allows us to compute $\hat{M}$ efficiently for systems where the transition relation R is in a functional form, e.g. sequential circuits. For these systems, $\hat{M}$ can be computed directly from the program text, by removing the logic that defines the invisible variables and treating them as inputs.

3.2   Checking the Counterexample

For safety properties, the counterexample generated by the model checker is a path $\langle \hat{s}_1, \hat{s}_2, \ldots \hat{s}_m \rangle$. The set of concrete paths that corresponds to this counterexample is given by

$$\psi_m = \{\langle s_1 \ldots s_m \rangle \mid I(s_1) \wedge \bigwedge_{i=1}^{m-1} R(s_i, s_{i+1}) \wedge \bigwedge_{i=1}^{m} h(s_i) = \hat{s}_i\} \qquad (1)$$

According to section 3.1, $h(s_i)$ is simply a projection of s_i to the visible variables. The right-most conjunct is therefore a restriction of the visible variables in step i to their values in the counterexample.

The counterexample is spurious if and only if the set ψ_m is empty. We check for that by solving ψ_m with a SAT solver. This formula is very similar in structure to the formulas that arise in Bounded Model Checking(BMC)[ ]. However, ψ_m is easier to solve because the path is restricted to the counterexample. Most model checkers treat inputs as latches, and therefore the counterexample includes assignments to inputs. While simulating the counterexample, we also restrict the values of the (original) inputs that are part of the definition (lie on the RHS) of the visible variables, which further simplifies the formula.

If a satisfying assignment is found, we know that the counterexample corresponds to a concrete path, which means that we found a real bug. Otherwise, we try to look for the 'failure' index f, i.e. the maximal index f, $f < m$, such that ψ_f is satisfiable. Given f, $\langle \hat{s}_1, \ldots \hat{s}_f \rangle$ is the longest prefix of the counterexample that corresponds to a concrete path. Our implementation sequentially searches in the range $1..m$ for the highest value f such that ψ_f is satisfiable. For long counterexample traces, we also have an option of performing a binary search over this range, in which case the number of SAT instances we solve is bounded by $\log m$.

3.3   Refining the Abstraction

As before, let f denote the failure index. Let D denote the set of all states d_f such that there exists some $\langle d_1 \ldots d_f \rangle$ in ψ_f. We call D the set of *deadend* states. By definition, there is no concrete transition from D to $h^{-1}(\hat{s}_{f+1})$.

Since there is an abstract transition from $\hat{s}_f$ to $\hat{s}_{f+1}$, there is a non-empty set of transitions ϕ_f from $h^{-1}(\hat{s}_f)$ to $h^{-1}(\hat{s}_{f+1})$ that agree with the counterexample.

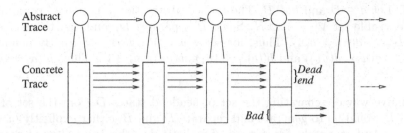

Fig. 1. A spurious counterexample corresponds to a concrete path that 'breaks' in the failing state. The failing state unites concrete 'deadend' and 'bad' states

The set of transitions ϕ_f is defined as follows:

$$\phi_f = \{\langle s_f, s_{f+1}\rangle \mid R(s_f, s_{f+1}) \wedge h(s_f) = \hat{s}_f \wedge h(s_{f+1}) = \hat{s}_{f+1}\} \tag{2}$$

Given the definition of h, ϕ_f represents all concrete paths from step f to step $f + 1$, where the visible variables in these steps are restricted to their values in the counterexample. Let B denote the set of all states b_f such that there exists some $\langle b_f, b_{f+1}\rangle$ in ϕ_f. We call B the set of *bad* states (see figure 1).

The counterexample exists because there is an abstract transition from s_f to s_{f+1} that does not correspond to any concrete transition. The transition exists because the deadend and bad states lie in the same abstract state. This suggests a mechanism to refine the abstraction. The abstraction h is refined to a new abstraction h' such that $\forall d \in D, \forall b \in B\ (h'(d) \neq h'(b))$. The new abstraction puts the deadend and bad states into separate abstract states and therefore eliminates the spurious transition from the abstract system.

3.4   Refinement by Separation and Learning

Let $S = \{s_1...s_m\}$ and $T = \{t_1...t_n\}$ be two sets of states (binary vectors) of size l, representing assignments to a set of variables W.

Definition 4. (The state separation problem) *Find a minimal set of variables* $U = \{u_1...u_k\}$, $U \subset W$, *such that for each pair of states* (s_i, t_j), $1 \leq i \leq m$, $1 \leq j \leq n$, *there exists a variable* $u_r \in U$ *such that* $s_i(u_r) \neq t_j(u_r)$.

Let D_I and B_I denote the restriction of D and B, respectively, to their invisible parts, i.e., $D_I = \{s^I | s \in D\}$ and $B_I = \{s^I | s \in B\}$. Let $H \in \mathcal{I}$ be a set of variables that separates D_I from B_I. The refinement is obtained by adding H to $\mathcal{V}$. Minimality of H is not crucial, rather it is a matter of efficiency. Smaller sets of visible variables make it easier to model check the abstract system, but can also be harder to find. In fact, it can be shown that computing the minimal separating set is NP-hard[5].

Lemma 1. *The new abstraction function h' separated D from B in the abstract system.*

Proof. Let $d \in D$ and $b \in B$. The refined abstraction function h' corresponds to the visible set $\mathcal{V}' = \mathcal{V} \cup H$. Since H separates D_I and B_I, there exists a $u \in H$ s.t. $d(u) \neq b(u)$. Thus, for some $u \in \mathcal{V}'$, $d(u) \neq b(u)$. By definition, $h'(d) = (d(u_1)...d(u_k))$ and $h'(b) = (b(u_1)...b(u_k))$, $u_i \in \mathcal{V}'$. Thus, $h'(d) \neq h'(b)$.
□

The naive way of separating the set of deadend states D from the set of bad states B would be to generate and separate D and B, either explicitly or symbolically. Unfortunately, for systems of realistic size, this is usually not possible. For all but the simplest examples, the number of states in D and B is too large to enumerate explicitly. For systems with moderate complexity, these sets can be computed symbolically with BDDs. However, even this is not possible for larger systems. Moreover, even if it were possible to generate D and B, it would still be computationally expensive to identify the separating variables.

Instead, we select *samples* from D and B and try to infer the separating variables for the entire sets from these samples. Of course, there is a tradeoff between the computational complexity of generating the samples, and the quality of the separating variables. Without a complete separation of D and B it can not be guaranteed that the counterexample will be eliminated. However, our algorithm is complete, because the counterexample will eventually be eliminated in subsequent refinement iterations. Our experience shows that state of the art SAT solvers like Chaff[11] can generate many samples in a short amount of time. The fact that D and B are large makes it relatively easy for SAT solvers to find satisfying assignments to equations 1 and 2 compared to typical SAT instances of similar size.

The idea of learning from samples has been studied extensively in the machine learning literature. A number of learning models and algorithms have been proposed. In the next two sections, we describe the techniques that we used to separate sets of samples of deadend and bad states, denoted by S_{D_I} and S_{B_I} respectively.

4   Separation as an Integer Linear Programming Problem

A formulation of the problem of separating S_{D_I} from S_{B_I} as an Integer Linear Programming (ILP) problem is depicted in Figure 2.

$$\text{Min } \sum_{i=1}^{|\mathcal{I}|} v_i$$

$$\text{subject to: } (\forall s \in S_{D_I})\, (\forall t \in S_{B_I}) \sum_{\substack{1 \leq i \leq |\mathcal{I}|, \\ s(v_i) \neq t(v_i)}} v_i \geq 1$$

Fig. 2. State separation with integer linear programming

The value of each integer variable[1] $v_1...v_{|\mathcal{I}|}$ in the ILP problem is interpreted as: $v_i = 1$ if and only if v_i is in the separating set. Every constraint corresponds to a pair of states (s_i, t_j), stating that at least one of the variables that separates (distinguishes) between the two states should be selected. Thus, there are $|S_{D_I}| \times |S_{B_I}|$ constraints.

Example 1. Consider the following two pairs of states: $s_1 = (0,1,0,1), s_2 = (1,1,1,0)$ and $t_1 = (1,1,1,1), t_2 = (0,0,0,1)$. The corresponding ILP problem will be

$$\text{Min } \sum_{i=1}^4 v_i$$
$$\text{subject to:}$$

$v_1 + v_3$	≥ 1	/* Separating s_1 from t_1 */
v_2	≥ 1	/* Separating s_1 from t_2 */
v_4	≥ 1	/* Separating s_2 from t_1 */
$v_1 + v_2 + v_3 + v_4$	≥ 1	/* Separating s_2 from t_2 */

The optimal value of the objective function in this case is 3, corresponding to one of the two optimal solutions (v_1, v_2, v_4) and (v_3, v_2, v_4).

5 Separation Using Decision Tree Learning

The ILP-based separation algorithm outputs the minimal separating set. However, the algorithm has a high complexity and cannot handle a large number of variables or samples. In this section, we formulate the separation problem as a Decision Tree Learning(DTL) problem, which is polynomial both in the number of variables and the number of samples.

Learning with decision trees is one of the most widely used and practical methods for approximating discrete-valued functions. A DTL algorithm inputs a set of examples and generates a decision tree that classifies them. An example is described by a set of attributes and the corresponding classification. Each internal node in the tree specifies a test on some attribute, and each branch descending from that node corresponds to one of the possible values for that attribute. Each leaf in the tree corresponds to a classification.

Data is classified by starting at the root node of the decision tree, testing the attribute specified by this node, and then moving down the tree branch corresponding to the value of the attribute. The process is repeated for the subtree rooted at the branch until one of the leafs is reached, which is labeled with the classification. The problem of separating S_{D_I} from S_{B_I} can be formulated as a DTL problem as follows:

- The attributes correspond to the invisible variables.
- The classifications are $+1$ and -1, corresponding to S_{D_I} and S_{B_I}.
- The examples are S_{D_I} labeled $+1$, and S_{B_I} labeled -1.

---

[1] Although the ILP problem is stated for integer variables, the constraints and objective function guarantees that their value will be either 0 or 1. Thus, they can be thought of as Boolean variables.

We generate a decision tree for this problem. The separating set that we output contains all the variables present at an internal nodes of the decision tree.

Lemma 2. *The above algorithm outputs a separating set for S_{D_I} and S_{B_I}.*

Proof. Let $d \in S_{D_I}$ and $b \in S_{B_I}$. The decision tree will classify d as $+1$ and b as -1. So, there exists a node n in the decision tree, labeled with a variable v, such that $d(v) \neq b(v)$. By construction, v lies in the output set.   □

Example 2. Going back to example 1, the corresponding DTL problem has 4 attributes (v_1, v_2, v_3, v_4) and as always, two classifications $(+1, -1)$. The set of examples is $E = \{((0,1,0,1), +1)$, $((1,1,1,0), +1)$, $((1,1,1,1), -1)$, $((0,0,0,1), -1)\}$. The following tree corresponds to the separating set (v_1, v_2, v_4).

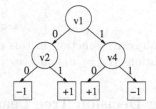

A number of algorithms have been developed for learning decision trees, e.g. ID3[12], C4.5[13]. All these algorithms essentially perform a simple top-down greedy search through the space of possible decision trees. We implemented a simplified version of the ID3 algorithm, which is described in Figure 3[10]. At each recursion, the algorithm has to pick an attribute to test at the root. We need a measure of the quality of an attribute. We start with defining a quantity called *entropy*, which is a commonly used notion in information theory. Given a set S containing $n_\oplus$ positive examples and $n_\ominus$ negative examples, the entropy of S is given by:

$$Entropy(S) = -p_\oplus log_2 p_\oplus - p_\ominus log_2 p_\ominus$$

where $p_\oplus = (n_\oplus)/(n_\oplus + n_\ominus)$ and $p_\ominus = (n_\ominus)/(n_\oplus + n_\ominus)$. Intuitively, entropy characterizes the variety in a set of examples. The maximum value for entropy

---

DecTree(Examples, Attributes)

1. Create a *Root* node for the tree.
2. If all examples are classified the same, return *Root* with this classification.
3. Let $A = BestAttribute(Examples, Attributes)$. Label *Root* with attribute A.
4. For $i \in \{0, 1\}$, let $Examples_i$ be the subset of *Examples* having value i for A.
5. For $i \in \{0, 1\}$, add an i branch to the *Root* pointing to subtree generated by $Dectree(Examples_i, Attributes - \{A\})$.
6. Return *Root*.

Fig. 3. Decision tree learning algorithm

is 1, which corresponds to a collection that has an equal number of positive and negative examples. The minimum value of entropy is 0, which corresponds to a collection with only positive or only negative examples. We can now define the quality of an attribute A by the reduction in entropy on partitioning the examples using A. This measure, called the *information gain* is defined as follows:

$$Gain(E, A) = Entropy(E) - (|E_0|/|E|) \cdot Entropy(E_0) - (|E_1|/|E|) \cdot Entropy(E_1)$$

where E_0 and E_1 are the subsets of examples having the value 0 and 1, respectively, for attribute A. The *BestAttribute(Examples, Attributes)* procedure returns the attribute $A \in Attributes$ that has the highest $Gain(Examples, A)$.

Example 3. We illustrate the working of our algorithm with an example. Continuing with our previous example, we calculate the gains for the attributes at the top node of the decision tree.

$$Entropy(E) = -(2/4)log_2(2/4) - (2/4)log_2(2/4) = 1.00$$
$$Gain(E, v_1) = 1 - (2/4) \cdot Entropy(E_{v_1=0}) - (2/4) \cdot Entropy(v_1=1) = 0.00$$
$$Gain(E, v_2) = 1 - (1/4) \cdot Entropy(E_{v_2=0}) - (3/4) \cdot Entropy(v_2=1) = 0.31$$
$$Gain(E, v_3) = 1 - (2/4) \cdot Entropy(E_{v_3=0}) - (2/4) \cdot Entropy(v_3=1) = 0.00$$
$$Gain(E, v_4) = 1 - (1/4) \cdot Entropy(E_{v_4=0}) - (3/4) \cdot Entropy(v_4=1) = 0.31$$

The *DecTree* algorithm will pick v_2 or v_4 to label the *Root*.

6   Efficient Sampling of States

Sampling D_I and B_I does not have to be arbitrary. As we now show, it is possible to direct the search for samples that contain more information than others. Let $\delta(D_I, B_I)$ denote the minimal separating set for D_I and B_I. Finding $\delta(D_I, B_I)$ by explicitly computing D_I and B_I and separating them is too computationally expensive, because both the size of these sets and the optimal separation techniques are worst-case exponential. We therefore look for samples S_{D_I} and S_{B_I} that are small enough to compute and separate, and, on the other hand, maintain $\delta(S_{D_I}, S_{B_I}) = \delta(D_I, B_I)$. Finding these sets is what we refer to as efficient sampling.

We suggest an iterative algorithm for efficient sampling. Let *SepSet* denote the current separating set. Initially, $SepSet = \emptyset$. In each step, the algorithm finds samples that are not separable by *SepSet* that was computed in the previous iteration. Computing a new pair of dead-end and bad states that are not separable by *SepSet*, can be done by solving $\Phi(SepSet)$, as defined below:

$$\Phi(SepSet) \doteq \psi_f \wedge \phi'_f \wedge \bigwedge_{v_i \in SepSet} v_i = v'_i \tag{3}$$

where ψ_f and ϕ_f are the formulas representing the deadend and bad states as defined in equations 1 and 2. The prime symbol over ϕ_f denotes the fact that we replace each variable $v \in \phi_f$ with a new variable v' (note that otherwise, by

```
SepSet = ∅;
i = 0;
repeat forever {
    If Φ(SepSet) is satisfiable, derive dᵢ and bᵢ from solution; else
exit;
    SepSet = δ(⋃ⱼ₌₀ⁱ{dⱼ}, ⋃ⱼ₌₀ⁱ{bⱼ});
    i = i + 1; }
```

Fig. 4. Algorithm *Sample-and-Separate* implements efficient sampling by iteratively searching for states that are not separable by the current separating set

definition, the conjunction of ψ_f with ϕ_f is unsatisfiable). The right-most clause in the above formula guarantees that the new samples of deadend and bad states are not separable by the current separating set.

Algorithm *Sample-and-Separate*, described in Figure 6, uses formula 3 to compute the minimal separating set of D_I and B_I without explicitly computing or separating them. In each step i, it finds samples $d_i \in D_I$ and $b_i \in B_I$ that are not separable by the current separating set *SepSet*. It then re-computes *SepSet* for the union of sets that were computed up to the current iteration. By repeating this process until no such samples exist, it guarantees that the resulting separating set separates D_I from B_I. Note that the size of *SepSet* can either increase or stay unchanged in each iteration.

The algorithm in Figure 6 finds a single solution to $\Phi(SepSet)$ and hence a single pair of states d_i and b_i. However, the size of each sample can be larger. Larger samples may reduce the number of iterations, but also require more time to derive and separate. The optimal number of new samples in each iteration depends on various factors, like the efficiency of the SAT solver, the separation technique and the examined model. Our implementation lets the user control this process by adjusting two parameters: the number of samples generated in each iteration, and the maximum number of iterations.

7   Experimental Results

We implemented our framework inside NuSMV[4]. We use NuSMV as a front-end, for parsing SMV files and for generating abstractions. However, for actual model checking, we use Cadence SMV, which implements techniques like cone-of-influence reduction, cut-points, etc. We implemented a variant of the ID3[12] algorithm to generate decision trees. We use a public domain LP solver[9] to solve our integer linear programs. We use Chaff[11] as our SAT solver. Some modifications were made to Chaff to efficiently generate multiple state samples in a single run. Our experiments were performed on the "IU" family of circuits, which are various abstractions of an interface control circuit from Synopsys. All experiments were performed on a 1.5GHz Dual Athlon machine with 3Gb RAM

Circuit	SMV		Sampling - ILP				Sampling - DTL				Eff. Samp. - DTL			
	Time	BDD	Time	BDD	S	L	Time	BDD	S	L	Time	BDD	S	L
$IU30$	0.7	116909	0.1	1731	0	1	0.1	1731	0	1	**0.1**	1731	0	1
$IU35$	0.6	149496	0.1	2357	0	1	0.1	2357	0	1	**0.1**	2357	0	1
$IU40$	1.2	225544	6.3	21249	3	4	0.9	18830	5	6	**0.6**	11028	2	3
$IU45$	37.5	2554520	6.1	17702	3	4	1.1	18847	5	6	**0.7**	10634	2	3
$IU50$	23.3	2094723	19.7	100647	13	14	**9.8**	90691	13	14	24.0	1274240	4	17
$IU55$	-	-	-	-	-	-	2072	51703825	6	9	**3.0**	64386	1	6
$IU60$	-	-	7.8	183811	4	7	7.8	183811	4	7	**4.5**	109393	1	6
$IU65$	-	-	7.9	192806	4	7	7.9	192806	4	7	**3.8**	47546	1	5
$IU70$	-	-	8.1	192806	4	7	8.2	192806	4	7	**3.8**	47546	1	5
$IU75$	102.9	7068752	32.0	142546	9	10	24.5	397620	13	14	**24.1**	550872	2	7
$IU80$	603.7	39989682	31.7	215404	9	10	44.0	341018	13	14	**24.1**	186662	2	7
$IU85$	2832	76232788	33.1	230979	9	10	44.6	443785	13	14	**25.2**	198359	2	7
$IU90$	-	-	33.0	230979	9	10	44.6	443785	13	14	**25.4**	198359	2	7

Fig. 5. Model checking results for property 1

and running Linux. No pre-computed variable ordering files were used in the experiments.

The results are presented in Figure 5 and Figure 6. The two tables correspond to two different properties. We compared the following techniques: 1) 'SMV': Cadence SMV, 2) 'Sampling-ILP': Sampling, separation using Integer Linear Programming, 50 samples per refinement iteration, 3) 'Sampling-DTL': Sampling, separation using Decision Tree Learning, 50 samples per refinement iteration, 4) 'Eff. Samp.-DTL': Efficient sampling, separation using Decision Tree Learning. For each run, we measured the total running time ('Time'), the maximum number of BDD nodes allocated ('BDD'), the number of refinement steps ('S'), and the number of latches in the final abstraction ('L'). The original number of latches in each circuit in indicated in its name. A '$-$' symbol indicates that we ran out of memory. We could not solve Property 2 for circuits $IU55...IU70$ with any of the methods.

The experiments indicate that our technique expedites standard model checking, both in terms of execution time and required memory. As predicted, the number of iterations is generally reduced when either ILP or efficient sampling is applied. In most cases, this translates to a reduction in the total execution time. There were cases, however, when smaller sets of separating variables resulted in larger BDDs. Such 'noise' in the experimental results is typical of BDD based techniques.

8   Conclusions and Future Work

We have presented an automatic counterexample guided abstraction-refinement algorithm that uses SAT, ILP and techniques from machine learning. Our algorithm outperforms standard model checking, both in terms of execution time and memory requirements. Our refinement technique is very general and can be extended to a large variety of systems. For example, in conjunction with predicate abstraction, we can apply our techniques to software model checking. There are several future research directions to our work. We are currently exploring

Circuit	SMV		Sampling - ILP				Sampling - DTL				Eff. Samp. - DTL			
	Time	BDD	Time	BDD	S	L	Time	BDD	S	L	Time	BDD	S	L
*IU*30	7.3	324268	8.0	113189	3	20	7.5	113189	3	20	**6.5**	113189	3	20
*IU*35	19.1	679224	11.8	186097	4	21	12.7	186097	4	21	**11.0**	186097	4	21
*IU*40	53.6	1100956	25.9	260299	6	23	19.0	207199	5	22	**16.1**	207199	5	22
*IU*45	226.1	6060256	28.3	411952	5	22	25.3	411952	5	22	**22.1**	411952	5	22
*IU*50	1754	25102082	160.4	2046981	13	32	**85.1**	605501	10	27	15120	3791826	7	31
*IU*75	-	-	1080	3716255	21	38	586.7	1178039	16	33	**130.5**	1050007	5	26
*IU*80	-	-	1136	3378860	21	38	552.5	1158076	16	33	**153.4**	1009030	5	26
*IU*85	-	-	1162	3493143	21	38	581.2	1272915	16	33	**167.7**	1079043	5	26
*IU*90	-	-	965	3712477	20	37	583.3	1271915	16	33	**167.1**	1079043	5	26

Fig. 6. Model checking results for property 2

criteria other than the size of the separating set for characterizing a good refinement. We also want to explore other machine learning techniques to solve the state separation problem.

References

1. F. Balarin and A. Sangiovanni-Vinventelli. An iterative approah to language containment. In C. Courcoubetis, editor, *Proc. 5th Intl. Conference on Computer Aided Verification (CAV'94)*, volume 697 of *Lect. Notes in Comp. Sci.*, pages 29–40. Springer-Verlag, 1993. 267
2. M. Berkelaar. lpsolve, version 2.0. Eindhoven Univ. Tech., The Netherlands. 276
3. A. Biere, A. Cimatti, E. Clarke, and Y. Zhu. Symbolic model checking without BDDs. In *Proc. of the Workshop on Tools and Algorithms for the Construction and Analysis of Systems (TACAS'99)*, LNCS. Springer-Verlag, 1999. 270
4. A. Cimatti, E. Clarke, F. Giunchiglia, and M. Roveri. NuSMV: a new symbolic model checker. *Int. Journal of Software Tools for Technology Transfer (STTT)*, 1998. 276
5. E. Clarke, O. Grumberg, S. Jha, Y. Lu, and H. Veith. Counterexample-guided abstraction refinement. In E. A. Emerson and A. P. Sistla, editors, *Proc. 12th Intl. Conference on Computer Aided Verification (CAV'00)*, volume 1855 of *Lect. Notes in Comp. Sci.* Springer-Verlag, 2000. 266, 267, 271
6. E. M. Clarke, O. Grumberg, and D. E. Long. Model checking and abstraction. *ACM Trans. Prog. Lang. Sys.*, 16(5):1512–1542, 1994. 268, 270
7. Satyaki Das and David L. Dill. Successive approximation of abstract transition relations. In *Proceedings of the Sixteenth Annual IEEE Symposium on Logic in Computer Science*, 2001. June 2001, Boston, USA. 267
8. R. Kurshan. *Computer aided verification of coordinating processes*. Princeton University Press, 1994. 267
9. J. Lind-Nielsen and H. Andersan. Stepwise CTL model checking of state/event systems. In N. Halbwachs and D. Peled, editors, *Proc. 11th Intl. Conference on Computer Aided Verification (CAV'99)*, volume 1633 of *Lect. Notes in Comp. Sci.*, pages 316–327. Springer-Verlag, 1999. 267
10. Tom M. Mitchell. *Machine Learning*. WCB/McGraw-Hill, 1997. 266, 274
11. M. Moskewicz, C. Madigan, Y. Zhao, L. Zhang, and S. Malik. Chaff: Engineering an efficient SAT solver. In *Proc. Design Automation Conference 2001 (DAC'01)*, 2001. 272, 276

12. J. R. Quinlan. Induction of decision trees. *Machine Learning*, 1986. 274, 276
13. J. R. Quinlan. *C4.5: Programs for Machine Learning.* Morgan Kaufmann, San Mateo, CA, 1993. 274
14. Dong Wang, Pei-Hsin Ho, Jiang Long, James Kukula, Yunshan Zhu, Tony Ma, and Robert Damiano. Formal property verification by abstraction refinement with formal, simulation and hybrid engines. In *Proc. Design Automation Conference 2001 (DAC'01)*, 2001. 267

Semi-formal Bounded Model Checking*

Jesse D. Bingham and Alan J. Hu

Department of Computer Science, University of British Columbia
{jbingham,ajh}@cs.ubc.ca

Abstract. This paper presents a novel approach to bounded model checking. We replace the SAT solver by an extended simulator of the circuit being verified. Compared to SAT-solving algorithms, our approach sacrifices some generality in selecting splitting variables and in the kinds of learning possible. In exchange, our approach enables compiled simulation of the circuit being verified, while our simulator extension allow us to retain limited learning and conflict-directed backtracking. The result combines some of the raw speed of compiled simulation with some of the search-space pruning of SAT solvers. On example circuits, our preliminary implementation is competitive with state-of-the-art SAT solvers, and we provide intuition for when one method would be superior to the other. More importantly, our verification approach continuously knows its coverage of the search space, providing useful semi-formal verification results when full verification is infeasible. In some cases, very high coverage can be attained in a tiny fraction of the time required for full coverage by either our approach or SAT solving.

1 Introduction

Model checking [4,10] has revolutionized formal hardware verification. The underlying engine for model checking has evolved from the original explicit state enumeration to symbolic model checking [3], and then bounded model checking [1]. Although none of these approaches strictly dominates the others, each new approach has enabled applying formal verification to problems that were previously intractable.

In this paper, we present a novel approach to bounded model checking. The basic bounded model checking construction reduces temporal logic model checking into the problem of finding a satisfying input assignment for a combinational circuit. Normally, this combinational circuit is converted to CNF and handed to a SAT-solver. Our approach, in contrast, searches for a satisfying assignment by explicitly simulating input vectors on the constructed circuit. The advantage of a simulation-based engine is that the circuit itself can be compiled into efficient machine code, resulting in very fast simulation. Furthermore, our simulation-based engine can be extended to handle non-Boolean devices (i.e. tri-state drivers)

* This work was supported in part by a research grant and a graduate fellowship from the Natural Science and Engineering Research Council of Canada. Experiments were conducted on a machine donated by Intel Corporation.

D. Brinksma and K. G. Larsen (Eds.): CAV 2002, LNCS 2404, pp. 280–294, 2002.
© Springer-Verlag Berlin Heidelberg 2002

without the cost of encoding such variables using multiple Booleans, as is required for SAT-solvers. The obvious disadvantage of a simulation-based approach is the exponential number of possible input vectors. A key contribution of this work is our extended simulation algorithm that prunes the search space analogously to the learning and conflict-directed backtracking of modern SAT-solvers, while still being amenable to compiled simulation.

As with previous model-checking innovations, our approach is inferior to existing methods on some types of problems. On other problems, though, our new approach is competitive with the state-of-the-art in bounded model checking. More importantly, our bounded model-checking engine continuously maintains a conservative bound on the fraction of the search space that has been verified, allowing our method to be used in a **semi-formal** manner when full, formal verification is infeasible. In some cases, very high coverage can be attained in a tiny fraction of the time required for full coverage by either our approach or SAT solving.

2   Background

Bounded model checking [1] forms the front-end for our verification approach, so we start with a brief review. Bounded model checking consists of three key insights. First, temporal logic with only bounded temporal semantics is still practically useful — both for checking bounded-time properties and also as an approximation to the unbounded semantics. Doing so avoids expensive fixpoint computations in the model checking algorithms. Second, since the temporal logic has bounded-time semantics, it is possible to convert the temporal logic model checking problem into a non-temporal logic problem, and a bounded model checking algorithm for some temporal logic must specify how to perform this conversion for any formula in that logic. For example, to verify that pUq holds for the next three clock cycles in a sequential circuit, one could "unroll" the circuit three times, creating a purely combinational circuit with three copies of the inputs and outputs (one for each clock cycle), and then build a small combinational network to check that pUq holds in all three cycles. (See Figure 1.) The third key insight is that modern SAT solvers have become efficient enough to solve the resulting combinational problem in many instances of practical importance. This third insight is simply enabling technology for the practical relevance of bounded model checking and is not integral to the idea. Indeed, a similar approach has been reported using an ATPG tool rather than a SAT solver [2]. In the present work, we rely on the first two insights of bounded model checking, but replace the SAT solver with an engine that offers competitive performance (but with different strengths and weaknesses), and also provides coverage information to allow semi-formal, incomplete verification.

Although our method replaces the SAT solver, the motivation, algorithms, and weaknesses in our approach can be better understood against the backdrop of the techniques and inefficiencies in typical, modern Boolean SAT solvers. The field of Boolean satisfiability checking has a long and extensive research litera-

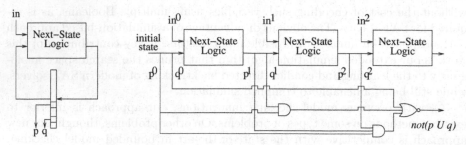

Fig. 1. Converting a Temporal Property to a Combinational One. To verify pUq over three clock cycles on a sequential circuit, we can unroll the circuit three times and create a combinational circuit whose output is true for any counterexample sequence

ture, but all of the leading, freely available, non-commercial SAT solvers used for bounded model checking (e.g., [8,12,9]) are based on the approach of Davis, Putnam, Logemann, and Loveland [6,5]. The basic idea is to **choose** heuristically a good variable on which to case split, assign a value to that variable and **propagate any constraints** that can be logically deduced from the assignment, **backtrack** if our choices and deductions lead to an obviously unsatisfiable formula, and possibly **learn** relationships among the variables by memorizing variable choices that guarantee a non-satisfying truth assignment. This process is repeated until either a satisfying assignment is found, or the entire search space has been exhausted. For example, consider the simple combinational circuit:

Standard SAT solvers work on formulas in conjunctive normal form (CNF), so if we wish to find an input assignment that makes the output true, the typical translation creates the CNF formula:[1]

$$(a + \overline{d})(b + \overline{d})(\overline{a} + \overline{b} + d)(\overline{c} + e)(\overline{d} + e)(c + d + \overline{e})e.$$

The first three clauses ensure the AND gate behaves as an AND gate, the next three clauses handle the OR gate, and the last clause specifies that the output must be true. The last clause has only the single literal e. Such clauses are called "unit clauses", and all SAT solvers immediately assign unit clauses to their forced values, simplify the resulting formula, and look for newly generated unit clauses to continue this process. For example, after the unit clause e has

---

[1] For such a small example, it is tempting to build the CNF for the output as a function of the circuit inputs. However, the CNF for a function given as a circuit is in general exponentially larger than the circuit. The typical translation we show here is linear in the size of the circuit, but introduces variables for each internal wire.

been propagated, we get the simpler CNF formula:

$$(a + \overline{d})(b + \overline{d})(\overline{a} + \overline{b} + d)(c + d).$$

At this point, the choice heuristic might choose to try making d true, and unit clause propagation will result in the satisfying assignment in which a and b are true as well.

The basic SAT algorithm appears to be little more than an explicit search through the possible truth assignments. Progress on SAT solving, however, has produced intelligent heuristics for choosing the variables for case-splitting, faster implementations for propagating constraints, clever ways to backtrack more efficiently, and heuristics for adding new clauses in order to learn not to repeat previous mistakes [8,12,9]. The resulting tools can be amazingly efficient on many SAT instances.

Let us now compare SAT-solving to a brute-force attack for the problem of finding an input assignment that satisfies a combinational circuit. The brute-force approach would be to systematically try all possible input assignments to the circuit, evaluating the circuit on each input assignment and looking for a satisfying assignment. Such an approach actually has an advantage over the SAT solver. Namely, given an input assignment, propagating the results of that assignment from inputs to outputs can be implemented extremely efficiently — for example, the circuit could be compiled into straight-line code that needs at most a few machine instructions to evaluate each gate. In contrast, constraint propagation for a SAT solver dominates the run time (over 90% [9]), and is slow, typically requiring several non-sequential (i.e., cache-miss-prone) memory accesses to walk through the data structures storing the formula, and several data-dependent (i.e., hard-to-predict) branches. On modern processors, the penalty for an L2 cache miss is around 50–100 cycles, and on a Pentium 4, the branch mispredict penalty is at least 19 cycles, so the compiled circuit simulation enjoys an enormous speed advantage. On the other hand, the SAT solver has several advantages over the brute-force attack. First, the SAT solver has the freedom to choose any variable in the system for case-splitting, and the choice of the right splitting variable can sometimes simplify a problem enormously. Empirical results, however, suggest that for bounded model checking, an excellent strategy is usually to choose the variables in a breadth-first manner moving exclusively forward from the inputs to the outputs, or exclusively backwards from the outputs to the inputs [11]. In the forward case, the strategy is essentially a very slow implementation of circuit simulation. The backward case, on the other hand, does give the SAT solver an option unavailable to the brute-force solver. The important advantages in favor of the SAT solver are the backtracking and learning strategies. In particular, modern SAT solvers use some form of non-chronologic or conflict-directed backtracking, in which the tool backtracks all the way back to a relevant decision that could avoid the unsatisfiable sub-problem, rather than simply to the most recent decision. Learning allows the SAT solver to remember combinations of decisions that led to unsatisfiable sub-problems, so that they can be avoided in the future. Our work essentially adds non-chronologic backtracking and learning to the brute-force solver, in a manner that still permits compiled simulation.

3   Verification Algorithm

3.1   Brute-Force Compiled Simulation

We first present the brute-force compiled simulation algorithm, and then show how it can be modified to incorporate intelligent backtracking and learning.

We assume we are given a gate-level sequential circuit, an initial state, a verification wire, and a time bound k. The verification problem is to find a sequence of inputs that causes the verification wire to be true at time k. Different bounded model checking constructions can be handled by pre-unrolling the circuit into a combinational circuit, and then using our algorithm with $k = 0$.

More formally, let C be a sequential circuit with n input variables $\{x_0, \ldots, x_{n-1}\}$ and m state variables $\{s_0, \ldots, s_{m-1}\}$. We use superscripts to denote time indices, so the initial state I is an assignment of Boolean values to s_i^0, for $i = 0, \ldots, m - 1$. Label the verification wire f, so we seek an input sequence that causes $f^k = 1$.

The brute-force approach would take an instance of the verification problem and generate a program with the following structure:

```
while (vector=choose_an_untried_vector()) {
  set_inputs(vector);  // Assign vector to circuit inputs
  simulate_circuit(k); // Simulate time 0 through k
  if (circuit.f.value==TRUE) return SATISFIABLE;
  record_unsuccessful_trial(vector,...);
}
return UNSATISFIABLE;
```

The heart of the program is the `simulate_circuit` function. The code generator declares a variable for each wire in the circuit, then does a topological sort on the gates, and generates code that evaluates the output of each gate as a function of its inputs. For example, if our circuit contains the gate `a = AND(b,c)`, the emitted code could be as simple as:

```
circuit.a.value = circuit.b.value & circuit.c.value;
```

which would compile to at most a few instructions in machine code. The generated simulator has no expensive data structure for storing and manipulating the circuit and performs no traversals over the circuit; instead, the only representation of the circuit is embedded in the evaluation code itself.

3.2   Skip Cubes

The key idea behind the advanced backtracking techniques used in modern SAT solvers is that many of the decisions (assignments to variables) made before reaching a conflict have no effect at all on that conflict. Therefore, the backtrack should not bother revising irrelevant decisions. Analogously, we will now introduce a mechanism, which we call "skip cubes", by which the circuit simulator can tell which input variables did not affect the value of f^k, thereby pruning the search space. Note that this is more specific than the cone-of-influence reduction, which can only eliminate portions of the circuit which do not affect f^k for **any** possible input vector.

Define the universal set U to consist of all binary vectors of length $N = n(k+1)$. An element $v = v_0 \ldots v_{N-1} \in U$ corresponds to an input sequence over $k+1$ time steps with $x_i^t = v_{tn+i}$, so we will use the terms "vector" and "input sequence" interchangeably. Starting in initial state I and given some $v \in U$, let w_v^t represent the value on a wire w of the circuit C at time step t.

Definition 1 (Skip Set) *The skip set of a wire w at time t with respect to input vector v is defined $\mathcal{S}_v(w^t) = \{u \mid u \in U \wedge w_v^t = w_u^t\}$.*

Intuitively, $\mathcal{S}_v(w^t)$ is the set of all vectors that cause w^t to have the same value as when C is simulated with the input sequence v. Specifically, simulating the circuit with a vector v will drive f^k to the same value as any other vector in $\mathcal{S}_v(f^k)$, so if f_v^k is false, we may skip any subset of these vectors when searching for a satisfying assignment.

Computing $\mathcal{S}_v(w^t)$ for each gate output could be done in a straightforward manner at the same time that the output value is computed. For example, if w is the output of an AND or NAND gate with inputs a and b, then

$$\mathcal{S}_v(w^t) = \begin{cases} \mathcal{S}_v(a^t) \cup \mathcal{S}_v(b^t) & \text{if } a_v^t = 0 \wedge b_v^t = 0 \\ \mathcal{S}_v(a^t) \cup \overline{\mathcal{S}_v(b^t)} & \text{if } a_v^t = 0 \wedge b_v^t = 1 \\ \overline{\mathcal{S}_v(a^t)} \cup \mathcal{S}_v(b^t) & \text{if } a_v^t = 1 \wedge b_v^t = 0 \\ \mathcal{S}_v(a^t) \cap \mathcal{S}_v(b^t) & \text{if } a_v^t = 1 \wedge b_v^t = 1 \end{cases}$$

Other gate rules are similar. Note, however, that $\mathcal{S}_v(w^t)$ is simply either the on-set or the off-set of w^t, so any exact computation of skip sets amounts to computing the exact functionality of each wire, which will blow-up for many practical examples.

Instead, in our approach we propagate conservative approximations $\mathcal{A}_v(w^t)$ such that $\{v\} \subseteq \mathcal{A}_v(w^t) \subseteq \mathcal{S}_v(w^t)$ and where $\mathcal{A}_v(w^t)$ has a succinct representation. The conservative approximations to the skip sets are special sets called *cubes*:

Definition 2 (Cube) *A cube is simply the Boolean subspace generated by assigning constants to some variables. Specifically, a set $B \subseteq U$ is a cube if $B = \{v \mid v_{i_1} = b_1, v_{i_2} = b_2, \ldots v_{i_\ell} = b_\ell\}$, where $0 \le i_1 < i_2 < \cdots i_\ell \le N - 1$ and the b_i are arbitrary Boolean constants. The indices $i_1, i_2, \ldots, i_\ell$ are called the specified bits; all others are called unspecified. If bit i_j is specified, then b_j is called the specified value.*

We may express a cube B as a length N vector over the alphabet $\{0, 1, -\}$, where B_i is the specified value of bit i if specified, or "$-$" if unspecified. We now define the *skip cube* of a wire:

Definition 3 (Skip Cube) *The skip cube $\mathcal{A}_v(w^t)$ of a wire w at time t with respect to input vector v is defined depending on the type of gate driving w:*

1. *If w is a two-input gate with controlling value μ (e.g., an AND gate with $\mu = 0$ or an OR gate with $\mu = 1$) and input wires a and b, then*

$$\mathcal{A}_v(w^t) = \begin{cases} \mathcal{A}_v(a^t) \cap \mathcal{A}_v(b^t) & \text{if } a_v^t = \overline{\mu} \wedge b_v^t = \overline{\mu} \\ \mathcal{A}_v(b^t) & \text{if } a_v^t = \overline{\mu} \wedge b_v^t = \mu \\ \mathcal{A}_v(a^t) & \text{if } a_v^t = \mu \wedge b_v^t = \overline{\mu} \\ \max(\mathcal{A}_v(a^t), \mathcal{A}_v(b^t)) & \text{if } a_v^t = \mu \wedge b_v^t = \mu \end{cases}$$

where $\max(\ldots)$ returns the set of greater cardinality.
2. *If w is the output of an inverter with input a, then $\mathcal{A}_v(w^t) = \mathcal{A}_v(a^t)$.*
3. *If w is a state-holding element with next-state signal a, then $\mathcal{A}_v(w^0) = U$ and $\mathcal{A}_v(w^t) = \mathcal{A}_v(a^{t-1})$ for $t > 0$.*
4. *If w is an input x_i, then $\mathcal{A}_v(w^t) = (B_0, \ldots, B_{N-1})$, where $B_j = w_v^t$ if $j = tn + i$, or $B_j = $ "$-$" otherwise.*
5. *If w is a two-input gate without a controlling value (i.e., exclusive-OR or exclusive-NOR), with input signals a and b, then $\mathcal{A}_v(w^t) = \mathcal{A}_v(a^t) \cap \mathcal{A}_v(b^t)$*

Larger gates can be handled similarly. Our implementation supports 3-input sum and carry gates.

Theorem 1. *$\mathcal{A}_v(w^t)$ as defined in Definition 3 is always a cube.*

Proof: The intersection of two cubes is always either another cube or the empty set. The latter case occurs only if the two cubes disagree on at least one specified bit. In Definition 3, all specified bits always agree with the input vector v.   □

Theorem 2. *Let $\mathcal{S}_v(w^t)$ and $\mathcal{A}_v(w^t)$ be defined as in Definitions 1 and 3. Then, $\{v\} \subseteq \mathcal{A}_v(w^t) \subseteq \mathcal{S}_v(w^t)$.*

Proof sketch: Structural induction on the circuit using the rules of definition 3.
□

Corollary 1. *Let $B = \mathcal{A}_v(w^t)$. For all $i = 0, \ldots, N - 1$, if B_i is specified, then $B_i = v_i$.*

The above results establish the correctness of the optimization that, upon completion of simulating vector v and finding $f_v^k = 0$, skips simulation of all vectors in $\mathcal{A}_v(f^k)$.

We now consider how the computation of the skip cubes can be efficiently integrated into compiled simulation. During simulation of C against input v, we store v as a string of N bits in memory, padded to the nearest machine word boundary. A skip cube B can also be stored as a same-sized bit string, with bit $i = 1$ in memory if and only if bit i is specified in B. If B_i is specified, the specified value is v_i by Corollary 1 and is thus readily available. Note from Definition 3 that the skip cube computation propagates from the inputs to the outputs of each gate, exactly as the value computation does. Accordingly, the code generator can allocate a (value, skip cube) pair for each wire in the original circuit, and the `simulate_circuit` function will contain code to compute both the value and the skip cube for each wire. In most cases, computing the skip cube of w^t is a straightforward copy of the array storing the skip cube of one of the gate inputs. The cases pertaining to a primary input or an initial state variable are also trivial to compute. The cube intersection operations required in cases 1 and 5 of Definition 3 can be achieved by computing a bitwise OR of the bit strings for the respective gate input skip cubes. The max operation of case 1 is the only slower operation, consisting of selecting the skip cube with the fewer specified bits. We implement this step by performing a population count on the skip cube bit strings. Figure 2 gives an example of skip cube computation.

3.3 Learning and Coverage

Upon simulating any vector v and finding that the value at time k of the verification wire f_v^k is false, the skip cube $\mathcal{A}_v(f^k)$ that we have simultaneously computed gives us a set of vectors that also would have made f_v^k false. The search procedure should remember this skip cube to ensure that it will never again try any vectors in this cube, thereby pruning the search space analogously to the learning and non-chronologic backtracking of conventional SAT procedures. For example, if some input x_i^0 always causes the verification wire to be false regardless of the other inputs, the first vector that we simulate with x_i^0 true will generate a skip cube for f_v^k that shows this fact, and our search procedure will never try any other vectors with x_i^0 true. Thus, the search procedure has effectively backtracked non-chronologically to the decision for x_i^0, and learned the relationship that x_i^0 implies $\overline{f^k}$.

Our current implementation maintains a BDD which represents the covered set V of input vectors that have been either explicitly simulated already or else covered via skip cubes.[2] After each simulation iteration, the resulting skip cube $\mathcal{A}_v(f^k)$ is disjoined into V, and the next simulation vector is chosen randomly from the complement set $\overline{V}$. Note that V is not directly related to the functionality of the circuit under verification, and thus the BDD for V does not necessarily blow up even when the BDD for the circuit would have exponential size. The algorithm completes when the entire space U is covered, or when an input sequence is discovered to make f^k true.

The use of a BDD to store the covered set has several advantages. First, all the operations needed by the algorithm can be done efficiently: converting a cube to a BDD, disjoining a BDD for the cube into the BDD for the covered set, and retrieving a random vector not in the covered set. BDDs also provide an easy way to incorporate input don't-cares into the verification method, by initializing V to include all don't-care vectors. Most important is the fact that the ratio $c = | S | / | U |$ can be computed in time linear in the number of BDD nodes. The coverage ratio c tells us the fraction of the search space that has been explored and eliminated by our algorithm. Periodically computing c allows the algorithm to communicate a progress metric to the user. Furthermore, in the event of a

---

[2] Several reviewers suggested using a ZBDD instead, which seems like a very promising idea.

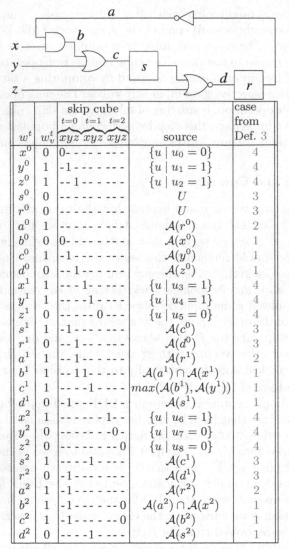

w^t	w^t_v	skip cube $t=0$ xyz	$t=1$ xyz	$t=2$ xyz	source	case from Def. 3
x^0	0	0--	---	---	$\{u \mid u_0 = 0\}$	4
y^0	1	-1-	---	---	$\{u \mid u_1 = 1\}$	4
z^0	1	--1	---	---	$\{u \mid u_2 = 1\}$	4
s^0	0	---	---	---	U	3
r^0	0	---	---	---	U	3
a^0	1	---	---	---	$\mathcal{A}(r^0)$	2
b^0	0	0--	---	---	$\mathcal{A}(x^0)$	1
c^0	1	-1-	---	---	$\mathcal{A}(y^0)$	1
d^0	0	--1	---	---	$\mathcal{A}(z^0)$	1
x^1	1	---	1--	---	$\{u \mid u_3 = 1\}$	4
y^1	1	---	-1-	---	$\{u \mid u_4 = 1\}$	4
z^1	0	---	--0	---	$\{u \mid u_5 = 0\}$	4
s^1	1	-1-	---	---	$\mathcal{A}(c^0)$	3
r^1	0	--1	---	---	$\mathcal{A}(d^0)$	3
a^1	1	--1	---	---	$\mathcal{A}(r^1)$	2
b^1	1	--1	1--	---	$\mathcal{A}(a^1) \cap \mathcal{A}(x^1)$	1
c^1	1	---	-1-	---	$max(\mathcal{A}(b^1), \mathcal{A}(y^1))$	1
d^1	0	-1-	---	---	$\mathcal{A}(s^1)$	1
x^2	1	---	---	1--	$\{u \mid u_6 = 1\}$	4
y^2	0	---	---	-0-	$\{u \mid u_7 = 0\}$	4
z^2	0	---	---	--0	$\{u \mid u_8 = 0\}$	4
s^2	1	---	-1-	---	$\mathcal{A}(c^1)$	3
r^2	0	-1-	---	---	$\mathcal{A}(d^1)$	3
a^2	1	-1-	---	---	$\mathcal{A}(r^2)$	2
b^2	1	-1-	---	--0	$\mathcal{A}(a^2) \cap \mathcal{A}(x^2)$	1
c^2	1	-1-	---	--0	$\mathcal{A}(b^2)$	1
d^2	0	---	-1-	---	$\mathcal{A}(s^2)$	1

Fig. 2. This circuit has two latches s and r with initial states $s^0 = r^0 = 0$. The table gives the skip cubes for all relevant wires with respect to the input vector $v = 011110100$, where the bits of v from left to right respectively give the input values for $x^0, y^0, z^0, x^1, y^1, z^1, x^2, y^2$, and z^2. The leftmost two columns give the wire name/time index and the bit value, respectively. The column labeled "skip cube" gives the skip cube for the wire. The rightmost two columns state the source of the skip cube and the rule from Definition 3 applied to obtain the skip cube. This example demonstrates the power of the skip cube technique. Suppose we wish to verify that latch r must be 0 at time 2, i.e., $r^2 = 0$. Observe that the skip cube for r^2 is $\mathcal{A}_v(r^2) = \{v \mid y^0 = 1\}$ and $r_v^2 = 0$. Thus, we know that any vector with $y^0 = 1$ implies $r_v^2 = 0$, so we can skip all other vectors with $y^0 = 1$. Hence, our search space has been reduced by a factor of 2

time-out or space-out, the coverage ratio provides an informative verification result and increases confidence that the property being verified holds. Having an accurate measure of progress and coverage greatly enhances the usability of verification tools, especially on challenging problems that can't be verified quickly or completely.

4   Experimental Results

We have implemented our algorithm to test its performance. The tool takes a sequential circuit in a slightly modified version of ISCAS89 format and outputs the simulator for that circuit as a C++ program. This translation step is virtually instantaneous. The simulator is then compiled and run to perform the verification. We report compile and run times for the simulator.[3]

For comparison, we ran against a leading, free, non-commercial SAT solver for bounded model checking, Z-Chaff. Our experiments were conducted with version Z2001.2.17. We used our own translator from ISCAS89 format to CNF, but ignore the negligible translation time. We believe our translator produces CNF comparable to other bounded model checking tools. For example, the multiplier in Section 4.1 is closely modeled on the example presented by Biere et al. [1], and Chaff is able to solve our generated CNF formulas slightly faster than the ones supplied by Biere.

4.1   Original 16×16 Multiplier Example

Our first example is a 16×16-bit multiplier with 16-bit output. We designed this problem instance closely following the one reported in the original bounded model checking paper [1]. The specification verified was

$$(done \land \neg overflow) \rightarrow (out_b = out'_b) \tag{1}$$

where $done$ is asserted when the output register has converged to the final value, $over flow$ is asserted if the product exceeds 16 bits, and out_b and out'_b are the bth output bits of a reference combinational multiplier and the sequential multiplier under verification, respectively. Separate runs were performed for $b = 0, \ldots, 15$, and the time bound used in each case was $k = b + 1$.

Table 1 gives the results for our tool and for Chaff. For semi-formal verification (rightmost three columns), our tool gives very high coverage extremely quickly. This illustrates the effectiveness of the skip cube propagation at quickly

---

[3] All experiments were conducted on a PC with a 1.5Ghz Intel Pentium 4 processor and 1GB of RDRAM. Memory usage is not reported, as it was never significant. The operating system was Linux 2.4.9, and the compiler was g++ version 2.95.2 using the -O3 optimization level. The compiler missed an obvious peephole optimization (two adjacent addl instructions modifying the stack pointer), so we used a simple Perl script to perform this optimization, resulting in a performance improvement of a couple percent.

Table 1. 16×16 Multiplier Results with Original Specification (Eq. 1). Compile and run times are in seconds. The column labeled "compile" gives the compilation time for the simulation program, while the rightmost four columns give the running time required of our tool to reach the indicated coverages, e.g., 126.4 seconds to fully verify bit 9, and only 2.2 seconds to attain 99.99% coverage

b	Chaff	compile	full	0.9999	0.999	0.99
		Compiled Simulation with Skip Cubes				
0	0.0	0.0	0.0	0.0	0.0	0.0
1	0.0	8.5	0.0	0.0	0.0	0.0
2	0.0	8.9	0.0	0.0	0.0	0.0
3	0.0	9.7	0.1	0.0	0.0	0.0
4	0.1	11.0	0.2	0.1	0.1	0.0
5	0.4	12.5	0.8	0.1	0.1	0.0
6	2.4	14.6	4.0	0.2	0.2	0.1
7	16.1	17.1	19.6	0.4	0.3	0.1
8	89.7	20.1	71.3	0.8	0.6	0.1
9	234.6	24.0	126.4	2.2	0.8	0.2
10	221.4	28.9	222.3	5.8	1.4	0.2
11	165.4	34.5	332.7	11.4	1.2	0.3
12	134.8	41.5	502.2	28.7	2.8	0.4
13	99.2	48.6	662.6	48.3	2.7	0.5
14	34.9	58.8	840.4	74.9	4.4	0.6
15	26.3	69.5	946.7	115.3	3.9	0.7

eliminating large parts of the search space. For complete, formal verification, our tool is competitive with Chaff up to bit 9, but then, surprisingly, the Chaff run times drop sharply. One normally expects output bit $n-1$ of an $n \times n$ multiplier to be the most difficult bit, but this curious behavior can be explained by the presence of $\neg overflow$ in the antecedent of the specification (Eq. 1) in conjunction with the time bound $b+1$. Although the circuit correctly computes the values of all output bits for all input values, almost all input word pairs actually raise $overflow$, making the specification vacuously true. A SAT solver can propagate constraints backwards from the overflow flag, quickly pruning the circuit down to essentially an 8×8 multiplier, making the high-order bits easy to verify.

4.2   Full-Size 16×16 Multiplier Example

In the preceding multiplier example, the combinational reference multiplier is actually a full-size 16×16 multiplier with 32-bit output. Similarly, the sequential multiplier would correctly compute all 32 output bits if the output register were wider. Accordingly, we removed the overflow logic from the preceding example, creating a true, full-sized 16×16 multiplier, and verified the specification:

$$done \rightarrow (out_b = out'_b) \tag{2}$$

Table 2. Full-Sized 16×16 Multiplier Results with Specification (Eq. 2). "time" indicates timeout after 1 hour. When our tool times out, the attained coverage is indicated in parentheses. For bit 10, we actually ran Chaff to completion, which took over 17 hours. Our result for bit 10 with 0.9999 coverage is anomalous, taking slightly longer than full coverage. This might be explained by extra floating-point comparisons performed by our tool when a target coverage is specified, and we have also observed slightly different page fault behavior, but we are still investigating

b	Chaff	compile	Compiled Simulation with Skip Cubes			
			full	0.9999	0.999	0.99
0	0.0	8.1	0.0	0.0	0.0	0.0
1	0.0	8.4	0.0	0.0	0.0	0.0
2	0.0	8.9	0.0	0.0	0.0	0.0
3	0.0	9.7	0.0	0.0	0.0	0.0
4	0.1	10.7	0.1	0.1	0.0	0.0
5	0.4	12.3	0.7	0.5	0.0	0.0
6	2.2	14.4	3.6	3.1	0.0	0.0
7	17.1	16.9	18.2	17.5	7.4	0.0
8	111.3	20.2	102.1	100.5	69.9	0.0
9	1081.2	23.9	533.7	519.4	447.6	0.0
10	time	28.4	2797.9	2928.4	2667.0	855.2
11	time	34.1	time(0.9776)	time(0.9776)	time(0.9776)	time(0.9776)
12	time	40.8	time(0.9418)	time(0.9418)	time(0.9418)	time(0.9418)
13	time	48.8	time(0.8769)	time(0.8769)	time(0.8769)	time(0.8769)
14	time	58.2	time(0.7509)	time(0.7509)	time(0.7509)	time(0.7509)
15	time	68.9	time(0.5004)	time(0.5004)	time(0.5004)	time(0.5004)

Table 2 presents the results for this experiment. This problem is much more difficult than that of Section 4.1. Here, we observe our approach running about as fast as Chaff for the low-order bits, and beating Chaff for bits 8, 9, and 10. For the higher-order bits, both tools timeout, but the compiled simulator provides a high coverage while the SAT solver reveals no information.

4.3   SRT Divider Example

Our last experiment is the most difficult. We verify a $2n$-bit by n-bit radix-2 SRT divider with redundant quotient representation [7] against a combinational divider. The specification asserts that if the SRT divisor is normalized, and if the the combinational divider does not overflow, then the two dividers produce the same result. In particular, we verify all bits of the quotient and remainder in a single run.

The results for $n = 4, \ldots, 8$ are given in Table 3, which clearly demonstrate that our approach is more effective than Chaff on this problem. For $n = 7$, we find our approach to be almost 4 times faster than Chaff even when compilation

Table 3. $2n$-bit by n-bit Radix-2 SRT Divider Results

n	Chaff	Compiled Simulation with Skip Cubes	
		compile	full
4	1.2	7.2	0.4
5	7.5	10.8	4.7
6	98.1	15.7	56.8
7	2848.4	22.3	735.2
8	time	30.4	time(0.7737)

time is included. For $n = 8$, both tools time-out (again set at 1 hour), but our tool reports the coverage attained.

5   Conclusion and Future Work

We have presented a novel approach to bounded model checking. Our search procedure has competitive performance with state-of-the-art SAT solvers on many problems. Intuition and experimental results suggest that SAT solvers have the advantage on smaller circuits and on circuits in which clever case-splitting heuristics can quickly establish unsatisfiability, whereas our new method has the advantage for larger circuits that aren't amenable to such attacks. Further experimentation will be needed to understand exactly when our technique is most effective. For instance, the examples in this paper are highly regular arithmetic circuits, and it is unclear how effective skip cubes would be on very unstructured control logic. A key advantage of our method is that it continually provides coverage information, which is useful as a progress indicator for lengthy verification runs, and as a semi-formal verification result for runs that time out. Our work provides a valuable additional tool for model checking when other methods (e.g., BDDs, SAT) fail.

We believe our implementation could be substantially optimized. For example, our implementation generates C++, which introduced many inefficiencies. A production tool should generate the simulator machine code directly, bypassing the compiler, which is not tuned for the very large, simply structured `simulate_circuit` function that we generate. There is little need for global optimizations, so the code generation would be straightforward.

More algorithmic directions for further research are to explore various design trade-offs. For example, we could compute more conservative approximations of the skip cubes using branchless code, which might run faster, but need more vectors. Alternatively, we could compute more accurate approximations of the skip sets, reducing the number of vectors needed, but slowing down the simulation as well. In some cases, it would be useful to shift between strategies, starting with skip cubes, for example, and then switching to an alternative if the skip cubes become too small. More generally, one could even try a hybrid approach combining the fast simulation of our method with the more sophisticated analysis of a SAT engine.

From a theoretical perspective, we would like to understand what factors influence the rate of convergence of the coverage ratio. Intuitively, if there exists a vector that produces a large skip cube, it is plausible that many other vectors (such as the other vectors in the skip cube) would also generate a large skip cube, so large skip cubes would be covered early. If this intuition is true, one could estimate statistically the total run time based on the first few coverage ratios computed, which would further enhance the usability of the model checker.

Acknowledgments

We would like to thank Armin Biere for supplying examples and details on the experimental procedures reported in [ ], and Sally McKee for discovering that the g++ optimizer was missing an obvious optimization and for suggesting a work-around.

References

1. Armin Biere, Alessandro Cimatti, Edmund M. Clarke, and Yunshan Zhu. Symbolic model checking without BDDs. In *Tools and Algorithms for Construction and Analysis of Systems*, pages 193–207. LNCS 1579. Springer, 1999. 280, 281, 289, 293

2. Vamsi Boppana, Sreeranga P. Rajan, Koichiro Takayama, and Masahiro Fujita. Model checking based on sequential ATPG. In *Computer-Aided Verification: Eleventh International Conference*, pages 418–430. LNCS 1633. Springer, 1999. 281

3. J. R. Burch, E. M. Clarke, K. L. McMillan, D. L. Dill, and L. J. Hwang. Symbolic model checking: 10^{20} states and beyond. In *Conference on Logic in Computer Science*, pages 428–439, 1990. 280

4. Edmund M. Clarke and E. Allen Emerson. Design and synthesis of synchronization skeletons using branching time temporal logic. In Dexter Kozen, editor, *Workshop on Logics of Programs*, pages 52–71, May 1981. Published as LNCS 131. Springer, 1982. 280

5. Martin Davis, George Logemann, and Donald Loveland. A machine program for theorem proving. *Communications of the ACM*, 5(7):394–397, July 1962. 282

6. Martin Davis and Hilary Putnam. A computing procedure for quantification theory. *Journal of the ACM*, 7(3):201–215, July 1960. 282

7. David Goldberg. *Computer Arithmetic*. Appendix A in D. A. Patterson and J. L. Hennessy, *Computer Architecture: A Quantitative Approach*, 2nd Ed., Morgan Kaufmann, 1996. 291

8. João P. Marques Silva and Karem A. Sakallah. GRASP — a new search algorithm for satisfiability. In *International Conference on Computer-Aided Design*, pages 220–227. IEEE/ACM, 1996. 282, 283

9. Matthew W. Moskewicz, Conor F. Madigan, Ying Zhao, Lintao Zhang, and Sharad Malik. Chaff: Engineering an efficient SAT solver. In *38th Design Automation Conference*, pages 530–535. ACM/IEEE, 2001. 282, 283

10. Jean-Pierre Queille and Joseph Sifakis. Specification and verification of concurrent systems in Cesar. In *5th International Symposium on Programming*, pages 337–351. LNCS 137. Springer, 1981. 280

11. Ofer Shtrichman. Tuning SAT checkers for bounded model checking. In *Computer-Aided Verification: 12th International Conference*, pages 480–494. LNCS 1855. Springer, 2000. 283

12. Hantao Zhang. SATO: An efficient propositional prover. In *14th Conference on Automated Deduction*, pages 272–275. LNAI 1249. Springer, 1997. 282, 283

Algorithmic Verification
of Invalidation-Based Protocols

Marco Bozzano and Giorgio Delzanno

Dipartimento di Informatica e Scienze dell'Informazione
Università di Genova, via Dodecaneso 35, 16146 Italy
giorgio@disi.unige.it

Abstract. We propose an extension of the model of Broadcast Protocols in which individual processes are allowed to have *unbounded local data* and to communicate via *value passing*. Our specification language is based on *multiset rewriting over first order atomic formulas* enriched with a mechanism for *global synchronization* to model broadcasts, and *constraints* to model the relations over *internal data* and *value passing*. For this new class of parameterized systems, we provide a symbolic validation procedure for checking safety properties, and *termination conditions* defined on special classes of multiset rewriting systems with linear constraints. We report here on practical experiments with coherence protocols for virtual shared memory, and multiprocessors systems in which the number of processors, pages or cache lines are left as parameters.

1   Introduction

Broadcast protocols [15] represent a very natural formalism to specify abstractions of *invalidation-based* protocols. In [16], Esparza, Finkel and Mayr have defined automated verification procedures to check *parameterized safety properties* (safety properties that are supposed to hold for any possible number of individual processes) for this class of infinite-state systems. The techniques of [16] exploit the property that the operational semantics of Broadcast Protocols can be given via extensions of Petri Nets with transfer arcs. *Backward reachability* always terminates for this class of Petri Nets when the seed of the computation consists of an upward-closed set of markings. The previous property reveals however a limitation of this model: processes must be represented here as indistinguishable *black tokens*. Thus, the algorithm of [16] can be applied only to analyze functional properties that can be formulated over *finite-state abstractions* of individual processes. As an example, in the models of cache coherence protocols given in [15,16] each individual process (cache) is modeled via a finite-state automata, obtained by forgetting cache identifiers and by considering a single cache line and a single memory location. However, the original formulation of these protocols (see [5]) as well as of other invalidation-based protocols (see [20]) depends on several parameters like cache lines or entries in a page table. To obtain more *concrete* models, we need specification languages in which

D. Brinksma and K. G. Larsen (Eds.): CAV 2002, LNCS 2404, pp. 295–308, 2002.
© Springer-Verlag Berlin Heidelberg 2002

individual processes are allowed to carry along information ranging over a possibly infinite domain, as in the formal models proposed in [18,21]. In order to specify and validate these class of protocols, we will combine three different lines of research: *multiset rewriting* [11], *constraints* [14], and the *theory of well-quasi orderings* of [1,17].

Multiset rewriting over first-order atomic formulas (MSR) [11] naturally extends the connection between rewriting and Petri Nets to nets with *colored tokens*, the colors being first-order terms attached to atomic formulas representing tokens. If we annotate rules with *constraints*, as proposed in [14], we achieve a clear separation between process structure and declaration of data relations, with advantages that will become clearer later. In this setting shared variables play the role of communication channels as shown in [10].

Suppose now we try to apply this paradigm to atomically specify invalidation phases as in the Broadcast Protocols model. We first note that the number of processes involved in a broadcast cannot be fixed a priori (it depends on the current configuration). However, by the *locality* of rewriting, a multiset rewriting rule allows us to specify only the behavior of a fixed number of processes.

As first contribution, we propose here an extension of the MSR specification language of [11] in which we introduce a mechanism for *global synchronization* that can be used to model broadcasts. To explain our idea, let us consider the *invalidation phase* caused by a *write miss* in the model of the M.E.S.I. cache coherence protocol (with a single cache line and memory location) given in [15]. In this example, every cache is modeled via a finite-state net. A token in a given place (*inv*, *modified*, *exclusive*, etc.) represents a cache in that state. On a write miss, the cache requesting to write its (unique) line first broadcasts a *signal* to invalidate all other caches (all other tokens move to place *inv*). In a Broadcast Protocol this behavior is captured by associating a set of *reactions* (e.g. cache invalidation) to a given action (e.g. broadcast sending). We obtain a similar effect in the MSR setting as follows. Let us model an action via a multiset rewriting rule, and any of the corresponding reactions as a rewriting rule $A \hookrightarrow B$ defined over two atomic formulas A and B. A reaction describes the behavior of a process in state A upon the reception of the broadcast. Using the syntax that we will formally introduce in Section 2, we formulate then the M.E.S.I. invalidation phase via rule like

$$inv \longrightarrow dirty \, [\, shared \hookrightarrow inv, \, dirty \hookrightarrow inv, \dots \,]$$

(the set of reactions associated to an MSR rule is written between square brackets). Furthermore, we will extend the operational semantics so as to enforce the application of reactions to the maximal multiset of atomic formulas matching their left-hand side.

In the formalism we will propose in this paper, that we call $\hookrightarrow$MSR(C), we will extend this idea to tokens colored with data. We achieve this aim by annotating an action and its reactions with a constraint (over a constraint system C that is a parameter of the language) defined over variables occurring in the corresponding atomic formulas. For instance, we refine the previous invalidation phase leaving the number of cache lines as a parameter as follows

$$inv(p, m) \longrightarrow dirty(p, m) \; [\; shared(q, n) \; \hookrightarrow \; inv(q, n), \ldots \;] : p \neq q, m = n, \ldots$$

where $p, q, m, n, \ldots$ denote universally quantified variables (ranging over integers), indicating the identifiers of processors (p, q) and memory addresses (m, n).

Following [ ], the method we use to check *parameterized properties* for the resulting models is based on *symbolic backward reachability*. In this paper we will focus on safety properties whose violations can be expressed via *upward-closed sets* of configurations. Our symbolic representation is based on the notion of *constrained configuration* introduced in [ ], i.e., *multisets of first-order atomic formulas annotated with constraints*. Multisets represent minimal requirements over the distribution of tokens in the net, whereas constraints provide a natural symbolic representation for relations over data of different processes. Based on this *rich assertional language*, we provide *symbolic* operations needed to implement *backward reachability*, namely we define a *symbolic predecessor operator* for $\hookrightarrow$MSR(C)-specifications, which is sound and complete for any constraint system. Furthermore, we will show that it is possible to algorithmically verify *safety properties* for a class of $\hookrightarrow$MSR-specifications equipped with a subclass of linear integer constraints. Under the previous hypotheses and following the general theory of [,], we obtain an extension of Broadcast Protocols with unbounded local data and value passing for which we can check algorithmically interesting safety properties.

Our work enlarges the target of the method presented in [ ] as well as of its predecessors [,] to new or simply more concrete examples of *invalidation-based* protocols. We report here on an interesting experiment with a coherence protocol for virtual shared memory proposed by Li and Hudak in [ ] and previously analyzed in [ ]. Using our technique, we have automatically verified the protocol in which the number of threads, processors, and pages of virtual memory are unbounded parameters. Finally, we have automatically validated coherence protocols for multiprocessors systems (M.S.I., M.E.S.I., Synapse) in which number of processors, cache lines and memory locations are left as parameters. In the following sections we will turn the previous intuitions into formal definitions.

2 Synchronous Multiset Rewriting

A *constraint system* is a tuple $C = \langle V, L, D, S \rangle$ where: V is a denumerable set of variables; L is a *first-order* language with variables in V and closed with respect to *existential quantification, conjunction,* and with *equality;* $\varphi \in L$ is called a *constraint;* D the *domain* of interpretation of constraints; a solution of a constraint φ is a mapping $V \rightsquigarrow D$ that satisfies φ; finally, $S(\varphi)$ is the set of solutions of φ. A constraint φ is *satisfiable* whenever $S(\varphi) \neq \emptyset$. Given a solution σ, we will use $\sigma_{|V}$ to indicate the restriction of σ to the variables in $V \subseteq V$.

Let P be a set of symbols, an *atomic formula* $p(x_1, \ldots, x_n)$ is such that $p \in P$, and $x_1, \ldots, x_n \in \mathrm{V}$ are *distinct* variables. A *ground* atomic formula $p(d_1, \ldots, d_n)$ is obtained by applying a solution σ to $p(x_1, \ldots, x_n)$ so that $\sigma(x_i) = d_i$ for $i : 1, \ldots, n$. A *multiset* of atomic formulas is indicated as $A_1 \mid \ldots \mid A_k$, where A_i and A_j have distinct variables, $\mid$ is an associative and commutative constructor, and ϵ denotes the empty multiset.

Definition 1. A *configuration* is a multiset of *ground atomic formulas*.

Intuitively, a configuration denotes a multiset of colored tokens. In the rest of the paper will use $\mathcal{M}, \mathcal{N}, \mathcal{H}, \mathcal{B}, \ldots$ to denote *multisets* of atomic formulas.

Definition 2. An *action* is a rewrite rule $\mathcal{H} \longrightarrow \mathcal{B}$, where $\mathcal{H}$ and $\mathcal{B}$ are two multisets of atomic formulas with distinct variables. A *reaction* is a rewrite rule $A \hookrightarrow B$ where A and B are two atomic formulas with *distinct* variables.

Definition 3 (Rules). Given $C = \langle \mathrm{V}, \mathrm{L}, \mathrm{D}, \mathrm{S} \rangle$, an $\hookrightarrow\mathrm{MSR}(C)$ *rule* has the form $\mathcal{H} \longrightarrow \mathcal{B} \, [A_1 \hookrightarrow B_1, \ldots, A_k \hookrightarrow B_k] : \varphi$, where

1. $\mathcal{H} \longrightarrow \mathcal{B}$ is an action, and $A_i \hookrightarrow B_i$ is a reaction for $i : 1, \ldots, k$; action and reactions have distinct variables from each other;
2. the constraint $\varphi \in \mathrm{L}$ is such that $\varphi = \varphi_a \wedge \varphi_1 \wedge \ldots \wedge \varphi_k$, where φ_a is defined over the variables of the action, and the constraint $\varphi_i \in \mathrm{L}$ is defined over the variables of the action and of the i-th reaction $A_i \hookrightarrow B_i$ for $i : 1, \ldots, k$;
3. the constraint $A_i = B_j$ is not satisfiable for $i \neq j$;
4. the constraint $A_i = A_j \wedge \varphi_a \wedge \varphi_i \wedge \varphi_j$ is not satisfiable for $i \neq j$.

In the following $\mathcal{H} \longrightarrow \mathcal{B} : \varphi$ will denote a rule without reaction. The variables shared between an action and a reaction, and occurring in φ_i are the *communication channels* between the sender and a receiver. Condition 3 rules out cyclic reactions, and condition 4 ensures the determinism of reactions.

For instance, let be R the following *invalidation step* of a coherence protocol $invalid(p, m) \longrightarrow modified(p', m') \, [modified(q, n) \hookrightarrow invalid(q', n')] : \varphi$, where φ is defined as $p \neq q, m' = m = n' = n, p' = p, q' = q$; p, q can be interpreted as processor identifiers, and m, n as addresses of data stored in the local caches.

Definition 4. An $\hookrightarrow\mathrm{MSR}(C)$ *specification* is a tuple $\langle \mathrm{P}, \mathrm{C}, \mathrm{I}, \mathrm{R} \rangle$, where P is a set of predicate symbols, C is a constraint system, I is a set of configurations (initial configurations), and R is a set of $\hookrightarrow\mathrm{MSR}(C)$ rules built over P.

Let $\oplus$ and $\ominus$ denote *multiset union* and *difference*, respectively. Furthermore, let $\preccurlyeq$ indicate the *multiset ordering*: $\mathcal{M} \preccurlyeq \mathcal{N}$ if $\zeta_A(\mathcal{M}) \leq \zeta_A(\mathcal{N})$ for every ground atom A, where $\zeta_A(\mathcal{M})$ is the number of occurrences of A in $\mathcal{M}$. The operational semantics of an $\hookrightarrow\mathrm{MSR}(C)$ specification $\langle \mathrm{P}, \mathrm{C}, \mathrm{I}, \mathrm{R} \rangle$ is defined as follows.

Definition 5 (Enabling a Rule). A rule $\mathcal{H} \longrightarrow \mathcal{B} \, [A_1 \hookrightarrow B_1, \ldots, A_k \hookrightarrow B_k] : \varphi$ from R is *enabled at* a configuration $\mathcal{M}$ *via* $\sigma \in \mathrm{S}(\varphi)$ if $\sigma(\mathcal{H}) \preccurlyeq \mathcal{M}$.

Definition 6 (Firing a Rule). Suppose the rule R defined as $\equiv \mathcal{H} \longrightarrow \mathcal{B}[A_1 \hookrightarrow B_1, \ldots, A_k \hookrightarrow B_k] : \varphi$ is enabled at $\mathcal{M}$ via $\sigma \in \mathrm{S}(\varphi)$. Firing it at $\mathcal{M}$ yields the configuration $\mathcal{M}'$, written $\mathcal{M} \Rightarrow_R \mathcal{M}'$, if there exists $n \geq 0$ such that

1. $\mathcal{M} = \sigma(\mathcal{H}) \oplus (C_1 \mid \ldots \mid C_n) \oplus \mathcal{Q}$, and $\mathcal{M}' = \sigma(\mathcal{B}) \oplus (C_1' \mid \ldots \mid C_n') \oplus \mathcal{Q}$;
2. $C_1 \mid \ldots \mid C_n$ is the *maximal* multiset contained in $\mathcal{M} \ominus \sigma(\mathcal{H})$ such that: for every $i : 1, \ldots, n$ there exists $\sigma_i \in S(\varphi)$ with $\sigma_{i|V} = \sigma_{|V}$, $V \subseteq \mathrm{V}$ being the set of variables of the *action* $\mathcal{H} \longrightarrow \mathcal{B}$, and there exists a *reaction* $A_{j_i} \hookrightarrow B_{j_i}$ $j_i \in \{1, \ldots k\}$, such that $\sigma_i(A_{j_i}) = C_i$ and $\sigma_i(B_{j_i}) = C_i'$.

The values associated to the variables occurring in the action are fixed by condition 1. Condition 2 allows the same reaction to be applied to different processes (atomic formulas) with possibly different values of the variables not in V, the only constraint being for the resulting mapping to satisfy the constraint φ. From condition 2, it follows that Q has no occurrences of atomic formulas that can be unified (so that all the resulting constraints are satisfied) with the left-hand side of a reaction, in other words every process ready to react *must react*.

Let $\mathcal{M}$ be $invalid(5,2) \mid modified(1,2) \mid modified(1,3) \mid modified(3,2)$. The rule R of the previous example is enabled at $\mathcal{M}$, and, since the reactions can be applied only for $m = n = 2$, when fired, it yields the new configuration defined as $modified(5,2) \mid invalid(1,2) \mid modified(1,3) \mid invalid(3,2)$.

We conclude this section defining the predecessor operator.

Definition 7 (Pre-Image). Let S be a set of configurations. The *predecessor* operator Pre is defined as $Pre(S) = \{\mathcal{M} \mid \mathcal{M} \Rightarrow_R \mathcal{M}', \mathcal{M}' \in S, R \in \mathrm{R}\}$.

3   A Consistency Protocol for Virtual Shared Memory

In this section we will focus our attention on the *broadcast distributed manager* protocol for maintaining a virtual shared memory consistent, proposed by Li and Hudak in [20]. In [18], Fisler and Girault modeled this protocol as a Colored Petri Net (CPN) parametric on numbers of threads, processors, and pages. They manually validated the parametric model, and they automatically validated some of its finite-state instances. Our aim will be to automatically validate a parametric model. In this protocol the virtual shared memory is organized into *pages*. Every processor has a *page table* used to maintain the status of each page relative to the processor. The status indicates the processor access rights to the page, namely *nil*, *read*, or *write* (that includes *read*), and whether or not the processor is the *owner* of the page. Intuitively, the owner is the last one that modified the page. Several processors may have read access to a page at once, whereas write access is exclusive. An important feature of this case-study is that the owner *changes over time*. The owner takes care of providing the page contents to any other processor that requests them and keeps track of all other processes that have read access to the page in a *copy-set*. Every processor must be told to invalidate its own copy before a write to the page occurs. Following [18], we consider a system in which: processors may contain several threads, but only one thread per processor is capable of faulting (this thread has it own handler); each processor has a single server; furthermore, broadcast is atomic (broadcast messages arrive before all other messages). When a processor wants to gain privileges it does not

Read and Write Faults

1. $\epsilon \longrightarrow rf(i,p)$: $true$ 2. $\epsilon \longrightarrow wf(i,p)$: $true$

Read Handler

3. $rf(i,p) \mid pt(j,q,l,o,a) \longrightarrow hrp(i,p) \mid pt(j,q,l',o,a)$:
$$i=j, p=q, l=\neg\mathbf{lck}, o=\neg\mathbf{own}, a=\mathbf{nil}, l'=\mathbf{lck}$$

4. $hrp(i,p) \mid pt(k,q,l,o,a) \longrightarrow hre(i,p) \mid pt(k,q,l',o,a) \mid sr(k,p)$:
$$k \neq i, p=q, l=\neg\mathbf{lck}, o=\mathbf{own}, l'=\mathbf{lck}$$

5. $hre(i,p) \mid pt(j,q,l,o,a) \longrightarrow pt(j,q,p,l',o,a')$:
$$i=j, p=q, l=\mathbf{lck}, l'=\neg\mathbf{lck}, a'=\mathbf{rd}$$

Read Server

6. $sr(i,p) \mid pt(j,q,l,o,a) \longrightarrow pt(j,q,l',o,a')$:
$$i=j, p=q, l=\mathbf{lck}, l'=\neg\mathbf{lck}, a'=\mathbf{rd}$$

Write Miss

7. $wf(i,p) \mid pt(j,q,l,o,a) \longrightarrow hwp(i,p) \mid pt(j,q,l',o,a)$:
$$i=j, p=q, l=\neg\mathbf{lck}, a=\mathbf{nil}, l'=\mathbf{lck}$$

8. $wf(i,p) \mid pt(j,q,l,o,a) \longrightarrow hwp(i,p) \mid pt(j,q,l',o,a)$:
$$i=j, p=q, l=\neg\mathbf{lck}, o=\neg\mathbf{own}, a=\mathbf{rd}, l'=\mathbf{lck}$$

9. $wf(i,p) \mid pt(j,q,l,o,a) \longrightarrow hwi(i,p) \mid pt(j,q,l',o,a)$:
$$i=j, p=q, l=\neg\mathbf{lck}, o=\mathbf{own}, a=\mathbf{rd}, l'=\mathbf{lck}$$

10. $hwp(i,p) \mid pt(k,q,l,o,a) \longrightarrow hwi(i,p) \mid pt(k,q,l',o,a) \mid sw(k,q)$:
$$k \neq i, p=q, l=\neg\mathbf{lck}, o=\mathbf{own}, l'=\mathbf{lck}$$

Invalidation

11. $hwi(i,p) \mid pt(j,q,l,o,a) \longrightarrow pt(j,q,l',o',a') \; [pt(k,r,m,s,b) \hookrightarrow pt(k,q,m,s,b')]$:
$$i=j, p=q, l=\mathbf{lck}, l'=\neg\mathbf{lck}, o'=\mathbf{own}, a'=\mathbf{wrt}, k \neq i, p=r, b'=\mathbf{nil}$$

Write Server

12. $sw(i,p) \mid pt(j,q,l,o,a) \longrightarrow pt(j,q,l',o',a')$:
$$i=j, p=q, l=\mathbf{lck}, o=\mathbf{own}, l'=\neg\mathbf{lck}, o'=\neg\mathbf{own}, a'=\mathbf{nil}$$

Fig. 1. Broadcast distributed manager

have, it faults and invokes a *handler* to request the page. Requests are broadcast to all other processors. The owner responds running a *server* while entries in the page table are locked to avoid conflicts between handlers and servers on the same processor.

In Fig 1 we illustrate an $\hookrightarrow$MSR-specification based on *linear arithmetic constraints* where conjunctions are like $x > z, x > y, t = 3$. The logic of the specification follows the CPN model of [18] from which we borrow the names of some places as described below. *Faulting threads* (the only one being interesting) are represented via atomic formulas $rf(i,p)$ (a read fault on processor i relative to page p) and $wf(i,p)$ (a write fault). Furthermore, entries in the page table of processor i will be represented via the atomic formula $pt(i,p,l,o,a)$, p being the page identifier, $l \in \{\mathbf{lck}, \neg\mathbf{lck}\}$ denoting whether the page entry for p is locked on i; $o \in \{\textbf{own}, \neg\textbf{own}\}$ denoting whether or not processor i is the owner of p; and $a \in \{\textbf{nil}, \textbf{rd}, \textbf{wrt}\}$ denoting the access rights of i for page p. Page contents are not relevant for the properties we consider here (mutual-exclusion). All free variables range over integers and may get unbounded values in a derivation starting from $init$, whereas the previous constants (**lck** etc.) must be read as fixed integer values. In the CPN model of [18] each entry of a page table has a local copy-set. However, as formally proved on the CPN model in [18], only the copy-set of the owner is of interest for the logic of the protocol. Taking this assumption, we model the *copy-set* via the multiset of entries with **rd** access rights contained in the current configurations. Only the current owner can modify it.

The first block of rules in Fig 1 non-deterministically simulates *write* and *read* faults. The second and third block define the behavior of read handlers and servers. On a read fault rf, the processor invokes the *read handler* (hrp=handler-read-prepare) that takes care of contacting the current owner of the page. Before terminating its execution, the (hre=handler-read-end) the handler modifies the rights of the processor entry page. The *read server* (modeled as sr) takes care of updating the rights of the owner entry page. The last blocks define the behavior of write handlers and servers. On a write fault wf, we distinguish two cases. If the processor on which the processor runs is the owner, then the thread directly goes to the invalidation state hwi (this avoids Error 2 of [18]). Otherwise, the processor invokes a *write handler* (hwp=handler-write-prepare) and locks the entry of the page table, while the handler moves to the invalidation-phase (hwi=handler-write-invalidate). At this stage the handler acquires the ownership of the page, updates his rights to *write*, while invalidating all processors reading that page. We model the invalidation-phase atomically using an action-reaction rule. The *write server* (modeled as sw) of the owner downgrades its rights to the page, relinquishes the ownership (this avoids Error 1 of [18]) of the page and then terminates. The initial states I are the configurations in which one processor is the owner (with read access) of all pages. Note that in our specification the values of the processor identifiers and pages are left unbounded.

The *safety property* we would like to establish on our specification is *mutual exclusion*. Specifically, we would like to ensure that the *write* access is *exclusive* for *any number of threads, processors, and pages*. We will come back to this verification problem after describing our method to handle this kind of parameterized invalidation-based protocols with unbounded local data.

4   Symbolic Verification Procedures

A parameterized safety property like mutual exclusion for our case study holds if and only if $I \cap Pre^*(U) = \emptyset$, where U is the infinite collection of *unsafe* configurations (infinite because of the number of processes and values of local data). In our example (as in many other practical situations [1,16,13]) unsafe states turn out to be *upward-closed* w.r.t. multiset inclusion $\preccurlyeq$.

Definition 8. A set of configurations S is *upward-closed* whenever $Up(S) = S$, where $Up(S) = \{\mathcal{N} \mid \mathcal{M} \preccurlyeq \mathcal{N}, \ \mathcal{M} \in S\}$.

To finitely represent the *generators* of an upward closed set of configurations, in [14] we introduced the notion of *constrained configuration* whose *rich denotation* consists of the *upward closure* of its *ground instances*. As an example, the *violations* to readers-writers mutual exclusion for Li-Hudak's protocol can be represented via

$$pt(i, p, l, o, a) \mid pt(k, q, m, s, b) \ : \ i \neq k, p = q, a = \mathbf{rd}, b = \mathbf{wrt}$$

whose denotations are: $(pt(u, v, w, y, \mathbf{rd}) \mid pt(u', v', w', y', \mathbf{wrt})) \oplus \mathcal{M}$ for any integers $u, v, u', v', \ldots \in \mathbb{Z}$, with $u \neq u'$, and for any other configuration $\mathcal{M}$. This example explains the reason why we introduced constraints in our specification language: they provide a natural symbolic representation for relations over data of different processes. Constrained configurations are defined as follows.

Definition 9 (Constrained Configuration). A *constrained configuration* has the form $p_1(x_{11}, \ldots, x_{1k_1}) \mid \ldots \mid p_n(x_{n1}, \ldots, x_{nk_n}) \ : \ \varphi$ where $p_1, \ldots, p_n \in$ P, $x_{i1}, \ldots, x_{ik_i} \in$ V for $i : 1, \ldots n$ and $\varphi \in$ L; the variables $x_{11}, \ldots$ are distinct each other.

The *set of ground instances* of a constrained configuration $\mathcal{M} : \varphi$ is defined as $Inst(\mathcal{M} : \varphi) = \{\sigma(\mathcal{M}) \mid \sigma \in \mathrm{S}(\varphi)\}$. The previous definition can be extended to *sets of constrained configurations* with *disjoint variables*, written $\mathbf{S}$, $\mathbf{S}'$, etc., in the natural way. *Rich denotations* are built as follows.

Definition 10 (Rich Denotation). Given a set $\mathbf{S}$ of constrained configurations (with disjoint variables), its denotation is defined as $[\![\mathbf{S}]\!] = Up(Inst(\mathbf{S}))$.

We will define next a symbolic pre-image operator **Pre** working on our assertional language according to the *rich* denotation of constrained configurations. Let us first introduce the notion of *unification* between two multisets of atomic formulas (with disjoint variables). The relation $(A_1 \mid \ldots \mid A_n) =_\theta (B_1 \mid \ldots \mid B_m)$ holds provided $m = n$ and the constraint $\theta = \bigwedge_{i=1}^{n} A_i = B_{j_i}$ is *satisfiable*, $j_1, \ldots, j_n$ being a permutation of $1, \ldots, n$. Finally, a *variant* of an formula is obtained by renaming its free variables with *fresh names*. We are ready now to define the operator **Pre**.

Definition 11 (Symbolic Pre-image). Let $\mathbf{S}$ be a set of C-constrained configurations. The symbolic predecessor operator **Pre** is defined as follows: $(\mathcal{N} : \xi) \in \mathbf{Pre}(\mathbf{S})$ if and only if there exists a *variant* $(\mathcal{M} : \psi)$ of a constrained configuration in $\mathbf{S}$, a *variant* $\mathcal{H} \longrightarrow \mathcal{B} \ [\ A_1 \hookrightarrow B_1, \ldots, A_k \hookrightarrow B_k \ ] : \varphi$ of a rule in R (recall that $\varphi = \varphi_a \wedge \varphi_1 \wedge \ldots \wedge \varphi_k$ as from Def. 3), and multisets $\mathcal{M}', \mathcal{B}', \mathcal{Q}$ and $n \geq 0$ such that

1. $\mathcal{M} = \mathcal{M}' \oplus (C_1 \mid \ldots \mid C_n) \oplus \mathcal{Q}$;
2. $\mathcal{B}' \preccurlyeq \mathcal{B}$ and $\mathcal{M}' =_\theta \mathcal{B}'$;
3. for all $i : 1, \ldots, n$ there exist $j_i \in \{1, \ldots, k\}$ and *variants* $A'_{j_i} \hookrightarrow B'_{j_i}$ and φ'_{j_i} of a reaction $A_{j_i} \hookrightarrow B_{j_i}$ and of the associated constraint φ_{j_i} (both obtained via the renaming ι_i) such that: $C_{j_i} =_{\theta_i} B'_{j_i}$ holds, the constraint $\gamma_i \equiv \psi \wedge \theta \wedge \varphi_a \wedge \varphi'_{j_i} \wedge \theta_i$ is satisfiable;

4. Q does not contain occurrences of atomic formulas D for which there exist $q \in \{1, \ldots, k\}$ (i.e. a reaction $A_q \hookrightarrow B_q$) such that $D =_\tau A_q$ holds, and $\psi \wedge \theta \wedge \varphi_a \wedge \varphi_q \wedge \tau$ is satisfiable;
5. $\mathcal{N} = \mathcal{H} \oplus (A'_{j_1} \mid \ldots \mid A'_{j_n}) \oplus Q$;
6. the constraint ξ defined as $\exists x_1 \ldots \exists x_u. \gamma_1 \wedge \ldots \wedge \gamma_n$ is satisfiable, where $x_1, \ldots, x_u$ are all the variables of $\gamma_1, \ldots, \gamma_n$ that do not occur in $\mathcal{N}$.

The symbolic operator **Pre** returns a set of constrained configurations and it is correct and complete with respect to Pre, i.e., $[\![\mathbf{Pre}(\mathbf{S})]\!] = Pre([\![\mathbf{S}]\!])$ for any $\mathbf{S}$.

As an example, consider the constrained multiset $M \equiv (\mathcal{M} : \varphi)$, where $\mathcal{M}$ is the multiset $modified(p,m) \mid modified(q,n)$, and φ is the constraint $m = n$ and the rule R we introduced in previous examples. Then, by selecting $\mathcal{M}' = \epsilon$ and $\mathcal{B}' = \epsilon$ in Def. 11, we obtain M itself. However, all other attempts of matching R with M fail (M does not satisfy the maximality of reaction applications). Contrary, $(invalid(r,l) \mid invalid(p,m) \mid modified(q,n) : l = m = n)$ has several predecessors like $(modified(r,l) \mid modified(p,m) \mid invalid(q,n) : l = m, m = n)$ as well as $(invalid(r,l) \mid modified(p,m) \mid invalid(q,n) : l = m = n)$; the latter expresses the fact that cache r was already invalid before firing R.

To define a symbolic reachability algorithm, we still need a comparison operator between constrained configurations.

Definition 12. An *entailment* $\sqsubseteq$ between constrained configurations is a relation such that $M \sqsubseteq N$ implies $[\![N]\!] \subseteq [\![M]\!]$.

We can now rephrase *backward reachability* as follows. Let $\mathbf{U}$ be a set of constrained configurations. We first compute $Pre^*(\mathbf{U})$: starting from $\mathbf{U}$, we repeatedly apply **Pre** to all stored constrained configurations. We stop when it is not possible to store new constrained configurations (i.e. for each new constrained configuration M we already computed N such that $N \sqsubseteq M$). If the fixpoint computation terminates we check that the initial configurations representing the *initial states* of the system are not contained in the denotation of the resulting set of constrained configurations (e.g. $init \notin [\![\mathbf{Pre}^*(\mathbf{U})]\!]$).

5 Sufficient Conditions for Termination

As shown in Section 3, our examples make use of arithmetic constraints. Thus, the termination of the symbolic backward reachability procedure cannot be guaranteed in general. To obtain sufficient conditions for termination, we need severe restrictions on the form of constraints and rewrite rules we allow in the specification. Let us first introduce the class NC of linear constraints defined as conjunctions of atomic formulas either of the form $x > y$ or $x = y$. Let us assume that all predicates in P have arity n. Given a constrained configuration $\mathcal{M} : \varphi$ let V_i be the set of variables occurring in position i in atoms of M for $i : 1, \ldots, n$. Finally, let $Var(\varphi)$ be the set of variables occurring in φ. Then, we further restrict NC-constrained configurations as follows.

Definition 13. An NC-constrained configuration $(\mathcal{M} : \varphi)$ is k-separable if φ can be partitioned into $\varphi_1, \ldots, \varphi_n$ such that $Var(\varphi_i) \subseteq V_i$ for $i : 1, \ldots, n$, and $x = y$ follows from φ_i for all $x, y \in V_i$, $i \neq k$.

Without loss of generality, we restrict our attention to k-separable constrained configurations in which all variables in position k (thus, the corresponding atomic formulas) are *totally ordered* w.r.t. to the $=$ and $>$ relations induced by φ_k. Given a k-separable constrained configuration C defined as $(\mathcal{M} : \varphi)$, C can be uniquely represented as a *string* $Str(C)$ of *multisets* of symbols in P built as follows. We first group together all atomic formulas in which the corresponding variables in position k are related via equality constraints. Then, we order the resulting groups according to the $>$ relation induced by φ_k. Since φ is satisfiable, we obtain an acyclic path. Finally, we represent every group of atomic formulas as the multiset obtained by selecting the corresponding predicate symbols.

For instance, given $C = p(a, x) \mid p(b, y) \mid q(c, z) : a = b = c, x > y, y = z$ we first group together the atomic formulas as follows: $C_1 = \{p(a, x)\}$, and $C_2 = \{p(b, z), q(c, y)\}$. $S(C)$ is then the string of multisets: $p \cdot pq$.

Definition 14. Given two k-separable constrained configurations C and D such that $S(C) = \mathcal{M}_1 \cdot \ldots \cdot \mathcal{M}_k$ and $S(D) = \mathcal{N}_1 \cdot \ldots \cdot \mathcal{N}_r$, let $C \sqsubseteq^* D$ iff there exists an *injective* mapping h from $1, \ldots, k$ to $1, \ldots, r$ such that if $i < j$ then $h(i) < h(j)$, and $\mathcal{M}_i \preccurlyeq \mathcal{N}_{h(i)}$ for $i : 1, \ldots, k$ ($\preccurlyeq$ denotes *multiset inclusion*).

It turns out that $\sqsubseteq^*$ is an entailment. Furthermore, following from the properties of the multiset and string embeddings [19], $\sqsubseteq^*$ is a *well-quasi-ordering*. Now, let us impose the following restriction on $\hookrightarrow$MSR(NC)-specifications.

Definition 15. A k-*separable specification* is such that the multisets occurring in the action and reactions of a rule $\mathcal{H} \longrightarrow \mathcal{B} \, [A_1 \hookrightarrow B_1, \ldots, A_n \hookrightarrow B_n] : \varphi$, are k-separable constrained configurations w.r.t. $\varphi_a, \varphi_1, \ldots, \varphi_n$.

Then, we obtain the following results.

Theorem 1. The class of k-separable constrained configuration is closed under applications of **Pre** associated to a k-separable specification. The symbolic backward reachability algorithm always terminates when taking in input a k-separable specification and a set of k-separable constrained configurations.

6   Experimental Results

We have implemented the backward reachability algorithm using the SICStus term manipulation and constraint solving libraries (e.g. for linear constraints). We used our prototype to analyze the Li-Hudak protocol of Fig. 1. We recall that our specification is a reformulation of the CPN model of [18] formally validated via static analysis and model checking. However, as shown in Fig. 2, we automatically discovered after 11 steps the following *error-trace*:

1. on a read fault a thread t (not running on the owner) invokes its handler and then suspends;

2. the server of the owner grants the request and updates its entry page;
3. a thread s running on the owner faults for write access;
4. the owner grants it;
5. the handler of s invalidates all other processors and the owner's rights upgrade to *write*;
6. finally, the suspended thread t updates its entry page to *read*.

This error trace uncovers a violation to writer exclusivity in the CPN model of [18]. From personal communication, Kathi Fisler informed us that this model was validated only manually (via static analysis). The analysis uncovered other errors but not the previous critical one. The models automatically verified with Cospan and Murϕ in [18] were based instead on different assumptions on interprocessor communication. Interestingly, the error we uncovered matches the Error 3 of [18] that Fisler and Girault only discovered using a more refined CPN model with explicit queue channels. However, the previous error occurs even in the more abstract model: it is caused, in fact, by a missing synchronization between handlers and servers. The nature of this error also reveals an ambiguity in the original, informal specification [20]: the notation used by Li and Hudak does not clarify, in fact, whether or not a broadcast should be *blocking* for the sender. This case study reveals once again the difficulties in using manual abstractions (i.e. to pass from the CPN model to another one) when modeling complex protocols.

To correct the error, the handler must wait for an acknowledgment from the server. We have encoded the corrected model in our framework, and we have automatically verified mutual exclusion (we computed the fixpoint in 7 steps and 0.8s on a Pentium II 450Mhz) as well as other properties (e.g. the owner (of unlocked pages) is unique, there is only one page entry for each page and node), whose violations can be naturally expressed in our assertional language) for an *arbitrary number* of *threads*, *processors*, and *pages*.

Finally, we have also modeled and automatically verified mutual exclusion for three cache coherence protocols for multi-processor systems (M.S.I., Synapse, and M.E.S.I. see Fig. 2) that, differently from previous models given via Broadcast protocols [15,16,13], we formulated for an *arbitrary number* of cache and memory lines (see the rule example of the introduction).

Model	Verification Problem	Steps	Size	Time	Verified?
Li-Hudak model Fig. 1	Read/write mutex	11	3600	6609s	Error found
Correct Li-Hudak model	Read/write mutex	7	24	0.8s	Yes
M.S.I. with many cache lines	Read/write mutex	1	2	0.01s	Yes
Synapse N+1 "	Read/write mutex	1	2	0.01s	Yes
M.E.S.I. "	Read/write mutex	3	7	0.1s	Yes

Fig. 2. Experimental results on a Pentium II 450Mhz

7 Conclusions and Related Works

With this work we have enlarged the scope of parameterized verification to invalidation-based protocols formulated at a greater level of detail than Broadcast Protocols: processes may have here unbounded local data and communicate via value passing. This way, we were able to analyze and observe interesting properties in different formal models of cache coherence protocols.

The model presented here can neither be formulated nor analyzed in the framework we proposed in [10], in which only rendez-vous is allowed as synchronization mechanism for colored tokens. Furthermore, contrary to what we claimed in [10], the class of separable specifications isolated in [10] must be futher restricted (e.g. using the notion of k-separability) to obtain the termination of backward reachability. Together with the automated analysis of a parameterized formulation of the *ticket algorithm* considered in [10], the preliminary results of our work show the potential interest of this line of research. Another possible way to model invalidation-phases in multiset rewriting would be to introduce tests for the emptiness of a place as in Gamma [21] or as in Petri Nets with inhibitor arcs. However, in [21] the authors need to use conservative *counting* abstractions to validate their Gamma specifications. In [21] they apply this method to verify a manually constructed abstract model of Li-Hudak protocol, in which, e.g., they do not distinguish between owners and writers. At this level of abstraction it is not possible to uncover the ambiguities in the original informal specification. In [8] a combination of manual abstractions, theorem proving (PVS), and automated abstractions (PAX [7]) has been used to verify Li-Hudak's protocol. The authors considered assumptions different from those taken in the first CPN model of [18]. Our work is inspired to the approach of [2,4], where *existential regions* are proposed as symbolic representation of configurations for parameterized Timed Petri Nets. In [3], Abdulla and Jonsson have used similar techniques to prove termination for backward reachability of *Unordered Channel Systems* in which messages can vary over an infinite *name* domain. However, they do not provide any mechanism for invalidation-phases. Networks of *finite-state* processes can be analyzed using the automata theoretic approach of [9,12,23], where sets of global states are represented as *regular languages*, and transitions as relations on languages. Symbolic exploration can then be performed using operations over automata with ad hoc accelerations (see e.g. [9]), or with automated abstractions techniques (see e.g. [7]).

Our work is complementary to the approach based on the *deductive method* with *invisible invariants* of [6], in which invariants are first generated and then proved to be inductive. We follow here, in fact, the paradigm of *symbolic model checking with rich assertional languages* [22]. The two approaches can be used to attack similar problems using different point-of-views.

As future work we plan to investigate techniques for handling liveness properties, more realistic broadcast with message queues, and more complex properties like sequential consistency.

Acknowledgements

We would like to thank Moshe Vardi for having helped us to find new directions in our research, and Kathi Fisler for fruitful discussions.

References

1. P. A. Abdulla, K. Cerāns, B. Jonsson, Y.-K. Tsay. General Decidability Theorems for Infinite-State Systems. In *Proc. LICS'96*, pp. 313–321, 1996. 296, 297, 301
2. P. A. Abdulla, B. Jonsson. Verifying Networks of Timed Processes (Extended Abstract). In *Proc. TACAS '98*, pp. 298–312. Springer, 1998. 306
3. P. A. Abdulla, B. Jonsson. Channel Representations in Protocol Verification. In *Proc. CONCUR 2001*, pp. 1–15. Springer, 2001. 306
4. P. A. Abdulla, A. Nylén. Better is Better than Well: On Efficient Verification of Infinite-State Systems. In *Proc. LICS 2000*, pp. 132–140, 2000. 306
5. P. A. Archibald, J. Baer. Cache Coherence Protocols: Evaluation Using a Multi-processor Simulation Model. *TOCS* 4(4): 273–298. 1986. 295
6. T. Arons, A. Pnueli, S. Ruah, Y. Xu, L. Zuck Parameterized Verification with Automatically Computed Inductive Assertions. In *Proc. CAV '01*, pp. 221-234, 2001. 306
7. K. Baukus, S. Bensalem, Y. Lakhnech, K. Stahl. Abstracting WS1S Systems to Verify Parameterized Networks. In *Proc. TACAS '00*, pp. 188-203, 2000. 306
8. K. Baukus, K. Stahl, S. Bensalem, Y. Lakhnech. Networks of Processes with Parameterized State Space. In *Proc. VEPAS '01*, ENTCS vol. 50, issue 4, 2001. 306
9. A. Bouajjani, B. Jonsson, M. Nilsson, T. Touilli. Regular Model Checking. In *Proc. CAV'00*, pp. 403-418, 2000. 306
10. M. Bozzano, G. Delzanno. Beyond Parameterized Verification. In *Proc. TACAS'02*, April 2002. 296, 297, 306
11. I. Cervesato, N. A. Durgin, P. Lincoln, J. C. Mitchell, A. Scedrov. A Meta-notation for Protocol Analysis. In *Proc. CSFW 1999*, pp. 55–69, 1999. 296
12. E. Clarke, O. Grumberg, S. Jha. Verifying Parameterized Networks. *TOPLAS* 19(5): 726–750, 1997. 306
13. G. Delzanno. Automatic Verification of Parameterized Cache Coherence Protocols. In *Proc. CAV 2000*, pp. 53–68, 2000. 297, 301, 305
14. G. Delzanno. An assertional language for systems parametric in several dimensions. In *Proc. VEPAS 2001*, ENTCS 50(4), 2001. 296, 297, 302
15. E. A. Emerson, K. S. Namjoshi. On Model Checking for Non-deterministic Infinite-state Systems. In *Proc. LICS '98*, pp. 70–80, 1998. 295, 296, 305
16. J. Esparza, A. Finkel, R. Mayr. On the Verification of Broadcast Protocols. In *Proc. LICS'99*, pp. 352–359, 1999. 295, 297, 301, 305
17. A. Finkel, P. Schnoebelen. Well-structured transition systems everywhere! *TCS*, 256(1-2):63–92, 2001. 296, 297
18. K. Fisler, C. Girault. Modelling and Model Checking a Distributed Shared Memory Consistency Protocol. In *Proc. ICATPN '98*, pp. 84-103, 2001. 296, 297, 299, 300, 301, 304, 305, 306
19. G. Highman. Ordering by Divisibility in Abstract Algebras. *Proc. London Math. Soc.*, 2:326–336, 1952. 304

20. K. Li, P. Hudak. Memory Coherence in Shared Virtual Memory Systems. TOCS 7(4): 321-359, 1989. 295, 297, 299, 305
21. D. Mentré, D. Le Métayer, T. Priol. Formalization and Verification of Coherence Protocols with the Gamma Framework. In *Proc. PDSE 2000*, pp. 105-113, 2000. 296, 306
22. Y. Kesten, O. Maler, M. Marcus, A. Pnueli, E. Shahar. Symbolic Model Checking with Rich Assertional Languages. In *Proc. CAV'97*, pp. 424–435, 1997. 306
23. A. P. Sistla, V. Gyuris. Parametrized Verification of Linear Networks using Automata as Invariants. *Formal Aspects of Computing*, 11(4):402–425, 1999. 306

Formal Verification of Complex Out-of-Order Pipelines by Combining Model-Checking and Theorem-Proving

Christian Jacobi*

IBM Deutschland Entwicklung GmbH, Processor Development II
71032 Boeblingen, Germany
cjacobi@de.ibm.com

Abstract. We describe a methodology for the formal verification of complex out-of-order pipelines as they may be used as execution units in out-of-order processors. The pipelines may process multiple instructions simultaneously, may have branches and cycles in the pipeline structure, may have variable latency, and may reorder instructions internally. The methodology combines model-checking for the verification of the pipeline control, and theorem proving for the verification of the pipeline functionality. In order to combine both techniques, we formally verify that the FairCTL operators defined in μ-calculus match their intended semantics expressed in a form where computation traces are explicit, since this form is better suited for theorem proving. This allows the formally safe translation of model-checked properties of the pipeline control into a theorem-proving friendly form, which is used for the verification of the overall correctness, including the functionality. As an example we prove the correctness of the pipeline of a multiplication/division floating point unit with all the features mentioned above.

1 Introduction

As microprocessor designs become increasingly complex, validation using traditional simulation becomes more and more insufficient to ensure the correctness of the design. Over the last years, formal methods have proved to be applicable to very complex systems such as out-of-order processors [10, 17, 14, 3, 13]. However, except for [13], these processors only contain very simple execution units. They can process only one instruction at a time, and their pipelines have a simple structure. Furthermore, the delay of the execution units is often assumed to be fixed. In contrast, modern execution units process multiple instructions simultaneously, may have branches and cycles in the pipeline structure (e.g., for iterative division algorithms), may have variable latency for each instruction, and may reorder instructions internally, i.e., instructions do not need to leave the pipeline in the order they entered it. In [13], a Tomasulo scheduler [19] has

---

* The work reported here was done while the author was affiliated with Saarland University.

D. Brinksma and K. G. Larsen (Eds.): CAV 2002, LNCS 2404, pp. 309–323, 2002.

been verified which is capable of using such execution units; however, neither the design nor the verification of the actual execution units is described in [13].

In this paper we describe a methodology for the verification of pipelined execution units with the features described above. As an example we describe the verification of the pipeline of a multiplication/division floating point unit, whose combinatorial datapaths have been verified in [4]. The pipeline can process up to six instructions simultaneously. The difficulty in the verification of such complex pipelines arises from the fact that pipelines consist of a control-dominated part which schedules the processing of the instructions in the pipeline, while simultaneously the effect of the datapaths on the data of each instruction has to be considered in order to guarantee *functional* correct behavior of the execution unit.

The use of theorem proving for the verification of complex pipelines would involve the construction of an inductive invariant to cope with the control-dominated part. The construction usually has to be performed manually, which is considered the hard part of the verification of out-of-order systems [10, 17, 13]. On the other hand, model-checking is suitable for the automatic verification of control-dominated systems, but becomes infeasible for the verification of complete pipelines due to the data part. Even if one uses abstract datapaths, e.g. uninterpreted functions [6], the state space grows huge due to the large number of (nested) function applications (e.g., due to possible cycles in the pipeline structure).

We propose a methodology which combines the best of both worlds: we use model-checking to verify the control part of the pipelines, and then use theorem proving to conclude overall correctness, including data correctness. We use the PVS theorem proving system [15] with its built-in model-checker [16].

In order to use model-checked properties for the further verification by theorem proving, the model-checked properties have to be translated into a form which is easy to use for theorem proving. In PVS, the FairCTL operators are defined as fixpoints in μ-calculus, which in turn are defined in terms of higher-order logic. These definitions are hard to use in theorem proving. It is more suitable for theorem proving to define computation traces explicitly, and to express temporal properties using standard mathematical quantifiers, e.g., $\forall t: p(t)$ to express a property p to hold for all times t. In order to translate model-checked properties safely from FairCTL to $\forall t$ form, we have proved theorems which relate the FairCTL operators defined in μ-calculus with their intended semantics expressed in $\forall t$ form. These relations are well known [7], but have not been verified using formal methods before.

The mathematics in this paper has been formalized and verified in PVS. For the sake of readability we use standard mathematical notation throughout the paper. All PVS specifications and proofs are available at our web site.[1]

Paper Outline. In the following section, we define the correctness criterion which the execution units shall obey. The correctness criterion is defined in terms of computation traces of a next-state function under a given input se-

---

[1] http://www-wjp.cs.uni-sb.de/projects/verification/{pvsctl,fpu}

quence. We then describe in section 3 how model-checked properties of a system can be translated into the computation trace form. In section 4 we show how model-checking and theorem proving is combined for the verification of complex pipelines. The discussion of related work is postponed to section 5. Section 6 gives a summary.

2   Pipeline Correctness Criterion

In this section we describe the correctness criterions which our execution units (EU, also called *pipelines* in this paper) shall obey. An execution unit can be seen as a black box with inputs and outputs interconnecting the EU with the Tomasulo scheduled processor core. The core *dispatches* instructions by passing the instruction data (operands, op-code, etc.) to the EU along with a tag used to identify the instruction. The EU executes the instruction and returns the result with the corresponding tag to the core. The EU may process several instructions simultaneously, instructions may have variable latency, and the EU may reorder instructions internally, i.e., instructions do not need to leave the pipeline in the order they have entered it. The Tomasulo scheduler from [13] can cope with these possibilities.

The Tomasulo scheduler only dispatches in-struction whose operands are available. There-fore, the pipelines do not have to cope with *data hazards*. The only hazards occurring in the pipelines are *structural hazards*, i.e., multiple in-structions requiring the same resources in the pipeline.

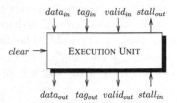

Fig. 1. Execution unit inter-face

Figure 1 shows a black-box view of an execution unit. The *clear* input is activated at power-up and during interupts in order to clear the pipeline. Instructions are dispatched into the EU by activating the $valid_{in}$ signal along with the instruction's $data_{in}$ and tag_{in}. The EU then computes the result and returns it by activating $valid_{out}$ along with the proper $data_{out}$ and tag_{out}. The $stall_{out}$ signal is activated if the EU cannot take further instructions; in this case, the scheduler must not dis-patch instructions. Analogously, if the core activates the $stall_{in}$ signal, the EU must not return any instructions. In the following, we ignore the *clear* signal since the implementation and verification of *clear* is simple.

Formalization of the EU Interface. Let S denote the state set of the EU (usually the set of possible contents of the registers in the EU). Let $\mathcal{D}_i$, $\mathcal{D}_o$, and $\mathcal{T}$ denote the set of the input data, output data, and tags, respectively. The *valid* and *stall* signals are booleans. The EU is specified by the following five functions:

1. $ns(S_{cur}, data_{in}, tag_{in}, valid_{in}, stall_{in}) \rightarrow S$: the next-state function, which computes the next state given the current state S_{cur} and the current inputs.
2. $data_{out}(S_{cur}, data_{in}, valid_{in}, stall_{in}) \rightarrow \mathcal{D}_o$: computes the data output of the EU given current state and inputs.

3. $tag_{out}(S_{cur}, tag_{in}, valid_{in}, stall_{in}) \rightarrow \mathcal{T}$: computes the output-tag.
4. $valid_{out}(S_{cur}, valid_{in}, stall_{in}) \rightarrow \mathbb{B}$: computes the valid output.
5. $stall_{out}(S_{cur}, stall_{in}) \rightarrow \mathbb{B}$: computes the stall output.

The functions $data_{out}$, tag_{out}, $valid_{out}$, and $stall_{out}$ model the combinatorial circuits computing the corresponding outputs from the (registered) state and the current inputs. Note that not all outputs may depend on all inputs. This is necessary to model absence of *combinatorial* dependencies between some inputs and outputs. For example, $stall_{out}$ only depends on the state and the current $stall_{in}$, i.e., whether the EU accepts a further instruction may not depend on the instruction data or tag.

Let $\mathcal{I} := \mathcal{D}_i \times \mathcal{T} \times \mathbb{B} \times \mathbb{B}$ denote the combination of the inputs of the EU. We recursively define the behavior of a pipeline under an infinite input sequence $I := (i_0, i_1, \ldots) \in \mathcal{I}^{\infty}$. We assume the pipeline to be in some initial state $init \in \mathcal{S}$ at time $t = 0$. The state $s^t(I)$ at time t is recursively defined as

$$s^0(I) := init, \quad s^{t+1}(I) := ns(s^t(I), i_t).$$

We define $data_{out}^t(I)$, $tag_{out}^t(I)$, $valid_{out}^t(I)$, and $stall_{out}^t(I)$ to be the outputs of the pipeline during cycle t, e.g., $stall_{out}^t(I) := stall_{out}(s^t(I), i_t.stall_{in})$. For the sake of convenience, we omit the parameter I if it is clear from the context.

We say a tag $tg \in \mathcal{T}$ is dispatched at time t (denoted by $disp(tg, t)$), if $valid_{in}^t$ and $tag_{in}^t = tg$ hold. The tag is returned at time t (denoted by $ret(tg, t)$), if $valid_{out}^t$ and $tag_{out}^t = tg$ hold. The tag is in use at time t (denoted by $inuse(tg, t)$), if the tag was dispatched and not yet returned, i.e.,

$$inuse(tg, t) := \exists t' < t \colon disp(tg, t') \text{ and } \forall t'' \in \{t', \ldots, t-1\} \colon \neg ret(tg, t'').$$

Correctness Criterion. We can now define the correctness criterions for execution units. A $valid_{out}$ may only be signaled if $stall_{in}$ is not active:

$$\forall t \colon stall_{in}^t \implies \neg valid_{out}^t. \tag{P1}$$

The $stall_{out}$ signal is live, i.e., at each point in time t, it will eventually become inactive (at time t'):

$$\forall t \colon \exists t' \geq t \colon \neg stall_{out}^{t'}. \tag{P2}$$

Instructions dispatched into the EU at time t will eventually be returned (at time t'). We call this property *liveness* of the EU.

$$\forall t \colon disp(tg, t) \implies \exists t' \geq t \colon ret(tg, t'). \tag{P3}$$

The last property, called *tag-consistency*, states that instructions returned at time t by the EU have already been dispatched before (at time t'), and have not already been returned in between (at time t''):

$$\forall t \colon ret(tg, t) \implies \exists t' \leq t \colon disp(tg, t') \text{ and}$$
$$\forall t'' \in \{t', \ldots, t-1\} \colon \neg ret(tg, t''). \tag{P4}$$

Note that the right side of the above definition does not exactly match $inuse(tg, t)$, since here $t' = t$ is allowed. However, it is sufficient to prove $\forall t\colon ret(tg, t) \implies inuse(tg, t)$ in order to assert tag-consistency. Note further that liveness and tag-consistency together yield a one-to-one mapping between dispatched and returned instructions.

Of course the execution unit cannot satisfy these properties if the input sequence does not satisfy some properties itself. The first required input property is that no instruction is dispatched if the $stall_{out}$ is active, analogously to (P1):

$$\forall t\colon stall_{out}^t \implies \neg valid_{in}^t. \tag{I1}$$

The analogue to (P2) is that the $stall_{in}$ signal is live:

$$\forall t\colon \exists t' \geq t\colon \neg stall_{in}^{t'}. \tag{I2}$$

The third input property is called *tag-uniqueness* and requires that no tag tg is dispatched into the EU if it is already in use:

$$\forall t\colon disp(tg, t) \implies \neg inuse(tg, t) \tag{I3}$$

We call an execution unit correct iff for all input sequences I and tags tg the properties (P1) to (P4) hold under the assumptions (I1) to (I3), where not all properties need all assumptions:

$$
\begin{aligned}
EU\,correct &:= (I1) \implies (P1) \text{ and} \\
&\quad (I1) \wedge (I2) \implies (P2) \wedge (P3) \text{ and} \\
&\quad (I1) \wedge (I2) \wedge (I3) \implies (P4).
\end{aligned} \tag{C}
$$

This definition of correctness only covers the correct termination of instructions. In order to cover the input/output data relation, we introduce the notion of *functional correct execution units*. An EU is called *functional correct* with respect to a function $dp\colon \mathcal{D}_i \to \mathcal{D}_o$, iff $dp(data_{in}) = data_{out}$ holds for corresponding inputs and outputs. For example, a floating point unit can be described by a function dp reflecting the combinatorial datapaths, and the pipelined hardware shall compute this function. In order to model functional correctness, we strengthen the liveness property (P3) to cover the relation between data input and output of an instruction:

$$\forall t\colon disp(tg, t) \implies (\exists t' \geq t\colon ret(tg, t') \text{ and } dp(data_{in}^t) = data_{out}^{t'}). \tag{P3'}$$

Formally, we call an execution unit *functional correct* with respect to dp iff (C) holds where (P3) is replaced by (P3').

Note that the definition of (functional) correctness allows multiple instructions (with distinct tags) in the EU simultaneously, and that no restriction on the order in which instructions leave the EU is imposed. Note further that not all EUs have a functional description; a memory unit, e.g., cannot be described by a function dp, since functions are by definition memory-less.

The correctness criterions of the EUs have been arranged with Kröning in order to allow the integration of our EUs into Kröning's Tomasulo core [13].

Example Pipeline. In [4], the verification of the combinatorial datapaths of an IEEE compliant floating point unit (FPU) is reported. Here, we aim at verifying the pipeline of this FPU as an example of our verification approach. Pipelining is not considered in [4]. Figure 2 shows the structure of the pipeline of the multiplication/division floating point unit.

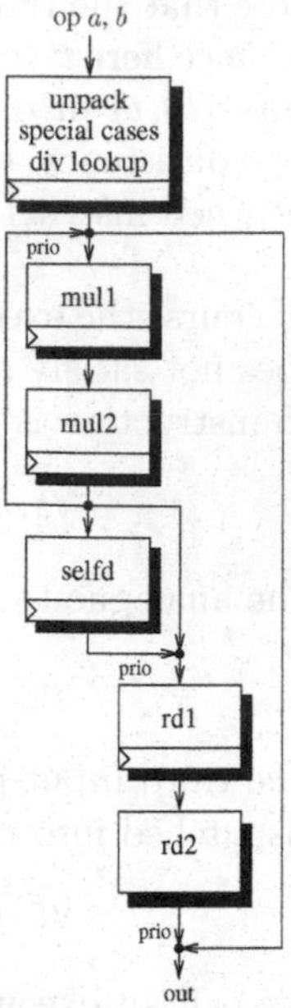

The first pipeline stage performs unpacking of floating point operands, handles special cases (e.g., operations on $\pm\infty$), and initial approximation lookup in case of division. The next two stages comprise a pipelined multiplier. For division, the instructions have to iterate through these stages up to 8 times, depending on the precision of the floating point operation. The *selfd* stage is used for divisions only, multiplications skip this stage. Finally, the results are rounded by a two-stage rounder. Special cases do not flow through the pipeline, but are bypassed from the unpacker to the output.

Each instruction flows through the pipeline until it cannot flow further due to structural hazards, i.e., other instructions in the pipeline require the same resources. For example, if two divisions are iterating simultaniously through the two multiplication stages, a multiplication in the unpack stage has to be stalled. Out-of-order completion in this pipeline can occur in various ways: for example, an operation involving special cases is bypassed to the output while other operations are still in the pipeline. Another example is a multiplication which overtakes a division that iterates through the *mul1* and *mul2* stages.

The FPU from [4] is given as a function md. We have partitioned the computation of this function into sub-functions corresponding to the datapaths of the individual pipeline stages, e.g, functions unp, $mul1$, …. For multiplications on non-special operands $md = rd2 \circ rd1 \circ mul2 \circ mul1 \circ unp$ holds, i.e., multiplication can be performed by consecutive execution of the pipeline stage functions. Analogously, for non-special divisions $md = rd2 \circ rd1 \circ selfd \circ (mul2 \circ mul1)^i \circ unp$ holds, where i is the number of iterations depending on the precision. For the verification of the pipeline, the actual implementation of the datapaths is not important, i.e., the functions can be left uninterpreted. We only have to prove that instructions take the correct path through this pipeline, and that the correct stage functions are applied to the instruction data.

Fig. 2. FPU pipeline

3   Translating FairCTL to $\forall t$ Form

Our goal is to use the PVS built-in model-checker for the verification of temporal properties of the pipeline control, and then to use the theorem prover to conclude overall correctness of the pipeline, including the datapaths. In PVS, the FairCTL operators are defined as fixpoint in μ-calculus [16], whereas we have used temporal properties in $\forall t$ form in the previous section. In order to transform model-checked statements from FairCTL to $\forall t$ form, we formally verify that the FairCTL operators defined as fixpoints in μ-calculus match their intended semantics expressed in $\forall t$ form. These theorems have first been proved in [8] and are well known. However, they have not been verified using formal methods, which is necessary to transform between μ-calculus and $\forall t$ form in a formally safe way. The formal verification depends on the definition of fixpoints and FairCTL operators in the PVS library, and on the Tarski-Knaster argument, which has been verified in PVS in [16]. We omit the proofs in this section, since they follow the very detailed "paper & pencil" proofs from [7].

In this section, systems are described by a state set S and a total next-state *relation* $N \subseteq S \times S$ which models a non-deterministic choice of the next state. In contrast, in the previous section systems were modeled by next state *functions* which deterministically compute the next state from the current state and some inputs. It is easy to transform between the two kinds of systems by "simulating" inputs by non-deterministic choice and vice versa. We come back to this difference at the end of this section.

Let $f \in 2^S$ be a predicate on S, and let ν denote the greatest fixpoint operator. In PVS, the **EX** and **EG** operators, for example, are defined as predicates

$$\mathbf{EX}(N, f) := \lambda s \in S \colon \exists s' \in S \colon f(s') \wedge N(s, s'),$$

$$\mathbf{EG}(N, f) := \nu(\lambda Q \in 2^S \colon f \wedge \mathbf{EX}(N, Q)).$$

An *N-path* is an infinite sequence $(p_0, p_1 \dots) \in S^\infty$ where successive states respect the next-state relation, i.e., $\forall t \colon N(p_t, p_{t+1})$ holds. We have proved the following theorem:

Theorem 1. $\mathbf{EG}(N, f)(s)$ *iff there exists an N-path* $p_0, p_1, \dots$ *starting in s, i.e.* $p_0 = s$, *where all states satisfy f, i.e.,* $\forall t \colon f(p_t)$.

We omit the definitions and theorems or the other FairCTL operators due to lack of space. Instead, we restate the theorems for the **AG** and **fairAF** operators with respect to the semantics of deterministic systems with input sequences below.

Non-Determinism versus Input Sequences. As mentioned above, FairCTL is defined in the context of non-deterministic systems without inputs, whereas deterministic systems with inputs have been used in the previous section to define the correctness of execution units. The use of deterministic next state functions is better suited for the definition of execution units since it is closer to the actual implementation; furthermore, we believe it is simpler to handle in theorem proving. However, the definition of FairCTL in PVS imposes the use of non-deterministic systems for model-checking. It is easy to bridge this gap:

Let $\mathcal{S}$ be the state type, $\mathcal{I}$ be the input type, and $ns : \mathcal{S} \times \mathcal{I} \to \mathcal{S}$ be the deterministic next-state function of a system as in section 2. Further, let $Ip \subseteq \mathcal{S} \times \mathcal{I}$ be an input predicate (e.g., $Ip \equiv stall_{out} \implies \neg valid_{in}$ to model the pipeline input property (I1)). Let $init \in \mathcal{S}$ be the initial state. We define a new state type $\mathcal{S}' := \mathcal{S} \times \mathcal{I}$ and a non-deterministic next-state relation $N \subseteq \mathcal{S}' \times \mathcal{S}'$ by

$$N\left((s_1, i_1), (s_2, i_2)\right) := \left(s_2 = ns(s_1, i_1) \wedge Ip(s_2, i_2)\right).$$

Read the new state type as current state and input. Then there is a transition from (s_1, i_1) to (s_2, i_2), iff the next-state function ns takes the transition $s_1 \to s_2$ under input i_1. Furthermore, the next-state relation N non-deterministically chooses the next input i_2, which has to satisfy the input-predicate Ip. We define $init' := \{(s, i) \mid s = init \wedge Ip(s, i)\}$ as the initial state set of the new system.

We now state the theorems for the **AG** and **fair AF** operators with respect to deterministic systems:

Theorem 2. $(\forall s' \in init' \colon \mathbf{AG}(N, f)(s'))$ *iff for all input sequences* $I = (i_0, i_1, \ldots) \in \mathcal{I}^\infty$ *satisfying the input predicate, the predicate* f *holds globally:*

$$\left(\forall t \colon Ip(s^t(I), i_t)\right) \implies \left(\forall t \colon f(s^t(I))\right),$$

where s^t *is defined as in section 2.*

Theorem 3. *Let fair be a predicate.* $(\forall s' \in init' \colon \mathbf{fair AF}(N, f)(fair)(s'))$ *iff for all input sequences* $I := (i_0, i_1, \ldots) \in \mathcal{I}^\infty$ *satisfying the input predicate and yielding a path on which fair holds infinitely often, the predicate* f *holds eventually. Formally: for all input sequences* I *holds*

$$\left((\forall t \colon Ip(s^t(I), i_t)) \wedge (\forall t \colon \exists t' \geq t \colon fair(s^t(I)))\right) \implies \left(\exists t \colon f(s^t(I))\right).$$

In the following, we do not explicitly distinguish between systems stated as next-state function or relation. Of course, one has to deal with the differences in PVS, but for reasons of readability we omit this in the rest of this paper.

4   Pipeline Verification

4.1   Separating Pipeline Control and Datapaths

In order to use model-checking on the pipeline control we have to separate the control and datapath circuits in the pipeline. Figure 3 shows a simple pipeline example. The control registers consist of valid bits indicating that a stage contains a valid instruction, the tags, and some auxiliary control data, e.g., a counter to keep track of the number of iterations to go through during divisions. The control circuit maintains the control registers, and computes the control outputs $valid_{out}, tag_{out}$, and $stall_{out}$.

The control interacts with the datapaths by computing the clock-enables ce for each stage and the multiplexer control signals where multiple inputs lead to the same pipeline stage (e.g, to the *mul1* stage in Fig. 2). The clock-enables control whether the register keeps its data from the previous cycle, or if new data is clocked into the register. If a stage i contains no valid

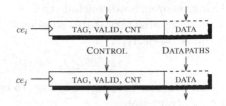

Fig. 3. Separating Control and Datapaths

instruction, it is always clocked ($ce_i = 1$), i.e., a potentially valid instruction is taken over from the preceeding stage. Otherwise, if stage i contains a valid instruction, it is only clocked if itself can pass its instruction to the succeeding stage j. This may not be possible due to several reasons: 1) the stage j may itself contain a valid instruction which it is unable to pass to the next stage. 2) there are multiple valid instructions aiming for stage j, and the instruction in stage i has lower priority. For instance, this may occur above stage $rd1$ in the FPU pipeline. 3) the instruction result has to be returned to the CPU from stage i, but the CPU has asserted the $stall_{in}$ signal. We refer the reader to [12] for details on the pipeline control.

According to the separation of control and data in the pipeline, we split the next-state function ns of the pipeline into a next-state function ns_{ctrl} of the control part, and a next-state function ns_{data} of the data part.

4.2 Verification of the Pipeline

In the following, we describe how we verify the liveness (P3) and tag-consistency (P4) properties of pipelines. We will not discuss the (P1) and (P2) properties, since these are fairly simple in comparison. Furthermore, we will only give the idea of the actual verification, since the mathematical details are tedious and straightforward.

Liveness. We start with the verification of liveness. In order to prove *functional* correctness of the pipelines, we will prove the strengthened liveness (P3') covering the functionality of the pipeline. The verification idea is as follows: we first use model-checking to show that each pipeline stage is live, i.e., that its clock-enable becomes eventually active. We then use theorem-proving to show that the instruction take the correct path through the pipeline and hence the correct result is computed.

For model-checking the liveness of each of the clock-enables, the liveness of $stall_{in}$ is presumed. We model-check the following property for each stage i and an arbitrary, not necessarily initial control state s:

$$\mathbf{fair\,AF}(ns_{ctrl}, ce_i)(\neg stall_{in})(s).$$

Using theorem 3 we conclude that the clock-enable ce_i is live in all computations starting in arbitrary states s under all input sequences where $stall_{in}$ is live, i.e., for all $I := (i_0, i_1, \ldots)$:

$$\left(\forall t \colon \exists t' \geq t \colon \neg stall_{in}^{t'}\right) \implies \left(\exists t \colon ce_i^t\right). \tag{1}$$

Using theorem proving, it is easy to extend 1 to 2 by exploiting that (1) holds for arbitrary states:

$$\left(\forall t \colon \exists t' \geq t \colon \neg stall_{in}^{t'}\right) \implies \left(\forall t \colon \exists t' \geq t \colon ce_i^{t'}\right). \tag{2}$$

Note that the left-hand side of the equation matches the pipeline input property (I2).

Having proved the liveness of the clock-enables, it is relatively easy to verify liveness of the complete pipeline including the datapaths by pushing instructions through the pipeline stage by stage. This is done using theorem proving. We exemplarily prove the liveness property (P3′) of the multiplicative FPU for multiplication instructions:

Theorem 4. *Assume that the input properties (I1) and (I2) hold. Assume further that a multiplication with tag tg is dispatched at time t, i.e., $disp(tg, t)$ holds. Then there exists $t' \geq t$ such that $ret(tg, t')$ and $data_{out}^{t'} = rd2 \circ rd1 \circ mul2 \circ mul1 \circ unp(data_{in}^t)$ hold, i.e., the multiplication eventually terminates with the correct data.*

Proof. We only sketch the proof, because its details are long and tedious. By input property (I1) we know that $stall_{out}^t$ is inactive, since otherwise the instruction cannot be dispatched. Since the definition of $stall_{out}$ directly depends on ce_{unp} (cf. [12, App. D]), one trivially concludes that the instruction is clocked into the register stage unp at time t. The data in this register are the outputs of the combinatorial unpack circuit.

From (2) we know that there exists a (minimal) time $t_1 > t$ such that $ce_{unp}^{t_1}$ is active, i.e., the unp stage is clocked at time t_1, and is not clocked in between. Hence, the data at time $t_1 - 1$ in the register stage unp is the same as at time t.

The unp stage is only clocked if its valid instruction proceeds to the next stage (this follows trivially from the definition of ce_{unp}^t). We conclude that the instruction with tag tg is clocked from the unp stage into stage $mul1$ at time t_1. The data at this time is computed from $mul1 \circ unp$, i.e., the composition of the first two combinatorial stages.

Analogously, we derive times $t_2 > t_1$, $t_3 > t_2$, and $t_4 > t_3$ where the instruction proceeds to $mul2$, $rd1$, $rd2$, respectively. When the instruction is in stage RD2, it is returned to the CPU immediately when the $stall_{in}$ signal becomes inactive. Hence, there exists $t' > t$ where the instruction is returned with $data_{out}^{t'}$ computed from $data_{in}^t$ by the combinatorial circuits between the register stages.

Note that the actual computation performed in the datapaths plays no role in the above proof, and hence the datapath functions may be left uninterpreted. □

Tag-Consistency. We now describe the verification of tag-consistency. We want to express tag-consistency (P4) in FairCTL in order to allow model-checking. Therefore we need a FairCTL formalization of "tag has been dispatched previously", and a formalization of tag-uniqueness. It would be useful to have temporal operators reaching in the past; however, FairCTL does not provide such operators. In order to circumvent this problem, we introduce an auxiliary variable $inuse_{tg}$ for each tag $tg \in \mathcal{T}$ representing that an instruction with tag tg is currently in the pipeline. The meaning of this variable is exactly the same as the predicate $inuse$ from section 2. The variable $inuse_{tg}$ is set whenever an instruction with tag tg enters the pipeline, and it is cleared whenever the tag tg leaves the pipeline. Tag-uniqueness can hence be modeled as input predicate Ip checking that the tag tg is not dispatched when the variable $inuse_{tg}$ is already set. Vice versa, tag-consistency can be modeled as an invariant stating that a tag tg can only leave the pipeline if $inuse_{tg}$ is set.

Let $\tilde{n}s_{ctrl}$ denote the next-state function of the modified model including the $inuse$ variables, and let Ip denote the input predicate modeling tag-uniqueness (I3). We verify the property

$$\forall tg\colon \mathbf{AG}\big(\tilde{n}s_{ctrl}, (valid_{out} \wedge tag_{out} = tg) \implies inuse_{tg}\big)(init),$$

where $init$ is an initial state in which all pipeline stages are empty (i.e., $valid_i = 0$), and all $inuse_{tg}$ variables are cleared. From this we conclude using theorem 2: for all input sequences $I = (i_0, i_1, \ldots) \in \mathcal{I}^\infty$ and for all tags tg

$$\big(\forall t\colon (valid_{in}^t \wedge tag_{in}^t = tg) \implies \neg inuse_{tg}^t\big) \implies$$
$$\big(\forall t\colon (valid_{out}^t \wedge tag_{out}^t = tg) \implies inuse_{tg}^t\big).$$

One can see (and easily verify in PVS) that the left-hand side of the implication matches tag-uniqueness, and that the right-hand side implies tag-consistency.

4.3   Some Practical Considerations

In order to verify tag-consistency, we have changed the model and added the auxiliary variables $inuse_{tg}$. It is easy to prove that these auxiliary variables do not affect the outputs of the actual pipeline implementation and hence can be omitted. They are used solely to prove the correctness of the pipeline.

The state-space for model-checking becomes very large due to the tags and the $inuse_{tg}$ variables. Of course, one can abstract the tags by means of scalar-sets [11] in the sense of data-type reduction as in SMV [14]. Model-checkers such as SMV support this as a built-in feature. In PVS the abstraction has to be done manually. We have abstracted the tags and proved the correctness of this abstraction, but omit the details since they are well known.

A major disadvantage of the PVS model-checker is that it is not capable of providing counter-examples when the verification of a FairCTL formula fails. Since the design of complex pipelines is very error-prone and debugging is hard, such counter-examples are very useful. We therefore developed and debugged the pipelines (without datapaths) in SMV, and then manually translated the pipeline control to PVS. We then used the PVS model-checker to re-check the properties.

We have manually performed the "pushing through the pipeline" in theorem 4 stage by stage during liveness verification. The proofs for each stage are very similar. We therefore believe that it is possible to create a proof strategy which performs the "pushing through the pipeline" automatically. This would result in a mostly automatic method for the verification of complex pipelines.

5   Related Work

There are some papers which report on the verification of out-of-order processors, e.g., by Hosabettu et.al. [10], by Sawada and Hunt [17], by McMillan [14], and by Berezin et.al. [4]. None of the cited papers mentions multi-cycle execution units, or even execution units which have a cycle in the pipeline structure or may reorder instructions internally. Kröning is the first who reports on the verification of a Tomasulo scheduler capable of handling such complex pipelines [13], although the design and the verification of the actual pipelines is not part of Kröning's work. In this paper we have presented a methodology to verify complex pipelines, and have presented the pipeline of a multiplication/division floating point unit as an example. Kröning is currently integrating this example (among other pipelined FPUs for other operations) into his Tomasulo CPU.

Aagaard and Leeser [2] propose a methodology for the verification of pipelines: they decompose pipelines into segments, and then further decompose the correctness proof of individual segments into smaller proof goals. Their work describes only how one *could* employ a theorem prover for the verification of pipelines, but they do not actually use formal methods (in the sense of a computer tool). We have tried a similar approach to the verification of our pipelines using solely theorem proving, but failed because very complex inductive invariants had to be constructed manually [12].

Another approach to the verification of pipelines is the use of a logic with uninterpreted functions that are used to model the datapath functionality. The use of uninterpreted functions is comparable to the separation of the EU into pipeline control and datapaths, since the actual datapath implementation has no impact on the pipeline verification (cf. sect. 4). Bryant et.al. [5] describe how a logic with equality and uninterpreted functions can be reduced to propositional logic. In [20], Velev and Bryant describe how this reduction can be used to verify in-order microprocessors with variable-latency EUs. They do not verify the actual EU, but use an abstract execution unit model in order to verify the processor core. The EUs modeled by the abstraction process only one instruction at a time, and hence do not reorder instructions internally. Velev and Bryant only verify in-order processors; the verification of out-of-order designs would probably require the manual construction of a complex inductive invariant, and hence automation would be lost. In our approach, this is not the case due to the use of model-checking.

Another approach is the use of uninterpreted functions within a model-checker such as SMV. Data-type reduction and case-splitting is used in order to reduce the state space [14]. This is used in [14] to verify a Tomasulo scheduler, where the functionality of the EUs is defined by uninterpreted functions. The state space and the number of cases to be checked grows rapidly in the number of function applications, which is large in our example due to the cycle in the pipeline structure. We have modeled the FPU pipeline in SMV with uninterpreted functions for the datapaths, and have tried to verify liveness with functional correctness using model-checking. This was infeasible due to the huge state space and number of cases. The verification of some cases aborted with a memory usage of >2GB, other cases ran for more than 5 days without terminating.

In [3], Berezin et.al. prove the correctness of a simple Tomasulo processor by combining model-checking with uninterpreted functions and theorem proving. They use SMV to verify an invariant of an abstraction of the processor, and then use PVS to conclude overall correctness of the concrete machine. Their translation from SMV to PVS is not formally safe in the sense that they introduce a new, manually written axiom in PVS which hopefully reflects exactly the model-checked property. In contrast, we use the PVS built-in model-checker, and then use the theorems from section 3 to safely translate the model-checked properties to a form suitable for theorem proving.

In [9], Ho et.al. use the abstraction of the datapaths of pipelines to token nets for the automatic verification of pipeline control properties. Their approach is not applicable to pipelines with cycles in the pipeline structure, and is not suitable to verify functional correctness of the pipelines.

In [1], Aagaard et.al. verify iterative circuits using Intel's Forte system. They use symbolic simulation and LTL model-checking for the verification of bit-level invariants of iterative floating point circuits, and then use theorem proving to conclude "numerical" correctness of the floating point results. Though Intel's circuits are most probably much more complex than ours in terms of gate count, the verified pipelines are simple in the sense that they seem to support only one instruction at a time and hence do not reorder instructions. Moreover, the work from [1] is not reproducible since Intel's Forte system is not publicly available.

Schneider and Hoffmann [18] report on the definition of LTL in the theorem prover HOL, and on the automatic translation of LTL to ω-automata within HOL. The ω-automata are used as input for a model-checker. Their definition of LTL is close to our $\forall t$ form. Hence, their work could be used to verify pipelines in HOL in a similar way as described here.

6   Summary

We have presented a methodology for the verification of complex pipelines. The pipelines may process several instructions simultaneously, may have variable latency, cycles and branches in the pipeline structure, and may reorder instructions internally. The pipelines are used as execution units in the Tomasulo scheduler

verified by Kröning [13]. As an example, we have presented the pipeline of a
floating point unit, whose combinatorial correctness has been proved in [4].

Verification of the pipelines using solely theorem proving is hard since one
has to manually construct a complex inductive invariant. The verification of the
pipelines using solely model-checking is infeasible due to the large state space
which arises from the datapaths, even if these are modeled as uninterpreted
functions (cf. sect. 5). We therefore combine model-checking and theorem proving
for the verification of the pipelines. Model-checking is used to verify properties of
the pipeline control, theorem proving is then used to conclude overall correctness
of the pipeline including the datapaths.

The correctness criterions for the execution units are given as temporal properties of the form $\forall t: p(t)$ (cf. sect. 2), which is suitable for theorem proving. In
contrast, the FairCTL operators used for model-checking are defined as fixpoints
in μ-calculus. We therefore have formally proved that the FairCTL operators, as
defined in μ-calculus, match their intended semantic expressed in $\forall t$ form. This
has been shown previously with "paper & pencil" proofs [8], but it has never
been proved using formal methods before. Having proved the correspondence of
the FairCTL operators expressed in μ-calculus and $\forall t$ form allows us to translate between both languages in a formally safe way. This is necessary to prevent
errors which may be introduced by translating properties between two systems
or languages by hand.

Acknowledgements

The author would like to thank Michael Backes, Christoph Berg, Sven Beyer,
Daniel Kröning, Wolfgang Paul, and Jochen Preiß for valuable discussions.

References

1. M. Aagaard, R. B. Jones, R. Kaivola, K. R. Kohatsu, and C.-J. H. Seger. Formal
   verification of iterative algorithms in microprocessors. In *DAC-00*. ACM/IEEE,
   2000. 321
2. M. Aagaard and M. Leeser. Reasoning about pipelines with structural hazards. In
   TPCD'94, volume 901 of *LNCS*. Springer, 1994. 320
3. S. Berezin, A. Biere, E. Clarke, and Y. Zhu. Combining symbolic model checking
   with uninterpreted functions for out-of-order processor verification. In *FMCAD
   '98*, LNCS 1522. Springer, 1998. 309, 320, 321
4. C. Berg and C. Jacobi. Formal verification of the vamp floating point unit. In
   CHARME 2001, LNCS 2144. Springer, 2001. 310, 314, 322
5. R. E. Bryant, S. German, and M. N. Velev. Processor verification using efficient
   reductions of the logic of uninterpreted functions to propositional logic. *ACM
   Trans. on Computational. Logic (TOCL)*, 2(1):1–41, Jan 2001. 320
6. J. R. Burch and D. L. Dill. Automatic verification of pipelined microprocessor
   control. In *CAV'94*, LNCS 818. Springer, 1994. 310
7. E. M. Clarke, O. Grumberg, and D. A. Peled. *Model Checking*. MIT Press, Cambridge, Massachusetts, 1999. 310, 315

8. E. A. Emerson and E. M. Clarke. Characterizing correctness properties of parallel programs using fixpoints. In *Automata, Languages and Programming*, LNCS 85. Springer, 1980. 315, 322

9. P.-H. Ho, A. J. Isles, and T. Kam. Formal verification of pipeline control using controlled token nets and abstract interpretation. In *ICCAD-98*. ACM, 1998. 321

10. R. Hosabettu, G. Gopalakrishnan, and M. Srivas. Verifying microarchitectures that support speculation and exceptions. In *CAV '00*, volume 1855 of *LNCS*. Springer, 2000. 309, 310, 320

11. C. N. Ip and D. L. Dill. Better verification through symmetry. *Formal Methods in System Design*, 9(1–2):41–75, 1996. 319

12. C. Jacobi. *Formal Verification of a Fully IEEE Compliant Floating Point Unit*. PhD thesis, Saarland University, Germany, 2002. handed in; draft available at www-wjp.cs.uni-sb.de/~cj/phd.ps. 317, 318, 320

13. D. Kroening. *Formal Verification of Pipelined Microprocessors*. PhD thesis, Saarland University, Computer Science Department, 2001. 309, 310, 311, 314, 320, 322

14. K. L. McMillan. A methodology for hardware verification using compositional model checking. *Science of Computer Programming*, 37(1-3):279–309, 2000. 309, 319, 320, 321

15. S. Owre, N. Shankar, and J. M. Rushby. PVS: A prototype verification system. In *CADE 11*, volume 607 of *LNAI*, pages 748–752. Springer, 1992. 310

16. S. Rajan, N. Shankar, and M. K. Srivas. An integration of model checking with automated proof checking. In *CAV'95*, volume 939. Springer, 1995. 310, 315

17. J. Sawada and W. A. Hunt, Jr. Processor verification with precise exceptions and speculative execution. In *CAV '98*, volume 1427 of *LNCS*. Springer, 1998. 309, 310, 320

18. K. Schneider and D. W. Hoffmann. A HOL conversion for translating linear time temporal logic to ω-automata. In *TPHOL 99*, volume 1690 of *LNCS*. Springer, 1999. 321

19. R. M. Tomasulo. An efficient algorithm for exploiting multiple arithmetic units. In *IBM Journal of Research and Development*, volume 11 (1), pages 25–33. IBM, 1967. 309

20. M. N. Velev and R. E. Bryant. Formal verification of superscalar microprocessors with multicycle functional units, exception, and branch prediction. In *DAC '00*. ACM/IEEE, 2000. 320

Automated Unbounded Verification
of Security Protocols

Yannick Chevalier and Laurent Vigneron*

LORIA - UHP - UN2, Campus Scientifique, B.P. 239
54506 Vandœuvre-lès-Nancy Cedex, France
{chevalie,vigneron}@loria.fr

Abstract. We present a new model for automated verification of security protocols, permitting the use of an unbounded number of protocol runs. We prove its correctness, completeness and also that it terminates. It has been implemented and its efficiency is clearly shown by the number of protocols successfully studied. In particular, we present an attack previously unreported on the *Denning-Sacco symmetric key protocol*.

Among the methods used for studying security protocols, model-checking has been successfully used in many different ways. The common point to all these methods is to consider *principals* who exchange *messages* that have a pattern described by a *protocol*. A security protocol designer aims at providing security properties to the principals who use the protocol. These methods use an *intruder*, someone who tries to violate the security properties, to find an *attack*. The model-checking methods diverge on the handling of an infinite number of principals. In this case, the problem of whether there exists an attack is undecidable [10] if principals can create new values different at each session. Some methods [18,13] give bounds on the number of principals that need to be considered. The drawback is that those bounds are obtained by assumptions on the shape of the messages exchanged during a protocol run.

Other methods abstract the execution of a protocol so that it is not necessary to give the number of participants. This abstraction can be done using tree-automata [11,15,8], or by simplifications either on the nonces creation model [4], or on the complexity of the keys used [17]. In all these models, the assumptions are done uniformly over all principals, making them less expressive than model-checking. A more complete comparison of the tools is given in Section 6.

We propose a new model for handling an infinite number of sessions by assuming two different types of principals. Some *regular* principals create nonces, and can only participate to a bounded number of runs of the protocol, the bound being given before the execution. Besides these regular principals, we add *in parallel* a finite number of *puppet* principals, who are allowed to conduct as many runs of the protocol as the *intruder* wishes them to. The model for these principals is simplified, and these simplifications permit to show the termination

---

* Supported by the Information Society Technologies (IST) Programme, FET Open Assessment Project IST-2000-26410, and the ACI Cryptology Vernam.

D. Brinksma and K. G. Larsen (Eds.): CAV 2002, LNCS 2404, pp. 324–337, 2002.

of the system as a whole. The intruder uses these puppet principals to find an attack on the regular principals. Having two different models permits to keep the expressiveness of model-checking while studying specification with an infinite number of principals.

This paper is organized as follows. We first describe the model used (Section 1), then we sketch the proof of completeness of our method in this abstracted model of the principals (Section 2). The construction of the Oracle's rules is explained in Section 3, and in Section 4 we sketch the proofs of correctness and termination of this system. We then present experimental results on the protocol library given in [7], and comparison with the results of [9] in Section 5. These experimental results include an attack previously unreported on the *Denning-Sacco symmetric key protocol*. We end this paper with a detailed comparison of our method with other ones (Section 6).

The system presented in this paper is an extension of the "lazy intruder" one given in [5] (see also [14], and [1,16] for related theoritical results) by the addition of the Oracle's rules. Other systems using different lazy strategies (but without Oracle) are presented in [3].

All the proofs sketched here can be found in [6].

1   Model Description

1.1   Overview of the Study of a Protocol

A protocol defines roles and messages, both finite. We study a finite number of different instances of roles. The regular instances, played by honest principals, are run only once. The other instances, called puppets, are run *in parallel*. There is a finite number of them, but they can be duplicated as many times as needed, providing a potentially infinite number of runs. We model an intruder who tries to find a flaw in the regular instances with the help of those puppet instances.

Regular Principals. For a principal, there is a finite number of runs of the protocol. Considering one run for one principal, its step k in the protocol can be written: $Step_k : M \to R$, meaning that it waits for a message M and when received, sends a response R. The messages M and R depend on the knowledge of this principal, denoted w_k: this knowledge is used for analyzing M, and for composing R. Some **variables** are used in w_k for representing the parts of the received messages whose value cannot be inferred unambiguously by the principal. A step is therefore:

$$Step_k : w_k, M \to w_{next(k)}, R$$

Applying this rule to a received message, unification permits to analyze this message by recognizing its known parts. The knowledge acquired from M is added to the principal's knowledge for its next step, yielding $w_{next(k)}$.

Since there is a finite number of principals, messages and runs, the number of w terms is also finite.

Intruder. His role is to try to compose the messages m_k of the protocol using his knowledge. This is written: $\text{COMP}(m_k)$ FROM $\text{KNOW}(I)$, where I is a set of terms. Following the Dolev-Yao's model, the intruder diverts all the messages sent by the principals, and tries to compose the messages awaited by the principals (see Section 1.3).

1.2 Protocol State and User Rules

Initial State and Transitions. The *current state* of a protocol is written: $B \parallel \mathcal{E}$. B is a multiset of terms that models both the principals (by their w term) and the knowledge of the intruder. $\mathcal{E}$ is a set of constraints of the shape:

$$\text{COMP}(m_{1,1}), \ldots, \text{COMP}(m_{1,k_1}) \text{ FROM } \text{KNOW}(I_1);$$
$$\ldots; \text{COMP}(m_{n,1}), \ldots, \text{COMP}(m_{n,k_n}) \text{ FROM } \text{KNOW}(I_n)$$

The *initial state* of the protocol is $B_0 \parallel \emptyset$, where $\emptyset$ denotes the empty set of constraints, and B_0 is a ground set containing the initial knowledge of the regular principals and of the intruder ($\text{KNOW}(I_0)$).

The actions of a principal receiving a message at step k (m_k) and replying to it (r_k) are modeled by the following rule on the current state of the protocol:

(Message) $\quad w_k, \text{KNOW}(I), B \parallel \mathcal{E} \rightarrow$
$\qquad w_{next(k)}, \text{KNOW}(I \cup r_k), B \parallel \mathcal{E}; \text{COMP}(m_k) \text{ FROM } \text{KNOW}(I)$

noindent*Rule description:* this rule adds in the constraints set $\mathcal{E}$ the constraint that the intruder must be able to compose the message m_k from the knowledge he has inferred so far, and that he may add the message r_k, sent by the principal and intercepted, to his knowledge.
We assume that, for all **Message** rules, the following inclusion of sets of variables stands: $\text{Var}(r_k) \subseteq \text{Var}(m_k) \cup \text{Var}(\mathcal{E})$
Informally, this inclusion reflects the fact that the messages sent by a principal are composed from the initial knowledge of this principal (which is ground information), the nonces created during the current protocol run (which are constants), and the messages the principal has already received. As the principal may not be able to verify all of the contents of those received messages, it may introduce variables in constraints.

Knowledge Properties. Let $I_1, \ldots, I_n$ be the n intruder's knowledge multisets inserted successively in $\mathcal{E}$ after n uses of the **Message** rule. Let $m_1, \ldots, m_n$ be the corresponding n messages to compose. We shall note that, at the time a knowledge multiset has been inserted into the constraints set, we have:

$$I_{i+1} = I_i \cup m_i, \quad i \in \{1, \ldots, n-1\}$$

Thus, at the time the $\text{KNOW}(I_i)$ terms were inserted into the constraints set, the I_i multisets formed a growing sequence for inclusion. We shall see later that this growth property can be kept during the constraints resolution.

1.3 Constraints Resolution Rules

The intruder is modeled by a set of rules. We took the classical Dolev-Yao intruder's model, in which one assumes *a)* you have to know the corresponding key in order to decompose a cipher, *b)* the intruder may compose *any* messages from the terms he already knows. The major difference so far is that we describe the actions of an intruder trying to decompose a message in order to prove he can compose it, whereas the original Dolev-Yao rules were only concerned with adding some new terms to the knowledge of the intruder. For conciseness, we note APPLY(t_1, t_2) the result of the creation of a new term from t_1 and t_2.

The construction operations that are handled are hash function application, in which case APPLY$(h, t) = h(t)$, symmetric encryption (APPLY$(t_1, t_2) = \{t_1\}^{sym}t_2$), asymmetric encryption $\{t_1\}^{pub}t_2$ and messages concatenation $< t_1, t_2 >$. We also use an operator INV() which maps an asymmetric key t to the key that is able to decode a message encrypted with t. We always assume that INV(INV$(t)) = t$.

Intruder's Model Rules. The following rules model the intruder's possible actions:

$(\mathcal{C}_{unif})$ T, COMP(t) FROM KNOW$(s \cup I); \mathcal{E} \rightarrow$
$\qquad\qquad T\sigma$ FROM KNOW$((s \cup I)\sigma); \mathcal{E}\sigma$ $(\sigma = mgu(t, s))$

$(\mathcal{C}_{dec})$ T, COMP(APPLY(t_1, t_2)) FROM KNOW$(I); \mathcal{E} \rightarrow$
$\qquad\qquad T$, COMP(t_1), COMP(t_2) FROM KNOW$(I); \mathcal{E}$

$(\mathcal{A}_{pub})$ T FROM KNOW$(\{t_1\}^{pub}t_2 \cup I); \mathcal{E} \rightarrow$
$\qquad\qquad$ COMP(INV(t_2)) FROM KNOW$(\{t_1\}^{pub}t_2 \cup I)$;
$\qquad\qquad T$ FROM KNOW$(\{t_1\}^{pub}t_2 \cup t_1 \cup I); \mathcal{E}$

$(\mathcal{A}_{sym})$ T FROM KNOW$(\{t_1\}^{sym}t_2 \cup I); \mathcal{E} \rightarrow$
$\qquad\qquad$ COMP(t_2) FROM KNOW$(\{t_1\}^{sym}t_2 \cup I)$;
$\qquad\qquad T$ FROM KNOW$(\{t_1\}^{sym}t_2 \cup t_1 \cup I); \mathcal{E}$

$(\mathcal{A}_{pair})$ T FROM KNOW$(< t_1, t_2 > \cup I); \mathcal{E} \rightarrow$
$\qquad\qquad T$ FROM KNOW$(t_1 \cup t_2 \cup < t_1, t_2 > \cup I); \mathcal{E}$

We restrict the application of these rules to rules *applicable* on the current state.

Rules description and applicability:

- $\mathcal{C}_{unif}$: using this rule, the intruder unifies a term he knows (s) with a term he has to compose (t). This rule is *applicable* if, in the current state, neither s nor t are variables;
- $\mathcal{C}_{dec}$: it is applied when the intruder, trying to compose a term APPLY(t_1, t_2), tries first to compose t_1 and t_2;
- $\mathcal{A}_{pub}, \mathcal{A}_{sym}$: these rules are applied when the intruder tries to decompose an encrypted term. In order to decompose this cipher, the intruder has to show he can compose the corresponding key from his current knowledge;

– $\mathcal{A}_{pair}$: this rule is applied when the intruder tries to decompose a message
built by the concatenation of two terms t_1 and t_2. No assumptions on his
knowledge is needed.

The last four rules are *applicable* only if $\text{APPLY}(t_1, t_2)$ is not unified with a
variable of the current state.

Oracle's Rules. The former rules correspond to the Dolev-Yao's intruder
model. In our model, the intruder has also the possibility to be helped by interacting with puppet principals. The main difference with regular principals is that
they always create the same nonces. We will explain in Section 3 how the rules
describing the results of these interactions are built. This construction ensures
the property $\text{Var}(r) \subseteq \bigcup_{i=1}^{n_r} \text{Var}(m_i^r)$ for the rules describing these interactions.
They are of the shape

$$(\text{Oracle}(r)) \quad B \parallel T, \text{COMP}(s) \text{ FROM } \text{KNOW}(I); \mathcal{E} \rightarrow$$
$$B\sigma \parallel T\sigma, \text{COMP}(m_1^r\sigma), \dots, \text{COMP}(m_{n_r}^r\sigma) \text{ FROM } \text{KNOW}(I\sigma); \mathcal{E}\sigma$$
$$\text{where } \sigma = mgu(r, s)$$

meaning that for composing a term s that unifies with the term r, the intruder
has to be able to compose the terms $m_1^r, \dots, m_{n_r}^r$. The Oracle rules already take
into account all the possible decompositions on the added constraints, or the use
of another Oracle rule. Thus, we only need to use the $\mathcal{C}_{unif}$ rule to simplify a
constraint added by an Oracle rule. The oracle rules are *applicable* if s is not
unified with a variable of the current state.

Growth of the Knowledge Multisets. We have already noted as a knowledge
property (Section 1.2) that the multisets of knowledge $(I_i)_{i \in \{1,\dots,n\}}$ are forming
a growing sequence for the inclusion ordering at the time they were added to
the constraints set. Then, considering the rules used for the decomposition of
intruder's knowledge, one sees that whenever a rule can be applied to I_i, it can
also be applied to I_j, $j \geq i$. This remark leads to the following result:

Proposition 1. *Let $B \parallel \mathcal{E}$ be a state derived. Let T_1 FROM $\text{KNOW}(I_1)$ and
T_2 FROM $\text{KNOW}(I_2)$ be two constraints inserted in $\mathcal{E}$ by the Message rule, and
such that $I_1 \subset I_2$. If T_1 FROM $\text{KNOW}(I_1) \rightarrow^* C_1$ FROM $\text{KNOW}(I_{1,1}); \dots; C_n$
FROM $\text{KNOW}(I_{1,n}); T_1$ FROM $\text{KNOW}(I_1')$, then there exists a sequence of transi-
tions: T_2 FROM $\text{KNOW}(I_2) \rightarrow^* C_1$ FROM $\text{KNOW}(I_{2,1}); \dots; C_n$ FROM
$\text{KNOW}(I_{2,n}); T_2$ FROM $\text{KNOW}(I_2')$, where $I_1' \subset I_2'$ and $I_{1,i} \subseteq I_{2,i}$, $i \in \{1, \dots, n\}$.*

This proposition permits to make the following hypothesis:

$(\mathcal{P}_1)$ Let T_1 FROM $\text{KNOW}(I_1)$, ..., T_n FROM $\text{KNOW}(I_n)$ be the constraints inserted in the constraints set by the Message rule. By Proposition 1, we always
assume that if a knowledge decomposition rule is applied on I_i, it is also applied on I_j, for all $j > i$.

Moreover, and for each state $B \parallel \mathcal{E}$ accessible from the initial state, the constraints set $\mathcal{E}$ satisfies the next proposition.

Proposition 2. *Let $B \parallel \mathcal{E}$ be an accessible state from the initial state of the protocol. For each variable $v \in Var(I)$, with $\textsc{Know}(I)$ appearing in $\mathcal{E}$ or B, there exists a constraint T' FROM $\textsc{Know}(I')$ in $\mathcal{E}$ such that $v \in Var(T') \setminus Var(I')$.*

The proof is done by induction on the constraints resolution system steps. It relies on the fact that all variables are created by the principals in the received messages, and thus appear first in the $\textsc{comp}()$ part of a constraint.

Remark: Applying further knowledge decomposition steps if necessary, let us assume (by $(\mathcal{P}_1)$) that the knowledge multisets $I_1, \dots, I_n$ form a growing sequence for inclusion. In this case, we write I_v the smallest knowledge multiset on which there is a constraint $\textsc{comp}(t)$, with $v \in Var(t)$. The previous proposition ensures that $v \notin Var(I_v)$. In other words, in the environment, each variable first appears in the $\textsc{comp}()$ part of a constraint.

1.4   Final State for the Constraints Resolution System

A constraint is *eliminated* when the rule $\mathcal{C}_{unif}$ deletes its last $\textsc{comp}()$ term. A constraints set $\mathcal{E}$ is *satisfiable* if there exist a ground substitution σ and a sequence τ of transitions that eliminates all the constraints of $\mathcal{E}\sigma$, denoted $\sigma \vdash \mathcal{E}$. A constraints set $\mathcal{E}$ is *simple* if, for all the terms $\textsc{comp}(t)$ in $\mathcal{E}$, t is a variable.

Proposition 3. *If $\mathcal{E}$ is simple, $\mathcal{E}$ is satisfiable.*

To prove this proposition, we only need to assume that the intruder knows one constant, his name for instance. Then, considering the substitution σ that maps all variables of $\mathcal{E}$ to this constant, σ is ground and $\sigma \vdash \mathcal{E}$. As a consequence, to show that all the constraints in $\mathcal{E}$ can be resolved, it is sufficient to prove that there is a sequence of transitions leading from $\mathcal{E}$ to $\mathcal{E}'$, with $\mathcal{E}'$ simple. Note that the assumption $(\mathcal{P}_1)$ does not prevent from reaching a simple constraints set.

A state $B \parallel \mathcal{E}$ reachable from the initial state and where $\mathcal{E}$ is simple, corresponds to a *possible state of a protocol run.*

Proposition 3 is essential for stating completeness, correctness and termination.

2   Completeness of the Constraints Resolution Rules

Let $B \parallel \mathcal{E}$ be a state reached from the initial state $B_0 \parallel \emptyset$, after applying some Message rules. We want to prove that if there exists a ground substitution σ such that $\sigma \vdash \mathcal{E}$, there exists a state $B' \parallel \mathcal{E}'$, reachable from $B \parallel \mathcal{E}$ using only *applicable* transitions, such that $\mathcal{E}'$ is simple. This proof will be obtained by showing that if there exists a sequence of transitions τ such that $B\sigma \parallel \mathcal{E}\sigma \rightarrow_\tau^* B''\sigma \parallel \emptyset$, then there also exists a sequence τ' of applications of *applicable* constraints simplification rules leading from $\mathcal{E}$ to a simple constraints set $\mathcal{E}'$.

First, we remove or alter the *applicability* condition of the rules. We prove, under these alterations, the reachability of a simple constraints set. Then, we prove that we can deduce, from the constructed transition sequence τ', a sequence of *applicable* transitions.

Alterations. We consider only the sequences of transitions that satisfy the property:

($\mathcal{P}_2$) If, in order to eliminate a constraint COMP(t), one has the choice between an application of the rule $\mathcal{C}_{unif}$ and of the rule $\mathcal{C}_{dec}$, we choose the sequence with the application of $\mathcal{C}_{dec}$.

We postpone the $\mathcal{C}_{unif}$ and Oracle(r) applications, and as the $\mathcal{C}_{unif}$ commute, we consider blocks beginning with an application of an Oracle rule, followed by the applications of the $\mathcal{C}_{unif}$ that eliminate the newly introduced constraints.

The decomposition rules cannot be postponed, and we have to consider two cases for building the sequence τ': if the rule is *applicable*, we apply it *as is* in τ'; else, it is applied to a variable. The solution in this last case is to add a constraint describing the shape of the awaited instance of this variable, and the rule is applied in τ', using the new variables (considered as *ghost* terms) introduced in this constraint.

Completeness. The changes done in the decomposition rules now make it possible to follow a sequence of transitions τ from $\mathcal{E}\sigma$, for generating a corresponding sequence of transitions τ' from $\mathcal{E}$. But some transitions of τ may still be postponed and not applied in τ'. In the following, we first show how the postponed rules can be used to reach a simple constraints set $\mathcal{E}'$; then we show that the transitions creating ghost terms can be removed without affecting the reachability of a simple constraints set.

Once there are only postponed transitions left, we repeat the procedure described in Figure 1 until there is no suitable transition left. This procedure ends because there is only a finite number of postponed transitions.

We prove in [ ] that it is always possible, when choosing a $\mathcal{C}_{unif}$ rule, to find s' in I such that s' is not a variable and can be unified with t. This is done by induction on the intruder's knowledge sets, and using ($\mathcal{P}_1$) and ($\mathcal{P}_2$).

Once the procedure of Figure 1 ends, either there are no more postponed rules and the set of constraints is empty (and therefore *simple*). Or there are still some postponed rules; the algorithm of Figure 1 implies that we have reached a simple

---

1. Choose an *applicable* postponed transition:
   − either $\mathcal{C}_{unif}$, such that:
      (a) this transition is not in an Oracle rule block;
      (b) all the variables v in $Var(s \cup I)$ are in at least one constraint
          T, COMP(v) FROM KNOW(I_v) of $\mathcal{E}$ where $v \notin Var(I_v)$.
   − or Oracle(r).
2. **Case** $\mathcal{C}_{unif}$: find s' in I such that s' is not a variable and $s'\rho = s\rho = t\rho$; apply the transition by replacing s with s';
   Case Oracle(r): apply the transition and free the $\mathcal{C}_{unif}$ rules of its block;
3. Apply all the postponed transitions that become applicable.

Fig. 1. Application of postponed transitions

constraints set $\mathcal{E}'$. Thus, we have found a sequence of transitions that reaches a simple constraints set $\mathcal{E}'$ from the satisfiable set $\mathcal{E}$.

This sequence of transitions may contain ghost terms. These terms are not used in the knowledge sets, and removing them does not affect the simple property of $\mathcal{E}'$. Transitions creating these terms are of no use and can be removed. Therefore we have built a sequence of applicable transitions leading to a simple constraints set.

Theorem 1 (Completeness). $\forall \mathcal{E},\ \exists \sigma,\ \sigma \vdash \mathcal{E}\ \Rightarrow\ \exists \mathcal{E}'\ simple,\ \exists \tau',\ \mathcal{E} \rightarrow^*_{\tau'} \mathcal{E}'$

3 Building the Oracle Rules

We now define how to build the rules describing the knowledge the intruder may yield by interacting with *puppet* principals. There is a finite number of *different* instances of these principals, but the total number of instances is not bounded. Each puppet principal receives a message and replies to it according to the rule $w_k, M \rightarrow w_{next(k)}, R$. In these rules, variables are used to denote ambiguous values. In this case, when a compound term has an ambiguous value, it is not represented by a single variable, but by a variable at each position of this term. Moreover, the new values created by such rules depend only on the instance of the principal. Thus, there is only a finite number of constants, and variables in messages may only be instantiated by constants or other variables.

In the following, we describe an algorithm building constraints over the set of knowledge I of the intruder, so that if these constraints are satisfied, the intruder may yield a term t after interaction with the puppet principals.

Building the Rules for Receiving/Sending Messages.

In the puppet principals rules, we first eliminate the w term. This cannot be done without other changes, since we do not have, in general, $Var(R) \subseteq Var(M)$. In addition, just removing the w term would imply that the intruder can start to communicate with a principal at a step that is not the first one of the principal. The set of $M \rightarrow R$ rules are transformed using the following algorithm:

Let $\mathcal{R}' = \emptyset$
For each puppet principal instance P
    Let $(L_1 \rightarrow R_1, \ldots, L_p \rightarrow R_p)$
    be the rules describing the received/sent messages by P.
    For $i = 1$ to p
        $\mathcal{R}' := \mathcal{R}' \cup \{(\bigcup_{j=1}^{i} L_j) \rightarrow R_i\}$

A rule $\bigcup_{j=1}^{i} L_j \rightarrow R_i$ of $\mathcal{R}'$ means that the intruder must compose all the L_j messages (the messages awaited by the principal before step i) for receiving the message R_i (sent at step i by the considered principal). These rules also have the following property: $Var(R_i) \subseteq \bigcup_{j=1}^{i} Var(L_j)$.

Building Constraint Rules over the Intruder Knowledge.
From the rules of $\mathcal{R}'$, with the help of constraints over the intruder's knowledge, we want to describe all the different ways for the intruder to get a subterm of R, for $L \rightarrow R \in \mathcal{R}'$. In this purpose, we build a new set of rules $\mathcal{R}''$ from $\mathcal{R}'$:

> Let $\mathcal{R}'' = \mathcal{R}'$
> Repeat
>   To choose $L \rightarrow R \in \mathcal{R}''$,
>   To choose one of the following actions:
>   – If $L = \text{APPLY}(t_1, t_2) \cup L'$, then $\mathcal{R}'' := \mathcal{R}'' \cup \{t_1 \cup t_2 \cup L' \rightarrow R\}$,
>   – If $R = <t_1, t_2>$, then $\mathcal{R}'' := \mathcal{R}'' \cup \{L \rightarrow t_1, \ L \rightarrow t_2\}$,
>   – If $R = \{t_1\}^{pub} t_2$, then $\mathcal{R}'' := \mathcal{R}'' \cup \{L \cup \text{INV}(t_2) \rightarrow t_1\}$,
>   – If $R = \{t_1\}^{sym} t_2$, then $\mathcal{R}'' := \mathcal{R}'' \cup \{L \cup t_2 \rightarrow t_1\}$.

As there is only a finite number of rules in $\mathcal{R}'$, and since a finite number of decompositions can be applied on each rule, $\mathcal{R}''$ is finite.

Searching for all the Constraints over the Intruder Knowledge.
We first initialize $\mathcal{R}'''$ with $\mathcal{R}''' = \mathcal{R}''$. A rule $L \rightarrow R \in \mathcal{R}'''$ expresses that the intruder must compose the terms in L in order to be able to know R. Let $l \in L$. He can compose l in two ways:

1. l may be in the intruder's knowledge at the time he started to look for a term;
2. l may be composed using the knowledge given by another rule of $\mathcal{R}'''$. That is, we have to find a rule $L' \rightarrow R' \in \mathcal{R}'''$, and a substitution ρ such that $R'\rho = l\rho$. The result is that the intruder may know $R\rho$ if he is able to compose $L'\rho \cup (L \setminus l)\rho$: the rule $L'\rho \cup (L \setminus l)\rho \rightarrow R\rho$ is added in $\mathcal{R}'''$.

If we iterate 2 from an initial rule $L \rightarrow R$, we find, at every step, a set of terms the intruder has to be able to compose in order to know a term $R\rho$. However, applications of 2 may loop. In order to ensure termination, we add a subsumption rule: suppose the applications of rule 2 results in $L \rightarrow R$; if $\exists L' \rightarrow R' \in \mathcal{R}'''$, $\exists \rho$ such that $R'\rho = R$ and $L'\rho \subseteq L$, the rule $L \rightarrow R$ can be rejected. Moreover, we reject all rules $L \rightarrow R$ such that $R \in L$, as they cannot help to obtain R.

There is only a finite number of constants, therefore only a finite number of rules can be generated using 2 and subsumption. They are the **Oracle rules**. The subsumption rule does not remove any useful rule from $\mathcal{R}'''$, since for two rules $L \rightarrow R$ and $L' \rightarrow R\rho$ in $\mathcal{R}'''$, if $R\rho$ can be unified with a term t, R can be unified with the term t, and if the constraint $\{\text{COMP}(l)\}_{l \in L'}$ FROM $\text{KNOW}(I)$ is satisfiable, then the constraint $\{\text{COMP}(l)\}_{l \in L}$ FROM $\text{KNOW}(I)$ is also satisfiable if $L\rho \subseteq L'$.

4   Correctness and Termination

The correctness and termination of our system of rules is stated as follows:

Theorem 2 (Correctness). *If $B \parallel \mathcal{E} \to^* B' \parallel \mathcal{E}'$, with $\mathcal{E}'$ simple, then $\mathcal{E}$ is satisfiable.*

Theorem 3 (Termination). *Starting from an initial state $B_0 \parallel \emptyset$, the rules Message, $\mathcal{C}_{unif}$, $\mathcal{C}_{dec}$, Oracle, $\mathcal{A}_{pub}$, $\mathcal{A}_{sym}$ and $\mathcal{A}_{pair}$ can be applied only a finite number of times.*

Correctness. The correctness is proved by induction on the number of steps necessary to reach a simple constraints set $\mathcal{E}'$ from $\mathcal{E}$. At step 0, this theorem corresponds to Proposition 3; the induction is then straightforward.

Termination. For the termination, since only a finite number of Message rules can be applied, this is sufficient to prove the termination of the constraints resolution rules. Second, this is enough to prove the termination of the system without the Oracle's rules, since only $\mathcal{C}_{unif}$ can be applied on the COMP() terms created by these rules.

The application of the constraints resolution rules terminates because at each step, either the number of different variables decreases, or multisets of terms are decreasing w.r.t. the subterm ordering.

5   Experimental Results

In order to test the efficiency of our system, we have analyzed a library of authentication protocols. Because of the inherent limitation of our tool, we have focused on protocols that were reported to be flawed in [9,7].

The introduction of an Oracle partially removes this limitation, as one can indicate that some principals (puppets) may run an unbounded number of sessions in parallel. As termination is ensured, and since the simplifications done on the puppet principals help the intruder, it becomes possible to *validate* a protocol. This validation is weaker than the one described in [17,4], since we have to provide an execution environment under which flaws are looked for. Moreover, the static analysis done while building the Oracle rules forbids to look for type flaws during the interaction between the intruder and the *puppet* principals.

The study of a protocol is done in two steps. First, a high-level protocol specification is compiled into a set of rewrite rules [12]. This protocol compiler is also used by other teams, for example in the AVISS project [2]. It can also be used to express that some principals (puppets) can be used *in parallel*. In this case, it calculates the Oracle rules. A more complete description is given in [5].

The second tool we use is daTac [19], a generic theorem prover using narrowing. The main reason for its use is that it permits to handle associative-commutative properties, used for example to express commutativity of RSA encryption. Its poor time performance should not conceal that our algorithm permits to visit only a very limited number of different states.

A Novel Attack on Denning Sacco Symmetric Key Protocol. The *Denning Sacco symmetric key protocol* was thought to be secure in several surveys [9,7]. In this protocol, A wants to communicate with B using a secret key generated by a keyserver S. The sequence of messages is:

$$
\begin{aligned}
A &\rightarrow S : A, B \\
S &\rightarrow A : \{B, K_{ab}, T, \{A, K_{ab}, T\}K_{bs}\}K_{as} \\
A &\rightarrow B : \{A, K_{ab}, T\}K_{bs}
\end{aligned}
$$

where T is a timestamp. The problem is that messages 2 and 3 are of the same global shape. This fact can be exploited in the following sequence of messages:

$$
\begin{aligned}
I(B) &\rightarrow S : B, A \\
S &\rightarrow I(B) : \{A, K_{ab}, T, \{B, K_{ab}, T\}K_{as}\}K_{bs} \\
I(A) &\rightarrow B : \{A, K_{ab}, T, \{B, K_{ab}, T\}K_{as}\}K_{bs} \quad (\equiv \{A, K_{ab}, T\}K_{bs})
\end{aligned}
$$

After this sequence of messages, B accepts a new value for the symmetric key he shares with A, whereas A is not aware a protocol run took place. This attack relies on a type flaw, and this kind of attack is sometimes considered to be dubious. In this case, one shall note this is very unlikely that B, as he receives the whole message, considers $T, \{B, K_{ab}, T\}K_{as}$ to be a timestamp. But the implementation of this protocol could lead to a real flaw in two cases:

1. in a flawed implementation, B might not check the tail of the last message. Since the last two messages begin with the same data type, there is a real risk of confusion here;
2. if a bloc-ciphering algorithm such as DES is used, the second message may be split into parts, from which the intruder will be able to construct a message acceptable by B, however cautious B is.

Therefore this flaw can occur in the implementation of this protocol. Its detection permits to give guidelines for the practical design of the protocol.

6   Comparison and Conclusion

Although there are still protocols that cannot be expressed in our high-level language, one shall note that our approach, in comparison with other classical results, seems rather efficient, and for two reasons.

Firstly, a look at Table 1 shows that we are able to correctly find out whether a protocol is flawed. Moreover, we were able to find type flaws in addition to other flaws. This is the case, for example, of the *Otway Rees protocol*. In contrast with Lowe's approach, we do not have to specify the type flaw looked for.

Secondly, one shall note that we do not find any "artifact" error. In the case of the *Yahalom protocol*, we do not find any flaw. In this case, the flaw reported in [7] cannot occur in our setting, because the last message of the attack cannot be composed by the Intruder. We do not claim to find all type flaws, since some of them rely on the associative property of the pairing. We only consider that

Table 1. Comparison of our approach with others

Protocol	Our tool	Lowe	Clark&Jacob	Brackin	Time
Protocols using symmetric encryption					
ISO Sym.Key One-Pass Unilat. Auth. Proto.	Attack	Attack	No attack	No attack	2s
ISO Sym. Key Two-Pass Mutual Auth. Proto.	Attack	Attack	No attack	No attack	14s
Andrew Secure RPC Protocol	Attack	Attack	Attack	Attack	14s
Davis Swick Private Key Certificates, Proto. 1	Attack	Attack	Attack	Attack	32s
Davis Swick Private Key Certificates, Proto. 2	Attack	Attack	Attack	Attack	1073s
Davis Swick Private Key Certificates, Proto. 3	Attack	Attack	No attack	No attack	6s
Davis Swick Private Key Certificates, Proto. 4	Attack	Attack	No attack	No attack	80s
Denning Sacco Symmetric Key Protocol	Attack	No attack	No attack	No attack	6s
Needham Schroeder Proto. with Convent. Key	Attack	No attack	Attack	Attack	20s
Otway Rees Key exchange Protocol	Attack	Attack	Attack	No attack	12s
Yahalom Protocol	No attack	No attack	Attack	Attack	
Woo&Lam Auth. Protocol Π_1	Attack	Attack	Attack	No attack	4s
Woo&Lam Auth. Protocol Π_2	Attack	Attack	Attack	No attack	3s
Woo&Lam Auth. Protocol Π_3	Attack	Attack	Attack	No attack	3s
Woo&Lam Auth. Protocol Π	Attack	Attack	Attack	No attack	2s
Woo&Lam Mutual Auth.	Attack	Attack	Attack	No attack	635s
Needham Schroeder Signature Protocol	Attack	Attack	No attack	Attack	18s
Kao Chow Repeated Auth. Protocol	Attack	No attack	Attack	Attack	4s
Kehne Langendorfer Schoenewalder	Attack	Attack	Attack	Attack	4s
Neumann Stubblebine	Attack	Attack	Attack	No attack	3s
Protocols using hash functions					
ISO One-Pass Unilat. Auth. Proto. with CCFs	Attack	Attack	No attack	No attack	3s
ISO Two-Pass Mutual Auth. Proto. with CCFs	Attack	Attack	No attack	No attack	5s
Protocols using public key encryption					
ISO Public Key One-Pass Unilat. Auth. Proto	Attack	Attack	No attack	No attack	4s
ISO Public Key Two-Pass Mutual Auth. Proto	Attack	Attack	No attack	No attack	10s
Needham Schroeder Public Key Protocol	Attack	Attack	Attack	No attack	7s
SPLICE/AS Auth. Protocol	Attack	Attack	Attack	No attack	12s
Hwang&Chen's mod. SPLICE/AS Auth. Proto	Attack	Attack	Attack	No attack	21s
Denning Sacco Key Distrib. with Public Key	Attack	Attack	Attack	No attack	57s
Shamir Rivest Adelman Three Pass Protocol	Attack	Attack	Attack	Unanalyzed	5s
Encrypted Key Exchange Protocol	Attack	Attack	Attack	No attack	6s
TMN Key Exchange Protocol	Attack	Unanalyzed	Unanalyzed	Unanalyzed	80s

pairing is right-associative, which permits us to find type flaws in the *tail* of messages (as in the *Denning-Sacco symmetric key protocol* case).

The tool used by Lowe in [9] is probably one of the best, up to date, for the complete study of security protocols. In contrast with our tool, it does not handle type flaws and is restricted to bounded number of sessions systems.

Blanchet proposed in [4] a tool that also permits model-checking with an unbounded number of principals. On one hand, this method handles nonces better than in our Oracle's rules, and it does not require a scenario. On the other hand, it cannot be used to detect replay attacks, short term secrecy and, in general, everything that is session dependent. For example, in this nonces setting, *every* protocol is subject to a replay attack.

The method used in Athena [17] also has the advantage of not requiring the declaration of instances of principals, and can handle an unbounded number of principals. Its drawback are that this method needs atomic keys, which make it inapplicable to protocols like SSL, and it requires that keys used for encryption are known by the receiver. This rules out protocols like SET Card-holder registration, which uses fresh keys in every message. Finally, Athena is not able to handle type flaws.

About these last two systems, we can note that the one described in [4] does not ensure termination because of problems that might arise from the *shape* of messages of the protocol. On the other hand, the model of [17] does not ensure termination because of an unrestricted nonce model. We have ensured termination by restricting the model of nonces and by rejecting type flaws during the building of the Oracle's rules. We feel that the model for the puppet principals can be improved toward either one or the other setting, thus permitting to study a protocol without having to specify instances for those puppet principals.

Our model was developped as part of the AVISS project [2] in the CL part, but is also partly used in the on-the-fly model-checker. Results obtained by both systems show its efficiency.

References

1. R. Amadio and D. Lugiez. On the reachability problem in cryptographic protocols. In *CONCUR'2000*, pages 380–394, 2000. 325
2. A. Armando, D. Basin, M. Bouallagui, Y. Chevalier, L. Compagna, S. Mödersheim, M. Rusinowitch, M. Turuani, L. Vigano, and L. Vigneron. The AVISS Security Protocol Analysis Tool. In *CAV'02*, 2002. Tool presentation. 333, 336
3. D. Basin. Lazy Infinite-State Analysis of Security Protocols. In R. Baumgart, editor, *Secure Networking — CQRE (Secure)'99*, LNCS 1740, pages 30–42, Heidelberg, Germany, 1999. Springer-Verlag. 325
4. B. Blanchet. An Efficient Cryptographic Protocol Verifier Based on Prolog Rules. In *14th IEEE Computer Security Foundations Workshop*, June 2001. 324, 333, 335
5. Y. Chevalier and L. Vigneron. Towards Efficient Automated Verification of Security Protocols. In *Verification Workshop (VERIFY'01) (in connection with IJCAR'01)*, *Università degli studi di Siena, TR DII 08/01*, pages 19–33, 2001. 325, 333
6. Y. Chevalier and L. Vigneron. Automated Unbounded Verification of Security Protocols. Research Report 4369, Institut National de Recherche en Informatique et Automatique, Nancy (France), January 2002. 325, 330
7. J. Clark and J. Jacob. A Survey of Authentication Protocol Literature: Version 1.0, 17 Nov. 1997. URL http://www.cs.york.ac.uk/~jac/papers/drareview.ps.gz. 325, 333, 334
8. H. Comon, V. Cortier, and J. Mitchell. Tree Automata with one Memory, Set Constraints and Ping-Pong Protocols. In *28th Int. Coll. Automata, Languages, and Programming (ICALP'2001)*, LNCS 2076, pages 682–693. Springer, 2001. 324
9. B. Donovan, P. Norris, and G. Lowe. Analyzing a Library of Security Protocols using Casper and FDR. In *W. on Formal Methods and Security Protocols*, 1999. 325, 333, 334, 335
10. N. Durgin, P. Lincoln, J. Mitchell, and A. Scedrov. Undecidability of Bounded Security Protocols. In *FLOC'99 Workshop on Formal Methods and Sec. Protocols (FMSP'99)*, 1999. 324
11. J. Goubault-Larrecq. A Method for Automatic Cryptographic Protocol Verification. In *IPDPS 2000 Workshops, Cancun, Mexico*, LNCS 1800, pages 977–984. Springer, May 2000. 324
12. F. Jacquemard, M. Rusinowitch, and L. Vigneron. Compiling and Verifying Security Protocols. In M. Parigot and A. Voronkov, editors, *Proceedings of LPAR'2000*, LNCS 1955, pages 131–160, Heidelberg, 2000. Springer-Verlag. 333
13. G. Lowe. Towards a Completeness Result for Model Checking of Security Protocols. *Journal of Computer Security 7*, 1, 1999. 324

14. J. Millen and V. Shmatikov. Constraint Solving for Bounded-Process Cryptographic Protocol Analysis. In *8th ACM Conference on Computer and Communication Security*, pages 166–175, November 2001. 325

15. D. Monniaux. Abstracting Cryptographic Protocols with Tree Automata. In *6th Int. Static Analysis Symposium (SAS'99)*, LNCS 1694. Springer-Verlag, 1999. 324

16. M. Rusinowitch and M. Turuani. Protocol Insecurity with Finite Number of Sessions is NP-complete. In *Proceedings of the 14th IEEE Computer Security Foundations Workshop*. IEEE Computer Society Press, 2001. 325

17. D. Song, S. Berezin, and A. Perrig. Athena, a Novel Approach to Efficient Automatic Security Protocol Analysis. *J. of Computer Security*, 9((1,2)):47–74, 2001. 324, 333, 335

18. S. Stoller. A Bound on Attacks on Authentication Protocols. Technical Report 526, Indiana University, Computer Science Dept, February 2000. 324

19. L. Vigneron. Positive Deduction modulo Regular Theories. In Hans Kleine-Büning, editor, *Computer Science Logic*, LNCS 1092, pages 468–485, Berlin, 1995. Springer-Verlag. URL: http://www.loria.fr/equipes/protheo/SOFTWARES/DATAC/. 333

Exploiting Behavioral Hierarchy for Efficient Model Checking

Rajeev Alur, Michael McDougall, and Zijiang Yang

Department of Computer and Information Science
University of Pennsylvania

1 Introduction

Inspired by the success of model checking in hardware and protocol verification, model checking techniques for software have been the focus of a lot of research in the last few years [5, 3, 2, 6]. Model checking can be applied only to relatively small models due to its inherently high computational requirements, and there are two complementary trends to address scalability. The *model extraction* approach, exemplified by projects such as Bandera [6] and SLAM [3], involves constructing inputs to model checkers by abstracting programs written in languages such as C and Java. The *model-based design* approach, exemplified by modeling notations such as Statecharts [7], promotes design using high-level models that are compiled into code. Our research agenda is to develop model checking techniques for model-based design of software.

Modern software design languages promote *hierarchy* as one of the key constructs for structuring complex specifications. The input language to our model checker is based on *hierarchic reactive modules* [1]. This choice was motivated by the fact that, unlike STATECHARTS and other languages, in hierarchic reactive modules, the notion of hierarchy is *semantic* with an observational trace-based semantics and a notion of refinement with assume-guarantee rules. The first contribution of this paper is the *Hermes* toolkit that implements hierarchic reactive modules. Our implementation has a *visual* front-end and XML-based back-end, consistent with modern software design tools, and is in Java.

There are two basic techniques for reachability analysis. Enumerative model checkers such as SPIN [8] perform an on-the-fly exploration of the state-space using a depth-first search, while symbolic model checkers such as SMV [9] perform a breadth-first search by manipulating sets of states, rather than individual states, encoded typically by ordered binary (or multi-valued) decision diagrams. Since the two approaches are incomparable, and have been shown to be successful, *Hermes* supports both enumerative and symbolic reachability analysis. In this paper, we report progress on exploiting the structuring information in the behavioral hierarchy of the input model to speed up the the exploration of reachable state-space of the model for both the approaches. More information about the tool is available at http://www.cis.upenn.edu/sdrl/hermes/

D. Brinksma and K. G. Larsen (Eds.): CAV 2002, LNCS 2404, pp. 338-342, 2002.
© Springer-Verlag Berlin Heidelberg 2002

4   Symbolic Checker

Figure 3 (a) shows a mode M_1 with two submodes M_2 and M_3. M_1 has a local variable x, M_2 has local variables y_1, y_2 and M_3 has y_3, y_4. There are 8 transitions $t_1..t_8$ and 8 control points $c_1..c_8$. Given a typical symbolic model checker, the

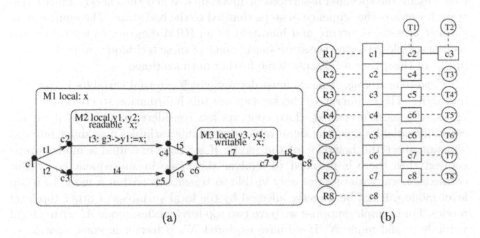

(a)   (b)

Fig. 3. (a): A hierarchical design. (b): Hierarchical symbolic representation

transition t_3 is denoted by an MDD representing $T_3 = (h = c_2 \wedge g_3 \wedge h' = c_4 \wedge y_1' = x \wedge x' = x \wedge y_2' = y_2 \wedge y_3' = y_3 \wedge y_4' = y_4)$, where the variable h is used to encode the control location. The transition relation of M_1, $T = \wedge_{i=1}^{8} T_i$, is represented by a single MDD or in conjunctively partitioned format.

In Hermes, the transition relation is represented as a map from control points to a list of pairs containing destinations of edges along with MDDs encoding guarded commands. Figure 3 (b) shows such a map for mode M_1. For each transition t_k from control point c_i to control point c_j, we build the MDD T_k' that encodes the guarded command of t_k. Then the pair (c_j, T_k') is added to the list associated with the control point c_i. Note that each T_k' is much smaller than the counterpart T_k used in a flat representation. For example, $t_3 = (c_2, c_4)$ can be denoted by a smaller MDD $T_3' = (g_3 \wedge y_1' = x \wedge y_2' = y_2)$. This is possible because local variables of M_2 and M_3 are not simultaneously active, therefore, y_3 and y_4 never appear in T_3' or other MDDs representing transitions in M_2. Since x is not writable in M_2, the term $x' = x$ can be dropped. The variables h is not needed in T_3' because the mapping provides information on control points. In other words, typing and scoping information of the original model is maintained during compilation of the transition relation using MDDs.

Like transition relations, the reachable state-sets in Hermes are not represented by a single MDD. A state region represented by an MDD is associated with each control point. As shown in figure 3 (b), there is an MDD R_i associated with each control point c_i. Such a representation allows us to partition the state

3   Enumerative Checker

The enumerative checker performs a depth first search of all reachable states of an HRM diagram. The search will check for states that are deadlocked or that violate the specified assertions or invariants. When the checker finds a bad state it outputs the sequence of steps that led to the bad state. The enumerative checker uses the structure and hierarchy of an HRM diagram to save time and memory while exploring the state space. Some of these techniques were described in [2]. In this paper we discuss some further optimizations.

Exploiting Hiding. A mode must declare which external variables it can read and write. The enumerative checker can use this information to create abstract views of a mode's context. Two contexts are considered equivalent if all the readable variables have the same value; unreadable variables may differ but this will not affect the behavior of the mode. If we have executed a mode in one context then there is no need to analyze the mode in subsequent equivalent contexts. Local variables are only visible to transitions within a mode so a top level mode will not be directly affected by the local variables of other top level modes. For example, suppose we have two top level modes: mode M with a local variable x, and mode N. If we have explored N's behavior in some context c_1 where $x = 3$, and we see another context c_2 which is the same as c_1 except that $x = 6$, then we do not need to compute N's behavior in context c_2. To exploit this, the enumerative checker keeps track of how each top level mode will behave in a context. When that context is seen again the old behavior is projected onto the current context to find the next reachable state.

Exploiting Sharing. This optimization exploits the fact that a mode can be shared by various parent modes. Recall that one mode may be instantiated in many places in an HRM diagram. Each instantiation will exhibit the same behavior when its global variables are the same. For example, Figure 2 shows a

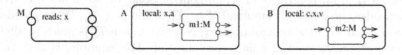

Fig. 2. Exploiting Sharing

mode M that is instantiated in two other modes A and B. Mode M only reads one variable x. The behavior of M will only depend on the value of x when its entry point becomes active. Once we have explored M in A with $x = 2$, we note which of the two exit points results from $x = 2$. When we encounter M in B with $x = 2$ we can just jump straight to the appropriate exit point. By suitable book-keeping, checker avoids recomputing a mode's behavior if another instance of that mode has already been searched for an equivalent context.

2   Hierarchical Modeling in Hermes

Hierarchical Reactive Modules (HRM) is a graphical language for describing and analyzing systems. Our goal in using HRM is to find verification algorithms that leverage the modularity that is present in so many modern designs.

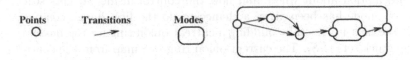

Fig. 1. The building blocks of the HRM language and a simple Mode diagram.

A simple HRM diagram resembles a finite state machine (FSM); it consists of states, called *points* in HRM, and transitions between points. HRM extends FSM by adding variables which can be read and updated as in normal programming languages. Each transition is enabled when its *guard*, a boolean expression over the diagram's variables, evaluates to true. Transitions can be annotated with *actions* which update the values of variables.

A set of points and transitions can be grouped into a *mode*. A mode's interaction with its surroundings is mediated by two interfaces: a *control* interface and a *data* interface. The control interface is a set of entry and exit points on the boundary of a mode. A mode can be embedded in other modes.

The data interface determines which data is available to a mode through a set of *global* variables. Each global variable is designated as *readable, writable* or both. Any external data that is not contained in a global variable will be hidden from the mode. Modes can also have their own *local* variables which are visible only to transitions within that mode or its submodes. A designer can re-use a mode by creating a *reference mode* which instantiates a copy of a mode that is defined elsewhere. Figure 1 shows a mode that contains some border points, internal points and one submode.

Certain modes are designated as *top level modes* that behave as separate processes or threads. We model concurrency by interleaving so that at any one time there is only one active top level mode. Top level modes communicate with each other through shared variables. HRM has a well-defined formal semantics [1].

HRM has two mechanisms for describing the requirements of a system. A point or mode can be given an *assertion condition*, which must be true whenever that point or mode is active. A system can also be given an *invariant*, which must be satisfied for all states of the system.

We have implemented a toolkit, called Hermes, which allows users to create, edit, type-check and verify HRM diagrams. The toolkit is implemented in Java and has a graphical user interface (GUI) for editing HRM diagrams. The GUI also acts a front-end to the model checking algorithms. Hermes also has command-line and scripting front-ends for environments where a GUI is impractical. The Hermes toolkit uses an XML file format to store HRM diagrams.

space intuitively with each region containing all the states with the same control point.

The reachability computation in Hermes computes reachable states at each control point. When a top mode M_i gets control for the first time, it starts the image computation from its entry point by following the transitions until the control gets stuck. The image computation returns an MDD S_i that contains the information about where and how the control inside M_i gets stuck. After each top mode has been given a chance to do the first image computation, it starts the next iteration by building a current onion ring for top mode M_i based on the stuck sets $\cup_i S_i$. The current onion ring is a map from the control points where the control became stuck during last image computation at M_i to newly reached states obtained from image computations at top modes other than M_i. By applying the image computation to the current onion ring of M_i, the control may continue from those stuck control points. The algorithm terminates if all the onion rings for top modes are empty, i.e., no new states can be reached at any control point.

In order to make Hermes work on existing sequential circuits designs we translate sequential circuits in BLIF format to XML that can be parsed by Hermes. The translation produces a Hermes model consisting of a single top-level mode. Besides having no concurrency, the model is linear rather than a tree or a DAG. Thus, the main structural feature that current Hermes exploits is the scoping of variables allowing for early quantification.

Acknowledgments. We thank Radu Grosu for helpful discussions. This research was supported in part by NSF award CCR99-70925, SRC award 99-TJ-688, and NSF CAREER award CCR97-34115.

References

1. R. Alur and R. Grosu. Modular refinement of hierarchic reactive machines. In *Proc. 27th POPL*, pages 390–402, 2000.
2. R. Alur, R. Grosu, and M. McDougall. Efficient reachability analysis of hierarchical reactive machines. In *Proc. 12th CAV*, LNCS 1855, pages 280–295, 2000.
3. T. Ball and S. Rajamani. The SLAM toolkit. In *Proc. 13th CAV*, 2001.
4. R. Brayton, G. Hachtel, A. Sangiovanni-Vincentell, F. Somenzi, et. al. VIS: A system for verification and synthesis. In *Proc. 8th CAV*, LNCS 1102, pages 428–432, 1996.
5. W. Chan, R. Anderson, P. Beame, S. Burns, F. Modugno, D. Notkin, and J. Reese. Model checking large software specifications. *IEEE Trans. on Software Engg.*, 24(7):498–519, 1998.
6. J. Corbett, M. Dwyer, J. Hatcliff, S. Laubach, C. Pasareanu, Robby, and H. Zheng. Bandera: Extracting finite-state models from Java source code. In *Proc. 22nd ICSE*, pages 439–448. 2000.
7. D. Harel. Statecharts: A visual formalism for complex systems. *Science of Computer Programming*, 8:231–274, 1987.
8. G. Holzmann. The model checker SPIN. *IEEE Trans. on Software Engg.*, 23(5):279–295, 1997.
9. K. McMillan. *Symbolic model checking: an approach to the state explosion problem.* Kluwer Academic Publishers, 1993.

IF-2.0: A Validation Environment for Component-Based Real-Time Systems*

Marius Bozga, Susanne Graf, and Laurent Mounier

VERIMAG, Centre Equation
2 avenue de Vignate, F-38610 Gières

1 Introduction

It is widely recognised that the automated validation of complex systems can hardly be achieved without tool integration. The development of the IF-1.0 toolbox [3] was initiated several years ago, in order to provide an open validation platform for timed asynchronous systems (such as telecommunication protocols or distributed applications, in general). The toolbox was built upon an *intermediate representation* language based on extended timed automata. In particular, this representation allowed us to study the semantics of real-time primitives for asynchronous systems. Currently, the toolbox contains dedicated tools on the intermediate language (such as compilers, static analysers and model-checkers) as well as front-ends to various specification languages and validation tools (academic and commercial ones). Among the dedicated tools, we focused on static analysis (such as slicing and abstraction) which are mandatory for an automated validation of complex systems. Finally, the toolbox was successfully used on several case studies, the most relevant ones being presented in [4].

In spite of the interest of this toolbox on specific applications, it appears that some of the initial design choices, which were made to obtain a maximal efficiency, are sometimes too restrictive. In particular they may prevent its applicability to a wider context:

- the *static* nature of the intermediate representation prevents the analysis of dynamic systems. More exactly, primitive operations like object (or thread) creation and destruction, which are widely and naturally used both in specification formalisms like UML or programming languages like Java, were not supported.
- the architecture of the exploration engine allowed only the exploration of pure IF-1.0 specifications. This is too restrictive for complex system specifications which mix formal descriptions and executable code (e.g, for components already implemented and tested).

This situation motivated the extension of the IF-1.0 intermediate representation and, in turn, to re-consider the architecture of the exploration engine.

* This work was supported in part by the European Commission FET projects ADVANCE, contract No IST-1999-29082 and AGEDIS, contract No IST-1999-20218

D. Brinksma and K. G. Larsen (Eds.): CAV 2002, LNCS 2404, pp. 343–348, 2002.

Some of the language extensions are derived from existing specification formalisms (UML [10] and SDL-2000 [8]) and object oriented programming languages (like Java). Concerning the exploration engine architecture, the approach we follow is influenced both by traditional model-checkers such as Spin [7] and Open/Caesar [5] and more recent runtime validation tools such as Verisoft [6], Java PathFinder [12] and SystemC [11]. The originality of this architecture is to preserve exhaustive exploration capabilities while supporting heterogeneous specifications (with external code invocations and dynamic object creations). These extensions are described in more details in the following sections, together with some running experiments and perspectives.

2   Dynamic Extended Automata

The formal basis for the IF-2.0 intermediate representation is a dynamic version of extended timed automata.

We focus on systems composed of several components (called *processes*), running in parallel and interacting through message-passing, either via communication channels (called *signalroutes*), or by direct addressing. The number of processes and signalroutes may change over time: they may be created and deleted dynamically, during the lifetime of the system.

Each process is described by an extended timed automaton. It has a unique process identifier (*pid*) value, a local memory consisting of variables (including clocks), control states and a queue of pending messages (received and not yet consumed). As usual, processes move from one control state to another by executing transitions, which are triggered by messages in the input queue and/or some (possibly timed) guards. Transition bodies are *sequential programs* consisting of elementary actions (like variable or clock assignments, message sending, process creation/destruction, external code invocation, etc) structured using elementary control-flow statements (like if-then-else, while-do, etc). Control states may be nested (as in statecharts) in order to factorize common behaviour and obtain modular automata descriptions. Signalroutes are specialised communication media that transport messages between processes. The behaviour of the signalroute is defined by its storing policy (FIFO or multiset), its delivery policy (peer to peer, unicast or multicast), its delaying policy ("zero delay", "delay" or "rate") and finally its reliability (reliable or lossy).

The semantics of the extended automata model is defined by the graph of its executions [1]. This graph is obtained by the *interleaved* execution of processes, where process transitions define *atomic* non-interruptive execution steps.

The semantics of time is similar to the one of timed automata: time progresses in states (i.e, all running processes wait in some state before selecting and executing some transition) and transitions take zero time to be executed. In order to control the time progress, or equivalently, the waiting time in states, we rely on transition urgencies [2] – explicit deadlines *eager*, *lazy* or *delayable*

---

[1] For pure IF-2.0 specifications there exists also a formal operational semantics, however, for specifications using external code we rely on runtime execution results.

attached to transitions defining when they *must* be executed. More precisely, *eager* transitions must be executed as soon as they are enabled and waiting is not allowed; *lazy* transitions are never urgent, that is, when a lazy transition is enabled the transition may be executed or, alternatively, the process may wait without any restriction; finally, when a *delayable* transition is enabled, waiting is allowed as long as time progress does not disable it.

Example 1. Consider a multi-threaded server which can handle at most N simultaneous requests. Thus, if possible, for a `request` message (received from the environment) a `thread` is created. The server keeps in the `thc` variable the number of running threads. Thread processes are quite simple: once created, they work (calling an external C procedure), and when finished they send a `done` message back to the server. These messages are delayed through a unique signalroute `cs` (which is passed as a parameter when creating a `thread` process).

```
signalroute cs(1) #delay[1,2]              task thc := thc - 1;
  from thread to server                       nextstate idle;
  with done;                                endstate;
                                          endprocess;
process server(1);
    var thc integer;                      process thread(0);
  state idle #start ;                         fpar parent pid, route pid;
    deadline lazy;                        state init #start ;
    provided thc < N;                        deadline lazy;
    input request();                         call work();
      fork thread(self, cs0);                output done()
      task thc := thc + 1;                      via route to parent;
      nextstate idle;                        stop;
    deadline eager;                        endstate;
    input done();                        endprocess;
```

3   State-Space Exploration

State-space exploration is one of the successful techniques used for the analysis of concurrent systems and also the core component of many model-based validation tool (i.e, model-checker, test-generator, etc). Nevertheless, exploration is far from being trivial for dynamic systems that, in addition, use complex data, involve various communication mechanisms, mix several description languages, and moreover, depend on time constraints. The solution we propose is an *open*, *modular* and *extensible* exploration platform designed to cope with the complexity and the heterogeneity of actual concurrent systems.

The IF-2.0 exploration platform relies on a clear separation between the individual behaviour of processes (i.e, memory update, transition firing) and the coordination mechanisms between processes (i.e, communication, creation, destruction). More precisely, each process or signalroute is represented as an object (in the sense of object-oriented languages) that has an internal state and may have one or more fireable (local) transitions, depending on its current state.

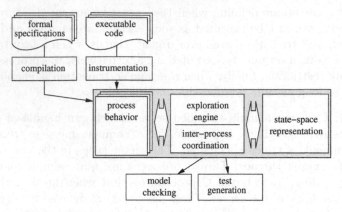

Fig. 1. Functional view of IF-2.0 exploration platform

Time is also a specialised process dealing with the management of all (running) clocks. Coordination is then realised by a kind of *process manager*: it scans the set of local transitions, choose the fireable one(s) with respect to global (system) constraints, ask the corresponding processes to execute these transitions and update the global state accordingly.

This architecture provides the possibility to validate complex heterogeneous systems. Exploration is not limited to IF-2.0 specifications: any kind of processes may be run in parallel on the exploration platform as long as they implement the interface required by the process manager. It is indeed possible to use code (either directly, or instrumented accordingly) of already implemented components, instead of extracting an intermediate model to be put into some global specification.

Another advantage of the architecture is the *extensibility* concerning coordination primitives and exploration strategies. Presently, the exploration platform supports asynchronous (interleaved) execution and asynchronous point-to-point communication between processes. Different execution modes, like synchronous or run-to-completion, or additional communication mechanisms, such as broadcast or rendez-vous, can be obtained by simply extending the process interfaces and the process manager functionality. Concerning the exploration strategies, reduction heuristics such as partial-order reduction or symmetry reduction are currently incorporated into the process manager. More specific heuristics may be added depending on the application domain.

4   Ongoing Work and Perspectives

The IF-2.0 representation and the associated environment are currently being used in several research projects. As example, we mention AGEDIS (see http://www.agedis.de) where we develop a testing environment for distributed systems. In this project, IF-2.0 plays a central role, both as an (operational) representation for system's behaviour (described in UML at the user level) and as an exploration engine used by a model-based test generator (an extension of TGV [9]).

In the near future we plan to upgrade the (most effective) static analysis techniques, already implemented for IF-1.0, to the new intermediate representation IF-2.0. In particular, *slicing* and *abstraction* techniques are mandatory to keep tractable the state-space exploration. However, due to the dynamic features of IF-2.0, some of these techniques have to be revisited.

Another perspective is the integration of the scheduling framework of [1] in order to improve the standard execution modes provided by the exploration engine (e.g, asynchronous or synchronous). Based on *dynamic priorities*, this scheduling framework is flexible and general enough to ensure a fine-grained control of execution of real-time systems, depending on various constraints. This framework fits also well in our exploration engine architecture. For instance, it is possible to extend the process manager with scheduling capabilities, in order to evaluate dynamic priorities at run-time and to restrict the set of fireable transitions accordingly.

The IF-2.0 package can be downloaded at
`http://www-verimag.imag.fr/~async/IF/`.

References

1. K. Altisen, G. Gößler, and J. Sifakis. A Methodology for the Construction of Scheduled Systems. In Mathai Joseph, editor, *Proceedings of FTRTFT 2000*, number 1926 in LNCS, pages 106–120. Springer-Verlag, September 2000. 347
2. S. Bornot, J. Sifakis, and S. Tripakis. Modeling Urgency in Timed Systems. In *International Symposium: Compositionality - The Significant Difference (Holstein, Germany)*, volume 1536 of *LNCS*. Springer, September 1997. 344
3. M. Bozga, J.Cl. Fernandez, L. Ghirvu, S. Graf, J. P. Krimm, and L. Mounier. IF: A Validation Environment for Timed Asynchronous Systems. In E. A. Emerson and A. P. Sistla, editors, *Proceedings of CAV'00 (Chicago, USA)*, volume 1855 of *LNCS*. Springer, July 2000. 343
4. M. Bozga, S. Graf, and L. Mounier. Automated Validation of Distributed Software using the IF Environment. In *Workshop on Software Model-Checking*, volume 55. TCS, July 2001. 343
5. H. Garavel. OPEN/CÆSAR: An Open Software Architecture for Verification, Simulation, and Testing. In B. Steffen, editor, *Proceedings of TACAS'98 (Lisbon, Portugal)*, volume 1384 of *LNCS*, pages 68–84. Springer, March 1998. 344
6. P. Godefroid. VeriSoft: A Tool for the Automatic Analysis of Concurrent Reactive Software (short paper). In *Proceedings of CAV'97 (Haifa, Israel)*, volume 1254 of *LNCS*, pages 476–479. Springer, June 1997. 344
7. G. J. Holzmann. *Design and Validation of Computer Protocols*. Prentice Hall Software Series, `http://cm.bell-labs.com/cm/cs/what/spin`, 1991. 344
8. ITU-T. Recommendation Z.100. Specification and Description Language (SDL). Technical Report Z-100, International Telecommunication Union – Standardization Sector, Genève, November 1999. 344
9. T. Jéron and P. Morel. Test Generation Derived from Model Checking. In N. Halbwachs and D. Peled, editors, *Proceedings of CAV'99 (Trento, Italy)*, volume 1633 of *LNCS*, pages 108–122. Springer, July 1999. 347

10. OMG. Unified Modeling Language Specification. Technical Report OMG UML v1.3 – ad/99-06-09, Object Management Group, June 1999. 344
11. S. Swan. An Introduction to System-Level Modeling in Systemc 2.0. Technical report, Open SystemC Initiative, 2001. 344
12. W. Visser, K. Havelund, G. Brat, and S. Park. Model checking programs. In *Proceedings of ASE'00*. IEEE Computer Society, September 2000. 344

The AVISS Security Protocol Analysis Tool*

Alessandro Armando[1], David Basin[2], Mehdi Bouallagui[3], Yannick Chevalier[3],
Luca Compagna[1], Sebastian Mödersheim[2], Michael Rusinowitch[3],
Mathieu Turuani[3], Luca Viganò[2], and Laurent Vigneron[3]

[1] Mechanized Reasoning Group, DIST
Università di Genova, Italy
[2] Institut für Informatik
Universität Freiburg, Germany
[3] LORIA-INRIA-Lorraine, Nancy, France

Abstract. We introduce AVISS, a tool for security protocol analysis
that supports the integration of back-ends implementing different search
techniques, allowing for their systematic and quantitative comparison
and paving the way to their effective interaction. As a significant example, we have implemented three back-ends, and used the AVISS tool
to analyze and find flaws in 36 protocols, including 31 problems in the
Clark-Jacob's protocol library and a previously unreported flaw in the
Denning-Sacco protocol.

1 Introduction

We describe the AVISS (Automated Verification of Infinite State Systems) tool
for security protocol analysis, which supports the simple integration of different
back-end search engines. As example back-ends, we have implemented an on-the-
fly model-checker, an analyzer based on constraint logic, and a SAT-based model-
checker. Although each of these back-ends can work independently, integrating
them into a single tool allows for the systematic and quantitative comparison
of their relative strengths, and paves the way for their effective interaction. As
an initial experiment, we have used the tool to analyze and find flaws in 36
protocols, including a previously unknown flaw in the Denning-Sacco protocol
and previously reported attacks (see [1]) to 31 protocols of [2].

The AVISS tool has a web-based graphical user-interface (accessible at
the URL: www.informatik.uni-freiburg.de/~softech/research/projects/
aviss) that aids protocol specification and allows one to select and configure different back-ends.

2 The System

The AVISS tool supports automatic protocol analysis in the presence of an active
intruder. As illustrated in Fig. 1, the system consists of different, independent

---

* This work was supported by the FET Open Assessment Project IST-2000-26410,
"AVISS: Automated Verification of Infinite State Systems".

D. Brinksma and K. G. Larsen (Eds.): CAV 2002, LNCS 2404, pp. 349–354, 2002.
© Springer-Verlag Berlin Heidelberg 2002

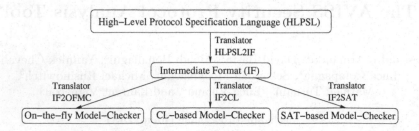

Fig. 1. The AVISS system architecture

modules. Protocols are formulated in a high-level protocol specification language
(HLPSL). The translator HLPSL2IF performs a static analysis to check the
executability of the protocol (i.e. whether each principal has enough knowledge
to compose the messages he is supposed to send), and then compiles the protocol
and intruder activities into an intermediate format (IF) based on first-order
multiset rewriting. The IF unambiguously specifies an infinite state transition
system. Afterwards, different translators are employed that translate the IF into
the input language of different analysis tools. The IF can be also generated in
a typed variant (the untyped one is the default), which leads to smaller search
spaces at the cost of abstracting away type-flaws (if any) from the protocol.

The input language HLPSL supports the declaration of protocols using standard "Alice&Bob" style notation indicating how messages are exchanged between principals [ ]. Additionally, one specifies type information, initial knowledge of principals, possible intruder behavior (e.g. variants of the Dolev-Yao
model), and information about session instances (given explicitly or implicitly
by declaring roles, with possibly several instances in parallel).[1] Security objec-
tives (authentication and secrecy) can also be declared. For example, the HLPSL
specification of (the authentication part of) the well-known Needham-Schroeder
Public Key (NSPK) protocol [ ] is:

```
PROTOCOL NSPK;
Identifiers                    Messages
  A, B: user;                    1.  A -> B:  {A,Na}Kb
  Na, Nb: nonce;                 2.  B -> A:  {Na,Nb}Ka
  Ka, Kb: public_key;            3.  A -> B:  {Nb}Kb
Intruder_knowledge I, a, b, ka, kb, ki;
Goal B authenticate A on Na;
```

Ease of tool integration was an important design consideration for the AVISS
tool. We currently have implemented three back-ends for performing complementary automated protocol analysis techniques.

The On-the-Fly Model-Checker (OFMC): The transition relation specified by the IF is unrolled starting from the initial state producing an infinite

---

[1] Note also that the tool handles several types of keys: symmetric (atomic or non-
atomic), asymmetric (public), and arrays of asymmetric keys are supported.

tree that is model-checked on-the-fly. We use Haskell, a compiled lazy functional programming language, to modularly specify the search space, reduction methods, heuristics, and procedures, generalizing the method of [ ]. When an attack is found, it is reported to the user by means of the sequence of exchanged messages.

Constraint-Logic-Based Model-Checker (CL): The IF is translated into a first-order theory which is input to the daTac prover [ ]. The CL backend combines rewrite-based first-order theorem proving with constraint logic in order to handle properties such as associativity/commutativity of operators for representing sets of messages. Message exchanges and intruder activities are directly translated from the IF rewrite rules into clauses; searching for a flaw then amounts to searching for an incoherence in the resulting formula.

The SAT-Based Model-Checker (SATMC): The SAT-based model-checker builds a propositional formula encoding a bounded unrolling of the transition relation specified by the IF, the initial state, and the set of states representing a violation of the security properties. The propositional formula is then fed to a state-of-the-art SAT solver (currently Chaff, SIM, and SATO are supported) and any model found by the solver is translated back into an attack, which is reported to the user.

There are other tools for protocol analysis providing similar features, e.g. [, ,]. To our knowledge, only CAPSL [ ], with its intermediate language CIL, is designed to support multiple analysis techniques. There are however several important differences between CAPSL/CIL and the AVISS tool. First, the CAPSL translator does not generate attacker rules, whereas we are able to produce IF rules from the specification of the intruder behavior. Second, we test a more general notion of executability (useful for e-commerce protocols such as non-repudiation protocols). CAPSL is unable to translate protocols where a principal receives a cipher, say $\{Na\}_K$, and later receives the key K and then uses Na in some message. In our case, the principal will store $\{Na\}_K$ and will decrypt it when he later receives the key. Finally, based on the available published experiments, the AVISS tool and its back-ends are considerably more effective on the Clark-Jacob's library than CAPSL and its current connectors.

3   Experiments

We have run successfully the AVISS tool to find flaws in 36 protocols, including 32 protocols from the Clark-Jacob's library [,]. Of the 36 protocols analyzed, 31 were already reported to be insecure in [ ] whereas for 1, namely the Denning Sacco protocol, no flaw was previously found. Table 1 lists the performance of the three back-ends on these problems.[2] Preliminary to the execution of the back-ends we generated both the untyped and the typed version of the IF specifications by means of the HLPSL2IF translator. The OFMC and the CL back-end were run against the untyped and the typed IF specifications of each protocol. The

---

[2] The protocols marked with a "*" are variants of protocols in [ ] that we have additionally analyzed. Times are obtained on a PC with a 1.4GHz Pentium III processor and 512Mb of RAM. The SATMC timings are obtained using the Chaff solver [ ].

kind of the attack found (if any) and the time spent by each back-end are given in the corresponding columns. For SATMC we give a pair of values t_e/t_s, where t_e is the *encoding time*, i.e. the time spent to generate the propositional formula, and t_s is the *search time*, i.e. the time spent by the SAT solver to check the formula. Note that the analysis of the untyped and typed IF specifications may lead to the detection of different kinds of attacks. Since SATMC is not suited to analyze untyped IF specifications, we applied it to typed specifications only (and thus not on protocols suffering from type flaw attacks).

Table 1 allows us also to analyze and compare the performance of the individual back-ends. The OFMC model-checker performs uniformly well on all the protocols: most of the attacks are found in a fraction of a second, and detecting all the attacks requires a total time of less than one minute. The poorer timings of the CL back-end are balanced by the fact that it is based on an off-the-shelf prover (daTac) and it offers other advantages such as the simple integration of algebraic relations on message constructors (e.g. commutativity of encryptions in RSA). For SATMC, the experiments show that the time spent to generate the SAT formula largely dominates the time spent to check the satisfiability of the SAT instance. Nevertheless, in many cases the overall timing is not too far from that of OFMC and it is better than that of CL. It is also interesting to observe that in many cases the time spent by the SAT solver is smaller than the time spent by OFMC for the same protocol.

We have begun experimenting with larger e-commerce protocols and the first results are very promising. For example, we have been able to compile and analyze the card-holder registration phase of SET protocol. Since our tool can only detect attacks (and for a correct protocol it only terminates when checking a finite number of sessions), we are also working on implementing back-ends that can find security proofs for correct protocols.

References

1. D. Basin. Lazy infinite-state analysis of security protocols. In *Secure Networking — CQRE'99*, LNCS 1740, pp. 30–42. Springer, 1999. 351
2. J. Clark and J. Jacob. A Survey of Authentication Protocol Literature: Version 1.0, 17. Nov. 1997. URL http://www.cs.york.ac.uk/~jac/papers/drareview.ps.gz. 349, 350, 351
3. G. Denker and J. Millen. CAPSL Intermediate Language. In *Proc. of FMSP'99*. URL for CAPSL and CIL: http://www.csl.sri.com/~millen/capsl/. 351
4. B. Donovan, P. Norris, and G. Lowe, Analyzing a library of protocols using Casper and FDR. In *Proc. of FMSP'99*. 349, 351
5. F. Jacquemard, M. Rusinowitch, and L. Vigneron. Compiling and Verifying Security Protocols. In *Proc. of LPAR'00*, LNCS 1955, pp. 131–160. Springer, 2000. 351
6. G. Lowe. Casper: a compiler for the analysis of security protocols. *J. of Computer Security*, 6(1):53–84, 1998. URL for Casper: http://web.comlab.ox.ac.uk/oucl/work/gavin.lowe/Security/Casper/index.html. 351
7. C. Meadows. The NRL protocol analyzer: An overview. *J. of Logic Programming*, 26(2):113–131, 1996. http://chacs.nrl.navy.mil/projects/crypto.html. 351

8. M. W. Moskewicz, C. F. Madigan, Y. Zhao, L. Zhang, and S. Malik. Chaff: Engineering an Efficient SAT Solver. In *Proc. of DAC'01*. 2001.   351

Table 1. Performance of the AVISS tool back-ends over the testsuite

Protocol Name	Kind of Attack	AVISS		
		OFMC	CL	SATMC
ISO symm. key 1-pass unilateral auth.	Replay	0.0	2.0	0.2/0.0
ISO symm. key 2-pass mutual auth.	Replay	0.0	3.9	0.4/0.0
Andrew Secure RPC prot.	Type flaw	0.0	4.3	NA
	Replay	0.1	32.7	80.6/2.7
ISO CCF 1-pass unilateral auth.	Replay	0.0	2.2	0.2/0.0
ISO CCF 2-pass mutual auth.	Replay	0.0	4.6	0.5/0.0
Needham-Schroeder Conventional Key	Replay STS	0.3	63.4	29.3/0.4
Denning-Sacco (symmetric)	Type flaw	0.0	16.0	NA
Otway-Rees	Type flaw	0.0	10.7	NA
Yahalom with Lowe's alteration	Type flaw	0.0	44.1	NA
Woo-Lam Π_1	Type flaw	0.0	0.8	NA
Woo-Lam Π_2	Type flaw	0.0	0.8	NA
Woo-Lam Π_3	Type flaw	0.0	0.8	NA
Woo-Lam Π	PS	0.2	1075.0	3.3/0.0
Woo-Lam Mutual auth.	PS	0.3	245.6	1024.1/8.0
Needham-Schroeder Signature prot.	MITM	0.1	53.9	3.8/0.1
* Neuman Stubblebine initial part	Type flaw	0.0	6.2	NA
* Neuman Stubblebine rep. part	Replay STS	0.0	3.5	15.2/0.2
Neuman Stubblebine (complete)	Type flaw	0.0	46.8	NA
Kehne Langendorfer Schoenwalder (rep. part)	PS	0.2	199.4	MO/-
Kao Chow rep. auth., 1	Replay STS	0.5	76.8	16.3/0.2
Kao Chow rep. auth., 2	Replay STS	0.5	45.3	339.7/2.1
Kao Chow rep. auth., 3	Replay STS	0.5	50.1	1288.0/MO
ISO public key 1-pass unilateral auth.	Replay	0.0	4.2	0.3/0.0
ISO public key 2-pass mutual auth.	Replay	0.0	11.1	1.2/0.0
* Needham-Schroeder Public KeyNSPK	MITM	0.0	12.9	1.8/0.1
NSPK with key server	MITM	1.1	TO	4.3/0.0
* NSPK with Lowe's fix	Type flaw	0.0	31.1	NA
SPLICE/AS auth. prot.	Replay	4.0	352.4	5.5/0.1
Hwang and Chen's modified SPLICE	MITM	0.0	13.1	NS
Denning Sacco Key Distr. with Public Key	MITM	0.5	936.9	NS
Shamir Rivest Adelman Three Pass prot.	Type flaw	0.0	0.7	NA
Encrypted Key Exchange	PS	0.1	240.8	75.4/1.8
Davis Swick Private Key Certificates, prot. 1	Type flaw	0.1	106.2	NA
	Replay	1.2	TO	1.4/0.0
Davis Swick Private Key Certificates, prot. 2	Type flaw	0.2	348.5	NA
	Replay	0.9	TO	2.7/0.0
Davis Swick Private Key Certificates, prot. 3	Replay	0.0	2.7	1.5/0.0
Davis Swick Private Key Certificates, prot. 4	Replay	0.0	36.0	8.2/0.1

Legenda: MITM: Man-in-the-Middle. PS: Parallel-Session. Replay STS: Replay attack based on a Short-Term Secret. NA: Not Attempted. NS: Not Supported. MO: Memory Out. TO: Time Out (> 1 hour).

SPeeDI – A Verification Tool for Polygonal Hybrid Systems[*]

Eugene Asarin[1], Gordon Pace[2], Gerardo Schneider[1], and Sergio Yovine[1]

[1] VERIMAG, 2 av. Vignate
38610 Gières, France
{asarin,gerardo,yovine}@imag.fr
[2] INRIA Rhone-Alpes / VASY
655 av. de l'Europe, 38330 Montbonnot, France
gordon.pace@inria.fr

1   Introduction

Hybrid systems combining discrete and continuous dynamics arise as mathematical models of various artificial and natural systems, and as an approximation to complex continuous systems. A very important problem in the analysis of the behavior of hybrid systems is reachability. It is well-known that for most non-trivial subclasses of hybrid systems this and all interesting verification problems are undecidable. Most of the proved decidability results rely on stringent hypothesis that lead to the existence of a finite and computable partition of the state space into classes of states which are equivalent with respect to reachability. This is the case for classes of rectangular automata [4] and hybrid automata with linear vector fields [9]. Most implemented computational procedures resort to (forward or backward) propagation of constraints, typically (unions of convex) polyhedra or ellipsoids [1, 6, 8]. In general, these techniques provide semi-decision procedures, that is, if the given final set of states is reachable, they will terminate, otherwise they may fail to. Maybe the major drawback of set-propagation, reach-set approximation procedures is that they pay little attention to the geometric properties of the specific (class of) systems under analysis. An interesting and still decidable class of hybrid system are the (2-dimensional) polygonal differential inclusions (or SPDI for short). An *SPDI* (Fig. 1) is defined by giving a finite partition $\mathbb{P}$ of the plane into convex polygonal sets, and associating with each $P \in \mathbb{P}$ a couple of vectors $\mathbf{a}_P$ and $\mathbf{b}_P$.

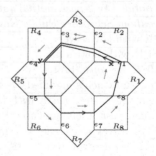

Fig. 1. SPDI

[*] Partially supported by Projet IMAG "Modélisation et Analyse de Systèmes Hybrides", by Projet CNRS MathSTIC "Analyse Qualitative de Systèmes Hybrides" and by the European Research Consortium in Informatics and Mathematics (ERCIM).

D. Brinksma and K. G. Larsen (Eds.): CAV 2002, LNCS 2404, pp. 354–359, 2002.
© Springer-Verlag Berlin Heidelberg 2002

The SPDI is $\dot{\mathbf{x}} \in \angle_{\mathbf{a}_P}^{\mathbf{b}_P}$ for $\mathbf{x} \in P$, where $\angle_{\mathbf{a}}^{\mathbf{b}}$ denotes the angle on the plane between the vectors $\mathbf{a}$ and $\mathbf{b}$. In [2] we have proved that (point-to-point, edge-to-edge and polygon-to-polygon) reachability is decidable and we have proposed a decision procedure that exploits the topological properties of the plane. Our procedure is not based on the computation of the reach-set but rather on the exploration of a finite number of types of qualitative behaviors obtained from the edge-signatures of trajectories (i.e., the sequences of their intersections with the edges of the polygons). Such types of signatures may contain loops which can be very expensive (or impossible) to explore naively. However, we have shown that loops have structural properties that are exploited by our algorithm to efficiently compute the effect of such loops. In summary, the novelty of the approach is the combination of several techniques, namely, (1) the representation of the two-dimensional continuous dynamics as a one-dimensional discrete dynamical system, (2) the characterization of the set of qualitative behaviors of the latter as a finite set of types of signatures, and (3) the "acceleration" of the iterations in the case of cyclic signatures.

2   SPeeDI

The tool SPeeDI is a collection of utilities to manipulate and reason mechanically about SPDIs, completely implemented in 5000 lines of Haskell [7], a general-purpose, lazy, functional language.

Visualization Aids: To help visualize systems, the tool can generate graphical representations of the SPDI, and particular trajectories and signatures within it.

Information Gathering: SPeeDI calculates edge-to-edge successor function composition and enlist signatures going from one edge to another.

Verification: The most important facet of the tool suite is that of verification. At the lowest level, the user may request whether, given a signature (with a possibly restricted initial and final edge), it is a feasible one or not. At a more general, and useful level, the user may simply give a restricted initial edge and restricted final edge, and the tool attempts to answer whether the latter is reachable from the former.

Trace Generation: Whenever reachability succeeds SPeeDI generates stripes of feasible trajectories using different strategies and graphical representation of them.

This typical usage sequence of the tool suite is captured in Figure 2.

Figure 3 illustrates a typical session of the tool on an example SPDI composed of 63 regions. The left part of the diagram shows selected portions of the input file, defining vectors, named points on the x-y plane, and regions (as sequences of point names, and pairs of differential inclusion vectors). The lower right-hand panel shows the signature generated by the tool `reachable` which satisfies the user's demand. The signature has two loops which are expressed with the star symbol. A trace is then generated from the signature using `simsig`. It traverses

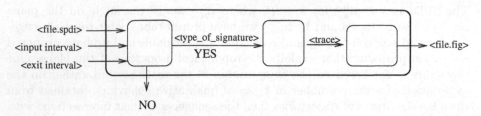

Fig. 2. Workflow of the tool

Input file

Generated Figure

```
Points: 0. 0.0, 0.0
* ...
33. -5.0, -35.0
34. -5.0, -25.0
35. -5.0, -15.0
36. -5.0, -5.0
37. -5.0, 5.0
38. -5.0, 15.0
39. -5.0, 25.0
* ...
Vectors:
* ...
v3. -1,0.1833333333
v8. 1,0
v9. 1,1
v12. 1, 1.5
v20. -1, 0.001
v22. 1,-0.001
v25. -1,0.7
v28. 1, 0.001
*...
Regions:
* ...
* R29
33 ? 41 ! 42 ! 34 ? 33, v9, v9
* R30
34 ! 42 ! 43 ? 35 ? 34, v22, v22
* R31
35 ? 36 ? 0 ! 44 ! 43 ! 35, v8, v8
* R32
44 ! 45 ! 0 ? 44, v12, v12
* R33
0 ? 45 ? 46 ! 38 ! 37 ! 0, v3, v20
* R34
38 ? 46 ? 47 ! 39 ! 38, v25, v20
* ...
```

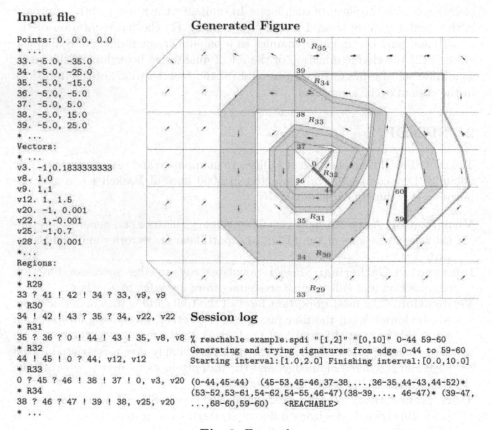

Session log

```
% reachable example.spdi "[1,2]" "[0,10]" 0-44 59-60
Generating and trying signatures from edge 0-44 to 59-60
Starting interval:[1.0,2.0] Finishing interval:[0.0,10.0]
(0-44,45-44) (45-53,45-46,37-38,...,36-35,44-43,44-52)*
(53-52,53-61,54-62,54-55,46-47)(38-39,..., 46-47)* (39-47,
...,68-60,59-60)  <REACHABLE>
```

Fig. 3. Example

three times the first loop and two times the second one. The graphical representation of the SPDI and the trace is generated automatically using simsig2fig. The execution time for this example is a few seconds.

3   Comparing and Contrasting with HyTech

While SPeeDI is, as far as we know, the only verification tool for hybrid systems implementing a decision algorithm (with the exception of timed automata), it is interesting to compare it to "semi-algorithmic" hybrid system verification tools such as HyTech [5]. HyTech is a tool capable of treating hybrid linear systems of any dimension, making it much more general than SPeeDI, which is limited to two-dimensional systems without resets. On the other hand, SPeeDI implements acceleration techniques (based on the resolution of fix-point equations) which yield a complete decision procedure for SPDIs. Also, SPeeDI does not handle arbitrary polyhedra, but only polygons and line segments. For these reasons, comparing the performance of the two tools is meaningless and no fair benchmarking is really possible.

We can only compare the two tools is we restrict ourselves to SPDIs. From some experiments we have run, we have reached a number of qualitative conclusions:

- It is well known that since HyTech uses exact rational arithmetic, it can it easily run into overflow problems. This is particularly an issue when the path to the target passes through a large number of regions. This makes verification of non-trivial sized SPDIs (eg the one in figure 3) impossible.
- In the case of loops, SPeeDI calculates the limit interval without repeatedly iterating the loop. It makes use of this interval to accelerate the reachability analysis, avoiding time consuming loop traversals. In contrast, HyTech performs these iterations. Following the loops explicitly, easily leads to overflow problems, and, more seriously, in certain (even simple) configurations, this analysis never terminates.

While the first issue is limited to HyTech, the second is inherent to any tool based on non-accelerated reachability analysis. On examples which HyTech can handle, the two tools take approximately the same amount of time (a fraction of a second) to reach the result. SPeeDI, however, can handle much larger examples.

4   Discussion

We have presented a prototype tool for solving the reachability problem for the class of polygonal differential inclusions. The tool implements the algorithm published in [2] which is based on the analysis of a finite number of qualitative behaviors generated by a discrete dynamical system characterized by positive affine Poincaré maps. Since the number of such behaviors may be extremely big, the tool uses several powerful heuristics that exploit the topological properties of planar trajectories for considerably reducing the set of actually explored signatures. When reachability is successful, the tool outputs a visual representation (in the form of an Xfig file) of the stripe of trajectories that go from the initial point (edge, polygon) to the final one.

Despite the fact that functional languages, especially lazy ones, have a rather bad reputation regarding performance (see for example, [10] for a report on the experiences of writing verification tools in functional languages), we found that the performance we obtained was more than adequate for the magnitude of examples we had in mind. Furthermore, we feel that with the gain in the level of abstraction of the code, we have much more confidence in the correctness of our tool had we used a lower level language. We found laziness particularly useful in separating control and data considerations. Quite frequently, optimizations dictated that we evaluate certain complex expressions at most once, if at all. In most strict languages, this would have led to complex code which mixes data computations (which use the values of the expressions) with control computation (to decide whether this is the first time we are using the expression and, if so, evaluate it). Thanks to shared expressions and laziness, all this came for free — resulting in cleaner code, where the complex control is not done by the programmer.

Future work previews the integration of SPeeDI into a large tool suite for qualitative analysis of hybrid systems. We plan to extend its functionality beyond reachability verification. In particular, we are currently working on the implementation of the algorithm developed in [3] for constructing the phase portrait of an SPDI which is composed of viability and controllability kernels.

References

[1] E. Asarin, O. Bournez, T. Dang, and O. Maler. Reachability analysis of piecewise-linear dynamical systems. In *HSCC'00*, pages 20–31. LNCS 1790, Springer, 2000. 354

[2] E. Asarin, G. Schneider, and S. Yovine. On the decidability of the reachability problem for planar differential inclusions. In *HSCC'01*. LNCS 2034, Springer, 2001. 355, 357

[3] E. Asarin, G. Schneider, and S. Yovine. Towards computing phase portraits of polygonal differential inclusions. In *HSCC'02*, pages 49–61. LNCS 2289, Springer, 2002. 358

[4] T. A. Henzinger, P. W. Kopke, A. Puri, and P. Varaiya. What's decidable about hybrid automata? In *STOC'95*, pages 373–382. ACM Press, 1995. 354

[5] T. A. Henzinger, P.-H.Ho, and H.Wong-toi. Hytech: A model checker for hybrid systems. *Software Tools for Technology Transfer*, 1(1), 1997. 357

[6] Thomas A. Henzinger, Pei-Hsin Ho, and Howard Wong-Toi. Hytech: A model checker for hybrid systems. *Software Tools for Technology Transfer*, 1:110–122, 1997. 354

[7] Simon Peyton Jones and John Hughes. Report on Haskell 98: A non-strict, purely functional language, 1999. available from http://www.haskell.org. 355

[8] A. B. Kurzhanski and P. Varaiya. Ellipsoidal techniques for reachability analysis. In *HSCC'00*. LNCS 1790, Springer, 2000. 354

[9] G. Lafferriere, G. Pappas, and S. Yovine. Symbolic reachability computation of families of linear vector fields. *Journal of Symbolic Computation*, 32(3):231–253, September 2001. 354

[10] M. Leucker, T. Noll, P. Stevens, and M. Weber. Functional programming languages for verification tools: Experiences with ML and Haskell. In *Proceedings of the Scottish Functional Programming Workshop (SFPW'01)*, 2001. 358

NuSMV 2: An OpenSource Tool for Symbolic Model Checking

Alessandro Cimatti[1], Edmund Clarke[2], Enrico Giunchiglia[3],
Fausto Giunchiglia[4], Marco Pistore[1], Marco Roveri[1],
Roberto Sebastiani[4], and Armando Tacchella[3]

[1] ITC-IRST
Via Sommarive 18, 38050 Trento, Italy
{cimatti,pistore,roveri}@irst.itc.it
[2] Carnegie Mellon University
5000 Forbes Avenue, Pittsburgh (PA), USA
emc@cs.cmu.edu
[3] DIST – Università di Genova
Viale Causa 13, 16145 Genova, Italy
{enrico,tac}@mrg.dist.unige.it
[4] Università di Trento
Via Sommarive 14, 38050 Trento, Italy
{fausto,rseba}@science.unitn.it

1 Introduction

This paper describes version 2 of the NuSMV tool. NuSMV is a symbolic model
checker originated from the reengineering, reimplementation and extension of
SMV, the original BDD-based model checker developed at CMU [15]. The Nu-
SMV project aims at the development of a state-of-the-art symbolic model
checker, designed to be applicable in technology transfer projects: it is a well
structured, open, flexible and documented platform for model checking, and is
robust and close to industrial systems standards [6].

The first version of NuSMV, referred with NuSMV1 in the following, basically implements BDD-based symbolic model checking. The new version of
NuSMV (NuSMV2 in the following) inherits all the functionalities of the previous version, and extend them in several directions. The main novelty in NuSMV2
is the integration of model checking techniques based on propositional satisfiability (SAT) [1]. SAT-based model checking is currently enjoying a substantial
success in several industrial fields (see, e.g., [10], but also [5]), and opens up new
research directions. BDD-based and SAT-based model checking are often able to
solve different classes of problems, and can therefore be seen as complementary
techniques.

Starting from NuSMV2, we are also adopting a new development and license
model. NuSMV2 is distributed with an OpenSource license [17], that allows
anyone interested to freely use the tool and to participate in its development.
The aim of the NuSMV OpenSource project is to provide to the model checking community a common platform for the research, the implementation, and

D. Brinksma and K. G. Larsen (Eds.): CAV 2002, LNCS 2404, pp. 359–364, 2002.

the comparison of new symbolic model checking techniques. NuSMV2 has been released in November 2001. Since then, the NuSMV team has received code contributions for different parts of the system. Several research institutes and commercial companies have express interest in collaborating to the development of NuSMV.

In this paper we describe the goals of the NuSMV OpenSource project (Section 2), we give an overview of the system (Section 3), and we end with some concluding remarks (Section 4). Further information on NuSMV can be found at http://nusmv.irst.itc.it/.

2   The NuSMV Open Source Project

Enormous progress has been carried out over the last decade in the applicability of symbolic model checking to practical verification problems. However, most of the state-of-the-art model checkers are proprietary. Moreover, several important techniques have been implemented only in prototype tools and have not been further maintained or developed (see e.g., the very nice results described in [8]). This is a clear disadvantage in terms of scientific progress, and is slowing down the introduction of model checking in non-traditional application domains.

With the OpenSource model [17], a whole community participates in the development of a software systems, with a distributed team and independent peer review. This may result in a rapid systems evolution, and in increased software quality and reliability. The OpenSource model has boosted the take-up of notable software systems, such as Linux and Apache. With the NuSMV Open-Source project, we would like to reach the same goals within the model checking community, providing a publicly available state-of-the-art symbolic model checker, and opening to anybody interested in the development of the tool.

NuSMV2 is distributed under GNU Lesser General Public License 2.1 (LGPL in brief; see [14]). This license grants full right to use and modify a program, for research and commercial applications, stand-alone or as part of a larger software system. On the other hand, this license is "copyleft": any improvement to NuSMV should be made freely available, under the terms of the LGPL. In this way, we achieve the goals of allowing for a free usage of NuSMV and to guarantee that the extensions become available to the whole community.

3   Overview of NuSMV2

In order to integrate SAT-based and BDD-based model checking, a major architectural redesign was carried out in NuSMV2, with the goal of making as many functionalities as possible independent of the actual model checking engine used. This allows for the effective integration of the new SAT-based engine, and opens up towards the implementation of other model checking procedures. A high level description of the internal structure of NuSMV2 is given in Figure 1.

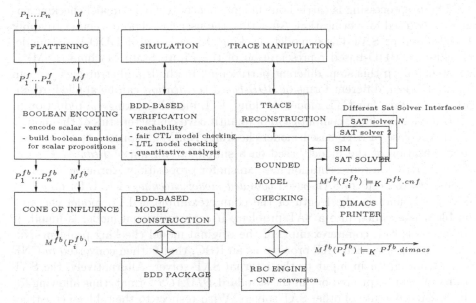

Fig. 1. The internal structure of NuSMV2

NuSMV is able to process files written in an extension of the SMV language. In this language, it is possible to describe finite state machines by means of declaration and instantiation mechanisms for modules and processes, corresponding to synchronous and asynchronous composition, and to express a set of requirements in CTL and LTL. NuSMV can work batch or interactively, with a textual interaction shell.

An SMV file is processed in several phases. The first phases require to analyze the input file, in order to construct an internal representation of the system. NuSMV2 neatly separates the input language in different layers, of increasing complexity, that are incrementally eliminated. The construction starts from the modular description of a model M and of a set of properties $P_1, \ldots, P_n$. The first step, called *flattening*, performs the instantiation of module types, thus creating modules and processes, and produces a synchronous, flat model M^f, where each variable is given an absolute name. The second step, called *boolean encoding*, maps a flat model into a boolean model M^{fb}, thus eliminating scalar variables. This second step takes into account the whole SMV language, including the encoding of bounded integers, and all the set-theoretic and arithmetic functions and predicates. It is possible to print out the different levels of the input file, thus using NuSMV2 as a flattener. The same reduction steps are applied to the properties P_i, thus obtaining the corresponding flattened boolean versions P_i^{fb}. In addition, by means of the *cone of influence* reduction [2], it is possible to restrict the analysis of each property to the relevant parts of the model $M^{fb}(P_i^{fb})$. This reduction can be extremely effective in tackling the state explosion problem.

The preprocessing is carried out independently from the model checking engine to be used for verification. After this, the user can choose whether to apply BDD-based or SAT-based model checking. In the case of BDD-based model checking, a BDD-based representation of the Finite State Machine (FSM) is constructed. In this step, different partitioning methods and strategies [18] can be used. Then, different forms of *BDD-based verification* can be applied: reachability analysis, fair CTL model checking, LTL model checking via reduction to CTL model checking, computation of quantitative characteristics of the model.

In the case of SAT-based model checking, NuSMV2 constructs an internal representation of the model based on a simplified version of *Reduced Boolean Circuit* (RBC), a representation mechanism for propositional formulae. Then, it is possible to perform SAT-based *bounded model checking* of LTL formulae [4]. Given a bound on the length of the counterexample, a LTL model checking problem is encoded into a SAT problem. If a propositional model is found, it corresponds to a counterexample of the original model checking problem. NuSMV2 represents each SAT problem as an RBC, that is then converted in CNF format and given in input to the internal SAT solver. Alternatively, the SAT problems can be printed out in the standard *DIMACS* format, thus allowing for the stand-alone use of other SAT solvers. With respect to the tableau construction in [4], enhancements have been carried out that can significantly improve the performances of the SAT solver [7]. In bounded model checking, NuSMV2 enters a loop, interleaving problem generation and solution attempt via a call to the SAT solver, and iterates until a solution is found or the specified maximum bound is reached.

NuSMV2 uses SIM [13] as the internal SAT solver. SIM is a SAT solver based on the Davis-Logemann-Loveland procedure. The features provided by SIM can produce dramatic speed-ups in the overall performances of the SAT checker, and thus of the whole system (see e.g., [19,10] for a discussion). It is currently under development a generic interface to SAT solvers to allow for the use of new state of the art SAT solvers like e.g. CHAFF [16].

The different properties that are checked on a FSM are handled and shown to the user by a property manager, that is independent of the model checking engine used for the verification. This means that it is possible for the user to decide what solution method to adopt for each property. Furthermore, the counterexample *traces* being generated by both model checking modules are presented and stored into a unique format. Similarly, the user can *simulate* the behavior of the specified system, by generating traces either interactively or randomly. Simulation can be carried out both via BDD-based or SAT-based techniques.

4   Concluding Remarks

NuSMV is a robust, well structured and flexible platform for symbolic model checking, designed to be applicable in technology transfer projects. In this paper, we have shown how BDD-based and SAT-based model checking are integrated in the new version of NuSMV, that significantly extends the previous version.

In particular, we have discussed the functionalities and the architecture of NuSMV2, that integrates SAT-based state of the art verification techniques, is able to work as a problem flattener in DIMACS format, and tackles the state explosion with cone of influence reduction. In the future, we plan to investigate a tighter integration between BDD-based and SAT-based technologies. The new internal architecture also opens up the possibility to integrate different boolean encodings (e.g. [8]) and verification engines (e.g. [1], allowing for Bounded Model Checking of Timed Automata.)

NuSMV2 has been used as the starting framework for the implementation and the evaluation of new verification techniques (see, e.g., [9] in this volume). It has also been used as the verification engine for tools in different application areas, ranging from the formal validation of software requirements [12], to the verification of StateChart models [11], to automated task planning [3]. Several of these applications have required the development of new functionalities and improvements to NuSMV2. The code for these extensions is currently being included in the mainstream NuSMV2 distribution.

References

1. G. Audemard, P. Bertoli, A. Cimatti, A. Kornilowicz, and R. Sebastiani. A SAT based approach for solving formulas over boolean and linear mathematical propositions. In *Proc. of CADE'02*, 2002. 363
2. S. Berezin, S. Campos, and E. M. Clarke. Compositional reasoning in model checking. In *Proc. COMPOS*, 1997. 361
3. P. Bertoli, A. Cimatti, M. Pistore, M. Roveri, and P. Traverso. MBP: a Model Based Planner. In *Proc. of the IJCAI'01 Workshop on Planning under Uncertainty and Incomplete Information*, Seattle, August 2001. 363
4. A. Biere, A. Cimatti, E. M. Clarke, and Y. Zhu. Symbolic model checking without BDDs. In *Proc. of the Fifth International Conference on Tools and Algorithms for the Construction and Analysis of Systems (TACAS'99)*, 1999. 359, 362
5. A. Borälv. A Fully Automated Approach for Proving Safety Properties in Interlocking Software Using Automatic Theorem-Proving. In S. Gnesi and D. Latclla, editors, *Proc. of the Second International ERCIM FMICS*, Pisa, Italy, July 1997. 359
6. A. Cimatti, E. M. Clarke, F. Giunchiglia, and M. Roveri. NuSMV : a new symbolic model checker. *International Journal on Software Tools for Technology Transfer (STTT)*, 2(4), March 2000. 359
7. A. Cimatti, M. Pistore, M. Roveri, and R. Sebastiani. Improving the Encoding of LTL Model Checking into SAT. In *Proc. WMCAI 2002*, number 2294 in LNCS, pages 182–195, 2002. 362
8. E. Clarke and X. Zhao. Word Level Symbolic Model Checking: A New Approach for Verifying Arithmetic Circuits. Technical Report CMU-CS-95-161, School of Computer Science, Carnegie Mellon University, Pittsburgh, PA 15213-3891, USA, May 1995. 360, 363
9. E. M. Clarke, A. Gupta, J. Kukula, and O. Strichman. Sat based abstraction-refinement using ILP and machine learning techniques. In *Proc. of Conference on Computer-Aided Verification (CAV'02)*, LNCS, 2002. To appear in this volume. 363

10. F. Copty, L. Fix, E. Giunchiglia, G. Kamhi, A. Tacchella, and M. Vardi. Benefits of bounded model checking at an industrial setting. In *Proc. of CAV 2001*, LNCS, pages 436–453, 2001. 359, 362
11. R. Eshuis and R. Wieringa. Verification support for workflow design with UML activity graphs. In *Proc. of ICSE*, 2002. To appear. 363
12. A. Fuxman, M. Pistore, J. Mylopoulos, , and P. Traverso. Model checking early requirements specifications in Tropos. In *Proc. of the Fifth IEEE International Symposium on Requirements Engineering (RE'01)*, Toronto, August 2001. 363
13. E. Giunchiglia, M. Maratea, A. Tacchella, and D. Zambonin. Evaluating search heuristics and optimization techniques in propositional satisfiability. In *Proc. of IJCAR 2001*, volume 2083 of *LNCS*, pages 347–363. Springer, 2001. 362
14. The Gnu Lesser General Public License: http://www.fsf.org/licenses/lgpl.html. 360
15. K. L. McMillan. *Symbolic Model Checking*. Kluwer Academic Publ., 1993. 359
16. M. Moskewicz, C. Madigan, Y. Zhao, L. Zhang, and S. Malik. Chaff: Engineering an Efficient SAT Solver. In *Proc. of the 39th Design Automation Conference*, June 2001. 362
17. The Open Source Organization. http://www.opensource.org. 359, 360
18. R. K. Ranjan, A. Aziz, B. Plessier, C. Pixley, and R. K. Brayton. Efficient BDD algorithms for FSM synthesis and verification. In *Proc. IEEE/ACM International Workshop on Logic Synthesis*, Lake Tahoe (NV), May 1995. 362
19. O. Shtrichman. Tuning SAT checkers for bounded model-checking. In *Proc. 12th International Computer Aided Verification Conference (CAV'00)*, 2000. 362

The d/dt Tool for Verification of Hybrid Systems

Eugene Asarin, Thao Dang, and Oded Maler

VERIMAG, 2, av de Vignate, Centre Equation
38610 Gières, France
{asarin,tdang,maler}@imag.fr

Abstract. In this paper we describe the tool **d/dt** which provides automatic safety verification of hybrid systems with linear continuous dynamics with uncertain input. The verification procedure is based on a method for overapproximating reachable sets by orthogonal polyhedra. The tool also allows to synthesize a controller which switches the system between continuous modes in order to satisfy a safety specification.

1 Introduction

Hybrid systems are dynamical systems whose state space is based on discrete variables, evolving by taking transitions, and continuous variables evolving according to some differential equation that depends on the discrete variables. When hybrid systems were first introduced to the verification community [10], they were viewed as an extension of timed systems in the sense that while in the latter all the continuous variables are clocks with a uniform slope in every discrete state, the former admit variables that may evolve according to an arbitrary continuous dynamics. The algorithmic verification approach for hybrid systems [2], developed together with that for timed systems, is based on the following principles:

1. Global configurations of a system consist of tuples of the form $(q, \mathbf{x})$ where q is a discrete state and $\mathbf{x} \in \mathsf{R}^n$ is a point in the continuous state space. Sets of reachable configurations can be written as unions of tuples of the form (q, F) where F is a subset of R^n. Such tuples are called symbolic states.
2. On such symbolic states one can define successor (or predecessor) operators that decompose into *transition-successor* and *time-successor*.
3. Equipped with a representation scheme for symbolic states and an implementation of these operators, one can apply standard verification algorithms.

The decidability results for timed automata [1] are based on the fact that there is a *finite* class of simple subsets of R^n which is closed under the above operations. The elements of this class, which are roughly sets definable by finite Boolean combinations of inequalities of the form $x_i \leq k$ or $x_i - x_j \leq k$ for an integer k, admit an efficient representation using difference bound matrices to which the time-successor operator can be easily applied (the computation of transition-successors is usually reduced to applying Boolean operations and

D. Brinksma and K. G. Larsen (Eds.): CAV 2002, LNCS 2404, pp. 365–370, 2002.
© Springer-Verlag Berlin Heidelberg 2002

does not pose major additional problems). This approach has been implemented in timed automata verification tools such as Kronos [19] and Uppaal [15]. The tool HyTech [13] took this idea further and applied to the more general class of "linear hybrid automata", in which the slope of every continuous variable is constant (but arbitrary) in every discrete state. Although the continuous dynamics in every discrete state is trivial, the combination with discrete transitions (and changes of the slope) makes the verification problem undecidable, apart from some special cases [12]. However, one can still compute the time-successors of a convex polyhedron using linear algebra, but the class of such polyhedra is infinite and the verification algorithms are not guaranteed to terminate. The tool presented in this paper attempts to go further and apply reachability-based verification techniques to systems where the continuous dynamics is defined by a differential equation $\dot{\mathbf{x}} = f(\mathbf{x})$. Under such dynamics, the time-successors of a set usually form curved objects and, except for some special cases [17], cannot be computed exactly. Instead, we take an approximation approach, that is, for a given initial polyhedron F we compute another polyhedron which contains all the time-successors of F. In [11] we presented a method to do so for arbitrary f, while in this tool we concentrate on the class of systems with linear continuous dynamics. Our reachability techniques can be seen as an extension of numerical integration from points to polyhedral sets and they are of interest even for purely continuous systems.

An outline of the paper is as follows. Section 2 is devoted to a brief description of our reachability techniques, the kernel algorithms of $\mathbf{d/dt}$, and their application to safety verification and switching controller synthesis for hybrid systems (see [3,4] for more details). In Section 3 we present the tool $\mathbf{d/dt}$ and some case studies treated using the tool.

2   Reachability Techniques

We use hybrid automata [2] as a modeling formalism for hybrid systems. In the model we consider, continuous dynamics are *linear with uncertain, bounded input* of the form $f(\mathbf{x}) = A\mathbf{x} + B\mathbf{u}$ where $\mathbf{u}$ ranges inside a convex polyhedron. All the *staying conditions* (or "invariant") and *transition guards* are specified as conjunctions of linear inequalities. The *resets* associated with discrete transitions are *affine, set-valued maps* of the form $R(\mathbf{x}) = D\mathbf{x} + J$ where D is a matrix and J is a convex polyhedron.

To *prove a safety property* (never reaching a set of bad states), we overapproximate the reachable set of the system on a step-by-step basis and check for its intersection with the set of bad states. Given a time step r, each iteration k computes a convex polyhedron overapproximating the set of states reachable during the time interval $[kr, (k + 1)r]$. While convex polyhedra allow to obtain reasonably good approximations for each time interval, the accumulation of reachable states often form a highly non-convex set. Therefore, to store reachable sets we use non-convex orthogonal polyhedra[1] [9] since they can be manipulated more easily than unions of arbitrary polyhedra. We consider first systems with continuous dynamics of the form $\dot{\mathbf{x}} = A\mathbf{x}$. Given an initial convex polyhedron F, the set F_r of reachable states at time r is the convex hull of the successors at time r of the vertices of F. The states reachable during the time interval $[0, r]$ are approximated by the convex hull $C = conv(F \cup F_r)$ which is enlarged by an appropriate amount to ensure overapproximation. Then, C is overapproximated by an orthogonal polyhedron. To handle staying conditions, we need to intersect F_r with the staying set and start the next iteration from the resulting polyhedron. For continuous dynamics with uncertain input $\dot{\mathbf{x}} = A\mathbf{x} + \mathbf{u}$, to compute F_r, we simulate the evolution of the faces of F. Since the dynamics of the normal vector of a face, governed by the adjoint system, is independent of the input, we use the Maximum Principle from optimal control to find the input that steers this face "farthest" allowing to cover all possible reachable states.

Concerning *switching controller synthesis*, the problem we consider is to find a controller that switches the system between continuous modes to avoid some bad states. The synthesis of such a controller is based on the *maximal invariant set* (i.e. the set of "winning" states). To compute this set, we make use of the *one-step predecessor* operator π. Given a set $\mathcal{F}$ of safe states, $\pi(\mathcal{F})$ consists of states from which the system *either* can stay in $\mathcal{F}$ indefinitely without switching *or* can stay in $\mathcal{F}$ for some time and then make a transition to another state which is still in $\mathcal{F}$. Intuitively, from all states which are not in $\pi(\mathcal{F})$ the system will leave $\mathcal{F}$ after not more than one switching; therefore, by iteratively removing all such states from $\mathcal{F}$ until convergence, we obtain an underapproximation of the maximal invariant set. Note that the operator π can be computed using our reachability operators for hybrid automata.

3   The Tool d/dt

We present first the implementation of the tool and then some applications. One important component of our reachability algorithms are procedures for manipulating convex and orthogonal polyhedra. For common operations on convex polyhedra (e.g. Boolean operations, membership testing), we combine two standard libraries cdd and Qhull (which allows to better handle degenerate cases) and use the library Cubes [9] for operations on orthogonal polyhedra. In addition, we implemented the geometric operations specific to our approach (e.g. orthogonal approximation, intersection detection). For run-time visualization, the tool provides an option to interface with the 3D viewer Geomview. Given an input hybrid automaton, a safety specification, and optionally some user-defined approximation parameters (e.g. time step, granularity of orthogonal approximations), the tool can work in the following three modes: *reachability* (compute an overapproximation of the reachable set); *verification* (check whether the system can

---

[1] Orthogonal polyhedra can be described as unions of closed full-dimensional hyperrectangles.

reach the bad set); *controller synthesis* (synthesize a safety switching controller by computing an underapproximation of the maximal invariant set).

We have successfully applied the tool to some case studies inspired from real-life applications. The first case study involves the verification of a longitudinal controller for platoons on automated highways. This controller consists of several modes with different control laws and we first proved the absence of collision for single modes [6] and also for a model with mode switching. For the latter model which has 4 continuous variables and 2 discrete states, the computation took 5 minutes on a Pentium 2. The second case study concerns a control method for under-actuated mechanical systems and its application to a double pendulum modeling the leg of a biped robot. As part of the design process we use the tool to find switching sequences which can drive the system to a desired periodic orbit [5]. We have also used the tool to analyze a model of bacterial quorum-sensing systems, more precisely, to determine whether the system can reach a equilibrium point corresponding to a steady state of luminescence [7].

4   Conclusion and Related Work

We have presented the tool **d/dt** for safety verification and switching controller synthesis for hybrid systems with linear differential inclusions. To our knowledge, at current time **d/dt** is the only existing tool that supports switching controller synthesis for hybrid systems. This work contributes a novel approach to the analysis and control of hybrid systems by exploiting the ideas of algorithmic methodology in computer science. In order to increase the applicability of **d/dt**, we intend to integrate in the tool our reachability technique for nonlinear continuous dynamics [11]. In addition, as verification is often expensive, we are considering an extension of the tool to include the analysis in a simulation fashion, that is, instead of exploring the whole state space, one can guide the reachability computation according to some strategy taking into account the property to be proved.

It is not easy to compare our tool to other tools in the domain for the following reason. The hybrid systems research is still young and, moreover, due to the complexity of the problem and the approximate nature of the solution, it is still hard to define performance measures and to compare tools according to standard benchmarks. In the remainder of the paper we discuss only the relationship between **d/dt** and two other tools: CheckMate [10] and VeriShift [8]. The reader is refered to [18] for a survey on hybrid systems verification tools. CheckMate can verify polyhedral invariant hybrid automata (where all the guard sets lie on the boundary of the staying sets and the reset maps are the identity). Unlike our tool, CheckMate takes an indirect approach, that is, it computes a finite-state abstraction of the original system using approximate reachability analysis and then verify the resulting discrete model. The reachability algorithm of CheckMate for linear continuous dynamics is similar to ours, but it is not easy to extend to systems with uncertain input. The tool VeriShift is designed to perform bounded time verification on hybrid automata with linear differential inclusions. It employs the ellipsoidal techniques [14] to approximate reachable sets. Note that in these tools reachable sets are represented in a non-canonical way (as unions of convex polyhedra or ellipsoids), which limits their applicability to high dimensional systems. The tool **d/dt** has been designed with generality in mind, and hence the problem of representing polyhedra of arbitrary dimension has been tackled and solved before the development of the rest of the algorithms. Therefore, one positive feature of **d/dt** is that it extends easily to more general systems (in terms of the complexity of dynamics and the dimensionality).

References

1. R. Alur and D. L. Dill, A Theory of Timed Automata, *Theoretical Computer Science* 126, 183–235, 1994. 365
2. R. Alur, C. Courcoubetis, N. Halbwachs, T. A. Henzinger, P.-H. Ho, X. Nicollin, A. Olivero, J. Sifakis and S. Yovine, The Algorithmic Analysis of Hybrid Systems, *Theoretical Computer Science* 138, 3–34, 1995. 365, 366
3. E. Asarin, O. Bournez, T. Dang and O. Maler, Reachability Analysis of Piecewise-Linear Dynamical Systems, *HSCC*, 20-31 LNCS 1790, Springer, 2000. 366
4. E. Asarin, O. Bournez, T. Dang, O. Maler and A. Pnueli, Effective Synthesis of Switching Controllers for Linear Systems, *Proc. of the IEEE*, July, 2000. 366
5. E. Asarin, S. Bansal, B. Espiau, T. Dang and O. Maler, On Hybrid Control of Under-actuated Mechanical Systems, *HSCC*, 77-88 LNCS 2034, Springer, 2001. 368
6. E. Asarin, T. Dang and O. Maler, **d/dt**, a Tool for Reachability Analysis of Continuous and Hybrid Systems, *Proc. IFAC Nonlinear Control Systems*, 20-31, 2001. 368
7. C. Belta, J. Schug, T. Dang, V. Kumar, G. J. Pappas, H. Rubin and P. Dunlap, Stability and reachability analysis of a hybrid model of luminescence in the marine bacterium *Vibrio Fisheri*, *Proc. 40th IEEE Conf. on Decision and Control*, 2001. 368
8. O. Botchkarev and S. Tripakis, Verification of Hybrid Systems with Linear Differential Inclusions Using Ellipsoidal Approximations, *HSCC*, 73-88 LNCS 1790, Springer, 2000. 368
9. O. Bournez, O. Maler and A. Pnueli, Orthogonal Polyhedra: Representation and Computation, *HSCC*, 46-60 LNCS 1569, Springer, 1999. 367
10. A. Chutinan and B. H. Krogh, Verification of Polyhedral Invariant Hybrid Automata Using Polygonal Flow Pipe Approximations, *HSCC*, 76-90 LNCS 1569, Springer, 1999. 368
11. T. Dang and O. Maler, Reachability Analysis via Face Lifting, *HSCC*, 96-109 LNCS 1386, Springer, 1998. 366, 368
12. T. A. Henzinger, P. W. Kopke, A. Puri and P. Varaiya, What's decidable about hybrid automata?, *J. of Computer and System Sciences* 57, 94-124, 1998. 366
13. T. A. Henzinger, P.-H. Ho and H. Wong-Toi, HyTech: A Model Checker for Hybrid Systems, *Software Tools for Technology Transfer* 1, 110-122, 1997. 366
14. A. Kurzhanski and P. Varaiya, Ellipsoidal Techniques for Reachability Analysis, *HSCC*, 202-214 LNCS 1790, Springer, 2000. 369
15. K. Larsen, P. Pettersson and W. Yi, Uppaal in a nutshell, *Software Tools for Technology Transfert* 1-1, 1997. 366

16. O. Maler, Z. Manna and A. Pnueli, From Timed to Hybrid Systems, *Real-Time: Theory in Practice*, 447-484 LNCS 600, Springer, 1992. 365
17. G. Pappas, G. Lafferriere and S. Yovine, A New Class of Decidable Hybrid Systems, *HSCC*, 7-12 LNCS 1569, Springer, 1999. 366
18. B. I. Silva, O. Stursberg, B. H. Krogh and S. Engell, An Assessment of the Current Status of Algorithmic Approaches to the Verification of Hybrid Systems, *Proc. IEEE Conf. on Decision and Control*, 2867-2874, 2001. 368
19. S. Yovine, Kronos: A Verification Tool for Real-time Systems, *Software Tools for Technology Transfer* 1-1, 123-133, 1997. 366

Model Checking Linear Properties
of Prefix-Recognizable Systems

Orna Kupferman[1]*, Nir Piterman[2], and Moshe Y. Vardi[3]**

[1] Hebrew University, School of Engineering and Computer Science
Jerusalem 91904, Israel
orna@cs.huji.ac.il
http://www.cs.huji.ac.il/~orna
[2] Weizmann Institute of Science, Department of Computer Science
Rehovot 76100, Israel
nirp@wisdom.weizmann.ac.il
http://www.wisdom.weizmann.ac.il/~nirp
[3] Department of Computer Science, Rice University
Houston, TX 77251-1892, U.S.A.
vardi@cs.rice.edu
http://www.cs.rice.edu/~vardi

Abstract. We develop an automata-theoretic framework for reasoning about *linear properties of infinite-state sequential systems*. Our framework is based on the observation that states of such systems, which carry a finite but unbounded amount of information, can be viewed as nodes in an infinite tree, and transitions between states can be simulated by finite-state automata. Checking that the system satisfies a temporal property can then be done by an alternating two-way automaton that navigates through the tree. We introduce *path automata on trees*. The input to a path automaton is a tree, but the automaton cannot split to copies and it can read only a single path of the tree. In particular, *two-way* nondeterministic path automata enable exactly the type of navigation that is required in order to check linear properties of infinite-state sequential systems.

We demonstrate the versatility of the automata-theoretic approach by solving several versions of the model-checking problem for LTL specifications and prefix-recognizable systems. Our algorithm is exponential in both the size of (the description of) the system and the size of the LTL specification, and we prove a matching lower bound. This is the first optimal algorithm for solving the LTL model-checking problem for prefix recognizable systems. Our framework also handles systems with regular labeling.

* Supported in part by BSF grant 9800096.
** Supported in part by NSF grants CCR-9988322, IIS-9908435, IIS-9978135, and EIA-0086264, by BSF grant 9800096, and by a grant from the Intel Corporation.

1 Introduction

In temporal-logic *model checking*, we verify the correctness of a finite-state system with respect to a desired behavior by checking whether a labeled state-transition graph that models the system satisfies a temporal logic formula that specifies this behavior (for a survey, see [CGP99]). An important research topic over the past decade has been the application of model checking to infinite-state systems. Notable successes in this area has been the application of model checking to real-time and hybrid systems (cf. [HHWT95, LPY97]). Another active thrust of research is the application of model checking to *infinite-state sequential systems*. These are systems in which a state carries a finite, but unbounded, amount of information, e.g., a pushdown store. The origin of this thrust is the important result by Müller and Schupp that the monadic second-order theory of *context-free graphs* is decidable [MS85]. As the complexity involved in that decidability result is nonelementary, researchers sought decidability results of elementary complexity. This started with Burkart and Steffen, who developed an exponential-time algorithm for model-checking formulas in the *alternation-free* μ-calculus with respect to context-free graphs [BS92]. Researchers then went on to extend this result to the μ-calculus, on one hand, and to more general graphs on the other hand, such as *pushdown graphs* [BS95, Wal96], *regular graphs* [BQ96], and *prefix-recognizable graphs* [Cau96]. The most powerful result so far is an exponential-time algorithm by Burkart for model checking formulas of the μ-calculus with respect to prefix-recognizable graphs [Bur97b]. See also [BCMS00, BE96, BEM97, BS99, Bur97a, FWW97].

In [KV00], Kupferman and Vardi develop an automata-theoretic framework for reasoning about infinite-state sequential systems. The automata-theoretic approach uses the theory of automata as a unifying paradigm for system specification, verification, and synthesis [WVS83, EJ91, Kur94, VW94, KVW00]. Automata enable the separation of the logical and the algorithmic aspects of reasoning about systems, yielding clean and asymptotically optimal algorithms. Kupferman and Vardi use two-way alternating tree automata in order to reason about branching properties of infinite state sequential systems. The idea is based on the observation that states of such systems can be viewed as nodes in an infinite tree, and transitions between states can be simulated by finite-state automata. Checking that the system satisfies a branching temporal property can then be done by an alternating two-way automaton. The two-way alternating automaton starts checking the input tree from the root. It then spawns several copies of itself that may go in different directions in the tree. Each new copy can spawn other new copies and so on. The automaton accepts the input tree if all spawned copies agree on acceptance. Thus, copies of the alternating automaton navigate through the tree and check the branching temporal property. The method in [KV00] handles prefix-recognizable systems, and properties specified in the μ-calculus. The method appears to be very versatile, and it has further applications: the μ-calculus model-checking algorithm can be easily extended to graphs with *regular labeling* (that is, graphs in which each atomic proposition p has a regular expression describing the set of states in which p holds) and *reg-*

ular fairness constraints, to μ-calculus with *backward modalities*, to checking *realizability* of μ-calculus formulas with respect to infinite-state sequential environments, and to computing the set pre^* ($post^*$) of predecessors (successors) of a regular set of states. All the above are achieved using a reduction to the emptiness problem for alternating two-way tree automata where the location of the alternating automaton on the infinite tree indicates the contents of the pushdown store.

The μ-calculus is sufficiently strong to express all properties expressible in the linear temporal logic LTL (and in fact, all properties expressible by an ω-regular language) [Dam94]. Thus, the framework in [KV00] can be used in order to solve the problem of LTL model-checking for prefix-recognizable systems. The solution, however, is not optimal. This has to do both with the fact that the translation of LTL to the μ-calculus is exponential, as well as the fact that the framework in [KV00] is based on tree automata. A tree automaton splits into several copies when it runs on a tree. While splitting is essential for reasoning about branching properties, it has a computational price. For linear properties, it is sufficient to follow a single computation of the system, and tree automata seem too strong for this task. For example, while the application of the framework in [KV00] to pushdown systems and LTL properties results in a doubly-exponential algorithm, the problem is known to be EXPTIME-complete [BEM97].

In this paper, we develop an automata-theoretic framework to reason about linear properties of infinite-state sequential systems. We introduce *path automata on trees*. The input to a path automaton is a tree, but the automaton cannot split to copies and it can read only a single path of the tree. In particular, *two-way* nondeterministic path automata enable exactly the type of navigation that is required in order to check linear properties of infinite-state sequential systems. We study the expressive power and the complexity of the decision problems for (two way) path automata. The fact that path automata follow a single path in the tree makes them very similar to two-way nondeterministic automata on infinite words. This enables us to reduce the membership problem (whether an automaton accepts the tree obtained by unwinding a given finite labeled graph) of two-way nondeterministic path automata to the emptiness problem of one-way alternating weak automata on infinite words, which was studied in [KVW00]. This leads to a quadratic upper bound for the membership problem for two-way nondeterministic path automata.

As usual, the automata-theoretic framework proves to be very helpful. We are able to solve the problem of LTL model checking with respect to pushdown systems by a reduction to the membership problem of two-way nondeterministic path automata. This is in contrast to [KV00], where the emptiness problem for two-way alternating tree automata is being used. We note that both simplifications, to the membership problem vs. the emptiness problem, and to path automata vs. tree automata are crucial: as we prove, the emptiness problem for two-way nondeterministic Büchi path automata is EXPTIME-complete, and the membership problem for two-way alternating Büchi automata is also EXPTIME-complete[1]. Our automata-theoretic technique matches the known upper bound for model checking LTL properties on pushdown systems [BEM97, EHRS00]. In addition, the automata-theoretic approach provides the first solution for the case the system is prefix recognizable. Specifically, we show that we can solve the model-checking problem of an LTL formula φ with respect to a prefix-recognizable system R of size n in time and space $2^{O(n+|\varphi|)}$. We also prove a matching EXPTIME lower bound.

Our framework also handles regular labeling (in both pushdown and prefix-recognizable systems). The complexity is exponential in the nondeterministic automata that describe the labeling, matching the known bound for pushdown systems [EKS01]. The automata-theoretic techniques for handling regular labeling and for handling the regular transitions of a prefix-recognizable system are very similar. In both settings, the system has to be able to check the membership of the word in the store in a regular expression. This leads us to the understanding that regular labeling and prefix recognizability have exactly the same power. In the full version, we prove that LTL model checking in a prefix recognizable system and LTL model checking in a pushdown system with regular labeling are intereducible. Since the latter problem is known be EXPTIME-complete [EKS01], our reductions suggest an alternative proof of the exponential upper and lower bounds for the problem of LTL model checking in prefix-recognizable systems.

2   Preliminaries

We consider finite or infinite sequences of symbols from some finite alphabet Σ. Given a *word* $w = w_0 w_1 w_2 \cdots \in \Sigma^* \cup \Sigma^\omega$, we denote by by $w_{\geq i}$ the suffix of w starting at w_i hence $w_{\geq i} = w_i w_{i+1} w_{i+2} \cdots$. The *length* of w is denoted by $|w|$ and is defined to be ω for infinite words.

Nondeterministic Automata. A *nondeterministic automaton on words* is $N = \langle \Sigma, Q, q_0, \eta, F \rangle$, where Σ is a finite alphabet, Q is a finite set of states, $q_0 \in Q$ is an initial state, $\eta : Q \times \Sigma \to 2^Q$ is a transition function, and $F \subseteq Q$ is a set of accepting states. We can run N either on finite words (*nondeterministic finite automaton* or *NFA* for short) or on infinite words (*nondeterministic Büchi automaton* or *NBW* for short). A *deterministic* automaton is an automaton for which $|\eta(q, a)| = 1$ for all $q \in Q$ and $a \in \Sigma$. We denote by N^q the automaton N with initial state q. A *run* of N on a finite word $w = w_0, \ldots, w_{l-1}$ is a finite sequence of states $p_0, p_1, \ldots, p_l \in Q^{l+1}$ such that $p_0 = q_0$ and for all $0 \leq j < l$, we have $p_{j+1} \in \eta(p_j, w_j)$. A run is *accepting* if $p_l \in F$. A *run* of N on an infinite word $w = w_0, w_1, \ldots$ is defined similarly as an infinite sequence. For a run $r = p_0, p_1, \ldots$, let $inf(r) = \{q \in Q \mid q = p_i \text{ for infinitely many } i\text{'s}\}$ be the set of

---

[1] In contrast, the membership problem for one-way alternating Büchi tree automata can be solved in quadratic time. Indeed, the problem can be reduced to the emptiness problem of the 1-letter alternating word automaton obtained by taking the product of the labeled graph that models the tree with the one-way alternating tree automaton [KVW00]. This technique cannot be applied to two-way automata, since they can distinguish between a graph and its unwinding. For a related discussion regarding past-time connectives in branching temporal logics, see [KP95].

all states occurring infinitely often in the run. A run r of an NBW is *accepting* if it visits the set F infinitely often, thus $inf(r) \cap F \neq \emptyset$. A word w is *accepted* by N if N has an accepting run on w. The *language* of N, denoted $L(N)$, is the set of words accepted by N. The size $|N|$ of a nondeterministic automaton N is the size of its transition function, thus $|N| = \Sigma_{q \in Q} \Sigma_{\sigma \in \Sigma} |\eta(q, \sigma)|$.

We are especially interested in cases where $\Sigma = 2^{AP}$, for some set AP of atomic propositions AP, and in languages $L \subseteq (2^{AP})^\omega$ definable by NBW or formulas of the linear temporal logic LTL [Pnu77]. For an LTL formula φ, the *language* of φ, denoted $L(\varphi)$, is the set of infinite words that satisfy φ.

Theorem 1. [VW94] *For every LTL formula φ, there exists an NBW N_φ with $2^{O(|\varphi|)}$ states, such that $L(N_\varphi) = L(\varphi)$.*

Labeled Rewrite Systems. A *labeled transition graph* is $G = \langle \Sigma, S, L, \rho, s_0 \rangle$, where Σ is a finite set of labels, S is a (possibly infinite) set of states, $L : S \to \Sigma$ is a labeling function, $\rho \subseteq S \times S$ is a transition relation, and $s_0 \in S_0$ is an initial state. When $\rho(s, s')$, we say that s' is a *successor* of s, and s is a *predecessor* of s'. For a state $s \in S$, we denote by $G^s = \langle \Sigma, S, L, \rho, s \rangle$, the graph G with s as its initial state. An s-*computation* is an infinite sequence of states $s_0, s_1, \ldots \in S^\omega$ such that $s_0 = s$ and for all $i \geq 0$, we have $\rho(s_i, s_{i+1})$. An s-computation $s_0, s_1, \ldots$ induces the s-*trace* $L(s_0) \cdot L(s_1) \cdots$. The set $\mathcal{T}_s$ is the set of all s-traces. We say that s satisfies an LTL formula φ, denoted $(G, s) \models \varphi$, iff $\mathcal{T}_s \subseteq \mathcal{L}(\varphi)$. A graph G satisfies an LTL formula φ, denoted $G \models \varphi$, iff its initial state satisfies it; that is $(G, s_0) \models \varphi$. The *model-checking problem* for a labeled transition graph G and an LTL formula φ is to determine whether G satisfies φ. Note that the transition relation need not be total. There may be finite paths but satisfaction is determined only with respect to infinite paths. In particular, if the graph has only finite paths, its set of traces is empty and the graph satisfies every LTL formula (It is also possible to consider finite paths. In this case, the NBW in Theorem 1 has to be modified so that it can recognize also finite words. Our results are easily extended to consider also finite paths).

A *rewrite system* is $R = \langle \Sigma, V, Q, L, T, q_0, x_0 \rangle$, where Σ is a finite set of labels, V is a finite alphabet, labeling function, T is a finite set of rewrite rules, to be defined below, q_0 is an initial state, and $x_0 \in V^*$ is an initial word. The set of *configurations* of the system is $Q \times V^*$. Intuitively, the system has finitely many control states and unbounded store. Thus, in a configuration $(q, x) \in Q \times V^*$ we refer to q as the *control state* and to x as the *store*. A configuration $(q, x) \in Q \times V^*$ indicates that the system is in control state q with store x. We consider here two types of rewrite systems. In a *pushdown* system, each rewrite rule is $\langle q, A, x, q' \rangle \in Q \times V \times V^* \times Q$. Thus, $T \subseteq Q \times V \times V^* \times Q$. In a *prefix-recognizable* system, each rewrite rule is $\langle q, \alpha, \beta, \gamma, q' \rangle \in Q \times reg(V) \times reg(V) \times reg(V) \times Q$, where $reg(V)$ is the set of regular expressions over V. Thus, $T \subseteq Q \times reg(V) \times reg(V) \times reg(V) \times Q$. For a word $w \in V^*$ and a regular expression $r \in reg(V)$ we write $w \in r$ to denote that w is in the language of the regular expression r. We note that the standard definition of prefix-recognizable systems does not include control states. Indeed, a prefix-recognizable system without states can simulate a prefix-recognizable system with states by having the state as the first letter of the unbounded store. For uniformity, we use prefix-recognizable systems with control states.

We consider two types of labeling functions, *simple* and *regular*. The labeling function associates with a configuration $(q, x) \in Q \times V^*$ a symbol from Σ. A simple labeling function depends only on the first letter of x. Thus, we may write $L : Q \times (V \cup \{\epsilon\}) \to \Sigma$. Note that the label is defined also for the case that x is the empty word ϵ. A regular labeling function considers the entire word x but can only refer to its membership in some regular set. Formally, for every state q there is a partition of V^* to $|\Sigma|$ regular languages $R_1, \ldots R_{|\Sigma|}$, and $L(q, x)$ depends on the regular set that x belongs to. We are especially interested in the cases where the alphabet Σ is the powerset 2^{AP} of the set of atomic propositions. In this case, we associate with every state q and proposition p a regular language $R_{q,p}$ that contains all the words x for which the proposition p is true in configuration (q, x). Thus $p \in L(q, x)$ iff $x \in R_{q,p}$.

The rewrite system R induces the labeled transition graph $G_R = \langle \Sigma, Q \times V^*, L', \rho_R, (q_0, x_0) \rangle$. The states of G_R are the configurations of R and $\langle (q, z), (q', z') \rangle \in \rho_R$ if there is a rewrite rule $t \in T$ leading from configuration (q, z) to configuration (q', z'). Formally, if R is a pushdown system, then $\rho_R((q, A \cdot y), (q', x \cdot y))$ if $\langle q, A, x, q' \rangle \in T$; and if R is a prefix-recognizable system, then $\rho_R((q, x \cdot y), (q', x' \cdot y))$ if there are regular expressions α, β, and γ such that $x \in \alpha$, $y \in \beta$, $x' \in \gamma$, and $\langle q, \alpha, \beta, \gamma, q' \rangle \in T$. In order to apply a rewrite rule in state $(q, z) \in Q \times V^*$ of a pushdown graph, we only need to match the state q and the first letter of z with the second element of a rule. On the other hand, in an application of a rewrite rule in a prefix-recognizable graph, we have to match the state q and find a partition of z to a prefix that belongs to the second element of the rule and a suffix that belongs to the third element. A labeled transition graph that is induced by a pushdown system is called a *pushdown graph*. A labeled transition system that is induced by a prefix-recognizable system is called a *prefix-recognizable graph*. We say that a rewrite system R satisfies an LTL formula φ if $G_R \models \varphi$. [2]

Example 1. The pushdown system $\langle 2^{\{p_1, p_2\}}, \{A, B\}, \{q_0\}, L, T, q_0, A \rangle$, with $T = \{\langle q_0, A, AB, q_0 \rangle, \langle q_0, A, \varepsilon, q_0 \rangle, \langle q_0, B, \varepsilon, q_0 \rangle\}$, and L defined by $R_{q_0, p_1} = \{A, B\}^* \cdot B \cdot B \cdot \{A, B\}^*$ and $R_{q_0, p_2} = A \cdot \{A, B\}^*$, induces the labeled transition graph below.

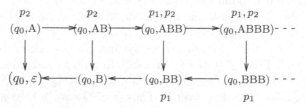

[2] Some work on verification of infinite-state system (e.g., [EHRS00]), consider properties given by nondeterministic Büchi word automata, rather than LTL formulas. Our algorithm actually handles properties given by automata. We translate an LTL formula to an automaton and use the automaton in our algorithm.

Consider a prefix-recognizable system $R = \langle \Sigma, V, Q, L, T, q_0, x_0 \rangle$. For a re-write rule $t_i = \langle s, \alpha_i, \beta_i, \gamma_i, s' \rangle \in T$, let $\mathcal{U}_\lambda = \langle V, Q_\lambda, q_\lambda^0, \eta_\lambda, F_\lambda \rangle$, for $\lambda \in \{\alpha_i, \beta_i, \gamma_i\}$, be the nondeterministic automaton for the language of the regular expression λ. We assume that all initial states have no incoming edges and that all accepting states have no outgoing edges. We collect all the states of all the automata for α, β, and γ regular expressions. Formally, $Q_\alpha = \bigcup_{t_i \in T} Q_{\alpha_i}$, $Q_\beta = \bigcup_{t_i \in T} Q_{\beta_i}$, and $Q_\gamma = \bigcup_{t_i \in T} Q_{\gamma_i}$. We assume that we have an automaton whose language is $\{x_0\}$. We denote the initial state of this automaton by x_0 and add all its states to Q_γ. Finally, for a regular labeling function L, a state $q \in Q$, and a proposition $p \in AP$, let $\mathcal{U}_{q,p} = \langle V, Q_{p,q}, q_{p,q}^0, \rho_{p,q}, F_{p,q} \rangle$ be the nondeterministic automaton for the language of $R_{q,p}$.

We define the *size* $\|T\|$ of T as the space required in order to encode the rewrite rules in T and the labeling function. Thus, in a pushdown system, $\|T\| = \sum_{\langle q, A, x, q' \rangle \in T} |x|$, and in a prefix-recognizable system, $\|T\| = \sum_{\langle q, \alpha, \beta, \gamma, q' \rangle \in T} |\mathcal{U}_\alpha| + |\mathcal{U}_\beta| + |\mathcal{U}_\gamma|$. In the case of a regular labeling function, we also measure the labeling function $\|L\| = \sum_{q \in Q} \sum_{p \in AP} |\mathcal{U}_{q,p}|$.

Theorem 2. *The model-checking problem for a pushdown system R and an LTL formula φ is solvable*

- *in time $O(\|T\|^3) \cdot 2^{O(|\varphi|)}$ and space $O(\|T\|^2) \cdot 2^{O(|\varphi|)}$ in the case that L is a simple labeling function* [EHRS00].
- *in time $O(\|T\|^3) \cdot 2^{O(\|L\|+|\varphi|)}$ and space $O(\|T\|^2) \cdot 2^{O(\|L\|+|\varphi|)}$ in the case that L is a regular labeling function. The problem is EXPTIME-hard in $\|L\|$ even for a fixed formula* [EKS01].

3   Two-Way Path Automata on Trees

Given a finite set Υ of directions, an Υ-*tree* is a set $T \subseteq \Upsilon^*$ such that if $\upsilon \cdot x \in T$, where $\upsilon \in \Upsilon$ and $x \in \Upsilon^*$, then also $x \in T$. The elements of T are called *nodes*, and the empty word ε is the *root* of T. For every $\upsilon \in \Upsilon$ and $x \in T$, the node If $z = x \cdot y \in T$ then z is a descendant of y. Each node $x \neq \varepsilon$ of T has a *direction* in Υ. The direction of the root is the symbol $\perp$ (we assume that $\perp \notin \Upsilon$). The direction of a node $\upsilon \cdot x$ is υ. We denote by $dir(x)$ the direction of the node x. An Υ-tree T is a *full infinite tree* if $T = \Upsilon^*$. A *path* π of a tree T is an infinite set $\pi \subseteq T$ such that $\varepsilon \in \pi$ and for every $x \in \pi$ there exists a unique $\upsilon \in \Upsilon$ such that $\upsilon \cdot x \in \pi$. Note that our definitions here reverse the standard definitions (e.g., when $\Upsilon = \{0, 1\}$, the successors of the node 0 are 00 and 10, rather than 00 and 01[3].

Given two finite sets Υ and Σ, a Σ-*labeled* Υ-*tree* is a pair $\langle T, \tau \rangle$ where T is an Υ-tree and $\tau : T \to \Sigma$ maps each node of T to a letter in Σ. When Υ and Σ are not important or clear from the context, we call $\langle T, \tau \rangle$ a labeled tree. A tree is *regular* if it is the unwinding of some finite labeled graph. More

---

[3] As will get clearer in the sequel, the reason for that is that rewrite rules refer to the prefix of words.

formally, a *transducer* $\mathcal{D}$ is a tuple $\langle \varUpsilon, \varSigma, Q, q_0, \eta, L \rangle$, where $\varUpsilon$ is a finite set of directions, $\varSigma$ is a finite set alphabet, Q is a finite set of states, $q_0 \in Q$ is a start state, $\eta : Q \times \varUpsilon \to Q$ is a deterministic transition function, and $L : Q \to \varSigma$ is a labeling function. We define $\eta : \varUpsilon^* \to Q$ in the standard way: $\eta(\varepsilon) = q_0$ and $\eta(ax) = \eta(\eta(x), a)$. Intuitively, a transducer is a labeled finite graph with a designated start node, where the edges are labeled by $\varUpsilon$ and the nodes are labeled by $\varSigma$. A $\varSigma$-labeled $\varUpsilon$-tree $\langle \varUpsilon^*, \tau \rangle$ is regular if there exists a transducer $\mathcal{D} = \langle \varUpsilon, \varSigma, Q, q_0, \eta, L \rangle$, such that for every $x \in \varUpsilon^*$, we have $\tau(x) = L(\eta(x))$. We denote by $\|\tau\|$, the number $|Q|$ of states of $\mathcal{D}$.

Path automata on trees are a hybrid of nondeterministic word automata and nondeterministic tree automata: they run on trees but have linear runs. Here we describe *two-way* nondeterministic Büchi path automata. For a set $\varUpsilon$ of directions, the *extension* of $\varUpsilon$ is the set $ext(\varUpsilon) = \varUpsilon \cup \{\varepsilon, \uparrow\}$ (we assume that $\varUpsilon \cap \{\varepsilon, \uparrow\} = \emptyset$). A *two-way nondeterministic Büchi path automaton* (2NBP, for short) on $\varSigma$-labeled $\varUpsilon$-trees is $\mathcal{S} = \langle \varSigma, P, \delta, p_0, F \rangle$, where $\varSigma$, P, p_0, and F are as in an NBW, and $\delta : P \times \varSigma \to 2^{(ext(\varUpsilon) \times P)}$ is the transition function. A path automaton that visits the state p and reads the node $x \in T$ chooses a pair $(\varDelta, p') \in \delta(p, \tau(x))$, and then follows direction $\varDelta$ and moves to state p'.

Formally, a *run* of a 2NBP $\mathcal{S}$ on a labeled tree $\langle \varUpsilon^*, \tau \rangle$ is a sequence of pairs $r = (x_0, p_0), (x_1, p_1), \ldots$ where for all $i \geq 0$, $x_i \in \varUpsilon^*$ is a node of the tree and $p_i \in P$ is a state. The pair (x, p) describes a copy of the automaton that reads the node x of $\varUpsilon^*$ and is in the state p. Note that many pairs in r may correspond to the same node of $\varUpsilon^*$; Thus, $\mathcal{S}$ may visit a node several times. The run has to satisfy the transition function. Formally, $(x_0, p_0) = (\varepsilon, q_0)$ and for all $i \geq 0$ there is $\varDelta \in ext(\varUpsilon)$ such that $(\varDelta, p_{i+1}) \in \delta(p_i, \tau(x_i))$ and

- If $\varDelta \in \varUpsilon$, then $x_{i+1} = \varDelta \cdot x_i$.
- If $\varDelta = \varepsilon$, then $x_{i+1} = x_i$.
- If $\varDelta = \uparrow$, then $x_i = \upsilon \cdot z$, for some $\upsilon \in \varUpsilon$ and $z \in \varUpsilon^*$, and $x_{i+1} = z$.

Thus, ε-transitions leave the automaton on the same node of the input tree, and $\uparrow$-transitions take it up to the parent node. Note that the automaton cannot go up the root of the input tree, as whenever $\varDelta = \uparrow$, we require that $x_i \neq \varepsilon$. A run r is *accepting* if it visits $\varUpsilon^* \times F$ infinitely often. An automaton accepts a labeled tree if and only if there exists a run that accepts it. We denote by $\mathcal{L}(\mathcal{A})$ the set of all $\varSigma$-labeled trees that $\mathcal{A}$ accepts. The automaton $\mathcal{A}$ is *nonempty* iff $\mathcal{L}(\mathcal{A}) \neq \emptyset$. We measure the size of a 2NBP by two parameters, the number of states and the size, $|\delta| = \varSigma_{p \in P} \varSigma_{a \in \varSigma} |\delta(s, a)|$, of the transition function.

Readers familiar with tree automata know that the run of a tree automaton starts in a single copy of the automaton reading the root of the tree, and then the copy splits to the successors of the root and so on, thus the run simultaneously follows many paths in the input tree. In contrast, a path automaton has a single copy at all times. It starts from the root and it always chooses a single direction to go to. In two-way path automata, the direction may be "up", so the automaton can read many paths of the tree, but it cannot read them simultaneously. The fact that a 2NBP has a single copy influences its expressive power and the complexity of its nonemptiness and membership problems. In the full version we study the expressive power of 2NBP. We show that a 2NBP cannot recognize even very simple properties that refer to all the branches of the tree. However, when a universal property considers only a bounded prefix of the branch, it can be recognized by a 2NBP. We now turn to study the emptiness and membership problems of 2NBP.

Given a 2NBP $\mathcal{S}$, the *emptiness problem* is to determine whether $\mathcal{S}$ accepts some tree, or equivalently whether $\mathcal{L}(\mathcal{S}) = \emptyset$. The *membership problem* of $\mathcal{S}$ and a regular tree $\langle \Upsilon^*, \tau \rangle$ is to determine whether $\mathcal{S}$ accepts $\langle \Upsilon^*, \tau \rangle$, or equivalently $\langle \Upsilon^*, \tau \rangle \in \mathcal{L}(\mathcal{S})$. The fact that 2NBP cannot spawn new copies makes them similar to word automata. Thus, the membership problem for 2NBP can be reduced to the emptiness problem of one-way weak alternating automata on infinite words (1AWW) over a 1-letter alphabet (cf. [KVW00]). The reduction yields a polynomial time algorithm for solving the membership problem. In contrast, the emptiness problem of 2NBP is EXPTIME-complete.

In the full version, we show that we can reduce the membership problem of 2NBP to the emptiness problem of alternating word automata. The reduction generalizes the construction in [PV01a, PV01b, Pit00]. We combine this reduction with an algorithm for checking the emptiness of alteranting word automata [KVW00]. Formally, we have the following.

Theorem 3. *Consider a 2NBP $\mathcal{S} = \langle \Sigma, P, p_0, \delta, F \rangle$.*

- *The membership problem of the regular tree $\langle \Upsilon^*, \tau \rangle$ in the language of $\mathcal{S}$ is solvable in time $O(|P|^2 \cdot |\delta| \cdot \|\tau\|)$ and space $O(|P|^2 \cdot \|\tau\|)$.*
- *The emptiness problem of $\mathcal{S}$ is EXPTIME-complete.*

We note that the membership problem for 2-way alternating Büchi automata on trees (2ABT) is EXPTIME-complete. Indeed, CTL model-checking of pushdown systems, proven to be EXPTIME-hard in [Wal00], can be reduced to the membership problem of a regular tree in a 2ABT. The size of the regular tree is linear in the size of the alphabet of the pushdown system and the size of the 2ABT is linear in the size of the CTL formula. Thus, path automata capture the computational difference between linear and branching specifications.

4 LTL Model Checking

In this section we solve the LTL model-checking problem by a reduction to the membership problem of 2NBP. We start by demonstrating our technique on LTL model-checking for pushdown systems. Then we show how to extend it to prefix-recognizable systems and to systems with regular labeling. For an LTL formula φ, we construct a 2NBP that navigates through the full infinite V-tree and simulates a computation of the rewrite system that does not satisfy φ. Thus, our 2NBP accepts the V-tree iff the rewrite system does not satisfy the specification. Then, we use the results in Section 3: we check whether the given V-tree is in the language of the 2NBP and conclude whether the system satisfies the property.

Consider a rewrite system $R = \langle \Sigma, V, Q, L, T, q_0, x_0 \rangle$. Recall that a configuration of R is a pair $(q, x) \in Q \times V^*$. Thus, the store x corresponds to a node in the full infinite V-tree. An automaton that reads the tree V^* can memorize in its state space the state component of the configuration and refer to the location of its reading head in V^* as the store. We would like the automaton to "know" the location of its reading head in V^*. A straightforward way to do so is to label a node $x \in V^*$ by x. This, however, involves an infinite alphabet, and results in trees that are not regular. We show that it is possible to label V^* with a regular labeling that is sufficiently informative to provide the 2NBP with the information it needs in order to simulate the transitions of the rewrite system. For pushdown systems with a simple labeling function, we show that it is enough to label a node x by its direction. For prefix-recognizable systems or systems with regular labeling, the label is more complex and reflects the membership of x in the regular expressions that are used in the transition rules and the regular labeling.

Pushdown Systems. Recall that in order to apply a rewrite rule of a pushdown system from configuration (q, x), it is sufficient to know q and the first letter of x. Let $\langle V^*, \tau_V \rangle$ be the V-labeled V-tree such that for every $x \in V^*$ we have $\tau_V(x) = dir(x)$. Note that $\langle V^*, \tau_V \rangle$ is a regular tree of size $|V| + 1$. We construct a 2NBP $\mathcal{S}$ that reads $\langle V^*, \tau_V \rangle$. The state space of $\mathcal{S}$ contains a component that memorizes the current state of the rewrite system. The location of the reading head in $\langle V^*, \tau_V \rangle$ represents the store of the current configuration. Thus, in order to know which rewrite rules can be applied, $\mathcal{S}$ consults its current state and the label of the node it reads (note that $dir(x)$ is the first letter of x). Formally, we have the following.

Theorem 4. *Given a pushdown system $R = \langle 2^{AP}, V, Q, L, T, q_0, x_0 \rangle$ and an LTL formula φ, there is a 2NBP $\mathcal{S}$ on V-trees such that $\mathcal{S}$ accepts $\langle V^*, \tau_V \rangle$ iff $G_R \not\models \varphi$. The automaton $\mathcal{S}$ has $O(|Q| \cdot \|T\|) \cdot 2^{O(|\varphi|)}$ states and the size of its transition function is $O(\|T\|) \cdot 2^{O(|\varphi|)}$.*

Proof. According to Theorem 1, there is an NBW $\mathcal{M}_{\neg\varphi} = \langle 2^{AP}, W, \eta_{\neg\varphi}, w_0, F \rangle$ such that $\mathcal{L}(\mathcal{M}_{\neg\varphi}) = (2^{AP})^\omega \setminus \mathcal{L}(\varphi)$. The 2NBP $\mathcal{S}$ tries to find a trace in G_R that satisfies $\neg\varphi$. The 2NBP $\mathcal{S}$ runs $\mathcal{M}_{\neg\varphi}$ on a guessed (q_0, x_0)-computation in R. Thus, $\mathcal{S}$ accepts $\langle V^*, \tau_V \rangle$ iff there exists an (q_0, x_0)-trace in G_R accepted by $\mathcal{M}_{\neg\varphi}$. Such a (q_0, x_0)-trace does not satisfy φ, and it exists iff $R \not\models \varphi$. We define $\mathcal{S} = \langle V, P, p_0, \delta, F' \rangle$, where

- $P = W \times Q \times tails(T)$, where $tails(T) \subseteq V^*$ is the set of all suffixes of words $x \in V^*$ for which there are states $q, q' \in Q$ and $A \in V$ such that $\langle q, A, x, q' \rangle \in T$. Intuitively, when $\mathcal{S}$ visits a node $x \in V^*$ in state $\langle w, q, y \rangle$, it checks that R with initial configuration $(q, y \cdot x)$ is accepted by $\mathcal{M}_{\neg\varphi}^w$. In particular, when $y = \varepsilon$, then R with initial configuration (q, x) needs to be accepted by $\mathcal{M}_{\neg\varphi}^w$. States of the form $\langle w, q, \varepsilon \rangle$ are called *action states*. From these states $\mathcal{S}$ consults $\eta_{\neg\varphi}$ and T in order to impose new requirements on $\langle V^*, \tau_V \rangle$. States of the form $\langle w, q, y \rangle$, for $y \in V^+$, are called *navigation states*. From these states $\mathcal{S}$ only navigates downwards y to reach new action states.

- $p_0 = \langle w_0, q_0, x_0 \rangle$. Thus, in its initial state $\mathcal{S}$ checks that R with initial configuration (q_0, x_0) contains a trace that is accepted by $\mathcal{M}$ with initial state w_0.
- The transition function δ is defined for every state in $\langle w, q, x \rangle \in W \times Q \times tails(T)$ and letter in $A \in V$ as follows.
    • $\delta(\langle w, q, \epsilon \rangle, A) = \{(\langle w', q', y \rangle, \uparrow) : w' \in \eta_{\neg\varphi}(w, L(q, A))$
       and $\langle q, A, y, q' \rangle \in T \}$.
    • $\delta(\langle w, q, B \cdot y \rangle, A) = \{(\langle w, q, y \rangle, B)\}$.
   Thus, in action states, $\mathcal{S}$ reads the direction of the current node and applies the rewrite rules of R in order to impose new requirements according to $\eta_{\neg\varphi}$. In navigation states, $\mathcal{S}$ needs to go downwards $B \cdot y$, so it continues in direction B.
- $F' = \{\langle w, q, \epsilon \rangle : w \in F$ and $q \in Q\}$. Note that only action states can be accepting states of $\mathcal{S}$.

We show that $\mathcal{S}$ accepts $\langle V^*, \tau_V \rangle$ iff $R \not\models \varphi$. Assume first that $\mathcal{S}$ accepts $\langle V^*, \tau_V \rangle$. Then, there exists an accepting run $(p_0, x_0), (p_1, x_1), \ldots$ of $\mathcal{S}$ on $\langle V^*, \tau_V \rangle$. Extract from this run the subsequence of action states $(p_{i_1}, x_{i_1}), (p_{i_2}, x_{i_2}), \ldots$. As the run is accepting and only action states are accepting states we know that this subsequence is infinite. Let $p_{i_j} = \langle w_{i_j}, q_{i_j}, \varepsilon \rangle$. By the definition of δ, the sequence $(q_{i_1}, x_{i_1}), (q_{i_2}, x_{i_2}), \ldots$ corresponds to an infinite path in the graph G_R. Also, by the definition of F', the run $w_{i_1}, w_{i_2}, \ldots$ is an accepting run of $\mathcal{M}_{\neg\varphi}$ on the trace of this path. Hence, G_R contains a trace that is accepted by $\mathcal{M}_{\neg\varphi}$, thus $R \not\models \varphi$.

Assume now that $R \not\models \varphi$. Then, there exists a path $(q_0, x_0), (q_1, x_1), \ldots$ in G_R whose trace does not satisfy φ. There exists an accepting run $w_0, w_1, \ldots$ of $\mathcal{M}_{\neg\varphi}$ on this trace. The combination of the two sequence serves as the subsequence of the action states in an accepting run of $\mathcal{S}$. It is not hard to extend this subsequence to an accepting run of $\mathcal{S}$ on $\langle V^*, \tau_V \rangle$.

Prefix-Recognizable Systems. We now turn to consider prefix-recognizable systems. Again the configuration of a prefix-recognizable system $R = \langle \Sigma, V, Q, L, T, q_0, x_0 \rangle$ consists of a state in Q and a word in V^*. So, the store content is still a node in the tree V^*. However, in order to apply a rewrite rule it is not enough to know the direction of the node. Recall that in order to represent the configuration $(q, x) \in Q \times V^*$, our 2NBP memorizes the state q as part of its state space and it reads the node $x \in V^*$. In order to apply the rewrite rule $t_i = \langle q, \alpha_i, \beta_i, \gamma_i, q' \rangle$, the 2NBP has to go up the tree along a word $y \in \alpha_i$. Then, if $x = y \cdot z$, it has to check that $z \in \beta_i$, and finally guess a word $y' \in \gamma_i$ and go downwards y' to $y' \cdot z$. Finding a prefix y of x such that $y \in \alpha_i$, and a new word $y' \in \gamma_i$ is not hard: the 2NBP can emulate the run of the automaton $\mathcal{U}_{\alpha_i}$ backwards while going up the tree and the run of the automaton $\mathcal{U}_{\gamma_i}$ while going down the guessed y'. How can the 2NBP know that $z \in \beta_i$? Instead of labeling each node $x \in V^*$ only by its direction, we can label it also by the regular expressions β for which $x \in \beta$. Thus, when the 2NBP run $\mathcal{U}_{\alpha_i}$ up the tree, it can tell, in every node it visits, whether z is a member of β_i or not. If $z \in \beta_i$, the 2NBP may guess that time has come to guess a word in γ_i and run $\mathcal{U}_{\gamma_i}$ down the guessed word.

Thus, in the case of prefix-recognizable systems, the nodes of the tree whose membership is checked are labeled by both their directions and information about the regular expressions β. Let $\{\beta_1, \ldots, \beta_n\}$ be the set of regular expressions β_i such that there is a rewrite rule $\langle q, \alpha_i, \beta_i, \gamma_i, q' \rangle \in T$. Let $\mathcal{D}_{\beta_i} = \langle V, D_{\beta_i}, q^0_{\beta_i}, \eta_{\beta_i}, F_{\beta_i} \rangle$ be the deterministic automaton for the language of β_i. For a word $x \in V^*$, we denote by $\eta_{\beta_i}(x)$ the unique state that $\mathcal{D}_{\beta_i}$ reaches after reading the word x. Let $\Sigma = V \times \Pi_{1 \leq i \leq n} D_{\beta_i}$. For a letter $\sigma \in \Sigma$, let $\sigma[i]$, for $i \in \{0, \ldots n\}$, denote the i-th element in σ (that is, $\sigma[0] \in V$ and $\sigma[i] \in D_{\beta_i}$ for $i > 0$). Let $\langle V^*, \tau_\beta \rangle$ denote the Σ-labeled V-tree such that $\tau_\beta(\epsilon) = \langle \bot, q^0_{\beta_1}, \ldots, q^0_{\beta_n} \rangle$, and for every node $A \cdot x \in V^+$, we have $\tau_\beta(A \cdot x) = \langle A, \eta_{\beta_1}(A \cdot x), \ldots, \eta_{\beta_n}(A \cdot x) \rangle$. Thus, every node x is labeled by $dir(x)$ and the vector of states that each of the deterministic automata reach after reading x. Note that $\tau_\beta(x)[i] \in F_{\beta_i}$ iff x is in the language of β_i. Note also that $\langle V^*, \tau_\beta \rangle$ is a regular tree whose size is exponential in the sum of the lengths of $\beta_1, \ldots, \beta_n$.

Theorem 5. *Given a prefix-recognizable system $R = \langle \Sigma, V, Q, L, T, q_0, x_0 \rangle$ and an LTL formula φ, there is a 2NBP $\mathcal{S}$ such that $\mathcal{S}$ accepts $\langle V^*, \tau_\beta \rangle$ iff $R \not\models \varphi$. The automaton $\mathcal{S}$ has $O(|Q| \cdot (|Q_\alpha| + |Q_\gamma|) \cdot |T|) \cdot 2^{O(|\varphi|)}$ states and the size of its transition function is $O(\|T\|) \cdot 2^{O(|\varphi|)}$.*

The proof resembles the proof for pushdown systems. This time, the application of a rewrite rule $t_i = \langle q, \alpha_i, \beta_i, \gamma_i, q' \rangle$ involves an emulation of the automata $\mathcal{U}_{\alpha_i}$ (upwards) and $\mathcal{U}_{\gamma_i}$ (downwards). Accordingly, one of the components of the states of the 2NBP is a state of either $\mathcal{U}_{\alpha_i}$ or $\mathcal{U}_{\gamma_i}$. Action states are states in which this component is a final state of $\mathcal{U}_{\gamma_i}$. From action states, the 2NBP chooses a new rewrite rule $t_{i'} = \langle q', \alpha_{i'}, \beta_{i'}, \gamma_{i'}, q'' \rangle$, and it applies it as follows. First, it chooses a final state of $\mathcal{U}_{\alpha_{i'}}$, and run $\mathcal{U}_{\alpha_i}$ backwards up the tree until it reaches the initial state. It then verifies that the current node is in the language of β_i, in which case it moves to the initial state of $\mathcal{U}_{\gamma_i}$ and runs it forward down the tree until it reaches a new action state.

Regular Labeling. Handling regular labels for pushdown systems or prefix-recognizable systems is similar to the above. We add to the label of every node in the tree V^* also the states of the deterministic automata that recognizes the languages of the regular expressions of the labels. The navigation through the V-tree proceeds as before, and whenever the 2NBP needs to know the label of the current configuration (that is, in action states, when it has to update the state of $\mathcal{M}_{\neg\varphi}$), it consults the labels of the tree.

If we want to handle a prefix-recognizable system with regular labeling we have to label the nodes of the tree V^* by both the deterministic automata for regular expressions β_i and the deterministic automata for regular expressions $R_{q,p}$. Let $\langle V^*, \tau_{\beta,L} \rangle$ denote this tree. Again note that $\langle V^*, \tau_{\beta,L} \rangle$ is a regular tree of exponential size.

Theorem 6. *Given a prefix-recognizable system $R = \langle \Sigma, V, Q, L, T, q_0, x_0 \rangle$ and an LTL formula φ, there is a 2NBP $\mathcal{S}$ such that $\mathcal{S}$ accepts $\langle V^*, \tau_{\beta,L} \rangle$ iff $R \not\models \varphi$. The automaton $\mathcal{S}$ has $O(|Q| \cdot (|Q_\alpha| + |Q_\gamma|) \cdot |T|) \cdot 2^{O(|\varphi|)}$ states and the size of its transition function is $O(\|T\|) \cdot 2^{O(|\varphi|)}$.*

Note that Theorem 6 differs from Theorem 5 only in the labeled tree whose membership is checked. Also, all the three labeled trees we use are regular, with $\|\tau_v\| = O(|V|)$, $\|\tau_\beta\| = 2^{O(|Q_\beta|)}$, and $\|\tau_{\beta,L}\| = 2^{O(|Q_\beta|+\|L\|)}$. Combining Theorems 4, 5, 6, and 3, we get the following.

Theorem 7. *The model-checking problem for a rewrite system R and an LTL formula φ is solvable*

- *in time $O(\|T\|^3) \cdot 2^{O(|\varphi|)}$ and space $O(\|T\|^2) \cdot 2^{O(|\varphi|)}$ when R is a pushdown system with simple labeling.*
- *in time $O(\|T\|^3) \cdot 2^{O(|\varphi|+|Q_\beta|)}$ and space $O(|T|^2) \cdot 2^{O(|\varphi|+|Q_\beta|)}$ when R is a prefix-recognizable system with simple labeling. The problem is EXPTIME-hard in $|Q_\beta|$ even for a fixed formula.*
- *in time $O(\|T\|^3) \cdot 2^{O(|\varphi|+|Q_\beta|+\|L\|)}$ and space $O(|T|^2) \cdot 2^{O(|\varphi|+|Q_\beta|+\|L\|)}$ when R is a prefix-recognizable system with regular labeling L.*

For pushdown systems with simple labeling (the first setting), our complexity coincides with the one in [EHRS00]. In the full version, we prove the EXPTIME lower bound in the second setting by a reduction from the membership problem of a linear space alternating Turing machine. An alternative proof is given in Theorem 2. This, together with the lower bound in [EKS01], implies EXPTIME-hardness in terms of $|Q_\beta|$ and $\|L\|$ in the the third setting. Thus, our upper bounds are tight.

References

[BCMS00]   O. Burkart, D. Caucal, F. Moller, and B. Steffen. Verification on infinite structures. Unpublished manuscript, 2000. 372

[BE96]   O. Burkart and J. Esparza. More infinite results. *Electronic Notes in TCS*, 6, 1996. 372

[BEM97]   A. Bouajjani, J. Esparza, and O. Maler. Reachability analysis of pushdown automata: Application to model-checking. In *8th Concur*, LNCS 1243, 135–150, 1997. 372, 373, 374

[BLM01]   P. Biesse, T. Leonard, and A. Mokkedem. Finding bugs in an alpha microprocessors using satisfiability solvers. In *13th CAV*, LNCS 2102, 454–464, 2001.

[BQ96]   O. Burkart and Y.-M. Quemener. Model checking of infinite graphs defined by graph grammers. In *1st Infinity*, ENTCS 6, 1996. 372

[BS92]   O. Burkart and B. Steffen. Model checking for context-free processes. In *3rd Concur*, LNCS 630, 123–137, 1992. 372

[BS95]   O. Burkart and B. Steffen. Composition, decomposition and model checking of pushdown processes. *Nordic J. Comut.*, 2:89–125, 1995. 372

[BS99]   O. Burkart and B. Steffen. Model checking the full modal μ-calculus for infinite sequential processes. *Theoretical Computer Science*, 221:251–270, 1999. 372

[Bur97a]   O. Burkart. Automatic verification of sequential infinite-state processes. LNCS 1354. 372

[Bur97b]   O. Burkart. Model checking rationally restricted right closures of recognizable graphs. In *2nd Infinity*, 1997. 372

[Cau96]   D. Caucal. On infinite transition graphs having a decidable monadic theory. In *23rd ICALP*, LNCS 1099, 194–205, 1996. 372

[CFF⁺01]   F. Copty, L. Fix, R. Fraer, E. Giunchiglia, G. Kamhi, A. Tacchella, and
            M. Y. Vardi. Benefits of bounded model checking at an industrial setting.
            In *13th CAV*, LNCS 2102, 436–453, 2001.
[CGP99]   E. M. Clarke, O. Grumberg, and D. Peled. *Model Checking*. MIT Press,
            1999. 372
[CKS81]   A. K. Chandra, D. C. Kozen, and L. J. Stockmeyer. Alternation. *J. of
            ACM*, 28(1):114–133, January 1981.
[Dam94]   M. Dam. CTL* and ECTL* as fragments of the modal μ-calculus. *TCS*,
            126:77–96. 373
[EHRS00]   J. Esparza, D. Hansel, P. Rossmanith, and S. Schwoon. Efficient algo-
            rithms for model checking pushdown systems. In *12th CAV*, LNCS 1855,
            232–247, 2000. 374, 376, 377, 383
[EJ91]   E. A. Emerson and C. Jutla. Tree automata, μ-calculus and determinacy.
            In *Proc. 32nd FOCS*, 368–377, October 1991. 372
[EKS01]   J. Esparza, A. Kucera, and S. Schwoon. Model-checking LTL with regular
            valuations for pushdown systems. In *4th STACS*, LNCS 2215, 316–339,
            2001. 374, 377, 383
[EL86]   E. A. Emerson and C.-L. Lei. Efficient model checking in fragments of
            the propositional μ-calculus. In *1st LICS*, 267–278, 1986.
[FWW97]   A. Finkel, B. Willems, and P. Wolper. A direct symbolic approach to
            model checking pushdown automata. In *2nd Infinity*, 1997. 372
[HHWT95]   T. A. Henzinger, P.-H. Ho, and H. Wong-Toi. A user guide to HYTECH.
            In *TACAS*, LNCS 1019, 41–71, 1995. 372
[KP95]   O. Kupferman and A. Pnueli. Once and for all. In *10th LICS*, 25–35,
            1995. 374
[Kur94]   R. P. Kurshan. *Computer Aided Verification of Coordinating Processes*.
            Princeton Univ. Press, 1994. 372
[KV00]   O. Kupferman and M. Y. Vardi. An automata-theoretic approach to
            reasoning about infinite-state systems. In *12th CAV*, LNCS 1855, 36–52,
            2000. 372, 373
[KV01a]   O. Kupferman and M. Y. Vardi. On clopen specifications. In *8th LPAR*,
            LNCS 2250, 24–38, 2001.
[KV01b]   O. Kupferman and M. Y. Vardi. Weak alternating automata are not that
            weak. *ACM Trans. on Computational Logic*, 2001(2):408–429, July 2001.
[KVW00]   O. Kupferman, M. Y. Vardi, and P. Wolper. An automata-theoretic ap-
            proach to branching-time model checking. *Journal of the ACM*, 47(2):312–
            360, March 2000. 372, 373, 374, 379
[LPY97]   K. G. Larsen, P. Petterson, and W. Yi. UPPAAL: Status & developments.
            In *9th CAV*, LNCS 1254, 456–459, 1997. 372
[Lyn77]   N. Lynch. Log space recognition and translation of parenthesis languages.
            Journal ACM, 24:583–590, 1977.
[MS85]   D. E. Muller and P. E. Schupp. The theory of ends, pushdown automata,
            and second-order logic. *TCS*, 37:51–75, 1985. 372
[Pit00]   N. Piterman.   Extending temporal logic with ω-automata.
            M.Sc. Thesis, The Weizmann Institute of Science, Israel, 2000.
            http://www.wisdom.weizmann.ac.il/home/nirp/public_html/
            publications/msc_thesis.ps. 379
[Pnu77]   A. Pnueli. The temporal logic of programs. In *18th FOCS*, 46–57, 1977.
            375
[PV01a]   N. Piterman and M. Vardi. From bidirectionality to alternation. In *26th
            MFCS*, LNCS 2136, 598–609, 2001. 379

[PV01b]   N. Piterman and M. Vardi. From bidirectionality to alternation. *TCS*, 2001. to appear. 379

[Var98]   M. Y. Vardi. Reasoning about the past with two-way automata. In *25th ICALP*, LNCS 1443, 628–641, 1998.

[VW94]   M. Y. Vardi and P. Wolper. Reasoning about infinite computations. *Information and Computation*, 115(1):1–37, November 1994. 372, 375

[Wal96]   I. Walukiewicz. Pushdown processes: games and modal logic. In *8th CAV*, LNCS 1102, 62–74, 1996. 372

[Wal00]   I. Walukiewicz. Model checking ctl properties of pushdown systems. In *20th FSTTCS*, LNCS 1974, 127–138, 2000. 379

[WVS83]   P. Wolper, M. Y. Vardi, and A. P. Sistla. Reasoning about infinite computation paths. In *24th FOCS*, 185–194, 1983. 372

Using Canonical Representations of Solutions to Speed Up Infinite-State Model Checking

Tatiana Rybina and Andrei Voronkov

University of Manchester
{rybina,voronkov}@cs.man.ac.uk

Abstract. In this paper we discuss reachability analysis for infinite-state systems in which states can be represented by a vector of integers. We propose a new algorithm for verifying reachability properties based on canonical representations of solutions to systems of linear inequations over integers instead of decision procedures for integer or real arithmetic. Experimental results demonstrate that problems in protocol verification which are beyond the reach of other existing systems can be solved completely automatically.

1 Introduction

Reachability properties arise is many applications of verification. In this paper we discuss reachability analysis for infinite-state systems in which state can be represented by vectors of integers. We propose a new algorithm for verifying reachability properties based on canonical representations of solutions to systems of linear inequations over integers instead of decision procedures for integer or real arithmetic. Experiments carried out with our infinite-state model checker BRAIN demonstrate that hard problems in protocol verification which are beyond the reach of other existing systems can be solved completely automatically.

This paper is organized as follows. In Section 2 we introduce our model of transition systems over integers and their symbolic representation. We define the reachability problem and a special kind of transition systems used in BRAIN,[1] called the guarded assignment systems. In Section 3 we introduce the so-called local backward reachability algorithm. In Section 4 we define the notion of basis of a constraint which is used in all main operations on constraints in BRAIN. In Section 5 we explain how, using bases, we implement all these operations, for example, entailment-checking for constraints. In Section 6 we give experimental evidence that our approach results in an efficient model-checker. In Section 7 we discuss related and future work.

The system BRAIN and all the examples of this paper can be found on the Web page www.cs.man.ac.uk/~voronkov/BRAIN/.

---

[1] BRAIN is an acronym for Backward Reachability Analysis with INtegers.

D. Brinksma and K. G. Larsen (Eds.): CAV 2002, LNCS 2404, pp. 386–400, 2002.

2   Preliminaries

We use a formal model of transition systems presented in [15]. In this model symbolic representations of transition system are formulas interpreted over a first-order structure, whose domain is the set of values for the state variables of the transition system. In this section we recall the main definitions of [15] specialized to the domain of integers and a particular first-order structure with this domain. We also define the reachability problem and guarded assignment systems used in our system BRAIN.

Denote by I the set of integers. We will formalize transition systems as follows. A transition system has a finite number of integer-valued variables. A state is a mapping from variables to integers. Transitions may change values of variables. A symbolic representation of such a system uses first-order formulas interpreted in a structure with the domain I.

We call an *integer transition system* a pair $\mathbb{S} = (\mathcal{V}, \mathcal{T})$, where $\mathcal{V}$ is a finite set of *state variables*. A *state* of the transition system $\mathbb{S}$ is a function $s : \mathcal{V} \to I$. We define the second component of transition systems as follows: $\mathcal{T}$ is a set of pairs of states, called the *transition relation* of $\mathbb{S}$. In the sequel we assume a fixed integer transition system $\mathbb{S} = (\mathcal{V}, \mathcal{T})$. We call a *transition* any set of pairs of states.

Consider the structure $\mathbb{I} = (I, >, <, \geq, \leq, +, -, 0, 1, 2, \ldots)$, where all the function and predicate symbols (for example $>$) have their standard interpretation over the integers.

A *valuation* for a set of variables V in $\mathbb{I}$ is any mapping $s : V \to I$. We will use the standard model-theoretic notation $\mathbb{I}, s \vDash A$ to denote that the formula A is true in the structure $\mathbb{I}$ under a valuation s. When we use this notation, we assume that s is defined on all free variables of A. A formula A with free variables V is said to be *satisfiable* (respectively, *valid*) in $\mathbb{I}$ if there exists a valuation s for V in $\mathbb{I}$ such that $\mathbb{I}, s \vDash A$.

A formula A is called *quantifier-free* if A contains no quantifiers. A formula A is called a *simple constraint* if A is a conjunction of atomic formulas, that is linear equations and inequations over integers.

We will often use the following simple property of $\mathbb{I}$.

Lemma 1. *In $\mathbb{I}$ every quantifier-free formula A is equivalent to a disjunction of simple constraints.*

In addition to the set of state variables $\mathcal{V}$, we also introduce a set $\mathcal{V}'$ of *next state variables* of the same cardinality as $\mathcal{V}$. We fix a bijection $' : \mathcal{V} \to \mathcal{V}'$ such that for all $v \in \mathcal{V}$ we have $v' \in \mathcal{V}'$. We can treat the variables in $\mathcal{V} \cup \mathcal{V}'$ also as logical variables. Then any mapping $s : \mathcal{V} \to I$ can be considered as both a state of the transition system $\mathbb{S}$ and a valuation for $\mathcal{V}$, and similarly for $s' : \mathcal{V}' \to I$.

Let S be a set of states and A be a formula with free variables in $\mathcal{V}$. We say that A *symbolically represents*, or simply *represents* S if for every valuation s for $\mathcal{V}$ we have $s \in S \Leftrightarrow \mathbb{I}, s \vDash A$. Likewise, we say that a formula B with free variables in $\mathcal{V} \cup \mathcal{V}'$ (symbolically) represents a transition T if for every pair of valuations (s, s') for $\mathcal{V}$ and $\mathcal{V}'$ respectively we have $(s, s') \in T \Leftrightarrow \mathbb{I}, s, s' \vDash B$.

$$drinks > 0$$
$$\land \; customers > 0 \Rightarrow drinks \; := \; drinks - 1 \qquad (* \; \texttt{dispense-drink} \; *)$$
$$true \Rightarrow drinks \; := \; drinks + 64 \qquad (* \; \texttt{recharge} \; *)$$
$$true \Rightarrow customers \; := \; customers + 1 \; (* \; \texttt{customer-coming} \; *)$$
$$customers > 0 \Rightarrow customers \; := \; customers - 1 \; (* \; \texttt{customer-going} \; *)$$

Fig. 1. Guarded assignment system

In the sequel we will follow the following convention. We will often identify a symbolic representation of a transition with the transition itself. For example, when T is a formula with free variables in $\mathcal{V} \cup \mathcal{V}'$ we can refer to T as a transition.

Let us introduce an important special case of transition systems, called the *guarded assignment systems*. The current version of BRAIN works with quantifier-free guarded assignment systems. To define guarded assignment systems, let us first introduce a syntax sugar for representing transitions. We assume that the set of state variables of the transition system is $\mathcal{V}$.

We call a *guarded assignment* any formula (or transition) of the form

$$P \land v_1' = t_1 \land \ldots \land v_n' = t_n \land \bigwedge_{v \in \mathcal{V} - \{v_1, \ldots, v_n\}} v' = v,$$

where P is a formula with free variables $\mathcal{V}$, $\{v_1, \ldots, v_n\} \subseteq \mathcal{V}$, and $t_1, \ldots, t_n$ are terms with variables in $\mathcal{V}$. We will write guarded assignments as

$$P \; \Rightarrow \; v_1 \; := \; t_1, \ldots, v_n \; := \; t_n. \qquad (1)$$

The formula P is called the *guard* of this guarded assignment.

A guarded assignment is *quantifier-free* if so is its guard. A guarded assignment is called *simple* if its guard is a simple constraint.

Formula (1) represents a transition which applies to the states satisfying P and changes the values of variables v_i to the values of the terms t_i before the transition. Note that a guarded assignment T is a deterministic transition: for every state s there exists at most one state s' such that $(s, s') \in T$. Moreover, such a state s' exists if and only if the guard of this guarded assignment is true at s, i.e., $\mathbb{I}, s \vDash P$.

A transition system is called a *guarded assignment system*, or simply *GAS* if its transition relation is a union of a finite number of guarded assignments. A GAS is called *quantifier-free* (respectively *simple*) if every guarded assignment in it is also quantifier-free (respectively *simple*). An example integer guarded assignment system for modelling a drink dispenser is given in Figure 1. This GAS is simple.

Note that a guarded assignment system may represent a non-deterministic transition system because several guards may be true in the same state.

Theorem 1. *One can effectively transform every quantifier-free guarded assignment over* $\mathbb{I}$ *into an equivalent union of simple guarded assignments. Hence, every integer quantifier-free GAS is also a simple GAS.* $\Box$

The notion of a guarded assignment system is not very restrictive. Indeed, broadcast protocols of Esparza, Finkel, and Mayr [ ] and Petri nets can be represented as integer simple guarded assignment systems. All transition systems for cache coherence protocols described in Delzanno [ ] are integer simple GAS. Not every transition system is a GAS. Indeed, every GAS has the following property: for every state s there exists a finite number of states s' such that $(s, s') \in \mathcal{T}$. Evidently, there are systems which do not satisfy this property.

We say that a state s_n is *reachable* from a state s_0 w.r.t. a transition T if there exists a sequence of states $s_1, \ldots, s_{n-1}$ such that for all $i \in \{0, \ldots, n-1\}$ we have $(s_i, s_{i+1}) \in T$. In this case we also say that s_n is reachable from s_0 *in n steps* and that s_0 is *backward reachable* from s_n in n steps. When T is clear from the context (for example, when T is the transition relation $\mathcal{T}$ of a transition system) we will simply write "reachable".

The reachability problem can now be defined as follows. We call the (integer) *reachability problem* the following decision problem. Given formulas *In*, *Fin*, and *Tr* such that (i) *In* represents a set of states, called the set of *initial states*; (ii) *Fin* represents a set of states, called the set of *final states*; and (iii) *Tr* represents the transition relation of a transition system $\mathbb{S}$, do there exist an initial state s_1 and a final state s_2 such that s_2 is reachable from s_1 w.r.t. *Tr*?

When we discuss instances of the reachability problem, we will call the formulas *In* and *Fin* the *initial* and *final conditions*, respectively, and *Tr* the *transition formula*.

The integer reachability problem for infinite-state systems is, in general, undecidable, even for simple GAS with three variables (because such GAS can easily represent two-counter machines, see, e.g., [ ]). Various results on reachability are discussed in many papers, including Esparza, Finkel, and Mayr [ ], Abdulla et.al. [ ], Kupferman and Vardi [ ].

3   Local Backward Reachability Algorithm

There are various (semi-decision) procedures for checking reachability. For example, a classification of reachability algorithms is undertaken in [ ]. The current version of BRAIN uses an algorithm called the *local backward reachability algorithm*. The algorithm is called local because it is based on a local entailment test rather than a global one. For a discussion of local algorithms see [,].

Before defining these algorithms, let us discuss symbolic representations of reachable states. We assume fixed initial and final conditions $In(\mathcal{V})$, $Fin(\mathcal{V})$ and the transition formula $Tr(\mathcal{V}, \mathcal{V}')$.

Let $A(\mathcal{V})$ be a formula which represents a set of states S. It is not hard to argue that the set of states reachable in one step from a state in S can be represented by the formula $\exists \mathcal{V}_1(A(\mathcal{V}_1) \wedge Tr(\mathcal{V}_1, \mathcal{V}))$.

Likewise, the set of states backward reachable in one step from a state in S is represented by the formula $\exists \mathcal{V}_1(A(\mathcal{V}_1) \wedge Tr(\mathcal{V}, \mathcal{V}_1))$. The last formula can be considerably simplified when the transition Tr is a guarded assignment. Let u be a guarded assignment of the form $P(v_1, \ldots, v_n) \Rightarrow v_1 := t_1, \ldots, v_n := t_n$. For simplicity we assume that $\mathcal{V} = \{v_1, \ldots, v_n\}$. This can be achieved by adding "dummy" assignments $v := v$ for every variable $v \in \mathcal{V} - \{v_1, \ldots, v_n\}$. Let also $A(v_1, \ldots, v_n)$ be a formula whose free variables are in $\mathcal{V}$. For every term t denote by t' the term obtained from t by replacing every occurrence of every state variable v_i by v_i'.

Define the following formulas:

$$A^u(v_1, \ldots, v_n) \stackrel{\text{def}}{=} \exists \mathcal{V}'(A(v_1', \ldots, v_n') \wedge P(v_1', \ldots, v_n') \wedge v_1 = t_1' \wedge \ldots \wedge v_n = t_n');$$
$$A^{-u}(v_1, \ldots, v_n) \stackrel{\text{def}}{=} P(v_1, \ldots, v_n) \wedge A(t_1, \ldots, t_n).$$

Lemma 2. *Let a formula* $A(v_1, \ldots, v_n)$ *represent a set of states* S. *Then (i) the formula* $A^u(v_1, \ldots, v_n)$ *represents the set of states reachable in one step from* S *using* u; *(ii) the formula* $A^{-u}(v_1, \ldots, v_n)$ *represents the set of states backward reachable in one step from* S *using* u. $\square$

These formulas explain the choice of backward reachability in BRAIN: the formula A^{-u} contains only quantifiers which are already contained in $P(v_1, \ldots, v_n)$ and $A(v_1, \ldots, v_n)$. In particular, if $P(v_1, \ldots, v_n)$ and $A(v_1, \ldots, v_n)$ are simple constraints then A^{-u} is a simple constraint too.

The *local backward reachability algorithm* LocalBackward is given in Figure 2. It is parametrized by a function select which selects a simple constraint in a set of simple constraints. The function $\mathrm{pdnf}(A)$ returns a set S of simple constraints such that A is equivalent to $\bigvee_{C \in S} C$ in $\mathbb{I}$. To apply this algorithm to a quantifier-free GAS, we first transform it to a simple GAS using Theorem 1.

Theorem 2 (Soundness and Semi-completeness). LocalBackward *has the following properties:*

1. *there is a final state reachable from an initial state if and only if the algorithm returns "reachable";*
2. *if the algorithm returns "unreachable", then there is no final state reachable from an initial state.* $\square$

On some inputs the algorithm does not terminate.

Note that termination of the local algorithms may depend on a the selection function select. Let us call the selection function *fair* if no formula remains in *unused* forever.

Theorem 3. *If the local forward (respectively backward) algorithm terminates for some selection function, then it terminates for every fair selection function.*

To implement the LocalBackward one has to implement procedures for the following problems:

procedure LocalBackward
input: quantifier-free formulas In, Fin,
          finite set of simple guarded assignments U
output: "reachable" or "unreachable"
begin
  IS := pdnf(In); FS := pdnf(Fin)
  if there exist $I \in IS, F \in FS$ such that $\mathbb{I} \vDash \exists \mathcal{V}(I \wedge F)$ **then** **return** "reachable"
  $unused$:= FS; $used$:= $\emptyset$
  while $unused \neq \emptyset$
    S := select($unused$)
    $used$:= $used \cup \{S\}$; $unused$:= $unused - \{S\}$
    forall $u \in U$
      (* backward application of u *)
      N := S^{-u}
      (* satisfiability-check for the new constraint N *)
      if $\mathbb{I} \vDash \exists \mathcal{V}(N)$ **then**
        (* intersection-checks *)
        if there exists $I \in IS$ such that $\mathbb{I} \vDash \exists \mathcal{V}(N \wedge I)$ **then** **return** "reachable"
        (* entailment-checks *)
        if for all $C \in used \cup unused$ we have $\mathbb{I} \nvDash \forall \mathcal{V}(N \to C)$ **then**
          $unused = unused \cup \{N\}$
          forall $C' \in used \cup unused$
            (* more entailment-checks *)
            if $\mathbb{I} \vDash \forall \mathcal{V}(C' \to N)$ **then** remove C' from $used$ or $unused$
  return "unreachable"
end

Fig. 2. Local backward reachability algorithm used in BRAIN

1. *Backward application of guarded assignments*: given a simple constraint S and guarded assignment u, compute S^{-u}.
2. *Satisfiability of simple constraints*: given a simple constraint C, is C satisfiable in $\mathbb{I}$?
3. *Entailment of simple constraints:* given simple constraints N and C, is the formula $N \to C$ valid in $\mathbb{I}$?

To implement the reachability algorithm efficiently, one has to implement efficiently these three procedures. As our experimental data show, for hard problems the number of entailment-checks is considerably larger than the number of transition applications and satisfiability-checks. Therefore, entailment-checking should be implemented especially efficiently.

A simple constraint over $\mathbb{I}$ can be considered as a system of linear equations and inequations over integers with variables in $\mathcal{V}$. Since ever equation $u\mathcal{V} + l = 0$ can be equivalently replaced by two inequations $u\mathcal{V} + l \leq 0$ and $-u\mathcal{V} - l \leq 0$, in the sequel we will only discuss inequations. Satisfiability of simple constraints is known to be NP-complete and entailment coNP-complete. If one uses relaxation (see Delzanno [7] or [15]) to use real numbers instead of integers, then both problems can be solved in polynomial time.

4   Hilbert's Basis

In this section we present some properties of the set of non-negative solutions to a simple constraint. Proofs can be found in, e.g., Schrijver [16]. In this section we consider $\mathcal{V}$ as a vector of variables rather than a set and restrict ourselves to simple constraints with the variables $\mathcal{V}$. Denote by $\mathbf{0}$ a vector of 0's. Every simple constraint C with variables in $\mathcal{V}$ can be written as a system of linear inequations with integer coefficients:

$$L\mathcal{V} + l \leq \mathbf{0}. \tag{2}$$

where L is a matrix with integer coefficients and l is a integer vector. We call a *solution* to such a system any vector V of non-negative integers which satisfies all inequations in the system. Let us emphasize that in this section we will only consider non-negative solutions. We will show below in Section 5 how to treat arbitrary integer solutions. For every system C of the form (2) denote by C^{hom} the corresponding system of homogeneous linear Diophantine inequations

$$L\mathcal{V} \leq \mathbf{0}. \tag{3}$$

We call a solution v to (2) *non-decomposable* if it cannot be represented in the form $v_1 + v_2$, where v_1 is a solution to (2) and v_2 is a non-zero solution to (3). Likewise, we call a solution to (3) non-decomposable if and only if it cannot be represented as a sum of two non-zero solutions to (3).

A pair of sets of vectors (N, H) is called a *basis* for a simple constraint C if the following conditions hold.

1. Every vector in N is a non-decomposable solution to C.
2. Every vector in H is a non-zero non-decomposable solution to C^{hom}.
3. Every solution v to C can be represented as a sum $v = w + \sum_{i=1...k} m_i w_i$, where $w \in N$, $k \geq 0$ and for all $i = 1...k$ m_i is a non-negative integer and $w_i \in H$.
4. Every solution v to C^{hom} can be represented as a sum $v = \sum_{i=1...k} m_i w_i$, where $k \geq 0$ and for all $i = 1...k$ m_i is a non-negative integer and $w_i \in H$. $\square$

This definition is a modification of the standard definition of Hilbert's basis [12] for the case of systems of linear inequations.

Theorem 4. *Every simple constraint has a basis, and this basis is unique.*

Algorithms for finding the basis of systems of linear Diophantine inequations are described in, e.g., Contejean and Devie [6], Ajili and Contejean [2], and Tomas and Filgueiras [17]. BRAIN uses a novel algorithm [18]. This algorithm, as well as other algorithms for funding Hilbert's basis, is too complex to be described here. In general, it is more difficult to find the basis of a simple constraint than to check its solvability.[2] The solvability problem is NP-complete, but the number of vectors in the basis can be exponential in the size of the system. Nevertheless, we will show that the construction of the basis may speed up reachability-checking.

BRAIN uses an *incremental algorithm* for building the basis. We call an *incremental basis-finding function* any function ibff of two arguments, such that for every pair of simple constraints (C_1, C_2), if B is the basis for C_1, then $\text{ibff}(B, C_2)$ is the basis of $C_1 \wedge C_2$. Essentially, an incremental basis-funding function uses a basis computed previously for C_1 to find a basis for $C_1 \wedge C_2$.

5   BRAIN

In this section we explain how BRAIN implements the three important procedures used in the local backward reachability algorithm: backward application of guarded assignments, satisfiability and entailment. All three algorithms are implemented using repeated calls to an incremental basis-finding function ibff. In order to use the basis incrementally, BRAIN stores the basis together with every computed simple constraint. This technique is similar to a technique used by Halbwachs, Proy, and Roumanoff [10] for real-valued systems. We assume that all variables range over non-negative integers and show how to handle arbitrary integers later. We call an *augmented constraint* a pair (C, B) consisting of a simple constraint C and its basis B.

Entailment-checking. The algorithm for entailment-checking in BRAIN is based on the following theorem.

Theorem 5. *Let $(C_1, (N_1, H_1))$ be an augmented constraint and C_2 be a simple constraint. Then $\mathbb{I} \models \forall \mathcal{V}(C_1 \to C_2)$ if and only if the following two conditions hold: (i) every vector $v \in N_1$ is a solution to C_2; (ii) every vector $w \in H_1$ is a solution to C_2^{hom}.*   □

This theorem gives us an algorithm for entailment-checking: to check the entailment problem for augmented constraints, one has to check that the vectors of the basis of C_1 are solutions to C_2 or to the corresponding homogeneous system C_2^{hom}. Checking that a particular vector is a solution to a system can obviously be solved in time polynomial in the size of the vector and the system. As a consequence, we obtain the following theorem.

Theorem 6. *Entailment of augmented constraints can be solved in polynomial time.*   □

---

[2]   Strangely enough, our experiments have shown that the existing algorithms for building the basis often outperform some well-known algorithms for checking solvability taken from integer programming packages. This could probably be explained by the fact that these packages are mostly intended for optimization and do not cope well with systems having several unbounded variables.

The algorithm implicit in Theorem 5 is used in BRAIN to check the entailment. To check entailment in polynomial time one can use instead of the basis any pair of sets of vectors (N, H) satisfying conditions (3) and (4) of the definition of basis, that is non-decomposability is not necessary. However, it is easy to prove that every pair of vectors (N, H) with these properties contains the basis, and thus using only non-decomposable vectors saves both space and time.

Satisfiability-checking. Evidently, a simple constraint C is satisfiable if for its basis (N, H) we have $N \neq \emptyset$. So satisfiability-checking for augmented constraints is trivial. Note that the reachability algorithm makes two kinds of satisfiability-checks:

1. checking whether the new formula N (i.e., S^{-u}) is satisfiable;
2. *intersection-checks*, when we check satisfiability of the formula $N \wedge I$.

The latter kind of satisfiability-checking can be performed by any satisfiability-checking procedure. But the first kind of satisfiability checks in BRAIN is combined with the backward applications of transitions for the reasons mentioned below.

Backward application of transitions. Repeated backward applications of transitions in the reachability algorithm may create too large constraints. To explain this, let us consider the formula for computing the set of states backward reachable from the set states presented by a simple constraint $C_1(v_1, \ldots, v_n)$. If the guarded assignment u has the form $C_2 \Rightarrow v_1 := t_1, \ldots, v_n := t_n$, then by Lemma 2 the formula C_1^{-u} is $C_2 \wedge C_1(t_1, \ldots, t_n)$. The number of atomic formulas in this simple constraint is the number of atomic formulas in C_1 plus the number of atomic formulas in C_2. Every iteration of the reachability algorithm yields longer constraints in which, for hard examples described below in Section 6, the number of atoms may be over a hundred. It is often the case that a large number of these atoms are a consequence of the remaining atoms in the constraint and can be safely removed (in our hardest examples the number of non-redundant atoms usually does not exceed ten). Redundant atoms in constraints do not change the basis, but they slow down entailment, since our algorithm for checking validity of $(C_1 \rightarrow C_2)$ is, roughly speaking, linear in the number of atoms in C_2.

We can get rid of redundant constraints in $C_2 \wedge C_1(t_1, \ldots, t_n)$ together with checking satisfiability of this constraint and building a basis for it using an incremental basis-finding function. The procedure for this is given in Figure 3. The input to this procedure is the sequence of atoms in $C_2 \wedge C_1(t_1, \ldots, t_n)$ in any order. When a new atom A_i should be added to the constraint, it is first checked whether the addition of this atom changes the basis. If it does not, then the atom is redundant.

The current version of BRAIN only works with variables ranging over nonnegative integers. Integers can be implemented using the same technology as follows. If an integer-valued variable is restricted by $v \leq n$ (or respectively by $n \leq v$), then it can be replaced by a variable $w = n - v$ (or respectively by $w =$

```
procedure Basis
input: sequence of atoms A₁, ..., Aₙ,
output: pair (C, B), where C is equivalent to A₁ ∧ ... ∧ Aₙ,
                      and B is the basis for A₁ ∧ ... ∧ Aₙ
begin
  C := true; B := the basis of C
  for i = 1 ... n
    B' = ibff(B, Aᵢ)
    if B' contains no solution then return (false, B')
    if B' ≠ B then(C, B) := (C ∧ Aᵢ, B')
  return (C, B)
end
```

Fig. 3. Incremental building of the basis

$v - n$) ranging over non-negative integers. For every unrestricted integer-valued variable v one can introduce two variables w_1, w_2 ranging over non-negative integers and replace all occurrences of v by $w_1 - w_2$.

6 Experiments

In this section we present the results of experiments carried out on a number of benchmarks taken from several Web pages. The examples can be found on the Web page www.cs.man.ac.uk/~voronkov/BRAIN/. We compare the performance of our system BRAIN with that of the following systems: HyTech (Henzinger, Ho, and Wong-Toi [11]), Action Language Verifier (Bultan [4]), and DMC (Delzanno and Podelski [8]).

All benchmarks were carried out on the same computers (Sparc 300 with 2G of RAM memory). These computers are slow (about 8–10 times slower than the modern PCs), but we did not have access to a network of PCs with large RAM. The systems HyTech, Action Language, and BRAIN are implemented in C++ or C, and were compiled using the same version 2.92 of the GNU C/C++ compiler. DMC is implemented in Sicstus Prolog. In several cases we had to interrupt the systems because they consumed over 2G of memory. DMC never consumed more than 14M of memory, but was interrupted after several weeks of running. We were interested in hard benchmarks, but occasionally, for the sake of comparison, included figures for relatively easy benchmarks, because only HyTech and BRAIN could solve some of the hard ones. All runtimes are given in seconds.

Note that HyTech and DMC use relaxation, i.e., they solve real reachability problems instead of integer reachability problems. Therefore, they are correct only when they report non-reachability. Among the systems compared with BRAIN only Action Language Verifier checks for integer reachability.

We took most of the benchmarks presented in this paper from Giorgio Delzanno's Web page www.disi.unige.it/person/DelzannoG/. The problems specified in these benchmarks were used to verify cache coherence protocols, properties of Java programs, and some other applications. The results are presented in Table 1 For each we present the runtimes and memory consumption (in megabytes). We write − when the compared system could not solve the problem because of the time or memory limit.

The table shows that BRAIN is normally faster than HyTech, and sometimes considerably faster. It also consumes less memory than HyTech. There are three problems (with the suffix -inv in the name) on which HyTech was faster (denoted by negative numbers in the speedup column). We will comment on these problems below. Considering that HyTech's implementation uses a polyhedra library based on [10] we cannot explain a considerable difference in the memory consumption between BRAIN and HyTech.

For non-trivial problems BRAIN is normally several hundred times faster than DMC, except for problems with invariants, where the difference is not so high. On non-trivial problems BRAIN without invariants is also normally at least 500 times faster than Action Language Verifier, on problems with invariants the difference is not so high. BRAIN also uses less memory than Action Language Verifier.

The problems with invariants were obtained from the original problems by adding *invariants*: some simple properties obtained by forward reachability analysis. A typical invariant has the form $v_1 + \ldots + v_k = m$, where m is a natural number. In fact, it bounds the variables $v_1, \ldots, v_k$ to a finite region. Such invariants cause a problem to BRAIN, because the basis for problems with such an invariant usually contains all, or a large portion, of the points in this region explicitly. We believe that this problem is not essential for the approach, but is rather particular to the current implementation of BRAIN in which the basis is stored explicitly, point-wise. A symbolic representation of this finite region, or the use of suitable datastructures for presenting finite-domain variables should solve this problem.

There are several problems which could only be solved by BRAIN, but not by any of the other systems. However, we would like to note that all of these systems are on some benchmarks more powerful than BRAIN since they can use techniques such as widening or transitive closure which the current version of BRAIN does not have. Examples are some versions of the ticket protocol.

To give the reader an idea of the complexity of the problems solved by BRAIN, we present statistics about the number of operations such an entailment-checks performed by BRAIN during each run. This statistics shows why DMC is hopelessly slow on some of these problems: for example, in the case of csm15 one can hardly check almost 10^9 entailment problems in reasonable time using general-purpose constraint-solving tools. BRAIN solves them in less than 2 hours (on a fast PC with Intel this time would be less than 15 minutes). The table shows that, for most of the benchmarks, entailment seems to be the most important operation. It also demonstrates slowdown of BRAIN on the problems with in-

problem	variables	intersections	entailment operations	transitions	3RAIN time	3RAIN memory	HyTech time	HyTech memory	HyTech speedup	ALV time	ALV memory	ALV speedup	DMC time	DMC memory	DMC speedup
csm5	13	3,313	790,119	3,576	9.26s	2	40.32s	18	4.35	87m32s	297	567	13h15m	11	5165
csm10	13	27,308	60,803,697	29,736	457s	11	868s	140	1.9	—	—	—	—	—	—
csm15	13	107,503	990,874,884	117,496	119m13s	60	154m32s	509	1.3	—	—	—	—	—	—
csm5-inv	13	106	835	152	0.37s	1	0.96s	2	2.6	2.87s	28	7.77	3.2s	10	8.6
csm10-inv	13	106	835	152	0.89s	1	0.96s	2	1.07	2.87s	28	3.22	3.2s	10	3.59
csm15-inv	13	106	835	152	1.88s	1	0.96s	2	-1.95	2.87s	28	1.52	3.2s	10	1.7
consistencyprot	12	813	30,557	880	0.96s	1	17.66s	10	18.4	17.66s	10	18.4	888s	10	925
consistencyprot-inv	12	813	29,803	880	7.25s	1	0.13s	2	-55	164.8s	73	22.7	19m52s	11	164.4
consprod	18	162,817	698,478,060	181,650	175m31s	22	—	—	—	—	—	—	—	—	—
consprod-inv	18	187	5,126	742	1.19s	1	1.2s	4	1.01	25.87s	68	21.7	4.9s	10	4.12
incdec	32	41,971	12,762,257	42,252	170.3s	10	—	—	—	—	—	—	—	—	—
incdec-inv	32	873	54,824	4,004	22.9s	1	120.9s	80	5.3	10h20m	846	1625	96.3s	10	4.2
bigjava	44	122,516	93,410,447	134,828	171m31s	25	—	—	—	—	—	—	—	—	—
bigjava1	44	127,185	95,800,396	139,688	189m16s	25	—	—	—	—	—	—	—	—	—
bigjava-inv	44	7,581	3,378,979	45,103	40m2s	11	32m5s	849	-1.25	—	—	—	—	—	—
bigjava1-inv	44	49,531	48,384,856	104,538	744m14s	19	—	—	—	—	—	—	—	—	—

Table 1. Statistics

variants: indeed the number of operations per second in these problems is much smaller than that for their original formulations without the invariants.

7   Related and Future Work

In this section we briefly overview related work on systems for infinite-state model checking and algorithms. We do not overview numerous papers related to reachability analysis.

Our technique of using Hilbert's basis is similar to a technique used to deal with real-valued systems described in Halbwachs, Proy and Roumanoff [10]. They represent convex polyhedra using *systems of generators*, i.e., two finite sets of vectors (called *vertices* and *rays*). This representation allows one to perform efficient entailment checks using a property similar to that of Theorem 5.

One can implement satisfiability- and entailment-checking using the decision procedure for the first order theory of $\mathbb{I}$. In some cases, one can even use off-the-shelf decision procedures or libraries. For example, Bultan, Gerber, and Pugh [5] use the Omega Library [14] for deciding Presburger arithmetic, Bultan [4] uses the Composite Library (Yavuz-Kahveci, Tuncer and Bultan [19]), Delzanno and Podelski [8] use the CLP(R) library of Sicstus Prolog. The use of decision procedures for Presburger arithmetic has several advantages, since formulas more general than simple constraints can be handled. As a consequence, one can use non-local reachability algorithms (see [15]), forward reachability, and apply techniques such as widening and transitive closure which cannot be handled by the current version of BRAIN. However, the use of general-purpose algorithms to decide specific classes of formulas may be inefficient, which is confirmed by our experiments.

Berard and Fribourg [3] report that HyTech shows better performance on Petri nets than integer-based systems. Moreover, they prove that for Petri nets using relaxation is exact. As we have shown, BRAIN is usually faster than HyTech on integer problems, even without the use of relaxation.

In the future we are going to develop BRAIN into an advanced infinite-state model-checker based on the implementation method proposed here, which will be both faster and more flexible. In particular, we will include in BRAIN other reachability algorithms and techniques such as widening. This will, however, require an implementation of quantifier elimination and an extension of our method, and especially Theorem 5, to constraints with existentially quantified variables and divisibility constraints.

To cope with the problem of large finite regions, one has to introduce their convenient symbolic representation, which may require reworking of all algorithms. It would also be interesting to apply our method to real-valued systems, or systems with both integer- and real-valued variables.

References

1. P. A. Abdulla, K. Cerans, B. Jonsson, and Y.-K. Tsay. Algorithmic analysis of programs with well quasi-ordered domains. *Information and Computation*, 160(1-2):109–127, January 2000. 389
2. F. Ajili and E. Contejean. Avoiding slack variables in the solving of linear Diophantine equations and inequations. *Theoretical Computer Science*, 173(1):183–208, 1997. 392
3. B. Bérard and L. Fribourg. Reachability analysis of (timed) Petri nets using real arithmetic. In J. C. M. Baeten and S. Mauw, editors, *CONCUR'99: Concurrency Theory, 10th International Conference*, volume 1664 of *Lecture Notes in Computer Science*, pages 178–193. Springer Verlag, 1999. 398
4. T. Bultan. Action Language: a specification language for model checking reactive systems. In *ICSE 2000, Proceedings of the 22nd International Conference on Software Engineering*, pages 335–344, Limerick, Ireland, 2000. ACM. 395, 398
5. T. Bultan, R. Gerber, and W. Pugh. Model-checking concurrent systems with unbounded integer variables: symbolic representations, approximations, and experimental results. *ACM Transactions on Programming Languages and Systems*, 21(4):747–789, 1999. 398
6. E. Contejean and H. Devie. An efficient incremental algorithm for solving of systems of linear diophantine equations. *Information and Computation*, 113(1):143–172, 1994. 392
7. G. Delzanno. Automatic verification of parametrized cache coherence protocols. In A. E. Emerson and A. P. Sistla, editors, *Computer Aided Verification, 12th International Conference, CAV 2000*, volume 1855 of *Lecture Notes in Computer Science*, pages 53–68. Springer Verlag, 2000. 389, 392
8. G. Delzanno and A. Podelski. Constraint-based deductive model checking. *International Journal on Software Tools for Technology Transfer*, 3(3):250–270, 2001. 389, 395, 398
9. J. Esparza, A. Finkel, and R. Mayr. On the verification of broadcast protocols. In *14th Annual IEEE Symposium on Logic in Computer Science (LICS'99)*, pages 352–359, Trento, Italy, 1999. IEEE Computer Society. 389
10. N. Halbwachs, Y.-E. Proy, and P. Roumanoff. Verification of real-time systems using linear relation analysis. *Formal Methods in System Design*, 11(2):157–185, 1997. 393, 396, 398
11. T. A. Henzinger, P.-H. Ho, and H. Wong-Toi. Hy-tech: a model checker for hybrid systems. *International Journal on Software Tools for Technology Transfer*, 1(1-2):110–122, 1997. 395
12. D. Hilbert. Über die Theorie der algebraischen Formen. *Mathematische Annalen*, 36:473–534, 1890. 392
13. O. Kupferman and M. Vardi. Model checking of safety properties. *Formal Methods in System Design*, 19(3):291–314, 2001. 389
14. W. Pugh. Counting solutions to Presburger formulas: how and why. *ACM SIGPLAN Notices*, 29(6):121–134, June 1994. Proceedings of the ACM SIGPLAN'94 Conference on Programming Languages Design and Implementation (PLDI). 398
15. T. Rybina and A. Voronkov. A logical reconstruction of reachability. submitted, 2002. 387, 389, 392, 398
16. A. Schrijver. *Theory of Linear and Integer Programming*. John Wiley and Sons, 1998. 392

17. A. P. Tomás and M. Filgueiras. An algorithm for solving systems of linear diophantine equations in naturals. In E. Costa and A. Cardoso, editors, *Progress in Artificial Intelligence, 8th Portugese Conference on Artificial Intelligence, EPIA'97*, volume 1323 of *Lecture Notes in Artificial Intelligence*, pages 73–84, Coimbra, Portugal, 1997. Springer Verlag. 392
18. A. Voronkov. An incremental algorithm for finding the basis of solutions to systems of linear Diophantine equations and inequations. unpublished, January 2002. 392
19. T. Yavuz-Kahveci, M. Tuncer, and T. Bultan. A library for composite symbolic representations. In T. Margaria, editor, *Tools and Algorithms for Construction and Analysis of Systems, 7th International Conference, TACAS 2001*, volume 1384 of *Lecture Notes in Computer Science*, pages 52–66, Genova, Italy, 2001. Springer Verlag. 398

On Discrete Modeling and Model Checking
for Nonlinear Analog Systems

Walter Hartong, Lars Hedrich, and Erich Barke

Institute of Microelectronic Circuits and Systems, University of Hannover
Appelstrasse 4, 30167 Hannover, Germany
{hartong,hedrich,barke}@ims.uni-hannover.de
http://www.ims.uni-hannover.de

Abstract. In this contribution we present a new method for developing discrete models for nonlinear analog systems. Using an adaptive state space intersection method the main nonlinear properties of the analog system can be retained. Consequently, digital model checking ideas can be applied to analog systems. To describe analog specification properties an extension to the standard model checking language CTL and the appropriate, algorithmic modifications are needed. Two nonlinear examples are given to show the feasibility and the advantages of this method.

1 Introduction

Formal verification for digital systems has a relatively long academic tradition. However, only a few years ago the capability of these tools has been raised to real world circuit sizes. Today, there are several commercial formal verification tools available and formal verification is used in many different disciplines.

There are also some tools which have been extended from digital to hybrid systems, i.e. to digital systems connected to some analog blocks or to an analog environment [1]. For some system classes these tools are quite successful, but they remain focused on the digital part of the system. The analog behavior is mostly restricted and the verification results are not appropriate to assess the functionality of the analog part. Furthermore, model checking languages used are not able to describe analog system properties.

One important paper to be named in this context is written by R. P. Kurshan and K. L. McMillan [2]. It is focused on digital system behavior but the circuit model used is based on transistors. Using a uniform state space intersection a discrete model is developed. The transition between state space regions is generated by following trajectories in the state space. We will see that these basic ideas are quite similar to the algorithms described in this contribution. Differences of these two approaches will be discussed later in more detail. Beyond that, the reachability analysis for nonlinear differential equations has been described in [3,4]. As far as we know, there is only one approach on equivalence checking for nonlinear analog systems [5].

D. Brinksma and K. G. Larsen (Eds.): CAV 2002, LNCS 2404, pp. 401–414, 2002.

This contribution presents a new model checking environment and a CTL extension which enables the work on pure nonlinear analog systems. The following chapter defines analog systems used in this context. The next part presents a discrete model for an analog system. Finally, a CTL extension is developed and the resulting changes in the model checking algorithms taken from well known digital tools are described. At the end, some experimental results are presented using small nonlinear examples.

2   System Description

The systems we will consider in this context are analog systems on the one hand and transition systems - as used in actual model checking tools - on the other hand. As we will see, an analog system is a transition system but the infinite number of states and the continuously defined state transition make these systems hardly accessible in an automatic way.

2.1   Analog Systems

The standard way to describe an analog system is a set of nonlinear first order differential algebraic equations

$$f(\dot{x}(t), x(t), u(t)) = 0 \tag{1}$$

where $x(t)$ is the vector of system variables and $u(t)$ denotes the vector of input variables. In general, the function $f(\cdot)$ is arbitrarily nonlinear. However, in practice the nonlinearities are restricted by the device models used. There are several ways to build such equations for example from a transistor netlist or a behavioral model. The most common method is the modified nodal analysis (MNA). The set of state variables in an analog system is given by Equation (2).

$$x_s = \{x \mid \dot{x} \in f(\dot{x}(t), x(t), u(t))\} \tag{2}$$

The coding of state variables spanning the state space depends on the way to build up Equation (1). It is not unique for one system [6]. Moreover, some state variables might be linearly dependent, so that the effective number of state variables may be smaller than the size of the set given in Equation (2). However, the number of independent state variables n is constant for a given system.

The link between state variables and system variables is not necessarily obvious like in the ODE case where $\dot{x}(t) = f(x(t), u(t))$. Mathematically, it is described by the system's differential index [7]. The initial value problem for differential algebraic equations can relatively easily be solved for systems of index 0 and 1. There are some approaches in solving systems with higher index, however this topic is still under research. Since we focus on basic model checking methods, this issue will not be discussed here. We assume the equation systems to be of index 0 or 1 with n linearly independent state variables. The state space spanned by the state variables $x_s \in \mathcal{R}^n$ is a continuous infinite Euclidean space.

2.2 Transition Systems

Digital and hybrid model checking tools are often based on transition systems.

Definition 1. *A state transition system* $T = (Q, Q_0, \sum, R)$ *consists of*
 - *a set of states* Q,
 - *a set of initial states* Q_0,
 - *a set of generators or events* $\sum$ *and*
 - *a state transition relation* $R \subseteq Q \times \sum \times Q$.

In fact, the analog system given above is also a state transition system. The set of states Q can be represented by the continuous state space $\mathcal{R}^n$. The number of states $x \in Q$ is always infinity, due to the continuous definition of the state variables. The initial state Q_0 is a single point or a region in the state space. Often, but not necessarily, this is the DC operating point. There are only $i + 1$ generators $\sum$ causing state transitions, namely, the time t and the i input values $u(t)$. The state transition relation $R \subseteq (\mathcal{R}^n \times \mathcal{R}^{i+1} \times \mathcal{R}^n)$ is a continuous function given by the time derivation $\dot{x}(t)$ in Equation (1). The actual state transition can be calculated by integrating this function.

$$g(x(t_0), u(t), \delta t) = x(t_0) + \int_{t_0}^{t_0 + \delta t} \left\{ \dot{x}(t) \,\middle|\, f\left(\dot{x}(t), x(t), u(t)\right) = 0 \right\} \, dt \quad (3)$$

Equation (3) has no direct time dependency but it depends on the input signals $u(t)$. Thus, the generators $\sum$ are not time t and input values but rather a time difference δt and the input values. Without losing generality, the time difference δt might be either an infinitesimal small or a finite value.

Thus, digital and analog systems can be described by transition systems. Unfortunately, the representation of states in the two system classes is totally different, so that an easy extension of digital tools to analog system seems to be difficult. Published model checking tools are already able to access discrete and partly linear system descriptions [1]. However, since our focus is on nonlinear analog behavior this is not sufficient.

Therefore, a new method has to be developed. Some of the following algorithms have been inspired by research in the area of approximating dynamical behavior [8]. Despite the similarities, there are a lot of differences, mainly caused by the overall target of the algorithms. Algorithms from this area have not been used, but some of the ideas have been adopted. We have already mentioned the work of Kurshan and McMillan [2] which is also linked to following algorithms.

3 Discrete Model Generation

As we have seen, the continuous variables in an analog system - state values and time - have to be transfered into a discrete state space description and a state transition relation. The next sections illustrate this process.

3.1   Discrete Time Steps

In Section 2.2 we found that the transition relation $R \subseteq \left(\mathcal{R}^n \times \mathcal{R}^{i+1} \times \mathcal{R}^n \right)$ for an analog system is given as a continuous function and the actual state transition can be calculated by integrating this function. In general, Equation (3) can only be solved using numerical integration. This problem is well known in analog simulators, like Spice, Spectre, Saber, etc. During transient simulation the differential equation system is solved using discrete time steps. Given a small time step $\Delta t = t_1 - t_0$, the transition between the actual state $x(t_0)$ and the next state $x(t_1)$ is determined by a numerical integrator, e.g. the backward Euler formula:

$$\mathrm{g_{num}}\left(x(t_0), u(t_1), \Delta t\right) = \left\{ x(t_1) \,\middle|\, f\left(\frac{x(t_1) - x(t_0)}{\Delta t}, x(t_1), u(t_1) \right) = 0 \right\} \qquad (4)$$

Disregarding numerical problems, there will always be an error due to the finite length of Δt. To bound this error, a local step size control mechanism is needed. The algorithm used take the second derivation with respect to time for a local measurement of the integration error. If the given error threshold is exceeded, step size is reduced otherwise the transient step is accepted. This method can be used directly in the analog model checking tool. An arbitrary test point $x(t)$ in the state space is mapped to its successor state $x(t + \Delta t)$, depending on the actual step size Δt and the input signals $u(t)$. In contrast to transient simulation, there is no temporal predecessor state for a test point. A second time step has to be calculated for each point to determine the second derivation, enabling a local error control.

In general, the time step Δt will vary throughout the state space, due to the step size control. As we will see later, this makes the checking of explicit time dependencies difficult because one has to store Δt for each transition separately. To make this easier, the time step is chosen to be equal for each point within one state space region (to be defined in Section 3.3). Kurshan and McMillan [2] proposed a constant time step Δt for the whole space developed by several small numerical integration steps (segments of trajectories). Despite the advantage of a constant time step, this is not suitable for all circuits since the step size variation in terms of state variable values may be large throughout the state space.

Thus, every state space point $x(t)$ can be mapped to its successor point $\mathrm{s}(x(t)) = \mathrm{g_{num}}(x(t), u_{const}, \Delta t_{length\_control})$ including a local step length control and assuming given input values. The resulting tuple of test and target point is represented by a successor vector $\mathrm{sv}(x(t)) = \mathrm{s}(x(t)) - x(t)$ in the state space.

3.2   Input Value Model

To solve Equation (3) or (4) the input value $u(t)$ is needed. Until now we have not defined this value. In principle, the input signals might be defined explicitly. However this is not really useful since the model checking result will only be true for one specific input signal and this is a contradiction the formal verification idea. Let us therefore assume some conditions for the input signal without defining it explicitly. To do this, the state space is extended by the input variables $x_{si} = \{x_s, u\} \in \mathcal{R}^{n+i}$. It is called extended state space. Thus, every state within the extended state space contains information about the actual input values. However, there is no information on the input value change with respect to time. Moreover, it is theoretically impossible to predict the input value variation because the input values are not determined by the system itself but rather from some outside systems.

There are two extreme assumptions: The input values do not change at all and the input values may change instantaneously over the whole input value range. For the first assumption, the model is build up as described before for several constant input values. There will be no transition between states with different input values. In the second approach, a state space region has not only transitions to regions at the same input level but additional transitions to the neighbor regions in terms of input values. By using the extended state space and the described input model the transition relation changes to $R \subseteq \left(\mathcal{R}^{n+i} \times \mathcal{R}^1 \times \mathcal{R}^{n+i}\right)$.

As we will see later, both of these input models are useful for certain conditions to be checked. Between these two extreme models it possible to assume the input values to vary within a given frequency range or within a maximum input voltage slope. This is the most suitable assumption for real world systems but it has not been considered in the prototype tool yet.

3.3 State Space Subdivision

To get a discrete and finite state description, the continuous and infinite state space has to be bounded and subdivided. This is done by rectangular boxes. In general, boxes are not necessarily the best choice [9], however, for implementation reasons boxes are the far most convenient data structure. Other subdivision geometries might be considered during future improvements.

The restriction to a finite region is simply done by a user defined start area, comprising the considered system behavior. This causes special border problems, which will be discussed later. However, it does not impact the correctness of the model checking result because in real world systems there is alway a natural bound for the state variable values.

Since we do not have a digital environment, a natural subdivision for the start area, given for example by threshold values of digital state transitions, is missing [1]. Furthermore, to retain the analog system behavior correctly, a sufficient number of subdivisions is needed, especially in state space regions with highly nonlinear behavior. This purpose differs from approaches focusing on digital circuit behavior [2]. However, the number of discrete regions should be kept as small as possible to reduce the total runtime.

We start with a user controlled uniform subdivision in all state space dimensions. Then, an automatic subdivision strategy is used to react on different system dynamics, depending on the actual state space region. The main target is to get a uniform behavior in each state space box. The uniformity is measured by the variation of the successor vectors (sv($\cdot$)), calculated in the state space (Section 3.1 and 3.4). Namely, vector length variation l_m and angle a_m between different vectors are considered. Equations (5) and (6) give the definition of these values. The function L($\cdot$) gives the length of the delivered vector or vector component. Input value variations are not taken into account.

$$l_m = 1 - \frac{\min_{y \in p_{test}} L(sv(y))}{\max_{y \in p_{test}} L(sv(y))} \tag{5}$$

$$a_m = \max_{\substack{y \in p_{test} \\ k \in n}} \frac{L(sv(y)_k)}{L(sv(y))} - \min_{\substack{y \in p_{test} \\ k \in n}} \frac{L(sv(y)_k)}{L(sv(y))} \tag{6}$$

Box subdivision is continued recursively until l_m and a_m drop under a given threshold or a given subdivision depth is exceeded.

Within the expected accuracy, all boxes fulfilling the l_m and a_m thresholds do not contain fix points. This is, because fix points are always surrounded by regions with nonuniform behavior in terms of Equations (5) and (6). This information is stored and used in the transition relation algorithm (Section 3.4).

Additional subdivisions are applied if the successor vectors in a region are too short in relation to the box size. This occurs mainly in regions where the system is strongly nonlinear, which implies Δt to be very small. Each box in the state space will represent a single state in the discrete model. Thus, the set of i states is given by $Q = \{box_1, box_2, ..., box_i\}$.

3.4 Transition Relation

The last step in getting a discrete system model is the transition relation between state space regions. In Section 3.1 successor points for single state space points have been defined (s($\cdot$)). Using this point to point relation, the target region r_{target} is given by the set of all target points associated with a test point within the state space region r_{test} (see Equation (7)), as illustrated by the gray regions in Figure 1. We call this exact transformation $T_1(\cdot)$.

$$r_{target1} = \{s(y) \mid y \in r_{test}\} = T_1(r_{text}) \tag{7}$$

Since it is not practical to calculate a huge or - mathematically - infinite number of successor points for each box, a good estimation or inclusion of the target region is needed. Three different approaches will be discussed.

An inclusion $r_{target2}$ can be calculated using interval analysis [10]. This approach provides an overestimated solution. That means, the correct solution $r_{target1}$ is fully included within $r_{target2}$. However, $r_{target2}$ might be much larger than $r_{target1}$. This effect is called overestimation and might be a serious problem especially for large systems [7].

Interval analysis has already successfully been used for hybrid systems [11].

$$r_{target2} = \mathrm{T}_{interval}(r_{test}) = \mathrm{T}_2(r_{test}) \supseteq r_{target1} \qquad (8)$$

A more practical but also less accurate way to approximate the target region is to choose a number of test points p_{test} within the test region (e.g. randomly, grid based, or corner values) and to calculate the dedicated target points p_{target}. The target region $r_{target3}$ can be approximated using an appropriate inclusion of these points. As we will see below, an inclusion operation is also needed while expanding the target regions to the actual state space regions. These two steps can be combined. Even a few test points may give a reasonable target approximation, but the region $r_{target3}$ might be under- or overestimated.

$$p_{test3} = \{s_1, s_2, ..., s_n\}, \; s_i \in r_{test} \qquad (9)$$
$$r_{target3} = \{\mathrm{inclusion}(s(y)) \mid y \in p_{test3}\} = \mathrm{T}_3(r_{test}) \simeq r_{target1} \qquad (10)$$

There are two approaches making this process rigorous which means that the target region $r_{target1}$ is fully included in the target approximation. At first, it is shown in [2] that T_3 is surely overestimated if all corner values are used as test points and if s($\cdot$) can be assumed to be monotonic. Secondly, following the argumentation in [8], this is done using Lipschitz constants L in each state space dimension. Using a grid of test points, spaced by h, one can calculate an extension diameter $d_{ex} = Lh$ for the target points. Expanding each target point by this diameter d_{ex} in each dimension gives a set of boxes. The union of these boxes is an overestimated target approximation $r_{target4}$. In Figure 2 three test and target points and the dedicated extension boxes are shown.

$$r_{target4} = \left\{\mathrm{expand}_{(Lh)}(s(y)) \mid y \in \mathrm{grid}\,(h, r_{test})\right\} = \mathrm{T}_4(r_{test}) \supseteq r_{target1} \;(11)$$

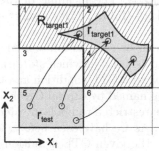

Fig. 1. State space transition relation using T_1

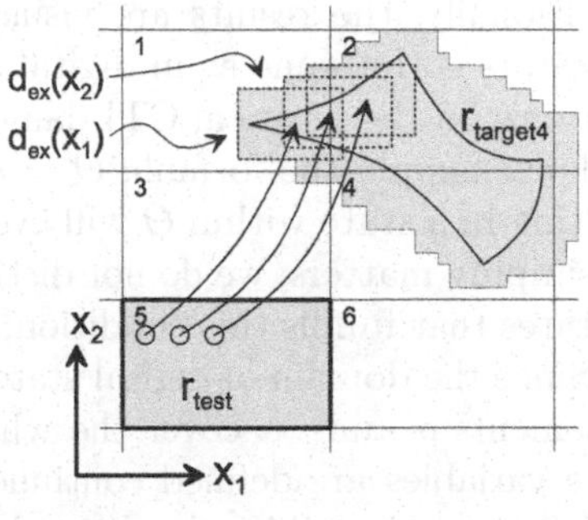

Fig. 2. Rigorous approach using Lipschitz constants

All discussed target regions ($r_{target1}$, $r_{target2}$, $r_{target3}$, and $r_{target4}$) do not fit into the state space subdivisions used. Therefore, a second step is needed to extend these regions to legal sets of boxes. For example, region $R_{target1}$ (hatched areas in Figure 1) is given by the set of all boxes having contact with the target region $r_{target1}$. Fortunately, this operation is always an overestimation and does therefore not impact the correctness of the above results. Until now, only the third operation $T_3(\cdot)$ has been implemented. $T_2(\cdot)$ and $T_4(\cdot)$ will follow in further implementation steps.

Some additional steps are needed to optimize the transition relation for some corner cases. Namely, these are prevention of long successor vectors, resulting in a box over-jump, boxes with self-connection and boxes with no transitions to other boxes due to short successor vectors. The last two conditions are unphysical if the box does not contain fix points (Section 3.3). As we have already mentioned in Section 3.1, no explicit time relations are considered. It might be useful or necessary in future implementations to store not only the transition relation $R \subseteq Q \times Q$ but rather this relation combined with the related transition time delays $R \subseteq Q \times Z \times Q$ where Z denotes the set of all transition time delays used.

4   Model Checking Algorithms

Due to the developed discrete model, the analog system is accessible by discrete algorithms. In this contribution a CTL model checker will be discussed but the foregoing approach can also be used for other formal verification approaches.

As we will see, existing model checking tools and languages are not well suited for the generated models and the description of analog properties. In particular, the intensively used BDD structures are not helpful for this kind of models, because the set of states can not efficiently be described by binary state variable combinations. Therefore, a modified model checker has been developed, based on the basic CTL algorithms described in [12]. A simple tree structure is used to store the discrete state regions. There are some algorithmic modifications due to the special need of the analog model, explained below. The language has been extended by a minimal set of operations enabling the work on analog models. Additionally, the results are visualized graphically. The meaning of the CTL operators is the same as in digital model checkers. Table 1 gives a short syntax overview on the classical CTL language.

For example the formula $\Theta = \mathsf{AF}(state_1)$ can be read as follows: All paths starting in a state within Θ will eventually reach a state in which $state_1$ is true. To simplify matters, we do not distinguish between a CTL condition and the set of states that fulfills this condition, both will be named by capital Greek letters.

Since the domain of digital state variables is restricted to boolean values, the statements a and $\neg a$ cover the whole domain. As we have seen before, analog state variables are defined continuously. Thus, the given CTL definition is not sufficient for describing condition in analog variables. To solve this problem, we introduce a greater and smaller operator in the language definition (Table 4). Thereby, half planes can be described in a continuous space e.g. ($x_1 > -13.2546$).

Table 1. Classical CTL syntax

$$\phi := a \mid \phi \circ \phi \mid \neg \phi \mid \triangleright \diamond \phi \mid \triangleright \phi \, U \, \phi$$

a	boolean variable	
○	boolean	$\vee \to$ or
	operators	$\wedge \to$ and
¬		$\neg \to$ not
▷	path	$E \to$ on some path
	quantifiers	$A \to$ on all paths
◇	temporal	$X \to$ next-time
	operators	$F \to$ eventually
		$G \to$ always
U		$U \to$ until

Table 2. CTL syntax extension

$$\phi := b * v \mid \phi \circ \phi \mid \neg \phi \mid \triangleright \diamond \phi \mid$$
$$\triangleright \phi \, U \, \phi \mid iv\phi$$

b	continuous variable	
v	real value	
*	analog	$> \to$ greater
	operators	$< \to$ smaller
iv	inverse time	

The combination of several half planes with boolean operators enables the definition of arbitrary Manhattan polytopes in a continuous n-dimensional space. Boolean variables are left out in this definition, because only pure analog system are considered in this contribution. However, an extension to hybrid systems seems to be possible.

Moreover, we have introduced the inverse time operator iv. It simply inverses all transition relations with respect to time. By this, we assume a branching (also known as non-Ockhamist) infinite past. A collection of other past time definitions and languages can be found in [13]. As we will see in the experimental results, this operator is useful for some analog properties to be checked. Due to these extensions, the meaning of all operators has to be reviewed to find out the necessary changes in known digital or hybrid model checking algorithms.

- If the threshold values v used in the greater/smaller operations are not subdivision values in the state space, they have to be added and the transition relation has to be reconstructed due to this change before executing the CTL formula. This makes the discrete model not only dependent on the analog system but also on the CTL formula used.
- The boolean operators $\neg$, $\vee$, and $\wedge$ are obviously defined for state space regions. However, as we will see later, not only the restricted state space has to be considered but also the outside area. In this context the definition will be extended.
- In contrast to the original analog model the discrete model will be nondeterministic due to the abstraction of the state space, namely because a state space region may be connected to several successor regions even without changing the input values. This does not effect the path quantifier definition but it has to be considered while using them in a CTL formula. Since the model is nondeterministic, the inverse time operator does not change the model structure in respect thereof.
- The last group comprises temporal operators. As we have seen before, the time step Δt may vary throughout the state space. Thus, the time quan-

tifier X has only a qualitative meaning. To enable checking of quantitative time dependencies the discrete model and the language needs further extensions (e.g. $X_{(3\mu s)}$, see also [14]). The other operations can be used in the same manner as in digital applications.

Obviously, this language is not very powerful describing analog design specifications. This is because we want to follow the digital model checking ideas as far as possible without major changes. It will be shown below that it is possible to check some analog properties even with this minimal set of operations.

4.1   Border Problems

Consider for example differential equation $\{\dot{x} = (1,0)^T\}$ and CTL formula $EG(\Theta)$ where $\Theta = ((x_2 > 1.0)\ \&\ (x_2 < 2.0))$. For this example Equation (3) is easy to solve symbolically $x(t_0 + \delta t) = x(t_0) + \int_{t_0}^{t_0+\delta t} \dot{x}\, dt = x(t_0) + \binom{1}{0} \delta t$.

It is obvious, that $EX(\Theta) = (\Theta)$ for all δt because a time step causes only a shift in x_1 direction and since region Θ is not restricted there, the EX operator does not affect that area. Furthermore, $EG(\Theta)$ is the largest fix point of the sequence $\{\Theta_0 = \Theta; \Theta_{i+1} = \Theta_i \wedge EX(\Theta_i)\}$. Consequently, the theoretical result of $EG(\Theta)$ is Θ. If a restricted state space - for example $([-5 .. 5], [-5 .. 5])^T$ - is applied to this example the result changes dramatically. Using the solution of $x(t_0 + \delta t)$ we find $EX(\Theta)$ to be $([-5 .. (5 - \delta t)], [1 .. 2])^T$. Thus, the largest fix point for the sequence defining EG is $\emptyset$.

Is that the expected result? To answer this question the meaning of $\Psi = EG(\Theta)$ has to be studied again: "For each state ψ within Ψ there is a path starting in ψ such that Ψ is invariantly true on this path." In the given example, every path leaves the restricted state space after some time but that does not necessarily mean that Ψ is not fulfilled on that path since Ψ is also restricted to the given state space. Thus, it has to be defined whether a path leaving the restricted state space fulfills that condition or not.

In other words, it has to be defined whether the area outside the restricted state space is part of the actual region or not. In the above example we have simply assumed that the outside area is not part of the region. Under this assumption the given result is correct. But if we assume the outside area to be part of the region $\Theta = \left(([-5 .. 5], [1 .. 2])^T + Outside\right)$ we get $EG(\Theta) = \Theta$.

To implement that, an outside area flag is stored for each region used. The border boxes are treated specially, they keep the value given by the border flag. As a result, the border boxes are not part of the model checking result and have to be omitted during interpretation. Every new region to be introduced has an outside flag set to false. All boolean operations are not only applied to the state space but also to the outside flag. Thus, it is possible to define all constellations.

5   Experimental Results

5.1   Biquad Lowpass Filter Example

The first example, a 2nd order Biquad lowpass filter, is shown in Figure 3. The opamp model has an open loop gain of 10000. The output voltage restriction is ±1.5 V and the maximum output current is 80 mA. Due to these restrictions the whole system is nonlinear. This circuit has two state variables, namely the capacitor voltages V_{c1} and V_{c2}. Using a charge oriented capacitor model will normally lead to the two charges as state variables. We changed this, because we found it more convenient to think in voltages than in charges. The corner frequency ω_c and the damping factor d are given by $\omega_c = \sqrt{R_1 R_2 C_1 C_2}^{-1}$ and $d = 0.5 C_1 \omega_c (R_1 + R_2)$. We use two different value sets for the resistors and capacitors, one with $\omega_c = 100\ s^{-1}$ and $d = 0.5$ and the second one at the same frequency but with $d = 2$. Thus, we get two equivalent lowpass filters differing only by the damping factor. The property to be checked in this example is the occurrence of overshooting in the two filters. Since these properties should be proved for arbitrary input signals, the appropriate input value model is chosen. The input signal range is $V_{in} = [-2 .. 2]$, so that the nonlinearity due to the restricted output voltage will effect the system behavior. The state space is restricted to $V_{c1} = [-4 .. 4]$ and $V_{c2} = [-2.5 .. 2.5]$.

The initial state in this example is assumed to be the DC operating point at $V_{in} = 0$. The question is: Which states are reachable from this point for arbitrary input signals within the given range? Instead of a single start point a start area is used, that is for example a box surrounding the initial point. Next, operation EF is used to check which states have a path that will eventually reach the starting area. However, the direction of this operation is wrong. Inverting the time gives the correct formula $\{\Phi_3 = \text{iv}(\text{EF}((V_{c2} < 0.5)\ \&\ (V_{c2} > -0.5)\ \&\ (V_{c1} < 0.5)\ \&\ (V_{c1} > -0.5)\ \&\ (V_{in} < 0.5)\ \&\ (V_{in} > -0.5)))\}$.

This equation is applied to both circuits. The result for the highly damped circuit is shown in Figure 4. The black box indicates the state space borders. The input voltage axis is perpendicular to the paper. As expected, the state V_{c1}

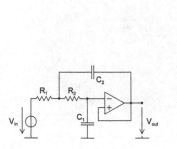

Fig. 3. 2nd order lowpass filter

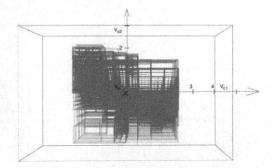

Fig. 4. Model checking result Φ_3

remains within a range of ± 2 V whereas it has been shown that it reaches higher levels in the less damped case. However, the output voltage V_{out} remains within the ± 1.5 V range for both circuits due to the opamp nonlinearities. It turns out that the opamp output restriction of ± 1.5 V does not have an impact on this result because states V_{c1} and V_{c2} are not restricted by the opamp output.

5.2   Tunnel Diode Oscillator Example

The analog system used in our second example is a simple tunnel diode oscillator circuit shown in Figure 5. The input voltage V_{in} is set to 2.6 V. In this operating point the circuit starts an oscillation automatically. The bounded state space is given by $V_C = [-0.2 .. 4.4]$ and $I_L = [-0.2 .. 4.0]$.

According to digital systems a stable oscillation might be proved by the following CTL equation $\Phi_5 = \{\mathsf{AG}(\mathsf{AF}(I_L > 2.2))\ \&\ \mathsf{AG}(\mathsf{AF}(I_L < 1.6))\}$. The collection of boxes fulfilling this condition is shown in Figure 6 in light gray. Except of some border boxes and the middle region, the whole state space is covered.

We can conclude that nearly the whole plane will float into an stable orbit. The next question might concern the possible orbit geometry. We generate this by applying $\Phi_6 = \{\mathsf{iv}(\mathsf{EG}(\Phi_5))\}$. The result Φ_6 contains the whole orbit calculated by an ordinary simulation (black line in Figure 6).

6   Conclusion

To apply digital model checking ideas to analog systems a discrete system model is needed. The main algorithmic task is to develop a state transition model in such a manner that the main nonlinear and dynamic properties of the analog system are retained. This is done using an automatic state space subdivision method and an algorithm developing the transition relation.

The implemented CTL model checker is based on digital algorithms, but it is extended by some operations, enabling the definition of analog properties in

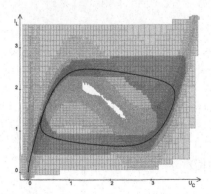

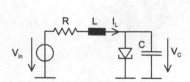

Fig. 5. Tunnel diode oscillator   **Fig. 6.** Model checking results Φ_5 and Φ_6

CTL. Some applications of this language are shown by the experimental results. However, applying CTL to analog systems, seems even more uncommon than doing so in digital. It is clear that the language is not sufficient for all analog properties. Especially, explicit time dependent properties, like slew rates or delays, are not covered in the prototype implementation.

As far as we know, the presented tool is the first approach to model checking for nonlinear analog systems. That opens a wide range of possibilities in applying formal methods not only to digital and hybrid systems but also to analog systems. Therefore, it is a step towards a more formalized analog design flow.

References

1. Alur, R., Henzinger, T., Lafferriere, G., Pappas, G.: Discrete abstractions of hybrid systems. Proceedings of IEEE (2000 971-984 401, 403, 405
2. Kurshan, R., McMillan, K.: Analysis of digital circuits trough symbolic reduction. IEEE Transactions on Computer-Aided Design of Integrated Circuits and Systems 10 (1991 1356-71 401, 403, 404, 405, 407
3. Dang, T., Maler, O.: Reachability analysis via face lifting. HSCC '98: Hybrid Systems: Computation and Control, LNCS (1998 96-109 401
4. Asarin, E., Bournez, O., Dang, T., Maler, O.: Approximate reachability analysis of piecewise-linear dynamical systems. HSCC '00: Hybrid Systems: Computation and Control, LNCS (2000 76-90 401
5. Hedrich, L., Hartong, W.: Approaches to formal verification of analog circuits. In Wambacq, P., ed.: Low-Power Design Techniques and CAD Tools for Analog and RF Intergrated Circuits. Kluwer Academic Publishers, Boston (2001 155-191 401, 400
6. Günther, M., Feldmann, U.: Cad-based electric circuit modeling in industry, part is Mathemetical structure and index of network equations. Suveys on Mathematics for Industry 8 (1999 97-129 402
7. März, R.: Numerical methods for differential algebraic equations. Acta Numerica (1991 141-198 402
8. Dellnitz, M., Froyland, G., Junge, O.: The algorithms behind gaio - set oriented numerical methods for dynamical systems. Ergodic Theory, Analysis, and Efficient Simulation of Dynamical Systems (eds. B. Fiedler, Springer (2001 145-174 403, 407
9. Henzinger, T., Ho, P.H.: Algorithmic analysis of nonlinear hybrid systems. CAV '95: International Conference on Computer-Aided Verification, LNCS 939 (1995 225-238 405
10. Neumaier, A.: Interval methods for systems of equations. Cambridge University Press, Cambridge (1990 406
11. Henzinger, T., Horowitz, B., Majumdar, R., Wong-Toi, H.: Beyond hytech: Hybrid systems analysis using interval numerical methods. HSCC '00: Hybrid Systems: Computation and Control, LNCS (2000 130-144 406
12. Burch, J., Clarke, E., Long, D., McMillian, K., Dill, D.: Symbolic model checking for sequential circuit verification. IEEE Transactions on Computer-Aided Design of Integrated Circuits and Systems 13 (1994 401-424 408
13. Laroussinie, F., Schnoebelen, P.: Specification in ctl+past for verification in ctl. Information and Computation 156 (2000 236-263 409

414   Walter Hartong et al.

14. Emerson, E., Mok, A., Sistla, A., Srinivasan, J.: Quantitytive temporal reasoning.
    CAV '90: International Conference on Computer-Aided Verification, LNCS (1990
    136-145   410

Synchronous and Bidirectional Component Interfaces*

Arindam Chakrabarti[1], Luca de Alfaro[2],
Thomas A. Henzinger[1], and Freddy Y. C. Mang[3]

[1] Department of Electrical Engineering and Computer Sciences
University of California, Berkeley, CA 94720-1770, USA
{arindam,tah}@eecs.berkeley.edu
[2] Department of Computer Engineering
University of California, Santa Cruz, CA 95064, USA
luca@soe.ucsc.edu
[3] Advanced Technology Group, Synopsys Inc.
fmang@synopsys.com

Abstract. We present *interface models* that describe both the input assumptions of a component, and its output behavior. By enabling us to check that the input assumptions of a component are met in a design, interface models provide a *compatibility* check for component-based design. When refining a design into an implementation, interface models require that the output behavior of a component satisfies the design specification only when the input assumptions of the specification are satisfied, yielding greater flexibility in the choice of implementations. Technically, our interface models are games between two players, Input and Output; the duality of the players accounts for the dual roles of inputs and outputs in composition and refinement. We present two interface models in detail, one for a simple synchronous form of interaction between components typical in hardware, and the other for more complex synchronous interactions on bidirectional connections. As an example, we specify the interface of a bidirectional bus, with the input assumption that at any time at most one component has write access to the bus. For these interface models, we present algorithms for compatibility and refinement checking, and we describe efficient symbolic implementations.

1 Introduction

One of the main applications of modeling formalisms is to capture designs. We present *interface models* that are specifically geared to support the component-based approach to design. Interface models describe both the inputs that can be accepted by a component, and the outputs it can generate. As an interface

---

* This research was supported in part by the AFOSR grant F49620-00-1-0327, the DARPA grant F33615-00-C-1693, the MARCO grant 98-DT-660, the NSF grant CCR-9988172, the SRC grant 99-TJ-683.003, and the NSF CAREER award CCR-0132780.

D. Brinksma and K. G. Larsen (Eds.): CAV 2002, LNCS 2404, pp. 414–427, 2002.
© Springer-Verlag Berlin Heidelberg 2002

constrains the acceptable inputs, the underlying component fits into some design contexts (which meet the constraints), but not into others. Interface models provide a means for answering four questions that arise in component-based design: the *well-formedness question* (can a component be used in some design, i.e., are the input constraints satisfiable?), the *verification question* (does a component satisfy a given property in all designs?), the *compatibility question* (do two components interact in compatible ways in a design?), and the *refinement question* (can a component be substituted for another one in every design context without violating compatibility?).

For each of the questions of well-formedness, verification, compatibility, and refinement, there are two basic choices for treating inputs and outputs. The *graph* view quantifies inputs and outputs with the same polarity; the *game* view quantifies inputs and outputs with opposite polarities. In the graph view, both inputs and outputs can be seen as labels in a nondeterministic state transition graph; in the game view, inputs and outputs are chosen by different players and the result of each combination of choices determines the state transition. For example, the graph view is appropriate for the verification question: does a component satisfy a given property for all acceptable inputs and all possible outputs? On the other hand, the game view is necessary for the well-formedness question [1,11]: are there acceptable inputs for all possible choices of outputs? We argue that also for compatibility and refinement, the game view is the appropriate one.

1.1   The Graph View

The graph view is taken by many process algebras (e.g., [12,17]) and state-based models (e.g., [15,13,7,4]). These frameworks are aimed at verification. Indeed, also refinement is typically viewed as a verification question: does a more detailed description of a component generate only behaviors that are permitted by a more abstract description? Refinement is usually defined as a form of trace containment or simulation: when quantifying universally over both inputs and outputs, we say that a component N refines a component M (written $N \preceq M$) if, for all input and output choices, the behaviors of N are a subset of those of M. In particular, N can only produce outputs that are also produced by M, and N can only accept inputs that are also accepted by M. This ensures that every language-theoretic property (such as safety) that holds for M also holds for N. The graph view of refinement, however, becomes problematic when we interpret refinement as substitutivity. The output clause is still appropriate: by requiring that the output behavior of N is a subset of that of M, it ensures that if the outputs of M can be accepted by the other components of the design, so can those of N. The input clause instead is questionable: it states that the implementation N should be able to accept a *subset* of the inputs accepted by the specification M. This raises the possibility that, when N is substituted for M in a design, N cannot accept some inputs from other components that could be accepted by M. Hence, *substitutivity of refinement* does not hold in the graph view. Indeed, in process algebras and the modeling language SMV [7], if $N \preceq M$ and $M \| P$ is deadlock-free, it is possible that $N \| P$ deadlocks [3]. To remedy this situation, some models, such as *I/O automata* [14] and *reactive modules* [4], require that components be able to accept *all* possible inputs; this condition is known as *input-enabledness* or *receptivity*. This requirement forces models to specify the outputs generated in response to *all* possible inputs, including inputs that the designers know cannot occur in the actual design.

The graph view is also limited in its capability to analyze component compatibility. If models specify explicitly which inputs can be accepted, and which ones are *illegal*, then it is possible to ask the compatibility question generically: do illegal inputs occur? If we quantify universally over both inputs and outputs, we obtain a verification question: two components M and N are compatible if, once composed, they accept all inputs. This is not a natural phrasing of the compatibility question: it requires $M\|N$ to accept all inputs, even though M and N could have illegal inputs. A more compositional definition is to call M and N compatible if there are *some* input sequences that ensure that all illegal inputs of M and N are avoided, and to label all other sequences as illegal for $M\|N$. This definition of compatibility leads to a dual treatment of inputs (quantified existentially) and outputs (quantified universally), and to the game view.

1.2   The Game View

According to the game view, inputs and outputs play dual roles. In trace theory [11], a trace model consists in two sets, of accepted and rejected traces, and games are used to solve the realizability and compatibility questions. In the game semantics of [2,3] and the interface models of [9,10], components are explicitly modeled as games between two players, Input and Output. The moves of Input represent the inputs that can be accepted, and the moves of Output the outputs that can be generated. To model the fact that these sets can change in time, after the input and output moves are chosen, the game moves to a new state, with possibly different sets of accepted inputs and possible outputs.

In the study of compatibility, game-based approaches quantify inputs existentially, and outputs universally. When two components M and N are composed, their composition may have illegal states, where one component emits outputs that are illegal inputs for the other one. Yet, M and N are considered *compatible* as long as there is *some* input behavior that ensures that, for all output behaviors, the illegal states are avoided: in other words, M and N are compatible if there is some environment in which they can be used correctly together. In turn, the input behaviors that ensure compatibility constitute the legal behaviors for the composition $M\|N$: when composing component models, both the possible output behaviors, and the legal input behaviors, are composed.

The game view leads to an *alternating* view of refinement [5]: a more detailed component N refines an abstract component M if all legal inputs of M are also legal for N and if, when M and N are subject to the same (legal) inputs, N generates output behaviors that are a subset of those of M. This definition ensures that, whenever $N \preceq M$, we can substitute N for M in every design without creating any incompatibility: in the game view, substitutivity of refinement holds. The alternating definition of refinement also mirrors the contravariant definition of subtyping in programming languages, which also supports substitutivity [18]. Indeed, the game framework can be viewed as a generalization of type theory to behaviors.

1.3 Synchronous Interface Models

In this paper, we adopt the game view to modeling, and we introduce two interface models for *synchronous* components. We begin with the simple model of *Moore interfaces*: in addition to the usual transition relation of a synchronous system, which describes the update rules for the outputs, a Moore interface has a symmetrically-defined transition relation for the inputs, which specifies which input transitions are acceptable. Our second model, *bidirectional interfaces*, illustrate how game-based models can be richer than their graph-based counterparts. Bidirectional connections cannot be modeled in the input-enabled setting: there are always environments that use such connections as input, and environments that use them as output, so that no component can work in all environments. Bidirectional connections, however, can be naturally modeled as a game between Input and Output players. As an example, we encode the access protocol to the PCI bus, in which several components share access to a multi-directional bus. By checking the compatibility of the component models, we can ensure that no conflicts for bus access arise. We have implemented tools for symbolic compatibility and refinement checking for both Moore and bidirectional interfaces, and we discuss how the game-based algorithms can be implemented with minor modifications to the usual symbolic machinery for graph-based algorithms, and yield a similar efficiency.

2 Compatibility and Composition

2.1 Moore Interfaces

Moore interfaces model both the behavior of a system component, and the interface between the component and its environment. The state of a module is described by a set of *state variables,* partitioned into sets of *input* and *output* variables. The possible changes of output variables are described by an *output transition relation*, while the legal changes of input variables are described by an *input transition relation.* Hence, the output transition relation describes the module's behavior, and the input transition relation describes the input assumptions of the interface.

Example 1   We illustrate the features of Moore interfaces by modeling a ± 1 adder driven by a binary counter. The adder *Adder* has two control inputs q_0 and q_1, data inputs $i_7 \cdots i_0$, and data outputs $o_7 \cdots o_0$. When $q_0 = q_1 = 1$, the adder leaves the input unchanged: the next value of $o_7 \cdots o_0$ is equal to $i_7 \cdots i_0$. When $q_0 = 0$ and $q_1 = 1$, the next outputs are given by $[o_7' \cdots o_0'] = [i_7 \cdots i_0] + 1 \bmod 2^8$, where primed variables denote the values at the next clock cycle, and $[o_7' \cdots o_0']$ is the integer encoded in binary by $o_7' \cdots o_0'$. Similarly, when $q_1 = 0$ and $q_0 = 1$, we have $[o_7' \cdots o_0'] = [i_7 \cdots i_0] - 1 \bmod 2^8$. The adder is designed with the assumption that q_1 and q_0 are not both 0: hence, the input transition relation of *Adder* states that $q_0' q_1' \neq 00$. In order to cycle between adding $0, +1, -1$, the control inputs q_0 and q_1 are connected to the outputs q_1 and q_0 of a two-bit count-to-zero counter *Counter*. The counter has only one input, cl: when $cl = 0$, then $q_1' q_0' = 11$; otherwise, $[q_1' q_0'] = [q_1 q_0] - 1 \bmod 4$.

When we compose *Counter* and *Adder*, we synthesize for their composition *Counter* $\|$ *Adder* a new input assumption, that ensures that the input assumptions of both *Counter* and *Adder* are satisfied. To determine the new input assumption, we solve a game between Input, which chooses the next values of cl and $i_7 \cdots i_0$, and Output, which chooses the next values of q_0, q_1, and $o_7 \cdots o_0$. The goal of Input is to avoid a transition to $q_1 q_0 = 00$. At the states where $q_1 q_0 = 01$, Input can win if $cl = 0$, since we will have $q_1' q_0' = 11$; but Input cannot win if $cl = 1$. By choosing $cl' = 0$, Input can also win from the states where $q_1 q_0 = 10$. Finally, Input can always win from $q_1 q_0 = 11$, for all cl'. Thus, we associate with *Counter* $\|$ *Adder* a new input assumption encoded by the transition relation requiring that whenever $q_1 q_0 = 10$, then $cl' = 0$. The input requirement $q_1 q_0 \neq 00$ of the adder gives rise, in the composite system, to the requirement that the reset-to-1 occurs early in the count-to-zero cycle of the counter. □

Given a set $\mathcal{W}$ of typed variables with finite domain, a state s over $\mathcal{W}$ is a function that assigns to each $x \in \mathcal{W}$ a value $s[\![x]\!]$ of the appropriate type; we write $\mathcal{S}[\mathcal{W}]$ for the set of all states over $\mathcal{W}$. We denote by $\mathcal{W}' = \{x' \mid x \in \mathcal{W}\}$ the set obtained by priming each variable in $\mathcal{W}$; given a predicate φ on $\mathcal{W}$, we denote by φ' the predicate on $\mathcal{W}'$ obtained by replacing in φ every $x \in \mathcal{W}$ with $x' \in \mathcal{W}'$. Given a state $s \in \mathcal{S}[\mathcal{W}]$ and a predicate φ on $\mathcal{W}$, we write $s \models \varphi$ if φ is satisfied under the variable interpretation specified by s. Given two states $s, s' \in \mathcal{S}[\mathcal{W}]$ and a predicate φ on $\mathcal{W} \cup \mathcal{W}'$, we write $(s, s') \models \varphi$ if φ is satisfied by the interpretation that assigns to $x \in \mathcal{W}$ the value $s[\![x]\!]$, and to $x' \in \mathcal{W}'$ the value $s'[\![x]\!]$. Moore interfaces are defined as follows.

Definition 1 (Moore interface) A *Moore interface* $M = \langle \mathcal{V}_M^i, \mathcal{V}_M^o, \theta_M^i, \theta_M^o, \tau_M^i, \tau_M^o \rangle$ consists of the following components:

- A finite set $\mathcal{V}_M^i$ of *input variables,* and a finite set $\mathcal{V}_M^o$ of *output variables.* The two sets must be disjoint; we define $\mathcal{V}_M = \mathcal{V}_M^i \cup \mathcal{V}_M^o$.
- A satisfiable predicate θ_M^i on $\mathcal{V}_M^i$ defining the legal initial values for the input variables, and a satisfiable predicate θ_M^o on $\mathcal{V}_M^o$ defining the initial values for the output variables.
- An *input transition predicate* τ_M^i on $\mathcal{V}_M \cup (\mathcal{V}_M^i)'$, specifying the legal updates for the input variables, and an *output transition predicate* τ_M^o on $\mathcal{V}_M \cup (\mathcal{V}_M^o)'$, specifying how the module can update the values of the output variables. We require that the formulas $\forall \mathcal{V}_M . \exists (\mathcal{V}_M^i)' . \tau_M^i$ and $\forall \mathcal{V}_M . \exists (\mathcal{V}_M^o)' . \tau_M^o$ hold. □

The above interfaces are called *Moore* because the next value of the output variables can depend on the current state, but not on the next value of the input variables, as in Moore machines. The requirements on the input and output transition relations ensure that the interface is non-blocking: from every state there is some legal input and possible output. Given a Moore interface $M = \langle \mathcal{V}_M^i, \mathcal{V}_M^o, \theta_M^i, \theta_M^o, \tau_M^i, \tau_M^o \rangle$, we let $Traces(\mathcal{V}_M^i, \mathcal{V}_M^o, \theta_M^i, \theta_M^o, \tau_M^i, \tau_M^o)$ be the set of traces of M, consisting of all the infinite sequences $s_0, s_1, s_2, \dots$ of states of $\mathcal{S}[\mathcal{V}_M]$ such that $s_0 \models \theta_M^i \wedge \theta_M^o$, and $(s_k, s_{k+1}) \models \tau_M^i \wedge \tau_M^o$ for all $k \geq 0$.

Composition of Moore interfaces. Two Moore interfaces M and N are *composable* if $\mathcal{V}_M^o \cap \mathcal{V}_N^o = \emptyset$. If M and N are composable, we merge them into a single interface P as follows. We let $\mathcal{V}_P^o = \mathcal{V}_M^o \cup \mathcal{V}_N^o$ and $\mathcal{V}_P^i = (\mathcal{V}_M^i \cup \mathcal{V}_N^i) \setminus \mathcal{V}_P^o$. The output behavior of P is simply the joint output behavior of M and N, since each interface is free to choose how to update its output variables: hence, $\theta_P^o = \theta_M^o \wedge \theta_N^o$ and $\tau_P^o = \tau_M^o \wedge \tau_N^o$. On the other hand, we cannot simply adopt the symmetrical definition for the input assumptions. A syntactic reason is that $\theta_M^i \wedge \theta_N^i$ and $\tau_M^i \wedge \tau_N^i$ may contain variables in $(\mathcal{V}_P^o)'$. But a deeper reason is that we may need to strengthen the input assumptions of P further, in order to ensure that the input assumptions of M and N hold. If we can find such a further strengthening θ^i and τ^i, then M and N are said to be *compatible*, and $P = M \| N$ with θ_P^i and τ_P^i being the weakest such strengthenings; otherwise, we say that M and N are incompatible, and $M \| N$ is undefined. Hence, informally, M and N are compatible if they can be used together under some assumptions.

Definition 2 (Compatibility and composition of Moore interfaces) For any two Moore interfaces M and N, we say that M and N are *composable* if $\mathcal{V}_M^o \cap \mathcal{V}_N^o = \emptyset$. If M and N are composable, let $\mathcal{V}_P^o = \mathcal{V}_M^o \cup \mathcal{V}_N^o$, $\mathcal{V}_P^i = (\mathcal{V}_M^i \cup \mathcal{V}_N^i) \setminus \mathcal{V}_P^o$, $\mathcal{V}_P = \mathcal{V}_P^o \cup \mathcal{V}_P^i$, $\theta_P^o = \theta_M^o \wedge \theta_N^o$, and $\tau_P^o = \tau_M^o \wedge \tau_N^o$.

The interfaces M and N are *compatible* (written $M \wr\wr N$) if they are composable, and if there are predicates θ^i on $\mathcal{V}_P^i$ and τ^i on $\mathcal{V}_P \cup (\mathcal{V}_P^i)'$ such that (i) θ^i is satisfiable; (ii) $\forall \mathcal{V}_P . \exists (\mathcal{V}_P^i)'. \tau^i$ holds; (iii) for all $s_0, s_1, s_2, \dots \in Traces(\mathcal{V}_P^i, \mathcal{V}_P^o, \theta^i, \theta_P^o, \tau^i, \tau_P^o)$ we have $s_0 \models \theta_M^i \wedge \theta_N^i$ and, for all $k \geq 0$, $(s_k, s_{k+1}) \models \tau_M^i \wedge \tau_N^i$.

The *composition* $P = M \| N$ is defined if and only if $M \wr\wr N$, in which case P is obtained by taking for the input predicate θ_P^i and for the input transition relation τ_P^i the weakest predicates such that the above condition holds.   □

To compute $M \| N$, we consider a game between Input and Output. At each round of the game, Output chooses new values for the output variables $\mathcal{V}_P^o$ according to τ_P^o; simultaneously and independently, Input chooses (unconstrained) new values for the input variables $\mathcal{V}_P^i$. The goal of Input is to ensure that the resulting behavior satisfies $\theta_M^i \wedge \theta_P^i$ at the initial state, and $\tau_M^i \wedge \tau_N^i$ at all state transitions. If Input can win the game, then M and N are compatible, and the most general strategy for Input will give rise to θ_P^i and τ_P^i; otherwise, M and N are incompatible. The algorithm for computing θ_P^i and τ_P^i proceeds by computing iterative approximations to τ_P^i, and to the set C of states from which Input can win the game. We let $C_0 = \top$ and, for $k \geq 0$:

$$\tilde{\tau}_{k+1} = \forall (\mathcal{V}_P^o)'. \left(\tau_P^o \rightarrow (\tau_M^i \wedge \tau_N^i \wedge C_k') \right) \qquad C_{k+1} = C_k \wedge \exists (\mathcal{V}_P^i)'. \tilde{\tau}_{k+1}. \tag{1}$$

Note that $\tilde{\tau}_{k+1}$ is a predicate on $\mathcal{V}_P^o \cup \mathcal{V}_P^i \cup (\mathcal{V}_P^i)'$. Hence, $\tilde{\tau}_{k+1}$ ensures that, regardless of how $\mathcal{V}_P^o$ are chosen, from C_{k+1} we have that (i) for one step, τ_M^i

and τ_N^i are satisfied; and (ii) the step leads to C_k. Thus, indicating by $C_* = \lim_{k \to \infty} C_k$ and $\widetilde{\tau}_* = \lim_{k \to \infty} \widetilde{\tau}_k$ the fixpoints of (1) we have that C_* represents the set of states from which Input can win the game, and $\widetilde{\tau}_*$ represents the most liberal Input strategy for winning the game. This suggests us to take $\tau_P^i = \widetilde{\tau}_*$. However, this is not always the weakest choice, as required by Definition 2: a weaker choice is $\tau_P^i = \neg C_* \vee \widetilde{\tau}_*$, or equivalently $\tau_P^i = C_* \to \widetilde{\tau}_*$. Contrary to $\tau_P^i = \widetilde{\tau}_*$, this weaker choice ensures that the interface P is non-blocking. We remark that the choices $\tau_P^i = \widetilde{\tau}_*$ and $\tau_P^i = C_* \to \widetilde{\tau}_*$ differ only at non-reachable states. Since the state-space of P is finite, by monotonicity of (1) we can compute the fixpoint C_* and $\widetilde{\tau}_*$ in a finite number of iterations. Finally, we define the input initial condition of P by $\theta_P^i = \forall \mathcal{V}^o.(\theta_P^o \to (\theta_M^i \wedge \theta_N^i \wedge C_*))$. The following algorithm summarizes these results.

Algorithm 1   Given two composable Moore interfaces M and N, let $C_0 = \top$, and for $k > 0$, let the predicates C_k and $\widetilde{\tau}_k$ be as defined by (1). Let $\widetilde{\tau}_* = \lim_{k \to \infty} \widetilde{\tau}_k$ and $C_* = \lim_{k \to \infty} C_k$; the limits can be computed with a finite number of iterations, and let $\theta_*^i = \forall \mathcal{V}^o.(\theta_P^o \to (\theta_M^i \wedge \theta_N^i \wedge C_*))$. Then the interfaces M and N are *compatible* iff θ_*^i is satisfiable; in this case their composition $P = M \| N$ is given by

$$\mathcal{V}_P^o = \mathcal{V}_M^o \cup \mathcal{V}_N^o \qquad\qquad \tau_P^o = \tau_M^o \wedge \tau_N^o \qquad\qquad \theta_P^o = \theta_M^o \wedge \theta_N^o$$
$$\mathcal{V}_P^i = (\mathcal{V}_M^i \cup \mathcal{V}_N^i) \setminus \mathcal{V}^o \qquad \tau_P^i = C_* \to \widetilde{\tau}_* \qquad\qquad \theta_P^i = \theta_*^i. \qquad\qquad \square$$

Implementation considerations. We have implemented composition and compatibility checking for Moore interfaces by extending the Mocha model checker [ ] to interfaces. To obtain an efficient implementation, we represent both the input and the output transition relations using a conjunctively decomposed representation, where a relation τ is represented by a list of BDDs $\tau_1, \tau_2, \ldots, \tau_n$ such that $\tau = \wedge_{i=1}^n \tau_i$. When computing $P = M \| N$, the list for τ_P^o can be readily obtained by concatenating the lists for τ_M^o and τ_N^o. Moreover, assume that τ_P^o is represented as $\bigwedge_{i=1}^n \tau_i^o$, and that $\tau_M^i \wedge \tau_N^i$ is represented as $\bigwedge_{j=1}^m \tau_j^i$. Given C_k, from (1) we obtain the conjunctive decomposition $\bigwedge_{j=1}^{m+1} \widetilde{\tau}_{k+1,j}$ for $\widetilde{\tau}_{k+1}$ by taking $\widetilde{\tau}_{k+1,m+1} = \neg \exists(\mathcal{V}_P^o)'.(\tau_P^o \wedge \neg C_k')$ and, for $1 \le j \le m$, by taking $\widetilde{\tau}_{k+1,j} = \neg \exists(\mathcal{V}_P^o)'.(\tau_P^o \wedge \neg \tau_j^i)$. We also obtain $C_{k+1} = \exists(\mathcal{V}_P^o)'. \bigwedge_{j=1}^{m+1} \widetilde{\tau}_{k+1,j}$. All these operations can be performed using image computation techniques. Once we reach k such that $C_k \equiv C_{k+1}$, the BDDs $\widetilde{\tau}_{k,1}, \ldots, \widetilde{\tau}_{k,m+1}$ form a conjunctive decomposition for $\widetilde{\tau}_*$. Since the two transition relations $\widetilde{\tau}_*$ and $C_* \to \widetilde{\tau}_*$ differ only for the behavior at non-reachable states, in our implementation we take directly $\tau_P^i = \widetilde{\tau}_*$, obtaining again a conjunctive decomposition. With these techniques, the size (number of BDD variables) of the interfaces that our tool is able to check for compatibility, and compose, is roughly equivalent to the size of the models that Mocha [ ] can verify with respect to safety properties.

2.2   Bidirectional Interfaces

Bidirectional interfaces model components that have bidirectional connections. To model bidirectionality we find it convenient to add to the Moore model a set Q

of *locations*. Informally, each location $q \in Q$ partitions the interface variables into inputs and outputs, and determines what values are legal for the inputs, and what values can be assigned to the outputs. At each location $q \in Q$, a particular choice of output and input values determines the successor location q'. The precise definition is as follows.

Definition 3 (Bidirectional interfaces) A *bidirectional interface* M is a tuple $\langle \mathcal{V}_M, Q_M, \hat{q}_M, v_M^o, \phi_M^i, \phi_M^o, \rho_M \rangle$ consisting of the following components:

- A finite set $\mathcal{V}_M$ of input or output *(inout)* variables.
- A finite set Q_M of locations, including an initial location $\hat{q}_M \in Q_M$.
- A function $v_M^o : Q_M \to 2^{\mathcal{V}_M}$, that associates with all $q \in Q_M$ the set $v_M^o(q)$ of variables that are used as outputs at location q. For all $q \in Q_M$, we denote by $v_M^i(q) = \mathcal{V}_M \setminus v_M^o(q)$ the set of variables that are used as inputs.
- Two labelings ϕ_M^i and ϕ_M^o, which associate with each location $q \in Q_M$ a predicate $\phi_M^i(q)$ on $v_M^i(q)$, called the input assumption, and a predicate $\phi_M^o(q)$ on $v_M^o(q)$, called the output guarantee. For all $q \in Q_M$, both $\phi_M^i(q)$ and $\phi_M^o(q)$ should be satisfiable.
- A labeling ρ_M, which associates with each pair of locations $q, r \in Q_M$ a predicate $\rho_M(q,r)$ on $\mathcal{V}_M$, called the *transition guard*. We require that for every location $q \in Q_M$, (i) the disjunction $\bigvee_{r \in Q_M} \rho_M(q,r)$ is valid and (ii) $\forall r, r' \in Q_M$, $(r \neq r') \Rightarrow \neg(\rho_M(q,r) \wedge \rho_M(q,r'))$. Condition (i) ensures that the interface is non-blocking, and condition (ii) ensures determinism. $\square$

We let $\mathcal{V}_M^i = \bigcup_{q \in Q_M} v_M^i(q)$ and $\mathcal{V}_M^o = \bigcup_{q \in Q_M} v_M^o(q)$ be the sets of all variables that are ever used as inputs or outputs (note that we do not require $\mathcal{V}_M^i \cap \mathcal{V}_M^o = \emptyset$). We define the set $Traces(\langle \mathcal{V}_M, Q_M, \hat{q}_M, \phi_M^i, \phi_M^o, \rho_M \rangle)$ of *bidirectional traces* to be the set of infinite sequences $q_0, s_0, q_1, s_1, \ldots$, where $q_0 = \hat{q}_M$, and for all $k \geq 0$, we have $q_k \in Q_M$, $s_k \in \mathcal{S}[\mathcal{V}_M]$, and $s_k \models (\phi_M^i(q_k) \wedge \phi_M^o(q_k) \wedge \rho_M(q_k, q_{k+1}))$. For $q_0, s_0, q_1, s_1, \ldots \in Traces(\langle \mathcal{V}_M, Q_M, \hat{q}_M, \phi_M^i, \phi_M^o, \rho_M \rangle)$ and $k \geq 0$, we say that q_k is *reachable* in $\langle \mathcal{V}_M, Q_M, \hat{q}_M, \phi_M^i, \phi_M^o, \rho_M \rangle$.

Composition of bidirectional interfaces is defined along the same lines as for Moore interfaces. Local incompatibilities arise not only when one interface output values do not satisfy the input assumptions of the other, but also when the same variable is used as output by both interfaces. The formal definition follows.

Definition 4 (Composition of bidirectional interfaces)
Given two bidirectional interfaces M and N, let $\mathcal{V}_\otimes = \mathcal{V}_M \cup \mathcal{V}_N$, $Q_\otimes = Q_M \times Q_N$, and $\hat{q}_\otimes = (\hat{q}_M, \hat{q}_N)$. For all $(p,q) \in Q_M \times Q_N$, let $\phi_\otimes^o(p,q) = \phi_M^o(p) \wedge \phi_N^o(q)$, and for all $(p',q') \in Q_M \times Q_N$, let $\rho_\otimes((p,q),(p',q')) = \rho_M(p,p') \wedge \rho_N(p,p')$. The interfaces M and N are *compatible* (written $M \wr\wr N$) if there is a labeling ψ associating with all $(p,q) \in Q_\otimes$ a predicate $\psi(p,q)$ on $\mathcal{V}_\otimes \setminus (\mathcal{V}_M^o(p) \cup \mathcal{V}_N^o(q))$ such that (i) $\psi(p,q)$ is satisfiable at all $(p,q) \in Q_\otimes$, and (ii) all traces $(p_0, q_0), s_0, (p_1, q_1), s_1, (p_2, q_2), s_2, \ldots \in Traces(\mathcal{V}_\otimes, Q_\otimes, \hat{q}_\otimes, \psi, \phi_\otimes^o, \rho_\otimes)$ satisfy, for all $k \geq 0$, the conditions (a) $\mathcal{V}_M^o(p_k) \cap \mathcal{V}_N^o(q_k) = \emptyset$ and (b) $s_k \models \phi_M^i(p_k) \wedge \phi_N^i(q_k)$. The composition $P = M \| N$ is defined if and only if M and N are compatible; if they are, then $P = M \| N$ is obtained by taking for ϕ_P^i the weakest predicate

ψ such that the above conditions (a) and (b) on traces hold, by taking for Q_P the subset of locations of $Q_\otimes$ that are reachable in $\langle \mathcal{V}_\otimes, Q_\otimes, \hat{q}_\otimes, \mathcal{V}_\otimes^o, \phi_P^i, \phi_\otimes^o, \rho_\otimes \rangle$, by taking $\mathcal{V}_P = \mathcal{V}_\otimes$ and $\hat{q}_P = \hat{q}_\otimes$, and by taking for $\mathcal{V}_P^o, \phi_P^i, \phi_P^o$, and ρ_P the restrictions of $\mathcal{V}_\otimes^o, \phi_\otimes^i, \phi_\otimes^o$, and $\rho_\otimes$ to Q_P. $\qquad \square$

Algorithm 2   Given two bidirectional interfaces M and N, let $\mathcal{V}_\otimes = \mathcal{V}_M \cup \mathcal{V}_N$, $Q_\otimes = Q_M \times Q_N$, and $\hat{q}_\otimes = (\hat{q}_M, \hat{q}_N)$. For all $(p, q) \in Q_M \times Q_N$, let $\phi_\otimes^i(p, q) = \phi_M^i(p) \wedge \phi_M^i(q)$, and for all $(p', q') \in Q_M \times Q_N$, let $\rho_\otimes((p, q), (p', q')) = \rho_M(p, p') \wedge \rho_N(p, p')$. The input labeling $\phi_\otimes^i(p, q)$ is computed by repeating the following steps, that progressively strengthen the input assertions:

[Step 1] For all $(p, q) \in Q_M \times Q_N$, if $v_M^o(p) \cap v_N^o(q) \neq \emptyset$, then initialize $\phi_\otimes^i(p, q)$ to F; otherwise initialize $\phi_\otimes^i(p, q)$ to the predicate $\forall v_\otimes^o(p, q)$. $(\phi_\otimes^o(p, q) \to (\phi_M^i(p) \wedge \phi_N^i(q))$.

[Step 2] For all (p, q) and (p', q') in $Q_M \times Q_N$, if $\phi_\otimes^i(p', q')$ is unsatisfiable, then replace $\phi_\otimes^i(p, q)$ with $\phi_\otimes^i(p, q) \wedge \forall v_\otimes^o(p, q).(\phi_\otimes^o(p, q) \to \neg \rho_\otimes((p, q), (p', q'))$.

Repeat [Step 2] until all input assumptions are replaced by equivalent predicates, i.e., are not strengthened.

We have that $M \mathcal{U} N$ iff $\phi_\otimes^i(\hat{q}_M, \hat{q}_N)$ is satisfiable. If $M \mathcal{U} N$ then their composition P is defined by taking Q_P to be the subset of locations of $Q_\otimes$ that are reachable in $\langle \mathcal{V}_\otimes, Q_\otimes, \hat{q}_\otimes, v_\otimes^o, \phi_P^i, \phi_\otimes^o, \rho_\otimes \rangle$, by taking $\mathcal{V}_P = \mathcal{V}_\otimes$ and $\hat{q}_P = \hat{q}_\otimes$, and by taking for $v_P^o, \phi_P^i, \phi_P^o$, and ρ_P the restrictions of $v_\otimes^o, \phi_\otimes^i, \phi_\otimes^o$, and $\rho_\otimes$ to Q_P. $\qquad \square$

We have developed and implemented symbolic algorithms for composition and compatibility and refinement checking of bidirectional interfaces. The tool, written in Java, is based on the CUDD Package used in JMocha [8]. In our implementation, the locations are represented explicitly, while the input assumptions and output guarantees at each location are represented and manipulated symbolically. This hybrid representation is well-suited to the modeling of bidirectional interfaces, where the set of input and output variables depends on the location.

Example 2 (PCI Bus)   We consider a PCI bus configuration with two PCI-compliant master devices and a PCI arbiter as shown in Figure 1(a). Each PCI master device has an *gnt* input and a *req* output to communicate with the arbiter, and a set of shared (read-write) signals, the IRDY and the FRAME, which are used to communicate with target devices. The arbiter ensures that at most one master device can write to the shared signals. Figure 1(b) shows a graphical description of the interface representing a master device. The figure shows for each location, the assumption ("a"), the guarantee ("g"), the set of inout variables that the interface writes to, and guarded transitions between locations. Composing two such interfaces we obtain the interface shown in Figure 1(c). Location Owner_Owner is illegal because both components write the shared variables FRAME and IRDY. Input assumptions of locations Req_Req, Owner_Req and Req_Owner are strengthened to make the illegal location unreachable. Note that this propagates the PCI master's assumptions about its environment to an assumption

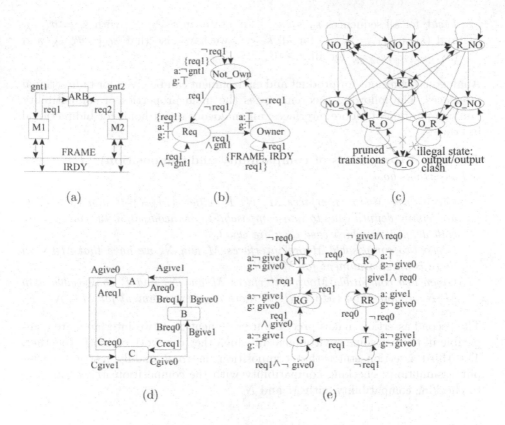

(a)   (b)   (c)

(d)   (e)

Fig. 1. PCI and Token-ring Protocols 1(a) PCI Local Bus Structural Diagram 1(b) PCI Master Interface 1(e) Composite interface for two PCI Master Modules 1(d) Token Ring Network Configuration 1(e) Token-ring NT Interface

on the behavior of the arbiter (which is the environment of the composite module): the arbiter should never assert gnt1 (gnt2) during or after asserting gnt2 (gnt1), until req2 (req1) is de-asserted at least once.   □

2.3   Properties of Compatibility and Composition

If M and N are composable Moore interfaces, we define their *product* $M \otimes N$ by $\mathcal{V}^o_{M \otimes N} = \mathcal{V}^o_M \cup \mathcal{V}^o_N$ and $\mathcal{V}^i_{M \otimes N} = (\mathcal{V}^i_M \cup \mathcal{V}^i_N) \setminus \mathcal{V}^o_{M \otimes N}$, and by letting $\theta^o_{M \otimes N} = \theta^o_M \wedge \theta^o_N$, $\theta^i_{M \otimes N} = \theta^i_M \wedge \theta^i_N$, $\tau^o_{M \otimes N} = \tau^o_M \wedge \tau^o_N$, and $\tau^i_{M \otimes N} = \tau^i_M \wedge \tau^i_N$. Intuitively, an *environment* for a Moore interface M is an interface that drives all free inputs of M, ensuring that all the input assumptions are met. Precisely, we say that a Moore interface N is an environment for a Moore interface M if M and N are composable and closed (i.e., $\mathcal{V}^o_M \cap \mathcal{V}^o_N = \emptyset$, and $\mathcal{V}^i_{M \otimes N} = \emptyset$), and if the following conditions hold:

– *Non-blocking:* $\theta^i_{M \otimes N}$ is satisfiable, and $\forall \mathcal{V}^o_{M \otimes N}.(\exists \mathcal{V}^i_{M \otimes N})'.\tau^i_{M \otimes N}$ holds.

– *Legal:* for all sequences $s_0, s_1, s_2, \ldots$ of states in $\mathcal{S}[\mathcal{V}_{M \otimes N}]$ with $s_0 \models \theta^o_{M \otimes N}$ and $(s_k, s_{k+1}) \models \tau^o_{M \otimes N}$ for all $k \geq 0$, we have also that $s_0 \models \theta^i_{M \otimes N}$ and $(s_k, s_{k+1}) \models \tau^i_{M \otimes N}$ for all $k \geq 0$.

Analogous definitions for product and environment can be given for bidirectional interfaces. The following theorem states the main properties of compatibility and composition of Moore interfaces; an analogous result holds for bidirectional interfaces.

Theorem 1 (properties of compatibility and composition) *The following assertions hold:*

1. *Given three Moore interfaces M, N, P, either $(M\|N)\|P$ and $(M\|N)\|P$ are both undefined (due to non-composability or incompatibility), or they are both defined, in which case they are equal.*
2. *Given two composable Moore interfaces M and N, we have that $M \wr\wr N$ iff there is an environment for $M \otimes N$.*
3. *Given two compatible Moore interfaces M and N, and P composable with $M\|N$, we have that $(M\|N)\wr\wr P$ iff there is an environment for $M \otimes N \otimes P$.*

The second assertion makes precise our statement that two interfaces are compatible iff there is some environment in which they can work correctly together. The third assertion states that composition does not unduly restrict the input assumptions: checking compatibility with the composition $M\|N$ amounts to checking compatibility with M and N.

3 Refinement

We define refinement as alternating simulation [ ]: roughly, a component N refines M (written $N \preceq M$) if N can simulate all inputs of M, and if M can simulate all outputs of N. Encoding the relation between the states of two Moore interfaces M and N by a predicate R, we can state the definition of refinement as follows.

Definition 5 (Refinement of Moore interfaces) Given two Moore interfaces M and N, we have that $N \preceq M$ if $\mathcal{V}^i_N \subseteq \mathcal{V}^i_M$ and $\mathcal{V}^i_M \cap (\mathcal{V}^o_M \cup \mathcal{V}^o_N) = \emptyset$, and if there is a predicate R on $\mathcal{V}_M \cup \mathcal{V}_N$ such that the following formulas are valid:

$$\theta^i_M \wedge \theta^o_N \;\rightarrow\; \exists(\mathcal{V}^o_M \setminus \mathcal{V}^o_N).(\theta^i_N \wedge \theta^o_M \wedge R)$$
$$R \wedge \tau^i_M \wedge \tau^o_N \;\rightarrow\; \exists(\mathcal{V}^o_M \setminus \mathcal{V}^o_N)'.(\tau^i_N \wedge \tau^o_M \wedge R') \qquad \square$$

As for normal simulation, there is a unique largest refinement relation between any two Moore interfaces. Hence, Definition 5 provides an iterative algorithm for deciding refinement: let $R_0 = \mathrm{T}$, and for $k \geq 0$, let

$$R_{k+1} = R_k \wedge \forall(\mathcal{V}_M \cup \mathcal{V}_N)'.(\tau^i_M \wedge \tau^o_N \rightarrow \exists(\mathcal{V}^o_M \setminus \mathcal{V}^o_N)'.(\tau^i_N \wedge \tau^o_M \wedge R'_k)). \qquad (2)$$

Denoting with $R_* = \lim_{k\to\infty} R_k$ the fixpoint (that again can be computed in a finite number of iterations), we have that $N \preceq M$ if and only if (i) $\mathcal{V}_N^i \subseteq \mathcal{V}_M^i$ and $\mathcal{V}_M^i \cap (\mathcal{V}_M^o \cup \mathcal{V}_N^o) = \emptyset$, and (ii) $\theta_M^i \wedge \theta_N^o \to \exists(\mathcal{V}_M^o \setminus \mathcal{V}_N^o).(\theta_N^i \wedge \theta_M^o \wedge R)$. In order to obtain an efficient implementation, we can again take advantage for the computation of (2) of list representations for the transition relations, and apply image-computation techniques.

Refinement of bidirectional interfaces is defined similarly, except that the refinement relation relates the locations of the two interfaces, rather than the states. The definition is as follows.

Definition 6 (Refinement of bidirectional interfaces) Given two bidirectional interfaces M and N, N refines M ($N \preceq M$) iff there is a binary relation $\preceq \subseteq Q_N \times Q_M$ such that $\hat{q}_N \preceq \hat{q}_M$, and such that for all $q \preceq p$ we have (i) $v_N^i(q) \subseteq v_M^i(q)$, (ii) $v_N^o(q) \supseteq v_M^o(p)$, (iii) $\phi_M^i(p) \to \phi_N^i(q)$, (iv) $\phi_N^o(q) \to \phi_M^o(p)$, (v) for all $s \in \mathcal{S}[v_M^i(p)]$ and all $t \in \mathcal{S}[v_N^o(q)]$, if $s \models \rho_M(p,p')$ and $t \models \rho_N(q,q')$, then $q' \preceq p'$. □

We can check whether $N \preceq M$ by adapting the classical iterative refinement check [10]. We start with the total relation $\preceq_0 = Q_N \times Q_M$, and for $k \geq 0$, we let $\preceq_{k+1}$ be the subset of $\preceq_k$ such that conditions (i)–(v) hold, with $\preceq_k$ in place of $\preceq$ in condition (v). Once we reach $m \geq 0$ such that $\preceq_{m+1} = \preceq_m$, we have that $N \preceq M$ iff $\hat{q}_N \preceq \hat{p}_N$. Since bidirectional interfaces are deterministic we can reduce the refinement checking problem to graph reachability on the product interface and hence $N \preceq M$ can be decided in $O(|Q_N| \times |Q_M|)$ time.

Example 3 (Token Ring) The IEEE 802.5 (Token Ring) is a widely used deterministic LAN protocol. Figure 1(e) shows an interface modeling a node that initially does not have the token. The same diagram with T as initial state would represent a node that initially has the token. We call these two interfaces NT and T, respectively. The token ring components are connected in a cyclic network; each pair of adjacent nodes communicate by req and gnt signals (Figure 1(d)). The req signal flows clockwise, and is used to request the token; the signal $give$ flows counterclockwise, and is used to grant the token. The protocol fails if more than one node has the token simultaneously: indeed, we can verify that two T interfaces are not compatible, while an NT interface is compatible with a T interface. Moreover, the protocol works for any number of participating nodes. To verify this, we check two refinements: first, an open-ring configuration consisting entirely of NT nodes is a refinement of the configuration consisting in just one NT node; second, an open-ring configuration with any number of NT nodes and one T node is a refinement of a configuration consisting in a single T node. Our implementation is able to perform the above compatibility and refinement checks in a fraction of a second. □

The notion of refinement, in addition to implementation, captures also substitutivity: if N refines M, and M is compatible with the remainder P of the design, then P is also compatible with N.

Theorem 2 (Substitutivity of refinement)   *Consider three bidirectional Moore or bidirectional interfaces M, N, P, such that $M \wr\!\wr P$, and $N \preceq M$. If $(\mathcal{V}_N^o \cap \mathcal{V}_P^i) \subseteq (\mathcal{V}_M^o \cap \mathcal{V}_P^i)$, then $N \wr\!\wr P$ and $(N \| P) \preceq (M \| P)$.*

The result has a proviso: all the variables that are output by N and input by P should also be output by M. If this were not the case, it would be possible for the additional outputs of N to violate the input assumptions of P.

References

1. M. Abadi, L. Lamport, and P. Wolper. Realizable and unrealizable concurrent program specifications. In *Proc. 16th Int. Colloq. Aut. Lang. Prog.*, volume 372 of *Lect. Notes in Comp. Sci.*, pages 1–17. Springer-Verlag, 1989. 415
2. S. Abramsky. Games in the semantics of programming languages. In *Proc. of the 11th Amsterdam Colloquium*, pages 1–6. ILLC, Dept. of Philosophy, University of Amsterdam, 1997. 416
3. S. Abramsky, S. Gay, and R. Nagarajan. A type-theoretic approach to deadlock-freedom of asynchronous systems. In *TACS'97: Theoretical Aspects of Computer Software. Third International Symposium*, 1997. 415, 416
4. R. Alur and T. A. Henzinger. Reactive modules. *Formal Methods in System Design*, pages 7–48, 1999. 415, 416
5. R. Alur, T. A. Henzinger, O. Kupferman, and M. Y. Vardi. Alternating refinement relations. In *CONCUR 97: Concurrency Theory*, volume 1466 of *Lect. Notes in Comp. Sci.*, pages 163–178. Springer-Verlag, 1998. 416, 424
6. R. Alur, T. A. Henzinger, F. Y. C. Mang, S. Qadeer, S. K. Rajamani, and S. Tasiran. Mocha: modularity in model checking. In *CAV 98: Proc. of 10th Conf. on Computer Aided Verification*, volume 1427 of *Lect. Notes in Comp. Sci.*, pages 521–525. Springer-Verlag, 1998. 420
7. E. Clarke, K. McMillan, S. Campos, and V. Hartonas-Garmhausen. Symbolic model checking. In *CAV 96: Proc. of 8th Conf. on Computer Aided Verification*, volume 1102 of *Lect. Notes in Comp. Sci.*, pages 419–422. Springer-Verlag, 1996. 415
8. L. de Alfaro, R. Alur, R. Grosu, T. Henzinger, M. Kang, R. Majumdar, F. Mang, C. Meyer-Kirsch, and B. Y. Wang. Mocha: A model checking tool that exploits design structure. In *ICSE 01: Proceedings of the 23rd International Conference on Software Engineering*, 2001. 422
9. L. de Alfaro and T. A. Henzinger. Interface automata. In *Proc. of 8th European Software Engineering Conference and 9th ACM SIGSOFT Symposium on Foundations of Software Engineering (ESEC/FSE)*, pages 109–120. ACM Press, 2001. 416
10. L. de Alfaro and T. A. Henzinger. Interface theories for component-based design. In *EMSOFT 01: Proc. of First Int. Workshop on Embedded Software*, volume 2211 of *Lect. Notes in Comp. Sci.*, pages 148–165. Springer-Verlag, 2001. 416
11. D. L. Dill. *Trace Theory for Automatic Hierarchical Verification of Speed-Independent Circuits.* MIT Press, 1988. 415, 416
12. C. A. R. Hoare. *Communicating Sequential Processes.* Prentice-Hall, 1985. 415
13. N. A. Lynch. *Distributed Algorithms.* Morgan-Kaufmann, 1996. 415
14. N. A. Lynch and M. Tuttle. Hierarcical correctness proofs for distributed algorithms. In *Proc. of 6th ACM Symp. Princ. of Dist. Comp.*, pages 137–151, 1987. 416

15. Z. Manna and A. Pnueli. *The Temporal Logic of Reactive and Concurrent Systems: Specification.* Springer-Verlag, New York, 1991. 415
16. R. Milner.   An algebraic definition of simulation between programs.   In *Proc. of Second Int. Joint Conf. on Artificial Intelligence*, pages 481–489. The British Computer Society, 1971. 425
17. R. Milner. *Communication and Concurrency.* Prentice-Hall, 1989. 415
18. J. C. Mitchell. *Foundations for Programming Languages.* MIT Press, 1996. 417

Interface Compatibility Checking for Software Modules[*]

Arindam Chakrabarti[1], Luca de Alfaro[2], Thomas A. Henzinger[1],
Marcin Jurdziński[1], and Freddy Y.C. Mang[3]

[1] EECS, University of California, Berkeley
[2] CE, University of California, Santa Cruz
[3] Advanced Technology Group, Synopsys Inc.

Abstract. We present a formal methodology and tool for uncovering errors in the interaction of software modules. Our methodology consists of a suite of languages for defining software interfaces, and algorithms for checking interface compatibility. We focus on interfaces that explain the method-call dependencies between software modules. Such an interface makes assumptions about the environment in the form of call and availability constraints. A call constraint restricts the accessibility of local methods to certain external methods. An availability constraint restricts the accessibility of local methods to certain states of the module. For example, the interface for a file server with local methods **open** and **read** may assert that a file cannot be read without having been opened. Checking interface compatibility requires the solution of games, and in the presence of availability constraints, of pushdown games. Based on this methodology, we have implemented a tool that has uncovered incompatibilities in TinyOS, a small operating system for sensor nodes in adhoc networks.

1 Introduction

In structured software design, functionality and data is arranged in software modules. Each module has a set of procedures, or *methods*, for accessing the encapsulated data. Modules can be treated as components, for example, taken from libraries, or implemented by different vendors. This raises the question of when two modules are *compatible*. A limited answer to this question is given by traditional type systems. For example, if method a of module A calls method b of module B, then the number and types of the actual parameters of the call of b in A must match the number and types of the formal parameters of the implementation of b in B; otherwise, the modules A and B are incompatible. This weak form of compatibility is resolved by type checking. Note that the type of an external method call in module A, say b(n:int), is an *assumption* about

[*] This research was supported in part by the AFOSR grant F49620-00-1-0327, the DARPA grant F33615-00-C-1693, the MARCO grant 98-DT-660, the NSF grants CCR-9988172, CCR-0085949, CCR-0132780, the SRC grant 99-TJ-683, and the Polish KBN grant 7-T11C-027-20.

the environment of A, namely, that it provides an implementation of b with a single formal parameter, which is an integer. The assumption is checked when the environment is provided.

We define and check two stronger forms of software module (SM) compatibility. The first is called *stateless SM interface compatibility*. Stateless SM interfaces can express assumptions about the call graph of the environment. For example, a common design requirement is that an initialization method must not call itself recursively. Consider again module A, this time with the two local methods a-init and a-update. Suppose that the implementation of a-init calls the external method b, and the designer of A wants to make sure that whatever b does, it causes no recursive call-back of a-init. This constraint about the environment can be written as a *call assumption* for module A, namely, b:not{a-init}. In general, the call assumption b:not{a_1,...,a_k} for a module A with external method b and local methods a_1, ..., a_k has the following interpretation: every chain of method calls that can be caused by an invocation of b must *not* contain any method in {a_1,...,a_k}. In particular, the default call assumption for an external method b is b:not{}; this does not constrain the implementation of b.

A second, even stronger form of software module compatibility is called *stateful SM interface compatibility*. Stateful SM interfaces can express assumptions about the state of the module when local methods are called by the environment. For example, a common design requirement is that an update method must not be called before the corresponding initialization method is called. Consider again module A with the local methods a-init and a-update. Suppose that the state variable x of A records whether or not the method a-init has been called: initially $x = 0$, and x changes to 1 with the first call of a-init, where it remains. The constraint that the environment calls a-update only when $x = 1$ can be written as a pair of *availability assumptions* for module A, namely, a-init:true and a-update:x=1, with the following interpretation: when $x = 0$, then only a-init may be called by the environment; when $x = 1$, then both a-init and a-update may be called. In general, the availability assumption a:p for a module A asserts that the local method a of A can be called only when the predicate p is true in the current state of A. The default availability assumption for a local method a, which does not constrain the environment, is a:true.

It is obviously undecidable to check if call and availability assumptions for module A are satisfied by the *code* for environment module B.[1] We therefore require the designer of a module to explicitly provide an interface. An SM interface makes *guarantees* about how the local methods interact with the environment, in addition to the assumptions about how the environment is expected to interact with the local methods. Then, two modules A and B are compatible if the guarantees of A meet the assumptions of B, and vice versa. Consider again the stateless case, where the interface of module A makes the call assumption b:not{a-init}. If the interface of module B, which owns the method b, provides the call guarantee b:{}, meaning that the implementation of b calls no other methods, then the modules A and B are compatible. On the other hand, if the

---

[1]   Static analysis may be used for conservative estimations.

interface of B has the call guarantee b:{a-init}, meaning that the implementation of b calls a-init, then the modules A and B are incompatible.

The interesting case is the third possibility, that the implementation of b calls some methods other than a-init. Suppose that the interface of B provides the call guarantee b:{c}, meaning that the implementation of b calls the new method c, which is external to both modules A and B. In this case, the call assumption b:not{a-init} of A may or may not be satisfied, depending on whether or not the implementation of c calls (directly or indirectly) a-init. While a pessimistic approach would reject the composition of A and B, because compatibility is not ensured for *all* environments —i.e., implementations of c— we instead take the optimistic approach to compatibility [ ] and compute the derived call assumption c:not{a-init} for the combined interface of $A\|B$. In other words, A and B are considered compatible, because there is *some* environment that makes A and B work together properly, namely, the environment that implements c without calling a-init. Note that only the chosen, optimistic approach to compatibility is associative. Suppose that a third module C provides an implementation of method c with call guarantee c:{}; that is, c calls no further methods. Then the composition $A\|B\|C$ is well-formed. While the optimistic approach permits all ways of assembling this system, namely, $(A\|B)\|C$ and $A\|(B\|C)$ and $(A\|C)\|B$, the pessimistic approach rejects the first one.

The optimistic approach to compatibility is made possible by the ability of interfaces to express environment assumptions, which can then be propagated when composing interfaces. In the stateless case, SM interface compatibility checking, as well as the derivation of call assumptions for the composite interface, are graph problems that can be solved in quadratic time. If state is involved, checking optimistic compatibility between two interfaces A and B requires the solution of a two-player *game* [, ,]. Player 1 represents both A and B, and player 2 represents the environment. If player 2 has a strategy of satisfying the call and availability assumptions of both A and B, then the two interfaces are compatible (because there is a "helpful" environment); otherwise they are incompatible. Note that if the composition of A and B is *closed*, i.e., calls no external methods, then the game disappears, and compatibility checking simply resolves the assumptions of A against the guarantees of B, and vice versa. As call chains may be recursive, we need to solve *pushdown* games, rendering compatibility checking and composition for stateful SM interfaces exponential. However, SM interfaces tend to be much smaller than the underlying module implementations: for instance, in the stateful example from above, the interface has only two states ($x = 0$ and $x = 1$), whereas the state of module A itself may be arbitrarily complex (depending on which data structures A contains).

We have modified the JBuilder programming environment to permit the annotation of Java objects with interfaces. When defining a Java object, the programmer may specify its interface as commentary, and our tool automatically checks its compatibility with the interfaces of other objects that have already been defined. The tool implements the compatibility check for the interface automata of [ ], as well as the stateless and stateful SM interfaces presented here.

Interface automata are based on finite-state games, and do not support recursive call-backs between modules. This is insufficient for many software applications, including our software driver TinyOS [13], a small operating system for sensor nodes in adhoc networks. TinyOS is structured into six modules, which represent different service layers. We have defined stateful SM interfaces for two of the layers, and discovered two incompatilities in their interaction. The notion of interface state that needs to be considered in this example is considerably less complex than the full state of the implementation, bearing out the promise of our methodology. In other words, by aiming at certain limited but common classes of module interaction errors, rather than intra-module errors, we are able to avoid many of the obstacles to fully automatic and complete software verification.

We are not the first to propose a formalization of software module interfaces. Many researchers have addressed this issue by developing languages for writing software specifications and contracts, e.g., [16,15,17,5,11]. These languages are typically based on pre- and postconditions, and therefore related in expressiveness to stateful SM interfaces (an availability assumption is a restricted kind of precondition, which cannot refer to the parameters of method calls). The key difference between our interfaces and software contracts is that contract violations are detected at run-time, while interface incompatibilities are uncovered at compile-time. In this respect, interfaces are *types*, and the stateful SM interfaces are related to recent trends in type systems to capture behavioral aspects of software [12,8,14], and type systems for module interaction [1]. Indeed, the latter also advocates a game-theoretic view. Architecture description languages (e.g., [3]) and software modeling languages (e.g., UML) also support various degrees of formality in specifying module interactions, but to our knowledge, none of these languages capture the optimistic, game-based approach to compatibility.

2   Stateless Software Module Interfaces

A *stateless SM interface* $I = (M^L, M^E, \mathcal{C}, \mathcal{B})$ consists of the following:

- A set M^L of *local methods*. These are the methods that are defined within the module.[2]
- A set M^E of *external* (or *imported*) *methods*. These are the methods that are not defined within the module, but called from method definitions within the module. We write M for the set of all methods known by the interface, i.e., we define $M = M^L \cup M^E$.
- A set $\mathcal{C} = \{C(l) \mid l \in M^L\}$ of *call guarantees*. For each local method $l \in M^L$, the call guarantee $C(l) \subseteq M$ specifies the (local and external) method calls that occur in the definition of l.
- A set $\mathcal{B} = \{B(m) \mid m \in M\}$ of *call assumptions*. For each method $m \in M$, the call assumption $B(m) \subseteq M^L$ specifies the local methods whose execution is forbidden as a result of an invocation of m.

---

[2] We assume that all local methods can be called by other modules. It is straightforward to further differentiate between *hidden* and *exported* local methods.

Note that call guarantees refer only to direct calls, that is, $m \in C(l)$ asserts that m is called directly by the definition of l. Call assumptions, on the other hand, refer to direct as well as indirect calls, that is, $l \in B(m)$ asserts that there must not be a sequence $m_0, m_1, \ldots, m_k$ of (local, known external, or unknown external) methods such that $m_0 = m$ and $m_k = l$ and for all $0 \leq i < k$, the definition of m_i calls m_{i+1}. Call guarantees and call assumptions may be inconsistent. For example, for local l and m, it must not happen that both $m \in C(l)$ and $m \in B(l)$. Consistency is defined formally below.

Call guarantees must conform with the module implementation[3]; call assumptions are constraints that the module designer puts on the implementation of external methods. For example, for local l and external e, if $l \in B(e)$, then e is expected to be implemented in a way that does not cause a direct or indirect call of l. Similarly, for local l and m and external e such that $e \in C(m)$, that is, e is called by m, if $l \in B(m)$, then e is again expected not to cause a direct or indirect call of l. In the latter case, the call assumption $l \in B(e)$ can be derived. If an interface contains all derived call assumptions, then it is called complete.

Consistent and Complete Interfaces For a local method $l \in M^L$ and a method $m \in M$, we say that l *calls* m, and write $m \in C^*(l)$ if there is a sequence $m_0, m_1, \ldots, m_k$ of methods $m_i \in M$ such that $m_0 = l$ and $m_k = m$, and $m_{i+1} \in C(m_i)$ for all $0 \leq i < k$. Note that m_i must be local for all $i < k$, and m_k may be either local or external. We say that l *properly calls* m, and write $m \in C^+(l)$, if $k > 0$. For a method $m \in M$ and local method $l \in M^L$, we say that m *must not call* l if $l \in B(m)$. The call assumption $B(m)$ of a method $m \in M$ is *complete* in the interface I if for all methods $m' \in M$, and all local methods $l, l' \in M^L$, if l must not call m', and l calls m, and l' calls m', then m must not call l'. The interface I is *complete* if the call assumptions of all methods in M are complete in I. The *completion* $I^c = (M^L, M^E, C, \mathcal{B}^c)$ of I is the (unique) stateless SM interface whose set $\mathcal{B}^c$ of call assumptions is the component-wise smallest family of sets $B^c(m)$ such that for all methods $m \in M$, both $B(m) \subseteq B^c(m) \subseteq M^L$ and $B^c(m)$ is complete in I^c.

The call assumption $B(l)$ of a local method $l \in M^L$ is *satisfied* in the interface I if l does not properly call any method that it must not call. The interface I is *consistent* if the call assumptions of all local methods in M^L are satisfied in I. Note that consistency can be checked in time required to compute the transitive closure C^+ of C, which is quadratic in the size of the interface (i.e., in the number of edges of a graph). Also note that for consistency, it does not matter whether I is complete, because if some call assumption $B^c(l)$ is not satisfied in the completion I^c, then there is a local method $l' \in M^L$ such that the call assumption $B(l')$ is not satisfied in the original interface I. Hence we need not insist on completeness in stateless SM interfaces.

---

[3] Indeed, it would not be difficult to derive call guarantees automatically from the module implementation by parsing method definitions.

Interface Compatibility and Composition Two stateless SM interfaces $I = (M_I^L, M_I^E, C_I, B_I)$ and $J = (M_J^L, M_J^E, C_J, B_J)$ are *proto-compatible* if their local methods are disjoint: $M_I^L \cap M_J^L = \emptyset$. If I and J are proto-compatible, then the *composition* of I and J is the stateless SM interface $I||J = (M^L, M^E, C, B)$ with

- $M^L = M_I^L \cup M_J^L$ and $M^E = (M_I^E \cup M_J^E) \setminus M^L$;
- for all $l \in M^L$, we have $C(l) = C_I(l)$ if $l \in M_I^L$, and $C(l) = C_J(l)$ if $l \in M_J^L$;
- for all $m \in M$, we have $B(m) = B_I(m) \cup B_J(m)$.

Note that composition is associative. The stateless SM interfaces I and J are *compatible* if they are proto-compatible, and the composition $I||J$ is consistent.

Theorem 1. *The compatibility of two stateless SM interfaces can be checked in quadratic time.*

3 Background: Pushdown Games

A *labeled pushdown game* $\mathcal{G} = (Q, \Sigma, \sigma, \Gamma, c_0, \hookrightarrow)$ consists of the following:

- a finite set Q of (*control*) *states*, partitioned into the *existential* states $Q_\exists$ and the *universal* states $Q_\forall$;
- a finite *stack alphabet* Γ;
- an initial configuration $c_0 \in Q \times \Gamma^+$;
- a transition relation $\hookrightarrow \subseteq (Q \times \Gamma) \times (Q \times Cmd(\Gamma))$, where $Cmd(\Gamma) = \{skip, pop\} \cup \{push(\gamma) \mid \gamma \in \Gamma\}$.

The *game tree* $\mathcal{T}(\mathcal{G})$ is a the labeled tree of configurations of $\mathcal{G}$ with the root c_0 such that each vertex $(q, \gamma \cdot w) \in Q \times \Gamma^+$ has the following successors:

- $(q', \gamma \cdot w)$ if $(q, \gamma) \hookrightarrow (q', skip)$;
- (q, w) if $(q, \gamma) \hookrightarrow (q', pop)$;
- $(q', \gamma' \cdot \gamma \cdot w)$ if $(q, \gamma) \hookrightarrow (q', push(\gamma'))$.

Furthermore, the vertex (q, w) is existential if $q \in Q_\exists$, and universal otherwise.

A two-player game is played on a game tree as follows. The game starts at the root. At an existential vertex, the existential player chooses a successor, and at a universal vertex, the universal player chooses a successor. The *reachability problem* for pushdown games asks, given a labeled pushdown game $\mathcal{G}$ and a control state $f \in Q$, if the existential player has a strategy to direct the play on the game tree $\mathcal{T}(\mathcal{G})$ to a node (f, w), for some $w \in \Gamma^*$.

Theorem 2. [18] *The reachability problem for labeled pushdown games is complete for DEXPTIME.*

4   Stateful Software Module Interfaces

When equipping SM interfaces with state, we use interface programs to specify the state transitions. An interface program is an abstraction of the code implementing a method and must be provided by the software designer. We represent interface programs by *flow graphs*, whose nodes represent control locations and whose edges are labeled with instructions, including method calls [10]. Nondeterministic branching is allowed and can be the result of abstraction. More formally, for a set X of typed variables and a set M of methods, an *interface program* $P = (L, E, \vdash, \dashv, \mu)$ over X and M is a labeled graph, consisting of the following:

– A finite set L of *program locations*. Every program has an *initial location* $\vdash \in L$ and a terminal location $\dashv \in L$.
– A set of edges $E \subseteq V \times V$, and a labeling function $\mu \colon E \to Instr(X, M)$, where $Instr(X, M)$ is the set containing assignment and conditional instructions over the variables in X, and calls to the methods in M.

We write $Progs(X, M)$ for the set of interface programs over X and M. A *stateful SM interface* $F = (X, M^L, M^E, \mathcal{P}, \mathcal{A}, \mathcal{B})$ consists of the following:

– A finite set $X = \{x_1 : D_1, \ldots, x_k : D_k\}$ of typed *interface variables*, where $D_1, \ldots, D_k$ are finite sets of values. We refer to the type-respecting valuations of the variables in X as *interface states*, and write $States(X)$ for the set of interface states.
– A finite set M of methods, partitioned into the set M^L of *local methods* and the set M^E of *external methods*.
– For every local method $l \in M^L$, an *interface program* $P(l) \in Progs(X, M)$ over the variables X and methods M. The interface program $P(l)$ abstracts the implementation of l by recording method calls, and the (nondeterministic) changes in the interface state between method calls.
– For every local method $m \in M^L$, an *availability assumption* $A(m) \in \mathcal{A}$, such that $A(m) \subseteq States(X)$. The availability assumption $A(m)$ states the expectation on the environment that m is invoked only when the interface state is in $A(m)$.
– For every method $m \in M$, a *call assumption* $B(m) \in \mathcal{B}$, such that $B(m) \subseteq M^L$. As for stateless SM interfaces, the call assumption $B(m)$ states the expectation on the environment that no method in $B(m)$ is invoked as a (direct or indirect) result of invoking m.

For the stateful SM interface F, we define the corresponding stateless SM interface $I_F = (M^L, M^E, \mathcal{C}, \mathcal{B})$, where $m \in C(l)$ iff some edge of the interface program $P(l)$ is labeled with a call of method m.

Pushdown Game Semantics Our aim in modeling the behaviour of a software module is to capture its possible interactions with the environment (i.e., the implementations of the external methods). While the environment cannot directly change the interface state, it can do so by calling a local method. Our notion of an error is a call of a local method m when the interface state is not in $A(m)$; such a call violates the availability assumption. For every local method m and interface state $s \in A(m)$, we want to check that there is a "helpful" environment, so that along every behavior of the interface that can result from calling m in state s, no error occurs. That is, we ask if there is a way of resolving the nondeterministic choices of the environment such that for all nondeterministic choices of the interface, an error never occurs. The environment has the choice, when an external method is called, to call back any sequence of local methods; the interface has the choice, when executing a local method l, to pursue any path in the nondeterministic interface program $P(l)$. As mutually recursive procedures are naturally modeled as pushdown systems [10], we need pushdown games, with the two players Interface and Environment. Given a stateful SM interface $F = (X, M^L, M^E, \mathcal{P}, \mathcal{A}, \mathcal{B})$, a local method $m_0 \in M^L$, and an interface state $s_0 \in S$, we define the following pushdown game $\mathcal{G}(F, m_0, s_0) = (Q, \Sigma, \sigma, \Gamma, c_0, \hookrightarrow)$:

- First, for every external method $m \in M^E$ with call assumption $B(m)$, we define the interface program with two locations: the initial location $\vdash_m$ and the terminal location $\dashv_m$, an edge $(\vdash_m, \dashv_m)$ labeled by a vacuously true condition, and an edge $(\vdash_m, \vdash_m)$ for each local method $m \in M^L \setminus B(m)$, labeled by the call of method m. In other words, we allow player Environment to choose an arbitrary implementation of m by making any sequence of local method calls that are permitted by the call assumption $B(m)$.
- Let $\mathcal{L}$ be the disjoint union of the sets of program locations of $P(m)$ for all methods $m \in M$, where $M = M^L \cup M^E$. We write $\vdash_m$ for the initial location of $P(m)$, and we write $\dashv_m$ for the terminal location of $P(m)$. The set of control states of the pushdown game is $Q - States(X) \times \mathcal{L}$, and the stack alphabet is $\Gamma = \mathcal{L} \cup \{\bot\}$. The control state (s, ℓ) is existential (i.e., player Environment moves) if ℓ is a nonterminal location of $P(m)$ for some external method $m \in M^E$, and (s, ℓ) is universal (i.e., player Interface moves) otherwise. The initial configuration is $c_0 = ((s_0, \vdash_{m_0}), \bot)$; that is, the stack contains only the bottom marker $\bot$.
- The stack records the return locations for a sequence of method calls. The transition relation $\hookrightarrow$ of the pushdown game is defined by the following rules.
  - *Method call.* For every state $s \in States(X)$, edge (ℓ, ℓ') labeled with a call of method m, and stack symbol $\gamma \in \Gamma$, we have $((s, \ell), \gamma) \hookrightarrow ((s, \vdash_m), push(\ell'))$ iff $s \in A(m)$.
  - *Return from method call.* For every state $s \in States(X)$, method $m \in M$, and location $\ell \in \mathcal{L}$, we have $((s, \dashv_m), \ell) \hookrightarrow ((s, \ell), pop)$.
  - *Conditional.* For every state $s \in States(X)$, edge (ℓ, ℓ') labeled with a condition c over $States(X)$, and stack symbol $\gamma \in \Gamma$, we have $((s, \ell), \gamma) \hookrightarrow ((s, \ell'), skip)$ if the state s satisfies the condition c.
  - *Assignment.* For every state $s \in States(X)$, edge (ℓ, ℓ') labeled with an assignment $x := d$ and a stack symbol $\gamma \in \Gamma$, we have $((s, \ell), \gamma) \hookrightarrow ((s[d/x], \ell'), skip)$.

A *play* of the pushdown game $\mathcal{G}(F, m_0, s_0)$ is a maximal sequence of configurations $c_0 \hookrightarrow c_1 \hookrightarrow c_2 \hookrightarrow \cdots$ starting from the initial configuration c_0. Player Environment *wins* the play if it is finite, and the last configuration is $((s, \dashv_{m_0}), \bot)$, for some state $s \in States(X)$; otherwise, player Interface is the winner. Note that if a finite play is won by player Interface, then the last configuration exhibits an error: it corresponds to a call of a local method in a state in which the method is not available. Note also that player Environment has a winning strategy in the game $\mathcal{G}(F, m_0, s_0)$ if it can interact with the interface F in such a way that if method m_0 is called in state s_0, then it can run to termination without ever violating an availability assumption. We say that (F, m_0, s_0) is *safe* if player Environment has a winning strategy in the pushdown game $\mathcal{G}(F, m_0, s_0)$.

Availability Consistency and Strengthening A stateful SM interface $F = (S, M^L, M^E, \mathcal{P}, \mathcal{A}, \mathcal{B})$ is *availability consistent* if (F, m, s) is safe for all local methods $m \in M^L$ and states $s \in A(m)$. Note that the notion of availability consistency is independent of the call assumptions $\mathcal{B}$, which are not modeled by the game semantics defined above. For every stateful SM interface F, it can be shown that there is a unique most general stateful SM interface $Safe(F) = (S, M^L, M^E, \mathcal{P}, \mathcal{A}', \mathcal{B})$ which is availability consistent, and obtained from F by strengthening the availability assumptions; namely, $A'(m) = \{s \in S \mid (F, m, s) \text{ is safe}\}$ for all local methods $m \in M^L$. From Theorem 2 it follows that the availability consistency of a stateful SM interface F can be checked, and $Safe(F)$ constructed, in exponential time.

Composition Two stateful SM interfaces $F = (X_F, M_F^L, M_F^E, \mathcal{P}_F, \mathcal{A}_F, \mathcal{B}_F)$ and $G = (X_G, M_G^L, M_G^E, \mathcal{P}_G, \mathcal{A}_G, \mathcal{B}_G)$ are *proto-compatible* if $M_F^L \cap M_G^L = \emptyset$. If F and G are proto-compatible, then the *proto-composition* $F \oplus G = (X, M^L, M^E, \mathcal{P}, \mathcal{A}, \mathcal{B})$ is defined as follows:

- $X = X_F \uplus X_G$.
- $M^L = M_F^L \cup M_G^L$ and $M^E = (M_F^E \cup M_G^E) \setminus M^L$.
- For all local methods $l \in M^L$, we have $P(m) = P_F(m)$ if $m \in M_F^L$, and $P(m) = P_G(m)$ if $m \in M_G^L$.
- For all local methods $m \in M^L$, we have $A(m) = A_F(m) \times States(X_G)$ if $m \in M_F^L$, and $A(m) = States(X_F) \times A_G(m)$ if $m \in M_G^L$.
- For all methods $m \in M$, we have $B(m) = B_F(m) \cup B_G(m)$.

The proto-compositon $F \oplus G$ may violate call assumptions as well as availability assumptions. We first remove all violations of call assumptions by making unavailable all local methods whose call assumptions are not satisfied, and then we remove all violations of availability assumptions by strengthening. Define $F \oplus^e G = (S, M^L, M^E, \mathcal{P}, \mathcal{A}^e, \mathcal{B})$, where for each local method $l \in M^L$, we have $A^e(l) = A(l)$ if the call assumption $B(l)$ is satisfied in the stateless SM interface $I_{F \oplus G}$ (which is the same as $I_F \| I_G$), and otherwise $A^e(l) = \emptyset$. The *composition* of two proto-compatible SM interfaces F and G is $F \| G = Safe(F \oplus^e G)$.

Proposition 1. *The composition of stateful SM interfaces is associative.*

Theorem 3. *Computing the composition of two stateful SM interfaces is in DEXPTIME.*

As in the stateless case, one might define a notion of compatibility for stateful SM interfaces, but a meaningful definition often depends on the application scenario. For example, one might say that two stateful SM interfaces F and G are *compatible* if they are proto-compatible, and the composition $F\|G$ has a local method m with $A_{F\|G}(m) \neq \emptyset$; that is, at least one method is available in at least one state of the composition. In practice, as in the TinyOS case study below, one often adopts a stronger notion of compatibility, which requires that certain methods must be available in certain states.

An Alternative Definition of Composition If the call assumption $B(l)$ of a local method l is violated in the above definition of composition, then l is made unavailable in all states, that is, $A(l)$ is set to the empty set. However, if a call of method $m \in B(l)$ occurs in the interface program $P(l)$, it does not necessarily mean that m is going to be invoked when l is called; whether or not this happens may depend on the state in which l is called. This suggests the following way of relaxing the definition of composition for stateful SM interfaces.

We modify the pushdown game semantics in such a way that a configuration of the pushdown game (i.e., control state and stack contents) is an error configuration if it violates a call assumption, i.e., if the method called in this configuration must not be called by a method that occurs on the stack. Note that by collecting all methods that occur on the stack in the control state of the pushdown game, we can define an error configuration by referring only to the control state. Let $\mathcal{G}^s(F \oplus G, m, t)$ be the modified pushdown game for local method m and state t of the proto-composition $F \oplus G$, and define $A^s(m) = \{t \in S_{F\oplus G} \mid$ player Environment has a winning strategy in $\mathcal{G}^s(F \oplus G, m, t)\}$ for each local method $m \in M_{F\oplus G}^L$. The alternative composition is defined as $F\|^s G = (S_{F\oplus G}, M_{F\oplus G}^L, M_{F\oplus G}^E, \mathcal{P}_{F\oplus G}, \mathcal{A}^s, \mathcal{B}_{F\oplus G})$. Note that $F\|^s G$ is harder to compute than $F\|G$, because the set of control states of the modified pushdown game $\mathcal{G}^s(F \oplus G, m, t)$ can be exponentially larger than that of the original game $\mathcal{G}(F \oplus G, m, t)$; this is why we chose our original definition of composition. On the other hand, the alternative composition is "better" (i.e., less constraining) in the following sense.

Proposition 2. *If a local method is available at a state t in $F\|G$, then it is available at t in $F\|^s G$. Moreover, for all stateful interfaces H proto-compatible with $F\|G$, if a local method is available at a state t in $(F\|G)\|H$, then it is available at t in $(F\|^s G)\|^s H$.*

Example 1. Consider the following two stateful SM interfaces F and G. Interface F has two states, $\{1, 2\}$; two local methods, a and b; the program for method a is empty; the program for method b makes the deterministic choice that if in

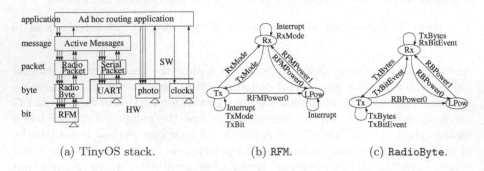

(a) TinyOS stack.   (b) RFM.   (c) RadioByte.

Fig. 1. 1(a) TinyOS communication stack for adhoc networking. 1(b) State transitions for RFM interface. 1(c) State transitions for RadioByte interface

state 1, it calls method a, and if in state 2, it calls an external method x; the call assumption for method b is that it must not (indirectly) call itself; and both methods a and b are available in both states. Interface G has two states, $\{1, 2\}$; a local method x; the program for x makes the deterministic choice that if in state 1, it changes the state to 2 and then calls b, and if in state 1, it calls a; there are no call assumptions; and method x is available in both states. In the composition $F\|G$ method b is not available in any state, because its call assumption is not satisfied in the stateless interface $I_{F\oplus G}$, and method x is available only in states $(1, 2)$ and $(2, 2)$, because in the other states it calls method b and thus violates the availability assumption for b. In the composition $F\|^s G$, method b is unavailable only in state $(2, 1)$ (only when called in this state does it violate its call assumption), and method x is available in all states. □

5   Case Study: TinyOS

The Tiny Microthreading Operating System (TinyOS) [13] is an event-driven operating system for networked embedded sensors. The design of TinyOS uses a state-machine programming model. It consists of a scheduler and a fixed number of finite-memory modules that are arranged in layers and communicate with each other via *events* and *commands*, which cause state transitions in the modules. Events are initiated at the lowest layer by hardware interrupts. Each event may cause higher-layer events and invoke lower-layer commands, but the TinyOS design requires that commands cannot cause events. A typical application is shown in Figure 1(a), consisting of a low-power radio stack, a UART serial port stack, sensor stacks, and adhoc routing.

We have used stateful SM interfaces to model the interfaces of two of the modules of TinyOS version 4.3, namely, RFM and RadioByte. Both commands and events are modeled as method calls; the local storage is modeled using state variables. The availability assumptions were obtained from the designers of TinyOS; the call assumptions are immediate from the TinyOS call conventions. The actual implementation of the modeled modules comprises about 460 lines of C code, with eight variables of type byte. Instead, each interface has only one variable, which can take three values. The modules RFM and RadioByte are the lowest two layers of the TinyOS stack. They both have three operating modes (states): transmitting (Tx), receiving (Rx), and low-power (LowPow). The state transitions are shown in Figure 1(b) and Figure 1(c).(Note, however, that the figures have no formal meaning and are only intended to help with the intuitive understanding of the TinyOS interfaces.) Invoking a local method can start a command-event chain. For example, Interrupt may be invoked due to a hardware interrupt when RFM is in states Tx or Rx, indicating that a bit has been transmitted or received, and triggering the event TxBitEvent or RxBitEvent, respectively. A detailed description of the two interfaces can be found in a technical report that accompanies this paper.

We have implemented a tool for checking the compatibility of stateful SM interfaces in Java (JDK 1.3). Composition of the two TinyOS interfaces gives a pushdown game with 117 control states and 5 stack symbols, which induces a state space of the size $5 \cdot 117 \cdot 2^{117}$. Our tool runs for about 30 minutes of CPU time on a Sun workstation with 256 MB RAM and two 200 MHz UltraSPARC CPUs. It reports an interface incompatibility at the composite state (LowPow, LowPow); that is, when both modules are in low-power mode. The incompatibility is that when the module RadioByte is in LowPow mode, invoking the only available method RBPower1 would in turn invoke RxMode. However, the method RxMode is not available when RFM is in LowPow mode. This incompatibility has been removed from the design in later distributions.

6 Implementation

We adapt and optimize Walukiewicz's algorithm for solving parity games on pushdown systems [18] to the special case of reachability pushdown games. Given a pushdown game $\mathcal{G}$, Walukiewicz constructs a finite game $\mathcal{F}$ of size exponential in the size of the pushdown system such that winning strategies in the finite game correspond to winning strategies in the pushdown game, and vice versa. There is a state of $\mathcal{F}$ for every triple consisting of a state of $\mathcal{G}$, a stack symbol of $\mathcal{G}$, and a state set of $\mathcal{G}$. Player 1 has a winning strategy from such a state (s, γ, T) in $\mathcal{F}$ iff he has a winning strategy to either win from s in $\mathcal{G}$ with the symbol γ on the top of the stack while never popping this copy of γ from the stack, or to enter a state in the set T while popping the symbol γ from the top of the stack. If player 1 has a winning strategy from (s, γ, T) in $\mathcal{F}$, then we say that T is a target set for s and γ. Player 1 has a winning strategy from $(s, \perp)$ in $\mathcal{G}$ iff he has a winning strategy from $(s, \perp, \emptyset)$ in $\mathcal{F}$.

We avoid the explicit construction of $\mathcal{F}$ by developing a symbolic algorithm for computing the solutions of the game. Let $\{1, 2, \ldots, n\}$ be the states of the pushdown system $\mathcal{G}$. For every state s and stack symbol γ, we construct a BDD $\mathcal{B}_{s,\gamma}(\overline{x})$, where $\overline{x} = x_1, \ldots, x_n$, to represent the set of target sets for s and γ. The function *Apply* gives for every pushdown rule of $\mathcal{G}$ a BDD over the variables $\overline{x}$:

$$Apply(r) = \begin{cases} x_{s'} & \text{if } r\colon (s,\gamma) \hookrightarrow (s',pop), \\ \mathcal{B}_{s',\gamma} & \text{if } r\colon (s,\gamma) \hookrightarrow (s',skip), \\ \exists \overline{z}.(\mathcal{B}_{s',\gamma'}[\overline{z}/\overline{x}] \wedge \bigwedge_{i=1}^{n}(z_i \Rightarrow \mathcal{B}_{i,\gamma})) & \text{if } r\colon (s,\gamma) \hookrightarrow (s',push(\gamma')). \end{cases}$$

Our algorithm initializes all BDDs $\mathcal{B}_{s,\gamma}$ to `false` and then keeps updating their values by applying the pushdown rules in the following way:

$$\mathcal{B}_{s,\gamma} := \begin{cases} \mathcal{B}_{s,\gamma} \vee \bigvee_{r \text{ is a rule for } (s,\gamma)} Apply(r) & \text{if } s \text{ is existential}, \\ \mathcal{B}_{s,\gamma} \vee \bigwedge_{r \text{ is a rule for } (s,\gamma)} Apply(r) & \text{if } s \text{ is universal}. \end{cases}$$

We briefly discuss the *pop*, *skip*, and *push* rules when s is an existential state; the universal case is similar. A rule $(s,\gamma) \hookrightarrow (s',pop)$ allows player 1 to instantly win by popping the top symbol γ from the stack while reaching state s'; every set containing s' is then a target set for s and γ. If there is a rule $(s,\gamma) \hookrightarrow (s',skip)$, then player 1 can apply it without any change to the stack contents, and so every target set for s' and γ is also a target set for s and γ. If there is a rule $(s,\gamma) \hookrightarrow (s',push(\gamma'))$, then T is a target set for s and γ if there is a set U such that U is a target set for s' and γ', and T is already known to be a target set for u and γ, for all $u \in U$.

The symbolic implementation of Walukiewicz's algorithm has several advantages over an enumerative solution. First, it can give substantial space savings due to the compact representation of target sets by BDDs. Second, the running time can be significantly reduced by avoiding the explicit manipulation of large state sets, as in the "saturation" algorithm of [4]. Third, the above simple BDD expressions allow for a straightforward and succinct implementation of a reachability pushdown games solver using any BDD package. In our implementation, we use the CUDD package [19] with Java wrappers provided by JMocha [2].

References

1. S. Abramsky. *Semantics of Interaction.* Lecture Notes, Oxford University, 2002. 431
2. R. Alur et al. jMocha: A model-checking tool that exploits design structure. *Proc. Int. Conf. Software Engineering*, pp. 835–836. IEEE, 2001. 440
3. R. Allen and D. Garlan. A formal basis for architectural connection. *ACM Trans. Software Engineering & Methodology*, 6:213–249, 1997. 431
4. A. Boujjani, J. Esparza, and O. Maler. Reachability analysis of pushdown automata: Application to model checking. *Concurrency Theory*, LNCS 1243, pp. 135–150. Springer, 1997. 440
5. A. Beugnard, J.-M. Jézéquel, N. Plouzeau, and D. Watkins. Making components contract aware. *IEEE Software*, 16:38–45, 1999. 431
6. L. de Alfaro and T. A. Henzinger. Interface automata. *Proc. Symp. Foundations of Software Engineering*, pp. 109–120. ACM, 2001. 430
7. L. de Alfaro and T. A. Henzinger. Interface theories for component-based design. *Embedded Software*, LNCS 2211, pp. 148–165. Springer, 2001. 430

8. R. DeLine and M. Fähndrich. Enforcing high-level protocols in low-level software. *Proc. Conf. Programming Language Design & Implementation*, pp. 59–69. ACM, 2001. 431
9. D. L. Dill. *Trace Theory for Automatic Hierarchical Verification of Speed-independent Circuits*. MIT Press, 1989. 430
10. J. Esparza and S. Schwoon. A BDD-based model checker for recursive programs. *Computer-Aided Verification*, LNCS 2102, pp. 324–336. Springer, 2001. 434, 435
11. R. B. Findler, M. Latendresse, and M. Felleisen. Behavioral contracts and behavioral subtyping. *Proc. Symp. Foundations of Software Engineering*, pp. 229–236. ACM, 2001. 431
12. J. Foster, M. Fändrich, and A. Aiken. A theory of type qualifiers. *Proc. Conf. Programming Language Design & Implementation*, pp. 192–203. ACM, 1999. 431
13. J. Hill, R. Szewczyk, A. Woo, S. Hollar, D. Culler, and K. Pister. System architecture directions for networked sensors. *Proc. Conf. Architectural Support for Programming Languages & Operating Systems*, pp. 93–104. ACM, 2000. 431, 438
14. J. R. Larus, S. K. Rajamani, and J. Rehof. *Behavioral Types for Structured Asynchronous Programming*. Technical Report, Microsoft Research, 2001. 431
15. D. C. Luckham and F. von Henke. An overview of Anna, a specification language for Ada. *IEEE Software*, 2:9–23, 1985. 431
16. D. L. Parnas. A technique for software module specification with examples. *Communications of the ACM*, 15:330–336, 1972. 431
17. D. S. Rosenblum. A practical approach to programming with assertions. *IEEE Trans. Software Engineering*, 21:19–31, 1995. 431
18. I. Walukiewicz. Pushdown processes: Games and model checking. *Information and Computation*, 164:234–263, 2001. 433, 439
19. F. Somenzi. CUDD: CU decision diagram package. Technical Report, University of Colorado at Boulder, 1997. 440

Practical Methods for Proving Program Termination

Michael A. Colón and Henny B. Sipma*

Computer Science Department, Stanford University
Stanford, CA 94305-9045
{colon,sipma}@cs.stanford.edu

Abstract. We present two algorithms to prove termination of programs by synthesizing linear ranking functions. The first uses an invariant generator based on iterative forward propagation with widening and extracts ranking functions from the generated invariants by manipulating polyhedral cones. It is capable of finding subtle ranking functions which are linear combinations of many program variables, but is limited to programs with few variables.

The second, more heuristic, algorithm targets the class of structured programs with single-variable ranking functions. Its invariant generator uses a heuristic extrapolation operator to avoid iterative forward propagation over program loops. For the programs we have considered, this approach converges faster and the invariants it discovers are sufficiently strong to imply the existence of ranking functions.

1 Introduction

Proving total program correctness consists of two tasks: proving partial correctness, that is, proving that the relation between inputs and outputs satisfies its specification, and proving termination. While many techniques have been proposed to automatically establish termination of term rewriting systems [9], logic programs [15] and functional programs [12], the problem of demonstrating termination of imperative programs has received much less attention. Clearly, one possible strategy is to reduce the problem to one of the well-studied cases by program transformation, but such an approach often introduces additional complexities. For example, when translating an imperative program into a functional program, the recursive functions introduced to encode loops often fail to terminate for all inputs, necessitating the development of automatic methods to approximate the domains of these functions [2].

In [4], we presented a method for generating linear ranking functions to prove termination of program loops. The approach taken was to represent program invariants and transition relations as polyhedral cones and to construct

---

* This research was supported in part by NSF(ITR) grant CCR-01-21403, by NSF grant CCR-99-00984-001, by ARO grant DAAD19-01-1-0723, and by ARPA/AF contracts F33615-00-C-1693 and F33615-99-C-3014.

D. Brinksma and K. G. Larsen (Eds.): CAV 2002, LNCS 2404, pp. 442–454, 2002.
© Springer-Verlag Berlin Heidelberg 2002

linear ranking functions by manipulating these cones. The method made the tacit assumption that the loops are unnested. As such, it could generate complex ranking functions for simple control structures, but was unable to construct even simple ranking functions for complex structures. Furthermore, it could not establish termination of unnested loops with multiple paths in which different paths require different ranking functions, i.e., loops which can be proved terminating using lexicographic ranking functions all of whose components are linear. The aim of the present work is to generalize the approach and address these shortcomings.

In this paper we propose two algorithms for proving termination of programs. The first is capable of finding complex linear ranking functions to prove termination, and uses iterative forward propagation with widening to derive invariants to justify the ranking functions. The second is more heuristic in nature, but is faster for structured programs and is capable of handling larger programs.

2   Preliminaries

2.1   Program Representation and Computational Model

We present programs using SPL (Simple Programming Language) [ ], a Pascal-like programming language with well-defined semantics. As an underlying computational model we use transition systems, a flexible first-order representation of programs.

A program $P : \langle V, L, \mathcal{T}, L_0, \Theta \rangle$ consists of the following components:

- V, a finite set of program variables; a *state* σ is an assignment to all variables in V. An *assertion* is a first-order formula over V.
- L, a finite set of program *locations*.
- $\mathcal{T}$, a finite set of *transitions*, where each transition τ is represented by a triple $\langle \ell, \ell', \rho \rangle$ consisting of a *prelocation* ℓ, a *postlocation* ℓ', and an assertion ρ over V and V', where V' denote the variables in the next state. By $post(\rho, \varphi)$ we denote the *postcondition* of τ with respect to an assertion φ, which is defined as the set of states reachable by taking transition τ from a state satisfying φ, that is, the set of states satisfying $\exists V_0 . \rho(V_0, V) \wedge \varphi(V_0)$.
- $L_0 \subseteq L$, the set of *initial locations*.
- Θ, an assertion characterizing the *initial states*.

A *configuration* is a pair $\langle \ell, \sigma \rangle$ consisting of a location and a state. A *computation* π is a potentially infinite sequence $\langle \ell_0, \sigma_0 \rangle, \langle \ell_1, \sigma_1 \rangle, \ldots$ of configurations such that ℓ_0 is an initial location, $\sigma_0 \models \Theta$, and for each adjacent pair of configurations $\langle \ell_i, \sigma_i \rangle$ and $\langle \ell_{i+1}, \sigma_{i+1} \rangle$, there exists a transition $\tau = \langle \ell_i, \ell_{i+1}, \rho \rangle$ such that $\sigma_i, \sigma_{i+1} \models \rho$.

2.2   Flow Graphs

Flow graphs are convenient for representing the control structure of programs. Recall that a *directed graph* $G = \langle V, E \rangle$ consists of a finite set of *vertices* V and a finite set of *edges* E, where each edge of E is a pair $\langle v, v' \rangle$ of vertices of V. A *path* of G is a potentially infinite sequence $v_1, v_2, \ldots$ of vertices such that for all $i > 0$, $\langle v_i, v_{i+1} \rangle \in E$. A finite path $v_1, \ldots, v_n$ is a *cycle* if $v_1 = v_n$. A graph is *acyclic* if none of its paths are cycles and *strongly-connected* if there is a path between every pair of vertices. A *strongly-connected subgraph* (SCS) of G is a subgraph of G which is strongly connected. An SCS S is a *maximal* SCS (MSCS) if it is not a proper subgraph of an SCS of G. An MSCS consisting of a single vertex and no edges is said to be *trivial*.

A *flow graph* is a directed graph in which a subset of the vertices are distinguished as being initial. A path of a flow graph is said to be *proper* if its first vertex is initial. The *control flow graph* (CFG) of a program is the flow graph whose vertices are the control locations and which contains an edge $\langle \ell, \ell' \rangle$ for each transition $\tau = \langle \ell, \ell', \rho \rangle$. The CFG of a program can be viewed as an abstraction of the program in which all variables are ignored: each computation of the program induces a path in the flow graph. However, not all paths of the flow graph correspond to computations of the program. Invariants and ranking functions are needed to refine this abstraction.

2.3 Ranking Functions

A binary relation $\prec$ is called *well-founded* over a domain $\mathcal{D}$ if there is no infinite descending chain, that is, no infinite sequence of elements $d_0, d_1, d_2, \ldots$ of $\mathcal{D}$ such that $d_i \succ d_{i+1}$ for all $i \geq 0$. The most commonly used well-founded domain is that of the natural numbers with the $>$ relation.

Well-founded relations can be used to show that a certain set of program locations cannot be visited infinitely often. Let π be an infinite computation of a program P. Since there are only finitely many locations, π must visit some subset of the locations infinitely often. This subset must be an SCS of the CFG of P. To prove termination of the program, then, it suffices to show that no SCS of the CFG can be visited infinitely often. To do so, we exhibit a ranking function for each SCS of the CFG.

A *ranking function* δ for an SCS S is a mapping from program states into a well-founded domain such that no transition associated with an edge of S increases the measure assigned by δ, and some transition decreases it. Thus the existence of a ranking function for S implies that any infinite computation can take the decreasing transitions only finitely many times, and therefore, if it remains within S, it must eventually confine itself to a proper sub-SCS of S which does not contain the decreasing transitions. If removal of these decreasing transitions from the SCS results in an acyclic graph, the SCS admits no infinite computations. If for each SCS of the CFG we can find a ranking function, we have shown that the program terminates.

2.4 Invariant Assertions

An assertion $\mathcal{I}$ is said to be *invariant* at location ℓ of a program P if, for any computation π of P, $\mathcal{I}$ holds whenever π reaches ℓ. An *invariant map* μ is any assignment of assertions to the locations of P such that $\mu(\ell)$ is invariant at ℓ. An invariant map μ is said to be *inductive* if, for every transition $\tau = \langle \ell, \ell', \rho \rangle$, $\text{post}(\rho, \mu(\ell)) \models \mu(\ell')$. Thus inductive invariant maps can be verified locally, provided the assertion language is decidable.

It is often possible to compute non-trivial invariants for a program by iterative forward propagation in an abstract domain, a method known as *abstract interpretation* [6]. Given a program P and a map μ, the operator $\mathcal{F}$ is defined as follows:

$$\mathcal{F}(\mu, P) = \bigcup_{\ell \in L} \{\ell \mapsto \mathcal{G}(\mu, \ell)\}.$$

with

$$\mathcal{G}(\mu, \ell') = \begin{cases} \bigsqcup_{\langle \ell, \ell', \rho \rangle \in T} \text{post}(\rho, \mu(\ell)) \sqcup \Theta & \text{if } \ell' \text{ is initial}, \\ \bigsqcup_{\langle \ell, \ell', \rho \rangle \in T} \text{post}(\rho, \mu(\ell)) & \text{otherwise} \end{cases}$$

Iterative application of $\mathcal{F}$ to an initial map assigning *false* to each location yields the strongest map of inductive invariants expressible in the given assertion language, provided it converges. If the assertion language contains infinite ascending chains, a heuristic *widening* operator is employed to ensure convergence for programs containing loops. The use of abstract interpretation to generate invariants expressible as systems of linear constraints was first proposed in [7].

When reasoning about infinite computations, it is often necessary to make use of assertions that may not hold every time a location is reached, but are guaranteed to hold in the limit. Given an SCS S with location ℓ, an assertion φ is said to be *tail invariant* at ℓ if, for any infinite computation π that never leaves S, φ fails to hold when π reaches ℓ only finitely many times. In other words, φ is an invariant of a suffix (or tail) of π. Tail invariants allow us to ignore the program states in the first pass of iterative structures such as **repeat** – **until** loops, in which the loop condition is evaluated at the end of each iteration.

Given an SCS S and an invariant map μ, μ can be strengthened to a map of tail invariants of S by forward propagation restricted to S. With each iteration, $\mathcal{F}$ is applied to μ and the resulting map is conjoined to the invariants of μ. It is sound, and usually sufficient, to terminate the forward propagation before a fixed point is reached.

2.5 Polyhedral Cones and Systems of Linear Constraints

Our invariant generator and our algorithm for generating ranking functions are based on polyhedral cones and systems of linear constraints.

A vector w is a *linear combination* of vectors $v_1, \ldots, v_n$ if $w = \lambda_1 v_1 + \cdots + \lambda_n v_n$ and a *conic combination* if $\lambda_1, \ldots, \lambda_n \geq 0$. The set of linear combinations of a set V is denoted $\mathcal{L}in(V)$, while $\mathcal{C}on(V)$ denotes its conic combinations. A *cone* is any set of vectors closed under conic combination. A pair $\langle L, R \rangle$ of sets of vectors is a *generator* of the cone C if $C = \mathcal{L}in(L) + \mathcal{C}on(R)$. The vectors in L are known as the *lines* of the generator, while the members of R are the *rays*. A cone is *polyhedral* if it possesses a finite generator. In this paper, we consider only polyhedral cones.

The *polar* C^* of a cone C is the set of vectors forming non-acute angles with every member of C, i.e., $C^* = \{w \mid w \cdot v \leq 0 \text{ for all } v \in C\}$. A cone is polyhedral iff its polar is polyhedral. A *double description* is a pair of cones $\langle C, D \rangle$ satisfying $D = C^*$, and the *double description method* is an algorithm for computing polars of polyhedral cones based on this dual representation [10].

A *linear constraint* is an assertion of the form $\alpha_1 x_1 + \ldots + \alpha_d x_d + \beta \; \rho \; 0$, where ρ is $=$ or $\leq$. A conjunction of linear constraints is known as a *system*. The *theory* of a system S is the set of constraints satisfied by every solution of S. It was proven by Farkas that the theory of a system S of linear constraints is the cone it generates, where the equalities are interpreted as lines and the inequalities are treated as rays.

The polar of a system S of linear constraints viewed as a cone admits two interpretations: It can be seen as the generator of solutions of S or as a homogeneous system of constraints on the coefficients of the consequences of S. This second interpretation allows us to impose syntactic restrictions on the consequences of a system. For example, a variable x_i can be eliminated from a system by adding the constraint $\alpha_i = 0$ to its polar. That is, $\alpha_i = 0$ is added to the cone D in the representation $\langle C, D \rangle$ of S using the double description method pair $\langle C', D' \rangle$ with C' representing precisely those consequences of S in which the variable x_i does not appear.[1] Given two systems S_1 and S_2, their *convex hull* $S_1 \sqcup S_2$, i.e., the intersection of their consequences, can be computed by adding the constraints of the polar of S_2 to the polar of S_1.

3   An Algorithm for Generating Ranking Functions

3.1   Algorithm

The algorithm, of which a schematic outline is shown in Figure 1, consists of two phases. The first phase prepares the program for computing the ranking functions: invariants of P are generated and its CFG G is extracted. Then G is pruned by eliminating vertices from G that have an invariant of *false* and edges that can never be taken due to the unsatisfiability of the enabling condition of the corresponding transition relation given the generated invariants.

The ranking functions are computed in the second phase by the mutually recursive procedures **rank1** and **rank2**. Given a flow graph G, **rank1** decomposes it into its MSCS's and invokes **rank2** on each non-trivial MSCS. If all MSCS's are trivial, **rank1** succeeds immediately.

Given an MSCS S, **rank2** first partitions the variables of the program into those that are modified by some transition of S and those that are preserved by all transitions of S. Next it computes the tail invariants. It then computes the set N of all linear expressions over the modified variables that do not increase under any transition of S. To do so, it first computes, for each transition $\tau = \langle \ell, \ell', \rho \rangle$ of S, the set of expressions e over modified variables such that

$$\mu(\ell) \wedge \rho \models e \geq e',$$

---

[1]   In essence, the double description method is used to simulate Fourier's elimination.

Input: program P
Output: ranking functions for each SCS or **fail**
1. Generate invariants μ for P; Extract the CFG G of P; Prune G using μ
2. call **rank1**(G)

procedure rank1(G)
1. decompose G into a list L of MSCS's
2. for each non-trivial $S \in L$ call **rank2**(S)

procedure rank2(S)
1. partition the variables for S
2. generate tail invariants of S
3. compute set N of non-increasing expressions for S
4. for each $\tau \in S$ do
   5. compute the set D of bounded decreasing expressions for τ
   6. if $N \cap D \neq \emptyset$ do
      7. output any expression of $N \cap D$ as a ranking function for S
      8. remove τ from S
9. if no transitions were removed from S then fail
10. call **rank1**(S)

Fig. 1. General algorithm for generating ranking functions

where e' denotes e with unprimed variables replaced by their primed versions. The computation is performed by representing the systems of linear inequalities $\mu(\ell)$ and ρ as polyhedral cones, taking their union, then adding equations to the polar of the combined system, to eliminate the unmodified variables and to ensure that the primed and unprimed versions of the same modified variable appear with opposite sign. Projecting this cone onto the primed variables then yields the generator of the non-increasing linear expressions for τ. (The precise details of this construction are presented in [4].) Taking the intersection of these cones over all $\tau \in S$ yields the set of expressions that are non-increasing over the entire MSCS.

Then, **rank2** computes for each transition $\tau = \langle \ell, \ell', \rho \rangle$ the set of expressions that both decrease under and are bounded from below by τ. That is, it computes the set of expressions e over the modified variables for which there exists a positive constant β and an expression Λ over the unmodified variables such that

$$\mu(\ell) \wedge \rho \models e \geq e' + \beta \quad \text{and} \quad \mu(\ell) \wedge \rho \models e' \geq \Lambda.$$

The restriction of the lower bound Λ to unmodified variables is necessary to ensure that the range of the purported ranking function is in fact well-founded. Again, **rank2** performs this computation by manipulating systems of linear inequalities represented as polyhedral cones.

Finally, for each transition τ possessing an expression δ which is bounded and decreasing under τ and non-increasing over the entire MSCS S, **rank2** outputs δ as a ranking function for S and removes τ from S. If no such transition exists, **rank2** fails. Otherwise, **rank2** invokes **rank1** to find ranking functions for the MSCS's created by the removal of these transitions.

in n : **integer where** $n \geq 0$
in A : **array** $[1 \ldots n]$ **of integer**
local i, j : **integer**

ℓ_0: $i := n$
ℓ_1: **while** $i \geq 0$ **do**
$\begin{bmatrix} \ell_2: \ j := 0 \\ \ell_3: \ \textbf{while } j \leq i - 1 \ \textbf{do} \\ \quad \begin{bmatrix} \ell_4: \ \textbf{if } A[j] > A[j+1] \ \textbf{then} \\ \quad \ell_5: \ \langle A[j], A[j+1] \rangle := \langle A[j+1], A[j] \rangle \\ \ell_6: \ j := j + 1 \end{bmatrix} \\ \ell_7: \ i := i - 1 \end{bmatrix}$

Fig. 2. Program BUBBLESORT

Notice that it is sound to make use of tail invariants of an SCS S when generating its ranking functions. If δ can be shown to be both non-increasing over S and decreasing under τ assuming tail invariants, then for any infinite computation which remains in S, after finitely many steps in which δ changes arbitrarily, δ will attain a maximum value and then decrease whenever τ is taken.

3.2 Examples

Consider the program BUBBLESORT shown in Figure 2. **rank1** decomposes the CFG G of this program into the non-trivial MSCS $S_1 : \{\ell_1, \ldots, \ell_7\}$, and the trivial MSCS ℓ_0. Given S_1, **rank2** finds that i is non-increasing over the MSCS and is bounded and decreasing under τ_7, using the invariant $i = j \land j \geq 0$ generated for ℓ_7.

Eliminating τ_7 and decomposing the resulting graph yields a single new non-trivial MSCS $S_2 : \{\ell_3 \ldots \ell_6\}$. For S_2, **rank2** finds that $-j$ is non-increasing over the MSCS and bounded and decreasing under τ_6. Note that partitioning the variables enables i to appear in the lower bound on $-j$. Otherwise, the ranking function $i - j$, involving more than one variable, would be needed to show termination of S_2.

Figure 3.2 shows a program with a slightly more complicated control structure which was derived from McCarthy's 91 function [13]. Given input x, the function returns $x - 10$ if $x > 100$ and 91 otherwise. For this program, **rank2** generates $-y_1$ for the MSCS $\{\ell_3, \ell_4\}$ and $-y_1 + 11 * y_2$ for the MSCS $\{\ell_5 \ldots \ell_{11}\}$.

3.3 Some Experimental Results

We have implemented our algorithm in Java using the invariant generator and polyhedral cone library of STeP [1] and have applied it to several programs taken from [13] and [5], obtaining the results presented in Table 1. Note that most of the execution time is spent in the invariant generator.

Table 1. Run times for general algorithm on a 1GHz Xeon Pentium III processor with 2GB RAM, running Linux and Java 1.3.1

Program	no. of variables	no. of statements	no. of loops	inv.gen. (msec)	rank gen. (msec)
BUBBLESORT	3	8	2	88	101
PERFECT	4	10	2	2328	149
MCCARTHY91	4	11	2	235	154
DETERMINANT	5	13	3	570	351
MATRIX-CHAIN	5	19	4	836	504
LUP-DECOMPOSITION	4	28	5	691	439

in x : **integer**
local y_1, y_2, z : **integer**

ℓ_0: $(y_1, y_2) := (x, 1)$;
ℓ_1: **if** $(y_1 > 100)$ **then** ℓ_2: $z := y_1 - 10$
    else
$\begin{bmatrix} \ell_3\text{: \textbf{while} } y_1 \leq 100 \textbf{ do } \ell_4\text{: } (y_1, y_2) := (y_1 + 11, y_2 + 1); \\ \ell_5\text{: \textbf{while} } y_2 > 1 \textbf{ do} \\ \quad \begin{bmatrix} \ell_6\text{: } (y_1, y_2) := (y_1 - 10, y_2 - 1); \\ \ell_7\text{: \textbf{if} } y_1 > 100 \wedge y_2 = 1 \textbf{ then } \ell_8\text{: } z := y_1 - 10 \\ \textbf{else} \\ \quad \begin{bmatrix} \ell_9\text{: \textbf{if} } y_1 > 100 \textbf{ then } \ell_{10}\text{: } (y_1, y_2) := (y_1 - 10, y_2 - 1); \\ \ell_{11}\text{: } (y_1, y_2) := (y_1 + 11, y_2 + 1) \end{bmatrix} \end{bmatrix} \end{bmatrix}$

Fig. 3. Program derived from McCarthy's 91 function

Encouraged by these results, we then applied the algorithm to a larger program – an implementation of mergesort taken from [16] and shown in Fig.6. For this example, the initial results were disappointing. The invariant generator failed to converge in a reasonable amount of time. We then re-ran the algorithm, restricting the invariant generator to consider only the variables i, m, n, p, q and r, which we knew *a priori* to be the only variables relevant to termination. With this restriction, the invariant generator converged in 5 seconds, generating invariants sufficiently strong to demonstrate termination in 2.5 sec. The generated ranking functions are $-p, m, r, q$, and $-i$ for the loops at $\ell_2, \ell_{14}, \ell_{33}, \ell_{38}$, and ℓ_{49}, respectively, and the ranking functions q and r for the loop at ℓ_{23}.

Unsatisfied with an algorithm that requires guidance in the form of a list of relevant variables to ensure convergence for a somewhat large, but not unduly complex program, we devised a more heuristic algorithm targeted at structured programs with simple ranking functions, which we present in the next section.

Input: program P
Output: invariant map μ
1. construct CFG G of P; initialize μ to $\emptyset$
2. call inv1(G)

procedure inv1(G)
1. decompose G into an ordered list L of MSCS's
2. for each $S \in L$ in order do
   3. if S is trivial then propagate assertions to S's vertex
   4. else call **inv2**(S)

procedure inv2(S)
1. let v be the header of S
2. if $\mu(v)$ is undefined then
   3. forward propagate assertions to v
   4. extrapolate $\mu(v)$ over S
5. remove from S all edges to v
6. call **inv1**(S)

Fig. 4. Algorithm for generating invariants

4 An Alternate Algorithm for Generating Ranking Functions

Our heuristic algorithm is based on two observations concerning the programs we have considered. First, they are all written in structured programming languages and, therefore, have reducible CFG's. Recall that a vertex v *dominates* a vertex w if every proper path to w passes through v; a flow graph G is *reducible* if every SCS S contains a vertex v that dominates it, called its *header*. Reducible flow graphs are well-structured: Their loops are properly nested.

Based on this observation, we devised an invariant generator that takes advantage of reducible CFG's. The algorithm, shown in Figure 4, propagates assertions through the CFG. However, upon encountering a non-trivial SCS, rather than iterating with widening until convergence, the algorithm attempts to extrapolate an over-approximation of the fixed point, which it then propagates into and past the SCS.

The extrapolation algorithm used is simple. Given an assertion, represented as a system of linear inequalities, it first computes those consequences of the system involving only variables not modified in the SCS, that is, it eliminates the modified variables. Then an attempt is made to refine the (now invariant) assertion by preserving any bounds on the modified variables implied by the original system. The approach taken is to determine for each modified variable whether the original system implies a bound on that variable which is linear in the unmodified variables and which is preserved by each transition. If so, the approximation is strengthened by including this bound.

The second observation concerning the programs we consider is that, provided care is taken to distinguish between those variables that are modified in

Input: program P
Output: ranking functions for each SCS
1. Generate invariants μ for P; Extract CFG G of P; Prune G using μ
2. call **rank1**(G)
3. if any SCS does not have a ranking function, fail

procedure rank1(G)
1. decompose G into a list L of MSCS's
2. for each non-trivial $S \in L$ call **rank2**(S)

procedure rank2(S)
1. partition the variables for S
2. generate tail invariants of S
3. for each variable v modified in S do
    4. if v is non-increasing/non-decreasing over S then
      5. for each $\tau \in S$ do
        6. if v is bounded and decreasing/increasing under τ then
          7. record τ and $v/-v$
8. remove from S all edges to its header
9. call **rank1**(S)

Fig. 5. Algorithm for generating ranking functions

an SCS and those that are preserved, all SCS's of these programs possess single-variable ranking functions. Thus, a heuristic algorithm that restricts itself to ranking functions of this form is likely to prove termination of most loops while avoiding the overhead of manipulating polyhedral cones. An algorithm for generating ranking functions incorporating this idea is presented in Figure 5.

The algorithm visits the loops of the program and attempts to find single-variable ranking functions that justify the elimination of transitions of the loop that are not transitions of any inner loop. It records, for any ranking function discovered, both the function and the set of transitions whose removal is justified by the function. It then breaks all cycles of the loop from the loop header and invokes itself recursively. Note that, unlike the algorithm of Section 3, this algorithm continues to search for ranking functions of inner loops even if it fails to prove termination of the outer loops. The structure of reducible CFG's makes this possible. If, after visiting all loops, removing the decreasing transitions from the CFG results in an acyclic graph, the algorithm reports success.

We have implemented this second algorithm and applied it to the programs considered in Section 3, obtaining the results shown in Table 2. As expected, this algorithm fails on MCCARTHY91, since no single-variable ranking function exists for the second MSCS. However, invariant generation is much faster than the iterative forward propagation with widening used in the previous section.

in n : **integer where** $n > 0$
local i, j, k, l, t : **integer**
local h, m, p, q, r : **integer**
local up : **boolean**
local a : **array** $[1..2 * n]$ **of integer**

ℓ_0: $up := \text{T};$
ℓ_1: $p := 1;$

ℓ_2: **repeat**
$\quad\begin{bmatrix}\ell_3: & h := 1; \\ \ell_4: & m := n; \\ \ell_5: & \textbf{if } up \textbf{ then} \\ & \quad [\ell_6: i := 1; \ \ell_7: j := n; \ \ell_8: k := n + 1; \ \ell_9: l := 2 * n] \\ & \textbf{else} \\ & \quad [\ell_{10}: k := 1; \ \ell_{11}: l := n; \ \ell_{12}: i := n + 1; \ \ell_{13}: j := 2 * n]; \\ \\ \ell_{14}: & \textbf{repeat} \\ & \begin{bmatrix} \ell_{15}: \textbf{if } m \geq p \textbf{ then } \ell_{16}: q := p \textbf{ else } \ell_{17}: q := m; \\ \ell_{18}: m := m - q; \\ \ell_{19}: \textbf{if } m \geq p \textbf{ then } \ell_{20}: r := p \textbf{ else } \ell_{21}: r := m; \\ \ell_{22}: m := m - r; \\ \\ \ell_{23}: \textbf{while } (q > 0 \wedge r > 0) \textbf{ do} \\ \quad \begin{bmatrix} \ell_{24}: \textbf{if } a[i] < a[j] \textbf{ then} \\ \quad \begin{bmatrix} \ell_{25}: a[k] := a[i]; \\ \ell_{26}: k := k + h; \ \ell_{27}: i := i + 1; \ \ell_{28}: q := q - 1 \end{bmatrix} \\ \textbf{else} \\ \quad \begin{bmatrix} \ell_{29}: a[k] := a[j]; \\ \ell_{30}: k := k + h; \ \ell_{31}: j := j - 1; \ \ell_{32}: r := r - 1 \end{bmatrix} \end{bmatrix}; \\ \\ \ell_{33}: \textbf{while } (r > 0) \textbf{ do} \\ \quad \begin{bmatrix} \ell_{34}: a[k] := a[j]; \\ \ell_{35}: k := k + h; \ \ell_{36}: j := j - 1; \ \ell_{37}: r := r - 1 \end{bmatrix}; \\ \\ \ell_{38}: \textbf{while } (q > 0) \textbf{ do} \\ \quad \begin{bmatrix} \ell_{39}: a[k] := a[i]; \\ \ell_{40}: k := k + h; \ \ell_{41}: i := i + 1; \ \ell_{42}: q := q - 1 \end{bmatrix}; \\ \\ \ell_{43}: h := -h; \ \ell_{44}: t := k; \ \ell_{45}: k := l; \ \ell_{46}: l := t \end{bmatrix} \\ & \textbf{until } m \leq 0; \\ \\ \ell_{47}: & up :=!up; \ \ell_{48}: p := 2 * p; \end{bmatrix}$
$\quad$**until** $p \geq n;$

ℓ_{49}: **if** $!up$ **then**
$\quad\begin{bmatrix} \ell_{50}: i := 1; \\ \ell_{51}: \textbf{while } i \leq n \textbf{ do} \\ \quad [\ell_{52}: a[i] := a[i + n]; \ \ell_{53}: i := i + 1] \end{bmatrix}$

Fig. 6. Program MERGESORT

Table 2. Run times for heuristic algorithm on a 1GHz Xeon Pentium III processor with 2GB RAM, running Linux and Java 1.3.1

Program	no. of variables	no. of statements	no. of loops	inv.gen. (msec)	rank gen. (msec)
BUBBLESORT	3	8	2	67	72
PERFECT	4	10	2	76	75
MCCARTHY91	4	11	2	-	-
DETERMINANT	5	13	3	169	186
MATRIX-CHAIN	5	19	4	216	233
LUP-DECOMPOSITION	4	28	5	186	208
MERGESORT	11	54	6	2665	3781

5   Conclusions

We present two algorithms to prove termination of programs. The first, more powerful algorithm is capable of finding subtle ranking functions which are linear combinations of many program variables, but is limited to short programs with few variables. The second, more heuristic algorithm, finds single-variable ranking functions in structured programs of larger size.

The approach taken by our first method bears resemblance to methods for automatically synthesizing *polynomial interpretations* [9] for establishing termination of term rewriting systems. For example, [11] extracts a system of nonlinear constraints on the coefficients of low-degree polynomials which guarantee correctness, then uses a combination of heuristic instantiation and a variant of *cylindrical algebraic decomposition* [3] to solve these constraints. Our algorithm can be seen as employing the double description method to solve a system of linear constraints on the coefficients of a linear expression which guarantee monotonicity of the defined function and the well-foundedness of its range. Our second method is similar to the heuristic approach proposed in [8], which identifies candidate single-variable ranking functions based on bounds appearing in the program, then verifies them using decision procedures. Our heuristic algorithm combines these two steps, using the double description method as a decision procedure. In addition, by making use of an invariant generator, our algorithm is able to discover ranking functions whose bounds do not appear explicitly in the program, but are implicit.

We see the utility of our algorithms in their potential to be incorporated into light-weight static analysis tools to identify potentially nonterminating loops. Preliminary analysis of a Web server, implemented by some 30,000 lines of Java code, indicated that one third of the loops could be proved terminating directly with our methods. Combined with static analysis to identify loop invariants our methods would be able to handle about half of the loops. If in addition we augmented our methods with some simple mechanisms to keep track of the size of collections, more than 80% of the loops could be handled. Thus, incorporated in an analysis tool, our methods could potentially relieve the programmer from checking 80% of the loops manually, if termination was a critical requirement.

References

1. Nikolaj S. Bjørner, Anca Browne, Michael Colón, Bernd Finkbeiner, Zohar Manna, Henny B. Sipma, and Tomás E. Uribe. Verifying temporal properties of reactive systems: A STeP tutorial. *Formal Methods in System Design*, 16(3):227–270, June 2000. 448

2. J. Brauburger and J. Giesl. Approximating the domains of functional and imperative programs. *Science of Computer Programming*, 35:113–136, 1999. 442

3. G. E. Collins. Quantifier elimination for real closed fields by cylindrical algebraic decomposition. In H. Brakhage, editor, *Proc. Second GI Conf. Autamata Theory and Formal Languages*, volume 33 of *Lecture Notes in Computer Science*, pages 134–183, 1975. 453

4. Michael Colón and Henny Sipma. Synthesis of linear ranking functions. In Tiziana Margaria and Wang Yi, editors, *7th International Conference on Tools and Algorithms for the Construction and Analysis of Systems (TACAS)*, volume 2031 of *LNCS*, pages 67–81. Springer Verlag, April 2001. 442, 447

5. T. Cormen, C. Leiserson, and R. Rivest. *Introduction to Algorithms*. McGraw-Hill, New York, 1990. 448

6. Patrick Cousot and Rhadia Cousot. Abstract interpretation: A unified lattice model for static analysis of programs by construction or approximation of fixpoints. In 4th *ACM Symp. Princ. of Prog. Lang.*, pages 238–252. ACM Press, 1977. 445

7. Patrick Cousot and Nicholas Halbwachs. Automatic discovery of linear restraints among the variables of a program. In 5th *ACM Symp. Princ. of Prog. Lang.*, pages 84–97, January 1978. 445

8. Dennis Dams, Rob Gerth, and Orna Grumberg. A heuristic for the automatic generation of ranking functions. In *Workshop on Advances in Verification (WAVe'00)*, pages 1–8, 2000. 453

9. N. Dershowitz. Termination of rewriting. *Journal of Symbolic Computation*, 3:69–116, 1987. 442, 453

10. K. Fukuda and A. Prodon. Double description method revisited. In *Combinatorics and Computer Science*, volume 1120 of *Lecture Notes in Computer Science*, pages 91–111. Springer-Verlag, 1996. 446

11. J. Giesl. Generating polynomial orderings for termination proofs. In J. Hsiang, editor, *Proc. 6th Intl. Conf. Rewriting Techniques and Applications*, volume 914 of *Lecture Notes in Computer Science*, pages 426–431. Springer-Verlag, 1995. 453

12. J. Giesl, C. Walther, and J. Brauburger. Termination analysis for functional programs. In W. Bibel and P. H. Schmitt, editors, *Automated Deduction – A Basis for Applications, Volume III: Applications*, chapter 6, pages 135–164. Kluwer Academic, 1998. 442

13. Zohar Manna. *Mathematical Theory of Computation*. McGraw-Hill, 1974. 448

14. Zohar Manna and Amir Pnueli. *Temporal Verification of Reactive Systems: Safety*. Springer-Verlag, New York, 1995. 443

15. D. de Schreye and S. Decorte. Termination of logic programs: The never ending story. *Journal of Logic Programming*, 19, 20:199–260, 1994. 442

16. Niklaus Wirth. *Algorithms + Data Structures = Programs*. Prentice-Hall, 1976. 449

Evidence-Based Model Checking*

Li Tan and Rance Cleaveland

Department of Computer Science
State University of New York at Stony Brook
Stony Brook, NY 11794-4400 USA
Phone: +1 703 534 6458
tt{tanli, rance}@cs.sunysb.edu

Abstract. This paper shows that different "meta-model-checking" analyses can be conducted efficiently on a generic data structure we call a *support set*. Support sets may be viewed as abstract encodings of the "evidence" a model checker uses to justify the yes/no answers it computes. We indicate how model checkers may be modified to compute supports sets without compromising their time or space complexity. We also show how support sets may be used for a variety of different analyses of model-checking results, including: the generation of diagnostic information for explaining negative model-checking results; and certifying the results of model checking (is the evidence internally consistent?).

Keywords: Model checking; diagnostic information; mu-calculus; temporal logic

1 Introduction

Temporal-logic model checking [CE81, QS82, CES86] refers to an array of techniques for automatically determining whether or not a system satisfies a property expressed in some temporal logic. Traditionally, model checkers have been viewed as decision procedures that return yes/no answers reflecting the "correctness" of the system being analyzed. However, researchers have also realized that the information collected by model checkers in order to compute their answers can also be of great interest to the users of model checkers. *Diagnostic information* [CGMZ95, Sti95] explaining answers to users represents one use of such information; others include coverage analysis [CKV01], vacuity checking [BBDER97] (is (part of) a formula "trivially true", and hence probably erroneous?), and result certification [Nam01] (does the evidence collected indeed support the conclusion returned, i.e. can the model checker be trusted?).

Existing "meta-model-checking" research is generally model-checker dependent: routines utilize algorithm-specific information computed during model-checking and hence are tightly bound to the infrastructure of checkers being

---

* Research supported by NSF grants CCR-9988489 and CCR-0098037 and Army Research Office grants DAAD190110003 and DAAD190110019.

D. Brinksma and K. G. Larsen (Eds.): CAV 2002, LNCS 2404, pp. 455–470, 2002.

used. In this paper we propose a generic framework for the analysis of model-checking results that uses a uniform encoding of the *evidence* collected by a model checker as it executes. In particular, we show how this evidence may be abstractly encoded in a special data structure, called a *support set*, that existing model checkers may be easily modified to generate. We then illustrate how support sets can be used to support different analyses of model-checking results in a model-checker independent fashion. Using our results, builders of model-checking tools can factor out diagnostic-information generation, or justification generation, or coverage analysis, from their model checkers and into special support-set analyzers computing the answers in question. The result is uncluttered model-checking code and an extensible implementation in which different support-set-based "meta-model-checking" analyzers may be added without modifying the underlying model-checking engine.

The rest of paper is organized as follows. Section 2 contains mathematical preliminaries, while Section 3 defines support sets. The section following illustrates how model checkers may be altered to compute support sets efficiently. The next few sections show how support sets may be used in support of different "meta-model-checking" analyses. Section 7 concludes and discusses related work.

2   Preliminaries

This section defines the system models and temporal logics used in the rest of the paper. In the remainder of the report we fix a set $\mathcal{A}$ of *atomic propositions*.

2.1   Kripke Structures and CTL*

Definition 1. *A Kripke structure is a tuple* $\langle S, s_I, \rightarrow, V \rangle$, *with* S *the set of states,* $s_I \in S$ *the start state,* $\rightarrow \subseteq S \times S$ *is transition relation and* $V : \mathcal{A} \rightarrow 2^S$ *the valuation.*

A Kripke structure encodes a system's operational behavior, with S being the possible set of system states and $\rightarrow$ the (atomic) state transitions. For atomic proposition $A \in \mathcal{A}$, $V(A)$ indicates in which states A is true. We usually write $s \rightarrow s'$ in lieu of $\langle s, s' \rangle \in \rightarrow$.

Given Kripke structure $\langle S, s_I, \rightarrow, V \rangle$, a *path* from $s \in S$ is a maximal sequence $\sigma = s_0 s_1 \ldots$ where $s = s_0$ and $s_i \rightarrow s_{i+1}$ for all $i < |\sigma|$. (Here $|\sigma| = n$ if $\sigma = s_0 s_1 \ldots s_n$ and ∞ if σ is infinite.) We use $\sigma[i]$ for s_i and $\sigma^{(i)}$ for $s_i s_{i+1} \ldots$ if $i \leq |\sigma|$.

CTL*. Formulas in the logic CTL* are given via the following grammar, where $A \in \mathcal{A}$.

$$\phi ::= A \mid \neg A \mid \phi \wedge \phi \mid \phi \vee \phi \mid \mathsf{A}\,\psi \mid \mathsf{E}\,\psi$$
$$\psi ::= \phi \mid \psi \wedge \psi \mid \psi \vee \psi \mid \mathsf{X}\,\psi \mid \psi\,\mathsf{U}\,\psi \mid \psi\,\mathsf{R}\,\psi$$

We refer to the formulas generated from ϕ as *state formulas* and those from ψ as *path formulas*. The CTL* formulas consist of the state formulas. We call A and

E *path quantifiers* and the X, U, R *path modalities*. The sublogic CTL consists of those CTL* formulas in which every path modality is immediately preceded by a path quantifier.

CTL* formulas are interpreted with respect to Kripke structures $T = \langle S, s_I, \rightarrow, V \rangle$ where $\rightarrow$ is *total*: for every $s \in S$ there exists $s' \in S$ with $s \rightarrow s'$. Given such a T, the semantics of CTL* formulas is given via a relation $\models_T$ associating states s in T to state formulas and paths σ in T to path formulas and which is defined below.

1. $s \models_T A(\neg A)$ iff $s \in V(A)$ $(s \notin V(A))$.
2. $s \models_T \phi_1 \wedge \phi_2$ $(\phi_1 \vee \phi_2)$ iff $s \models_T \phi_1$ and (or) $s \models_T \phi_2$.
3. $s \models_T A\psi$ $(E\psi)$ iff for every (some) path σ from s, $\sigma \models_T \psi$.
4. $\sigma \models_T \phi$, where ϕ is a state formula, iff $\sigma[0] \models \phi$.
5. $\sigma \models_T \psi_1 \wedge \psi_2$ $(\psi_1 \vee \psi_2)$ iff $\sigma \models_T \psi_1$ and (or) $\sigma \models_T \psi_2$.
6. $\sigma \models_T X\psi$ iff $\sigma^{(1)} \models \phi$.
7. $\sigma \models_T \psi_1 U \psi_2$ iff for some $i \geq 0$, $\sigma^{(i)} \models \psi_2$ and $\sigma^{(j)} \models \psi_1$ for all $j < i$.
8. $\sigma \models_T \psi_1 R \psi_2$ iff for all $i \geq 0$ $\sigma^{(i)} \models \psi_2$ or $\sigma^{(j)} \models \psi_1$ some $j < i$.

The release modality R is the dual of the until operator U. Intuitively, $\psi_1 R \psi_2$ holds of a path if ψ_2 is kept true until "released" from this obligation by the truth of ψ_1.

2.2   The Modal Mu-Calculus and Boolean Equation Systems

We define the modal mu-calculus and boolean equation systems by first giving a general account of fixpoint equation systems over complete lattices [Mad97].

Lattices and Environments A *complete lattice* is a partially ordered set $\langle Q, \sqsubseteq \rangle$ with the following property: every subset $Q' \subseteq Q$ has a least upper bound $\bigsqcup Q'$ in Q. It can be shown that arbitrary upper bounds $\bigsqcap Q$ also exist and that any complete lattice has a unique least element $\perp$ and maximum element $\top$. In addition, the Tarski-Knaster theorem guarantees the existence of unique least and greatest fixpoints for any monotonic function $f : Q \rightarrow Q$. Given monotonic f, we write $\mu f \in Q$ for the least "solution" to $f(x) = x$ and $\nu f \in Q$ for the greatest. These fixpoints are characterized as follows.

$$\mu f = \bigsqcup \{q \in Q \mid f(q) \sqsubseteq q\} \qquad \nu f = \bigsqcap \{q \in Q \mid q \sqsubseteq f(q)\}$$

Let $\langle Q, \sqsubseteq \rangle$ be a complete lattice and $\mathcal{X}$ be a finite set of *variables*. Then an *environment* over $\mathcal{X}$ is a function from $\mathcal{X}$ to Q. We use $Q^{\mathcal{X}}$ to represent the set of all environments over $\mathcal{X}$. Environments constitute a complete lattice under the pointwise extension of $\sqsubseteq$ to $Q^{\mathcal{X}}$: $\theta \sqsubseteq \theta'$ if and only if for all $X \in \mathcal{X}, \theta(X) \sqsubseteq \theta'(X)$.

If $\theta \in Q^{\mathcal{X}}$ and $\mathcal{X}' \subseteq \mathcal{X}$, then $\theta | \mathcal{X}' \in Q^{\mathcal{X}'}$ is defined by $(\theta | \mathcal{X}')(X) = \theta(X)$ for all $X \in \mathcal{X}'$. If $\theta' \in Q^{\mathcal{X}'}$ then $\theta[\theta']$ denotes the environment obtained by *updating* θ by θ':

$$\theta[\theta'] = \begin{cases} \theta'(X) \text{ if } X \in \mathcal{X}' \\ \theta(X) \text{ otherwise} \end{cases}$$

Fixpoint Equation Systems We now develop a general framework for systems of equations over a complete lattice. Throughout the remainder of this subsection we fix a complete lattice $\langle Q, \sqsubseteq \rangle$ and a finite set $\mathcal{X}$ of variables.

Syntax An *equation block* B is a set of equations $\{X_1 = f_1, \ldots, X_l = f_l\}$, where the f_i are monotonic functions in $Q^{\mathcal{X}} \to Q$, $\{X_1, \ldots X_l\} \subseteq \mathcal{X}$, and the X_i are distinct. We use $lhs(B) = \{X_1, \ldots, X_l\}$ for the left-hand side variables of B, and $rhs(B, X_i) = f_i$ for the right-hand side for X_i in B, respectively. The f_i are often represented syntactically as expressions involving free occurrences of the variables from $\mathcal{X}$. In this case, we use $vars(f_i)$ to refer to the set of variables occurring freely in f_i, and we define $vars(B) = lhs(B) \cup \bigcup_{i=1}^{l} vars(f_i)$ as the *variables* in equation block B. We refer to the variables in $lhs(\mathcal{B})$ as *bound* and the variables in $vars(\mathcal{B}) - lhs(\mathcal{B})$ as *free*.

A *parity block* E has form $\langle \sigma, B \rangle$, where $\sigma \in \{\mu, \nu\}$ is a *parity indicator* and B is an equation block. We lift the notions lhs, rhs, $vars$, free variable, and bound variable to parity blocks in the straightforward manner.

A *fixpoint equation system* is a nonempty sequence $\mathcal{E} = E_1 \ldots E_m$ of parity blocks whose left-hand sides are pairwise disjoint. If $\mathcal{E}'$ is an equation system and E is a parity block whose left-hand side variables are disjoint from those in $\mathcal{E}'$ then we write $E :: \mathcal{E}'$ for the equation system obtained by adding E to the front of $\mathcal{E}'$. We use $\mathcal{E}^{(k)} = E_k E_{k+1} \cdots$ to refer to the subsequence of $\mathcal{E}$ starting from k-th parity block. The operations lhs, rhs, $vars$, etc., are generalized in the straightforward manner. We call $\mathcal{E}$ *closed* if every $X \in vars(\mathcal{E})$ is bound, i.e. an element of $lhs(\mathcal{E})$. We also define $h_{\mathcal{E}}(X) = k$ when $X \in lhs(E_k)$ and refer to $h_{\mathcal{E}}(X)$ as the *depth* of X in $\mathcal{E}$. We write $h(X)$ when $\mathcal{E}$ is clear from context. We say X_i is *shallower* or *higher* than X_j if $h(X_i) < h(X_j)$, and *deeper* (or *lower*) if $h(X_i) > h(X_j)$. If X is a left-hand side variable in $\mathcal{E}$ we define $\sigma_{\mathcal{E}}(X)$ to be the parity of the unique parity block E in $\mathcal{E}$ such that $X \in lhs(E)$. We omit reference to $\mathcal{E}$ and write $\sigma(X)$ when $\mathcal{E}$ is clear from context.

In a fixpoint equation system $\mathcal{E}$, we say that X_i syntactically depends on X_j, written as $X_i \lhd X_j$, if $X_j \in vars(rhs(X_i))$. We write $\overset{*}{\lhd}$ for the transitive and reflexive closure of $\lhd$; so $X_i \overset{*}{\lhd} X_j$ if there is a path of syntactic dependencies from X_i to X_j.

Semantics Let $\theta \in Q^{\mathcal{X}}$ be an environment; then a single block $B = \{X_1 = f_1, \ldots, X_l = f_l\}$, where $\mathcal{X}' = \{X_1, \ldots, X_l\}$, may be seen as inducing a function $f_{B,\theta} : Q^{\mathcal{X}'} \to Q^{\mathcal{X}'}$ mapping environments over $\mathcal{X}'$ to environments over $\mathcal{X}'$ as follows.

$$f_{B,\theta}(\theta') = (X_1 \mapsto f_1(\theta[\theta'])) \cdots [X_l \mapsto f_l(\theta[\theta'])]$$

That is, $f_{B,\theta}(\theta')$ returns an environment over $\mathcal{X}'$ in which each X_i is mapped to the result of evaluating f_i on environment $\theta[\theta']$. Note that in $\theta[\theta']$ θ' "overwrites" the values for the X_i in θ. Consequently, θ may be seen as providing values only for variables that are not in $\mathcal{X}'$. It follows from the monotonicity of the f_j that for any θ, $f_{B,\theta}$ is a monotonic function over $Q^{\mathcal{X}'}$, and consquently, least and greatest fixpoints, $\mu f_{B,\theta}$ and $\nu f_{B,\theta}$, which are environments over $\mathcal{X}'$, exist. Given $\theta \in Q^{\mathcal{X}}$, we then define the semantics of a parity block in terms of these fixed points: $[\![\langle \sigma, B \rangle]\!]\theta = \sigma f_{B,\theta}$. So $[\![\langle \sigma, B \rangle]\!]$ maps environments over $\mathcal{X}$ to environments over $lhs(B)$.

Fixpoint equation systems are now interpreted as follows. For an environment $\theta \in Q^{\mathcal{X}}$ and equation system $\mathcal{E}$ with $lhs(\mathcal{E}) = \mathcal{X}_{\mathcal{E}} \subseteq \mathcal{X}$ we define a function $f_{\mathcal{E},\theta}$ that maps environments in $Q^{\mathcal{X}_{\mathcal{E}}}$ to environments in $Q^{\mathcal{X}_{\mathcal{E}}}$. We then use an appropriate fixpoint of this function to arrive at the meaning of $\mathcal{E}$. We define $f_{\mathcal{E},\theta}$ by induction on the structure of $\mathcal{E}$. When $\mathcal{E} = \langle \sigma, B \rangle$ (i.e. $\mathcal{E}$ contains one block), then we take $f_{\mathcal{E},\theta} = f_{B,\theta}$. In this case $f_{\mathcal{E},\theta}$ is clearly monotonic, and we define $[\![\mathcal{E}]\!]\theta = [\![\langle \sigma, B \rangle]\!]\theta$. When $\mathcal{E} = \langle \sigma, B \rangle :: \mathcal{E}'$ contains two or more blocks, $f_{\mathcal{E},\theta}$ is defined as

$$f_{\mathcal{E},\theta}(\theta') = ([\![\mathcal{E}']\!](\theta[\theta']))[f_{B,\theta[[\![\mathcal{E}']\!](\theta[\theta'])]}(\theta'|\mathcal{X}_B)],$$

where $\mathcal{X}_B = lhs(B)$. This expression may be understood via its subexpressions.

$[\![\mathcal{E}']\!](\theta[\theta'])$ is the environment defined by $\mathcal{E}'$ in environment θ updated with bindings in θ'. This environment assigns a "fixpoint value" to every left-hand variable in $\mathcal{E}'$.

$f_{B,\theta[[\![\mathcal{E}']\!](\theta[\theta'])]}$ is the function on environments defined by block B and the environment obtained by updating θ with the bindings in $\mathcal{E}'$.

$\theta'|\mathcal{X}_B$ is the subenvironment of θ' obtained by restricting variables to those that appear as left-hand sides in B.

It is easy to show that $f_{\mathcal{E},\theta}(\theta')$ is monotonic over the lattice $Q^{\mathcal{X}_{\mathcal{E}}}$ and hence has unique least and greatest fixpoints. We then define $[\![\mathcal{E}]\!]\theta$ as: $[\![\langle \sigma, B \rangle :: \mathcal{E}']\!]\theta = \sigma f_{\langle \sigma, B \rangle :: \mathcal{E}',\theta}$.

If $\mathcal{E}$ is closed then for any θ, θ' we have that $[\![\mathcal{E}]\!]\theta = [\![\mathcal{E}]\!]\theta'$. In this case we often omit reference to θ and write $[\![\theta]\!]$ for this (unique) environment.

We conclude this general treatment of fixpoint equation systems with a the definition of *alternation depth*. Here we adopt the convention that $max\emptyset = 0$.

Definition 2. *Let $\mathcal{E} = E_1 E_2 \cdots E_m$ be an equation system and X a left-hand side variable in $\mathcal{E}$. Then the alternation depth, $ad(X)$ of X is given as:*

$$ad(X) = 1 + max\{ad(X') \mid \sigma(X) \neq \sigma(X'), h(X') < h(X), X \overset{*}{\lhd} X' \overset{*}{\lhd} X\}$$

The Modal Mu-Calculus In this paper we define modal mu-calculus formulas using fixpoint equation systems whose right-hand sides are formulas built as follows.

$$f = A \mid \neg A \mid \bigwedge \mathcal{X}' \mid \bigvee \mathcal{X}' \mid \langle\rangle X \mid [] X$$

Here $A \in \mathcal{A}$ and $\mathcal{X}' \subseteq \mathcal{X}$. The lattice $\langle Q, \sqsubseteq \rangle$ used to interpret variables is given by fixing a Kripke structure $T = \langle S, s_I, \rightarrow, V \rangle$ and taking $Q = 2^S$ and $\sqsubseteq = \subseteq$. We adopt the usual semantics of modal formulas given below; note that $\theta \in (2^S)^{\mathcal{X}}$

maps variables to sets of states in T. For any f, $[\![f]\!]_T$ is a monotonic function from $(2^S)^{\mathcal{X}}$ to 2^S.

$$[\![A]\!]_T\theta = V(A) \qquad\qquad [\![\neg A]\!]_T\theta = S - V(A)$$
$$[\![\bigvee \mathcal{X}']\!]_T\theta = \bigcup\{\theta(X) \mid X \in \mathcal{X}'\} \qquad [\![\bigwedge \mathcal{X}']\!]_T\theta = \bigcap\{\theta(X) \mid X \in \mathcal{X}'\}$$
$$[\![\langle\rangle X]\!]_T\theta = \{s \mid \exists s \to s'.\ s' \in \theta(X)\} \qquad [\![[]X]\!]_T\theta = \{s \mid \forall s \to s'.\ s' \in \theta(X)\}$$

Mu-calculus fixpoint equation systems in essence define a collection of formulas, one for each $X \in lhs(\mathcal{E})$. This notation is clumsy for users, but more user-friendly logics such as CTL, LTL and CTL* may be translated efficiently into it [Dam94, BC96b].

Boolean Equation Systems Boolean equation systems are fixpoint equation systems defined over the boolean lattice $\langle\{\mathbf{0},\mathbf{1}\}, \sqsubseteq\rangle$, where $\mathbf{0}$ and $\mathbf{1}$ are the boolean values "false" and "true", respectively, and $\mathbf{0} \sqsubset \mathbf{1}$. In this setting environments may be viewed as characteristic functions of subsets of $\mathcal{X}$, so we use set operators $\cup$, $\cap$, and $-$ on such environments. The right-hand sides of equations are the formulas given by the following, where $\mathcal{X}' \subseteq \mathcal{X}$.

$$f := \bigvee \mathcal{X}' \mid \bigwedge \mathcal{X}'$$

We often write tt for $\bigwedge \emptyset$ and ff for $\bigvee \emptyset$. The definition of $[\![f]\!]\theta$ is standard: $[\![\bigvee \mathcal{X}']\!]\theta = \mathbf{1}$ iff $\mathcal{X}' \cap \theta \neq \emptyset$, and $[\![\bigwedge \mathcal{X}']\!]\theta = \mathbf{1}$ iff $\mathcal{X}' \subseteq \theta$.

Boolean equation systems may be derived from mu-calculus equation systems and Kripke structures. Intuitively, this is done by assigning a boolean variable to each state / mu-calculus variable pair; the boolean variable is intended to indicate whether or not the state is in the set of states associated with the mu-calculus variable. The resulting boolean equation system has alternation depth no greater than the mu-calculus equation system from which it is derived.

3 Support Sets

When a model-checking problem is encoded as a boolean equation system, the goal is typically to determine the value of a single distinguished variable ("does the start state satisfy the formula?"). A support set stores the evidence for such a variable's value as an abstract "proof" recording how values of variables depend on values of other variables.

Definition 3 (Support Set). *Let $\mathcal{E} = E_1 \ldots E_m$ be a closed boolean equation system with $\mathcal{X} = lhs(\mathcal{B})$, let $X \in \mathcal{X}$, and let $r \in \{\mathbf{0},\mathbf{1}\}$. Then a support set for r and X is a triple $\Gamma = \langle r, X, \Xi\rangle$, where $\Xi : \mathcal{X} \to 2^{\mathcal{X}}$ is a partial function such that $\Xi(X)$ is defined and such that the following properties hold for each X_i where $\Xi(X_i)$ is defined ($X_i \xrightarrow[\Gamma]{} X_j$ if $(\Xi(X_i))(X_j) = r$).*

I. (Direct Inference) $[\![f_i]\!](\Xi(X_i)) = r$
II. (Inclusion) If $X_i \xrightarrow[\Gamma]{} X_j$, then $\Xi(X_j)$ is defined.

III.(Circularity Restriction) If there exists a loop $\rho \equiv X_{p_1} \xrightarrow{r} \cdots \xrightarrow{r} X_{p_1}$
and X_i *is the shallowest variable on* ρ, *then* $(r = 1 \Rightarrow \sigma_i = \nu) \wedge (r = 0 \Rightarrow \sigma_i = \mu)$.

If $\Gamma = \langle r, X, \Xi \rangle$ then we call r the *support value* and X the *support variable* of Γ.

Support sets may be understood as follows. Recall that environments over the boolean lattice are isomorphic to sets of variables. Thus Ξ may be seen as associating an environment to each variable X_i on which it is defined. The existence of an edge $X_i \xrightarrow{r} X_j$ indicates a dependency of the value of X_i on X_j. Thus Condition I asserts that if $\Xi(X_i)$ is defined then under the interpretation $\Xi(X_i)$ of its variables, f_i evaluates to r, the boolean result of the support set. Condition II requires all variables on which X_i depends to be in the domain of Ξ. The last condition imposes restrictions on cyclic dependencies: the parity of the "shallowest" variable on the cycle must be consistent with r.

We may define an environment $g(\Gamma)$ for $\Gamma = \langle r, X, \Xi \rangle$ as follows.

$$(g(\Gamma))(X_i) = \begin{cases} r & \text{if } \Xi(X_i) \text{ is defined} \\ \bar{r} & \text{otherwise} \end{cases}$$

Theorem 1 states that the environment defined by a support set constitues a *partial model* of $\mathcal{E}$ in the following sense: if $r = 1$ then $g(\Gamma) \subseteq [\![\mathcal{E}]\!]$, and if $r = 0$ then $g(\Gamma) \cap [\![\mathcal{E}]\!] = \emptyset$. Since $\Xi(X)$ is always defined, it follows that $[\![\mathcal{E}]\!](X) = r$.

Theorem 1. *Let $\mathcal{E}$ be a closed boolean equation system with $X \in lhs(\mathcal{E})$ and a support set $\Gamma = \langle r, X, \Xi \rangle$. Then $g(\Gamma)$ is a partial model for $\mathcal{E}$.*

The next theorem guarantees the existence of support sets.

Theorem 2. *Given closed boolean equation system $\mathcal{E}$ and $X \in lhs(\mathcal{E})$, let $r = [\![\mathcal{E}]\!](X)$. Then there exists a support set for $\mathcal{E}$ with support value r and support variable X.*

Support Sets for Temporal Logics The previous definition introduces support sets in the context of boolean equation systems. At their lowest level many model checkers may be seen to manipulate such equation systems. However, conveying support-set-based information to users of model checkers requires the translation of boolean variables into user-level notations. The remainder of this section sketches how this can be done.

Users of model checkers typically input a (representation of) a Kripke structure and a formula in a temporal logic; the boolean variables used by the model checker represent assertions about whether or not a given state in the Kripke structure satisfies a given temporal formula derived from the formula input by the user. A *decorated support set* includes functions for extracting this information from boolean variables.

Definition 4. *Let $T = \langle S, s_I, \rightarrow, V \rangle$ be a Kripke structure, ϕ be a formula in a temporal logic Φ (i.e. Φ is the set of formulas) with satisfaction relation*

$\models_T \subseteq S \times \Phi$. Also let $\mathcal{E}$ be a boolean equation system with $\mathcal{X} = lhs(\mathcal{E})$. Then $\langle \Gamma, \pi_T, \pi_\Phi \rangle$ is a decorated support set if $\Gamma = \langle r, X, \Xi \rangle$ is a support set over $\mathcal{X}$ and $\pi_T : \mathcal{X} \to S$, $\pi_\Phi : \mathcal{X} \to \Phi$ satisfy the following for all X_i such that $\Xi(X_i)$ is defined.

1. $\pi_S(X) = s_I$ and $\pi_\Phi(X) = \phi$.
2. If $\Xi(X_i)$ is defined then $\pi_S(X_i) \models_T \pi_\Phi(X_i)$ iff $r = \mathbf{1}$.
3. If $X_j \in \Xi(X_i)$ then either $\pi_T(X_i) = \pi_T(X_j)$ or $\pi_T(X_i) \to \pi_T(X_j)$.

In a decorated support set, π_T and π_Φ extract state and temporal-formula information from the boolean variables in Γ. Condition 1 requires that the support variable of Γ be mapped to the start state of T and the initial formula ϕ, while Condition 2 stipulates that the value returned in Γ respect the semantics of the temporal logic. Condition 3 requires dependencies among boolean variables to "respect" T's transition relation.

4   Extracting Support Sets

As a generic vehicle for conveying model-checker reasoning, support sets are only useful to the extent that existing model checkers can be modified to compute them. In this section we show how this may be done by presenting an extended example.

We begin by noting that for explicit-state mu-calculus model checkers, whether global [And94, CS93, EL86] or local [And94, BC96a, LRS98], the extraction of support sets is straightforward, since such procedures typically work by implicity or explicitly converting a mu-calculus model-checking problem into a boolean equation system as described in Section 2. For reasons of space we do not consider these further. Instead, in the remainder of this section we show how an automaton-based algorithm for CTL* may be modified to construct support sets [KVW00]. This algorithm is not obviously mu-calculus-related; nevertheless, support-set information may be extracted without damaging the time or space complexity of the procedure.

In automaton-based model checking for CTL*, formulas are converted into tree automata accepting the trees that make the formula true. Checking whether a Kripke structure satisfies a formula involves determining whether or not the (infinite) tree obtained by unwinding the Kripke structure is accepted by the formula's tree automaton. This acceptance check is typically performed by viewing the Kripke structure itself as a tree automaton accepting the (single) tree obtained by the unwinding process just mentioned, computing a product with it and the automaton for the formula in question, and then checking whether or not the resulting product automaton is nonempty.

The automaton-based model checker considered below comes from [KVW00], although for technical convenience the definitions of the automata used borrow ideas from [BCG01] as well. Recall that $\mathcal{A}$ is the (fixed) set of atomic propositions.

Definition 5.

1. *An* alternating tableau transition system *is a tuple* $\langle Q, \rightarrow, q_I, \ell \rangle$, *where* Q *is a finite set of states,* $\rightarrow \subseteq Q \times Q$ *is the transition relation,* $q_I \in Q$ *is the start state, and* $\ell \in Q \rightarrow \mathcal{A} \cup \{\neg A \mid A \in \mathcal{A}\} \cup \{\wedge, \vee, [], \langle\rangle\}$ *is the labeling, and the following holds for all* $q \in Q$.

$$|\{q' \mid q \rightarrow q'\}| \begin{cases} = 0 \text{ if } \ell(q) \in \mathcal{A} \cup \{\neg A \mid A \in \mathcal{A}\} \\ \geq 1 \text{ if } \ell(q) \in \{\wedge, \vee\} \\ = 1 \text{ if } \ell(q) \in \{[], \langle\rangle\} \end{cases}$$

2. *Alternating tableau transition system* $\langle Q, \rightarrow, q_I, \ell \rangle$ *is* hesitant *if for every non-trivial[1] strongly connected component* $Q_i \subseteq Q$ *of the graph* $\langle Q, \rightarrow \rangle$ *and every* $q \in Q_i$, *either* $\ell(q) \in \{\wedge, []\}$ *or* $\ell(q) \in \{\vee, \langle\rangle\}$. *In the former case* Q_i *is called* existential, *while in the latter it is called* universal.

3. *A* hesitant alternating tableau automaton (HATA) *is a tuple* $\langle Q, \rightarrow, q_I, \ell, \langle G, B \rangle \rangle$ *where* $\langle Q, \rightarrow, q_I, \ell \rangle$ *is a hesitant alternating tableau transition system and* $G, B \subseteq Q$ *constitute the acceptance condition.*

HATAs are very similar to the hesitant automata in [KVW00]; the only real difference is the use of labels on states rather than transitions to record "alternation information".

HATAs generate "runs" as they process Kripke structures.

Definition 6. *Given HATA* $M = \langle Q, \rightarrow, q_I, F, \ell, \langle G, B \rangle \rangle$ *and a Kripke structure* $T = \langle S, s_I, \rightarrow, V \rangle$, *a run of* M *on* T *is a maximal tree in which the nodes are are labeled by elements of* $S \times Q$ *as follows. (1) The root of the tree is labeled by* $\langle s_I, q_I \rangle$. *(2) For each node* σ *labeled by* $\langle s, q \rangle$:

1. *If* $\ell(q) \in A$ *then* σ *is a leaf.*
2. *If* $\ell(q) = \wedge$ *and* $\{q' \mid q \rightarrow q'\} = \{q_1, \cdots, q_m\}$, *then* σ *has children* $\sigma_1, \cdots, \sigma_m$, *with* σ_i *labeled by* $\langle s, q_i \rangle$.
3. *If* $\ell(q) = \vee$ *then* σ *has one child,* σ', *which is lableled by* $\langle s, q' \rangle$ *for some* $q' \in \{q' \mid q \rightarrow q'\}$.
4. *If* $\ell(q) = []$, $q \rightarrow q'$, *and* $\{s' \mid s \rightarrow s'\} = \{s_1, .., s_m\}$ *then* σ *has children* $\sigma_1, .., \sigma_m$, *with* σ_i *is labeled by* $\langle s_i, q' \rangle$.
5. *If* $\ell(q) = \langle\rangle$ *and* $q \rightarrow q'$ *then* σ *has one child* σ', *and* σ' *is labeled by* $\langle s', q' \rangle$ *for some* s' *such that* $s \rightarrow s'$.

Note that any infinite path in a run eventually consists only of states from the same nontrivial strongly connected component. We call such an infinite path *existential* if this component is existential and *universal* otherwise. Because the transition relation of T is total, the only leaves in a run must be labeled either by $\langle s, A \rangle$ or $\langle s, \neg A \rangle$ for some $A \in \mathcal{A}$. We call leaves *successful* if they are labeled $\langle s, A \rangle$ and $s \in V(A)$ or $\langle s, \neg A \rangle$ and $s \notin V(A)$. A run is *successful* iff: every leaf is successful; every existential infinite path contains infinitely many occurrences of

---

[1] A strongly connected component Q_i is nontrivial if there exist $q, q' \in Q_i$ such that $q \rightarrow q'$.

states in G; and every universal infinite path contains finitely many occurrences of states in B.

In order to determine whether or not a HATA M has a successful run on Kripke structure T, [KVW00] advocates checking the nonemptiness of a product automaton built from M and T. In the slightly revised setting considered here the nonemptiness check may be defined on an and-or graph $G_{T,M}$ defined as follows.

- The vertex set of $G_{T,M}$ is $S \times Q$.
- The edge relation E is defined by: $\langle \langle s, q \rangle, \langle s', q' \rangle \rangle \in E$ iff $\langle s', q' \rangle$ satisfies the conditions of being a child of $\langle s, q \rangle$ in some run of M on T.
- Labeling function $f \in S \times Q \to \{\wedge, \vee\}$ is defined as follows.

$$f(\langle s, q \rangle) = \begin{cases} \wedge \text{ if } \ell(q) \in \{\wedge, []\} \text{ or } \langle s, q \rangle \text{ would be a successful leaf in some} \\ \quad \text{run} \\ \vee \text{ otherwise} \end{cases}$$

The model-checking routine works by assigning truth values 0 and 1 to vertices in $G_{T,M}$. Details may be found in [KVW00], but the rough idea is to process the strongly connected components in $G_{T,M}$ in reverse topological order, starting with components containing no edges to other components. Strongly connected components in $G_{T,M}$ have the property that all nodes share the same label ($\wedge$ or $\vee$). Sink nodes in the graph correspond to successful or unsuccessful leaves in some run and are assigned 1 in the first case and 0 in the latter. The following process is then repeated for each component. First, values in lower components that the current component has edges into are "propagated upwards" into the current component, and new boolean values assigned to nodes in the current component in the obvious manner (i.e. a $\vee$-labeled node is assigned 1 if it has an edge to a node assigned boolean value 1, etc.). This propagation process is continued until no more is possible. If the component still has unlabeled nodes then all nodes are assigned 1 if the component is labeled $\vee$ and there exists a vertex in the component of form $\langle s, q \rangle$ for some $q \in G$, or if the component is labeled $\wedge$ and there is no vertex of form $\langle s, q \rangle$ for some $q \in B$; and 0 otherwise. It may be shown that $\langle s_I, q_I \rangle$ is assigned 1 if HATA M accepts Kripke structure T and 0 otherwise.

In order to extract support sets from the information computed by this model-checking algorithm, we first define a boolean equation rom $G_{T,M}$ as follows. *Variables* correspond to vertices in $G_{T,M}$, while *right-hand sides* are constructed from labels and edges in $G_{T,M}$: if the label of a vertex v is $\wedge$, then the right-hand side for the variable v is $\bigwedge\{v' \mid \langle v, v' \rangle \in E\}$, and similary for $\vee$. *Blocks* are constructed from the strongly connected components of $G_{T,M}$. Let $G_1, \ldots, G_m$ be these components listed in topographical order: if $i < j$ then there is no edge from any node in G_j to G_i. For each G_i we construct two parity blocks E_i, E_i' as follows.

If G_i's label is $\vee$: Let E_i contain the equations whose left-hand sides $\langle s, q \rangle$ are nodes in G_i and with the property that $q \in G$. Let E_i' consist of the other equations whose left-hand sides are in G_i. Assign ν as the parity of E_i and μ as the parity of E_i'.

If G_i's label is $\wedge$: Let E_i contain the equations whose left-hand sides $\langle s, q \rangle$ are nodes in G_i and with the property that $q \in B$. Let E_i' consist of the other equations whose left-hand sides are in G_i. Assign μ as the parity of E_i and ν as the parity of E_i'.

The boolean equation system $\mathcal{E}_{T,M}$ is the sequence $E_1 E_1' \dots E_m E_m'$. One may prove the following.

Theorem 3. *Let T be a Kripke structure and M a HATA, and let s be a state in T and q a state in M. Then $[\![\mathcal{E}_{T,M}]\!](\langle s, q \rangle) = 1$ iff the value assigned to node $\langle s, q \rangle$ in $G_{T,M}$ by the model-checking algorithm of [KVW00] is 1.*

The evaluation procedure then computes the dependency set, denoted as $\xi(\langle s_k, q_k \rangle)$, for every vertex $\langle s_k, q_k \rangle$ in $G_{T,M}$. Recall that vertices in a strongly-connected component G_i are evaluated in two steps. Variable $\langle s_k, q_k \rangle$ is assigned a value in the first step if the values of its children determines permit; in this case we define $\xi(\langle s_k, q_k \rangle)$ to contain the children whose value matches $\langle s_k, q_k \rangle$. In the second step, the remaining vertices in G_i are evaluated. We consider the case that G_i is existential; the case that G_i is universal can be handled similarly. If there is a vertex $\langle s', q' \rangle$ in G_i with $q' \in G$, then the other vertices in G_i have value 1. We build a spanning tree rooted at $\langle s', q' \rangle$ for the unassigned variables in G_i using the inverse edge relation E^{-1}. For each node $\langle s'', q'' \rangle \neq \langle s', q' \rangle$ in the tree, we assign $\xi(\langle s'', q'' \rangle)$ the singleton set containing the parent of $\langle s'', q'' \rangle$ in the tree. We then make $\xi(\langle s', q' \rangle)$ contain one of its children in G_i with respect to E (the choice is abitrary). If there does not exist a $\langle s', q' \rangle$ such that $q' \in G$, then every remaining vertex $\langle s_k, q_k \rangle$ on G_i is assigned 0 and $\xi(s_k, q_k) = \{\langle s_l, q_l \rangle \mid \langle \langle s_k, q_k \rangle, \langle s_l, q_l \rangle \rangle \in E\}$. We now construct a support set $\Gamma = \langle r, \langle s, q \rangle, \Xi_{T,M} \rangle$ after $\langle s, q \rangle$ is labeled, where r is the label of $\langle s, q \rangle$, $\Xi(\langle s_k, q_k \rangle) = \xi(\langle s_k, q_k \rangle)$ if $\langle s_k, q_k \rangle$ is assigned r and $r = 1$, and $\Xi(\langle s_k, q_k \rangle) = \overline{\xi(\langle s_k, q_k \rangle)}$ if $\langle s_k, q_k \rangle$ is assigned r and $r = 0$ (this assignment in effect assigns the truth value 0 to every variable in $\xi(\langle s_k, q_k \rangle)$). One may check that Γ satisfies the requirements of being a support set and that "extracting" this support set does not affect the time or space complexity of the procedure.

We close this section with some comments about decorated support sets. In CTL* automaton-based model checking the HATA is constructed from a CTL* formula provided by the user. As the model checker should return a decorated support set, one may wonder how to define the functions π_T and π_Φ. In the procedure just outlined the mapping π_T is straightforward, since every boolean variable corresponds to a pair $\langle s, q \rangle$, where s is a system state. As for π_ϕ, the HATA constructions in [BCG01, KVW00] work by associating HATA states with (sets of) CTL* propositions. These CTL* propositions can then be returned by π_Φ.

5   Diagnostic Information

In the remainder of the paper we study two different applications for support sets. In this section we show how support sets may be used to compute *diagnostic information* in general, and *linear witnesses* in particular. We note that support sets may also be used to compute winning strategies for the purposes of diagnostic routines based on game-based model checking [SS98], although we do not pursue this point here.

Counterexamples are used to indicate why a Kripke structure fails to satisfy a temporal property. Intuitively, a counterexample is a part of system "responsible" for the property being violated. Dually, when system satisfies a temporal property, a user may still desire some explanation given as a portion of the system, called a *witness*, responsible for the property being satisfied. Although counterexample generators have existed for a number of years, to the best of our knowledge [CGMZ95] represents the first systematic explanation of how they work. Their definitions in the setting of CTL require that counterexamples and witnesses to be *linear*, i.e., execution paths of the system. In general the existence of linear counterexamples / witnesses depends on the structure of formulas as well as the Kripke structure being checked. In the case of CTL, for example, linear counterexamples (witnesses) exist if the primary path quantifier used is A (E). [KV99] gives more general conditions for CTL* and shows show that judging whether a CTL* formulae admits such counterexamples / witnesses is PSPACE-complete.

Here we show how support sets may be used to generate linear counterexamples / witnesses without reference to the temporal logic in which system properties are formulated. In the rest of this section we restrict our attention to Kripke structures that are *self-loop-free*: no state s has the property that $s \to s$.

Definition 7. *Support set* $\langle r, X, \Xi \rangle$ *is* linear *if for all* X_i *such that* $\Xi(X_i)$ *is defined,* $|\Xi(X_i)| \leq 1$. *Decorated support set* $\langle \Gamma, \pi_T, \pi_\Phi \rangle$ *is* linear *if* Γ *is.*

If a decorated support set is linear then one may extract a *linear witness* to the result contained in the support set as follows. Let $\Gamma = \langle \Gamma' = \langle r, X, \Xi \rangle, \pi_T, \pi_\Phi \rangle$ be a linear decorated support set for Kripke structure T. Then the *state projection* $\pi_S(\Gamma')$ is defined as follows: let $X_1 X_2 \ldots X_n$ be a depth-first search of the graph induced by Ξ beginning at $X = X_1$. Then $\pi_S(\Gamma) = \pi_T(X_1) \ldots \pi_T(X_n)$. In general, $\pi_S(\Gamma)$ is not an execution sequence of T, since the definition of decorated support set allows the states associated with adjacent variables in Γ to be the same, and hence not connected by a transition. However, a subsequence of $\pi(\Gamma)$ is guaranteed to be a computation path of T: delete all but one occurrence of a state in contigous subsequences containing only this state. Let $\pi(\Gamma)$ be this sequence; it is easy to show that it is a computation path in T that is a linear model of the result reported by the model checker.

In general support sets are not linear, but they can *minimized* in the following sense. A support set $\Gamma = \langle r, X, \Xi \rangle$ is *minimal* if the following conditions hold.

1. For every X' such that $\Xi(X')$ is defined, $X \xrightarrow{\Gamma}^* X'$ (i.e. X' affects X).
2. If $r = \mathbf{1}$ then for every variable X' whose right-hand side uses $\bigvee$ such that $\Xi(X')$ is defined, $|\Xi(X')| = 1$, and dually for $r = \mathbf{0}$.

Intuitively, a support set is minimal if it contains no extraneous information. It is straightforward to convert a support set $\Gamma = \langle r, X, \Xi \rangle$ into a minimal support set $\Gamma_{\min} = \langle r, X, \Xi_{\min} \rangle$. The witness-extraction procedure can be applied to support sets that, while not linear themselves, minimize to linear support sets. Finally, we note that even when minimial support sets are not linear, they may be used to generate "recursive" linear witnesses à la [CGMZ95] when all but one element in $\Xi(X')$ are guaranteed to belong to different strongly connected components than X' for any X'.

6   Certifying Model-Checking Results

In this section we give an efficient algorithm to check the validity of a support set submitted by a model checker. Such a routine has several practical motivations [Nam01]:

- It can be used to check for bugs in model checkers: if a support set returned by a checker is in fact not a support set, then the checker's reasoning is faulty.
- Support sets can be used as "certificates" for system correctness. A validity checker can then be used to check the "internal consistency" of such a certificate.

In what follows we fix boolean equation system $\mathcal{E} = E_1 \dots E_n$. Let $\Gamma = \langle r, X, \Xi \rangle$ be a support set for $\mathcal{E}$ submitted by a checker. Without loss of generality, assume $r = \mathbf{1}$. Validating Γ amounts to checking that Properties I, II and III in Definition 3 hold. Properties I and II Γ can be easily ascertained with routines that execute in $O(|\Gamma|)$. Checking Property III on Γ can be reduced to an *even-cycle* problem on labeled directed graphs. A labeled directed graph is a tuple $G = \langle D, V, E, \ell \rangle$, where $\ell : V \to D$ labels each vertex with a element from D. The *even-cycle* problem is given as follows: given a labeled directed graph $G = \langle \{1, 2, \cdots, k\}, V, E, \ell \rangle$, determine whether there is a cycle ρ in it such that $min_{v \in \rho}\{\ell(v)\}$ is even.

Γ induces a labeled directed graph $G = \langle \{1, 2, \cdots, k\}, V, E, \ell \rangle$ as follows. V is the set of all variables defined on Ξ, E is the relation $\xrightarrow{\Gamma}$. ℓ satisfies the following criteria.

- If $X', X'' \in lhs(E_i)$ then $\ell(X') = \ell(X'')$.
- If $i < j$ then $\ell(E_i) \leq \ell(E_j)$. (Here $\ell(E_i)$ is the common value shared by all left-hand sides in E_i.)
- If the parity of E_i is μ then $\ell(E_i)$ is even; otherwise, $\ell(E_i)$ is odd.

A labeling satisfying these properties can easily be constructed in $|\mathcal{E}|$ time with $k \leq n$, where n is the number of blocks. Checking III on Γ is equivalent to checking whether there is an even cycle in G. [KKV01] shows that the even-cycle problem can be solved in $O((|V| + |E|)log(\lceil \frac{k}{2} \rceil))$. Their approach is a variant of an algorithm for hierarchical clustering [Tar82]. As our construction of ℓ above restricts $k \le n$, checking property III can be done in $O(|\Xi|log(\lceil \frac{n}{2} \rceil))$, where n is the number of parity blocks of $\mathcal{E}$.

The complexity can be improved by noticing that an even-cycle can only exist in a strongly-connected component of G_Γ. Therefore, we can check each strongly-connected component independently. By Definition 2, the maximal labeling number k won't exceed the alternation depth of $\mathcal{E}$. Thus, the overall time complexity is $O(|\mathcal{E}| \cdot |\mathcal{T}| \cdot log(\lceil \frac{ad(\mathcal{E})}{2} \rceil))$, which is less than the lower bound of μ-calculus model-checking. This suggests that the certifier will not in general increase the cost of overall complexities of a verification tool.

7   Conclusions and Related Work

In this paper we have presented support sets as a generic data structure for conveying "meta-model-checking" results, i.e. results regarding the means by which model-checking answers are arrived at. We showed how model checkers may be modified to return support sets and how support sets may be used to generate diagnostic information and may be efficiently checked for internal consistency. We have also studied other uses for support sets not mentioned in this paper, including vacuity checking [KV99]. Prototype implementations of these results are being investigated in the context of the CWB-NC verification tool [CS96].

The idea of retaining evidence during model checking as a basis for justifying the result has appeared in several recent publications. In [PZ01, PPZ01] ideas in the setting of linear-time temporal-logic are presented. Regarding the mu-calculus, [Mat00] uses a distinguised solution to alternation-free boolean equation system, called *extended boolean graphs* (EBGs), to encode the proof structures. EBGs can be viewed as a special case of support set in the alternation-free fragment of the mu-calculus. Even closer to this work is that in [Nam01], which uses deductive proofs to encode evidence for model-checking in the modal mu-calculus. That paper also discusses some of the same applications mentioned here for deductive information; a technical point of departure, however, is that deductive proofs in that setting require extra information in form of *ranking information* which records information on the number of "approximations" of outer variables that an inner variable depends on. This requirement plays the same role as the circularity restriction for support sets: in fact, the ranking information specifies the position of a variable in a dependency loop. With this extra information verifying the validity of proofs is easier than the verification for support sets. An obvious drawback is that storing ranking information requires additional space, and it also requires model checkers to maintain the information about numbers of approximations for variables. This information is not typically computed by on-the-fly (local) algorithms due to its top-down evaluation fashion. Therefore, it is not clear how ranking information can be collected for local algorithms. On the other hand, support sets require only dependency information, which is computed by both global and local algorithms.

References

[And94]   H. R. Andersen. Model checking and boolean graphs. *Theoretical Computer Science*, 126(1):3–30, April 1994. 462

[BBDER97] I. Beer, S. Ben-David, C. Eisner, and Y. Rodeh. Efficient detection of vacuity in ACTL formulas. In *Proceedings of the Ninth International Conference on Computer Aided Verification (CAV '97), LNCS 1254*. Springer-Verlag, 1997. 455

[BC96a]   G. S. Bhat and R. Cleaveland. Efficient local model checking for fragments of the modal μ-calculus. In *Proceedings of the Second International Workshop on Tools and Algorithms for the Construction and Analysis of Systems (TACAS '96), LNCS 1055*. Springer-Verlag, March 1996. 462

[BC96b]   G. S. Bhat and R. Cleaveland. Efficient model checking via the equational μ-calculus. In E. M. Clarke, editor, *11th Annual Symposium on Logic in Computer Science (LICS '96)*, pages 304–312, New Brunswick, NJ, July 1996. Computer Society Press. 460

[BCG01]   G. Bhat, R. Cleaveland, and A. Groce. Efficient model checking via büchi tableau automaton. In *Proceedings of the Seventh International Conference on Tools and Algorithms for the Construction and Analysis of Systems (TACAS '01), LNCS 2031*. Springer-Verlag, 2001. 462, 465

[CE81]   E. M. Clarke and E. A. Emerson. Design and synthesis of synchronization skeletons using branching-time temporal logic. In *Proceedings of the Workshop on Logic of Programs*, Yorktown Heights, volume 131 of *Lecture Notes in Computer Science*. Springer-Verlag, 1981. 455

[CES86]   E. M. Clarke, E. A. Emerson, and A. P. Sistla. Automatic verification of finite-state concurrent systems using temporal logic specifications. *ACM TOPLAS*, 8(2), 1986. 455

[CGMZ95]   E. Clarke, O. Grumberg, K. McMillian, and X. Zhao. Efficent generation of counterexamples and witnesses in symbolic model checking. In *Proc. 32nd Design Automaton Conference*, San Francisco, CA, 1995. 455, 466, 467

[CKV01]   H. Chockler, O. Kupferman, and M. Vardi. Coverage metrics for temporal logic model checking. In *Proceedings of the Seventh International Conference on Tools and Algorithms for the Construction and Analysis of Systems (TACAS '01), LNCS 2031*. Springer-Verlag, April 2001. 455

[CS93]   R. Cleaveland and B. U. Steffen. A linear-time model checking algorithm for the alternation-free modal mu-calculus. *Formal Methods in System Design*, 2:121–147, 1993. 462

[CS96]   R. Cleaveland and S. Sims. The NCSU concurrency workbench. In R. Alur and T. A. Henzinger, editors, *Computer Aided Verification (CAV '96)*, volume 1102 of *Lecture Notes in Computer Science*, pages 394–397, New Brunswick, New Jersey, July 1996. Springer-Verlag. 468

[Dam94]   M. Dam. CTL* and ECTL* as fragement of the modal μ-calculus. *Theoretical Computer Science*, 126:77–96, 1994. 460

[EL86]   E. A. Emerson and C.-L. Lei. Efficient model checking in fragments of
           the propositional mu-calculus. In *Symposium on Logic in Computer Science (LICS '86)*, pages 267–278, Cambridge, Massachusetts, June 1986.
           Computer Society Press. 462

[KKV01]   V. King, O. Kupferman, and M. Y. Vardi. On the complexity of parity
           word automaton. In *The 4th International Conference on Foundations of
           Software Science and Computation Structures*, Vol. 2030 of *Lecture Notes
           in Computer Science*, 2001. 468

[KV99]   O. Kupferman and M. Y. Vardi. Vacuity detection in temporal model
           checking. In *Proceedings of the Tenth Conference on Correct Hardware
           Design and Verification Mothods, LNCS 1703*, 1999. 466, 468

[KVW00]   O. Kupferman, M. Y. Vardi, and P. Wolper. An automata-theoretic approach to branching-time model checking. *Journal of the ACM*, 47(2):312–
           360, March 2000. 462, 463, 464, 465

[LRS98]   X. Liu, C. R. Ramakrishnan, and S. A. Smolka. Fully local and efficient
           evaluation of alternating fixed points. In *Proceedings of the Fourth International Conference on Tools and Algorithms for the Construction and
           Analysis of Systems (TACAS '98), LNCS 1389*. Springer-Verlag, 1998.
           462

[Mad97]   A. Mader. *Verification of Modal Properties Using Boolean Equation Systems*. PhD thesis, Müchen, Techn-Univ., 1997. 457

[Mat00]   R. Mateescu. Efficient diagnostic generation for boolean equation system. In *Proceedings of the Sixth International Conference on Tools and
           Algorithms for the Construction and Analysis of Systems (TACAS '00)*,
           Vol. 1785 of *Lecture Notes in Computer Science*. Springer-Verlag, March
           2000. 468

[Nam01]   K. Namjoshi. Certifying model checkers. In *Proceedings of the 13th International Conference on Computer Aided Verification (CAV '01), LNCS
           2102*. Springer-Verlag, 2001. 455, 467, 468

[PPZ01]   D. Peled, A. Pnueli, and L. Zuck. From falsification to verification. In
           FST&TCS, volume 2245 of *Lecture Notes in Computer Science*. Springer-
           Verlag, 2001. 468

[PZ01]   D. Peled and L. Zuck. From model checking to a temporal proof. In
           M. Dwyer, editor, *SPIN 2001*, volume 2057 of *Lecture Notes in Computer
           Science*, pages 1–14, Toronto, May 2001. Springer-Verlag. 468

[QS82]   J. P. Queille and J. Sifakis. Specification and verification of concurrent
           systems in Cesar. In *Proceedings of the International Symposium in Programming*, volume 137 of *Lecture Notes in Computer Science*, Berlin, 1982.
           Springer-Verlag. 455

[SS98]   P. Stevens and C. Stirling. Practical model checking using games. In *Proceedings of the Fourth International Conference on Tools and Algorithms
           for the Construction and Analysis of Systems (TACAS '98), LNCS 1389*.
           Springer-Verlag, 1998. 466

[Sti95]   C. Stirling. Local model checking games. In I. Lee and S. A. Smolka,
           editors, *Proceedings of the Sixth International Conference on Concurrency
           Theory (CONCUR '95)*, Vol. 962 of *Lecture Notes in Computer Science*.
           Springer-Verlag, 1995. 455

[Tar82]   R. E. Tarjan. A hierarchical clusting algorithm using strong components.
           Information Processing Letters, 14:26–29, 1982. 468

Mixing Forward and Backward Traversals in Guided-Prioritized BDD-Based Verification

Gianpiero Cabodi, Sergio Nocco, and Stefano Quer

Dip. di Automatica e Informatica, Politecnico di Torino
Turin, Italy
{cabodi,nocco,quer}@polito.it
http://www.polito.it/~{cabodi,quer}

Abstract. Over the last decade BDD-based symbolic manipulations have been among the most widely used core technologies in the verification domain. To improve their efficiency within the framework of *Unbounded Model Checking*, we follow some of the most successful trends proposed in this field.

We present a very promising approach based on: Mixing forward and backward traversals, dovetailing approximate and exact methods, adopting guided and partitioned searches, efficiently using conjunctive decompositions and generalized cofactor based BDD simplifications. One of the main contributions of this paper is a backward verification procedure based on a prioritized traversal. We call the method "inbound-path-search". Initially, an approximate forward traversal produces over-approximate onion-ring frontier sets. After that, these rings are used as distance estimators and guides to partition state sets in terms of the *estimated* distance from the "target" set of states. Finally, while the subsequent search is performed, the higher priority is given to the subset with the smallest estimated distance.

We experimentally compare our methodology with a state-of-the-art technique (*approximate-reachability don't cares model checking*) implemented in the freely available VIS tool. Results show interesting improvements in terms of both efficiency and power.

1 Introduction

Binary Decision Diagrams (BDDs[1]) are one of the most widely used core techniques in the field of Formal Verification. They provide a compact implicit representation and manipulation formats for functions with a support varying from a few tens to a few hundreds of Boolean variables. Albeit many optimized procedures and variants of the original BDD representation format have been introduced over the years, most of the existing techniques are limited by the well-known memory explosion problem.

Recently, BDD-based tools have been challenged by approaches based on propositional satisfiability (SAT) such as Bounded Model Checking (BMC).

---

[1] Reduced Ordered BDDs (ROBDDs), or simply BDDs whenever no ambiguity arises.

D. Brinksma and K. G. Larsen (Eds.): CAV 2002, LNCS 2404, pp. 471–484, 2002.

While traditional BDD-based model checking searches for counter-examples of *unbounded* length, SAT-based model checking drops the requirement for a fix-point computation, and only targets bounded execution runs. As a consequence SAT methods search for counter-examples of *bounded* length, by working on a combinational unrolling of given length of the sequential system under check. For that reason BMC targets falsification and partial verification rather than full verification.

Some recent papers, e.g., [1, 2], have compared BDD and SAT based model checking. SAT methods have often been considered more efficient even though part of the gain is a direct consequence of comparing SAT based *bounded* against traditional BDD based *unbounded* model checking. As a consequence, in [2] the authors adapt a BDD-based model checker to bounded model checking in order to make a fair comparison between the BDD and SAT engines. Some works also address unbounded model checking using SAT solvers [3], but so far their practical impact has been much less relevant than BMC tools. In other cases mixed strategies have been proposed to cope with advantages and disadvantages of both the techniques [4].

Albeit representing a good compromise for bug hunting in large models, BMC is unfortunately a partial verification method in practice, since a complete verification would require computing the "diameter"[2] of the system, which is often impossible. Another major problem of semi-exhaustive verification is that it shows a severe degradation in usability for corner-case bugs, where the tuning effort becomes higher and recovery more difficult.

Our main goal is to find bugs, since we address the verification of large designs under development, but we are also interested in complete algorithms, able to efficiently handle both verification and falsification cases. In order to achieve the above goals, we explore possible enhancements of BDD based symbolic verification, following some of the trends proposed in the past years to face the BDD explosion problem.

We exploit *approximate traversals* [5] to simplify exact verification; we follow the *guided search* [6,7] paradigm when combining *forward and backward* [8,9] traversals to mutually focus and narrow their search area; we finally exploit conjunctive partitioning and cofactor based simplifications to keep BDD sizes under control. More specifically, we present what we call "inbound-path-search", i.e., a backward search approach based on partitioning and prioritized traversal. We first derive from an over-approximated breadth-first traversal an onion-ring partitioning of the state space. Each ring (or frontier) is a set of states at a given distance from the initial state. Distances are based on approximate computations, so we just use them as estimates of correct measures, in order to drive a backward search to its "target", i.e., the initial state. To do so, state sets in backward traversal are partitioned by the onion-ring frontiers, and higher priorities are given to partitions with smallest distance from the target set of states.

---

[2] We call "diameter" of a system its sequential depth, or the maximum shortest path connecting an initial state to any reachable state.

1.1   Related Works and Contributions

Our approach shares goals and underlying ideas with recent works in two main research paths.

On the first path, partitioning and guided searches, as *"divide-and-conquer"* methodologies, are used to attack large problems [10,11,12,13]. In the present work we do partition set of states, in order to operate smaller traversals from individual partitions, and we do adopt a priority based selection strategy. However, our partitioning strategy is driven by a traversal related heuristic, instead of mere BDD based measures (e.g., BDD size [11,12,13] or density [10]). We partitions state sets and we assign them priorities based on their estimated distance from the target set of states. We call our prioritized traversal "inbound-path-search", as we first explore space regions with smaller estimated distance from the target set.

On the second path, approximate, exact, forward, and backward traversals [8,9,14] are mixed and adopted together. Our work shares with this set of papers the general idea of focusing and guiding more accurate traversals with previous approximate ones. We follow [8] in its idea of combining approximate forward and exact backward traversals, using frontier sets computed in the forward direction to guide and simplify backward traversals. Our sequence of traversals always ends up with an exact traversal, i.e., we do not have false negatives. We share with [14] the idea of using an over-approximation of the reachable state set to simplify exact verification. This is the term of comparison we choose in the experimental section, as a complete and exact model checking approach using approximate traversals. Our main contribution is to propose more sophisticated and efficient simplification strategy for BDD representation of state sets. We use individual frontier sets, i.e., the onion-rings, instead of fix-point reached states as tighter constraints for symbolic search.

The overall verification method we present is able to check invariant properties[3] on large problems made up of some hundreds of memory elements. We compare our methodology with the approximate reachability don't care model checking [14] as implemented in the VIS tool [15]. Our experimental results show that we are able to check properties on circuits outside the scope of state-of-the-art BDD based verification tools.

To sum up, some of the major contributions of our approach are the following:

- A new BDD based property verification strategy for Unbounded Model Checking.
- A technique for exact verification (without false negatives), exploiting approximate traversals as a way to drive and drastically simplify bug hunting efforts in exact symbolic traversals.
- A set of optimizations within image and pre-image procedures, sharing the common goal of keeping BDDs as much partitioned and simplified as possible, in order to avoid memory blow-ups.

---

[3] The extension to more general temporal logic (e.g., CTL) formulas is possible, and it has been partially implemented, but it is just mentioned in the sequel.

As a final remark it is worth pointing out that the present work extends the one presented in [16]. In that work we show that BDD-based verification can deal with large circuit and problem sizes in the *bounded* verification domain and we compare our approach with SAT-based BMC. Here we work in the *unbounded* verification domain, i.e., we propose a complete verification procedure, and we compare our results with a state-of-the-art BDD-based unbounded model checker.

2   Preliminaries

Our verification framework handles Finite State Machines described by their transition relation TR with initial state set S. We check an invariant property P by attempting to prove (or disprove) the reachability of the target state set T, i.e., the complement of P (T = ¬P), from S. Extending our approach to temporal logic formulas (e.g., CTL model check) is possible, provided that the simplification and partitioning are properly embedded within backward CTL evaluation procedures. We limit our description to invariant properties both for their practical relevance and for sake of simplicity in the explanation: support for the outermost AG or EX operators in CTL formulas is trivial, whereas nested operators would require *ad-hoc* simplifications.

```
FWDVER (TR, S, T)
    i = 0
    R₀ = S
    repeat
        if ((T ∧ Rᵢ) ≠ ∅)
            return (COUNTEREX(TR, R))
        i = i + 1
        Rᵢ = S∨ IMG (TR,Rᵢ₋₁)
    until (Rᵢ ≠ Rᵢ₋₁)
    return (PASS)
```

The procedure is based on the iterated application of the IMG function, to compute symbolic images of the set of state R_{i-1}. The state sets generated at each traversal iteration, i.e., R_i, are often called frontier sets. Notice that the pseudo-code shows a particular case, the one we adopt for approximate forward traversals: The whole reached state set is given as input to the image procedure, whereas any state set in the interval between the newly reached states and the reached states could be used. On the fly tests for intersection with target are done at each iteration, thus avoiding full computation of reachable states whenever T is reached before the fix-point. A counter-example is possibly computed starting from the array R of frontier sets R_i.

Fig. 1. Breadth-first exact forward verification

A standard BDD-based *exact forward verification* (Figure 1) is a breadth-first least fix-point visit of the state space that starts from S and tries to find a path to T. CTL model checking procedures are often implemented (as well as our exact search) as backward traversal procedures, so let us also mention here that an invariant (or an AG CTL property) can be verified by proving/disproving the mutual reachability of S and T in the backward direction. This is easily expressed by swapping the S and T sets, and changing the IMG function with the PREIMG computation in Figure 1.

Let us finally put a remark on the generalized cofactor operator. The generalized cofactor of f with respect to g is expressed as $f \downarrow g$. Whereas the "constrain" cofactor may introduce new variables and BDD nodes in the result, the "restrict" cofactor does not. After some experimental comparison between constrain and restrict, we selected the latter one for our implementation because of its BDD simplification properties.

3   Prioritized Forward-Backward Verification

Our approach follows [14] in its main purpose of exploiting over-approximations of reachable states as care set for backward model checking procedures. However, we address more aggressive simplification strategies: We exploit cofactoring based simplifications and decomposed representations for state sets, whereas [14] simply conjoins (Boolean AND operator) state sets with the pre-computed over-approximation. Some of our optimizations work at the level of traversal iterations, and they are shown in this section. The other ones are related to inner steps of image/pre-image computations and are discussed in the next section.

Our starting idea is to combine approximate forward and exact backward search, as done in [8] for equivalence check and in [16] for bounded model check. An initial approximate traversal is used to guide and simplify an exact backward verification task. In order to represent (and differentiate) the various state sets involved in different traversal strategies, we adopt the following notations:

- F_i (B_i): Frontier set in exact forward (backward) traversal starting from initial state set $F_0 = S$ ($B_0 = T$). We do not compute F (B) in our approach, but we use it as a term of comparison while proving the correctness of the combined forward-backward traversals.
- F_i^+: Frontier set in the over-approximate forward traversal, starting from the initial state set S ($F_0 = S$).
- R (R^+): Set of exact (over-approximate) forward reachable states, representing the least fix point value of F (F^+).
- FB_i: Frontier set in exact backward traversal over-approximate forward states (R^+) and/or frontiers (F_i^+). Computation of FB sets is guided and simplified using previously computed R^+ and F^+ sets.
- RB: Reached state set in exact backward traversal over approximate forward states (computed as union of FB frontiers).

Let us first introduce a model check procedure (FWDBWDMC, Figure 2) sharing similarities with [8,14].

The FWDBWDMC procedure is able to check invariants (or AG($\neg$T) CTL specifications) in the backward direction, using the fix-point over-approximation R^+ to simplify backward state sets FB. It is known that all CTL formulas can

FwdBwdMC (TR, S, T)
$F_0^+ = S$
$i = 0$
/* approximate forward */
repeat
    $i{+}{+}$
    $F_i^+ = S \vee \text{Img}^+ (\text{TR}, F_{i-1}^+)$
until $(F_i^+ = F_{i-1}^+)$
$R^+ = F_i^+$
$RB = FB_0 = T {\downarrow} R^+$
$i = 0$
/* exact backward */
while $((FB_i \wedge R^+ \wedge \neg RB) \neq 0)$
    if $(FB_i \wedge S \neq 0)$
        return (counterEx (TR, FB))
    $i{+}{+}$
    $CARE = R^+ \wedge \neg RB$
    $FB_i = \text{PreImg} (\text{TR}, FB_{i-1}) {\downarrow} CARE$
    $RB = (RB \vee FB_i) {\downarrow} R^+$
return (PASS)

The procedure proceeds in two steps. Firstly, it computes the set of over-approximate forward frontier sets, i.e., F_i^+. Each entry in the F^+ array over-estimates the frontier set of an exact traversal:

$$F_i^+ \supseteq F_i$$

Secondly, it performs a backward traversal. The fix point value ($R^+ = F_i^+$) is taken as care set when computing backward frontiers FB. More specifically, each new frontier FB_i is evaluated taking into account only newly reached states in the care space ($R^+ \wedge \neg RB$). The restrict cofactor is adopted for generalized cofactor simplifications. A counter-example is possibly evaluated.

Fig. 2. Forward backward for invariant model checking

be rewritten (and evaluated) in terms of just three operators: EX, EG, and EU. Variants of FwdBwdMC can be adapted to cover all of them, by properly simplifying state sets with the R^+ care set.

Cofactor based simplifications are extensively applied though inner steps of the procedure. The correctness of the result is based on the following observations. Let us express a standard backward traversal from T by the following pre-image computation step

$$FB_i = \text{PreImg}(\text{TR}, FB_{i-1})$$
$$RB = RB \vee FB_i$$

A first way of using care set based simplifications (as done in [14]) is

$$FB_i = \text{PreImg}(\text{TR}, FB_{i-1}) \wedge R^+ \wedge \neg RB$$
$$RB = RB \vee FB_i$$

where frontier sets FB_i are conjoined (Boolean AND) with the care set R^+ (so that part of the states unreachable from S are not considered) and with $\neg RB$ (only newly reached states are taken into account). A problem with this approach arises from the fact that conjunction often means producing larger BDDs, so our solution is using the *restrict* generalized cofactor:

$$FB_i = \text{PreImg}(\text{TR}, FB_{i-1}) {\downarrow} (R^+ \wedge \neg RB)$$
$$RB = (RB \vee FB_i) {\downarrow} R^+$$

We use both the over-approximation of (forward) reachable states (R^+) and the complement of backward reached states ($\neg RB$) as care set for frontier computation. In other words, frontiers are arbitrarily simplified over (forward) unreachable states and already reached (backward) states (included in RB). Cofactor simplification with previously reached states ($\neg RB$) is common to many BDD based traversal tools, whereas the simplification with R^+ is usually performed only for TR, not for reached states. Making it on frontier sets may add unreachable states to FB_i sets, but this does not affect the correctness of the overall process (by introducing false paths to S) since the (exact) pre-image of unreachable states ($U = \neg R$) is outside the set of reachable states:

$$U \subseteq \neg R^+ \subseteq \neg R \;\Rightarrow\; \text{PreImg}(\text{TR}, U) \subseteq \neg R \tag{1}$$

The set of backward reachable states is also simplified by R at each new iteration introducing new values by means of disjunction (Boolean OR with the new FB_i frontier).

A second approach we introduce is more oriented to falsify the property under check (i.e., finding bugs), and it does not merely use the fix point R^+, set, but individual F^+ rings in order to simplify and guide the backward search to the target S set. The outer procedure (FwdBwdPMC) and the recursive step BwdPMCStep are shown in Figure 3.

FwdBwdPMC (TR,S,T)	BwdPMCStep (TR,From,T,F^+,Care,i)
$F_0^+ = S$	if (From $\wedge$ T$\wedge$ Care $\neq 0$)
i = 0	return (T)
/* approximate forward */	Care = Care $\wedge\neg$ From
repeat	/* inbound-path-search */
i++	To = PreImg (TR, From $\downarrow F_i^+$) $\downarrow F_{i-1}^+$
$F_i^+ = $ S$\vee$ Img$^+$ (TR, F_{i-1}^+)	if (To $\neq 0$)
until ($F_i^+ = F_{i-1}^+$)	FB = BwdPMCStep (
$R^+ = F_i^+$	TR,To$\wedge F_{i-1}^+$,T,F^+,Care,i-1)
i = 0	if (FB $\neq$ NULL)
/* locate innermost intersection	FB = (From, FB)
frontier – target */	return (FB)
while ($F_i^+ \wedge$ T= 0)	/* global-path-search */
i++	To = PreImg(TR,From) $\downarrow$Care
if (i > size(F^+))	if (To $\neq 0$)
return (PASS)	while ($F_i^+ \wedge$ To = 0)
/* exact backward */	i++
FB = BwdPMCStep (	FB = BwdPMCStep (
TR, T, S, F^+, R^+, i)	TR,To,T,F^+,Care,i)
if (FB = NULL)	if (FB $\neq$ NULL)
return (PASS)	FB = (From, FB)
else	return (FB)
return (counterEx(TR,FB))	return (NULL)

Fig. 3. Forward backward prioritized model check

Approximate forward frontier sets F_i^+ are initially computed in FWDB-WDPMC as in FWDBWDMC, then backward traversal is achieved recursively by BWDPMCSTEP receiving, as parameters, the transition relation TR, a local starting state From (a frontier set at the generic call, S at the outer one), the target set T, the forward over-approximated frontiers (F^+), a care subspace (R^+ at the outer call), and the index of i the innermost F_i^+ frontier intersecting From. Since the method is particularly oriented to to seek for a backward path connecting From to S, the generic recursion tries to find it by first looking for a path through the inner frontier F_{i-1}^+:

$$\text{To} = \text{PREIMG}(\text{TR}, \text{From}\downarrow F_i^+)\downarrow F_{i-1}^+$$

This step combines cofactor simplifications both on the domain and image sets. More specifically, the result set To is simplified using the inner F_{i-1}^+ frontier as care set, whereas From is simplified with F_i^+. The result is correct since no states outside F_i^+ can have a pre-image in F_{i-1}^+. In case the computed pre-image To is not void, i.e., a step to the inner frontier has been done, a recursive call is activated to complete the path to S: The procedure receives as initial set To $\wedge F_{i-1}^+$, where the conjunction is kept indicated (no product BDD is computed), so that the second term will disappear when recursively computing the pre-image to the F_{i-2}^+ frontier and so on so forth.

As far as pre-images succeed reaching inner frontiers, the approach shows its best guiding and simplification power, since the search is driven by approximate frontiers into sub-spaces where the chance to attain the goal is higher. Of course the chance relies in the goodness of the (forward) approximation process, so the search might fail, either for errors in the approximations, or simply because no paths to S exist (property is not falsifiable). This is the case where backward search is completed by a local wider exploration from the From set to the whole CARE, which is equal to R^+, with the exclusion of all From sets up in the recursion tree. This attempt is done both to explore the complete search space when no *inbound* path is found, so that starting states for new searches are generated, or the absence of a path to S is finally proved. In order to avoid an excessive amount of partitioning, with consequent exponential degradation of time performance, we have two heuristic controls on the activation of the *inbound* path search: the BDD size threshold on From (no inbound search is done if From is under the threshold) and a maximum amount of partitionings up in the recursion tree. The above controls are common to several techniques adopting partitioning with BDDs, and they are not shown in Figure 3 for sake of simplicity.

Recursions stop whenever the target set T is intersected by From, or a dead end is attained because no success was locally found by both inbound and global attempts.

The correctness of the procedure is guaranteed by the following theorem.

Theorem 1. *Let F^+ be an array of k over-approximated forward frontiers such that $F_0^+ = S$, $\forall_{0<i<k} F_i^+ \supseteq F_i$, and $F_{k-1}^+ = R^+ \supseteq R$. Let T be the complement*

of an invariant under check. Then the FWDBWDPMC *is correct, i.e., it finds a path from* T *back to* S *if and only such a path exists.*

Sketch of Proof The proof is achieved in two steps:

- We first prove that no false negatives are generated by the procedure, i.e., that any counter-example generated is correct. This is guaranteed by the fact that partitioning and prioritized visit does not introduce states unreachable from S. The only unreachable states considered are those generated by co-factor simplifications, that do not generate backward paths to S (see Equation (1)).
- We then show that the procedure is complete, i.e., it fully explores a subspace able to prove or falsify the property. We do this by showing that the "global-path-search" section of BWDPMCSTEP is just a recursive version of FWDBWDMC (and it explores the same state sets) in case the "inbound-path-search" fails.

A key issue for performance in the above procedures is keeping BDD sizes under control by means of generalized cofactor simplifications and threshold based control over conjunctions.

- Frontier sets in approximate forward traversals (F_i^+) are "clustered" on a threshold basis. Each set is a conjunction of terms with disjoint[4] support: $F_i^+ = \prod_{j \in Groups} f_i^j$ (see Section 4). As in transition relation clustering, we partially compute products as far as the generated products is under a chosen threshold.
- Accuracy of the over-approximate forward traversal is not as important as in approximate model check [9], where the goodness of a verification task heavily relies on the ability of an approximate model to represent the exact behavior. The main purpose of approximate traversal in our solution is to generate good care sets for effective BDD simplifications throughout an exact traversal. Since accuracy often implies larger BDDs, even in approximate traversals, we achieve better results with intermediate solutions (trading off accuracy for BDD size).
- Frontier sets in exact backward traversal (FB_i) are always computed and manipulated in their cofactored form, i.e., the PREIMG procedure directly works with the F_i^+ set in order to simplify $FB_i = B_i \downarrow F_i^+$ while computing it (see next paragraph). Furthermore, FB_i sets are generated in conjunctively decomposed forms, using a technique derived from [18].

4 Performance Issues in Image and Pre-image Computations

Let us concentrate now on the inner steps of image and pre-image computations, involving some of the most effective optimizations for the overall performance.

---

[4] Overlapping projections are also possible, as adopted in [8,17], but we presently limit our implementation to approximate images with non-overlapping components.

We will describe approximate image, exact and approximate pre-image, under a general attempt to control BDD sizes by means of conjunctive partitioning and clustering[5], combined with generalized cofactor simplifications.

Approximate image is computed as

$$F_i^+ = \text{IMG}^+(\text{TR}, F_{i-1}^+) = \prod_{j \in Groups} \text{IMG}(\text{TR}_j, F_{i-1}^+)$$

where $\text{TR} = \prod_{j \in Groups} \text{TR}_j$ is the clustered transition relation (each group is in turn a statically generated product of clusters). The partial images of each group are conjoined under threshold control, so the result F_i^+ is a conjunctively partitioned BDD.

Exact pre-image exploits two levels of partitioning and cofactor simplifications. First of all, the cofactoring term (CARE in Figure 2 and Figure 3) is given as a parameter to the PREIMGWITHCARE function, in order to be used as a care set for inner operations:

$$FB_i = \text{PREIMG}(\text{TR}, FB_{i-1}) \downarrow \text{CARE}$$
$$= \text{PREIMGWITHCARE}(\text{TR}, FB_{i-1}, \text{CARE}) \downarrow \text{CARE}$$

The latter function is implemented as the classical linear "and-exist" or "relational product" with early quantification, where the generic step (computing a new intermediate product $P_j = \exists_{x_j}(P_{j-1} \wedge \text{TR}_j)$) is optimized as follows

$$P_j = \exists_{x_j}(P_{j-1} \wedge tr_j) \downarrow \text{CARE}$$
$$P_j = \exists_x P_j \wedge (P_j \downarrow \exists_x P_j)$$

Each partial product is first cofactored with the care set CARE, then the basic decomposition step of [18] is applied, exploiting the sets of early quantification variables as variable layers driving the decomposition (instead of the variable ordering). The latter step produces a conjunctively decomposed pre-image, that is finally clustered under threshold control.

5   Experimental Results

The presented technique is implemented in a program called FBV (Forward-Backward Verifier), running on top of the Colorado University Decision Diagram (CUDD) package.

We describe an experimental comparison between this tool and VIS [15] using the technique described in [14] as implemented with the command "model_check -D 3". Our experience with VIS shows that within the proposed set of experiments this choice is more efficient than other special purpose techniques, e.g., approximate model checking (command "approximate_model_check"), and forward

---

[5] We denote with clustering a partial computation of a product (AND), controlled by a BDD size threshold. The technique is derived from partitioned transition relation manipulation: Whenever the size of an intermediate product is too high, the product is aborted, a cluster is put aside and product computation resumes.

invariant checking (command "check_invar") (both unable to complete most of the experiments). The experiments are performed on a 1.7 GHz Pentium IV Workstation with a 1 GByte main memory, running RedHat Linux.

We present data on two sets of circuits:

- ISCAS'89 and ISCAS'89-addendum benchmarks (upper part of Table 1). In this case the verified properties are automatically generated as described in [16][6].
- Models taken from [0] (lower part of Table 1). In this case the verified properties are available with the original descriptions.

Each line in Table 1 describes one or more checks on a given model. Models are sorted by number of state variables (column # SV). Column # reports the number of checked properties. Whenever # is larger than one, we report overall results for the verified set of properties. Properties are either proved correct, and denoted by *Pass*, or they are falsified and labeled by *Fail*. Depth indicates the maximum sequential depth explored (i.e., the length of the counter-example or the amount of breadth-first backward iterations done to prove correctness) over the set of checked properties.

Overall, the circuits presented have different sizes, some of them outside the range of problems manageable by state-of-the-art BDD based verifiers. Circuit philo is a synchronous version of the Philosopher problem, where the asynchronous behavior is modeled by a scheduler enabling just one philosopher at the time. We check safety properties in all the cases. The Cone-Of-Influence reduction is always applied before starting the verification process.

The FwDBwDPMC procedure is used for the s3330, s3384, and s35932, FwDBwDMC in all other cases. Data shows how our technique is more efficient in terms of memory usage (since our optimizations primarily target BDD size reduction). As far as execution time is concerned, in some cases the two tools are comparable (usually on experiments where BDDs could be enough easily deal with the VIS tool), whereas in other cases our optimizations are the key to complete the verification task. On the one hand, minor differences in "easier" experiments are related to different settings and partitions used in approximate reachability. On the other hand, performance in "difficult" experiments is largely dominated by backward traversals, where cofactor based simplifications provides much smaller BDDs in FBV than the corresponding AND based simplifications in VIS.

6   Conclusions and Future Works

BDD-based symbolic manipulation has been one of the most widely used core technologies in the synthesis and verification domain, over the last decade. Nevertheless, existing algorithms are still limited by memory resources in practice.

---

[6] Notice however that [16] refers to bounded verification whereas we present here only data on unbounded verification.

Table 1. Experimental comparison between FBV and the Approximate Reachability Don't Cares strategy of VIS. ovf means overflow on time (time limit = 10800 seconds). In this case Mem. indicates maximum memory usage before aborting verification

Model	# SV	#	Pass/Fail	Depth	VIS Mem. [MByte]	VIS Time [sec]	FBV Mem. [MByte]	FBV Time [sec]
s3330	132	5	Fail	5	45	640	20	17
s3384	183	3	Fail	11	203	ovf	65	2993
s9234	211	5	Fail	241	23	198	30	427
s15850.1	534	3	Fail	76	143	1230	118	700
s13207.1	638	5	Fail	430	120	1748	60	1824
s38584.1	1426	1	Fail	11	342	ovf	180	456
s35932	1728	1	Fail	32	315	ovf	60	831
vsaR	66	2	Fail	20	21	29	17	21
am2901	68	1	Fail	17	36	116	28	81
FIFOs	142	1	Pass	16	121	2618	35	823
$philo_{20}$	40	1	Pass	35	16	4	20	13
$philo_{60}$	120	1	Pass	115	251	ovf	29	78
$philo_{100}$	200	1	Pass	195	383	ovf	159	6220
$Palu_{16}$	317	1	Fail	3	37	196	23	110
		1	Pass	3	38	271	23	82

Following some of the most promising techniques proposed over the last a few years, we present in this paper an approach to face very large *Unbounded Model Checking* problems. We propose to mix forward and backward approximate and exact traversals, guided search, conjunctive decompositions and generalized cofactor based BDD simplifications, to obtain relevant performance enhancements.

We experimentally compare our tool with a state-of-the-art BDD based model checker. Our experience leads to the conclusion that we are able to deal with problems outside the present scope of other BDD-based tools.

Among the possible future works we need some effort on heuristics, to make our approach more self-tuning, and to obtain a common framework for experiments and comparisons with different tools and sets of models.

Acknowledgment

The authors would like to thank Fabio Somenzi for the source descriptions of some circuits used in the experiments.

References

1. A. Biere, A. Cimatti, E. M. Clarke, M. Fujita, and Y. Zhu. Symbolic Model Checking using SAT procedures instead of BDDs. In *Proc. 36th Design Automat. Conf.*, pages 317–320, New Orleans, Louisiana, June 1999. 472
2. F. Copty, L. Fix, R. Fraer, E. Giunchiglia, G. Kamhi, A. Tacchella, and M. Y. Vardi. Benefits of Bounded Model Checking at an Industrial Setting. In Gérard Berry, Hubert Comon, and Alan Finkel, editors, *Proc. Computer Aided Verification*, volume 2102 of *LNCS*, pages 435–453, Paris, France, July 2001. Springer-Verlag. 472
3. P. F. Williams, A. Biere, E. M. Clarke, and A. Gupta. Combining Decision Diagrams and SAT Procedures for Efficient Symbolic Model Checking. In E. Allen Emerson and A. Prasad Sistla, editors, *Proc. Computer Aided Verification*, volume 2102 of *LNCS*, pages 124–138, Chicago, Illinois, July 2000. Springer-Verlag. 472
4. A. Gupta, Z. Yang, P. Ashar, and A. Gupta. SAT–Based Image Computation with Application in Reachability Analysis. In *Proc. Formal Methods in Computer-Aided Design*, volume 1954 of *LNCS*, Austin, TX, USA, 2000. 472
5. H. Cho, G. D. Hatchel, E. Macii, B. Plessier, and F. Somenzi. Algorithms for Approximate FSM Traversal Based on State Space Decomposition. *IEEE Transactions on CAD*, 15(12):1465–1478, December 1996. 472
6. K. Ravi and F. Somenzi. Hints to Accelerate Symbolic Traversal. In *Correct Hardware Design and Verification Methods (CHARME'99)*, pages 250–264, Berlin, September 1999. Springer-Verlag. LNCS 1703. 472, 481
7. M. K. Ganai, A. Aziz, and A. Kuehlmann. Enhancing Simulation with BDDs and ATPG. In *Proc. 36th Design Automat. Conf.*, pages 385–390, New Orleans, LA, November 1999. 472
8. G. Cabodi, P. Camurati, and S. Quer. Efficient State Space Pruning in Symbolic Backward Traversal. In *Proc. Int'l Conf. on Computer Design*, pages 230–235, Cambridge, Massachussetts, October 1994. 472, 473, 475, 479
9. S. G. Govindaraju and D. L. Dill. Verification by Approximate Forward and Backward Reachability. In *Proc. Int'l Conf. on Computer-Aided Design*, pages 366–370, San Jose, California, November 1998. 472, 473, 479
10. K. Ravi and F. Somenzi. High–Density Reachability Analysis. In *Proc. Int'l Conf. on Computer-Aided Design*, pages 154–158, San Jose, California, November 1995. 473
11. G. Cabodi, P. Camurati, and S. Quer. Improving the Efficiency of BDD-based Operators by means of Partitioning. *IEEE Transactions on CAD*, 18(5):545–556, May 1999. 473
12. G. Cabodi, P. Camurati, and S. Quer. Improving Symbolic Reachability Analisys by means of Activity Profiles. *IEEE Transactions on CAD*, 19(9):1065–1075, September 2000. 473
13. R. Fraer, G. Kamhi, B. Ziv, M. Y. Vardi, and L. Fix. Prioritized Traversal: Efficient Reachability Analysis for Verification and Falsification. In E. Allen Emerson and A. Prasad Sistla, editors, *Proc. Computer Aided Verification*, volume 1855 of *LNCS*, pages 389–402, Chicago, Illinois, July 2000. Springer-Verlag. 473
14. I. Moon, J. Jang, G. D. Hachtel, F. Somenzi, J. Yuan, and C. Pixley. Approximate Reachability Don't Cares for CTL Model Checking. In *Proc. Int'l Conf. on Computer-Aided Design*, pages 351–358, San Jose, California, November 1998. 473, 475, 476, 480

15. R. K. Brayton et al. VIS. In Mandayam Srivas and Albert Camilleri, editors, *Proc. Formal Methods in Computer-Aided Design*, volume 1166 of *LNCS*, pages 248–256, Palo Alto, California, November 1996. Springer-Verlag. 473, 480

16. G. Cabodi, P. Camurati, and S. Quer. Can BDDs compete with SAT solvers on Bounded Model Checking? In *Proc. 39th Design Automat. Conf.*, New Orleans, Louisiana, June 2002. 474, 475, 481

17. S. G. Govindaraju, D. L. Dill, A. Hu, and M. A. Horowitz. Approximate Reachability Analysis with BDDs using Overlapping Projections. In *Proc. 35th Design Automat. Conf.*, pages 451–456, San Francisco, California, June 1998. 479

18. G. Cabodi. Meta-BDDs: A Decomposed Representation for Layered Symbolic Manipulation of Boolean Functions. In Gérard Berry, Hubert Comon, and Alan Finkel, editors, *Proc. Computer Aided Verification*, volume 2102 of *LNCS*, pages 118–130, Paris, France, July 2001. Springer-Verlag. 479, 480

Vacuum Cleaning CTL Formulae*

Mitra Purandare and Fabio Somenzi

University of Colorado at Boulder
{Mitra.Purandare,Fabio}@Colorado.EDU

Abstract. Vacuity detection in model checking looks for properties that hold in a model, and can be strengthened without causing them to fail. Such properties often signal problems in the model, its environment, or the properties themselves. The seminal paper of Beer et al. [1] proposed an efficient algorithm applicable to a restricted set of properties. Subsequently, Kupferman and Vardi [15] extended vacuity detection to more expressive specification mechanisms. They advocated a more minute examination of temporal logic formulae than the one adopted in [1]. However, they did not address the issues of practicality and usefulness of this more scrupulous inspection. In this paper we discuss efficient algorithms for the detection of vacuous passes of temporal logic formulae, showing that a thorough vacuity check for CTL formulae can be carried out with very small overhead, and even, occasionally, in less time than plain model checking. We also demonstrate the usefulness of such a careful analysis with the help of case studies.

1 Introduction

The basic function of a model checker [9, 16] is to establish whether a certain property holds (or passes) in a given system; otherwise, to produce an error trace. By systematically exploring the state space of the system to be verified, a model checker relieves the user of the burden of generating test cases. However, the thoroughness of verification depends on the properties examined, and hence, ultimately, on the user.

In an effort to increase the efficacy of model checking as a debugging and verification approach, recent work has therefore considered how to assess the quality and comprehensiveness of a given set of properties. Two approaches have emerged: One consists of measuring the *coverage* of a set of properties [13, 14, 7, 6], defined in such a way that incomplete coverage exposes features of the model not adequately verified. As is commonly done in Automatic Test Pattern Generation [12], in this case one relates coverage to the fraction of alterations to the model that would be detected by the given set of properties.

The second approach to assess the quality of properties, which is the focus of this paper, is the detection of *vacuous passes* in temporal logic formulae [1, 15]. Following the definition of [1], a formula φ passes vacuously in a model K if it

---

* This work was supported in part by SRC contract 2001-TJ-920 and NSF grant CCR-99-71195.

passes in K, and there is a subformula φ' of φ that can be changed arbitrarily without affecting the outcome of model checking.

The vacuous pass of a formula often signals problems in any combination of the model, its environment, and the formula itself. Both in the approach based on measuring coverage, and in the one that checks for vacuous passes, the quality of a set of properties is related to "how snugly the properties fit the model." In coverage measurements one checks for modifications of the model that do not turn any passing properties into failing ones. In vacuity detection, by contrast, one looks for changes in the passing properties themselves that restrict the sets of states that satisfy them, without causing them to fail.

The authors of [ ] identify a subset of ACTL called w-ACTL for which vacuity detection can be done efficiently. That is, vacuity detection for a w-ACTL formula φ amounts to model checking a *witness formula* that is obtained by replacing a subformula of φ with either true or false, and is therefore no more complex than φ. The definition of w-ACTL makes it possible to designate at most one operand of a binary operator as *interesting*. Vacuity detection is then restricted to replacement of the (unique) smallest interesting subformula of φ.

In [ ] vacuity detection is extended to full CTL*. Furthermore, the restriction to interesting subformulae is lifted. The length of the witness formula for φ, however, is quadratic in the length of φ. Thus, an increase in the expressiveness of the logic and in the thoroughness of analysis is paid with an increase in the worst-case complexity of the algorithm.

The approach of [ ] owes its efficiency to two factors. On the one hand, exactly one subformula is replaced for each formula. On the other hand, in the parse tree of φ, all the temporal operators are on the path connecting the root to the smallest interesting subformula, which is replaced by false. As a consequence, the witness formula for φ is very often trivial. This second factor does not show up in the worst-case complexity analysis, but is quite important in practice.

While the simplicity of the witness formulae for w-ACTL is an obvious advantage from the standpoint of speed, it is also the inherent limitation of the approach of [ ], because drastic changes in the formula have only slight chances of detecting non-major flaws. Though in the initial stages of debugging, vacuity detection for w-ACTL has proved very useful, a more careful analysis may substantially improve the effectiveness of a model checker as a debugging tool.

In this paper we show that a thorough vacuity check as the one advocated in [ ] can be implemented efficiently for Computational Tree Logic (CTL) formulae [ ], so that the overhead relative to plain model checking is in practice very limited in spite of the worse complexity bound. Indeed, our algorithm may occasionally outperform plain model checking.

Instead of checking φ and the witness formulae generated by various replacements in a sequential fashion, we check φ and all its replacements in a single bottom-up pass over the parse tree of φ. At each node we exploit the relationships between the sets of states satisfying the various formulae. Depending on the number of negations along the path connecting a node to the root of the parse tree, the satisfying set of a witness subformula is either a lower bound or an upper bound on the satisfying set of the corresponding subformula of φ. This allows us to speed up fixpoint computations by accelerating convergence, or simplifying the computation of preimages.

As demonstrated in [18, 3], starting a fixpoint computation from a good approximation may drastically reduce the time to convergence, especially with symbolic algorithms that may be greatly affected by the sizes of the Binary Decision Diagrams (BDDs [5]). In our approach to vacuity detection, the bounds on the fixpoints are not obtained by modifying the transition relation of the model. Hence, the effects are less dramatic, but sufficient to often allow several formulae to be model checked in about the same time as just one of them.

Other devices that help our algorithm limit the overhead are the detection of cases in which different replacements lead to equivalent formulae, or at least to identical computations; and the sharing of don't care and early termination conditions between φ and its witness formulae. The details of the algorithm are discussed in Sections 4 and 5.

A practical algorithm for thorough vacuity detection is only of limited import unless the analysis it performs is also useful: Presenting the user of a model checker with much information of scarce relevance is likely to decrease her productivity. Our experiments, however, indicate that a more minute examination of formulae than that based on replacement of just one subformula leads to the the discovery of more bugs and to the detection of weaknesses in formulae that would otherwise go unnoticed. The "signal to noise" ratio is also quite good, with most vacuous passes leading to improved verification. This is illustrated by the case studies described in Section 2, and the experiments summarized in Section 6.

2   The Case for Thorough Vacuity Detection

Fpmpy is a floating-point multiplier included among the examples distributed with VIS [20]. It implements a simplified version of the IEEE 754 standard for floating point arithmetic. Several CTL formulae test properties primarily related to the handling of special cases like infinities, NaNs, and denormals (which are not implemented by the model). The multiplier takes three clock cycles to complete an operation. Hence, it is natural for properties checked on its model to have the form

$$AG(p \rightarrow AX\,AX\,AX\,q) \ ,$$

where p and q are propositional formulae. These formulae are in w-ACTL, and their witness formulae according to [1] have the form

$$AG(p \rightarrow AX\,AX\,AX\,\text{false}) \ .$$

These witness formulae fail trivially because the model has fair paths—hence the formulae reduce to $AG\,\neg p$—and p, albeit different from formula to formula, holds in the first cycle of a computation. Accordingly, vacuity detection for w-ACTL reports no problems. By contrast, when replacing each leaf of the parse tree with either true or false depending on the number of negations along the path from the leaf to the root, many replacements result in vacuous passes. This is especially true of the following formula

$$\text{AG}(\text{START} \wedge \text{valid}(x) \wedge \text{valid}(y) \rightarrow \text{valid}(z)) , \qquad (1)$$

where START holds in the first clock cycle of a computation, and valid() tells whether the inputs (x and y) or the output (z) are not denormals. Out of 24 replacements, 20 produce vacuous passes. Examination of the passing witness formulae revealed that:

1. The environment of the model lacks an assignment to a primary input to the multiplier (start).
2. The MSB of the exponent could be incorrect due to overflow during its computation.
3. The multiplier maintains the invariant $\text{AG}\,\text{valid}(z)$. Hence, (1) can be strengthened by replacing the antecedent of the implication with true.

Two features of the more extensive analysis based on replacing all leaves are instrumental in highlighting the bugs and weaknesses of fpmpy: the replacement of non-interesting formulae (to prove the antecedent redundant), and the replacement of individual atomic propositions (to expose the problem with the MSB of the exponent).

The MinMax parameterized circuit [19, 10] computes the average of the minimum and maximum of a stream of n-bit numbers. The following property

$$\text{AG}((\min = 2^n - 1 \wedge \max = 0) \rightarrow$$
$$\text{AX}((\min = 2^n - 1 \wedge \max = 0) \vee (\min = \text{last} \wedge \text{last} = \max))) \qquad (2)$$

states that from a reset state, in which min holds the largest possible n-bit integer, and max is 0, it is only possible to transit to another reset state, or to a state in which both min and max have the same value as the last input (last). This time, thorough vacuity detection uncovers no errors in the model, but it points out that the system satisfies the invariant

$$\text{AG}((\min[n-1] = 1 \wedge \max[n-1] = 0) \rightarrow (\min = 2^n - 1 \wedge \max = 0)) , \qquad (3)$$

where $n - 1$ is the index of the most significant bit. The set of properties can be enhanced by adding (3) or by strengthening (2) to

$$\text{AG}((\min[n-1] = 1 \wedge \max[n-1] = 0) \rightarrow$$
$$\text{AX}((\min[n-1] = 1 \wedge \max[n-1] = 0) \vee (\min = \text{last} \wedge \text{last} = \max))) .$$

Our last example illustrates a possible drawback of exhaustively replacing all the leaves of the parse tree with either true or false. In a model of n dining philosophers [11], each philosopher may be in one of four states: thinking, left, right, and both, depending on which chopsticks she is holding. Mutual exclusion requires that a philosopher may not hold the chopstick to her right if her right neighbor holds the one to his left. This may be written as

$$\mathsf{AG}\,\neg((p[i] = \texttt{right} \vee p[i] = \texttt{both}) \wedge$$
$$(p[(i+1) \bmod n] = \texttt{left} \vee p[(i+1) \bmod n] = \texttt{both})) \ . \qquad (4)$$

Suppose the state $p[i]$ of the i-th philosopher is encoded by two binary variables, $l[i]$ and $r[i]$, each one indicating possession of one chopstick. Then thorough vacuity detection will report vacuous passes, indicating that (4) can be rewritten as

$$\mathsf{AG}\,\neg(r[i] \wedge l[(i+1) \bmod n]) \ . \qquad (5)$$

Since the two formulations are equivalent, the quality of verification is not affected by this change, and, depending on the description style, converting (4) into (5) may require extensive modifications of the model. Therefore, report of vacuous passes in this case may be regarded as noise. However, this appears a reasonable price to pay for the advantages afforded by a careful examination the properties.

3   Preliminaries

The logic CTL [8] is defined over an alphabet A of atomic propositions: Any atomic proposition is a CTL property, and if φ and ψ are CTL properties, then so are $\varphi \wedge \psi$, $\varphi \vee \psi$, $\neg\varphi$, and $\mathsf{E}\,\varphi\,\mathsf{U}\,\psi$, $\mathsf{EG}\,\varphi$, and $\mathsf{EX}\,\varphi$. The semantics of CTL are defined over a Kripke structure $K = \langle S, T, S_0, A, L \rangle$, where S is the set of states, $T \subseteq S \times S$ is the transition relation, $S_0 \subseteq S$ is the set of initial states, A is the set of atomic propositions, and $L : S \to 2^A$ is the labeling function. The semantics of CTL are defined in Figure 1. If fairness constraints are specified, the path quantifiers are restricted to *fair paths*, that is, paths that intersect every fairness constraint infinitely often. A formula is said to hold in K if it is satisfied by every initial state of K. An ECTL formula is a CTL formula in which negation is only applied to the atomic propositions. An ACTL formula is the negation of an ECTL formula. A property that is neither ECTL nor ACTL is a *mixed property*.

$K, s_0 \models \varphi$ iff $\varphi \in L(s_0)$ for $\varphi \in A$
$K, s_0 \models \neg\varphi$ iff $K, s_0 \not\models \varphi$
$K, s_0 \models \varphi \vee \psi$ iff $K, s_0 \models \varphi$ or $K, s_0 \models \psi$
$K, s_0 \models \varphi \wedge \psi$ iff $K, s_0 \models \varphi$ and $K, s_0 \models \psi$
$K, s_0 \models \mathsf{EX}\,\varphi$ iff there exists a path $s_0, s_1, \ldots$ in K such that $K, s_1 \models \varphi$
$K, s_0 \models \mathsf{EG}\,\varphi$ iff there exists a path $s_0, s_1, \ldots$ in K such that for $i \geq 0$,
           $K, s_i \models \varphi$
$K, s_0 \models \mathsf{E}\,\varphi\,\mathsf{U}\,\psi$ iff there exists a path $s_0, s_1, \ldots$ in K such that there exists
           $i \geq 0$ for which $K, s_i \models \psi$, and for $0 \leq j < i$, $K, s_j \models \varphi$.

Fig. 1. Semantics of CTL

Boolean operators other than $\wedge$, $\vee$, and $\neg$, and the operators EF, AX, AG, AF, and AU can be defined as abbreviations, e.g., $\text{EF}\,\varphi = \text{E}(\varphi \vee \neg\varphi)\,\text{U}\,\varphi$, $\text{AX}\,\varphi = \neg\,\text{EX}\,\neg\varphi$, $\text{AG}\,\varphi = \neg\,\text{EF}\,\neg\varphi$, $\text{AF}\,\varphi = \neg\,\text{EG}\,\neg\varphi$, and $\text{A}\,\varphi\,\text{U}\,\psi = \neg(\text{E}\,\neg\psi\,\text{U}\,\neg(\varphi \vee \psi)) \wedge \neg\,\text{EG}\,\neg\psi$. Clearly, the abbreviations should be expanded before checking whether a formula is an ECTL or ACTL formula.

The model checking problem for CTL with fairness constraints can be translated into the computation of fixpoints of appropriate functionals [17]:

$$\text{E}\,\varphi\,\text{U}\,\psi = \mu Z \,.\, \psi \vee (\varphi \wedge \text{EX}\,Z),$$
$$\text{EG}\,\varphi = \nu Z \,.\, \varphi \wedge \text{EX}\,Z,$$
$$\text{E}_C\,\text{G}\,\varphi = \nu Z \,.\, \varphi \wedge \text{EX} \bigwedge_{c \in C} (\text{E}\,Z\,\text{U}(Z \wedge c)) \,,$$

where C is a set of sets of states that must be traversed infinitely often by a fair path, and where with customary abuse of notation, we identify a formula and the set of states where it is satisfied. Also, we often do not distinguish between a set and its characteristic function. Thus, $p \wedge \neg\{s_0\}$ stands for the characteristic function of the set consisting of the states in the set whose characteristic function is p, except for s_0. When we want to mark the difference between a formula and its satisfying set, we let $[\![\varphi]\!]$ denote the satisfying set of φ.

Note that EU, EG, and EX are monotonic both in their arguments and in the transition relation.

In vacuity detection we replace an occurrence of subformula φ' in φ with another formula ψ; this is denoted by $\varphi[\varphi' \leftarrow \psi]$ and is called the *witness* of φ'. We write $\varphi[\varphi' \leftarrow \bot]$ for $\varphi[\varphi' \leftarrow \text{false}]$ if φ' appears in φ under an even number of negations. Otherwise, $\varphi[\varphi' \leftarrow \bot]$ stands for $\varphi[\varphi' \leftarrow \text{true}]$.

A formula φ passes vacuously in K if $K \models \varphi$, and there exists an occurrence of a subformula φ' of φ such that $K \models \varphi[\varphi' \leftarrow \bot]$. If this holds, then $K \models \varphi[\varphi' \leftarrow \psi]$ for any ψ. This follows from the monotonicity of the operators involved in model checking [15].

4   Combining Model Checking and Vacuity Detection

In this section we describe an efficient algorithm that combines the model checking of a CTL formula φ with thorough detection of vacuous passes. We assume that φ is given as a parse *tree* (as opposed to a parse *graph*). That is, each occurrence of a given subformula is considered separately.

We assume that φ only contains existential quantifiers. The only operators that label the internal nodes of the parse tree are therefore $\neg$, $\wedge$, EX, EU, and EG. This choice prevents us from putting formulae in negation normal form. Instead, each node of the parse tree is annotated with its *negation parity*, that is the number of nodes labeled $\neg$ on the path connecting the root of the tree to the parent of the node itself.[1]

---

[1] Our implementation also allows nodes of the parse tree labeled by $\vee$, $\rightarrow$ and $\oplus$. An implication node counts as a negation for its antecedent child, but not for its conse-

Let $\Pi = (N, E, \lambda)$ be the parse tree of a CTL formula φ with atomic propositions from $A \neq \emptyset$, where $N = \{i : 1 \leq i \leq n\}$ is the set of nodes; $E \subseteq N \times N$ is the set of edges; and $\lambda : N \to A \cup \{\neg, \wedge, \mathsf{EX}, \mathsf{EU}, \mathsf{EG}\}$ labels each node of the parse tree with either an atomic proposition or an operator. The root of the parse tree is node n.

The outdegree of a node i obeys the obvious restrictions: if $\lambda(i) \in A$ it is 0; if $\lambda(i) \in \{\neg, \mathsf{EX}, \mathsf{EG}\}$ it is 1; otherwise, it is 2. Let $\nu : N \to \{0, 1\}$ map each node to its negation parity: $\nu(n) = 0$, and if $(i, j) \in E$, then $\nu(i) = \nu(j)$ if and only if $\lambda(i) \neq \neg$. If $\nu(i) = 0$, i is an *even-parity* node; otherwise, it is an *odd-parity* node. For $1 \leq i \leq n$ let Π_i denote the subtree of Π rooted at node i, and φ_i denote the CTL formula represented by Π_i.

To check whether subformula φ_j of φ affects the truth value of φ in K, we replace φ_j with $\bot$. If $\nu(i) = 0$, $[\![\varphi_i[\varphi_j \leftarrow \bot]]\!] \subseteq [\![\varphi_i]\!]$, whereas if $\nu(i) = 1$, $[\![\varphi_i]\!] \subseteq [\![\varphi_i[\varphi_j \leftarrow \bot]]\!]$. This observation is the basis for our algorithm.

Given a *replacement function* $\rho : N \to \{\emptyset, \bot\}$, let

$$\Psi(\Pi, \rho) = \{\varphi\} \cup \{\varphi[\varphi_i \leftarrow \bot] : \rho(i) = \bot\} .$$

A *vacuity detection experiment* for φ in K is defined by a triple (K, Π, ρ): It consists of answering, for each $\psi \in \Psi(\Pi, \rho)$ the model checking question $K \models \psi$. If $K \models \varphi$, each additional affirmative answer is a *vacuous pass*.

Let $\delta : N \to 2^N$ map node i to the set of nodes that are reachable from i and such that $j \in \delta(i)$ implies $\rho(j) = \bot$. That is, $\delta(i)$ is the set of descendants of i that have been marked for replacement. Our algorithm computes for each $i \in N$ a function $\sigma_i : \delta(i) \cup \{0\} \to (\delta(i) \cup \{0\}) \times 2^Q$ such that $\sigma_i(j) = (k, S)$ satisfies the following conditions.

1. $k \leq j$;
2. $\sigma_i(0) = (0, [\![\varphi_i]\!])$;
3. if $k = j \neq 0$, then $S = [\![\varphi_i[\varphi_j \leftarrow \bot]]\!]$;
4. if $k < j$, then $S = \emptyset$ and $[\![\varphi_i[\varphi_j \leftarrow \bot]]\!] = [\![\varphi_i[\varphi_k \leftarrow \bot]]\!]$.

The computation is performed by post-order traversal of the parse tree. At each node i, first we compute a "draft" of σ_i, that we call σ_i', and then derive σ_i from it by a *reduction* process. The details of the computation of σ_i' depend on $\lambda(i)$ as follows, except for $\sigma_i'(i)$, which is always $(i, \bot)$ if $\rho(i) = \bot$, and undefined otherwise.

1. If $\lambda(i) \in A$, $\sigma_i'(0) = (0, [\![\varphi_i]\!])$.
2. If $\lambda(i) \in \{\neg, \mathsf{EX}\}$, let c be the child of i, and, for $j \in \delta(i) \cup \{0\} \setminus \{i\}$, let $\sigma_c(j) = (k, P)$. Then, if $k = j$, $\sigma_i'(j) = (j, \lambda(i)P)$; otherwise $\sigma_i'(j) = (k, \emptyset)$.
3. If $\lambda(i) = \wedge$, let l and r the two children of i and, for $j \in \delta(l) \cup \{0\}$, let $\sigma_l(j) = (k, P)$. Then, if $k = j$, $\sigma_i'(j) = (j, P \wedge [\![\varphi_r]\!])$; otherwise $\sigma_i'(j) = (k, \emptyset)$. Note that $i \notin \delta(l)$, $\delta(l) \subseteq \delta(i)$, and $\delta(l) \cap \delta(r) = \emptyset$. The case for $j \in \delta(r)$ is similar.

---

quent child. The exclusive-or requires special treatment, because it is not monotonic: We do not allow replacements of the descendants of a node labeled $\oplus$. Since these are implementation details, we shall not discuss them further.

4. If $\lambda(i) = \mathsf{EG}$ the computation proceeds as in the case of EX. However, the order in which the values of σ_i' are determined is relevant: $\sigma_i'(0)$ is computed last. If $\nu(i) = 1$,

$$U = \bigwedge \{P : \sigma_i'(j) = (j, P), j \in \delta(i) \setminus \{0\}\}$$

is used as an upper bound in computing $[\![\varphi_i]\!]$. Otherwise,

$$L = \bigvee \{P : \sigma_i'(j) = (j, P), j \in \delta(i) \setminus \{0\}\}$$

is used as lower bound. (The use of lower bounds in greatest fixpoint computations is discussed in Section 5.)

5. Finally, if $\lambda(i) = \mathsf{EU}$, the computation proceeds as in the case of EX. However, the order in which the values of σ_i' are determined is relevant: if $\nu(i) = 1$, $\sigma_i'(0)$ is computed first, and $[\![\varphi_i]\!]$ is used as lower bound in the other fixpoint computations; otherwise $\sigma_i'(0)$ is computed last, and

$$L = \bigvee \{P : \sigma_i'(j) = (j, P), j \in \delta(i) \setminus \{0\}\}$$

is used as a lower bound in computing $[\![\varphi_i]\!]$.

The reason for computing $\sigma_i'(0)$ last in case of greatest fixpoint, regardless of $\nu(i)$ is that the BDD for $[\![\varphi[\varphi_j \leftarrow \bot]]\!]$ are likely to be smaller than that for $[\![\varphi]\!]$ because the formula is simpler.

The reduction process that derives σ_i from σ_i' sets $\sigma_i(j) = (k, \emptyset)$ if $\sigma_i'(j) = (j, P)$, there is $k < j$ such that $\sigma_i'(k) = (k, P)$, and k is the least number that satisfies this condition. Furthermore, if $\sigma_i'(j) = (k, \emptyset)$, and $\sigma_i(k) = (k', \emptyset)$, then $\sigma_i(j) = (k', \emptyset)$.

The following result states that the solution to a vacuity detection experiment is contained in σ_n.

Theorem 1. *If $\sigma_n(j) = (j, P)$ then $[\![\varphi[\varphi_j \leftarrow \bot]]\!] = P$; otherwise, if $\sigma_n(j) = (k, \emptyset)$, then $\sigma_n(k) = (k, P)$, $P \neq \emptyset$, and $[\![\varphi[\varphi_j \leftarrow \bot]]\!] = P$.*

4.1   Early Termination and Don't Cares

It is sometimes possible to avoid computing either $[\![\varphi]\!]$ or $[\![\varphi[\varphi' \leftarrow \bot]]\!]$. Suppose a set of care states is given at the current node of the parse tree. At the root of the parse tree, this set of states is all the initial states. If we ignore vacuity detection, the computation can be terminated early as soon as it is known that all the care states satisfy the formula, or as soon as it is known that at least one of the care states does not satisfy it. Hence, if the root of the parse tree is a least fixpoint, then computation can be terminated as soon as it is known that the formula passes; if it is a greatest fixpoint, early termination occurs as soon as it is known that the formula fails.

Another source of care states is the satisfying set of the sibling of the current node when the parent is labeled $\wedge$. The computation of the second child of such a node r can be stopped as soon as all the states satisfying the sibling are known to satisfy r as well, or when it is known that no state satisfying r satisfies its sibling.

These observations can be extended to vacuity detection. For instance, if the negation parity of the node is even, and $[\![\varphi[\varphi' \leftarrow \bot]]\!]$ contains all the care states, then the computation of $[\![\varphi]\!]$ can be skipped. Likewise, if the negation parity is odd and $[\![\varphi[\varphi' \leftarrow \bot]]\!]$ contains no care state, neither does $[\![\varphi]\!]$.

4.2   Complexity

In practice, sharing partial results between the evaluation of the given formula and the evaluation of its witness formula is beneficial. However, in the worst case, we still have a quadratic bound (cf.[15]). To make things more precise, we consider the number of node evaluations as our metric. If a formula and all the witness formulae obtained by replacing a subformula with $\bot$ are model checked independently, then the number of node evaluations is quadratic in the length of the formula.

When sharing takes place, if we assume that replacements are limited to the leaves, the number of evaluations of each node in the CTL parse tree is bounded by the number of leaves below the node plus 1 (for the original formula).

For a balanced binary tree the total number of node evaluations is $O(n \log n)$, but for generic 2-restricted trees (each node has at most two children), the number of evaluations is $O(n^2)$. To see this, consider a binary tree such that at least one child of each node is a leaf.

5   Updating Greatest Fixpoints Using Lower Bounds

In this section we show how knowledge of a lower bound to a greatest fixpoint can be used to speed up its computation. It is well-known how use a lower bound for the computation of least fixpoints as follows. Let $l = \mathsf{E}\, q\, \mathsf{U}\, p$ and $u \leq l$. Then,

$$l = \mathsf{E}\, q\, \mathsf{U}(p \vee u) \ . \tag{6}$$

We can similarly use an upper bound to compute a greatest fixpoint. Now suppose $g = \mathsf{E}\, q\, \mathsf{R}\, p$ and $u \leq g$. Then,

$$g = u \vee \mathsf{E}(q \vee \mathsf{EX}\, u)\, \mathsf{R}(\neg u \wedge p) \ . \tag{7}$$

In words, (7) says that a state in g is either a state in u, or a state on an infinite path entirely contained in $\neg u \wedge p$, or a state with a finite path in $\neg u \wedge p$ that leads to a state still in $\neg u \wedge p$ that satisfies q or has a successor in u.

The iterates of the fixpoint in (7) are all contained in $\neg u \wedge p$; hence, they can be regarded as frontiers. While using (6) may speed up convergence, (7) may decrease the cost of the image computations, but does not affect the number of iterations.

As in the case of least fixpoints, frontiers can be optimized using u as don't care. We can apply this approach also to the computation of greatest fixpoints under fairness constraints.

$$\mathsf{E}_C\,\mathsf{G}\,p = u \vee \mathsf{E}(\neg u \wedge p)\,\mathsf{U}(\neg u \wedge p \wedge \mathsf{EX}\,u) \vee \mathsf{E}_C\,\mathsf{G}(\neg u \wedge p) \ . \tag{8}$$

Equation (8) says that if the states in u are on fair paths contained in p, then a state on a fair path contained in p is either a state in u, or a state on a fair path entirely contained in $\neg u \wedge p$, or a state on a finite path reaching a state in $\neg u \wedge p$ that has a successor in u. In the absence of fairness constraints, one can show that (7) and (8) are equivalent.

This result can be combined with [2, Theorem 4]: In guided search, u must be a lower bound on the final fixpoint, not necessarily on the one that is being computed.

Example 1. Consider the structures of Fig. 2, adapted from [2]. Part (3) shows the original structure, while Parts (1) and (2) show structures obtained by the application of hints. Suppose we want to compute $\mathsf{EG}\,p$. Let $\mathsf{EX}_i\,Z$ the operator that computes the predecessors of the states in Z in the structure of Part (i) of Fig. 2. (The other temporal logic operators are similarly annotated.) From the graph of Part (1) we compute

$$\eta_1 = \nu Z\,.\,p \wedge \mathsf{EX}_1\,Z = \{s_4\}\ .$$

From the graph of Part (2) we compute:

$$\eta_2 = \{s_4\} \vee \mathsf{E}(\mathsf{EX}_2\{s_4\})\,\mathsf{R}_2(p \wedge \neg\{s_4\}) = \{s_0, s_3, s_4\}\ .$$

The fixpoint computation requires three preimages:

$$\mathsf{EX}_2\{s_4\},\mathsf{EX}_2\{s_0, s_1, s_3\}, \text{ and } \mathsf{EX}_2\{s_0, s_3\}\ .$$

By contrast, the non-incremental approach computes

$$\eta_2 = \nu Z\,.\{s_4\} \vee (\{s_0, s_1, s_3, s_4\} \wedge \mathsf{EX}_2\,Z)\ ,$$

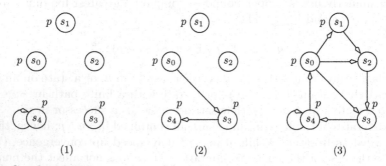

(1)   (2)   (3)

Fig. 2. Combining Theorem 4 of [2] with incremental greatest fixpoint computation

which requires the following preimages:

$$\mathsf{EX}_2\{s_0, s_1, s_3, s_4\} \text{ and } \mathsf{EX}_2\{s_0, s_3, s_4\} .$$

Finally, from the graph of Part (3) of Fig. 2, we compute:

$$\eta_3 = \{s_0, s_3, s_4\} \vee \mathsf{E}(\mathsf{EX}_3\{s_0, s_3, s_4\}) \, \mathsf{R}_3(p \wedge \neg\{s_0, s_3, s_4\}) = \{s_0, s_3, s_4\} ,$$

The fixpoint computation converges after one iteration with $Z = \emptyset$, having computed $\mathsf{EX}_3\{s_0, s_3, s_4\}$ and $\mathsf{EX}_3\{s_1\}$. By contrast, the non-incremental approach computes

$$\eta_3 = \nu Z .\{s_0, s_3, s_4\} \vee (\{s_0, s_1, s_3, s_4\} \wedge \mathsf{EX}_3 \, Z) ,$$

which in turn requires the computation of $\mathsf{EX}_3\{s_0, s_1, s_3, s_4\}$.   □

In general, we see that the incremental approach leads to more EXs (because $\mathsf{EX}\,u$ must be computed). On the other hand, each EX is applied to a smaller set.

6 Experiments

In this section we present preliminary results obtained with an implementation of the proposed algorithms in VIS 1.4 [4]. The CPU times were measured on an IBM IntelliStation running Linux with a 1.7 GHz Pentium 4 CPU and 1 GB of RAM. We checked a total of 588 formulae on 88 models.

Fig. 3 compares the run times for model checking without vacuity detection (Plain), checking all witnesses serially (Naive), and our algorithm (Vacuum). For reference, the time spent for reachability analysis is also shown (Reach). Only the experiments in which plain model checking took more than one second are shown in this plot. The replacements affected all the leaves of all formulae. (If no witnesses for the leaves pass, then no other witnesses will pass.) Though usually the witnesses are easier to model check than the given formula, this is not always the case. (See, for instance, vending.) However, in most cases, the time for a thorough vacuity detection is close to that for plain model checking. Our algorithm clearly dominates the naive approach.

Of the 588 formulae, 470 (80%) passed. A total of 2880 witnesses was generated, and 547 passed; the percentage of vacuous passes was therefore 19%. These vacuous passes were found in 35 different models (40%) and in a total of 100 formulae (17%). These results are detailed in Table 1. For each of the 88 designs, the table gives the number of properties that were checked, and how many passed; it also gives how many witnesses were generated and how many resulted in vacuous passes.

Of the 588 formulae, 411 (70%) are w-ACTL. For these we also ran the algorithm of [1]. We found that 34 formulae (6%) in 8 models (9%) caused vacuous passes.

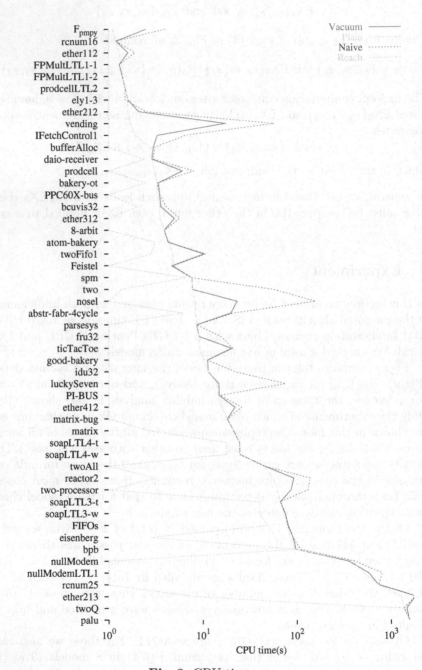

Fig. 3. CPU times

Table 1. Statistics for vacuity detection experiments

Design	Passed/Total	Vacuous Passes/Witnesses	Design	Passed/Total	Vacuous Passes/Witnesses
abp	3/3	5/19	nullModem	1/1	0/2
arbiter	4/4	0/12	nullModemLTL1	1/1	1/1
arbiter_bug	4/4	0/12	PI_BUS	19/25	6/43
eisenberg	9/9	0/18	PPC60X_bus	24/30	3/38
good_bakery	9/10	0/18	palu	1/2	0/1
bakery_ot	1/1	0/1	pf	0/2	0/0
atom_bakery	1/1	0/4	peterson	3/3	2/6
synch_bakery	4/6	0/8	philo	1/2	40/80
bpb	2/3	0/143	nosel	2/2	1/260
bufferAlloc	1/1	5/22	philo4	8/8	0/16
two_processor	5/13	0/11	drop4	4/8	0/8
coherence	8/10	9/32	ping_pong_new	3/5	1/6
counter	1/1	0/1	prodcell	9/10	0/19
crd	3/3	1/6	prodcellLTL2	1/1	1/1
ctlp3	1/1	0/2	rcnum16	1/1	0/15
daio_receiver	3/4	0/13	rcnum25	1/1	0/24
dcnew	3/7	1/6	reactor2	2/3	0/5
ely1-3	0/1	0/0	reqAck	2/2	3/13
ether112	6/6	2/20	reqAckRed	2/2	3/13
ether212	6/6	2/20	reset	0/1	0/0
ether312	6/6	2/20	rgraph	0/1	0/0
ether412	6/6	2/20	twoFifo1	3/4	6/19
FIFOs	1/1	0/1	twoQ	5/7	7/25
Fpmpy	5/8	24/99	short	2/3	1/4
FPMultLTL1-1	1/1	0/1	bcuvis32	10/10	43/66
FPMultLTL1-2	1/1	1/1	fru32	11/11	128/167
abstr_fabr_4cycle	8/8	0/62	idu32	21/21	69/126
Feistel	1/1	0/2	controlvis	17/17	28/103
two	1/2	0/2	pcuv	17/17	42/80
twoAll	5/5	0/35	spm	1/2	0/3
luckySeven	1/3	0/25	soapLTL3-t	0/1	0/0
gigamax	9/9	0/12	soapLTL3-w	0/1	0/0
gray	3/4	2/10	soapLTL4-t	1/1	0/1
ibuf	1/1	0/21	soapLTL4-w	1/1	1/1
IFetchControl1	15/22	17/89	solitaireVL	0/1	0/0
island	3/3	0/6	spinner4	3/6	0/18
jam	2/3	0/4	syncarb	33/33	0/300
lock	9/9	3/75	tcp	1/2	0/2
packstart	1/4	0/2	ticTacToe	29/42	0/107
parsepack	4/4	0/15	tlc	4/5	0/8
parsesys	4/4	0/8	4-arbit	3/3	0/6
matrix	30/32	0/45	8-arbit	2/3	0/4
matrix_bug	14/32	0/25	vending	12/15	53/132
minMax	4/5	32/200	sbc	3/3	0/9

7 Extensions to the Basic Algorithm

In this section we discuss possible extensions to our algorithm for vacuity detection. One of the main advantages of a through analysis of the formulae is the ability to identify weak properties. It is possible to extend this idea to include more cases than those created by replacements with $\bot$. Consider the following example. Once we know that $\psi = \mathsf{AG}(p \to \mathsf{AF}\,q)$, passes in a certain model, we already know that $\varphi = \mathsf{AG}(p \to \mathsf{EF}\,q)$ passes as well, because $\psi \to \varphi$. Also, the satisfying sets computed for φ are bounds for those of ψ. In our example, we have $[\![\neg\,\mathsf{EF}\,q]\!] \subseteq [\![\mathsf{EG}\,\neg q]\!]$. In general, if $\psi \to \varphi$, and φ is checked before ψ, we have two cases:

1. φ fails: then ψ also fails.
2. φ passes: we can use the satisfying sets computed for φ as bounds for those of ψ.

We can produce strengthened formulae by extending the replacement function to specify a change of existential quantifier, or temporal operator.

Failing formulae are excluded by definition from vacuity checking. However, if $\mathsf{AF}\,p$ fails in a model, it is useful to know whether $\mathsf{EF}\,p$ fails as well. (It signals a bigger discrepancy between expectations and actual behavior of the model.) The mechanism that strengthen passing formulae for vacuity detection can be employed also to weaken them and help debug them if they fail.

We have presented and implemented our algorithm for CTL model checking. Extension to LTL and CTL* is possible. We briefly discuss the case of LTL. For each replacement formula, a different Büchi automaton is generated. The automaton is for the negation of the witness formula, and hence its language is larger than the language of the automaton for original formula. The result of the language emptiness check is therefore an upper bound on the result for the original formula.

References

[1] I. Beer, S. Ben-David, C. Eisner, and Y. Rodeh. Efficient detection of vacuity in ACTL formulas. In O. Grumberg, editor, *Ninth Conference on Computer Aided Verification (CAV'97)*, pages 279–290. Springer-Verlag, Berlin, 1997. LNCS 1254. 485, 486, 487, 495

[2] R. Bloem, K. Ravi, and F. Somenzi. Efficient decision procedures for model checking of linear time logic properties. In N. Halbwachs and D. Peled, editors, *Eleventh Conference on Computer Aided Verification (CAV'99)*, pages 222–235. Springer-Verlag, Berlin, 1999. LNCS 1633. 494

[3] R. Bloem, K. Ravi, and F. Somenzi. Symbolic guided search for CTL model checking. In *Proceedings of the Design Automation Conference*, pages 29–34, Los Angeles, CA, June 2000. 487

[4] R. K. Brayton et al. VIS: A system for verification and synthesis. In T. Henzinger and R. Alur, editors, *Eighth Conference on Computer Aided Verification (CAV'96)*, pages 428–432. Springer-Verlag, Rutgers University, 1996. LNCS 1102. 495

[5] R. E. Bryant. Graph-based algorithms for Boolean function manipulation. *IEEE Transactions on Computers*, C-35(8):677–691, August 1986. 487

[6] H. Chockler, O. Kupferman, R. P. Kurshan, and M. Y. Vardi. A practical approach to coverage in model checking. In G. Berry, H. Comon, and A. Finkel, editors, *Thirteenth Conference on Computer Aided Verification (CAV'01)*, pages 66–78. Springer-Verlag, Berlin, July 2001. LNCS 2102. 485

[7] H. Chockler, O. Kupferman, and M. Y. Vardi. Coverage metrics for temporal logic model checking. In *Tools and algorithms for the construction and analysis of systems (TACAS)*, pages 528–542. Springer, 2001. LNCS 2031. 485

[8] E. M. Clarke and E. A. Emerson. Design and synthesis of synchronization skeletons using branching time temporal logic. In *Proceedings Workshop on Logics of Programs*, pages 52–71, Berlin, 1981. Springer-Verlag. LNCS 131. 489

[9] E. M. Clarke, O. Grumberg, and D. A. Peled. *Model Checking*. MIT Press, Cambridge, MA, 1999. 485, 486

[10] O. Coudert, C. Berthet, and J. C. Madre. Verification of sequential machines using Boolean functional vectors. In L. Claesen, editor, *Proceedings IFIP International Workshop on Applied Formal Methods for Correct VLSI Design*, pages 111–128, Leuven, Belgium, November 1989. 488

[11] E. W. Dijkstra. Cooperating sequential processes. In Genuys, editor, *Programming Languages*, pages 43–112. Academic Press, 1968. 488

[12] H. Fujiwara. *Logic Testing and Design for Testability*. MIT Press, Cambridge, MA, 1985. 485

[13] Y. Hoskote, T. Kam, P.-H. Ho, and X. Zhao. Coverage estimation for symbolic model checking. In *Proceedings of the Design Automation Conference*, pages 300–305, New Orleans, LA, June 1999. 485

[14] S. Katz, O. Grumberg, and D. Geist. "Have I written enough properties?" — A method of comparison between specification and implementation. In *Correct Hardware Design and Verification Methods (CHARME'99)*, pages 280–297, Berlin, September 1999. Springer-Verlag. LNCS 1703. 485

[15] O. Kupferman and M. Y. Vardi. Vacuity detection in temporal model checking. In *Correct Hardware Design and Verification Methods (CHARME'99)*, pages 82–96, Berlin, September 1999. Springer-Verlag. LNCS 1703. 485, 486, 490, 493

[16] R. P. Kurshan. *Computer-Aided Verification of Coordinating Processes*. Princeton University Press, Princeton, NJ, 1994. 485

[17] K. L. McMillan. *Symbolic Model Checking*. Kluwer Academic Publishers, Boston, MA, 1994. 490

[18] K. Ravi and F. Somenzi. Hints to accelerate symbolic traversal. In *Correct Hardware Design and Verification Methods (CHARME'99)*, pages 250–264, Berlin, September 1999. Springer-Verlag. LNCS 1703. 487

[19] D. Verkest, L. Claesen, and H. De Man. Special benchmark session on formal system design. In L. Claesen, editor, *Proceedings IFIP International Workshop on Applied Formal Methods for Correct VLSI Design*, pages 75–76, Leuven, Belgium, November 1989. 488

[20] URL: http://vlsi.colorado.edu/~vis. 487

CVC: A Cooperating Validity Checker

Aaron Stump, Clark W. Barrett, and David L. Dill

Computer Systems Laboratory, Stanford University
Stanford, CA 94305, USA
Phone: +1 650 725 3646, Fax: +1 650 725 6949
{stump,barrett,dill}@cs.stanford.edu

Abstract. Decision procedures for decidable logics and logical theories have proven to be useful tools in verification. This paper describes the CVC ("Cooperating Validity Checker") decision procedure. CVC implements a framework for combining subsidiary decision procedures for certain logical theories into a decision procedure for the theories' union. Subsidiary decision procedures for theories of arrays, inductive datatypes, and linear real arithmetic are currently implemented. Other notable features of CVC are the incorporation of the high-performance Chaff solver for propositional reasoning, and the ability to produce independently checkable proofs for valid formulas.

1 Introduction

Decision procedures for decidable logics and logical theories have been used successfully in several approaches to verification. They play an important role in verification based on interactive theorem provers (e.g., PVS [ ]), where decidable subgoals that arise in proofs of system correctness can be automatically discharged by decision procedures, thus reducing the burden on the user. They have also been used in more automatic approaches to verification, where verification problems are reduced to validity checking problems, typically involving very large formulas (e.g., [ ]).

CVC is a high-performance system for checking validity of formulas in a relatively rich decidable logic. Atomic formulas are applications of predicate symbols like $<$ and $=$ to first-order terms like $x + 2 * y$ and $car(cons(x, L))$. Formulas are then the usual boolean combinations (built using AND, OR, NOT, etc.) of atomic formulas. CVC's language provides predicate and function symbols which are convenient for modelling systems like hardware, protocols, and software. CVC is implemented in around 150K lines of C++.

CVC is the successor to the Stanford Validity Checker (SVC) [ ]. In addition to the ability to produce proofs and the incorporation of an efficient SAT solver, CVC has many improvements over SVC. The codebase is much more robust and extensible. The C++ Standard Template Library (STL) is used for efficient data structures. Such seemingly minor features as the syntax for the input language and the quality of the error messages have been greatly improved, resulting in a

D. Brinksma and K. G. Larsen (Eds.): CAV 2002, LNCS 2404, pp. 500–504, 2002.
© Springer-Verlag Berlin Heidelberg 2002

much more usable system. The following is an example of CVC input:

```
list : TYPE = DATATYPE cons (car : REAL, cdr : list), null END;
L1, L2 : list;
x, y : REAL;
P : [ [REAL, REAL]− > BOOLEAN];

QUERY (x = 2 ∗ y − 1) AND (L1 = L2 WITH car := x) =>
      P(x + y, car(L1)) => P(3 ∗ y − 1, x);
```

The example first declares an inductive datatype of lists. Then it declares some uninterpreted constants and an uninterpreted binary predicate P. It then queries a formula, which in this case is valid. The WITH operator performs functional updating of a data structure.

2   Cooperating Decision Procedures

Early work by Nelson and Oppen showed that under certain restrictions, independent decision procedures for quantifier-free logical theories in classical first-order logic with equality can be combined to obtain a decision procedure for the union of the theories [7]. The most basic restriction is that the theories may not share function and predicate symbols other than the equality symbol. The union of the theories can contain terms like $car(L) + 3 \ast x$ which have function symbols from the signatures of more than one theory. A variant of the Nelson-Oppen approach is implemented in CVC [ ]. The subsidiary decision procedures currently implemented are for the following theories.

Arrays: The theory of arrays implemented [ ] has function symbols for reading from a location i in an array a (syntax: a[i]) and functionally updating an array a to contain a given value v at a given index i (syntax: a WITH [i] := v). Arrays are extensional, which leads to validity of non-trivial equalities between updated arrays such as (assuming a is an array)

$$((\text{a WITH } [1] := 100) \text{ WITH } [2] := 200) =$$
$$((\text{a WITH } [2] := 200) \text{ WITH } [1] := 100).$$

Inductive Datatypes: CVC allows the user to declare inductive datatypes like lists and trees. Inductive datatypes are determined by a set of constructors, like *cons* and *null*, which construct members of the datatype out of some constituent elements (possibly none at all); and selectors, like *car* and *cdr*, which retrieve constituent elements from members of the datatype. Selectors are considered partial functions, so car(null) is considered to be undefined. When a datatype is declared, testers like cons? and null? are automatically added. c?(x) is true iff x was constructed using constructor c. CVC's language has special syntax for tuples and records, which are special cases of inductive datatypes.

Linear Real Arithmetic: The theory of linear real arithmetic has the usual function symbols for addition, subtraction, and arithmetic negation, as well as for multiplication and division by a constant. There are also the usual predicate symbols for arithmetic comparison. CVC implements a version of Fourier-Motzkin variable elimination to handle inequalities.

3   Proofs

CVC can optionally produce proofs for every formula it reports valid. The proofs are represented using a variant of the Edinburgh Logical Framework (LF) [5], extended with features for more conveniently representing multi-arity functions like the tuple-forming operator and n-ary addition [12]. The proofs can be efficiently checked by a proof checker called **flea** [11], which ships with CVC.

4   Chaff

Given the great advances that have been made in propositional SAT solving tools in the last decade, much greater performance on problems with boolean structure can be achieved by incorporating a modern SAT solver. CVC incorporates the Chaff SAT solver [6] to do its propositional reasoning. The Chaff code is modified to assert CVC literals (atomic formulas or their negations) in its search for a satisfying assignment. When the rest of CVC discovers a contradiction, a conflict clause is added to Chaff containing the relevant assertions. CVC determines which assertions are relevant to the contradiction by reusing the infrastructure that produces proofs in order to track assumptions [3]. This approach greatly improves performance.

5   Performance

Figure 5 compares CVC and its predecessor SVC on benchmarks from processor verification. Size is the size in kilobytes of the formula represented with maximal sharing of common subexpressions in ASCII. Running times are in seconds on an 850MHz PIII. CVC is faster than SVC on all but a handful of the examples. All but the last three examples were part of SVC's suite of benchmarks, and hence are among the examples that SVC could be expected to perform best on.

6   Related Work

CVC is similar to the ICS system [4]. ICS implements a version of Shostak's algorithm for combining decision procedures, which is less general than the framework implemented in CVC. Other features of CVC that distinguish it from ICS are

- incorporation of a state-of-the-art SAT solver
- the ability to produce independently verifiable proofs

test	size (Kb)	SVC time	CVC time
fb_12_11	10	1.0	0.2
fb_5_12	11	4.2	0.3
fb_6_12	8	1.1	0.2
dlx-dmem	71	0.2	1.8
dlx-pc	87	0.2	0.9
dlx-regfile	71	0.2	3.8
pp-bloaddata-a	32	0.6	1.6
pp-bloaddata	31	8.8	4.1
pp-dmem2	30	8.6	1.4
pp-invariant	29	0.3	0.2
ibm-full-5	350	16.1	2.3
ibm-full-10	370	15.0	2.3
bool_dlx2_aa	238	> 10000	0.7

- support for arbitrary inductive datatypes
- implementation in C++ (ICS is written in Ocaml)

Other cooperating decision procedures include:

- Simplify at Compaq SRC (http://research.compaq.com/SRC/esc/ Simplify.html)
- STeP at Stanford (http://www-step.stanford.edu/)
- Vampyre at Berkeley (http://www-cad.eecs.berkeley.edu/ rupak/Vampyre/)

7   Final Remarks

A Linux executable together with basic examples and documentation is freely available at http://verify.stanford.edu/CVC. We thank the anonymous reviewers for their comments. This work was supported under ARPA/Air Force contract F33615-00-C-1693 and NSF grants CCR-9806889 and CCR-0121403.

References

1. C. Barrett, D. Dill, and J. Levitt. Validity checking for combinations of theories with equality. In M. Srivas and A. Camilleri, editors, *Formal Methods In Computer-Aided Design*, volume 1166 of *LNCS*, pages 187–201. Springer-Verlag, 1996. 500
2. C. Barrett, D. Dill, and A. Stump. A Framework for Cooperating Decision Procedures. In David McAllester, editor, *17th International Conference on Computer Aided Deduction*, volume 1831 of *LNAI*, pages 79–97. Springer-Verlag, 2000. 501
3. C. Barrett, D. Dill, and A. Stump. Checking Satisfiability of First-Order Formulas by Incremental Translation to SAT. In *14th International Conference on Computer-Aided Verification*, 2002. 502
4. J. Filliâtre, S. Owre, H. Rueß, and N. Shankar. ICS: integrated canonizer and solver. In G. Berry, H. Comon, and A. Finkel, editors, *13th International Conference on Computer-Aided Verification*, 2001. 502

5. R. Harper, F. Honsell, and G. Plotkin. A Framework for Defining Logics. *Journal of the Association for Computing Machinery*, 40(1):143–184, January 1993. 502
6. M. Moskewicz, C. Madigan, Y. Zhaod, L. Zhang, and S. Malik. Chaff: Engineering an Efficient SAT Solver. In *39th Design Automation Conference*, 2001. 502
7. G. Nelson and D. Oppen. Simplification by cooperating decision procedures. *ACM Transactions on Programming Languages and Systems*, 1(2):245–57, 1979. 501
8. S. Owre, J. Rushby, and N. Shankar. PVS: A Prototype Verification System. In D. Kapur, editor, *11th International Conference on Automated Deduction*, volume 607 of *LNAI*, pages 748–752. Springer-Verlag, 1992. 500
9. J. Skakkebæk, R. Jones, and D. Dill. Formal verification of out-of-order execution using incremental flushing. In *10th International Conference on Computer Aided Verification*, 1998. 500
10. A. Stump, C. Barrett, D. Dill, and J. Levitt. A Decision Procedure for an Extensional Theory of Arrays. In *16th IEEE Symposium on Logic in Computer Science*, pages 29–37. IEEE Computer Society, 2001. 501
11. A. Stump and D. Dill. Faster Proof Checking in the Edinburgh Logical Framework. In *18th International Conference on Automated Deduction*, 2002. 502
12. A. Stump and D. Dill. Producing Proofs from an Arithmetic Decision Procedure in Elliptical LF. In *3rd International Workhsop on Logical Frameworks and Meta-Languages*, 2002. (acceptance pending). 502

χChek: A Multi-valued Model-Checker

Marsha Chechik, Arie Gurfinkel, and Benet Devereux

Department of Computer Science, University of Toronto,
Toronto, ON M5S 3G4, Canada.
Email: {chechik,arie,benet}@cs.toronto.edu

1 Introduction

χChek is a multi-valued symbolic model-checker [CDE01a,CDEG01]. It is a generalization of an existing symbolic model-checking algorithm to an algorithm for a multi-valued extension of CTL (χCTL). Given a system and a χCTL property, χChek returns the *degree* to which the system satisfies the property. By multi-valued logic we mean a logic whose values form a *finite quasi-boolean distributive lattice*. The meet and join operations of the lattice are interpreted as the logical *and* and *or*, respectively. The negation is given by a lattice dual-automorphism with period 2, ensuring the preservation of involution of negation ($\neg\neg a = a$) and De Morgan laws. For example, a 3-valued logic of abstraction (**3**), consisting of values *true* (T), *maybe* (M), and *false* (F), is given in Figure 1(a), where the negation operator is defined as: $\neg$T = F, $\neg$F = T, and $\neg$M = M.

Multi-valued logics have a wide range of uses in modeling. For example, the logic **3** allows for a natural representation of abstract or partial systems. In this case, the value *maybe* is used to represent state variables that are not known to be either *true* or *false*. Furthermore, additional values can be added to the logic to support better granularity, often useful for iterative refinement of partial systems. Although there are several techniques for verifying such systems [BG99], to our knowledge, χChek is the first symbolic model-checker that attacks this problem directly, without reducing it to several classical model-checking problems first.

Since a product of quasi-boolean logics is also quasi-boolean, these logics are the natural choice for reasoning about disagreements and inconsistencies between different viewpoints (also known as aspects, or features). With quasi-boolean logics, it is possible to combine different viewpoints into a single system without first resolving their inconsistencies or assigning priorities to them [EC01]. For example, if we are interested in combining two partial viewpoints, each specified using the logic **3**, we can use the product logic **3x3** (see Figure 1(b)) to represent their composition. In this case, the logic value TF represents information specified to be *true* in the first viewpoint, and *false* in the second; MT represents information that is underspecified in the first viewpoint, and is *true* in the second, etc. Properties of such a composition can then be verified using χChek. Furthermore, counter-examples can help the analyst identify the *important* disagreements, that is, disagreements that affect the properties of interest. The results of this analysis can guide a negotiation between stakeholders to resolve the important disagreements first, leaving resolution of other disagreements until later stages of the design process.

D. Brinksma and K. G. Larsen (Eds.): CAV 2002, LNCS 2404, pp. 505–509, 2002.
© Springer-Verlag Berlin Heidelberg 2002

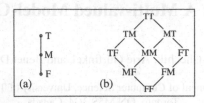

Fig. 1. Some multi-valued logics: (a) **3** – 3-valued logic of abstraction; (b) **3x3** – a product logic.

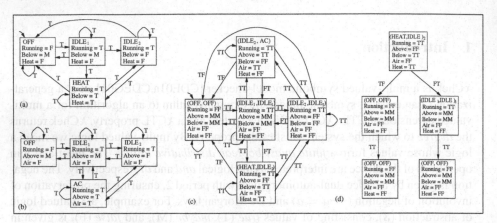

Fig. 2. Models of the thermostat. (a) Heater aspect; (b) AC aspect; (c) a combined model over logic **3x3**; (d) witness for a temporal logic property.

Furthermore, $\mathcal{X}$Chek does not require that the logic values be interpreted as truth values. For example, the logic values can be interpreted as sets of propositional formulae, thus making $\mathcal{X}$Chek a solver for CTL query checking problems [BG01,GDC02].

Verification using $\mathcal{X}$Chek proceeds similarly to verification using a classical model-checker, with the most complicated part being the correct formalization of the properties. Although $\mathcal{X}$Chek does not provide any tools to address this problem, all of the standard techniques, such as property patterns of Dwyer et al [DAC99], can be used with it. This is possible because $\mathcal{X}$CTL is syntactically equivalent to CTL, and semantically derived from CTL by replacing existential quantification by disjunction, and universal quantification by conjunction. This definition of $\mathcal{X}$CTL ensures that $\mathcal{X}$Chek is equivalent to a classical model-checker when the classical boolean logic is used for the analysis [CDEG01].

2   Overview and Example

We illustrate the use of $\mathcal{X}$Chek on a simple example of a thermostat controller. The thermostat is described using two aspects: Heater and Air Conditioner (AC). The Heater aspect is responsible for activating the heat when the temperature drops below desired, and the AC aspect is responsible for activating the air conditioning. We first model each of the aspects individually, and then merge them to produce the final model of the thermostat.

Property	Result
$E[\neg\texttt{Below}\ U\ (\neg\texttt{Below} \wedge \texttt{Heat})]$	FF
$AG(\texttt{Heat} \rightarrow \neg\texttt{Air})$	TT
$EX(EX\ \texttt{Running} = \text{FF})$	TT

Table 1. Verification results.

The Heater aspect, described in Figure 2(a), consists of a switch to turn the thermostat on and off (Running), one temperature indicator (Below), and a variable indicating whether the heater is on (Heat). Notice that in the states OFF and $\texttt{IDLE}_1$, the current temperature is unknown. This can be modeled by splitting these states, assigning Below a value T in one copy and F in another. Alternatively, we model this using the logic **3**, assigning Below the value M, as shown in Figure 2(a). The AC aspect, shown in Figure 2(b), is similar. The resulting models are generalized Kripke structures, called χKripke structures, where both transitions and state variables are assigned values from a multi-valued logic.

In the final step of our construction, we merge the two aspects to construct a monolithic model of the thermostat, shown in Figure 2(c). The composition that was chosen for this example is similar to parallel asynchronous composition with a special treatment of global (or shared) states. First, we identify the states OFF and $\texttt{IDLE}_1$ as global, thus requiring that they can only be merged with themselves. Second, we add an environmental constraint that Above $\wedge$ Below is not *true*, making the state (Heat, AC) unreachable in the composition.

As a logic of composition, we choose the logic **3x3**, shown in Figure 1(b). Values of state variables in a merged state are computed as follows: a value of a shared variable is a tuple formed from values of this variable in the original aspects. For example, the value of Running in state (OFF, OFF) is (F,F), which we write as FF. A value of a variable that is local to one aspect is a tuple where all elements are equal to the value this variable has in the "host" aspect. For example, the value of Below in state $(\texttt{IDLE}_2, \texttt{AC})$ is MM because Below has value M in the Heater aspect and is not present in the AC aspect. A transition between two states (s_1, t_1) and (s_2, t_2) is also multi-valued, and defined as $(R_1(s_1, s_2), R_2(t_1, t_2))$, where $R_i(x, y)$ is the value of the transition between states x and y in system i. For example, the transition between $(\texttt{IDLE}_2, \texttt{IDLE}_2)$ and $(\texttt{IDLE}_1, \texttt{IDLE}_1)$ is FT because the transition between $\texttt{IDLE}_2$ and $\texttt{IDLE}_1$ in the Heater aspect is F and in the AC aspect is T. This value denotes disagreement between the two aspects on the value of the transition. We annotate transitions with their values, omitting FF transitions. The resulting composition is shown in Figure 2(c).

For the purpose of this example, we identify the following three properties: (1) Is the heat ever turned on before the temperature falls below desired? (2) Is heat on only if air conditioning is off? (3) When the system is in the state $(\texttt{HEAT}, \texttt{IDLE}_2)$, can it reach the state (OFF, OFF) in two steps? The formalization of these properties in χCTL is given in Table 1.

Finally, we use χChek to verify the properties. The results of the verification on the combined system are summarized in Figure 1. The first property can be verified directly on the Heater aspect, the second can only be verified on the combined model, and the third can be verified on either aspect. Thus, the result TT for the third property is interpreted to mean that the property is T in either of the aspects. However, since the combined system still contains disagreements, it is possible that the two aspects agree on the value of the property but disagree on the *reason* why it holds. $\mathcal{X}$Chek helps us discover this problem by generating a witness, shown in Figure 2(d). A witness in the multi-valued case does not necessarily correspond to a single execution – it might instead be a tree, as in Figure 2(d). This witness shows that the property is satisfied in the Heater aspect because it is possible for the system to evolve into the OFF state via a single transition from the HEAT state, and then remain in the OFF state indefinitely. On the other hand, the AC aspect requires the system to first evolve into the $IDLE_1$ state, and only then proceed to the OFF state. Moreover, since our counter-example generator is guaranteed to produce a single common execution if one exists, it follows that this disagreement is important, and additional negotiation is required. Further analysis shows that the source of the problem is our decision to make $IDLE_1$ a global (or shared) state across the aspects.

3   Implementation

$\mathcal{X}$Chek is implemented in Java, and provides support for both model-checking with fairness and the generation of counter-examples (or witnesses). The tool consists of three components: (1) the model-checking engine itself ($\mathcal{X}$Chek); (2) a counter-example generator (KEG); (3) a web-based front-end for interactive exploration and visualization of counter-examples (KegVis).

$\mathcal{X}$Chek receives a $\mathcal{X}$Kripke structure (a multi-valued generalization of a Kripke structure) K and a $\mathcal{X}$CTL formula φ, and produces a value of φ at every state of K. The modular implementation of $\mathcal{X}$Chek allows it to support a wide variety of specification languages for $\mathcal{X}$Kripke structures. Currently, these structures can be specified either explicitly, as directed graphs in XML, or as compositions of modules expressed in an SMV-like notation. The later enables $\mathcal{X}$Chek to verify SMV models as well as abstractions and merges of these models.

The actual analysis is performed using different decision diagrams: MDDs and MBTDDs implemented as a custom decision diagram package [CDE+01b], as well as BDDs and ADDs using the standard CUDD library. The complexity of model-checking of a $\mathcal{X}$CTL formula φ, under the assumption that all operations on decision diagrams take constant time, is $O(|h| \times |S| \times |\varphi|)$, where h is the height of the lattice used in the model, and S is its state space. Depending on the problem at hand, choosing the right type of a decision diagram may significantly improve the performance of the algorithm. A detailed comparison between different decision diagrams is available in [CGD+02].

It is important to note that any multi-valued model-checking problem can be reduced to several classical model-checking problems. In fact, if a property φ does not contain negation, then model-checking of this property using $\mathcal{X}$Chek with BDDs is exactly equivalent to solving several classical problems. If φ does contain negation, then one must expand the state space by introducing a variable $\bar{a}$ for every atomic proposition a, and require the assertion $\bar{a} = \neg a$ to hold in every state [BG00]. Then, for every property with negation over the original model, there is an equivalent property without negation over the expanded model. Alternatively, a more memory-efficient solution can be achieved if all of the classical problems are solved at the same time. The description of this approach is available in [CGD+02].

Please see [CDEG01,CGD+02] for a more detailed description of the architecture of χChek and its application to several realistic case studies. The tool itself can be downloaded from http://www.cs.toronto.edu/fm.

References

[BG99]   G. Bruns and P. Godefroid. "Model Checking Partial State Spaces with 3-Valued Temporal Logics". In *Proceedings of CAV'99*, volume 1633 of *LNCS*, pages 274–287, 1999.

[BG00]   G. Bruns and P. Godefroid. "Generalized Model Checking: Reasoning about Partial State Spaces". In *Proceedings of CONCUR'00*, volume 877 of *LNCS*, pages 168–182, August 2000.

[BG01]   G. Bruns and P. Godefroid. "Temporal Logic Query-Checking". In *Proceedings of 16th Annual IEEE Symposium on Logic in Computer Science (LICS'01)*, pages 409–417, 2001.

[CDE01a]   M. Chechik, B. Devereux, and S. Easterbrook. "Implementing a Multi-Valued Symbolic Model-Checker". In *Proceedings of TACAS'01*, volume 2031 of *LNCS*, pages 404–419. Springer, April 2001.

[CDE+01b] M. Chechik, B. Devereux, S. Easterbrook, A. Lai, and V. Petrovykh. "Efficient Multiple-Valued Model-Checking Using Lattice Representations". In *Proceedings of CONCUR'01*, volume 2154 of *LNCS*, pages 451–465. Springer, August 2001.

[CDEG01]   M. Chechik, B. Devereux, S. Easterbrook, and A. Gurfinkel. "Multi-Valued Symbolic Model-Checking". CSRG Tech Report 448, University of Toronto, October 2001.

[CGD+02]   M. Chechik, A. Gurfinkel, B. Devereux, A. Lai, and S. Easterbrook. "Symbolic Data Structures for Multi-Valued Model-Checking". CSRG Tech Report 446, University of Toronto, January 2002.

[DAC99]   M. Dwyer, G. Avrunin, and J. Corbett. "Patterns in Property Specifications for Finite-State Verification". In *Proceedings of 21st International Conference on Software Engineering*, May 1999.

[EC01]   S. Easterbrook and M. Chechik. "A Framework for Multi-Valued Reasoning over Inconsistent Viewpoints". In *Proceedings of International Conference on Software Engineering (ICSE'01)*, pages 411–420, May 2001.

[GDC02]   A. Gurfinkel, B. Devereux, and M. Chechik. "Model Exploration with Temporal Logic Query Checking". CSRG Technical Report 445, University of Toronto, Department of Computer Science, March 2002.

PathFinder: A Tool for Design Exploration

Shoham Ben-David, Anna Gringauze, Baruch Sterin, and Yaron Wolfsthal

IBM Research Laboratory in Haifa
{shoham,vanna,baruch,wolfstal}@il.ibm.com

1 Introduction

In this paper we present a tool called PathFinder[1], which exploits the power of model checking for developing and debugging newly-written hardware designs. Our tool targets the community of design engineers, who—in contrast to verification engineers—are not versed in formal verification, and therefore have traditionally been distant from the growing industry momentum in the area of model checking[2].

PathFinder provides a means for the designer to explore, debug and gain insight into the behaviors of the design at a very early stage of the implementation—even before their design is complete. In the usage paradigm enabled by PathFinder, which we call *Design Exploration*, the design engineer specifies a behavior of interest, and the tool then finds and demonstrates—graphically—a set of execution *traces* compliant with the specified behavior, if any exist. When presented with each such execution sequence, the designer is essentially furnished with an insight into the design behavior, and specifically with an example of a concrete scenario in which the behavior of interest occurs. This scenario can then be closely inspected, refined, or abandoned in favor of another scenario.

Technically, PathFinder works by translating scenarios specified by the designer into safety properties, and then challenging an underlying model checker with proving the negation of those properties. If the property presented to the model checker turns out to be false, the counter example is a *trace* demonstrating the scenario requested by the designed. Thus, with PathFinder, designers can harness the power of static analysis - without being subjected to the learning curve involved with formal specification and verification.

2 The Visual Specification Interface

Path Specification. To specify a design behavior of interest (a *scenario*), the user of PathFinder creates a graphical representation of the scenario as an

---

[1] There is no connection between our tool and the Java PathFinder tool from NASA.

[2] In the hardware industry, there is an age-old practical separation between the roles of design engineer and verification engineer. Designers implement chip specifications, while verification engineers check the compliance of the implementation to the specifications.

D. Brinksma and K. G. Larsen (Eds.): CAV 2002, LNCS 2404, pp. 510–514, 2002.
© Springer-Verlag Berlin Heidelberg 2002

ordered sequence of *phases*. Each phase is represented by Boolean expressions which define the beginning and the termination conditions of the phase.

As a simple example, consider a state machine "machine(0:3)", with 16 possible values. Suppose the designer is interested in seeing a scenario where the state machine passes through states 4 and 6 and then reaches state 1—not necessarily in consecutive clock cycles. The specification is expressed by a graphical path description as shown in Figure 1 below.

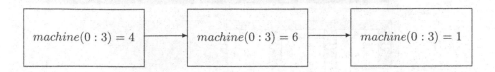

Fig. 1. Simple path specification

This path specification drives the underlying model checker to look for a trace with a state where $machine(0 : 3)$ has the value of 4, then in a later state the value is 6, and then on the final state of the trace, $machine(0 : 3)$ has the value of 1. Although restrictive, we found that this path specification formalism is expressive enough to describe behaviors of interest. More important, it incurs a minimal learning curve.

Controlling Input Behavior.   A basic design principle of PathFinder has been that the user should be able to produce first traces with minimal effort. Input signals therefore have default values, to save the effort of assigning a behavior to each of them. We chose this default behavior to be non-deterministic behavior. Thus, with minimal effort, the user is able to generate initial traces. The user then moves to restrict input behavior–essentially, debugging the environment model. The more the user is willing to invest in this process, the more accurate the input behavior will be.

PathFinder offers the user a variety of ways to restrict input signal behavior. These include the ability to describe a deterministic behavior through a graphical timing diagram editor, and the use of predefined state machines. Unless a very complicated input behavior is needed, in which case it should be modeled using either Verilog or VHDL with non-deterministic extension, the user can easily define the desired behavior through graphical means.

A screen capture of the PathFinder GUI is shown in Figure 2. The path specification panel is just below the center of the GUI, where a path scenario—in the form of a sequence of phases as described above—can be visually entered by the user. Below that, we see the path constraints panel, where the user can impose constraints—specified in the Sugar [2] language—to further restrict the paths

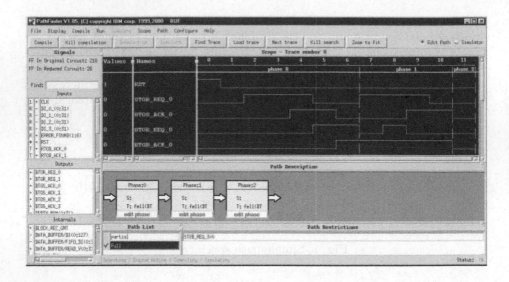

Fig. 2. Screen capture of the PathFinder GUI

he/she wants shown. The left part of the GUI is where the signals of the design are managed; in particular, input variables are controlled from here. Above the path specification panel, we see the timing diagram panel, where traces are displayed and can be further manipulated (to be presented in the next section).

3   More Key Features of PathFinder

As described in Section 1, the central theme in PathFinder is to visually demonstrate a set of execution traces of the design, which match an abstract path specified by the user. PathFinder also offers a host of additional features aimed at computing useful information on the design's behavior and making it rapidly accessible to the user. These features include:

Generation of Disjoint Multiple Traces.   PathFinder includes an algorithm which, for a given path description, produces multiple traces which comply with the path specification. The generation of such multiple traces—while maintaining many variations between them—provides the user with additional information, which proved to be useful in practice. The number of traces can be specified by the user.

The Disjoint Multiple Traces algorithm [ ] is heuristic, and therefore is not guaranteed to find disjoint traces. However, our practical experience shows that it almost always does.

Detection of Maximal Partial Trace.   In design exploration (contrast to "bug hunting" with Model Checking), the user always expects to be presented with a trace as a result of the search. Accordingly, PathFinder produces a maximal *partial trace* (maximal in terms of *events* encountered), when no full trace exists for the given path. The algorithmic details of this feature are described in [3]. The user furthermore can interrupt the search at any time, and be presented with the maximal partial trace found in the search thus far.

Interactive Design Exploration Mode.   The main purpose of this feature is to let the user gain additional information about the design as quickly as possible. In *interactive mode*, the underlying model checker does not terminate after finding the desired traces. Rather, it saves all information in memory (reachable state set, traces etc.), and interactively serves new requests coming from the user, thereby providing the user with new information as desired. The primary types of user requests supported by our experimental exploration system are presented below.

1. **Additional Cycles.**   With this type of request, the user can specify a number, N, of additional cycles to extend the current trace(s). The algorithm then performs N forward steps from the final state of each trace previously computed for the path specification.
2. **Additional Traces.**   This type of request allows the user to ask for N more traces, different from all the others previously produced.
3. **Longer Trace.**   This type of request allows the user to ask the model checker to search for a longer trace than those already produced.

Simulation Engine.   A very useful feature of PathFinder is its integrated simulator, which provides insights on design behavior and in particular can help in the debugging of traces. Once a trace is produced and displayed for the user as a timing diagram, the user can modify the values of input variables by directly manipulating the timing diagram; clicking on the input signal at the cycle to be changed will toggle the value. Then, the user can explore the different scenarios made possible by the introduction of these changes ("what-if" analysis).

4   Related Work and Experience

The problem of making formal specification and verification techniques easier to access has been addressed before. Fisler in [4] and Amla et al in [1] discuss the usage of *timing diagrams* for specification, as those are a commonly used and visually appealing specification method for designers. Hardin et al [5], in the model checker COSPAN, have implemented a feature called "check-pointing", which provides for path exploration. The contribution of PathFinder is in that unlike more common property verification tools, it provides for interactive exploration and debugging by designers, in a highly intuitive way.

Initial experiments with PathFinder reveal a good level of designer acceptance. PathFinder is used on a newly written designs with a few hundred state variables for 3–4 days, and finds 10–15 bugs on the average. We are therefore optimistic about the prospects of the Design Exploration paradigm embodied in the tool, which we feel can open new frontiers in making the power of model checking accessible to engineers at large.

References

[1] N. Amla, E. A. Emerson, R. P. Kurshan, and K. S. Namjoshi. Model checking synchronous timing diagrams. In *Formal Methods in Computer-Aided Design*, pages 283–298, 2000. 513

[2] I. Beer, S. Ben-David, C. Eisner, D. Fisman, A. Gringauze, and Y. Rodeh. The temporal logic sugar. In *Computer Aided Verification, Proc. 13th International Conference*, volume 2102 of *Lecture Notes in Computer Science*, pages 363–367. Springer, 2001. 511

[3] S. Ben-David, A. Gringauze, S. Keidar, B. Sterin, and Y. Wolfsthal. Design exploration through model checking. Technical Report H0097, IBM Haifa Research Laboratory, December 2001. 512, 513

[4] K. Fisler. Timing diagrams: Formalization and algorithmic verification. *Journal of Logic, Language and Information*, 8(3):323–361, 1999. 513

[5] R. H. Hardin, Z. Har'El, and R. P. Kurshan. COSPAN. In *Computer Aided Verification, Proc. 8th International Conference*, volume 1102 of *Lecture Notes in Computer Science*, pages 423–427. Springer, 1996. 513

Abstracting C with abC

Dennis Dams[1], William Hesse[2], and Gerard Holzmann[1]

[1] Bell Labs, Lucent Technologies
600 Mountain Ave, Murray Hill, NJ 07974, USA
[2] Dept. of Computer Science, Univ. of Massachusetts
Amherst, MA 01003, USA

Abstract. A conceptually simple and practically very useful form of data abstraction in model checking is *variable hiding*, which amounts to suppressing all information about a given set of variables. The abC tool automates this for programs written in the C programming language. It features an integrated demand-driven pointer analysis, and has been implemented as an extension of GCC.

1   Introduction

The starting point for a model checker [2] is a *verification model*. The construction of a suitable such model comprises a major part of the overall verification effort. A well-chosen model may indeed eliminate the sources of the notorious state-explosion problem. Tools for *automated abstraction* assist in the extraction of verification models from system descriptions that are otherwise too detailed. The FeaVer tool [4], based on the explicit-state model checker Spin [4,5], enables the checking of C source code through a conversion into Spin's input language. Case studies with FeaVer have indicated that *data hiding* and *narrowing* are promising candidates for automated abstraction. In data hiding, variables are removed from the program and their value is assumed to be unknown. In narrowing, the types of variables are replaced by smaller types. In both cases, nondeterminism is introduced at the level of the model checker so that the model's behaviour over-approximates the original program, which is needed to ensure preservation of universal temporal properties. Data hiding and narrowing were the most effective types of abstractions used in the verification of Lucent's PathStar call-processing software [6]. In this case study, about 30 so-called "class 5" telephony features were checked mechanically with a method based on model extraction from the call-processing source code. Over a period of roughly two years, FeaVer caught 70 errors in the code. The types of abstraction used, and hiding in particular, are simple enough to justify elaborate tool support, and also to be readily understood and applied by non-expert users.

These findings motivated the development of abC, a tool that automates most of the process of hiding data in C code. Given an initial set of variables to be abstracted, abC performs an analysis to find dependent variables that must additionally be hidden, and then performs the actual program transformation in which all such variables are removed from the program. While both tasks

D. Brinksma and K. G. Larsen (Eds.): CAV 2002, LNCS 2404, pp. 515–520, 2002.
© Springer-Verlag Berlin Heidelberg 2002

are simple in concept, implementing them for the full (ANSI) C language is a non-trivial effort. The variable-dependency analysis is complicated by the presence of pointers and arrays. In their presence, a *pointer analysis* is necessary in order to still be able to (over)approximate variable dependencies with reasonable precision. abC integrates such an analysis into the algorithm for inference of abstraction, in a demand-driven fashion: Points-to information is only computed when needed for the abstraction inference. The program transformation can in general not just remove entire assignment statements, because a single expression may manipulate both abstract and concrete variables—any concrete side-effects will have to be filtered out and retained in such a case.

The tool has been implemented as an extension to the front end of the GNU Compiler Collection (GCC version 3.0.1, [ ]). GCC's representation of the parsed C code is relatively well documented and comes with an extensive API offering many access and utility functions. Furthermore, this representation is shared between compilers of various other languages (including an extension of C that has become commonly used among many programmers), thus facilitating any extension of abC to such languages.

Various other verification platforms offer facilities for data abstraction. Bandera [ ] comes with a library of abstractions for Java data types which includes the point abstraction, which is similar to hiding. Reference types are currently not handled but work on this extension is underway [ ]. Also the PET tool [ ] implements a limited form of variable hiding for Pascal programs that does not handle pointers. Other techniques for abstraction, employed in Bandera, Java Pathfinder (JPF, [ ]), and the BeBop tool set [ ] are *slicing*[1] and *predicate abstraction*. Whereas hiding starts from a given set of variables to be abstracted, in slicing and predicate abstraction one specifies variables (or, more generally, conditions) that need to be retained, which are then propagated backwards through the program in order to find all code (generally: predicates) that they depend on. Being dual, both approaches may be used in a complementary fashion.

2   Overview of the Tool

In abC, the objects of abstraction[2] are *memory locations as specified by variable names*. The intuition is that neither the value, nor the address of such a variable is known. This design decision determines the granularity of abstraction. Aggregate variables like arrays and structures can only be abstracted as a whole, not per element or member; in these cases the location of such a variable will be understood to comprise that whole region of memory. Given a set of abstract variables, we call an expression (and also its value) abstract if it contains an abstract variable. When an expression is abstract, its value is unknown. Ultimately, in the *transformation phase*, this will lead to that expression being replaced by the special token NONDET, that signifies a nondeterministic choice to the model

---

[1] Slicing originates in the area of compiler-optimization algorithms, as do many other techniques used by these verification tools.

[2] We refer to objects that are not abstract as *concrete*.

checker. In order to avoid the introduction of too much nondeterminism, which could easily cancel any positive effect of the abstraction on the state space, an *abstraction inference phase* takes place first.

Abstraction inference phase This is a flow-insensitive, context-insensitive interprocedural static analysis that finds additional variables to be abstracted, for example because abstract values are stored to concrete locations. Due to the presence of reference types, locations may be denoted by expressions whose value is not determined at compile time (like in *p=...). In order not to abstract too many additional variables due to this, the abstraction inference is combined with a pointer analysis. The algorithm is based on 4 inference rules, presented below, that are applied whenever the value of an expression e2 is stored in a location denoted by e1. This typically happens as the result of an assignment e1=e2, but values are also stored e.g. when a function with arguments is called. With every expression that denotes a location[3], we associate a *key*—intuitively this a variable in the expression that needs to be abstract if that location must be abstract. For example, the keys of p, p->f, p++, and q=*p are all p, and the key of a[i] is a. The definition follows the inductive scheme defining valid expressions in C and is beyond the scope of this paper.

1. The key of e1 must be abstract if (a) the value of e2 is abstract, or (b) the value of e1 is abstract.
2. In addition, the key of e2 must be abstract if e2 is of pointer type and (a) the value of e1 is abstract, or (b) the value of e2 is abstract.

Rules 1 reflect pure abstraction inference. 1(a) says that an abstract value may only be assigned to an abstract location. 1(b) deals with cases such as a[i]=3 when i is abstract. Even when a is concrete, the value 3 is stored to an unknown element of the array. The rule then prescribes to also make a abstract[4]. Rules 2 combine abstraction inference with pointer analysis. For example, if the program contains a pointer assignment q=p then further operations on q may influence p, like *q=x. Rule 2(a) captures such aliasing by requiring that p must be abstract whenever q is. Finally, rule 2(b) captures the combined effect of 1(a) and 2(a) and is thus merely a shortcut.

Pointer arithmetic (including certain casts) and out-of-bounds array indexing invalidate the rules. Occurrences of the former are flagged by the tool so that they can be manually processed. Wrong array indexing is harder to catch—a separate tool like UNO [7] or FlexeLint [1] may be used. abC also flags calls through function pointers as these disable the inter-procedural inference; abstraction of function pointers is disallowed. An example run is given in the appendix.

---

[3] Examples of expressions that denote a location are x, *p, p->f, and &y. Expressions that do not denote a location are e.g. 3, x+y, p=y, a==b, and y++ when x and y are not pointers.

[4] If the array is short, then an alternative would be to leave a concrete and replace this assignment by a[NONDET]=3 signifying that 3 has to be stored to a nondeterministic element in the array. This option could be easily added to the tool if deemed useful.

Transformation phase If the application of the inference rules does not abstract additional variables, the set of abstract variables is closed under dependencies in the sense that in no execution of the program, an abstract value will be stored to a concrete location. At this point[5], the program transformation will remove all code that stores values to abstract variables ("abstract assignments"), as well as declarations of abstract variables (unless they contain initializers). Furthermore, abstract expressions that occur as tests in if, while, etc. are replaced by the token NONDET.

This transformation has to take into account the fact that abstract assignments may contain concrete side effects[6]. The transformation of an expression is therefore a recursive procedure. For example, denoting by tr(e) the result of transforming expression e, tr(e1+e2) is defined as e1+e2 if both operands are concrete, and as the comma expression ((tr(e1),tr(e2)),NONDET) when either one is abstract. Intuitively, in the latter case tr first evaluates any side effects contained inside e1 and e2 before returning NONDET. The full inductive definition of tr is again beyond the scope of this paper.

Example: If the variables a, m, and n are abstract, then the code fragment
    if (k<m) { int n; a[i++] = b[j++] = (n = k++, k); }
is transformed into
    if (NONDET) { (i++, b[j++] = (k++, k)); }.

Acknowledgements

We thank Ilya Shlyakhter for many discussions on the topic and Kedar Namjoshi for his assistance with GCC.

References

1. **Bandera**:   http://www.cis.ksu.edu/santos/bandera   **BeBop**:   http://www.research.microsoft.com/projects/slam **FeaVer**: http://cm.bell-labs.com/cm/cs/what/feaver **GCC**: http://gcc.gnu.org **JPF**: http://ase.arc.nasa.gov/visser/jpf **FlexeLint**: http://www.gimpel.com **Spin**: http://netlib.bell-labs.com/netlib/spin/whatispin.html 515, 516, 517
2. E. M. Clarke, O. Grumberg, and D. A. Peled. *Model Checking*. MIT Press, 1999. 515
3. Elsa Gunter, Robert Kurshan, and Doron Peled. PET: An interactive software testing tool. In *Proc. CAV2000*, Springer Verlag, LNCS 1855, pp. 552–556. 516
4. J. Hatcliff. Personal communication. 516
5. G. J. Holzmann. Logic Verification of ANSI-C Code with Spin. *Proc. SPIN2000*, Springer Verlag, LNCS 1885, pp. 131–147. 515

---

[5] The transformation may also be invoked with a non-closed set of abstract variables—this will not be further discussed here.

[6] Two common sources of this are the fact that the C assignment statement is really an expression and hence has a value (equal to the value of the right-hand side), and the presence of the comma expression (e1,e2) that evaluates and returns the value of e2, but only after evaluating e1 including any possible side effects.

6. G. J. Holzmann and M. H. Smith. Automating software feature verification. *Bell Labs Technical Journal*, Vol. 5, No. 2, April-June 2000, pp. 72–87. 515

7. G. J. Holzmann. Static source code checking for user-defined properties. Proc. IDPT June 2002, Pasadena, CA, USA. 517

Appendix

The abstraction inference phase of abC is demonstrated on the following (contrived) C program (line numbers added for convenience).

```
1 char *nametab[2][2] = { { "(none)", "(none)" }, { "pi2", "xxxxxxxx" } };
2 typedef struct { float x; float y; char *name; } NamedPoint;
3 short i = 1;
4
5 NamedPoint move(NamedPoint q, short *d)
6 { float xx = q.x+*d, yy = q.y+*d;
7   NamedPoint r = { xx, yy };
8   r.name = nametab[i][i];
9   return r;
10 }
11
12 int main(void)
13 { char *nullstr = "";
14   NamedPoint newp, p = { 3.1415F, 3.1415F, nametab[i][0] };
15   nametab[i][i] = "movedpi2";
16   newp = move(p,&i);
17   p.name = nullstr;
18   printf("%s: (%f,%f)\n", newp.name, newp.x, newp.y);
19 }
```

Besides this program, the input to abC consists of a file specifying the initial set of variables to be abstracted. Each variable occupies one line and is preceded by its scope, i.e. the name of the function to which it is local, or the specifier (global). We let this file contain the single line move d, indicating that the formal parameter d of function move is to be abstracted. Instructing abC to perform one abstraction inference step yields a new file containing, besides move d, the lines (global) i, move xx, and move yy. A log file explaining the newly inferred abstractions is also produced:

```
line     6: move xx        <--- move d
line     6: move yy        <--- move d
line    16: (global) i     <--- move d
```

The first line says that xx has to be abstracted because it depends on d in line 6—it is the initializer of xx that causes rule 1(a) to apply. The inference given in the third line is because the call to move on line 16 causes the argument &i to be stored in formal parameter d; rule 2(a) applies here.

The next iteration takes the file giving the four currently abstracted variables and produces again a longer list. The log file now contains the following inferences:

```
line     7: move r                <--- move xx, move yy
line     8: move r                <--- (global) i, (global) i
line     8: (global) nametab      <--- (global) i, (global) i
line    14: main p                <--- (global) i
line    14: (global) nametab      <--- (global) i
line    15: (global) nametab      <--- (global) i, (global) i
```

Several variables occur on the right-hand side of an inference in those cases where a single expression (whose storing causes a new abstraction) contains multiple variables, like the (incomplete) initializer on line 7 and the double indexes on lines 8 and 15. Note that `nametab` must be abstracted for three reasons: rule 2(b) applies to the pointer assignment on line 8 and to the initialization in line 14, and rule 1(b) applies to the assignment in line 15.

In the next iteration we get:

```
line    9: (global) move      <--- move r
line   16: move q         <--- main p
line   17: main nullstr      <--- main p
```

Here, the return on line 9 causes the function name `move` to be abstracted. One can think of the return statement as assigning the returned expression, `r`, to the function name, `move`. The ensuing abstraction of `move` will then flow back into the calling context, causing (in this case) also the variable `newp`, to which the return value is assigned, to become abstract. This happens in the next iteration:

```
line   16: main newp    <--- (global) move
```

Another iteration does not produce any inferences, so the current list of abstract variables is closed under dependencies. Some care has to be taken; abC also warns that it cannot analyze the definition of the function printf which is called on line 18. It is easily checked however that the call to printf cannot cause any dependencies.

AMC: An Adaptive Model Checker

Alex Groce[1], Doron Peled[2], and Mihalis Yannakakis[3]

[1] Computer Science Department, Carnegie Mellon University
[2] Department of Elec. and Comp. Eng., University of Texas at Austin
[3] Avaya Laboratories

Abstract. The AMC (for adaptive model checking) system allows one to perform model checking directly on a system, even when its internal structure is unknown or invisible. It also allows one to perform model checking using an inaccurate model, incrementally improving the model each time that a false negative (i.e., not an actual) counterexample is found.

1 Introduction

Inconsistencies are often present between a system and a corresponding finite state model that is used for the verification of the system. Such inconsistencies can be the result of modeling (or implementation) errors or changes made to the system after the model was finalized. Our tool, AMC, attempts to perform automatic verification of full LTL properties despite such discrepancies. Previous work proposed the idea of *black box checking* (BBC) [6], in which the verification is performed directly on the system, without a model being presented in advance. Moreover, in BBC we may not have access to the internal structure of the system and may not be able to record the different states while performing the verification; we are restricted to performing interactions with the system, from a given predefined vocabulary (which must include a reliable *reset* action that returns the system to its initial state from any other state). We have also extended this framework to *adaptive model checking* (AMC) [5], where rather than beginning from scratch, we may use finite state learning algorithms to improve the accuracy of a possibly faulty model.

AMC takes as input a (possibly erroneous) model of a system and an LTL property or specification automaton. We currently handle, in addition to the format used by AMC itself, input of models or specification automata produced by the Concurrency Workbench [3]. AMC must also be equipped with an interface to the actual system. AMC alternates between model checking runs on the current model, and incremental learning for improving the model (see Figure 1). The usual output of model checking is either a counterexample for the given property or a statement that no error was found. In our system, we may also use the model and a false negative counterexample generated during verification to improve the model used for verification. The learning algorithm of Angluin [1] and the conformance testing of Vasilevskii and Chow [2,7] (VC) are used in order to compare the given model to the actual system and improve it if a discrepancy occurs.

The AMC system fills the gap between verifying a model of the system (as is done usually in model checking), and the direct verification of finite state

D. Brinksma and K. G. Larsen (Eds.): CAV 2002, LNCS 2404, pp. 521–525, 2002.
© Springer-Verlag Berlin Heidelberg 2002

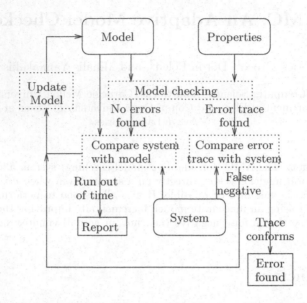

Fig. 1. The adaptive model checking strategy

systems [4,6]. The user can either start with an empty model, in which case
the system will attempt to learn the model while performing the verification, or
enter a model that may be an approximation of the actual system.

2   The Principle of AMC

Angluin's Learning Algorithm. Angluin's learning algorithm [1] plays an
important role in our adaptive model checking approach. The learning algorithm
performs experiments on a finite state system $\mathcal{S}$ and produces a *minimized* finite
automaton representing it.

The basic data structure of Angluin's algorithm consists of two finite sets of
finite strings V and W over the alphabet Σ, and a table f. The set V is prefix
closed (and contains thus in particular the empty string ε). The rows of the
table f are the strings in $V \cup V.\Sigma$, while the columns are the strings in W. The
set W must also contain the empty string. Let $f(v, w) = 1$ when the sequence of
transitions vw is a successful execution of $\mathcal{S}$, and 0 otherwise. The entry $f(v, w)$
can be computed by performing the experiment vw after a **Reset**.

We call the sequences in V the *access* sequences, as they are used to access
the different states of the automaton we are learning from its initial state. The
sequences in W are called the *separating sequences*, as their goal is to separate
between different states of the constructed automaton. Namely, if $v, v' \in V$ lead
from the initial state into different states, than we will find some $w \in W$ such
that $\mathcal{S}$ allows either vw or $v'w$ as a successful experiment, but not both.

We define an equivalence relation $\equiv mod(W)$ over strings in Σ^* as follows: $v_1 \equiv v_2\ mod(W)$ when the two rows, of v_1 and v_2 in the table f, are

the same. Denote by $[v]$ the equivalence class that includes v. A table f is *closed* if for each $va \in V.\Sigma$ such that $f(v, \varepsilon) \neq 0$ there is some $v' \in V$ such that $va \equiv v' \bmod(W)$. A table is *consistent* if for each $v_1, v_2 \in V$ such that $v_1 \equiv v_2 \bmod(W)$, either $f(v_1, \varepsilon) = f(v_2, \varepsilon) = 0$, or for each $a \in \Sigma$, we have that $v_1 a \equiv v_2 a \bmod(W)$. Notice that if the table is not consistent, then there are $v_1, v_2 \in V$, $a \in \Sigma$ and $w \in W$, such that $v_1 \equiv v_2 \bmod(W)$, and exactly one of $v_1 a w$ and $v_2 a w$ is an execution of S. This means that $f(v_1 a, w) \neq f(v_2 a, w)$. In this case we can add aw to W in order to separate v_1 from v_2.

Given a closed and consistent table f over the sets V and W, we construct a *proposed automaton* $M = \langle S, s_0, \Sigma, \delta \rangle$ as follows: The set of states S is $\{[v] | v \in V, f(v, \varepsilon) \neq 0\}$. The initial state s_0 is $[\varepsilon]$. The transition relation δ is defined as follows: for $v \in V, a \in \Sigma$, the transition from $[v]$ on input a is enabled iff $f(v, a) = 1$ and in this case $\delta([v], a) = [va]$.

The facts that the table f is closed and consistent guarantee that the transition relation is well defined. In particular, the transition relation is independent of which state v of the equivalence class $[v]$ we choose; if v, v' are two equivalent states in V, then for all $a \in \Sigma$ we have that $[va]$ coincides with $[v'a]$ (by consistency) and is equal to $[u]$ for some $u \in V$ (by closure). There are two basic steps used in the learning algorithms for extending the table f:

add_rows(v) : Add v to V. Update the table by adding a row va for each $a \in \Sigma$ (if not already present), and by setting $f(va, w)$ for each $w \in W$ according to the result of the experiment **Reset** $v\,a\,w$.

add_column(w) : Add w to W. Update the table f by adding the column w, i.e., set $f(v, w)$ for each $v \in V \cup V.\Sigma$, according the the experiment **Reset** $v\,w$.

The Angluin algorithm is executed in phases. After each phase, a new proposed automaton M is generated. The proposed automaton M may not agree with the system S. We need to compare M and S (we present later a short description of the VC black box testing algorithm for performing the comparison). If the comparison succeeds, the learning algorithm terminates. If it does not, we obtain a run σ on which M and S disagree, and add all its prefixes to the set of rows V. We then execute a new phase of the learning algorithm, where more experiments due to the prefixes of σ and the requirement to obtain a closed and consistent table are called for.

The subroutine in the Angluin learning algorithm is an incremental step of learning. Each call to this subroutine starts with either an empty table f, or with a table that was prepared in the previous step, and a sequence σ that distinguishes the behavior of the proposed automaton (as constructed from the table f) and the actual system. The subroutine ends when the table f is closed and consistent, hence a proposed automaton can be constructed from it.

Black Box Testing. Comparing a model $M = (S, s_0, \Sigma, \delta)$ with a finite state system S can be performed using the Vasilevskii-Chow [7,2] algorithm. As a preparatory step, we require the following:

– A spanning tree $G : S \to 2^{\Sigma^*}$ for M, and its corresponding runs T.
– A *separation function* ds. That is, for every pair of distinct states $s, s' \in S$, we have that $ds(s) \cap ds(s')$ contains at least one sequence that is enabled

from exactly one of s or s'. Furthermore, for each $s \in S$, $|ds(s)| \leq n$, and for each $\sigma \in ds(s)$, $|\sigma| \leq n$.

Let $\Sigma^{\leq k}$ be all the strings over Σ with length smaller or equal to k. Further, let m be the number of states of the automaton M. We do the experiments with respect to a conjectured maximal size n of S. That is, our comparison is correct as long as representing S faithfully (using a finite automaton) does not need to have more than n states. The black box testing algorithm prescribes experiments of the form **Reset** $\sigma \rho$, performed on S, as follows:

- The sequence σ is taken from $T.\Sigma^{\leq n-m+1}$.
- Run σ from the initial state s_0 of M. If σ is enabled from s_0, let s be the state of M that is reached after running σ. Then ρ is taken from the set $ds(s)$.

Adaptive Model Checking. The BBC algorithm involves applying Angluin's algorithm until a candidate model is found. Then this model is used for model checking against the given LTL specification. If a counterexample is found, it is compared against the actual system S. If this is found to be an actual execution of S, an error is reported. Otherwise, Angluin's algorithm is executed again, starting with the counterexample as a first experiment (since the counterexample separates the behavior of the candidate model and the actual system). If no counterexample is found, we use the VC algorithm to compare the model and the system and upon finding a discrepancy use it as a new experiment in a new iteration of Angluin's algorithm. This iterative process terminates when a true counterexample is found, or when the VC algorithm finds no difference between the model and the actual system.

Since the complexity of the VC algorithm is prohibitive when dealing with large systems, we try to eliminate its use as much as possible. The AMC strategy starts with an estimated model and, provided that a false negative counterexample is found, attempts to refine it. The Angluin algorithm is started, but not from scratch; we generate a separation function for the given model M and use the union of its sequences as the initial value for the separating sequences in W. We also generate a spanning tree for M, and use its sequences as the initial value of the access sequences V. In this fashion, if the model is not changed (as shown in [5], we can obtain it back without calling the VC algorithm. We have performed experiments in which this strategy was capable of changing the model in such a way that actual errors could be found [5].

3   The AMC System

The AMC system is written in Standard ML of New Jersey (SML). It includes around 5000 lines of code. It allows three different modes of interfacing with the actual system:

1. Each process of the system is an independent Unix process, written in C, and the AMC system is another process that interacts with all the other processes. Inspired by the Verisoft system [4], we observe the interprocess communication operations. We replace each communication operation (and

any other operation that can affect the checked property, such as a nondeterministic choice or a timeout) with a macro expansion that interacts with the AMC verifier using a shared file.

2. The direct verification of a system. The system is a single Unix process, or an external device whose input and (binary) output can interface with our AMC system. We interact with a system using a Unix bidirectional pipeline, which in one direction emits the sequence of inputs (or a **Reset**), and in the other direction waits for a response of 0 or 1 (for *enabled*, or *disabled*, respectively).

3. The verified system is a single SML process, which is compiled together with our AMC system. The SML interface to foreign code could also be used in this case.

The above modes of operation of AMC lend themselves to different capabilities and difficulties. Mode 1 allows one to check C programs directly, without modeling them (or verifying a model while improving its accuracy against actual C code). The speed of the execution is highly affected by the frequent interprocess interaction. Each communication between processes is replaced with a sequence of commands in which the communicating process notifies the AMC process about its intention to communication, and preempts itself until the communication is scheduled.

Mode 2 allows us to interact with an external device directly and perform the verification or the update on an actual device. The speed of the interaction depends on the actual device involved and the speed of using (Unix) pipelines. Since a physical device is involved, the automatic scheduling of the AMC by the operating system is also an important factor.

Mode 3 involves only one process and hence reflects the actual speed of the adaptive model checking algorithm. As was shown in [5], this may be, in the worst case of verification without a model, exponential time in the (estimated minimized) size of the system, although the average case complexity of finding errors in a system (if they exist) is polynomial.

References

1. D. Angluin, Learning Regular Sets from Queries and Counterexamples, Information and Computation, 75, 87–106 (1978). 521, 522
2. T. S. Chow, Testing software design modeled by finite-state machines, IEEE transactions on software engineering, SE-4, 3, 1978, 178–187. 521, 523
3. R. Cleaveland, J. Parrow, B. Steffen, The Concurrency Workbench: a semantic-based tool for the verification of concurrent systems, TOPLAS 15(1993), 36–72. 521
4. P. Godefroid, Model checking for programming languages using VeriSoft, Proc. 24th ACM Symp. on Progr. Lang. and Sys., 174-186, 1996. 522, 524
5. A. Groce, D. Peled, M. Yannakakis, Adaptive Model Checking, TACAS 2002, LNCS 2280, Springer, 357–370. 521, 524, 525
6. D. Peled, M. Y. Vardi, M. Yannakakis, Black Box Checking, FORTE/PSTV 1999, Beijing, China, 225–240. 521, 522
7. M. P. Vasilevskii, Failure diagnosis of automata, Kibertetika, no 4, 1973, 98–108. 521, 523

Temporal-Safety Proofs for Systems Code*

Thomas A. Henzinger[1]   Ranjit Jhala[1]   Rupak Majumdar[1]
George C. Necula[1]   Grégoire Sutre[2]   Westley Weimer[1]

[1] EECS Department, University of California, Berkeley
[2] LaBRI, Université de Bordeaux, France

Abstract. We present a methodology and tool for verifying and certifying systems code. The verification is based on the *lazy-abstraction* paradigm for intertwining the following three logical steps: construct a predicate abstraction from the code, model check the abstraction, and automatically refine the abstraction based on counterexample analysis. The certification is based on the *proof-carrying code* paradigm. Lazy abstraction enables the automatic construction of small proof certificates. The methodology is implemented in BLAST, the Berkeley Lazy Abstraction Software verification Tool. We describe our experience applying BLAST to Linux and Windows device drivers. Given the C code for a driver and for a temporal-safety monitor, BLAST automatically generates an easily checkable correctness certificate if the driver satisfies the specification, and an error trace otherwise.

1   Introduction

An important goal of software engineering is to facilitate the construction of *correct* and *trusted* software. This is especially important for low-level systems code, which usually cannot be shielded from causing mischief by runtime protection mechanisms. Correctness requires technologies for the *verification* of software, which enable engineers to produce programs with few or no bugs. Trust requires technologies for the *certification* of software, which assure users that the programs meet their specifications, e.g., that the code will not crash, or leak vital secrets. Both verification and certification are most effective when performed for actual code, not for separately constructed abstract models.

For verification, *model-checking* based approaches have the advantages of being, unlike most theorem-proving based approaches, fully automatic and, unlike most program-analysis based approaches, capable of checking path-sensitive properties. The main obstacle to model checking is, of course, scalability. Recently, *abstraction-refinement* based techniques have been developed for (mostly) automatically constructing and model checking abstract models derived directly from code [3, 7, 25, 16]. However, the main problem faced by such techniques is

* This work was supported in part by the NSF ITR grants CCR-0085949,CCR-0081588, the NSF Career grant CCR-9875171, the DARPA PCES grant F33615-00-C-1693, the MARCO GSRC grant 98-DT-660, the SRC contract 99-TJ-683, a Microsoft fellowship, and gifts from AT&T Research and Microsoft Research.

D. Brinksma and K. G. Larsen (Eds.): CAV 2002, LNCS 2404, pp. 526-538, 2002.

still scalability: for large software systems and complicated specifications, the abstraction process can take too much time and space, and the resulting model may again be too large to be model checked. The technique of *lazy abstraction* [15] is an attempt to make counterexample-guided abstraction refinement for model checking [6, 3] scalable by localizing the abstraction process and avoiding unnecessary work. Lazy abstraction builds an abstract model on-the-fly, during model checking, and on demand, so that each predicate is used only in abstracting those portions of the state space where it is needed to rule out spurious counterexamples. This is unlike traditional predicate-abstraction based model checking [13, 8, 1], which constructs a uniform predicate abstraction from a given system and a given set of predicates. The result is a nonuniform abstract model, which provides for every portion of the state space just as much detail as is necessary to prove the specification. Also, lazy abstraction short-circuits the traditional abstract-verify-refine loop [3], and avoids the repetition of work in successive abstraction phases and in successive model-checking phases.

For certification, *proof-carrying code* (PCC) [18] has been proposed as a mechanism for witnessing the correct behavior of untrusted code. Here, the code producer sends to the consumer the code annotated with loop invariants and function pre- and postconditions, as well as a proof of correctness of a verification condition, whose validity guarantees the correctness of the code with respect to the specification. From the code and the annotations, the consumer can build the verification condition and check the supplied proof for correctness. The checking of the proof is much simpler than its construction. In particular, by encoding the proof, proof checking becomes a type-checking problem. Proof-carrying code has the advantages of avoiding trusted third parties, and of being tamper-proof, because tampering with either the proof or the code will result in an invalid proof. The main problem faced by PCC is that a user may have to supply annotations such as loop invariants. In [18] it is shown how loop invariants can be inferred automatically for proofs of type and memory safety, but the problem of inferring invariants for behavioral properties, such as temporal safety, remains largely open [11].

We show that lazy abstraction can be used naturally and efficiently to construct small correctness proofs for temporal-safety properties in a PCC based framework. The proof generation is intertwined with the model-checking process: the data structures produced by lazy abstraction automatically supply the annotations required for proof construction, and provide a decomposition of the proof which leads to a small correctness certificate. In particular, using abstraction predicates only where necessary keeps the proof small, and using the model checker to guide the proof generation eliminates the need for backtracking, e.g., in the proof of disjunctions. Our strategy to generate proofs from model-checking runs is different from [17, 22]. We exploit the structure of sequential code so that the proof is an invariant for every control location, along with local checks for every edge of the control-flow graph that the invariants are sound. Both [17, 22] work at the transition-system level. On the other hand, they generate proofs for properties more general than safety.

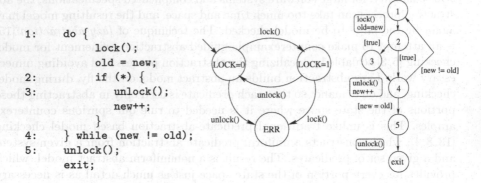

```
1:    do {
          lock();
          old = new;
2:        if (*) {
3:            unlock();
              new++;
          }
4:    } while (new != old);
5:    unlock();
      exit;
```

Fig. 1. (a) The program `Example`. (b) Locking specification. (c) CFA.

We have implemented proof generation in the tool BLAST [15] for model checking C programs. BLAST has been inspired by the Microsoft SLAM project [3], and attempts to improve on the abstract-verify-refine methodology by the use of lazy abstraction for model construction, and the use of theorem proving for predicate discovery. We focus here on the automatic verification and certification of device drivers. Device drivers are written at a fairly low level, but must meet high-level specifications, such as locking disciplines, which are difficult to verify without path-sensitive analysis. They are critical for the correct functioning of modern computer systems, but are written by untrusted third-party vendors. Some studies show that device drivers typically contain 7 times as many bugs as the rest of the OS code [5]. Using BLAST, we have run 10 examples of Linux and Windows device drivers, of up to 60K lines of C code. We have been able to discover several errors, and construct, fully automatically, small proofs of correctness, each less than 150K. This demonstrates that lazy-abstraction based verification and proof generation scales well to large software systems.

2   An Example

We consider a small example to give an overview of lazy abstraction and proof generation. Consider the program in Figure 1(a). A temporal-safety specification is a monitor automaton with error locations. Consider the locking discipline specified by the automaton of Figure 1(b). The monitor uses a global variable *LOCK*, which is 1 when the lock is held, and 0 otherwise. An error occurs if the function `lock` is called with the lock held (*LOCK* = 1) or `unlock` is called without the lock held (*LOCK* = 0). The program and specification are input to BLAST as C code, which are then combined to get a single sequential program with a special error location that is reachable iff the specification is not met. Thus we assume that the program has a special error label, and safety checking is checking whether the error label is reachable.

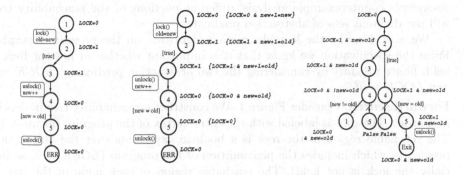

Fig. 2. Forward search.   **Fig. 3.** Backward counter- **Fig. 4.** Search with new
                                example analysis.   predicate.

We represent programs as *control flow automata* (CFA). A CFA is a directed
graph with vertices corresponding to control points of the program (begins and
ends of basic blocks), and edges corresponding to program operations. An edge
is labeled either by a *basic block* of instructions that are executed along that
edge, or by an *assume predicate* that represents the condition that must hold
for the edge to be taken. Figure 1(c) shows the CFA for the program `Example`.
The program labels correspond to CFA vertices with the same label. The edges
labeled with boxes represent basic blocks; those labeled with [·] represent assume
predicates. The condition of the `if (*)` statement is not modeled. We assume
that either branch can be taken, hence both outgoing edges are labeled with
[`true`], which stands for the assume predicate `true`.

2.1   Verification

The lazy abstraction algorithm comprises two phases. In the forward-search
phase, we build a *reachability tree*, which represents a portion of the reachable,
abstract state space of the program. Each node of the tree is labeled by a vertex
of the CFA and a boolean formula, called the *reachable region*, constructed as a
combination of a finite set of *abstraction predicates*. Each edge of the tree is labeled by a basic block or an assume predicate. Each path in the tree corresponds
to a path in the CFA. The reachable region of a node describes the reachable
states of the program in terms of the abstraction predicates, assuming execution
follows the sequence of instructions labeling the edges from the root of the tree
to the node. If we find that an error node is reachable in the tree, then we go to
the second phase, which checks if the error is real or results from our abstraction
being too coarse (i.e., if we lost too much information by restricting ourselves to
a particular set of abstraction predicates). In the latter case, we ask a theorem
prover to suggest additional abstraction predicates which rule out that particular spurious counterexample. By iterating the two phases of forward search and

backwards counterexample analysis, different portions of the reachability tree will use different sets of abstraction predicates.

We now describe the lazy-abstraction algorithm on the program Example. From the specification we know that it is important whether or not the lock is held, hence we start by considering the two abstraction predicates[1] $LOCK = 1$ and $LOCK = 0$[2].

Forward search. Consider Figure 1. We construct a reachability tree in depth-first order. The root is labeled with the entry vertex of the program (location 1). The reachable region of the root is a boolean expression over the abstraction predicates which includes the precondition of the program ($LOCK = 0$, as initially the lock is not held). The reachable region of each node in the tree is obtained from the reachable region of the parent and the instructions labeling the edge between the parent and the node, by an overapproximate successor computation with respect to the set of abstraction predicates. This computation involves calls to a theorem prover and is also used in the generation of correctness certificates. In the example, the search finds a path to an error node, namely, $(1, 2, 3, 4, 5)$.

Backwards counterexample analysis. We check if the path from the root to the error node is a genuine counterexample or results from the abstraction being too coarse. To do this, we symbolically simulate the error trace backwards in the original program. As we go backwards from the error node, we try to find the first node in the reachability tree where the abstract trace fails to have a concrete counterpart. If we find such a *pivot node*, then we conclude that the counterexample is spurious and refine the abstraction from the pivot node on. If the analysis goes back to the root without finding a pivot node, then we have found a real error in the program.

Figure 3 shows the result of this phase. In the figure, for each node, the formula in the curly braces, called the *bad region*, represents the set of states that can go from the corresponding control location to an error by executing the sequence of instructions labeling the path from the node to the error node. Formally, the bad region of a node is the intersection of the reachable region of the node with the weakest precondition of *true* with respect to the sequence of instructions labeling the path in the reachability tree from the node to the error node. It is computed inductively, starting backwards from the error node, which has the bad region *true*. Note that unlike the search phase, the counterexample analysis is precise: we track all predicates obtained along a path. In Figure 3, we find that the bad region at location 1 is *false*, which implies that the counterexample is spurious. In [15] we show how the *proof* that the bad region at a node is empty (i.e., unsatisfiable) can be used to extract additional abstraction predicates which rule out the spurious counterexample. In the example, we find that *new = old* is such an important predicate.

Search with new predicates. We again start the forward-search phase, starting from the pivot node, but this time we track the predicate *new = old* in

---

[1] Predicates are written in *italics*, code in typewriter font.

[2] This is not necessary; we can also start with the empty set of abstraction predicates.

addition to $LOCK = 0$ and $LOCK = 1$. The resulting search tree is shown in Figure 4. Notice that we can stop the search at the leaf labeled 1: as the states satisfying the reachable region $LOCK = 0 \land new = old$ are a subset of those satisfying the reachable region $LOCK = 0$ of root, the subtree constructed from the leaf would be included in the subtree of the root. In the new reachability tree, no error node is reachable. Hence we conclude that the program Example satisfies the locking specification.

2.2 Certification

To certify that a program satisfies its specification, we use a standard *temporal-safety rule* from deductive verification: given a transition system, if we can find a set I of states such that (1) I contains all initial states, (2) I contains no error states, and (3) I is closed under successor states, then the system cannot reach an error state from an initial state. If (1)–(3) are satisfied, then I is called an *invariant* set. In our setting, the temporal-safety rule reduces to supplying for each vertex q of the CFA an invariant formula $I(q)$ such that

1. $(LOCK = 0) \Rightarrow I(1)$;
2. $I(\text{ERR}) = false$;
3. for each pair of CFA vertices q and q' with an edge labeled op between them, $sp(I(q), \text{op}) \Rightarrow I(q')$, where sp is the strongest-postcondition operator [10].

Thus, to provide a proof of correctness, it suffices to supply a location invariant $I(q)$ for each vertex q of the CFA, and proofs that the supplied formulas meet the above three requirements.

The location invariants can be mined from the reachability tree. In particular, the invariant for q is the disjunction of all reachable regions that label the nodes in the tree which correspond to q. For example, $I(4)$ is $(LOCK = 0 \land \neg new = old) \lor (LOCK = 1 \land new = old)$. It is easy to check that $(LOCK = 0) \Rightarrow I(1)$, since the root of the reachability tree is labeled by the precondition of the program $(LOCK = 0)$. Also, as there is no node labeled ERR in the tree, we get the second requirement by definition. The interesting part is checking that the third requirement, that for each edge $q \xrightarrow{\text{op}} q'$ of the CFA, $sp(I(q), \text{op}) \Rightarrow I(q')$. Consider the edge $4 \xrightarrow{[\text{new!=old}]} 1$. We need to show that

$$sp((LOCK = 0 \land \neg new = old) \lor (LOCK = 1 \land new = old), [\text{new!} = \text{old}]) \Rightarrow (LOCK = 0).$$

By distributing sp over $\lor$, we are left with the proof obligation $((LOCK = 0) \lor false) \Rightarrow (LOCK = 0)$. To prove this, notice that the disjuncts on the left can be broken down into subformulas obtained from the reachable regions of individual nodes. Hence we can show the implication by matching each subformula with the appropriate successor on the right. So we get the two obligations $(LOCK = 0) \Rightarrow (LOCK = 0)$ and $false \Rightarrow (LOCK = 0)$. Exactly these obligations were generated in the forward-search phase when computing abstract successors. Each obligation is discharged, and the whole proof assembled, using a proof-generating theorem prover.

3 From Lazy Abstraction to Verification Conditions

3.1 Control flow automata

Syntax. A *control flow automaton* C is a tuple $\langle Q, q_0, X, \mathtt{Op}, \rightarrow \rangle$, where Q is a finite set of control locations, q_0 is the initial control location, X is a finite set of typed variables, $\mathtt{Op}$ is a set of operations, and $\rightarrow \subseteq (Q \times \mathtt{Op} \times Q)$ is a finite set of edges labeled with operations. An edge $(q, \mathtt{op}, q')$ is also denoted $q \xrightarrow{\mathtt{op}} q'$. The set $\mathtt{Op}$ of operations contains (1) *basic blocks* of instructions, i.e., finite sequences of assignments $\mathtt{lval} = \mathtt{exp}$, where $\mathtt{lval}$ is an lvalue from X (i.e., a variable, structure field, or pointer dereference), and $\mathtt{exp}$ is an arithmetic expression over X; and (2) *assume predicates* $\mathtt{assume(p)}$, where $\mathtt{p}$ is a boolean expression over X (arithmetic comparison or pointer equality), representing a condition that must be true for the edge to be taken. For ease of exposition we describe our method only for CFAs without function calls; the method can be extended to handle function calls in a standard way (and function calls are handled by the BLAST implementation). A program written in an imperative language such as C can be transformed to a CFA [21].

Semantics. The set $\mathcal{V}_X$ of *(data) valuations* over the variables X contains the type-preserving functions from X to values. A *state* is a pair in $Q \times \mathcal{V}_X$. A *region* is a set of states; let $\mathcal{R}$ be the set of regions. We use first-order formulas over some fixed set of relation and function symbols to represent regions. The semantics of operations is given in terms of the strongest-postcondition operator [10]: $sp(r, \mathtt{op})$ of a formula r with respect to an operation $\mathtt{op}$ is the strongest formula whose truth holds after $\mathtt{op}$ terminates when executed in a valuation that satisfies r. For a formula $r \in \mathcal{R}$ and operation $\mathtt{op} \in \mathtt{Op}$, the formula $sp(r, \mathtt{op}) \in \mathcal{R}$ is syntactically computable. However, we leave certain relation and function symbols (e.g., multiplication) uninterpreted, and the set of states denoted by $sp(r, \mathtt{op})$ may be overapproximate. A location $q \in Q$ is *reachable* from a precondition $Pre \in \mathcal{R}$ if there is a path $q_0 \xrightarrow{\mathtt{op}_1} q_1 \xrightarrow{\mathtt{op}_2} \cdots \xrightarrow{\mathtt{op}_n} q_n$ in the CFA and a sequence of formulas r_i, for $i \in \{0, \ldots, n\}$, such that $q_n = q$, $r_0 = Pre$, $r_n \not\Rightarrow false$, and $sp(r_i, \mathtt{op}_{i+1}) = r_{i+1}$ for all $0 \le i < n$. The witnessing path is called a *feasible* path from (q_0, Pre) to q.

3.2 Verification conditions

Let $C = \langle Q, q_0, X, \mathtt{Op}, \rightarrow \rangle$ be a CFA with a precondition $Pre \in \mathcal{R}$ and a special *error location* $q_{\mathcal{E}} \in Q$. We consider the specification that there is no feasible path in C from (q_0, Pre) to the error location $q_{\mathcal{E}}$. Such a path is called an *error trace*. Note that every temporal-safety property can be checked in this way, using a product with a suitable monitor automaton. A *verification condition* (VC) [10] for a program and a specification is a first-order formula r such that the validity of r ensures that the program adheres to the specification. In order to produce the VC we require that every location q of the CFA is annotated with a formula, the *invariant region* $I(q)$. Given the invariants $I: Q \rightarrow \mathcal{R}$, the verification condition

$\mathcal{VC}(C, Pre, q_\mathcal{E}, I)$ that asserts the correctness of the CFA is

$$(Pre \Rightarrow I(q_0)) \; \wedge \; (I(q_\mathcal{E}) = \mathit{false}) \; \wedge \bigwedge_{q \xrightarrow{\mathrm{op}} q'} \left(sp(I(q), \mathrm{op}) \Rightarrow I(q') \right),$$

which contains one conjunct for each edge of C. In other words, the VC states that the invariant of each location is an inductive overapproximation of the states that can be reached at that location. Formally, if $\mathcal{VC}(C, Pre, q_\mathcal{E}, I)$ is valid, then the error location $q_\mathcal{E}$ is not reachable in C from Pre [10].

3.3   Invariant generation via lazy abstraction

The invariants required for the VC are got automatically from the data structure built by the lazy-abstraction algorithm [15]. We assume that both the code producer and consumer are working at the CFA level. Consider a CFA $C = \langle Q, q_0, X, \mathrm{Op}, \to \rangle$. Let T be a rooted tree, where each node is labeled by a pair $(q, r) \in Q \times \mathcal{R}$, and each edge is labeled by an operation $\mathrm{op} \in \mathrm{Op}$. We write $\mathrm{n}\colon(q, r)$ if node n is labeled by control location q and region r. If there is an edge from $\mathrm{n}\colon(q, r)$ to $\mathrm{n}'\colon(q', r')$ labeled by op, then node n' is a (op, q')-*son* of node n. We write $Leaves_T$ for the set of leaf nodes, and Int_T for the set of internal nodes. The tree T is a *reachability tree* for the CFA C if (1) each internal node $\mathrm{n}\colon(q, r)$ has a (op, q')-son $\mathrm{n}'\colon(q', r')$ for each edge $q \xrightarrow{\mathrm{op}} q'$ of C; (2) if $\mathrm{n}'\colon(q', r')$ is a (op, q')-son of $\mathrm{n}\colon(q, r)$, then $sp(r, \mathrm{op}) \Rightarrow r'$; and (3) for each leaf node $\mathrm{n}\colon(q, r)$, there are internal nodes $\mathrm{n}_1\colon(q, r_1), \ldots, \mathrm{n}_k\colon(q, r_k)$ such that $r \Rightarrow (r_1 \vee \ldots \vee r_k)$. The reachability tree is *safe* w.r.t. to precondition $Pre \in \mathcal{R}$ and error location $q_\mathcal{E} \in Q$ if (1) the root has the form $\mathrm{n}\colon(q_0, Pre)$ and (2) for all nodes of the form $\mathrm{n}\colon(q_\mathcal{E}, r)$, we have $r \Leftrightarrow \mathit{false}$.

Theorem 1. [15] *Let C be a CFA with precondition Pre and error location $q_\mathcal{E}$. If the lazy-abstraction algorithm $\mathsf{LA}(C, Pre, q_\mathcal{E})$ terminates, then it returns either an error trace, or a safe reachability tree.*

The reachability problem for CFAs is undecidable, so LA may not terminate on all inputs. However, it terminates on all our examples (and [15] contains some termination criteria). A safe reachability tree witnesses the correctness of the CFA, and the reachable regions that label its nodes provide invariants. In particular, if T is a safe reachability tree for $(C, Pre, q_\mathcal{E})$, then the *invariant region* $I(q)$ of each control location q of C is defined to be the union of all reachable regions of *internal* nodes of T labeled by q, that is, $I(q) = \bigvee_{\mathrm{n}\colon(q, r) \in Int_T} r$. From these invariants, we will generate a proof of the verification condition $\mathcal{VC}(C, Pre, q_\mathcal{E}, I)$. In fact, we modify the lazy-abstraction algorithm to guide, during the construction of a safe reachability tree, the generation of the correctness proof.

4   Proof Generation

Representing proofs. We encode the proof of the verification condition in LF [14], so that proof checking reduces to a linear-time type-checking problem.

The logic we encode in LF is first-order logic with equality and special relation and function symbols for arithmetic and memory operations. The encoding is standard [14, 18], and is omitted. The inference rules of the proof system include the standard introduction and elimination rules for the boolean connectives used in natural deduction with hypothetical judgments [23], together with special rules for equality, arithmetic, and memory operations. In BLAST, proofs are represented in binary form using Implicit LF [20]. We use the proof encoding and checking mechanism of an existing PCC implementation to convert proofs from a textual representation to binary, and to check proofs.

Generating proofs. Given a safe reachability tree T for a CFA C with precondition Pre and error location $q_{\mathcal{E}}$, we must prove the three conjuncts of the verification condition $\mathcal{VC}(C, Pre, q_{\mathcal{E}}, I)$, namely, that (1) the precondition implies the invariant of the initial location, (2) the invariant of the error location is false, and (3) the invariants are closed under postconditions. We prove each conjunct separately. The first conjunct of the VC is $Pre \Rightarrow I(q_0)$. Since the root of T is labeled with the control location q_0 and the reachable region Pre, the precondition Pre is a disjunct of the invariant $I(q_0)$. Hence, the first conjunct follows from simple propositional reasoning. The second conjunct is $I(q_{\mathcal{E}}) = false$. This is again true by the construction of T and the invariants. For the third conjunct, it suffices to show a proof obligation for each edge of the CFA. We use distributivity of postconditions and implication over disjunction to break the obligation for a CFA edge into individual obligations for the edges of the safe reachability tree that correspond to the CFA edge. Then we discharge the smaller proof obligations by relating them to the construction of the reachable regions during the forward-search phase of the lazy-abstraction algorithm.

Consider the edge $q \xrightarrow{\text{op}} q'$ of C, and the corresponding proof obligation $sp(I(q), \text{op}) \Rightarrow I(q')$. Recall that $I(q)$ is the union of all reachable regions of nodes of T labeled by q. Since sp distributes over disjunction, it suffices to prove $\left(\bigvee_{\text{n}:(q,r_n) \in Int_T} sp(r_n, \text{op}) \right) \Rightarrow \left(\bigvee_{\text{m}:(q',r_m) \in Int_T} r_m \right)$, or equivalently, to prove $\bigwedge_{\text{n}:(q,r_n) \in Int_T} \left(sp(r_n, \text{op}) \Rightarrow \bigvee_{\text{m}:(q',r_m) \in Int_T} r_m \right)$. Hence, it suffices to prove one obligation for each internal node labeled by q. For every internal node $\text{n}:(q, r_n)$ of T, there is a unique (op, q')-son $\text{m}:(q', r_m)$ of n. This observation is essential for guiding the proof generation. We break the proof of $sp(r_n, \text{op}) \Rightarrow I(q')$ into two cases, corresponding to whether m is an internal node or a leaf.

If m is an internal node of T, then it suffices to prove $sp(r_n, \text{op}) \Rightarrow r_m$. We generate a proof for this by considering the computation that put the edge from n to m into the safe reachability tree. Assume that $r_n = \bigvee R_i$, where each disjunct R_i is a conjunction of literals, and each literal is either an abstraction predicate or its negation. Then $r_m = \bigvee R_i'$, where for each i, the disjunct R_i' is computed as an overapproximate (abstract) successor region of R_i as follows [15]: the literal p (resp., $\neg p$) appears in R_i' iff $sp(R_i, \text{op}) \Rightarrow p$ (resp., $sp(R_i, \text{op}) \Rightarrow \neg p$) is valid. Distributing sp over disjunction, it suffices to prove $sp(R_i, \text{op}) \Rightarrow r_m$, which further reduces to proving $sp(R_i, \text{op}) \Rightarrow R_i'$ for each i. This is proved by putting together exactly the proofs used in the abstract successor computation.

If m is a leaf of T, then we break the proof into three parts. First, we generate a proof for $sp(r_n, \mathbf{op}) \Rightarrow r_m$ as above. Second, we check why the node m is a leaf of the safe reachability tree. There must be a set $S = \{\mathbf{k} \mid \mathbf{k} : (q', r_k)\}$ of nodes of T such that $r_m \Rightarrow \bigvee_{k \in S} r_k$; this set can be obtained from the lazy-abstraction algorithm. We extract the proof of the above implication. Third, we notice that $\bigvee_{k \in S} r_k \Rightarrow I(q')$, by the definition of $I(q')$. These three proofs are combined into a proof of $sp(r_n, \mathbf{op}) \Rightarrow I(q')$.

Our proof generation is optimized in two ways. First, we use the intermediate steps of the model checker to break a proof that invariants are closed under post-conditions into simpler proofs about the disjuncts that make up the invariants. Moreover, these proofs are available from the forward-search phase of the model checker. Second, we reduce the size of the proof by using a coarse, nonuniform abstraction sufficient for proving correctness, as provided by the lazy-abstraction algorithm. This eliminates predicates that are not essential to correctness and submits fewer obligations to the proof generator than would a VC obtained by direct symbolic simulation of all paths.

5   Experiments

5.1   The BLAST toolkit

We have implemented a tool that applies lazy abstraction and proof generation for temporal-safety properties of C programs. The input to BLAST is a C program and a safety monitor written in C; these are compiled into a CFA with a special error state. The lazy-abstraction algorithm runs on the CFA and returns either a genuine error trace or a proof of correctness (or fails to terminate). Our handling of C features follows that of [1]. We handle all syntactic constructs of C, including pointers, structures, and procedures (leaving the constructs not in the predicate language uninterpreted). However, we model integer arithmetic as infinite-precision arithmetic (no wraparound), and we assume a *logical* model of the memory. In particular, we model the expression $p + i$, where p is a pointer and i is an integer, as yielding a pointer value that points to the object pointed to by p. Hence, we do not model pointer arithmetic precisely.

BLAST makes use of several existing tools. We use the CIL compiler infrastructure [21] to construct CFAs from C programs. We use the CUDD package [24] to represent regions as BDDs over sets of abstraction predicates. Finally, we use the theorem prover Simplify [9] for abstract-successor computations and inclusion checks, and the (slower) proof-generating theorem prover Vampyre [4] where proofs are required. The cost of verification and certification is dominated by the cost of theorem proving, so we incorporate automatic lemma extraction by caching theorem prover calls. Our experiments show that many atomic proof obligations that arise during the entire process are identical, and so the size of the proof in dag representation is considerably smaller than a derivation tree.

5.2   Checking device drivers with BLAST

The Linux kernel has two primitive locking functions, spin_lock and spin_unlock, which are used extensively by device drivers to ensure mutual exclusion. We checked the locking specification from Figure 1(b) on the Linux drivers listed in the top part of Table 1. We modeled the behavior of the kernel using a non-deterministic main function which calls all possible device functions registered with the kernel. Column 2 shows the code size. Column 3 gives the total number of abstraction predicates; the number of active predicates is the maximum number of predicates considered at any one point in the model-checking process. The times are for a 700 MHz Pentium III processor with 256M RAM, and for verification only; in all cases parsing time is less than a second. Column 5 shows the part of verification time spent in counterexample analysis. We found several interprocedural bugs in the locking behavior. For example, we found paths in aha152x.c where a lock can be acquired twice; see also [12]. On the other hand, some correctness proofs use nontrivial data dependencies involving conditional locking (e.g., tlan.c), or unlocking based on some status code (e.g., ide.c), and come up as false positives in [12].

We also ran BLAST on an I/O request packet (IRP) completion specification for several device drivers included in the Microsoft Windows NT DDK[3]; this is shown in the bottom part of Table 1. The Windows OS uses an IRP data structure to communicate with a kernel-mode device driver. The IRP completion specification gives correct ways for Windows device drivers to handle IRPs by specifying a sequence of functions to be called in a certain order, and specific return codes. The entire specification is captured by a safety-monitor automaton with 22 states. To check this specification against some drivers from the DDK, we wrote a model of the rest of the kernel as nondeterministic functions modeling the interface, and we wrote a driver main function that calls the dispatch routines nondeterministically. We found several bugs in the drivers involving incorrect status codes. These bugs were independently confirmed by SLAM [2].

5.3   Experiences with BLAST

We conjecture that the following are the main reasons for the efficiency of the lazy-abstraction algorithm.

1. *Sparse reach set.* While the state space of programs is huge, the set of states that are *reachable* is often very small. Traditional abstraction schemes compute the abstract transition relation for the entire state space. Lazy abstraction, on the other hand, considers only the reachable part of the state space. We believe that this is the single most important advantage of lazy abstraction.
2. *Local structure.* Instead of building a uniform predicate abstraction, the lazy-abstraction algorithm exploits the control-flow structure of the program by using predicates only where required. This ensures that abstract successors

---

[3] Available from http://www.microsoft.com/ddk.

Program	Postprocessed LOC	Predicates		BLAST Time (sec)	Ctrex analysis (sec)	Proof Size (bytes)
		Total	Active			
qpmouse.c	23539	2	2	0.50	0.00	175
ide.c	18131	5	5	4.59	0.01	253
aha152x.c	17736	2	2	20.93	0.00	
tlan.c	16506	5	4	428.63	403.33	405
cdaudio.c	17798	85	45	1398.62	540.96	156787
floppy.c	17386	62	37	2086.35	1565.34	
[fixed]		93	44	395.97	17.46	60129
kbfiltr.c	12131	54	40	64.16	5.89	
		48	35	256.92	165.25	
[fixed]		37	34	10.00	0.38	7619
mouclass.c	17372	57	46	54.46	3.34	
parport.c	61781	193	50	1980.09	519.69	102967

Table 1. Verification times with BLAST. A blank proof size indicates a bug was found.

are computed only to the necessary precision, and recomputed only in parts of the state space where the abstraction changes. Large parts of the state space that are known to be error free are not searched again. This also helps in producing compact proofs.

3. *Cartesian post.* Our experiments show that we can replace the most precise but computationally expensive abstract-postcondition computation [8] by an imprecise one [1, 15], and still prove all properties of interest. This speeds up the computation significantly.[4]

While our running times and proof sizes are encouraging, we feel there is a lot of room for improvement. We are transitioning to an oracle-based representation of proofs [19], which we expect, based on previous experience, to further reduce the size of the proofs by an order of magnitude. The times taken by the counterexample analysis often dominates the verification time. We believe that a faster theorem prover and optimization techniques from program analysis will be useful in speeding up the process.

Acknowledgments. We thank Tom Ball and Sriram Rajamani for many fruitful discussions and for the IRP completion specification. We thank Microsoft Research for hosting R. Majumdar and W. Weimer as summer interns, which gave them the opportunity to learn about SLAM.

References

1. T. Ball, R. Majumdar, T. Millstein, and S.K. Rajamani. Automatic predicate abstraction of C programs. *Conf. Programming Language Design and Implementation*, pp. 203–213. ACM, 2001.

---

[4] For the Windows examples, [8] failed to finish even after 24 hours.

2. T. Ball and S.K. Rajamani. Personal communication.
3. T. Ball and S.K. Rajamani. The SLAM project: debugging system software via static analysis. *Symp. Principles of Programming Languages*, pp. 1–3. ACM, 2002.
4. D. Blei, C. Harrelson, R. Jhala, R. Majumdar, G.C. Necula, S.P. Rahul, W. Weimer, and D. Weitz. *Vampyre: A Proof-generating Theorem Prover*. http://www.eecs.berkeley.edu/~rupak/Vampyre.
5. A. Chou, J. Yang, B. Chelf, S. Hallem, and D. Engler. An empirical study of operating system bugs. *Symp. Operating System Principles*, pp. 78–81. ACM, 2001.
6. E.M. Clarke, O. Grumberg, S. Jha, Y. Lu, and H. Veith. Counterexample-guided abstraction refinement. *Computer-Aided Verification*, LNCS 1855, pp. 154–169. Springer-Verlag, 2000.
7. J. Corbett, M. Dwyer, J. Hatcliff, C. Pasareanu, Robby, S. Laubach, and H. Zheng. Bandera: extracting finite-state models from Java source code. *Int. Conf. Software Engineering*, pp. 439–448. ACM, 2000.
8. S. Das, D. L. Dill, and S. Park. Experience with predicate abstraction. *Computer-Aided Verification*, LNCS 1633, pp. 160–171. Springer-Verlag, 1999.
9. D. Detlefs, G. Nelson, and J. Saxe. *The Simplify Theorem Prover*. http://research.compaq.com/SRC/esc/Simplify.html.
10. E. Dijkstra. *A Discipline of Programming*. Prentice-Hall, 1976.
11. M.D. Ernst. *Dynamically Discovering Likely Program Invariants*. Ph.D. Thesis. University of Washington, Seattle, 2000.
12. J.S. Foster, T. Terauchi, and A. Aiken. Flow sensitive type qualifiers. *Conf. Programming Languages Design and Implementation* (to appear), ACM, 2002.
13. S. Graf and H. Saïdi. Construction of abstract state graphs with PVS. *Computer-Aided Verification*, LNCS 1254, pp. 72–83. Springer-Verlag, 1997.
14. R. Harper, F. Honsell, and G. Plotkin. A framework for defining logics. *Journal of the ACM*, 40:143–184, 1993.
15. T.A. Henzinger, R. Jhala, R. Majumdar, and G. Sutre. Lazy abstraction. *Symp. Principles of Programming Languages*, pp. 58–70. ACM, 2002.
16. G. Holzmann. Logic verification of ANSI-C code with Spin. *SPIN Workshop*, LNCS 1885, pp. 131–147. Springer-Verlag, 2000.
17. K. Namjoshi. Certifying model checkers. *Computer-Aided Verification*, LNCS 2102, pp. 2–13. Springer-Verlag, 2001.
18. G.C. Necula. Proof carrying code. *Symp. Principles of Programming Languages*, pp. 106–119. ACM, 1997.
19. G. Necula and S.P. Rahul. Oracle-based checking of untrusted software. *Symp. Principles of Programming Languages*, pp. 142–154. ACM, 2001.
20. G.C. Necula and P. Lee. Efficient representation and validation of proofs. *Symp. Logic in Computer Science*, pp. 93–104. IEEE Computer Society, 1998.
21. G.C. Necula, S. McPeak, S.P. Rahul, and W. Weimer. CIL: intermediate language and tools for analysis and transformation of C programs. *Compiler Construction*, LNCS 2304, pp. 213–228. Springer-Verlag, 2002.
22. D. Peled and L. Zuck. From model checking to a temporal proof. *SPIN Workshop*, LNCS 2057, pp. 1–14. Springer-Verlag, 2001.
23. F. Pfenning. *Computation and Deduction*. Lecture notes, CMU, 1997.
24. F. Somenzi. *Colorado University Decision Diagram Package*. http://vlsi.colorado.edu/pub.
25. W. Visser, K. Havelund, G. Brat, and S. Park. Model Checking Programs. *Conf. Automated Software Engineering*, pp. 3-12. IEEE, 2000.

Extrapolating Tree Transformations

Ahmed Bouajjani and Tayssir Touili

LIAFA, Univ. of Paris 7, Case 7014, 2 place Jussieu, F-75251 Paris 5, France
{Ahmed.Bouajjani,Tayssir.Touili}@liafa.jussieu.fr

Abstract. We consider the framework of *regular tree model checking* where sets of configurations of a system are represented by regular tree languages and its dynamics is modeled by a term rewriting system (or a regular tree transducer). We focus on the computation of the reachability set $R^*(L)$ where R is a regular tree transducer and L is a regular tree language. The construction of this set is not possible in general. Therefore, we present a general acceleration technique, called *regular tree widening* which allows to speed up the convergence of iterative fixpoint computations in regular tree model checking. This technique can be applied uniformly to various kinds of transformations.

We show the application of our framework to different analysis contexts: verification of parametrized tree networks and data-flow analysis of multithreaded programs. Parametrized networks are modeled by relabeling tree transducers, and multithreaded programs are modeled by term rewriting rules encoding transformations on control structures.

We prove that our widening technique can emulate many existing algorithms for special classes of transformations and we show that it can deal with transformations beyond the scope of these algorithms.

1 Introduction

Regular Model Checking has been proposed as a general and uniform framework for reasoning about infinite-state systems [KMM+97, WB98, BJNT00, Bou01]. In this framework, systems are modeled and analyzed using automata-based symbolic representations: configurations of the system are encoded as words or trees (of arbitrary sizes). This suggests the use of regular finite-state word/tree automata to represent sets of configurations, and the use of regular relations represented as word/tree transducers (or rewriting systems) to model the dynamics of the system, i.e., the transition relation between configurations. Then, verification problems based on performing reachability analysis are reduced to the computation of closures of regular languages under regular word/tree transducers (rewriting systems), i.e., given a regular relation R and a regular language L, compute $R^*(L)$, where R^* is the reflexive-transitive closure of R. A more general problem is to construct a representation of the relation R^* as a finite transducer. This problem is harder than the previous one: there are regular relations having nonregular transitive closures, but under which subclasses of regular languages are effectively closed (see, e.g., [BMT01]). Computing $R^*(L)$ is impossible in general since the transition relation of any Turing machine is a regular word

D. Brinksma and K. G. Larsen (Eds.): CAV 2002, LNCS 2404, pp. 539–554, 2002.
© Springer-Verlag Berlin Heidelberg 2002

transduction. Therefore, the main issue in regular model checking is (1) to determine classes of regular languages L and relations R such that the closure $R^*(L)$ is effectively constructible, and (2) to find accurate and powerful fixpoint acceleration techniques which help the convergence of language closures (reachability analysis) in the general case.

During the last three years, several authors addressed this issue, essentially in the case of Regular Word Model Checking where configurations are encoded as words (see, e.g., [ABJN99, JN00, BJNT00, PS00, DLS01, Tou01]). In this paper, we consider the more general case of Regular Tree Model Checking. Indeed, tree-like structures are very common and appear naturally in many modeling and verification contexts. We consider in this paper two of such contexts: verification of parametrized networks with tree-like topologies, and data flow analysis of multithreaded programs.

Indeed, in the case of parametrized tree networks, labeled trees of arbitrary height represent configurations of networks of arbitrary numbers of processes: each vertex in a tree corresponds to a process, and the label of a vertex is the current control state of its corresponding process. Typically, actions in such parametrized systems are communications between processes and their sons or fathers. These actions correspond in our framework to tree relabeling rules (transformations which preserve the structure of the trees). Examples of such systems are multicast protocols, leader election protocols, mutual exclusion protocols, etc.

In the case of multithreaded programs, trees represent control structures recording the names of the procedures to call, and the sequential/parallel order in which they must be called. These structures are of unbounded sizes and are transformed dynamically after the execution of each action of the program (e.g., recursive call, launching a new thread, etc.). Such actions correspond in our framework to tree transformations represented as tree transductions (or tree rewriting rules). Notice that, in contrast with the previous case (parametrized systems), these tree transformations are not tree relabelings, but transformations which modify the structures of the trees (non structure-preserving transformations).

Therefore, our aim in this work is to provide algorithmic techniques which allow to compute automatically closures of regular tree languages under regular tree transformations, and when possible, to compute transitive closures of regular tree transformations. Moreover, we want to define *general* techniques which can deal with different classes of relations, and which can be applied *uniformly* in many verification and analysis contexts such as those mentioned above.

The main contribution of our work is the definition of a general acceleration technique on tree automata called *regular tree widening*. Our technique, is based on comparing languages (automata) obtained by successive applications of a transformation R to a language L in order to guess automatically the limit $R^*(L)$. The guessing technique we introduce is based on detecting regular growths in the structures of the automata. A test is performed to check automatically whether the guess covers all the reachable configurations, i.e., whether the set $R^*(L)$ is included in the guessed language. The same test ensures in many interesting cases that the guess is exact i.e., that the guessed language is precisely $R^*(L)$. This technique can also be applied in order to compute iteratively transitive closures of relabeling transducers.

We show that the iterative computation of closures enhanced with regular tree widening yields a quite general and accurate reachability analysis procedure which can be applied uniformly to various analysis problems. We illustrate this by showing the application of this procedure to the analysis of parametrized systems and to the analysis of multithreaded programs. Moreover, we prove that this procedure is powerful and accurate enough to compute precisely the reachability sets for many significant classes of systems, covering several classes for which there exist different specialized algorithms.

First, we consider the case of parametrized networks. We consider a particular class of models based on term rewriting systems called *Well-Oriented Systems*. These models correspond to systems where, typically, informations are exchanged between a set of processes (the leaves of the tree) and another process (the root of the tree) through a tree-like network, assuming that the state of each process is modified after the transmission of a message (this correspond for instance to the fact that paths followed by messages are marked, messages are memorized by routers, etc.). We assume moreover that the system has a finite number of ascending and descending phases. These assumptions are quite realistic and many protocols and parallel algorithms running on tree-like topologies (e.g., leader election protocols, mutual exclusion protocols, parallel boolean algorithms, etc.) have these features (for instance, requests are generated by leaves and go up to the root, and then answers or acknowledgements are generated by the root and go down to leaves following some marked paths).

We prove that for every well-oriented system, the transitive closure is regular and we provide a transducer characterizing this closure. Then, we prove that our widening techniques can simulate the direct construction we provide for well-oriented system.

Then, we address the issue of analyzing multithreaded programs using regular tree model checking. We consider programs with recursive calls, dynamic creation of processes, and communication. We adopt the approach advocated in [EK99] which consists in reducing data flow analysis to reachability analysis problems for Process Rewriting Systems (PRS) [May98]. Programs are described as term rewriting rules of the form $t \rightarrow t'$ where t and t' are terms built up from process variables, sequential composition, and asynchronous parallel composition.

We give a construction of a tree automaton recognizing the set of immediate successors/predecessors of any regular tree language by a PRS transition, and then, the reachability sets of PRSs can be computed iteratively using regular tree widening. We illustrate our approach on the example of a concurrent server which can launch an unbounded number of threads.

Then, we show that our techniques are at least as general as the known algorithms in this context. Namely, we show that reachability analysis with regular tree widening terminates and computes precisely the sets of forward/backward reachable configurations in the case of PA rewriting systems (when all the left-hand-sides of the rules are process variables). Hence, our techniques cover the case considered in [LS98, EP00] and can handle programs which are beyond the scope of these algorithms (e.g., the concurrent server). Actually, we prove a more general result. We prove that our procedure terminates and computes the exact reachability set (at least in the case) of any PRS R such that R or R^{-1} is Noetherian. This is for instance the case of the concurrent server. The completeness result for PA follows from the fact that we can transform any PA into an equivalent one which has this property.

For lack of space we omit the details and refer to the full version of this paper [BT02].

Related Work: The idea of widening operation is inspired by works in the domain of abstract interpretation [CC77] where it is mainly used for systems with numerical data domains (integer or reals) [CH78]. There are numerous works on tree-like representations of program configurations or schemes. Probably the first work using tree automata and tree transducers for symbolic reachability analysis of systems (especially parametrized systems) is [KMM+97]. However, no acceleration techniques are provided in that work. In [LS98, EP00], tree automata are used for symbolic reachability analysis of PA processes and its applications in model-checking and static analysis of programs. Works on acceleration techniques for regular model checking concern mainly the case of word automata and transducers [ABJN99, JN00, BJNT00, PS00, Tou01]. Our regular tree widening technique is an extension of the widening techniques for word automata defined in [BJNT00, Tou01]. In [DLS01], techniques are presented for computing transitive closures for tree transducers, but no completeness results are provided. The problem of finding subclasses of term rewriting systems (tree transducers) which effectively preserve regularity has also been considered in the automata-theory community by several authors (see, e.g., [GT95] where it is proved that ground tree rewrite systems preserve regularity).

2   Preliminaries

2.1   Trees and Terms

An alphabet Σ is ranked if it is endowed with a mapping $rank : \Sigma \to \mathbb{N}$. For $k \geq 0$, Σ_k is the set of elements of rank k. The elements of Σ_0 are called constants. Let $\mathcal{X}$ be a denumerable set of symbols called variables. Let $T_\Sigma[\mathcal{X}]$ denote the set of terms over Σ and $\mathcal{X}$. T_Σ will stand for $T_\Sigma[\emptyset]$. Terms in T_Σ are called *ground terms*. A term in $T_\Sigma[\mathcal{X}]$ is *linear* if each variable occurs at most once.

As usual, a term in $T_\Sigma[\mathcal{X}]$ can be viewed as a rooted labeled tree where an internal node with n sons is labeled by a symbol from Σ_n, and the leaves are labeled with variables and constants.

Definition 1. *A **bottom-up tree automaton** (we shall omit 'bottom-up') is a tuple $\mathcal{A} = (Q, \Sigma, F, \delta)$ where Q is a finite set of states, Σ is a ranked alphabet, $F \subseteq Q$ is a set of final states, and δ is a set of rules of the form*

$$f(q_1, \ldots, q_n) \to_\delta q \tag{1}$$
$$a \to_\delta q \tag{2}$$
$$q \to_\delta q' \tag{3}$$

where $a \in \Sigma_0$, $n \geq 1$, $f \in \Sigma_n$, and $q_1, \ldots, q_n, q, q' \in Q$.

Let t be a ground term. A run of $\mathcal{A}$ on t can be done in a bottom-up manner as follows: first, we assign a state to each leaf according to the rules (2), then for each node, we must collect the states assigned to all its children and then associate a state to the node itself according to the rules (1). Formally, if during the state assignment process the subterms $t_1, \ldots, t_n$ are labeled with states $q_1, \ldots, q_n$, and if the rule $f(q_1, \ldots, q_n) \to_\delta q$ is in δ then the term $f(t_1, \ldots, t_n)$ is labeled with q. A term t is accepted if $\mathcal{A}$ reaches the root of t in a final state.

The language accepted by the automaton $\mathcal{A}$ is the set of ground terms that it accepts: $\mathcal{L}(\mathcal{A}) = \bigcup_{q \in F} L_q$.

Definition 2. *A **bottom-up tree transducer** (we shall omit 'bottom-up') is a tuple $\mathcal{T} = (Q, \Sigma, \Sigma', F, \delta)$ where Q is a finite set of states, Σ and Σ' (the sets of input and output symbols) are ranked alphabets, $F \subseteq Q$ is a set of final states, and δ is a set of rules of the form:*

$$f(q_1(x_1), \ldots, q_n(x_n)) \to_\delta q(u), u \in T_{\Sigma'}[\{x_1, \ldots, x_n\}] \tag{4}$$
$$q(x) \to_\delta q'(u), u \in T_{\Sigma'}[\{x\}] \tag{5}$$
$$a \to_\delta q(u), u \in T_{\Sigma'} \tag{6}$$

where $a \in \Sigma_0$, $n \geq 1$, $f \in \Sigma_n$, $x, x_1, \ldots, x_n \in \mathcal{X}$, and $q_1, \ldots, q_n, q, q' \in Q$.

Given an input term t, $\mathcal{T}$ proceeds as previously: it begins by replacing some leaves according to the rules (6). For instance, if a leaf is labeled a and the rule $a \to_\delta q(u)$ is in δ, then a is replaced by $q(u)$. The substitution proceeds then towards the root. If the rule $f(q_1(x_1), \ldots, q_n(x_n)) \to_\delta q(u)$ is in δ, then $\mathcal{T}$ replaces an occurrence of a subtree $f(q_1(t_1), \ldots, q_n(t_n))$ by the term $q(u[x_1 \leftarrow t_1, \ldots, x_n \leftarrow t_n])$, where each occurrence of the variable x_i in t is replaced by t_i. The computation continues until the root of t is reached.

The transducer $\mathcal{T}$ defines the following *regular* relation between trees $R_\mathcal{T} = \{(t, t') \in T_\Sigma \times T_{\Sigma'} \mid t \xrightarrow{*}_\delta q(t')$, for some $q \in F\}$. We denote by $R_\mathcal{T}^n$ the composition of $R_\mathcal{T}$, n times. As usual, $R_\mathcal{T}^* = \bigcup_{n \geq 0} R_\mathcal{T}^n$ denotes the reflexive-transitive closure of $R_\mathcal{T}$.

Let $L \subseteq T_\Sigma$ be a tree language. Then, we define the set $\mathcal{R}_\mathcal{T}(L) = \{t' \in \Sigma' \mid \exists t \in L, (t, t') \in R_\mathcal{T}\}$.

Definition 3. *A transducer is* **linear** *if all the right hand sides of its rules are linear (no variable occurs more than once).*

We restrict ourselves to linear tree transducers since they are closed under composition whereas general transducers are not [Eng75, CDG+97].

Proposition 1. *Let T be a linear tree transducer and $\mathcal{L}$ be a regular tree language. Then, $R_T(\mathcal{L})$ and $R_T^{-1}(\mathcal{L})$ are regular and effectively constructible.*

Particular cases of linear transducer are *relabeling tree transducers*.

Definition 4. *A transducer is called a* **relabeling** *if all its rules are of the form*

$$f\big(q_1(x_1),\ldots,q_n(x_n)\big) \rightarrow_\delta q\big(g(x_1,\ldots,x_n)\big) \tag{7}$$

$$a \rightarrow_\delta q(b) \tag{8}$$

$$q(x) \rightarrow_\delta q'(x) \tag{9}$$

where $f, g \in \Sigma_n$ and $a, b \in \Sigma_0$.

Notice that relabeling tree transducers preserve the structure of the input tree. A relabeling $(Q, \Sigma, \Sigma', F, \delta)$ can be seen as a tree automaton over the product alphabet $\Sigma \times \Sigma'$. The rules (7) can then be written $f/g(q_1,\ldots,q_n) \rightarrow q$, the rules (8) can be written $a/b \rightarrow q$, and the rules (9) can be written $q \rightarrow q'$.

2.2   Tree Automata and Hypergraphs

Definition 5. *Let V be a set of vertices and Σ be a ranked alphabet. Let $f \in \Sigma_n$ and $v, v_1, \ldots, v_n \in V$, the tuple $(v, f, v_1, \ldots, v_n)$ is a* **hyperedge** *labeled by f and connecting in order v to the vertices $v_1, \ldots, v_n$. We will write $v \xrightarrow{f} v_1, \ldots, v_n$ for every hyperedge $(v, f, v_1, \ldots, v_n)$, or just $v \xrightarrow{a}$ if $a \in \Sigma_0$. A* **hypergraph** *is a pair $\mathcal{G} = (V, H)$ where V is a set of vertices and H a set of hyperedges on V.*

Given a bottom-up tree automaton $\mathcal{A} = (Q, \Sigma, F, \delta)$, the transition relation δ can be represented by the hypergraph $\mathcal{G}_\delta = (Q, H_\delta)$, where H_δ is defined by:

- $q \xrightarrow{f}_\delta q_1, \ldots, q_n \in H_\delta$ for every rule $f(q_1,\ldots,q_n) \rightarrow_\delta q$.
- $q \xrightarrow{a}_\delta \in H_\delta$ for every initial rule $a \rightarrow_\delta q$.
- $q \rightarrow_\delta q' \in H_\delta$ for every rule $q \rightarrow_\delta q'$.

All operations on tree automata can be defined on hypergraphs. In the remainder of the paper, a tree automaton (tree relabeling transducer) will be represented by a pair $(\mathcal{G}, F)$, where $\mathcal{G}$ is the hypergraph that represents its transition relation and F is the set of final states.

3   Widening Techniques on Tree Automata

We define hereafter an extrapolation technique on tree automata called *regular tree widening* which allows to compute the limit of a sequence of tree sets obtained by iterating tree transformations.

3.1   Principle

The technique we present generalizes the one we have introduced in [BJNT00, Tou01] in the case of word automata. The principle proposed in these previous works is based on the detection of growths during the iterative computation of the sequence $L, R(L), R^2(L), \ldots$, in order to guess $R^*(L)$. For instance, if the situation $L = L_1 L_2$ and $R(L) = L_1 \Delta L_2$ occurs, then we guess that iterating R will produce $L_1 \Delta^* L_2$. In some cases, it is possible to decide whether our guess is correct. Here, we extend this principle to the case of tree languages. The detection of growths is performed on the hypergraph structures of the tree automata recognizing the computed sequence of languages.

Definition 6. *Let $\mathcal{G} = (V, H)$ be a hypergraph and $F \subseteq V$ be a set of accepting vertices. Then, a **hypergraph bisimulation** is a symmetrical binary relation $\rho \subseteq V \times V$ such that, for every $v, v' \in V$, $(v, v') \in \rho$ iff*

- *$v \in F$ iff $v' \in F$,*
- *for every hyperedge $v \xrightarrow{f} v_1, \ldots, v_n \in H$, there exists a hyperedge $v' \xrightarrow{f} v'_1, \ldots, v'_n \in H$ such that, for every $i \in \{1, \ldots, n\}$, $(v_i, v'_i) \in \rho$. We write $v \sim v'$ if there exists a hypergraph bisimulation relating v and v'.*

Given two tree automata $\mathcal{A} = (\mathcal{G}, F)$ and $\mathcal{A}' = (\mathcal{G}', F')$, we write $\mathcal{A} \sim \mathcal{A}'$ iff every vertex in F is bisimilar to a vertex in F' and vice versa.

Definition 7. *Suppose that we are given:*

- *a sub-hypergraph of $\mathcal{G}$: $\Delta = (V_\Delta, H_\Delta)$ ($V_\Delta \subseteq V$, and $H_\Delta \subseteq H$),*
- *two subsets of V_Δ: $\mathcal{I}_\Delta$ and $\mathcal{O}_\Delta$ called entry and exit vertices,*
- *φ: a partition of $\mathcal{I}_\Delta \cup \mathcal{O}_\Delta$.*

Let $\sim_\varphi$ denote the equivalence relation induced by φ. We assume moreover that $(\sim_\varphi \cap \, \mathcal{O}_\Delta \times \mathcal{O}_\Delta) \subseteq \sim$ (i.e., non bisimilar exit vertices are not $\sim_\varphi$-equivalent). Then, we define two hypergraphs $\mathcal{G}\backslash_\varphi \Delta$ and $\mathcal{G}[\Delta \leftarrow \Delta^+]$ as follows:

- *$\mathcal{G}\backslash_\varphi \Delta$ is the hypergraph (V', H') such that*
    - *$V' = V\backslash V_\Delta \cup \{[v]_\varphi \mid v \in \mathcal{I}_\Delta \cup \mathcal{O}_\Delta\}$ and*
    - *$H' = H\backslash H_\Delta \cup \{v'_0 \xrightarrow{f} v'_1, \ldots, v'_n \mid v_0 \xrightarrow{f} v_1, \ldots, v_n \in H\backslash H_\Delta$ and if $v_i \in \mathcal{I}_\Delta \cup \mathcal{O}_\Delta$ then $v'_i = [v_i]_\varphi$, otherwise $v'_i = v_i\}$*
    where $[v]_\varphi$ denotes the $\sim_\varphi$-equivalence class of the vertex v. Intuitively, $\mathcal{G}\backslash_\varphi \Delta$ is the hypergraph obtained from $\mathcal{G}$ by removing all hyperedges in Δ, and collapsing $\sim_\varphi$-equivalent vertices.
- *$\mathcal{G}[\Delta \leftarrow \Delta^+]$ is the hypergraph (V, H'') where:*
    $H'' = H \cup \{v_0 \xrightarrow{f} v'_1, \ldots, v'_n \mid v_0 \xrightarrow{f} v_1, \ldots, v_n \in \Delta$ and $\forall i$, if $v_i \in \mathcal{O}_\Delta$ then $v'_i \in [v_i]_\varphi \cap \mathcal{I}_\Delta$, otherwise $v'_i = v_i\}$.
    Intuitively, $\mathcal{G}[\Delta \leftarrow \Delta^+]$ is obtained by adding loops allowing to iterate Δ (by going back to entry vertices).

Now, we are able to define the *regular widening* operation on tree automata:

Definition 8 (Regular tree widening). *Let $\mathcal{A} = (\mathcal{G}, F)$ and $\mathcal{A}' = (\mathcal{G}', F')$ be two tree automata. Then, given a sub-hypergraph Δ of $\mathcal{G}'$, sets of entry and exit vertices $\mathcal{I}_\Delta$ and $\mathcal{O}_\Delta$, and a partition φ of $\mathcal{I}_\Delta \cup \mathcal{O}_\Delta$ such that $(\sim_\varphi \cap\, \mathcal{O}_\Delta \times \mathcal{O}_\Delta) \subseteq \sim$, if*

$$(\mathcal{G}, F) \sim (\mathcal{G}' \setminus_\varphi \Delta, F') \tag{10}$$

then we define $\nabla(\mathcal{A}, \mathcal{A}', \Delta, \varphi) = (\mathcal{G}'[\Delta \leftarrow \Delta^+], F')$.

Notice that the same widening principle can be applied in the case of relabeling tree transducers (in order to compute iteratively transitive closures of relabeling transducers).

Example 1. Consider the following term rewriting rule: $R = a \rightarrow f(a, b)$ and assume we want to compute $R^*(a)$. Let $(\mathcal{G}_0, \{q_0\})$, $(\mathcal{G}_1, \{q_2\})$, and $(\mathcal{G}_2, \{q_3\})$ be tree automata recognizing a, $R(a)$, and $R^2(a)$. Their corresponding hypergraphs are depicted in Figure 1.

By comparing $\mathcal{G}_1$ and $\mathcal{G}_2$, we detect a widening situation where Δ is the hypergraph $(\{q_1, q_2, q_3\}, \{q_3 \xrightarrow{f} q_2, q_1\})$, $\mathcal{I}_\Delta = \{q_3\}$, $\mathcal{O}_\Delta = \{q_1, q_2\}$, and $\varphi = \{\{q_1\}, \{q_2, q_3\}\}$. Then, the widening operator ∇ yields an automaton $(\mathcal{G}, \{q_3\})$ obtained by adding the loop drawn by thick lines to $\mathcal{G}_2$. This automaton defines precisely $R^{\geq 3}(a)$ (its union with the automata of the previous steps corresponds to $R^*(a)$).

Performing a widening operation requires finding a widening situation, i.e., a subgraph Δ and a partition φ satisfying the condition (10).

Proposition 2. *The problem of finding widening situations is NP-complete.*

The detection of candidates Δ can be done effectively by performing a product between the two compared hypergraphs $\mathcal{G}$ and $\mathcal{G}'$, and guessing nondeterministically the entries and the exits of Δ. Efficient (but uncomplete) strategies can be adopted in order to reduce nondeterminism (the number of candidates Δ).

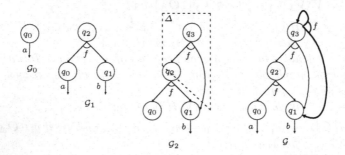

Fig. 1. Illustration of the regular tree widening mechanism

3.2   Exact Widening

We give hereafter a test which allows for some relations R to check automatically whether a widening operation computes the *exact* reachability set $R^*(L)$.

Definition 9. *A relation R is nœtherian if there is no infinite sequence of terms $t_0, t_1, \ldots$ such that for every $i \geq 0$, $(t_i, t_{i+1}) \in R$.*

Proposition 3. *If R or R^{-1} is nœtherian then $L' = R^*(L)$ iff*

$$L' = R(L') \cup L \tag{11}$$

Proof: In [FO97], a proof for the case where R^{-1} is nœtherian is given. The proof for the other case can be found in the full paper.   □

Therefore, when R or R^{-1} is nœtherian, we can use our widening technique to generate automatically closure candidates, and use the test (11) to check automatically that a candidate is indeed equal to $R^*(L)$.

4   Parametrized Networks with Tree-Like Topologies

We show the application of regular tree model checking in the analysis of parametrized networks of identical processes arranged in a tree-like topology.

We model such systems by relabeling tree transducers. Indeed, the set of configurations of a parametrized tree network can be represented by a set of trees (of arbitrary size) where nodes correspond to control location of processes, and therefore, actions in the network can be seen as transformations which modify the labels in the trees.

Then, given a set of initial configurations represented by a finite tree automaton $\mathcal{A}$ and a finite tree transducer $\mathcal{T}$ representing the dynamics in the network, we can apply reachability analysis with regular widening in order to compute (an upper-approximation of) the set of reachable configurations $\mathcal{T}^*(\mathcal{A})$. We can also apply the same procedure in order to compute a finite transducer corresponding to the transitive closure of $\mathcal{T}$.

4.1   Example : Parallel OR Algorithm

To illustrate our approach, we show the example of a parallel boolean program, called PERCOLATE [KMMt97], which computes the OR of a set of boolean values: we consider an arbitrary number of processes arranged in a binary tree architecture. Each process has a variable *val* ranging over $\{0, 1, \bot\}$. Initially, all the leaves have *val* $\in \{0, 1\}$, and all the others have *val* $= \bot$. The purpose of the program is to percolate to the root the value 1 if at least one of the leaves has *val* $= 1$. A transition of the system consists in assigning 1 to a node if one of its children has $val = 1$, and 0 otherwise. This corresponds to the term rewriting system $R_{percolate}$ given by the following rewriting rules:

$$\bot(1(x_1, x_2), 1(x_3, x_4)) \to 1(1(x_1, x_2), 1(x_3, x_4))$$
$$\bot(1(x_1, x_2), 0(x_3, x_4)) \to 1(1(x_1, x_2), 0(x_3, x_4))$$
$$\bot(0(x_1, x_2), 1(x_3, x_4)) \to 1(0(x_1, x_2), 1(x_3, x_4))$$
$$\bot(0(x_1, x_2), 0(x_3, x_4)) \to 0(0(x_1, x_2), 0(x_3, x_4))$$

The property to check is that the root is labeled by 1 if and only if at least one of the leaves is labeled by 1. This property can be represented by a regular tree automaton. Hence, we can check the satisfaction of this property if we are able to compute the set of reachable configurations in the system.

Actually, our approach allows to construct automatically the transitive closure of $R_{percolate}$ after two iterations (see Theorems 1 and 2).

4.2 Well-Oriented Systems

We prove hereafter that with our widening techniques reachability analysis terminates and computes exactly the transitive closure of (at least) a kind of relabeling transducers, called *Well-Oriented Systems*, which correspond to a significant class of parametrized networks.

It can be observed that many protocols and parallel algorithms which are defined on networks with a tree-like topology satisfy the following features: (1) informations go from leaves upward to the root and vice versa, which means that each node communicates directly either with its children or with its father, (2) there is a finite number of alternating phases of upward and downward information propagation (e.g., requests are sent by leaves, and then answers are sent by the root, and son on), (3) the state of each process is modified after each transmission of information, i.e., at each phase, when a node of the network is crossed, it is marked by a new label. This corresponds for instance to marking paths, memorizing sent messages, etc.

We introduce a model to describe the dynamics of such parametrized tree networks which consists of term rewriting systems called *well-oriented systems*. To simplify the presentation, we shall restrict ourselves in this section to binary trees, the general case is similar.

Definition 10. *Let $S = S_0 \cup S_1 \cup \cdots \cup S_n$, where the S_i's are disjoint finite sets of symbols. We denote by $S_{\leq i}$ the set $\bigcup \{S_j \mid j \leq i\}$.*

A n-phase well-oriented system (n-phase WOS) over S is a set of rewriting rules of the form:

$$b(a(x_1, x_2), c_1(x_3, x_4)) \to a(b'(x_1, x_2), c_1(x_3, x_4)) \tag{12}$$
$$a(b(x_1, x_2), c_2(x_3, x_4)) \to b'(a(x_1, x_2), c_2(x_3, x_4)) \tag{13}$$
$$a(b(x_1, x_2), c_2(x_3, x_4)) \to b'(a(x_1, x_2), a(x_3, x_4)) \tag{14}$$
$$b \to d \tag{15}$$

$$b(a(x_1, x_2), c_1(x_3, x_4)) \rightarrow d(a(x_1, x_2), c_1(x_3, x_4)) \tag{16}$$

$$a(b(x_1, x_2), c_2(x_3, x_4)) \rightarrow a(d(x_1, x_2), c_2(x_3, x_4)) \tag{17}$$

$$a(b(x_1, x_2), c_2(x_3, x_4)) \rightarrow a(d(x_1, x_2), d(x_3, x_4)) \tag{18}$$

as well as the symmetrical forms of these rules obtained by commuting the children, where $a, b' \in S_{i+1}$, $b \in S_i$, $d \in S_{i+2}$, $c_1 \in S_{\leq i+1}$, *and* $c_2 \in S_{\leq i}$, *such that* $0 \leq i \leq n-1$ *for the rules (12), (13), and (14), and* $0 \leq i \leq n-2$ *for the last rules.*

In the definition above, the variables x_1, x_2, x_3 and x_4 represent the subtrees hanging under the nodes a and c_1 in the rules (12) and (16), and b and c_2 in the other rules.

Intuitively, a rule (12) corresponds to the upward propagation of a. When a crosses b, it takes its place and labels its old place with b' in order to mark its path. Similarly, a rule (13) corresponds to the downward propagation of a, and a rule (14) corresponds to the broadcasting of a. Finally, the four last rules allow to pass from one phase to the next one. More precisely, the rule (15) corresponds to a nonconditionnal passage, and the rules (16) (resp. (17) and (18)) to a conditionnal passage towards a descending (resp. an ascending) phase.

Several examples can be modeled using well-oriented systems. For instance, the system $R_{percolate}$ given above is a 1-phase WOS where $S_0 = \{\perp\}$, and $S_1 = \{0, 1\}$. Other examples such as the *Parity Tree* [CGJ95] and the *asynchronous tree arbiter* mutual exclusion protocol [ABH⁺97] can be found in the full version of the paper [BT02].

4.3 Analyzing Well-Oriented Systems

In order to prove that regular widening allows to construct transitive closures of WOSs, we give first a direct construction of these transitive closures, and show that regular widening can simulate this construction.

Theorem 1. *Let R be a well-oriented system, then R^* is regular and effectively representable by a tree transducer.*

Proof (Sketch): Let R be a n-phase well-oriented system. Let us denote by $R_{i+1}^{\uparrow}$ (resp. $R_{i+1}^{\downarrow}$) the set of rules of the form (12) (resp. the set of rules of the form (13) and (14)) corresponding to the upward (resp. downward) propagation of the letters a of S_{i+1}.

We let $R_i = R_i^{\uparrow} \cup R_i^{\downarrow}$ for every $1 \leq i \leq n$. The set R_i corresponds to the phase i of the system since its rules propagate the letters of S_i. Finally, the rules (15), (16), (17), and (18) are called $R_{i+1 \rightarrow i+2}$ (they correspond to the passage from the phase $i+1$ to the phase $i+2$, i.e., from the propagation of the symbols of S_{i+1} to the propagation of the symbols of S_{i+2}).

The main observation is that the application of the previous rules always increases the index of the label of any node in the tree. This property together with the fact that c_1 and c_2 are in $S_{\leq i+1}$ ensure that the phase $i+1$ ($a \in$

$\mathcal{S}_{i+1}$) depends only on the earlier phases $j \leq i+1$. Therefore, it is easy to see that $R^* = R_n^* \circ R_{n-1 \to n}^* \circ R_{n-1}^* \circ \cdots \circ R_{1 \to 2}^* \circ R_1^*$. Moreover, the fact that $c_2 \in \mathcal{S}_{\leq i}$ ensures that during the phase $i+1$, there is no interaction between the ascending rules $R_{i+1}^\uparrow$ and the descending ones $R_{i+1}^\downarrow$. This infers that $R_i^* = (R_i^\uparrow)^* \circ (R_i^\downarrow)^*$. Then, the proof consists in giving direct constructions of the transducers $(R_i^\uparrow)^*$, $(R_i^\downarrow)^*$, and $R_{i \to i+1}^*$ for every $1 \leq i \leq n$ (see [BT02] for details).

□

We show also that regular tree widening is able to compute the transitive closure of any well-oriented system (it can emulate the construction given above).

Theorem 2. *Let R be a well-oriented system, then a tree transducer that represents R^* can be computed using regular tree widening.*

5   Multithreaded Programs as Process Rewrite Systems

We show in this section the application of regular tree model checking in the analysis of multithreaded programs modeled as term rewriting systems. We consider here multithreaded programs with recursive calls, dynamic creation of parallel processes, and communication. These programs are modeled by *Process Rewrite Systems* [May98].

5.1   Process Rewrite Systems

Let $Act = \{a, b, c, \ldots\}$ be a set of actions, $Var = \{X, Y, \ldots\}$ be a set of process variables, and T_p be the set of process terms t defined by the following syntax:

$$t ::= 0 \mid X \mid t \cdot t \mid t \| t$$

Intuitively, "0" is the null process, "·" (resp. "$\|$") denotes sequential composition (resp. parallel composition).

Definition 11 ([May98]). *A* Process Rewriting System *(PRS for short) is a finite set of rules R of the form $t_1 \xrightarrow{a} t_2$, where $t_1, t_2 \in T_p$ and $a \in Act$. A PA declaration is a PRS where all the rules have the form $X \xrightarrow{a} t$.*

A PRS induces a transition relation $\xrightarrow{a}_R$ over T_p defined by:

$$\frac{t_1 \xrightarrow{a} t_2 \in R}{t_1 \xrightarrow{a}_R t_2} \; ; \quad \frac{t_1 \xrightarrow{a}_R t_1'}{t_1 \| t_2 \xrightarrow{a}_R t_1' \| t_2} \; ; \quad \frac{t_1 \xrightarrow{a}_R t_1'}{t_1 . t_2 \xrightarrow{a}_R t_1' . t_2} \; ;$$

$$\frac{t_2 \xrightarrow{a}_R t_2'}{t_1 \| t_2 \xrightarrow{a}_R t_1 \| t_2'} \; ; \quad \frac{t_2 \xrightarrow{a}_R t_2'}{t_1 . t_2 \xrightarrow{a}_R t_1 . t_2'} (t_1 \approx 0)$$

where $t \approx 0$ means that t is a terminated process.

5.2   Example: A Concurrent Server

The JAVA code below corresponds to a typical concurrent server who launches a new thread to deal with each new client request. The number of launched threads is unbounded.

```java
public void server() {
    Socket socket;
    while(true) {
        try{
            socket=serverSocket.accept();
        } catch (Exception e){
            System.err(e);
            continue;
        }
        Thread t=new thread(runnableService(socket));
        t.start();
    }
}
```

Let us model this program by a PRS system. An instance of the procedure server() is represented by the process variable X, the instruction try is represented by the variable Y, and an instance of t.start() is represented by the variable Z. The variables T and F correspond to the booleans true and false meaning that the try instruction (represented by Y) succeeded or failed, respectively. The program is modeled by the following PRS rules:

- $R_1 = X \rightarrow Y.X$ (the procedure starts by executing Y),
- $R_2 = Y \rightarrow T$ (Y returns true),
- $R_3 = Y \rightarrow F$ (Y returns false),
- $R_4 = T.X \rightarrow X \| Z$ (if Y returns true, then a new thread is launched),
- $R_5 = F \rightarrow 0$ (otherwise, the request is ignored after failure).

5.3   Reachability Analysis of PRSs

PRS terms can be naturally represented as trees. Indeed, the set T_p can be seen as T_Σ where $\Sigma_0 = \{0\} \cup Var$ and $\Sigma_2 = \{\cdot, \|\}$. Thus, we can use finite tree automata to represent regular sets of PRS configurations. Therefore, we can apply regular tree model checking to perform reachability analysis of PRSs. We use iterative computation of reachable configurations enhanced with regular tree widening steps.

As in [LS98, EP00], we do not take into account the structural equivalence between terms defined by the properties of neutrality of 0 w.r.t. "$\cdot$ and "$\|$", associativity and commutativity of "$\|$", and associativity of "$\cdot$". Indeed, introducing this equivalence makes the set of reachable configurations nonregular [LS98]. Moreover, since terms represent program control structures, it may be legitimate to ignore structural equivalence since for instance informations about the hierarchy between procedures are lost when reasoning modulo associativity.

We prove that when applied to PA systems, our widening technique yields the termination of forward and backward reachability analysis and produces the exact sets of all reachable successors and predecessors. Moreover, we prove that our technique is applicable beyond the PA case (e.g., for the server above). Furthermore, we prove that our technique allows to construct the exact reachability set for each PRS system R such that R or R^{-1} is Noetherian. For instance, it can be seen that the system corresponding to the concurrent server defined in Section 5.2 is such that R^{-1} is Noetherian. Then, the completeness result concerning PA follows from the fact that we can transform any PA system to an equivalent one having this property.

Theorem 3. *For every PRS system R, and every regular tree language L, $R^*(L)$ is effectively computable using regular tree widening, provided that we are given a test that checks whether some language is equal to $R^*(L)$.*

An immediate consequence of this theorem is:

Corollary 1. *For every PRS system R, if R or R^{-1} is nœtherian then for every regular tree language L, the sets $R^*(L)$ and $(R^{-1})^*(L)$ are effectively computable using regular tree widening.*

Theorem 4. *For every PA system R, and every regular tree language L, the sets $R^*(L)$ and $(R^{-1})^*(L)$ are effectively computable using regular tree widening.*

Let us mention that Theorem 3 holds also for the class of *ground term rewrite* (GTR) systems which is known to preserve regularity [GT95]. Actually, PRS systems are sets of *ground* term rewriting rules (contrary to, e.g., WOSs used to model parametrized systems in Section 4.2). However, semantically, PRSs are not standard GTR systems due to the semantics of the operator "·" which imposes a particular rewriting strategy on the trees. To establish our results for this class, we proceed as for PRS: we provide a new direct construction of the reachability sets and we show that the widening technique allow to simulate this construction. The direct construction we provide constitutes an alternative and actually simpler proof of the result in [GT95].

6   Conclusion

We have defined a general framework for reasoning about many kinds of infinite-state systems. Indeed trees are very common data structures and can be used to encode configurations of many classes of systems.

In this paper we have considered the case of parametrized tree networks and the case of multithreaded programs modeled as transformers of tree control structures. Of course many other cases can be considered since we can consider all systems modeled as term rewriting systems, e.g., systems manipulating abstract data types, logic programs, process calculi, etc. In particular, our algorithmic techniques could be applied in the analysis of cryptographic protocols following the approach in [Mon02, GL00, CCM01] where such systems are represented as term rewriting systems and sets of configurations of such protocols are represented by means of tree automata.

We have defined an acceleration technique (regular tree widening) based on detecting regular growths in sequences of tree sets. Hence, this technique can be applied uniformly regardless from the class of tree transformations since it is based on comparing hypergraph structures of tree automata. In particular, it can be used for structure-preserving as well as for non structure-preserving transformations. We have also shown that this technique is accurate and powerful enough to emulate existing specialized algorithms for symbolic reachability analysis (such as the one for PA systems). In [Tou01], it has already been shown that regular *word* widening (defined on word automata) can simulate existing constructions such as those in [ABJN99, BMT01]. We can actually show that regular widening simulates many other constructions such as, e.g., those in [BEM97, ABJ98] concerning pushdown systems and lossy fifo-channel systems.

Finally, the widening principle we have defined here on trees can be extended easily to graphs using graph grammars. This would allow to deal with systems having more complex control or data structures. However, the problem is then to determine a class of graph grammars having nice closure and decision properties, which can be used as symbolic representation structures.

References

[ABH+97]   Rajeev Alur, Robert K. Brayton, Thomas A. Henzinger, Shaz Qadeer, and Sriram K. Rajamani. Partial-order reduction in symbolic state space exploration. In *Computer Aided Verification*, pages 340–351, 1997. 549

[ABJ98]   P. Abdulla, A. Bouajjani, and B. Jonsson. On-the-fly Analysis of Systems with Unbounded, Lossy Fifo Channels. In *CAV'98*. LNCS 1427, 1998. 553

[ABJN99]   P. A. Abdulla, A. Bouajjani, B. Jonsson, and M. Nilsson. Handling global conditions in parametrized system verification. *Lecture Notes in Computer Science*, 1633:134–150, 1999. 540, 542, 553

[BEM97]   A. Bouajjani, J. Esparza, and O. Maler. Reachability Analysis of Pushdown Automata: Application to Model Checking. In *CONCUR'97*. LNCS 1243, 1997. 553

[BJNT00]   A. Bouajjani, B. Jonsson, M. Nilsson, and T. Touili. Regular model checking. In *CAV'00*. LNCS, 2000. 539, 540, 542, 545

[BMT01]   A. Bouajjani, A. Muscholl, and T. Touili. Permutation Rewriting and Algorithmic Verification. In *LICS'01*. IEEE, 2001. 539, 553

[Bou01]   A. Bouajjani. Languages, Rewriting systems, and Verification of Infinte-State Systems. In *ICALP'01*. LNCS 2076, 2001. invited paper. 539

[BT02]   A. Bouajjani and T. Touili. Extrapolating tree transformations. Technical report, LIAFA, May 2002. http://verif.liafa.jussieu.fr/~touili. 542, 549, 550

[CC77]   P. Cousot and R. Cousot. Static Determination of Dynamic Properties of Recursive Procedures. In *IFIP Conf. on Formal Description of Programming Concepts*. North-Holland Pub., 1977. 542

[CCM01]   H. Comon, V. Cortier, and J. Mitchell. Tree automata with one memory, set constraints and ping-pong protocols. In *ICALP'2001*. LNCS 2076, 2001. 553

[CDG⁺97]   H. Comon, M. Dauchet, R. Gilleron, F. Jacquemard, D. Lugiez, S. Tison, and M. Tommasi. Tree automata techniques and applications. Available on: http://www.grappa.univ-lille3.fr/tata, 1997. 544

[CGJ95]   E. M. Clarke, O. Grumberg, and S. Jha. Verifying parameterised networks using abstraction and regular languages. *Lecture Notes in Computer Science*, 962:395–407, 1995. 549

[CH78]   Patrick Cousot and Nicholas Halbwachs. Automatic discovery of linear restraints among variables of a program. In *POPL'78*. ACM, 1978. 542

[DLS01]   Dennis Dams, Yassine Lakhnech, and Martin Steffen". Iterating transducers. In *CAV'01*. LNCS, 2001. 540, 542

[EK99]   J. Esparza and J. Knoop. An automata-theoretic approach to interprocedural data-flow analysis. In *FOSSACS'99*, volume LNCS 1578, 1999. 541

[Eng75]   Joost Engelfriet. Bottom-up and top-down tree transformations – a comparison. In *Mathematical Systems Theory*, volume 9(3), 1975. 544

[EP00]   Javier Esparza and Andreas Podelski. Efficient algorithms for pre * and post * on interprocedural parallel flow graphs. In *Symposium on Principles of Programming Languages*, pages 1–11, 2000. 542, 551

[FO97]   L. Fribourg and H. Olsen. Reachability sets of parametrized rings as regular languages. In *Infinity'97*. volume 9 of Electronical Notes in Theoretical Computer Science. Elsevier Science, 1997. 547

[GL00]   J. Goubault-Larrecq. A method for automatic cryptographic protocol verification. In *15th IPDPS 2000 Workshops*. LNCS 1800, 2000. 553

[GT95]   R. Gilleron and S. Tison. Regular tree languages and rewrite systems. In *Fundamenta Informaticae*, volume 24, pages 157–175, 1995. 542, 552

[JN00]   B. Jonsson and M. Nilsson. Transitive closures of regular relations for verifying infinite-state systems. In *TACAS'00*. LNCS, 2000. 540, 542

[KMM⁺97]   Y. Kesten, O. Maler, M. Marcus, A. Pnueli, and E. Shahar. Symbolic model checking with rich assertional languages. In O. Grumberg, editor, *Proc. CAV'97*, volume 1254 of *LNCS*, pages 424–435. Springer, 1997. 539, 542, 547

[LS98]   D. Lugiez and Ph. Schnoebelen. The regular viewpoint on PA-processes. In *Proc. 9th Int. Conf. Concurrency Theory (CONCUR'98), Nice, France, Sep. 1998*, volume 1466, pages 50–66. Springer, 1998. 542, 551

[May98]   R. Mayr. Decidability and Complexity of Model Checking Problems for Infinite-State Systems. Phd. thesis, TUM, 1998. 541, 550

[Mon02]   D. Monniaux. Abstracting cryptographic protocols with tree automata. *Science of Computer Programming*, 2002. 553

[PS00]   A. Pnueli and E. Shahar. Liveness and acceleration in parametrized verification. In *CAV'00*. LNCS, 2000. 540, 542

[Tou01]   T. Touili. Widening Techniques for Regular Model Checking. In *Vepas Workshop*. Volume 50 of Electronic Notes in TCS, 2001. 540, 542, 545, 553

[WB98]   Pierre Wolper and Bernard Boigelot. Verifying systems with infinite but regular stae spaces. In *CAV'98*. LNCS 1254, 1998. 539

Regular Tree Model Checking*

Parosh Aziz Abdulla, Bengt Jonsson, Pritha Mahata, and Julien d'Orso

Dept. of Computer Systems. P.O. Box 337, S-751 05 Uppsala, Sweden
{parosh,bengt,pritha,juldor}@docs.uu.se

Abstract. In this paper, we present an approach for algorithmic verification of infinite-state systems with a parameterized tree topology. Our work is a generalization of regular model checking, where we extend the work done with strings toward trees. States are represented by trees over a finite alphabet, and transition relations by regular, structure preserving relations on trees. We use an automata theoretic method to compute the transitive closure of such a transition relation. Although the method is incomplete, we present sufficient conditions to ensure termination. We have implemented a prototype for our algorithm and show the result of its application on a number of examples.

1 Introduction

Regular model checking has recently been advocated for model checking of *parameterized systems*, i.e. systems whose description is parameterized by the number of components in them (e.g. [KMM+97, KMM+01, WB98, DJNT00]).

In regular model checking, states are represented by strings over a finite alphabet, while sets of states are represented by regular sets. Regular relations specified by finite-state transducers are used to describe actions between states. Regular model checking has been used to verify several classes of protocols with linear or ring-formed topologies, such as mutual exclusion protocols and cache coherence protocols (e.g. [BJNT00, Mai01, PRZ01, APR+01, FP01]).

On the other hand, there are several classes of systems which are beyond the capability of regular model checking, either because the behaviour of the system cannot be captured by a regular relation [FP01], or because the topology of the system is not linear. In this paper, we extend the work in [JN00, BJNT00] in order to obtain a model checking algorithm for tree-formed protocols. We propose *regular tree languages* as a symbolic representation of state spaces and *regular tree relations*, characterized by finite-state *tree transducers*, as a symbolic representation of the transition relation.

A major problem in model checking of parameterized systems is that the depth of the state space is in general not bounded. This means that standard iteration based symbolic reachability algorithms [BCMD92, McM93] are not guaranteed to terminate for these systems. Therefore, an important challenge is how

---

* This work was supported in part by the European Commission (FET project ADVANCE, contract No IST-1999-29082).

to *accelerate* the standard algorithm in order to make it terminate more often on practical examples. One way to achieve that is to augment the algorithm by adding the effect of arbitrarily long sequences of actions. Since an action in our case is modelled by a regular tree relation, this amounts to computing the transitive closure of a regular tree relation. For instance, the effect of an action which sends a token upwards in a tree is that the token is propagated an arbitrary number of steps toward the root of the tree.

The main contribution of this paper is to show how to compute the transitive closure for a large class of actions. Starting from a tree transducer corresponding to an action, we compute a new (symbolic) transducer corresponding to the transitive closure. We also classify a class of actions for which the construction of the symbolic transducer always terminates. We do that by extending the notion of *local depth* [JN00] to trees. Intuitively, an action has local depth k if repeated applications of the action changes each node of the tree at most k times. We show that, for any action with a finite local depth, we can compute a finite-state tree transducer corresponding to the transitive closure of the action.

We have implemented a prototype for computing such a transitive closure and verification. We show the result of running our algorithm for verification of parameterized versions of a number of protocols: two token tree protocols, the PERCOLATE protocol [KMM+97], and a tree arbiter described in [ABH+97].

Related Work   Regular model checking has been proposed by [KMM+97, KMM+01] and [WB98]. Several techniques have been proposed for accelerating reachability analysis for parameterized systems such as bisimulation [DLS01], widening [BJNT00, Tou01], automatic invariant generation [PRZ01, APR+01], and transitive closure [ABJN99, JN00, BJNT00, PS00].

The paper [FP01] goes beyond regular languages using context-free languages as a symbolic representation. The paper [BMT01] proposes a subclass of regular languages closed under a larger set of operations than regular languages.

The difference between the above works and the work of this paper is that they all consider systems with linear topologies. Our work can be seen as a generalization of the techniques described in [JN00] for word transducers. The work in [KMM+97] also considers tree-formed protocols. However, [KMM+97] only considers transducers that represent the effect of a single application of an action rather than the transitive closure.

2   Words

In this section, we recall some standard definitions and results for word languages. The concepts of *finite* automata and *regular languages* are defined as usual. For a word w, and $i : 1 \leq i \leq |w|$, we let $w(i)$ denote the ith element of w. For words $w_1, \ldots, w_m$ of equal length k over an alphabet Σ, we let $w_1 \times \cdots \times w_m$ be the word w over Σ^m such that $w(i) = (w_1(i), \ldots, w_m(i))$ for $i : 1 \leq i \leq k$. An m-ary *relation* on the alphabet Σ is a set of tuples of the form $(w_1, \ldots, w_m)$, where $w_1, \ldots, w_m \in \Sigma^*$ and $|w_1| = \cdots = |w_m|$. We observe that a language K over Σ^m characterizes an m-ary relation $[K]$ on Σ in the sense that $(w_1, \ldots, w_m) \in [K]$ if and only if $(w_1 \times \cdots \times w_m) \in K$. A relation R is *regular* if $R = [K]$ for some regular language K.

For relations R and R', we define $R \otimes R'$ as the relation $(w_1, \ldots, w_k, w'_1, \cdots, w'_m)$ where $(w_1, \ldots, w_k) \in R$, $(w'_1, \ldots, w'_m) \in R'$, and $|w_1| = |w'_1|$. Notice that the third condition ensures $|w_1| = \cdots = |w_k| = |w'_1| = \cdots = |w'_m|$. For a relation R of arity m and $i : 1 \leq i \leq m$, we let $R|_i$ denote the relation $\{(w_1, \ldots, w_{i-1}, w_{i+1}, \ldots, w_m)| (w_1, w_2, \ldots, w_m) \in R\}$. The operation is generalized in the obvious manner to $R|_I$, where I is a subset of $\{1, \ldots, m\}$.

It is straightforward to show that regular relations are closed under $\otimes$ and $|_I$.

Sometimes, we use the term *word language* instead of *language* to avoid confusion with *tree languages* (defined later). The same applies to other concepts, e.g. automata, relations, etc.

3   Trees

In this section, we introduce some preliminaries on trees and tree relations.

A *ranked alphabet* is a pair (Σ, ρ), where Σ is a finite set of symbols and ρ is a mapping from Σ to $\mathbb{N}$. We call $\rho(f)$ the *arity* of f. We let Σ_p denote the set of symbols in Σ with arity p. Intuitively, each node in a tree is labelled with a symbol in Σ with the same arity as the out-degree of the node. Sometimes, we abuse notation and use Σ to denote the ranked alphabet (Σ, ρ).

Trees Following the standard notation (e.g. found in [CDG+99]), the nodes in a tree are represented by strings over $\mathbb{N}$. More precisely, the empty string ϵ represents the root of the tree, while a node $b_1 b_2 \ldots b_k$ is a child of the node $b_1 b_2 \ldots b_{k-1}$. Also, nodes are labelled by symbols from Σ.

Formally, a *tree* T over a ranked alphabet Σ is a pair (S, λ), where

- S, called the *tree structure*, is a finite set of sequences over $\mathbb{N}$ (i.e, a finite subset of $\mathbb{N}^*$). Each sequence n in S is called a *node* of T. If S contains a node $n = b_1 b_2 \ldots b_k$, then S will also contain the node $n' = b_1 b_2 \ldots b_{k-1}$, and the nodes $n_r = b_1 b_2 \ldots b_{k-1} r$, for $r : 0 \leq r < b_k$. We say that n' is the *parent* of n, and that n is a *child* of n'. A *leaf* of T is a node n which does not have any child, i.e., there is no $b \in \mathbb{N}$ with $nb \in S$.
- λ is a mapping from S to Σ. The number of children of n is equal to $\rho(\lambda(n))$. Observe that if n is a leaf then $\lambda(n) \in \Sigma_0$.

We use $T(\Sigma)$ to denote the set of all trees over Σ.

We let $n \in T$ indicate that $n \in S$, and let $f \in T$ denote that $\lambda(n) = f$ for some $n \in T$.

For a tree $T = (S, \lambda)$ and a node $n \in T$, the *subtree* of T rooted at n is the tree $T_n = (S_n, \lambda_n)$, where $S_n = \{b| nb \in S\}$ and $\lambda_n(b) = \lambda(nb)$.

Tree Relations We generalize the definition of a relation from words to trees.

For a ranked alphabet Σ and $m \geq 1$, we let $\Sigma^\bullet(m)$ be the ranked alphabet which contains all tuples $(f_1, \ldots, f_m)$ such that $f_1, \ldots, f_m \in \Sigma_p$ for some p. We define $\rho((f_1, \ldots, f_m)) = \rho(f_1)$. In other words, the set $\Sigma^\bullet(m)$ contains the m-tuples, where all the elements in the same tuple have equal arities. Furthermore, the arity of a tuple in $\Sigma^\bullet(m)$ is equal to the arity of any of its elements. For trees $T_1 = (S_1, \lambda_1)$ and $T_2 = (S_2, \lambda_2)$, we say that T_1 and T_2 are *structurally equivalent*, denoted $T_1 \cong T_2$, if $S_1 = S_2$.

Consider structurally equivalent trees $T_1, \ldots, T_m$ over an alphabet Σ, where $T_i = (S, \lambda_i)$ for $i : 1 \leq i \leq m$. We let $T_1 \times \cdots \times T_m$ be the tree $T = (S, \lambda)$ over $\Sigma^\bullet(m)$ such that $\lambda(n) = (\lambda_1(n), \ldots, \lambda_m(n))$ for each $n \in S$. An m-ary *relation* on the alphabet Σ is a set of tuples of the form $(T_1, \ldots, T_m)$, where $T_1, \ldots, T_m \in T(\Sigma)$ and $T_1 \cong \cdots \cong T_m$. In a similar manner to the case of words, a tree language K over $\Sigma^\bullet(m)$ characterizes an m-ary tree relation $[K]$ on $T(\Sigma)$. Notice that the condition of being structurally equivalent is a generalization of the condition of having the same length in the case of words (Section 2). Furthermore, in the case of words we worked with Σ^m (rather than $\Sigma^\bullet(m)$) since symbol arities were not relevant there.

The operations of intersection $\cap$ and union $\cup$ are defined as usual. The operation $|_i$ and its generalization $|_I$ are defined in a similar manner to words. For regular tree relations R and R', we define $R \otimes R'$ as the set of tuples $(T_1, \cdots, T_m, T_1', \cdots, T_n')$ such that $(T_1, \cdots, T_m) \in R$, $(T_1', \cdots, T_n') \in R'$, and $T_1 \cong T_1'$. Observe that the third condition is again a generalization of the corresponding condition in the case of words. We use $\circ$ to denote the composition of two binary relations as usual. We use R^i to denote i compositions of the relation R and define $R^* = \cup_{i \geq 0} R^i$ and $R^+ = \cup_{i \geq 1} R^i$.

4   Tree Automata

In this section, we introduce tree automata and use them to recognize regular tree languages and regular tree relations.

A *tree language* is a set of trees.

A *tree automaton* over a ranked alphabet Σ is a tuple $A = (Q, F, \delta)$, where Q is a finite set of *states*, $F \subseteq Q$ is a set of *final states*, and δ is the *transition relation*, represented by a set of rules each of the form $(q_1, \ldots, q_p) \xrightarrow{f} q$ where $f \in \Sigma_p$ and $q_1, \ldots, q_p, q \in Q$. Unless stated otherwise, we assume Q and δ to be finite.

The automaton A takes a tree $T \in T(\Sigma)$ as input. It proceeds from the leaves to the root, annotating states to the nodes of T. A transition rule of the form shown above tells us that if the children of a node n are already annotated from left to right with $q_1, \ldots, q_p$ respectively, and if $\lambda(n) = f$ (with $f \in \Sigma_p$), then the node n can be annotated by q. As a special case, a transition rule of the form $\xrightarrow{f} q$ implies that a leaf labeled with $f \in \Sigma_0$ can be annotated by q.

Formally, a *run* r of A on a tree $T = (S, \lambda) \in T(\Sigma)$ is a mapping from S to Q such that for each node $n \in T$ with children $n_1, \ldots, n_k$: $(r(n_1), \ldots, r(n_k)) \xrightarrow{\lambda(n)} r(n) \in \delta$.

For a state q, we let $T \xRightarrow{r}_A q$ denote that r is a run of A on T such that $r(\epsilon) = q$. We use $T \Longrightarrow_A q$ denote that $T \xRightarrow{r}_A q$ for some r. For a set $S \subseteq Q$ of states, we let $T \xRightarrow{r}_A S$ ($T \Longrightarrow_A S$) denote that $T \xRightarrow{r}_A q$ ($T \Longrightarrow_A q$) for some $q \in S$. We say that A *accepts* T if $T \Longrightarrow_A F$. We define $L(A) = \{T \mid T \text{ is accepted by } A\}$. A tree language K is said to be *regular* if there is a tree automaton A such that $K = L(A)$.

We use tree automata also to characterize relations: An automaton A over $\Sigma^\bullet(m)$ characterizes an m-ary relation on $T(\Sigma)$, namely the relation $R = [L(A)]$. A relation R is said to be *regular* if there is a tree automaton A with $R = [L(A)]$. Sometimes, we denote R by $R(A)$.

In [CDG+99], it is shown that regular tree languages are closed under the Boolean operations. Closedness under the operators $\otimes$ and $R|_I$ is straightforward. From the fact that $R \circ R' = ((R \otimes T(\Sigma)) \cap (T(\Sigma) \otimes R'))|_2$ we get the following

Lemma 1. *Regularity is closed under composition.*

Although Lemma 1 states that regularity is preserved by a finite number of applications of the $\circ$ operator, it is well-known that regularity is not preserved by $*$ even in the case of words (i.e. R^* need not be regular even if R is).

Transducers In the special case where D is a tree automaton over $\Sigma^\bullet(2)$, we call D a *tree transducer* over Σ

Example 1. Let B be a tree automaton over $\Sigma = \{0, 1, and, or\}$ (with $\rho(and) = \rho(or) = 2$ and $\rho(1) = \rho(0) = 0$), where $Q = \{q_0, q_1\}$, $F = \{q_1\}$ and δ:

$$\xrightarrow{0} q_0 \quad \xrightarrow{1} q_1 \quad (q_0, q_0) \xrightarrow{or} q_0 \quad (q_0, q_1) \xrightarrow{or} q_1 \quad (q_1, q_0) \xrightarrow{or} q_1$$
$$(q_1, q_1) \xrightarrow{or} q_1 \quad (q_0, q_0) \xrightarrow{and} q_0 \quad (q_0, q_1) \xrightarrow{and} q_0 \quad (q_1, q_0) \xrightarrow{and} q_0 \quad (q_1, q_1) \xrightarrow{and} q_1$$

B recognizes the tree language which is the set of true Boolean expressions over Σ.

Example 2. **Token Tree Protocol** As a running example in this paper, we consider a tree transducer modelling the behaviour of a simple token tree protocol. The system consists of processes that are connected in a binary tree-like fashion. Each process stores a single bit which reflects whether the process has a token or not. The token tree passes a token from a leaf to the root. We represent the system by a tree transducer over an alphabet consisting of $t, n \in \Sigma_0$ representing processes at the leaves, and $N, T \in \Sigma_2$ representing processes at the inner nodes of the tree. Processes labeled by $\{n, N\}$ are those which do not have a token, while those labeled by $\{t, T\}$ are those which do have the token. The set of states is $\{q_0, q_1, q_2\}$ where q_2 is the (single) final state. The transition relation is given by:

$$\xrightarrow{(n,n)} q_0 \qquad\qquad \xrightarrow{(t,n)} q_1 \qquad (q_0,q_0) \xrightarrow{(T,N)} q_1 \qquad (q_1,q_0) \xrightarrow{(N,T)} q_2$$

$$(q_0,q_1) \xrightarrow{(N,T)} q_2 \qquad (q_0,q_0) \xrightarrow{(N,N)} q_0 \qquad (q_0,q_2) \xrightarrow{(N,N)} q_2 \qquad (q_2,q_0) \xrightarrow{(N,N)} q_2$$

Intuitively, the states correspond to the following

q_0 the node is idle, i.e., the token is not in the node, nor in the subtree below the node;

q_1 the node is releasing the token to the node above it in the tree;

q_2 the token is either in the node or in a subtree below the node.

5   Symbolic Transducers

In this section we show how to compute the transitive closure of regular tree relations. More precisely, given a tree transducer D, we generate a new infinite tree transducer H, called the *history transducer* of D, such that $R(H) = (R(D))^*$. We also introduce *symbolic transducers* which are compact representations of history transducers.

History Transducers With a transducer D we associate a *history transducer* which corresponds to the reflexive transitive closure of $R(D)$. Each state of H is a word of the form $q_1 \cdots q_k$ where $q_1, \ldots, q_k$ are states in D. Intuitively, for each $(T,T') \in (R(D))^*$, the history transducer H encodes the successive runs of D needed to derive T' from T. The term "history transducer" reflects the fact that the transducer encodes the histories of all such derivations.

Formally, consider a tree transducer $D = (Q, F, \delta)$ over a ranked alphabet Σ. The *history (tree) transducer* H for D is an (infinite) transducer (Q_H, F_H, δ_H), where $Q_H = Q^*$, $F_H = F^*$, and δ_H contains all rules of the form $(w_1, \ldots, w_p) \xrightarrow{(f,f')} w$ such that there is $k \geq 0$ where the following conditions are satisfied

- $|w_1| = \cdots = |w_p| = |w| = k$.

- there are $f_1, f_2, \ldots, f_{k+1}$, with $f = f_1, f' = f_{k+1}$, and $(w_1(i) \ldots, w_p(i)) \xrightarrow{(f_i, f_{i+1})} w(i)$ belongs to δ, for each $i : 1 \leq i \leq k$.

Observe that all the symbols $f_1, \ldots, f_{k+1}$ are of the same arity p. We also notice that if $(T \times T') \overset{r}{\Longrightarrow}_H w$, then there is a $k \geq 0$ such that $|r(n)| = k$ for each $n \in (T \times T')$. In other words, any run of the history transducer assigns states (words) of the same length to the nodes.

From the definition of H we derive the following lemma which states that H characterizes the reflexive transitive closure of $R(D)$.

Lemma 2. *For a transducer D and its history transducer H, we have $R(H) = (R(D))^*$.*

Symbolic Transducers For a transducer D, the symbolic transducer S of D is a compact representation of the history transducer H of D. More precisely, each state of S is a (word) regular expression over the states of D. A state ϕ in S represents all states in the history transducer which are (words) belonging to the language of ϕ.

Formally, we assume a transducer $D = (Q, F, \delta)$ and the corresponding history transducer $H = (Q_H, F_H, \delta_H)$. To define symbolic transducers, we first need the following definition.

For regular expressions $\phi_1, \ldots, \phi_p$ and symbols f, f', define $(\phi_1, \ldots, \phi_p) \xrightarrow{(f,f')}$ to be the set $\{w| \ \exists w_1 \in \phi_1 \ldots . \exists w_p \in \phi_p. \ (w_1, \ldots, w_p) \xrightarrow{(f,f')} w \in \delta_H\}$.

Lemma 3. *For regular expressions $\phi_1, \ldots, \phi_p$ and symbols f, f', the set $(\phi_1, \ldots, \phi_p) \xrightarrow{(f,f')}$ is effectively regular.*

Consider a tree transducer $D = (Q, F, \delta)$ over a ranked alphabet Σ. We define the *symbolic (tree) transducer S* for D to be the (possibly infinite-state) transducer (Q_S, F_S, δ_S), where Q_S is a set of regular expressions over Q, F_S is a set of regular expressions over Q, and δ_S contains a set of rules each of the form $(\phi_1, \ldots, \phi_p) \xrightarrow{(f,f')} \phi$. The transducer S is derived from D according to Algorithm 1 (see Figure 1). Observe that, by Lemma 3, the regular expression ϕ at line 4 of the code is always computable. Notice that in the first iteration, we have to choose $p = 0$ at line 3.

Input: Tree Transducer $D = (Q, F, \delta)$
Output: Symbolic Transducer $S = (Q_S, F_S, \delta_S)$
begin
    1. $Q_S = \emptyset, F_S = \emptyset, \delta_S = \emptyset,$
    2. **repeat**
       3. **for each** $p, f, f' \in \Sigma_p,$ and $\phi_1, \ldots, \phi_p \in Q_S$ **do**
       4. $\phi := (\phi_1, \ldots, \phi_p) \xrightarrow{(f,f')}$
       5. $Q_S := Q_S \cup \{\phi\}$
       6. $\delta_S := \delta_S \cup \{(\phi_1, \ldots, \phi_p) \xrightarrow{f,f'} \phi\}$
      7. **od**
    8. **until** no new states or rules can be added to Q_S and δ_S
    9. $F_S := \{\phi \in Q_S| \ (\phi \cap F^*) \neq \emptyset\}$
end

Fig. 1. Algorithm 1 : Computing symbolic transducer

The following lemmas state the relationship between symbolic and history transducers.

Lemma 4. *Consider a transducer D and its corresponding history and symbolic transducers H and S. For trees T and T'*

- *if $(T \times T') \Longrightarrow_S \phi$ then $(T \times T') \Longrightarrow_H w$ for each $w \in \phi$.*
- *if $(T \times T') \Longrightarrow_H w$ then $(T \times T') \Longrightarrow_S \phi$ for some ϕ with $w \in \phi$.*

Corollary 1. *For a transducer D and its corresponding history and symbolic transducers H and S, we have $R(S) = R(H)$.*

From Lemma 2 and Corollary 1 we get

Theorem 1. *For a transducer D and its corresponding symbolic transducer S, we have $R(S) = (R(D))^*$.*

Termination Since there are infinitely many regular expressions over the set of states of D, the algorithm in Figure 1 may in general not terminate.

Example 3. Consider the token tree transducer of Example 2.

A transition of the corresponding history transducer is $(q_0 q_0 q_0, q_1 q_0 q_0) \xrightarrow{(N,N)} q_2 q_1 q_0$ corresponding to the three transductions $(q_0, q_1) \xrightarrow{(N,T)} q_2$, followed by $(q_0, q_0) \xrightarrow{(T,N)} q_1$, followed by $(q_0, q_0) \xrightarrow{(N,N)} q_0$.

When we run Algorithm 1 on the protocol, we get e.g. $\phi_0 = q_0^* = \xrightarrow{(n,n)}$ and $\phi_1 = q_1 q_0^* = \xrightarrow{(t,n)}$. If we consider the pair of symbols (N, N) and the regular expressions (ϕ_0, ϕ_1), we get, in the next step of the algorithm, the new expression $\phi_2 = q_2 q_1 q_0^* = (\phi_0, \phi_1) \xrightarrow{(N,N)}$. These steps give the rules $\xrightarrow{(n,n)} \phi_0$, $\xrightarrow{(t,n)} \phi_1$, and $(\phi_0, \phi_1) \xrightarrow{(N,N)} \phi_2$, respectively.

6   Saturation

In order to make the algorithm in Figure 1 terminate more often, we present in this section a method to accelerate the iterations of the algorithm. We do that by defining the notion of *idempotent states* and then *saturating* all generated regular expressions by such states.

Idempotent States To define idempotent states, we need some preliminaries. First, we define the notion of context. Intuitively, a context is a tree with a single "hole" at one of its leaves. Formally, we consider a special symbol $\Box \notin \Sigma$ with arity 0. A *context* over Σ is a tree (S_C, λ_C) over $\Sigma \cup \{\Box\}$ such that there is exactly one $n_c \in S_C$ with $\lambda_C(n_c) = \Box$. In the sequel, we will always assume $n_c \in S_C$ to be the unique node with $\lambda_C(n_c) = \Box$.

For a context $C = (S_C, \lambda_C)$ and a tree $T = (S, \lambda)$, we define $C[T]$ to be the tree (S_1, λ_1), where

- $S_1 = S_C \cup \{n_c \cdot n \mid n_c \in S_C \text{ and } \lambda_C(n_c) = \square \text{ and } n \in S\}$.
- for each $n \in S_C$ with $n \neq n_c$ we have $\lambda_1(n) = \lambda_C(n)$.
- for each $n_1 = n_c \cdot n$ with $n \in S$ we have $\lambda_1(n_1) = \lambda(n)$.

Notice that the above operation represents a substitution, where we replace the hole in C by T.

Consider a tree transducer $D = (Q, F, \delta)$ over a ranked alphabet Σ. We extend the notion of runs to contexts. Let q be a state and $C = (S_C, \lambda_C)$ a context. A *run* r of D on C from q is defined in a similar manner to a run (Section 4) except that $r(n_c) = q$. In other words, the leaf labeled with $\square$ is annotated by q. We use $C(q_1) \overset{r}{\Longrightarrow}_A q_2$ to denote that r is a run of A on C from q_1 such that $r(\epsilon) = q_2$. The notation $C(q_1) \Longrightarrow_A q_2$ and the extension to sets of states are explained in a similar manner to runs on trees.

A context $C = (S_C, \lambda_C)$ over $\Sigma^\bullet(2)$ is said to be *copying* if for each $n \in S_C$ with $n \neq n_c$ we have $\lambda_C(n) = (f, f)$ for some $f \in \Sigma$. In other words, the context corresponds to a copy operation on all its nodes.

For an automaton $A = (Q, F, \delta)$ we define the *suffix* of a state $q \in Q$ as follows:

$$suff(q) = \{C : \text{context} \mid C(q) \Longrightarrow_A F\}$$

For a set $X \subseteq Q$, we define its suffix: $suff(X) = \bigcup_{q \in X} suff(q)$.

Then, we define a state q to be *idempotent* if and only if $suff(q)$ contains only copying contexts. Intuitively, idempotent states denote states from which the transducer only accepts contexts corresponding to a copy operation on nodes. Note that idempotent states can be syntactically characterized (see full version of the paper).

Saturation Consider a transducer $D = (Q, F, \delta)$, its history transducer $H = (Q_H, F_H, \delta_H)$, and its symbolic transducer $S = (Q_S, F_S, \delta_S)$. Consider $W \subseteq Q_H$ and $X \subseteq Q$. We define the *saturation* of W by X, denoted $\lceil W \rceil_X$ as the smallest set W' containing W and closed under the following two rules for each $q \in X$

- if $w_1 \cdot w_2 \in W'$ then $w_1 \cdot q \cdot w_2 \in W'$.
- if $w_1 \cdot q \cdot q \cdot w_2 \subset W'$ then $w_1 \cdot q \cdot w_2 \subset W'$.

Let $Q_{idm} \subseteq Q$ to be the set of all idempotent states in Q. For $W \subseteq Q_H$, we use $\lceil W \rceil$ to denote the set $\lceil W \rceil_{Q_{idm}}$. The saturation operation obviously defines an equivalence relation on sets of states of H, and therefore also the states Q_S of the symbolic transducer S. This allows us to derive a new transducer S_{SAT} by merging all equivalent states in S. We can achieve that by changing the termination condition of Algorithm 1 (line 8), so that the algorithm stops if all new states generated are equivalent to the previous ones. Notice that this guarantees termination in case the number of equivalence classes is finite. The following theorem states that saturation does not affect the relation recognized by the symbolic transducer.

Theorem 2. $R(S) = R(S_{SAT})$.

We devote the rest of this subsection to the proof of Theorem 2 (achieved through Lemmas 5 to 7).

The following lemma states that the saturation operation does not add any element to the suffix of a set of states in H.

Lemma 5. *Let $w_1, w_2 \in Q_H$ and let $q \in Q$ be an idempotent state.*

- $suff(w_1 \cdot q \cdot w_2) \subseteq suff(w_1 \cdot w_2)$.
- $suff(w_1 \cdot q \cdot w_2) \subseteq suff(w_1 \cdot q \cdot q \cdot w_2)$.

From Lemma 5 we get the next lemma stating that equivalent states have identical suffixes.

Lemma 6. *For $W_1, W_2 \subseteq Q_H$, if $\lceil W_1 \rceil = \lceil W_2 \rceil$ then $suff(W_1) = suff(W_2)$.*

A consequence of Lemma 6 follows in the next lemma. This lemma states that the equivalence relation we consider is in fact a congruence. In the proof of the lemma, we will assume that S contains no useless states (ϕ_u with $suff(\phi_u) = \emptyset$) since these states do not change the language recognized by S and can be removed.

Lemma 7. *If $(\phi_1, \ldots, \phi_i, \ldots, \phi_p) \xrightarrow{(f,f')} \phi \in \delta_S$, and $suff(\phi_i) = suff(\phi_i')$ for some $i : 1 \leq i \leq p$, then there exists ϕ' such that $suff(\phi) = suff(\phi')$ and $(\phi_1, \ldots, \phi_i', \ldots, \phi_p) \xrightarrow{(f,f')} \phi' \in \delta_S$.*

The fact that our equivalence relation is a congruence (Lemma 7) implies that we can apply the extension of the MyHill-Nerode theorem to trees (described in [CDG+99]).

Example 4. When we run Algorithm 1 on our token tree protocol, we get expressions like $\phi_0 = q_0{}^*$ and $\phi_1 = q_1 q_0{}^*$. Their saturated version (q_2 being the idempotent state) is $\lceil \phi_0 \rceil = (q_0 + q_2)^*$ and $\lceil \phi_1 \rceil = q_2^* \cdot q_1 \cdot (q_0 + q_2)^*$.

7   Termination

As noted earlier, saturation enables us to define an equivalence relation on regular expressions, and thus to collapse several states of S together. However, to have termination of Algorithm 1, we need to make sure that we generate only a finite number of equivalence classes. In this section, we introduce a class of transducers which include all the protocols we consider in this paper, and for which termination is guaranteed.

More precisely, we consider transducers where the set of states can be partitioned into three parts: states whose prefixes only perform copy operations, states which are idempotent i.e. states whose suffixes only perform copy operations (Section 6), and states which perform the changes. For the latter, we require that they satisfy the *finite local depth* property (described below).

To simplify the proofs, we first consider the class of *well-behaved transducers* satisfying the above condition on state partitioning. In the full version of this paper, we indicate how to lift these restrictions to a larger class of systems.

Notice that well-behaviour is just one sufficient condition for termination. The algorithm may still terminate even in cases where the given transducer is not well-behaved.

Through this section, we let $D = (Q, F, \delta)$ be a transducer, and H and S be its history and symbolic transducers. We first need some definitions.

Copying Prefix States For a state $q \in Q$, its prefix is the set of trees:

$$pref(q) = \{T : tree|\ T \Longrightarrow_D q\}$$

We now define the notion of *copying tree*: a tree $T = (S, \lambda)$ is copying if for each node $n \in S$ we have $\lambda(n) = (f, f)$ for some symbol f. We say that q is a *copying prefix state* if $pref(q)$ only contains copying trees.

Local Depth

Let $Q_1 \subseteq Q$. For a regular relation $R(D)$ and a natural number k, we say that R has *local depth* k with respect to Q_1 if R satisfies the following condition: Consider any two trees $T = (S, \lambda)$ and $T' = (S, \lambda')$, with $(T, T') \in R^m$. Then, there are trees $T_i = (S, \lambda_i)$ for $i : 0 \leq i \leq m$ such that $T_0 = T$, $T_m = T'$, related by accepting runs $T_i \times T_{i+1} \xRightarrow{r_i}_D F$, and for each node $n \in S$, there are at most k different j with $r_j(n) \in Q_1$.

We are now ready to state the conditions that will allow us to ensure termination.

Well-Behaved Transducer A transducer $D = (Q, F, \delta)$ is said to be *well-behaved* if Q contains a single copying prefix state q_{cpy}, a single idempotent state q_{idm}, and $R(D)$ has a finite local depth with respect to $Q \setminus \{q_{cpy}, q_{idm}\}$.

We devote the rest of this section to proving that if the transducer we are considering is *well-behaved*, then Algorithm 1 terminates.

The following lemma means that a state q_{cpy} can only appear as q_{cpy}^* in the regular expressions we generate.

Lemma 8. *For any regular expression ϕ generated by Algorithm 1, if $w^l \cdot q_{cpy} \cdot w^r \in \phi$ then $w^l \cdot z \cdot w^r \in \phi$ for any $z \in q_{cpy}^*$.*

We recall (Theorem 2) that we can assume that all sets generated in Algorithm 1 are saturated with q_{idm}. This (together with Lemma 8) leads to the the following Lemma.

Lemma 9. *Let ϕ be a regular expression generated by Algorithm 1. If $\phi \subseteq \{q_{cpy}, q_{idm}\}^*$ then $\lceil \phi \rceil_{\{q_{idm}\}}$ is the union of one or more of the following seven regular expressions:*

1. q_{idm}^* 2. q_{idm}^+ 3. $(q_{cpy} + q_{idm})^*$

4. $q_{idm} (q_{cpy} + q_{idm})^*$ 5. $(q_{cpy} + q_{idm})^* q_{idm}$

6. $q_{idm} (q_{cpy} + q_{idm})^* q_{idm}$ 7. $(q_{cpy} + q_{idm})^* q_{idm} (q_{cpy} + q_{idm})^*$

Lemma 9 and finite local depth imply that we only need to consider regular expressions of a restricted form:

Lemma 10. *For a well-behaved transducer D with local depth k, Algorithm 1 needs only consider regular expressions of the form*

$$\phi_0 \cdot q_1 \cdot \phi_1 \cdot q_2 \cdots \phi_{n-1} \cdot q_n \cdot \phi_n$$

with $n \leq k$, each $\lceil \phi_i \rceil$ is the union of one or more of the seven regular expressions described in Lemma 9, and $q_i \notin \{q_{cpy}, q_{idm}\}$.

Consequently, we can conclude that for a well-behaved system, Algorithm 1 terminates.

Theorem 3. *Algorithm 1 terminates for any well-behaved transducer.*

Example 5. In Example 2, we have $q_{cpy} = q_0$ and $q_{idm} = q_2$. The local depth of $R(D)$ with respect to $\{q_1\}$ is 1.

8   Experimental Results

We have implemented a prototype based on Algorithm 1 and its modifications described in Section 6 and Section 7. In this section, we give a description of the protocols we have verified with our algorithm.

We describe and report more thoroughly these examples in the full version of this paper.

1. Simple Token Protocol This porotocol is detailed in Example 2.

2. Two-Way Token Protocol This example is a generalization of the previous one. Here, we allow the token to move downwards as well as upwards.

3. The PERCOLATE *Protocol* The protocol PERCOLATE, described in [KMM+97], operates on a tree of processes. Each process has a local variable with values $\{0,1\}$ for the leaf nodes and $\{U,0,1\}$ for internal nodes[1] (U is interpreted as "undefined yet"). The system percolates the disjunction of values in the leaves up to the root.

---

[1] To simplify the notation, we do not distinguish between the nullary and binary versions of the symbols 0 and 1.

4. Tree Arbiter The tree arbiter protocol [ABH⁺97] operates on a tree of processes and aims at preserving mutual exclusion. The leaf nodes try to access a shared resource, while the interior nodes are used to manage the resource. Access to the resource is represented by a token which can move inside the tree.

References

[ABH⁺97] R. Alur, R.K. Brayton, T.A. Henzinger, S. Qadeer, and S.K. Rajamani. Partial-order reduction in symbolic state space exploration. In O. Grumberg, editor, *Proc. 9ᵗʰ Int. Conf. on Computer Aided Verification*, volume 1254, pages 340–351, Haifa, Israel, 1997. Springer Verlag. 556, 567

[ABJN99] Parosh Aziz Abdulla, Ahmed Bouajjani, Bengt Jonsson, and Marcus Nilsson. Handling global conditions in parameterized system verification. In *Proc. 11ᵗʰ Int. Conf. on Computer Aided Verification*, volume 1633 of *Lecture Notes in Computer Science*, pages 134–145, 1999. 556

[APR⁺01] T. Arons, A. Pnueli, S. Ruah, J. Xu, and L. Zuck. Parameterized verification with automatically computed inductive assertions. In *Proc. 13ᵗʰ Int. Conf. on Computer Aided Verification*, pages 221–234, 2001. 555, 556

[BCMD92] J.R. Burch, E.M. Clarke, K.L. McMillan, and D.L. Dill. Symbolic model checking: 10^{20} states and beyond. *Information and Computation*, 98:142–170, 1992. 555

[BJNT00] A. Bouajjani, B. Jonsson, M. Nilsson, and T. Touili. Regular model checking. In Emerson and Sistla, editors, *Proc. 12ᵗʰ Int. Conf. on Computer Aided Verification*, volume 1855 of *Lecture Notes in Computer Science*, pages 403–418, 2000. 555, 556

[BMT01]   A. Bouajjani, A. Muscholl, and T. Touili. Permutation rewriting and algorithmic verification. In *Proc. LICS' 01 17ᵗʰ IEEE Int. Symp. on Logic in Computer Science*. IEEE, 2001. 556

[CDG⁺99] H. Common, M. Dauchet, R. Gilleron, F. Jacquemard, D. Lugiez, S. Tison, and M. Tommasi. *Tree Automata Techniques and Applications*. October 1999. 557, 559, 564

[DLS01]   D. Dams, Y. Lakhnech, and M. Steffen. Iterating transducers. In G. Berry, H. Comon, and A. Finkel, editors, *Computer Aided Verification*, volume 2102 of *Lecture Notes in Computer Science*, 2001. 556

[FP01]   Dana Fisman and Amir Pnueli. Beyond regular model checking. In *Proc. 21th Conference on the Foundations of Software Technology and Theoretical Computer Science*, Lecture Notes in Computer Science, December 2001. 555, 556

[JN00]   Bengt Jonsson and Marcus Nilsson. Transitive closures of regular relations for verifying infinite-state systems. In S. Graf and M. Schwartzbach, editors, *Proc. TACAS '00, 6ᵗʰ Int. Conf. on Tools and Algorithms for the Construction and Analysis of Systems*, volume 1785 of *Lecture Notes in Computer Science*, 2000. 555, 556

[KMM⁺97] Y. Kesten, O. Maler, M. Marcus, A. Pnueli, and E. Shahar. Symbolic model checking with rich assertional languages. In O. Grumberg, editor, *Proc. 9ᵗʰ Int. Conf. on Computer Aided Verification*, volume 1254, pages 424–435, Haifa, Israel, 1997. Springer Verlag. 555, 556, 566

[KMM⁺01] Y. Kesten, O. Maler, M. Marcus, A. Pnueli, and E. Shahar. Symbolic model checking with rich assertional languages. *Theoretical Computer Science*, 256:93–112, 2001. 555, 556

568   Parosh Aziz Abdulla et al.

[Mai01]   M. Maidl. A unifying model checking approach for safety properties of parameterized systems. In *Proc. 13th Int. Conf. on Computer Aided Verification*, pages 324–336, 2001. 555

[McM93]   K.L. McMillan. *Symbolic Model Checking*. Kluwer Academic Publishers, 1993. 555

[PRZ01]   A. Pnueli, S. Ruah, and L. Zuck. Automatic deductive verification with invisible invariants. In *Proc. TACAS '01, 7th Int. Conf. on Tools and Algorithms for the Construction and Analysis of Systems*, volume 2031, pages 82–97, 2001. 555, 556

[PS00]   A. Pnueli and E. Shahar. Liveness and acceleration in parameterized verification. In *Proc. 12th Int. Conf. on Computer Aided Verification*, volume 1855 of *Lecture Notes in Computer Science*, pages 328–343, 2000. 556

[Tou01]   T. Touili. Regular Model Checking using Widening Techniques. *Electronic Notes in Theoretical Computer Science*, 50(4), 2001. Proc. Workshop on Verification of Parametrized Systems (VEPAS'01), Crete, July, 2001. 556

[WB98]   Pierre Wolper and Bernard Boigelot. Verifying systems with infinite but regular state spaces. In *Proc. 10th Int. Conf. on Computer Aided Verification*, volume 1427 of *Lecture Notes in Computer Science*, pages 88–97, Vancouver, July 1998. Springer Verlag. 555, 556

Compressing Transitions for Model Checking

Robert Kurshan[1], Vladimir Levin[2], and Hüsnü Yenigün[3]

[1] Cadence Design Systems, New Providence, NJ 07974
rkurshan@cadence.com
[2] Lucent Technologies, Mount Olive, NJ 07828
vlevin@lucent.com
[3] Sabancı University, İstanbul, Turkey
yenigun@sabanciuniv.edu

Abstract. An optimization technique is presented that compresses a chain of transitions into a single jump transition, thus making a model smaller prior to model checking. We give compression algorithms, together with conditions that allow such compressions to preserve next-time-free LTL. Experimental results are presented and discussed.

1 Introduction

In model checking a multi-component system, memory or/and time necessary to explore the system's state space may often grow too fast, even exponentially in the number of system's components. This is known as the state space explosion problem. Methods to fight it, often called "reductions", constitute one of the most important directions in formal verification and their effectiveness largely determines the size of systems manageable by model checking.

This paper suggests a reduction method that attempts to compress a sequence of transitions into a single transition, eliminating the interim states. A simple example of the compression method in the case of a sequential program is to replace the consecutive assignments $x := 1; x := x + 1$ with one assignment $x := 2$. Although this substitution might seem always possible, it is not so. Consider the property **always**$(x = 2)$: it holds on the compressed code, but fails on the original code. The paper formulates rules for correct compression and suggests simple reduction algorithms based on those rules.

When applied to a multi-process system with interleaving semantics, this compression method can augment partial order reduction. Partial order reduction gets its effect by ignoring redundant interleavings. Given two or more executions that only differ in the interleaving orders of their transitions (for example, a, b and b, a), it suffices to check the property on only one of those executions provided that its truth value can be guaranteed to be the same on any other one. The conditions which guarantee this kind of insensitivity to a particular interleaving order make up the heart of partial order reduction. In general ([16,4,13,10]), these conditions require that the transition selected to be executed be irrelevant to the property and independent (i.e. commutative) with all other transitions,

D. Brinksma and K. G. Larsen (Eds.): CAV 2002, LNCS 2404, pp. 569–582, 2002.
© Springer-Verlag Berlin Heidelberg 2002

and also, it cannot close a state-transition cycle. However, the very same conditions suggest that interim states between the transitions (e.g., between a and b) are also irrelevant to the property. Hence, there is no reason to execute the selected sequence (a, b) in steps, transition-by-transition. Instead, it can be executed as an atomic jump transition. Thus, the compression method completes the partial order reduction approach.

The compression is performed as a program transformation of the same sort required for static partial order reduction (SPOR) [10,7]. The model checker operates on the compressed program, which is equivalent (relative to the property being checked) to the original program.

SDLCheck [12] is a model checking tool developed for verification of SDL programs [6]. Given an SDL program and a property in a subset of Linear Temporal Logic (LTL) [15], they are both translated into S/R, the input language of the model checking tool COSPAN [9]. SDLCheck treats each SDL statement (an assignment, an output, etc.) as an atomic transition and reflects this view in the S/R model it produces: global states are generated before and after each SDL statement is executed. SDLCheck implements SPOR in the translation phase from SDL to S/R. Thus, the S/R model is optimized to have partial order reduction realized in the model checking phase. The combined tool, SDLCheck+COSPAN, utilizes all enhancements of COSPAN, including BDD-based symbolic verification. SDLCheck also implements the compression technique given in this paper.

SPOR is used to analyze the SDL system, and gather the information required for the compression.

For instance, it can detect if x is an important variable for the correctness of the verification, and if it is not, then the compression algorithm replaces the consecutive assignments $x := 1; x := x+1$ with $x := 2$. COSPAN, therefore, does not generate the interim state after executing $x := 1$, avoiding many possible interleavings that would be caused by the transitions of the other processes at this interim state. After transitions are compressed, SPOR is applied again, but this time, to the compressed S/R model.

2 Preliminaries

2.1 Modeling Programs by Transition Systems

We model a finite state program by *a transition system* $M = (S, \varsigma, T, \mathcal{P}, L)$ where S is a finite set of states, $\varsigma \in S$ is the initial state, T is a set of deterministic transitions, each transition $t \subseteq S \times S$, $\mathcal{P}$ is a finite set of propositional variables, and $L : S \mapsto 2^{\mathcal{P}}$ is an interpretation function: for every state s, $L(s)$ is the set of all propositional variables which are *true* at s.

For a transition t, the set $start(t)$ (the set $final(t)$) include all states that appears in a pair $(s_1, s_2) \in t$ as s_1 (respectively, s_2). Since transition t is assumed deterministic, we associate it with a function $t : start(t) \mapsto final(t)$ such that $t(s_1) = s_2$ iff $(s_1, s_2) \in t$. For a state s, the set of transitions *enabled* at s is

$enabled(s) = \{t \in T \mid s \in start(t)\}$. We assume for simplicity that for every state s, $enabled(s) \neq \emptyset$.

A *state-transition path* of M is an infinite or finite alternating sequence of states and transitions $\sigma = s_1, t_1, s_2, t_2, \ldots$ (ends in a state if it is finite) in which $t_i(s_i) = s_{i+1}$. Let $\sigma|_K$ be the projection of σ on a set K. An infinite state-transition path is called a *run* of M if it starts from the initial state ς.

To specify properties of a system M, we use LTL_x, which is LTL without the next–time operator. M satisfies an LTL_x formula ϕ, denoted by $M \models \phi$, iff for every run σ of M, the proposition sequence $L(\sigma|_S)$ satisfies ϕ, denoted by $\sigma|_S \models \phi$, — we refer the reader to the literature for the exact definition (see, for example, [15]). Checking if $M \models \phi$ is performed by a model checking procedure.

2.2   Static Partial Order Reduction

Model checking algorithms construct reachable state space of M, by starting from the initial state and by successively exploring all the transitions enabled at a state. Partial order reduction techniques calculate, for each state s, a set of transitions called *stamper(s)*, which is a subset of the enabled transitions at s. Only the transitions in *stamper(s)* are used to generate the next states of s, rather than using all the enabled transitions, thus omitting some runs of M. Stamper[1] sets must satisfy certain conditions, so that at least one run that does not satisfy ϕ (if such a run existed in M in the first place) is not omitted.

Partial order reduction follows the observation that the correctness of ϕ on a proposition sequence $\pi = p_1, p_2, \ldots$ (where $p_i \subseteq \mathcal{P}$) does not depend on how many times one and the same subset $\mathcal{P}$ appears as adjacent elements (hence stutters) in π. An integer $i \geq 2$ is said to be a *visible index* for π if $p_i \neq p_{i-1}$. Let $i_1 < i_2 < \ldots$ be all the visible indices of π. By taking the *fluent projection* of π defined as $fluent(\pi) = p_1, p_{i_1}, p_{i_2} \ldots$, we define *stuttering equivalence* relation on two proposition sequences π and π' as, $\pi \sim_{st} \pi'$ if $fluent(\pi) = fluent(\pi')$. Two systems $M = (S, \varsigma, T, \mathcal{P}, L)$ and $M' = (S', \varsigma', T', \mathcal{P}, L')$ with common $\mathcal{P}$ are said to be stuttering equivalent, denoted by $M \sim_{st} M'$, iff for each run σ of M, there exists a run σ' of M' such that $L(\sigma|_S) \sim_{st} L'(\sigma'|_{S'})$, and vice versa.

In [10,7], the stamper set conditions were modified into the static partial order reduction (SPOR) form, making it possible to select the stamper sets prior to actual model checking, and, hence, syntactically convert M into a (reduced) system M'. The following is a SPOR variation of the main partial order reduction theorem [13].

Theorem 1. [2]. *If SPOR reduces M to M', then $M \sim_{st} M'$.*

Since any LTL_x formula ϕ is *stuttering-closed* [11] (i.e. if $\pi \sim_{st} \pi'$ then $\pi \models \phi$ iff $\pi' \models \phi$), the following holds too.

---

[1] Different names have been used in the literature for different but similar conditions [16,4,13]. The term "stamper" is introduced in [14] to unify "stubborn", "ample", "persistent", etc. sets of transitions.

[2] The proof is given in detail in [17].

Corollary 1. *For any LTL_x formula ϕ, $M \models \phi$ iff $M' \models \phi'$.*

The implementation of SPOR algorithm is defined for a transition system M given in the form of process control flow graphs (supplied with additional information from the source program, which characterizes the data effects of transitions). The SPOR algorithm, in this setting, returns (identifies) a subset of stamper transitions $\mathcal{A} \subseteq T$, such that if $A \subseteq \mathcal{A}$ is a subset of enabled transitions of a single process, then $A = stamper(s)$ is a stamper set at s.

3   Compressing Links into Jump Transitions

Since the correctness of an LTL_x property actually depends on $fluent(L(\sigma|_S))$, the stuttering states, and the transitions outgoing from these states are not needed at all. We take this view, and try to identify such stuttering states, and the outgoing transitions from these states. We then combine a chain of stuttering transitions into a single *jump* transition, so that the intermediate stuttering states disappear. As an introductory example, assume that we have the following transitions $t_1 = \{(s_1, s_2)\}$ and $t_2 = \{(s_2, s_3)\}$. If s_1 is reachable, then so is s_2 and s_3, and a model checker has to generate all these states. If $L(s_2) = L(s_3)$, then t_1 and t_2 can be safely replaced with the transition $j_{(t_1, t_2)} = \{(s_1, s_3)\}$ in M, s_1 and s_3 will still be reachable, but s_2 is no longer reachable. This is the basic idea, however there are certain conditions under which such a transition compression can be done.

Below, we define the rules for compressing a transition system M. Also we claim the correctness of the rules by a number of lemmas. The proofs of the lemmas are given in [ ] and omitted here due to the space limitations. We assume that a transition system M has been analyzed for static partial order reduction (hence, the stamper transitions are known), but has not been reduced yet. Applying compression rules to M may modify it into a different transition system M', which we can show is then stuttering-equivalent to M.

Definition 1. *Given two transitions $a, b \in T$ of a system $M = (S, \varsigma, T, \mathcal{P}, L)$, the pair (a, b) is called a* link *in M if the following conditions hold:*
   (1) $final(a) = start(b)$
   (2) $\{b\}$ is a stamper set at all the states in $start(b)$
   (3) For any run σ, $\sigma|_{\{a,b\}}$ is either
      (i) a finite sequence of the form $(ab)^\star$ or $(ab)^\star a$; or
      (ii) an infinite sequence of the form $(ab)^\omega$
Given a link (a, b), we define the jump *transition relation as*
   $j_{(a,b)} = \{(s_a, s_b) | s_a \in start(a) \wedge s_b = b(a(s_a))\}$

Intuitively, conditions 1 and 3 guarantee that we only produce a jump transition for a pair of transitions that follow each other, in the sense that b cannot get enabled before a on any run of M. They further impose that a is the only enabler for b. Removing the transitions a and b, and inserting the new transition $j_{(a,b)}$, will end up in missing some reachable states. Condition 2 guarantees that such states are either at the start or in the middle of some stuttering sequence of states, and thus safe to remove. The conditions of Definition 1 can further be relaxed, but this formulation is relatively easier to explain and implement.

Lemma 1. *Given a transition system* $M = (S, \varsigma, T, \mathcal{P}, L)$ *and a link* (a, b) *in* M, *let* $M' = (S, \varsigma, T \cup \{j_{(a,b)}\} \setminus \{a, b\}, \mathcal{P}, L)$. *Then,* $M \sim_{st} M'$.

Lemma 2. *Given a transition system* $M = (S, \varsigma, T, \mathcal{P}, L)$, *and a link* (a, b) *in* M, *let* $M' = (S, \varsigma, T \cup \{j_{(a,b)}\} \setminus \{a, b\}, \mathcal{P}, L)$. *Then if* $\{a\}$ *is stamper in* M *and* $start(a) \cap final(b) = \emptyset$, *then* $\{j_{(a,b)}\}$ *is stamper in* M'.

Lemma 3. *Given a transition system* $M = (S, \varsigma, T, \mathcal{P}, L)$, *and two transitions* $t_1, t_2 \in T$, *such that* $start(t_1) \cap start(t_2) = \emptyset$, *let* $t_0 \notin T$ *be defined as* $t_0 = t_1 \cup t_2$. *Then for* $M' = (S, \varsigma, T \cup \{t_0\} \setminus \{t_1, t_2\}, \mathcal{P}, L)$, $M \sim_{st} M'$.

Lemma 4. *Given a transition system* $M = (S, \varsigma, T, \mathcal{P}, L)$, *and a transition* $t_0 \in T$, *let* $t_1, t_2 \notin T$ *be two transitions such that* t_1 *and* t_2 *are a partitioning for* t_0. *Then for* $M' = (S, \varsigma, T \cup \{t_1, t_2\} \setminus \{t_0\}, \mathcal{P}, L)$, $M \sim_{st} M'$.

4   Compressing Transitions in a Multi-process System

A transition system $M = (S, \varsigma, T, \mathcal{P}, L)$ is a model for a multi-process program with an inter-process communication through message exchange, such as an SDL program [6]. The Algorithm 2 given below compresses local, input and output transitions with other local, input and output transitions, which all belong to one and the same process. The Algorithm 1 attempts to convert (to some extent) a pair of corresponding output and input transitions into a rendezvous transition. Thus, the interim and final transition systems which the algorithm produces may be associated with a multi-process program having both message exchange and two-process rendezvous synchronization. Below we explain specific features of such transition systems.

4.1   A Multi-process Transition System

In a multi–process transition system M, processes P are subsets of transitions: $P \subseteq 2^T$. Transitions T are partitioned into two sets, T^1 and T^2, that contain, respectively, "private" and "rendezvous" transitions. Each private transition belongs to only one process $p \in P$, which performs this transition (yet, a private transition may access variables of other processes too: consider, for example, an output action that updates a buffer variable of a receiving process). A rendezvous transition belongs to exactly two different processes $p, q \in P$. For each process p, we may produce (by translation from the source program) a graph G^p, called the *control flow graph* of p. The graph's nodes N are called *locations*. Multiple edges are allowed between two locations. However, there exist two mappings from the graph edges E into the locations N that give for each edge $e \in E$ its starting and final locations, $sloc(e)$ and $floc(e)$[3]. The edges in G^p are associated with the transitions p, i.e. there exists a one-to-one mapping $p \mapsto E$. We denote t the edge associated with transition t. If t is a rendezvous transition shared by processes p and q then it is associated with edge t^p in graph G^p and edge t^q in graph G^q. We will also apply edge specific notations (fanin, fanout, starting and final nodes, etc.) to transitions. In p, the following conditions are assumed to hold:

– All transitions in p which are enabled at the initial state ς have the common starting location, let loc_ς^p. No other transition may leave this location.

– For every run σ of M, $\sigma|_p$ corresponds to a (infinite or finite) path in G^p.

Lemma 5. *If a is the only fanin transition of a location and b is the only fanout transition of the same location then for a and b the condition 3 of Definition 1 is true.*

As explained above, the SPOR algorithm analyzes the process control flow graphs of system M (enriched with the data effects of transitions) and returns the set of stamper transitions $\mathcal{A} \subseteq T$. Thus, a *multi-process (transition) system M* can be represented by a tuple $(S, \varsigma, T = T^1 \cup T^2, \mathcal{P}, L, P, (G^p)_{p \in P}, \mathcal{A})$.

We also introduce a multi–process system with message exchange. In such systems, the set of private actions T^1 is further partitioned into subsets of local, output and input transitions, denoted respectively by, T^l, T^o and T^i. We assume that the output transitions $p^o \subseteq p$ of process p, are partitioned into subsets, called *output signals*. Respectively, the input transitions $q^i \subseteq q$ of process q, are partitioned into subsets called *input signals*. There exists a matching mapping from the set of (all) output signals to the set of (all) input signals such that at most one output signal of process p matches a given input signal of process q. This gives us a relation $\mathcal{C} \subseteq T^o \times T^i$ that connects every output transition of process p with one or more input transitions which all belong to process q. Relation $\mathcal{C}$ reflects, for example, a communication topology of SDL programs. Below, we refer to $\mathcal{C}$ as to *the signal connection* of system M.

4.2   Syntactic Manipulations with Transitions

In the implementation of the compression algorithms, we have to deal with syntactic representation of transitions of a system M. An example of syntax that fits well our purpose is Dijkstra guarded command $g(X) \hookrightarrow U := e(X)$, where guard $g(X)$ is a boolean expression, and $U := e(X)$ is a parallel assignment of values produced by expressions $e(X)$ to variables U. In the context of this syntax, states of the system M are given as valuations of program's variables X, among which we assume to have not only data variables D of the source program, but also the program counters of the processes, i.e. control variables, which model the control flow graphs of M. For example, if a is a local (input or output) transition of process p that starts in location c_1 and finishes in location c_2 then it can be

---

[3] Through introducing interim nodes, graph G^p can be explained as a traditional graph, where edges are pairs of nodes.

expressed by the command $p.c = c_1 \wedge g(D) \hookrightarrow V, p.c := e(D), c_2$, where $p.c$ is the program counter of process p and V is a list of (different) data variables. In a case of a local transition, all data variables used in this command must be local variables of process p. Additionally, in a case of an input or output action, one shared data variable is involved, which models the input buffer of the receiving process. A rendezvous transition we will deal with is represented by the following command:

$$p.c = c_1^p \wedge q.c = c_1^q \wedge g(D) \hookrightarrow V, p.c, q.c := e(D), c_2^p, c_2^q$$

where c_1^p, c_2^p and c_1^q, c_2^q are, respectively, locations in processes p and q.

When representing a transition a by a guarded command $g(X) \hookrightarrow U := e(X)$, $g(X)$ defines the set of states where a is enabled $(start(a))$. If $g(X) = g_1(X) \vee g_2(X)$ and $g_1(X) \wedge g_2(X) = false$, then the command can immediately be split into two commands as, $g_1(X) \hookrightarrow U := e(X)$ and $g_2(X) \hookrightarrow U := e(X)$, cf. Lemma 4. Merging two transitions, cf. Lemma 3, whose guards are disjoint is a bit more complicated, since, a variable, say, x may be updated in the both commands, say, by expression $f_1(X)$ in one and expression $f_2(X)$ in the other one. Yet, this is still simple: in the merged command, x will be updated by the conditional expression if $g_1(X)$ then $f_1(X)$ else $f_2(X)$ fi.

Merging commands (which represent transitions) as explained above can be utilized in an implementation of the algorithms given below. However, we need a more complicated splitting method. Consider two consecutive output transitions a, b of process p that send messages to two different processes q_1 and q_2. In general, we cannot make a jump transition $j_{(a,b)}$ that implements the both outputs in one step, i.e. simultaneously sends messages to q_1 and q_2, because the output b may be disabled (for example, the input buffer of process q_2 is full) when output a is enabled. However, if we split a into two outputs a_1 and a_2 such that a_1 is enabled iff output b is enabled, then we can make the jump transition $j_{(a_1,b)}$ (note that a copy of transition b must be preserved to work as a partner of transition a_2). Thus, we need a method to split transition a in such a way that $s \in start(a_1)$ iff $s \in start(a)$ and $a(s) \in start(b)$. Since, $start(a)$ is expressed by the guard of the command for transition a — let it be $g^a(X) \hookrightarrow U^a := e^a(X)$, the problem is only to express the predicate $a(s) \in start(b)$.

Fortunately, this problem can be approached through a well studied technique of manipulation with program actions and predicates. Namely, we refer to the *weakest liberal precondition* predicate transformer [ ] $wlp(\alpha, \pi)$, where α is a program action and π is a predicate. In our context, α is the update function of transition a, i.e. the parallel assignment $U^a := e^a(X)$, and π stands for $start(b)$, which is already expressed by the guard $g^b(X)$ of the transition b command. Thus, the predicate $a(s) \in start(b)$ can be syntactically expressed as $wlp(U^a := e^a(X), g^b(X))$. This wlp expression can then be unfolded into an ordinary boolean expression through substitution of the expression $e^a(X)$ for occurrences of variables U^a in the guard $g^b(X)$.

A harder task would be to express the set of final states of transition a. However, in order, to obtain good compression it may suffice to under-approximate this set with a big enough set $F \subseteq final(a)$, which is expressible by a boolean expression in a chosen syntax. The first approximation set F can always be given by the expression $p.c = floc(a)$ provided that a belongs to process p.

4.3   Compression Algorithms

Next are two compression algorithms, presented in a pseudo-algorithmic form. These algorithms can be implemented, by embedding the steps into the traversal of the control flow graph. The algorithms perform syntactic modification of control flow graphs (and related components) of a multi-process system M.

Algorithm 1 deals with output/input pairs of (connected) transitions. It splits output o and input i in such a way that reveals the rendezvous sub-case of their interaction: namely, an output sub-transition o_1 makes a link with input sub-transition i_1, whereas the remaining private sub-transitions o_2 and i_2 take care of the asynchronous sub-case of the original output/input interaction.

Algorithm 1. Revealing a rendezvous component of an output/input pair.
Input: Multi–process system M augmented with a signal connection C.
Action: Modify M as follows. In each pair of processes (p, q), $p, q \in P$, such that an output signal of p matches an input signal of q, for each pair of transitions $(o, i) \in C$ such that i is a stamper transition, do the following:

1. Choose an approximation set $F \subseteq final(o)$, using available heuristics (for example, the set expressed by condition $p.c = floc(o)$).
2. Split input transition i into i_1 and i_2, and output transition o into o_1 and o_2 in such a way that $s \in start(i_1)$ iff $s \in start(i) \cap F$ and $s \in start(o_1)$ iff $o(s) \in start(i_1)$.
3. (Fact: the pair (o_1, i_1) is a link.) Make a jump transition $j = j_{(o_1, i_1)}$. (Note that j is a rendezvous transition shared by processes p and q.)
4. In process p, replace o by j, o_2. In process q, replace i by j, i_2.
5. In graph G^p, replace edge o by two new edges o_2, j^p which both have the same starting and final locations as o. In graph G^q, replace edge i by two new edges i_2, j^q which both have the same starting and final locations as i.
6. In the set of stamper transitions $\mathcal{A}$, replace i by i_2 and, if transition $o \in \mathcal{A}$ then also replace o by o_2, j. In relation C replace pair (o, i) by (o_2, i_2).

Return the modified system M' and the signal connection C'. The sets T^l, T^o, T^i, T^2 are changed according to the changes in processes P and their control flow graphs $(G^p)_{p \in P}$.

A *hammock* is a set of $n > 1$ edges (or associated transitions) such that they all start at one location, let, s and finish at one location, let, f, not necessarily different from s. We say that an edge (a transition) b *follows* a if $sloc(b) = floc(a)$. A *chain* is a set of $n > 1$ edges (or associated transitions) such that (i) they form an acyclic path, i.e. may be ordered into a sequence $e_1, \ldots e_n$ where e_{i+1} follows e_i and e_1 does not follow e_n, and (ii) each of them has either one fanin or one fanout edge. A hammock (chain) is maximal if it would not be a hammock (respectively, chain) any more if any other edge (transition) is included into it. Below, whenever a hammock (chain) of edges $\{e_1, \ldots e_n\}$ is said to be replaced by a new edge e, it is meant that $sloc(e) = sloc(e_1)$ and $floc(e) = floc(e_n)$ (if the edges form a chain, e_1 and e_n are, respectively, the first and last elements).

Algorithm 2 compresses chains and hammocks in each process of system M. For simplicity, it only deals with private transitions and ignores rendezvous transitions. Algorithm 2 utilizes Procedure 1 that basically (though not exclusively) targets output transitions, for which making a link with a preceeding transition, say, a, is a problem: the set of final states of transition a does not necessarily (in a fact, almost never) coincides with the set of starting states of the following output transition. As an example, consider two consequtive outputs.

Algorithm 2. Compressing hammocks and chains.
Input: A multi-process system M.
Variables: C, H and R will keep temporary sets of (structures of) transitions of a current process p. C is designated for chains, H for hammocks, R contains those remaining transitions of process p that the algorithm has not rejected to deal with yet. Some pairs of transitions in chains of C can be marked as *bad*.

Action: Modify each process $p \in P$ and graph G^p, and the $\mathcal{A}$ as follows.

1. Initialize: $C :=$ the maximal chains of $p \setminus T^2$, $H :=$ the maximal hammocks of $p \setminus T^2$, $R := p \setminus (T^2 \cup \bigcup C \cup \bigcup H)$.
2. If no chain in C contains transitions a, b s.t. b follows a and (a, b) is not *bad* then do the following. If $H = \emptyset$ then select the next process in P and go to step 1. Otherwise, go to step 6.
3. Otherwise, pick up such a pair (a, b) in a chain of C, which is not marked *bad* and b follows a. If (a, b) is not a link then perform Procedure 1 given below and then go to step 2.
4. $((a, b)$ is a link.) In process p replace a and b by a jump transition $j = j_{(a,b)}$. In graph G^p replace the chain $\{a, b\}$ by a new edge j. Remove b from $\mathcal{A}$. If $a \in \mathcal{A}$ then replace a by j. Remove a and b from (a chain in) C.
5. If any fanin or fanout transition of j belongs to a chain in C then include j into this chain. Otherwise, include j into a hammock $h \in H$ such that $\{j\} \cup h$ is a hammock. If no such hammock is found, then, check if j makes a hammock with a transition $r \in R$. If it does, include the hammock $\{j, r\}$ into H and remove r from R. Otherwise, include j into R. Go to step 2.
6. If $H = \emptyset$ then go to step 2. Otherwise, choose a hammock, let, $\{a_1, \ldots a_n\} \in H$ and remove it from H. If the hammock cannot be merged into a single transition a (cf. Lemma 4), then repeat this step 6.
7. In process p replace $a_1, \ldots a_n$ by a. In graph G^p replace the hammock $\{a_1, \ldots a_n\}$ by a new edge a. If all $a_1, \ldots a_n \in \mathcal{A}$ then replace all of them by a; otherwice, $\mathcal{A} := \mathcal{A} \setminus \{a_1, \ldots a_n\}$.
8. If a makes a chain with transitions in the set $\{a\} \cup R \cup \bigcup C$ then form the maximal chain (in this set) that contains a and include it into C. Chains

from C are included into this new chain with their *bad* markings (if any). Remove from R the transitions which participate in this new chain. Go to step 6.

9. If a makes a hammock $\{a, r\}$ with transition $r \in R$ then include it into H and remove r from R. Otherwise, include a into R. Go to step 6.

Return the modified system M'

In Algorithm 2, each process p is modified within two loops that perform in one or more turns, one after another. The first loop (steps from 2 through 5 and Procedure 1) attempts to compress chains in C as much as possible. When nothing remains to compress in C, the second loop (steps from 6 through 9) attempts to merge hammocks in H as much as possible. Each of the loops may generate a new hammock for H. The first loop may also include a new transition into an existing hammock in H, whereas the second loop may generate a new chain for C with a transition in R. When nothing is left to compress (merge) in both C and H, modification of process p finishes and the next process is selected.

Procedure 1. (Performed for pair (a, b), if it is not a link.)

1. If $b \notin \mathcal{A}$ or a or b makes a link with a transition in the same chain of C that a, b belong to then go to step 2. Otherwise, go to step 3.
2. In C, mark the pair (a, b) as *bad*. If a follows c and (c, a) is *bad*, then remove a from C. If d follows b and (b, d) is *bad*, then remove b from C. Return to continue step 3 of Algorithm 2.
3. Split transition a into a_1, a_2 s.t. state $s \in start(a_1)$ iff $s \in start(a)$ and $a(s) \in start(b)$. In process p, replace a by a_1, a_2. In graph G^p, let $sloc(a) = \lambda$ and $floc(a) = \lambda_1$; then, make a new location λ_2 and replace the edge a by two new edges a_1, a_2 s.t. the both have λ as the starting location, whereas $floc(a_1) = \lambda_1$ and $floc(a_2) = \lambda_2$. Associate the edges a_1 and a_2 with transitions a_1 and a_2, respectively. (Fact: (a_1, b) is a link. Note that in G^p edge a_2 is not connected yet to edge b.)
4. Make the jump transition $j = j_{(a_1, b)}$. In process p replace a_1 by j. In graph G^p replace chain $\{a_1, b\}$ by a new edge j, and associate transition b with a new edge b' s.t. $sloc(b') = \lambda_2$ and $floc(b') = floc(b)$. (Thus, from now on, the new location λ_2 effectively replaces the old λ_1 — so that the new edge b' follows a_2). If $a \in \mathcal{A}$ then replace it by j, a_2. Remove a, b from (a chain in) C. Return to continue step 3 of Algorithm 2.

Theorem 2. *Given a multi-process transition system M (with signal connection C), Algorithm 2 (respectively Algorithm 1) returns a transition system M' such that $M \sim_{st} M'$.*

The proof of this theorem follows from the two facts: (i) each complete sequence of steps of the algorithm (Algorithm 2 or Algorithm 1, respectively) produces an intermediate system $\tilde{M}$ such that $\tilde{M} \sim_{st} M$, and (ii) the algorithm terminates. In Algorithm 1, a complete sequence of steps include all steps that deal with one output/input pair (o, i). In Algorithm 2, there are two types of complete step sequences: one deals with a pair of transitions (a, b) taken from a chain in C and the other one deals with a hammock taken from H.

5   Implementation and Experimental Results

Experimental results are presented in this section. Currently, revealing a rendezvous component of output/input transition pairs is not implemented. The table below summarizes our results.

Example	Experiments	
Leader(6)	Explicit, SPOR 1548 sec, 380M	Explicit, SPOR, Compression 1080sec, 204M
Sort(12)	Symbolic, SPOR 87 sec, 20M	Symbolic, SPOR, Compression 54 sec, 9.4M
HW/SW Elevator	–	Symbolic+SPOR+Compression 14403 sec, 415M
Triple Ring	Symbolic, SPOR 21 sec, 28M	Symbolic, SPOR, Compression 18 sec, 24M

A leader election protocol with 6 processes could only be verified using an explicit search, since the symbolic verification ran out of memory. The compressed system could be verified in a shorter time and using less memory than the uncompressed system. The sort example (a chain of SDL processes that runs as a parallel sorting algorithm), on the contrary, could not be verified (even with 7 processes) using explicit search after waiting 24 hours. However, the compression technique in this case also reduced the amount of time and memory required in symbolic search. As a HW/SW co-design example, we tried a simple elevator system as given in [10]. This example could only be verified using symbolic search, SPOR and compression all at the same time. It ran out of memory when compression was not used.

Fourth example is a ring consisting of three processes P, Q and R such that P sends messages to Q, Q to R and R to P. The property we checked is invisible in processes P and Q. Using SDLCheck with SPOR and no compression, we generated S/R code for this program. Then we manually modified this S/R code in such a way that one of the output/input pairs, namely, between P and Q, is split into the rendezvous action and non-rendezvous output and input (respectively, in P and Q.) The result of this small optimization, which is additional to SPOR, is not just 15% improvement. The more important is what it indeed demonstrates. Since, the cycle of inter-process communication [7] has been deliberately broken in process R (in SDLCheck, this is controllable), all local actions in P and Q appear stamper.

As a result, they are enforced to execute prior to any input and output actions. Therefore, neither of the two non-rendezvous actions (the output from P to Q and the corresponding input in Q), which remain after extraction of the rendezvous component, ever becomes enabled. In other words, communication between P and Q could be implemented as fully rendezvous, for this particular property. Remarkably, COSPAN recognizes and utilizes this situation. Before actual model checking, COSPAN applies the localization reduction, which eliminates state variables that fall out of the influence cone of the property. So, we can observe that this reduction indeed completely eliminates the buffer of the process Q. We emphasize that no such effect can be observed using only (any) one or even (any) two of the three reductions we applied in the sequence: compression of the output/input pair (based on SPOR), SPOR itself and (finally) localization reduction.

As the experimental results suggest, the transition compression may help reducing the required time and memory further, in addition to other relief techniques such as SPOR, localization reduction, symbolic verification, etc.

6   Conclusion and Related Work

A formal basis for the compression of transitions in a transition system is presented. The formalization of the method at the transition system level provides a more general framework than previous work. Recently, a similar approach was outlined in [5] and then elaborated in [18] that compresses transitions of one process. However, even within a single process, that approach does not compress consecutive output transitions. We show that consecutive transitions may be compressed, provided that the conditions of Definition 1 are satisfied. The other method does not suggest any technique for extracting a rendezvous component from asynchronous communication, as we do. Although the previous work states that their method is closely related to partial order reduction, the exact relationship is not made explicit. We show this relationship explicitly.

The compression method presented, may also make some of the variables in the system automatically removed, as in the case of the triple ring example. Live variable analysis, given in [1] can be considered as a similar approach. However, live variable analysis technique identifies the unused assignments to variables, and then removes these assignments from the model. Note that, in the triple ring example, the buffer of the process is actually used effectively in the original system. It becomes unused only after compressing the output and input transitions into a jump transition. Therefore, a live variable analysis on the original system would not recognize the process' buffer as a dead variable.

An observation that partial order reduction may be improved by jumping via a sequence of stamper (ample) transitions, was reported in [2], which suggests a different method (called a *leap*) that simultaneously executes transitions from all (current) stamper sets, rather than from one such set. This means merging independent concurrent transitions from different processes, hence, contrasts to compressing consecutive transitions from one or several processes. The leap and compression methods can be combined together, and SDLCheck implements this. However, our experiments do not show that the leap method consistently improves performance. For example, even after waiting eight hours, we could not verify the sorting algorithm with 12 processes when we used a compressed S/R model that realizes the leap technique. Apparently, such performance decline is due to the intrinsic complexity of the leap mechanism, which must deal (during the model checking, not statically) with the entire set of all current stamper sets.

Our method can benefit directly from any progress in the field of partial order reduction theory. Relaxing visibility conditions of transitions [14], for example, can directly be incorporated into our tool.

References

1. Marius Bozga, Jean-Claude Fernandez, and Lucian Ghirvu. State space reduction based on live variables analysis. In *Static Analysis Symposium*, pages 164–178, Venezia, Italy, 1999. 580
2. H. Van der Schoot and H. Ural. An improvement on partial order model checking with ample sets. Technical Report TR-96-11, Univ. of Ottawa, Canada, 1996. 580
3. E. W. Dijkstra. Guarded commands, nondeterminacy, and formal derivation of programs. *Communications of ACM*, 18(8):453–457, August 1975. 575
4. P. Godefroid. *Partial–Order Methods for the Verification of Concurrent Systems: An Approach to the State–Explosion Problem*. PhD thesis, University of Liège, Liège, Belgium, November 1994. 569, 571
5. G. J. Holzmann. The engineering of a model checker: The gnu i-protocol case study revised. In *6th Workshop on SPIN*, LNCS 1680, 1999. 580
6. ITU–T, Geneva. *Functional Specification and Description Language (SDL), Recommendation Z.100*, March 1993. 570, 573
7. R. P. Kurshan, V. Levin, M. Minea, D. Peled, and H. Yenigün. Combining hardware and software verification tecniques. *Formal Methods in System Design.* accepted for publication. 570, 571, 579
8. R. P. Kurshan, V. Levin, and H. Yenigün. Compressing transitions for model checking. Technical report, Bell Labs, Lucent Technologies, 2002. 572
9. R. P. Kurshan. *Computer–Aided Verification of Coordinating Processes: The Automata–Theoretic Approach*. Princeton University Press, 1994. 570
10. R. P. Kurshan, V. Levin, M. Minea, D. Peled, and H. Yenigun. Static partial order reduction. In *4th International Conference Tools and Algorithms for the Construction and Analysis of Systems*, LNCS 1384, pages 345–357, Portugal, 1998. 569, 570, 571, 579
11. L. Lamport. What good is temporal logic? In R.E.A. Mason, editor, *Information Processing*, pages 657–668, Paris, September 1983. Elsevier Science Publishers. 571
12. V. Levin and H. Yenigun. SDLCheck : A model checking tool. In *13th CAV*, France, 2001. 570
13. D. Peled. All from one, one for all – on model checking using representatives. In *5th CAV*, LNCS 697, pages 409–423, Crete, June 1993. Springer–Verlag. 569, 571
14. D. Peled, A. Valmari, and I. Kokkarinen. Relaxed visibility enhances partial order reduction. *Formal Methods in System Design*, 19(3), November 2001. 571, 581
15. A. Pnueli. The temporal logics of programs. In *18th Annual IEEE–CS Symposium on Foundations of Computer Science*, pages 46–57, Cambridge, 1977. 570, 571
16. A. Valmari. A stubborn attack on state explosion. In *2nd CAV*, LNCS 531, pages 156–165, Rutgers, June 1990. Springer–Verlag. 569, 571
17. H. Yenigün. *Static Partial Order Reduction and Model Checking of HW/SW Co-Design Systems*. PhD thesis, Middle East Technical University, Turkey, 2000. 571

18. K. Yorav. *Exploiting Syntactic Structure for Automatic Verification.* PhD thesis, The Technion – Israel Institute of Technology, Haifa, Israel, 2000.   580

Canonical Prefixes of Petri Net Unfoldings

Victor Khomenko[1], Maciej Koutny[1], and Walter Vogler[2]

[1] Department of Computing Science, University of Newcastle
Newcastle upon Tyne NE1 7RU, U.K.
{Victor.Khomenko, Maciej.Koutny}@ncl.ac.uk
[2] Institut für Informatik, Universität Augsburg
D-86135 Augsburg, Germany
Walter.Vogler@informatik.uni-augsburg.de

Abstract. In this paper, we develop a general technique for truncating Petri net unfoldings, parameterised according to the level of information about the original unfolding one wants to preserve. Moreover, we propose a new notion of completeness of a truncated unfolding. A key aspect of our approach is an *algorithm-independent* notion of cut-off events, used to truncate a Petri net unfolding. Such a notion is based on a *cutting context* and results in the unique *canonical* prefix of the unfolding. Canonical prefixes are complete in the new, stronger sense, and we provide necessary and sufficient conditions for its finiteness, as well as upper bounds on its size in certain cases. A surprising result is that after suitable generalisation, the standard unfolding algorithm presented in [ ], and the parallel unfolding algorithm proposed in [ ], despite being non-deterministic, generate the canonical prefix. This gives an alternative correctness proof for the former algorithm, and a new (much simpler) proof for the latter one.

Keywords: Model checking, Petri nets, unfolding, canonical prefix.

1 Introduction

Computer aided verification tools implementing model checking (see, e.g., [ ]) verify a concurrent system using a finite representation of its state space, and thus may suffer from the state explosion problem. To cope with this, several techniques have been developed, which usually aim either at a compact representation of the full state space of the system, or at the generation of its reduced (though sufficient for a given verification task) state space. Among them, a prominent technique is McMillan's (finite prefixes of) Petri Net unfoldings (see, e.g., [,]). They rely on the partial order view of concurrent computation, and represent system states implicitly, using an acyclic net. More precisely, given a Petri net Σ, the unfolding technique aims at building a labelled acyclic net Unf_Σ (a *prefix*) satisfying two key properties:

- *Completeness.* Each reachable marking of Σ is represented by at least one 'witness', i.e., one marking of Unf_Σ reachable from its initial marking. (Similarly, for each possible firing of a transition in Σ there is a suitable 'witness' event in Unf_Σ.)

D. Brinksma and K. G. Larsen (Eds.): CAV 2002, LNCS 2404, pp. 582–595, 2002.

– *Finiteness.* The prefix is finite and thus can be used as input to model checking algorithms, e.g., those searching for deadlocks.

This paper presents a uniform treatment of both these aspects and provides a fresh impetus for further development of unfolding-based model checking techniques.

There are two fundamental issues which we wish to address here, namely the precise *semantical* meaning of completeness, and the *algorithmic* problem of generating complete prefixes.

Semantical Meaning of Completeness A direct motivation to re-examine the issue of completeness was provided by our own experience of dealing with unfoldings of Signal Transition Graphs (STGs) in [11], used to specify the behaviour of asynchronous circuits. Briefly, an STG (see [16]) is a Petri net together with a set of binary signals (variables), which can be set or reset by transition firings. A transition can either change the value of one specific signal, or affect no signals at all. Thus, the current values of the signals depend not on the current marking, but rather on the sequence of transition firings that leads to it. In effect, one is interested in a 'combined' system state which includes both the current marking and the current values of the binary signals. Therefore, if one wants to ensure that a prefix represents the entire state space, some additional information (in this case, the valuation of signal variables) must be taken into account. Clearly, the completeness as sketched above does not guarantee this.

We soon found that the situation can also be a totally opposite one, i.e., the standard notion of completeness can be unnecessarily strong. As an example, one can consider the building of a prefix when there is a suitable notion of symmetric (equivalent) markings, as described in [9]. The idea is then to ensure that each marking of Σ is represented in Unf_Σ either directly or by a symmetric marking. Such an approach may significantly reduce the size of the prefix.

Having analysed examples like these, we have concluded that the original notion of completeness, though sufficient for certain applications, may be too crude and inflexible if one wants to take into consideration more complex semantics of concurrent systems, or their inherent structural properties.

Algorithmics of Prefix Generation The essential feature of the existing unfolding algorithms (see, e.g., [5,8,13]) is the use of cut-off events, beyond which the unfolding starts to repeat itself and so can be truncated without loss of information. So far, cut-off events were considered as an algorithm-specific issue, and were defined w.r.t. the part of the prefix already built by an unfolding algorithm (in other words, at run-time). Such a treatment was quite pragmatic and worked reasonably well. But, in more complicated situations, the dynamic notion of a cut-off event may hinder defining appropriate algorithms and, in particular, proving their correctness. This has become apparent when dealing with a parallel algorithm for generating prefixes in [8], where the degree of possible non-determinism brought up both these issues very clearly. To conclude, the algorithm-dependent notion of a cut-off event is increasingly difficult to manage.

There is also an important aspect linking cut-off events and completeness, which was somewhat overlooked in previous works. To start with, the notion of a complete prefix given in [ ] did not mention cut-off events at all. But, with the development of model-checking algorithms based on unfoldings, it appeared that cut-off events are heavily employed by almost all of them. Indeed, the deadlock detection algorithm presented in [ ] is based on the fact that a Petri net is deadlock-free iff each configuration of its finite and complete prefix can be extended to one containing a cut-off event, i.e., a Petri net has a deadlock iff there is a configuration which is in conflict with all cut-off events. The algorithms presented in [, ,] use the fact that there is a certain correspondence between the deadlocked markings of the original net and the deadlocked markings of a finite and complete prefix, and cut-off events are needed to distinguish the 'real' deadlocks from the 'fake' ones, introduced by truncating the unfolding. Moreover, those algorithms need a stronger notion of completeness than the one presented in [ ], in order to guarantee that deadlocks in the prefix do correspond to deadlocks in the original Petri net.[1] Since all these algorithms make certain assumptions about the properties of a prefix with cut-off events, it is natural to formally link cut-off events with the notion of completeness, closing up a rather uncomfortable gap between theory and practice.

The New Approach In order to address issues of semantical meaning and algorithmic pragmatics relating to the finite prefixes of Petri net unfoldings, we propose a parametric set-up in which questions concerning, e.g., completeness and cut-off events, could be discussed in a uniform and general way. One parameter captures the information we intend to retain in a complete prefix, while the other two specify under which circumstances a given event can be designated as a cut-off event. Crucially, we decided to shift the emphasis from markings to the execution histories of Σ, and the former parameter, a suitably defined equivalence relation $\approx$, specifies which executions can be regarded as equivalent. Intuitively, one has to retain at least one representative execution from each equivalence class of $\approx$. (The standard case in [,] is then covered by regarding two executions as equivalent iff they reach the same marking.)

For efficiency reasons, the existing unfolding algorithms usually consider only local configurations when deciding whether an event should be designated as a cut-off event. But one can also consider arbitrary finite configurations for such a purpose if the size of the resulting prefix is of paramount importance (see, e.g., [ ]). As a result, the final definition of the set-up, called here a *cutting context*, contains besides an adequate order (as in [ ]) a parameter which specifies precisely those configurations which can be used to designate an event as a cut-off event. For a given equivalence relation $\approx$, we then define what it means for a

---

[1] According to the notion of completeness presented in [ ], a marking M enabling a transition t may be represented by a deadlocked configuration C in a complete prefix, as long as there is another configuration C' representing this marking and enabling an instance of t. This means that the prefix may contain a deadlock, which does not correspond to any deadlock in the original net system (see Figure 1).

prefix to be complete. In essence, we require that all equivalence classes of $\approx$ are represented, and that any history involving no cut-off events can be extended (in a single step) in exactly the same way as in the full unfolding.

The definition of a cutting context leads to our central result, the *algorithm-independent* notion of a cut-off event and the related unique *canonical* prefix; the latter is shown to be complete w.r.t. our new notion of completeness. Though the canonical prefix is always complete, it may still be infinite, making it unusable for model checking. We therefore investigate what guarantees the finiteness of the canonical prefix and, in doing so, formulate and prove a version of König's Lemma for unfoldings of (possibly unbounded) Petri nets.

To summarise, this paper addresses both semantical and algorithmic problems using a single device, namely the canonical prefix. The theoretical notion of a complete prefix is useful as long as it can be the basis of a practical prefix-building algorithm. We show that this is indeed the case, generalising the already proposed unfolding algorithm presented in [5] as well as the parallel algorithm from [8]. We believe that the above approach results in a more elegant framework for investigating issues relating to unfolding prefixes, and provides a powerful and flexible tool to deal with different variants of the unfolding technique. All proofs can be found in the technical report [10].

2   Basic Notions

In this section, we first present basic definitions concerning Petri nets, and then recall (see also [4,5]) notions related to net unfoldings.

A *net* is a triple $N \stackrel{\text{df}}{=} (P, T, F)$ such that P and T are disjoint sets of respectively *places* and *transitions*, and $F \subseteq (P \times T) \cup (T \times P)$ is a *flow relation*. A *marking* of N is a multiset M of places, i.e., $M : P \rightarrow \{0, 1, 2, \ldots\}$. As usual, ${}^\bullet z \stackrel{\text{df}}{=} \{y \mid (y, z) \in F\}$ and $z^\bullet \stackrel{\text{df}}{=} \{y \mid (z, y) \in F\}$ denote the *pre-* and *postset* of $z \in P \cup T$. We will assume that ${}^\bullet t \neq \emptyset \neq t^\bullet$, for every $t \in T$. A *net system* is a pair $\Sigma \stackrel{\text{df}}{=} (N, M_0)$ comprising a finite net N and an *initial* marking M_0. We assume the reader is familiar with the standard notions of the theory of Petri nets, such as the *enabledness* and *firing* of a transition, marking *reachability*, and net *boundedness* and (1-)*safeness*. We will denote the set of reachable markings of Σ by $\mathcal{M}(\Sigma)$.

Branching Processes Two nodes (places or transitions), y and y', of a net $N = (P, T, F)$ are in *conflict*, denoted by $y \# y'$, if there are distinct transitions $t, t' \in T$ such that ${}^\bullet t \cap {}^\bullet t' \neq \emptyset$ and (t, y) and (t', y') are in the reflexive transitive closure of the flow relation F, denoted by $\preceq$. A node y is in *self-conflict* if $y \# y$.

An *occurrence net* is a net $ON \stackrel{\text{df}}{=} (B, E, G)$, where B is the set of *conditions* (places) and E is the set of *events* (transitions), satisfying the following: ON is acyclic (i.e., $\preceq$ is a partial order); for every $b \in B$, $|{}^\bullet b| \leq 1$; for every $y \in B \cup E$, $\neg(y \# y)$ and there are finitely many y' such that $y' \prec y$, where $\prec$ denotes the transitive closure of G. $Min(ON)$ will denote the set of minimal (w.r.t. $\prec$)

elements of $B \cup E$. The relation $\prec$ is the *causality relation*. A $\prec$-*chain* of events is a finite or infinite sequence of events such that for each two consecutive events, e and f, it is the case that $e \prec f$. Two nodes are *concurrent*, denoted $y \ co \ y'$, if neither $y \# y'$ nor $y \preceq y'$ nor $y' \preceq y$.

A *homomorphism* from an occurrence net ON to a net system Σ is a mapping $h : B \cup E \to P \cup T$ such that: $h(B) \subseteq P$ and $h(E) \subseteq T$; for all $e \in E$, the restriction of h to $^\bullet e$ is a bijection between $^\bullet e$ and $^\bullet h(e)$; the restriction of h to $e^\bullet$ is a bijection between $e^\bullet$ and $h(e)^\bullet$; the restriction of h to $Min(ON)$ is a bijection between the multisets $Min(ON)$ and M_0; and for all $e, f \in E$, if $^\bullet e = {}^\bullet f$ and $h(e) = h(f)$ then $e = f$. If an event e is such that $h(e) = t$, then we will often refer to it as being t-*labelled*.

A *branching process* of Σ (see [ ]) is a quadruple $\pi \overset{\text{df}}{=} (B, E, G, h)$ such that (B, E, G) is an occurrence net and h is a homomorphism from ON to Σ. A branching process $\pi' = (B', E', G', h')$ of Σ is a *prefix* of a branching process $\pi = (B, E, G, h)$, denoted $\pi' \sqsubseteq \pi$, if (B', E', G') is a subnet of (B, E, G) (i.e., $B' \subseteq B$, $E' \subseteq E$ and $G' = G \cap (B' \times E' \cup E' \times B')$) containing all minimal elements and such that: if $e \in E'$ and $(b, e) \in G$ or $(e, b) \in G$ then $b \in B'$; if $b \in B'$ and $(e, b) \in G$ then $e \in E'$; and h' is the restriction of h to $B' \cup E'$. For each net system Σ there exists a unique (up to isomorphism) maximal (w.r.t. $\sqsubseteq$) branching process Unf_{Σ}^{max}, called the *unfolding* of Σ.

For convenience, we assume a branching process to start with a (virtual) *initial event* $\perp$, which has the postset $Min(ON)$, empty preset, and no label. We do not represent $\perp$ in figures nor treat it explicitly in algorithms.

Configurations and Cuts A *configuration* of an occurrence net ON is a set of events C such that for all $e, f \in C$, $\neg(e \# f)$ and, for every $e \in C$, $f \prec e$ implies $f \in C$; since we assume the initial event $\perp$, we additionally require that $\perp \in C$. For $e \in E$, the configuration $[e] \overset{\text{df}}{=} \{f \mid f \preceq e\}$ is called the *local configuration* of e, and $\langle e \rangle \overset{\text{df}}{=} [e] \setminus \{e\}$ denotes the set of *causal predecessors* of e. Moreover, for a set of events E' we denote by $C \oplus E'$ the fact that $C \cup E'$ is a configuration and $C \cap E' = \emptyset$. Such an E' is a *suffix* of C, and $C \oplus E'$ is an *extension* of C.

The set of all finite (resp. local) configurations of a branching process π will be denoted by $\mathcal{C}_{fin}^\pi$ (resp. $\mathcal{C}_{loc}^\pi$) — or simply by $\mathcal{C}_{fin}$ (resp. $\mathcal{C}_{loc}$) if $\pi = Unf_{\Sigma}^{max}$.

A *co-set* is a set of mutually concurrent conditions. A *cut* is a maximal (w.r.t. set inclusion) co-set. Every marking reachable from $Min(ON)$ is a cut.

Let C be a finite configuration of a branching process π. Then $Cut(C) \overset{\text{df}}{=} (Min(ON) \cup C^\bullet) \setminus {}^\bullet C$ is a cut; moreover, the multiset of places $h(Cut(C))$ is a reachable marking of Σ, denoted $Mark(C)$. A marking M of Σ is *represented* in π if there is $C \in \mathcal{C}_{fin}^\pi$ such that $M = Mark(C)$. Every such marking is reachable in Σ, and every reachable marking of Σ is represented in the unfolding of Σ.

In the rest of this paper, we assume that Σ is a fixed, though not necessarily bounded, net system, and that $Unf_{\Sigma}^{max} = (B, E, G, h)$ is its unfolding.

König's Lemma for Branching Processes König's Lemma (see [ ]) states that a finitely branching, rooted, directed acyclic graph with infinitely many nodes reachable from the root has an infinite path. It turns out that a version of such a result holds for branching processes of Petri nets.

Proposition 1. *A branching process π is infinite iff it contains an infinite $\prec$-chain of events.*

Note that the above result does not follow directly from the original König's Lemma [12], since the conditions of π can have infinitely many outgoing arcs.

3   Complete Prefixes of Petri Net Unfoldings

As explained in the introduction, there exist several different methods of truncating Petri net unfoldings. The differences are related to the kind of information about the original unfolding one wants to preserve in the prefix, as well as to the choice between using either only local configurations (which can improve the running time of an algorithm), or all finite configurations (which can result in a smaller prefix). Also, we need a more general notion of completeness for branching processes. Here we generalise the entire set-up so that it will be applicable to different methods of truncating unfoldings and, at the same time, allow one to express the completeness w.r.t. properties other than marking reachability.

Cutting Contexts For flexibility, our new set-up is parametric. The first parameter determines the information to be preserved in a complete prefix (in the standard case, the set of reachable markings). The main idea here is to shift the emphasis from the reachable markings of Σ to the finite configurations of Unf_Σ^{max}. Formally, the information to be preserved in the prefix corresponds to the equivalence classes of some equivalence relation $\approx$ on $\mathcal{C}_{fin}$. The other two parameters are more technical: they specify under which circumstances an event can be designated as a cut-off event.

Definition 2. A *cutting context* is a triple $\Theta \stackrel{\mathrm{df}}{=} \left(\approx, \lhd, \{\mathcal{C}_e\}_{e \in E} \right)$, where:

1. $\approx$ is an equivalence relation on $\mathcal{C}_{fin}$.
2. $\lhd$, called an *adequate* order (comp. [8]), is a strict well-founded partial order on $\mathcal{C}_{fin}$ refining $\subset$, i.e., $C' \subset C''$ implies $C' \lhd C''$.
3. $\approx$ and $\lhd$ are *preserved by finite extensions*, i.e., for every pair of configurations $C' \approx C''$, and for every suffix E' of C', there exists[2] a finite suffix E'' of C'' such that:
   (a) $C'' \oplus E'' \approx C' \oplus E'$, and
   (b) if $C'' \lhd C'$ then $C'' \oplus E'' \lhd C' \oplus E'$.
4. $\{\mathcal{C}_e\}_{e \in E}$ is a family of subsets of $\mathcal{C}_{fin}$, i.e., $\mathcal{C}_e \subseteq \mathcal{C}_{fin}$ for all $e \in E$. $\diamond$

---

[2] Unlike [8], we do not require that $E'' = I_1^2(E')$, where I_1^2 is the 'natural' isomorphism between the finite extensions of C' and C''. That isomorphism may be undefined if $Mark(C') \neq Mark(C'')$, and thus cannot be used in our generalised settings.

The main idea behind the adequate order is to specify which configurations will be preserved in the complete prefix; it turns out that all $\lhd$-minimal configurations in each equivalence class of $\approx$ will be preserved. The last parameter is needed to specify the set of configurations used later to decide whether an event can be designated as a cut-off event. For example, $\mathcal{C}_e$ may contain all finite configurations of Unf_Σ^{max}, or, as it is usually the case in practice, only the local ones. We will say that a cutting context Θ is *dense* (*saturated*) if $\mathcal{C}_e \supseteq \mathcal{C}_{loc}$ (resp. $\mathcal{C}_e = \mathcal{C}_{fin}$), for all $e \in E$.

In practice, Θ is usually dense (or even saturated, see [6]), and at least the following three kinds of the equivalence $\approx$ have been used:

- $C' \approx_{mar} C''$ if $Mark(C') = Mark(C'')$. This is the most widely used equivalence (see [5,6,8,13]). Note that the equivalence classes of $\approx_{mar}$ correspond to the reachable markings of Σ.
- $C' \approx_{code} C''$ if $Mark(C') = Mark(C'')$ and $Code(C') = Code(C'')$, where $Code(C)$ is the signal coding function. Such an equivalence is used in [10] for unfolding Signal Transition Graphs (STGs) specifying asynchronous circuits.
- $C' \approx_{sym} C''$ if $Mark(C')$ and $Mark(C'')$ are symmetric (equivalent) markings. This equivalence is the basis of the approach exploiting symmetries to reduce the size of the prefix, described in [3].

For an equivalence relation $\approx$, we denote by $\mathfrak{R}_\approx^{fin} \stackrel{\mathrm{df}}{=} \mathcal{C}_{fin}/_\approx$ the set of its equivalence classes, and by $\mathfrak{R}_\approx^{loc} \stackrel{\mathrm{df}}{=} \mathcal{C}_{loc}/_\approx$ the set of its equivalence classes on the local configurations. We will also denote by Θ_{ERV} the cutting context corresponding to the framework used in [5], i.e., such that $\approx$ is equal to $\approx_{mar}$, $\lhd$ is the total adequate order for safe net systems proposed there, and $\mathcal{C}_e = \mathcal{C}_{loc}$, for all $e \in E$.

We will write $e \lhd f$ whenever $[e] \lhd [f]$. Since $\lhd$ is a well-founded partial order on the set of events, we can use Noetherian induction (see [2]) for definitions and proofs, i.e., it suffices to define or prove something for an event under the assumption that it has already been defined or proven for all its $\lhd$-predecessors.

Proposition 3. *Let e and f be two events, and C be a finite configuration.*
  1. *If $f \prec e$ then $f \lhd e$.*
  2. *If $f \in C \lhd [e]$ then $f \lhd e$.*

In the rest of this paper, we assume that the cutting context Θ is fixed.

Completeness of Branching Processes We now introduce a new notion of completeness for branching processes.

Definition 4. A branching process π is *complete* w.r.t. a set E_{cut} of events of Unf_Σ^{max} if the following hold:

1. If $C \in \mathcal{C}_{fin}$, then there is $C' \in \mathcal{C}_{fin}^\pi$ such that $C' \cap E_{cut} = \emptyset$ and $C \approx C'$.
2. If $C \in \mathcal{C}_{fin}^\pi$ is such that $C \cap E_{cut} = \emptyset$, and e is an event such that $C \oplus \{e\} \in \mathcal{C}_{fin}$, then $C \oplus \{e\} \in \mathcal{C}_{fin}^\pi$.

A branching process π is *complete* if it is complete w.r.t. some set E_{cut}. $\diamond$

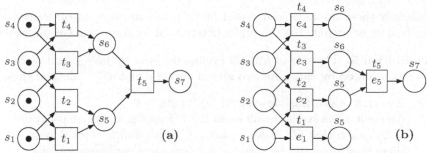

Fig. 1. A Petri net **(a)** and one of its branching processes **(b)**, which is complete according to [5], but not w.r.t. Definition 4: the configuration $\{e_1, e_4\}$ does not preserve firings and introduces a fake deadlock. To make the prefix complete w.r.t. Definition 4, one has to add an instance of t_5 consuming the conditions produced by e_1 and e_4

Note that π remains complete following the removal of all events e for which $\langle e \rangle \cap E_{cut} \neq \emptyset$, after which the events from E_{cut} (usually referred to as *cut-off* events) will be either maximal events of the prefix or not in the prefix at all. Note also that the last definition depends only on the equivalence $\approx$, and not on the other components of the cutting context.

For the relation $\approx_{mar}$, each reachable marking is represented by a configuration in C_{fin} and, hence, also by a configuration in C_{fin}^{π}, provided that π is complete. This is what is usually expected from a correct prefix. But even in this special case, our notion of completeness differs from that presented in [5], since it requires *all* configurations in C_{fin}^{π} containing no events from E_{cut} to preserve all transition firings, rather than the *existence* of a configuration preserving all firings. The justification why such a stronger property is desirable, e.g., for deadlock detection, was given in the introduction (see also Figure 1). Obviously, our notion is strictly stronger than the one in [5], i.e., it implies the completeness in the sense of [5], but not vice versa (see Figure 1). However, the proof of completeness in [5] almost gives the stronger notion; we have adopted it (see [10, Proposition 8]) with relatively few modifications.

4   Canonical Prefix

This and the next section develop our central results. First, we define cut-off events without resorting to any algorithmic argument. This yields a definition of the canonical prefix, and we then establish several of its relevant properties.

Static Cut-Off Events In [5], the definition of a cut-off event was algorithm-specific, and given w.r.t. the already built part of a prefix. Here we define cut-off events w.r.t. the whole unfolding instead, so that it will be independent of an algorithm (hence the term 'static'), together with *feasible* events, which are precisely those events whose causal predecessors are not cut-off events, and as such must be included in the prefix determined by the static cut-off events.

Definition 5. The sets of *feasible* events, denoted by $fsble_\Theta$, and *static cut-off* events, denoted by cut_Θ, are two sets of events e of Unf_Σ^{max} defined thus:

1. An event e is a feasible event if $\langle e \rangle \cap cut_\Theta = \emptyset$.
2. An event e is a static cut-off event if it is feasible, and there is a configuration $C \in \mathcal{C}_e$ such that $C \subseteq fsble_\Theta \setminus cut_\Theta$, $C \approx [e]$, and $C \lhd [e]$. Any C satisfying these conditions will be called a *corresponding* configuration of e.   ◇

Note that $fsble_\Theta$ and cut_Θ are well-defined sets due to Noetherian induction. Indeed, when considering an event e, by the well-foundedness of $\lhd$ and Proposition 3(1), one can assume that for the events in $\langle e \rangle$ it has already been decided whether they are in $fsble_\Theta$ or in cut_Θ. And, by Proposition 3(2), the same holds for the events in any configuration C satisfying $C \lhd [e]$.

Since $\langle \bot \rangle = \emptyset$, $\bot \in fsble_\Theta$ by the above definition. Furthermore, $\bot \notin cut_\Theta$, since $\bot$ cannot have a corresponding configuration. Indeed, $[\bot] = \{\bot\}$ is the smallest (w.r.t. set inclusion) configuration, and so $\lhd$-minimal by Definition 2(2).

Remark 1. A naïve attempt to define an algorithm-independent notion of a cut-off event as an event e for which there is a configuration $C \in \mathcal{C}_e$ such that $C \approx [e]$ and $C \lhd [e]$ fails. Indeed, suppose that $\Theta = \Theta_{ERV}$, as it is often the case in practice. Then a corresponding local configuration C of a cut-off event e defined in this way may contain another cut-off event. Though in this case Unf_Σ^{max} contains another corresponding configuration $C' \lhd C$ with no cut-off events and the same final marking, such a configuration is not necessarily local.

The approach proposed in this paper, though slightly more complicated, allows to deal uniformly with arbitrary cutting contexts. Moreover, it coincides with the naïve approach when Θ is saturated.   ◇

Canonical Prefix and Its Properties Once we have defined feasible events, the following notion arises quite naturally. The *canonical* prefix of Unf_Σ^{max} is the unique branching process Unf_Σ^Θ, whose set of events is $fsble_\Theta$, and whose conditions are the conditions adjacent to these events. Thus Unf_Σ^Θ is uniquely determined by the cutting context Θ.

In what follows, we present several fundamental properties of Unf_Σ^Θ. We stress that, unlike those given in [5], their proofs are not algorithm-specific (see [10]).

Theorem 6. Unf_Σ^Θ *is complete w.r.t.* $E_{cut} = cut_\Theta$.

Having established that the canonical prefix is always complete, we now set out to analyse its finiteness. A necessary and sufficient condition for the latter follows directly from our version of König's Lemma for branching processes.

Theorem 7. Unf_Σ^Θ *is finite iff there is no infinite* $\prec$-*chain of feasible events.*

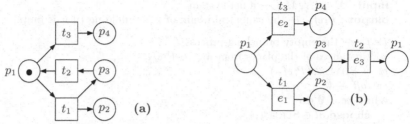

Fig. 2. An unbounded net system **(a)** and its canonical prefix **(b)**. The cutting context is such that $C' \approx C'' \Leftrightarrow Mark(C') \cap \{p_1, p_3, p_4\} = Mark(C'') \cap \{p_1, p_3, p_4\}$ and $\{\perp\} \in \mathcal{C}_{e_3}$, and so e_3 is a static cut-off event

Thus, in order to get a finite canonical prefix, one should choose a cutting context such that the $\mathcal{C}_e$'s contain enough configurations, and $\approx$ is coarse enough, to cut each infinite $\prec$-chain. Interestingly, certain cutting contexts sometimes give a finite canonical prefix even for unbounded net systems. Figure 2(a) shows a net modelling a loop, where place p_2, used for counting the number of iterations, is unbounded. If $\approx$ ignores the value of this 'counter' place, it is possible to build a finite and complete canonical prefix, shown in Figure 2(b).

The following result provides quite a tight and practical indication for deciding whether Unf_Σ^Θ is finite or not.

Proposition 8. *If $|\mathfrak{R}_\approx^{fin}| < \infty$ and Θ is dense, then Unf_Σ^Θ is finite. If $|\mathfrak{R}_\approx^{fin}| = \infty$, then Unf_Σ^Θ is infinite.*

Corollary 9. *Let $\approx$ be either of $\approx_{mar}$, $\approx_{code}$, $\approx_{sym}$. If Σ is bounded and Θ is dense, then Unf_Σ^Θ is finite. If Σ is unbounded, then Unf_Σ^Θ is infinite.*

In the important special case of a total adequate order $\lhd$, one can also derive an upper bound on the number of non-cut-off events in Unf_Σ^Θ. A specialised version of the following result (for $\Theta = \Theta_{ERV}$) was proven in [5] for the prefix generated by the unfolding algorithm presented there.

Theorem 10. *Suppose that $\lhd$ is total, $|\mathfrak{R}_\approx^{loc}| < \infty$, and the following holds: For every $\mathcal{R} \in \mathfrak{R}_\approx^{loc}$, there is $\gamma_\mathcal{R} > 0$ such that, for every chain $e_1 \lhd e_2 \lhd \cdots \lhd e_{\gamma_\mathcal{R}}$ of feasible events whose local configurations belong to $\mathcal{R}$, there is at least one $i \leq \gamma_\mathcal{R}$ such that $[e_i] \in \bigcap_{[e] \in \mathcal{R}} \mathcal{C}_e$. Then $|fsble_\Theta \setminus cut_\Theta| \leq \sum_{\mathcal{R} \in \mathfrak{R}_\approx^{loc}} \gamma_\mathcal{R}$.*

Note that if Θ is dense, then $\gamma_\mathcal{R} = 1$ for every $\mathcal{R} \in \mathfrak{R}_\approx^{loc}$, and $\sum_{\mathcal{R} \in \mathfrak{R}_\approx^{loc}} \gamma_\mathcal{R} = |\mathfrak{R}_\approx^{loc}| \leq |\mathfrak{R}_\approx^{fin}|$. The standard result of [5] is then obtained by taking $\Theta = \Theta_{ERV}$. Indeed, since the reachable markings of Σ correspond to the equivalence classes of $\approx_{mar}$, the upper bound on the number of non-cut-off events in Unf_Σ^Θ in this case is equal to $|\mathcal{M}(\Sigma)|$. Using the above theorem, one can easily derive the following upper bounds for the remaining two equivalences considered in this paper (in each case, we assume that Θ is dense):

input : $\Sigma = (N, M_0)$ — a net system
output : $Pref_\Sigma$ — the canonical prefix of Σ's unfolding (if it is finite)

$Pref_\Sigma \leftarrow$ the empty branching process
add instances of the places from M_0 to $Pref_\Sigma$
$pe \leftarrow$ POTEXT($Pref_\Sigma$)
$cut\_off \leftarrow \emptyset$
while $pe \neq \emptyset$ **do**
    choose $Sl \in$ SLICES(pe)
    if $\exists e \in Sl : [e] \cap cut\_off = \emptyset$
    then
        for all $e \in Sl$ in any order refining $\lhd$ **do**
            if $[e] \cap cut\_off = \emptyset$
            then
                add e and new instances of the places from $h(e)^\bullet$ to $Pref_\Sigma$
                if e is a cut-off event of $Pref_\Sigma$ **then** $cut\_off \leftarrow cut\_off \cup \{e\}$
            $pe \leftarrow$ POTEXT($Pref_\Sigma$)
    else $pe \leftarrow pe \setminus Sl$

Note: e is a cut-off event of $Pref_\Sigma$ if there is $C \in \mathcal{C}_e$ such that
the events of C belong to $Pref_\Sigma$ but not to cut_off, $C \approx [e]$, and $C \lhd [e]$.

Fig. 3. Unfolding algorithm with slices

$$- \left|\mathfrak{R}^{fin}_{\approx_{code}}\right| = \left|\{(Mark(C), Code(C))\}_{C \in \mathcal{C}_{fin}}\right| \leq |\mathcal{M}(\Sigma)| \cdot |Code(\mathcal{C}_{fin})| \leq$$
$$|\mathcal{M}(\Sigma)| \cdot 2^n, \text{ where } n \text{ is the number of signals.}$$
$$- \left|\mathfrak{R}^{fin}_{\approx_{sym}}\right| \leq \left|\mathfrak{R}^{fin}_{\approx_{mar}}\right| = |\mathcal{M}(\Sigma)|.$$

These upper bounds are rather pessimistic, particulary because we bound $\left|\mathfrak{R}^{loc}_\approx\right|$ by $\left|\mathfrak{R}^{fin}_\approx\right|$. In practice, the set $\mathfrak{R}^{fin}_\approx$ is usually exponentially larger than $\mathfrak{R}^{loc}_\approx$, and so prefixes are often exponentially smaller than reachability graphs.

5 Algorithms for Generating Canonical Prefixes

It turns out that canonical prefixes can be generated by straightforward gen-eralisations of the existing unfolding algorithms (see, e.g., [5, 8]). The *slicing* algorithm from [8], parameterised by a cutting context Θ, is shown in Figure 3. (The algorithm proposed in [5] is a special case.) It is assumed that the func-tion POTEXT($Pref_\Sigma$) finds the set of *possible extensions* of a branching process $Pref_\Sigma$, according to the following definition.

Definition 11. For a branching process π of Σ, a *possible extension* is a pair (t, D), where D is a co-set in π and t is a transition of Σ, such that $h(D) = {}^\bullet t$ and π contains no t-labelled event with preset D. We will take the pair (t, D) as a t-labelled event having D as its preset. $\diamond$

Compared to the standard unfolding algorithm in [5], the slicing algorithm has the following modifications in its main loop. A set of events Sl, called a *slice*, is chosen on each iteration and processed as a whole, without taking or adding any events from or to pe. A slice must satisfy the following conditions:

- Sl is a non-empty subset of the current set of possible extensions pe;
- for every $e \in Sl$ and every event $f \lhd e$ of Unf_Σ^{max}, $f \notin pe \setminus Sl$ and $pe \cap \langle f \rangle = \emptyset$.

In particular, if $f \in pe$ and $f \lhd e$ for some $e \in Sl$, then $f \in Sl$. The set $\text{SLICES}(pe)$ is chosen so that it is non-empty whenever pe is non-empty. Note that this algorithm, in general, exhibits more non-determinism than the one from [5]: it may be non-deterministic even if the order $\lhd$ is total. Since the events in the current slice can be processed completely independently, the slicing algorithm admits efficient parallelisation (along the lines proposed in [8]). A crucial property of the slicing unfolding algorithm is that it generates the canonical prefix.

Theorem 12. *If Unf_Σ^Θ is finite, then the slicing algorithm generates Unf_Σ^Θ in a finite number of steps.*

As far as this paper is concerned, the above theorem completes our investigation. What remains is to put this section in the context of the previous work. In the case $\Theta = \Theta_{ERV}$ the slicing algorithm is nothing more but the algorithm proposed in [8]. Moreover, by setting $\text{SLICES}(pe) \overset{\text{df}}{=} \{\{e\} \mid e \in \min_\lhd pe\}$, one can obtain the unfolding algorithm of [5]. For the slicing algorithm, the correctness was proven (in a very complicated way) in [8] by showing that it is equivalent to the unfolding algorithm of [5], in the sense that prefixes produced by arbitrary runs of these algorithms are isomorphic (and then relying on the correctness results developed in [5]). The theory developed in this paper allows for a much more elegant and general proof, essentially by showing that arbitrary runs of both these algorithms generate the canonical prefix. Moreover, one should not forget that the notion of completeness developed in this paper is strictly stronger than that used in previous works; in particular, algorithms shown correct here are also correct w.r.t. the weaker notion.

6   Conclusions

In this paper, we presented a general framework for truncating Petri net unfoldings. It provides a powerful tool for dealing with different variants of the unfolding technique, in a flexible and uniform way. In particular, by finely tuning the cutting contexts, one can build prefixes which better suit a particular model checking problem. A fundamental result is that, for an arbitrary Petri net and a cutting context, there exists a 'special' canonical prefix of its unfolding, which can be defined without resorting to any algorithmic argument.

We introduced a new, stronger notion of completeness of a branching process, which was implicitly assumed by many existing model checking algorithms employing unfoldings (see the introduction). The canonical prefix is complete w.r.t. this notion, and it is exactly the prefix generated by arbitrary runs of the non-deterministic unfolding algorithms presented in [5,8]. This gives a new correctness proof for the unfolding algorithms presented there, which is much simpler in the case of the algorithm developed in [ ]. As a result, relevant model checking tools can now make stronger assumptions about the properties of the prefixes they use. In particular, they can safely assume that for each configuration containing no cut-off events, *all* firings are preserved.

Finally, we gave conditions for the finiteness of the canonical prefix and, in certain cases, the upper bounds on its size, which are helpful in choosing problem-specific cutting contexts. To deal with the finiteness problem, we developed a version of König's Lemma for branching processes of (possibly unbounded) Petri nets. We believe that the results contained in this paper, on the one hand, will help to better understand the issues relating to prefixes of Petri net unfoldings, and, on the other hand, will facilitate the design of efficient model checking tools.

Acknowledgements

This research was supported by an ORS Awards Scheme grant ORS/C20/4, EPSRC grants GR/M99293 and GR/M94366 (MOVIE), and an ARC grant JIP.

References

1. E. M. Clarke, O. Grumberg, and D. Peled: *Model Checking*. MIT Press (1999). 582
2. P. M. Cohn: *Universal Algebra*. Reidel, 2nd edition (1981). 588
3. J.-M. Couvreur, S. Grivet and D. Poitrenaud: Unfolding of Products of Symmetrical Petri Nets. Proc. of *ICATPN'2001*. Springer LNCS 2075 (2001) 121–143. 583, 588
4. J. Engelfriet: Branching processes of Petri Nets. *Acta Inf.* 28 (1991) 575–591. 585, 586
5. J. Esparza, S. Römer and W. Vogler: An Improvement of McMillan's Unfolding Algorithm. Proc. of *TACAS'96*. Springer LNCS 1055 (1996) 87–106. 582, 583, 584, 585, 587, 588, 589, 590, 591, 592, 593
6. K. Heljanko: Minimizing Finite Complete Prefixes. Proc. of *CS&P'99*, Warsaw, Poland (1999) 83–95. 584, 588
7. K. Heljanko: Using Logic Programs with Stable Model Semantics to Solve Deadlock and Reachability Problems for 1-Safe Petri Nets. *Fund. Inf.* 37(3) (1999) 247–268. 584
8. K. Heljanko, V. Khomenko and M. Koutny: Parallelisation of the Petri Net Unfolding Algorithm. Proc. of *TACAS'02*. Springer LNCS 2280 (2002) 371–385. 582, 583, 585, 588, 592, 593, 594
9. V. Khomenko and M. Koutny: LP Deadlock Checking Using Partial Order Dependencies. Proc. of *CONCUR'2000*. Springer LNCS 1877 (2000) 410–425. 584
10. V. Khomenko, M. Koutny and W. Vogler: Canonical Prefixes of Petri Net Unfoldings. Techn. Rep. CS-TR-741, Dept. of Comp. Sci., Univ. of Newcastle (2001). 585, 589, 590
11. V. Khomenko, M. Koutny and A. Yakovlev: Detecting State Coding Conflicts in STGs Using Integer Programming. Proc. of *DATE'02*. IEEE (2002) 338–345. 583

12. D. König: Über eine Schlußweise aus dem Endlichen ins Unendliche. *Acta Litt. ac. sci. Szeged* 3 (1927) 121–130. Bibliography in: Theorie der endlichen und unendlichen Graphen. Teubner, Leipzig (1936, reprinted 1986) 586, 587
13. K. L. McMillan: Using Unfoldings to Avoid State Explosion Problem in the Verification of Asynchronous Circuits. Proc. of *CAV'92*. LNCS 663 (1992) 164–174. 582, 583, 584, 588
14. K. L. McMillan: *Symbolic Model Checking*. PhD thesis, CMU-CS-92-131 (1992).
15. S. Melzer and S. Römer: Deadlock Checking Using Net Unfoldings. Proc. of *CAV'97*. Springer LNCS 1254 (1997) 352–363. 584
16. A. Semenov: *Verification and Synthesis of Asynchronous Control Circuits Using Petri Net Unfolding*. PhD Thesis, University of Newcastle upon Tyne (1997). 583, 588

State Space Reduction by Proving Confluence

Stefan Blom and Jaco van de Pol

CWI, P.O.-box 94.079, 1090 GB Amsterdam, The Netherlands
{sccblom,vdpol}@cwi.nl

Abstract. We present a modular method for on-the-fly state space reduction. The theoretical foundation of the method is a new confluence notion for labeled transition systems. The method works by adding confluence information to the symbolic representation of the state space. We present algorithms for on-the-fly exploration of the reduced state space, for detection of confluence properties and for a symbolic reduction, called prioritization. The latter two algorithms rely on an automated theorem prover to derive the necessary information. We also present some case studies in which tools that implement these algorithms were used.

Keywords: Labeled transition systems, on-the-fly state space reduction, partial order reduction, confluence, theorem proving, symbolic transformation, branching bisimulation, μCRL tool set

1 Introduction

A popular approach to the verification of distributed systems is based on an exhaustive state space exploration. This approach suffers from the well-known *state space explosion* problem. Much research is devoted to algorithms that generate a reduced, but essentially equivalent, state space. Collectively, these methods are called partial-order reduction methods. In this paper we introduce a new method for generating a reduced state space that is branching bisimilar with the original one.

The method is based on a subtle variation on the *confluence*-notion for labeled transition systems (LTS). Invisible (τ) steps in the LTS may be confluent or not. All states in a subset connected by confluent steps are branching bisimilar. By virtue of our new confluence notion, this subset may be replaced by a particular *representative* state, and only transitions outgoing from this representative need to be explored. This is explained in Section 2.

In order to apply confluence for the immediate generation of the reduced state space, the confluent transitions must be detected before generating the LTS. This is solved in Section 3 by representing the system specification in an intermediate format, called *linear process*. A specification in this format consists of a finite number of symbolic transitions. The confluence property of each symbolic transition (or in fact a stronger approximation) can be expressed as a Boolean formula over the data types that occur in the specification. This formula is solved by a separate automated theorem prover. If the formula can be

D. Brinksma and K. G. Larsen (Eds.): CAV 2002, LNCS 2404, pp. 596–609, 2002.

proved, the transition is marked as confluent, allowing for some reduction of the corresponding state space.

In some cases it is even possible to feed the information on confluent symbolic transitions back to the symbolic level. This results in a transformation on linear processes, which we call *symbolic prioritization*, described in Section 4. Confluence detection and symbolic prioritization can be applied to infinite state spaces as well. In Section 5 we show a number of applications, to which we applied our state space reduction techniques. The example in Section 5.2 goes beyond traditional partial-order reduction methods, which are based on super-determinism.

Implementation. Our ideas are implemented in the context of the μCRL tool set [3]. The basic functionality of this tool set is to generate a state space (LTS) out of a μCRL specification. To this end *linear processes* are used as an intermediate representation. This contributes to the modularity of the tool set. In particular, several optimizations are implemented as separate tools that transform a linear process, aiming at a reduction of the state space to be generated.

To this tool set, we added symbolic prioritization as yet another optimizer on linear processes. Moreover, the on-the-fly reduction algorithm has been integrated in the state space generator of the tool set.

With the approach in this paper we further contribute to modularity. In particular, we defined a notion of confluence, which is quite liberal, but nevertheless sufficient to ensure correctness of the on-the-fly reduction algorithm. Finding confluent transitions is a separate task. In fact, while the maximal set of confluent transitions is hard to detect, it is perfectly acceptable if actual confluence detection algorithms only find a subset.

We have used an automated theorem prover to find a reasonable subset of confluent transitions, but an alternative approach could be to prove confluence by hand, or with interactive theorem provers. In cases where the specification is automatically generated from source code, it is sometimes even possible to know a priori that certain transitions are confluent.

Related Work. Several *partial order reduction* algorithms that preserve branching bisimilarity have been proposed in the literature [19,15,14,1]. These approaches also allow the reduction to a representative subset of all states. Some of these approaches restrict attention to deterministic transitions. All these approaches involve some notion of *determinacy*. We compare our approach with [19], where criteria Ä5 and Ä8 for obtaining branching bisimilar reduced state spaces are introduced.

Criterion Ä8 allows the selection of one outgoing transition from a state, provided it is an invisible *super-deterministic* transition. In our approach, such a transition need not be deterministic, but only confluent, which means that *eventually* the computation paths reach the same state. It can be proved that the set of super-deterministic transitions forms a confluent set of τ-transitions, but not vice versa. Criterion Ä5 prevents that a transition is postponed forever. This is implemented in [14] by the algorithm Twophase. In phase one, a state is expanded by repeatedly applying *deterministic* invisible transitions; the result is then fully expanded in phase two. Our algorithm can be seen as a modification: we take confluent transitions until a terminal strongly connected component (SCC) is reached, instead of deterministic transitions only.

Our method has some similarities with [1], where sequences of a component's local transitions are compressed to a single transition. Also, they have a detection phase and a generation phase. However, the setting is quite different because that paper aims at compositional model checking, whereas our method is independent of the structure of the specification. Moreover, they only prove preservation of weak-simulation equivalence.

Several confluence notions have been studied in the setting of branching bisimulation [12,20,9]. In [2] these notions are compared systematically. In summary, the notions in [12,20] only deal with *global confluence*, whereas we deal with *partial* confluence, i.e. it suffices to identify a confluent *subset* of the τ-transitions. In practical applications it is seldom the case that all τ-transitions are confluent. The confluence notion in [20] has the nice theoretical property that the τ-transition relation is confluent, if and only if it only connects states that are branching bisimilar. For reduction purposes, this would require to consider *all* outgoing transitions in each terminal SCC. Our notion of confluence is slightly stronger, and as a consequence we only have to take the outgoing transitions from a single member of each terminal SCC.

The confluence notion in [12] was adapted to partial confluence already in [9]. In order to apply it for state space reduction, this notion required the absence of τ-loops. [9] introduced an algorithm to reduce concrete state spaces as follows. First, all strongly connected τ-components are collapsed, in order to get rid of τ-cycles. Then, the *maximal* set of strongly confluent τ-steps is computed, and strongly confluent τ-transitions are given priority over other transitions. We note that these steps can only be applied *after* generating the unreduced state space. Especially absence of τ-loops is a severe obstacle for on-the-fly generation. In our paper, we use theorem proving to find (not necessarily all) confluent symbolic transitions in the *specification*. Our modified confluence notion works in the presence of τ-loops. So we provide a genuine on-the-fly reduction method. Our new method even allows to perform some optimization at specification level already.

2   Confluence and Reduction On-the-Fly

In this section we present the confluence property, a state space reduction method based on the confluence property and an algorithm that computes these reduced state spaces "on-the-fly".

We use labeled transition systems (LTS) to model states spaces. Confluence is a property of sets of invisible transitions in an LTS. Any set of transitions induces an equivalence relation on the set of states, which identifies states in the same component. If a set of invisible transitions is confluent then the induced equivalence relation is a branching bisimulation. Moreover, each finite equivalence class has a representative, whose transitions are the same as those of the whole equivalence class. Because of these representatives, we can give an algorithm that computes the reduced state space without computing the whole original state space.

Because the reduction preserves branching bisimilarity, the reduced state space can be used to check all properties of the original system that are expressible in action based CTL*-X (computation tree logic without next-time) or HML (Hennessy-Milner logic).

2.1 Confluence

The labels of our LTSs will be taken from a given set Act. We assume that Act contains a special element τ, representing the invisible action.

Definition 1 (LTS). *A labeled transition system is a triple* $(S, \rightarrow, s_0)$, *consisting of a set of states* S, *transitions* $\rightarrow \subseteq S \times \mathsf{Act} \times S$ *and an initial state* $s_0 \in S$.

We write $s \xrightarrow{a} t$ for $(s, a, t) \in \rightarrow$. Moreover, $\xrightarrow{a}$ denotes the transitive reflexive closure of $\xrightarrow{a}$, and $\xleftrightarrow{a}$ denotes the equivalence relation induced by $\xrightarrow{a}$, i.e. its reflexive, transitive, symmetric closure. We write $s \xRightarrow{a} t$ if either $s \xrightarrow{a} t$, or $a = \tau$ and $s = t$. Note that in $s \xRightarrow{a} t$ *only* invisible steps are optional. Given a subset of τ-transitions $c \subseteq \xrightarrow{\tau}$, we write $s \xrightarrow{\tau_c} t$ for $(s, t) \in c$. Finally, we write $S_1 \xleftrightarrow{}_b S_2$ to denote that LTSs S_1 and S_2 are branching bisimilar [ ].

The idea is that a subset c of the set of invisible transitions is confluent if the steps in c cannot make real choices. This is formalized with two conditions. First, if in a certain state two different sequences of c steps are possible then these sequences can be extended with more c steps to sequences that end in the same state. Second, if in a state both a c step and an a step are possible then after doing the c step, the a step is still possible (optional if $a = \tau$) and the results of the two a steps are in the same c equivalence class.

Definition 2 (confluence). *Let* c *be a subset of* $\xrightarrow{\tau}$. *Then* c *is* confluent *iff the following diagrams hold (for all* $a \in \mathsf{Act}$*):*

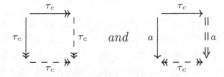

As a consequence, the equivalence relation $\xleftrightarrow{\tau_c}$ induced by a confluent c coincides with $\xrightarrow{\tau_c} \cdot \xleftarrow{\tau_c}$. We can view $\xrightarrow{\tau_c}$ as a directed graph. A strongly connected component (SCC) in this graph is a maximal set of states X, such that for all $s, t \in X$ we have $s \xrightarrow{\tau_c} t$ and $t \xrightarrow{\tau_c} s$. A terminal SCC (TSCC) is an SCC X without outgoing edges, i.e. for all $s \in X$, if $s \xrightarrow{\tau_c} t$ then $t \in X$.

2.2 Reduction

As mentioned before, the equivalence relation induced by a confluent set is a branching bisimulation. By taking the original state space modulo this equivalence one can reduce the state space. An effective way of computing the transitions of the reduced state space is to find a representative of each equivalence class, whose transitions are precisely the transitions of the equivalence class. As representative of a class, we can choose any element in a TSCC of this class, if that exists. Note that in finite graphs every equivalence class contains a TSCC. Because of confluence this TSCC is unique. The notion of *representation map* is based on this idea. The first condition forces every element in an equivalence class to have the same representative. The second condition forces this representative to be in the TSCC.

Definition 3 (representation map). *Given an LTS $S \equiv (S, \rightarrow, s_0)$ with a confluent subset of τ-steps labeled c, a map $\phi : S \rightarrow S$ is called a representation map if $\forall s, t \in S : s \xrightarrow{\tau_c} t \Rightarrow \phi(s) = \phi(t)$ and $\forall s \in S : s \xrightarrow{\tau_c}\!\!\!\twoheadrightarrow \phi(s)$.*

Based on the notion of representation map we can define a reduced LTS. The set of states of the reduced LTS will be the set of representatives. For every transition from a representative to a destination state in the original LTS, we include a transition from that representative to the representative of that destination in the reduced LTS. Finally, the new initial state is the representative of the old initial state. In [2] it is proven that the reduced LTS is branching bisimilar to the original LTS.

Definition 4 (LTS modulo ϕ). *Given a confluent $c \subseteq \xrightarrow{\tau}$ and a representation map ϕ, we define $S/_\phi = (\phi(S), \xrightarrow{}_\phi, \phi(s_0))$, where $s \xrightarrow{a}_\phi t$ if $a \neq \tau_c$ and $\exists t' : s \xrightarrow{a} t'$ and $\phi(t') = t$. As usual, $\phi(S) = \{\phi(s) \mid s \in S\}$.*

Theorem 5 ([2]). *Given a transition system S with a confluent subset of τ-steps labeled c and a representation map ϕ, we have that $S \underleftrightarrow{}_b S/_\phi$.*

2.3 Algorithm for Reduction On-the-Fly

The essential functions in an "on-the-fly" interface for an LTS are a function that yields the initial state and a function that computes outgoing transitions of a given state. Given an on-the-fly representation of an LTS and the label for confluent transitions, the key to providing an on-the-fly representation of the reduced LTS is a function that computes a representation map (see Figure 1).

Such a function must return a representative from the terminal strongly connected component of the τ_c graph. Moreover, this representative must be unique for all elements of an equivalence class. We implemented the latter requirement simply by maintaining a table of pairs $(s, Representative(s))$ that we have computed so far. To compute a representative if it is not in the table, we use a variation on Tarjan's algorithm for finding strongly connected components [18].

```
ReducedInit()
    return Representative(Init())

ReducedNext(state)
    return { (a,Representative(s)) | a ≠ τc, (a,s) ∈ Next(state) }
```

Fig. 1.

More precisely, we perform a depth first search of the graph of confluent transitions until we find a state with a known representative or until we backtrack from a node where we entered a strongly connected component. The first thus encountered component is the TSCC. In the latter case this node is chosen as the representative, and stored in the table (see [2] for a detailed algorithm).

The table consumes a significant amount of memory. If this is unacceptable, a total order on the set of states can be provided, and one can choose the least state in the TSCC as the representative and recompute the TSCC each time rather than storing it.

3   Confluence Detection by Theorem Proving

In the previous section we discussed a state space generation algorithm, which applies reduction on-the-fly, based on some information on confluent transitions. In this section we show how this information is obtained. In particular, by exploiting a special format for the specification, we show that (stronger approximations of) confluence properties can be expressed by quantifier-free first order formulae. These formulae can be solved by a separate automated theorem prover.

3.1   Symbolic Specifications in μCRL

We implemented our ideas in the setting of the μCRL formalism. A μCRL specification [11,3] consists of an *algebraic specification*, defining the data sorts, and a *process specification*, defining the system under scrutiny as the parallel composition of several components, each specified as a process algebra expression. We utilize the result in [10], that such specifications can be transformed to a *linear process*, without a considerable blow-up in size.

A linear process consists of a vector of global state variables d, an initial state vector d_0, and a set of program rules, traditionally called summands. These summands define the process behaviour in a condition/action/effect style, similar to I/O-automata or UNITY programs. These summands have the following form[1]:

$$\{\sum_{e_i}[b_i(d, e_i)] \Rightarrow a_i(d, e_i); d := g_i(d, e_i)\}_{i \in I}$$

---
[1] We focus on the essential ingredients, rather than concrete μCRL syntax.

We assume that the data algebra contains the special sorts Bool for booleans and Act for external actions. In the summands above, we have that:

- e_i is a vector of local variables, used for instance to model arbitrary input of this summand.
- $b_i(d, e_i)$ is a term of type Bool, with variables among d and e_i, denoting the condition or guard of the summand.
- $a_i(d, e_i)$ is a term of type Act, with variables among d and e_i, denoting the action executed by this summand.
- $g_i(d, e_i)$ is a vector of terms, whose sorts match the vector of global state variables. These denote the next state.

Each summand specifies a structural transition $\xrightarrow{i}$ as follows:

$$d \xrightarrow[i]{\alpha} d' \text{ iff } \exists e_i.\, b_i(d, e_i) \wedge d' = g_i(d, e_i) \wedge \alpha = a_i(d, e_i)$$

Together, a linear process specifies a *structural* labeled transition system $(\Sigma, (\xrightarrow{i})_{i \in I}, s_0)$, from which the ordinary LTS can be obtained by taking the union of all structural transitions. Here a state in Σ is a vector of data values for the global variables; s_0 is the initial state vector; I is the (index) set of the summands; $\xrightarrow{i}$ is the structural transition generated by summand i, which is a subset of the transitions of the whole LTS.

Note that a structural transition defined in this way is partial (due to the enabling condition b) and non-deterministic (due to choice involved in $\exists e$). Also note that one summand may generate transitions with various labels. A similar decoupling of action labels and structural transitions occurs in [10].

3.2   Generation of Confluence Formulae

Owing to the format of linear processes, commutation formulae can be generated. In order to facilitate automated theorem proving, we try to avoid quantifiers. The generated formulae will be Boolean expressions over the user defined abstract data types, with implicit universal quantification.

To get the formulae in this form, we only consider a special case, which occurs frequently in practice. So in fact we detect a stronger approximation of confluence. Consider two divergent steps of summands i and j:

$$\sum_{e_i} [b_i(d, e_i)] \Rightarrow a_i(d, e_i); d := g_i(d, e_i)$$

$$\sum_{e_j} [b_j(d, e_j)] \Rightarrow \tau; d := g_j(d, e_j)$$

The first simplification is that we only consider a closing of this diagram *in zero or one step* (strong confluence). Furthermore, we assume that the diagram is closed by using the same summands j and i again, and moreover we only try the same instance of summand i and j. This situation is depicted in the following picture (we left out the enabling conditions).

$$
\begin{array}{ccc}
d & \xrightarrow{\quad\tau\quad} & g_j(d, e_j) \\
& & \Big\downarrow a_i(g_j(d,e_j),e_i) \\
a_i(d,e_i)\Big\downarrow & & g_i(g_j(d, e_j), e_i) \\
& & = \\
g_i(d, e_i) \;-\!\!\dashrightarrow_{\tau}\; g_j(g_i(d, e_i), e_j)
\end{array}
\qquad\text{or}\qquad
\begin{array}{ccc}
d & \xrightarrow{\quad\tau\quad} & g_j(d, e_j) \\
\tau\Big\downarrow & & \Big\| = \\
g_i(d, e_i) & = & \cdot
\end{array}
$$

Commutation of τ-summand j with summand i can be expressed by the following Boolean expression over the algebraic data theory. Note that these formulae can be generated automatically for any linear process.

$$
\begin{pmatrix} b_i(d, e_i) \\ \wedge \\ b_j(d, e_j) \end{pmatrix}
\rightarrow
\begin{pmatrix}
b_i(g_j(d, e_j), e_i) & \wedge \\
b_j(g_i(d, e_i), e_j) & \wedge \\
a_i(d, e_i) = a_i(g_j(d, e_j), e_i) & \wedge \\
g_i(g_j(d, e_j), e_i) = g_j(g_i(d, e_i), e_j)
\end{pmatrix}
\vee
\begin{pmatrix}
a_i(d, e_i) = \tau \\
\wedge \\
g_i(d, e_i) = g_j(d, e_j)
\end{pmatrix}
$$

If τ-summand j commutes with all summands i (including j), it can be safely marked as a confluent τ-summand. As strong confluence implies confluence, the transitions generated by τ-summand j will form a confluent subset in the sense of Definition 2. Because the union of two confluent subsets constitutes a confluent subset, it is safe to label multiple summands in the same linear process.

3.3 Automated Theorem Prover

In order to prove formulae of the above kind, we have built a theorem prover for Boolean combinations over a user-defined algebraic data type. In [17] we show how an extension of binary decision diagrams (BDD) enhanced with term rewriting can be applied to these formulae. This is along the lines of the BDDs extended with equality developed in [8]. Given a formula, the prover returns an equivalent but ordered BDD. If this BDD equals TRUE, the pair (i,j) commutes.

If the resulting BDD doesn't equal TRUE, then the formula could not be proved, and τ-summand j cannot be marked as confluent. Note that this may be due to the fact that it is not confluent, or due to the fact that the prover is inherently incomplete (simple equalities over an abstract data type are undecidable already, let alone arbitrary Boolean expressions). In this case, the prover provides some diagnostics, on the basis of which user interaction is possible.

The user can add equations to the data specification, or provide an invariant. It is possible to add new equations, provided they hold in the initial model. Proving correctness of the new equations requires induction, which is beyond our theorem prover. The new equations could be proved either manually, or using a separate interactive theorem prover.

In some cases, the formula is not valid in the initial model, but it would hold for reachable states d. In this case, the user may supply an invariant Inv and the confluence formulae are proved under the assumption $Inv(d)$. Of course such an invariant must be checked separately. With our theorem prover, one can check whether Inv holds initially, and is preserved by all summands i:

$$Inv(d_0) \text{ and for all } i \in I : \ b_i(d, e_i) \wedge Inv(d) \rightarrow Inv(g_i(d, e_i))$$

4   Optimization by Symbolic Prioritization

Combining the previous sections, we can now mark certain transitions as being confluent by using an automated theorem prover, and subsequently generate a reduced state space by the on-the-fly reduction algorithm. However, the confluence marks can also be used to apply an optimization to the specification, i.e. on the symbolic level. Let transition j be a deterministic transition (i.e. without local variables) which is marked as confluent:

$$[b_j(d)] \Rightarrow \tau_c; d := g_j(d)$$

Now because the j summand is confluent, it may be given priority to other summands, as long as loops are avoided. To avoid loops, we will only give summand j priority just after a non-marked (visible or non-visible) transition. So let another summand i be given, which is not marked as confluent:

$$\sum_{e_i} [b_i(d, e_i)] \Rightarrow a_i(d, e_i); d := g_i(d, e_i)$$

Now, if we can prove that j is always enabled after the i-transition, we can combine the i and j summand in one step. Enabledness of j can be represented by the formula $b_i(d, e_i) \rightarrow b_j(g_i(d, e_i))$. This formula is sent to the prover, and upon success, we modify summand i to become:

$$\sum_{e_i} [b_i(d, e_i)] \Rightarrow a_i(d, e_i); d := g_j(g_i(d, e_i))$$

We call this transformation *symbolic prioritization*. One advantage of this symbolic optimization is that the intermediate state $g_i(d, e_i)$ doesn't have to be explored during state space generation. Another advantage is that this optimization often gives rise to a cascade of other possible optimizations, such as removal of dead code and unused variables. For instance, summand j might be unreachable after the optimization. This can be checked by proving that $\neg b_j$ is an invariant. Other summands may become unreachable as well, and variables used in them may become useless and can be removed or given a dummy value.

A very interesting effect is that we can now possibly mark more transitions as confluent. Recall that we only mark "strong confluence", where a diverging pair is closed in zero or one step. After symbolic prioritization, we might detect confluence also when the diverging pair can be closed in two steps, as illustrated in the diagram below. Of course, this process can be iterated.

| | original state space | | reduced state space | | total costs | |
system	states	transitions	states	transitions	states	transitions
abp	97	122	29	54	97	98
brp	1952	2387	1420	1855	1952	2275
mutex	96	192	26	46	56	75
DKR(3)	67	124	2	1	20	19
DKR(5)	864	2687	2	1	32	31
DKR(7)	18254	77055	2	1	72	71
Firewire(10)	72020	389460	6171	22668	8443	23326
Firewire(12)	446648	2853960	27219	123888	40919	127016
Firewire(14)	2416632	17605592	105122	544483	167609	557419
Lift1	38000	112937	12826	38151	27292	48684
Lift2	223720	712593	69987	231365	166645	300051
Lift1 + prio	38000	112937	12826	38151	16404	39991
Lift2 + prio	223720	712593	69987	231365	88741	239958

Fig. 2. Benchmarks for confluence detection and on-the-fly reduction

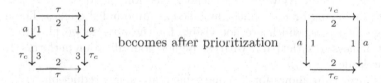

In the system on the left, automatic confluence marking will not detect the confluence of τ-summand (2), because the divergence with a-summand (1) cannot be closed in one step. However, typically τ-summand (3) will be detected to be confluent, because no other summands are enabled in its source state. The marking of summand (3) is denoted by the τ_c-label. Note that after a-summand (1) it is always possible to perform the marked τ_c-summand (3). Hence symbolic prioritization can be applied, and we obtain the system on the right. In the new situation summand (2) becomes strongly confluent, so it will be detected by a second application of automatic confluence detection. Due to the confluence of summand (2), the state space generation algorithm will now visit a single path through this graph. Also note that summand (3) becomes unreachable in this example.

5   Applications

We applied our method to finite instances of several distributed algorithms, protocols and industrial case studies. A number of experiments are described in detail in [17]. The μCRL-code is available via http://www.cwi.nl/~vdpol/

CAV02-experiments. Figure 2 shows the reduction obtained by confluence detection and on-the-fly reduction. For each system, we list the size of the original and the reduced state space, and also – in order to allow fair comparisons – the total costs including the number of nodes and transitions that are visited during the TSCC-computation.

The first rows refer to the alternating bit protocol, the bounded retransmission protocol, and a mutual exclusion algorithm. Furthermore, DKR(n) refers to the DKR leader election protocol with n parties; Firewire(n) to the Firewire Tree Identify protocol for n components from the IEEE 1394 bus standard; and the lift entries refer to a case study with distributed lifts [7], used for lifting car trucks by several lift legs. For the lift systems we also denote the cost reduction obtained after symbolic prioritization.

As a conclusion, we note that the contribution of confluence reduction to toy examples is rather modest. However, on the industrial case studies (Firewire, Lift) the reduction is notable. On the DKR protocol the reduction is even dramatic (the number of visited states goes from exponential down to $n \log n$). We now discuss two experiments in more detail.

5.1 Leader Election Protocol

In the DKR (Dolev-Klawe-Rodeh) leader election protocol [5], n parties are connected in a ring by n channels, modeled as unbounded queues. These parties exchange messages, which are not visible for the outside world. After a finite number of messages, the party with the highest identification performs the action "I'm the leader".

This algorithm allows for a remarkable state space reduction, viz. from exponential to linear in the number of parties. The theorem prover detects that all τ-summands are confluent, even when n is unknown. Given a concrete number of parties, the generation algorithm finds a completely deterministic path representing the whole state space. So the state space is immediately reduced to a single transition, labeled "I'm the leader". We remark that also the traditional partial order reduction methods have been successfully applied to this example (see also [1]).

5.2 Shared Data Space Systems

We also studied distributed systems based on shared data space architectures, such as Splice [4]. A Splice system consists of a number of application processes, that coordinate through agents, which are coupled via some network. The agents locally maintain multi-sets of data items (the distributed data space), into which applications can write new items, and from which applications can read items. The agents distribute their items by asynchronously sending messages to each other over the network.

Figure 3 depicts a simple Splice system, with a producer and a consumer. In between, several workers independently take input items from their local storage, perform some computation, and write output items back in the space. We want

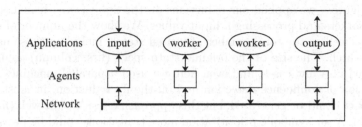

Fig. 3. Splice architecture

	original space	reduced state space		after prioritization	
		# states	cost	# states	cost
Splice(1,2)	85362	15	75	9	45
Splice(2,2)	18140058	69	644	9	65
Splice(3,2)	??	297	5151	9	101
Splice(1,4)	??	83	743	25	169
Splice(2,4)	??	1661	29936	25	249
Splice(3,4)	??	31001	1057187	25	393
Splice(1,6)	??	317	3657	56	425
Splice(2,6)	??	14387	326832	56	630
Splice(3,6)	??	??	??	56	999

Fig. 4. Splice benchmarks with symbolic prioritization

to prove transparency of the number of workers. See [13] for the full case study, which heavily relies on using our confluence reduction.

This communication mechanism is a-synchronous, and leads to much non-determinism: messages from one agent are sent to the others in any order. Consequently, the agents receive messages in various orders, even when they originate from the same agent. By proving confluence, it is detected that all these different orders are equivalent. In fact, the on-the-fly reduction algorithm computes a reduced state space, as if there were only one global multi-set of data items.

Another reduction is possible within the workers. They read any message from their agent, and write some computed result back. Note that such transactions cannot be represented by super-deterministic transitions, because a worker can start with any message in the current set of its agent. Therefore, traditional partial-order reduction methods, which are based on super-determinism, fail on this example. However, several such transactions commute, basically because $(A \cup \{a\}) \cup \{b\} = (A \cup \{b\}) \cup \{a\}$. Using confluence reduction, only a fixed transaction order is explored.

For this example, we also needed symbolic prioritization: although the transactions commute, the corresponding diagrams can only be closed in multiple steps. This corresponds to the diagram in Section 4.

In Figure 4 we applied our reductions on the Splice(m,n) benchmarks, having m workers and processing n input values. We show the number of generated states, as well as the total number of visited states, including those used in the TSCC search. The size of the original state space (first column) could only be computed in a few cases, and even here we used a parallel machine. After one application of confluence detection and on-the-fly reduction, in most cases the state space could be generated, but this approach doesn't scale well (middle two columns). After symbolic prioritization more transitions could be proven confluent, and running on-the-fly reduction again results in pretty small state spaces (last two columns).

As a final remark, we note that the size of the reduced space doesn't depend on the number of workers anymore. So this example has been solved nearly symbolically in the number of workers.

References

1. R. Alur and B.-Y. Wang. "Next" heuristic for on-the-fly model checking. In J. C. M. Baeten and S. Mauw, editors, *Proc. of CONCUR '99*, LNCS 1664, pages 98–113. Springer, 1999. 597, 598, 606
2. S. C. C. Blom. Partial τ-confluence for efficient state space generation. Technical Report SEN-R0123, CWI, Amsterdam, 2001. 598, 600, 601
3. S. C. C. Blom, W. J. Fokkink, J. F. Groote, I. van Langevelde, B. Lisser, and J. C. van de Pol. μCRL: A toolset for analysing algebraic specifications. In G. Berry, etal, editor, *Proc. of CAV 2001*, LNCS 2102, pages 250–254. Springer, July 2001. 597, 601
4. M. Boasson. Control systems software. *IEEE Transactions on Automatic Control*, 38(7):1094–1106, July 1993. 606
5. D. Dolev, M. Klawe, and M. Rodeh. An $O(n \log n)$ unidirectional distributed algorithm for extrema finding in a circle. *Journal of Algorithms*, 3(3):245–260, September 1982. 606
6. R. J. van Glabbeek and W. P. Weijland. Branching time and abstraction in bisimulation semantics. *Journal of the ACM*, 43(3):555–600, 1996. 599
7. J. F. Groote, J. Pang, and A. G. Wouters. A balancing act: Analyzing a distributed lift system. In S. Gnesi and U. Ultes-Nitsche, editors, *Proc. of FMICS*, pages 1–12, Paris, France, 2001. 606
8. J. F. Groote and J. C. van de Pol. Equational binary decision diagrams. In M. Parigot and A. Voronkov, editors, *Proc. of LPAR 2000*, LNAI 1955, pages 161–178. Springer, 2000. 603
9. J. F. Groote and J. C. van de Pol. State space reduction using partial τ-confluence. In M. Nielsen and B. Rovan, editors, *Proc. of MFCS 2000*, LNCS 1893, pages 383–393. Springer, 2000. 598
10. J. F. Groote, A. Ponse, and Y. S. Usenko. Linearization in parallel pCRL. *Journal of Logic and Algebraic Programming*, 48(1-2):39–70, 2001. 601
11. J. F. Groote and M. A. Reniers. Algebraic process verification. In J. A. Bergstra, A. Ponse, and S. A. Smolka, editors, *Handbook of Process Algebra*, chapter 17. Elsevier, 2001. 601
12. J. F. Groote and M. P. A. Sellink. Confluence for process verification. *Theoretical Computer Science*, 170:47–81, 1996. 598

13. J. M. M. Hooman and J. C. van de Pol. Formal verification of replication on a distributed data space architecture. In *Proceedings of SAC 2002 (Madrid)*, pages 351–358. ACM, 2002. 607

14. R. Nalumasu and G. Gopalakrishnan. An efficient partial order reduction algorithm with an alternative proviso implementation. *Formal Methods in System Design*, 20(3):231–247, 2002. 597

15. D. Peled. Partial order reduction: Linear and branching temporal logics and process algebras. In Peled et al. [16], pages 233–258. 597

16. D. A. Peled, V. R. Pratt, and G. J. Holzmann, editors. *Partial Order Methods in Verification*, DIMACS Series 29. AMS, July 1997. 609

17. J. C. van de Pol. A prover for the μCRL toolset with applications – Version 0.1. Technical Report SEN-R0106, CWI, Amsterdam, 2001. 603, 605

18. R. E. Tarjan. Depth first search and linear graph algorithms. *SIAM Journal on Computing*, 1(2):146–160, 1972. 600

19. A. Valmari. Stubborn set methods for process algebras. In Peled et al. [16], pages 213–232. 597, 602

20. M. Ying. Weak confluence and τ-inertness. *Theoretical Computer Science*, 238:465–475, 2000. 598

Fair Simulation Minimization[*]

Sankar Gurumurthy[1], Roderick Bloem[2], and Fabio Somenzi[1]

[1] University of Colorado at Boulder
{gurumurt,Fabio}@Colorado.EDU
[2] Technical University of Graz
rbloem@ist.tu-graz.ac.at

Abstract. We present an algorithm for the minimization of Büchi automata based on the notion of *fair simulation* introduced in [6]. Unlike direct simulation, fair simulation allows flexibility in the satisfaction of the acceptance conditions, and hence leads to larger relations. However, it is not always possible to remove edges to simulated states or merge simulation-equivalent states without altering the language of the automaton. Solutions proposed in the past consisted in checking sufficient conditions [11, Theorem 3], or resorting to more restrictive notions like *delayed simulation* [5]. By contrast, our algorithm exploits the full power of fair simulation by efficiently checking the correctness of changes to the automaton (both merging of states and removal of edges).

1 Introduction

Optimizing Büchi automata is an important step in efficient model checking for linear-time specification [13, 9]. It is usually cost-effective to invest time in the optimization of the automaton representing the negation of the LTL property because this small automaton is composed with the much larger system to be verified. Any savings obtained on the automaton are therefore amplified by the size of the system. As a side effect of minimizing the automaton, the acceptance conditions may also simplify, thus compounding the advantages of state space reduction. Omega-regular automata are also used to specify properties directly [8]; minimization techniques are applicable to this case as well.

An automaton $\mathcal{A}'$ can replace another automaton $\mathcal{A}$ in model checking if $\mathcal{A}$ and $\mathcal{A}'$ accept the same language. Since checking language equivalence is in general hard, practical approaches [11, 4, 5] resort to various notions of simulations [10] that account for the acceptance conditions of the automata. Simulation is a stronger notion than language containment because the simulating automaton cannot look ahead the moves of the simulated one. On the other hand, several variants of simulation relations can be computed in polynomial time; among them, direct simulation, fair simulation, and delayed simulation.

Direct simulation (BSR-aa in [2]) is the most restrictive of these notions: It requires that the simulating state satisfy all the acceptance conditions of the

---

[*] This work was supported in part by SRC contract 2001-TJ-920 and NSF grant CCR-99-71195.

simulated one.[1] *Fair simulation*, proposed in [6], relaxes the restriction on the acceptance condition, but it can still be computed in polynomial time. However, its use for minimization of a Büchi automaton is non-trivial because, unlike with direct simulation, one cannot always collapse two states that are fair-simulation equivalent without changing the language accepted by the automaton [5, Proposition 4]. It is also not always possible to remove an edge from state r to state p provided there is a edge from r to q and q fair simulates p. An example is the automaton for $\mathsf{G}\,\mathsf{F}\,a$ and the corresponding game automaton shown in Fig. 4 and discussed in Section 2.

Two approaches have been described in the literature to overcome these limitations of fair simulation. Theorem 3 of [11] says that it is safe to remove the edge described above, provided there is no path in the automaton from q to p. Indeed, the removed edge cannot be used in the accepting run going through q whose existence is guaranteed by the fact that q simulates p.

Etessami et al. [5], on the other hand, have proposed a new notion of simulation called *delayed simulation*, which guarantees that states that are simulation equivalent can be safely merged. Delayed simulation restricts fair simulation by imposing an additional constraint on the non-accepting runs from two related states: If q simulates p, and the i-th state of a run from p is accepting, then there must be a matching run from q such that its j-th state is accepting, and $j \geq i$.

Neither palliative dominates the other. Minimization of the automata family A_n of [5, Proposition 3] is not allowed by [11, Theorem 3] but is possible using delayed simulation, while for the automaton of Fig. 1 the situation is reversed. The word $a\neg a\neg aaa^\omega$ has (unique) infinite non-accepting runs from both n_2 and n_3. The run starting from n_3 has an accepting state in first position that is not matched in the run from n_2. Hence, n_2 does not delayed-simulate n_3. However, it does fair-simulate n_3, and [11, Theorem 3] leads to the removal of the edge from n_1 to n_3, effectively eliminating n_3 and n_5 from the automaton.

For the family of automata $\mathcal{A}_n$ exemplified in Fig. 2 for $n = 4$, neither method allows any reduction in the number of states. State n_{ij} delayed-simulates $n_{i'j}$ for $i > i'$, but not vice-versa; hence collapsing is impossible. The automata consist of one SCC, and thus [11, Theorem 3] does not apply either. However, the equivalence class of state n_{ij} according to fair simulation is $[n_{ij}] = \{n_{kj} : 1 \leq k \leq n\}$, and each such equivalence class can be collapsed reducing the number of states from $n^2 + 2$ to $n + 2$.

Another problem with delayed simulation is that it is not safe for edge removal. Consider the automaton of Fig. 3, which accepts the language $\Sigma^* \cdot \{a\}^\omega$. It is not difficult to see that q delayed-simulates p. Indeed, a run moving from p can only take the self-loop, which can be matched from q by going to p.

Even though q is a predecessor of both q and p, one cannot remove the edge (q, p). That is, one cannot use delayed simulation as one would use direct simulation. Since optimization methods based on removal and addition of edges are strictly more powerful than methods based on collapsing simulation equivalent

---

[1] *Reverse simulation* [11] is a variant of direct simulation that looks at runs reaching a state, instead of runs departing from it.

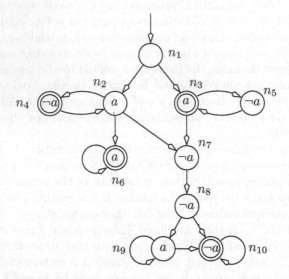

Fig. 1. A sub-optimal automaton that cannot be minimized by delayed simulation

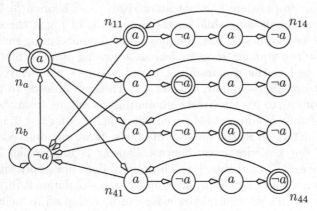

Fig. 2. An automaton that cannot be minimized by either delayed simulation or application of [11, Theorem 3]

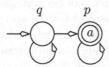

Fig. 3. An automaton showing that delayed simulation is not safe for edge removal

states (collapsing can be achieved by adding and removing edges), this inability limits the optimization potential of methods based on delayed simulation.

The method we propose overcomes the problems seen so far by using fair simulation to select states to be merged and edges to be removed, but checking for their validity before accepting them. The check amounts to verifying whether the modified automaton is still fair-simulation equivalent to the given one. To gain efficiency, we incrementally compute the new simulation relation from the self-simulation relation of the given automaton.

As in [6, 5], the computation of a fair simulation is reduced to the computation of the winning positions for the protagonist in a Streett game [3, 12]. Noting that in the case of non-generalized Büchi automata, the Streett game is equivalent to a parity game with three priorities, Etessami et al. [5] have applied to the problem the recent algorithm of Jurdziński [7], specialized for the case at hand.

Jurdziński's algorithm for parity games assigns a progress measure to the nodes of the game graph by computing the least fixpoint of a monotonic function. If the game graph is changed judiciously, it is therefore possible to update the new progress measure starting the fixpoint computation from the old one. We show how one can produce a locally optimal automaton by a sequence of state mergings or, alternatively, edge removals. Because of the incremental update of the simulation relation, the worst-case complexity of the resulting algorithm is within a factor of k from the complexity of computing the fair simulation once, where k is the number of attempted changes in the sequence that are rejected.

An automaton produced by our procedure is optimal in the sense that if any states are merged at the end of a sequence of mergings, or any edge removed at the end of a sequence of removals, the resulting automaton is not fair simulation equivalent to the old one.

We have implemented the new algorithm for fair simulation minimization in Wring [11], and we report the results of its evaluation in Section 5.

2   Preliminaries

Definition 1. *An* infinite game *is a tuple* $(Q_a, Q_p, \delta, \mathcal{F})$. *Here,* Q_a *and* Q_p *are finite, disjoint sets of antagonist and protagonist states, respectively. We write* $Q = Q_a \cup Q_p$ *for the set of all states. Furthermore,* $\delta \subseteq Q \times Q$ *is the transition relation, and* $\mathcal{F} \subseteq Q^\omega$ *is the acceptance condition.*

An infinite game is played by an antagonist and a protagonist. Starting from a given state $q_0 \in Q$, the antagonist moves from the states in Q_a and the protagonist moves from the states in Q_p. In this manner, the two build a *play* $\rho = q_0, q_1, \ldots$. The game ends if a state with no successors is reached, in which case the protagonist wins the game iff the last state is an antagonist state. If a state without successors is never reached, an infinite play results. In this case, the protagonist wins the game iff $\rho \in \mathcal{F}$. The antagonist wins iff the protagonist does not.

We shall consider Streett acceptance conditions, which depend on $\inf(\rho)$, the set of states that occur infinitely often in a play ρ. A *Streett acceptance condition* is described by a set of pairs of sets of states $\{(E_1, F_1), \ldots, (E_n, F_n)\} \subseteq 2^Q \times 2^Q$. A play is winning if for all $1 \leq i \leq n$, either $\inf(\rho) \cap E_i = \emptyset$ or $\inf(\rho) \cap F_i \neq \emptyset$. Of special interest to us are *1-pair Streett conditions*, Streett conditions for which $n = 1$. A *parity condition* is a sequence of sets of states $(F_0, F_1, \ldots)$ such that the sets listed form a partition of Q. A play is winning if the lowest index i such that $\inf(\rho) \cap F_i \neq \emptyset$ is even. The 1-pair Streett condition $\{(E, F)\}$ is equivalent to the parity condition $(F, E \setminus F, Q \setminus E \setminus F)$. We shall identify the description of an acceptance condition with the subset of Q^ω that it describes.

A *(memoryless) strategy* for the protagonist is a function $\sigma : Q_p \to Q$ such that for all $q \in Q_p$, $(q, \sigma(q)) \in \delta$. A state $q_0 \in Q$ is *winning* for the protagonist if there is a strategy for the protagonist such that any play $\rho = q_0, q_1, \ldots$ for which $q_i \in Q_p$ implies $q_{i+1} = \sigma(q_i)$ is winning for the protagonist. The definitions of a strategy and a winning state for the antagonist are analogous. For parity, and hence for 1-pair Streett games, there is a partition (Q_w, Q_l) of Q such that all states in Q_w are winning for the protagonist, and all states in Q_l are winning for the antagonist. Hence, a state is winning for one player iff it is *losing* for the other. As usual, we shall identify with the protagonist, and simply call a state winning if it is winning for the protagonist.

Definition 2. *A Büchi automaton* over a finite domain Σ is a tuple $\mathcal{A} = \langle V, V_0, T, C, \Lambda \rangle$, where V is the finite set of states, $V_0 \subseteq V$ is the set of initial states, $T : V \times V$ is the transition relation, $C \subseteq V$ is the acceptance condition, and $\Lambda : V \to 2^\Sigma$ is the labeling function.

As usual, for a set of states $V' \subseteq V$, we shall write $T(V')$ to mean $\{v' \mid \exists v \in V' : (v, v') \in T\}$, and we shall write $T(v)$ for $T(\{v\})$. A *run* of $\mathcal{A}$ is an infinite sequence $\rho = \rho_0, \rho_1, \ldots$ over V, such that $\rho_0 \in V_0$, and for all $i \geq 0$, $\rho_{i+1} \in T(\rho_i)$. A run ρ is *accepting* if $\inf(\rho) \cap C \neq \emptyset$.

The automaton accepts an infinite word $\sigma = \sigma_0, \sigma_1, \ldots$ in Σ^ω if there exists an accepting run ρ such that, for all $i \geq 0$, $\sigma_i \in \Lambda(\rho_i)$. The language of $\mathcal{A}$, denoted by $L(\mathcal{A})$, is the subset of Σ^ω accepted by $\mathcal{A}$. We write $\mathcal{A}^v$ for the Büchi automaton $\langle V, \{v\}, T, C, \Lambda \rangle$.

Simulation relations play a central role in this paper. A simulation relation is a relation between nodes of two graphs. If p is simulated by q, from state q we can mimic any run from p without knowing the input string ahead of time. Hence, simulation implies language inclusion. We recapitulate the notions of fair simulation [6] and delayed simulation [7].

Definition 3. *Given Büchi automata*

$$\mathcal{A}_1 = \langle V_1, V_{01}, T_1, C_1, \Lambda_1 \rangle \text{ and } \mathcal{A}_2 = \langle V_2, V_{02}, T_2, C_2, \Lambda_2 \rangle \ ,$$

we define the game automaton $\mathcal{G}_{\mathcal{A}_1,\mathcal{A}_2} = (Q_a, Q_p, \delta, \mathcal{F})$, *where*

$$Q_a = \{[v_1, v_2] \mid v_1 \in V_1,\ v_2 \in V_2,\ \text{and}\ \Lambda_1(v_1) \subseteq \Lambda_2(v_2)\},$$
$$Q_p = \{(v_1, v_2) \mid v_1 \in V_1\ \text{and}\ v_2 \in V_2\},$$
$$\delta = \{([v_1, v_2], (v_1', v_2)) \mid (v_1, v_1') \in \delta_1, [v_1, v_2] \in Q_a\} \cup$$
$$\{((v_1, v_2), [v_1, v_2']) \mid (v_2, v_2') \in \delta_2, [v_1, v_2'] \in Q_a\},$$
$$\mathcal{F} = \{\{(v, w) \mid v \in C_1, w \in V_2\}, \{(v, w) \mid v \in V_1, w \in C_2\})\}\ .$$

The first subscript in $\mathcal{G}_{\mathcal{A}_1,\mathcal{A}_2}$ identifies the antagonist, while the second identifies the protagonist. The style of brackets is used to differentiate between antagonist and protagonist states: Square brackets denote an antagonist state, while round parentheses indicate a protagonist state. Intuitively, the protagonist tries to prove the simulation relation by matching the moves of the antagonist. The antagonist's task is to find a series of moves that cannot be matched.

State v of automaton $\mathcal{A}$ is *fairly simulated* by v' of automaton $\mathcal{A}'$ if $[v, v']$ is winning in $\mathcal{G}_{\mathcal{A},\mathcal{A}'}$. For different simulation relations we adapt the acceptance criteria of the game graph. We say that v is *delayed simulated* by v' if there is a strategy such that for any play ρ starting from $[v, v']$, if $\rho_i = (w, w')$ with $w \in C_1$, then there is a $j \geq i$ such that $\rho_j = (w, w')$ and $w' \in C_2$.

Example 1. A Büchi automaton $\mathcal{B}$ for the LTL property $\mathsf{G}\,\mathsf{F}\,a$ and the corresponding game automaton $\mathcal{G}_{\mathcal{B},\mathcal{B}}$ are shown in Fig. 4. The set of winning antagonist states is

$$\{[1, 1], [1, 2], [2, 2]\}\ .$$

Therefore, State 2 fair-simulates State 1. However, $\mathcal{B}'$ obtained from $\mathcal{B}$ by removing transition $(2, 1)$, is not simulation equivalent to $\mathcal{B}$. Fig. 5 shows the modified automaton and the game graph required to prove that $\mathcal{B}'$ fair simulates $\mathcal{B}$. (The transition from $(1, 2)$ to $[1, 1]$ is missing.) Notice that, irrespective of the starting

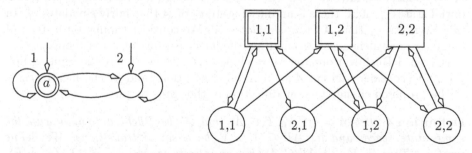

Fig. 4. Automaton for $\mathsf{G}\,\mathsf{F}\,a$ (left) and corresponding game automaton (right). Boxes are antagonist nodes, and circles are protagonist nodes. The label shows the antagonist and protagonist components, respectively. A double border on the left indicates antagonist acceptance; a double border on the right or on the entire node indicates protagonist acceptance

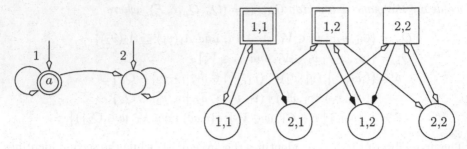

Fig. 5. Automaton $\mathcal{B}'$ (left) and game automaton $\mathcal{G}_{\mathcal{B},\mathcal{B}'}$ (right). Black arrow-heads identify the antagonist's winning strategy

state, the antagonist can constrain the play to the states $[1,2]$ and $(1,2)$ of $\mathcal{G}_{\mathcal{B},\mathcal{B}'}$, and therefore win from any initial position. One can verify that removal from $\mathcal{B}$ of the self-loop on State 1 corresponds to removing the transition from $(1,1)$ to $[1,1]$ from $\mathcal{G}_{\mathcal{B},\mathcal{B}}$. Since the protagonist still has a winning strategy from all states, the removal from $\mathcal{B}$ of the self-loop preserves simulation equivalence. $\quad\square$

3   Computing Fair Simulations Incrementally

In this section we shall describe the theory underlying the algorithm. We shall describe how we can use modifications of the game graph to verify proposed changes of a given automaton. Then, we shall quickly review Jurdziński's algorithm for parity games. We shall show that for a series of successful modifications of one kind, we can extend upon the evaluation of the original game graph with no overhead in complexity.

Our use of simulation relations is based on the fact that if v simulates w, then $L(\mathcal{A}^v) \supseteq L(\mathcal{A}^w)$. Hence, given two automata $\mathcal{A}$ and $\mathcal{A}'$, for the language of $\mathcal{A}'$ to be included in that of $\mathcal{A}$, it is sufficient (though not necessary) that for all initial states v_0' of $\mathcal{A}'$ there is an initial state v_0 of $\mathcal{A}$ that fairly simulates v_0'. In this case, we say that $\mathcal{A}$ *fairly simulates* $\mathcal{A}'$. We consider simulation instead of language equivalence since computing the latter is prohibitively expensive.

Given a Büchi automaton $\mathcal{A} = \langle V, V_0, T, C, \Lambda \rangle$, we build the game graph $\mathcal{G}_{\mathcal{A},\mathcal{A}}$. We consider edges of $\mathcal{A}$ for removal or addition , and we check correctness of the proposed change by a modification of the game graph.

Definition 4. *Let* $\mathcal{A} = \langle V, V_0, T, C, \Lambda \rangle$ *and* $\mathcal{A}'$ *be Büchi automata with the same state space, and let* $\Delta T \subseteq V \times V$ *be a set of transitions. We define* $\mathrm{rem}(\mathcal{A}, \Delta T) = \langle V, V_0, T \setminus \Delta T, C, \Lambda \rangle$. *For an infinite game* $\mathcal{G}_{\mathcal{A},\mathcal{A}'} = (Q_a, Q_p, \delta, \mathcal{F})$, $\mathrm{rem}(\mathcal{G}_{\mathcal{A},\mathcal{A}'}, \Delta T)$ *is the game graph* $(Q_a, Q_p, \delta', \mathcal{F})$, *where*

$$\delta' = \delta \setminus \{((v_1, v), [v_1, v']) \mid (v_1, v) \in Q_p, [v_1, v'] \in Q_a, (v, v') \in \Delta T\} \ .$$

Similarly, $\mathrm{add}(\mathcal{A}, \Delta T) = \langle V, V_0, T \cup \Delta T, C, \Lambda \rangle$, *and* $\mathrm{add}(\mathcal{G}_{\mathcal{A},\mathcal{A}'}, \Delta T)$ *is the game graph* $(Q_a, Q_p, \delta', \mathcal{F})$, *where*

$$\delta' = \delta \cup \{([v, v_2], (v', v_2)) \mid [v, v_2] \in Q_a, (v', v_2) \in Q_p, (v, v') \in \Delta T\} \ .$$

Intuitively, if we add transitions to the automaton, we know that the new automaton simulates the old one. We have to check whether simulation holds in the opposite direction. To do this, we add transitions to the antagonist states in the game, reflecting the new edges in the modified automaton. The following theorem is easily proven.

Theorem 1. *Let* $\mathcal{A}$ *be a Büchi automaton, and let* $\Delta T \subseteq V \times V$ *be a set of transitions. We have* $\mathcal{G}_{\mathcal{A},\mathrm{rem}(\mathcal{A},\Delta T)} = \mathrm{rem}(\mathcal{G}_{\mathcal{A},\mathcal{A}}, \Delta T)$. *Furthermore,*

$$\mathrm{rem}(\mathrm{rem}(\mathcal{G}_{\mathcal{A},\mathcal{A}}, \Delta T), \Delta T')) = \mathrm{rem}(\mathcal{G}_{\mathcal{A},\mathcal{A}}, \Delta T \cup \Delta T') \ .$$

Similarly, $\mathcal{G}_{\mathrm{add}(\mathcal{A},\Delta T),\mathcal{A}} = \mathrm{add}(\mathcal{G}_{\mathcal{A},\mathcal{A}}, \Delta T)$. *Furthermore,*

$$\mathrm{add}(\mathrm{add}(\mathcal{G}_{\mathcal{A},\mathcal{A}}, \Delta T), \Delta T')) = \mathrm{add}(\mathcal{G}_{\mathcal{A},\mathcal{A}}, \Delta T \cup \Delta T') \ .$$

This theorem says that we can obtain the game graph of the original automaton $\mathcal{A}$ and a modified version $\mathcal{A}'$, that is obtained by adding or removing edges, by modifying the game graph. Furthermore, it states that edges can be deleted a few at a time, or all at once. Hence, we can modify the game graph instead of building it from scratch. After a recapitulation of Jurdziński's algorithm, we shall show that this means that we can efficiently reuse information.

We use Jurdziński's algorithm [ ] for parity games as specialized in [ ] to compute the simulation relation. We can use this algorithm because 1-pair Streett conditions correspond to length-3 parity conditions. Let n_1 be the number of protagonist states (v_1, v_2) such that v_1 satisfies the fairness constraint of $\mathcal{A}_1$, but v_2 does not satisfy the fairness constraint of $\mathcal{A}_2$, i.e., $n_1 = |\{(v_1, v_2) \in Q \mid v_1 \in C_1, v_2 \notin C_2\}|$. Jurdziński's algorithm for three priorities computes a *progress measure* on the states of the game automaton: $r : Q \to \{0, \dots, n_1\} \cup \{\infty\}$, such that $r(q) \neq \infty$ iff n_1 is a winning state. The measure is computed as a least fixpoint of the following lifting function.

$$\mathrm{lift}(r, q) = \lambda p \, . \begin{cases} \mathrm{update}(r, q) & \text{if } p = q, \\ r(p) & \text{otherwise.} \end{cases}$$

Here, $\mathrm{update}(r, q)$ is a function that is monotonic in the measures of the successors of q, and hence lift is (pointwise) monotonic. Because of monotonicity, the measure can be updated at most $n_1 + 1$ times per node. Combined with the fact that $\mathrm{update}(r, q)$ can be performed in time proportional to the number of successors of q, this implies that the complexity of the algorithm is $O(|\delta| \cdot n_1) = O(|Q|^2 \cdot n_1)$.

To be more precise, if $q \in Q_a$, then $\mathrm{update}(r, q)$ is monotonic in $\max\{r(p) \mid (q, p) \in \delta\}$, and if $q \in Q_p$, then $\mathrm{update}(r, q)$ is monotonic in $\min\{r(p) \mid (q, p) \in \delta\}$.

It should be noted that the measure of an antagonist (protagonist) node without successors is 0 (∞).

We can check the validity of a proposed addition of an edge to, or removal of an edge from $\mathcal{A}$ by constructing the game graph $\mathcal{G}_{\mathcal{A},\mathcal{A}}$, and modifying it as described above. If for every initial state v there is an initial state w such that $[v, w]$ is winning, then the proposed modification does not change the language of the graph. In the naive implementation, this implies that for every modification Jurdziński's algorithm has to be rerun. We shall now show the modification of the game graph allows us to quickly evaluate a proposed modification.

Lemma 1. *If transitions from protagonist states are removed from the game graph, the measure of a node cannot decrease. Similarly, if transitions from antagonist states are added, the measure cannot decrease.*

Proof. Since the measure of a protagonist node is a monotonic function of the minimum of the measures of its successors, removing one successor cannot decrease the measure. Similarly for antagonist nodes.   □

Intuitively, if we add transitions from antagonist states, or remove transitions from protagonist states, the game becomes harder to win. This result has the advantage that for a given sequence of additions of transitions from antagonist states, the correctness of all additions can be checked within the same complexity bound that holds for the original algorithm: $O(|Q|^2 \cdot n_1)$, assuming that all such modifications are legal.

Given a sequence of additions or removals of sets of edges, there may be candidates that change the language of the automaton. Work done evaluating such modifications is lost, and hence the complexity of validating such a set of modifications is $O(|Q|^2 \cdot n_1 \cdot k)$, where k the number of failed modifications. Clearly, $k = O(|Q|^2)$.

To merge fair-simulation equivalent states, the algorithm will try to change the graph in such a way as to create states with the same predecessors and successors. One of such a pair of states can be dropped, assuming that either the remaining state is accepting or the dropped state is not.

Theorem 2. *Let $\mathcal{A} = \langle V, V_0, T, C, \Lambda \rangle$ be a Büchi automaton such that there are $v, v' \in V$ with $T(v) = T(v')$, $T^{-1}(v) = T^{-1}(v')$, $\Lambda(v) \subseteq \Lambda(v')$ and $v \in C$ implies $v' \in C$. Then, $L(\mathcal{A}) = L(\mathcal{A}')$, where $V' = V \setminus \{v\}$, $V_0' = V_0 \cup \{v'\} \setminus \{v\}$ if $v \in V_0$ and $V_0 = V_0$ otherwise, $T' = T \cap (V' \times V')$, and $C' = C \setminus \{v\}$.*

We do not have to consider changes to the graph more than once. This is another consequence of monotonicity of the measure. If $\mathrm{add}(\mathcal{A}, \Delta T)$ is not simulated by $\mathcal{A}$, then $\mathrm{add}(\mathrm{add}(\mathcal{A}, \Delta T'), \Delta T)$ is not simulated by $\mathrm{add}(\mathcal{A}, \Delta T')$. This follows because the measure of the game graph $\mathrm{add}(\mathcal{G}_{\mathcal{A},\mathcal{A}}, \Delta T')$ is not smaller than that of $G_{\mathcal{A},\mathcal{A}}$, and hence the measure of $\mathrm{add}(\mathrm{add}(\mathcal{G}_{\mathcal{A},\mathcal{A}}, \Delta T'), \Delta T)$ is not smaller than that of $\mathrm{add}(G_{\mathcal{A},\mathcal{A}}, \Delta T'), \Delta T)$. Recalling that a state is winning if its measure is smaller than ∞, it is clear that the latter game graph does not have more winning positions, and hence does not define a greater simulation relation.

A similar observation can be made for removing edges.

4   A Fair Minimization Algorithm

In this section we describe a method to minimize a Büchi automaton using the game graph. The proposed method uses the fair-simulation relation to find states that are candidates for merger and edges that are candidates for removal. By manipulating the game graph, the algorithm checks whether the proposed merger of two states or removal of an edge is correct, i.e., whether it results in a simulation-equivalent automaton. Because the simulation relation does not have to be recomputed every time from scratch, this method is efficient. Furthermore, it is more effective than known methods that can be applied statically, as discussed in Section 1.

The algorithm proceeds in two phases: First it tries to merge equivalent states, and then it tries to remove redundant edges.

The algorithm attempts to merge two fair-simulation equivalent states v and w by adding edges such that the successors of v become successors of w and vice-versa, and likewise for predecessors. Validation of the correctness of a modification is performed as described in Section 3.

In detail, we construct $\mathcal{G}_{\mathcal{A},\mathcal{A}}$ and compute the progress measure using Jurdziński's algorithm. Then, we pick a pair of states v, w that we wish to merge. We construct $\mathcal{G}' = \mathrm{add}(\mathcal{G}_{\mathcal{A},\mathcal{A}}, \Delta T)$, where $\Delta T = (\{v, w\} \times T(\{v, w\})) \cup (T^{-1}(\{v, w\}) \times \{v, w\}))$. We then update the progress measure, thereby computing the simulation relation between $\mathcal{A}$ and $\mathcal{A}'$, where $\mathcal{A}' = \mathrm{add}(\mathcal{A}, \Delta T)$. If we find that the $\mathcal{A}$ still simulates $\mathcal{A}'$, then the merge is accepted, a new pair is proposed for merger, $\mathcal{G}_{\mathcal{A}'',\mathcal{A}}$ is computed, etc.

As discussed, pairs of simulation-equivalent states are picked as candidates for merger. Though [ ] shows that fair-simulation equivalence is no guarantee for mergeability (and in fact the number of equivalent states that cannot be merged can be in the order of $|Q|^2$), the chances that two equivalent states are mergeable are quite high in practice. The number of rejected modifications is thus limited by the number of pairs of simulation-equivalent states that cannot be merged.

The second stage of the algorithm proceeds likewise to attempt to remove edges. The candidates for removal are edges (u, v) for which there is a state w that simulates v and an edge (u, w).

In Stage 1, if we find a pair of states (v, w) such that v and w are delayed-simulation equivalent, the merge is guaranteed to succeed. Similarly in Stage 2, if w direct-simulates v. Each stage of the algorithm leads to a graph that is optimal, in that no candidate for removal has to be checked again.

Backtracking can be implemented efficiently by using time stamps. Every assignment of a measure to a state receives a time stamp—initially 0. Before the measure is updated, the time stamp is increased. When $r(v)$ is changed, its time stamp is checked. If it is not the current timestamp, the value is saved. If one needs to backtrack, one looks for all the nodes such that $r(v)$ has the most recent timestamp. One replaces these values with the old values, and the old time stamp. Then, one decreases the current time stamp to the previous value. A list of nodes with new values is kept, so that the cost of undoing the changes is proportional to the extent of the changes, and not the size of the game graph.

Likewise, when an arc is added or removed from the game graph, a change record with the current time stamp is appended to the list. As pointed out in [7], another way to improve performance is to exploit the decomposition of the game graph into SCCs, processing them in reverse topological order.

5   Experiments

In this section we present preliminary experimental results for our algorithm. We have implemented the approach described in Section 4 in Wring [11], and compared it to other methods for the minimization of Büchi automata. As test cases we have used 1000 automata generated by translation of as many random LTL formulae distributed with Wring [11, Table 2]. In addition, we report results for 23 hard-to-minimize cases, partly derived from examples found in the literature [6, 11, 5].

In Wring, the sequence of optimization steps applied to a Büchi automaton starts with a pruning step (P) that removes states that cannot reach a fair cycle, and simplifies the acceptance conditions. This is followed by a pass of peep-hole minimization (M), which is of limited power, but is fast, and includes transformations that simulation-based methods cannot accomplish. After that, direct (D) and reverse (R) simulations are used to merge states and remove arcs. Finally, a second pruning step is applied. We refer to this standard sequence by the following abbreviation: PMDRP.

We compare this standard optimization sequence to others that use in addition or alternative to the other steps, fair simulation minimization (F), and delayed simulation minimization (d). Since neither of these two alternative methods can deal with generalized Büchi automata, they are applied only to the cases in which there is exactly one fairness condition. (For the 1000 automata of Table 1, this happens 465 times.) The notation F/D designates the application of fair simulation minimization to automata with one acceptance condition, and direct simulation to the other automata. Likewise for d/D.

The results for the automata derived from LTL formulae are summarized in Table 1. For each method, we give the total number of states, transitions,

Table 1. Experimental results for 1000 automata derived from LTL formulae

method	states	trans	fair	init	weak	term	time
PMDRP	5620	9973	487	1584	400	523	125.5
PMDRFP	5581	9827	487	1560	396	529	158.0
PMDRdP	5618	9980	488	1584	400	523	160.1
PMF/DRP	5587	9869	488	1556	395	529	162.5
PMd/DRP	5618	9980	488	1584	400	523	159.9
PDP	5704	10722	489	1587	396	523	114.7
PF/DP	5688	10625	489	1561	392	529	153.5
Pd/DP	5910	11522	488	1626	383	520	155.0

fairness conditions, initial states, and we report how many automata were weak or terminal [1]. Finally, we include the total CPU time. In comparing the numbers it should be kept in mind that the results are affected by a small noise component, since they depend on the order in which operations are attempted, and this order is affected by the addresses in memory of the data structure.

The result for PMDRFP shows that our algorithm can still improve automata that have undergone extensive optimization. The CPU times increase w.r.t. PMDRP, but remain quite acceptable. In spite of having to check each modification of the automata, fair simulation minimization is about as fast as delayed simulation.

There are several reasons for this. First, the time to build the game graph dominates the time to find the winning positions, and delayed simulation produces larger game graphs (up to twice the size, and about 10% larger on average) in which each state has four components instead of three. Second, most modification attempted by the fair simulation algorithm do not change the language of the given automaton (78% in our experiments); hence, as discussed in Section 3, their cost is low.

Finally, Jurdziński's algorithm converges faster for the fair simulation game when the delayed simulation relation is a proper subset of the fair simulation relation.

The shorter optimization sequences are meant to compare fair simulation minimization to delayed simulation minimization without too much interference from the other techniques. In particular, one can see from comparing PF/DP and Pd/DP that removal of transitions, as opposed to merging of simulation equivalent states, does play a significant role in reducing the automata. Indeed, direct simulation, which can be safely used for that purpose, does better than delayed simulation.

Finally, Table 2 summarizes the results for the hard-to-minimize automata.

Table 2. Experimental results for 23 hard-to-minimize automata

method	states	trans	fair	init	weak	term	time
PMDRP	131	219	21	29	3	2	0.49
PMDRFP	106	165	21	25	4	2	1.05
PMDRdP	128	212	21	29	3	2	1.22
PMF/DRP	106	167	21	25	4	2	1.38
PMd/DRP	138	229	21	29	3	2	1.40
PDP	133	222	22	30	3	2	0.47
PF/DP	106	168	21	25	4	2	2.60
Pd/DP	130	217	21	30	3	2	3.42

6   Conclusions

We have presented an algorithm for the minimization of Büchi automata based on fair simulation. We have shown that existing approaches are limited in their optimization power, and that our new algorithms can remove more redundancies than the other approaches based on simulation relations. We have presented preliminary experimental results showing that fair simulation minimization improves results even when applied after an extensive battery of optimization techniques like the one implemented in Wring [11]. Our implementation is still experimental, and we expect greater efficiency as it matures, but the CPU times are already quite reasonable.

The approach of checking the validity of moves by updating the solution of a game incrementally can be applied to other notions of simulation that do not allow safe collapsing of states or removal of edges. In particular, we plan to apply it to a relaxed versions of reverse simulation. We also plan to address the open issue of extending our approach to generalized Büchi automata, that is, to automata with multiple acceptance conditions.

Acknowledgment

We thank Kavita Ravi for many insightful observations on simulation minimization.

References

[1] R. Bloem, K. Ravi, and F. Somenzi. Efficient decision procedures for model checking of linear time logic properties. In N. Halbwachs and D. Peled, editors, *Eleventh Conference on Computer Aided Verification (CAV'99)*, pages 222–235. Springer-Verlag, Berlin, 1999. LNCS 1633. 621

[2] D. L. Dill, A. J. Hu, and H. Wong-Toi. Checking for language inclusion using simulation relations. In K. G. Larsen and A. Skou, editors, *Third Workshop on Computer Aided Verification (CAV'91)*, pages 255–265. Springer, Berlin, July 1991. LNCS 575. 610

[3] E. A. Emerson and C. S. Jutla. Tree automata, mu-calculus and determinacy. In *Proc. 32nd IEEE Symposium on Foundations of Computer Science*, pages 368–377, October 1991. 613

[4] K. Etessami and G. J. Holzmann. Optimizing Büchi automata. In *Proc. 11th International Conference on Concurrency Theory (CONCUR2000)*, pages 153–167. Springer, 2000. LNCS 1877. 610

[5] K. Etessami, T. Wilke, and A. Schuller. Fair simulation relations, parity games, and state space reduction for Büchi automata. In F. Orejas, P. G. Spirakis, and J. van Leeuwen, editors, *Automata, Languages and Programming: 28th International Colloquium*, pages 694–707, Crete, Greece, July 2001. Springer. LNCS 2076. 610, 611, 613, 614, 617, 619, 620

[6] T. Henzinger, O. Kupferman, and S. Rajamani. Fair simulation. In *Proceedings of the 9th International Conference on Concurrency Theory (CONCUR'97)*, pages 273–287. Springer-Verlag, 1997. LNCS 1243. 610, 611, 613, 614, 620

[7] M. Jurdziński. Small progress measures for solving parity games. In *STACS 2000, 17th Annual Symposium on Theoretical Aspects of Computer Science*, pages 290–301, Lille, France, February 2000. Springer. LNCS 1770. 613, 617, 620

[8] R. P. Kurshan. *Computer-Aided Verification of Coordinating Processes*. Princeton University Press, Princeton, NJ, 1994. 610

[9] O. Lichtenstein and A. Pnueli. Checking that finite state concurrent programs satisfy their linear specification. In *Proceedings of the Twelfth Annual ACM Symposium on Principles of Programming Languages*, pages 97–107, New Orleans, January 1985. 610

[10] R. Milner. *Communication and Concurrency*. Prentice Hall, Englewood Cliffs, NJ, 1989. 610

[11] F. Somenzi and R. Bloem. Efficient Büchi automata from LTL formulae. In E. A. Emerson and A. P. Sistla, editors, *Twelfth Conference on Computer Aided Verification (CAV'00)*, pages 248–263. Springer-Verlag, Berlin, July 2000. LNCS 1855. 610, 611, 612, 613, 620, 622

[12] W. Thomas. On the synthesis of strategies in infinite games. In *Proc. 12th Annual Symposium on Theoretical Aspects of Computer Science*, pages 1–13. Springer-Verlag, 1995. LNCS 900. 613

[13] P. Wolper, M. Y. Vardi, and A. P. Sistla. Reasoning about infinite computation paths. In *Proceedings of the 24th IEEE Symposium on Foundations of Computer Science*, pages 185–194, 1983. 610

Author Index

Lecture Notes in Computer Science

For information about Vols. 1–2315
please contact your bookseller or Springer-Verlag